INQUIZITIVE

InQuizitive is a new formative, adaptive online learning tool that is thoroughly informed by psychological research into how students learn.

InQuizitive is: Formative

InQuizitive's answer-specific feedback anticipates common mistakes and recognizes not only when students answer incorrectly but *how* they answered incorrectly. Personalized feedback helps students get back on track and learn from their mistakes.[1]

InQuizitive is: Game-like

Gaming elements engage students and keep them working. Students gain or lose points by adjusting the confidence slider, progress through three levels in each chapter, and win bonus points for hot streaks and bonus questions.[2]

InQuizitive is: Adaptive

InQuizitive is built to adapt to each student's needs. It offers more questions in areas where a student needs help, yet allows students who know the material to progress more quickly.

InQuizitive is: Motivating

InQuizitive guides students to the right answer after each response. This turns every question—even ones the students answer incorrectly—into a positive and motivating learning experience.[3]

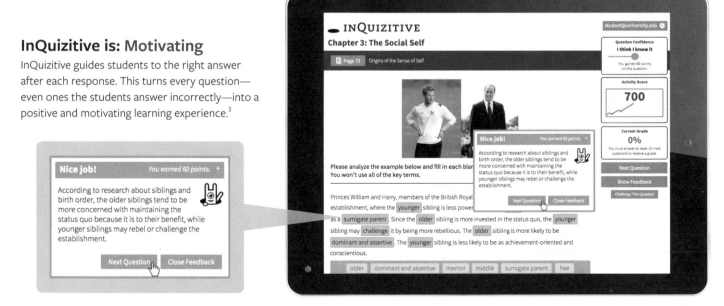

1 Research shows that formative quizzing is only as good as the feedback students get while completing activities (McTighe and O'Connor, 2005).
2 A study by Naceur and Schiefele (2005) found that information retention was more highly correlated with student interest than student ability.
3 To be maximally effective, a system also needs to turn failures into positive learning experiences (Gee, 2009).

Social Psychology

FOURTH EDITION

Not So Fast

A new feature in each chapter, "Not So Fast," encourages critical thinking by gently nudging the reader to uncover a common misconception, revealing a sounder approach to thinking about the topic.

- **Ch. 2: Critical Thinking about Correlation and Causation**
  Do claims such as "States with abstinence-only sex education have higher homicide rates" correctly imply that abstinence-only sex education increases homicide? More generally, how should a correlation between two variables be interpreted?

- **Ch. 3: Critical Thinking about Assuming a Single Explanation**
  Overly flattering self-assessments are not caused only by a need for self-enhancement; many people lack the skills and knowledge to accurately judge themselves. It's important to consider the possibility that behaviors may have more than one cause.

- **Ch. 4: Critical Thinking about Representativeness and the Regression Effect**
  Bad luck seems to follow athletes after they appear on the cover of *Sports Illustrated*, but this phenomenon—and many more—can be easily explained by a statistical regularity known as the regression effect.

- **Ch. 5: Critical Thinking about the Fundamental Attribution Error**
  While the people who stayed in New Orleans during Hurricane Katrina were often blamed for being irresponsible or foolish, a closer look reveals the situational factors that could have kept them from evacuating.

- **Ch. 6: Critical Thinking about What Micro-Analyses of Behavior Can Reveal**
  Smiles aren't always genuine. How can we detect real joy or affection in someone's facial expression?

- **Ch. 7: Critical Thinking about Surveys vs. Experiments**
  To test whether there is a causal relationship between, say, the severity of fraternity hazing and one's commitment to the fraternity, would it be adequate to simply survey fraternities about their hazing practices and how committed their members are?

- **Ch. 8: Critical Thinking about External Validity**
  In the lab, subliminal stimuli can influence participants, but in the real world, can they cause significant changes in attitude, such as voting for an opposite-party candidate or wanting to commit suicide?

- **Ch. 9: Critical Thinking about Conformity and Disagreement**
  Researchers must always keep in mind that people respond to their subjective interpretation of a situation, not the objective situation, especially when an experiment involves a potentially confusing scenario.

- **Ch. 10: Critical Thinking about the Variable Being Measured**
  When investigating variables, such as newlyweds' explicit attitudes toward each other, experimenters must be sure to avoid confusing the measures of those variables with the variables themselves.

- **Ch. 11: Critical Thinking by Finding the Proper Comparison**
  Finding the proper comparison in an experiment is critical but can be surprisingly challenging, as illustrated by a study about gender stereotypes that examined teachers' reactions to very similar male and female names on essays.

- **Ch. 12: Critical Thinking about Correlated Trends**
  What's the deeper meaning behind the simultaneous increase of yearly sales of salted caramel ice cream and legalized marijuana, or the number of search requests for "Kate Upton" and "jihad"?

- **Ch. 13: Critical Thinking about Third Variables and Spurious Associations**
  In studies that link two variables, such as the playing of violent video games and subsequent aggression, experimenters should be wary of the effects of third variables.

- **Ch. 14: Critical Thinking about Generalizing to the Real World**
  In response to concern about the external validity of economic games played in the lab, experimenters can investigate whether actions in such games predict real world behavior, or they can conduct field research that aims to replicate lab findings.

FOURTH EDITION

Social Psychology

Thomas Gilovich
Cornell University

Dacher Keltner
University of California, Berkeley

Serena Chen
University of California, Berkeley

Richard E. Nisbett
University of Michigan

W. W. Norton & Company · New York · London

W. W. Norton & Company has been independent since its founding in 1923, when William Warder Norton and Mary D. Herter Norton first published lectures delivered at the People's Institute, the adult education division of New York City's Cooper Union. The firm soon expanded its program beyond the Institute, publishing books by celebrated academics from America and abroad. By midcentury, the two major pillars of Norton's publishing program—trade books and college texts—were firmly established. In the 1950s, the Norton family transferred control of the company to its employees, and today—with a staff of four hundred and a comparable number of trade, college, and professional titles published each year—W. W. Norton & Company stands as the largest and oldest publishing house owned wholly by its employees.

EDITOR: Sheri Snavely

PROJECT EDITOR: Rachel Mayer

DEVELOPMENTAL DITOR: Betsy Dilernia

ASSISTANT EDITOR: Scott Sugarman

MANAGING EDITOR, COLLEGE: Marian Johnson

MANAGING EDITOR, COLLEGE DIGITAL MEDIA: Kim Yi

PRODUCTION MANAGER: Sean Mintus

MEDIA EDITOR: Patrick Shriner

ASSOCIATE MEDIA EDITOR: Stefani Wallace

MEDIA PROJECT EDITOR: Penelope Lin

ASSISTANT MEDIA EDITOR: George Phipps

MARKETING MANAGER, PSYCHOLOGY: Lauren Winkler

DESIGN DIRECTOR: Rubina Yeh

PHOTO EDITOR: Nelson Colon

PERMISSIONS MANAGER: Megan Jackson

COMPOSITION: Jouve

MANUFACTURING: Transcontinental Interglobe, Inc.

Permission to use copyrighted material is included beginning on page C-1.

ISBN 978-0-393-93896-8

W. W. Norton & Company, Inc., 500 Fifth Avenue, New York, NY 10110-0017

wwnorton.com

W. W. Norton & Company Ltd., 15 Carlisle Street, London W1D 3BS

3 4 5 6 7 8 9 0

We dedicate this book to

Karen, Ilana, and Rebecca Dashiff Gilovich

Mollie McNeil and Natalie and Serafina Keltner-McNeil

Sebastian and Stella Chen-McDermott

Sarah Nisbett

ABOUT THE AUTHORS

THOMAS GILOVICH is Professor of Psychology and Co-Director of the Center for Behavioral Economics and Decision Research at Cornell University. He has taught social psychology for over 30 years and is the recipient of the Russell Distinguished Teaching Award at Cornell. His research focuses on judgment, decision making, and well-being. He is a member of the American Academy of Arts and Sciences and a fellow of the American Psychological Society, the American Psychological Association, the Society for Personality and Social Psychology, the Society of Experimental Social Psychology, and the Committee for Skeptical Inquiry.

DACHER KELTNER is Thomas and Ruth Ann Hornaday Professor of Psychology and the Director of the Greater Good Science Center at the University of California, Berkeley. He has taught social psychology for the past 18 years and is the recipient of the Distinguished Teaching Award for Letters and Sciences. His research focuses on the prosocial emotions (such as love, sympathy, and gratitude), morality, and power. Other awards include the Western Psychological Association's award for outstanding contribution to research, the Positive Psychology Prize for excellence in research, and the Ed and Carol Diener mid-career award for research excellence in Social Psychology. He is a fellow of the American Psychological Association, the American Psychological Society, and the Society for Personality and Social Psychology. In 2008, the *Utne Reader* listed Dacher as one of the 50 visionaries changing the world.

SERENA CHEN is Professor of Psychology and the Marian E. and Daniel E. Koshland, Jr. Distinguished Chair for Innovative Teaching and Research at the University of California, Berkeley. She has taught social psychology for the past 18 years and is the recipient of the Distinguished Teaching Award from Berkeley's Social Science Division. Her research focuses on the social bases of the self and identity, and on the intrapersonal and interpersonal consequences of social power and other hierarchy-related dimensions (e.g., social class, income inequality). She is a fellow of the Society of Personality and Social Psychology, American Psychological Association, and the Association for Psychological Science, as well as the recipient of the Early Career Award from the International Society for Self and Identity. The Association for Psychological Science also identified her as a Rising Star.

RICHARD E. NISBETT is Theodore M. Newcomb Distinguished University Professor of Psychology at the University of Michigan and Research Professor at Michigan's Institute for Social Research. He has taught courses in social psychology, cultural psychology, cognitive psychology, and evolutionary psychology. His research focuses on how people reason and how reasoning can be improved. He also studies how people from different cultures think, perceive, feel, and act in different ways. He is the recipient of the Distinguished Scientific Contribution Award of the American Psychological Association and the William James Fellow Award of the American Psychological Society and is a member of the National Academy of Sciences and the American Academy of Arts and Sciences.

CONTENTS IN BRIEF

PREFACE

A FRESH PERSPECTIVE IN SOCIAL PSYCHOLOGY

Social psychology illuminates and clarifies the nature of human beings and their social world. It is a science that offers novel insights into the foundations of moral sentiments, the origins of violence, and the reasons people fall in love. It provides basic tools for understanding how people persuade one another, why people trust and cooperate with each other, and how people rationalize their undesirable actions. Social psychology offers scientifically grounded answers to questions human beings have been thinking about since we started to reflect on who we are: Are we rational creatures? How can we find happiness? What is the proper relationship of the individual to the larger society? How are we shaped by the culture in which we are raised?

After decades of collective experience teaching social psychology, we decided at the turn of the twenty-first century to put pen to paper (or fingers to keyboard) and write our own vision of this fascinating discipline. It was an ideal time to do so. Many new developments in the field were reshaping social psychology. Exciting new research had revealed how different kinds of culture—country of origin, regional culture, social class—shape human thought, feeling, and action. Evolutionary theory was helping to guide how social psychologists study things such as homicide, morality, and cooperation. Social psychologists were making inroads into the study of the brain. Specific areas of interest to us—judgment and decision making, emotion, altruism, and well-being—had emerged as well-defined areas of investigation that were producing important insights about human behavior. The lure of writing a textbook, and the challenge in doing so, was to capture all of these new developments and integrate them with the timeless classics of social psychology that make it such a captivating discipline.

It's a bit shocking to us to think that this is the fourth edition of the text; it seems like just yesterday when we first got together in Berkeley, California, to map out what an informative survey of social psychology should look like. Our work on all four editions has been deeply rewarding. Our fascination with the field, and our pride in being a part of it, has been rekindled and magnified with each edition. It is gratifying to have this book reach the minds of the next generation of social psychology students.

Whether students end up as teachers, salespeople, or talent agents, or as software designers, forest rangers, or book editors, other people are going to be the center of their lives. All of us grow up dependent on the members of our nuclear family (and in many cultural contexts, a larger extended family); we go through adolescence obsessed with our social standing and intensely focused on our prospects for romance and sexuality; and as adults we seek out others in the workplace, at clubs, in places of worship, and on holidays. Social psychologists spend their professional lives studying this intense sociality, examining how we act, think, and feel in all of these social encounters—and *why* we act, think, and feel that way. Above all, we want our book to capture the fundamentally social nature of human life and to present the clever, informative, and sometimes inspiring methods that social psychologists have used to study and understand the social life around us.

In our teaching, we have found that many great studies in social psychology are simple narratives: the narrative of the person who felt compelled to harm another person in the name of science, the narrative of the clergyman who did not help someone in need because he was in a hurry, the narrative of the Southerner whose blood pressure rose when he was insulted in a hallway, the story of the young researcher who lived among hunter-gatherers in New Guinea to discover universal facial expressions. In our experience, teaching social psychology brings forth so many "Aha!" moments precisely because of these stories that are embedded within, and that inspire, our science.

SOCIAL PSYCHOLOGY, THE SCIENTIFIC METHOD, AND CRITICAL THINKING

These narratives are different, though, from others that try to capture something important about the human condition: the story of the tortoise and the hare, the tale of the boy who cried wolf, and the anecdote of the child down the street who "took candy from a stranger" and paid a high price for doing so. The tales we tell in this book are all grounded in empirical evidence. It's the scientific foundation of their claims that distinguish social psychologists from other astute observers of the human condition, such as novelists, playwrights, clergymen, and parents, teachers, and coaches. The methods of social psychology are every bit as important as the insights they reveal.

In fact, we believe that social psychology is unparalleled as a means of teaching critical thinking. This new edition has been reworked to emphasize this message even more than the previous editions. The current version makes explicit the power of social psychology's methods and habits of thought for understanding the world and assessing the likely truth and value of what friends and the media tell us. To make sure students hone their critical-thinking skills, we approach the subject matter of social psychology in several ways.

First, in Chapter 2, The Methods of Social Psychology, we present an overview of the most important elements of conducting research. We tie the methods of social psychology together by showing how many of them can be applied to a single problem: the nature of the "culture of honor." That chapter, and much of the rest of the book, is oriented toward providing the critical-thinking skills that are the hallmark of social psychology. We show how the tools of social psychology can be used to critique research in the behavioral and medical sciences students encounter online and in magazines and newspapers. More importantly, we show how the methods of social psychology can be used to understand everyday life and to figure out how to navigate new situations.

Second, a new "Not So Fast" feature in each chapter highlights how easy it is to be fooled by the available evidence and to draw conclusions that seem solid but in fact don't stand up to scientific scrutiny. They show how even the smartest among us can be misled by what we experience and what we read or hear unless we've learned some fundamental principles of the scientific method. Another new feature of this edition is that each chapter ends with a set of open-ended "Think About It" questions that challenge students to think critically in the context of a research-related or real-life scenario.

Third, we embed discussion of methodological issues throughout the book, in the context of many lines of research. This melds the content of social psychology with the principles that underlie research that can be used to understand ordinary events in people's lives.

Fourth, our You Be the Subject figures invite students to get an insider's view of experimentation in social psychology. Annotated figures help students read data graphics and understand the take-away points of the research. We have tried to make sure that all our field's varied methods—such as archival analyses, semantic and affective priming, neuroimaging, and participant observation—are discussed in sufficient depth to give the reader an understanding of how they work, what their strengths and weaknesses are, and how they can be applied to events in everyday life.

Much of the subject matter of social psychology—attraction, conformity, prejudice—readily engages the student's attention and imagination. The material sells itself. But in most textbook summaries of the field, the presentation comes across as a list of unconnected topics—as one intriguing fact after another. As a result, students often come away thinking of social psychology as all fun and games. That's fine up to a point. Social psychology *is* fun. But it is much more than that, and we have tried to show how the highlights of our field—the classic findings and the exciting new developments—are part of a scientific study of human nature that can sit with pride next to biology, chemistry, and physics, and that is worthy of the most serious-minded student's attention.

THE APPLICATION OF SOCIAL PSYCHOLOGY TO EVERYDAY LIFE

Possibly the easiest part of writing a social psychology textbook is pointing out the enormous applied implications of what the field has to offer. We do a great deal of this throughout the text. Each chapter begins with events in the real world that drive home the themes and wisdom of social psychology. For example, Chapter 3, The Social Self, begins with the story of Eminem and his alter ego, Slim Shady. Chapter 12, Groups, begins with the harrowing story of the abduction of Middle East bureau chief Terry Anderson and his report that the time he spent in solitary confinement was worse than any physical torture he received. Chapter 14, Altruism, begins with the story of Wesley Autrey, who jumped onto the tracks in front of an oncoming subway train to save the life of Cameron Hollopeter. What better way for the student to ponder the findings of social psychology than by relying on them to understand current events? Interspersed throughout the text are Focus On boxes that profile real-world applications of the wisdom of social psychology—for example, in understanding how black uniforms make professional athletes more aggressive, or how meditation might shift a person's brain chemistry.

To bring into sharper focus the relevance of social psychology to daily living, we have four applied mini-chapters, or modules, at the end of the book. These modules bring science-based insight to bear on four areas of great importance to just about everyone: the latest findings on health and how science-based, practical techniques help us cope with stress during difficult times; the new science of behavioral economics and how it can help us lead more financially stable and rewarding lives; the latest discoveries in the study of human intelligence and education; and a review of social psychological insights into how the legal system functions and how it can be improved. The modules constitute dramatic evidence of the relevance of social psychological findings to advancing human welfare.

NEW CONTENT IN THE FOURTH EDITION

The cumulative nature of science requires that revisions do justice to the latest discoveries and evolving views of the field. This new edition has much to offer in this regard.

- Chapter 3: The Social Self. We incorporated additional theory and research developing the key notion that the self is fundamentally social and shifts as a function of the social context. New topics include introspection, the accuracy of self-knowledge, how social class shapes views of the self, varieties of high and low self-esteem, and online self-presentation.

- Chapter 4: Social Cognition: Thinking About People and Situations. We added a section that explores how the regression effect, and the corresponding regression fallacy, can distort people's judgments. We also provide even greater coverage than before to the many ways in which sights, sounds, and even smells that people not aware of can nonetheless have a significant influence on what they think and act.

- Chapter 5: Social Attribution: Explaining Behavior. We present important work on how people can recall their past behavior or simulate their future actions by imagining themselves from the "outside," much as an observer would, or from the "inside," looking out at the environment. This simple difference in perspective has great influence on people's thoughts, feelings, and behavior.

- Chapter 6: Emotion. We present new findings that document the social importance of touch, show how mimicry is crucial to friendships, and delineate how emotions like disgust are drivers of moral judgment.

- Chapter 7: Attitudes, Behavior, and Rationalization. We continue to cover key findings and theories on the relationship between attitudes and behavior, honing our discussion of cognitive dissonance theory and the principles that determine whether and how people reduce dissonance.
- Chapter 8: Persuasion. We cover the latest in social psychological approaches to political ideology, as well recent findings on barriers to persuasion. New topics include the role of meta-cognition on persuasion and the role of incidental factors such as font clarity and the context in which persuasion is attempted.
- Chapter 9: Social Influence. We added a new section on social networks and how people are influenced not only by what their friends do, but by what the friends of their friends do, and even the friends of the friends of their friends.
- Chapter 10: Relationships and Attraction. We include more in-depth coverage of the principles of social exchange theory and Rusbult's investment model of commitment, as well as an updated presentation of attachment theory. We have also streamlined the discussion of different types of love.
- Chapter 11: Stereotyping, Prejudice, and Discrimination. We have more coverage of what it's like to be a member of a stigmatized group, including recent work on the psychological and physiological costs of trying to conceal one's identity as a member of such a group. We also examine new field research devoted to finding ways for members of groups with a long history of conflict to see one another as individuals and overcome their mutual animosity.
- Chapter 12: Groups. There is a new section on the physiology that accompanies our exposure to other people that we think of as threats or as providers of opportunity.
- Chapter 13: Aggression. We present remarkable new evidence linking inequality within a culture to levels of aggression, and we consider in more depth the topics of violence against women and of barriers to conflict resolution.
- Chapter 14: Altruism and Cooperation. We present new findings on how people from the upper classes are less altruistic in many respects than those from lower-class backgrounds, and on how altruism and cooperation are contagious, spreading from one person to another.

In making these changes, we have preserved the approach in the previous editions that each chapter can stand alone, and chapters can be read in any order. We have done so stylistically by writing chapters that are complete narratives in their own right. Our chapters stand on their own theoretically as well, being organized around social psychology's emphasis on situationism, construal, and automaticity and highlighting important issues addressing what is universal about human behavior and what is variable across cultures. Although our table of contents suggests a particular order of covering the material, instructors will find it easy to present the topics in whatever order best suits their own preferences or needs.

ACKNOWLEDGMENTS

No book is written in a vacuum. Many people have helped us in the course of writing this text, starting with our families. Karen Dashiff Gilovich was her usual bundle of utterly lovable qualities that make the sharing of lives so enjoyable—and the difficulties of authorship so tolerable. Mollie McNeil was a steady source of kindness, enthusiasm, and critical eye and ear. Sebastian and Stella Chen-McDermott brought joy and inspiration daily, bringing to life so much of social psychology even in the context of their young lives. Sarah and Susan Nisbett were sounding boards and life-support systems. Mikki Hebl, Dennis Regan, and Tomi-Ann Roberts went well beyond the call of collegial duty by reading every chapter of early editions and providing us with useful commentary. In addition to giving us the considerable benefit of their good judgment and good taste, they also pointed out a few of our blind spots and saved us from an occasional embarrassing error. John H. Bickford, Jr. was an indispensable resource as we worked to improve our LGBT coverage in the fourth edition, guiding us to the appropriate terminology and helping us create a more inclusive book. We are grateful to Maya Kuehn, Juliana Breines, and Anna Luerssen for contributing the Think About It questions in each chapter and providing insightful reviews of the Not So Fast features and the test bank. Juliana and Anna also led the effort to revise and improve the test bank for the fourth edition. Sadie Leder Elder and Minda Oriña rigorously checked the accuracy of each chapter's proofs, suggesting helpful changes and corrections along the way.

We are indebted to Jon Durbin, Vanessa Drake-Johnson, and Paul Rozin for bringing us together on this project in the first place. And we owe enormous thanks to Sheri Snavely, who has steered us through chapter by chapter, for all but the first edition. The book would not be where it is today without her insights, talent, and sense of humor, not to mention her well-timed and well-calibrated nudges. We would also like to thank Scott Sugarman, who seems able to do just about anything, including keeping us and everyone at Norton sane when the inevitable difficulties of putting a four-author book together arise. We also owe a great deal to our developmental editor Betsy Dilernia, who literally read every line of every page with an eagle eye and a talented red marker. Thanks are also due to our tireless project editor Rachel Mayer, photo editor Nelson Colon, and production manager Sean Mintus. Our media editor, Patrick Shriner, together with associate editor Stefani Wallace, has worked diligently to develop modern and high-quality media for our book, including the new interactive instructors' suite, student eBook, InQuizitive adaptive assessment, video, and online labs. We also are grateful for the marketing efforts of Lauren Winkler and the Norton travelers who have worked to make this book a success.

Our thanks to the following people for their helpful suggestions and close reading of various chapters in the first, second, third, and fourth editions of the book.

Glenn Adams, *University of Toronto*

Craig Anderson, *Iowa State University*

Bob Arkin, *Ohio State University*

Clarissa Arms-Chavez, *Auburn University, Montgomery*

Joan Bailey, *New Jersey City University*

Miranda Barone, *University of Southern California*

Doris Bazzini, *Appalachian State*

Kristin Beals, *California State University, Fullerton*

Gordon Bear, *Ramapo College of New Jersey*

Elliott Beaton, *McMaster University*

Leonard Berkowitz, *University of Wisconsin–Madison*

Frank Bernieri, *Oregon State University*

Anila Bhagavatula, *California State University, Long Beach*

John H. Bickford Jr., *University of Massachusetts Amherst*

Susan Boon, *Calgary University*

Juliana Breines, *Brandeis University*

Tim Brock, *Ohio State University*

Don Carlston, *Purdue University*

Sandra Carpenter, *University of Alabama*

Bettina Casad, *California Polytechnic State University, Pomona*

Nicholas Christenfeld, *University of California, San Diego*

Charlene Christie, *Oneonta College*

Eric Cooley, *Western Oregon University*

Alita Cousins, *Eastern Connecticut State University*

Karen Couture, *Keene State College*

Traci Craig, *University of Idaho*

Ken Cramer, *University of Windsor*

Chris Crandall, *University of Kansas*

Susan Cross, *Iowa State University*

Fiery Cushman, *Harvard University*

George Cvetkovich, *Western Washington University*

Alex Czopp, *Western Washington University*

Deborah Davis, *University of Nevada, Reno*

Chris De La Ronde, *Austin Community College*

Ken DeMarree, *Texas Tech University*

Rachel Dinero, *Cazenovia College*

Pete Ditto, *University of California, Irvine*

Dan Dolderman, *University of Toronto*

John Dovidio, *Yale University*

David Duemler, *Lane Community College*

Richard P. Eibach, *Yale University*

Scott Eidelman, *University of Arkansas, Fayetteville*

Naomi Eisenberger, *University of California, Los Angeles*

Jack Feldman, *Georgia Institute of Technology*

Eli Finkel, *Northwestern University*

Marcia Finkelstein, *University of South Florida*

Madeleine Fugere, *Eastern Connecticut State University*

Azenett Garza-Caballero, *Weber State University*

Daniel Gilbert, *Harvard University*

Omri Gillath, *University of Kansas*

Erinn Green, *University of Cincinnati*

Tay Hack, *Angelo State University*

Jon Haidt, *University of Virginia*

Judith Harackiewicz, *University of Wisconsin, Madison*

Lisa Harrison, *California State University, Sacramento*

Todd Hartman, *Appalachian State University*

Lora Haynes, *University of Louisville*

Steve Heine, *University of British Columbia*

Marlone Henderson, *University of Texas at Austin*

Edward Hirt, *Indiana University*

Zach Hohman, *California State University, Fullerton*

Gina Hoover, *Ohio State University*

Amy Houlihan, *Texas A&M, Corpus Christi*

Matthew I. Isaak, *University of Louisiana at Lafayette*

Kareem Johnson, *Temple University*

Kimberly Kahn, *Portland State University*

Andy Karpinski, *Temple University*

Johan Karremans, *Radboud University*

Iva Katzarska-Miller, *University of Kansas*

Sulki Kim, *California State University, Fullerton*

Leslie Kirby, *Vanderbilt University*

Marc Kiviniem, *University of Nebraska, Lincoln*

Stan B. Klein, *University of California, Santa Barbara*

Catalina E. Kopetz, *University of Maryland*

Maya Kuehn, *University of California, Berkeley*

Ziva Kunda (deceased), *Waterloo University*

Marianne LaFrance, *Yale University*

Alan Lambert, *Washington University*

Jeff Larsen, *Texas Tech University*

Sadie Leder Elder, *High Point University*

Norman Li, *University of Texas, Austin*

Debra Lieberman, *University of Hawaii*

Anson (Annie) Long, *Indiana University of Pennsylvania*

Anna Luerssen, *Lehman College*

Debbie S. Ma, *California State University, Northridge*

Jon Maner, *Florida State University*

Doug McCann, *York University*

Connie Meinholdt, *Ferris State University*

Batja Mesquita, *University of Leuven*

Cynthia Mohr, *Portland State University*

Daniel Molden, *Northwestern University*

Mark Muravan, *University at Albany*

Mary Murphy, *University of California, Irvine*

Todd Nelson, *California State University, Stanislaus*

Angela J. Nierman, *University of Kansas*

Clark Ohnesorge, *St. Olaf College*

M. Minda Oriña, *St. Olaf College*

Bernadette Park, *University of Colorado*

Gerrod Parrott, *Georgetown University*

Ashby Plant, *Florida State University*

Jacqueline Pope-Tarrence, *Western Kentucky University*

Deborah Prentice, *Princeton University*

Mary Pritchard, *Boise State University*

Emily Pronin, *Princeton University*

David Rand, *Yale University*

Denise Reiling, *Eastern Michigan University*

Jessica Remedios, *Tufts University*

Jane Richards, *University of Texas, Austin*

Jennifer Richeson, *Northwestern University*

Robert D. Ridge, *Brigham Young University*

Neal Roese, *University of Illinois at Urbana–Champaign*

Regina Roof-Ray, *Hartford Community College*

Alex Rothman, *University of Minnesota, Twin Cities Campus*

Darcy Santor, *Dalhousie University*

Constantine Sedikides, *University of Southampton*

Sohaila Shakib, *California State University, Dominguez Hills*

Gregory P. Shelley, *Kutztown University*

J. Nicole Shelton, *Princeton University*

Jeff Sherman, *Northwestern University*

Colleen Sinclair, *University of Missouri, Columbia*

Elizabeth R. Spievak, *Bridgewater State College*

Sue Sprecher, *Illinois State University*

Emily Stark, *Minnesota State University, Mankato*

Jeff Stone, *University of Arizona*

Justin Storbeck, *Queens College*

Michael Strube, *Washington University, St. Louis*

Kate Sweeny, *University of California, Riverside*

Lisa Szafran, *Syracuse University*

Lauren A. Taglialatela, *Kennesaw State University*

Chuck Tate, *San Francisco State University*

Warren Thorngate, *Carleton University*

Zakary Tormala, *Indiana University, Bloomington*

Jeanne Tsai, *Stanford University*

Jim Uleman, *New York University*

Naomi Wagner, *San Jose State University*

Nathan Westbrook, *California State University, Fullerton*

David Wilder, *Rutgers University*

Ben Wilkowski, *University of Wyoming*

Edward Witt, *Michigan State University*

Connie Wolfe, *Muhlenberg College*

Cor van Halen, *Radboud University*

Joseph Vandallo, *University of South Florida*

Leigh Ann Vaughn, *Ithaca College*

Marcellene Watson-Derbigny, *Sacramento State University*

Aaron Wichman, *Western Kentucky University*

Nancy Yanchus, *Georgia Southern University*

Jennifer Yanowitz, *University of Minnesota, Twin Cities Campus*

Janice Yoder, *University of Akron*

Jason Young, *Hunter College*

Randy Young, *Bridgewater State University*

CONTENTS

Social Psychology

FOURTH EDITION

An Invitation to Social Psychology

Alan Turing, a British mathematician, logician, and philosopher educated at Princeton and Cambridge, is generally considered to be the founder of computer science. During World War II Turing was head of Hut 8, the British government agency responsible for breaking the Enigma code of the German Navy, an accomplishment that contributed greatly to the Allied war effort.

In January 1952, when Turing was 39, he was arrested for "gross indecency," a term the British used for homosexual conduct. Turing was convicted of the charge and allowed to choose between imprisonment and chemical castration to reduce his libido and cause impotence. He chose the latter punishment, which involved the administration of female hormones. Turing attempted to come to the United States but was considered a security risk and not allowed to enter. On June 8, 1954, Turing was found dead from cyanide poisoning in his apartment. The death was ruled a suicide.

At the time of Turing's death, homosexuality was illegal in most states of the U.S. In 1986, the U.S. Supreme Court, in a 5-4 decision, ruled that a Georgia sodomy law forbidding oral and anal sex between homosexual adults was constitutional. The majority opinion, written by Justice Byron White, asserted that the Constitution did not confer "a fundamental right to engage in homosexual sodomy." Seventeen years later, in *Lawrence* v. *Texas*, the Court reversed itself, declaring that homosexual conduct was permitted under the "due process" clause of the Fourteenth Amendment. Thereupon, all laws in the U.S. criminalizing homosexual acts became invalid.

Alan Turing
Founder of Modern Computer Science

Until 1974, the American Psychiatric Association held that homosexuality was a mental illness. Until 1994, homosexuality was a necessary and sufficient cause for discharge from the American military. President Clinton issued an order prohibiting discrimination against homosexual members of the armed forces, but also prohibiting people who "demonstrate a propensity or intent to engage in homosexual acts" from serving in the armed forces. This "don't ask, don't tell" ruling was overturned in 2011 by President Obama, and now it is possible for openly gay individuals to serve in the armed forces.

For many years, elections in the U.S. were won by politicians whose main platform planks were the banning of abortion and the outlawing of same-sex marriage. Until quite recently, public opinion ran strongly against gay marriage. Then, within an astonishingly brief period of time, public opinion swung toward general support for marriage equality. From 2012 to 2014, the percentage of Republicans who supported marriage equality increased from 24 to 40, a two-thirds increase. As of March 2014, 68 percent of 18–33-year-olds supported same-sex marriage. In 2014, Jon Stewart's *Daily Show* sent two men on a mission to a Waffle House in Alabama, one of the reddest states. One of the men loudly asked the other to marry him. The reaction of the patrons? Applause.

From mental illness and illegality of homosexual behavior to tolerance of same-sex marriage—in scarcely more than a generation. This fact, and a hundred others concerning homosexuality in relation to social norms and individual psychology, are the kinds of topics that deeply interest social psychologists.

Why was homosexuality ever such a threat to people in modern Western societies? In many cultures, homosexuality never was considered abnormal or reprehensible or even particularly worthy of notice; in others it has been punishable by death since time immemorial. Why has homosexuality for women in virtually every society always been more tolerated than homosexuality for men? To what degree is homosexual behavior, even sexual orientation, influenced by social norms and institutional settings? How is it possible for an entire society to change its attitudes toward a salient social phenomenon in, so to speak, the blink of an eye? What are the effects of societal rejection versus acceptance on the emotional, even physical, well-being of individuals who are gay or lesbian? How do stereotypes of gay people change over time? How do sexual-minority cultures and subcultures change over time, and what are the factors that influence such changes?

In this chapter, we explain what social psychology is and what social psychologists study. We also present some of the basic concepts of social psychology, especially the surprising degree to which social situations can influence behavior; the role of construal, or the interpretive processes people use to understand situations; and how two different kinds of thinking—one rapid, intuitive, and nonconscious, and the other slower, analytical, and conscious—contribute in tandem to understanding what is happening in social situations. We also describe some recent developments in social psychology that have changed the field—namely, the application of evolutionary concepts to human behavior, the use of the tools of neuroscience, and the discovery of some significant variations in human cultures that frequently lead people in diverse societies to respond to the "same" situation in very different ways.

Changing Attitudes toward Homosexuality
Same-sex marriage is now legal in the United States, and adoption of children by gays is legal in many states. Openly gay politicians such as Tammy Baldwin are being elected to national political office.

Characterizing Social Psychology

People have always sought explanations for human behavior. Stories, parables, and folk wisdom have been passed from generation to generation, in an attempt to explain why people do what they do and to prescribe behaviors to avoid or follow. Social psychologists go beyond folk wisdom and try to establish a scientific basis for understanding human behavior. **Social psychology** can be defined as the scientific study of the feelings, thoughts, and behaviors of individuals in social situations.

Why are people inclined to stereotype members of different groups? Why do people risk their lives to help others? Why do some marriages flourish and others fail? How do orderly crowds turn into violent mobs? These sorts of questions lie at the heart of social psychology, and careful research has provided at least partial answers to all of them. Some of the answers probably won't surprise you. For example, we tend to like people who like us, and the people we like generally have attitudes and interests that are similar to ours. When experimental findings reflect what our intuitions and folk wisdom say will happen, social psychologists expand upon that folk wisdom, seeking to discover what lies behind the phenomenon in question. In contrast, other answers have been so counterintuitive that they surprised even the social psychologists who conducted the research. As you will see throughout this book, many of our most strongly

social psychology The scientific study of the feelings, thoughts, and behaviors of individuals in social situations.

"The test of learning psychology is whether your understanding of situations you encounter has changed, not whether you have learned a new fact."

—NOBEL PRIZE-WINNING PSYCHOLOGIST DANIEL KAHNEMAN

held folk theories or intuitions fail to give complete answers to important questions, and others are just plain wrong. Social psychologists test these intuitions by devising studies and crafting experiments that reveal the causes of behavior in social situations.

Explaining Behavior

In April 2004, more than a year after the start of the war in Iraq, CBS broadcast a story on *60 Minutes II* that exposed American atrocities against Iraqi prisoners in the Abu Ghraib prison near Baghdad. CBS showed photos of naked prisoners with plastic bags over their heads, stacked up in a pyramid, and surrounded by laughing male and female American soldiers. Other photos showed hooded prisoners standing on narrow pedestals with their arms stretched out and electric wires attached to their bodies. CBS also reported that prisoners had been required to simulate sexual acts.

The reaction on the part of many Iraqis and others in the Arab world was to regard the acts as evidence that the United States had malevolent intentions toward Arabs (Hauser, 2004). Most Americans, too, were appalled at the abuse and ashamed of the behavior of the U.S. soldiers. Many of those who saw the photos on television or in the newspapers assumed that the soldiers who had perpetrated these acts were rotten apples—exceptions to a rule of common decency prevailing in the military and the general population.

Social psychologists, however, were not so quick to make such an assumption. Indeed, 30 years before the atrocities at Abu Ghraib, Philip Zimbardo and his colleagues paid 24 Stanford University undergraduate men, chosen for their good character and mental health, to be participants in a study of a simulated prison (Haney, Banks, & Zimbardo, 1973). The researchers flipped a coin to determine

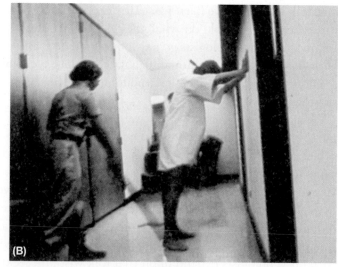

Prison Situations and Intimidation

(A) Military guards at the Abu Ghraib prison in Iraq used torture, humiliation, and intimidation to try to obtain information from the prisoners. This included stripping them and making them lie naked in the prison corridors. (B) Such degradation echoes what happened in the Zimbardo prison study, as shown in this photo of a "guard" seeking to humiliate one of his prisoners at the simulated prison.

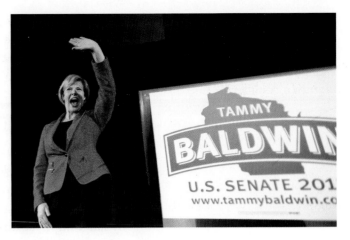

Changing Attitudes toward Homosexuality
Same-sex marriage is now legal in the United States, and adoption of children by gays is legal in many states. Openly gay politicians such as Tammy Baldwin are being elected to national political office.

Characterizing Social Psychology

People have always sought explanations for human behavior. Stories, parables, and folk wisdom have been passed from generation to generation, in an attempt to explain why people do what they do and to prescribe behaviors to avoid or follow. Social psychologists go beyond folk wisdom and try to establish a scientific basis for understanding human behavior. **Social psychology** can be defined as the scientific study of the feelings, thoughts, and behaviors of individuals in social situations.

Why are people inclined to stereotype members of different groups? Why do people risk their lives to help others? Why do some marriages flourish and others fail? How do orderly crowds turn into violent mobs? These sorts of questions lie at the heart of social psychology, and careful research has provided at least partial answers to all of them. Some of the answers probably won't surprise you. For example, we tend to like people who like us, and the people we like generally have attitudes and interests that are similar to ours. When experimental findings reflect what our intuitions and folk wisdom say will happen, social psychologists expand upon that folk wisdom, seeking to discover what lies behind the phenomenon in question. In contrast, other answers have been so counterintuitive that they surprised even the social psychologists who conducted the research. As you will see throughout this book, many of our most strongly

social psychology The scientific study of the feelings, thoughts, and behaviors of individuals in social situations.

held folk theories or intuitions fail to give complete answers to important questions, and others are just plain wrong. Social psychologists test these intuitions by devising studies and crafting experiments that reveal the causes of behavior in social situations.

Explaining Behavior

In April 2004, more than a year after the start of the war in Iraq, CBS broadcast a story on *60 Minutes II* that exposed American atrocities against Iraqi prisoners in the Abu Ghraib prison near Baghdad. CBS showed photos of naked prisoners with plastic bags over their heads, stacked up in a pyramid, and surrounded by laughing male and female American soldiers. Other photos showed hooded prisoners standing on narrow pedestals with their arms stretched out and electric wires attached to their bodies. CBS also reported that prisoners had been required to simulate sexual acts.

The reaction on the part of many Iraqis and others in the Arab world was to regard the acts as evidence that the United States had malevolent intentions toward Arabs (Hauser, 2004). Most Americans, too, were appalled at the abuse and ashamed of the behavior of the U.S. soldiers. Many of those who saw the photos on television or in the newspapers assumed that the soldiers who had perpetrated these acts were rotten apples—exceptions to a rule of common decency prevailing in the military and the general population.

Social psychologists, however, were not so quick to make such an assumption. Indeed, 30 years before the atrocities at Abu Ghraib, Philip Zimbardo and his colleagues paid 24 Stanford University undergraduate men, chosen for their good character and mental health, to be participants in a study of a simulated prison (Haney, Banks, & Zimbardo, 1973). The researchers flipped a coin to determine

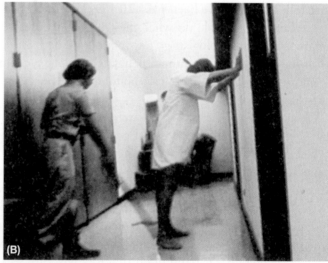

Prison Situations and Intimidation
(A) Military guards at the Abu Ghraib prison in Iraq used torture, humiliation, and intimidation to try to obtain information from the prisoners. This included stripping them and making them lie naked in the prison corridors. (B) Such degradation echoes what happened in the Zimbardo prison study, as shown in this photo of a "guard" seeking to humiliate one of his prisoners at the simulated prison.

who would be a "guard" and who would be a "prisoner." The guards wore green fatigue uniforms and reflective sunglasses. The prisoners wore tunics with nylon stocking caps and had a chain locked around one ankle. The "prison" was set up in the basement of the psychology department, and the researchers anticipated the study would last 2 weeks. Right away, the guards turned to verbal abuse and physical humiliation, requiring the prisoners to wear bags over their heads, stripping them naked, and requiring them to engage in simulated sex acts. As a result, the study had to be terminated after 6 days because the behavior of the guards produced extreme stress reactions in several of the prisoners.

Zimbardo today maintains that the balance of power in prisons is so unequal that they tend to be brutal places, unless the guards observe strict regulations, to curb their worst impulses. Thus, at both Abu Ghraib and Stanford, "It's not that we put bad apples in a good barrel. We put good apples in a bad barrel. The barrel corrupts anything that it touches" (quoted in Schwartz, 2004). Some might contend that the soldiers in Iraq were only following orders and that, left to their own devices, they would not have chosen to behave as they did. That may be the case, but it only pushes the question back one step: Why did they follow such orders?

Social psychologists seek to find answers to just such questions. They study situations in which people exert influence over one another, as well as the ways people respond to influence attempts of various kinds. Social psychologists are also interested in how people make sense of their world—how they decide what and whom to believe; how they make inferences about the motives, personalities, and abilities of other people; and how they reach conclusions about the causes of events.

Much of what social psychologists have learned about human behavior is invaluable. Social psychology now forms a significant part of the curriculum in many schools of business, public health, social work, education, law, and medicine. Social psychological research on such topics as judgment and decision making, social influence, and how people function in groups is relevant to all those fields. Social psychologists apply their knowledge to important questions concerning individuals and society at large, studying how to reduce stereotyping and prejudice in the classroom and workplace; how to make eyewitness testimony more reliable; how physicians can best use diverse sources of information to make a correct diagnosis; what goes wrong in airplane cockpits when there is an accident or near accident; and how businesses, governments, and individuals can make better decisions.

Research by social psychologists regularly influences government policy. For example, research on the effects of different kinds of welfare programs is used in shaping government assistance policies. Research also affects decisions by the courts. The landmark *Brown* v. *Board of Education* (1954) ruling that struck down school segregation in the United States drew heavily on social psychological research, which indicated that segregated schools were inherently unequal in their effects (and thus unconstitutional).

By the time you finish this book, you will have acquired a greater understanding of yourself and others. You will also have knowledge you can apply in your education, your career, and your interpersonal relationships.

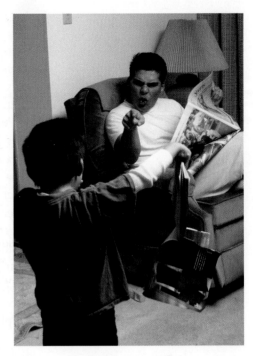

Explaining Situations
Social psychologists seek to understand how individuals act in relation to others in social situations and why. Is this father an especially impatient person, or is his son being particularly obnoxious? If the son is being particularly obnoxious, how might the father behave in order to encourage better behavior in his son?

Events like those at Abu Ghraib can be studied from many viewpoints, including those of anthropologists, criminologists, sociologists, and personality psychologists. Each type of professional takes a different approach to what happened and offers different kinds of explanations.

Personality psychology is a close cousin of social psychology, but it emphasizes individual differences in behavior rather than the social situation. Personality psychologists try to find a consistent pattern in the way a person behaves across situations—an individual's position on a trait dimension. Social psychologists would examine the general situation at Abu Ghraib, in which orders were not clear but the guards were pressured to "soften up" the prisoners to get information about other insurgents and future attacks. Personality psychologists would instead look at whether certain traits and dispositions—for example, sadism or hostility—would predict cruel behavior across a range of situations.

Social psychology is also related to cognitive psychology, the study of how people perceive, think about, and remember aspects of the world. In fact, many psychologists call themselves cognitive social psychologists. Social psychologists differ from cognitive psychologists primarily in that the topics they study are usually social, such as social behavior and perceptions of other people. Cognitive psychologists would be more likely to study categorization processes or memory for words or objects.

Sociology is the study of behavior of people in the aggregate. Sociologists study institutions, subgroups, bureaucracies, mass movements, and changes in the demographic characteristics of populations (for example, age, gender, socioeconomic status). Social psychologists sometimes do sociological work themselves, although they are likely to bring an interest in individual behavior to the study of aggregates. A sociologist might study how economic or government policy influences marriage and divorce rates in a population, whereas a social psychologist would be more likely to study why individuals fall in love, get married, and sometimes get divorced.

The Power of the Situation

Are we all capable of acts of brutality? In 1963 the philosopher Hannah Arendt suggested as much in her controversial book *Eichmann in Jerusalem* (Arendt, 1963). Arendt described the trial of Adolf Eichmann, the notorious architect of Hitler's plan to exterminate the Jews in Nazi-occupied Europe. Advancing a very provocative thesis, Arendt described Eichmann as little more than a bureaucrat doing his job. While not condoning his actions (Arendt herself was Jewish), she argued that Eichmann was not the demented, sadistic person everyone expected (and that the prosecutor claimed he was), but instead a boring, unimaginative cog in a machine that he served with a resigned (if nevertheless perverse) sense of duty. Perhaps even more disturbing, the logical conclusion of Arendt's theory is that any one of us is capable of performing acts of brutality. Look at the person sitting closest to you right now. Do you think that he or she is capable of atrocities? Do you think any situation could be so powerful that an ordinary person—even you—could act as Eichmann did in Nazi Germany or as the prison guards behaved at Abu Ghraib?

Arendt's book created a firestorm of indignant protests, and she was denounced for what many regarded as her attempt to exonerate a monster. But research has supported Arendt's unorthodox views about what she called "the banality of evil." This research raises a question that is central to the study of social psychology: How does the situation people find themselves in affect their behavior?

Kurt Lewin, the founder of modern social psychology, was a Jewish Berliner who fled Nazi Germany in the 1930s and became a professor at the University of Iowa and then at MIT. Lewin was a physicist before becoming a psychologist, and he applied a powerful idea from physics to an understanding of psychological existence. He believed that the behavior of people, like the behavior of objects, is always a function of the field of forces in which they find themselves (Lewin, 1935). To understand how fast a solid object will travel through a medium, for example, we must know such things as the viscosity of the medium, the force of gravity, and any initial force applied to the object. In the case of people, the forces are psychological as well as physical. Of course the person's own attributes are also important determinants of behavior, but these attributes always interact with the situation to produce the resulting behavior.

The field of forces in the case of human behavior is the role of the situation, especially the social situation, in guiding behavior. The main situational influences on our behavior, influences that we often misjudge or fail to see altogether, are the actions—and sometimes just the mere presence—of other people. Friends, romantic partners, even total strangers can cause us to be kinder or meaner, smarter or dumber, lazier or more hardworking, bolder or more cautious. They can produce drastic changes in our beliefs and behavior not only by what they tell us explicitly, but also by modeling through their actions what we should think and do, by subtly implying that our acceptability as a friend or group member depends on adopting their views or behaving as they do. We rely on other people for clues about what emotions to feel in various situations and even to define who we are as individuals. All these effects have been shown in numerous studies demonstrating the power of the situation.

The Milgram Experiment

One of the most striking and famous demonstrations of the power of situations is a classic experiment by psychologist Stanley Milgram (1963, 1974). Milgram advertised in the local newspaper for men to participate in a study on learning and memory at Yale University in exchange for a modest amount of money. (In subsequent experiments, women also participated; the results were similar.) When the volunteers—a mix of laborers, middle-class individuals, and professionals ranging in age from their 20s to their 50s—arrived at the laboratory, a man in a white lab coat told them they would be participating in a study about the effects of punishment on learning. There would be a "teacher" and a "learner," and the learner would try to memorize word pairs such as *wild/duck*. The volunteer and another man, a somewhat heavyset, pleasant-looking man in his late 40s, drew slips of paper to determine who would play which role. But things were not as they seemed: The pleasant-looking man was actually an

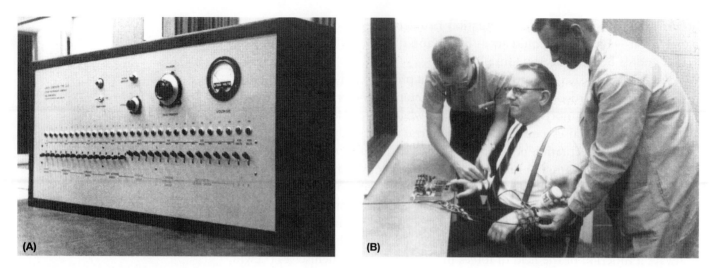

The Milgram Experiment

To examine the role of social influence, Stanley Milgram set up a study in which participants believed they were testing a learner (actually a confederate) and punishing him with shocks when he gave the wrong answer. (A) Milgram's "shock machine." (B) The participant and experimenter attaching electrodes to the "learner" before testing begins.

accomplice, or confederate, of the experimenter, and the drawing was rigged so that he was always the learner.

The participant "teacher" was then instructed to administer shocks—from 15 to 450 volts—to the "learner" each time he made an error. Labels under the shock switches ranged from "slight shock" through "danger: severe shock" to "XXX." The experimenter explained that the teacher was to administer shocks in ascending 15-volt magnitudes: 15 volts the first time the learner made an error, 30 volts the next time, and so on. The teacher was given a 45-volt shock so he would have an idea of how painful the shocks would be. What he didn't know was that the learner, who was in another room, was not actually being shocked.

Most participants became concerned as the shock levels increased and turned to the experimenter to ask what should be done, but the experimenter insisted they go on. The first time a teacher expressed reservations, he was told, "Please continue." If the teacher balked, the experimenter said, "The experiment requires that you continue." If the teacher continued to hesitate, the experimenter said, "It's absolutely essential that you continue." If necessary, the experimenter escalated to, "You have no other choice. You must go on." If the participant asked whether the learner could suffer permanent physical injury, the experimenter said, "Although the shocks may be painful, there is no permanent tissue damage, so please go on."

In the end, despite the learner's groans, pleas, screams, and eventual silence as the intensity of the shocks increased, 80 percent of the participants continued past the 150-volt level—at which point the learner mentioned that he had a heart condition and screamed, "Let me out of here!" Fully 62.5 percent of the participants went all the way to the 450-volt level, delivering everything the shock generator could produce. The *average* amount of shock given was 360 volts, *after* the learner let out an agonized scream and became hysterical.

Milgram and other experts did not expect so many participants to continue to administer shocks as long as they did. (A panel of 39 psychiatrists predicted that only 20 percent of the participants would continue past the 150-volt level and that only 1 percent would continue past the 330-volt level.) At first, some researchers even expressed suspicion about whether Milgram's participants really believed they were shocking the learner. To convince the scientific community that his participants took the situation seriously, Milgram invited social scientists to observe his experiments from behind a one-way mirror. The observers could scarcely believe what they were seeing. One of them reported:

> I observed a mature and initially poised businessman enter the laboratory smiling and confident. Within twenty minutes he was reduced to a twitching, stuttering wreck, who was rapidly approaching a point of nervous collapse. He constantly pulled on his earlobe and twisted his hands. At one point he pushed his fist into his forehead and muttered: "Oh God, let's stop it." And yet he continued to respond to every word of the experimenter and obeyed to the end.
>
> (Milgram, 1963, p. 377)

Milgram's study and its implications are described in more detail in Chapter 9. For now, the important question is: What made the participants in Milgram's study engage in behavior that they had every reason to suspect might seriously harm another person? Milgram's participants were not heartless fiends. Instead, the situation was extraordinarily effective in getting them to do something that would normally fill them with horror. For example, the experiment was presented as a scientific investigation—an unfamiliar situation for most participants. In all probability, the participants had never been in a psychology experiment before, and they had never been in a situation in which they were being asked to do something that could so severely harm another individual. The experimenter explicitly took responsibility for what happened. (Adolf Hitler frequently made similar pledges during the years he marched his nation over a precipice.) Moreover, participants could not have guessed at the outset what the experiment involved, so they were not prepared to resist anyone's demands. And as Milgram stressed, the step-by-step nature of the procedure was undoubtedly crucial. If the participant didn't quit at 225 volts, then why quit at 255? If not at 420, then why at 435?

"Evil is obvious only in retrospect."

—GLORIA STEINEM

Seminarians as Samaritans

A classic experiment by John Darley and Daniel Batson (1973) demonstrates the power of the situation even more simply. These investigators asked students at the Princeton Theological Seminary about the basis of their religious orientation to determine whether particular students were primarily concerned with religion as a means toward personal salvation or were more concerned with religion for its other moral and spiritual values. After determining the basis of their religious orientation, the psychologists asked each young seminarian to go to another building to deliver a short sermon. The seminarians were told what route to follow to get there most easily. Some were told that they had plenty of time to get to the building where they were to deliver the sermon, and some were told that they were already late and should hurry. On the way to deliver their sermon—on the topic of the Good Samaritan, by the way—each of the seminarians passed a man who was sitting in a doorway with his head down, coughing and groaning, and in apparent need of help.

It turned out that the nature of religious orientation was of no use in predicting whether the seminarians would offer assistance. But as you can see in

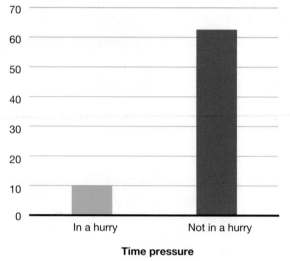

Percentage of seminarians offering help

70
60
50
40
30
20
10
0

In a hurry — Not in a hurry

Time pressure

Figure 1.1

The Power of the Situation and Helping
Princeton seminarians usually helped a "victim" if they were not in a hurry, but rarely helped if they were in a rush.

SOURCE: Darley & Batson, 1973.

dispositions Internal factors, such as beliefs, values, personality traits, and abilities, that guide a person's behavior.

fundamental attribution error The failure to recognize the importance of situational influences on behavior, and the corresponding tendency to overemphasize the importance of dispositions on behavior.

channel factors Situational circumstances that appear unimportant on the surface but that can have great consequences for behavior—facilitating it, blocking it, or guiding it in a particular direction.

Figure 1.1, whether seminarians were in a hurry or not was a very powerful predictor. The seminarians were pretty good Samaritans as a group—but only when they weren't in a rush.

The Fundamental Attribution Error

People are thus governed by situational factors—such as whether they are being pressured by someone or whether they are late—more than they tend to assume. At the same time, internal factors—the kind of person someone is—have much less influence than most people assume they do. You may be surprised by many of the findings reported in this book because most people underestimate the power of the external forces that operate on an individual, and tend to assume, often mistakenly, that the causes of behavior can be found mostly within the person.

Psychologists call internal factors **dispositions**—that is, beliefs, values, personality traits, and abilities that guide behavior. People tend to think of dispositions as the underlying causes of behavior, but that's not necessarily true. Upon seeing a prison guard humiliating a prisoner, we might assume the guard is a cruel person. Noticing a stranger in the street behaving angrily, maybe we'd assume that the person is aggressive or ill tempered. Such judgments are valid far less often than we think. Seeing an acquaintance give a dollar to a beggar may prompt us to assume that the person is generous, but subsequent observations of the person in different situations might show that we had overgeneralized from a single act.

The failure to recognize the importance of situational influences on behavior, together with the tendency to overemphasize the importance of dispositions, was labeled the **fundamental attribution error** by Lee Ross (1977). Many findings in social psychology indicate that people should look for situational factors that might be affecting someone's behavior before assuming that the person has dispositions that match the behavior. As you read this book, you will become more attuned to situational factors and less inclined to assume that behavior can be fully explained by characteristics inherent in the individual. The ultimate lesson of social psychology is thus a compassionate one. Social psychology encourages us to look at another person's situation—to try to understand the complex field of forces acting on the individual—in order to fully understand the person's behavior.

Channel Factors

Kurt Lewin (1952) introduced the concept of **channel factors** to help explain why certain circumstances that appear unimportant on the surface can have great consequences for behavior, either facilitating or blocking it. The term is also meant to reflect that such circumstances can sometimes guide behavior in a particular direction by making it easier to follow one path rather than another.

Consider a study by Howard Leventhal and his colleagues on how to motivate people to take advantage of health facilities' offerings of preventive care (Leventhal, Singer, & Jones, 1965). They attempted to persuade Yale students to get tetanus inoculations. To convince them that the inoculation was in their best interest, the researchers had them read scary materials about the number of ways a person could get tetanus (in addition to the proverbial rusty nail). To make sure they had the students' full attention, the team showed them photos of people in the last stages of lockjaw. But not to worry—the students could avoid this fate simply by going to the student health center at any time and getting a free inoculation. Interviews showed that most participants formed the intention to get an inoculation, but only 3 percent did so. Other participants were given a map of the Yale campus with a circle around the health center and were asked to review their weekly schedule and decide on a convenient time to visit the center and the route they would take to get there. Bear in mind that these were seniors who knew perfectly well where the health center was, so such condescending treatment might produce little more than annoyance. In fact, it increased the percentage of students getting an inoculation ninefold, to 28 percent.

The channel factor in this case was the requirement to shape a vague intention into a concrete plan. A similar channel factor accounts for the use of public health services more generally. Attitudes about health; personality tests; demographic variables such as age, gender, and socioeconomic status; and other individual differences don't do a very good job of predicting who will use these services. The most powerful determinant of usage yet discovered is the distance to the closest facility (Van Dort & Moos, 1976).

The channel factor notion was employed in the "Get Out the Vote" phone call on election eve in the Obama U.S. presidential campaign of 2008. Voters were called and first asked if they were Democrats. If yes, they were asked if they planned to vote (itself producing an increase in voting); if planning to vote, asked if they knew where their polling place was; if not, they were told where it was. In any case they were then asked if they needed help getting to the polling place; if yes, help was offered; if no, they were asked when they planned to vote. And then, the crucial intervention: "Where will you be just before you vote?" After the answer: "What route do you plan to use to get there?" This procedure is now considered "best practice," and both Republicans and Democrats use it.

The channel factor concept is central to a new field at the intersection of social psychology and economics known as behavioral economics. For example, economists have encouraged businesses to get as many of their employees as possible to participate in retirement plans, in which the employer puts money away for the employee's retirement. Rather than have their employees "opt in" to their retirement programs, by checking a box or signing a statement saying they wish to be enrolled in the retirement plan, they create an easy channel for participation by having it be automatic. Employees must check a box or sign a statement saying they *don't* want the retirement plan, or they are automatically enrolled (**Figure 1.2**). This trivial-seeming channel factor creates far more participation (and far happier retirements) than when the channel factor conspires against participation (Choi, Laibson, & Madrian, 2009; Madrian & Shea, 2001).

The Fundamental Attribution Error
If you knew a theology student had come across this person, who was coughing and groaning, and passed the person up without offering help, what would you think of him? Was he an uncaring person, or did some situational factor, such as being in a hurry, cause him to rush past without thinking about what action to take? If you're like most people, you would probably jump to an unfavorable conclusion about the student's personality.

"If you are like most people, then like most people, you don't know you're like most people."
—SOCIAL PSYCHOLOGIST DAN GILBERT

If you do not wish to take part in the retirement plan funded in part by the company, please indicate that by checking the box below.	If you wish to take part in the retirement plan funded in part by the company, please indicate that by checking the box below.
☐	☐

Figure 1.2
How to Have a Happy Retirement
If the box on your new employee form asks the question on the left, you are much more likely to be enrolled in the company's retirement plan than if the box asks the question on the right.

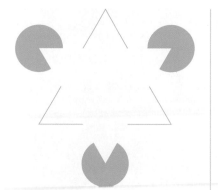

Figure 1.3
Gestalt Principles and Perception
When viewing this figure, known as the Kanizsa triangle, people fill in the empty spaces in their mind and perceive a white triangle.

The Role of Construal

Look at **Figure 1.3**. Do you see a white triangle? Most people do. But in fact there is no white triangle. We construct a triangle in our mind out of the *gaps* in the picture. The gaps are located just where they would be if a triangle were laid over the outlined triangle and a portion of each of the three circles. That makes a good, clear image, but it's entirely a creation of our perceptual apparatus and our background assumptions about the visual world. Both the perceptual process and the assumptions are automatic and nonconscious—that is to say, we're not consciously aware of them. Now that you know the triangle is in your mind's eye and not on the page, do you still see it? Now look at **Figure 1.4**, a painting by surrealist artist Salvador Dali. Dali was a master at using the mind's tendency to construct meaningful figures from the gaps in an image. He created a number of well-known double images—pictures that could be perceived in two different ways, as in this painting.

Interpreting Reality

Our perceptions normally bear a resemblance to what the world is really like, but perception requires substantial interpretation on our part and is subject to significant error under certain conditions. What we see is not necessarily what is actually there but what is plausible—what makes a good, predictable "figure" in light of stored representations we have of the world and what makes sense in light of the context in which we encounter something. German psychologists in the early part of the twentieth century convincingly argued for this view in the case of visual perception. The theoretical orientation of those psychologists centered on the concept of *gestalt*, German for "form" or "figure." The basic idea of **Gestalt psychology** is that objects are perceived not by means of some passive and automatic registering device, but by active, usually nonconscious interpretation of what the object represents. The belief we have that we see the world directly, without any complicated perceptual or cognitive machinery "doctoring" the data, is referred to by philosophers and social psychologists as "naïve realism" (Pronin, Gilovich, & Ross, 2004; Ross & Ward, 1996).

What's true for visual perception is even truer for judgments about the social world. Our judgments and beliefs are actively constructed from perceptions and thoughts. They are not simple readouts of reality.

In his study of obedience (discussed above), Milgram manipulated his participants' understanding of the situation they found themselves in by lulling

Gestalt psychology Based on the German word *gestalt*, meaning "form" or "figure," this approach stresses the fact that people perceive objects not by means of some automatic registering device but by active, usually nonconscious interpretation of what the object represents as a whole.

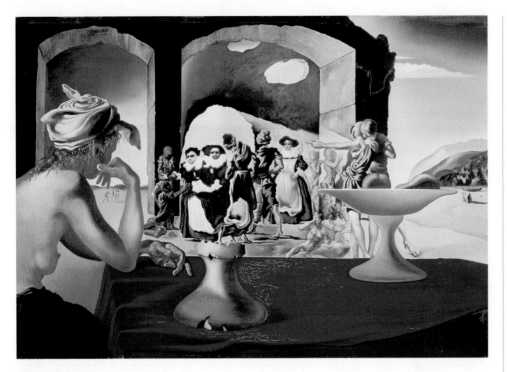

Figure 1.4
Gestalt Principles in Art

In his *Slave Market with Disappearing Bust of Voltaire*, Salvador Dali confronts the viewer with the bust of the French philosopher Voltaire (at center of painting). But on closer inspection, the bust is largely the product of the gap in the wall behind the two merchants. Their faces form Voltaire's eyes, and their collars form his nose and cheeks.

them with soothing interpretations of events that were designed to throw them off the scent of anything that could be regarded as sinister. A "study participant" who had "chosen" to be in the "experiment" was "learning" a list of words with "feedback" that was given by the real participant in the form of electric shock.

A *participant* is someone who is acting freely; *learning* is a normal activity that often depends on *feedback*, generally an innocuous form of information. All this was taking place in the context of an *experiment*, a benign activity carried out by trustworthy scientists. Our **construal** of situations and behavior refers to our interpretation of them and to the inferences, often nonconscious, that we make about them. Whether we regard people as free agents or victims, as freedom fighters or terrorists, as migrant workers or illegal aliens, will affect our perceptions of their actions. And our perceptions drive our behavior toward them.

Participants in the Milgram experiment were not simply registering what the situation was; they were interpreting it in ways that the experimenter was encouraging.

Schemas

How do we know how to behave in different kinds of situations? For example, suppose you're riding on an uncrowded train and someone asks you to give up

First umpire: "I call 'em as I see 'em."
Second umpire: "I call 'em as they are."
Third umpire: "They ain't nothin' till I call 'em."

construal An interpretation of or inference about the stimuli or situations people confront.

schema A knowledge structure consisting of any organized body of stored information.

"Without a profound simplification the world around us would be an infinite, undefined tangle that would defy our ability to orient ourselves and decide upon our actions. . . .We are compelled to reduce the knowable to a schema."

—NOVELIST PRIMO LEVI

your seat so the person can sit; what prompts you to respond in a particular way? Do you refuse, ask for an explanation, pretend not to hear, or promptly surrender the seat? For that matter, how do you know how to behave in even the most ordinary situations, such as attending a college seminar?

Although it usually seems as though we understand social situations immediately and directly, we actually depend on elaborate stores of systematized knowledge to understand even the simplest and most "obvious" situation. These knowledge stores are called **schemas**, generalized knowledge about the physical and social world, such as what kind of behavior to expect when dealing with a minister, a sales clerk, a professor, or a panhandler and how to behave in a seminar, at a funeral, at a McDonald's or a four-star restaurant, or when riding on a crowded or empty subway. There is even a schema—alleged to be universal—for falling in love.

Schemas capture the regularities of life and lead us to have certain expectations we can rely on so we don't have to invent the world anew all the time. There is a schema for "a party," for example: we expect people to act cheerful, excited, talkative, and maybe a little silly.

An early experiment by Solomon Asch (1940), another of the German founders of social psychology who immigrated to the United States in the 1930s, shows that schemas can sometimes operate very subtly to influence judgments. Asch asked two groups of undergraduates to rank various professions in terms of prestige. One of the professions was politician. Before they gave their own ratings, the participants in one group were told that a sample of fellow students had previously ranked politicians near the top in prestige, whereas the participants in the other group were told that their fellow students had ranked politicians near the bottom. This manipulation affected the participants' judgments substantially, but not because it changed their minds about politicians or because they were trying to conform. Asch was able to show that participants in the first

Schemas

Our schemas—generalized knowledge about the physical and social world—help us know what is expected of us and how to behave in particular situations. (A) Our schema of a pizza shop leads us to order at a counter, wait for the pizza to be ready, and then either take it to an empty table or take it home to eat. (B) In contrast, our schema of a high-end restaurant leads us to be seated at a table with silverware, glasses, and a tablecloth; to choose what we want from a menu; to order at the table; and to be served food and wine by a waiter.

group took the label *politician* to refer to statesmen of the caliber of Thomas Jefferson and Franklin D. Roosevelt. Participants in the second group were rating something closer to corrupt political hacks. It wasn't that the participants were blindly going along with the ratings of their peers. Rather, the different schemas activated by their peers' ratings served to define just what it was that participants were supposed to be judging.

Many of the persuasion attempts we are exposed to in the media have the goal not so much of changing our judgment about something, but rather of changing what it is that's being judged. Advocates of legal abortion try to call up schemas related to *free choice*, while anti-abortion activists try to activate schemas related to *murder*. Affirmative action advocates encourage schemas related to *diversity*, and those opposed to affirmative action try to activate schemas related to *fairness*.

Stereotypes

Much work in social psychology has been dedicated to the study of **stereotypes**—schemas that we have for people of various kinds. Research on stereotyping examines the content of these person schemas and how they are applied and sometimes misapplied in order to facilitate—or derail—the course of interaction. We tend to judge individuals based on particular person schemas we have—stereotypes about a person's nationality, gender, religion, occupation, neighborhood, or sorority. Such summaries may be necessary to function efficiently and effectively. But they can be wrong, they can be applied in the wrong way and to the wrong people, and they can be given too much weight in relation to more specific information we have about a particular person (or would have if we didn't assume that the stereotype is all we need to know). The frequently pernicious role of stereotypes is the subject of an entire chapter of this book (Chapter 11).

stereotype A belief that certain attributes are characteristic of members of a particular group.

Stereotypes and Construal
Stereotypes are schemas about people of a certain kind. We construe people in light of the stereotypes they call up. Would you be surprised to know that the fellow in this picture is a wealthy lawyer who plays polo and frequents trendy bars in Manhattan? None of these things is true, and you relied on your stereotypes to prevent you from entertaining those possibilities.

Automatic vs. Controlled Processing

How would you react if you saw a stranger at an airport carrying a backpack, looking agitated, and sweating profusely? In the post-9/11 world, you might fear that such a person might be carrying a bomb and that you could become a victim of a terrorist attack. The mind processes information in two ways when you encounter a social situation. One is automatic and nonconscious, often based on emotional factors, and the other is conscious and systematic and more likely to be controlled by careful thought. Often, emotional reactions occur before conscious thought takes over. Thus, your fearful reaction to the person with the backpack might automatically kick in without any special thought on your part. But when you start thinking systematically, you realize that he might have just come in from the summer heat, that he might be agitated because he's late for his plane, and that there's no reason to suspect he might be carrying a bomb or threatening your safety in any other way.

Research by Patricia Devine and her colleagues has shown how automatic and controlled processing can result in quite different attitudes in the same person toward members of outgroups (Devine, 1989a, 1989b; Devine, Monteith, Zuwerink, & Elliot, 1991; Devine, Plant, Amodio, Harmon-Jones, & Vance, 2002). People with low expressed prejudice toward an outgroup may nevertheless reveal feelings toward people in the outgroup that are almost as prejudiced as those of people who confess to explicit disliking of the group. For example, experimenters asked some white participants to read words reminiscent of African-Americans and then read a brief description of someone whose race was not specified. Those participants were more likely to report that the individual was hostile than were participants who hadn't read such words. And this was true whether or not they were willing to express anti-black attitudes in a questionnaire—in other words, whether or not they were openly prejudiced. The judgments of the "unprejudiced people" were revealed to be just as prejudiced as their explicitly prejudiced counterparts when studied by a technique that examines nonconscious processing of information.

In related research, Anthony Greenwald and his colleagues showed that the great majority of white people take longer to associate black faces with pleasant stimuli than to classify white faces with pleasant stimuli (Greenwald, McGhee, & Schwartz, 1998). This was true even for participants who showed no overt prejudice when asked about their attitudes.

In general, automatic processes give rise to *implicit* attitudes and beliefs that can't be readily controlled by the conscious mind; and controlled, conscious processing results in *explicit* attitudes and beliefs of which we are aware—though

these may become implicit or nonconscious over time. It's important to recognize, too, that participants in these experiments were not necessarily dissembling. They likely were genuinely ignorant of the extent of the bias that was revealed by the implicit measures of attitude.

As another example of nonconscious cognitive processes, consider the impact of social categories on judgments and behavior. Easily discernible personal features, such as gender, race, and age, tend to trigger stereotypes that a person uses in forming judgments about other people, even when the person is unaware that these social categories have influenced the judgment in question (Blair, Judd, & Fallman, 2004; Brewer, 1988; Macrae, Stangor, & Milne, 1994). Even behavior can be nonconsciously influenced by social categories. Bargh, Chen, and Burrows (1996) found that just mentioning words that call to mind elderly people (*cane, Florida*) causes college students to walk down a hall more slowly. And others have found that activating the concept of "professor" actually makes students do better on a trivia test (Dijksterhuis & van Knippenberg, 1998).

Types of Nonconscious Processing

Social psychologists have shown that much of our cognitive activity is hidden from us. In solving problems, sometimes we're well aware of the relevant factors we're dealing with and the procedures we're using to work with them. For example, when you solve a math problem ("Take half the base, multiply it by the height and . . ."), you generally know exactly what formula you're using. But these sorts of cognitive processes—where you are conscious of most of what is going on in your head—are rarer than you might think. Often we can't correctly explain the reasons for our judgments about other people, our understanding of the causes of physical and social events, or what led us to choose one job applicant over another (or one romantic partner over another, for that matter).

In one experiment making this point about awareness, researchers asked customers in a mall to evaluate the quality of four nightgowns laid out in a row on a table (Nisbett & Wilson, 1977). Customers were by far most likely to give the highest rating to the last nightgown they examined. Yet in response to whether the position of the nightgowns had influenced their judgments about quality, they were astonished that the questioner could think they might have been influenced by such a trivial, irrelevant factor!

Often we can't even identify some of the crucial factors that affect our beliefs and behavior. John Bargh and Paula Pietromonaco presented words on a computer screen for one-tenth of a second, and then to make sure the participants were unaware of what they had seen, they presented a "masking stimulus" consisting of a line of Xs where the word had been (Bargh & Pietromonaco, 1982). Some participants were exposed to words with a hostile meaning and some to neutral words. The participants then read about one "Donald," whose behavior was ambiguous as to whether it could be construed as hostile. ("A salesman knocked at the door, but Donald refused to let him enter.") Participants exposed to the hostility-related words rated Donald as being more hostile than participants exposed to the neutral words. Immediately after reading the paragraph, participants were unable to distinguish words they had seen from those they hadn't seen, and didn't even know that words had been flashed at all.

There are by now literally hundreds of demonstrations of influences on important judgments and behavior of which people are unaware. For example:

- If a freshman is assigned randomly to a dorm room in which the roommate is a drinker, he gets worse grades; if the student himself was a drinker in high school, the cost to his grades of the drinking roommate is very great (Kremer & Levy, 2003). (We use masculine pronouns advisedly. Women seem to be immune to this particular kind of influence.)

Types of Nonconscious Processing
There is much less violence in housing project buildings surrounded by greenery than in buildings surrounded by concrete.

- When people are surrounded by greenery they are less aggressive than when in an environment with lots of red in it (Kuo & Sullivan, 2001).
- When people read a persuasive communication in a room with a fishy smell, they are less likely to be persuaded by it than if there is no distinctive smell or an unpleasant smell that isn't fishy (Lee & Schwarz, 2012). (This works, though, only in cultures where dubious propositions are described as "fishy.")

Here's something you can try for yourself. Have a conversation with someone in which you deliberately change your body position from time to time. Fold your arms for a couple of minutes. Shift most of your weight to one side. Put one hand in a pocket. Watch what your conversation partner does after each change and try not to giggle. "Ideomotor mimicry" is something we engage in quite nonconsciously. When people don't do it, the encounter can become awkward and unsatisfying.

You will read countless examples in this book of the effects of various stimuli and situations that exert their effects without our conscious awareness. Indeed, if the effects in a given study were consciously produced, you wouldn't have to read about it in this book; you would already know about it.

Functions of Nonconscious Processing

Why does so much mental processing take place outside of our awareness? Partly, it's a matter of efficiency. Conscious processes are generally slow and can run only serially—one step or one problem at a time. Automatic processes are typically much faster and can operate in parallel. When we recognize a face as belonging to a fourth-grade classmate, we have done so by processing numerous features (forehead, eyes, chin, coloring, and so on) at the same time and holistically. Recognizing each feature one step at a time would leave us hopelessly mired in computation. And it's quite handy to be able to drive on autopilot while enjoying the scenery or carrying on a conversation. (Just make sure the conversation is with someone physically in the car with you. Talking on a hand-held or hands-free cell phone while driving is a very different type of activity in many respects, and one that substantially increases your risk of having an accident.)

We're not conscious of many of the stimuli that influence us, and we're not fully aware of the cognitive processes that underlie our judgments and behaviors. Conscious mental activity is slow, and it's no more essential to know what processes produce our behavior than it is to know what processes underlie perception or memory. The crucial thing is for us to respond rapidly and efficiently to a given situation.

A very important implication of the concept of nonconscious processing of stimuli is that research on human behavior should not normally depend on people's verbal reports about why they believe something or why they engaged in a particular behavior. Since people often can't really give accurate reports, what they say may mislead rather than enlighten the researcher. Instead, social psychologists have to craft experiments to isolate the true causes of people's behavior.

🔄 LOOKING BACK

Much of our behavior, and many kinds of construal processes, occur without our awareness, sometimes without an awareness of even the stimuli to which we are responding. We tend to overestimate how accessible our mental processes are to our consciousness.

Evolution and Human Behavior: How We Are the Same

Why do human beings generally live in family groups, assign roles to people on the basis of age and gender, own property, adorn their bodies, classify flora and fauna, and have rites of passage and myths? Evolution may explain such behaviors (Conway & Schaller, 2002).

Evolutionary theory has been around for about 150 years, ever since Charles Darwin published *The Origin of Species*. Darwin discovered many modifications in animal and plant characteristics that had occurred over time in the Galápagos Islands. The theory has proved invaluable in understanding why organisms of all kinds have the properties they do, and how they come to have them. The key idea is that a process of **natural selection** operates on animals and plants, so that adaptive traits—those that enhance the probability of survival and reproduction—are passed on to subsequent generations. Organisms that die before they reproduce may be unlucky, or they may possess survival characteristics that are less than optimal in their particular environments. And those organisms that don't reproduce won't pass on these nonadaptive characteristics (through their genes) to a new generation. Those that do survive and reproduce give their genes a chance to live on in their offspring, along with the possibility that their characteristics will be represented in at least one more generation. Disadvantageous characteristics are selected against; characteristics better adapted to the environment are selected for.

Darwin himself assumed that natural selection operates for behavioral inclinations, just as it does for physical characteristics such as size, coloring, or susceptibility to parasites. In addition, the number and importance of things that are universally true about humans is certainly consistent with the idea that much of what we share is at least partly the result of natural selection and is encoded in our genes. Recent developments in evolutionary theory and comparative biology, together with anthropological findings and studies by psychologists, have produced evidence that the theory of evolution can be quite helpful in explaining why people behave the way they do.

Human Universals

One theme that's consistent with evolutionary theory is that many human behaviors and institutions are universal, or very nearly so (Schaller, Simpson, & Kenrick, 2006). In the process of human evolution, we've acquired basic behavioral propensities, much as we've acquired physical features like bipedalism (having two legs), that help us adapt to the physical and social environment.

Table 1.1 contains a list of reputed universals. Two things are worth noting about the practices listed in the table, aside from their alleged universality. One is that humans share some of these characteristics with other animals, especially the higher primates. These include facial expressions (almost all of which we share with chimpanzees and some other animals), dominance and submission, food sharing, group living (true of all primates except orangutans), greater aggressiveness on the part of males (true of almost all mammals), preference

natural selection An evolutionary process that molds animals and plants so that traits that enhance the probability of survival and reproduction are passed on to subsequent generations.

TABLE 1.1 UNIVERSAL BEHAVIORS, REACTIONS, AND INSTITUTIONS

SEX, GENDER, AND THE FAMILY

Copulation normally conducted privately	Sexual jealousy	Sexual regulation
Live in family (or household)	Marriage	Husband usually older than wife
Sexual modesty	Division of labor by gender	Males more physically aggressive
Females do more child care	Mother-son incest unthinkable	Incest prevention and avoidance
Preference for own kin	Sex differences in spatial cognition	

SOCIAL DIFFERENTIATION

Age statuses	Classification of kin	Leaders
Ingroup distinguished from outgroup	Division of labor by age	

SOCIAL CUSTOMS

Baby talk	Pretend play	Group living
Dance	Rites of passage	Law (rights and obligations)
Dominance/submission	Taboo foods	Feasting
Practice to improve skills	Body adornment	Property
Hygienic care	Death rites	Rituals
Magic to sustain and improve life	Etiquette	Taboo utterances
Magic to win love	Gossip	Toys
Nonbody decorative art	Food sharing	

EMOTION

Childhood fear of strangers	Wariness around snakes	Rhythm
Facial expressions of fear, anger, disgust, happiness, sadness, and surprise	Envy	Melody

COGNITION

Aesthetics	Anthropomorphism of animals	Myths
Belief in supernatural, religion	Medicine	Taxonomy
Classification of flora and fauna	Language	Narrative

SOURCE: Compiled by Donald Brown, 1991; appearing in Pinker, 2002.

for own kin (almost surely true of all mammals), and wariness around snakes (true of all the large primates, including humans). The other, even more striking aspect of Table 1.1 is that the number of universals we share with other animals is quite small.

The bulk of Table 1.1 represents a large number of behaviors and institutions that appear to be effective adaptations for highly intelligent, group-living, upright-walking, language-using animals that are capable of living in almost any kind of ecology. These universals are compatible with an evolutionary interpretation

Universal Facial Expressions Chimpanzees and humans express dominance and submission, anger and fear, through similar facial expressions.

(we are a particular kind of creature, qualitatively different from any other, with many adaptations so effective that they have become wired into our biology). But some theorists believe that the commonalities can be accounted for as simply the result of our species' superior intelligence. For example, every human group figures out for itself that incest is a bad idea and that classification of flora is useful.

Group Living, Language, and Theory of Mind

Group living contributed to survival in ages past. Groups provided protection from predators and greater success in hunting game and finding foraging areas. The ability to produce and understand language has enabled people to live in groups and convey not only emotions and intentions to others, but also beliefs, attitudes, and complex thoughts.

There is strong evidence that infants are born with their brain "prewired" to acquire language, perhaps because of its importance to humans living together in groups (Pinker, 1994). Normal children learn language at developmental stages that are almost identical from one culture to another. At birth, all infants can produce the full range of possible sounds (phonemes) that exist in the totality of languages spoken anywhere on Earth, and they babble all these sounds in the crib. Language acquisition consists of dropping all the "wrong" phonemes that are not used by the child's particular language. Thus, children can learn to speak any language, depending on where they grow up; they can learn to speak their native language perfectly well even if they grow up with deaf parents who never speak at all; and twins can sometimes develop their own unique language in the crib, a language that follows rules of grammar in the same way as formally recognized languages do (Pinker, 1994, 2002). These findings indicate that there are general, inherited propensities to develop grammatical language.

Just as evolution has prepared humans to live together in groups and to communicate to promote survival and reproduction, it also may have provided humans with a **theory of mind**—the ability to recognize that other people have beliefs and desires. Children recognize before the age of 2 that the way to understand

theory of mind The understanding that other people have beliefs and desires.

Theory of Mind
Temple Grandin is a high-functioning autistic woman who is a doctor of animal science and professor. As a child, she was mocked with the epithet "tape recorder" for her habit of constantly repeating things. She has described her under-standing of the emotions and beliefs of other people as being so poor that she feels like "an anthropologist on Mars." She understands the pain and terror of animals sufficiently well, however, that she has been able to devise humane methods of slaughtering them.

other people's behavior is to understand their beliefs and desires (Asch, 1952; Kuhlmeier, Wynn, & Bloom, 2003; Leslie, 2000; Malle, Moses, & Baldwin, 2001). By the age of 3 or 4, theory of mind is sophisticated enough that children can recognize when other people's beliefs are false (Wellman, 1990).

Some of the most powerful evidence for a biologically based theory of mind comes from studying people who, through a genetic defect or physical or chemical trauma before or after birth, seem not to have a theory of mind, or to have only a weak version of one. Such a claim has been made about people with *autism*, a disorder characterized by the inability to adequately communicate with others and interact with them. Autistic individuals do not seem able to compre-hend others' desires or beliefs, including the fact that others' beliefs might be false (Perner, Frith, Leslie, & Leekam, 1989). Autistic children can have nor-mal or even superior intellectual functioning, but less comprehension of people's beliefs and desires, than children with Down syndrome, whose general intellec-tual functioning is far below normal. It seems plausible that evolution has pro-vided us with a kind of understanding that is too universally essential to leave to chance or laborious trial-and-error learning. Given the importance of accurately understanding other people's beliefs and intentions, it would not be surprising that a theory of mind comes prewired.

Evolution and Gender Roles

Why is polygyny (one man with several wives) more common than polyandry (one woman with several husbands)? Why do women tend to care more than men about a potential partner's financial prospects? The evolutionary approach provides a possible answer to such questions in its theory of **parental investment**. In almost all mammalian species, the two sexes have different costs and bene-fits associated with the nurturing of offspring, largely because the number of offspring a female can have over the course of her lifetime is limited. The value

parental investment The evolutionary principle that costs and benefits are associated with reproduction and the nurturing of offspring. Because these costs and benefits are different for males and females, one gender will normally value and invest more in each child than will the other.

of each child to her is therefore relatively high—her investment in each is great. And it's in the interest of her genes to see to it that each infant grows to maturity; therefore her mate's ability to support her is very important. For males, however, a nearly unlimited number of offspring is theoretically possible because so little energy is involved in creating them. (Fourteenth-century conqueror Ghengis Khan is reported to have impregnated literally thousands of women!) A male can walk away from copulation and never see his mate or offspring again. Even if the male stays with the female and their offspring, however, his investment in the offspring is less than that of the female. The economic resources of a female with whom he has reproduced are of less consequence to him. Evolution thus provides one way of looking at many seemingly universal tendencies related to gender roles and child rearing.

Avoiding the Naturalistic Fallacy

Evolutionary theory as applied to human behavior is controversial. The claim that there are biologically based differences between women and men in behaviors related to mate choice is particularly objectionable to some people. Such notions are controversial in part because they follow a long history of mistaken claims about biological differences that have been used to legitimize and perpetuate male privilege (Bem, 1993).

Even more objectionable, evolutionary theory has been invoked as justification for viewing the different human "races" almost as separate subspecies. Indeed, in the early twentieth century, Darwin's ideas were used to justify the struggle of some groups of people to achieve supremacy over others—the notion that might determines right. This so-called social Darwinist movement incorrectly interpreted "the survival of the fittest" to mean the survival of one human group in competition with another human group, rather than one individual's struggle to survive and reproduce in its environment. Similarly distorted versions of Darwin's theory were also used to justify fascism and the ruthless domination of the weak by the strong.

Evolutionary claims about human behavior can also lead people to assume, mistakenly, that biology is destiny—that what we are biologically predisposed to do is what we inevitably will do and perhaps even should do. This claim—that the way things *are* is the way they *should be*—is known as the **naturalistic fallacy**, and it has no logical foundation. We are predisposed to do many things that we can overcome. Virtually all human societies are plagued by violence in everyday life, for example, but the incidence of it over the past few centuries has declined astronomically. The chances of being killed in various parts of England declined from the thirteenth century to the twentieth by factors ranging from 10 to 100 (Pinker, 2011). The most horrendous forms of torture, such as breaking all the bones in a person's body on the rack, are no longer practiced in Europe. Even in the past century, political leaders like Theodore Roosevelt and Winston Churchill did not hesitate to praise colonial wars and the damage done by them to subject peoples. But it would be unthinkable for their modern successors to express such sentiments. Civilization can be regarded as the never-ceasing attempt to modify much of what comes naturally, reducing the extent to which human life, as seventeenth-century philosopher Thomas Hobbes put it, is "poor, nasty, brutish, and short."

naturalistic fallacy The claim that the way things *are* is the way they *should be*.

The fact that a theory can be misused is no reason to reject the theory itself in all its aspects. Caution about evolutionary claims is called for. What is not called for, however, is a rejection of evolutionary ideas out of hand.

Social Neuroscience

Evolutionary approaches to the study of social behavior alert us to the fact that everything humans do or think takes place on a biological substrate. In recent years, social psychologists have begun to examine the biological grounding for all behavior: the brain. There is a new field focusing on the neural underpinnings of social behavior called *social neuroscience.*

One of the chief tools of this new science is a technology known as functional magnetic resonance imaging (fMRI). While a person is experiencing different emotions or solving various problems, blood flows to the areas of the brain that are active. Scientists can take a picture of the brain that detects this blood flow, thus showing which brain regions mediate various feelings and behaviors.

Researchers in social neuroscience have reached intriguing conclusions about the areas of the brain that function most when we are feeling angry, fearful, or amorous (Heatherton, Macrae, & Kelley, 2004; Ochsner & Lieberman, 2001); when we're excited about the possibility of winning something valuable or worried about the prospect of losing it (Knutson et al., 2008; Tom, Fox, Trepel, & Poldrack, 2007); when we conclude that an action is morally reprehensible (Borg, Hyunes, Van Horn, Grafton, & Sinnott-Armstrong, 2006; Borg, Lieberman, & Kiehl, 2008; Greene, Sommerville, Nystrom, Darley, & Cohen, 2001); and when we're solving various kinds of cognitive and social problems.

New studies are finding the specific brain structures that are activated when we're rejected socially and when we're esteemed by others (Muscatell & Eisenberger, 2012). Research is also beginning to show which parts of the brain become active for different motivational and emotional states. Other studies have begun to clearly map the different regions involved in reading other people's mental states, referred to as the mentalizing network (Lieberman, 2007, 2013). You may be intrigued to discover that this region is less active when powerful people attempt to interpret the emotions of others than when people with little power attempt to interpret others' emotions. This finding makes sense in light of what we know about the effects of power on relationships, discussed in Chapter 10.

In other lines of research, neuroscientists have provided a window into the development of social behavior by tracing physical changes in the brain. For example, it turns out that a region of the brain that alerts people to danger is poorly developed until early adulthood (Decety & Michalska, 2010). This late development of an important brain region may help explain why adolescents take greater risks (in how they drive, for instance) than people in their mid-20s and beyond. Neuroscience has also revealed that later in life, the brain regions that mediate learning, notably the prefrontal cortex, decay particularly rapidly with increasing age. These findings help explain why older adults find it more difficult to learn than younger people (Dempster, 1992; Raz et al., 1997; Shimamura, 1994).

Neuroscience not only tells us which areas of the brain function most when certain kinds of activities are taking place. It also

"Young man, go to your room and stay there until your cerebral cortex matures."

informs us about how the brain, the mind, and behavior function as a unit and how social factors influence each of these components at the same time.

⬤ LOOKING BACK

Evolutionary theory informs our understanding of human behavior, just as it does our understanding of the physical characteristics of plants and animals. The many universals of human behavior suggest that some of these behaviors may be prewired—especially language and theory of mind. Differential parental investment of males and females may help us understand certain differences between women and men. Although misunderstandings and misapplications of evolutionary ideas sometimes make people suspicious of it, the theory has important implications for the field of social psychology.

Culture and Human Behavior: How We Are Different

The most important legacy of evolution for human beings is the great flexibility it allows for adaptation to different circumstances. The enormous range of behaviors that people exhibit is tied to the fact that humans, together with rats, are the most successful of all the mammals in our ability to live in virtually every type of ecosystem. Our adaptability and the range of environments we have evolved in have resulted in extraordinary differences between human cultures. Depending on the prevailing culture, humans may be more or less likely to cooperate with each other, to assign different roles to men and women, or to try to distinguish themselves as individuals.

Cultural Differences in Social Relations and Self-Understanding

Until fairly recently, psychologists regarded cultural differences as being limited primarily to differences in beliefs, preferences, and values. Some cultures regard the world as having been created by a supernatural force, some by impersonal natural forces, and some don't ponder the question much at all. The French like to eat fatty goose liver, the Chinese like to eat chicken feet, Americans like to eat cotton candy—and each group has trouble appreciating the tastes preferred by the other groups. These differences, while interesting, are not the sort of thing that would make anyone suspect that fundamentally different psychological theories are needed to account for the behavior of people in different societies.

Recent research, however, shows that cultural differences go far deeper than beliefs and values. In fact, they extend all the way to the level of fundamental forms of self-conception and social existence, and even to the perceptual and cognitive processes people use to develop new thoughts and beliefs (Henrich, Heine, & Norenzayan, 2010). Many of these differences are discussed throughout the book, but one set of interrelated tendencies is particularly central, and we introduce it here.

To get a feel for this set of tendencies, think about the following propositions. How plausible do you find each one?

- People have substantial control over their life outcomes, and they much prefer situations in which they have choice and control to those in which they do not.

- People want to achieve personal success. They find that relationships with other people can sometimes make it harder to attain their goals.

- People want to be unique, to be different from other people in significant respects.

- People want to feel good about themselves. Excelling in some ways and being assured of their good qualities by other people are important to personal well-being.

- People like their relationships with others to be based on mutuality and equality, but if some people have more power than others, most people prefer to be in the superior position.

- People believe that the same rules should apply to everyone; individuals should not be singled out for special treatment because of their personal attributes or connections to important people. Justice is, or should be, blind.

Hundreds of millions of people are reasonably well described by these propositions, but those people tend to be found in particular parts of the world—namely, Western Europe and many of the present and former nations of the British Commonwealth, including the United States, Canada, and Australia. These societies tend to be highly **independent** (or **individualistic**) **cultures** (Fiske, Kitayama, Markus, & Nisbett, 1998; Hofstede, 1980; Hsu, 1953; Markus & Kitayama, 1991; Triandis, 1995). Westerners think of themselves as distinct social entities, tied to each other by bonds of affection and organizational memberships to be sure, but essentially separate from other people and having attributes that exist in the absence of any connection to others. They tend to see their associations with other people, even their own family members, as voluntary and subject to termination once those associations become sufficiently troublesome or unproductive (**Table 1.2**).

But these characterizations describe other people less well. In fact, they provide a poor description of most of the world's people, particularly the citizens of East Asian countries such as China (Triandis, McCusker, & Hui, 1990), Japan

independent (individualistic) culture A culture in which people tend to think of themselves as distinct social entities, tied to each other by voluntary bonds of affection and organizational memberships but essentially separate from other people and having attributes that exist in the absence of any connection to others.

TABLE 1.2 INDEPENDENT VS. INTERDEPENDENT CULTURES	
INDEPENDENT CULTURES	INTERDEPENDENT CULTURES
Conception of the self as distinct from others, with attributes that are constant	Conception of the self as inextricably linked to others, with attributes depending on the situation
Insistence on ability to act on one's own	Preference for collective action
Need for individual distinctiveness	Desire for harmonious relations within group
Preference for egalitarianism and achieved status based on accomplishments	Acceptance of hierarchy and ascribed status based on age, group membership, and other attributes
Conviction that rules governing behavior should apply to everyone	Preference for rules that take context and particular relationships into account

BOX 1.1 **FOCUS ON *CULTURE***

Dick and Jane, Deng and Janxing

The first page of a reader for American children from the 1930s shows a little boy running with his dog. "See Dick run," the primer reads. "See Dick run and play." "See Spot run." The first page of a Chinese reader from the same era shows a little boy sitting on the shoulders of a bigger boy. "Big Brother loves Little Brother," reads the text. "Little Brother loves Big Brother." The difference between what

the American child and the Chinese child of the 1930s were exposed to on the first day of class says much about the differences between their worlds. The American child is taught to orient toward action and to be prepared to live in a world where control and individual choice are possible. The Chinese child is more likely to be taught to be attuned to relationships. To the Westerner, it makes sense to speak of the

existence of the person apart from any group. To East Asians (such as Chinese, Japanese, and Koreans) and to many of the world's other peoples, the person exists only as a member of a larger collective—family, friends, village, corporation. People are related to one another like ropes in a net, completely interconnected and having no real existence without the connections (Munro, 1985).

Attention to Action vs. Relationships

(A) The Dick and Jane readers of the United States emphasize action and individualism, as shown here with the drawing of Dick running and the words "See Dick. See Dick run." (B) East Asian readers are more likely to emphasize relationships, as seen in this Chinese reader in which two boys walk down the street with their arms around each other. The text says, "Xiao Zhiang is a very nice boy. He is my best friend. We always study together and play together. We have a lot of fun together."

(Bond & Cheung, 1983), and Korea (Rhee, Uleman, Lee, & Roman, 1995), as well as people from South Asian countries such as India (Dhawan, Roseman, Naidu, Thapa, & Rettek, 1995; Savani, Markus, & Conner, 2008) and Malaysia (Bochner, 1994), people from the Middle East (Greenberg, Eloul, Markus, & Tsai, 2012), people from many Latin American countries (Gabrielidis, Stephan, Pearson, & Villareal, 1997; Triandis, Bontempo, Villareal, Asai, & Lucca, 1988), and people from Eastern Europe (Grossmann & Kross, 2010; Varnum, Grossmann, Katunar, Nisbett, & Kitayama, 2008). These societies represent more

interdependent (or **collectivistic**) **cultures**. People in such cultures do not have as much freedom or personal control over their lives, and they do not necessarily want or need either (Sastry & Ross, 1998).

Such differences between people in independent and interdependent societies have important implications for the nature of their personal goals and strivings, values, and beliefs, as **Box 1.1** illustrates. Success is important to East Asians, but in good part because it brings credit to the family and other groups to which they belong, rather than merely as a reflection of personal merit.

Personal uniqueness is not very important to interdependent peoples and may in fact even be undesirable. In a clever experiment by Kim and Markus (1999), Korean and American participants were offered a pen as a gift for being in a study. Several of the pens were of one color and one pen was of another color. Americans tended to choose the unique color and Koreans the common color. Being unique and being better than others are not so important for interdependent people to feel good about themselves; moreover, feeling good about themselves is itself not as important a goal as it is for Westerners and other independent peoples (Heine, Lehman, Markus, & Kitayama, 1999).

Interdependent people tend not to expect or even value mutuality and equality in relationships; on the contrary, they're likely to expect hierarchical relations to be the rule (Hsu, 1953; Triandis, 1987, 1995). They tend not to be universalists in their understanding of social norms; instead, they believe in different strokes for different folks. Justice should keep her eyes wide open, paying attention to the particular circumstances of each case that comes before her.

Individualism and Collectivism in the Workplace

One of the first social scientists to measure independence (or individualism) versus interdependence (or collectivism) was Geert Hofstede (1980), who surveyed the values of tens of thousands of IBM employees around the world. **Table 1.3**

interdependent (collectivistic) culture A culture in which people tend to define themselves as part of a collective, inextricably tied to others in their group and placing less importance on individual freedom or personal control over their lives.

"Culture is an inherited habit."
—FRANCIS FUKUYAMA

Among traditional Kenyan tribespeople, the individualist is "looked upon with suspicion.... There is no really individual affair, for everything has a moral and social influence."
—JOMO KENYATTA (1938), FIRST PRESIDENT OF INDEPENDENT KENYA

TABLE 1.3 INDEPENDENT AND INTERDEPENDENT CULTURES ON THE JOB	
INDEPENDENT CULTURES	**INTERDEPENDENT CULTURES**
Want to get the recognition they deserve when they do a good job	Want the employer to have a major responsibility for their health and welfare
Want to have considerable freedom to adopt their own approach to the job	Want to work in a congenial and friendly atmosphere
Want to fully use their skills and abilities on the job	Want to be completely loyal to their company
Want to work in a department that is run efficiently	Believe that knowing influential people is more important than ability
Believe that decisions made by individuals are better than those made by groups	Believe that the better managers are those who have been with the company the longest time

SOURCE: Adapted from Hofstede, 1980.

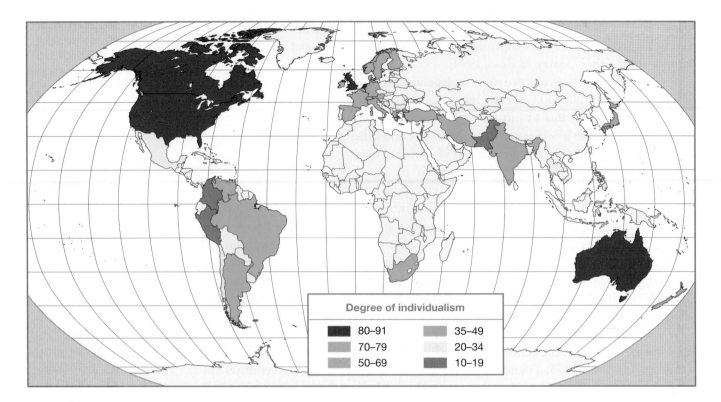

Figure 1.5
Individualism and Collectivism
This map shows the degree of individualism and collectivism among IBM employees around the world, indicating greater individualism in Great Britain and in the United States, Canada, Australia, and New Zealand, all former British colonies. People in the countries represented by gray were not surveyed by the researchers.

SOURCE: Sabini, 1995, p. 261; based on data from Hofstede, 1980.

shows the types of values and beliefs Hofstede examined and the differences he observed in individualistic and collectivistic cultures. **Figure 1.5** displays these results geographically, showing the average degree of individualism expressed by the citizens of 67 countries. You can see that the countries of British heritage are the most individualistic, followed by the countries of continental Europe. East Asia, South Asia, Asia Minor, and Latin America are all relatively collectivistic.

Although Hofstede himself studied few East Asian societies, there is now a great deal of evidence about them. The research to date indicates that those cultures are very different from Western cultures. In a survey similar to Hofstede's, two professors in a business school in the Netherlands, Charles Hampden-Turner and Alfons Trompenaars, examined independence and interdependence among 15,000 middle managers from the United States, Canada, Great Britain, Australia, Sweden, the Netherlands, Belgium, Germany, France, Italy, Japan, Singapore, and Korea (Hampden-Turner & Trompenaars, 1993). They presented these managers, who were attending seminars conducted by the investigators, with dilemmas in which individualistic values were pitted against collectivistic values. In line with Hofstede's results, they found that managers from East Asia, South Asia, and Latin America tended to hold collectivistic values; managers from British and former British colonies valued individualism; and managers from continental European nations valued a mix of individualism and collectivism. **Box 1.2** contains a sampling of the researchers' questions.

BOX 1.2 **FOCUS ON *CULTURE***

Individualism or Collectivism in Business Managers

Charles Hampden-Turner and Alfons Trompenaars (1993) studied individualism versus collectivism in thousands of business managers. To examine the value placed on individual distinctiveness and accomplishment versus harmonious relations within the group, they asked the business managers in their seminars whether business managers preferred

> jobs in which personal initiatives are encouraged and individual initiatives are achieved

or

> jobs in which no one is singled out for personal honor, but in which everyone works together.

To examine the acceptance of ascribed status (for example, age, family, religious background) as a basis for rewarding employees, the researchers asked the business managers whether they agreed with the following sentiment:

> It is important for a manager to be older than his subordinates. Older people should be more respected than younger people.

To see whether their respondents felt there should be universal rules governing employer-employee relations or whether instead circumstances and specific situations should be taken into account, they asked the business managers how they thought a manager should deal with an employee who had performed well for 15 years, but had recently become unproductive. If circumstances indicate it's unlikely that performance will improve, should the employee be dismissed on the grounds that

> job performance should remain the grounds for dismissal, regardless of the age of the person and his previous record

or instead do you feel that

> [it is] wrong to disregard the 15 years the employee has been working for the company. One has to take into account the company's responsibility for his life.

The cultures studied fell into three major clusters. East Asian managers were by far the most interdependent, or collectivistic, in their expressed values; managers from the British and former Commonwealth nations were the most independent, or individualistic (the United States and Canada were the most extremely independent); and managers from continental Europe were in between. What's more, the researchers found an interesting difference within Europe: People from the northwestern European nations of Sweden, the Netherlands, and Belgium were more individualistic than those from the more southern European nations of France, Italy, and Germany.

Some Qualifications

Societies differ in many ways, and it's not possible to put each society entirely in one box or another and say that some are independent in all respects and others are interdependent in all respects. Moreover, there are regional and subcultural differences within any large society. The U.S. South, for example, is more interdependent than much of the rest of the country in that family connections and community ties tend to be more important (Vandello & Cohen, 1999). However, the South has been described as more tolerant of character quirks and various kinds of social deviance than other regions of the country—clearly individualistic tendencies (Reed, 1990).

Moreover, the socialization within a given society of particular individuals or particular types of individuals may be oriented more toward independence or more toward interdependence. Gender socialization in our society is a good example (Kashima et al., 1995). While Dick is depicted in children's readers as running and playing (being independent), Jane is often shown caring for her dolls and cooking for others (being interdependent).

In many cultures, there are also social class differences in the independence versus interdependence dimension. Working-class people in modern societies are more interdependent than middle-class individuals. Working-class people have more interactions with their families than middle-class individuals do (Allan, 1979); their parenting styles emphasize conformity and obedience more than do those of middle-class individuals (Kohn, 1969); and they value personal uniqueness less than middle-class individuals do.

A study by Stephens and her colleagues provides a striking example of the different values placed on uniqueness (Stephens, Markus, & Townsend, 2007). The researchers asked people how they would feel if a friend bought a car just like one they themselves had just bought. Middle-class people were likely to report that they would be disappointed because they like to be unique; working-class people were more likely to say they would be very happy to share that similarity with a buddy. Middle-class people also appear to care much more about exercising choice than do working-class people. Middle-class people were found to like an object that they had chosen better than one they were given; the reverse was true for working-class people (Stephens, Fryberg, & Markus, 2011). Class differences seem to be broad and deep enough that it's reasonable to regard them as genuine cultural differences.

As a final qualification to these broad generalizations, researchers have found that the same person can have a relatively independent orientation in some situations (such as competing in a debate tournament) and a relatively interdependent orientation in others (such as singing in a choir) (Gardner, Gabriel, & Lee, 1999; Kühnen & Oyserman, 2002; Trafimow, Triandis, & Goto, 1991).

Culture and Gender Roles

Earlier, the discussion focused on some aspects of gender roles that are—or have been—universal. But gender roles vary greatly around the world, and even within subcultures in the same country. Male dominance is one of the most variable aspects of gender roles. Some preliterate peoples, living lives much like those of people during the thousands of years of recent human evolution, are hunter-gatherers. The predominant male role is to hunt; the predominant female role is to gather plants. Despite the sharp demarcation of gender roles, such societies are relatively gender-egalitarian. In fact, the social structures are characterized by weak hierarchies in general; leaders have little power over others. Modern Western cultures are also relatively gender-egalitarian, especially Northwestern European countries and most especially Scandinavian countries. Women constitute almost half the membership of the Parliament in Sweden. Relative status of women in the rest of the world ranges from the Scandinavian extreme of equality to near-slavery conditions for women.

The kinds of sexual relations that are considered normal and appropriate also vary enormously. Overwhelmingly, polygyny (one man with several wives) and serial monogamy are the most common expectations among the world's subcultures—and that may have been the case for thousands of years. The traditional U.S. ideal of lifetime monogamy is a rarity. The United States is considered decidedly prudish by many Western Europeans, for whom extramarital affairs are commonplace. The funeral of a recent president of France was attended by his wife and his mistress standing side by side. (Though the French do seem to have limits on this sort of thing. President François Hollande separated from

his long-time partner in 2006 after it was discovered that he was carrying on an affair with a married woman. He installed this woman in the Élysée Palace as his official mistress. Less than 2 years later he was spotted by the press on a motor scooter returning to the palace from an alleged tryst with yet another mistress, also married. This was considered, as the French say, *de trop*.)

In certain cultures, women (and sometimes even men) who are suspected of having extramarital affairs are put to death. Indeed, a woman who is raped might be expelled from the family circle or even killed. Gay and lesbian people in some societies may be put to death. Until just a generation or so ago, gays and lesbians in certain European countries were routinely sentenced to prison. In contrast, in some Native American cultures, bisexual men were admired as being "two-spirit" people. And in yet other cultures, homosexual behavior is so unremarkable that there is no term for either the practice or the type of person who engages in it.

It's a matter of some disagreement among social scientists whether the different sexual mores (norms) that characterize various cultures are merely arbitrary, or whether most of them have economic or other practical roots. An example of an economic explanation concerns farmers in Nepal and Tibet who practice a form of polyandry: one wife with many husbands who are brothers. This system serves the economic goal of keeping scarce agricultural land in one family and produces just one set of related heirs per generation. A similar purpose was served by primogeniture, a common rule in Western Europe that only the firstborn male could inherit land. Otherwise, estates would be broken up into ever-smaller units, and the original power of the landowning family would dwindle away to the status of ordinary peasants.

In this book, we frequently return to discussions of gender. Women and men differ in the way they understand themselves, as well as in their emotions and motivations. But these diverse patterns are far from being constant across cultures. There are many ways of constructing gender.

Culture and Evolution as Tools for Understanding Situations

Both evolution and culture affect how people see the world and behave within it. The two together are complementary ways of understanding social relations. For the first hundred thousand years or so of human existence, our ancestors were

Culture and Gender Roles
Women constitute almost 50 percent of politicians in Scandinavia. Their representation goes all the way to the top. (A) Jóhanna Sigurðardóttir, prime minister of Iceland (2009–2013). (B) Erna Solberg, prime minister of Norway (2013–present). (C) Mari Kiviniemi, prime minister of Finland (2010–2011). (D) Helle Thorning-Schmidt, prime minister of Denmark (2011–present).

largely concerned with the necessities of surviving, reproducing, and nourishing their young in a fundamentally social environment. Such challenges may have resulted in the evolution of prewired inclinations toward certain behaviors and ways of thinking. But such inclinations are tools that can be applied flexibly or not at all. And many, if not most, of these tools are highly modifiable by culture (Sperber, 1996). Different ecologies and economies placed people in situations that varied markedly from one another and in turn produced different social systems and practices.

Evolution has given us all the capacity for an astonishingly wide range of behaviors. Whether a society develops a particular prewired option or not may depend on how adaptive the behavior is for the circumstances that confront the people in it (Sperber, 1996). Nature proposes, but culture disposes. Far from making us rigidly programmed automatons, evolution has equipped us with a large repertoire of tools for dealing with the enormous range of circumstances that humans confront. Cultural circumstances and our high intelligence determine which tools we develop and which tendencies we try to override.

◔ LOOKING BACK

People in Western societies are characteristically individualistic, or independent, whereas people in other societies are more likely to be collectivistic, or interdependent. Westerners tend to define themselves as having attributes that exist apart from their relations with other people. Non-Westerners are more likely to define themselves in terms of their relations with others. These differences have important implications for many of the most important phenomena of social psychology. Gender roles and sexual mores are examples of behaviors that differ widely from one culture to another. Evolution and culture both make important contributions to understanding human social behavior. Evolution predisposes us to certain behaviors, but culture determines which behaviors are likely to be developed in particular situations.

Social Psychology and Critical Thinking

Many of your college courses teach not only facts and methods of research, but also how to reason (Nisbett, 2015). Mathematics courses, for example, teach rules of logic. Literature courses teach how to closely read a text to derive intended meanings that may not be obvious on the surface. Such reasoning tools can be applied broadly in everyday professional and personal life.

It's our belief that there is no better way to learn critical thinking than by learning about social psychology. Courses in social psychology present a great deal of information about scientific methods. Unlike most other sciences, though, social psychology presents those methods in the context of common everyday events. This makes it possible to apply them very broadly to daily problems.

Take, for example, statistics. Courses in statistics teach rules about how to calculate variation of some attribute in a population and rules about how to estimate the degree of relationship that exists between two kinds of events. But the examples used in statistics courses typically concern agricultural plots, IQ tests, and other phenomena that are not drawn from ordinary life. And that means statistics courses by themselves have a limited impact on critical reasoning (Nisbett, 2015). When knowledge about statistics is applied to everyday life events, the gain for reasoning in general is very great. People will come to apply statistical heuristics, or rules of thumb, to choices they make each day, to understanding the behavior of other people, and to criticism of scientific claims they encounter in the media. The same is true of many methodological concepts such as the need for control groups.

Two of the authors of this book have written a great deal about how to improve critical thinking (Belsky & Gilovich, 1999; Gilovich, 1991; Nisbett, 2015; Nisbett, Fong, Lehman, & Cheng, 1987; Nisbett & Ross, 1980) Much of what they have shown to be effective is achieved to a substantial extent in a social psychology course. But we believe that even more can be done to improve critical thinking skills by engaging you in exercises that make explicit use of the scientific tools you will develop by reading about research on particular topics. In order to bring home lessons in critical reasoning, we highlight in each chapter various ways of applying critical tools to everyday life events.

SUMMARY

Characterizing Social Psychology

- *Social psychology* is the scientific study of the feelings, thoughts, and behaviors of individuals in social situations.

The Power of the Situation

- Social psychology emphasizes the influence of situations on behavior. People often find it difficult to see the role that powerful situations can play in producing their own and others' behavior, and so are inclined to overemphasize the importance of personal dispositions in producing behavior. The two tendencies together are called the *fundamental attribution error*.

The Role of Construal

- Social psychology also focuses on the role of *construal* in understanding situations. People often feel that their comprehension of situations is direct, without much mediating thought. In fact, even the perception of the simplest objects rests on substantial inference and the complex cognitive structures that exist for carrying it out.
- The primary tool people use for understanding social situations, and physical stimuli for that matter, is the *schema*. Schemas are stored representations of numerous repetitions of highly similar stimuli and situations. They tell us how to interpret situations and how to behave in them. *Stereotypes* are schemas of people of various kinds—police officers, Hispanics, yuppies. Stereotypes serve to guide interpretation and behavior, but they can often be mistaken or misapplied, and they can lead to damaging interactions and unjust behaviors.

Automatic vs. Controlled Processing

- People's construals of situations are often largely automatic and nonconscious. As a consequence, people are sometimes in the dark about how they reached a particular conclusion or why they behaved in a particular way.
- People perceive many things nonconsciously and have little access to cognitive processes, in part because they have no need for conscious access to these things.

Evolution and Human Behavior: How We Are the Same

- The evolutionary perspective focuses on practices and understandings that are universal and seem to be indispensable to social life, suggesting that humans are pre-wired to engage in those practices. Natural selection has operated on human behaviors just as it has on physical traits.
- Some evolutionary theorists talk about universal characteristics that are cognitive in nature, including *language*, which appears at the same stage of development in all cultures, as well as a *theory of mind*, which also develops early in normal people of all cultures. Some have argued that differences between males and females may be explained by the differential *parental investment* required of the two sexes.
- Prewiring does not imply lack of modifiability. Human behavior is highly susceptible to being changed. To assume that humans have a genetic predisposition to behave in particular ways does not mean it is right to behave in those ways. Believing that because things are a particular way means they should be that way is to commit the naturalistic fallacy.

Culture and Human Behavior: How We Are Different

- Behaviors and meanings can differ dramatically across cultures. Many of these differences involve the degree to which a society is *independent*, or *individualistic* (having fewer social relationships of a looser sort), or whether it is *interdependent*, or *collectivistic* (having many relationships of a highly prescribed nature). These differences influence conceptions of the self and the nature of human relationships, as well as basic cognitive and perceptual processes.
- Gender roles and sexual mores differ enormously across cultures. Even within the West, gender and sexual practices

diverge significantly. Theorists differ in how strongly they believe this variability is arbitrary versus rooted in economic factors or some other aspect of the objective situation confronting the culture.

Social Psychology and Critical Thinking

- Scientific methods, when applied to everyday life events, provide reasoning skills that are very widely applicable. This text focuses on maximizing gains to critical thinking.

THINK ABOUT IT

1. How does social psychology differ from related disciplines, like personality psychology and sociology? How might a social psychologist, in contrast to researchers in other disciplines, try to understand the atrocities at Abu Ghraib?

2. What does the Milgram experiment on obedience demonstrate about the power of the situation? What features of the experimental situation might have increased the likelihood that participants would continue to shock the learner even after the learner showed signs of pain?

3. Why are schemas so important for social interaction? What is your schema for being a student in a classroom? What might happen if you didn't have that schema?

4. When trying to understand people's thoughts, feelings, and motivations, why don't researchers just ask them? What does research on automatic versus controlled processing tell us about people's awareness of their own mental states?

5. How does evolution help explain social behavior? Which types of behaviors seem most likely to be explained by evolution, and which ones seem less likely?

6. What is the naturalistic fallacy, and why is it so important to avoid when considering evolutionary explanations?

7. How do Western and Eastern countries differ in their beliefs about the role of the self in relation to the group? How might these beliefs lead to different behaviors in an academic setting?

8. Are evolutionary and cultural explanations for behavior compatible? How might these two perspectives complement each other when it comes to explaining gender differences in mate selection?

THE ANSWER GUIDELINES FOR THE THINK ABOUT IT QUESTIONS CAN BE FOUND AT THE BACK OF THE BOOK . . . ☞

The Methods of Social Psychology

Retail business owners across the Northern and Southern United States received the following letter from a job applicant who described himself as a hardworking 27-year-old man who was relocating to the letter-recipient's area from Michigan. Among a set of appropriate qualifications listed in the letter, the applicant described one rather striking blemish:

> There is one thing I must explain, because I feel I must be honest and want no misunderstandings. I have been convicted of a felony, namely manslaughter. You will probably want an explanation for this before you send me an application, so I will provide it. I got into a fight with someone who was having an affair with my fiancée. I lived in a small town, and one night this person confronted me in front of my friends at the bar. He told everyone that he and my fiancée were sleeping together. He laughed at me to my face and asked me to step outside if I was man enough. I was young and didn't want to back down from a challenge in front of everyone. As we went into the alley, he started to attack me. He knocked me down, and he picked up a bottle. I could have run away and the judge said I should have, but my pride wouldn't let me. Instead I picked up a pipe that was laying in the alley and hit him with it. I didn't mean to kill him, but he died a few hours later at the hospital.

Some business owners who received the letter replied and complied with the applicant's requests, providing a job application, the name of a contact person, or a phone number to call. Some even sent a note with their response.

Defending One's Honor
Duels, like the one shown here between Aaron Burr and Alexander Hamilton, were practiced in the United States well into the nineteenth century. They were called "affairs of honor."

In truth, however, the applicant was a fictional character created by two social psychologists in a carefully planned study (Cohen & Nisbett, 1997). The investigators measured the degree to which potential employers responded to the applicant's inquiry. If there was a note, the researchers rated how sympathetic it seemed—how encouraging it was, how personal it was, and whether it mentioned an appreciation for the applicant's candor.

Cohen and Nisbett found some distinct patterns in the replies. Retailers from the South complied with the applicant's requests more than the retailers from the North did. And the notes from Southern business owners were much warmer and more sympathetic than those from the North. One Southern retailer wrote the following in her letter:

As for your problem of the past, anyone could probably be in the situation you were in. It was just an unfortunate incident that shouldn't be held against you. Your honesty shows that you are sincere. . . .

I wish you the best of luck for your future. You have a positive attitude and a willingness to work. Those are the qualities that businesses look for in an employee. Once you get settled, if you are near here, please stop in and see us.

No letter from a Northern employer was remotely as sympathetic toward the applicant.

Why were the Southerners seemingly so accepting of murder? You will find out in this chapter. More important, you will find out *how* the investigators found out. They employed most of the methods at the disposal of social psychologists—methods that deepen our understanding of human behavior and help us improve many types of social outcomes.

The Value of Social Psychology Research

Why do social psychologists conduct research? Why is it useful to read about it? For the most part, people can get along perfectly well in everyday life without the benefit of findings from social psychology. The world is a reasonably predictable place: most of the situations we find ourselves in are similar to other familiar situations, and our observations about how people behave in those situations are accurate enough to allow us to navigate through the world with some confidence in the correctness of our predictions.

But many situations—interviews, initiations, dating—can contain surprises and pitfalls that social psychology research can help us anticipate and avoid. And even in familiar situations, our ideas about how people are likely to behave can be mistaken. Chapters 4, 5, and 12 describe some of these mistaken beliefs about social behavior and how those beliefs get formed.

Our opinions about *why* we behave as we do can also be mistaken (Nisbett & Wilson, 1977). As discussed in Chapter 1, many of the factors that influence our behavior are hidden from us: they aren't represented in conscious, verbal forms but in nonconscious, nonverbal forms that aren't accessible to introspection. Fortunately, social psychology research can tell us about the reasons not just for other people's behavior but for our own as well.

To see how social psychology research illuminates even ordinary aspects of human behavior and its causes, take a look at **Box 2.1**. Make your own guesses about the outcomes of the research described, and then see how accurate those guesses are by looking at pp. 48–49. When you have to predict the results of studies and *then* find out what they were, you avoid the **hindsight bias**, the tendency to believe that you could have predicted some outcome which in fact you couldn't have predicted accurately.

Once we hear some new fact, we can think of reasons why it might be expected to be true. It's a useful thing to do, except that dredging up those reasons often leaves us with the feeling that we could have predicted the outcome. Often we couldn't have. Social psychologists can demonstrate this hindsight bias by telling some people a fact and asking them if they would have predicted it, and not telling other people about the fact and asking for their predictions. It's very common that the people kept in ignorance make incorrect predictions, but those told the fact are confident they could have predicted it correctly (Bradfield & Wells, 2005; Fischhoff, Gonzalez, Lerner, & Small, 2005; Guilbault, Bryant, Brockway, & Posavac, 2004). Matching your predictions about Box 2.1 with the actual findings should counteract any tendency to assume that social psychology findings are obvious. They are often obvious only in hindsight, not in foresight.

> **hindsight bias** People's tendency to be overconfident about whether they could have predicted a given outcome.

🔙 LOOKING BACK

Social psychology research shows us that some of our stereotypes about how people behave are mistaken; it also shows us how such beliefs are formed with sometimes faulty procedures. Our beliefs about the reasons for our own behavior can also be mistaken. Social psychology findings sometimes seem obvious, but often only after we know what they are. Hindsight bias mistakenly tells us that we might have known the correct answer if we had been asked to predict the finding.

How Social Psychologists Test Ideas

Social psychologists use a wide variety of methods to test hypotheses about human behavior. As you read about these methods in this chapter and see them applied elsewhere in the book, keep in mind that their underlying logic is crucial for getting at the likely truth of propositions about social behavior. Even if you can't conduct a study to test a particular proposition because resources are insufficient or because it would be unethical, thinking through how you *would* test a given idea can lead you to new hypotheses that, on reflection, might seem preferable to your initial speculation. Such an exercise is called a *thought experiment,* and it's one of the most useful critical-thinking skills you'll learn from reading this book.

"The scientific method itself would not have led anywhere, it would not even have been born without a passionate striving for clear understanding."

—ALBERT EINSTEIN,
OUT OF MY LATER YEARS

BOX 2.1 **FOCUS ON *INTUITIVE SOCIAL PSYCHOLOGY***

Predicting Research Results

Make your own predictions about how people would behave in each of these situations. Put a check by the answer you believe to be correct before you see what actually is the right answer. If you don't commit yourself in that way you'll be vulnerable to the hindsight bias. (See pp. 48–49 for answers.)

1. Does familiarity breed liking or contempt? Would you be likely to prefer (a) a song you had heard many times on the radio or (b) one you had heard less often?

2. Suppose some people were persuaded to lie about their beliefs about a certain matter. Would those people be more inclined to adjust their beliefs in the direction of the lie if paid (a) a small amount of money, (b) a large amount of money, or (c) no money at all?

3. Suppose you knew that an acquaintance wanted a favor from you that was somewhat inconvenient for you to grant. Would you like him better if (a) he refrained from asking you the favor, (b) he asked you to do the favor and you complied, or (c) he asked you to do the favor and you regretfully turned him down?

4. Suppose you got a friend to think seriously for a few minutes about the inevitability of death. Would those thoughts be likely to make her feel (a) more helpless, (b) less favorably inclined toward her fellow human beings, or (c) more patriotic?

5. Suppose a person endured a painful medical procedure. Would he be less willing to undergo the procedure again if (a) the pain lasted for a long time, (b) the pain at its peak was particularly intense, (c) the first phase of the procedure was particularly painful, or (d) the final phase of the procedure was particularly painful?

6. Suppose male college students were asked to grade an essay written for an English class, and a picture of the female student who allegedly wrote the essay was attached to the essay. Would the grade be higher if (a) she was very pretty, (b) she was average looking, (c) she was quite plain looking, or (d) the student grading the essay was about as good looking as the person who allegedly wrote the essay?

7. Suppose people were asked what a person should do if given the choice between an option with substantial potential gain but also substantial risk, and another option that entails less potential gain but also less risk. Would people be more likely to recommend the risky choice if (a) they considered the choice by themselves or (b) they considered the choice in discussion with a small group; or (c) would it make no difference?

8. Suppose you asked one group of people to give their opinion about an issue after very brief consideration, and also asked another group to spend several minutes thinking about as many

aspects of the issue as possible and then give their opinion. Which group do you think would have more extreme views on the topic: (a) the group asked immediately about their opinion or (b) the group asked to ponder a while before answering; or (c) would the amount of time spent thinking about the question make no difference?

9. Suppose you offered an award to some nursery school children if they would draw with some special colored markers, and all the children who were offered the award drew with them. Would these children be (a) more likely to play with the markers at a subsequent time than the children who were never offered the award but got one anyway, (b) less likely, or (c) equally likely?

10. Suppose you asked a group of people to report 6 instances when they behaved in an assertive fashion, another group to report 12 instances when they behaved in an assertive fashion, and a third group to report 6 instances of some other behavior altogether, such as instances of introverted behavior. Which group would later report that they were most assertive: (a) the group asked for 6 instances of assertive behavior, (b) the group asked for 12 instances of assertive behavior, (c) the group asked about some other behavior; or (d) would it make little difference what the group was asked?

---

hypothesis A prediction about what will happen under particular circumstances.

theory A body of related propositions intended to describe some aspect of the world.

A **hypothesis** is a prediction about what will happen under particular circumstances. A **theory** is a body of related propositions intended to describe some aspect of the world. In speaking casually, people may say that something is "just a theory," meaning it's a notion largely unsupported by facts. In science, including social science, theories generally have support in the form of empirical data, and they often make predictions that are surprising except in light of the theory. In the history of science, many theories have led to a greater understanding of natural phenomena or to important real-life consequences. Evolutionary theory is supported by an enormous number of facts as well as nonintuitive predictions that have been confirmed by empirical observation. Bacterial adaptation to drugs, for example, is well understood in terms of evolutionary theory. Relativity theory in physics, which is also supported by a huge number of facts and accurate predictions, led to the development of the atomic bomb.

An example of a hypothesis born of a social psychological theory is the prediction that, if person A likes person B, who dislikes person C, person A will either come to dislike person C or begin to dislike person B. Such a hypothesis, which can be tested in a variety of ways, is an example of the sort of hypotheses that are generated by what is called *balance theory*, or the theory that people like their thoughts to be consistent with one another, and will do substantial mental work to achieve such cognitive consistency. Hypotheses are tested by studies, which examine predictions about what will happen in particular concrete contexts. Thus theories are more general than hypotheses, which are more general than findings from the studies that test them.

Observational Research

At the simplest level, research can be a matter of merely looking at a phenomenon in some reasonably systematic way, with a view to understanding what's going on and coming up with hypotheses about why things are happening as they are. Charles Darwin was first and foremost a great observer of natural life, and his observations of finches in the Galápagos Islands led to his theory of evolution by natural selection.

Social psychologists themselves learn a great deal from observation. One such method of research, used by both psychologists and cultural anthropologists, is called *participant observation* and involves observing some phenomenon at close range. An anthropologist may live with a group of people for a long time, just noting what they do and coming up with guesses—sometimes inspired by conversations with the people being studied—about why those people behave in certain ways or have certain beliefs.

In the 1970s, cultural anthropologist Shirley Brice Heath used participant observation to study preparation for schooling by middle-class and working-class families in a North Carolina town. She lived with the families, observing and taking part in their daily activities. She found remarkable differences between these two groups by living with them for long periods. The middle-class families read to their children a great deal, included them in dinner-table conversations, used the printed word to guide their behavior (recipes, game rules), and taught them how to categorize objects, how to answer "why" questions, and how to evaluate and make judgments about things. The working-class families didn't do those things as much, and although their children were reasonably well prepared for the early grades of school, their lack of preparation showed up in later grades, when they faced more complex tasks involving categorization and evaluation (Heath, 1982, 1983).

Observational Methods
The evolutionary psychologist and human behavioral ecologist Lawrence Sugiyama is shown here, with bow and arrow, involved in a particularly active form of participant observation.

In the 1950s, the social psychologists Roger Barker and Herbert Wright (1954) studied how children in a U.S. Midwestern town interacted with their surroundings. They followed children around as they delivered the morning paper, went to school, played kick the can, did their homework, and went to church suppers. The study revealed a great deal about the way young people interact with their environments, the opportunities and constraints that came with their environments, and the factors that molded their characters.

Social psychologists often observe social situations in a semiformal way, taking notes and interviewing participants. However, they typically design additional formal studies to verify the impressions they get from participant observation. Observations are often misleading, so any tentative conclusions gleaned from observation should ideally be tested using other methods.

Archival Research

One type of research can be conducted without ever leaving the library (or the laptop). Researchers can look at evidence found in *archives* of various kinds, including census reports, police records, sports statistics, newspaper articles, and databases containing historic and ethnographic (anthropological) descriptions of people in different cultures. For example, for their research on culture of honor, Nisbett and his colleagues (1993) studied FBI reports of homicides and found, as they had anticipated, that homicides were more common in the U.S. South than in the North. The FBI reports also included the circumstances of the homicides—murders committed in the context of another felony (such as while robbing a convenience store) versus murders that are crimes of passion (such as during a heated argument between neighbors or in the context of a lovers' triangle). In another study, Nisbett and Cohen (1996) analyzed the various types of murders and discovered that in the South, the most common kinds of homicide involved some type of insult—for example, barroom quarrels and cases of sexual infidelity. Indeed, other kinds of homicide not involving personal honor are actually less common in the South, leading a Southern sociologist (Reed, 1981) to say that you're safer in the South than the North if you stay out of the wrong bars and bedrooms!

Cultures of Honor
Homicides in cultures of honor can be the outcome of a quarrel over a $1 bet.

The observation that insult-related homicides are more common in the South led Nisbett and Cohen to begin a research program to study whether Southerners really do respond more aggressively to insults, or whether the higher rate of insult-related homicides was due to factors such as hotter temperatures or more lenient justice systems.

Surveys

One of the most common types of study in social psychology involves simply asking people questions. *Surveys* can be conducted using either interviews or written questionnaires. The participants can be a small collection of students or a large national population. When the investigator is trying to discern the beliefs or attitudes of some group of people—freshmen at a particular university, Hispanics living in Canada, or the population of Australia—*random sampling* is important. The people in the survey must be a random sample of the population as a whole. The only way to obtain a random sample is to give everyone in the population an equal chance of being chosen. If the university has a directory of students, a random sample can be obtained by finding out the total number of freshmen (say, 1,000), deciding how many to interview (say, 50), and then selecting every twentieth name from the directory and asking those people to participate in the survey (**Figure 2.1**).

Convenience sampling, such as contacting people as they enter the library or e-mailing fraternity and sorority members, is not random. A convenience sample may be *biased* in some way; that is, it might include too many of some kinds of people and too few of others. Information based on biased samples is sometimes worse than no information at all. One notable example is a survey by the *Literary Digest*, based on more than a million respondents, which erroneously predicted that the Republican Alf Landon would defeat Franklin Delano Roosevelt in the 1936 U.S. presidential election. In fact, the election was one of the most dramatic landslides in history: Landon carried only two states. How could the survey have been so far off the mark? The sample was biased because it was drawn from telephone directories and automobile registrations. In 1936, wealthy people were more likely to own phones and cars than were poorer people, as well as more likely to be Republicans. Polls in the 2012 national election differed significantly in their accuracy. One of the least accurate was the Rasmussen poll, which called only land lines, not cell phones. Can you guess the direction of error for the Rasmussen results? Too Obama or too Romney?

You've undoubtedly seen the results of reader surveys in various magazines. Two-thirds of *Cosmopolitan* readers who went on a vegan diet say they lost weight. Three-quarters of the readers of *Outside* magazine say that sex is more enjoyable outdoors. Sixty percent of respondents in a *Reader's Digest* poll claim they are happier after going to church than if they stay home and watch a football game on Sunday. Actually, all three results are fictional, and you should ignore each claim. In fact, you should ignore claims like these even if they aren't made up, because the people who take the time to respond to such polls are likely to be different from those who do not respond, and therefore are unlikely to represent the population as a whole. *Cosmo* readers who lost weight may be more likely to respond to a survey about weight loss than those who didn't lose weight. The criterion that everyone is equally likely to be in the sample is clearly not met, upping the odds that the survey results are misleading.

Nisbett and Cohen (1996) used surveys to pursue social psychological questions concerning attitudes toward violence. One hypothesis about why U.S. Southerners are more likely to commit homicide is that Southern attitudes might be more accepting of violence. But when these investigators looked at published national surveys of attitudes toward violence, they found few regional differences. For example, Southerners were no more likely than Northerners to agree with the sentiment that "an eye for an eye" is a justified retaliation, and Southerners were

Population
Group you want to know about
(e.g., U.S. college students)

Random samples
are likely to capture the proportions of given types of people in the population as a whole (i.e., U.S. college students).

Convenience samples
can produce proportions that are severely skewed away from the actual proportions in the population as a whole.

Figure 2.1
Random Sampling and Convenience Sampling

How accurate were your predictions? (See Box 2.1 on p. 44)

1. Familiarity, in general, breeds liking. The more a person has been exposed to a stimulus, within broad limits, the more the person likes it. See Chapter 10.

2. People are more persuaded by the lies they tell if they are paid nothing or a small amount than if they are paid a lot. See Chapter 7.

3. We like people more if we do them a favor. See Chapters 7 and 9.

4. When people are reminded of their own mortality, they focus on the values they hold most dear, such as religion and love of country. See Chapter 7.

5. The duration of pain has little effect on people's willingness to experience a procedure again. See Chapter 6.

6. Males give higher grades to females who are good looking. See Chapter 10.

7. When people discuss things in a group, they tend to shift their opinions about something further in the direction they were inclined to hold when thinking about it by themselves. Therefore, there's no general answer to the question of whether people are more likely to prefer risk when they discuss things in a group. The prefer risk more if that was their initial inclination before discussion and less if caution was their initial inclination. See Chapter 12.

8. Thinking more about an issue makes people's opinions about the issue more extreme. People who think about politics a lot aren't more moderate and balanced than people who are generally unconcerned about politics. They're more extreme, in either a leftward or a rightward direction. See Chapter 9.

9. Rewarding children for doing something they would do anyway makes them less interested in doing it. Contracts are likely to turn play into work. See Chapter 7.

actually more likely to agree that "when a person harms you, you should turn the other cheek and forgive him." However, the researchers found that Southerners were more likely to favor violence in response to insults and to think that a man would be justified to fight an acquaintance who "looks over his girlfriend and talks to her in a suggestive way." Southerners were also more likely to approve of violence in response to threats to home and family, thinking, for example, that "a man has a right to kill a person to defend his house." The investigators also found that Southerners were more approving of violence in socializing children: they were more likely to say that spanking was a reasonable way to handle a child's misdeeds, and more likely to say that they would encourage a child to beat up someone who was bullying him. (For examples of the kinds of questions the researchers asked participants, see **Figure 2.2**. See p. 49 for explanation of answers.)

In trying to explain this acceptance of violence in specific contexts, Nisbett and Cohen sought out anthropologists and historians. Several sources suggested that the South might be a "culture of honor." The U.S. North was settled by farmers from England, Holland, and Germany. Farmers in general are peace-loving folks; there's little reason for them not to be. The U.S. South was settled by herding peoples from the edges of Great Britain—Scottish, Irish, and Scotch-Irish from Ulster. Herding peoples throughout the world tend to be tough guys. They need to be because they can lose their livelihood—their herd—in an

---

FIGURE 2.2 **YOU BE THE SUBJECT**

Attitude toward Violence

Sometimes conflicts are resolved through fighting, and other times they are resolved nonviolently.

Imagine that a man named Fred finds himself in the following situations. In these situations, please indicate whether his starting a fight would be extremely justified, somewhat justified, or not at all justified.

1. Fred fights an acquaintance because that person looks over Fred's girlfriend and starts talking to her in a suggestive way.

2. Fred fights an acquaintance because that person insults Fred's wife, implying that she has loose morals.

3. Fred fights an acquaintance because that person tells others behind Fred's back that Fred is a liar and a cheat.

   On occasion, violent conflict involves shooting another person. Imagine that a man named Fred finds himself in the following situations. In these situations, indicate whether his shooting another person would be extremely justified, somewhat justified, or not at all justified.

4. Fred shoots another because that person steals Fred's wife.

5. Fred shoots another because that person sexually assaults Fred's 16-year-old daughter.

Results: See p. 49 to find out what your answers indicate.

SOURCE: Nisbett & Cohen, 1996.

instant. They cultivate a stance of being ready to commit violence at the merest hint that they might not be able to protect themselves, their homes, and their property. A man has to retaliate violently if insulted in order to establish that he is not to be trifled with. Parents teach their children not to fear violence, and to know how to protect themselves. This historical hypothesis guided the rest of Nisbett and Cohen's research.

In addition to the fringes of Britain, herding has traditionally been much more common in the Mediterranean countries than in northern Europe, and those countries in general have always been cultures of honor (the Corsican Napoleon and the Sicilian Mafia are examples). In Greek mythology (or perhaps in Greek history, we don't really know), Paris of Troy took beautiful Helen from her husband Menelaus of Sparta, provoking a war of 10 years' duration. "The face that launched a thousand ships" likely wouldn't have caused so many northern European vessels to set sail.

Correlational Research

One of the most important distinctions among different types of research is that between correlational and experimental research. In **correlational research**, psychologists simply determine whether a relationship exists between two or more variables. **Experimental research** goes a step further, by enabling investigators to make strong inferences about how different situations or conditions affect people's behavior.

Correlation Does Not Establish Causation Looking for correlations is an important way to begin a line of inquiry. However, once established, a correlation requires further exploration. Does variable 1 causally influence variable 2, or is it the other way around—reverse causation, in other words? Or does some **third variable** influence both? In correlational research, we can never be sure about causality.

For example, *TIME Magazine* (February 2004) published a cover story devoted to the proposition that love, sex, and marriage are good for physical and mental health. Although the article quoted statistics showing that married people are happier than unmarried people, it didn't consider a number of questions that should make a careful reader skeptical of the magazine's causal claims. Happier people may be more appealing to others and more likely to be married for that reason, so happiness may cause marriage rather than marriage causing happiness. This would be a case of reverse causation. Perhaps good physical and mental health leads to a greater likelihood of marriage, as well as a greater likelihood of being happy. In this case, the causal factor would be a third variable, namely health, operating on both of the other two.

Correlational research usually can't provide convincing evidence that there is a causal relationship because of the possibility of **self-selection**—that is, the investigator has no control over the level of a particular participant's score on a given variable. In effect, the participant has "chosen" the level of *all* variables—those that are measured and those that are not. For example, in the study reported by *TIME*, the researchers didn't assign people to be married or not; participants in the study either were or were not married. And the investigators didn't know what other qualities each participant brought along with his or her marital status—a sunny or gloomy disposition, good or bad physical health,

10. People report that they're more assertive if they're asked to think of a few instances of assertiveness rather than if they are asked to think of many. It's easier to come up with a few instances than many, and people use the effort they expend as an indicator of what they are really like. See Chapter 4.

correlational research Research that does not involve random assignment to different situations, or conditions, and that psychologists conduct to determine whether there is a relationship between the variables.

experimental research In social psychology, research that randomly assigns people to different conditions, or situations, and that enables researchers to make strong inferences about how these different conditions affect behavior.

third variable In correlational research, a variable that exerts a causal influence on both variable 1 and variable 2.

self-selection In correlational research, a problem that arises when the participant, rather than the researcher, selects his or her level on each variable, bringing with this value unknown other properties that make causal interpretation of a relationship difficult.

Answers to Figure 2.2

If you answered "extremely justified" or "justified" to most of these items, your attitudes toward violence as an appropriate response to an insult or affront resemble those of U.S. Southerners and members of other cultures of honor.

Correlations Cannot Establish Causation

A cover story appearing in *TIME Magazine* featured research on the benefits of sex, love, and marriage for physical and mental health. Undoubtedly those contentions are true, but most of the evidence reported was purely correlational, and therefore we can't accept the magazine's causal claims.

an easygoing or high-maintenance personality. These various qualities are self-selected as opposed to researcher-selected.

In correlational research, investigators can look at only the degree of relationship between two or more variables. Strength of relationship can range from 0, meaning that the variables have no relationship at all, to 1, meaning that the covariation is perfect: the higher the level on one variable, the higher the level on the other—without exception. (In the latter case, the correlation is +1. If it were the case that being higher on one variable was perfectly associated with being lower on the other, the correlation would be –1.) By convention, a correlation of .2 indicates a slight relationship, a correlation of .4 a moderately strong relationship, and a correlation of .6 or higher a very strong relationship. **Figure 2.3** shows what are called scatterplots. Variable 1 is on the x-axis (horizontal), and variable 2 is on the y-axis (vertical). Each dot represents a case—for example, a study participant for whom you have a score on variable 1 and a score on variable 2. Panel A shows a perfect negative correlation, and panel E shows a perfect positive correlation.

Panel B in Figure 2.3 shows a correlation of .3, which corresponds, for example, to the correlation between the percent fat content of a person's body and the degree of incipient cardiovascular illness. Both the marked spread of the dots (their scatter) and the relatively shallow slope of the line that best fits the scatterplot show that the association is relatively weak. Consider the causal possibilities for the relationship in panel B. It's possible that something about being overweight causes cardiovascular illness. But it's also possible that people who are under stress tend to gain weight and also to develop cardiovascular symptoms. And it's possible that some underlying syndrome—a particular constellation of genes, for example—makes people prone both to be overweight and to develop cardiovascular illness. In either case, being overweight might play no causal role in cardiovascular illness (Jeffery, 1996).

Panel C in Figure 2.3 shows a correlation of .5, which is approximately the degree of association between height and weight. This correlation helps us understand the ambiguity of correlational findings. Height predicts weight, and weight predicts height, but you wouldn't say that one *causes* the other. Rather, a wide range of genetic and environmental factors causes both. Some of those factors undoubtedly make some people larger than others—influencing both height and weight. But some factors influence weight more than height, and vice versa. In any case, height does not cause weight, nor does weight cause height.

Figure 2.3
Scatterplots and Correlations

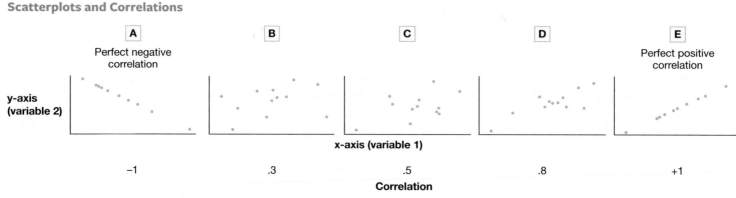

BOX 2.2

Not So Fast:
Critical Thinking about
Correlation and Causation

The items below are the findings of numerous correlational studies for which scientists or the media have implied a causal connection. To be a good consumer of correlational research, you need to be able to evaluate such causal claims carefully. For each of the findings in the list, consider alternatives to the stated or implied causal relationship, namely A causes B. Might it actually be the case that B causes A? Or that some variable C causes both? (Some possible responses to the original causality claims are presented on pp. 53–54.)

1. *TIME Magazine* reported that attempts by parents to control the size of portions their children eat will cause the children to become overweight (June 23, 2008,

p. 102). If the parents of overweight children stop controlling their portions, will the children get thinner?

2. Countries with higher average IQs have higher average wealth measured as average gross domestic product (GDP). Does being smarter make a country richer?

3. People who attend church have lower mortality rates than those who do not (Schnall et al., 2008). Does religion make people live longer?

4. People who have a dog are less likely to be depressed. If you give a dog to a depressed person, will the person become happier?

5. States with abstinence-only sex education have higher homicide rates. Does abstinence-only sex education cause aggression? If students in those states receive more informative sex education, will the homicide rate go down?

6. Intelligent men have better sperm, meaning higher sperm count and greater motility (Arden, Gottfredson, Miller, & Pierce, 2008). Does this finding suggest that attending college, which makes people smarter, also improves sperm quality?

7. People who smoke marijuana are subsequently more likely to use cocaine than people who do not smoke marijuana. Does marijuana use cause cocaine use?

Panel D in Figure 2.3 shows a correlation of .8. This is about the degree of correlation that you would find between a person's score on the math portion of the Scholastic Aptitude Test (SAT) on a first testing occasion and that obtained a year later. The association is quite strong, as indicated by the relatively slight scatter of the points around the line fitting the scatterplot and the relatively steep slope of that line. But it can't be said that the SAT score on the first occasion caused the score on the second occasion. Instead, it can be said that an underlying and undoubtedly highly complex set of factors involving genetics and social variables caused both scores to be similar for a given individual.

Scientific findings reported in the media are often based on correlational research. It's crucial to recognize the limits of such findings. They're often interesting, and they might *suggest* a particular causal connection, but by no means can correlational studies establish causation. To further develop your critical-thinking abilities, try your hand at interpreting the correlational results in **Box 2.2**.

The Value of Correlational Findings Correlational studies can be very helpful in alerting investigators to various possibilities for valid causal hypotheses about some aspect of the world. Moreover, correlational studies are sometimes a researcher's best option when an experimental study would be difficult or unethical. Researchers can't randomly assign people to the levels of certain variables (such as gender, socioeconomic status, and intelligence), and random assignment is a requirement of a well-designed experiment. In addition, researchers wouldn't

Longitudinal Studies
Three participants in the *Up* series of documentary films by Michael Apted. The films are an ongoing longitudinal study that has traced the development of 14 British people from various socioeconomic backgrounds since 1964.

independent variable In experimental research, the variable that is manipulated; it is hypothesized to be the cause of a particular outcome.

dependent variable In experimental research, the variable that is measured (as opposed to manipulated); it is hypothesized to be affected by manipulation of the independent variable.

random assignment Assigning participants in experimental research to different groups randomly, so they are as likely to be assigned to one condition as to another.

want to assign participants to a condition that held serious long-term risks. But correlational studies don't normally indicate the direction of causality or reveal whether some third variable is driving the association between the two variables of interest.

Even if correlational studies usually can't prove that a causal relationship exists, clever analysis of correlational data can be quite persuasive about the meaning of a relationship. Consider the following example: people who watch the local evening news—with reports of murders, fires, and other newsworthy mayhem—see more danger in the world than people who don't. The most obvious explanation is that watching dangers on TV makes people feel more at risk. But could it be that people who are anxious watch local TV to justify their fearfulness? Or is there some third variable? For example, elderly people may have more anxiety about their lives and may have more time to watch TV. This study could be refined so that it potentially rules out the latter hypothesis. For example, older adults may not be more likely to watch TV than younger people, and they may be no more anxious about their lives than younger people. These possibilities could be assessed by research. Ruling out alternative hypotheses isn't normally sufficient to prove that a given relationship is causal, but as more and more alternative explanations are tested and rejected, it becomes more and more plausible that there is indeed a causal relationship.

In this book, you'll see many illustrations of the different types of inferences that can be drawn from correlational studies. You'll also discover some of the clever ways that social psychologists have managed to circumvent the problems characteristic of correlational research.

Experimental Research

The best way to be sure about causality is to conduct an experiment. Experimental research requires an independent variable and a dependent variable. The **independent variable**, which the scientist manipulates, is presumed to be the cause of some particular outcome called the **dependent variable**, which is measured. In experiments, the researcher determines what the independent variable will be and what the levels for that variable will be. Dependent variables can be measured in many ways, including verbal reports (such as statements about degree of anger or anxiety); behavior (helping or not, getting an inoculation or not); physiological measures (heart rate or stress monitoring, such as cortisol levels); or neural measures (increased activity in certain brain areas).

The great power of experiments comes from their ability to expose participants to different levels of the independent variable by **random assignment**, which ensures that participants are as likely to be assigned to one condition as to another. It guarantees that, on average, except for the manipulation of the independent variable, there should be no differences across experimental groups. There will be as many men as women in each condition, as many liberals as conservatives, as many athletes as nonathletes. Random assignment thus rules out the possibility of self-selection biases in samples; the experimenter has done the selecting. Also critical to experiments is a carefully crafted **control condition**, which is comparable to the experimental condition in every way except that it lacks the one ingredient hypothesized to produce the expected effect on the dependent variable.

As an example of a carefully designed experiment, let's go back to two findings: U.S. Southerners are more likely to commit homicide in situations where there has been an insult, and Southerners are more likely to believe that violence is an appropriate response to an insult. Both of these findings are correlational: Southernness is associated with insult-related homicides, and Southernness is associated with the belief that violence is an appropriate response to an insult.

To study further whether Southerners actually do react more aggressively to an insult, Cohen and his colleagues conducted a series of experiments (Cohen, Nisbett, Bowdle, & Schwarz, 1996). The study participants were all middle-class students at the University of Michigan; some students were Southerners, and some were Northerners. All of them believed they were participating in a study on the effects of time constraints on judgments of various kinds. After filling out a questionnaire, they were asked to take it down a long, narrow hallway lined with filing cabinets and leave it on a table at the end.

For some participants, a nasty surprise awaited near the end of the hallway. Another student stood in the hallway with a file drawer pulled out. For the participant to pass by, the student had to push the drawer in and move out of the way. Moments later, when the participant started back down the hall, the student had to get out of the participant's way again. This time the student slammed the drawer shut, pushed into the participant's shoulder, and said, "Asshole." (He then quickly exited behind a door labeled Photo Lab to avoid a physical confrontation. One participant actually ran after the student and rattled the doorknob, trying to get at him. You can probably guess the region of the country that participant was from.) Subjects in a control condition simply left the questionnaire on the table without incident. (The participants were, of course, randomly assigned to one or the other condition.) The study therefore had two independent variables: whether the participant was Northern or Southern, and whether the participant was insulted or not.

Several dependent variables were examined after the insult either did or did not take place. First, observers were positioned so they could see the participant immediately after he was insulted. Insulted Southerners usually showed a flash of anger; insulted Northerners were more likely to shrug their shoulders or to appear amused. Second, participants were asked to read a story in which a man made a pass at another man's fiancée. Participants were asked to provide an ending for the story. Southerners who had been insulted were much more likely to provide a violent ending to the story than Southerners who had not been insulted, whereas the endings provided by Northerners were unaffected by the insult. Third, the participants' level of testosterone, the hormone that mediates aggression in males, was tested both before and after the insult. The level of testosterone increased for Southerners who had been insulted, but it did not increase for Southerners who had not been insulted or for Northerners, whether insulted or not.

Fourth, as the participant walked back down the narrow hallway, another assistant to the experimenter walked toward him. This assistant was very tall and muscular and his instructions were to walk down the middle of the hall, forcing the participant to dodge out of his way. The dependent variable was how far

control condition A condition comparable to the experimental condition in every way except that it lacks the one ingredient hypothesized to produce the expected effect on the dependent variable.

Possible Answers to Questions about Correlations
(See Box 2.2 on p. 51)

1   It could be that parents try to control the size of portions their children eat if they are overweight. If so, the direction of causation is the reverse of that hypothesized by *TIME Magazine*. It could also be the case that families with more stress in their lives have more controlling parents and more overweight children, but there is no causal connection between the two. Instead, a third variable, associated with stress, accounts for the correlation.

2. It could be that wealthier countries have better education systems and hence produce people who get higher IQ scores. In that case, wealth causes intelligence, rather than the other way around. In fact, we have good reason to believe that the correlation between IQ and wealth holds because of causality working in both directions: Greater intelligence leads to greater wealth, and greater wealth leads to greater intelligence (in part through better educational systems).

3. It could be that healthier people engage in more social activities of all kinds, including going to church. If so, the direction of causation runs opposite of the one implied. Or it could be that good social adjustment—a third variable—causes people both to engage in more social activities and to be healthier.

4. It could be that people who are depressed are less likely to do anything fun, like getting a pet. If so, the direction of causation is opposite to the one implied. (But in fact, giving a pet to a depressed person does improve the person's mood.)

5. It could be that states that are poorer are more likely to have higher homicide rates, and

away the participant was when he finally swerved out of the assistant's way. The investigators thought that the insulted Southerners would be put into such an aggressive mood that they would play "chicken" with the assistant, waiting until the last moment to swerve aside. And they did indeed. Northerners, whether insulted or not, swerved aside at a distance of about 5 feet (1.4 meters) from the assistant. Southerners, who are known for their politeness, stood aside at around 9 feet (2.75 meters) if not insulted, but pushed ahead until 3 feet (less than 1 meter) away if they had been insulted.

The experiment Cohen and his colleagues conducted was not an experiment in the full sense. Only one of the independent variables was created by random assignment—namely, whether the participant was insulted or not. The other independent variable was status as a Southerner or Northerner. Thus, technically, the Cohen study was correlational. The basic finding was that something about Southernness predisposes college men to respond aggressively to insults, but the study does not indicate what the causally relevant aspect of Southernness is.

In many cases, however, experimental research can establish a causal relationship between two variables. Recall from Chapter 1 the study in which Darley and Batson (1973) found that seminary students in a hurry were less likely to offer aid to a victim. In that experiment, the main independent variable was whether or not the student was in a hurry, and the dependent variable was whether or not the student stopped to help the victim. The seminary students were randomly assigned to either the "late" condition or the control ("not late") condition. This random assignment ensured that participants in the two conditions were, on average, the same kind of people, thereby demonstrating that something related to being late was what caused such a large proportion of seminarians in the late condition to fail to help the apparent victim.

Before we turn to other concepts that a smart consumer of research should know, it's worth noting that, although experimental research can provide answers to the causality questions that are left unclear by purely correlational research, experiments are not without their limits. One limit, alluded to earlier, is that sometimes an experiment is simply not possible or wouldn't be ethical to conduct. We wouldn't want to assign 10-year-old children to watch lots of violent TV over a long period of time, for example. And we couldn't randomly assign some people to be married and others to remain single. Can causality ever be established in important domains like these? Yes.

One way to get closer to establishing causality in such situations is by taking advantage of natural experiments. In a **natural experiment**, events occur that the investigator believes to have causal implications for some outcome. For example, we might measure people's happiness before and after they get married. It turns out that people are happier after marriage than they were before (Argyle, 1999). These findings are scarcely decisive, but they strongly suggest that married people are happier *because* they are married—not that they are married because they are cheerful.

Another example of a natural experiment occurred when television was first introduced in the United States. It didn't come to all regions of the country at the same time; some communities had TV and others didn't. Whether or not a

6. It could be that better physical health—a third variable—helps people to be smarter and helps sperm to be of better quality. Or some other factor could be associated with both intelligence and sperm quality, such as drug or alcohol use. So there might be no causal connection between intelligence and sperm quality.

7. It could be that people who take any kind of drug are more sensation seeking than other people and therefore engage in many kinds of stimulating behavior that are against the law. Smoking marijuana may not cause cocaine use, and cocaine use may not cause marijuana use. Rather, some third factor, such as sensation seeking, may influence both.

states that are poorer are more likely to have abstinence-only sex education. Indeed, both are true. So there may be no causal connection at all between sex education and homicide. Rather, a third variable, such as poverty or something associated with it, may be causally linked to both, thereby accounting for the correlation.

Honor Experiments
Researchers had U.S. Southern and Northern male students walk down a hallway where an accomplice shoved the student and called him an asshole. Southern students responded with more anger, as well as higher increases in their testosterone levels (Cohen, Nisbett, Bowdle, & Schwarz, 1996).

community received television was not determined by the community itself (and hence any results could not be attributed to self-selection). This natural experiment therefore allowed investigators to draw relatively strong conclusions about the impact of TV on people's habits and opinions.

"Science walks forward on two feet, namely theory and experiment. Sometimes it is one foot which is put forward first, sometimes the other, but continuous progress is only made by the use of both."

—ROBERT MILLIKAN, NOBEL PRIZE IN PHYSICS, 1946

⬆ LOOKING BACK

Social psychologists study phenomena by observational methods (though they usually do so to get an intuitive understanding with a view toward applying other methods), archival research involving records of various kinds, and surveys in which people are asked questions. The validity of surveys typically depends on using respondents who are randomly sampled from the population they represent. Correlational research, in which the investigator establishes whether there is a relationship between two variables, suffers from the problem of self-selection: the individuals being studied have "chosen" their level on each variable rather than being assigned a level by the investigator. Experimental research manipulates an independent variable and observes the effects of the manipulation on a dependent variable.

---

natural experiment A naturally occurring event or phenomenon having somewhat different conditions that can be compared with almost as much rigor as in experiments where the investigator manipulates the conditions.

external validity An indication of how well the results of a study generalize to contexts besides those of the study itself.

More Concepts for Understanding Research

All research is not created equal. Just because someone has conducted a study does not mean you should accept the results as fact. What sets a well-designed study apart from a flawed one? In an experiment, random assignment and a control group can go a long way toward eliminating potential problems. But in designing any study, researchers also need to carefully consider certain types of validity and reliability, as well as the statistical significance of their findings.

External Validity in Experiments

The previous section pointed out the weaknesses of correlational research, but experimental studies can have weaknesses too. Sometimes experiments can be so removed from everyday life that it can be hard to know how to interpret them (Aronson, Ellsworth, Carlsmith, & Gonzalez, 1990). **External validity** is an indication of how well the results of a study generalize to contexts besides those of the study itself. When researchers are unable to generalize the results to real-life situations, there is poor external validity. When the purpose of the research is to generalize directly to the outside world, external validity is critical. For example, if researchers are investigating whether watching violence on TV makes children more aggressive, the TV programs the children see in the study should resemble real TV shows, and the types of aggressive behavior examined should be behavior that children might actually engage in.

Poor external validity is not always a problem. Milgram's study of obedience (discussed in Chapters 1 and 9) had poor external validity in the sense that few people in our society are ever placed in a situation where an authority figure is commanding them to harm another person. Nevertheless, such things have happened in the world and will happen again.

field experiment An experiment conducted in the real world (not a lab), usually with participants who are not aware they are in a study of any kind.

Investigators sometimes deliberately strip down a situation to its bare essentials to make a theoretical point that would be hard to make in real-world circumstances. For example, to find out how familiarity with a stimulus affects its attractiveness, Robert Zajonc and his colleagues (1968) showed fictitious Turkish words and fake Chinese characters to Americans, presenting some of them many times and some of them only a few times (**Figure 2.4**). The more times participants saw a given stimulus, the more they thought the stimulus referred to something good. The experiment had poor external validity because the experimental situation was unlike something anyone would ever encounter in real life. But the simplicity of the situation and the initial unfamiliarity of the foreign words and characters ensured that it was the sheer number of repetitions of the words that affected their attractiveness, and not something else about the stimuli. In research like Zajonc's, where the purpose is to clarify a general idea or theory, external validity is not essential.

One of the best ways to ensure external validity is to conduct a field experiment. Similar conceptually to a laboratory experiment, a **field experiment** takes place in the real world, usually with participants who are unaware they are involved in a research study at all. An example would be an experiment in which researchers study the reactions of people who are asked to give up their seats on an uncrowded bus or train.

In the field experiment described at the beginning of this chapter, Cohen and Nisbett (1997) examined the reactions of U.S. Southern and Northern business owners to a letter allegedly written by a job applicant who had been convicted of

Figure 2.4
External Validity
In this study, researchers presented fictitious Turkish words and made-up Chinese characters to participants a varying number of times. After the presentation, the participants were asked to guess how positive the meaning was for each word or character. Those that were presented many times were more likely to be regarded as referring to something positive. Although this study has poor external validity because nobody in real life would be in such a situation, it was a good test of the hypothesis that mere familiarity with a stimulus makes it more attractive.

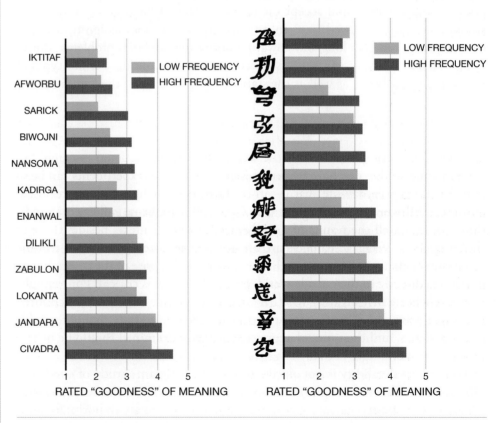

SOURCE: Adapted from Zajonc et al., 1968.

a felony. The felony in question was either a motor vehicle theft or, in the version you read, a homicide in the context of a love triangle. The dependent variable was the degree of responsiveness to the applicant's letter, ranging from no response at all to sending an encouraging letter and an application form. Southern retailers were much more encouraging of the man convicted of homicide than Northern retailers. The experiment provides, in a field setting, evidence that Southern norms concerning violence in response to an insult are more accepting than Northern norms. Because there was no difference in the reactions of Southerners and Northerners to the letter that mentioned a theft, we know that Southerners are not simply more forgiving of crimes generally. Thus, the theft letter constitutes a control condition in this field experiment. And because the participants were potential employers who believed they were responding to a real applicant, its external validity is much higher than it would be if the participants had been asked to assess fictional job applicants in a laboratory setting.

Internal Validity in Experiments

Whatever the goal of an experiment, internal validity is essential. **Internal validity** requires that only the manipulated variable—and no other external influence—could have produced the results. The experimental situation is held constant in all other respects, and participants in the various experimental conditions don't differ at all, on average, before they come to the laboratory. You'll remember the easy way to avoid the possibility that participants will differ from each other in some unanticipated way that might influence the results: by randomly assigning them to the various experimental conditions. For example, the investigators can flip a coin to determine the condition for each participant, or consult a random number table and assign each participant to the experimental condition if the next number is odd and to the control condition if the next number is even. Random assignment ensures that the participants in one condition will not be different, on average, from those in the other conditions—and this is essential for establishing internal validity.

Internal validity also requires that the experimental setup seem realistic and plausible to the participants. If participants don't believe what the experimenter tells them, or if they don't understand something crucial about the instructions or the nature of the task they are to perform, then internal validity will be lacking and the experimenter can have no confidence in the results. In such cases, participants are not responding to the independent variable as conceptualized by the experimenter, but to something else entirely.

Researchers can help ensure that their experimental design meets the criteria for internal validity by debriefing participants in pilot studies, which are preliminary versions of the experiment. **Debriefing** may involve directly asking participants whether they understand the instructions and whether they find the setup to be reasonable. Pilot study participants are generally told the purpose of the experiment and what the investigators expected to find. Pilot participants can often provide useful information about how well the experiment is designed when they are brought in as consultants, so to speak, in the debriefing. Even after the experimental setup is finalized, debriefing is routine for the purpose of education—to let the participants know what questions are being studied, how the research addresses those questions, and why the results might have social value.

internal validity In experimental research, confidence that only the manipulated variable could have produced the results.

debriefing In preliminary versions of an experiment, asking participants directly if they understood the instructions, found the setup to be reasonable, and so on. In later versions, debriefings are used to educate participants about the questions being studied.

"Inquiry is fatal to certainty."
—WILL DURANT, PHILOSOPHER

reliability The degree to which the particular way researchers measure a given variable is likely to yield consistent results.

measurement validity The correlation between some measure and some outcome the measure is supposed to predict.

regression to the mean The tendency of extreme scores on a variable to be followed by, or associated with, less extreme scores.

Reliability and Validity of Tests and Measures

Reliability refers to the degree to which a measure gives the same result on repeated occasions, or the degree to which two measuring instruments (such as human observers) yield the same result. If you take an IQ test twice, do you get roughly the same score? Do two observers agree in their ratings of the charisma of world leaders or fellow fraternity members? Reliability is typically measured by correlations between 0 and 1. As a rule of thumb, ability tests such as IQ tests are expected to have reliability correlations of about .8 or higher. Personality tests, such as verbal measures of extraversion, are expected to have that level of correlation or a little lower. People's degree of agreement about the kindness or charisma of another person would likely show a correlation of at least .5.

Measurement validity refers to the correlation between some measure and some outcome the measure is supposed to predict. For example, IQ test validity is measured by correlating IQ scores with grades in school and with performance in jobs. If IQ scores predict behavior that requires intelligence, it can be inferred that the test is a valid measure of intelligence. Validity coefficients, as they are called, typically do not exceed .5. Personality tests rarely correlate with behavior in a given situation better than about .3. This result is surprising to most people, who expect that a measure of extraversion should predict quite well a person's behavior at a party, and a measure of aggression should predict quite well a person's behavior in a hockey game.

Regression to the Mean

A very important and frequently misunderstood statistical regularity is known as **regression to the mean**: the tendency for extreme scores to be followed by, or to accompany, less extreme scores. This is a completely general point. Extreme scores on any variable are further away from the mean of a distribution of scores, and scores close to the mean of nearly all distributions are more common than scores further from the mean. This pattern is visible in **Figure 2.5**, which shows a *normal distribution*, sometimes called a bell curve.

Many types of variables are distributed in this fashion: IQ, physical height, income level, annual corn yield in Iowa, number of mistakes per day in the manufacturing of glass jars. Extremely tall fathers have sons who are typically closer to the mean, and extremely tall sons, in turn, tend to have fathers who are closer to the mean. The rookie of the year in baseball typically doesn't do as well his second year. The spectacularly successful investor in 2015 is not likely

Figure 2.5
A Normal Distribution: the Bell Curve
Variables distributed in this fashion, which include most human physical, mental, and personality variables, have a mean at the center of the distribution, and there are more cases at the center than at any other location. The more a value for a given observation of a variable departs from the mean, the more likely it is to regress toward the mean when observed subsequently, or at the same time by another kind of measure of the variable.

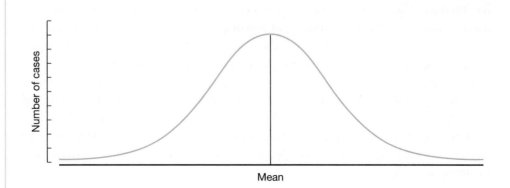

Mean

to be as successful in 2016. Your best tennis game ever, sad to say, is not likely to be so terrific the next time you're on the court. If you're unusually depressed, "this too shall pass," because (hopefully) an extremely low mood is not typical for you. Unfortunately, your happiest day is likely to be followed by one that's less happy.

When you go to the doctor with a bad cold, you'll likely get better even if all the doctor does is say "hello." The reason is that you probably went when your symptoms were close to their peak intensity and therefore had no place to go except down—in other words, back toward the mean of your health distribution. (This isn't true, of course, for progressive diseases such as arthritis or cardiovascular problems.)

An interesting application of the concept of regression to the mean was made by Daniel Kahneman and Amos Tversky (1973b) in their attempt to improve the training of Israeli pilots. The investigators told the instructors that a general principle of learning is that people benefit from positive feedback, which informs them about what they're doing right. The instructors insisted that principle didn't apply to pilot training: when they praised an usually good maneuver, the novice pilot typically performed worse the next time around. Moreover, if they shouted at the pilot for a particularly bad performance, the pilot nearly always performed better the next time around. But of course, the instructor could say nothing at all and get the same results simply due to regression to the mean: a particularly good performance would typically be worse the next time a maneuver was tried, and a particularly bad performance would typically be better the next time around. Once they understood this idea, the instructors got better results, and novice pilots had a more pleasant training experience.

The concept of regression is a statistical one at base, but the cause of regression isn't a statistical one. The reason that rookie of the year did so well is that the stars aligned just right for him. He was in perfect health and had no injuries. There were no family or girlfriend problems, and his team had just gotten the best coach in the league. The odds are against such a terrific pattern the next year.

Regression to the mean is an extremely important concept to have in your critical-thinking toolbox. Once you have it firmly in your mind, you'll see it crop up constantly as you observe and think about human behavior.

Statistical Significance

When researchers obtain an empirical result—such as finding a correlation between two variables, or observing that some independent variable affects a dependent variable in an experiment—they can test the relationship's statistical significance. A finding has **statistical significance** if the probability of obtaining the finding by chance is less than some quantity. By convention, this quantity is usually set at 1 in 20, or .05, but probabilities can be much lower. Statistical significance is primarily due to two factors: (1) the size of the difference between groups in an experiment or the size of a relationship between variables in a correlational study, and (2) the number of cases the finding is based on. The larger the difference or relationship and the larger the number of cases, the greater the statistical significance. All the findings reported in this book are statistically significant (though not all are based on large effects).

statistical significance A measure of the probability a given result could have occurred by chance.

basic science Science or research concerned with trying to understand some phenomenon in its own right, with a view toward using that understanding to build valid theories about the nature of some aspect of the world.

applied science Science or research concerned with solving important real-world problems.

intervention An effort to change a person's behavior.

↺ LOOKING BACK

External validity refers to how closely an experimental setup resembles what people find in the real world. Internal validity refers to the extent to which investigators know that only the manipulated variable could have produced the results. Reliability refers to the degree to which different measuring instruments, or the same instrument at different times, produce the same values for a given variable. Measurement validity refers to the extent to which a measure predicts outcomes that it is supposed to measure. Regression to the mean is the tendency of extreme scores on a variable to be followed by, or associated with, less extreme scores. Statistical significance is a measure of the probability that a result could have occurred by chance.

Basic and Applied Science

The practice of scientific research is of two broad types: basic science and applied science. **Basic science** (or basic research) is concerned with trying to understand some phenomenon in its own right, rather than using a finding to solve a particular real-world problem. Basic scientific studies are conducted with a view toward using the findings to build valid theories about the nature of some aspect of the world. For example, social psychologists investigating the obedience of people to an authority figure in the laboratory are doing basic science, attempting to understand the nature of obedience and the factors that influence it. They are not trying to find ways to make people less obedient to dubious authorities, though they may hope their research is relevant to such real-world problems. Social psychologists who study the effect of being in a hurry on helping another person are interested in how situational factors affect people's behavior. Although their objective is not to find ways of making people more inclined to help people in need, they would hope their research would be relevant to such a goal.

Applied Research

Tobacco companies spend a lot of money on advertising to encourage people to buy their cigarettes. Social psychologists can study how to counter that effect, as this public service advertisement by the California Department of Health Services is trying to do.

Applied science (or applied research) is concerned with solving a real-world problem of importance. An example of applied research in social psychology would be a study of how to make preteens less susceptible to cigarette advertising. (One way is to make them aware of the motives of tobacco companies and of their cynical desire to make chumps of kids by getting them to do something that is not in their best interest.) Another example would be an attempt o convince people to use condoms to prevent the spread of sexually transmitted diseases (STDs). (One way is to have characters in soap operas talk about the use of condoms—a form of product placement, as it's known in the advertising industry; Bandura, 2004.)

There is a two-way relationship between basic and applied research. Basic research can give rise to theories that can lead to **interventions**, or efforts to change certain behaviors. For example, social psychologist Carol Dweck found that people who believe intelligence is a matter of hard work study harder in school and get better grades than people who believe intelligence is a matter of genes; you're either intelligent or not, and you can't do much to change it (Dweck, Chiu, & Hong, 1995). Her basic research on the nature of beliefs about intelligence and their relationship to work in school prompted her to design an intervention with minority junior high students. She told some of them that their intelligence was under their control and gave them information about how working on school subjects actually changes the physical nature of the brain (Blackwell, Trzesniewski, & Dweck, 2007; Henderson & Dweck, 1990). Such students worked harder and got better grades than students who were not given such information. Joshua Aronson and his colleagues have obtained similar results (Aronson, Fried, & Good, 2002; Good, Aronson, & Inzlicht, 2003).

The direction of influence can also go the other way: applied research can produce results that feed back into basic science. For example, applied studies during World War II on how to produce effective propaganda led to an extensive program of basic research on attitude change. That program, in turn, gave rise to theories of attitude change and social influence that continue to inform basic science, and to generate new techniques of changing attitudes in applied, real-world contexts.

Replication

replication The reproducing of the results of a scientific study.

Although it wouldn't be obvious to you in reading the rest of this book, virtually every finding of any interest or importance in social psychology—in fact, in science in general—has been repeated. **Replication** is the reproducing of research results by the original investigator or by someone else. Some results do not replicate; attempts to duplicate the procedures of the study don't succeed in producing the same results. Sometimes the original investigator can show that the replication attempt was not carried out correctly, and the original investigator, or someone else, may show that the original result is found when the study is done properly. Sometimes, it's just by chance that a replication attempt fails: every result has a certain probability of being an error. Other times, the replication attempt fails because the original result was a fluke or not conducted with precision.

Scientific controversy is sometimes generated by failures to replicate and accusations of incompetence on the part of investigators. Such debate usually results in a consensus in the field as to whether a particular finding should be accepted or not. In this way, science is self-correcting. Errors are made and interpretations may be faulty, but the scientific enterprise usually manages to winnow out the wheat from the chaff.

🔄 LOOKING BACK

Basic science attempts to discover fundamental principles; applied science attempts to solve real-world problems. There is an intimate relationship between the two: Basic science can reveal ways to solve real-world problems, and applied science aimed at solving real-world problems can give rise to the search for basic principles that explain why the solutions work. Replication of results increases our confidence in them.

institutional review board
(IRB) A university committee that
examines research proposals and
makes judgments about the ethical
appropriateness of the research.

informed consent A person's signed
agreement to participate in a procedure
or research study after learning all the
relevant aspects.

deception research Research in
which the participants are misled about
the purpose of the research or the
meaning of something that is done to
them.

Ethical Concerns in Social Psychology Research

Most people of course would naturally want to conduct research geared to changing people's attitudes only if they believed the direction of change was for the better. We wouldn't support, or even want to allow, research that might have the effect of encouraging people to engage in unhealthy or dangerous behaviors. Most of us would not approve of a study in which participants were physically or psychologically harmed with little justification. For this reason, research conducted at universities has to be approved by an **institutional review board (IRB)**, a committee that examines research proposals and makes judgments about their ethical appropriateness. An IRB includes at least one scientist, one nonscientist, and one person who is not affiliated with the institution. If some aspect of the study procedures is deemed overly harmful, that procedure must be changed before the research can be approved.

The key to the previous sentence is the word *overly*. Research may be allowed even if it does make people uncomfortable or embarrassed or causes physical pain, as long as the research is deemed sufficiently likely to yield scientific information of significant value, and the discomfort or harm to the participants is not too great. For example, the Milgram studies on obedience (1963, 1974) were conducted before approval IRB committees existed. Today, Milgram's proposal would be thoroughly examined by an IRB, and it's not clear whether it would be approved. On the one hand, there is no question that Milgram's research did make some participants extremely uncomfortable; their psychological distress was manifest to observers. On the other hand, many (if not most) people would consider the knowledge gain to be enormous. It's impossible to think about Nazi Germany the same way after learning the results of the Milgram studies. Nor can we think the same way about the behavior of American soldiers involved in torturing Iraqi prisoners once we know about those studies. We can no longer blithely assume that ordinary, decent people would refuse to obey commands that are patently harmful. Different IRBs would undoubtedly reach different conclusions about the admissibility of the Milgram experiments today. What do you think? Would you permit research like Milgram's to be conducted?

In medical research, which is also governed by IRBs, the principle of informed consent governs the acceptability of research. Even if a given procedure is not known to be beneficial—indeed, even if there is a possibility that it will be less beneficial than other procedures, or actually harmful in the short term—an IRB might allow the research to be conducted if the knowledge gain relative to the risk is deemed great enough. But participants must give their **informed consent**—their agreement to participate in light of their knowledge about all relevant aspects of the procedure.

Informed consent is also required for much social psychology research. However, for certain types of studies, known as **deception research**, it's not possible to obtain informed consent from the participants. Darley and Batson (1973) could not have told their seminary participants the true nature of their study, or that the stated reason for their need to hurry was bogus and the apparent victim was actually a confederate who was merely pretending to be hurt as part of the experiment. Informed consent would have defeated the purpose of the study. If there's a good reason for deception, it's generally allowed by IRBs.

An IRB, for example, gave permission for Cohen and his colleagues (1996) to deceive their Southern and Northern participants, and even to shove them and call them a dirty name. In general, when asked their opinion about what they were put through, participants generally understand the reasons and often say they learned more, and enjoyed the study more, than subjects who were not deceived or made uncomfortable (Smith & Richardson, 1983). For example, participants in the insult condition of the Cohen study actually reported that they learned more and had a better time than participants in the control condition.

The debriefing procedure is particularly important when participants have been deceived or made uncomfortable. Experimenters owe them a full accounting of what was done, what aspects of the procedure involved deception, why they were made uncomfortable, what the experiment was intended to examine, and what the potential is for valuable social contributions based on the research.

An understanding of the methods and concepts discussed in this chapter is vital to appreciating the studies described in this book. When you read about an experiment, try to identify the independent and dependent variables, and think about whether the experiment has good external validity. Equally important, keep these methods in mind when you read about scientific findings in magazines and newspapers and on the Internet, because science reporting is often based on studies that employed dubious methodology. In addition, familiarity with these methodological principles can help you understand other people's behavior and guide your own.

🔄 LOOKING BACK

Ethical concerns about social psychology research are addressed by institutional review boards. Deception and even minor harm to participants are sometimes allowed when the potential gain to knowledge is considered to be great enough.

SUMMARY

The Value of Social Psychology Research

- Research by social psychologists teaches people how to interpret and predict the outcomes of various social experiences. Study results and findings help people understand their own behavior and that of others.

How Social Psychologists Test Ideas

- Social psychologists often use *participant observation*, placing themselves in real situations to understand a social phenomenon better and helping them plan research that will test the hypotheses developed in observational settings.
- Social psychologists use *archives* for information that helps them understand social phenomena; such records include census reports, police records, newspaper accounts, and historic and ethnographic records.
- *Surveys* ask people questions. *Random sampling* is essential for accurately describing the attitudes or behavior of people of a particular population, such as students at a certain university, residents of a town, or the population of a country as a whole.
- *Correlational research* examines relationships between variables, such as between age and support for welfare reform. Correlations can vary in strength from −1 to +1. Longitudinal studies examine the correlation between a measure at one time and the same or a different measure at a later time.

- The problem of *self-selection* in correlational research occurs when the investigator is unable to choose the level of any variable for participants. Consequently, it's impossible to know if something associated with one of the measured variables is causing the correlation between two variables, or if one of the variables is causing the other.
- In *experimental research*, the investigator manipulates different levels of the *independent variable* (the variable about which a prediction is made) and measures the effect of different levels on the *dependent variable*.

More Concepts for Understanding Research

- *External validity* refers to how closely the experimental setup resembles real-life situations. The greater the external validity, the more it is possible to generalize from the results obtained to real-life settings.
- *Field experiments* test hypotheses experimentally in real-life situations as opposed to the laboratory. Field experiments automatically have external validity.
- *Internal validity* refers to whether the experimenter can be confident that it is the manipulated variable only that accounts for the results, rather than some extraneous factor such as participants' failure to understand instructions.
- When *debriefing* study participants, investigators explain the purpose of the experiment and the likely knowledge gain.
- *Reliability* refers to the extent to which participants receive the same score when tested with a conceptually similar instrument or when tested at different times.
- *Measurement validity* is the degree to which some measure predicts what it is supposed to, such as the degree to which an IQ test predicts school grades.
- *Regression to the mean* is the tendency of extreme scores on a variable to be followed by, or accompanied by, less extreme scores.
- *Statistical significance* is a measure of the probability that a result could have occurred by chance.

Basic and Applied Science

- *Basic science* is research conducted for the purpose of testing theories. *Applied science* is research intended to solve real-world problems.
- *Replication* of research is repeating a study in order to determine whether the findings can be duplicated.

Ethical Concerns in Social Psychology Research

- *Institutional review boards* are committees that review research procedures to make sure that the privacy and safety of participants are protected.

- *Informed consent* refers to the willingness of participants to take part in a study based on information presented to them before the study begins, informing them of the procedures they will undergo and any possible risks.

Informed consent is not always possible, as when an experiment involves deception, in which participants are misled about the purposes of a study.

THINK ABOUT IT

1. After reading this chapter, do you think it's important for students of social psychology to have a basic understanding of research methods? Why or why not?

2. In an experiment on nonconscious processing, participants read a persuasive message in a room with either a fishy smell, an unpleasant smell that was not fishy, or no distinctive smell (Lee & Schwartz, 2012). The researchers measured the degree to which the participant was persuaded by the message, and discovered that participants were the least likely to be persuaded in the presence of a fishy smell (there was something "fishy" about the message). In this experiment, what was the independent variable? What was the dependent variable?

3. Suppose a group of researchers hypothesized that finding your romantic partner physically attractive contributes to feelings of satisfaction in your relationship. To evaluate this hypothesis, 100 participants completed a survey that included questions assessing their current relationship satisfaction, as well as ratings of how physically attractive they believed their partner to be. The researchers found that the more physically attractive participants rated their partners, the more satisfied they tended to be in their relationship. In this fictitious study, did the researchers employ a correlational or an experimental design? How do you know?

4. Consider the hypothetical study in question 3 again. The researchers found a relationship between perceptions of partner physical attractiveness and relationship satisfaction. With these data, can the researchers conclude that perceiving your partner as physically attractive causes you to become more satisfied in your

relationship? Are there other potential explanations for these findings?

5. In Chapter 3, you will learn about research on the self, including self-esteem. Suppose the scatterplot below displays the relationship between self-esteem and academic success. How might you interpret this graph? Is the correlation between these two variables positive or negative? Try guessing the correlation coefficient.

6. In this textbook, you will learn about various studies evaluating social psychological phenomena using functional magnetic resonance imaging (fMRI), which measures activation in the brain while the participant lies immobile in a large metal tube, looking at a small computer screen. For example, in studying relationships, researchers may measure brain activation while participants experience a social rejection, or may look at how brain activation during a stressful experience is affected if a close friend holds the participant's hand. How would you characterize the external validity of such research?

THE ANSWER GUIDELINES FOR THE THINK ABOUT IT QUESTIONS CAN BE FOUND AT THE BACK OF THE BOOK . . .

The Social Self

On October 17, 1972, Marshall Bruce Mathers III was born in Saint Joseph, a small town in Missouri. After being abandoned by his father, Marshall and his mother moved from city to city, often struggling to get by on welfare. Marshall was in his early teens when they finally settled in Detroit, Michigan. At around age 11, Marshall was introduced to hip hop music. By 14, he had dropped out of school and was performing amateur raps. In 1997, Marshall, increasingly known as Eminem, placed second in that year's Rap Olympics. A year later, he signed with the record label Aftermath Entertainment, headed by fellow rapper and record producer Dr. Dre. In 1999, Eminem introduced the world to his alter ego, Slim Shady, in his debut album, *The Slim Shady LP*. And, as the saying goes, the rest is (music) history. The album went triple platinum by the end of 1999 and catapulted Eminem to stardom.

Over the next decade, Eminem faced one controversy after another, due, among other things, to lyrics laced with profanity, as well as misogynist and homophobic sentiments, even as his record sales soared and he received multiple Grammy awards. During this same period, Eminem started an acting career, married and divorced the same woman twice, was arrested for assault and carrying a concealed weapon, nearly died from a drug overdose, and checked into and out of rehab.

Fans and critics alike eagerly awaited the 2008 release of Eminem's memoir, *The Way I Am*, chronicling the colorful life of the talented and controversial star. Unlike an autobiography, a memoir reflects a less formal account of the subject's life. As the writer Gore Vidal put it: "A memoir is how one remembers one's own life, while

Who Is Eminem?

Like most people, Eminem—pictured here during a performance, arriving at the premiere of his movie *8 Mile*, and sitting quietly in the audience at the 53rd Annual Grammy Awards show in 2011—has many different selves.

an autobiography is history, requiring research, dates, facts double-checked." Vidal's view of memoirs describes Eminem's well. At the same time, it illustrates a central theme in social psychology: that reality is subjective, a product of our construal of the social world. And that world includes ourselves. *The Way I Am* doesn't tell us who Eminem is in an objective sense; it sheds light on who Eminem thinks he is. It tells us how Eminem makes sense of his own qualities and behaviors that, to the outside observer, can seem utterly incompatible. For example, the average person might find it puzzling that Eminem can spew forth profanity after profanity, knowing that his audience is filled with young, impressionable ears—and yet he can be fiercely protective of his own children. But this seeming contradiction might make perfect sense to Eminem himself.

For each of us, as for Eminem, our self is in part a product of our construals, yet the self is fundamentally social in nature. We come to know ourselves through the immediate social environment, the surrounding culture, and our gender. Our self-esteem is often based on comparisons we make between ourselves and others. We regulate our behavior by initiating, altering, and controlling it in the pursuit of our goals, and we present ourselves to others in ways designed to get them to form particular impressions of us. Like Eminem's Slim Shady, most of us have alter egos— second (and third, and fourth) selves—that characterize who we are in the presence of relevant audiences. This chapter explores these notions to draw a portrait of the self as it is constructed, maintained, and negotiated in the social environment.

The Nature of the Social Self

The social psychological study of the self usually begins with William James. In his book *The Principles of Psychology* (1890), James introduced many concepts about the self that continue to inspire research today. One of his most enduring contributions is reflected in the title of this chapter, "The *Social* Self." James coined the term the *social me* to refer to the parts of self-knowledge that are derived from social relationships. James' term reflects his conviction that the self is not something to be distinguished from the social world, but rather that it's a social entity through and through. Who a person is in one social context (with soccer buddies) is often not the same as who the person is in another social environment (with a romantic partner). Recall from Chapter 1 that there are cultural differences in the self-conceptions that people hold dear—another illustration of the social nature of the self. In this chapter, we explore cultural and other key social origins of the self. As James articulated over a century ago, our sense of who we are is forged in large part by our interactions with others.

Introspection

Before we explore the social underpinnings of the self, let's address an intuition you're likely to have, namely that a major source of self-understanding is, well, ourselves. Indeed, the Ancient Greek admonition to "know thyself" seems to imply that self-knowledge can be acquired through introspection. People do indeed focus their attention on themselves in a deliberate attempt to enhance self-understanding. Dan McAdams (2008) even proposes that people often go beyond such basic introspective efforts to weave full-fledged stories about themselves, what he refers to as the narrated self.

McAdams' central claim is that we are continually telling a story about ourselves as we live our lives. Like a good novel, this narrated self has settings (where you grew up), characters (a generous mentor), plot twists and turns (your parents' divorce), dramatic themes (the quest for justice), and vivid images and scenes (when your "one and only" dumped you for your best friend). We construct these self-narratives, McAdams maintains, to integrate our many goals, to make sense of conflict, and to explain how we change over time. Eminem's memoir can be thought of as his narrated self, at least the version that existed when he wrote it. Your narrated self right now might focus on your choices for a particular life path—a career, a romantic partner, the pursuit of particular values. Vivid and engaging self-narratives, McAdams finds, enable people to feel happy and fulfilled as they age. The notion of the narrated self fits into a broad theme of this book—that our understanding of the social world, including ourselves, is often shaped by construal processes.

The Accuracy of Self-Knowledge

If self-knowledge is at least partly a product of construal processes, several questions arise about the accuracy of self-knowledge. To put it another way, if you wanted to find out who someone is, who would you ask? Most of us assume that the best person to ask is the person himself or herself (Pronin, Kruger, Savitsky, & Ross, 2001). After all, this person has privileged access to self-relevant information, such as past experiences, not to mention current thoughts, feelings, and intentions (Epley & Dunning, 2006). Yet we're also quick to recognize that people can sometimes possess a startling lack of self-insight. In fact, the reliability of introspection as a method of assessment has been debated for decades. Recall the research described in Chapter 1 in which Nisbett and Wilson (1977) set up situations that enabled these researchers to discover that people can readily provide explanations for their evaluations and behaviors that are not in fact accurate. Someone might say that the nightgown she likes best is the one with the

"A man has as many social selves as there are individuals who recognize him. As many different social selves as there are distinct groups about whose opinions he cares."

—WILLIAM JAMES

best texture or color, when in fact she picked it out because it was the last one she saw. Our ability to report accurately even on quite important questions—such as why we chose job candidate A over job candidate B, why we like Joe better than Jack, or how we solved a particular problem—can be wide of the mark (Nisbett & Wilson, 1977).

Sometimes we lack self-insight because of strong motives; there are certain things many of us would rather not know about ourselves. But much of the time, introspection leads to inaccurate conclusions about the self simply because we don't have access to certain mental processes, such as those that lead us to prefer, say, objects placed in the rightmost position of an array or that we've seen last (Wilson, 2002; Wilson & Dunn, 2004). Such mental processes are nonconscious, occurring outside of our awareness, leaving us to generate alternative, plausible accounts for our preferences and behaviors instead.

Given such roadblocks, how can a person gain accurate self-knowledge? Recent research suggests that other people can be good sources of knowledge about ourselves. Vazire and Mehl (2008) asked participants to rate how accurate they think people are at assessing how much they themselves perform 25 different behaviors (e.g., reading, singing, watching TV). The researchers also asked participants how accurate they think people are at predicting how often *other* people they know well perform the same types of behaviors. For every single behavior, the participants rated the accuracy of self-predictions to be greater than the accuracy of predictions about the behavior of others—again, reflecting a widespread assumption that each person is the best expert on himself or herself.

In a clever subsequent study, however, the same researchers again had participants report on their enactment of the 25 behaviors. They also recruited "informants"—close friends, parents, and romantic partners of the participants—to report on the participants' enactments of the same behaviors. Then, over a 4-day period, with participants wearing a device that records the ambient sounds of their daily lives, Vazire and Mehl measured the actual frequency of participants' behaviors. Contrary to the assumption that we know ourselves the best, they found that the reports of close others are as accurate as our own in anticipating our actual behavior.

But there is more to the story. Interestingly, ratings made by the self and ratings made by close others *independently* predicted the self's behavior. In other words, the two kinds of ratings had unique predictive power. Vazire and her colleagues argue that there are certain aspects of a person that are uniquely known to the self and certain aspects that are uniquely known to others (Vazire, 2010; Vazire & Carlson, 2011). Because we have greater information than others do about our inner states (such as our thoughts and feelings), we are better judges of our internal traits (being optimistic or pessimistic, for instance). Other people, though, have better information for judging our external traits, by observing our overt behavior, such as being boisterous or outspoken.

The Vazire researchers further point out that motivational forces can also be at play. As we will explore in depth later this chapter, most people want to think highly of themselves, so when it comes to value-laden traits, such as creativity, other people tend to know us better than we know ourselves—because their judgments are less likely to be tainted by the desire to arrive at favorable assessments of the self. Thus, introspection can yield accurate self-knowledge at least for certain aspects of the self, but for some aspects, other people can be a better source of information.

The Organization of Self-Knowledge

Regardless of its accuracy, there's no question that most of us have an enormous pool of self-knowledge. This includes the self-narratives we are constructing and updating on an ongoing basis, as well as all the inferences we've made about ourselves based on our life experiences. Collectively, all this self-knowledge is stored in our memories in some fashion, and it is capable of being retrieved, elaborated upon, and used as a source of information, continuity, comfort, or dismay.

Social psychologists assume that self-knowledge is stored in memory in cognitive structures known as self-schemas. Built from past experience, **self-schemas** represent people's beliefs and feelings about themselves, both in general and in particular kinds of situations (Greenwald, 1980; Markus, 1977; Markus & Wurf, 1987). Consider the domain of conscientiousness. Each of us has a self-schema representing our beliefs and feelings about how conscientious (or not) we are. These beliefs and feelings are based on our experiences in situations where conscientiousness was relevant (such as studying for exams or remembering a sibling's birthday). The relevant experiences are stored in memory as part of our conscientiousness self-schema.

People vary in the precise content of any self-schema and in how elaborated it is. The self-schema of a person who views himself as very high (or low) in conscientiousness is likely to include more (or fewer) instances of past conscientious behavior, along with more elaborate beliefs about what it means to be high (or low) in conscientiousness, compared with the self-schema of a person for whom conscientiousness is not part of her self-conception at all.

Like the schemas we have about personality traits, other people, situations, and objects, the schemas we have about ourselves serve as more than simple storehouses of self-knowledge. They also perform an organizing function, by helping us navigate, and make sense of, all the information that bombards us every day.

In one of the earliest papers exploring the concept of self-schemas, Hazel Markus (1977) hypothesized that if self-schemas exist, then a person who has a self-schema in a particular domain (a self-schema about extraversion or intellectual curiosity, perhaps) should process information in that domain more quickly, retrieve evidence consistent with the self-schema more rapidly, and readily reject information that contradicts the self-schema. To test these hypotheses, Markus first identified participants who labeled themselves as either quite dependent or quite independent. These participants she called "schematic" for the dimension of dependence. She also identified "aschematic" participants: those who rated themselves moderately on the independent-dependent dimension, and for whom neither dependence nor independence was important to their self-definition.

Several weeks later, the participants rated how well a series of traits presented on a computer screen described them. The schematic participants judged schema-relevant traits as true or not true of themselves much more quickly than aschematic participants, suggesting that people are particularly attuned to information that maps onto a self-schema. The schematic participants were also able to generate many more behaviors consistent with the schema-relevant traits, suggesting that past actions and experiences supporting the self-schema

self-schema A cognitive structure, derived from past experience, that represents a person's beliefs and feelings about the self in general and in specific situations.

"I don't know anybody here but the hostess—and, of course, in a deeper sense, myself."

are abundant in memory and come readily to mind. Finally, the schematic participants were more likely to refute feedback from a personality test that contradicted their self-schemas, such as independent participants being told they were actually dependent. In short, regardless of their accuracy, self-schemas serve as the basic units of organization for self-knowledge, and influence our interpretations and judgments of ourselves and the social world.

⏴ LOOKING BACK

The notion that the self is fundamentally social has long been recognized. As the immediate or broader social context shifts, so too may the nature of the self. Self-knowledge is derived in part from introspection, but this knowledge can be subject to construal processes, is limited by what people have introspective access to, and can be distorted by motivational forces. Self-knowledge is stored in memory in cognitive structures known as self-schemas.

Origins of the Sense of Self

Where does your sense of self come from? A social psychological answer focuses on specific ways the social situation shapes the nature of the self. The social situation can be as concrete as cues in the immediate social context, such as the presence of a close friend or a more academically successful classmate. It can also be rather abstract and diffuse, such as norms conveyed by key institutions in one's culture or by members of an important social group, such as one's gender group.

Family and Other Socialization Agents

We learn what attitudes and behaviors are socially appropriate from parents, siblings, teachers, peers, and other socialization agents. This process happens naturally and directly, as when parents insist that their children share, take turns, and say "thank you." It also occurs indirectly, through modeling appropriate behavior. Socialization agents can also shape our sense of self. By encouraging certain behaviors and providing opportunities for particular activities, socialization agents can influence the personality traits, abilities, and preferences we come to think of as our own. Imagine a woman whose Jewish parents took her to synagogue every week as a child, insisted she take Hebrew lessons, and made sure she had a Bat Mitzvah ceremony. Because her parents encouraged her to engage in such religious activities, it's not surprising that, as an adult, being Jewish became central to this woman's sense of self. **Box 3.1** provides another illustration of how family—in particular, siblings—can profoundly influence the nature of the self.

Another way that family and other socialization agents shape the self is captured by the notion that we come to know ourselves by imagining what others think of us. The sociologist Charles H. Cooley (1902) coined the phrase "looking-glass self," referring to the idea that other people's reactions to us serve as a mirror of sorts. The approval and disapproval of others, and their comments about our behavior, allow us to "see ourselves as others see us." In other words, self-knowledge is derived in part from **reflected self-appraisals**, our beliefs about others' reactions to us. Throughout our lives, we experience overt or subtle reactions and appraisals from others. For example, your parents praise your

reflected self-appraisal A belief about what others think of one's self.

BOX 3.1 **FOCUS ON *EVOLUTION***

Siblings and the Social Self

What do most U.S. presidents, English and Canadian prime ministers, Oprah Winfrey, Bette Davis, and all of the actors who have portrayed James Bond (except Daniel Craig) have in common? What do Virginia Woolf, Ben Franklin, Charles Darwin, Mohandas Gandhi, Vincent Van Gogh, and Madonna have in common? The first group are firstborns. The second are later-borns. What does birth order have to do with a person's sense of self? According to Frank Sulloway (1996, 2001), a great deal. Sulloway has looked at sibling dynamics from an evolutionary perspective and arrived at a "born-to-rebel" hypothesis. Across species, Sulloway theorizes, sibling conflict, especially when resources are scarce, is frequent, widespread, and occasionally deadly. Sand sharks devour one another before birth in the oviducts of the mother until one well-fed young shark emerges. Once a blue-footed booby drops below 80 percent of its body weight, its siblings exclude it from the nest, or worse, peck it to death. Infant hyenas are born with large canine teeth, which they often use to deadly effect on their newly born siblings. Even in humans, young siblings engage in frequent conflict, up to one squabble every 5 minutes (Dunn & Munn, 1985). You may remember long car trips in which the chief entertainment was sibling baiting.

Humans have evolved adaptations, or solutions, to threats to survival, and one such adaptation involves a means of resolving sibling conflict. According to the principle of diversification, siblings develop different personality traits, abilities, and preferences within the same family so that they can peacefully occupy different niches.

Throughout most of development, older siblings are larger and more powerful and often act as surrogate parents. They are invested in the status quo, which, not coincidentally, benefits them. ("Things were fine until you came along.") In contrast, younger siblings, with the "establishment" niche already occupied by their older sibling, develop in ways that make them inclined to challenge the family status quo. In a review of 196 studies of personality and birth order, Sulloway found that older siblings tend to be more assertive and dominant and more achievement-oriented and conscientious. These traits are consistent with older siblings' more assertive, powerful role in the family. In contrast, younger siblings tend to be more agreeable, and they are likely to be more open to novel ideas and experiences. This social self emerges as younger siblings learn to coexist with their more dominant older siblings (which accounts for their elevated agreeableness), and as they find imaginative ways to carve out their own niche in the world (which accounts for their increased openness to experience). Charles Darwin is an excellent case study for Sulloway's hypothesis. The fifth of six children, Darwin developed perhaps the most revolutionary scientific theory in human history, one that challenged religious ideas about the creation of life on Earth. To do so, he circumnavigated the globe on the ship HMS *Beagle*, often facing great dangers as he collected evidence that led to his original, paradigm-shifting theory of evolution.

Sibling Conflict

Firstborns like Prince William (right) are often more responsible and more likely to support the status quo than younger siblings like Prince Harry, who often are more mischievous, more open to novel experiences, and more likely to rebel against authority.

---

accomplishments; a romantic partner makes light of your fears; a teacher assigns you a challenging task; your peers laugh heartily at your jokes. Reactions and appraisals such as these convey that you're competent, neurotic, have potential, or have a good sense of humor. In short, we see ourselves partly through the eyes of those around us.

The idea that we gain self-knowledge through reflected self-appraisals might seem to suggest that we have little say in how we see ourselves. But the key concept here is that we internalize how we *think* others perceive us, not necessarily how they *actually* see us. In fact, our reflected self-appraisals often don't correlate highly with the way other people evaluate us (Felson, 1993; Kenny & DePaulo, 1993; Shrauger & Schoeneman, 1979; Tice & Wallace, 2005). Most people think they are somewhat shy—probably including even the guy who can be counted on to be the life of the party (Zimbardo, 1990).

Figuring out how, and to what degree, reflected self-appraisals influence a person's sense of self can be tricky. For example, Amy's view of herself as a clumsy person could stem from her perception that her family and friends see her this way and convey that impression to her. But it's also possible that her view of herself as clumsy has been detected by other people who then convey that impression back to her. Self-views often affect the perceptions of other people, who then reflect those views back to us, as much as the other way around (Felson, 1993; Kenny & DePaulo, 1993). The upshot, then, is that although other people influence our sense of self through reflected self-appraisals, their impact may not be as simple and direct as the idea of the looking-glass self originally suggested.

Jennifer Pfeifer and her colleagues explored a novel way to examine whether reflected appraisals influence self-views, or vice versa. She looked at the neural systems that are engaged when people think about and report on their self-views versus their reflected self-appraisals (Pfeifer et al., 2009). Research suggests that activity in certain areas of the brain, including the medial prefrontal cortex, is heightened when we think about the self, as when someone asks us to think about who we are (Lieberman, 2007). Reflected self-appraisal, however, also requires social perception—in particular, taking the perspective of others (what do others think about me?)—and thus brain regions that support perspective taking are also engaged (such as the temporal-parietal junction).

Pfeifer and her colleagues looked at activity in the brains of both early adolescent and adult participants (Pfeifer et al., 2009). This allowed them to see whether the influence of reflected self-appraisals on self-views is greater during adolescence, a developmental period during which the opinions and evaluations of others are of pronounced importance. And in fact, when asked to report their self-views, young adolescents exhibited greater activity than adults in neural systems relevant to *both* self-perception and perspective taking. In other words, adolescents, more than adults, spontaneously relied on reflected appraisals when reporting their self-views, suggesting that adolescents' sense of self is especially likely to be based on their beliefs about how others view them.

Situationism and the Social Self

In the film *Zelig*, Woody Allen plays a character who automatically takes on the appearance of the people around him. Surrounded by a group of African-Americans, he begins to look black; in the presence of a group of elderly Greeks, he takes on their Mediterranean appearance. The humor of the film stems from how it makes light of a deeper truth: that our social self shifts dramatically from one situation to another. This notion that the social self changes across different contexts is consistent with the principle of *situationism,* and it's supported by abundant empirical evidence.

Aspects of the Self That Are Relevant in the Social Context Students who are rebellious and free-spirited in the dorm will shift to a more sober and

conventional demeanor around parents or professors. Someone who sees herself as relaxed and outspoken when with her close friends may be shy and inhibited when interacting with a group of new acquaintances. In situations where people experience a failure of some kind—for example, learning they have performed poorly on an exam—negative beliefs and feelings about the self come to the fore (Brown, 1998). Markus and Wurf (1987) coined the term **working self-concept** to refer to the idea that only a subset of a person's vast pool of self-knowledge is brought to mind in any given context—usually the subset that's most relevant or appropriate in the current situation. Thus, for example, notions of the self related to one's relationship are likely to be on the top of the mind with a romantic partner, whereas notions of the self related to competition are likely to be at the forefront when you're engaged in an important sports match.

Aspects of the Self That Are Distinctive in the Social Context William McGuire and Alice Padawer-Singer (1978) proposed another perspective on the effects of the current situation on the social self. According to their distinctiveness hypothesis, we highlight what makes us unique in a given social situation. To test this hypothesis, they asked sixth-graders at different schools to describe themselves. On average, children wrote 12 statements referring to their recreational activities, attitudes, friends, and school activities. (The children, incidentally, were more likely to refer to their dog when defining themselves than to all other family members combined!)

McGuire and Padawer-Singer examined these descriptions to see whether children defined themselves according to how they differed from their classmates. They did indeed (**Figure 3.1**). Thirty percent of the children who were especially young or old compared with their classmates (that is, 6 months from the most common age of their classmates) mentioned

Context and the Sense of Self
In Woody Allen's film *Zelig*, the title character takes on the appearance of those with whom he interacts, providing a dramatic illustration of how we often express different characteristics when in different social contexts. (A) Zelig looks Chinese when he is next to a Chinese man. (B) Zelig takes on African-American features when he stands between two African-American men.

working self-concept A subset of self-knowledge that is brought to mind in a particular context.

Percentage of students who mention a particular fact in self-definition

American children define themselves according to how they are unique and different from their classmates.

■ Typical
■ Unusual

Figure 3.1
Distinctiveness and the Sense of Self

SOURCE: Adapted from McGuire & Padawer-Singer, 1978.

their age in their self-definition, whereas only 19 percent of the other children did. Forty-four percent of the children who were born outside the United States mentioned this biographical fact, whereas only 7 percent of those born in the United States mentioned that fact about themselves. Twenty-six percent of the children of the minority gender in their class mentioned their gender as part of their self-definition compared with 11 percent of the majority gender (see also Cota & Dion, 1986). At least in the Western world, what's most central to identity is what makes a person distinct. Being white, for example, is likely to be often on Eminem's mind given that the world he occupies is filled with black artists.

Malleability and Stability Most of us would readily agree that our sense of self shifts depending on the social context. Yet we also experience a sense of continuity in the self, the feeling that we have a stable, core self. How can we reconcile what appear to be dueling notions of malleability and stability in the social self?

There are several paths of reconciliation. First, although the content of the working self-concept varies across situations, there are nevertheless core aspects of self-knowledge that are likely to be on the top of the mind whenever a person thinks about the self (Markus, 1977). Thus, although Joo Young may see herself as painfully shy around members of the opposite sex but outgoing with her girl-friends, she sees herself as a good listener no matter who she is around. For LGBT (lesbian, gay, bisexual, and transgender) people, who frequently face the decision of whether or not to disclose their LGBT status, their sexual-minority identity is likely to be a core, cross-situationally salient aspect of the self (Cain, 1991).

Second, a person's overall pool of self-knowledge remains relatively stable over time, providing a sense of self-continuity even as different pieces of self-knowledge come to the fore in different contexts (Linville & Carlston, 1994). Thus, your belief that you're lazy may not be part of your working self-concept in a job interview (at least let's hope this isn't the case), but it's nonetheless stored in memory, ready to be retrieved when you're lounging around watching TV instead of doing the laundry.

Finally, although a person's sense of self may shift depending on the context, it's likely that these shifts conform to a predictable, stable pattern (Chen, Boucher, & Tapias, 2006; English & Chen, 2007; Mischel & Shoda, 1995). Take a person who sees herself as confident around her friends, but as insecure around her overly critical mother. Although this person's sense of self clearly shifts according to the social context, it's not as if she's confident around her friends one day and insecure around them the next. In other words, the malleability in this individual's self is itself *stable*. Whenever she is around her friends, she sees herself as confident, whereas being around her mother reliably shifts her self-concept to include being insecure. In short, the social self is defined by two truths: it is malleable, shifting from one context to another, and at the same time a person's social self has core components that persist across contexts.

Culture and the Social Self

The American Declaration of Independence and the *Analects* of the Chinese philosopher Confucius have shaped the lives of billions of people. Yet they reflect radically different ideas about the social self. The Declaration of Independence prioritized the rights and freedoms of the individual, and it protected those rights and liberties from infringement by others. Confucius emphasized the

"We hold these truths to be self-evident, that all men are created equal, that they are endowed by their Creator with certain unalienable rights, that among these are Life, Liberty, and the pursuit of Happiness."
—DECLARATION OF INDEPENDENCE

importance of knowing one's place in society, of honoring traditions, duties, and social roles, and of thinking of others before the self.

The differences reflected in these documents run deep in the cultures people inhabit. In Western societies, people are concerned about their individuality, about freedom, and about self-expression. Our adages reflect this: "The squeaky wheel gets the grease." "If you've got it, flaunt it." In Asian cultures, homilies and folk wisdom encourage a different view of the self: "The empty wagon makes the most noise." "The nail that stands up is pounded down." Hazel Markus, Shinobu Kitayama, and Harry Triandis have offered far-reaching theories about how cultures vary in the social selves they encourage and how these different conceptions of the self shape the emotions we feel, the motivations that drive us, and our ways of perceiving the social world (Markus & Kitayama, 1991; Triandis, 1989, 1994, 1995). Before reading about two distinct self-construals that tend to vary across cultures, complete the exercise in **Figure 3.2**. Really, do this. You'll get much more out of the following discussion if you do.

Independent and Interdependent Self-Construals Cultures that promote an *independent self-construal* include much of the West, especially northwestern Europe and former British colonies, such as Canada, the United States, Australia, and New Zealand. In these societies, the self is an autonomous entity that is distinct and separate from others (**Figure 3.3A**). It's important for people to assert their uniqueness and independence, and the focus is on internal causes of behavior. These imperatives lead to a conception of the self in terms of traits that are stable across time and social context.

In contrast, in cultures that foster *interdependent self-construals*, the self is fundamentally connected to other people (**Figure 3.3B**). The imperatives are to find a place within the community and to fulfill appropriate roles. There is close attention to social contexts and a recognition of the shifting demands of situations on behavior. These concerns lead to a conception of the self as something embedded within social relationships, roles, and duties. This kind of self-construal is prevalent in many Asian cultures, as well as in many Eastern European cultures (Grossmann & Varnum, 2011; Realo & Allik, 1999; Tower, Kelly, & Richards, 1997), South Asian cultures (Dhawan, Roseman, Naidu, Thapa, & Rettek, 1995; Savani, Markus, & Conner, 2008), African cultures (Ma & Schoeneman, 1997; Mwaniki, 1973), and Latin American cultures (Sanchez-Burks, Nisbett, & Ybarra, 2000).

In short, an independent self-construal promotes an inward focus on the self, whereas an interdependent self-construal encourages an outward focus on the social situation. Research shows that this difference in focus is reflected in the self-narratives of members of different

> *"A person of humanity wishing to establish his own character, also establishes the character of others."*
>
> —CONFUCIUS

FIGURE 3.2 **YOU BE THE SUBJECT**

Self-Definition

Write down ten things that describe who you are. You will have a chance to reflect on your answers later in this section.

1. I am
2. I am
3. I am
4. I am
5. I am
6. I am
7. I am
8. I am
9. I am
10. I am

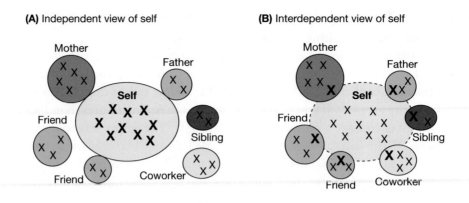

(A) Independent view of self

(B) Interdependent view of self

Figure 3.3

Views of the Self

(A) In the independent view of the self, the self is construed as a distinct, autonomous entity, separate from others and defined by distinct traits and preferences. (B) In the interdependent view of the self, the self is construed as connected to others and defined by duties, roles, and shared preferences and traits.

cultures. Cohen and Gunz (2002) asked Canadian and Asian students (a mixture of students from Hong Kong, China, Taiwan, Korea, and various South and Southeast Asian countries) to tell stories about ten different situations in which they were the center of attention—for example, being embarrassed. Canadians were more likely than Asians to reproduce the scene from their original point of view, looking outward from their own perspective. Asians were more likely to imagine the scene as an observer might, describing it from a third-person perspective. We might say that Westerners tend to experience and recall events from the inside out—with themselves at the center, looking out at the world. Easterners are more likely to experience and recall events from the outside in—starting from the social world, looking back at themselves as an object of attention. Westerners play the lead in their personal narratives; non-Westerners are more likely to be just one among many cast members. **Figure 3.4** provides another illustration of differences between Westerners and East Asians in the degree of attention they pay to the social context.

Who Are You? The common belief among Westerners that they are self-contained is shown by simply asking them to describe themselves (as you were asked to do in Figure 3.2). Kuhn and McPartland (1954) invented a simple "Who Am I?" exercise that asks people to list 20 statements that describe who they are. Americans' self-descriptions tend to be context-free responses referring to personality traits ("I'm friendly," "hardworking," "shy") and personal preferences ("I like camping"). The responses of interdependent participants tend to refer to relationships with other people or groups ("I am Jan's friend") and are often qualified by context ("I am serious at work"; "I am fun-loving with my friends") (Cousins, 1989; Ip & Bond, 1995; Markus & Kitayama, 1991). Take a minute to look back at your own answers on the ten-question Who Am I? exercise in Figure 3.2 and see what type of personal characterizations you emphasized.

Ma and Schoeneman (1997) gave the Who Am I? test to American university students and to four different groups living in Kenya: university students, workers in Nairobi (the capital city), and traditional Maasai and Samburu herding peoples. Kenya was for decades a colony of Great Britain, and city dwellers,

BOX 3.2 **FOCUS ON *CULTURE AND NEUROSCIENCE***

Culture and the Social Self in the Brain

As we saw in our discussion of reflected appraisals and the brain, when people are asked to judge the self with respect to various trait dimensions, a certain region of the brain known as the medial prefrontal cortex is particularly active (Heatherton et al., 2006). This suggests that this part of the frontal lobe is involved in processes that represent self-knowledge. Zhu and his colleagues conducted a study using an interesting twist on this paradigm to ascertain whether many of the cultural differences in self-construal discussed in this chapter would be reflected in differences in neural activation (Zhu, Zhang, Fan, & Han, 2007). They had Chinese participants and Western Europeans rate the applicability of different traits to themselves, their mothers, and another unrelated person. For members of both cultures, considering the applicability of the traits to themselves produced activation in the medial prefrontal cortex. But for Chinese participants, activation in this same region was also observed when participants were thinking about whether the traits characterized their mothers. For the Westerners, there was, if anything, a relative deactivation of the medial prefrontal cortex when they thought about their mothers. These findings seem to suggest that for people with interdependent self-construals, the same region of the brain represents the self and mother; they are merged within the brain. In contrast, for those with independent self-construals, the self and mother are quite distinct, all the way down to which neurons are activated in each person's brain.

Figure 3.4
Cultural Differences in Attention to the Social Context
In this study, American and Japanese participants were shown picture stimuli, a series of cartoons with either a Caucasian boy (for Americans) or an Asian boy (for Japanese) in the center, surrounded by four other people who were the same in all the pictures (Masuda et al., 2008). In some cartoons, the emotional expression of the boy (e.g., happy) matched the emotional expressions on the faces of the surrounding people (e.g., happy). In other cases, as in the two pictures shown above, there was a mismatch in the emotional expressions of the boy (e.g., angry) versus the others (e.g., happy). The findings demonstrate that when judging an individual's emotions, the Japanese are more likely to take into account the emotions of others in the surrounding social context.

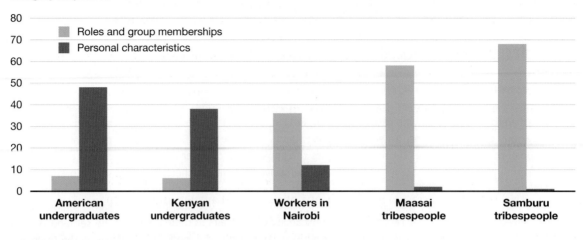

Percentage of category responses

Figure 3.5
Self-Characterization in Four African Groups
The results from this study suggest that Westernization is associated with the development of a more independent self-construal.

SOURCE: Ma & Schoeneman, 1997.

especially those who are educated, have had a great deal of exposure to Western culture. Kenyan students have been exposed still more to Western culture and are being educated in a Western tradition. In contrast, traditional African tribespeople are reputed to have little sense of themselves as individuals. Rather, their sense of self is defined by family, property, and position in the community. Tribespeople are constantly made aware of their roles and status in relation to family members and other groups (Mwaniki, 1973).

Figure 3.5 shows how differently these four African groups view themselves. Traditional Maasai and Samburu characterize themselves in terms of roles and group memberships, whereas Kenyan students are far more likely to mention personal characteristics. Kenyan students, in fact, differ only slightly from American students. Workers in Nairobi are in between the tribespeople and the students. This pattern of evidence, when considered in relation to the very large differences typically found between East Asian and Western students, suggests that modernization by itself does not produce substantial differences in self-conceptions. Rather, it is a Western orientation that seems essential to an independent conception of the self.

Gender and the Social Self

In a review of the literature on the self-concept and gender, Susan Cross and Laura Madson (1997) gathered evidence indicating that women in the United States tend to construe the self in more interdependent terms than men do—that is, in terms of connection to others. In contrast, men in the United States tend to prioritize difference and uniqueness, construing the self in more independent terms. The same gender differences are found among the Japanese (Kashima, Siegal, Tanaka, & Kashima, 1992).

The evidence for these basic differences in self-construal is diverse. When women describe themselves, they are more likely than men to refer to social characteristics and relationships (Maccoby & Jacklin, 1974). When selecting photographs that are most revealing of who they are, women are more likely than men to choose photos that include other people, such as friends and family members (Clancy & Dollinger, 1993). In social interactions, women tend to be more empathic and better judges of other people's personalities and emotions (Ambady, Hallahan, & Rosenthal, 1995; Bernieri, Zuckerman, Koestner, & Rosenthal, 1994; Davis & Franzoi, 1991; Eisenberg & Lennon, 1983; Hall, 1984). Men tend to be more attuned to their own internal responses, such as increased heart rate, whereas women are more attuned to situational cues, such as other people's reactions (Pennebaker & Roberts, 1992; Roberts & Pennebaker, 1995).

Where do these gender differences in self-construal come from? Socialization processes are one influential source. Many agents of socialization guide women and men into different self-construals. The media portray women and men differently, typically showcasing men in positions of power and agency and women in more nurturing roles. Parents raise girls and boys differently. For example, parents tend to talk with their girls more than their boys about emotions and being sensitive to others (Fivush, 1989, 1992). The friendships and groups that people form from the earliest ages also influence gender differences in self-construal. Starting at age 3 and continuing through the primary school years, girls and boys tend to play in gender-segregated groups that reinforce and amplify the differences in self-construal (Maccoby, 1990). Girls' groups tend to focus on cooperative games that are oriented toward interpersonal relationships (for example, mother and child). Boys' groups tend to emphasize competition, hierarchy, and distinctions among individuals. As adults, gender-specific roles further amplify these differences. For example, even today, Western women take on most of the responsibilities for raising children, which calls on interdependent tendencies.

In addition, certain gender differences in the social self may have originated in human evolutionary history. Men were equipped physically and psychologically for hunting and aggressive encounters with other groups, whereas women were equipped physically and psychologically for nurturing the young. Thus, an independent self-construal fits the roles largely fulfilled by males in our evolutionary history, and an interdependent self-construal is better tailored to the caregiving demands that fell disproportionately to females. Yet different cultures have very different ways of dealing with gender, and the past several generations have witnessed enormous changes in gender roles, especially in the West. To whatever degree evolution may have contributed to gender differences in self-construal, these sorts of sex differences are not inevitable, suggesting there are limits to any evolutionary account of the role of gender in the nature of the self-concept.

Social Comparison

Sometimes people actively seek out information about themselves through comparison with other people. This is the central tenet of **social comparison theory**, an influential and enduring theory in social psychology put forward by Leon Festinger in the early 1950s (Festinger, 1954; see also Suls & Wheeler, 2000; Wood, 1996). The essence of the theory is that when people have no objective standard by which to evaluate their traits or abilities, they do so largely by comparing themselves with others. Whether you are "physically strong" can be determined fairly objectively by simple tests of strength. But to be "honest" or "morally upright," dimensions that are less easy to quantify objectively, is to be more honest and morally upright than others.

social comparison theory The hypothesis that people compare themselves to other people in order to obtain an accurate assessment of their own opinions, abilities, and internal states.

BOX 3.3 **FOCUS ON *CULTURE***

Social Class Shapes the Social Self

Mounting evidence shows that a person's social class also shapes the self a person adopts. Markus and her colleagues propose that life in different social-class subcultures in the United States promotes the elaboration of distinct self-construals (Stephens, Markus, & Phillips, 2013). Living in relatively higher-class environments, characterized by more abundant resources, safer neighborhoods, greater education access, higher job security, and so on, affords people with the opportunity, if not the mandate, to develop selves that reflect the U.S. cultural ideal of independence. This independent self-construal emphasizes choice, freedom from constraint, the pursuit of opportunities, and self-expression. In contrast, the culture of lower-class individuals in the United States is characterized by fewer resources, less safe neighborhoods, limited education access, and tenuous job security. In such circumstances, the Stephens team argues, it makes sense that people would develop selves that are more sensitive to the social context, to the constraints in the environment, and to their dependence on others. Among

lower-class individuals, a more socially responsive, interdependent kind of self-construal is promoted.

The different self-construals of higher- and lower-class individuals matter. Because the norms and values of many U.S. institutions are grounded in the ideal of independence, people who hold an independent self-construal, and exhibit its corresponding psychological tendencies and behaviors, are at a distinct advantage—and one that serves to perpetuate social-class differences. For example, in the vast majority of American schools, administrators and teachers expect and reward behavior associated with an independent self-construal, such as working on one's own rather than in a group and standing out from the pack (Stephens et al., 2012). It's hardly surprising, then, that the children whose social class promotes an independent self-construal have better academic achievement outcomes than their counterparts raised in a social class that encourages interdependence.

Researchers have begun to explore ways to change institutions so that they promote the growth and development of lower-class individuals and,

accordingly, help close the social-class achievement gap. Stephens, Hamedani, and Destin (2014) studied a group of incoming first-generation college students (students who do not have parents with 4-year degrees and who are disproportionately in the lower class) and a group of continuing-generation students (those who have at least one parent with a 4-year degree). Both participant groups listened to one of two panels of first-generation and continuing-generation junior- and senior-year college students sharing stories about their college experiences. The two panels differed in whether they discussed how their social-class backgrounds influenced their college experiences. Panelists in the "difference-education" condition described the ways their social-class backgrounds had had both positive and negative effects, emphasizing the importance of using strategies that take into account their different social-class status. Panelists in the "standard control" condition also shared stories about their college experiences but did not highlight the role of their social class.

Class Differences and the Social Self
Higher- and lower-class individuals often inhabit very different environments, as shown by these pictures of an upper-class neighborhood on the left and a lower-class neighborhood on the right.

Remarkably, the typical academic achievement gap seen between first- and continuing-generation students was eliminated among students exposed to the difference-education panel. The researchers showed that the elimination of this gap occurred because the intervention increased the likelihood that first-generation students sought out college resources (such as e-mailing a professor for help) and, as a result, improved their grades. Exposure to the difference-education panelists also had broader benefits, such as decreasing stress and anxiety among both first- and continuing-generation students. It thus appears that even relatively simple interventions can help level the playing field for individuals, such as those with lower-class backgrounds, who tend to hold interdependent self-construals, yet are faced with tasks and situations tailored to reward independence. Social class shapes the nature of the social self, but does not have to determine life outcomes.

Festinger noted, however, that there is no point in comparing yourself with Steve Jobs or Serena Williams, nor is it very helpful to compare yourself with total novices. To get an accurate sense of how good you are at something, you must compare yourself with people who have roughly your level of skill. Numerous experiments have demonstrated that people are indeed especially drawn to comparisons with others roughly similar to themselves (Kruglanski & Mayseless, 1990; Suls, Martin, & Wheeler, 2002; Suls & Wheeler, 2000).

We like to feel good about ourselves, though, so our search for similar targets of comparison tends to be biased toward people who are slightly inferior to, or worse off than, ourselves. This is ironic because it puts us in the position of saying, "Compared with people who are slightly worse at tennis than I am, I'm pretty good!" or "Compared with people who are almost as conscientious as I am, I'm pretty darn conscientious!" These sorts of *downward* social comparisons help us define ourselves favorably, giving a boost to our self-esteem (Aspinwall & Taylor, 1993; Helgeson & Mickelson, 1995; Lockwood, 2002).

"It is not enough to succeed. Others must fail."

—GORE VIDAL

Social Comparisons
It's not informative to compare your intelligence or athletic skill to someone renowned for brilliance or celebrated for tennis-playing ability.

Do biased social comparisons like these come at a cost? After all, we can learn a lot from people who are better than we are in various domains of life, and we sacrifice opportunities for improvement if we only engage in downward social comparison. In fact, when our focus is on improving some skill or component of our personality, we tend to forgo the self-esteem benefits of downward social comparison and engage in *upward* social comparison instead (Blanton, Pelham, De Hart, & Kuyper, 1999). For example, in one study that examined the social comparisons made by a group of ninth-graders, researchers found that students usually chose to compare their grades with those of someone who had slightly better grades than they did, presumably with the hope that one day they might get higher grades themselves (Blanton, Buunk, Gibbons, & Kuyper, 1999).

We can also try to have it both ways. An important study of breast cancer patients showed how people get the emotional benefits of favorable comparisons without forfeiting the opportunity to learn from those who are better off (Taylor & Lobel, 1989). They do so by *comparing* themselves with those who are worse off ("I only had to have one set of lymph nodes removed") but *affiliating* with those who are better off ("She seems to be in good spirits all the time, and I'd like to ask her over for lunch to find out how she does it").

🔄 LOOKING BACK

The social self originates from a variety of sources. Parents and other socialization agents—by virtue of what they teach us, what they encourage in us, how they react to us—help define who we are. The current situation matters as well: the social self shifts from one context to another. A person's culture of origin shapes the social self in profound ways. People from Western cultures, especially men in these cultures, define the self in independent terms, emphasizing uniqueness and autonomy; people from East Asian cultures, and women in many cultures, define the self in interdependent terms, emphasizing connection to others. Finally, the social self is shaped by comparison to other people.

Self-Esteem

In 1987, California Governor George Deukmejian signed Assembly Bill 3659 into law. The bill allocated an annual budget of $245,000 for a self-esteem task force, charged with two goals: understanding the effects of self-esteem on drug use, teenage pregnancy, and high school dropout rates; and elevating the self-esteem of schoolchildren. The initiative was based on the assumption that strenghthening self-esteem would help cure society's ills.

Several findings would seem to support this assumption. People with low self-esteem are less satisfied with life, more hopeless, and more depressed (Crocker & Wolfe, 2001), and they are less able to cope with life's challenges, such as the social and academic demands of college (Cutrona, 1982). They tend to disengage from tasks following failure (Brockner, 1979), and they are more prone to anti-social behavior and delinquency (Donnellan, Trzesniewski, Robins, Moffitt, & Caspi, 2005). Raising self-esteem, the thinking was, just might produce healthier, more resilient children and a better society in the long run.

You probably recognize such a legislative act as something that could happen only in a Western culture (and perhaps only in California!). In fact, we examine some rather pronounced cultural differences in self-esteem later in this section.

In addition, it's important to note that the data the California legislators relied on were correlational in nature, which means causal conclusions about the role of self-esteem cannot be drawn on the basis of these data. Regardless of the merits (or shortcomings) of the California task force, the topic of self-esteem has attracted considerable attention by social psychologists.

Trait and State Self-Esteem

Self-esteem refers to the overall positive or negative evaluation people have of themselves. Researchers usually evaluate self-esteem with simple self-report measures like the scale in **Table 3.1**. As you can see from this scale, self-esteem represents how we feel about our attributes and qualities, our successes and failures, and our self in general. People with high self-esteem feel quite good about themselves. People with low self-esteem feel ambivalent about themselves; they tend to feel both good and bad about who they are. People who truly dislike themselves are rare and are typically found in specific clinical populations, such as severely depressed individuals.

Trait self-esteem is a person's enduring level of self-regard across time. Studies indicate that trait self-esteem is fairly stable: people who report high trait self-esteem at one point in time tend to report high trait self-esteem many years later; people who report low trait self-esteem at one point tend to report low trait self-esteem later (Block & Robins, 1993).

State self-esteem refers to the dynamic, changeable self-evaluations a person experiences as momentary feelings about the self (Heatherton & Polivy, 1991).

self-esteem The overall positive or negative evaluation an individual has of himself or herself.

TABLE 3.1 SELF-ESTEEM SCALE

Indicate your level of agreement with each of the following statements by using the scale below.

0 STRONGLY DISAGREE	1 DISAGREE	2 AGREE	3 STRONGLY AGREE

—— 1. At times I think I am no good at all.

—— 2. I take a positive view of myself.

—— 3. All in all, I am inclined to feel that I am a failure.

—— 4. I wish I could have more respect for myself.

—— 5. I certainly feel useless at times.

—— 6. I feel that I am a person of worth, at least on an equal plane with others.

—— 7. On the whole, I am satisfied with myself.

—— 8. I feel I do not have much to be proud of.

—— 9. I feel that I have a number of good qualities.

—— 10. I am able to do things as well as most other people.

To determine your score, first reverse the scoring for the five negatively worded items (1, 3, 4, 5, & 8) as follows: 0 = 3, 1 = 2, 2 = 1, 3 = 0. Then add up your scores across the 10 items. Your total score should fall between 0 and 30. Higher numbers indicate higher self-esteem.

SOURCE: Rosenberg, 1965.

Much as your working self-concept changes from one context to the next, so too does your state self-esteem, which rises and falls according to transient moods and specific construal processes that arise in different situations. For example, your current mood, either positive or negative, will shift your self-esteem up or down (Brown, 1998). When people experience a temporary setback, their self-esteem frequently takes a temporary dive—especially among those who have low self-esteem to begin with (Brown & Dutton, 1995). When college students watch their beloved college football team lose, their feelings of personal competence often drop (Hirt, Zillman, Erickson, & Kennedy, 1992). And children of average intelligence have lower self-esteem when they are in a classroom with academically talented children, rather than with children who have lower academic abilities (Marsh & Parker, 1984). Comparing themselves with highly talented children makes them feel less able. Self-esteem also shifts during different stages of development. As males move from early adolescence (age 14) to early adulthood (age 23), their self-esteem tends to rise. During the same period, females' self-esteem tends to fall (Block & Robins, 1993). Clearly, although one part of self-esteem is quite stable, another part shifts in response to a person's current social situation and broader life context.

Contingencies of Self-Worth

The domains in daily life that affect self-esteem differ from person to person. Jennifer Crocker and her colleagues have proposed a **contingencies of self-worth** account of self-esteem that captures this fact (Crocker & Wolfe, 2001; see also Crocker & Park, 2003). Self-esteem is contingent on—rises and falls with—successes and failures in domains on which a person has based his or her self-worth. These investigators have focused on several domains that are important for self-esteem among college students in particular: family support, school competence, competition, virtue, social approval, physical appearance, and religious identity (see also Crocker, Luhtanen, Cooper, & Bouvrette, 2003). A sample item measuring self-esteem contingency in the domain of academic competence is

contingencies of self-worth A perspective maintaining that self-esteem is contingent on successes and failures in domains on which a person has based his or her self-worth.

"My self-esteem gets a boost when I get a good grade on an exam or paper." An item measuring contingency in the domain of others' approval is "I can't respect myself if others don't respect me."

The key prediction of the contingencies of self-worth perspective is that self-esteem tends to rise when things are going well in domains that are personally important to us, but will drop when things go poorly in these domains. In a test of this prediction, researchers studied the self-esteem of University of Michigan students who had applied to graduate school (Crocker, Sommers, & Luhtanen, 2002). They asked students to go to a website and fill out a self-esteem questionnaire every day that they received a response from a graduate school—either an acceptance or a rejection. Not surprisingly, students in general had higher self-esteem on days when they received an acceptance and lower self-esteem on days when they received a rejection. However, these effects were much larger for those students whose self-esteem was heavily contingent on academic competence. These findings suggest that it's probably wise for people to base their sense of self-worth on performance in many domains, rather than put all their eggs in one basket. Indeed, studies have shown that to the extent we derive our sense of self-worth from multiple domains that are distinct from one another, the more likely we are to avoid feeling devastated by a setback or failure in any one domain (Linville, 1987; Showers, 1992).

Social Acceptance and Self-Esteem

Several of the domains that define people's self-worth—social approval, virtue, even competition—are highly social in nature. Mark Leary offered an especially social take on self-esteem, maintaining in his **sociometer hypothesis** that self-esteem is primarily a readout of our likely standing with others; that is, self-esteem is an internal, subjective index of how well we are regarded by others and hence how likely we are to be included or excluded by them (Leary, Tambor, Terdal, & Downs, 1995). Throughout most of evolutionary history, Leary reasons, we couldn't go it alone, and therefore we needed a way to quickly assess how we are doing socially. Our feelings of state self-esteem constitute just such an assessment.

"So, when he says, 'What a good boy am I,' Jack is really reinforcing his self-esteem."

Leary notes that those things that make us feel good about ourselves—feeling attractive, competent, likable, and morally upright—are precisely those things that make others accept us (or reject us if we fall short). High self-esteem indicates that we are thriving in our relationships; low self-esteem suggests that we are having interpersonal difficulties. In this sense, low self-esteem is not something to be avoided at all costs; rather, it provides useful information about when we need to attend to and shore up our social bonds.

Culture and Self-Esteem

East Asian languages have no word or phrase that captures the idea of feeling good about oneself. The Japanese have a term now, but like the Japanese rendering for *baseball*—namely, *beisoboru*—the word for *self-esteem* is simply borrowed from English: *serufu esutiimu*. The fact that it was Westerners who invented the

sociometer hypothesis The idea that self-esteem is an internal, subjective index or marker of the extent to which a person is included or looked on favorably by others.

"Who so would be a man must be a nonconformist. Hitch your wagon to a star. Insist on yourself; never imitate. The individual is the world."

—RALPH WALDO EMERSON

"Independence is happiness."

—SUSAN B. ANTHONY

term *self-esteem* reflects a long-standing concern in the West with the value of the individual. In the Enlightenment, during the eighteenth century, Western Europeans began to prioritize individuality, freedom, and rights—ideas that would weave their way into the U.S. Constitution (Baumeister, 1987; Seligman, 1988; Twenge, 2002). Nineteenth-century transcendentalist writers, including Ralph Waldo Emerson, Henry David Thoreau, and Margaret Fuller, continued this tradition and emphasized the dignity and power of the individual.

Today, the emphasis on self-esteem in the West is higher than ever. Bookstores are filled with children's books about the importance of having a strong sense of self-worth. Modern American parents want to raise independent and confident children—not the obedient children of 50 years ago (Remley, 1988). It comes as little surprise, then, that between 1968 and 1984, American college students reported greatly increased self-esteem (Twenge & Campbell, 2001).

Independent cultures foster higher levels of self-esteem than interdependent cultures. Compared with the world's more interdependent peoples—from Japan to Malaysia to India to Kenya—Westerners consistently report higher self-esteem and a more pronounced concern with evaluating the self (Dhawan, Roseman, Naidu, Thapa, & Rettek, 1995; Markus & Kitayama, 1991). It's not that Asians and other non-Westerners feel bad about themselves. Rather, they are more concerned with other ways of feeling good about themselves—for example, they are motivated toward self-improvement and commitment to collective goals (Crocker & Park, 2004; Heine, 2005; Norenzayan & Heine, 2004). Perhaps more dramatically, as people from interdependent cultures gain greater exposure to the West, this emphasis on self-worth rubs off on them and their self-esteem rises. As you can see in **Figure 3.6**, as Asian individuals become more immersed

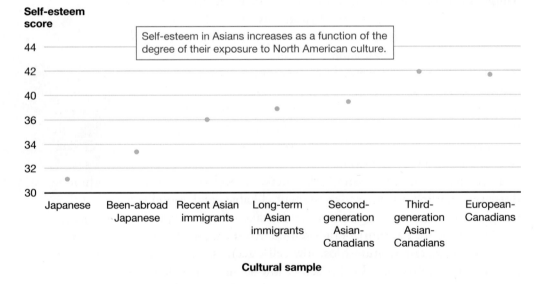

Figure 3.6

Cultural Change and Shifts in Self-Esteem

The graph represents the following groups. Japanese are those who live in Japan. Been-abroad Japanese are those who have spent time in a Western culture. Recent Asian immigrants are those who moved to Canada within the last 7 years (prior to the study). Long-term Asian immigrants have lived in Canada for more than 7 years. Second-generation Asian-Canadians were born in Canada but their parents were born in Asia. Third-generation Asian-Canadians were born in Canada, and their parents were born in Canada, but their grandparents were born in Asia. European-Canadians are Canadians whose ancestors were Europeans.

SOURCE: Adapted from Heine & Lehman, 2003.

in Canadian life, they become more like Canadians in general with respect to self-esteem (Heine & Lehman, 2003).

What is it about independent and interdependent cultures that creates these differences? A situationist hypothesis would be that people from Western cultures create social interactions that enhance self-esteem. Consistent with this notion, studies have found that situations described by Japanese as common daily experiences are regarded as less conducive of high self-esteem—by both Japanese and Americans—than daily situations in the United States (Kitayama, Markus, Matsumoto, & Norasakkunkit, 1997). For example, Japanese are more frequently encouraged to engage in "assisted" self-criticism than Americans are; Japanese math teachers and sushi chefs critique themselves in sessions with their peers—not the sort of activities that tend to build self-esteem, however beneficial they might be to skill development. Situations reported by Americans as typical in their country, by contrast, are regarded by both Americans and Japanese as more esteem-enhancing than situations common in Japan. For example, Americans are much more often praised for their achievements than Japanese people are.

These cultural differences in the emphasis on promoting self-esteem versus working to improve the self have important consequences for how people respond to failures and setbacks. Steven Heine and his colleagues asked Canadian and Japanese students to take a so-called creativity test and then gave them false feedback about their performance (Heine et al., 2001). Some were told they had performed very well, and others were told they had performed very badly. The experimenters then gave the participants the opportunity to work on a similar task. The Canadians worked longer on the second task if they had succeeded at the first; the Japanese worked longer if they had failed. Canadians thus avoided being reminded of failure, and Japanese used the occasion to improve.

More Than Just High vs. Low Self-Esteem

Research on high and low self-esteem has a long history, and increasing evidence indicates that there are multiple varieties of each. For example, although securely held high self-esteem is linked to positive outcomes, high self-esteem that is essentially inflated egotism—not warranted by any obvious facts and hence rather tenuous and insecure—tends to have negative, potentially even dangerous consequences (Baumeister, Smart, & Boden, 1996). In particular, people with inflated, more egotistical high self-esteem may react in a volatile fashion to threats to their self-esteem, sometimes resorting to violent actions to reassert their feelings of superiority, in an attempt to dominate those who challenge them.

The stability of a person's sense of self-worth is another dimension to consider. Some people have relatively stable (high or low) self-esteem, whereas in others it is relatively unstable. Researchers typically measure self-esteem stability by having participants complete the scale in Table 3.1 once or twice a day over the course of 4–7 days, under the instruction to base their responses on their current feelings (Kernis, 2005). They then compute an index of response variability over time, in addition to computing self-esteem levels. The correlation between stability and level tends to be small, indicating that self-esteem stability can have different effects for individuals who are relatively high versus low in self-esteem.

In one study (Kernis, Cornell, Sun, Berry, & Harlow, 1993), researchers measured the level and stability of participants' self-esteem and later had them read a speech in front of an evaluator, who subsequently gave positive or negative

"Men resemble the times more than they resemble their fathers."

—ARAB PROVERB

"America is a vast conspiracy to make you happy."

—JOHN UPDIKE

Dangers of High Self-Esteem
It is safe to say that Narcissus, the Greek mythological figure who fell in love with an image of himself, had high self-esteem. But not all types of high self-esteem involve the excessive—and ultimately tragic, in Narcissus's case—degree of fixation on the self that Narcissus displayed.

feedback (such as: "From the way she looked reading this speech, this person doesn't seem very socially skillful"). Participants indicated their reactions to the feedback (including their emotions and their perceptions of the evaluator). Stability had different effects among those with high versus low self-esteem. Among the high group, unstable self-esteem was associated with stronger reactions to the feedback. Unstable high self-esteem individuals reacted particularly favorably to positive feedback and particularly unfavorably (defensively) to negative feedback, whereas the reactions of those with stable high self-esteem were less extreme. Things looked differently for low self-esteem participants. In this group, stability of self-esteem had little influence on reactions to positive feedback and, if anything, greater instability predicted less defensive reactions to negative feedback.

🔄 LOOKING BACK

Self-esteem is a person's positive or negative evaluation of himself or herself. Trait self-esteem is fairly stable, whereas state self-esteem fluctuates across different situations. People have different contingencies of self-worth: some people are more invested in intellectual ability, others in religious orientation, still others in sociability. According to the sociometer hypothesis, self-esteem is a gauge of a person's standing with others, and thus a useful potential warning about the possibility of rejection. People in non-Western cultures are less concerned with feeling positively about their attributes than are modern Westerners, and non-Westerners are more likely to seek opportunities for self-improvement. Self-esteem may vary in more ways than level; for example, people may have either secure or insecure high self-esteem.

Motives Driving Self-Evaluation

Implicit in our discussion of self-esteem is the fact that people are motivated to view themselves positively. This motive, known as self-enhancement, influences many processes related to self-evaluation, including how people respond to negative feedback about their own personality, and what kinds of information they seek out. Another important motivating factor in evaluating oneself is self-verification.

Self-Enhancement

Suppose you just found out that your romantic interest in a coworker is not reciprocated, or you recently received a less than stellar performance appraisal at work. Naturally you're going to feel bad about yourself and will probably try to find ways to feel better. In other words, there will be a need for **self-enhancement**, the desire to maintain, increase, or protect positive views of the self (Leary, 2007; Sedikides & Gregg, 2008). To satisfy what can be a very powerful motive, people use various strategies.

self-enhancement The desire to maintain, increase, or protect one's positive self-views.

Self-Serving Construals As we've already discussed, most people—or at least most Westerners—tend to have a positive view of themselves and, on average, their level of self-esteem is high. In fact, when asked to indicate how they compare with others in general on various personality traits and abilities, people consistently exhibit a pronounced **better-than-average effect**; most people think they are above average in popularity, kindness, fairness, leadership, and the ability to get along with others, to name just a few characteristics (Alicke & Govorun, 2005). And it will probably not surprise you to learn that most people think they are above-average drivers (Svenson, 1981). A majority of drivers interviewed *while hospitalized for being in an automobile accident* rated their driving skill as closer to "expert" than "poor" (Preston & Harris, 1965; Svenson, 1981).

Why are people so upbeat about their talents and dispositions? Part of the answer has to do with how people interpret what it means to be kind, fair, athletic, or even a good driver. In short, self-serving construals are one means of pursuing self-enhancement. As Nobel Prize–winning economist Thomas Schelling once stated:

> Everybody ranks himself high in qualities he values; careful drivers give weight to care, skillful drivers give weight to skill, and those who think that, whatever else they are not, at least they are polite, give weight to courtesy, and come out high on their own scale. This is the way that every child has the best dog on the block.
>
> *(Schelling, 1978, p. 64)*

If people tend to construe particular personal characteristics in terms of those things at which they excel, most of them will end up convinced they are above average. Indeed, construed in such self-serving ways, most people *are* above average.

David Dunning and his colleagues have shown that people engage in just this sort of self-serving construal of what it means to be, say, artistic, athletic, or agreeable, and that such construals are an important part of the better-than-average effect. They have found, for example, that much stronger better-than-average effects are observed for ambiguous traits that are easy to construe in multiple ways (artistic, sympathetic, talented) than for unambiguous ones that are not (tall, punctual, muscular). Also, when people are given precise instructions about how they should interpret what it means to be, for instance, artistic or athletic, the magnitude of the better-than-average effect diminishes dramatically (Dunning, Meyerowitz, & Holzberg, 1989).

People also take advantage of another type of ambiguity that allows them to think highly of themselves, the ambiguity concerning which behaviors or characteristics "count" in determining what someone is like. People tend to judge *other* people—how kind, outgoing, or athletic they are—by the way they are on average, and yet define *themselves* in terms of how they behave when they're at their best. We generally think of John's kindness as some middle ground between his warmest, most giving moments and the times when he's been rather cold; but when we think of our own kindness, we recall the time when we *most* went out of our way to help someone else. If people (unknowingly) juggle the standards for what constitutes "talented," "considerate," or "agreeable," it should come as no surprise that they think of themselves as above average (Williams & Gilovich, 2012; Williams, Gilovich, & Dunning, 2012).

Self-Affirmation Affirmations are another strategy people can use to maintain positive views of themselves (Steele, 1988). **Self-affirmation theory** focuses on efforts to maintain an overall sense of self-worth when we are confronted with

better-than-average effect The finding that most people think they are above average on various personality trait and ability dimensions.

self-affirmation theory The idea that people can maintain an overall sense of self-worth following psychologically threatening information by affirming a valued aspect of themselves unrelated to the threat.

feedback or events that threaten a valued self-image, such as getting a poor test grade or health information indicating we are at risk for a specific illness. Under these circumstances, we can maintain an overall sense of self-worth by affirming ourselves in a domain unrelated to the threatened domain. For instance, if you learn of threatening health information, you could restore the blow to your self-esteem by reminding yourself of, say, your artistic abilities, your close friendships, or your academic accomplishments.

Empirical support for self-affirmation theory is abundant (McQueen & Klein, 2006; Sherman & Cohen, 2006). Moreover, self-affirmations have been shown to do more than simply help people maintain a general sense of self-worth. They also help minimize a wide range of defensive, and potentially harmful, behaviors people exhibit when faced with threat, such as the *self-serving attributional bias*, the tendency to attribute responsibility to themselves when they succeed, but to deny responsibility when they fail (Sherman & Cohen, 2006). (For more discussion, see Chapter 5.) Another defensive maneuver people show in response to a threat to self-esteem is derogating members of stereotyped groups (Fein & Spencer, 1997). This behavior does not occur if people affirm a valued aspect of themselves prior to evaluating stereotyped group members. In the domain of health awareness, studies have shown that, after affirming the self, people are more receptive to troubling, but potentially useful, health information, resulting in a greater likelihood of actually engaging in healthy behaviors (Sherman, Nelson, & Steele, 2000).

Comparing and Reflecting Let's look at one more manifestation of self-enhancement motives. Recall that people sometimes make downward social comparisons—comparing themselves to inferior or worse-off others—to feel better about themselves. This is self-enhancement at work. But what happens when the only available comparison target we have is superior or better off than we are? Can self-enhancement motives still be served in such situations? Yes they can, as captured by the **self-evaluation maintenance (SEM) model**. According to this theory, we shift between two processes—reflection and comparison—in a way that lets us maintain favorable self-views. In areas that are *not* especially relevant to our self-definition, we engage in *reflection*, whereby we flatter ourselves by association with others' accomplishments. Suppose you care very little about your own athletic skills, but when your friend scores the winning goal during a critical soccer match, you beam with pride, experience a boost to your self-esteem, and revel in her victory celebrations as if, by association, it were your victory too. The closer you are to the triumphant person, the more likely you are to bask in their reflected glory (see Chapter 11).

However, when a domain *is* relevant to our self-definition, we engage in *comparison*, assessing how our ability or performance stacks up to that of others. When we are superior to others, the comparison is downward, enabling us to maintain favorable self-views. But what if others outperform us? Comparing the self to outperforming others would have unflattering results. Moreover, such comparisons are particularly painful when the comparison target is a close associate. Is there anything we can do to protect our self-esteem in such challenging self-evaluative circumstances? There is indeed, but it takes some strategic maneuvering.

In one study that demonstrates these strategies, Tesser and Smith (1980) had two pairs of friends, seated in four individual booths, play a word game. Each participant had to guess four words based on clues provided by the three other participants. Each person chose clues for the others from a list of ten clues with

self-evaluation maintenance (SEM) model The idea that people are motivated to view themselves favorably, and that they do so through two processes: reflection and social comparison.

level of difficulty clearly marked; to keep participants from knowing the source of the clues, they were presented to the appropriate participant by the experimenter. In the high-relevance condition, the task was described as a measure of verbal skills. In the low-relevance condition, the task was described as a playful game. The researchers reasoned that the high-relevance condition should trigger comparison, leading participants to worry that others would succeed on the task and make their performance compare unfavorably. This concern should be stronger for a friend than a stranger, since unflattering comparisons sting more with friends. Reflection should be triggered in the low-relevance condition such that participants could enjoy the success of others, particularly if it was their friend who succeeded. Given all of this, what kinds of clues do you think participants chose for their friends versus strangers—easy or difficult ones?

As you can see in **Figure 3.7**, when the word game was not relevant to participants' self-concept (that is, a playful game), participants provided easier clues to a friend than to a stranger, presumably to elevate their friend's performance and, through reflection, their own self-regard. But when the word game was relevant to participants' self-concept, they provided clues to a friend that were every bit as hard as the clues they provided to a stranger. They did so, according to the SEM model, out of fear that a stellar performance by their friend, in particular, would make them look and feel bad in comparison. In short, one strategy for dealing with situations in which others may outperform you is to sabotage their performance. A nicer way to put this is that one way to ensure flattering comparisons is to close the gap between the level of your performance and that of others. Hurting someone else's performance can help close this gap, but so could improving your own performance.

The logic of the SEM model suggests two other strategies as well. You could decrease your closeness to people who outperform you, thereby minimizing the sting of unflattering comparisons with them. Or you could decrease the relevance of the domain in which they outperform you, thus increasing the appeal of reflection and dampening the sting of comparison (Erber & Tesser, 1994; Tesser, 1988).

Self-Enhancement and Well-Being All this talk about the strategizing people do to view themselves favorably may make you wonder whether self-enhancement strivings are beneficial to an individual. Isn't having an honest and accurate understanding of oneself a hallmark of a person's mental health and happiness? (Recall the ancient Greek induction to "know thyself.")

Many important movements in psychology, such as the humanistic movement of Abraham Maslow and Carl Rogers, encourage us to accept our weaknesses, foibles, and flaws. In a controversial line of work, Shelley Taylor and Jonathon Brown have challenged this position. They argue that self-knowledge often includes positive illusions about the self—that we are funnier, smarter, or warmer than we really are—and that such illusions, far from being detrimental, actually enhance well-being (Taylor & Brown, 1988, 1994; Updegraff & Taylor, 2000). Dozens of studies, carried out with Europeans and North Americans, have shown that people who are well-adjusted are more prone to various illusions about the self relative to those who suffer from low self-esteem and unhappiness.

"Anybody can sympathise with the sufferings of a friend, but it requires a very fine nature to sympathise with a friend's success."

—OSCAR WILDE

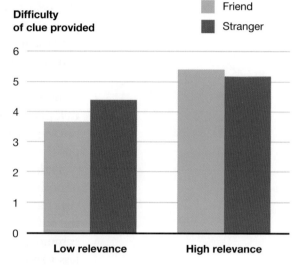

Figure 3.7
Comparison and Self-Esteem
When the game in this study was low in self-relevance, participants gave easier clues to a friend than a stranger, helping their friend perform better, thus setting themselves up for basking in their friend's glory. But when the game was high in relevance, a stranger was given easier clues than a friend, since a better-performing friend in an important domain is more threatening to one's own self-regard than a superior-performing stranger.

SOURCE: Adapted from Tesser & Smith, 1980.

In a laboratory context, Taylor and her colleagues examined whether positive illusions have protective or detrimental biological consequences in stressful situations (Taylor, Lerner, Sherman, Sage, & McDowell, 2003). Participants high in the tendency to self-enhance (to hold positive illusions about themselves) and participants low in that tendency faced several stress-inducing tasks (such as counting backward by sevens from 9,095), during which various indicators of their biological responses to stress were recorded. The results showed a healthier set of coping responses among high self-enhancers relative to low self-enhancers. For instance, high self-enhancers exhibited lower baseline levels of cortisol (the stress hormone) and also showed less autonomic nervous system arousal during the stressful tasks.

Other researchers have questioned the notion that positive illusions invariably promote adjustment and health, arguing instead that accurate rather than illusory self-beliefs foster well-being and other positive outcomes (Colvin & Block, 1994; Colvin & Griffo, 2008). They cite research showing that people who rate themselves more favorably than others do (that is, people who self-enhance) are seen by others as narcissistic (John & Robins, 1994). Additional studies demonstrate that people who hold relatively accurate views of themselves, in that their ratings of themselves are similar to others' ratings of them, are judged by others more positively than are people who self-enhance (Colvin, Block, & Funder, 1995).

Perhaps the greatest challenge to Taylor and Brown's thesis about the benefits of positive illusions comes from cross-cultural research. This work demonstrates that East Asians are less likely than Westerners to endorse positive illusions about the self (Heine, Lehman, Markus, & Kitayama, 1999; Kitayama, Markus, Matsumoto, & Norasakkunkit, 1997). In one study, Japanese college students were less likely than American students to assume they were better than average in important abilities, such as academic talent (Markus & Kitayama, 1991). Such cross-cultural evidence suggests that positive illusions do not automatically enhance well-being. They often do so for Westerners because a positive view of the self is a cherished cultural value. In contrast, personal well-being for East Asians appears to be more closely tied to interdependent values. Researchers have found that the well-being of East Asians is more dependent on fulfilling social roles and expectations, and this finding is consistent with an interdependent self-construal (Suh, Diener, Oishi, & Triandis, 1998).

So are self-enhancing tendencies adaptive or not? Do they benefit the individual? At present, the answer appears to be "it depends." For example, Robins and Beer (2001) showed that students who entered college with self-enhancing beliefs about their academic ability reported higher average levels of self-esteem and well-being over a 4-year period relative to their non-enhancing peers. However, self-enhancement tendencies were associated with a downward trajectory over the 4-year period for both self-esteem and well-being. In essence, although self-enhancement was linked to greater self-esteem and well-being in the short term, the advantages associated with engaging in self-enhancement erode over time. The safest conclusion to draw at this point is that self-enhancement provides a number of benefits, but it can be taken too far and exact significant costs.

Self-Verification

Although a wealth of evidence indicates that self-enhancement is a powerful motive that drives our self-evaluative pursuits, we don't always want to see ourselves through rose-colored glasses. The truth, at least our version of it, also

BOX 3.4

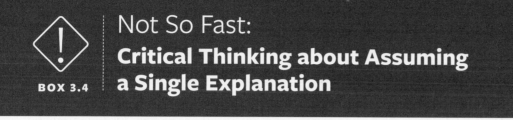

Not So Fast:
Critical Thinking about Assuming a Single Explanation

Consider what the following decisions have in common: applying only to highly selective law schools; auditioning for *The Voice*; ignoring the physical therapy your doctor prescribed; pursuing a career in art instead of accounting; asking one of the most popular girls on campus out on a date; signing up for the full marathon instead of the half marathon. Each decision involves an assessment of your traits and abilities—an assessment of your law school credentials, singing talent, physical condition, artistic gifts, attractiveness to potential dating partners, or running prowess. These decisions have something else in common: they follow from a decidedly favorable assessment of your traits and abilities. This should come as no surprise, given the research demonstrating how robust the desire for self-enhancement tends to be (especially among members of Western cultures), and how adept people are at satisfying that desire. It is also natural and tempting to assume that the desire for self-enhancement alone accounts for people's inflated self-assessments. But not so fast; other factors may be at play.

To be sure, there is ample evidence that self-enhancement often drives overly favorable self-appraisals, but it would be a mistake to assume that flattering self-appraisals are the product of motivational forces alone. Non-motivational cognitive deficits may be a major culprit as well.

One example of a cognitive barrier to accurate self-assessment is the simple fact that sometimes people don't have access to all the information required to appraise their traits and abilities accurately. We're not talking about a lack of access to nonconscious processes, which we discussed at the outset of this chapter. Instead, we are talking about a lack of basic knowledge related to the trait or ability in question. Kruger, Dunning, and their colleagues offer a particularly clear example of this deficiency, what they call the double curse of incompetence (Dunning, Heath, & Suls, 2004; Kruger & Dunning, 1999). The curse is that incompetent people—that is, those who tend to perform well below their peers in a given domain—are deficient not only in the skills needed to perform better, but also in the very knowledge necessary for accurately recognizing their incompetence. We all know those students (or, let's face it, we may have been one of them) who walk out of an exam room certain they've aced the test, only to find out a few days later that they bombed it. The skills and knowledge that would have led to a better test score are pretty much the same skills and knowledge required for having a more accurate prediction of how they did on the test in the first place.

So before concluding that someone's overly flattering self-assessment is a clear sign he or she has a hefty appetite for

self-enhancement, it's important to consider other, decidedly less motivational sources of flawed self-appraisal. We mentioned just one of these sources—lacking the skills and knowledge needed to make more accurate self-assessments in the first place—but other possibilities exist. For example, in an effort to be polite, other people tend to provide us with overly positive estimates of our abilities and traits. To the extent that's true, we can scarcely be blamed for overestimating our abilities and the attractiveness of our personality.

The broader lesson here is that a certain explanation for our own and other people's behaviors can jump out as obvious, and in fact may be correct some or even most of the time. However, it would be unwise not to consider the possibility that the behavior in question may have additional, albeit less obvious, causes.

matters. According to **self-verification theory**, we strive for stable, subjectively accurate beliefs about ourselves because they give us a sense of coherence (Swann, 1990). Stable, accurate, and coherent self-views make us more predictable to ourselves and others, which helps interactions with others go more smoothly. More concretely, we strive to get others to confirm or verify our preexisting beliefs about ourselves. To illustrate, if you see yourself as extraverted, self-verification theory would predict that you will seek to get others to see you as extraverted

self-verification theory The theory that people strive for stable, subjectively accurate beliefs about the self because such self-views give a sense of coherence.

as well. This holds true even for negative self-views. The idea is that if you truly believe you are, say, socially awkward, getting others to see this subjective truth bolsters your feelings of coherence and predictability.

People engage in a number of self-verification strategies. We selectively attend to and recall information that is consistent with (and therefore verifies) our self-views. People with negative self-views, for example, spend more time studying negative rather than positive feedback about themselves; they remember negative feedback better; and they prefer to interact with others who are likely to provide negative rather than positive feedback (Swann & Read, 1981; Swann, Wenzlaff, Krull, & Pelham, 1992).

Other self-verification strategies involve displaying identity cues—such as customary facial expressions, posture, gait, clothes, haircuts, and body decorations—to signal important facets of our identity and increase the likelihood that others' impressions of us will confirm our own self-view. Wearing a simple T-shirt conveys information about a person's political affiliation, music preferences, the clubs he belongs to, the type of holidays he takes, his university, his sexual attitudes. Samuel Gosling and his colleagues have found that even college students' dorm rooms—including the way clothes are folded (or not, as the case may be), the way books are arranged, and what is hanging on the walls—convey information about the self, thereby contributing to self-verification efforts (Gosling, Ko, Mannarelli, & Morris, 2002).

As many novels and movies vividly portray, people also choose to enter into relationships that maintain consistent views of the self, even when those views are dark, ruinous, and tragic. These sorts of preferences guarantee that our personal lives will probably confirm our self-views. In a study of intimate bonds, romantic partners who viewed each other in a congruent fashion—that is, whose perceptions of each other were in agreement—reported more commitment to the relationship, even when one partner viewed the other in a negative light (Swann, De La Ronde, & Hixon, 1994).

How might people integrate the self-enhancement and self-verification perspectives? One answer is that these two motives guide different processes related to self-evaluation. Self-enhancement seems to be most relevant to our emotional responses to feedback about the self, whereas self-verification determines our more cognitive assessment of the validity of the feedback (Swann, Griffin, Predmore, & Gaines, 1987). To test this hypothesis, the Swann team gave participants with negative or positive self-beliefs negative or positive feedback. In terms

Identity Cues and Self-Verification

We create self-confirming social environments through the clothes we wear, hairstyles, jewelry, tattoos, and other identity cues. Left: A high school student wears his varsity jacket off the field, signaling his identity as an athlete. Right: Girls signal their youth and trendiness by donning Harajuku-inspired fashion while hanging out in the Harajuku district of Tokyo.

of participants' evaluations of the accuracy and competence of the feedback—that is, the quality of the information—self-verification prevailed. Those with negative self-beliefs found the negative feedback most diagnostic and accurate, whereas participants with positive beliefs rated the positive feedback higher on these dimensions. All participants, however, felt good about the positive feedback and disliked the negative feedback. Our quest to verify our sense of ourselves, then, guides our assessment of the validity of self-relevant information, while our desire to think favorably about ourselves guides our emotional reactions to the same information.

⟲ LOOKING BACK

Self-evaluative activities such as seeking out evaluative feedback about ourselves can be driven by different motives, such as self-enhancement and self-verification. Self-enhancement strategies include self-serving construals and shifting back and forth between reflection and comparison processes, depending on the self-relevance of the domain. When self-verification is our priority, we seek out appraisals and relationship partners that confirm our preexisting self-views, and we display cues that increase the likelihood that others will see us as we see ourselves.

Self-Regulation: Motivating and Controlling Behavior

Self-regulation refers to the processes by which people initiate, alter, and control their behavior in pursuit of their goals—whether the goal is doing well in school, being a good friend, or getting in better shape (Carver & Scheier, 1982; Higgins, 1999; Muraven & Baumeister, 2000). Given that successful goal pursuit often requires resisting temptations, self-regulation also involves the ability to delay gratification—to prioritize long-term goals (getting into graduate school) by forgoing short-term immediate rewards (a weeknight out on the town). Let's take a look at what social psychologists have discovered about self-regulation efforts.

Self-Discrepancy Theory

One influential perspective on self-regulation is captured in a theory proposed by Tory Higgins (1987). According to the **self-discrepancy theory**, people hold beliefs about not only what they are *actually* like, but also what they would *ideally* like to be and what they think they *ought* to be. Your **actual self** is the self you believe you are. Your **ideal self** represents your hopes and wishes, and your **ought self** represents your duties and obligations.

According to the self-discrepancy theory, ideal and ought beliefs serve as self-guides, motivating people to regulate their behavior in order to close the gap between their actual self and their ideal and ought standards. When people feel they're failing to live up to these standards—in other words, when they perceive a discrepancy between their actual self and either their ideal or ought self—there are predictable emotional consequences. Specifically, discrepancies between the actual and the ideal self produce dejection-related emotions, and discrepancies between the actual and the ought self give rise to agitation-related emotions. Here are two examples. When the judges disparage Sameer's singing ability at an *American Idol* audition, the discrepancy between his actual self (a poor singer) and his ideal self (a rock star) arouses dejection-related emotions,

self-regulation Processes by which people initiate, alter, and control their behavior in the pursuit of goals, including the ability to resist short-term rewards that thwart the attainment of long-term goals.

self-discrepancy theory A theory that behavior is motivated by standards reflecting ideal and ought selves. Falling short of these standards produces specific emotions: dejection-related emotions for actual-ideal discrepancies, and agitation-related emotions for actual-ought discrepancies.

actual self The self that people believe they are.

ideal self The self that embodies people's wishes and aspirations.

ought self The self that is concerned with the duties, obligations, and external demands people feel they are compelled to honor.

promotion focus Self-regulation of behavior with respect to ideal self standards, or a focus on attaining positive outcomes and approach-related behaviors.

prevention focus Self-regulation of behavior with respect to ought self standards, or a focus on avoiding negative outcomes and avoidance-related behaviors.

ego depletion A state, produced by acts of self-control, in which people lack the energy or resources to engage in further acts of self-control.

such as disappointment and shame. When Mina loses patience with her ailing grandmother (actual self), she may feel agitation-related emotions, such as guilt and anxiety if her ought self includes being a patient and loving granddaughter.

Ideal and ought standards are associated with two fundamentally different approaches to goal pursuit. When people regulate their behavior with respect to ideal self standards, they tend to have a **promotion focus**, or a focus on attaining positive outcomes (Higgins, 1996). By contrast, when people regulate their behavior with respect to ought self standards, they tend to have a **prevention focus**, a focus on avoiding negative outcomes.

Wide-ranging evidence supports Higgins' account of how ideal and ought selves can have different emotional and motivational consequences. When people are subtly induced to think about how they might approximate their ideal self—for example, by reading personality trait terms that capture their ideal self—they generally exhibit elevated cheerful emotions (Higgins, Shah, & Friedman, 1997; Shah & Higgins, 2001) and heightened sensitivity to positive outcomes (Brendl, Higgins, & Lemm, 1995). But if they think they will never become their ideal self, they tend to experience dejection-related emotions, such as depression and shame, and show reduced physiological arousal. In contrast, associations to a person's ought self, and any deviation from it, activates agitated emotions (such as guilt or panic), elevated physiological arousal, avoidant behavior, and sensitivity to negative outcomes (Strauman & Higgins, 1987).

As you might expect, Westerners are more likely to have a promotion focus. They are more interested in attaining personal goals and more likely to feel that their own efforts are sufficient to achieve them. East Asians are more likely to exhibit a prevention focus. They are more concerned with the possible negative consequences of their actions for their relations with others (Lee, Aaker, & Gardner, 2000; Uskul, Sherman, & Fitzgibbon, 2009).

Ego Depletion

Trying to live up to ideal and ought self standards can be hard work. Often it requires controlling the impulse to engage in behavior that makes it harder to achieve our ideal and ought selves. In fact, acts of self-control can be downright exhausting. Roy Baumeister, Kathleen Vohs, and their colleagues argue that when we attempt to control our behavior to live up to important standards, we often experience what they call **ego depletion**; much as physical exercise can exhaust our muscles, exerting self-control can exhaust us psychologically (Baumeister, Vohs, & Tice, 2007). This claim is based on the idea that self-control draws on a limited resource (Muraven & Baumeister, 2000). When we exercise self-control, we use up that precious resource so that less of it is available to sustain further acts of self-control.

In one study demonstrating the costs of self-control, participants were asked to rein in their emotions while watching an emotionally evocative film clip (Muraven, Tice, & Baumeister, 1998). Afterward, they were not able to squeeze a hand grip as long as control participants could. In another study, participants who exercised their will by eating healthy radishes instead of delicious-smelling cookies later gave up on an unsolvable puzzle faster than participants who did not exercise self-control and were allowed to indulge in the cookies (Baumeister, Bratslavsky, Muraven, & Tice, 1998).

The notion that every time you engage in an act of self-control, your subsequent ability to regulate yourself suffers might make you want to throw in the towel. Not so fast. Researchers have discovered various ways to counteract ego depletion effects, such as cash incentives or other motivators (Muraven & Slessareva, 2003). In addition, being in a positive mood can offset the negative influence of using self-control, presumably because of the empowering and energizing effects of positive emotions (Tice, Baumeister, Shmueli, & Muraven, 2007).

People's lay theories about self-control also matter (Job, Dweck, & Walton, 2010). If you hold the theory that self-control is a limited resource, lo and behold, you tend to show the standard ego depletion effect. But if you don't believe that self-control is limited, and could even imagine that self-control is energized after having exerted self-control in an initial task, then you tend not to show ego depletion.

Research by Matthew Gailliot and his colleagues points to perhaps the most intriguing—and, without a doubt, most controversial—factor that may counteract ego depletion: glucose, or common sugar (Gailliot et al., 2007). These researchers hypothesized that self-regulation relies on circulating blood glucose levels. When people exercise self-control, their blood glucose levels drop, and they exhibit less self-control on subsequent tasks. And if blood glucose levels are somehow replenished after an initial self-control task, people no longer show ego depletion.

Supporting these provocative ideas, Gailliot and his colleagues found that engaging in an initial self-control task—suppressing one's emotions, for instance—does indeed appear to reduce circulating blood glucose levels; this, in turn, predicts poorer performance on subsequent self-control tasks (Gailliot et al., 2007). To test whether a boost in blood glucose can counteract ego depletion effects, they had participants first engage in a self-control task and then drink lemonade sweetened with either sugar (glucose) or an artificial sweetener (no glucose). Participants who drank the artificially sweetened beverage showed the standard ego depletion effect on a later self-control task, whereas participants who drank the glucose-containing beverage did not.

Does this mean the next time you face a task that requires self-control, you should reach for the nearest soda or candy bar? Maybe, maybe not. Attempts to replicate the Gailliott findings have been mixed, with some studies failing to demonstrate that exerting self-control lowers blood glucose levels (Molden et al., 2012). In addition, growing evidence suggests that simply rinsing the mouth with a glucose-laden liquid—*without actually ingesting it*—can counteract ego depletion

The Cost of Self-Control

In a study demonstrating ego depletion, participants who exercised their will power and ate radishes, instead of delicious-smelling cookies, subsequently worked less long on an unsolvable puzzle. The self-control required to eat radishes instead of cookies reduced their subsequent capacity for self-control (Baumeister et al., 1998).

effects (Hagger & Chatzisarantis, 2013). Results like these clearly suggest that more research is needed to explain the mechanisms underlying ego depletion effects when they occur. Glucose appears to be part of the story, but it may not be necessary that it be fully ingested and metabolized (Inzlich, Schmeichel, & Macrae, 2014).

At present, the most prudent conclusion to draw about this lively area of research appears to be that exerting self-control can be depleting, but most situations do not completely wipe out our self-regulatory resources. With particular kinds of inducements (such as monetary ones), we can override ego depletion.

Automatic Self-Control Strategies

The preceding discussion may make it seem like exercising self-control is a conscious, deliberate endeavor. Researchers Ayelet Fishbach and her colleagues have examined the self-control strategies people use to resist short-term temptations that would otherwise derail their long-term goals. Results from this work suggest that many such strategies can be deployed automatically, operating without our even realizing it.

Suppose you're trying to eat a healthier diet (long-term goal), but you're faced with a plate of warm, soft chocolate chip cookies (temptation). Surely the alluring properties of the cookies and the immediate gratification they offer will put thoughts about eating healthily on the back burner, right? Across a series of studies, Fishbach, Friedman, and Kruglanski (2003) showed that quite the opposite can happen: the cookies may actually make you think more about your goal to eat healthily. The idea is that temptations (unhealthy foods) may become linked in memory to your goal (eating well) so that when temptations are brought to mind, so too are thoughts of healthy eating. And the connection between the two can occur automatically. What's more, the Fishbach team found that bringing goals to mind first has the effect of *diminishing* thoughts about temptations. Thus, being faced with temptations reminds us of our goals, and thinking about our goals puts temptations out of mind. But before deciding you can abandon all deliberate efforts to resist temptations, note that the effects found in this research apply mainly to people for whom the goal is very important, and who have had substantial past success resisting goal-interfering temptations.

Automatic self-control strategies can influence behavior as well as thoughts, leading people to approach goals and to avoid temptations. In a clever set of studies demonstrating this effect, Fishbach and Shah (2006) measured how long it took participants to pull or push a lever in response to goal-related and temptation-related words (**Figure 3.8**). Pulling a lever toward oneself is thought to represent approach tendencies, bringing an object closer. In contrast, pushing a lever away represents avoidance tendencies, moving an object further from the self. You see where this is going? Participants' *pulling* responses were quicker in response to goal-related words, but their *pushing* responses were quicker in response to temptation-related words. And it's not as if participants were consciously deciding to pull and push more or less quickly; they were simply demonstrating automatic tendencies to approach goals and avoid temptations. Sound too good to be true? Well, there are some caveats. In particular, it's probably no surprise that these results held mainly for people who have been successful at regulating their behavior in the past. But on a more encouraging note, these results mainly held true when temptations were very high in attractiveness—precisely when the automatic deployment of self-control strategies is most needed.

"Lord grant me chastity and continence, but not yet."

—SAINT AUGUSTINE'S
(IRONIC) PRAYER

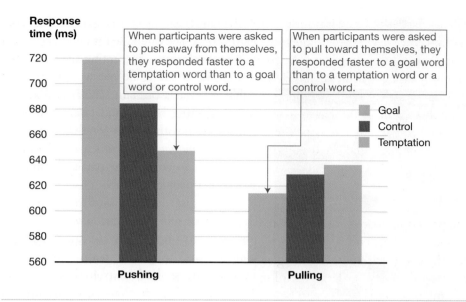

Figure 3.8
Automatic Self-Control Strategies
Participants' response times for pushing a lever away from themselves versus pulling the lever toward themselves in response to self-generated goal, control, and temptation target words.

🔄 LOOKING BACK

Self-regulation refers to how people go about initiating, changing, and controlling their behavior in pursuit of goals. Goal-directed actions can be motivated by standards in the form of ideal and ought selves. Such actions can be either promotion-focused or prevention-focused. People tend to experience dejection-related emotions when they fall short of their ideal standards, and agitation-related emotions when they fail to meet their ought standards. Acts of self-regulation can be depleting, such that an initial act of self-control diminishes performance on a subsequent task requiring self-control. Researchers continue to explore the underlying mechanisms and boundary conditions of ego depletion effects. People may have unintentional self-control strategies, such as automatic behavioral tendencies to approach goals and avoid temptations.

Self-Presentation

Alexi Santana entered Princeton University as a member of the class of 1993. His academic performance was impressive, he excelled in track, and he was admitted to one of Princeton's most exclusive eating clubs. He dazzled his dormmates with tales of being raised on a sheep farm in the wild canyons of southern Utah, and with his unusual habits, such as preferring to sleep on the floor and routinely arising at dawn.

The only trouble was that Alexi Santana was a fictitious identity. Santana was actually James Hogue, a 34-year-old drifter and former track star from Kansas City. Hogue had been convicted and served time for various crimes, including check forging and bicycle theft. He had gotten into Princeton thanks to a fraudulent application and had earned the admiration of his peers based on a completely fabricated identity. In the documentary film *Con Man*, Jessie Moss showed that Hogue had had a pattern of assuming false identities.

Hogue's story (or is it Santana's?) is an extreme version of a basic truth: our social self is often a dramatic performance in which we try to project a public self consistent with our hopes and aspirations. This public self is one that we actively create in our social interactions and that is shaped by the perceptions of other people and the perceptions we want others to have of us (Baumeister, 1982; Mead,

Self-Presentation

James Hogue attended Princeton University on an academic scholarship under the assumed name of Alexi Santana. He constructed a false identity for himself as a self-educated 18-year-old from Utah. Hogue was arrested for forgery, wrongful impersonation, and falsifying records at Princeton.

self-presentation Presenting the person we would like others to believe we are.

face The public image of ourself that we want others to believe.

1934; Schlenker, 1980; Shrauger & Schoeneman, 1979). The public self is concerned with **self-presentation**—presenting the person we would like others to believe we are. Hogue's public self was a brilliant scholar and athlete with a riveting history and fascinating idiosyncracies. Another term for this concept is *impression management,* which refers to how we attempt to control the particular impressions other people form about us.

Sociologist Erving Goffman inspired the study of self-presentation with his keen observations about how we stake out our identity in the public realm, something James Hogue had mastered (Goffman, 1959, 1967). Rather than doing controlled experiments, Goffman relied on naturalistic observations of how people behave in public settings. He spent time in mental institutions, noting how patients there seemed to ignore many rules of self-presentation, such as making unflattering comments about others and failing to observe common social courtesies. Goffman wrote an entire chapter on what he called response cries, like "Oops!," that we resort to after committing social gaffes and feel deeply embarrassed. These linguistic acts help reestablish social order when we have violated the rules of self-presentation, and show how committed we are to preserving the self we want others to accept.

Such observations led Goffman to what has been called a dramaturgic perspective on the social self. Social interaction can be thought of as a drama of self-presentation, in which we attempt to create and maintain an impression of ourselves in the minds of others (Baumeister, 1982; Brown, 1998; Goffman, 1959; Leary & Kowalski, 1990; Schlenker & Leary, 1982). Critical to this drama, in Goffman's terms, is **face**, the public image of ourselves that we want others to have. For instance, someone may want others to think she's a gifted, temperamental artist; someone else might want to come across as a person with intellectual gifts that enable him to excel without studying; yet another individual might

Private and Public Faces

People may present themselves differently in public and private. (A) Lily Allen is not showing a carefully constructed public face as she is getting in a car after doing some shopping in London, but (B) she does present a public face when she arrives at the Cannes Film Festival in Cannes, France in 2014.

(A)

(B)

want to give the impression of being an object of romantic interest to more than a few people. Social interactions are the stage on which we play out these kinds of claims, regardless of how true they may be. Much like a play, the social drama of self-presentation is highly collaborative. We depend on others to honor our desired social identities, and others likewise depend on us to honor their face claims.

Goffman's insights have shaped the study of the social self in several lasting ways. For example, the concept of self-monitoring derives in part from Goffman's analysis of strategic self-presentation (Gangestad & Snyder, 2000; Snyder, 1974, 1979). **Self-monitoring** refers to the tendency to monitor one's behavior to fit the demands of the current situation. High self-monitors carefully scrutinize situations, and they shift their self-presentation and behavior to fit the prevailing context. High self-monitors, such as Hogue, are like actors, changing their behavior according to the present people and situation.

In contrast, low self-monitors are more likely to behave according to their own traits and preferences, regardless of the social context. This suggests admirable candor and honesty. However, in one study, patients in a psychiatric hospital scored low on a self-monitoring scale, and these findings are consistent with Goffman's early observations and his theory that effective social functioning requires participation in some degree of strategic self-presentation (Snyder, 1974).

Self-Handicapping

One of the complexities of strategic self-presentation is that people often don't live up to the public self they are trying to portray. For example, your claim about being the next great American writer will eventually be put to the test when you submit your prose for publication; your claim about being the next great tri-athlete will eventually face the truth of the stopwatch and the performance of competitors. The obvious drawback of the public self is that we might not live up to it, and we risk embarrassing ourselves when that happens. To protect the self in these circumstances, we engage in various self-protective behaviors.

Self-handicapping is the tendencey to engage in self-defeating behavior to protect the public self and prevent others from making unwanted inferences based on poor performance (Arkin & Baumgardner, 1985; Deppe & Harackiewicz, 1996; Hendrix & Hirt, 2009; Hirt, McCrea, & Kimble, 2000; Jones & Berglas, 1978). Think of how often people engage in self-destructive behaviors when their

self-monitoring The tendency to monitor one's behavior to fit the current situation.

self-handicapping The tendency to engage in self-defeating behavior in order to have an excuse ready should one perform poorly or fail.

BOX 3.5 FOCUS ON *HEALTH*

Dying to Present a Favorable Self

You might assume that self-presentation is always a good thing. Erving Goffman himself wrote about how people's strategic self-presentation and their honoring of other people's public claims are essential ingredients of harmonious communities. But self-presentational concerns can sometimes be dangerous to our health (Leary, Tchividjian, & Kraxberger, 1994). Many practices that promote health are awkward or embarrassing and pose problems for our public identity. As a consequence, we avoid them. We sacrifice physical health to maintain a public identity defined by composure and aplomb. In one study, for example, 30–65 percent of respondents reported embarrassment when buying condoms (Hanna, 1989). Embarrassment could deter sexually active teenagers from buying condoms, thus increasing their risk of sexually transmitted diseases and unwanted pregnancies. Similarly, the fear of embarrassment at times prevents obese individuals from pursuing physical exercise programs or taking needed medications (Bain, Wilson, & Chaikind, 1989).

In other instances, we engage in risky behavior to enhance our public image and identity. Concerns about others' impressions of us and concerns about our physical appearance are good predictors of excessive sunbathing, which increases the likelihood of skin cancer (Leary & Jones, 1993). Moreover, adolescents typically cite social approval as one of the most important reasons for starting to drink alcohol and smoke cigarettes (Farber, Khavari, & Douglass, 1980). And the same need for an enhanced public image motivates many cosmetic surgeries, which carry with them a variety of health risks.

public selves are on the line. Students sometimes irrationally put too little effort into studying for an exam. Athletes party all night before the championship game. You may act too casually at a job interview, or say shockingly inappropriate things on a first date. Why do we engage in such self-defeating behaviors? In Goffman's view, these actions provide an explanation for possible failure, thereby protecting the desired public self. If you don't perform as well as expected on an exam you didn't prepare for, there's no threat to the claim you would like to make about your academic talents. Of course, some "self-handicap" claims are bogus. Classrooms are filled with students who act as though they haven't studied terribly hard when in fact they did. The phenomenon is so common that students at Dartmouth College have given the people who do it a name: "sneaky bookers."

In one of the first experimental studies of self-handicapping, male participants were led to believe that they were either going to succeed or going to have difficulty on a test they were scheduled to take (Berglas & Jones, 1978). Participants were given the chance to ingest one of two drugs: the first would enhance their test performance, and the second would impair it. Participants who felt they were likely to fail the test preferred the performance-inhibiting drug, even though it was likely to diminish their chances of success. Apparently, people would sometimes rather fail and have a ready excuse for it than go for success and have no excuse for failure.

Presenting the Self Online

Online social networking sites are a common part of an astounding number of people's daily lives. As of 2012, Facebook alone had over 845 million users, who collectively spent an estimated 9.7 billion minutes per day using it (Wilson, Gosling, & Graham, 2012). There is no question that, these days, a good deal of social life happens online. What does self-presentation in the online social world look like?

Given that most of the information on social networking sites, such as Facebook, is provided by the users themselves, there is ample opportunity for people to manage others' impressions of them. Do people tend to present themselves authentically online, posting accurate information about who they are, what they've accomplished, their beliefs, and their likes and dislikes? Or do people take advantage of the opportunity that social networking sites offer to convey especially positive self-images?

Self-presentation researchers are beginning to tackle these questions. In one study, researchers had observers rate the personality traits (including extraversion, neuroticism, and openness) of 236 American and German users of online social networking sites—Facebook in the United States and similar sites called StudiVZ and SchuelerVZ in Germany—based on the information provided on their profile pages (Back et al., 2010). Observers' ratings were compared to an accuracy criterion made up of an average of users' own ratings of their personality and the ratings of four well-acquainted friends. Users were also asked to provide ratings reflecting who they would ideally like to be. Would you expect observer ratings to correlate more highly with the users' own and friends' ratings, thus suggesting that people present themselves relatively accurately online, or with users' ideal self ratings, suggesting instead that people try to present themselves in an ideal light online? You may be surprised to learn that the findings supported the former view, that online, people tend to present their offline selves fairly accurately, a conclusion bolstered by other studies as well (Waggoner, Smith, & Collins, 2009).

Why would people present themselves accurately online when it seems so easy, not to mention tempting, to paint a positive image of the self in the sphere of online social life? Recall that although self-enhancement motives are robust (particulary among members of Western, more individualistic cultures), other self-evaluative motives may prevail at times. In particular, online self-presentations may be driven as much or more by self-verification motives, the desire to be known and understood by others (Swann, 1990), and crafting accurate online profiles of the self would serve that need. A less flattering explanation is that overly favorable online presentations of the self often need to withstand offline scrutiny. You can probably relate to having offline interactions with people who have read your profile, making it difficult (or at least awkward) to post blatantly inaccurate statements about yourself online. Given such difficulty, you would think that when it comes to physical features, people would be inclined to tell the truth—for example, posting selfies that capture what they typically look like, and reporting accurately on their height, weight, and age. But research suggests otherwise (Toma & Hancock, 2010). While we may present our personality and other attributes (such as our occupation) fairly accurately online, this is less the case for our physical attributes, perhaps because of the vital role that physical appearance plays in attraction (see Chapter 10).

🔄 LOOKING BACK

Self-presentation involves people's efforts to get others to form particular impressions of them. These strategies are more characteristic of high self-monitors, people who change their behavior based on the situation in which they find themselves. Low self-monitors attend more to their own preferences and dispositions, with little regard for the situation or what others think. People may engage in self-defeating behaviors, or self-handicapping, to have an excuse available should they fail or perform poorly. Self-presentation is also relevant in online social networking, where it appears people are more inclined to provide accurate information about some aspects of themselves, such as their personality traits, over others, such as their physical features.

Chapter Review

Online Study Materials

INQUIZITIVE   EBOOK

SUMMARY

The Nature of the Social Self

- The self is fundamentally social, and it shifts according to changes in the social situation.
- Introspection for gaining self-knowledge is not always accurate, and the perceptions of other people are often a better assessment of one's behavior.
- *Self-schemas*, organizing structures that help guide the construal of social information, represent a person's beliefs and feelings about the self in general and in specific situations.

Origins of the Sense of Self

- Socialization by family members and other important people is one of the foundations of the social self. *Reflected self-appraisals* are beliefs about what others think of one's social self.
- The social self is shaped by the current situation in many ways, and different selves are evoked in different situations.
- The social self is profoundly shaped by whether people live in independent or interdependent cultures.
- Women generally emphasize their relationships and define themselves in an interdependent way, and men generally emphasize their uniqueness and construe themselves in an independent way.
- People rely on *social comparisons* to learn about their own abilities, attitudes, and personal traits.

Self-Esteem

- *Trait self-esteem* is a stable part of one's identity, whereas *state self-esteem* changes according to different contextual factors.
- Self-esteem is defined by particular domains of importance, or *contingencies of self-worth*, and by being accepted by others.
- Self-esteem is more important, and is higher, in Western cultures than East Asian cultures.
- Self-esteem can be characterized by more than just whether it is high or low, suggesting there are qualitatively different forms of high and low self-esteem.

Motives Driving Self-Evaluation

- The motives for self-evaluation include the desire for self-enhancement and self-verification.
- The motivation to think well of oneself guides the maintenance of relationships that let people make favorable social comparisons, and that provide the opportunity to bask in the successes of relationship partners.
- Having a stable set of self-beliefs gives people a sense of coherence and predictability.

Self-Regulation: Motivating and Controlling Behavior

- *Self-discrepancy theory* investigates how people compare their *actual self* to both their *ideal self* and *ought self* and the emotional consequences of such comparisons.
- When people regulate their behavior with respect to ideal self standards, they have a *promotion focus* for attaining positive outcomes. When people regulate their behavior with respect to ought self standards, they have a *prevention focus* for avoiding negative outcomes.
- Self-control can produce a state of *ego depletion*, which makes it harder to exert further self-control.
- Self-control strategies can be implemented automatically, such as when long-term goals automatically spring to mind when people face temptations that can thwart these goals.

Self-Presentation

- *Self-presentation* is related to the public self; people present themselves the way they want others to see them. *Face* refers to the image people want others to have about them. *Self-monitoring* ensures that a person's behavior fits the demands of the social context.
- People protect their public self through *self-handicapping*, behavior that can excuse a poor performance or a failure.
- Self-presentation happens online, just as it does in face-to-face interactions. Different motives can guide online self-presentation, including the desire for others to see the self accurately.

THINK ABOUT IT

1. According to research on the accuracy of self-knowledge, for what qualities are we the best judges of ourselves? For what qualities are others superior judges of us? How does motivation contribute to this asymmetry?

2. Josie is a 13-year-old girl who thinks she's a funny person, and her friends and family generally think Josie is funny too. How would Cooley's notion of the "looking-glass self" explain how Josie's sense of herself as funny developed? As an adolescent, what does research suggest is likely occurring in Josie's brain when she thinks about her self-views?

3. How might a female undergraduate's working self-concept regarding her gender shift during a day on campus, as she attends her advanced math class (in which she is the only female), has a low-key lunch with a friend, and attends her gender studies class? Will her frequently shifting self-concept undermine her sense of having a coherent self?

4. How do an individual's daily experiences in his or her contingent versus noncontingent domains affect his or her state self-esteem? Over time, how might these experiences translate to trait self-esteem?

5. Do people from Eastern cultures generally feel worse about themselves than people from Western cultures? How do researchers interpret self-reported self-esteem differences between cultures?

6. Should people be more likely to display the better-than-average effect for their own intelligence before or after learning how intelligence is measured in scientific research? How do construals contribute to this process?

7. If you're fairly sure you are scatterbrained, but a friend tells you that you're organized and put-together, what will your cognitive reaction likely be? What will your emotional reaction likely be? Which motive (self-enhancement or self-verification) drives which set of reactions?

8. Suppose two friends both have an actual self that is relatively happy, and a potential self that is extremely happy (happier than their actual self). If this discrepancy in happiness leads one friend to experience agitation, and the other friend to experience dejection as a result, what does this tell you? What theory would this evidence support?

THE ANSWER GUIDELINES FOR THE THINK ABOUT IT QUESTIONS CAN BE FOUND AT THE BACK OF THE BOOK . . .

Social Cognition: Thinking about People and Situations

Early in the morning on June 28, 1993, New York State troopers on Long Island's Southern State Parkway noticed a Mazda pickup truck with no license plates. When they motioned for the driver to pull over, he sped off, leading them on a 25-minute chase that ended when the Mazda slammed into a utility pole. After arresting the driver, the officers noticed a foul odor emanating from under a tarp in the back of the truck. When the tarp was removed, the officers discovered the badly decomposed body of a 22-year-old woman. Subsequent investigation implicated the driver, Joel Rifkin, in the murders of 16 other women, making him the most prolific serial killer in New York State history.

Those who knew Rifkin expressed shock at the news. One neighbor told reporters, "When I would come home at 1 or 2 in the morning, if I saw the garage light on, I'd feel safe because I knew Joel was around." A second neighbor said he was "simply a gentle young man." Classmates asserted he was "not the kind of guy who would do something like this."

As this story makes clear, social judgments can have serious consequences. Mistaking a serial killer as someone who's "gentle" and "safe" to be around can be a lethal error. More generally, effective action requires sound judgment about the world around us. "How will my professor react if I ask for more time?" "Are they developing nuclear weapons?" "Will my boyfriend be faithful?" "Is it worth it?"

This chapter's discussion of social cognition—and sources of error in judgment about the social world—proceeds in five parts. Each focuses on a critical aspect of social judgment: (1) Our judgments are only as accurate as the quality of the

Errors in Social Judgment
Although Joel Rifkin was the most prolific serial killer in New York's history, his neighbors insisted that he was "a gentle young man" who was "not the kind of guy who would do something like this."

information on which they are based, yet the information available to us in everyday life is not always representative or complete. (2) The way information is presented, including the order in which it is presented and how it is framed, can affect the judgments we make. (3) We don't just passively take in information. We often actively seek it out, and a pervasive bias in our information-seeking strategies can distort the conclusions we reach. (4) Our preexisting knowledge, expectations, and mental habits can influence the construal of new information and thus substantially influence judgment. (5) Two mental systems, reason and intuition, underlie social cognition, and their complex interplay determines the judgments we make.

Studying Social Cognition

The field of social cognition is the study of how people think about the social world and arrive at judgments that help them interpret the past, understand the present, and predict the future. Social psychologists have long been interested in cognition. Indeed, one of the earliest and most fundamental principles of social psychology is the construal principle introduced in Chapter 1: if we want to know how a person will react in a given situation, we must understand how the person experiences that situation. Social stimuli rarely influence people's behavior directly; they do so indirectly through the way they're interpreted and construed.

The story that opened this chapter does more than testify to the importance of social judgments in everyday life. It also highlights the fact that our judgments are not always flawless. We trust some people we shouldn't. We make some investments that turn out to be unwise. Some of our mistakes are harmless and others have dire consequences, but all of them can help us figure out how to do better next time.

Mistakes are informative to psychologists because they provide particularly helpful clues about how people think about others and make inferences about them. Errors provide hints about the strategies, or rules, people follow to make judgments—both those that turn out to be successful and those that lead to disaster. The strategy of scrutinizing mistakes has a long tradition in psychology. Perceptual psychologists study illusions because they help reveal general principles of perception. Psycholinguists study speech errors to learn about speech production. Mistakes can reveal a great deal about how a system works by showing its limitations. Thus, researchers interested in social cognition have often explored the limitations of everyday judgment.

"Many complain about their memory; few about their judgment."

—LA ROCHEFOUCAULD

The Information Available for Social Cognition

Social cognition depends first of all on information. Understanding other people depends on accurate information. But sometimes people have little or no information on which to base their assessments; sometimes the available information is misleading; sometimes the way people acquire information affects their thinking unduly. Each of these circumstances presents special challenges to achieving an accurate understanding of others.

Minimal Information: Inferring Personality from Physical Appearance

A lack of sufficient information on which to base a judgment rarely stops people from making inferences about a person or situation. Consider the impressions we form of complete strangers based on the briefest glances. One of the most interesting things about such impressions is how quickly we make them. The term *snap judgment* exists for a reason. In a telling empirical demonstration of this fact, Janine Willis and Alex Todorov (2006) showed participants a large number of faces and had them rate how trustworthy, competent, likable, aggressive, or attractive each person seemed. Some participants were given as much time as they wanted to make each rating, and their trait judgments were used as the "gold standard" of comparison—the most telling impressions an individual could form based solely on photographs. Other participants were also asked to rate the photos, but after seeing each face for only a second (1,000 milliseconds), half a second (500 ms), or a tenth of a second (100 ms). How well did these hurried trait judgments correspond with the more reflective assessments? As you can see in **Table 4.1**, remarkably well. A great deal of what we conclude about people based on their faces is determined almost instantaneously. In fact, the correlation between judgments made at leisure and those made under time pressure was almost as high for participants given a tenth of a second for their ratings as for those given a full second!

Perceiving Trust and Dominance What is it that people think they see in brief glances at another person's face? To find out, Todorov and his colleagues had participants rate a large number of photographs of different faces, all with neutral expressions, on the personality dimensions people most often spontaneously mention when describing faces (Todorov, Said, Engell, & Oosterhof, 2008). When they looked at how all these judgments correlated with one another, they found that two dimensions tend to stand out. One is a positive-negative dimension,

TABLE 4.1 CORRELATIONS BETWEEN TIME-CONSTRAINED AND UNCONSTRAINED TRAIT JUDGMENTS

TRAIT JUDGMENT	EXPOSURE TIME		
	100 MS	500 MS	1,000 MS
Trustworthiness	.73	.66	.74
Competence	.52	.67	.59
Likability	.59	.57	.63
Aggressiveness	.52	.56	.59
Attractiveness	.69	.57	.66

NOTE: All correlations were significant, $p < .001$.

SOURCE: Adapted from Willis & Todorov, 2006.

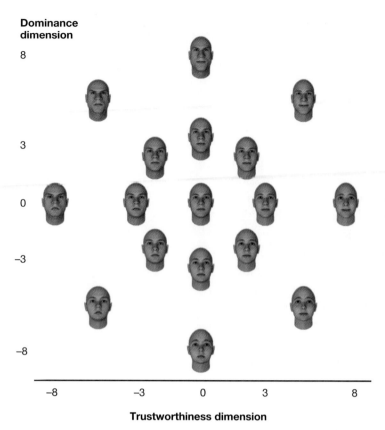

Dominance dimension

8

3

0

−3

−8

−8   −3   0   3   8

Trustworthiness dimension

Figure 4.1

Judging Faces

These computer-generated faces show variations on the two independent dimensions of trustworthiness (x-axis) and dominance (y-axis).

SOURCE: Adapted from Todorov, Said, Engell, & Oosterhof, 2008.

involving such assessments as whether someone is seen as trustworthy or untrustworthy, aggressive or not aggressive. The other dimension centers around power, involving assessments such as whether someone seems confident or bashful, dominant or submissive. It appears, then, that people are set to make quite important judgments about others: whether they should be approached or avoided (dimension 1), and whether they're likely to be top dog or underdog (dimension 2). Todorov used computer models to generate faces that represent various combinations of these two dimensions, including faces that are more extreme on each trait dimension than would ever be encountered in real life (**Figure 4.1**). In these faces, you can see the hypermasculine features, such as a very pronounced jaw, that make someone look dominant, and the features, such as the shape of the eyebrows and eye sockets, that make someone look trustworthy.

If you look at the faces that are seen as trustworthy and not dominant, you'll notice that they tend to look like baby faces. Indeed, extensive research by Leslie Zebrowitz and her colleagues has shown that adults with such baby-faced features as large round eyes, a large forehead, high eyebrows, and a rounded, relatively small chin are assumed to possess many of the characteristics associated with the very young (Berry & Zebrowitz-McArthur, 1986; Zebrowitz & Montepare, 2005). They are judged to be relatively weak, naive, and submissive, whereas adults with small eyes, a small forehead, and an angular, prominent chin tend to be judged as strong, competent, and dominant (**Figure 4.2**).

It makes sense that we consider adults with baby faces to be relatively harmless and helpless. The renowned ethologist Konrad Lorenz (1950) speculated that the cuteness of the young in many mammalian species triggers a hardwired, automatic reaction that helps ensure the young and helpless receive adequate care. The automatic nature of our response to infantile features makes it more likely that we would overgeneralize and come to see even adults with such features as trustworthy and friendly. These assessments have dramatic consequences: baby-faced individuals receive more favorable treatment as defendants in court (Zebrowitz & McDonald, 1991), but they have a harder time being seen as appropriate for "adult" jobs, such as banking (Zebrowitz, Tenenbaum, & Goldstein, 1991).

The Accuracy of Snap Judgments How accurate are the snap judgments we make of people based on their appearance, or upon witnessing very brief samples of their behavior? Are people with baby faces, for example, really more likely to be weak or submissive? It's easy to imagine how being treated by others as weak and submissive might encourage something of a dependent disposition. It's also easy to imagine how a strong jaw might elicit deference from others, thereby encouraging a forceful, dominant stance toward the world. But are the facial features people associate with different personality traits valid cues to those traits? Are brief samples of people's behavior—psychologists call them "thin slices" of behavior—reliable guides to what they're really like?

FIGURE 4.2 **YOU BE THE SUBJECT: PERSONALITY RATINGS BASED ON APPEARANCE**

Review these photos and circle where you think each person would fall on the personality scales below.

Personality Rankings

	Weak	1	2	3	4	5	6	7	8	9	10	Strong
	Naive	1	2	3	4	5	6	7	8	9	10	Competent
	Submissive	1	2	3	4	5	6	7	8	9	10	Dominant

	Weak	1	2	3	4	5	6	7	8	9	10	Strong
	Naive	1	2	3	4	5	6	7	8	9	10	Competent
	Submissive	1	2	3	4	5	6	7	8	9	10	Dominant

Results: If you're like most people, you judged the person in the top photo, who is more baby-faced according to the criteria the researchers used, to be lower on these personality dimensions than the person in the bottom photo.

SOURCE: Adapted from Zebrowitz, Tenenbaum, & Goldstein, 1991.

Note first that sometimes it's as important to know what other people *think* someone is like as it is to know that person's true characteristics. In those cases, the pertinent question boils down to how well snap judgments predict more considered consensus opinion. And the evidence indicates that they predict rather well. For example, in one study, participants were shown, for 1 second, pictures of the Republican and Democratic candidates in U.S. congressional elections and asked to indicate which candidates looked more competent. Those judged to be more competent by most of the participants won 69 percent of the races

Infantile Features in Young Mammals

Do you find these baby animals cute? Do you feel warmth and compassion toward them? You should. Psychologists and ethologists argue that the features associated with the very young in virtually all mammalian species trigger emotions that encourage caregiving, and hence survival.

(Todorov, Mandisodza, Goren, & Hall, 2005). The person judged to be more competent might not actually be more competent. Their judgment might lack validity, in other words. However, what matters in predicting the outcome of elections is not what is really true, but what the electorate believes to be true.

In another line of research, participants were shown thin slices of professors' performance in the classroom (that is, three 10-second silent video clips) and asked to rate the professors on a variety of dimensions, such as how anxious, competent, active, and warm they seemed. A composite of these relatively quick assessments correlated significantly with students' evaluations of their professors at the end of the semester (Ambady & Rosenthal, 1993). This finding indicates that judgments based on thin slices of behavior have a certain sort of validity. Such reactions do a decent job of predicting judgments based on exposure to much larger samples of behavior. But we don't know that the reactions are valid in the sense that they tell us what the professors are really like—how competent they might be perceived to be by educational experts, for example, or how well their students do on an exam compared to how well students in another professor's class do.

Experimenters in another study showed participants 5-, 10-, or 20-second clips of inmates in a medium-security prison and asked them to assess whether each inmate was a psychopath. Their judgments correlated significantly with trained assessments made on the basis of extensive interviews (Fowler, Lilienfeld, & Patrick, 2009). Presumably, the latter assessments based on more extensive exposure to the inmates are accurate indicators of their true level of psychopathy. If so, this indicates that people can make reasonably accurate judgments from thin slices of behavior. In another study, students could tell whether people on speed dates were interested in seeing each other again after watching a mere 10-second clip of their interaction. The effect was not huge, but it was significant. The judges were 9 percent more accurate than they would have been had they just blindly used the base rate of the males' interest in another date, and 2 percent more accurate if they had used the females' base rate (Place, Todd, Penke, & Asendorpf, 2009). In still another study, participants were able to determine sexual orientation, at beyond chance levels, on the basis of 10-second clips of gay, lesbian, and heterosexual individuals sitting in a chair (Ambady, Hallahan, & Conner, 1999).

The available evidence thus indicates there is often some validity to even extremely brief exposure to other people's behavior. However, it's probably unwise to hire, reject, or make commitments to people based on snap judgments, because in general they contain only a kernel of truth (Pound, Penton-Voak, & Brown, 2007; Zebrowitz, Voinescu, & Collins, 1996). But they do provide a kernel.

Misleading Firsthand Information: Pluralistic Ignorance

Some of the information we have about the world, including our immediate impressions of others, comes to us through direct experience. The rest comes to us secondhand, through gossip, the mass media, biographies, textbooks, and so on. In many cases, the information collected firsthand is more accurate because it has the advantage of not having been filtered by someone else, who might slant things in a particular direction. But firsthand experiences can also be deceptive, as when we fail to pay close attention to information about events that occur before our eyes, or when we misconstrue their true meaning. Our firsthand experience can also be unrepresentative, as it tends to be when judging what the students at a given university are like based on the one or two encountered during a campus tour. We can be similarly misled when we judge what "the locals" in a foreign country are like from the few we encounter at hotels, restaurants, or museums.

Some of the firsthand information we acquire about people is inaccurate because it's intended to be. People's behavior sometimes springs from a desire to create an impression that is not a true reflection of their beliefs or traits. The gap between inner reality and outer behavior can lead to predictable errors in judgment. Consider the following familiar scenario (Miller & McFarland, 1991). A professor finishes a discussion of a difficult topic by asking, "Are there any questions?" Many students are completely mystified, but no hands are raised. The befuddled students conclude that everyone else understands the material, and that they alone are confused.

Inner Reality vs. Outer Behavior
Students who don't understand what the teacher is saying might act like they do because they think everyone else understands, and they don't want to be seen as a bit "slow." But when everyone acts this way, it reinforces the false impression that everyone else understands the teacher, and it becomes even harder for anyone to speak up. This is a classic example of pluralistic ignorance.

This is just one example of a phenomenon known as **pluralistic ignorance**. This misperception occurs whenever people act in ways that conflict with their private beliefs because of a concern for the social consequences. It's embarrassing to admit you didn't understand a lecture when you suspect that everyone else did. However, when everyone follows that logic, an illusion is created and everyone misperceives the group norm.

Pluralistic ignorance is particularly common in situations where "toughness" is valued, and people are afraid to show their kinder, gentler impulses. Gang members, for example, have been known privately to confess their objections to brutal initiation procedures and the lack of concern for human life, but they are afraid to say so because of the fear of being ridiculed by their peers. The result is that few of them realize how many of their fellow gang members share their private reservations (Matza, 1964).

More recently, Nicole Shelton and Jennifer Richeson (2005) examined another form of pluralistic ignorance, one with profound implications for interactions among members of different ethnic groups. The researchers predicted that individuals might worry that someone from another ethnic group would not be interested in talking to them. Initiating conversation would therefore seem risky, something they might want to avoid out of fear of being rejected. As a result, no opening gesture is made and no contact is established. But how do people interpret the missed opportunity? When Shelton and Richeson asked students a series of focused questions to probe this issue, they found that although the students generally attributed their own failure to initiate contact to their fear of rejection, they assumed the other person didn't initiate contact because of a lack of interest in establishing friendships across ethnic lines. And when both people assume the other is not interested, neither one makes the effort to become friends.

Misleading Firsthand Information: Self-Fulfilling Prophecies

In early January of 1981, Joseph Granville, financial writer and author of the *Granville Market Letter*, wrote that the stock market was headed for a steep decline and advised his readers to "sell everything." Remarkably, stocks tumbled

pluralistic ignorance Misperception of a group norm that results from observing people who are acting at variance with their private beliefs out of a concern for the social consequences; those actions reinforce the erroneous group norm.

self-fulfilling prophecy The tendency for people to act in ways that bring about the very thing they expect to happen.

the very next day, in what was then the biggest day of trading in the history of the New York Stock Exchange. Had Granville seen something that other analysts missed? Or did his advice lead to a sell-off that helped cause the very decline he predicted? This question highlights another way in which firsthand information can be misleading: we can fail to notice that our own behavior has brought about what we're seeing. This phenomenon is called the **self-fulfilling prophecy**: our expectations lead us to behave in ways that elicit the very behavior we expect from others. If we think someone is unfriendly, we're likely to offer something of a cold shoulder ourselves, which is likely to elicit the very coldness we anticipated.

The most famous demonstration of the impact of self-fulfilling prophecies is a study in which researchers told elementary schoolteachers that aptitude tests indicated that several of their students could be expected to "bloom" intellectually in the coming year (Rosenthal & Jacobson, 1968). In reality, the students so described were chosen randomly. Nevertheless, the expectation that certain students would undergo an intellectual growth spurt set in motion a pattern of student-teacher interaction that led those students to score higher on IQ tests administered at the end of the year (Jussim, 1986; Smith, Jussim, & Eccles, 1999).

In another notable study, Saul Kassin, Christine Goldstein, and Ken Savitsky (2003) had some students commit a mock crime (stealing $100 from a locked laboratory cabinet) and other students simply visit the scene of the crime. These students were then questioned by student interrogators who were led to believe they were likely to be guilty or innocent. The interrogators who thought their suspects were likely to be guilty asked more incriminating questions and generally conducted more vigorous and aggressive interrogations. This in turn led these suspects to act more defensively, which made them appear guilty to a group of uninformed observers who listened to tapes containing only the suspects' comments (with the interrogators' questions removed). When the interrogators thought someone was guilty, he or she acted in ways that elicited apparent evidence of guilt.

Note that if a prophecy is to be self-fulfilling, there must be some mechanism that translates a given expectation into action that would tend to confirm the prophecy. In the study of teachers' expectations, the mechanism was the teachers' behavior. In particular, the teachers tended to challenge the students they thought were about to "bloom," giving them more material, and more difficult material, to learn. Not all prophecies have that link. Someone might think you're rich, but it's hard to imagine how that belief would help make it so. In fact, some prophecies can even be self-negating, as when a driver believes "nothing bad can happen to me" and therefore drives recklessly (Dawes, 1988).

Misleading Secondhand Information

Self-Fulfilling Prophecies
If teachers believe a student is capable, they are likely to act toward the student in ways that bring out the best in him or her, thereby confirming their initial belief.

Do you believe that global warming is caused by humans? That Walt Disney was anti-Semitic? That your roommate's father is a good parent? Opinions like these are based to a large extent on secondhand information. Few of us have any firsthand knowledge of the links between industrialization and climatological data. None of us knows firsthand what Walt

Disney thought about Jews. Similarly, for most people, knowledge of their roommate's father is restricted to whatever stories the roommate has told about him.

Because so many of our judgments are based on secondhand information, a comprehensive understanding of social cognition requires an analysis of how accurate this information is likely to be. What are some of the variables that influence the accuracy of secondhand information? What factors reduce the reliability of secondhand information, and when do these factors tend to come into play?

Ideological Distortions People who transmit information often have an ideological agenda—a desire to foster certain beliefs or behaviors—that leads them to accentuate some elements of a story and suppress others. Sometimes such motivated distortion is relatively "innocent": the person relaying the message fervently believes it but chooses to omit certain inconvenient details that might detract from its impact. For example, when preparing U.S. President Harry Truman for his 1947 speech on the containment of the Soviet Union, Undersecretary of State Dean Acheson remarked that it was necessary to be "clearer than the truth."

"Here it is—the plain, unvarnished truth. Varnish it."

Of course, not all distortions are so innocent. People often knowingly provide distorted accounts for the express purpose of misleading. In American politics, Republicans call attention to all kinds of misleading statistics to make Democrats look bad, and the Democrats return the favor. In areas of intense ethnic strife, such as Kashmir, the Congo, Gaza, and Rwanda, all sides wildly exaggerate their own righteousness and inflate tales of atrocities committed against them (even though the reality is often bad enough).

Distortions in the Service of Entertainment: Overemphasis on Bad News
One of the most pervasive causes of distortion in secondhand accounts is the desire to entertain. On a small scale, this happens in the stories people tell one another, sometimes embellished to make them more interesting. Being trapped in an elevator with 20 people for an hour is more intriguing than being trapped with 6 people for 15 minutes. So we round up, generously.

On a larger scale, the desire to entertain distorts the messages people receive through the mass media. One way print and broadcast media can attract an audience is to report—indeed, overreport—negative, violent, and sensational events. Bad news tends to be more newsworthy than good news—or, as the news world puts it, "If it bleeds, it leads."

The media do indeed provide a distorted view of reality. In the world as the media present it, 80 percent of all crime is violent; in the real world, only 20 percent of reported crimes are violent (Center for Media and Public Affairs, 2000; Marsh, 1991; Sheley & Askins, 1981). In addition, news coverage of crime doesn't correlate with the rise and fall of the crime rate. There is just as much coverage during the best of times as there is during the worst of times (Garofalo, 1981; Windhauser, Seiter, & Winfree, 1991). The world presented in motion pictures and television dramas is even more violent than TV news coverage (Gerbner, Gross, Morgan, & Signorielli, 1980).

Positive and Negative Information In the Media

The media are more likely to report negative than positive information because the public seems more interested in the negative. Starting on March 8, 2014, the media devoted nearly round-the-clock coverage to the missing Malaysia Airlines Flight 370, continuing for several weeks. In contrast, the media rarely cover any of the more than 87,000 flights that take place without incident every day in the United States alone.

Effects of the Bad-News Bias The bad-news bias can lead people to believe they are more at risk of victimization than they really are. Investigators have conducted surveys that ask people how much television they watch and their impressions of the prevalence of crime: "How likely do you think it is that you or one of your close friends will have their house broken into during the next year?" "If a child were to play alone in a park each day for a month, what do you think that child's chances are of being the victim of a violent crime?"

TV Violence and Belief in Victimization

Viewing crime shows such as *Criminal Minds* makes people feel unsafe. People who don't watch much TV feel safer than those living in the same neighborhood who do watch TV frequently.

Such studies have consistently found a positive correlation between the amount of time spent watching TV and the fear of victimization. As with all correlational studies, however, this finding by itself is difficult to interpret. Perhaps there is something about the kind of people who watch a lot of television, besides their viewing habits, that makes them feel vulnerable. To address this problem, researchers have collected data from a variety of other measures (income, gender, race, residential location) and examined whether the findings hold up when these other variables are statistically controlled. An interesting pattern emerges. The correlation between TV viewing habits and perceived vulnerability is substantially reduced among people living in low-crime neighborhoods, but it remains strong among those living in high-crime areas (Doob & MacDonald, 1979; Gerbner et al., 1980). People who live in dangerous areas and don't watch much TV feel safer than their neighbors who watch a lot. Thus, the violence depicted in TV programs can make the world appear to be a dangerous place, especially when the televised images are similar to what people see in their own environment.

How Information Is Presented

To understand the powerful impact of how information is presented, we only need to consider the marketing and advertising of products. In an economy of abundance, companies can easily produce enough to satisfy the needs of society, but they find it useful to stimulate sufficient "need" so that there will be a larger demand for their products. By manipulating the messages people receive about various products through marketing, producers hope to influence consumers' buying impulses. The key to successful marketing, in turn, is not simply the selection of *what* information to present, but *how* to present it. It is an article of faith among advertisers that the way information is presented has a powerful influence on what people think and how they behave.

Social psychologists have confirmed the validity of this conviction. Countless studies have demonstrated that slight variations in the presentation of information—*how* it is presented and even *when* it is presented—can have profound effects on people's judgments.

Order Effects

How happy are you with your life in general? How many dates have you been on in the past month?

If you are like most people, there may have been some connection, but not a strong one, between your responses to the two questions. After all, there is much more to life than dating. Indeed, when survey respondents were asked these two questions in this order, the correlation between their responses was only .32. But when another group was asked the two questions in the opposite order, the correlation between their responses was twice as strong: .67. Asking about their recent dating history in the first question made them very aware of how that part of their life was going, which then had a notable effect on how they answered the second question (Strack, Martin, & Schwarz, 1988; see also Haberstroh, Oyserman, Schwarz, Kiihnen, & Ji, 2002; Tourangeau, Rasinski, & Bradburn, 1991).

Results such as these provide striking confirmation of something many people grasp intuitively—that the order in which items are presented can have a

primacy effect A type of order effect: the disproportionate influence on judgment by information presented first in a body of evidence.

recency effect A type of order effect: the disproportionate influence on judgment by information presented last in a body of evidence.

framing effect The influence on judgment resulting from the way information is presented, such as the order of presentation or the wording.

powerful influence on judgment. This is why we worry so much about whether we should go first or last in any kind of performance. Sometimes the information presented first exerts the most influence, a phenomenon known as a **primacy effect**. On other occasions, the information presented last has the most impact, a phenomenon known as a **recency effect**. These two are collectively referred to as *order effects*.

As a rough general rule, primacy effects most often occur when the information is ambiguous, so that what comes first influences how the later information is interpreted. Consider a study in which Solomon Asch (1946) asked people to evaluate a hypothetical individual described by the following terms: intelligent, industrious, impulsive, critical, stubborn, and envious. The individual was rated favorably, no doubt because of the influence of the two very positive terms that began the list—*intelligent* and *industrious*. A second group read the same trait adjectives in the opposite order and formed a much less favorable impression. *Stubborn* and *envious* are not getting off to a good start. Thus, there was a substantial primacy effect. Traits presented at the beginning of the list had more impact than those presented later on. Etiquette books (and your parents) are right: first impressions are crucial. Note that all the traits in Asch's experiment have different shades of meaning, and how each is construed depends on the information already encountered. Take the word *stubborn*. When it follows positive traits, such as *intelligent* and *industrious*, people interpret it charitably, as steadfast or determined. However, when it follows *envious*, it is seen more negatively, as closed-minded or rigid (Asch & Zukier, 1984; Biernat, Manis, & Kobrynowicz, 1997; Hamilton & Zanna, 1974).

Recency effects, in contrast, typically result when the last items come more readily to mind. Information remembered obviously receives greater weight than information forgotten, so later items sometimes exert more influence on judgment than information presented earlier.

Framing Effects

Order effects like those just discussed are a type of **framing effect**; the way information is presented, including the order of presentation, can "frame" the way it is processed and understood. Asking survey respondents first about how many dates they've had recently frames the question about life in a way that highlights the importance of one's dating life to overall well-being.

Order effects are a type of "pure" framing effect. The frame of reference is changed even though the content of the information is exactly the same in the two versions; only the order is different. Consider the (probably apocryphal) story of the monk whose request to smoke while he prayed was met with a disapproving stare by his superior. When he mentioned this to a friend, he was told: "Ask a different question. Ask if you can pray while you smoke." The request is the same in both versions. But there is a subtle difference in the frame of reference. The latter presupposes smoking; the former does not.

Spin Framing Framing effects are not limited to the order in which information is presented. Advertisers, for example, try to induce consumers to frame a buying decision in terms favorable to the product being advertised. They do so by using what might be called *spin framing*, a less pure form of framing that varies the content, not just the order, of what is presented. A company with a competitive edge in quality will introduce information that frames the issue as one of quality. Another company with an edge in price will feature information that frames the issue as one of savings.

Participants in political debates use spin framing to highlight some aspects of the relevant information and not others. Thus, we hear advocates of different positions talk of "pro-choice" versus "the right to life," "terrorists" versus "freedom fighters," "illegal aliens" versus "undocumented workers," even "torture" versus "enhanced interrogation." The power of such terms to frame, or spin, the relevant issues led the United States in 1947 to change the name of the War Department to the more benign-sounding Defense Department.

Spin Framing
Are these U.S. soldiers in Afghanistan "liberators" or members of an "occupying army"? The words used to describe them highlight different information, which affects how people react to them.

Politicians (and some polling organizations with a political mission) engage in spin framing when they conduct opinion polls to gather support for their positions. People are more likely to say they are in favor of repealing a "death" tax than an "inheritance" tax. And asking people whether they are in favor of "tax relief" is almost guaranteed to elicit strong support because the very word *relief* implies that taxes are a burden from which relief is needed (Lakoff, 2004). Framing survey questions in particular ways can influence public opinion dramatically on a host of policy issues. Because it is so easy to slant public opinion in a given direction, it is important to know who sponsored the poll, as well as the exact wording of the questions. As former Israeli Prime Minister Shimon Peres noted, opinion polls are "like perfume—nice to smell, dangerous to swallow."

Positive and Negative Framing Nearly everything in life is a mixture of good and bad. Ice cream tastes great, but it is full of saturated fat. Loyalty is a virtue, but it can make a person blind to another's faults. The mixed nature of most

80% Lean

20% Fat

Positive vs. Negative Framing
A piece of meat that is 80% lean is no different from one that is 20% fat, but one label emphasizes the negative and makes it seem less appealing and the other emphasizes the positive.

things means that they can be described, or framed, in ways that emphasize the good or the bad, with predictable effects on people's judgments. A piece of meat described as 75 percent lean seems more appealing than one described as 25 percent fat (Levin & Gaeth, 1988); students feel much safer using a condom described as having a 90 percent success rate than one described as having a 10 percent failure rate (Linville, Fischer, & Fischhoff, 1993). Notice that the exact same information is provided in each frame (pure framing); only the focus is different. Also note that there is no "correct" frame. It is every bit as valid to state that a piece of meat is 75 percent lean as it is to state that it is 25 percent fat.

These sorts of framing effects influence judgments and decisions of the greatest consequence, even among individuals with considerable expertise on the topic in question. In one study, for example, over 400 physicians were asked whether they would recommend surgery or radiation for patients diagnosed with a certain type of cancer (McNeil, Pauker, Sox, & Tversky, 1982). Some were told that of 100 previous patients who had the surgery, 90 lived through the postoperative period, 68 were still alive after a year, and 34 were still alive after 5 years. Eighty-two percent of these physicians recommended surgery. Others were given exactly the same information, but it was framed in different language: that 10 died during surgery or the postoperative period, 32 had died by the end of the first year, and 66 had died by the end of five years. Only 56 percent of the physicians given the information in this form recommended surgery.

Because negative information tends to attract more attention and have greater psychological impact than positive information (Baumeister et al., 2001; Rozin & Royzman, 2001), information framed in negative terms tends to elicit a stronger response. To some extent, the results just described reflect that tendency. Ten people dying sounds more threatening than 90 out of 100 surviving. More direct support for this idea comes from studies that have examined people's reactions to losses versus unrealized gains (Tversky & Kahneman, 1981). People hate losing things much more than failing to have them in the first place.

Temporal Framing

Suppose one of your friends e-mails you today and asks if you can come over next Saturday morning at 9:00 to help him move. You're free that day and he's a good friend, so of course you say you'll help him out. Now suppose that on a Saturday morning at 8:30, your friend e-mails to ask if you can come over in half an hour and help him move. It's cold out and you still feel sleepy, so you write back saying you're not feeling well—or maybe you don't write back at all, pretending you never saw the e-mail. Why were you so eager to help when asked a week in advance, but so reluctant when asked on the day in question?

You probably have had similar feelings of being at odds with a decision made by an earlier version of yourself. Your earlier self might have thought it was a good idea to take an extra-heavy course load this semester, but now your present self is frazzled, sleep deprived, and overworked. How could you have thought this would be a good idea? Or an earlier self might have thought that an Outward Bound experience would be the perfect way to spend a chunk of your precious summer vacation, but once you are up in the mountains, the bad food and the onslaught of mosquitoes makes you wonder what you were thinking.

Why do things often seem like brilliant ideas at one time and terrible ideas at another? The key to understanding these sorts of disagreements within ourselves is to recognize that we think about actions and events within a particular time perspective—a *temporal frame*. They belong to the distant past, the present moment, the immediate future, and so on.

According to **construal level theory**, the temporal perspective from which people view events has important and predictable implications for how they construe them (Fiedler, 2007; Liberman, Sagristano, & Trope, 2002; Trope & Liberman, 2003, 2010). Any action or event can be thought of at a low level of abstraction, rich in concrete detail—for example, chewing your food, carrying a friend's chair up the stairs, or giving a panhandler a dollar. But it can also be thought of at a higher level of abstraction, rich in meaning but stripped of detail—dining out, helping a friend, or being generous. It turns out that we tend to think of distant events, those from long ago or far off in the future, in abstract terms, and of events close at hand in concrete terms. Next week you'll be dining out, or helping a friend move; but right now you're chewing your food, or later this afternoon you'll be carrying your friend's chair up the stairs.

This difference in construal has important implications for what people think and how they act in their everyday lives, and it explains many inconsistent preferences. Things that sound great in the abstract are sometimes less thrilling when fleshed out in all their concrete detail, so we regret making some commitments. You think of a heavy course load a year from now as "furthering my education" or "expanding my horizons." That sounds great, so you accept the challenge. But you experience the heavy course load during the semester itself as "studying" or "spending time in the library," which is less inspiring, so you question your earlier decision to take on this burden. In contrast, sometimes the abstract level can be less desirable than the concrete, producing the opposite sort of inconsistency. You might swear that you'll stick to your diet no matter what (because you don't want to "pig out"), yet when you're standing in front of the buffet, you find it easy to indulge (because you're only "sampling the different options").

This influence of near and far events applies to dimensions other than time (Trope & Liberman, 2010). Something can be near or far in space (at your college

construal level theory A theory about the relationship between psychological distance and abstract or concrete thinking: psychologically distant actions and events are thought about in abstract terms; actions and events that are close at hand are thought about in concrete terms.

Temporal Distance and Construal

When an event is far away, we think of it in broad, abstract terms like "exploring foreign lands." When an event is close at hand, we think about it in narrower, more concrete terms, like "packing."

campus versus in Barbados), or it can be near or far socially (something that will happen to you versus something that will happen to a distant acquaintance). Far or near on these other dimensions has the same effect on construal as far or near in time. In one study, for example, NYU students tended to think of "climbing a tree" as "holding onto branches" when the climbing was to take place 3 miles from campus, but as "getting a good view" when it was to take place 3,000 miles away on the West Coast. Similarly, "going to the dentist" was seen as "getting a cavity filled" nearby but as "protecting one's teeth" in far-off Los Angeles (Fujita, Henderson, Eng, Trope, & Liberman, 2006).

🔄 LOOKING BACK

The way information is presented, including the order in which it is presented, can affect judgment. Primacy effects occur when information presented first has more impact than information presented later, often because the initial information influences the way later information is construed. Recency effects occur when information presented later is better remembered and thus has more impact. People are susceptible to how information is framed. Sometimes people deliberately spin information so as to influence our judgment by changing our frame of reference. The temporal framing of an event—whether it will occur soon or far in the future—also influences how we think of it; far-off events are construed in more abstract terms, and imminent events are construed more concretely.

How We Seek Information

Suppose a friend gives you several potted plants for your dorm room or apartment and says, "I'm not sure, but they might need frequent watering. You should check that out." How would you do that? If you are like most people, you would water them often and see how they do. What you would *not* do is give a lot of water to some, very little to the others, and compare the results.

Confirmation Bias

When evaluating a proposition (a plant needs frequent watering; a generous allowance spoils a child; Hispanics place a high value on family life), people more readily, reliably, and vigorously seek out evidence that would support the proposition rather than information that would contradict the proposition. This tendency is known as the **confirmation bias** (Klayman & Ha, 1987; Skov & Sherman, 1986).

In one study that examined the confirmation bias, Jennifer Crocker asked one group of participants to determine whether working out the day before an important tennis match makes a player more likely to win (Crocker, 1982). Another group was asked to determine whether working out the day before a match makes a player more likely to lose. Both groups could examine any of four types of information before coming to a conclusion: the number of players in a sample who worked out the day before and won their match, the number of players who worked out and lost, the number of players who did not work out the day before and won, and the number of players who did not work out and lost. In fact, all four types of information are needed to make a valid determination. You have to calculate and compare the success rate of those who worked out the day before

confirmation bias The tendency to test a proposition by searching for evidence that would support it.

the match with the success rate of those who did not. If the first ratio is higher than the second, then working out the day before increases the chances of winning.

But participants tended not to seek out all the necessary information. Instead, as **Figure 4.3** makes clear, participants exhibited the confirmation bias: they were especially interested in examining information that could potentially confirm the proposition they were investigating. Those trying to find out whether practicing leads to winning were more interested in the number of players who practiced and won than those trying to find out whether practicing leads to losing—and vice versa (Crocker, 1982).

This tendency to seek confirming information can lead to all sorts of false beliefs, because a person can find supportive evidence for almost anything (Gilovich, 1991; Shermer, 1997). Are people more likely to come to harm when there is a full moon? There will certainly be many months in which hospital ERs are unusually busy during the full moon. Do optimistic people live longer? You can probably think of some very elderly people who are unusually upbeat. But evidence consistent with a proposition is not enough to draw a firm conclusion, as there might be even more evidence against it—more days with empty ERs during the full moon, more pessimists living long lives ("grumpy old men"). The danger of the confirmation bias, then, is that if we look mainly for one type of evidence, we are likely to find it. To truly test a proposition, we must seek out the evidence against it as well as the evidence for it.

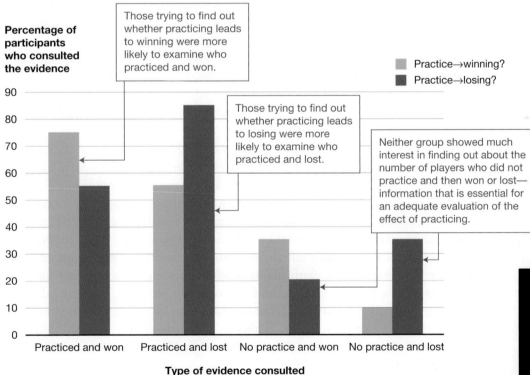

Figure 4.3
The Confirmation Bias
Light green bars represent the responses of participants trying to determine whether practicing the day before a tennis match makes a player more likely to win. Dark green bars represent the responses of participants trying to find out whether practicing the day before makes a player more likely to lose.

SOURCE: Adapted from Crocker, 1982.

Searching for Evidence That Fits Our Beliefs
People who deny the reality of global warming often seize on episodes like these to support their skepticism ("Would we have periods like this if the planet were really getting warmer?"). Those who are worried about climate change are likely to seize on them to support their view ("This is just the extreme weather we can expect as a result of climate change").

In the social realm, the confirmation bias often leads people unwittingly to ask questions that shape the answers they get, thereby providing illusory support for the very thing they're trying to find out. In one telling study, researchers asked one group of participants to interview someone and determine whether the target was an extravert; another group was asked to determine whether the target was an introvert (Snyder & Swann, 1978). Participants selected their interview questions from a list provided. Those charged with determining whether the target was an extravert tended to ask questions that focused on sociability ("In what situations are you most talkative?"). Those charged with determining whether the target was an introvert tended to ask questions that focused on social withdrawal ("In what situations do you wish you could be more outgoing?"). Of course, if you ask people about times when they are most sociable, they are likely to answer in ways that will make them seem relatively outgoing, even if they are not. And if you ask about their social reticence, they will almost certainly answer in ways that make them seem relatively introverted—again, even if they are not. In a powerful demonstration of this tendency, the investigators tape-recorded the interview sessions, edited out the questions, and then played the responses to another, uninformed set of participants. These latter participants rated those who had been interviewed by someone testing for extraversion as more outgoing than those who had been interviewed by someone testing for introversion.

Motivated Confirmation Bias

In the preceding examples, and fairly often in daily life, the individuals who fall prey to the confirmation bias have no particular motivation to confirm a particular outcome. As far as they are concerned, they are simply testing a proposition. Even so, they end up engaging in a biased, and potentially misleading, search for evidence.

But sometimes, of course, people deliberately search for evidence that supports their preferences or expectations. Someone who wants a given proposition to be true may energetically sift through the pertinent evidence in an effort to uncover information that confirms its validity. In such cases, information that supports what a person wants to be true is readily accepted, whereas information that contradicts what the person would like to believe is subjected to critical scrutiny and often discounted (Dawson, Gilovich, & Regan, 2002; Ditto & Lopez, 1992; Gilovich, 1983, 1991; Kruglanski & Webster, 1996; Kunda, 1990; Pyszczynski & Greenberg, 1987).

In one notable examination of this type of motivated confirmation bias, proponents and opponents of capital punishment read about studies of the death penalty's effectiveness as a deterrent to crime (Lord, Ross, & Lepper, 1979). Some read state-by-state comparisons purportedly showing that crime rates are not any lower in states with the death penalty than in states without the death penalty, but they also read about how crime rates within a few states decreased as soon as the death penalty was put in place. Other participants read about studies showing the exact opposite: state-by-state comparisons that made the death penalty look effective and before-and-after comparisons that made it look ineffective. Those who favored the death penalty interpreted the evidence, whichever set they were exposed to, as strongly supporting their position. Those opposed to the death penalty thought the evidence warranted the opposite conclusion. Both sides jumped on the problems associated with the studies that contradicted their positions, but they readily embraced the studies that supported them. Their preferences tainted how they viewed the pertinent evidence.

⬱ LOOKING BACK

Efforts to acquire needed information are often compromised by two pronounced types of confirmation bias. One type occurs when we look for evidence consistent with propositions or hypotheses we wish to evaluate. To evaluate a proposition satisfactorily, however, it is necessary to examine evidence both for it and against it. The other type of confirmation bias occurs when we want a given proposition to be true, and we seek evidence that confirms our beliefs or preferences and explain away evidence that contradicts them.

Top-Down Processing: Using Schemas to Understand New Information

What is being described in the following paragraph?

> The procedure is quite simple. First you arrange things into different groups. Of course, one pile may be sufficient, depending on how much there is to do. If you have to go somewhere else due to lack of facilities, that is the next step; otherwise you are pretty well set.
>
> (Bransford & Johnson, 1973, p. 400)

Not so easy to figure out, is it? *What* is arranged into different groups? *What* facilities might be lacking? Most people find it difficult to discern what the paragraph is about. But suppose it had the title "Washing Clothes." Now read the paragraph again. Suddenly it is no longer so mystifying. Each sentence makes perfect sense when construed from the perspective of doing laundry.

Understanding the paragraph involves using what we already know to make sense of new information. What we know about doing laundry helps us comprehend what it means to "arrange things into different groups" and to "go somewhere else due to lack of facilities." Similarly, what we know about human nature and about different contexts allows us to determine whether another person's tears are the product of joy or sadness. What we know about norms and customs enables us to decide whether a gesture is hostile or friendly.

Perceiving and understanding the world involves the simultaneous operation of bottom-up and top-down processes. **Bottom-up processes** consist of taking in relevant stimuli from the outside world, such as text on a page, gestures in an interaction, or sound patterns at a cocktail party. At the same time, **top-down processes** filter and interpret bottom-up stimuli in light of preexisting knowledge and expectations. The meaning of stimuli is not passively recorded; it is actively *construed*.

Preexisting knowledge is necessary for understanding, and it is surely required for judgment. Indeed, as the laundry example makes clear, understanding and

bottom-up processes "Data-driven" mental processing, in which an individual forms conclusions based on the stimuli encountered in the environment.

top-down processes "Theory-driven" mental processing, in which an individual filters and interprets new information in light of preexisting knowledge and expectations.

judgment are inextricably linked. They both involve going beyond currently available information and extrapolating from it. Psychologists who study human judgment, then, have been interested in how people use their stored knowledge.

One principle psychologists have discovered is that information is not filed away bit by bit. Instead, information is organized in coherent configurations, or schemas, in which related information is stored together. Information about Hillary Rodham Clinton, Democratic candidate for president, is tightly connected to information about Hillary Rodham Clinton, Wellesley graduate; Hillary Rodham Clinton, former First Lady; Hillary Rodham Clinton, former secretary of state; and Hillary Rodham Clinton, best-selling author (Bartlett, 1932; Markus, 1977; Nisbett & Ross, 1980; Schank & Abelson, 1977; Smith & Zarate, 1990). You no doubt have schemas for all sorts of things, such as a fast-food restaurant (chain, so-so food, bright primary colors for decor, limited choices, cheap), a party animal (boisterous, drinks to excess, exuberant but clumsy dancer), and an action film (good guy establishes good guy credentials, bad guy gains the upper hand, good guy triumphs and bad guy perishes in eye-popping pyrotechnical finale).

The Influence of Schemas

The various schemas we all possess affect our judgments in many ways: by directing our attention, structuring our memories, and influencing our interpretations (Brewer & Nakamura, 1984; Hastie, 1981; Taylor & Crocker, 1981). Without schemas, our lives would be a buzzing confusion. But schemas can sometimes lead us to mischaracterize the world.

Attention Attention is selective. We cannot focus on everything, and the knowledge we bring to a given situation enables us to direct our attention to what's most important and ignore everything else. The extent to which our schemas and expectations guide our attention was powerfully demonstrated by an experiment in which participants watched a videotape of two teams of three people, each passing a basketball back and forth (Simons & Chabris, 1999). The members of one team wore white shirts, and the members of the other team wore black shirts. The researchers asked each participant to count the number of passes the members of one of the teams made. Forty-five seconds into the action, a person wearing a gorilla costume strolled into the middle of the action. Although a large gorilla might seem hard to miss, only half the participants noticed it! The participants' schemas about what is likely to happen in a game of catch directed

Expectations Guide Attention
Because people don't expect to see a gorilla in the middle of a game of catch, only half the participants who watched this video saw it. Schemas can be so strong they can prevent us from seeing even very dramatic stimuli we don't expect to see.

© 2005, Daniel J. Simons

their attention so intently to some parts of the videotape that they failed to see a rather dramatic stimulus they weren't expecting.

Memory Because schemas influence attention, they also influence memory. We are most likely to remember stimuli that have captured our attention. Indeed, former *New York Times* science writer Daniel Goleman has referred to memory as "attention in the past tense" (Goleman, 1985). The influence of schemas on memory is also important for judgment—and hence subsequent action. After all, many judgments are not made immediately; they are made down the road, on the basis of information retrieved from memory.

Researchers have documented the impact of schemas on memory in many experiments (Fiske & Taylor, 1991; Hastie, 1981; Stangor & McMillan, 1992). In one study, students watched a videotape of a husband and wife having dinner together (Cohen, 1981). Half of them were told that the wife was a librarian, the other half that she was a waitress. The students later took a quiz that assessed their memory of what they had witnessed. The central question was whether their memories were influenced by their stereotypes (schemas about particular groups in society) of librarians and waitresses. The researchers asked them, for example, whether the woman was drinking wine (librarian stereotype) or beer (waitress stereotype), and whether she had received a history book (librarian) or romance novel (waitress) as a gift. The tape had been constructed to contain an equal number of items consistent and inconsistent with each stereotype.

Did the participants' preexisting knowledge influence what they recalled? It did indeed. Students who thought the woman was a librarian recalled librarian-consistent information more accurately than librarian-inconsistent information; those who thought she was a waitress recalled waitress-consistent information more accurately than waitress-inconsistent information. Information that fits a preexisting schema often enjoys an advantage in recall (Carli, 1999; Zadny & Gerard, 1974).

This study shows that schemas can influence memory by affecting the **encoding** of information, or the filing away of information in memory. Schemas affect what information people pay attention to and how they initially interpret and store that information. But schemas can also influence the **retrieval** of information, or how information is extracted from memory.

Social psychologists have good reason to believe that schemas influence encoding because we know that they direct attention. One way to find out whether schemas influence retrieval as well would be to provide people with a schema *after* they have been exposed to the relevant information, when it obviously cannot influence encoding. Many experiments have used this tactic. The typical result is that providing a schema after participants have encountered the relevant information does not affect memory as much as providing it beforehand (Bransford & Johnson, 1973; Howard & Rothbart, 1980; Rothbart, Evans, & Fulero, 1979; Wyer, Srull, Gordon, & Hartwick, 1982; Zadny & Gerard, 1974). Nonetheless, sometimes schemas provided after information has been encountered do have a substantial effect (Anderson & Pichert, 1978; Carli, 1999; Cohen, 1981; Hirt, 1990). Thus, the appropriate conclusion seems to be that schemas influence memory through their effect on both encoding and retrieval, but the effect on encoding is typically much stronger.

Construal Schemas influence not only what information we focus on and remember, but also the way we interpret, or construe, that information. To understand how this works, meet Donald, who may seem to you like a contestant in an extreme sports competition. Actually, Donald is a fictitious person

encoding Filing information away in memory based on what information is attended to and the initial interpretation of the information.

retrieval The extraction of information from memory.

who has been used as a stimulus in numerous experiments on the effect of prior knowledge on social judgment:

Donald spent a great amount of his time in search of what he liked to call excitement. He had already climbed Mt. McKinley, shot the Colorado rapids in a kayak, driven in a demolition derby, and piloted a jet-powered boat—without knowing very much about boats. He had risked injury, and even death, a number of times. Now he was in search of new excitement. He was thinking, perhaps, he would do some skydiving or maybe cross the Atlantic in a sailboat. By the way he acted one could readily guess that Donald was well aware of his ability to do many things well. Other than business engagements, Donald's contacts with people were rather limited. He felt he didn't really need to rely on anyone. Once Donald made up his mind to do something it was as good as done no matter how long it might take or how difficult the going might be. Only rarely did he change his mind even when it might well have been better if he had.

(Higgins, Rholes, & Jones, 1977, p. 145)

In one early study featuring Donald as the stimulus, students participated in what they thought were two unrelated experiments (Higgins, Rholes, & Jones, 1977). In the first, they viewed a number of trait words projected on a screen as part of a perception experiment. Half the participants were shown the words *adventurous, self-confident, independent,* and *persistent* listed among a set of ten traits. The other half were shown the words *reckless, conceited, aloof,* and *stubborn.* After completing the ostensible perception experiment, the participants moved on to the second study on reading comprehension, in which they read the short paragraph about Donald and rated him on a number of trait scales. (The paragraph is intentionally ambiguous about whether Donald is an adventurous, appealing sort or a reckless, unappealing person.) The investigators were interested in whether the words that participants encountered in the first experiment would lead them to apply different schemas and thus affect their evaluations of Donald.

As the investigators expected, participants who had previously been exposed to the words *adventurous, self-confident, independent,* and *persistent* formed more favorable impressions of Donald than did those who were shown the less flattering words. Thus, participants' schemas about traits like adventurousness and recklessness influenced the kind of inferences they made about Donald.

The broader point is that information that is most accessible in memory can influence how we construe new information. This is most likely when the stimulus, like many of Donald's actions, is ambiguous (Trope, 1986). In such cases, we must rely more heavily on top-down processes to compensate for the inadequacies of the information obtained from the bottom up.

Behavior We've seen how schemas influence our attention, memory, and construal. Can they also influence behavior? The answer is a resounding yes. Many studies have shown that certain types of behavior are elicited automatically when people are exposed to stimuli in the environment that bring to mind a particular schema.

In one especially notable experiment, described as an investigation of language proficiency, the investigator had participants perform a sentence completion task

Adventurous or Reckless?
Whether it seems bold or foolish to eat a tarantula might be influenced by whether you earlier read about someone taking a gamble that paid off or ended in disaster.

(Bargh, Chen, & Burrows, 1996). They were given 30 sets of 5 words each, and had to form a grammatical English sentence using 4 of the words from each 5-word set. For half the participants, embedded within these 150 words were many that are stereotypically associated with older adults: *gray, wrinkle, Florida, bingo*, and so on. These words were chosen to bring to mind the schema of older people. The remaining participants were exposed to neutral words that are not associated with elderly people, so their old-age schema was not primed. **Priming** is the term researchers use to refer to procedures that momentarily activate a particular idea or schema.

The experimenter thanked the participants for their efforts, and the study appeared to be over. But it had just begun. A second experimenter covertly timed how long it took each participant to walk from the threshold of the laboratory to the elevator down the hall. The investigators had predicted that merely activating the concept of older adults for some of the participants would make them walk more slowly down the hallway because "slow" is a trait associated with elderly people. Amazingly, it did. Participants who had performed the sentence completion task using numerous words associated with older adults took 13 percent longer to walk to the elevator (Bargh, Chen, & Burrows, 1996; see also Cesario, Plaks, & Higgins, 2006).

Further studies of this sort have found that activating the trait of rudeness makes people behave more assertively (Bargh, Chen, & Burrows, 1996), and activating the goal of achievement leads people to persevere longer at difficult tasks (Bargh, Gollwitzer, Lee-Chai, Barndollar, & Trotschel, 2001). Playing German music in a liquor store appears to boost sales of German wine at the expense of French wine, whereas playing French music appears to boost sales of French wine— even if customers don't realize what type of music is being played (North, Hargreaves, & McKendrick, 1999).

In another set of demonstrations, Dutch social psychologists Ap Dijksterhuis and Ad van Knippenberg exposed students to stimuli meant to bring to mind the schema for a social group associated with intellectual accomplishment (professors) or the schema for a social group not noted for refined habits of mind (soccer hooligans). Those exposed to the professor cues subsequently performed better on a test of general knowledge than those shown cues associated with soccer hooligans (Dijksterhuis & van Knippenberg, 1998).

More remarkable still, this same team of researchers demonstrated that priming the stereotype of professor or supermodel led participants to perform in a manner *consistent* with the stereotype, but activating a specific (extreme) example of the stereotyped group (Albert Einstein or Claudia Schiffer, for instance) led participants to perform in a manner *inconsistent* with the stereotype. In other words, they performed worse on the general knowledge test when Einstein was brought to mind and better when Claudia Schiffer was (Dijksterhuis & van Knippenberg, 1998).

priming The presentation of information designed to activate a concept and hence make it accessible. A prime is the stimulus presented to activate the concept in question.

Priming
Activating stereotypes, such as professor and supermodel, may lead people to construe themselves along the lines of the stereotyped group, and act the way they think someone in the group would act. Activating a specific extreme instance of the group, however, such as (A) Albert Einstein or (B) Claudia Schiffer, tends to have the opposite effect; people compare themselves to these individuals and realize they aren't much like them at all.

These results fit the general tendency for the priming of schemas to produce behavior in line with the schema in question, because the activated schema affects construal. People think of themselves as more intelligent (and act that way) when viewing themselves, however implicitly, through the lens of a professor than the lens of a fashion model. The priming of *specific members* of a stereotyped group, in contrast, tends to yield behavior that contrasts with the stereotype in question (Herr, 1986; Schwarz & Bless, 1992). Individual examples tend to serve as standards of judgment—in this case, Einstein serves as a very high standard (making people feel unintelligent), and Claudia Schiffer serves as a relatively low standard (making people feel smart).

Which Schemas Are Activated and Applied?

In the librarian/waitress study described earlier, there is little doubt about which schema participants applied to the information in the videotape. The experimenter informs them that the woman is a librarian (or waitress), and they know nothing else about her. It stands to reason, then, that they would view the videotape through the lens of their librarian (or waitress) schema. In real life, however, the situation is often more complicated. You might know that besides being a librarian, the woman is a triathlete, a Republican, and a gourmet cook. Which schema (or combination of schemas) is likely to be thought of, or activated?

Recent Activation Schemas can be brought to mind, or activated, in various ways. Recent activation is one of the most common and important ways of doing so. If a schema has been brought to mind recently, it tends to be more accessible and hence ready for use (Ford & Kruglanski, 1995; Herr, 1986; Sherman, Mackie, & Driscoll, 1990; Srull & Wyer, 1979, 1980; Todorov & Bargh, 2002).

Recall the "Donald" study described earlier (Higgins et al., 1977). Participants who had previously been exposed to trait adjectives such as *adventurous* formed more favorable impressions of the fictional Donald than those who had been exposed to adjectives such as *reckless*. By exposing participants to words implying adventurousness or recklessness, the researchers were trying to prime participants' schemas for the traits *adventurous* and *reckless*. Of course, schemas can become activated by exposure to stimuli other than words. People's judgments and behavior have been shown to be influenced by schemas primed by features of the surrounding environment (Aarts & Dijksterhuis, 2003; Gosling, Ko, Mannarelli, & Morris, 2002; Kay, Wheeler, Bargh, & Ross, 2004); cultural symbols, such as a country's flag (Carter, Ferguson, & Hassin, 2011; Ehrlinger et al., 2011; Hassin, Ferguson, Shidlovsky, & Gross, 2007); the pursuit of a goal (Aarts, Gollwitzer, & Hassin, 2004); a significant other (Shah, 2003); feedback from one's own body (Jostmann, Lakens, & Schubert, 2009; Lee & Schwarz, 2011); even a passing smell (Holland, Hendricks, & Aarts, 2005).

Frequent Activation and Chronic Accessibility You may have noticed that people differ in the schemas they tend to use when evaluating others. Employers at high-tech firms are often concerned with whether job candidates are smart, sales managers with whether employees are persuasive, and those involved in the entertainment business with whether an actress or actor has charisma. As these examples illustrate, the role of the evaluator, or the context in which a target person is encountered, often influences which traits or schemas are used.

But sometimes it's simply a matter of habit. If a person uses a particular schema frequently, it may become chronically accessible and therefore likely to be used still more often in the future. A frequently activated schema functions much like a recently activated one: its heightened accessibility increases the likelihood that it will be applied to understanding a new stimulus.

In one study that examined the impact of chronic accessibility on information processing, researchers recruited participants for two supposedly unrelated experiments (Higgins, King, & Mavin, 1982). First they were asked to list the personality traits of five people: two male friends, two female friends, and themselves. This part of the experiment was designed to identify what schemas were most accessible for each participant. Any trait schema that was listed in three or more of a given participant's descriptions was considered a highly accessible, or chronically accessible, schema.

About 2 weeks later, the participants returned for the second, supposedly unrelated experiment and were greeted by a different experimenter. They read a brief description of another person, but they didn't know the description had been individually crafted for each participant to include certain behaviors reflecting some traits that were highly accessible for them and other behaviors reflecting less accessible traits. After reading the description, the participants wrote their own characterization of the target person. These descriptions were then scored for whether they included behaviors that exemplified the chronically accessible and relatively inaccessible traits for each participant. Consistent with the idea that people's chronically accessible schemas strongly influence their evaluations of others, participants' descriptions of the target person contained more behaviors reflecting their chronically accessible traits (55 percent) than behaviors exemplifying their less accessible traits (31 percent). The chronically accessible schemas each of us brings to a given situation have a significant impact on how we interpret what we encounter.

The Influence of Chronically Accessible Schemas on Perception and Judgment If certain schemas, such as "smuggling" or "threat," are used a lot, they tend to be highly accessible and are therefore readily applied to new situations.

Consciousness of Activation: Necessary or Not? Carefully conducted interviews with participants at the end of many priming experiments have found that very few (and, in many cases, none) of them suspected that there was any connection between the two parts of the study—the initial priming phase and the subsequent judgment phase. This finding raises the question of how conscious a person must be of a stimulus for it to effectively prime a given schema. Research suggests a clear-cut answer: not at all. A great many studies have shown that stimuli presented outside of conscious awareness can prime a schema sufficiently to influence subsequent information processing (Bargh, 1996; Debner & Jacoby, 1994; Devine, 1989b; Dijksterhuis, Preston, Wegner, & Aarts, 2008; Draine & Greenwald, 1998; Ferguson, 2008; Ferguson, Bargh, & Nayak, 2005; Greenwald, Klinger, & Liu, 1989; Klinger, Burton, & Pitts, 2000; Lepore & Brown, 1997; Shah, 2003).

In one study, researchers showed a set of words to participants on a computer screen so quickly that it was impossible to discern what the words were

BOX 4.1 **FOCUS ON *EVERYDAY LIFE***

Subtle Situational Influence

Social psychologists have recently been busy exploring ways in which our behavior can be influenced by stimuli of which we are unaware. Words, sights, sounds, and even smells can influence how we act, for good or for ill. These investigations make it clear that social influence is pervasive, and yet we're often unaware that we're being influenced. Consider the following findings.

- Want to make your employees be more creative? Have them work in a green or blue environment—and be sure they don't work in a red environment (Lichtenfield, Elliot, Maier, & Pekrun, 2012; Mehta & Zhu, 2009).

- Green, as in environmental greenery, can help reduce violence. People living in public housing surrounded by greenery commit many fewer violent crimes than people in nearby public housing surrounded by concrete (Kuo & Sullivan, 2001).

- Want to get lots of hits on your dating website? Wear a red shirt in your profile photo, or at least put a red border around your picture. Both men and women are considered to be sexier when dressed in red, or just surrounded by red (Elliot et al., 2010).

- Want taxpayers to support education bond issues? Lobby to make schools the primary voting location. Want to get the voters to outlaw late abortion? Lobby to have voters cast their ballots in churches. The associations people have to the buildings that serve as polling stations influence how people vote (Berger, Meredith, & Wheeler, 2008).

- Want to get people to pay more consistently for the office tea or coffee they use by putting the agreed-upon fee in the "honest box"? On the wall near the box, put up a poster with anything with eyes (even a symbolic, stick-figure face). A nonconscious sense of being observed makes people more likely to be on their best behavior (Bateson, Nettle, & Roberts, 2006; Haley & Fessler, 2005).

- Want someone to reject a proposition? Have the person entertain the idea in a seafood store or on a wharf. If the person is from a culture that uses the expression "fishy" to mean "dubious," the association will make it more likely that the proposition will be doubted (Lee & Schwarz, 2012).

- Want someone to be deeply concerned about the threat posed by climate change? Have them fill out a survey about carbon emissions in an especially hot room. People take the threat of global warming more seriously when they are feeling uncomfortably warm themselves (Risen & Critcher, 2011).

This list might remind you of the stand-up comic who follows a rapid-fire series of one-liners with the statement, "I've got a million of these." Social psychologists have no shortage of demonstrations of the influence of incidental stimuli on people's behavior. The most obvious implication of this research is that we can exert some influence over people's behavior by attending to the details of their surrounding physical environment. A less obvious implication is that if we want to free ourselves of these kinds of influences, we should try to consider important propositions and potential courses of action in a number of different settings, if possible. That way, incidental stimuli associated with the different environments are likely to cancel each other out, resulting in more sound judgments and decisions.

(Bargh & Pietromonaco, 1982). (In a control condition in which participants were asked simply to guess what each word was, they were unable to do so, guessing fewer than 1 percent correctly.) The words were either mainly hostile (*hate, whip, stab, hostile*) or mainly nonhostile (*water, long, together, every*). Next, the researchers had the participants read a short paragraph about an individual who had committed a number of moderately hostile acts, and then rate that person on a number of trait dimensions. The participants who had previously been exposed to predominantly hostile words rated the target person more negatively than those exposed to predominantly nonhostile words. They did so, mind you, even though they were not consciously aware of the words to which they had been exposed. Thus, schemas can be primed even when the presentation of the activating stimuli is subliminal, or below the threshold of conscious awareness (**Box 4.1**). In other words, a **subliminal stimulus** is one that is below the threshold of conscious awareness.

Expectations Sometimes people apply a schema because of a preexisting expectation about what they will encounter (Hirt, MacDonald, & Erikson, 1995; Sherman et al., 1990; Stangor & McMillan, 1992). The expectation activates the schema, and the schema is then readily applied. If the expectation is warranted, it saves considerable mental energy. For example, applying a "haggling" schema to a given commercial transaction allows us to dismiss the stated price without much thought or anxiety, and it frees us to make a counteroffer. Misapplying the haggling schema, however, can lead to the embarrassment of making a counteroffer when it is not appropriate.

Expectations thus influence information processing by lowering the threshold for the application of a given schema. The expectation essentially primes the schema, and the schema is readily applied at the slightest hint that it is applicable.

⬅ LOOKING BACK

Knowledge structures, or schemas, play a crucial role in judgment. Schemas influence judgment by guiding attention, influencing memory, and determining how information is construed. Schemas can also directly influence behavior. Schemas are particularly likely to exert an influence if they have been recently activated (and hence primed) or are habitually used, and people need not be aware of the recent or chronic activation of a schema for it to exert its effects. Schemas normally allow us to make judgments and to take action quickly and accurately, but they can also mislead.

Reason, Intuition, and Heuristics

Suppose you were offered a chance to win $10 by picking, without looking, a red marble from a bowl containing a mixture of red and white marbles. You can make your selection from either of two bowls: a small bowl with 1 red marble and 9 white marbles, or a large bowl with 9 red marbles and 91 white marbles. Which bowl would you choose?

If you're like most people, you might experience some conflict here. The rational thing to do is to select the small bowl because it offers better odds: 10 percent versus 9 percent (**Figure 4.4**). But there are 9 potential winning marbles in the large bowl and only 1 in the other. The greater number of winning marbles gives many people a gut feeling that they should select from the large bowl, regardless of the objective odds. Indeed, in one experiment, 61 percent of those who faced this decision chose the larger bowl, the one with the lower odds of winning (Denes-Raj & Epstein, 1994).

These results show that we're often "of two minds" about certain problems. Indeed, a great deal of research suggests that our responses to stimuli are guided by two systems of thought, analogous to intuition and reason (Epstein, 1991; Evans, 2007; Kahneman & Frederick, 2002; Sloman, 2002; Stanovich & West, 2002; Strack & Deutsch, 2004). The intuitive system operates quickly and automatically, is based on associations, and performs many of its operations simultaneously—*in parallel*. The rational system is slower and more controlled, is based on rules and deduction, and performs its operations one at a time—*serially*.

"I know too well the weakness and uncertainty of human reason to wonder at its different results."

—THOMAS JEFFERSON

Figure 4.4
Intuition and Reason

Even though a small bowl with just one red marble and a few whites provides a better chance of choosing a winning (red) marble, people often select the larger bowl, with more red marbles, and many more white marbles, knowing full well that they're giving themselves lower odds of winning, thereby letting intuition override reason.

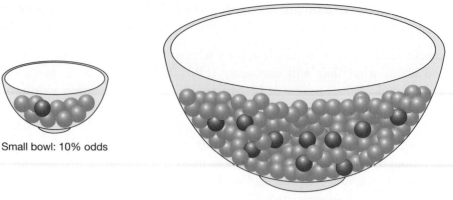

Small bowl: 10% odds

Large bowl: 9% odds

The rapid, parallel nature of the intuitive system means that it virtually always produces some output—an "answer" to the prevailing problem. That output is sometimes overridden by the output of the slower, more deliberate rational system. For instance, if you had to predict the outcome of the next coin flip after witnessing five heads in a row, your intuitive system would quickly tell you that six heads in a row is rare and that you should therefore bet on tails. But then your rational system might remind you of a critical feature of coin flips that you may have learned in a statistics or probability course: the outcomes of consecutive flips are independent, so you should ignore what happened on the earlier flips (**Figure 4.5**).

Note that several things can happen with the output of these two systems. (1) They can agree. For example, you might have a good feeling about one job candidate over another, and the former's qualifications might fit your rule to "always go with the person with more experience." (2) As in the coin-flip example, they can disagree, and the message from the rational system can override the message from the intuitive system. (3) Finally, the intuitive system can produce a response that "seems right" and can do so with such speed that the rational system is never engaged. In that case, you simply go with the flow—that is, with the quick output of the intuitive system.

The rest of the chapter focuses on this last pattern, drawing from Amos Tversky and Daniel Kahneman's work on the heuristics of judgment. This work has had a

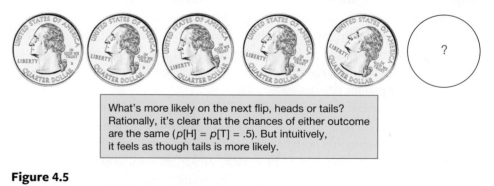

What's more likely on the next flip, heads or tails? Rationally, it's clear that the chances of either outcome are the same ($p[H] = p[T] = .5$). But intuitively, it feels as though tails is more likely.

Figure 4.5
Intuitive Processing and Mistaken Judgment
When watching a series of coin flips and seeing several heads in a row, nearly everyone has an intuitive feeling that the next flip is going to be a tail. With the right education, however, that intuitive impulse is suppressed in light of a rational realization that the outcomes of coin flips are independent of one another, and the chances of heads on the next flip are the same as they always are, 50–50.

great impact—not only in psychology, but also in economics, management, law, medicine, political science, and statistics (Gilovich, Griffin, & Kahneman, 2002; Kahneman, Slovic, & Tversky, 1982; Tversky & Kahneman, 1974). Tversky and Kahneman have argued that the intuitive system automatically performs certain mental operations—assessments of how easily something comes to mind, or of how similar two entities are—that powerfully influence judgment. They refer to these mental operations as **heuristics**: mental shortcuts that provide serviceable, if usually rather inexact, answers to common problems of judgment. They yield answers that feel right and therefore often are not overridden by more effortful, rational considerations.

Tversky and Kahneman have argued that although these heuristics generally serve us well, they sometimes distort our judgments. Our intuitive system generates an assessment relevant to the task at hand and suggests what may seem like a perfectly acceptable answer to the problem. But when this initial intuitive assessment is not modified or overridden by a more considered analysis, important considerations might be ignored, and our judgments systematically biased. Let's examine how such biases can arise in the context of two of the most important and extensively researched heuristics: the availability heuristic and the representativeness heuristic. We rely on the **availability heuristic** when we judge the frequency or probability of some event by how readily pertinent instances come to mind. We use the **representativeness heuristic** when we try to categorize something by judging how similar it is to our conception of the typical member of the category.

The Availability Heuristic

Which of these two American states has more tornadoes each year: Nebraska or Kansas? Even though they both average the same number, you, like most people, may have answered Kansas. If so, then you were guided by the availability heuristic. For most people, thinking about the frequency of tornadoes in Kansas immediately brings to mind the one in the classic film *The Wizard of Oz*.

We can't prevent ourselves from assessing the ease with which we can think of examples from Nebraska and Kansas, and once we've made such assessments, they seem to give us our answer. It is easier to think of a tornado in Kansas (even though it was fictional) than one in Nebraska, so we conclude that Kansas

heuristics Intuitive mental operations, performed quickly and automatically, that provide efficient answers to common problems of judgment.

availability heuristic The process whereby judgments of frequency or probability are based on how readily pertinent instances come to mind.

representativeness heuristic The process whereby judgments of likelihood are based on assessments of similarity between individuals and group prototypes, or between cause and effect.

The Availability Heuristic
People often judge the likelihood of an event by how readily pertinent examples come to mind. (A) While tornadoes occur with equal frequency in both Nebraska and Kansas, people tend to think they are more common in Kansas because of familiarity with (B) *The Wizard of Oz*, in which a tornado in Kansas whisks Dorothy and her dog Toto to the land of Oz.

(A) (B)

probably has more tornadoes. The implicit logic seems compelling: if examples can be quickly recalled, there must be many of them. Usually that's true. It's easier to think of male presidents of Fortune 500 companies than female presidents, successful Russian novelists than successful Norwegian novelists, and instances of German military aggression than Swiss military aggression precisely because there are more male presidents, more successful Russian novelists, and more instances of German military aggression. The availability heuristic, therefore, normally serves us well. The ease with which relevant examples can be brought to mind—how available they are—is indeed a reasonably accurate guide to overall frequency or probability.

The availability heuristic, however, is not an infallible guide. Certain events may simply be more memorable or retrievable than others, making availability a poor indicator of true number or probability. Nebraska has as many tornadoes as Kansas, but none is as memorable as the one in *The Wizard of Oz*. In an early demonstration of the availability heuristic, Kahneman and Tversky (1973a) asked people whether there are more words that begin with the letter *r* or more words that have *r* in the third position. A large majority thought more words begin with *r*, but in fact more words have *r* in the third position. Because words are stored in memory in some rough alphabetical fashion, words that begin with *r* (*rain, rowdy, redemption*) are easier to recall than those with *r* as the third letter (*nerd, harpoon, barrister*). The latter words, although more plentiful, are harder to access.

Distinguishing Ease of Retrieval from Amount Retrieved As just noted, the availability heuristic involves judging the frequency of an event, the size of a category, or the probability of an outcome by how *easily* relevant instances can be brought to mind (Schwarz & Vaughn, 2002). Note that it is not simply an assessment of the *number* of instances that are retrieved. But how do we know that? After all, not only do people have an easier time thinking of words that begin with *r*, but they also can think of many more of them. How do we know people arrive at their answers by consulting their experience of how *easy* it is to think of examples, rather than by simply comparing the *number* of examples they can generate? It's difficult to distinguish between these two explanations because they're so tightly intertwined. If it's easier to think of examples of one category, we will almost certainly think of more of them.

An ingenious experiment by Norbert Schwarz and his colleagues managed to untangle the two interpretations (Schwarz et al., 1991). In the guise of gathering material for a relaxation-training program, they asked students to review their lives for experiences relevant to assertiveness. The experiment involved four conditions. One group was asked to list 6 occasions when they had acted assertively, and another group was asked to list 12 such examples. A third group was asked to list 6 occasions when they had acted unassertively, and the final group was asked to list 12 such examples. The requirement to generate 6 or 12 examples of either behavior was carefully chosen; thinking of 6 examples would be easy for nearly everyone, but thinking of 12 would be extremely difficult.

Notice how this experimental setup disentangles the *ease* of generating examples and the *number* of examples generated. Those who have to think of 12 examples of either assertiveness or unassertiveness will think of more examples, but it will be hard to do so. What, then, has a greater effect on judgment? To find out, the investigators had the participants rate their own assertiveness. As Kahneman and Tversky would have predicted, the results indicated that it is the ease of

TABLE 4.2 THE AVAILABILITY HEURISTIC

Participants' average ratings of how assertive they are after thinking of 6 or 12 examples of their assertiveness or unassertiveness.

	TYPE OF BEHAVIOR	
NUMBER OF EXAMPLES	ASSERTIVE	UNASSERTIVE
6	6.3	5.2
12	5.2	6.2

SOURCE: Adapted from Schwarz et al., 1991.

generating examples that seems to guide people's judgments. Those who provided 6 examples of their assertiveness subsequently rated themselves as more assertive than those who provided 12 examples, even though the latter thought of more examples (**Table 4.2**). Similarly, those who provided 6 examples of their failure to be assertive subsequently rated themselves as less assertive than those who provided 12 examples. Indeed, the effect of ease of generation was so strong that those who thought of 12 examples of unassertiveness rated themselves as more assertive than those who thought of 12 examples of assertiveness! Apparently, the difficulty of coming up with 12 occasions when they acted unassertively convinced participants in the former group that they must be pretty assertive after all.

Biased Assessments of Risk One area where the availability heuristic can lead to trouble in everyday life harks back to the earlier discussion of negative information being overreported in the news. Such overreporting has the unfortunate effect of making many people more fearful than necessary. But not all hazards are equally overreported; some receive more news coverage than others. As a result, if people assess their risk by how easily they can bring to mind various hazards, they should be especially worried about those hazards they hear a lot about in the media, and not as worried about hazards that receive less attention, even if they are equally (or more) lethal (Slovic, Fischoff, & Lichtenstein, 1982).

For example, do more people die each year by homicide or suicide? As you have surely noticed, homicides receive much more media coverage, so most people think they are more common. In reality, suicides outnumber homicides in the United States by a ratio of 3 to 2. Are people more likely to die by accident or from disease? Statistics indicate that disease claims more than 16 times as many lives as accidents, but because accidents (being more dramatic) receive disproportionate media attention, most people erroneously consider them to be responsible for as many deaths as disease. Finally, do more people die each year in fires or drownings? Again, fires receive disproportionate media coverage, so most people think fires cause more fatalities than drownings, but in reality the reverse is true.

People typically overestimate the frequency of dramatic events that claim the lives of many people at once. Deaths due to plane crashes, earthquakes, and tornadoes are good examples. In contrast, people underestimate the commonness of silent individual deaths, such as those resulting from emphysema and stroke. People also underestimate the lethality of maladies they frequently encounter in nonfatal form—deaths from vaccinations, diabetes, and asthma. Because everyone knows healthy asthmatics and healthy diabetics, it's easy to

TABLE 4.3 BIASED ASSESSMENTS OF PERCEIVED CAUSES OF DEATH	
MOST OVERESTIMATED	MOST UNDERESTIMATED
All accidents	Smallpox vaccination
Motor vehicle accidents	Diabetes
Tornadoes	Lightning
Flood	Stroke
All cancers	Asthma
Fire	Emphysema
Homicide	Tuberculosis

SOURCE: Adapted from Slovic, Fischoff, & Lichtenstein, 1982.

lose sight of the number of lives that are lost to these afflictions. **Table 4.3** lists the most overestimated and underestimated hazards; death from accidents tends to be overestimated and death from disease underestimated.

Biased Estimates of Contributions to Joint Projects Another example of how the availability heuristic can distort everyday judgment involves the dynamics of joint projects. People sometimes work together on a project and then afterward decide who gets the bulk of the credit. Suppose you work with someone on a class project and turn in a single paper. Whose name is listed first? What if you and an acquaintance are hired to write a computer program for a lump-sum payment. How do you split the money?

With the availability heuristic in mind, social psychologist Michael Ross predicted that people would tend to overestimate their own contributions to such projects. After all, we devote a lot of energy and attention to our own contributions, so they should be more available than the contributions of everyone else. Ross and Sicoly (1979) conducted several studies that verified this prediction. In one study, they asked married couples to apportion responsibility for various tasks or outcomes in their daily life: how much each contributed to keeping the house clean, maintaining the social calendar, starting arguments, and so on. The respondents tended to give themselves more credit than their partners did. In most cases, when the estimates made by the two participants were summed, they exceeded the logically allowable maximum of 100 percent. (In our favorite example, a couple was asked to estimate their relative contributions to making breakfast. The wife said her share was 100 percent, on the reasonable grounds that she bought the food, prepared it, set the table, cleared the table, and washed the dishes. The husband estimated his contribution to be 25 percent—because he fed the cat!)

How do we know it's the availability heuristic rather than a motivational bias that gives rise to this phenomenon? In other words, maybe people overestimate

Overestimating the Frequency of Dramatic Deaths

People tend to overestimate the likelihood of dramatic causes of death that kill many people at once, such as plane crashes. Because these catastrophes receive a great deal of coverage in the media, they come to mind easily when considering the relative risk of different hazards.

their contributions simply because they want to see themselves, and have others see them, in the most favorable light. This would certainly be the logical conclusion if the effect held true only for positive items. But Ross and Sicoly found that the overestimation of a person's own contributions held for negative outcomes (such as starting arguments) as well as positive outcomes (such as taking care of the house), making it clear that availability plays a large role in this effect.

Availability's Close Cousin: Fluency Just as examples of some categories are easier to think of than others, some individual stimuli are easier to process than others. Psychologists use the term **fluency** to refer to the ease (or difficulty) associated with information processing. A clear image is easy to process, or fluent. An irregular word (like *imbroglio*) is hard to process, or disfluent.

Overestimating Contributions Because people's own contributions are much more salient than those of their coworkers, they tend to overestimate how much of a contribution they make to the group's overall output. Each of these workers is likely to think that they have done more to maintain this garden than their co-workers think they have.

The subjective experience of fluency, much like the subjective sense of availability, influences all sorts of judgments people are called on to make (Jacoby & Dallas, 1981; Oppenheimer, 2008). For example, we judge fluent names to be more famous, fluent objects to be more prototypical members of their categories, and common adages that rhyme to be more valid and truthful than those that don't (Jacoby, Woloshyn, & Kelley, 1989; McGlone & Tofighbakhsh, 2000; Whittlesea & Leboe, 2000). Fluency also influences the perceived difficulty of a task that's being described. When the font (typeface) of a recipe is hard to read, people assume the dish would be harder to cook (Song & Schwarz, 2008).

In addition to such direct effects on judgment, fluency appears to influence *how* people process relevant information. In many respects, the feeling of fluency (or disfluency) has the same effect as being in a good (or bad) mood (see Chapter 6). A feeling of disfluency while processing information leads people to take something of a "slow down, be careful" approach to making judgments and decisions. Researchers have examined this tendency using the Cognitive Reflection Test (Frederick, 2005). In one study, the test was printed in either a normal, highly readable font or a degraded, hard-to-read font (**Figure 4.6**). Performing well on the Cognitive Reflection Test requires stifling an immediate gut feeling to get the correct answer to each question. For example: "A bat and ball cost $1.10 in total. The bat costs $1 more than the ball. How much does the ball cost?" You need to think beyond the immediate response of 10 cents to arrive at the correct response of 5 cents ($0.05 + $1.05 = $1.10). Participants gave more correct answers when the questions were presented in a degraded, and hence disfluent, font (Alter, Oppenheimer, Epley, & Eyre, 2007). The difficulty of merely reading the question caused them to slow down, giving their more analytical, reflective cognitive processes a chance to catch up with their immediate intuitive response.

The Representativeness Heuristic

We all sometimes find ourselves wondering whether someone is a member of a particular category. Is he gay? Is she a Republican? In making such assessments,

fluency The feeling of ease (or difficulty) associated with processing information.

FIGURE 4.6 **You Be the Subject: Cognitive Reflection Test**

Some participants answered the following questions, presented in an easily readable font. Try it. What are the answers?

1. In a lake, there is a patch of lily pads. Every day, the patch doubles in size. If it takes 48 days for the patch to cover the entire lake, how long would it take for the patch to cover half the lake?_____ days

2. If it takes 5 machines 5 minutes to make 5 widgets, how long would it take 100 machines to make 100 widgets?_____ minutes

Other participants were given the same questions in a font that was hard to read. Try them again.

1. IN A LAKE, THERE IS A PATCH OF LILY PADS. EVERY DAY, THE PATCH DOUBLES IN SIZE. IF IT TAKES 48 DAYS FOR THE PATCH TO COVER THE ENTIRE LAKE, HOW LONG WOULD IT TAKE FOR THE PATCH TO COVER HALF THE LAKE? _____DAYS

2. IF IT TAKES 5 MACHINES 5 MINUTES TO MAKE 5 WIDGETS, HOW LONG WOULD IT TAKE 100 MACHINES TO MAKE 100 WIDGETS? _____ MINUTES

Conclusion: The effort required to read the degraded, disfluent font can carry over to solving the problems, putting people into a more reflective mindset. They are therefore more likely to see that it would take 47 days for the lily pads to cover half the lake, and 5 minutes for 100 machines to make 100 widgets.

SOURCE: Adapted from Alter et al., 2007.

we automatically assess the extent to which the person in question *seems* gay or Republican. In so doing, we rely on what Kahneman and Tversky (1972) have dubbed the representativeness heuristic. Instead of focusing on the true question of interest—"Is it likely that this person is a Republican?"—we ask, "Does this person seem like a Republican?" or "Is this person similar to my prototype of a Republican?" The use of the representativeness heuristic thus reflects an implicit assumption that *like goes with like*. A member of a given category ought to resemble the category prototype; an effect ought to resemble its cause.

The representativeness heuristic is generally useful in making accurate judgments about people and events. Members of certain groups often resemble the group prototype (the prototype must come from somewhere), and effects often

The Representativeness Heuristic

Images like this (A) can give people a specific sense of what a representative Republican is like. But many Republicans aren't at all like the stereotype, so we can be surprised when we learn that a person who doesn't fit the stereotype (B) is a Republican.

resemble their causes. The degree of resemblance between person and group, or between cause and effect, can thus be a helpful guide to group membership and causal status. The strategy is effective to the extent that the prototype has some validity and the members of the category cluster around the prototype.

But even when the prototype is valid, the representativeness heuristic can create difficulties if we rely on it exclusively. The problem is that a strong sense of resemblance can blind us to other potentially useful sources of information. One source of useful information, known as **base-rate information**, concerns knowledge about relative frequency. How many members of the category in question are there relative to the members of all other categories? The individual in question is more likely to be a Republican if the local population includes a lot of Republicans. But a strong sense of representativeness sometimes leads us to ignore base-rate likelihood, which could (and should) be put to good use.

The Resemblance between Members and Categories: Base-Rate Neglect

Many studies have documented this tendency to ignore or underutilize base-rate information when assessing whether someone belongs to a particular category (Ajzen, 1977; Bar-Hillel, 1980; Ginosar & Trope, 1980; Tversky & Kahneman, 1982). In one of the earliest studies, Kahneman and Tversky (1973b) asked participants to consider the following description of Tom W., supposedly written during Tom's senior year in high school by a psychologist who based his assessment on Tom's responses on personality tests. The participants were also told that Tom is now in graduate school.

> Tom W. is of high intelligence, although lacking in true creativity. He has a need for order and clarity and for neat and tidy systems in which every detail finds its appropriate place. His writing is rather dull and mechanical, occasionally enlivened by somewhat corny puns and by flashes of imagination of the sci-fi type. He has a strong drive for competence. He seems to have little feel and little sympathy for other people and does not enjoy interacting with others. Self-centered, he nonetheless has a deep moral sense.
>
> (*Kahneman & Tversky, 1973b, p. 238*)

One group of participants ranked nine academic disciplines (including computer science, law, and social work) in terms of the likelihood that Tom chose them as his field of specialization. A second group ranked the nine disciplines in terms of how similar they thought Tom was to the typical student in each discipline. A final group did not see the description of Tom; they merely estimated the percentage of all graduate students in the United States who were enrolled in each of the nine disciplines.

How should the participants assess the likelihood that Tom would choose each discipline for graduate study? They should certainly assess how similar Tom is to the type of person who pursues each field of study—that is, they should consider how representative Tom is of the people in each discipline. But representativeness is not a perfect guide. Some of the least lawyerly people study law, and some of the least people-oriented individuals pursue social work. Therefore, any additional useful information should also be considered, such as the proportion of all graduate students in each field (or base-rate information). Clearly, Tom is more likely to be in a discipline that has 1,000 students on campus than one that has 10. A savvy judgment, then, would somehow combine representativeness with an assessment of the popularity of each field.

Table 4.4 lists the rankings of the nine disciplines by each of the three groups of participants, those assessing likelihood, similarity, and base rate. Notice that the

TABLE 4.4 THE REPRESENTATIVENESS HEURISTIC

Participants ranked nine academic disciplines in terms of the likelihood that Tom W. chose that particular field, the perceived similarity between Tom W. and the typical student in that field, or the number of graduate students enrolled in that field.

DISCIPLINE	LIKELIHOOD	SIMILARITY	BASE RATE
Business administration	3	3	3
Computer science	1	1	8
Engineering	2	2	5
Humanities and education	8	8	1
Law	6	6	6
Library science	5	4	9
Medicine	7	7	7
Physical and life sciences	4	5	4
Social science and social work	9	9	2

SOURCE: Adapted from Kahneman & Tversky, 1973b.

rankings of the *likelihood* that Tom chose to study each of the disciplines are virtually identical to the rankings of Tom's *similarity* to the students in each discipline. In other words, the participants' responses were based entirely on how much the description of Tom resembled the typical student in each field. By basing their responses exclusively on representativeness, the participants failed to consider the other useful source of information: base-rate frequency. As you can also see from Table 4.4, the likelihood rankings did not correspond at all to what the participants knew about the overall popularity of each of the fields. Useful information was ignored.

It's important to note, however, that although base-rate neglect is often observed, it is not inevitable (Bar-Hillel & Fischhoff, 1981). Certain circumstances encourage the use of base-rate information, and two stand out as having the greatest impact. The first is whether the base-rate information has some causal significance to the task at hand (Ajzen, 1977; Tversky & Kahneman, 1982). For example, if you were given a description of an individual's academic strengths and weaknesses and were asked to predict whether the person passed an exam, you would not be indifferent to the fact that 70 percent of the students who took the exam failed (that the base rate of failure was 70 percent). Note that the base rate has causal significance in this case: the fact that 70 percent of the students failed means the exam was difficult, and the difficulty of the exam is part of what *causes* a person to fail. People use the base rate in such contexts because its relevance is obvious. When the base rate is not causally relevant, as in the Tom W. experiment, its relevance is less obvious. If twice as many people major in business as in the physical sciences, it would be *more likely* that Tom W. is a business major, but it would not *cause* him to be a business major. The relevance of the base rate is thus less apparent.

A second way to improve people's use of base-rate information is to change their fundamental approach to the problem. People typically try to assess whether someone belongs to a particular category by taking an "inside" view of the task and focusing on details of the case at hand. Who is this person, and what "type" does he or she resemble? But it is possible to take an "outside" view of the problem. Suppose you want to predict the undergraduate majors of a large number

Not So Fast:
Critical Thinking about Representativeness and the Regression Effect

To cut back on illegal driving practices (such as speeding, running red lights, and driving in bus lanes), local authorities have been installing more and more safety cameras at especially hazardous locations. Some people feel it's just a way for municipalities to increase revenue from the fines they charge for violations. But others passionately maintain that they have increased road safety. One group estimated that safety cameras in the United Kingdom save over 100 lives a year and result in over 4,000 fewer collisions (PA Consulting Group, 2005).

Alas, the purported safety benefit is substantially overstated. It fails to take into account a statistical regularity that plagues sound judgment in all walks of life: the regression effect. The **regression effect** is the statistical tendency, when any two variables are imperfectly correlated, for extreme values on one of them to be associated with less extreme values on the other. Tall parents tend to have tall kids, but not as tall as the parents themselves. Extremely attractive people tend to marry attractive partners, but not as attractive as they are themselves. Students with the worst scores on the midterm tend to do badly on the final, but not as badly as they did initially.

What does this have to do with traffic safety? Cameras are installed where they are most needed—in locations with a poor recent collision history. Given that the number of accidents at one time are imperfectly correlated with the number of accidents afterward, locations where there were an unusually large number of accidents are likely to have fewer accidents afterward, regardless of the presence of safety cameras. When the regression effect is taken into account, the best estimate is that safety cameras in the UK save 24 lives a year, not over 100. They work, in other words, but not as well as they *seem* to work.

People often fail to see the regression effect for what it is, and instead conclude that they've encountered some important phenomenon (like an exaggerated effect of safety cameras). Psychologists refer to this as the **regression fallacy**. If you're a sports fan, for example, you've probably heard of the *Sports Illustrated* jinx. The idea is that appearing on the cover of *Sports Illustrated* is bad luck—it's often followed by an unfortunate outcome, such as an injury, the end of a winning streak, or a loss in a key game or match. Of course it is! People appear on the cover of *Sports Illustrated* precisely when they're at their peak and so, on average, they will tend not to do as well in the near future. It's pure statistical regression, not a jinx.

The lesson for research should be clear. We're often most interested in helping people who are most in need, such as those who have been depressed for a long time and finally seek treatment, individuals whose arthritis has become unbearable, or students sent to the counselor's office for classroom disruption. Because these people are at such a low point, on average, they are likely to experience improvement, whether or not their problems are addressed. That can make it tricky to assess the effectiveness of any treatment they receive. Among other things, the regression effect reinforces the importance of conducting research with a suitable control group: it allows researchers to determine whether the improvement seen in the treatment group is greater than that in the control group (which, if chosen correctly, should also benefit from the regression effect).

Why do people so often overlook the regression effect and commit the regression fallacy? One explanation is that regression runs counter to the representativeness heuristic. The most representative outcome for an athlete pictured on the cover of *Sports Illustrated* is success, not failure; the most representative outcome for someone who is extremely depressed is further sadness, not an uptick in mood. Because the mind makes predictions based on representativeness, we often find results that regress toward the mean surprising, and we invent explanations having nothing to do with regression to make sense of the surprise.

---

of students, not just Tom W. The details about each student might now seem less important, and the significance of other, purely "statistical" considerations, such as base-rate frequency, might become more apparent. In the extreme case, if everyone in a sample of 20 resembled a pre-law student, most people would nevertheless hesitate to guess that all were pre-law students. Indeed, circumstances that encourage an outside perspective have been shown to reduce base-rate neglect and other biases of human judgment (Gigerenzer, 1991; Griffin & Tversky, 1992; Kahneman & Lovallo, 1993; Kahneman & Tversky, 1982b, 1995).

regression effect The statistical tendency, when two variables are imperfectly correlated, for extreme values on one of them to be associated with less extreme values on the other.

regression fallacy The failure to recognize the influence of the regression effect and to offer a causal theory for what is really a simple statistical regularity.

"The plan is nothing. Planning is everything."

—GENERAL
DWIGHT D. EISENHOWER

The Planning Fallacy

People typically estimate that projects will be completed sooner than they actually are, even when they're aware of past efforts that took much longer than originally planned. (A) It took 10 years longer than estimated to complete construction of the Sydney Opera House. (B) Conceived in 1995, the F-35 Joint Strike Fighter plane was estimated to cost $89 million per plane when the production contract was signed and is now estimated to be $207.6 million per plane. Although the F-35 is being flown by test pilots, it is not yet operational.

The Planning Fallacy A common pitfall that results from adopting an inside view is the tendency to be unrealistic about how long it takes to complete a project. This tendency, known as the **planning fallacy**, is something of a paradox because people's overly optimistic views about their ability to finish a current project exist side by side with their knowledge that the amount of time needed in the past has typically exceeded their original estimate. Students, for example, often confidently assert that they will have all assignments done well in advance of an exam, so they can calmly and thoroughly review the material beforehand. However, it is distressingly common for this anticipated calm review to give way to feverish cramming. Students aren't the only victims of the planning fallacy. Even your textbook authors, who know about the planning fallacy, have fallen prey to it when estimating how long it would take to write an article. And don't even ask how long they thought it would take to finish this book.

The error is illustrated more dramatically by setbacks in large-scale building projects. When the people of Sydney, Australia, decided in 1957 to build their iconic opera house, the original estimates were that it would be completed by 1963 and cost $7 million. It opened in 1973 at a cost of $102 million. Similarly, when Montreal was named host of the 1976 Summer Olympics, the mayor announced that the entire Olympiad would cost $120 million, and that many events would take place in a stadium with a first-of-its-kind retractable roof. The Olympics, of course, went on as planned in 1976, but the stadium did not get its roof until 1989. Moreover, the final cost of the stadium was $120 million, the amount budgeted for the entire Olympics!

To shed light on the planning fallacy, Roger Buehler, Dale Griffin, and Michael Ross (1994) conducted a number of studies of people's estimates of completion times. In one study, they asked students in an honors program to predict as accurately as possible when they would turn in their theses. They also estimated what the completion date would be "if everything went as poorly as it possibly could." Fewer than a third of the students finished by the time they had estimated. More remarkably, fewer than half finished by the time they had estimated for the worst-case scenario.

Follow-up experiments laid the blame for people's optimistic forecasts on the tendency to approach the task from an exclusively inside perspective. One study had participants verbalize their thoughts as they were trying to estimate how

BOX 4.3 **FOCUS ON *CULTURE***

Predictions East and West

The philosopher Ludwig Wittgenstein had this to say about the direction of the future:

> When we think about the future of the world, we always have in mind its being where it would be if it continued to move as we see it moving now. We do not realize that it moves not in a straight line . . . and that its direction changes constantly.

As it turns out, Wittgenstein was a little too ready to say "we." Whereas Westerners are indeed inclined to predict that the world will move in whatever direction it now moves, East Asians are likely to expect the world to reverse direction. Ji, Nisbett, and Su (2001) point to a tradition in the East, dating back thousands of years, that emphasizes change. The *Tao* (the Way) envisions the world as existing in one of two states at any given time—*yin* and *yang* (light and dark, weak and strong, and so on)—that alternate with one another. The fact that the world is in one state is a strong indication that it is

about to be in the other state. The black dot inside the white swirl and the white dot inside the black swirl of the Tao symbol are reminders that the seed of the future is to be found in the present.

Ji and her colleagues reasoned that the tradition of the *Tao* would cause East Asians to judge events as being likely to reverse course rather than continue moving in their current direction. They tested this hypothesis in several ways. In one study, they asked participants to read brief stories and predict how they would turn out. For example, participants read about a poor young man and were asked how likely it was that he would become rich. The Americans thought it was not very likely; the Chinese thought it was more likely.

In another study, the researchers showed participants various time trends they were unlikely to know anything about, such as the world economic growth rate and the world cancer death rate. These trends were shown as either decidedly increasing or decidedly decreasing. American respondents were overwhelmingly likely to predict that the trends would

The Tao Symbol

continue in the same direction they were going. Chinese respondents were much more likely than Americans to predict that the trends would reverse course—to move down if they had been going up, and to move up if they had been going down. And who do you think bets that the stock market will go up when it's in a bullish mood and down when it's in a bearish mood? You guessed it: the Americans bet the current direction; the Chinese bet the opposite (Ji, Zhang, & Guo, 2008).

long a task would take (Buehler et al., 1994). Nearly all their thoughts were about various plans and scenarios for finishing the project. Only a precious few dealt with the participants' track record on previous tasks. Thus, the inside perspective (What steps are required to complete *this* project?) crowds out the potentially informative outside perspective (How often do I get such things done on time?) People have personal histories that would be helpful in accurately estimating completion times; they just don't use them. When Buehler and his colleagues asked people how often they completed tasks by the time they initially expected, the average response was only a third of the time.

The Resemblance between Cause and Effect The representativeness heuristic also affects people's assessments of cause and effect (Downing, Sternberg, & Ross, 1985; Gilovich & Savitsky, 2002). In particular, people are predisposed to look for and accept causal relationships in which like goes with like. Big effects are thought to have big causes, small effects to have small causes, complicated effects to have complicated causes, and so on. This assumption is often valid. Being hit with a small mallet typically produces a smaller bruise than being hit with a large mallet. Resolving the complicated mess in the Middle East will probably require complex, sustained negotiation, not some simple suggestion that has yet to be made. But sometimes small causes create big effects, and vice versa: tiny viruses give rise to devastating diseases like ebola and AIDS; splitting the nucleus of the atom releases an awesome amount of energy.

Health and medicine are areas in which the impact of representativeness on causal judgments is particularly striking. Many people think you should avoid milk (or other dairy products) if you have a cold, and potato chips if you have acne. Why? Because milk seems representative of phlegm, and the greasiness of potato chips seems representative of the oily skin that often accompanies acne. For centuries, Western physicians believed that yellow vegetables were good for people with jaundice (which turns the skin yellow). To be sure, people are affected by what they eat—they gain weight by eating lots of fat, and develop an orange tint to the skin by consuming too much carotene.

Sometimes, however, we take this belief that "you are what you eat" to magical extremes. In one experiment, college students were asked to make inferences about the attributes of members of (hypothetical) tribes (Nemeroff & Rozin, 1989). One group read about a tribe that ate wild boar and hunted sea turtles for their shells, a second group about a tribe that ate sea turtles and hunted wild boar for their tusks. The students' responses indicated that they assumed the characteristics of the food would "rub off" on the tribe members. Members of the turtle-eating tribe were considered better swimmers and more generous; those who ate wild boar were thought to be more aggressive and more likely to have beards.

Another area where representativeness affects causal judgments is the realm of pseudoscientific belief systems. Consider, for example, the case of astrological signs and representative personality traits. A central tenet of astrology is that an individual's personality is influenced by the astrological sign under which the person was born. The personalities associated with 9 out of the 12 astrological signs are listed in **Table 4.5**. Notice the resemblance between the features we associate with each sign's namesake and those that supposedly characterize individuals born under that sign.

The personality profiles that supposedly accompany various astrological signs have been shown time and again to have absolutely no validity (Abell, 1981; Schick & Vaughn, 1995; Zusne & Jones, 1982). Why, then, is astrology so popular? Part of the reason is that astrology takes advantage of people's use of the representativeness heuristic. Each of the personality profiles has some superficial appeal because each draws on the intuition that like goes with like. Who is more inclined to be vacillating than a Gemini (a Twin)? Who is more likely to be fair and well balanced than a Libra (the Scales)?

The Joint Operation of Availability and Representativeness

The availability and representativeness heuristics sometimes operate in tandem. For example, a judgment that two things belong together—that one is representative of the other—can make an instance in which they do occur together particularly available. The joint effect of these two heuristics can thus create an **illusory correlation** between two variables, or the belief that they are correlated

illusory correlation The belief that two variables are correlated when in fact they are not.

TABLE 4.5 REPRESENTATIVENESS AND ASTROLOGICAL SIGNS

Purported personality characteristics of people born under particular astrological signs. Notice the resemblance between the characteristics of each sign and the personalities thought to characterize people with that sign.

	ASTROLOGICAL SIGN	PERSONALITY CHARACTERISTICS
	Aries (the Ram)	Quick-tempered; headstrong
	Taurus (the Bull)	Plodding; prone to rage
	Gemini (the Twins)	Vacillating; split personality
	Cancer (the Crab)	Attached to their homes
	Leo (the Lion)	Proud; leader
	Virgo (the Virgin)	Modest; retiring
	Libra (the Scales)	Well balanced; fair
	Scorpio (the Scorpion)	Sharp; secretive
	Capricorn (the Goat)	Hardworking; down to earth

SOURCE: Adapted from Huntley, 1990; Read et al., 1978.

when in fact they are not. A judgment of representativeness leads us to expect an association between the two entities, and this expectation in turn makes instances in which they are paired unusually memorable.

A classic set of experiments by Loren and Jean Chapman (1967) highlights how readily people form illusory correlations, and how consequential they can be. The Chapmans were struck by a paradox observed in the practice of clinical psychology. Clinicians often claim that they find projective personality tests helpful in making clinical diagnoses, but systematic research has shown most of these tests to be completely lacking in validity. (Projective tests require people respond to unstructured and ambiguous stimuli, such as the famous Rorschach inkblots, thus "projecting" their personalities onto what they see.) Why would intelligent, conscientious, and well-trained clinicians believe that such tests can diagnose mental or emotional problems when they cannot? Why, in other words, do some clinicians perceive an illusory correlation between their clients' conditions and their responses on such tests?

To find out, the Chapmans first asked numerous clinicians about which of their clients' specific test responses tended to indicate the presence of which specific pathological conditions. Much of their work focused on the Draw-a-Person Test, in which the client draws a picture of a person, and the therapist interprets the picture for signs of various psychopathologies. The clinicians reported that they observed many connections between particular drawings and specific conditions—drawings and pathologies that seem, intuitively, to belong together. People suffering from paranoia, for example, were thought to be inclined to draw unusually large or small eyes. People excessively insecure about their intelligence were thought to be likely to draw a large (or small) head.

"For what it's worth, next week all your stars and planets will be in good aspect for you to launch an invasion of England."

To investigate these illusory correlations further, the Chapmans gathered a sample of 45 Draw-a-Person pictures: 35 drawn by psychotic patients in a nearby hospital and 10 drawn by graduate students in clinical psychology. They then attached a phony statement to each picture that supposedly described the condition of the person who drew it. Some came with the description "is suspicious of other people," others with the description "has had problems of sexual impotence," and so on. The researchers were careful to avoid any correlation between the nature of a drawing and the condition attached to each one. For example, "is suspicious of other people" appeared just as often on pictures with average eyes as on pictures with large or small eyes.

These pictures (with accompanying pathologies) were then shown to college students who had never heard of the Draw-a-Person Test. Although the study was carefully designed so there was no connection between the pictures and specific conditions, the students nonetheless "saw" the same relationships reported earlier by the clinical psychologists. To the students, too, it seemed that prominent eyes were likely to have been drawn by individuals who were suspicious of others. This finding suggests, of course, that the clinical psychologists were not detecting any real correlations between pathological conditions and responses on the Draw-a-Person Test. Instead, they were "detecting" the same nonexistent associations that the undergraduate students were seeing—illusory correlations produced by the joint operation of availability and representativeness. Certain pictures are representative of specific pathologies (for example, prominent eyes and paranoia), and therefore instances in which the two are observed together (a paranoid individual drawing a person with large eyes) are particularly noteworthy and memorable.

In a final study, the Chapmans asked another group of students to indicate the extent to which various conditions (suspiciousness, impotence, dependence) "called to mind" different parts of the body (eyes, sexual organs, mouth). Tellingly, their responses matched the correlations reported by the earlier groups of clinicians and students. In addition to highlighting the joint influence of availability and representativeness, these findings exemplify a much broader point about human judgment: when associations or propositions seem plausible, people often believe them, regardless of what the evidence shows to be the case.

⬆ LOOKING BACK

Two mental systems guide our judgments and decisions: one akin to intuition and the other akin to reason. The intuitive system operates quickly and automatically, while the rational system tends to be more deliberate and controlled. These systems can lead to the same judgments, they can lead to opposite judgments, or the intuitive system may produce a satisfying judgment so quickly that the rational system is never engaged. The quick assessments made by the intuitive system are often based on heuristics, which can sometimes bias judgment. The availability heuristic may lead to biased assessments of risk and biased estimates of people's contributions to joint projects. The representativeness heuristic may result in base-rate neglect and mistaken assessments of cause and effect. When these two heuristics operate together, they can lead to an illusory correlation between two variables.

Chapter Review

SUMMARY

Studying Social Cognition

- By studying errors of judgment, psychologists can understand how people make judgments and learn what can be done to avoid mistakes.

The Information Available for Social Cognition

- Sometimes people make judgments on the basis of very little information, such as making personality judgments based on physical appearance.
- Mistaken inferences can arise from *pluralistic ignorance*, which tends to occur when people are reluctant to express their misgivings about a perceived group norm; their reluctance in turn reinforces the false norm.
- People's judgments can seem to them more accurate than they really are because of the *self-fulfilling prophecy*. More specifically, people can draw mistaken inferences about others that seem valid because they act in ways that elicit the very behavior they were expecting—behavior that wouldn't have happened otherwise.
- Information received secondhand often does not provide a full account of what happened, instead stressing certain elements at the expense of others.
- Negative information is more likely to be reported than positive information, which can lead people to believe they are more at risk of various calamities than they actually are.

How Information Is Presented

- The way information is presented, such as the order of presentation, can affect judgment. A *primacy effect* arises when the information presented first is more influential, because it affects the interpretation of subsequent information. A *recency effect* arises when information presented last is more influential, often because it is more available in memory.
- Order effects are a type of *framing effect*. Other framing effects involve varying of the language or structure of the information presented to create a desired effect.
- The temporal framing of an event can also influence how it is interpreted. Far-off events are construed in more abstract terms, and imminent events are construed more concretely.

How We Seek Information

- People tend to examine whether certain propositions are true by searching for information consistent with the proposition in question. This *confirmation bias* can lead people to believe things that aren't true because evidence can generally be found to support even the most questionable propositions.
- People are sometimes motivated to find evidence supporting a preexisting conclusion and so they do so disproportionately, coming to the conclusion that their preferred conclusion is more valid than it really is.

Top-Down Processing: Using Schemas to Understand New Information

- Schemas influence the interpretation of information. They are important *top-down* tools for understanding the world, as opposed to the *bottom-up* processing of information from the world.
- Schemas guide attention, memory, and the construal of information, and they can directly prompt behavior.
- Being exposed to certain stimuli (such as a plastic shovel) often has the effect of *priming* the concepts with which they're associated (the beach), making them momentarily more accessible.
- In general, the more recently and the more frequently a schema has been activated, the more likely it is to be applied to new information. Conscious awareness of a schema is not required in order to be influenced by it.

Reason, Intuition, and Heuristics

- People have two systems for processing information: an intuitive system and a rational system. Intuitive responses are based on rapid, associative processes, whereas rational responses are based on slower, rule-based reasoning.

- Intuitive *heuristics*, or mental shortcuts, provide people with sound judgments most of the time, but they sometimes lead to errors in judgment.
- People use the *availability heuristic* when judging the frequency or probability of some event by how readily relevant instances come to mind. It can cause people to overestimate their own contributions to group projects, and it can lead to faulty assessment of the risks posed by memorable hazards.
- The sense of *fluency* people experience when processing information can influence the judgments they make about it. Disfluent stimuli lead to more reflective thought.
- People use the *representativeness heuristic* when trying to categorize something by judging how similar it is to their conception of the typical member of a category, or when trying to make causal attributions by assessing how similar an effect is to a possible cause. Sometimes this leads people to overlook highly relevant considerations such as *base-rate information*, or how many members of the category there are in a population.
- The inside perspective on judgment leads to errors such as the *planning fallacy*, which can be avoided by taking an outside perspective and attending to a past record of finishing similar tasks in a given time frame.
- Operating together, availability and representativeness can produce potent *illusory correlations*, which result from thinking that two variables are correlated, both because they resemble each other and because the simultaneous occurrence of two similar events stands out more than that of two dissimilar events.

THINK ABOUT IT

1. How valid are snap judgments? Do brief exposures to a person's physical appearance or "thin slices" of their behavior provide meaningful information about what they are really like?

2. What role might pluralistic ignorance play in the problem of binge drinking on college campuses? What could school administrators do to reduce pluralistic ignorance in this context?

3. How does the desire to entertain tend to bias the kinds of stories that are reported most frequently in the media? What effects might this bias have on people's beliefs about the world?

4. If you were developing an advertising campaign for a fitness class, what kinds of framing strategies might you use to increase the chances of people signing up for the class? In particular, consider spin framing, positive and negative framing, and temporal framing.

5. Suppose you're about to go on a blind date when a mutual friend warns you that your date can be a little cold and unfriendly. According to research on the confirmation bias, how might this information influence the impression you ultimately form about your date?

6. Research on priming suggests that it is possible for a stimulus to activate a schema even if a person is not consciously aware of the stimulus. Can you think of ways that you might be able to use priming to influence others' behavior?

7. Imagine you're working on a group project with three other students and you are all asked to indicate your individual contribution to the project, relative to the other group members' contributions, in the form of a percentage. If you were to sum the individual percentages reported by each group member, would you expect it to add up to roughly 100%? Why or why not?

THE ANSWER GUIDELINES FOR THE THINK ABOUT IT QUESTIONS
CAN BE FOUND AT THE BACK OF THE BOOK . . .

Social Attribution: Explaining Behavior

Bill Gates is the richest person in the world. Having dropped out of Harvard at the ripe old age of 19, he started a company called Microsoft (you might have heard the name). Why was he able to invent tremendously creative and powerful software at such a young age and build such a hugely successful company? Most people would say he must be one of the smartest people who ever lived. But Bill Gates would not likely be one of the people who would say that.

Instead, as science writer Malcolm Gladwell informs us in his book *Outliers,* Gates would tell you that in 1968, when he was in eighth grade, he was bored with his Seattle public school (Gladwell, 2008). His parents were well-off enough to enroll him in a private school called Lakeside, which just happened to have a time-sharing computer terminal that linked the school's computer club (at a time when few colleges, let alone high schools, had computer clubs) to a mainframe computer in downtown Seattle. Back then, most computers still required a clumsy punch-card system for data entry; but Lakeside's terminal, like those today, used a more efficient keyboard system. Gates became one of a tiny handful of teenagers in the world who were able to do real-time programming in 1968.

His luck kept on running for the next 6 years. Lakeside was rich but soon ran out of money to pay for expensive mainframe time. By coincidence, Monique Rona, one of the founders of a company called Computer Center Corporation (CCC), had a son at Lakeside. Her company offered to let the Lakeside Computer Club have free programming time in exchange for testing the company's software. CCC went bankrupt shortly thereafter, but by then Gates and his friends managed to persuade a local firm, Information Sciences, Inc. (ISI), to let them have free

Bill Gates

(A) A fledgling entrepreneur. (B) After he became primarily a philanthropist.

computer time as payment for helping the firm develop a payroll program. Gates by this time was spending 20–30 hours a week programming.

Gates also established a connection with the University of Washington, which happened to have one computer that was free for the little-used period from 3 a.m. to 6 a.m. Living close to the university, he could sneak out of bed at night and walk to the computer center. (Years later, Gates explained to his mother why she had found it so difficult to wake him up in the mornings.)

The next fortuitous event was that one day ISI needed programmers who were familiar with a particular type of software to handle a new job setting up a computer system for a power station in Bonneville, Washington. Being familiar with the software, Gates and his pals went to work at Bonneville under the supervision of a brilliant master of programming. (Gates's high school allowed him to skip the spring term of his senior year to do the work.) By the time he got to Harvard, he had spent many thousands of hours programming—almost certainly more than any freshman there, and probably more than any freshman anywhere. Bill Gates was a brilliant guy, but he couldn't have started Microsoft at 19 if he hadn't had such unusually fortunate experience with programming beginning when he was 13.

This kind of difference between the explanations—or "causal attributions"—of the observer (that's you) and the actor (Bill Gates) is commonplace. The observer is inclined to attribute actions, especially highly distinctive ones, to properties of the actor, such as personality traits and abilities. The actor is more inclined to attribute the same action to situational factors. In this chapter, you'll read about a particularly important element of construal, namely the process of causal attribution for events—how people understand why others, as well as they themselves, behave the way they do.

People make causal attributions because they need to draw inferences about others (and themselves) in order to make predictions about future behavior. Was Robert kind to his new employer because he's a caring person or because he was just currying favor? Did the congresswoman visit the new senior citizens' center because she has a real interest in older adults, or was she just trying to win votes?

This chapter examines how people explain the behavior they witness (or hear about) in others, and the effect of their explanations on the judgments they make about them. We'll also explore how people understand the causes of their own behavior, as well as the way this understanding influences both their immediate emotional experience and their subsequent behavior. These are the concerns of **attribution theory**, the study of how people understand the causes of events.

attribution theory A set of concepts explaining how people assign causes to the events around them and the effects of people's causal assessments.

causal attribution Linking an event to a cause, such as inferring that a personality trait is responsible for a behavior.

From Acts to Dispositions: Inferring the Causes of Behavior

In class one day, you listen as a student gives a long-winded answer to a question your professor asks. When the student is finally finished, your professor says, "Good point," and then proceeds to expand on the topic. You can't help wondering, "Did the professor really think it was a good point, or was she just trying to encourage student participation? Or was she trying to boost her standing on ratemyprofessors.com?" The way you answer these questions—the way you construe the meaning of the professor's behavior—explains her particular action. It also helps make sense of many of her other actions in the course, such as whether she calls on this student often, or whether she consistently praises students' opinions in general. And your attributions may affect your own behavior toward your professor in the future.

Causal attribution is the construal process people use to explain both their own and others' behavior. Understanding causal attributions is crucial to understanding everyday social behavior because we all make causal attributions many times a day, and the attributions we make can greatly affect our thoughts, feelings, and future behavior.

The Pervasiveness and Importance of Causal Attribution

When you ask someone out for a date but are rebuffed ("No thanks, I have a cold"), you don't simply take the response at face value. You wonder whether the person really has a cold or is just giving you the brush-off. Similarly, when you

Causal Attribution
Causal attribution is central to much of social life, ranging from off-the-cuff speculation to formal decision-making situations, such as a trial. Often, the core question the jury must answer is what caused a given event or series of events.

get an exam back, you're not simply happy or sad about the grade you received. You make an attribution. If the grade is a good one, you might decide this is just another example of how smart and hardworking you are, or you might attribute the grade to luck or easy grading. If the grade is a bad one, you might decide you're not so good at this subject, or you might conclude that the test was unfair.

Attributions are a constant part of mental life. You may ask yourself such questions as: "Why was my interview so short? Did the interviewers conclude that I obviously have what it takes, or were they just not interested?" "Why does everything work out so well for my roommate, while I have to struggle to get by?"

Concluding that someone won't go out with you because she's sick leads to an entirely different set of emotional reactions than concluding that she finds you unappealing. And attributing a bad grade on an exam to a lack of ability leads to unhappiness and withdrawal, whereas attributing failure to a lack of effort often leads to more vigorous attempts to study harder and more effectively in the future. Indeed, systematic research on causal attribution has shown that people's explanations have tremendous consequences in a number of areas, including health and education.

Explanatory Style and Attribution

A group of investigators led by Chris Peterson and Martin Seligman has examined the impact of attributions on academic success by relating a person's explanatory style to long-term academic performance. **Explanatory style** refers to a person's habitual way of explaining events, and it's assessed along three dimensions: internal/external, stable/unstable, and global/specific. To assess explanatory style, researchers ask participants to imagine six different good events that might happen to them ("You do a project that is highly praised") and six bad events ("You meet a friend who acts hostilely toward you") and to provide a likely cause for each (Peterson & Barrett, 1987). The participants then say whether each cause (1) is due to something about them or something about other people or circumstances (internal/external), (2) will be present again in the future or not (stable/unstable), and (3) is something that influences other areas of their lives or just this one (global/specific). An explanation that mentions an *internal* cause implicates the self ("There I go again"), but an *external* cause does not ("That was the pickiest set of questions I've ever seen"). A *stable* cause implies that things will never change ("I'm just not good at this"), whereas an *unstable* cause implies that things may improve ("The cold medicine I was taking made me groggy"). Finally, a *global* cause is something that affects many areas of life ("I'm stupid"), while a *specific* cause applies to only a few ("I'm not good with names").

In the research by Peterson, Seligman, and their colleagues, the three dimensions of internal/external, stable/unstable, and global/specific are combined to form an overall explanatory style index, which is then correlated with an outcome variable of interest, such as students' GPAs. A tendency to explain negative events in terms of internal, stable, and global causes is considered a pessimistic explanatory style, and it's related to a variety of undesirable life outcomes. For example, students with a pessimistic explanatory style tend to get lower grades than those with a more optimistic style (Peterson & Barrett, 1987).

Peterson and Seligman have also studied the association between different explanatory styles and health. In one study, they examined whether a person's

"A pessimist sees the difficulty in every opportunity; an optimist sees the opportunity in every difficulty."

—SIR WINSTON CHURCHILL

explanatory style as a young adult could predict physical health later in life (Peterson, Seligman, & Vaillant, 1988; see also Peterson, 2000). The study took advantage of the fact that members of Harvard's graduating classes from 1942 to 1944 took part in a longitudinal study that required them to complete a questionnaire every year and submit medical records of periodic physical examinations. Using the medical records, judges scored each person's physical health on a 5-point scale, where 1 means the person was in good health and 5 means the person was deceased. This was done for all participants when they reached the ages of 25, 30, 35, and so on.

The physical health of the men at each of these ages was then correlated with their explanatory style as young men, which was assessed by having judges score the descriptions they gave in 1946 of their most difficult experiences during World War II. The correlations, after statistically controlling for the participants' initial physical condition at age 25, are reported in **Table 5.1**. As a quick glance at the table indicates, optimistic explanatory style during younger adulthood is a significant predictor of physical health in later life. (Explanatory style does not correlate with health between ages 30 and 40, most likely because nearly all participants were in generally good health at those ages, so there was nothing to predict.)

Thus, regarding one of the most important outcomes there can be—whether we are vigorous or frail, alive or dead—our causal attributions seem to matter. The optimistic tendency to make external, unstable, and specific attributions for failure presumably makes us less prone to despair and encourages more of a can-do outlook that promotes such behaviors as exercising regularly, visiting the doctor, and even flossing our teeth—behaviors that can lead to a longer, healthier life.

Attributions about Controllability Another group of researchers, led by Bernard Weiner and Craig Anderson, has also shown that people's attributional style has a powerful effect on their long-term outcomes. But these investigators emphasize whether an attribution implies that a given outcome is controllable. On the one hand, attributions for failure that imply controllability—for example, a lack of effort or a poor strategy—make it easier to persevere because we can always

TABLE 5.1 EXPLANATORY STYLE EARLIER IN LIFE PREDICTS LATER PHYSICAL HEALTH

AGE	CORRELATION
30	.04
35	.03
40	.13
45	.37*
50	.18
55	.22*
60	.25*

SOURCE: Adapted from Peterson, Seligman, & Vaillant, 1988.
*Denotes statistically significant correlation.

Productive Attributional Style
Franklin Delano Roosevelt was elected U.S. president for four terms. FDR's optimistic attributional style undoubtedly contributed to his being one of the most successful political figures in U.S. history, despite having a severe physical handicap.

try harder or try a new strategy (Anderson, 1991; Anderson & Deuser, 1993; Anderson, Krull, & Weiner, 1996). If we view outcomes as beyond our control, on the other hand, it's tempting to simply give up—indeed, it's often rational to do so.

Research inspired by findings such as these has shown that people can be trained to adopt more productive attributional tendencies for academic outcomes—in particular, an inclination to attribute failure to a lack of effort—and that doing so has beneficial effects on subsequent academic performance (Dweck, 1975; Forsterling, 1985). The effects are both substantial and touching. Blackwell, Dweck, and Trzesniewski (2004) report tough junior high school boys crying when made to realize that their grades were due mainly to a lack of effort rather than a lack of brains. Making people believe they can exert control over events that they formerly believed to be beyond their control restores hope and unleashes the kind of productive energy that makes future success more likely (Crandall, Katkovsky, & Crandall, 1965; Dweck & Reppucci, 1973; Peterson, Maier, & Seligman, 1993; Seligman, Maier, & Geer, 1968).

Gender and Attributional Style This type of training might be put to good use to undo some inadvertent attributional training occurring in elementary school classrooms across the United States that appears to give rise to a troubling gender difference in attributional style. Research shows that boys are more likely than girls to attribute their failures to lack of effort, and girls are more likely than boys to attribute their failures to lack of ability (Dweck, 1986; Dweck, Davidson, Nelson, & Enna, 1978; Lewis & Sullivan, 2005; Ryckman & Peckham, 1987; Whitley & Frieze, 1985).

Carol Dweck and her colleagues have found that this difference likely results in part from teachers' feedback patterns in fourth-grade and fifth-grade classrooms (Dweck et al., 1978). The researchers found that although girls, on average, outperform boys in school, negative evaluation of girls' performance was almost exclusively restricted to intellectual inadequacies ("This is not right, Lisa"). In contrast, almost half of the criticism of boys' work referred to nonintellectual factors ("This is messy, Bill"). Positive evaluation of girls' performance was related to the intellectual quality of their performance less than 80 percent of the time; for boys, it was 94 percent of the time. From these data, Dweck and her colleagues argue that girls learn that criticism means they may lack intellectual ability, whereas boys learn that criticism may just mean they haven't worked hard enough or paid enough attention to detail. Similarly, girls are likely to suspect that praise may be unrelated to the intellectual quality of their performance, whereas boys learn that praise means their intellectual performance was excellent (Good, Rattan, & Dweck, 2012).

Dweck and her colleagues performed an experiment in which they gave students feedback of the kind girls typically receive or the kind boys typically get (Dweck et al., 1978). They found that both girls and boys who got the kind of comments girls usually receive (criticism almost exclusively for intellectual failing and praise only sometimes for intellectual success) tended to view subsequent failure as a reflection of their ability. Both girls and boys who got the kind of feedback boys usually receive (criticism often for nonintellectual failing but praise that almost always referred to the high intellectual quality of the work) were inclined to view subsequent failure feedback as a reflection of their lack of effort and attention to detail.

Therefore, whatever other reasons there may be for boys crowing about their successes and dismissing their failures, this pattern is reinforced by the treatment they receive in the classroom. And whatever motivational factors operate for girls, their more modest attributions are likewise shaped by the feedback they receive in school (Espinoza, Areas da Luz Fontes, & Arms-Chavez, 2014).

⟲ LOOKING BACK

People differ in their explanatory styles; that is, they differ in whether they tend to make attributions that are external or internal, stable or unstable, global or specific. Attributional style predicts academic success as well as health and longevity. Belief in the controllability of outcomes is important, and beliefs about the controllability of academic outcomes can be altered by training. Boys and girls learn to draw different conclusions about academic outcomes. Boys receive feedback indicating that success is due to ability and failure is due to insufficient effort or to incidental factors, whereas girls receive feedback indicating the reverse.

The Processes of Causal Attribution

Does she really like me, or is she just pretending she does because she's after my best friend? Does that salesman really believe the turbo boost is essential to performance or is he just saying that to get a bigger commission? Is he really that selfish, or is he just under a lot of pressure? These types of questions run through people's heads every day. How we answer them—how we assess the causes of observed or reported behavior—is not capricious; rather, such assessments follow rules that make the answers predictable. These rules serve several purposes. They help us understand the past, illuminate the present, and predict the future. Only by knowing the cause of a given event can we grasp the true meaning of what has happened and anticipate what's likely to happen next.

For example, our perception of how much control another person has over his or her actions is one important factor in how we judge that person. When a person offers an excuse for problematic behavior, it typically yields more sympathy and forgiveness if the excuse involves something beyond the person's control ("I had a flat tire") than if it involves something controllable ("I needed to take a break") (Weiner, 1986). Gay people are viewed more favorably by those who believe they are "born this way" rather than choosing to be gay (Whitely, 1990).

When we're trying to figure out the cause of something, a particularly important question to answer is whether an outcome is the product of something within the person (that is, an internal, or "dispositional," cause) or a reflection of something about the context or circumstances (an external, or "situational," cause). Ever since Kurt Lewin pointed out that behavior is always a function of both the person and the situation (see Chapter 1), theories of attribution have focused on how people assess the relative contributions of these two types of causes (Heider, 1958; Hilton & Slugoski, 1986; Hilton, Smith, & Kim, 1995; Jones & Davis, 1965; Kelley, 1967; Medcoff, 1990). How do we figure out why someone acted a certain way? Was it primarily because that's who he is, or largely because of the situation he faced?

Frequently, the distinction between internal and external causes is straightforward. You might win the pot in your weekly poker game because you're a

"If we're being honest, it was your decision to follow my recommendation that cost you money."

better player than everyone else (internal cause), or maybe you simply were lucky and got the best cards (external cause). Knowledge and skill clearly reside within a person, and luck is something completely beyond a person's influence. In the case of poker, the internal/external dichotomy is easy to grasp.

In other contexts, however, the distinction isn't as clear. We might say that someone became a rock-and-roll guitarist because of a deep love of the instrument (internal cause) or because of the desire for fame and fortune (external cause). But aren't love of the instrument and desire for fame both inner states? And if so, why is the love of playing the guitar considered an internal cause, whereas the desire for fame and fortune considered an external cause? The answer is that loving to play the guitar is not something shared by everyone, or even most people, so it tells us something characteristic and informative about the person. It thus makes sense to refer to the cause as something personal or internal. Many people, however, seem to find the prospect of fame attractive. (Why else would there be so many reality TV shows?!) And even more find the prospect of wealth attractive. Doing something to achieve fame and fortune, then, tells us little about the person in hot pursuit of either. So in this case, it makes sense to refer to the cause as something impersonal or external. Determining whether certain actions are the product of internal versus external causes thus requires assessments of what most people are like and what most people are likely to do.

Attribution and Covariation

When scientists attempt to nail down the cause of some phenomenon, they try to isolate the one cause that seems to make a difference in producing the effect. In other words, they try to identify the cause that seems always to be present when the effect or phenomenon occurs, and always seems to be absent when the phenomenon does not occur. For example, to determine whether ulcers are caused by a bacterium, a medical researcher might determine whether people who are given the bacterium develop ulcers and whether people who have ulcers improve after taking an antibiotic to fight the bacterium.

To a considerable degree, this is how people assess causality in their everyday lives (Cheng & Novick, 1990; Fiedler, Walther, & Nickel, 1999; Forsterling, 1989; Hewstone & Jaspers, 1987; Kelley, 1973; Nisbett & Ross, 1980; White, 2002). When your friend states that she likes her statistics class, you automatically try to figure out why: "Is she a math fan?" "Is the class taught by a gifted teacher?" What does your friend say about other math classes, or about her classes in general? What do other students in her statistics class say about it?

In considering these questions, people use what attribution theorists have dubbed the **covariation principle** (Kelley, 1973). We try to determine what causes—internal or external, symptomatic of the person in question or applicable to nearly everyone—"covary" with the observation or effect we're trying to explain. Psychologists believe that three types of covariation information are particularly significant: consensus, distinctiveness, and consistency.

1. **Consensus** refers to what most people would do in a given situation. Does everyone behave the same way in that situation, or do few other people behave that way? Is your friend one of a precious few who likes her statistics

---

"The logic of science is also that of business and life."

—JOHN STUART MILL

"The whole of science is nothing more than refinement of everyday thinking."

—ALBERT EINSTEIN

covariation principle The idea that behavior should be attributed to potential causes that occur along with the observed behavior.

consensus A type of covariation information: what most people would do in a given situation; that is, whether most people would behave the same way, or few or no other people would behave that way.

class, or do most students like the class? All else being equal, the more an individual's reaction is shared by others (when consensus is high), the less it says about that individual and the more it says about the situation.

2. **Distinctiveness** refers to what an individual does in different situations. Is a particular behavior unique to a specific situation, or does it occur in many situations? Does your friend seem to like all math classes, or even all classes in general, or does she just like her statistics class? The more someone's reaction is confined to a particular situation (when distinctiveness is high), the less it says about that individual and the more it says about the specific situation.

3. **Consistency** refers to what an individual does in a given situation on different occasions. Is the behavior the same now as in the past, or does it vary? Does your friend have favorable things to say about today's statistics class only, or has she raved about the course all semester? The more an individual's reaction varies across occasions (when consistency is low), the harder it is to make a definite attribution either to the person or to the situation. The effect is likely due to some less predictable combination of circumstances.

distinctiveness A type of covariation information: what an individual does in different situations; that is, whether the behavior is unique to a particular situation, or occurs in all situations.

consistency A type of covariation information: what an individual does in a given situation on different occasions; that is, whether next time, under the same circumstances, the person would behave the same or differently.

Putting the three types of covariation information together, a *situational attribution* is called for when consensus, distinctiveness, and consistency are all high (**Table 5.2**). When everyone you know likes your friend's statistics class, when your friend claims to like few other math classes, and when she has praised the class all semester, there must be something special about that class. In contrast, a *dispositional attribution* is called for when consensus and distinctiveness are low but consistency is high. When few other students like her class, when she claims to like all math courses, and when she has raved about the statistics class all semester, her fondness for the course must reflect something about her.

When psychologists have given research participants these three types of covariation information and asked them to attribute a reported effect to a particular cause, they do indeed use the logic of covariation (Forsterling, 1989; Hewstone & Jaspers, 1983; Hilton et al., 1995; McArthur, 1972; White, 2002). They make situational attributions when consensus, distinctiveness, and consistency are high, and make dispositional attributions when consensus and distinctiveness

TABLE 5.2 COVARIATION INFORMATION

ATTRIBUTION	CONSENSUS	DISTINCTIVENESS	CONSISTENCY
An **external attribution** is likely if the behavior is:	High in **consensus**: Everyone raves about the class.	High in **distinctiveness**: Your friend does not rave about many other classes.	High in **consistency**: Your friend frequently raves about the class.
An **internal attribution** is likely if the behavior is:	Low in **consensus**: Hardly anyone raves about the class.	Low in **distinctiveness**: Your friend raves about all classes.	High in **consistency**: Your friend has raved about the class on many occasions.

Covariation and Attribution
If your roommate laughs at Chris Rock but doesn't laugh at many other comedians on TV (high distinctiveness), and most people you know laugh at Chris Rock (high consensus), and both your roommate and most other people you know almost always laugh at a Chris Rock performance (high consistency), you're going to think your roommate laughs at Chris Rock because of the situation, namely because it's a Chris Rock performance. If your roommate laughs at pretty much every comic on the tube (low distinctiveness), every time he sees one (high consistency), and, of course, you know that's not true of everyone you know (low consensus), you're going to think your roommate laughs at any comedian because he's a pushover for comedians; in other words, he has a disposition to be very fond of them.

discounting principle The idea that people should assign reduced weight to a particular cause of behavior if other plausible causes might have produced it.

augmentation principle The idea that people should assign greater weight to a particular cause of behavior if other causes are present that normally would produce a different outcome.

are low but consistency is high. The only surprising finding is that people are sometimes only modestly influenced by consensus information. They respond to whether or not everyone laughed at the comedian, but rather mildly. This reflects a common tendency to focus more on information about the person (distinctiveness and consistency) at the expense of information that speaks to the influence of the surrounding context (consensus).

Attribution and Imagining Alternative Actors and Outcomes

The judgments people make aren't always based on what's actually happened; sometimes they base them on what they *imagine* would happen under different situations, or if a different individual were involved. For example, in considering the high rates of obedience in Milgram's experiment (see Chapters 1 and 9), you might try to imagine what you would do if you were a participant (Milgram, 1963, 1974). You might find it difficult to imagine administering so much electric shock to the victim (the "learner"). In other words, you would believe that a change in the participant—in particular, if *you* were the participant—would lead to a change in the outcome. Hence, you would conclude that it must have been the person (or rather the people who delivered so much shock), not the situation, that was responsible for the behavior.

The Discounting and Augmentation Principles Sometimes the information available to us suggests that either of two (or more) causes might be responsible for a given behavior. Someone interviews for a job and seems quite personable. Is that the way she really is, or is she just putting on a good face for the interview? We're not well equipped to make an attribution when we haven't had the opportunity to see how this person behaves in other situations, or to witness how other people behave in exactly the same situation.

In circumstances like these, people typically use their general knowledge about the world to infer how most people would behave in the situation in question, and they combine that knowledge with a bit of logic to arrive at an attribution. The logic is known as the **discounting principle**, according to which our confidence that a particular cause is responsible for a given outcome must be reduced (discounted) if there are other plausible causes that might have produced it (Kelley, 1973). Either a sunny disposition or the desire to land a job is sufficient to make someone act personably in an interview. By pure logic, then, we can't make a confident attribution. But we supplement the pure logic with our knowledge of what people are like. That knowledge tells us that nearly everyone would act in a personable manner to get the job offer, so we can't be confident that the applicant's disposition is all that sunny. We thus discount the possibility that what we've seen (a personable demeanor) tells us something about the person involved (she's personable) because we imagine that nearly everyone would act similarly in that context.

Extending that logic just a bit leads to a complementary **augmentation principle**, by which we can have greater (augmented) confidence that a particular cause is responsible for a given outcome if other causes are present that we imagine would produce a *different* outcome. Typically, we can be more certain that a person's actions reflect what that person is really like if the circumstances would seem to discourage such actions. If someone advocates a position despite being threatened with torture for doing so, we can safely conclude that the person truly believes in that position.

One important implication of the discounting and augmentation principles is that it can be difficult to know what to conclude about someone who behaves "in role," but easy to figure out what to think about someone who acts "out of role." In one of the earliest attribution studies, participants witnessed another person acting in either an extraverted or introverted manner during an interview (Jones, Davis, & Gergen, 1961). Half the participants were led to believe the person was interviewing for a job as a submariner, a position that required close contact with many people over a long period of time and thus favored extraverted personalities. The other participants thought the person was interviewing for a job as an astronaut, which involved long periods of solitude and thus favored an introverted personality. (Note that this study was published in 1961, when space flight involved a single astronaut in a tiny capsule.)

In short, half the participants witnessed behavior that conformed to the dictates of the situation. The person exhibited the appropriate trait for the job. Because the behavior fit the situation in these instances, it should be difficult to judge whether the behavior truly reflected the person being interviewed. In contrast, the other half of the participants witnessed behavior that defied the dictates of the situation. The person behaved in a way that was inappropriate for the job. As a result, the behavior should be seen as a clear reflection of the interviewee's true self.

When the participants subsequently rated the interviewee on a host of trait dimensions related to introversion/extraversion, their judgments closely followed the logic of the discounting and augmentation principles. As shown in **Figure 5.1**,

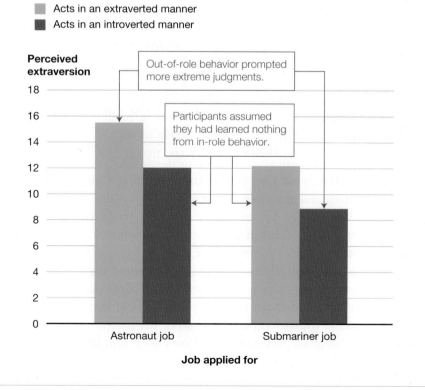

SOURCE: Adapted from Jones, Davis, & Gergen, 1961.

Figure 5.1
Discounting and Augmentation
Out-of-role behavior is seen as more informative of a person's true self than in-role behavior. This bar graph shows the perceived extraversion of a person who acted in an introverted or extraverted manner while interviewing for a position that favored introversion (astronaut) or extraversion (submariner).

counterfactual thoughts Thoughts of what might have, could have, or should have happened "if only" something had occurred differently.

emotional amplification An increase in an emotional reaction to an event that is proportional to how easy it is to imagine the event not happening.

"Of all sad words of tongue or pen, the saddest are these, 'It might have been.'"

—JOHN GREENLEAF WHITTIER, NINETEENTH-CENTURY QUAKER POET AND ABOLITIONIST

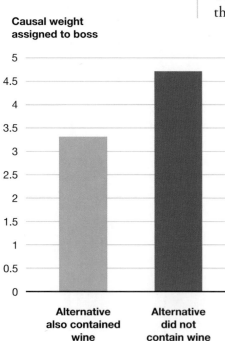

Causal weight assigned to boss

Figure 5.2

The Role of Imagined Outcomes in Causal Attribution

The graph shows the causal significance of the menu choice according to participants who read that the boss almost ordered a different dish that did or did not also contain wine.

SOURCE: Adapted from Wells & Gavanski, 1989.

participants responded as if they had learned nothing about the person's degree of extraversion if he behaved in a fashion that would be considered "in role" (the middle two bars). Out-of-role behavior prompted more extreme judgments (the two outer bars). Someone who acts outgoing when he should be subdued is assumed to be a true extravert; someone who acts withdrawn when he should be outgoing is assumed to be a true introvert.

The Influence of What Almost Happened In making causal assessments, we sometimes consider whether a given outcome is likely to have happened if the circumstances were slightly different. Our attributions are thus influenced by our knowledge of what has actually happened in the past, as well as by **counterfactual thoughts** (thoughts *counter* to the facts)—considerations of what might have, could have, or should have happened, "if only" a few minor things were done differently (Johnson, 1986; Kahneman & Tversky, 1982a; Roese, 1997; Roese & Olson, 1995). "If only I had studied harder" implies that a lack of effort was the cause of a poor test result. "If only the Republicans had nominated a different candidate" implies that the candidate, not the party's principles, was responsible for defeat.

Consider, for example, an experiment in which participants read about a woman who went to lunch with her boss to celebrate her promotion (Wells & Gavanski, 1989). The woman's boss ordered for her; but not knowing she suffered from a rare allergy to wine, he ordered a dish made with a wine sauce. The woman fell ill shortly after the meal, went into convulsions, and died en route to the hospital. Some participants read a version of this story in which the boss had considered ordering a different dish that did not contain wine. The others read a version in which the alternative dish the boss had considered also contained wine. The participants then answered several questions about the cause of the woman's death.

The investigators predicted that the participants' attributions would be influenced not only by what happened in the scenario, but by what *almost* happened. Those who read that the woman's boss almost ordered a dish without wine could readily imagine a chain of events in which she was just fine, and thus they would come to view the boss's choice of meals as quite causally significant. In contrast, if the dish the boss almost ordered also contained wine, the participants would not so readily imagine a different outcome, and consequently would be likely to see the menu choice as less causally significant. As **Figure 5.2** indicates, that is exactly what happened.

Emotional Effects of Counterfactual Thinking Our attributions influence our emotional reactions to events, and therefore our counterfactual thoughts do as well. An emotional reaction tends to be more intense if the event almost didn't happen—a phenomenon known as **emotional amplification**. Would you feel worse, for example, if someone you loved died in a plane crash after switching her assigned flight at the last minute, or after sticking with her assigned flight? Most people say that a last-minute switch would make the loss harder to bear because of the thought that it "almost" didn't happen. In general, the pain or joy we derive from any event tends to be proportional to how easy it is to imagine the event not happening.

Given that our thoughts about "what might have been" exert such a powerful influence on our reactions and attributions, a key question becomes:

What determines whether a counterfactual event seems like it "almost" happened? Some of the most common determinants are time and distance. Imagine, for example, that someone survives a plane crash in a remote area and then tries to hike to safety. Suppose he hikes to within 75 miles (120 kilometers) of safety before dying of exposure. How much should the airline pay his relatives in compensation? Would your estimate of the proper compensation change if he'd made it to within a quarter of a mile (402 meters) to safety? It would for most people. In this study, those who were led to believe he died a quarter mile from safety recommended an average of $162,000 more in compensation than those who thought he died 75 miles away (Miller & McFarland, 1986). Because he almost made it (within a quarter mile), his death seems more tragic and thus more worthy of compensation.

This psychology of coming close leads to a kind of paradox in the emotional reactions of Olympic athletes to winning a silver or bronze medal, instead of the gold. An analysis of the smiles and grimaces athletes exhibited on the medal stand at the 1992 Summer Olympics in Barcelona, Spain, revealed that second-place silver medalists seemed to be less happy than the third-place bronze medalists they had outperformed (Medvec, Madey, & Gilovich, 1995). This finding was replicated at the 2004 Olympics in Athens, Greece (Matsumoto & Willingham, 2006). Since when is bronze better than silver? The reversal of reasonable expectations about medals results from silver medalists being consumed by what they did not receive (the coveted gold medal), whereas bronze medalists focus on what they did receive (a medal). (Those who finish fourth in Olympic competition receive no medal at all.) Indeed, analyses of the athletes' comments during postevent interviews confirmed the suspected difference in their counterfactual thoughts. Silver medalists were more focused on how they could have done better "if only" a few things had gone differently, whereas bronze medalists were more inclined to state that "at least" they received a medal. Second place can thus be a mixed blessing. The triumph over many can get lost in the defeat by only one.

The Influence of Exceptions vs. Routines Another determinant of how easy it is to imagine an event not happening is whether it resulted from a routine action or a departure from the norm. In a study that examined this idea, participants read about a man who was severely injured when a store he happened to be in was robbed (Miller & McFarland, 1986). In one version of the story, the robbery took place in the store where the man typically shopped. In another version, the robbery took place in a store he decided to visit for "a change of pace." When participants considered how much the victim should be compensated for his injuries, those who thought the injuries were sustained in an unusual setting recommended over $100,000 more than those who thought the injuries occurred in the victim's usual store. The injuries were presumably more tragic because it was so easy to see how they could have been avoided.

This kind of reasoning helps explain why those who put themselves in considerable danger, such as bullfighters and fighter pilots, often have informal rules against changing places with someone else. Switching places is thought to be asking for trouble. The death some years ago of the Spanish matador Yiyo seemed particularly tragic, in part because he violated the unwritten code of

Counterfactual Emotions on the Olympic Podium
Students who didn't know anything about the 1992 Olympic Games in Barcelona rated the apparent happiness of the three medalists. The happy athlete on the right won the bronze medal. The unhappy one on the left won the silver medal. The happy bronze medal winner is undoubtedly comparing the result with a failure to win a medal at all. The gloomy silver medalist is probably contemplating how close she came to the gold.

The Anguish of What Might Have Been
It's especially upsetting when someone dies who was not supposed to be in a particular situation. (A) The matador José Cubero, known as Yiyo, died in the bullring after substituting at the last minute for another bullfighter. (B) In the Israeli army, soldiers are forbidden to trade missions, no matter how compelling the circumstances. The reasoning is that if a soldier dies on a mission that he was not supposed to go on, the family will feel even greater anguish at his "needless death," and the soldier who should have gone may feel guilt over still being alive.

his profession and served as a last-minute replacement for another bullfighter (Miller & Taylor, 1995). The extra anguish that accompanies such tragedies may make them particularly memorable, thereby reinforcing the superstition that switching spots somehow increases the chances of disaster by "tempting fate" (Risen & Gilovich, 2007, 2008).

In less ominous circumstances, the same processes are at work in the belief that you should never change lines at the grocery store, or depart from your initial hunch on a multiple-choice test. Because we "kick ourselves" when our new line slows to a crawl or when our initial hunch was right, such occasions may be particularly memorable, and we may overestimate how often a change of heart leads to a bad outcome (Kruger, Wirtz, & Miller, 2005; Miller & Taylor, 1995).

> ### ❶ LOOKING BACK
>
> A primary aspect of causal attribution involves assessing how much the person or the situation is responsible for a given event. People make such assessments by employing the logic of covariation. We consider the distinctiveness and consistency of a person's behavior, as well as whether others would have behaved similarly. When the person's behavior is not unique to a particular situation, when the person behaves consistently in those circumstances, and when not everyone behaves in that way, we feel confident it's something about the person that caused the behavior. When behavior is distinctive and consistent and most people behave in the same way as that person, we tend to attribute the behavior to the situation. We also rely on our psychological insight to make attributions. When someone stands to gain from a particular behavior, we attribute the behavior to what the person stands to gain, and not to the person's underlying dispositions. But when someone behaves in a way that conflicts with self-interest, we are inclined to attribute the behavior to the person's dispositions. Counterfactual thoughts about events that "almost" occurred influence our causal attributions and emotional reactions to events that did occur.

Errors and Biases in Attribution

The attributions people make are sometimes less than fully rational. Our hopes and fears sometimes color our judgment; we sometimes reason from faulty premises; we're occasionally misled by information of questionable validity. In other words, our causal attributions are occasionally subject to predictable errors and biases. Indeed, since the initial development of attribution theory in the late 1960s and early 1970s, social psychologists have made considerable progress in illuminating some of the pitfalls of everyday causal analysis.

The Self-Serving Attributional Bias

One of the most consistent biases in causal assessments is one you have no doubt noticed time and time again: people are inclined to attribute their own failure and other bad events to external circumstances, but to attribute their successes and other good events to themselves—that is, they're subject to a **self-serving attributional bias** (Carver, DeGregorio, & Gillis, 1980; Greenberg, Pyszczynski, & Solomon, 1982; Mullen & Riordan, 1988). Think for a moment about two of your classes, the one in which you've received your highest grade and the one in which you've received your lowest. In which class would you say the exams were the most "fair" and constituted the most accurate assessment of your knowledge? If you're like most people, you'll find yourself thinking that the exam on which you performed well was the better test of your knowledge (Arkin & Maruyama, 1979; Davis & Stephan, 1980; Gilmour & Reid, 1979). Students tend to make external attributions for their failures ("The questions were ambiguous"; "The professor is a sadist"), and internal attributions for success ("The hard work paid off"; "I'm smart"). Research shows that professors do the same thing when their manuscripts are evaluated for possible publication (Wiley, Crittenden, & Birg, 1979). "Of course they accepted this brilliant paper." "They obviously sent this to reviewers who are morons." (But note that papers by the authors of this textbook truly are rejected only because of theoretical bias, unfair evaluation procedures, or the simple narrow-mindedness of reviewers.)

Consider your favorite athletes and their coaches. How do they explain their wins and losses, their triumphs and setbacks? Richard Lau and Dan Russell (1980) examined newspaper accounts of the postgame attributions of professional athletes and coaches and found that attributions to one's own team were much more common for victories than for defeats. In contrast, attributions to external elements (bad calls, bad luck, and so on) were much more common for defeats than for victories. Overall, 80 percent of all attributions for victories were to aspects of one's own team, but only 53 percent of all attributions for defeats were to one's own team. Only 20 percent of attributions for victories were to external elements, whereas 47 percent of attributions for defeats were to external elements (see also Roesch & Amirkhan, 1997).

self-serving attributional bias The tendency to attribute failure and other bad events to external circumstances, and to attribute success and other good events to oneself.

"Success has a thousand fathers; failure is an orphan."
—OLD SAYING

"There might have been some carelessness on my part, but it was mostly just good police work."

"First, I'd like to blame the Lord for causing us to lose today."

Self-Serving Attributional Bias

(a) When the San Francisco Giants won their third World Series title in 5 years in 2014, they tended to attribute their success to internal causes, such as deft trades by their front office, and clutch performances by their stars, like Madison Baumgardner, Pablo Sandoval, and Buster Posey. (b) Players on the Kansas City Royals, and other teams defeated by the Giants during this period, are more likely to cite other factors, like luck, for the Giants' success.

You've no doubt observed the tendency to attribute success internally and failure externally (**Box 5.1**), and it's easy to explain why it happens: people are prone to a self-serving bias in their attributions because doing so makes them feel good about themselves (or at least prevents them from feeling bad about themselves). The self-serving attributional bias, then, is a motivational bias—motivated by the desire to maintain self-esteem. What could be simpler?

Actually, things are not so simple. Even a completely rational person, unaffected by motivations to feel good, might make the same pattern of attributions and be justified in doing so (Wetzel, 1982). After all, when we try to succeed at something, any success is usually at least partly due to our efforts and thus warrants our taking some of the credit. Failure, on the other hand, usually occurs *despite* our efforts and therefore requires looking elsewhere, perhaps externally, for its cause. A fully rational individual, then, might exhibit an apparently self-serving pattern of attribution because success is generally so much more tightly connected than failure to our intentions and effort.

To see this pattern more clearly, consider a series of experiments that reliably elicits the self-serving attributional bias (Beckman, 1970). Participants tutor a student who is having difficulty mastering some material. (In some of these studies, the participants are real teachers, and in others they're college students.) After an initial round of tutoring, the student is assessed and found to have done poorly. A second round of tutoring follows, and then an additional assessment. For half the participants, the student's performance on the second assessment remains poor; for the other half, the student shows marked improvement. Such studies typically reveal that the teachers tend to take credit if the student improves from session to session, but they tend to blame the student if the student continues to perform poorly. In other words, people make an internal attribution for success (improvement) but an external attribution for failure (continued poor performance).

It may seem as if the teachers are trying to feel good about themselves and are making less than rational attributions to do so. But that's not necessarily the case. Suppose researchers programmed a computer, devoid of any feelings and hence having no need to feel good about itself, with software that let it use the covariation principle. What kind of attributions would it make if the programmers gave the computer these inputs? (1) The student did poorly initially, (2) the teacher redoubled his or her efforts or changed teaching strategy (as most people do after an initial failure), and (3) the student did well or poorly in the second session. The computer would then look for a pattern of covariation between the outcome and the potential causes that would tell it what sort of attribution to make. When the student failed both times, there would be no correlation between the teacher's efforts and the student's performance (some effort at time 1 and poor performance by the student; increased effort at time 2 and continued poor performance). Because an attribution to the teacher couldn't easily be justified, the attribution would be made to the student. When the student succeeded the second time, however, there would be an association between the teacher's efforts and the student's performance (some effort at time 1 and poor performance; increased effort at time 2 and improved performance). An attribution to the teacher would therefore be fully justified.

As this example indicates, we shouldn't be too quick to accuse others of making self-serving attributions just to make themselves feel good. It can be difficult to tell from the pattern of attributions alone whether someone has made an attribution to protect self-esteem; such a pattern could be the result of a purely rational analysis.

"We permit all things to ourselves, and that which we call sin in others, is experience for us."

—RALPH WALDO EMERSON, *EXPERIENCE*

The Fundamental Attribution Error

Try to recall your initial thoughts about the individuals who delivered the maximum level of electric shock in Milgram's studies of obedience (as mentioned earlier; see also Chapters 1 and 9). The participants had to deliver more than

400 volts of electricity to another person, over the victim's protests, as part of a learning experiment (Milgram 1963, 1974). Nearly two-thirds of all participants followed the instructions. In this case, a straightforward application of the covariation principle would lead to a situational attribution, not an inference about the participants' character or personality. Because virtually all participants delivered a high level of shock in the face of protests by the "learner," and nearly two-thirds were willing to deliver everything the machine could produce (that is, consensus was high), their behavior doesn't say much about the individual people involved, but rather speaks to something about the situation that made their behavior (surprisingly) common.

If you're like most people, however, you formed a rather harsh opinion of the participants, thinking of them as unusually cruel and callous, perhaps, or as unusually weak. If so, your judgments reflect a second way that everyday causal attributions often depart from the general principles of attributional analysis. There seems to be a pervasive tendency to see people's behavior as a reflection of the kind of people they are, rather than as a result of the situation they find themselves in.

The tendency to attribute people's behavior to elements of their character or personality, even when powerful situational forces are acting to produce the behavior, is known as the **fundamental attribution error** (Ross, 1977). It's called "fundamental" because the problem being solved (figuring out what someone is like from a sample of behavior) is so basic and essential, and because the tendency to think dispositionally (to attribute behavior to the person while ignoring important situational factors) is so common and pervasive.

Experimental Demonstrations of the Fundamental Attribution Error

Social psychologists have devised a number of experimental paradigms to examine the fundamental attribution error (Gawronski, 2003; Gilbert & Malone, 1995; Lord, Scott, Pugh, & Desforges, 1997; Miller, Ashton, & Mishal, 1990; Miller, Jones, & Hinkle, 1981; Vonk, 1999). In one of the earliest studies, students at Duke University read an essay about Fidel Castro's Communist regime in Cuba (Jones & Harris, 1967). Half the participants read a pro-Castro essay, and half read an anti-Castro essay, supposedly written in response to a directive to "write a short, cogent essay either defending or criticizing Castro's Cuba as if you were giving the opening statement in a debate." Afterward, the participants rated the essayist's general attitude toward Castro's Cuba. Because the essayist was presumably free to write an essay that was either supportive or critical of Castro's Cuba, it's not surprising that those who read a pro-Castro essay rated the writer's attitude as being much more favorable toward Communist Cuba than those who read an anti-Castro essay (see the left-hand portion of **Figure 5.3**).

However, the results from other participants in this experiment *are* surprising. Although they read the same essays, the researchers told them that the essayist's stance (pro- or anti-Castro) had been assigned, not freely chosen. These participants' ratings of the essayist's true attitude were less extreme. Nevertheless, they still drew inferences about the essayist's attitude: those who read a pro-Castro essay thought the author was relatively pro-Castro, and those who read an anti-Castro essay thought the author was relatively anti-Castro (see the right-hand portion of Figure 5.3). From a purely logical perspective, these inferences are

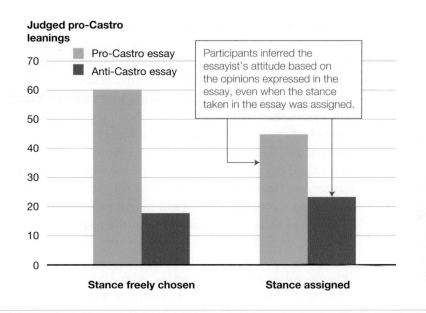

Judged pro-Castro leanings

- Pro-Castro essay
- Anti-Castro essay

Participants inferred the essayist's attitude based on the opinions expressed in the essay, even when the stance taken in the essay was assigned.

Stance freely chosen | Stance assigned

SOURCE: Adapted from Jones & Harris, 1967.

Figure 5.3
The Fundamental Attribution Error
Participants rated the essayist's true attitude toward Castro's Cuba; higher numbers indicate more of an assumed pro-Castro attitude.

unwarranted. If people are instructed to write on a given topic, what they write can't be taken as an indication of what they really believe. In thinking that the essays reflected the authors' true beliefs, participants were committing the fundamental attribution error.

You might object to this conclusion and question how much support such studies provide for the fundamental attribution error. After all, when people are compelled to say something that is inconsistent with their beliefs, they normally distance themselves from their statements by subtly indicating they don't really believe what they're saying (Fleming & Darley, 1989). But the essays contained no distancing cues, so participants legitimately may have inferred that the written viewpoints reflected something of the true attitudes of the authors.

Other demonstrations of the fundamental attribution error get around these problems by allowing plenty of room for such distancing behaviors. In those studies, participants are randomly assigned to one of two roles: questioner or responder (Gilbert & Jones, 1986; Van Boven, Kamada, & Gilovich, 1999). The questioner's job is to read a series of questions over an intercom to the responder, who then answers with one of two entirely scripted responses. Thus, the responders' answers are not their own and shouldn't be considered informative about their true personalities. The added twist in these studies is that, after reading each question, the questioners themselves, with instructions from the experimenter, indicate to the responder which of the two responses he or she is to make. Thus, the questioners are determining the responders' behavior. For example, in response to the question, "Do you consider yourself to be sensitive to other people's feelings?" the questioner signals to the responder which of these two answers to give: "I try to be sensitive to others' feelings all the time. I know it is important to have people one can turn to for sympathy and understanding. I try to be that person whenever possible" (altruistic response) or "I think there are too many sensitive, 'touchy-feely' people in the world already. I see no point in trying to be understanding of another if there is nothing in it for me" (selfish response).

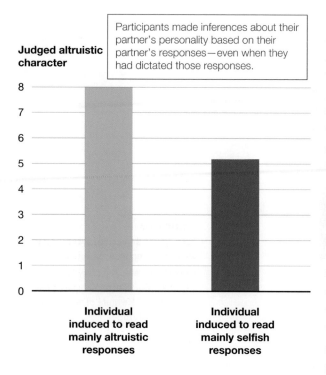

Judged altruistic character

Participants made inferences about their partner's personality based on their partner's responses—even when they had dictated those responses.

Individual induced to read mainly altruistic responses

Individual induced to read mainly selfish responses

Figure 5.4

Perceivers "Learn" from Behavior They Demanded from Another Person

This graph shows participants' average trait ratings of individuals that *they themselves* had directed to respond in an altruistic or selfish manner. Higher numbers indicate greater assumed altruism.

SOURCE: Adapted from Van Boven et al., 1999.

After reading a list of these questions to the responder and eliciting a particular response, the questioners in one such study rated the responder on a set of personality traits: trustworthiness, greediness, and kindheartedness (Van Boven, Kamada, & Gilovich, 1999). The investigators found that the questioners drew inferences about the responders—even though they themselves had directed the responders to answer as they did! Responders led to recite mainly altruistic responses were rated more favorably than those led to recite mainly selfish responses (**Figure 5.4**). Note also that this occurred even though the responders could have (and may have) tried through tone of voice to distance themselves from the responses they had to give.

The Fundamental Attribution Error and Perceptions of the Advantaged and Disadvantaged An inferential problem we face in our daily lives is deciding how much credit to give to those who are succeeding in life and how much blame to direct at those who are not. How much praise and respect should we give to successful entrepreneurs, film stars, and artists? And to what degree should we hold the impoverished accountable for their condition? The discussion thus far about the fundamental attribution error suggests that people tend to assign too much responsibility to the individual for great accomplishments and terrible mistakes, and not enough responsibility to the particular situation, broader societal forces, or pure dumb luck.

An ingenious laboratory experiment showed that people are indeed quick to commit the fundamental attribution error in such situations (Ross, Amabile, & Steinmetz, 1977). The study shows that we can sometimes fail to see the advantages some people enjoy in life and the disadvantages others must overcome. Participants took part in a quiz-game competition, much like the television show *Jeopardy*. Half of them were assigned the role of questioner and the other half the role of contestant. The questioner's job was to think of challenging, but not impossible, general-knowledge questions ("Who were the two coinventors of calculus?" "Who played the role of Victor Laszlo in the film *Casablanca*?"), and the contestant would answer the questions (see answers on p. 177).

From a self-presentation standpoint, the questioners had a tremendous advantage. It was relatively easy for them to come off well because they could focus on whatever personal knowledge they happened to have and ignore their various pockets of ignorance. Everybody has *some* areas of expertise, and the questioners could focus on theirs. The contestants, however, suffered from the disadvantage of having to field questions about the questioners' store of knowledge, which typically didn't match their own.

If participants were thinking logically, they should correct for the relative advantages and disadvantages enjoyed by the questioners and contestants, respectively. If asked to rate the questioners' and contestants' general knowledge and overall intelligence, anyone watching the quiz show should be reluctant to make any distinction between the participants in these two roles; any difference in their *apparent* knowledge and intelligence could easily be explained by

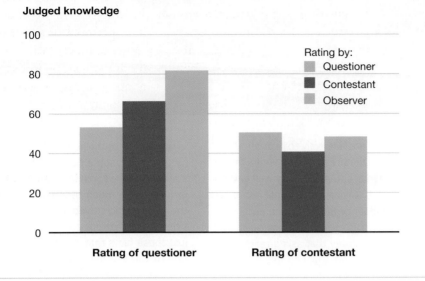

Judged knowledge

SOURCE: Adapted from Ross et al., 1977.

Figure 5.5
Role-Conferred Advantage and Disadvantage
The bars show ratings of the general knowledge of the questioner and contestant in the quiz-show experiment. Participants thought the questioners were more knowledgeable than the contestants, even though they knew they had been randomly assigned to their roles and that the questioners had a much easier task.

their roles. But that was not what happened. Predictably, the hapless contestants failed to answer many of the questions correctly. The contestants came away quite impressed by the questioners' abilities, rating them more highly than their own. And when the quiz game was later reenacted for a group of observers, they, too, rated the questioners' general knowledge more highly than that of the contestants (**Figure 5.5**). Notice that the only people not fooled by the questioners' performance were the questioners themselves, who rated their own general knowledge and intelligence as roughly equal to the average of the student body. The questioners knew they had skipped over yawning gaps in their knowledge base in order to come up with whatever challenging questions they could offer.

The quiz-game study has profound relevance to everyday life (Ross et al., 1977). Organizational psychologist Ronald Humphrey set up a laboratory microcosm of a business office (Humphrey, 1985). He told participants he was interested in "how people work together in an office setting." All participants witnessed a random procedure whereby some of the participants were selected to be "managers" and to assume supervisory responsibilities, while others were selected to be mere "clerks" who followed orders. Humphrey gave the managers time to study manuals describing their tasks. While they were studying them, the experimenter showed the clerks the mailboxes, filing system, and so on. The newly constructed office team then went about their business for 2 hours. The clerks were assigned to work on a variety of low-skilled, repetitive jobs and had little autonomy. The managers, as in a real office, performed reasonably high-skill-level tasks and directed the clerks' activities.

At the end of the work period, managers and clerks rated themselves and each other on a variety of role-related traits, such as leadership, intelligence, motivation for hard work, assertiveness, and supportiveness. For all these traits, managers rated their fellow managers more highly than they rated their clerks. For all but hardworkingness, clerks rated their

Attributions to Ability
The trappings of an office can prompt us to see competence when there isn't actually a great deal of it.

BOX 5.2

Not So Fast:
Critical Thinking about the Fundamental Attribution Error

When Hurricane Katrina devastated the city of New Orleans in 2005, people across the United States and around the world were surprised that thousands of residents stayed in the city rather than evacuate—costing the lives of nearly 1,500 of them, and leading to a harrowing several days for many more. Why would so many people have chosen to stay and risk their lives rather than evacuate, as they were told to do by numerous authorities and media sources? Viewers were puzzled because they thought of staying as *choosing* to stay. As Secretary of Homeland Security Michael Chertoff put it, "Officials called for a mandatory evacuation. Some people chose not to obey that order. That was a mistake on their part." Michael Brown (who ended up losing his job as head of the Federal Emergency Management Agency [FEMA] as a result of his handling of the federal response to the hurricane) echoed the same sentiment when he stated that " . . . a lot of people . . . chose not to leave."

But how many really "chose" to stay? It's not hard to detect the influence of the fundamental attribution error here when one considers that those who stayed behind were poorer, probably didn't own a car, had minimal access to news, and had weaker social networks and therefore less opportunity to discuss the situation and how to deal with it. If you don't have a car to get you out of the city, don't have the money to pay for lodging wherever you flee to, and are less likely to hear about the gravity of the threat from friends, family, or the media, you might very well end up, as they did, staying and sticking it out.

The influence of the fundamental attribution error is even more obvious in the results of a survey that asked relief workers from around the country (doctors, counselors, firefighters, police officers) to provide three words to describe those who evacuated in advance of the hurricane and those who stayed behind. Those who left were most often described as "intelligent," "responsible," and "self-reliant," whereas those who stayed behind were described as "foolish," "stubborn," and "lazy" (Stephens, Hamedani, Markus, Bergsieker, & Eloul, 2009). Being taken in by the fundamental attribution error is easy to do here because the raw facts are that some people left and some stayed, and the fortunes of those who left tended to be much better than those of the people who stayed behind. The dispositional explanations come easily when it's just those facts that command our attention. It takes some effort to look further and see the background influences that made it so much easier for some people to evacuate than others.

There's a general lesson from the Katrina tragedy and our mistaken causal attributions for the deaths of so many: we shouldn't be so fast to make dispositional attributions for others' behavior; we should hold off until we've made a serious attempt to assess the situation confronting them.

The Fundamental Attribution Error and Hurricane Katrina
Some people had ready means of escape from Katrina and some did not. Commenters typically ignored such differences when explaining the "choice" to evacuate in advance of the hurricane's arrival.

managers more highly than they rated their fellow clerks. And bear in mind that these attributions were made by people who knew their jobs were assigned by the proverbial flip of a coin. The attributions to ability are surely stronger in daily life where it's possible that bosses really have been selected for their greater ability and workers for their lesser ability.

Causes of the Fundamental Attribution Error

Why are people so quick to see someone's actions as a reflection of the person's inner traits and enduring character? A tendency so strong and so pervasive is probably the result of several causes acting jointly. Indeed, social psychologists have identified several psychological processes that appear to be responsible for the fundamental attribution error.

Motivational Influence and the Belief in a Just World One reason we're likely to attribute behavior to people's traits and dispositions is that dispositional inferences can be comforting. The twists and turns of life can be unsettling. A superbly qualified job candidate may be passed over in favor of a mediocre applicant with the right connections. A selfless Good Samaritan may be stricken with cancer and experience a gruesome death. Such events cause anxiety, and we're tempted to think such things couldn't possibly happen to us. But we can minimize perceived threats in several ways. One way is to attribute people's behaviors or life experiences to something about them, rather than to fate or chance (Burger, 1981; Walster, 1966). More broadly, by thinking that people "get what they deserve," that "what goes around comes around," or that "good things happen to good people and bad things happen to bad people," we can reassure ourselves that nothing bad will happen to us if we are the right kind of person living the right kind of life. Thus, we tend to attribute behavior and outcomes to dispositions in part because there is a *motive* to do so.

Social psychologists maintain that this motive lies behind what's called the **just world hypothesis**—the belief that people get what they deserve in life (Lambert, Burroughs, & Nguyen, 1999; Lerner, 1980; Lipkus, Dalbert, & Siegler, 1996). Victims of rape, for example, are often viewed as responsible for their fate (Abrams, Viki, Masser, & Bohner, 2003; Bell, Kuriloff, & Lottes, 1994), as are victims of domestic abuse (Summers & Feldman, 1984). This insidious tendency reaches its zenith in the claim that, if no defect in a victim's manifest character or past actions can be found, the tragic affliction must be due to some flaw or transgression in a "past life." Thus, for example, it has been argued that children who have been sexually abused are likely to have been sex offenders themselves in a past life (Woolger, 1988). Such beliefs show how far people will go to maintain their belief in a just world. Research in this area also shows that people tend to "derogate the victim"—that is, they rate unfavorably the character of those who suffer unfortunate experiences that are completely beyond their personal control (Jones & Aronson, 1973; Lerner & Miller, 1978; Lerner & Simmons, 1966). And, "since I'm a good person, I don't have to worry that I will have the terrible fate of that bad person."

Perceptual Salience and Causal Attributions What influences whether a potential cause springs to mind or how readily it springs to mind? One important determinant is how much the cause stands out perceptually, or how *salient* it is (Lassiter, Geers, Munhall, Ploutz-Snyder, & Breitenbecher, 2002; Robinson & McArthur, 1982; Smith & Miller, 1979). Features of the environment that more

Answers to Quiz-Show Game Questions p. 174

Isaac Newton and Gottfried von Leibnitz; Paul Henreid.

"The employees have to assume a share of the blame for allowing the pension fund to become so big and tempting."

just world hypothesis The belief that people get what they deserve in life and deserve what they get.

readily capture our attention are more likely to be seen as potential causes of an observed effect. And because people are so noticeable and interesting, they tend to capture our attention much more readily than other aspects of the environment. Situations, if attended to at all, may be seen as mere background to the person and his or her actions. This is particularly true of various social determinants of a person's behavior (customs, social norms) that are largely invisible. Attributions to the person, then, have an edge over situational attributions in everyday causal analysis. In other words, people are usually more salient than situations.

The importance of perceptual salience in our causal attributions has been demonstrated in many ways. In one study, participants watched a videotape of a conversation between two people (Taylor & Fiske, 1975). Some participants saw a version that showed only one of the individuals; others saw a version that let them see both people equally well. When the participants assigned responsibility for setting the tone of the conversation, those who could see only one person assigned more responsibility to that individual than those who could see both people in the conversation equally well.

Attribution and Cognition Perceptual salience explains some instances of the fundamental attribution error better than others. It explains the results of the quiz-show study, for example, because the decisive situational influence—that the questioner could avoid areas of ignorance but the contestant could not—was invisible and therefore had little impact on people's judgments. But what about the attitude attribution studies in which participants knew that a writer had been assigned to argue for the particular position advocated in an essay? Here, the situational constraints were far from invisible. Why didn't the participants discount appropriately and decide that the target person's behavior was perfectly well accounted for by the situational constraints, and thus refrain from making any inference about the person at all? The answer is that the cognitive machinery people draw on when using the discounting principle doesn't work that way.

Let's review the logic of the discounting principle, depicted in **Figure 5.6A**. That logic requires us to simultaneously weigh what we've seen (or heard or read) about the person's behavior, and the context of that behavior, to determine the kind of person we're dealing with—to decide whether to draw a dispositional inference. What's puzzling about the fundamental attribution error, then, is why we don't do that. Why don't we reject dispositional inferences when it should be clear that the situation is powerful enough to have induced the behavior?

The Influence of Perceptual Salience on Causal Attributions
People who are more salient—bigger, more brightly lit, more distinctively dressed—are typically seen as more influential in outcomes.

That would indeed be a puzzle if, in fact, we reasoned along the lines depicted in Figure 5.6A—simultaneously considering the behavior and the context in which it occurs. But research by Dan Gilbert (1989, 2002) makes it clear that we don't reason that way at all. Instead, we reason in the manner depicted in **Figure 5.6B**. We observe the behavior, identify what it is, and automatically characterize the person as having a disposition corresponding to the behavior

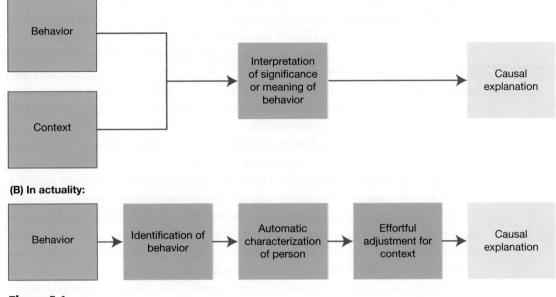

(A) In theory:

Behavior

Context

Interpretation of significance or meaning of behavior

Causal explanation

(B) In actuality:

Behavior → Identification of behavior → Automatic characterization of person → Effortful adjustment for context → Causal explanation

Figure 5.6
Inferring Dispositions
(A) In theory, people should simultaneously weigh both the observed behavior of a person and the surrounding context to arrive at an explanation for that behavior. (B) In actuality, people tend to spontaneously make a dispositional inference and adjust for the context only with effort.

observed. Only then do we consider the context of the behavior. But it's often too little and too late: the dispositional inference has been made, and revising it is effortful and therefore typically insufficient. Indeed, sometimes the adjustment is neglected altogether. In short, the situation is secondary and often slighted in the process of terms of establishing a causal explanation.

Ample evidence supports Gilbert's theory: we rapidly and automatically characterize other people based on their behavior (Carlston & Skowronski, 1994; Moskowitz, 1994; Newman, 1993; Todorov & Uleman, 2003; Uleman, 1987; Winter & Uleman, 1984). Initially, someone who acts in a hostile manner is considered hostile regardless of what prompted the hostility; someone who acts in a compassionate manner is seen as compassionate, despite what may have prompted the compassion. Then, but only if we are somehow prompted to reflect, do we consciously ponder what we know about the prevailing situational constraints and adjust our initial dispositional inference if it seems warranted. Thus, the situational information is taken into account only after an initial dispositional inference has already been made—if situational information is considered at all (see Figure 5.6B). This analysis suggests that when we are tired, unmotivated, or distracted, we should be more likely to commit the fundamental attribution error (or to make a larger error) because the adjustment stage is shortened or skipped.

And that's exactly what happens. In one study, participants watched a videotape, without the sound, of a young woman engaged in a conversation with another person. The woman appeared anxious throughout: "She bit her nails, twirled her hair, tapped her fingers, and shifted in her chair from cheek to cheek" (Gilbert, 1989, p. 194). Gilbert told half the participants that the woman was responding to a number of anxiety-inducing questions (about her sexual fantasies or personal failings, for example). He told the other participants that she was responding to questions about innocuous topics (world travel or great books, for example). Gilbert predicted that all participants, regardless of what they were told about the content of the discussion, would immediately and automatically assume she was an anxious person. Those told she was discussing anxiety-producing topics, however, would take that into account and adjust their initial characterization, concluding that maybe she was not such an anxious person after all. Those told she was discussing a series of bland topics would not make such an adjustment, and would conclude she was an anxious person.

So far, this is just a standard attribution experiment. But Gilbert added a twist. He gave another two groups of participants the same information he gave the first two, but he had these groups memorize a list of words while watching the videotape. Gilbert reasoned that this extra demand on their attention would make them less able to carry out the deliberative stage of the attribution process in which they would (ordinarily) adjust their initial characterization of the person to account for situational constraints. If so, then those who thought the woman was discussing anxiety-provoking topics should nevertheless rate her as being just as anxious as those who were told she was discussing innocuous topics. As **Figure 5.7** indicates, that's just what happened. When participants were busy memorizing a list of words, they didn't have the cognitive resources needed to adjust their initial impression, so they rated the woman as being just as anxious when they thought she was discussing anxiety-provoking topics as when discussing innocuous topics. The demonstration is important because many things in life may rob us of the cognitive resources needed to carry out the correction phase of attributional analysis (Geeraert, Yzerbyt, Corneille, & Wigboldus, 2004).

Salient Situations It stands to reason that we would focus initially on the person and only later adjust to account for the situation, because people are compelling stimuli of considerable importance to us. But what about those occasions when it's the situation that is more salient—that has the most importance? What happens, for example, when we see someone react to a new ride at an amusement park and we want to know whether the ride is scary or not? Do we immediately and automatically characterize the situation (the ride is terrifying) based on the behavior we've seen (these people are terrified), and only later correct this initial situational inference in light of what we know about the individuals involved (they're rookies who've never been to a first-rate amusement park)? Research suggests that in these circumstances we do indeed focus on the context when making causal attributions. When we're primarily interested in finding out about the situation a person is in (and are less interested in the person engaged in the behavior), Gilbert's attributional sequence is reversed. In such cases, we will

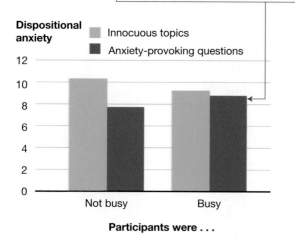

Observers who were kept busy by having to memorize a list of words did not correct their initial, automatic impression that the person was dispositionally anxious and did not take into account the nature of the material being discussed.

Figure 5.7

Adjusting Automatic Characterizations

Observers had to judge how generally anxious a person was who appeared anxious while discussing either innocuous or anxiety-provoking topics.

SOURCE: Adapted from Gilbert, 1989.

automatically and effortlessly draw strong inferences about the situation (Krull, 1993; Krull & Dill, 1996; Krull & Erickson, 1995).

Consequences of the Fundamental Attribution Error Does it matter that we're susceptible to the fundamental attribution error? Indeed it does. We make the error many times a day, and the results can be unfortunate. Here's just one example: People, including employers and college admissions officers, often assume they can learn a lot about a person's traits and abilities from a 30-minute unstructured interview. But interviews reveal only the person's *apparent* traits and abilities in a *single situation*. In fact, the validity of the unstructured interview is close to nil: the correlation between judgments based on interviews and the subsequent judgments based on performance on the job or in school is only .10 (Hunter & Hunter, 1984).

The Fallibility of Interviews
We tend to assume far more accuracy and utility for interviews than is really the case. The 30-minute interview—for college, medical school, executive positions, the Peace Corps, etc.—has almost no predictive validity.

A more accurate prediction of future performance would require information based on a wide array of situations: letters summarizing experience with the candidate in a range of situations, reports of previous job performance, high school GPA (which in turn is based on performance in everything from labs to ability to concentrate on homework to mastery of material as revealed by exams). Such information is far from infallible, but it often predicts future behavior with reasonable accuracy. Correlations between these types of "input" information and later outcomes are typically much higher than for interviews, on the order of .30 to .50. Relying on one or two interviews is a setup for disappointment; employees are hired and students admitted who aren't as terrific as initially thought, and more deserving people are passed up.

If the fundamental attribution error is so pervasive and consequential, why are we so susceptible to it and so unaware of it? For one thing, we're not very good at assessing the validity of our own judgments. We can explain after the fact almost any failure of prediction, and we do it so effectively that we're prevented from seeing our errors. Suppose, for example, you were the interviewer who hired Jane, who didn't work out very well. "True, but she had some personal problems that came up shortly after she was hired." Or "Jane's boss was the real problem; she's so difficult to get along with." Your decision to choose Jane prevented you from finding out that other candidates for that job might have been more satisfactory.

A second reason for the pervasiveness of the fundamental attribution error is that we often see a given individual only in particular kinds of situations. You see Rachel only at parties, when she seems nice and fun to be around, but you don't know about the trials she inflicts on her roommates. You see Professor Jones only in his statistics classroom, where he seems stiff and boring and none too pleasant, but you don't see him being kind, funny, and helpful with his student advisees. Such errors sometimes cause no harm, but sometimes they do; and it's difficult to trace the error back to the fact that dispositional inferences were formed on the basis of limited or biased information.

actor-observer difference A
difference in attribution based on who
is making the causal assessment: the
actor (who is relatively inclined to make
situational attributions) or the observer
(who is relatively inclined to make
dispositional attributions).

The Actor-Observer Difference in Causal Attributions

It may have occurred to you that the degree to which you're oriented toward the person versus the situation depends on whether you're engaged in the action yourself or just observing someone else. In the role of "actor," you're usually more interested in determining what kind of situation you're dealing with than assessing what kind of person you are. In the role of "observer," in contrast, you're often primarily interested in determining what kind of person you're dealing with. By this logic, actors should be more likely than observers to make situational attributions for a particular behavior—to see their own behavior as caused by the situation, when observers of the very same behavior are more likely to slight the situation and focus more exclusively on the actor's dispositions. Indeed, there's considerable evidence for just such a difference (Jones & Nisbett, 1972; Pronin, Lin, & Ross, 2002; Saulnier & Perlman, 1981; Schoeneman & Rubanowitz, 1985; Watson, 1982; see Malle, 2006, for a dissenting voice).

In one of the most straightforward demonstrations of this **actor-observer difference** in attribution, participants had to explain why they chose the college major that they did, or why their best friends chose the major that they did. When the investigators scored the participants' explanations, they found that participants more often referred to characteristics of the person when explaining someone else's choice than they did when explaining their own choice. They typically focused on the specifics of the major when explaining their own choice. You might attribute your own decision to major in psychology, for instance, to the facts that the material is fascinating, the textbooks beautifully written, and the professors dynamic and accessible. In contrast, you might attribute your friend's decision to major in psychology to "issues" he needs to work out (Nisbett, Caputo, Legant, & Maracek, 1973).

This phenomenon has significant implications for human conflict, both between individuals and between nations. Married couples, for example, often squabble over attributional differences. John may blame a late meeting or unusually heavy traffic to explain why an errand didn't get done, whereas his husband may be more inclined to argue that he's lazy, inattentive, or "just doesn't care." Similarly, at the national level, the United States is likely to explain the stationing of its troops in so many locations across the globe as a necessary defense against immediate and future threats. Other countries may be more inclined to see it as a manifestation of U.S. "imperialism."

Like the fundamental attribution error, the actor-observer difference has no single cause. Several factors give rise to it. First, assumptions about what needs explaining can vary for actors and observers. When asked, "Why did you choose the particular college that you did?" a person might reasonably interpret the question to mean "Considering you are who you are, why did you choose the particular college that you did?" The person is taken as a given and therefore need not be included as part of the explanation. This is much like Willie Sutton's explanation of why he robbed banks: "Because that's where the money is." He takes it as given that he's a crook and thus interprets the question as one about why he robs *banks* rather than gas stations. Notice, in contrast, that when asked about someone else ("Why did your roommate choose his particular college?"), the nature of the person can't be taken as a given, so it's reasonable to invoke the roommate's dispositions in offering an explanation (Kahneman & Miller, 1986; McGill, 1989).

BOX 5.3 **FOCUS ON *MEMORY AND IMAGINATION***

The Mind's Eye

As far back as the late nineteenth century, psychologists have noted that when people remember past experiences, they tend to do so from one of two perspectives. Sometimes we remember events from a first-person perspective, in which we "see" in our mind's eye what we saw when we actually experienced the event in question. We see our teacher praising us in front of the class, the look on our father's face when he uttered the words "getting divorced," the football as it sails toward us in the end zone. But sometimes we remember events from a third-person perspective, in which we see *ourselves* in the mental image, much like an observer would. We see ourselves beaming that day in the classroom, the tears on our cheeks when our parents split up, throwing our head back in exultation after the touchdown.

Do these different perspectives influence people's judgments in the same way that having an actor's or observer's perspective influences people's causal attributions? They do. People make more dispositional attributions for their own behavior when they recall the episode from a third-person perspective rather than a first-person perspective (Frank & Gilovich, 1989). First-person memories also tend to be more detail focused, so they encourage a bottom-up, low-level construal of the event in question, whereas third-person memories encourage a top-down, high-level construal (Libby & Eibach, 2011). If you remember going over Chapter 1 of this book from a first-person perspective, you're likely to think that you were "reading"; if you remember it from a third-person perspective, you're likely to think that you were "studying." This perspective difference can have all sorts of influences on people's attributions. For example, people who suffer from low self-esteem are more likely to make "I'm no good" overgeneralizations when recalling a failure experience from a third-person instead of a first-person perspective (Libby, Valenti, Pfent, & Eibach, 2011).

People may also adopt either of these same two perspectives when anticipating or imagining future events, and the consequences for prediction are similar to those for causal attribution. Students who imagine completing an academic assignment from a third-person perspective tend to think of it more as "pursuing my education" than "doing my homework," so they end up being more motivated to do the work (Vasquez & Buehler, 2007).

In the most remarkable demonstration of the influence of first-person versus third-person perspective, Lisa Libby, Richard Eibach, and their colleagues asked voters in Ohio to picture themselves voting in the 2004 presidential election from either a first- or a third-person perspective. Those who did so from a third-person perspective reported feeling more enthusiastic about the prospect of voting and saw themselves as more committed to this key element of participatory democracy (high-level construal). When the investigators followed up after the election to see who actually voted, they found that those who had earlier thought of voting from a third-person perspective were 25 percent more likely to do so than those who had thought of it from a first-person perspective (Libby, Shaeffer, Eibach, & Slemmer, 2007).

Second, the perceptual salience of the actor and the surrounding situation is different for the actor and the observer (Storms, 1973). The actor is typically oriented outward, toward situational opportunities and constraints. Observers, in contrast, are typically focused on the actor and the actor's behavior. Because, as we noted earlier, people tend to make attributions to potential causes that are perceptually salient, it makes sense that actors will tend to attribute their behavior to the situation, while observers will tend to attribute that same behavior to the actor.

Third, actors and observers differ in the amount and kind of information they have about the actor and the actor's behavior (Andersen & Ross, 1984; Jones & Nisbett, 1972; Prentice, 1990; Pronin, Gilovich, & Ross, 2004). Actors know what intentions influenced them to behave in a certain way; observers can only guess at those intentions. Actors are also much more likely to know whether a particular action is typical of them or not. An observer may see someone slam a door and conclude that he's an angry person. The actor, in contrast, may know that this is an unprecedented outburst and hence does not warrant such a sweeping conclusion. (In the attribution language used earlier, the actor is in a much better position to know if the behavior is *distinctive* and thus merits a situational rather than a dispositional attribution.)

↺ LOOKING BACK

Our attributions are subject to predictable errors and biases. We often exhibit a self-serving attributional bias, attributing success to the self and failure to the situation. We exhibit the fundamental attribution error when we attribute behavior to a person's dispositions rather than to the situation, even when there are powerful situational factors that we ought to consider. Actors are more likely than observers to attribute behavior to the situation, whereas observers are more likely than actors to attribute behavior to the actor's dispositions.

Culture and Causal Attribution

Much of what psychologists know about how people understand the behavior of others is undoubtedly universal. People everywhere are likely to engage in counterfactual thinking, imagining outcomes that might have occurred as an aid in understanding what did happen. People everywhere probably prefer to maintain the view that they live in a just world. All people undoubtedly perceive the causes of their own behavior somewhat differently than they perceive the causes of other people's behavior. But there are some basic differences in how people from different cultures understand the causes of behavior. Some of these differences could be anticipated on the basis of what has been discussed already about cultural differences in perception and in characteristic social relations.

Cultural Differences in Attending to Context

Most of the world's people tend to pay more attention to social situations and the people who are involved in them than Westerners do. The kinds of social factors that are merely background for North Americans appear to be more salient to people from other cultures (Hedden et al., 2000; Ji, Schwarz, & Nisbett, 2000). Recall from Chapters 1 and 3 that Westerners generally define themselves in terms of their relationships with others less often than other people throughout the world do. Westerners think about themselves more in the context of personal goals, attributes, and preferences than non-Westerners, whereas non-Westerners think about themselves more in terms of the social roles they occupy and their obligations to other people and institutions. Non-Westerners therefore have to pay more attention to others and to the details of the situations they find themselves in, because effective action typically requires coordinating their actions with those of other people.

Asians and Westerners do indeed differ in how much attention they give to context, even when perceiving inanimate objects. Kitayama, Duffy, Kawamura, and Larsen (2002) demonstrated this difference in a study with Japanese and American participants (**Figure 5.8**). After examining a square with a line drawn at the bottom, they went to another part of the room and saw a square of a

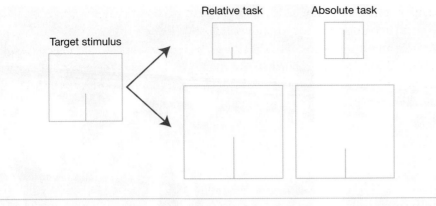

Relative task Absolute task

Target stimulus

SOURCE: Adapted from Kitayama, Duffy, Kawamura, & Larsen, 2002.

Figure 5.8
Sensitivity to Context and the Framed Line Task
After seeing the target stimulus, participants draw a vertical line at the bottom of an empty square. In the relative task, the line must be drawn in the same *proportion* to the square as it was originally. In the absolute task, the new line must be exactly the same length as the original line. Japanese participants performed better at the relative task, and Americans performed better at the absolute task.

different size; they had to draw either a line of the same length as the original or a line having the same length *in relation to* the original square. Americans were better at the absolute judgment, which required ignoring the context, whereas Japanese were better at the relative judgment, which required paying attention to the context.

Hedden and his colleagues used functional magnetic resonance imaging (fMRI) to examine activation of the fronto-parietal area of the brain, which is associated with difficult perceptual judgments (Hedden, Ketay, Aron, Markus, & Gabrieli, 2008). There was more activity in that region for East Asians when they made judgments about absolute line length and thus had to *ignore* the context, and more activity in that brain area for Westerners when they made proportional judgments and thus had to *attend to* the context.

Causal Attribution for Independent and Interdependent Peoples

Given the pronounced difference between Asians' and Westerners' attention to context, it should come as no surprise to learn that Asians are more inclined than Westerners to attribute behavior to the situation. For example, attributions for the outcomes of sports events are not the same in independent cultures as they are in interdependent cultures. Coaches and players on sports teams in the United States tend to see positive outcomes as the result of the abilities of individual players and the actions of coaches ("We've got a very good keeper in Bo Oshoniyi, who was defensive MVP of the finals last year") (Lau & Russell, 1980). In contrast, the attributions of Hong Kong coaches and players are more likely to refer to the other team and the context ("I guess South China was a bit tired after having played in a quadrangular tournament") (Lee, Hallahan, & Herzog, 1996).

Other research demonstrates that Westerners see dispositions and internal causes, where Asians see situations and contexts. Morris and Peng (1994) showed participants animated cartoons of an individual fish swimming in front of a group of fish. In some scenes, the individual fish scooted off from the approaching group; in other scenes, the fish was joined by the group and they swam off together; in still other scenes, the individual fish joined the group. Participants were asked why these events occurred. Americans tended to see the behavior of the individual fish as internally caused, and Chinese were more likely to see the

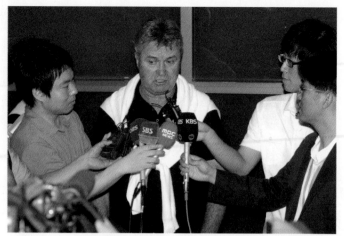

Attributions of Western reporters for outcomes of sporting events tend to emphasize the traits and abilities of individual players. Attributes of East Asian reporters tend to emphasize the setting, the recent history of the two teams' experience, and other contextual factors.

behavior of the individual fish as externally caused (see also Kashima, Siegal, Tanaka, & Kashima, 1992; Rhee, Uleman, Lee, & Roman, 1995; Shweder & Bourne, 1984).

These differences in causal perception are probably due to variations in cultural outlook that result in a different focus of attention. Asians think of themselves as part of a larger context in which they are connected to others, so they are inclined to see animals and even objects as behaving as they do because of their connections to other animals and objects (Markus & Kitayama, 1991). In contrast, Westerners see themselves as acting independently of social connections, so they tend to view all kinds of other things as acting in ways that are relatively unaffected by a larger context.

Culture and the Fundamental Attribution Error

Is it reasonable to assume that the fundamental attribution error occurs in all cultures? After all, nearly everyone wishes to live in a just world; other people and their dispositions are everywhere more salient than the situation; and therefore capture attention more readily, than the situation; and all people have the same basic cognitive machinery. The error does indeed seem widespread. For example, the finding of Jones and Harris (1967) that people assume a speech or an essay by another person represents that person's own opinion on the topic, despite the presence of obvious situational demands, has been demonstrated in many societies, including China (Krull et al., 1996), Korea (Choi & Nisbett, 1998), and Japan (Kitayama & Masuda, 1997).

Evidence indicates, however, that the fundamental attribution error is more widespread and pronounced for Westerners than for Easterners. Westerners pay little attention to situational factors in circumstances in which Asians pay considerable attention to them and grant their influence. Consider the results of the Jones and Harris study, in which students inferred that a person who was required to express certain beliefs actually held those beliefs (Jones & Harris, 1967). Koreans make the same error as Americans when they read essays written by other people. But in a variation of the Jones and Harris setup, participants had to write an essay favoring a position specified by the experimenter before seeing someone else write a similar essay (Choi & Nisbett, 1998). With this direct experience of being required to advocate a particular position, Koreans recognized how powerful the situation is, and therefore made no assumption about the attitudes of a target individual they subsequently observed. American participants, in contrast, learned nothing from the experience of being pressured to write what they did. They were just as likely as control participants to assume that the coerced target believed what he or she said.

Koreans are also more likely to recognize the implications of consensus information. If many people behave in a particular way in a given situation, they recognize that the situation is probably the main determinant of behavior (Cha & Nam, 1985). Americans' attributions tend to be less influenced by consensus information. Finally, evidence indicates that Asians are less likely to make an initial dispositional inference in circumstances where such inferences are made by the great majority of Westerners. Na and Kitayama (2011) presented participants with information about a person that could be expected to lead them to make an inference about the person's personality (such as "She checked twice to see if the gas was on in the stove before she left," which might lead a participant to infer that she was *careful*). When participants were later shown a picture of the person along with the word *reckless*, the American participants exhibited a pattern of brain activity associated with surprise, but the Korean participants did not. Thus, Asians are not just more likely to notice situational cues that might correct a dispositional inference; they might also be less likely to make a dispositional inference in the first place.

There are also differences in attributional tendencies among American subcultures. Puerto Rican children use fewer traits when describing themselves than Anglo-American children (Hart, Lucca-Irizarry, & Damon, 1986), and they are less likely to use traits to describe other people's behavior (Newman, 1991). Zarate, Uleman, and Voils (2001) found that Mexican-Americans and Mexicans were also less likely than Anglo-Americans to make trait inferences.

Priming Culture

In today's world of highly mobile populations, many people have spent significant parts of their lives in both independent and interdependent societies. Their experiences provide psychologists with an opportunity to better understand cultural influences on attribution. For example, Hong Kong has been the location for several fruitful cultural studies because the British governed Hong Kong for 100 years. The culture there is substantially Westernized, and children learn English when they are quite young, sometimes at the same time that they learn Cantonese.

People in Hong Kong, it turns out, can be encouraged to think in either an interdependent way or an independent way when presented with images that suggest one culture or the other. Hong, Chiu, and Kung (1997) showed some participants the U.S. Capitol building, a cowboy on horseback, and Mickey Mouse. They showed other participants a Chinese dragon, a temple, and men writing Chinese characters using a brush. They also showed a control group of participants neutral pictures of landscapes. Next the investigators showed all participants animated cartoons of an individual fish swimming in front of a group of other fish, behind the group, joining the group, departing from the group, and so on. They had the participants explain why the individual fish was behaving in these various ways. Participants who previously saw the American pictures gave more reasons relating to motivations of the individual fish, and fewer explanations relating to the other fish or the context, than participants

(A)   (B)   (C)   (D)

Priming Culture

To prime Western associations and individualistic attributions, investigators might show participants a photo of (A) the U.S. Capitol building or (B) an American cowboy roping a steer. To prime Asian associations and collectivist attributions, the investigators might show participants a photo of (C) a Chinese temple or (D) a Laotian dragon.

who saw the Chinese pictures. Participants who saw the neutral pictures gave explanations that were in between those of the other two groups.

Other natural experiments are made possible by the fact that many people living in North America are of Asian descent and think of themselves as partly Asian and partly Western. In one study, researchers asked Asian-American participants to recall either an experience that made their identity as an American apparent to them or an experience that made their Asian identity salient (Peng & Knowles, 2003; see also Benet-Martinez, Leu, Lee, & Morris, 2002). They then showed the students a group of highly abstract cartoon vignettes suggesting physical movements, such as an object falling to the bottom of a container of liquid, and had them rate how much they thought the object's movement was due to dispositional factors (shape, weight) versus contextual factors (gravity, friction). Participants who had their American identity primed rated causes internal to the objects as being more important, compared to participants who had their Asian identity primed.

It's also possible to prime religious concepts and affect the degree to which attributions are dispositional. Research shows that Protestants are more concerned than Catholics are with the state of their souls, and they are more likely to make internal, dispositional attributions for behavior (Li et al., 2011). When Protestants are primed to think about the soul, this increases their internal attributions still further. The same manipulation has no effect on the attributions of Catholics (Li et al., 2011).

Social Class and Attribution

So far in this section we've looked at how people from different countries, and from diverse ethnic and religious backgrounds, vary in their tendencies to attribute events and behavior to situational versus dispositional causes. Recent studies find that another form of culture—social class—influences attribution in important ways. **Social class** refers to the amount of wealth, education, and occupational prestige individuals and their families enjoy. Families with higher socioeconomic status enjoy greater wealth, education, and occupational prestige than those from less privileged backgrounds. And it turns out that within a particular culture or ethnicity, people from different levels on the socioeconomic ladder arrive at very different causal explanations for events.

Michael Kraus and his colleagues have found that lower-class or working-class individuals resemble individuals from interdependent cultures in their

social class The amount of wealth, education, and occupational prestige individuals and their families have.

attributional tendencies (Kraus, Piff, & Keltner, 2009). The investigators had participants make attributions for positive life events (getting into a desired graduate program) and negative life experiences (suffering with a health problem). Lower- and working-class people were more likely to invoke situational causes, whereas those higher up the socioeconomic ladder tended to invoke dispositional causes. When the investigators showed participants a person with a particular facial expression (smiling, sad, or angry) surrounded by people with the same or different expressions, those lower on the socioeconomic ladder were more likely to be swayed by the emotions of the faces in the surrounding context (also see Box 3.2). The lower social-class participants were less likely to rate a smiling target as happy when the other faces were frowning, for example. Investigators believe that these class differences are found because lower social-class people, like Asians, live in worlds where attention to other people is more necessary for effective functioning than it is for higher social-class people.

Dispositions: Fixed or Flexible?

Do Asians, Catholics, and people of lower social class think like "social psychologists," putting great emphasis on situational determinants of behavior, whereas Westerners, Protestants, and people of higher social class think like "personality psychologists," putting more emphasis on dispositional determinants? Not quite. It may be more accurate to say that everyone is inclined to think in both of these ways. We know that Asians and Westerners both understand their fellow human beings in terms of the so-called Big Five personality dimensions of extraversion, neuroticism, agreeableness, conscientiousness, and openness to experience. These dimensions play almost as big a role in judging people's personalities, including one's own personality, for Asians as they do for Westerners (Cheung et al., 2001; McCrae, Costa, & Yik, 1996; Piedmont & Chase, 1997; Yang & Bond, 1990). But Norenzayan, Choi, and Nisbett (1999) asked Korean and American college students a number of questions intended to tap their theories about the causes of behavior and found that although Koreans and Americans rated the importance of personality the same, the Koreans reported situations to be more important than did the Americans.

The Norenzayan team (1999) also asked their participants several questions about their beliefs regarding how fixed or flexible personality is, including whether it is something about a person that can't be altered much, or whether it can be changed. The Koreans considered personalities to be more changeable than the Americans did. The belief in the flexibility of personality is, of course, consistent with the view that behavior is substantially influenced by external factors.

The idea that personality is changeable is also consistent with the view—much more characteristic of interdependent people than independent people—that abilities can be changed by environmental factors and through effort (Dweck, 1999; Dweck, Chiu, & Hong, 1995; Dweck, Hong, & Chiu, 1993). Americans report valuing education more than Asians do, but American students spend much less time studying than Asian students do (Stevenson & Stigler, 1992). The belief in the value of effort to overcome inadequacy is deeply rooted in the cultures of China, Korea, and Japan.

Thus, making attributions and forming impressions are handled in many ways the same in different cultures and in other ways quite differently. Interdependent people live in more interconnected social worlds than independent people. And probably as a consequence, interdependent people are more attuned to their environment. Embedded in a social web themselves, interdependent people are inclined to see the contexts in which other people, and even animals and objects, exist. Asians, like Westerners, do tend to make the fundamental attribution error. But, being more attuned to situational contexts, they are more likely to correct their judgments when the context is highlighted in some way (Choi & Nisbett, 1998).

---

❶ LOOKING BACK

People in interdependent cultures pay more attention to social context than Western-ers do. Asians as well as Westerners are susceptible to the fundamental attribution error, but Westerners are more susceptible to it. For individuals reared in both interde-pendent and independent cultures, it is possible to prime the different ways of perceiving and attributing behavior. Social class also influences attributional tendencies: lower- and working-class people are more likely to attend to the surrounding circumstances, whereas upper-middle- and upper-class people tend to make dispositional attributions. Protestants, whose concerns focus on the soul, are more likely to make dispositional attributions than Catholics.

Beyond the Internal/External Dimension

Everyday causal analysis often requires people to determine whether a given action is mainly due to something about the person involved or to the surround-ing situational context. But this person/situation question is not the only one we ask, and it's not the whole story about everyday causal analysis. We often ask our-selves additional questions about someone's behavior to arrive at a more nuanced understanding of its meaning, and to enable us to make more refined predictions about future behavior. In particular, we're often interested in understanding a person's intentions (Heider, 1958; Jones & Davis, 1965; Malle, 1999).

Think of it this way: people engage in causal analysis to make the world more predictable—to find the "glue" that holds all sorts of varying instances of behavior together. Sometimes that glue is a trait in the person—for example, her kindness explains her long hours at the soup kitchen, her unfailing politeness to everyone in the residence hall, and her willingness to share her notes with others in her class. At other times the glue is provided by knowing someone's intentions—for example, the long hours in the library, the ingratiating behavior toward the professor, and the theft of another student's notes all come together and make sense if we know that the individual has a particularly strong desire to get good grades (Malle, Moses, & Baldwin, 2001; Searle, 1983). One study found that, across a wide range of circumstances, people explain intentional actions by referring to the actor's reasons (Malle, 2001). Reasons for action, of course, are many and varied, but the overwhelming majority of the reasons offered to explain behavior fall into two classes: desires and beliefs. Why did the senator endorse an amendment banning the burning of the American flag? Because she *wants* to be reelected, and she *believes* she needs to appease her constituents. Why does the neighbor put up with his wife's abusive insults? Because he doesn't *want* to be alone, and he *believes* no one else would be interested in him.

Beliefs and wants give rise to intentional action, so it stands to reason that to understand the behavior of others, we have to understand what they're seeking and what they believe will allow them to get it (or prevent them from getting it). Understanding others' beliefs and desires is central to the *theory of mind* that is so obviously necessary to a full comprehension of other people, and that understanding is manifested at such an early age that many people believe it is hardwired in the human brain (see Chapter 1).

⟲ LOOKING BACK

When we want to understand a person's intentions, the attributional question we are most inclined to ask concerns the *reason* for the person's behavior. Understanding a person's reasons for a particular action, in turn, often requires understanding the person's beliefs and desires.

Chapter Review

SUMMARY

From Acts to Dispositions: Inferring the Causes of Behavior

- People constantly search for the causes of events, and their attributions affect their behavior.
- People have different *explanatory styles*, which tend to be stable over time. A pessimistic style, attributing good outcomes to external, unstable, and local causes and bad outcomes to internal, stable, and global causes, is associated with poor health, poor performance, and depression.

The Processes of Causal Attribution

- The *covariation principle* is involved in making attributions. When a person engages in a given behavior across many situations and other people tend not to engage in the behavior, it's reasonable to attribute the behavior to the person. When the person engages in the behavior only in a particular situation and most others in the same situation also exhibit the behavior, it's reasonable to attribute the behavior to the situation.
- The ability to imagine what others would likely do in a given situation allows people to make use of the *discounting principle* and the *augmentation principle*. If situational constraints could plausibly have caused an observed behavior, people discount the role of the person's dispositions. If strong forces were present that would typically inhibit the behavior, they assume the actor's dispositions were particularly powerful.
- *Counterfactual thoughts* can powerfully affect attribution. People often perform mental simulations, adding or subtracting elements about the person or situation and estimating the likely effect on the outcome, then using these simulations to guide their attributions. Joy or pain in response to an event is amplified when counterfactual thinking encourages the thought that things might have turned out differently.

Errors and Biases in Attribution

- People's attributions are not always fully rational. They sometimes attribute events to causes that flatter themselves beyond what the evidence calls for, thus exhibiting the *self-serving attributional bias*.
- The *fundamental attribution error* is the tendency to attribute behavior to real or imagined dispositions of the person and to neglect influential aspects of the situation confronting the person. Even when it ought to be obvious that the situation is a powerful influence on behavior, people often attribute behavior to presumed traits, abilities, and motivations.
- One of the reasons people make such erroneous attributions is due to the *just world hypothesis*: thinking that people get what they deserve and that bad outcomes are brought about by bad or incompetent people.
- Another reason for the fundamental attribution error is that people and their behavior tend to be more salient than situations.
- A final reason for the fundamental attribution error is that attribution appears to be a two-step process. People typically characterize others immediately and automatically in terms consistent with their behavior, and only later, or perhaps not at all, do they adjust this initial characterization to account for the impact of prevailing situational forces.
- There are *actor-observer differences* in attributions. In general, actors tend to attribute their behavior much more to situations than observers do, partly because actors can usually see the situations they confront better than observers can.

Culture and Causal Attribution

- Marked cultural differences in susceptibility to the fundamental attribution error are common. Interdependent people are less likely to make the error than independent people, in part because their tendency to pay attention to context encourages them to look to the situation confronting the actor.

- When bicultural people are primed to think about one culture or the other, they make causal attributions consistent with the culture that is primed.
- Lower-class individuals, like people from interdependent cultures, tend to make more situational attributions compared to middle-class and upper-class individuals.

Beyond the Internal/External Dimension

- Much of the time, people are concerned with more than just whether to attribute behavior to the situation versus the person. They're interested in discerning the intentions and reasons that underlie a person's behavior.

THINK ABOUT IT

1. Carla was the last person to be picked for dodgeball teams in her gym class. She thinks to herself, "Jeez, no one wants me for their team. I'm terrible at dodgeball. In fact, I'm terrible at all sports. No matter how much I work out or how hard I try, I'm never going to get any better." What are the three attribution dimensions that comprise explanatory style? Describe where Carla falls on these three dimensions. How do you know? Overall, what is Carla's explanatory style?

2. Can you think of a time when you committed the fundamental attribution error? What happened? Why do you think you made this mistake?

3. Curtis, a busy guy with good taste in music, has a friend who raves about a new band. Curtis wants to know whether it's worth his time to listen: Is the band actually awesome (an external attribution) or is his friend not all that discerning about music (an internal attribution)? Curtis recalls that his friend raves about the band every time he listens to them, none of their other friends rave about the band, and his friend raves about every band. Describe the three components of the covariation principle, and explain how each one applies in this scenario. Based on this information, what should Curtis conclude? Is the band awesome or does his friend simply love all music?

4. Imagine you are single and decide to go to a speed-dating event, in which you will have a series of 5-minute dates with many people. You really care about getting to know what your dates are like. Given this situation, which types of behaviors would strongly signal the type of person your date is? What types of behaviors might you discount, that is, chalk up to the demands of the speed-dating situation? Apply the augmentation and discounting principles in your analysis.

5. Can you think of other aspects of one's identity (besides culture, religion, or social class) that might influence the types of attributions one makes? How so?

6. Mary, Travis, and Hussein stand to receive their awards at the National Spelling Bee. Mary, who won first place, receives her trophy with a smile on her face. The second-place winner, Travis, covers his face with his hands and sobs. Eventually, he politely receives his award despite the tears. When Hussein's name is called for the third-place prize, he grins and excitedly claims his award. Using what you learned in this chapter, explain Mary, Travis, and Hussein's (perhaps surprising) reactions to their respective prizes.

THE ANSWER GUIDELINES FOR THE THINK ABOUT IT QUESTIONS CAN BE FOUND AT THE BACK OF THE BOOK . . .

Emotion

One day in the Nazi concentration camp at Auschwitz, prisoners were clearing a gas chamber of corpses. As they disposed of the stiffening bodies, they discovered a 16-year-old girl, breathing and very much alive. A camp medical doctor, Miklos Nyiszli, was notified; he and his staff were immediately overwhelmed by feelings of sympathy for the girl. Instinctively, they offered her a coat to keep her warm. They fed her warm broth and tea. They plotted ways to help her escape and settled on the idea of hiding her among the German women working in the camp, hoping she might somehow eventually find her freedom. Nyiszli pitched this idea to the commandant at the concentration camp, but the officer was unmoved. He quickly disposed of the girl using his method of choice—she was shot in the back of the neck.

George Orwell, the English critic and novelist, also experienced such a "sympathy breakthrough" during his time in combat. Orwell fought against the fascists in the Spanish Civil War in the 1930s. One day in Spain, Orwell had a fascist in his sight. With gun loaded and aimed, he was poised to shoot his adversary. As the soldier raced by, panting, half dressed, clutching his pants with his hand and stumbling, Orwell simply could not pull the trigger. Later he reflected, "I did not shoot partly because of the detail of the trousers. I had come to shoot 'Fascists'; but a man who is holding up his trousers isn't a 'Fascist', he is visibly a fellow creature, similar to yourself, and you don't feel like shooting him" (quoted in Glover, 1999, p. 53).

George Orwell
Best known for the novels *Animal Farm* and *Nineteen Eighty-Four*, Orwell fought Fascists in the Spanish Civil War in the 1930s.

"We all know that emotions are useless and bad for our peace of mind and our blood pressure."

—B. F. SKINNER

Sympathy breakthroughs like the ones Nyiszli and Orwell experienced are surprisingly common during combat. Often in face-to-face encounters with adversaries, soldiers who have been trained to kill will abandon that mind-set and ignore the orders of superiors. They refuse to kill; or, having killed, they collapse in sorrow at the harm they have caused (Marshall, 1947).

We can learn many lessons from such sympathy breakthroughs. One is that sympathy is a powerful trigger of altruistic behavior (a theme we'll explore in Chapter 14). A more general lesson is that emotions are important guides for thoughts and behaviors. Emotions have a powerful influence on what people perceive, how they reason, what they value, what they deem right and wrong. As the dramatic examples above illustrate, soldiers sometimes radically shift how they think about combat; they no longer view their adversaries as enemies, but as fellow human beings. Once set in motion, emotions trigger action, impelling people to respond to specific goals, threats, and opportunities in the environment. Sympathy breakthroughs have led soldiers to shift from a fight-or-flight pattern of action to one of altruism and concern.

The philosopher Jean Paul Sartre called these effects of emotions "magical transformations." What do you think he meant? Here's one possibility. Any situation can be construed in multiple ways, thereby eliciting a variety of behaviors. Emotions are magical transformations in that they powerfully and immediately steer people to specific ways of thinking and acting. For over 2,000 years, philosophers and other keen observers of the human condition have been wary of the emotions, seeing them as an enemy of reason and disruptive of harmonious social bonds (Oatley, 2004). Social psychologists recognize a different perspective, having demonstrated that although emotions can indeed alter sound judgment and make people behave irrationally, they can also aid reason and are vital to healthy relationships and the effective pursuit of a good life.

This chapter explores several enduring questions: How are emotions universal, and how do they vary across cultures? What roles do emotions play in social relationships? How do emotions influence reasoning? And finally, what is happiness? Before tackling these questions, we'll first attempt to define emotion—not a simple task.

Characterizing Emotion

Light is something everybody knows about, but it's exceptionally hard to define. The same is true of emotions. When you experience cold feet before making a speech in class, what is that experience of fear like? What happens when a stranger's anonymous kindness moves you to tears? How would you characterize sympathy, an emotion so pivotal to Nyiszli's and Orwell's responses to their wartime enemies? What are emotions, and how do they differ from more general feelings of, say, well-being or despair?

Emotions can be defined as brief, specific, multidimensional responses to challenges or opportunities that are important to our goals, especially our social goals. Usually an emotion lasts for seconds or minutes, not hours or days. Facial expressions of emotion typically last for 1–5 seconds (Ekman, 1992). Many physiological responses that accompany emotion—sweaty palms, blushing, increased

emotion A brief, specific response, both psychological and physiological, that helps people meet goals, including social goals.

blood pressure—last dozens of seconds or minutes. In contrast, *moods*, such as feeling irritable or blue, can last for hours and even days. Emotional disorders, including depression and generalized anxiety, last for weeks or months or years.

Emotions are also specific: we have feelings about specific people and events—the politician whose rhetoric infuriates you, the kind friend whose act of generosity fills you with gratitude, the ill relative whose demise saddens you. Philosophers call the focus of an emotional experience its "intentional object." When you're angry, for instance, you usually have a very clear sense of what you're angry about (like the embarrassing story your dad told your friends about how you danced in fifth grade).

Emotions also help us achieve our social goals, in terms of responding to specific challenges and opportunities involving interactions with other people (DeSteno & Salovey, 1996; Frijda & Mesquita, 1994; Keltner & Haidt, 1999; McCullough, Kilpatrick, Emmons, & Larson, 2001; Oatley & Jenkins, 1992; Parrott, 2001; Salovey & Rodin, 1989; Salovey & Rothman, 1991; Tiedens & Leach, 2004). Gratitude motivates us to reward others for their generosity. Guilt prompts us to make amends when we have harmed someone. Anger impels us to right social wrongs and restore justice. Of course, not every episode of emotion has positive social results; some outbursts of anger, for example, produce undesirable outcomes. (If, in anger, you make sarcastic comments to a traffic cop, you might find yourself much worse off than if you'd stifled that particular emotion.) But in general, emotions motivate and guide appropriate goal-directed behavior that supports stronger and smoother social relationships.

The Components of Emotion

Having differentiated emotions from other affective states such as moods, let's consider how to distinguish different emotions from one another. How might the sympathy Orwell felt toward the enemy in Spain differ from sadness or fear? How do we distinguish between anger and disgust, or surprise and awe? Psychologists do so by studying five components of emotion.

The first component is what gives rise to emotions initially—namely, an **appraisal process**, consisting of patterns of construal by which we evaluate events and objects in our environment according to their relation to our current goals (Lazarus, 1991; Smith & Ellsworth, 1985). Fast, automatic appraisals of whether an event is consistent or inconsistent with our goals lead to general pleasant or unpleasant feelings (LeDoux, 1993; Mischel & Shoda, 1995; Zajonc, 1980). More deliberative appraisals about what caused an event, who is responsible for it, whether it is fair, and what might be done about it—appraisals of causality, responsibility, fairness, and likely courses of action—transform initial pleasant or unpleasant feelings into more specific emotions, such as fear, anger, pride, gratitude, or sympathy (Barrett, 2006; Lazarus, 1991; Roseman, 1991; Russell, 2003; Smith & Ellsworth, 1985). Every emotion involves a distinct appraisal process.

Appraisal processes initiate emotions. Once under way, emotions involve distinct *physiological responses*, such as the blush response of embarrassment or goosebumps that accompany awe, as well as activation of neurotransmitter systems in the brain (Davidson, Pizzagalli, Nitzschke, & Kalin, 2003). Emotions also involve *expressive behavior*, the focus of the next section, and *subjective feelings*, the qualities that define what the experience of a particular emotion is like,

appraisal process A component of emotion; patterns of construal for evaluating events and objects in the environment based on their relation to current goals.

described with words, metaphors, and narratives (Barrett, Mesquita, Ochsner, & Gross, 2007; Oatley, 2003; Niedenthal, 2008; Wilson & Gilbert, 2008).

Perhaps most importantly, emotions move us toward specific actions and behaviors (Frijda, 1986). *Action tendencies* constitute the fifth component of emotion. Without emotions, we would be inactive, lost in thought. Consider what researchers have learned about anger. Appraisals of unfairness trigger experiences of anger (Smith & Ellsworth, 1985), a response observed even in our primate relatives. In one study, Sarah Brosnan and Frans de Waal had two capuchin monkeys sit next to each other and trade tokens with an experimenter in exchange for food (Brosnan & de Waal, 2003). When both received cucumbers from the experimenter, they performed the task calmly. However, when one of the two received a more desirable grape, nearly half the monkeys still receiving bland cucumbers refused to exchange tokens for food, and many threw their cucumbers in angry protest.

Feelings of anger can motivate behavior that helps restore justice. For example, in studies examining protestors demonstrating against low wages, unemployment, discrimination, and police violence, anger consistently predicts which individuals will participate in collective efforts, such as going to a march or signing a petition (van Zomoren, Postmes, & Spears, 2008). Research shows that anger activates the left frontal lobes of the brain, leading to acts that bring about social change (Harmon-Jones, Sigelman, Bohlig, & Harmon-Jones, 2003). Thus, although anger raises the blood pressure, makes us see the proverbial red, and can lead to antisocial behavior, it can also prompt behaviors that restore justice when we perceive the world to be unfair.

With the five components of emotion in mind, let's return to the sympathy breakthroughs of Nyiszli and Orwell, and consider what researchers have learned about the emotion—sympathy—that led to their prosocial acts (Goetz, Keltner, & Simon-Thomas, 2010). Appraisals of harm, need, and vulnerability trigger experiences of sympathy, and activation in old regions of the brain (the

Emotions and Actions

(A) This angry-looking monkey shows a classic threat display, signaling aggressive intentions. (B) This demonstrator shows a similar pattern of expressive behavior, signaling anger at the injustice she is protesting.

periaqueductal gray), as well as a bundle of nerves running through the body known as the vagus nerve, support caregiving behavior. We express sympathy through verbal expressions of concern, soothing vocalizations, and comforting touch. The experience of sympathy is accompanied by an urge to help. In addition, there are shifts in how we construe the social environment; distinctions between "us and them" or "Democrat and Republican" diminish, and are replaced by a heightened awareness of our shared humanity with others (Oveis, Horberg, & Keltner, 2010). Perhaps most critically, sympathy is often what inspires us to take action, to reduce the suffering of others.

"Nothing's either good or bad but thinking makes it so."
—WILLIAM SHAKESPEARE,
HAMLET

🕐 LOOKING BACK

Emotions are brief, specific, multidimensional experiences that help people meet their (often social) goals. Emotions involve five components: the appraisal process, physiological responses, expressive behavior, subjective feelings, and action tendencies. Emotions guide our behavior and lead to action, enabling us to respond to the threats and opportunities we perceive in the environment.

Emotional Expression: Universal and Culturally Specific

An evolutionary approach to emotion proposes that the components of emotion—an appraisal process, physiological responses, expressive behavior, subjective feelings, and action tendencies—enable adaptive reactions to survival-related threats and opportunities all people face (Ekman, 1992; Nesse, 1990; Öhman, 1986; Tooby & Cosmides, 1992). Thus, we might expect that these components would be universal.

In contrast, a cultural approach assumes that emotions are strongly influenced by the values, roles, institutions, and socialization practices that vary across cultures (Ellsworth, 1994; Markus & Kitayama, 1991; Mesquita, 2003; Oatley, 1993). As a result, people in different cultures might be expected to express their emotions in very different ways.

Scientific studies of emotional expression reveal support for both perspectives. The ways we express emotions are both universal and subject to striking cultural differences.

Darwin and Emotional Expression

The science of emotional expression begins with the observations of Charles Darwin, in his own musings about where emotions come from. After his travels aboard the HMS *Beagle*, Darwin published *The Expression of Emotions in Man and Animals* in 1872, detailing his evolutionary perspective on emotional expression. In making his case, Darwin proposed what he called the "principle of serviceable associated habits," which maintains that the expressions of human emotion we observe today derive from actions that proved useful in our evolutionary past. For example, the observable signs of anger—the furrowed brow and display of teeth, the tightened posture and clenched fists, the fierce growl—are vestiges of

BOX 6.1

Not So Fast:
Critical Thinking about
What Micro-Analyses of Behavior Can Reveal

The English writer George Eliot, author of *Middlemarch*, had this to say about smiling: "Wear a smile and have friends." Parents often urge their children to smile when out in public, and there's no shortage of aphorisms advising us to smile to win friends and enjoy life. But is the smile necessarily a signal of positive emotion? Paul Ekman suggests not (1993). Based on his years of study of human emotion and facial anatomy, Ekman differentiates between felt and false smiles. Felt smiles accompany our experience of positive emotions such as joy, mirth, and affection, and are indeed catalysts of good feeling in others and friendship. False smiles, by contrast, rely on the upturn of the lip corners to hide negative emotions, and have little to do with positive emotion or an interest in being friends. We show a false smile, for example, when we feel physical pain, or mild disgust at a friend's bragging, or frustration at a politician who's behaving arrogantly, or sarcastic disapproval of someone to whom we feel superior.

How do we distinguish between felt and false smiles? Relying on language alone probably won't work. We only have a limited number of words—*smirk* or *grin* or *beam*—that differentiate different kinds of smiles. To think critically about how to detect felt and false smiles, we need to turn to an early anatomical analysis of different smiles found in *The Mechanism of Human Facial Expression*, published in 1862 by the French physician Duchenne de Boulogne. In this book, Duchenne detailed the results of his research on stimulating the facial muscles with electrical currents.

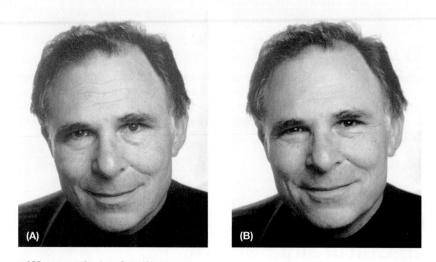

Different Kinds of Smiles
Paul Ekman demonstrates (A) a polite, non-Duchenne smile (false smile) and (B) a Duchenne, or enjoyment, smile (felt smile).

He identified the actions of two muscles: the zygomaticus major, which pulls the lip corners upward, and the orbicularis oculi, which surrounds the eye and when contracting, causes crow's-feet to form, the upper cheek to raise, and a pouch to form under the lower eyelid.

Based on this anatomical distinction, Ekman coined the term the *Duchenne smile* for the smile that involves the action of the orbicularis oculi and can be thought of as a felt smile. Duchenne smiles tend to last 1–5 seconds, and the lip corners turn up equally on both sides (Frank, Ekman, & Friesen, 1993). They are usually associated with activity in the left anterior portion of the brain, whereas non-Duchenne smiles (false smiles) are associated with activity in the right anterior portion of the brain (Ekman & Davidson, 1993; Ekman, Davidson, & Friesen, 1990).

This description is consistent with studies demonstrating that positive emotions are more strongly associated with activation in the left side of the brain (Davidson et al., 2003). When people are feeling positive emotions, they tend to display Duchenne smiles; when feeling negative emotions, they are more likely to show non-Duchenne smiles (Hess, Banse, & Kappas, 1995; Keltner & Bonanno, 1997; Ruch, 1995). Therefore, to determine whether someone is showing a felt or false smile, and is indeed wanting to be our friend, we can look for those crow's-feet, the lower eyelid pouches, the raised cheek, and the symmetrical raising of the lip corners.

threat displays and attack behavior observed in our mammalian relatives that were essential in adversarial encounters.

Darwin's detailed analysis generated three hypotheses about emotional expression. First, it posits universality. Darwin reasoned that because all humans have used the same 30–40 facial muscles to communicate similar emotions in our evolutionary past, people in all cultures should communicate and perceive emotion in a similar fashion. Second, Darwin reasoned that because humans share an evolutionary history with other mammals, most recently primates, our emotionally expressive behaviors should resemble those of other species. In support of this thesis, Darwin drew fascinating parallels between human emotion and the behaviors of animals in the London Zoo, as well as those of his dogs at home. Third, Darwin argued that blind individuals, lacking the rich visual input a culture provides related to how to display emotion, will still show expressions similar to those of sighted people because the tendency to express emotions in specific ways has been encoded by evolutionary processes.

The Universality of Facial Expression

Interested in the universality of emotional expression, Darwin asked British missionaries living in other cultures whether they had observed expressions not seen in contemporary Victorian England. The missionaries could come up with no such expressions. That evidence is anecdotal, but some 100 years later, the question of universality was pursued more systematically by Paul Ekman and Wallace Friesen, as well as Carroll Izard (Ekman, Sorenson, & Friesen, 1969; Izard, 1971; Tomkins, 1962, 1963).

Cross-Cultural Research on Emotional Expression To test Darwin's universality hypothesis, Ekman and Friesen took more than 3,000 photographs of people trained in nonverbal expression, such as actors, as they portrayed anger, disgust, fear, happiness, sadness, and surprise according to Darwin's descriptions of these expressions (Ekman et al., 1969). They then presented photos of these expressions to people in Japan, Brazil, Argentina, Chile, and the United States, who selected from six emotion terms the one that best matched the feeling the person appeared to be showing in each photo. Across these five cultures, accuracy rates were typically 70–90 percent for the six emotions. If participants had been merely guessing (which they would have been if they couldn't read the emotions with any accuracy), they would have succeeded only 6.0–16.7 percent of the time.

Critics of the Ekman and Friesen study were unconvinced. They noted a fundamental flaw in this study: the participants had all been exposed to Western media, and therefore might have learned how to identify the expressions through that exposure.

The investigators thus faced a stiff challenge: to find a culture that had little or no exposure to Westerners or to Western media. To accomplish this goal, Ekman traveled to Papua New Guinea to study the Fore (pronounced *FOR-ay*), an isolated hill tribe living in preindustrial, hunter-gatherer-like conditions. The Fore who participated in Ekman's study had seen no movies or magazines, did not speak English or pidgin (a combination of English and a native language), had never lived in Western settlements, and had never worked for Westerners. After getting approval for his study from the local witch doctor, Ekman devised

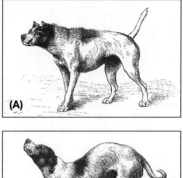

Signaling Intentions
Darwin believed animals signal their intentions through behavioral displays. (A) This dog is signaling his hostile intentions toward another dog. (B) This dog signals submission to another dog. Remind you of any other species? Our own, for instance?

Charles Darwin
In addition to developing the theory of evolution, Darwin studied emotional expressions in humans and nonhuman species. He sought to document that human emotional expressions have parallels in other species and are universal to people of all cultures.

Figure 6.1

Recognizing Facial Expressions of Emotion

Groups of Americans and Fore tribe members in New Guinea both reliably judged the emotions expressed in these photos at higher rates of accuracy than expected by chance. This study demonstrated that facial expressions of emotion have been shaped by evolution and are universal.

SOURCE: Adapted from Ekman, Sorenson, & Friesen, 1969.

an emotion-appropriate story for each of the six emotions. For example, the sadness story was: "The person's child had died, and he felt sad." For adult participants, he presented photos of three different expressions, along with a story that matched one of the expressions, and asked them to match the story to the appropriate expression (Ekman & Friesen, 1971). Here chance guessing would have yielded an accuracy rate of 33 percent. Children in the study had to select from two photos to match an expression to a story (in this case chance guessing would be 50 percent). The Fore adults achieved accuracy rates ranging from 68 to 92 percent in judging the six emotions; the children achieved accuracy rates ranging from 81 to 98 percent.

In another task, Ekman videotaped the posed expressions of Fore participants as they imagined being the person in the six emotion-specific stories, then presented these clips to American college students, who selected from six emotion terms the one that best matched the Fore's pose (**Figure 6.1**). The students labeled the posed expressions of the Fore with above-chance accuracy, with the exception of fear. Subsequent studies have consistently found that people from cultures that differ in religion, political structure, economic development, and independence versus interdependence nevertheless agree a great deal in how they label the photos depicting happiness, surprise, sadness, anger, disgust, and fear (Ekman, 1984, 1993; Elfenbein & Ambady, 2002, 2003; Izard, 1971, 1994).

Emotional Expression in Other Animals Darwin's second claim—that our emotional behaviors and expressions resemble those of our mammalian relatives—has helped explain their origins in humans. For example, chimps show threat displays and emit whimpers that are remarkably similar to our own displays of anger and sadness. When affiliating in a friendly fashion, nonhuman primates show the "silent bared-teeth display" that resembles our smile, and when playing and wrestling, they exhibit the "relaxed open-mouth display," the predecessor to the human laugh (Preuschoft, 1992).

Six Universal Facial Expressions of Emotion

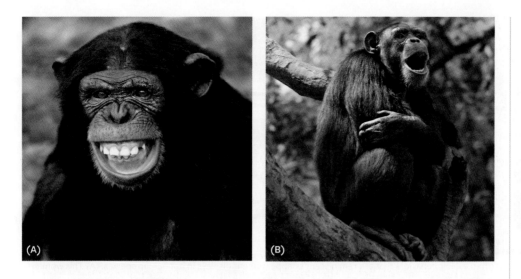

Origins of Our Emotional Expressions
These chimpanzees demonstrate two facial expressions that resemble those of humans. (A) The silent bared-teeth display, like a smile. (B) The relaxed open-mouth display, like a laugh.

Interest in the parallels between human and nonhuman expression has helped reveal why we express embarrassment as we do. Participants in various research studies have been led to experience embarrassment in various ways, such as by watching themselves on videotape sing the "Star-Spangled Banner" or having to suck on pacifiers in front of friends. When feeling embarrassed, people shift their gaze down, smile in a self-conscious way, move their heads down and to the side thus exposing their necks, and often touch their face or shrug their shoulders (Harris, 2001; Keltner, 1995). Why do we express embarrassment with this specific pattern of behavior? Cross-species comparisons reveal that our expression of embarrassment resembles appeasement displays in other mammals, often resulting in the effect of short-circuiting conflict and triggering affiliation (Keltner & Buswell, 1997).

In humans, embarrassment signals remorse for social transgressions, prompting forgiveness and reconciliation after someone has violated a social norm (Miller, 1992, 1996; Miller & Leary, 1992; Miller & Tangney, 1994; Parrott & Smith, 1991). For example, one study found that when strangers encounter someone who shows embarrassment or blushes visibly, as opposed to displaying no emotion or other emotions such as pride, they trust that stranger more and think he or she has a more upstanding character (van Dijk, de Jong, & Peters, 2009). Another study found that people will even give more lottery tickets to such an individual, thereby increasing his or her chances of winning a cash prize (Feinberg, Willer, & Keltner, 2012).

Well-timed displays of embarrassment can serve people well. Early in his presidency, John F. Kennedy approved a disastrous attempt to overthrow Cuban dictator Fidel Castro. He immediately took public ownership of the failure and apologized for his poor leadership. President Kennedy's approval ratings, already high, spiked following his apology and his honest and open signs of embarrassment.

The social benefits of embarrassment cast a new light on many everyday social phenomena. Think of how often you've embarrassed yourself by telling self-deprecating stories about something foolish you did when flirting or first getting

Social Benefits of Embarrassment
President Kennedy shows classic signs of embarrassment and remorse, including the head movements, downward gaze, and nervous face touching. Although conveying regret, this display causes others to trust the individual more.

Embarrassment, Appeasement, and Maintaining Social Bonds

To maintain harmonious social relations, humans often exhibit behaviors that are reminiscent of appeasement displays in nonhuman species. (A) This woman shows the typical elements of an embarrassment display—downward gaze, head movements down and to the side, a compressed smile, and face touching—that trigger others to forgive. (B) The chimp in the middle directs many similar submissive behaviors seen in human embarrassment, including the downward head movements, gaze aversion, and movements in the mouth, to the dominant chimp on the right, as a way to avoid conflict. Photograph by Frans de Waal.

to know someone you like. Now you can understand why: it's an opportunity to express embarrassment, thereby eliciting trust and positive feeling in others. When defendants first appear in a courtroom, their lawyers are concerned about the degree to which they show remorse, a self-conscious emotion related to embarrassment. (Some defendants are better at it than others. The talented actor Mark Wahlberg was an admitted delinquent who said the best acting he ever did was in juvenile court!) Defendants who express remorse are judged less harshly.

Emotional Expression among the Blind Recent studies of pride and shame bring together Darwin's ideas about universality, cross-species similarities, and the expressions of emotion by those born without eyesight. Pride is the feeling associated with gaining status through socially valued actions. The emotion is reliably signaled with dominance-related behaviors seen in other mammals: expansive posture, chest expansion, head movements up and back, upward arm thrusts (Tracy & Robins, 2004). When Jessica Tracy and Richard Robins traveled to Burkina Faso, in Africa, they found that a remote tribe there could readily identify displays of pride from static photos (Tracy & Robins, 2007).

Studies of blind individuals have shown that their expressions of emotion are remarkably similar to those of sighted people. Tracy and Matsumoto (2008) analyzed the emotional expressions of sighted and blind Olympic athletes from 37 countries just after they had either won or lost a judo competition. Congenitally blind athletes, who made up part of the sample, have received no visual input from their culture about how to express emotion nonverbally. Sure enough, after victory, both sighted and blind athletes, including those blind from birth, expressed pride with smiles and by tilting their heads back, expanding their chest, and raising their arms in the air. After losing, both groups of athletes dropped their heads and slumped their shoulders in shame.

Cultural Specificity of Emotional Expression

When anthropologists began writing about the emotional lives of people in different cultures, they noticed cultural variations in emotional expressions. In one well-known study, the Utku Inuit of Alaska (colloquially referred to as Eskimos) were never observed by visiting anthropologists to express anger (Briggs, 1960). Even when visiting Europeans stole their canoes or acted rudely, the Inuit showed no anger. How can we begin to understand such cultural variation in expression?

Culture and Emotion Accents One idea is that cultures develop **emotion accents**—highly stylized, culturally specific ways of expressing particular emotions (Elfenbein & Ambady, 2002). In a study conducted in India and the United States, for example, participants judged the two expressions of embarrassment shown in **Figure 6.2** (Haidt & Keltner, 1999). As you can see, members of both cultures were likely to interpret the expression on the left as embarrassment. But Indian participants also tended to see the tongue bite—an emotion accent in India—as embarrassment, whereas U.S. college students were bewildered by this display and saw little embarrassment in it.

Culture and Focal Emotions Cultures also seem to be defined by particular emotions. Tibet is a compassionate culture, Mexico a proud one, and Brazil an affectionate, flirtatious one. Batja Mesquita proposes that cultures vary in their

emotion accent A specific way people from different cultures express a particular emotion.

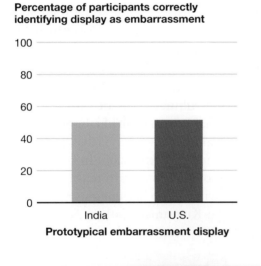

Percentage of participants correctly identifying display as embarrassment

Prototypical embarrassment display

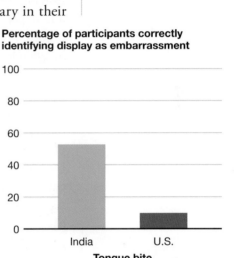

Percentage of participants correctly identifying display as embarrassment

Tongue bite

(A)   (B)

Figure 6.2
Universality and Cultural Variation in Emotional Expression
People in the United States and India agree in their judgments of (A) a typical embarrassment display, but only people in India recognize (B) the ritualized tongue bite as a display of embarrassment.

SOURCE: Adapted from Haidt & Keltner, 1999.

focal emotion An emotion that is especially common within a particular culture.

focal emotions, those that are relatively common in the everyday lives of the members of a culture, and are experienced and expressed with greater frequency and intensity (Mesquita, 2003). For example, in cultures that value honor, sexual slurs and insults to the family are highly charged events that trigger more anger than in cultures that don't prioritize honor (Rodriguez Mosquera, Fischer, & Manstead, 2000, 2004). Anger appears to be a more focal emotion in honor-based cultures.

Let's consider embarrassment and shame. Such emotions convey modesty and an appreciation of others' opinions—core concerns in interdependent cultures. Therefore, we might expect shame and embarrassment to be focal emotions in more interdependent cultures, and recent studies have confirmed these expectations. In China, a highly interdependent culture, there are at least 113 words to describe shame and embarrassment, far exceeding the 25 or so synonyms in the English language for these two words. This suggests that the self-conscious emotions are highly focal in the daily conversations of the Chinese (Li, Wang, & Fischer, 2004). The degree to which an emotion is focal is also manifested nonverbally. In the study of Olympic athletes we considered earlier, athletes from interdependent cultures, such as China and Japan, showed more intense head droops and shoulder shrugs of shame in response to losing than athletes from independent cultures, such as the United States (Tracy & Matsumoto, 2008).

Culture and Ideal Emotions Why do some emotions become focal in a particular culture? Jeanne Tsai and her colleagues have offered one answer in their *affect valuation theory* (Tsai, 2007; Tsai, Knutson, & Fung, 2006). They argue that emotions that promote important cultural ideals are valued and will tend to play a more prominent role in the social lives of individuals. For example, in the United States, excitement is greatly valued, because it enables people to pursue a cultural ideal of independent action and self-expression. In contrast, many East Asian cultures attach greater value to feelings of calmness and contentedness, because these emotions fold the individual into harmonious relationships (Kitayama, Karasawa, & Mesquita, 2004; Kitayama, Markus, & Kurokawa, 2000; Kitayama, Mesquita, & Karasawa, 2005; see also Mesquita, 2001; Mesquita & Karasawa, 2002).

These cultural differences in which emotions are most valued translate into striking variations in emotional behavior. Americans, for example, compared with East Asians, are more likely to participate in exciting but risky recreational practices (such as mountain biking); to advertise consumer products with intense smiles of excitement; to get addicted to excitement-enhancing drugs (cocaine); to express preferences for upbeat, exciting music rather than soothing, slower songs; and to read children's books that feature highly excited protagonists (Tsai, 2007). In responding to emotional stimuli, people from independent cultures are more likely to show intense smiles of excitement (Tsai & Levenson, 1997).

These descriptions of cultural variations are, of course, averages. You probably know (or may be) someone of East Asian ancestry who loves to bungee-jump, to listen to punk rock, and perhaps even to try "a little blow," as one notable American described his youthful experience with cocaine. And you probably also know someone of U.S. or European ancestry who'd rather read poetry or listen to Brahms than ride a mountain bike or go cliff diving. But these notable average differences in emotional behavior, Tsai maintains, derive from the value placed on excitement in the West. It's a value that leads people from many cultures to be bemused by American excitability. Indians, for example, sometimes refer affectionately to Americans as "dogs"—because they're always going "Wow, wow!"

It is striking, by the way, how certain East-West differences in the value placed on emotions like excitement and contentment correspond to emotional distinctions between the young and the old. Young people are more likely to pursue enjoyment through vigorous, exciting activities than their parents and grandparents, whose pursuit of happiness tends to take the form of quieter, calmer activities. This is presumably one of the things that inspired The Who's Pete Townshend to sing "I hope I die before I get old." He was almost certainly referring to the transition from a life of intensity and gusto to one of more sedate pleasures. But the research on happiness indicates that Townshend may have been unduly pessimistic about aging, as you'll learn in more detail in the last section of this chapter. Older people have a greater ability than the young to construe outcomes and events in ways that promote happiness (Carstensen, 2011; Carstensen et al., 2011; Charles & Carstensen, 2009). These differences between East and West, and young and old, come together in the value placed on youth in the West and the veneration of older adults in the East.

Culture and Display Rules Various cultures differ in their **display rules**—culturally specific rules that govern how, when, and to whom people express emotion (Ekman & Friesen, 1969). People can *de-intensify* their emotional expression—for example, suppressing the urge to laugh at a friend's fumbling on a romantic quest. People can *intensify* their expression—smiling widely upon taking the first bite of yet another culinary disaster concocted by a roommate, for instance. They can *mask* their negative emotions with a polite smile. And they can *neutralize* their expression with a poker face.

Here's one example of how culturally specific display rules shape emotional expression. In many Asian cultures, it's inappropriate to speak of personal enthusiasms; and in these cultures, people may also de-intensify their expressions of pleasure at personal success. In keeping with this thesis, across dozens of cultures, people from interdependent cultures report being more likely to suppress positive emotional expression than people from independent cultures, and to temper their experience of positive emotion with negative emotions (Matsumoto et al., 2008; Mesquita & Leu, 2007; Schimmack, Oishi, & Diener, 2002).

① LOOKING BACK

Darwin inspired dozens of studies finding that human emotional expression is universal, is seen in other species, and is evident in those blind from birth. At the same time, cultures have specific emotion accents, such as the tongue bite in India for embarrassment. Cultures vary in the emotions that are focal, having richer vocabularies and expressing them more in their nonverbal behavior. People of different cultures vary in the emotions they value. And cultures differ in how they regulate emotions with specific display rules, the rules governing how and when to express emotions.

Emotions and Social Relationships

Kirsten Lindsmith and Jack Robison are like many couples in their 20s, trying to navigate the complexities of a romantic relationship (Harmon, 2011). They haggle over the housework, struggle to communicate with each other, and fumble for words to describe their future together. Complicating their challenges is the fact

display rule A culturally specific rule that governs how, when, and to whom people express emotion.

Neutralizing Expressions
In accordance with the display rules of poker, this woman masks any feelings about her cards with a neutral poker face.

Emotions in Personal Relationships

Emotions often determine the quality and stability of romantic relationships. If this couple can maintain the humor and mirth and other positive emotions throughout their marriage, they will be less likely to divorce.

that both Kirsten and Jack have been diagnosed with Asperger's syndrome. People with Asperger's, who sometimes refer to themselves as Aspies, can reason like well-adjusted adults, and their language is untouched by their condition. What proves difficult for Aspies is emotion—expressing how they feel and understanding the feelings of others. Even the most straightforward interactions that involve emotion, such as giving each other constructive criticism or expressing encouragement, often escalate into conflict and misunderstanding.

Emotions are like a nonverbal language we use to carry out our social interactions (Eibl-Eibesfeldt, 1989; van Kleef, 2009). Our fleeting expressions of emotion are more than just momentary readouts of how we feel; they coordinate our interactions with others—whether soothing a distressed child, reconciling with a friend, or flirting with someone (**Box 6.2**). When we struggle to express our emotions, or fall short in knowing what others feel, our social interactions are undermined. In this section we follow the story of Kirsten and Jack to highlight the roles emotions play in social relationships.

Promoting Commitment

Young couples like Kirsten and Jack face a daunting challenge: to remain committed to each other while facing the daily struggles of romantic life. Economist Robert Frank refers to this as the "commitment problem": our long-term relationships require that we sacrifice for others and trust that others will do the same (Frank, 1988). When we consider how common divorce is (see Chapter 10), it's clear that this is no simple task.

Emotions solve the commitment problem in two ways. First, the expression of certain emotions signals our sincere commitment to others' well-being. For example, a timely expression of sympathy indicates we are concerned about the person's welfare, and will make sacrifices on his or her behalf if need be. Second, emotions can motivate us to put aside our own self interest and act in ways that prioritize the welfare of others. Feelings of guilt can be painful, but they often lead us to do things—apologize, make amends, sacrifice—that benefit others (Schaumberg & Flynn, 2012). Anger can be profoundly unpleasant, but it can motivate us to defend someone who has been wronged, even at great cost to ourselves (Fehr & Gachter, 2002).

It turns out there's a branch of our nervous system that actually fosters commitment in long-term relationships. A chemical called oxytocin is produced in the hypothalamus and released into the brain and bloodstream. In nonhuman species, oxytocin promotes commitment, or what is called pair bonding, the preference for one mate over desirable alternatives. This claim rests upon comparisons of prairie voles, which display pair bonding, and closely related montane voles, which do not (Carter, 1998; Insel, Young, & Zuoxin, 1997). When scientists give the promiscuous montane voles an injection of oxytocin, they stay close to a sexual partner, even when desirable voles are placed nearby (Williams, Insel, Harbaugh, & Carter, 1994).

In humans, oxytocin is associated with experiences and expressions of love, which promote commitment in long-term relationships (Keltner, Kogan, Piff, & Saturn, 2014). For example, when people express love nonverbally with Duchenne

BOX 6.2 **FOCUS ON *CULTURE***

Flirtation and the Five Kinds of Nonverbal Display

Flirting is the pattern of behavior—both verbal and nonverbal, conscious and at times nonconscious—that communicates our attraction to a potential romantic partner. Researchers Givens (1983) and Perper (1985) spent hundreds of hours in singles bars, charting the flirtatious behaviors that predict romantic encounters. They found that in the initial attention-getting phase, men roll their shoulders and engage in exaggerated motions to show off their physical size, raising their arms to let others admire their well-developed pecs and washboard abs. Women smile coyly, preen, flip their hair, and walk with arched back and swaying hips. In the recognition phase, the potential romantic partners lock their gaze on each other, expressing interest by raised eyebrows, singsong voices, and laughter. In the touching phase, the potential romantic partners move close, and they create opportunities to

Flirting
Can you tell from the woman's nonverbal language what she is trying to convey?

touch with provocative brushes of the arm, pats on the shoulder, or not-so-accidental bumps against one another. Finally, in the keeping-time phase, the potential partners express and assess each other's interest by lining up their actions. When they are mutually interested, their glances, gestures, and laughter mirror each other's, and their shoulders and faces are aligned.

What are the elements of the nonverbal language of flirtation, or of other interactions for that matter? Paul Ekman and Wallace Friesen (1969) have organized the rich language of nonverbal behavior, so evident in flirtation, into five categories. The first is *affective displays*, or emotional expressions. *Emblems* are nonverbal gestures that directly translate to words. Well-known emblems in English include the peace sign, the thumbs-up sign, the rubbing of one forefinger with the other to say "shame on you," and, during the Civil Rights Movement of the 1960s, the raised, clenched fist for Black Power. Emblems vary dramatically in their meaning in different cultures. For example, the gesture of forming a circle with the thumb and forefinger means "OK" in the United States, "money" in Japan, "zero" in France, and "let's have sex" in parts of Mediterranean Europe. When accepting an invitation to dinner in Greece, think carefully about whether you want to make this gesture.

Illustrators are nonverbal behaviors we use to make our speech vivid, engaging, and easy to visualize. We rotate our hands in the air and use dramatic fist shakes to indicate the power of our convictions. We raise our eyebrows to give emphasis to important words or phrases.

Black Power
The year 1968 will long be remembered as a time of civil unrest, as marches and gatherings in cities around the world protested against the Vietnam War, the deaths of Martin Luther King, Jr. and Robert Kennedy, and for civil rights. The Olympics in Mexico City that year will also be remembered for the student protests against an oppressive government, which ended in soldiers killing dozens of students at a march. In this photo taken from those summer Olympics, medal-winning American sprinters Tommie Smith and John Carlos raise their fists and display the emblem for Black Power.

Regulators are nonverbal expressions we use to coordinate conversation. We look at people to whom we want to speak. We look away and turn our bodies away from those we wish would stop speaking.

Finally, there are *self-adaptors*—the nervous, seemingly random behaviors we engage in when tense, as if to release nervous energy. We touch our nose, jiggle our legs, and rub our chin.

The Effect of Oxytocin on Commitment
Research demonstrating that oxytocin promotes commitment and love might have had something to do with the development of the new perfume Pheromax, whose selling feature is the oxytocin it includes in its chemical makeup.

(felt) smiles, open-handed gestures, and eye contact, their oxytocin levels rise. The same is true when people receive affectionate touches from another person. When couples kiss, men enjoy a rise in oxytocin levels. Sex also leads to a boost in oxytocin. In light of these findings, you might wonder whether oxytocin might be used as a therapy for struggling romantic couples, to heighten their love and commitment to one another. While that has not happened, one experiment did find that couples solved their conflicts more constructively after having inhaled oxytocin in a nasal spray, compared to inhaling a neutral solution (Ditzen et al., 2009).

Motivating Coordinated Action

Kirsten and Jack struggle to communicate emotion. Their voices can lack emotional intonation. Their faces are often expressionless. Kirsten doesn't like to be caressed. Jack is overwhelmed by the sweaty feeling of holding Kirsten's hand. Their interactions with each other are often missing what emotional expressions can provide: timely social rewards for other people's actions. Before infants can tell their parents what they like and don't like, they rely on their smiles, coos, and laughs to express delight to their parents for things they have done that are pleasing. The same is true in our adult social lives: smiles, laughs, warm pats on the back, and interested vocalizations are ways we express our approval of what others are doing (van Kleef, 2009).

Let's develop this idea that emotions coordinate interactions by examining another modality of expression: touch. With a deftly placed touch we can encourage people or dissuade them from inappropriate behavior. And we can communicate emotions such as gratitude and love that reward others for the actions we find desirable. In one study demonstrating this idea, a toucher and a touchee sat at a table with a black curtain between them, preventing all communication between the two participants other than touch (Hertenstein, Keltner, App, Bulleit, & Jaskolka, 2006). The toucher attempted to convey different emotions by making contact with the touchee for 1 second on the forearm. Upon being touched, the touchee selected which emotion had been communicated from a list of emotion terms. As you can see in **Figure 6.3**, participants could

Figure 6.3
Communicating Emotion through Touch
With a brief touch to the forearm, participants in this study could reliably communicate different emotions to a stranger.

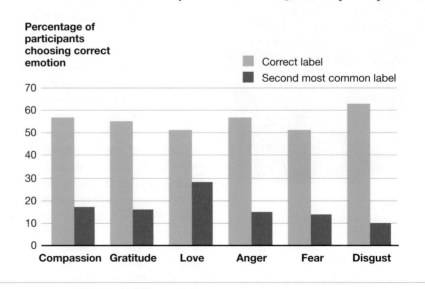

SOURCE: Adapted from Hertenstein et al., 2006.

reliably communicate love, sympathy, and gratitude with brief tactile contact, all emotions that convey commitment and provide rewarding experiences to others.

Other research reveals how the right kind of touch can prompt people to act in collaborative fashion. In one study, teachers touched some students in a friendly fashion and didn't touch others (Guéguen, 2004). Students who were touched were much more likely to go to the blackboard to solve a difficult problem the teacher had assigned. Touch may also help sports teams perform more collaboratively and efficiently. Michael Kraus and his colleagues coded all the touches—high fives, fist bumps, head slaps, and bear hugs—that basketball teammates in the NBA engaged in during one game at the beginning of the 2008 season (Kraus, Huang, & Keltner, 2010). Each player on average touched his teammates for only about 2 seconds during the game. Teams who touched more early in the season played better later in the season, even when controlling for how well the team was playing in the game in which the touch was coded, how much money the players were making, and the preseason expectations of the team.

Touch and Cooperation on the Basketball Court
Athletic teams in which teammates touch each other more play better. In 2000, the USA basketball team celebrated the Olympic gold medal with many kinds of touch.

Knowing Our Place in Groups

Kirsten and Jack, like many Aspies, see themselves as social outcasts. They feel awkward at parties and have little interest in joining in with others. Their emotional difficulties dampen their involvement with others because emotions are central to our affiliative tendencies. Emotions motivate us to join groups. They cause us to be inspired by other group members and leaders, and they lead us to protest on behalf of the group when injustices arise.

Emotions also help us know our place, or status, within social groups. Status hierarchies are seen in all mammalian species, and are surprisingly common in our own social lives. Join just about any kind of group—sorority or fraternity, a political or recreational group, or a team—and you'll quickly find that you have a rank, or position, within that group. In surprising ways, we, like other mammals, find our social rank in groups in face-to-face emotional exchanges. Non-human species rely on nonverbal displays to establish their rank. Apes pound their chests, chimps show submissive displays, dogs snarl and raise their hair, stags lock their horns.

People rely heavily on emotional expressions to signal their status in hierarchies, and to know their place. For example, when we see people—both ordinary citizens and politicians—expressing anger as opposed to other negative emotions, we attribute higher status to them (Knutson, 1996; Tiedens, 2001). When negotiators express anger, they are more likely to get their way and prompt more subordinate behaviors in their counterparts (Sinaceur & Tiedens, 2006; Van Kleef, De Dreu, Pietroni, & Manstead, 2006). An old adage of trial lawyers states that when you have the law on your side, you should argue the law; when you have the facts on your side, you should argue the facts; and when you have neither on your side, you should pound the table!

"I brought out the meekness in others."

emotional intelligence (EQ) The ability to express, recognize, and use emotions well within social interactions.

Emotional Intelligence

In the most general sense, the struggles of Kirsten and Jack reflect a deficit in what Peter Salovey and John Mayer call emotional intelligence (Salovey & Mayer, 1990). **Emotional intelligence (EQ)** is defined by four skills: (1) the ability to accurately perceive others' emotions, (2) the ability to understand one's own emotions, (3) the ability to use current feelings to aid in making good decisions, and (4) the ability to manage one's emotions in ways that fit the current situation. In his best-selling book *Emotional Intelligence*, Daniel Goleman made the case that EQ is as important as IQ in predicting success at work and in our personal lives (Goleman, 1995).

How do scientists measure EQ? In an emotion recognition test, people must label emotional expressions with appropriate emotion words. To give you a feel for this kind of test, we'd like you to take our own EQ test shown in **Figure 6.4**. The 10 drawings capture emotions of interest to Darwin in his *Expression of Emotions in Man and Animals*. Look at the words first, and then try to match each drawing with the appropriate word, as participants did in some of the Ekman studies discussed earlier.

Aspies like Kirsten and Jack tend to struggle on tests like these. In fact, Kirsten refers to her experiences of describing emotions as the "blue screen of death"—the screen one sees when a computer crashes. Describing her emotions,

EMOTION WORDS TO MATCH TO EMOTICONS

Admiration	Gratitude
Awe	Guilt
Coyness	Maternal Love
Disagreement	Sadness
Embarrassment	Sympathy

Answer: 1

Answer: 2

Answer: 3

Answer: 4

Answer: 5

Answer: 6

Answer: 7

Answer: 8

Answer: 9

Answer: 10

(Answers: 1. coy; 2. admiration; 3. gratitude; 4. disagreement; 5. sympathy; 6. awe; 7. embarrassment; 8. guilt; 9. maternal love; 10. sadness)

Figure 6.4
An EQ Test.
Illustrations by Matt Jones.

and perceiving the emotions of others, is hard, often painfully so. By contrast, people who score high on tests such as the one you just took (8 or more correct out of 10) we would call high-EQ individuals. At every stage of life, people with a high EQ tend to enjoy strong relationships (Brackett, Rivers, & Salovey, 2011; Mayer, Barsade, & Roberts, 2008). For example, high-EQ 5-year olds prove to be better adjusted socially, as rated by their teachers, 3 years later. High-EQ adolescents report having more friends. High-EQ young adults have more constructive and cooperative interactions with their romantic partners. In midlife, high-EQ adults enjoy greater respect and status at work and are perceived to be better workplace citizens.

> ### ↺ LOOKING BACK
>
> Emotions are a nonverbal language we use to carry out our social interactions. Emotions serve to communicate our commitment to others and build trust. Our emotional expressions, such as touch, serve as rewards in interactions, coordinating behavior between people. Emotions help us know our place within groups. The ability to know what others feel and to use emotions wisely is known as emotional intelligence, which predicts stronger social relationships of just about every kind.

Emotions and Social Cognition

Many of our most important decisions—what job to take, whom to marry, which neighborhood to live in—rely on gut feelings. Philosophers have long argued that this is not a desirable state of affairs. Our emotions, this line of thought goes, are less sophisticated than our logic and higher reasoning, and can lead to rash, misguided decisions (Haidt, 2001; Oatley, 2004). The metaphors we use to describe our feelings often reveal this belief about emotion: we speak of emotions as forms of insanity ("I'm madly in love") and disease ("I'm sick with envy") rather than forms of clarity and health. Perhaps we are better off when reason is the master of our passions.

It certainly is true that emotions bias how we see the world. But psychologists have made the case that this is often, and even typically, a good thing. Here's the argument. Any situation can be construed in a number of ways, and lead to various actions. Emotions prioritize the information we should focus on and factor into our actions, behavior, and decisions (Oatley & Johnson-Laird, 2011). Sometimes this leads to problematic biases; but often emotions guide perception, reasoning, and judgment in ways that enable quick and adaptive responses to challenges and opportunities in the environment. (Clore, Gasper, & Garvin, 2001; Clore & Parrott, 1991; Forgas, 1995, 2003; Isen, 1987; Lerner & Keltner, 2001; Loewenstein & Lerner, 2003; Rozin, 1996).

Emotions Influence Perception

After the death of a loved one, bereaved individuals experience recurrent feelings of profound sadness. For many months, and very often longer, their perceptions are tinged with the poignant qualities of loss: a piece of music may trigger recollections of a first date; a room or object in the house will prompt memories of the past; a falling leaf may elicit thoughts about the shortness of life. The idea

"Reason is and ought to be the slave of passion."

—DAVID HUME,
SCOTTISH PHILOSOPHER

that emotions influence perception is found in color-based metaphors portraying emotions as lenses through which we perceive our circumstances—sadness is blue, anger makes us see red, happiness has us looking at the world through rose-colored glasses.

To understand how emotions shape perception, let's return to an idea we considered earlier, that emotions involve distinct appraisals (Lazarus, 1991). When you're frightened, say from an encounter with a bear while camping, your mind is attuned to threat and uncertainty—core appraisals of fear—which bias what you perceive. You might take the crunching of twigs and branches nearby to be a sign of a bear's approach. You might sense the call of a coyote as closer than it really is. Your fear directs your attention to potential threats, triggered by your original encounter with the bear, preparing you to respond effectively.

We perceive events, in other words, in ways that are consistent with the emotions we're currently feeling (Oatley & Johnson-Laird, 2011). To provide evidence for this idea, researchers in one study had participants listen to uplifting music by Mozart or depressing music by Mahler (Niedenthal & Setterlund, 1994). Feeling either happy or sad, participants then completed a lexical decision task, judging whether strings of letters were words or nonwords. When feeling happy, participants were quicker to identify happy words (such as *delight*) than sad words (*weep*) or positive words unrelated to happiness (*calm*). When feeling sad, participants were quicker to identify the sad words than the happy words or the negative words unrelated to sadness (*injury*).

Emotions can also influence broader judgments, such as our sense that our circumstances are fair or safe, or unfair and dangerous. In one study conducted 2 months after the 9/11 terrorist attacks, participants were asked to write about either how the attacks had made them angry or how they had made them fearful. People primed to feel fear not only judged future terrorist attacks to be more likely than participants primed to feel anger, but they also reported that they themselves were more likely to be victimized by different threats, such as dying in a flu epidemic (Lerner & Gonzalez, 2005; Lerner, Gonzalez, Small, & Fischhoff, 2003).

It's important to note that the influences emotions have on perception can be disastrous. For example, we intuitively know our experiences of anger sometimes lower our threshold for seeing aggressive intentions in others, and lead to us to behave in adversarial ways that we may later regret. When we experience frustration at school or at work and return to our friends and loved ones at the end of the day, we may be quicker to perceive potential affront and hostile intent in others' actions. Here's a study that brings this notion to life (Baumann & DeSteno, 2010). Participants first wrote about a memory that made them feel anger or disgust or sadness. Then they briefly viewed a photograph of a man who was holding either a gun or a neutral object. Anger, but not disgust or sadness, made participants more likely to identify the neutral object as a gun, but not misidentify the gun as a neutral object. Anger primes us to perceive threat and aggression, a theme we'll continue to pursue to understand the causes of aggression in Chapter 13.

Anger and Perceived Threat
Police officers are known to experience high levels of stress, which interferes with sleep and can lead to irritability, frustration, and anger. There are some who believe that it is this anger that can lead police officers to misinterpret tense encounters with civilians, as in this photo, in erroneously hostile fashion, sometimes leading to disastrous results.

Emotions Influence Reasoning

People tend to assume that positive emotions are sources of simplistic or lazy thinking. Think of any highly creative person—such as Vincent van Gogh, Virginia Woolf, T. S. Eliot, or Charles Darwin—and you imagine their creative acts were produced during moments of struggle, tension, somberness, and even despair.

Alice Isen (1987, 1993) suggested that this view of creativity is wrong—that happiness instead prompts people to reason in ways that are flexible and creative. In her studies, Isen induced positive emotion in her participants with trivial events. She gave them little bags of candy, or they found a dime she had placed in their path. They watched amusing film clips. These subtle ways of making participants feel good produced striking changes in their reasoning. When given one word (such as *carpet*) and asked to generate a related word, people feeling positive emotions came up with more novel associations (*fresh* or *texture*) than people in a neutral state, who tended to produce more common responses (such as *rug*). People feeling positive categorized objects in more inclusive ways, rating fringe members of categories (like *cane* or *purse* as an example of clothing) as better members of that category than people in a neutral state, whose categories tended to be more narrowly defined. These effects of positive emotion have important social consequences, and studies have demonstrated this influence of emotions on reasoning. Negotiators in a positive mood are more likely to reach an optimal agreement that incorporates the interests of both sides, because positive moods allow opponents to think flexibly about the positions and interests of the other side (Carnevale & Isen, 1986; Forgas, 1998).

Extending Isen's findings, Barbara Fredrickson has advanced her **broaden-and-build hypothesis** regarding positive emotions (Fredrickson, 1998, 2001). Fredrickson proposes that positive emotions broaden our thoughts and actions to help us develop emotional and intellectual resources, such as empathy or the acquisition of knowledge. These increases in intellectual resources, in turn, build our social resources, such as friendships and social networks. Fredrickson and her colleagues have found that when people are led to experience positive emotions (such as by watching an amusing film clip), they broaden and build in many ways (Fredrickson, 2001; Waugh & Fredrickson, 2006). People who feel positive, for example, rate themselves as more similar to outgroup members, suggesting that they broaden their way of looking at themselves in relation to people from different groups. Within developing relationships, people feeling positive emotion see greater overlap between their self-concepts and the self-concepts of their friend or romantic partner.

Emotions Influence Moral Judgment

Near the end of legal trials, judges in the United States often caution jurors to put aside their emotions in deciding on the guilt or innocence of the defendant, sentence length, and punitive damages. In light of what we have learned thus far, this recommendation would seem to be at best unrealistic: emotions have powerful influences on perception and reasoning. This recommendation also ignores the essential role that emotions play in our moral judgments (Haidt, 2001). To begin to appreciate this role, read the following scenario, and decide whether you think the actions of the protagonists are right or wrong:

> Mark and Julie are brother and sister. They are traveling together in France on a summer vacation from college. One night they're staying alone in a cabin near the beach. They decide it would be interesting and fun if they tried making love. At the very least it would

broaden-and-build hypothesis The idea that positive emotions broaden thoughts and actions, helping people build social resources.

social intuitionist model of moral judgment The idea that people first have fast, emotional reactions to morally relevant events, and then rely on reason to arrive at a judgment of right or wrong.

moral foundations theory A theory proposing that there are five evolved, universal moral domains in which specific emotions guide moral judgments.

be a new experience for each of them. Julie was already taking birth control pills, but Mark uses a condom, too, just to be safe. They both enjoy making love, but they decide not to do it again. They keep that night as a special secret, which makes them feel even closer to each other.

When asked whether such actions are wrong, nearly all college students immediately say yes, typically with pronounced disgust (Haidt, 2001). They're in good company. All cultures around the world view incest as immoral (Brown, 1991). When pressed to explain why Julie and Mark's encounter is wrong, people may reason that it is dangerous to inbreed, only to remember that Julie and Mark are using contraception. They may contend that each would be hurt emotionally, but recall that it was clearly specified that Julie and Mark were not harmed in any way by the event. Eventually, when all of their possible reasons have been refuted, people may simply say, "I can't explain why, I just know this is wrong." Jonathan Haidt labels this kind of inarticulate but firm conviction that a given act is wrong (or right) "moral dumbfounding."

The way people respond to this kind of scenario illustrates the central thesis of Haidt's **social intuitionist model of moral judgment**, the idea that our moral judgments are the product of fast, emotional intuitions, like the gut feeling that incest is wrong, which then influence how we reason about the issue in question (Haidt, 2001). We feel our way to our moral judgments, in other words; we don't reason our way there. Our reasoning often serves merely to justify the moral conviction we arrived at intuitively or emotionally.

What, then, are our primarily emotion-based moral intuitions? In his related **moral foundations theory**, Haidt and his colleagues draw upon studies of different cultures, and evolutionary arguments about the "moral" responses observed in primates, to make a case for five moral domains, or foundations, characterized by different emotional reactions (Graham et al., 2013; Haidt, 2012; Haidt & Josephs, 2004). *Care/harm* centers on the suffering of others, especially vulnerable individuals. This moral intuition is triggered by signs of weakness and pain, and elicits emotions like sympathy, which we considered at the start of this chapter. *Fairness/cheating* focuses on concerns that others act in a just fashion, and is triggered by unfair acts—scamming, deceiving, failing to reciprocate a generous act, taking more than what one deserves. As we saw earlier, anger is the quintessential emotion associated with violations of fairness: it fuels our passion for justice. *Loyalty/betrayal* pertains to the commitments we make to groups. It's the foundation for strong, cohesive social collectives, and when violated, leads to experiences of emotions like group pride or rage. *Authority/subversion* is about finding one's place in social hierarchies. Our intuitions about authority and respect are founded, as we have seen, in experiences of emotions such as embarrassment, shame, fear, pride, and awe. Finally, *purity/degradation* centers on avoiding dangerous diseases and contaminants, and more metaphorically, socially impure ideas or actions. Disgust is the emotion at the core of such intuitions.

When we encounter people acting in ways that violate the rules within one of these five moral domains, specific emotions arise, which guide our initial judgments of right and wrong (Batson, Engel, & Fridell, 1999; Greene & Haidt, 2002; Haidt, 2003; Horberg, Oveis, & Keltner, 2011). After the initial gut feeling is underway, people rely on more deliberative processes—assessments of costs and benefits, causal attributions, considerations of prevailing social norms—to

BOX 6.3 **FOCUS ON *NEUROSCIENCE***

Trolleyology and the Moral Brain

Neuroscientist and philosopher Joshua Greene and his colleagues have provided one of the most compelling demonstrations of Haidt's social intuitionist model of moral judgment (Greene, Sommerville, Nystrom, Darley, & Cohen, 2001). They presented participants with morally compelling scenarios and asked for quick decisions about them. The participants worked through a variety of moral scenarios while their brains were scanned using fMRI. Participants judged different moral and nonmoral dilemmas in terms of whether they considered the action to be appropriate or not. Some of the moral dilemmas were likely to engage mainly impersonal, rational calculation, whereas others had more personal, emotional implications.

An example of the more impersonal type is the well-known "trolley dilemma," in which the participant imagines a runaway trolley headed for five people who will be killed if it proceeds on its present course. The only way to save them is to hit a switch that will turn the trolley onto another set of tracks, where, unfortunately, one person is located and will die as result of the switch. The participant is asked whether it is appropriate to hit the switch and save the five lives at the cost of the one. Most participants answer yes with only a little hesitation.

In the more emotionally evocative "footbridge dilemma," five people's lives are again threatened by a trolley, but in this case the participant is asked to imagine standing next to a very heavy stranger on a footbridge over the trolley tracks. The participant is told that pushing the stranger off the bridge and onto the tracks would kill the stranger, but his dead body would cause the train to veer off its course and thus would save the lives of the five other people. (The participant's own weight, it is explained, is insufficient to send the trolley off the track.) Is it appropriate to push the stranger off the footbridge? The same two options are presented in the trolley dilemma and the footbridge dilemma—one death or five—but in the footbridge dilemma, the action is highly visceral. The participant must imagine using his or her own hands to push the stranger to his death.

As participants responded to several different dilemmas of this sort in the Greene study, fMRI techniques indicated which parts of their brains were active. Consistent with Haidt's social intuitionist model, the personal moral dilemmas activated regions of the brain that previous research had found to be involved in emotional processing. The impersonal moral dilemmas and the nonmoral dilemmas activated brain regions associated with working memory, regions centrally involved in deliberative reasoning.

arrive at a final moral judgment of right or wrong. But emotions, according to Haidt, are the primary drivers of moral judgment (**Box 6.3**).

Moral foundations theory has inspired studies showing that experiences of disgust intensify judgments that "impure" acts are morally wrong. For example, people who feel high levels of disgust about a behavior—such as smoking or eating meat—strongly condemn the act as immoral (Rozin & Singh, 1999). Even when the original cause of the emotion has nothing to do with the action being judged, disgust still leads to more extreme moral judgments related to the purity/degradation domain. Researchers have found that people led to feel disgust by viewing images of gore are more likely to morally condemn impure acts, such as leaving sweat on an exercise machine (Horberg, Oveis, Keltner, & Cohen, 2009). Feeling disgusted by gross images has been found to heighten prejudice and bias toward groups that might be construed as "impure"—namely, gay men—but not other outgroups (Dasgupta, DeSteno, Williams, & Hunsinger, 2009). This incidental effect of disgust is so strong that people standing near a trash can sprayed with a putrid-smelling scent expressed more negative attitudes toward gay men (Inbar, Pizarro, & Bloom, 2012).

Moral foundations theory also helps us understand the so-called "culture wars" between political liberals and conservatives over issues like abortion, gun rights, same-sex marriage, and climate change. Survey research on tens of thousands of participants reveals that liberals and conservatives look at the world through different moral lenses. If you study **Figure 6.5**, you'll see that as people report more liberal political views, they attach increasing importance to the domains of harm and fairness. By contrast, as people endorse more conservative political views, they attach greater importance to the authority, loyalty, and purity domains. Stated differently, liberal morality is centered mainly on concerns about harm and fairness; conservative morality, it may surprise you (especially if you're liberal), is broader, involving concerns about harm and fairness, but also about authority, loyalty, and purity.

These differences in moral judgment help explain why liberals and conservatives diverge on important issues of our day. Consider the debate over climate change. Liberals are more likely than conservatives to believe that through the burning of fossil fuels, humans have caused a rising of Earth's surface temperature, which is causing the loss of species, more extreme weather, rising sea levels, and economic and political instability. How might Moral Foundations Theory make sense of such political differences? One answer has been pursued by Matthew Feinberg and Robb Willer, who propose that climate change is most often framed in public discourse as being about harm (to vanishing species) and care (of natural lands and oceans), a framing that liberals are more inclined to endorse (Feinberg & Willer, 2013). In keeping with this analysis, they find that public service announcements and editorial pieces in newspapers typically discuss environmental issues in terms of harm and care. When conservatives

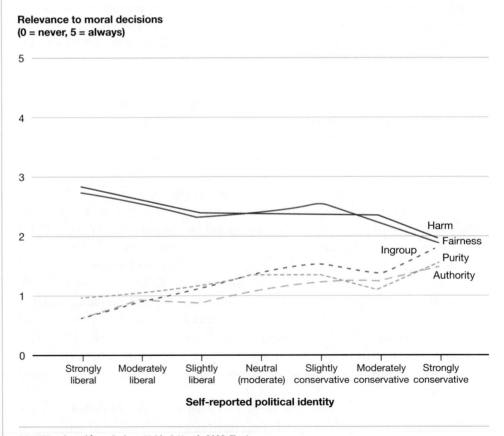

Figure 6.5
Moral Foundations Theory
Liberals and conservatives endorse different moral foundations.

SOURCE: Adapted from Graham, Haidt, & Nosek, 2009, Fig. 1.

read arguments for pro-environment policy changes couched in the language of purity and accompanied by images of toxic clouds, dirty drinking water, and a forest covered in garbage, they express pro-environment attitudes nearly equivalent to those expressed by liberal participants.

Interestingly, there's an asymmetry between liberals and conservatives in understanding the moral foundations underlying the views of their political opponents (Haidt, 2012). Conservatives realize that liberals value fairness and avoidance of harm more than they themselves do, and the other moral foundations less. But liberals often fail to realize that conservative views are frequently the result of emphasizing the values of authority, loyalty, and purity.

⤴ LOOKING BACK

Emotions prioritize certain construals of the environment over others, and shape our social cognition in profound ways. Emotions influence how we perceive the world, guiding what we focus on and categorize in emotion-congruent fashion. When feeling fear, for example, we exaggerate the perils, risks, and uncertainties around us. Emotions shape how we reason. Positive emotions broaden and build thought patterns, producing more creative thinking. Emotions are also powerful intuitions that feed into our moral judgments, shaping our views on punishment and wrongdoing and what we deem right and wrong.

Happiness

In its second sentence, the Declaration of Independence refers to inalienable rights that all citizens should enjoy, among them "life, liberty, and the pursuit of happiness." This well-known phrase makes a radical point: the most important task of a government is to ensure that people enjoy these three rights, including the pursuit of happiness. But what exactly are we pursuing when we pursue happiness?

Over time, the meaning of happiness has changed (McMahon, 2006). In classical Greek times, about 2,500 years ago, people believed happiness was achieved through ethical behavior—being temperate, fair, dutiful, and so on. During the Middle Ages, a period of frequent plagues and wars, people thought happiness was found in the afterlife, in communion with God when the soul was liberated from the turmoil of Earthly life. Philosophers of the eighteenth-century Enlightenment encouraged people to seek happiness in hedonistic experiences and in actions that advance the well-being of many (the idea of the greater good). As psychologists have turned their attention to the scientific study of happiness, they too have uncovered variations in its meaning. For Americans, personal achievement is a main pathway to happiness; for East Asians, harmonious interactions and the fulfillment of duties are regarded as the surest pathways to the good life (Kitayama, Karasawa, & Mesquita, 2004; Yuchida & Kitayama, 2009).

Psychologists now believe happiness has two measurable components (Diener, 2000). The first is life satisfaction, or how well you think your life is going in general. The second is emotional well-being, which refers to the tendency to experience more positive emotions than negative emotions at any moment in time, or over a given length of time. A recent review of hundreds of studies reveals that this mixture of life satisfaction and emotional well-being—happiness—matters in important ways (Lyubomirsky, King, & Diener, 2005). For example, marriage expert John Gottman has observed that marriages with greater emotional well-being—a higher ratio of positive to negative emotions—are more likely to last (Gottman, 1993).

Happiness is associated with creativity and high performance at work. It is also connected to better health, demonstrated by reduced pain, better sleep, and stronger cardiovascular and immune systems. Happiness may even increase life expectancy. One study found that nuns who at age 20 reported greater happiness in personal narratives as they entered the convent were more likely to live into their 80s and 90s than nuns who reported being less happy in their narratives from young adulthood (Danner, Snowdon, & Friesen, 2001).

In light of these considerations, let's address three questions people have been exploring for millennia. Do we know what makes us happy? How should we pursue happiness? What determines our recollections of what makes us happy?

Knowing What Makes Us Happy

Can we reliably predict what will make us happy and what will bring us despair? These kinds of predictions matter. We burn the midnight oil at work on the assumption that career success will bring lasting joy. We choose graduate school, career, vacations, and romantic partners based on the sense that one option will bring more happiness than others. A given decision process may begin with practical considerations, but we're very likely to come back to the basic question: What will make us happy? Unfortunately, our answers can sometimes be wide of the mark. Simply put, we're not always good at predicting what will make us happy.

In research on **affective forecasting**, Daniel Gilbert and Timothy Wilson have documented a variety of biases that undermine our attempts to predict what will make us happy (Gilbert, Brown, Pinel, & Wilson, 2000). One study examined the expected impact of breaking up with a romantic partner and compared it to its actual impact (Gilbert, Pinel, Wilson, Blumberg, & Wheatley, 1998). Students who had not experienced a romantic breakup, called "luckies," reported on their own overall happiness and then predicted how unhappy they would be 2 months after a breakup. The researchers compared this estimate with the happiness of people who had recently broken up, labeled "leftovers." As **Figure 6.6** shows, leftovers were just as happy as luckies, but luckies predicted they would be much *less* happy 2 months after a breakup than leftovers actually were. Although some breakups are indeed devastating, and divorce has many costs, people tend to overestimate how much a romantic breakup would diminish their life satisfaction.

A related study looked at the predicted and actual effects of getting tenure (Gilbert et al., 1998). As you may know, university and college professors are evaluated around 6 years into their employment period, and are either given tenure (thus securing them a permanent position) or sent packing. The tenure process is fraught with anxiety and doubt, but many such tenure-related anxieties may be misguided. Five years after the tenure decision, professors in the Gilbert study who did not get tenure were not significantly less happy than those who did. Once again, predictions differed from reality. Young assistant professors predicted a level of happiness after getting tenure that was far above what was actually observed in professors who did get tenure. And assistant professors expected a level of happiness after a denial of tenure that was far below what was actually observed in professors who had been recently denied tenure.

A variety of biases interfere with people's attempts to predict their future happiness. One is **immune neglect** (Gilbert et al., 1998). We are often remarkably

affective forecasting Predicting future emotions, such as whether an event will result in happiness or anger or sadness, and for how long.

immune neglect The tendency for people to underestimate their capacity to be resilient in responding to difficult life events, which leads them to overestimate the extent to which life's problems will reduce their personal well-being.

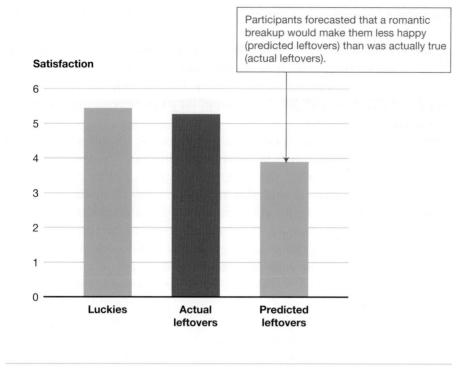

Satisfaction

Participants forecasted that a romantic breakup would make them less happy (predicted leftovers) than was actually true (actual leftovers).

Luckies   Actual leftovers   Predicted leftovers

SOURCE: Adapted from Gilbert et al., 1998.

Figure 6.6
Do We Know What Makes Us Happy?
This study demonstrated the accuracy of participants in their judgments of how happy they will be following a romantic breakup. The results were consistent with their claims about biased affective forecasting.

resilient in responding to painful setbacks, largely because of what Gilbert and Wilson call the "psychological immune system," which enables us to get beyond stressful experiences and trauma. Just as our biological immune system protects us from toxins and disease, our psychological immune system protects us from psychological distress. We have a great capacity to find the silver lining, the humor, the potential for insight and growth, in the face of painful setbacks and traumatic experiences; and these "immune-related" processes allow us to return to satisfying lives in the face of negative experiences. However, when estimating the effects of traumatic events like breakups or failures at work, we fail to consider these processes, how effectively they will take hold, or how quickly they will exert their effects. As a consequence, we inaccurately predict our future happiness.

Another bias is **focalism**: we focus too much on the most immediate and searing elements of significant events, such as the initial despair after learning our romantic partner is leaving us, and we neglect to consider how other aspects of our lives also shape our satisfaction (Wilson, Wheatley, Meyers, Gilbert, & Axson, 2000). We tend to assume that once a particular event happens—for example, acing the GREs or landing a dream job—we will be truly and enduringly happy. What we forget to consider is that after those exam scores arrive, or after we have the career we've always wanted, many other events—such as health problems, conflicts with our spouse, or difficulties with our children—will also influence our happiness.

Pursuing Happiness

If our beliefs about the influences of life events on happiness are often misguided, as the literature on affective forecasting suggests, what *does* influence our happiness? How might we sharpen our understanding of what makes us happy?

"Nothing in life is as important as you think it is at the moment you are thinking of it."

—PSYCHOLOGIST AND NOBEL LAUREATE DANIEL KAHNEMAN

focalism A tendency to focus too much on a central aspect of an event while neglecting the possible impact of associated factors or other events.

One answer comes from examining demographic factors of happier individuals, such as marital status, age, and income, as Angus Deaton and Daniel Kahneman did by surveying over 450,000 U.S. residents (Deaton & Kahneman, 2010). Participants reported not only on their life satisfaction, called "life evaluation," but also on their emotional well-being, indicating the intensity of the negative emotion, stress, and positive emotion they experienced the day before completing the questionnaire.

A first finding that emerged is that relationships matter. People who reported being alone the day before taking the survey reported lower life satisfaction and lower emotional well-being than those who had been with other people. More generally, studies of happiness find that relationships of all kinds—romantic partnerships, friendships, family connections, neighborhood ties, and links to teammates, fellow activists, or parishioners—tend to lift people's spirits (Lyubomirsky, 2007). Religious engagement is associated with greater happiness, probably in part because such involvement leads to a sense of community and trust in others (Helliwell & Putnam, 2004). Social bonds bring personal happiness.

Now we're going to ask you to do a little affective forecasting. As you get older, do you think you'll be happier than you are now? Less happy? Or about the same? In the Deaton and Kahneman study, and in others like it, older people reported *greater* personal life satisfaction than younger people. They also reported less negative emotion and stress. So much for our cultural beliefs about the incomparable joys of youth and the inevitable suffering of the midlife crisis! While it's true that as people age, their physical health declines, along with aging comes a greater capacity for happiness. Developmental psychologist Laura Carstensen argues that one of the reasons is improved relationships: as people age, their circle of acquaintances tends to shrink, mostly by limiting the relationships to family and valued friends (Carstensen, 2011). Acquaintances who don't make you happy occupy less prominent places in your daily life. And people who are retired don't have to deal daily with annoying "bad apples" in the workplace. Carstensen also argues, as noted earlier, that older people are better at construing events in ways that make them happy; they're better able than younger people to let things go and not be undone by the hassles of daily life.

What about money? Is it really true that "money doesn't buy happiness," or would it be wiser to live according to the dictum "greed is good"? The research evidence tells a nuanced story. First, having very little money is unambiguously associated with greater unhappiness. For example, people living in poor countries are not as happy as those living in wealthier, industrialized countries (Diener, 2000). This seems to be because people in disadvantaged countries are more likely to suffer from unemployment, poor nutrition, diseases, and civil strife. Increases in national wealth ameliorate these conditions. In the Deaton and Kahneman (2010) survey of U.S. residents, the poorest people were the least happy. With each increase in income above the poverty level, people reported greater life satisfaction. Poorer participants (those making less than $1,000 per month) were also twice as likely as better off participants (those making more than $3,000 per month) to feel intense sadness and worry when alone, or divorced, or from suffering from health issues. When people don't have enough money, life's difficulties, such as health problems and divorce, are more stressful.

Second, the impact of money on happiness is quite different for those who are better off financially. In the Deaton and Kahneman (2010) study, people's life satisfaction tended to increase the richer they were, but only up to an annual income of $75,000. Beyond that, more money did not buy them anything in terms of life satisfaction. Some have argued that this is due to longer commutes, diminished time with friends and family, and reduced opportunities for recreation and relaxation that comes with making more money (Frank & Levine, 2014; Myers, 2001). In terms of daily experiences of positive and negative emotions, however, the benefits of making more money continued to accrue beyond an income of $75,000 a year. Thus, money appears to buy more in terms of moment-to-moment experiences of pleasure and sorrow than in relation to overall satisfaction with life.

Beyond examining certain demographic correlates of happiness (income, relationship status, and age), social psychologists have investigated the practices and habits of happy people. First, you might try practicing gratitude. Try to develop a mind-set of appreciating the many things you've received from other people, like the opportunity to learn, to do meaningful work, or to express your ideas. Robert Emmons and Michael McCullough (2003) asked participants to write about what had made them feel grateful once a week for 9 weeks with the following prompt:

> There are many things in our lives, both large and small, that we might be grateful about. Think back over the past week and write down on the lines below up to five things in your life that you are grateful or thankful for.

Other participants wrote about a hassle during the week or a significant life event. Then, for each week of the study, participants reported on their life satisfaction and physical health. Simply writing about things to be grateful for once a week led to boosts in life satisfaction and reduced reports of problematic health symptoms. (Japanese psychotherapy, incidentally, involves encouraging clients to think of ways they have been helped by others. In contrast, Western therapy is more likely to emphasize digging up past traumas from the past, felt to be caused by the actions of other people. The implied clinical experiment might yield fascinating results.)

A second recommendation involves following the folk wisdom that says it's better to give than to receive—and folk wisdom in this case apparently got it right. Elizabeth Dunn and her colleagues tested this idea by asking participants to rate how happy they were and then giving them either $5 or $20 (Dunn, Aknin, & Norton, 2008). They had to spend the money either on themselves or on someone else by the end of the day, at which time they again rated how happy they were. The result? Spending money on others led to greater boosts in happiness than spending money on themselves, a finding that has since been replicated in 136 cultures (Aknin et al., 2013). To experience greater happiness, this study suggests, we would be well served by sharing, giving to charity, volunteering, or surprising others with gifts.

You're not likely to spend all your money on others, of course. What about the money you spend on yourself? Do some types of expenditures lead to more happiness than others? There's an easy answer: focus on experiences rather than possessions. Work by Tom Gilovich and his colleagues has found that if you're conflicted about whether to buy a material good (an attractive coat, a 3D TV) or to finance a personal experience (such as tickets to a concert or a trip to Mexico), you're better off opting for the experience (Carter & Gilovich, 2010; van Boven, Campbell, & Gilovich, 2010).

When people are asked to recall their most significant material purchase and most significant experiential purchase over the past 5 years, they report that the experiential purchase brought more joy, was a source of more enduring satisfaction, and was more clearly "money well spent." Why is this so? One reason is that we quickly adapt or habituate to the material good (the new smartphone is fun for a while but soon it feels no different than the old one), but the experience lingers. It lives on in the memories we cherish, in the stories we tell, and in the very sense of who we are. And experiences are also often more satisfying because we tend to evaluate them on their own terms, not in comparison to what others have. Jane and Jack both have cars like yours; but only you spent 2 weeks in Guatemala working on a farm and living with a peasant family.

Recalling Our Happy Moments

A great part of our emotional life involves reflecting on what has made us happy. We think back to listening to live music or having a great dinner with friends. As we age, we turn to thoughts of past vacations with our family, an afternoon with grandchildren, or game-changing times during our career. We rely on our memory to reconstruct past experiences. But what drives recollections of our happy moments?

Barbara Fredrickson (1998) and Daniel Kahneman (1999) have found some surprising answers. In their research, they have people experience positive emotion in different ways. In one study, participants watched a series of pleasurable film clips, such as a comedy routine, a puppy playing with a flower, or penguins diving into the water (Fredrickson & Kahneman, 1993). While viewing, they moved a dial to rate the intensity of their second-by-second experience of pleasure. At the end, they gave an overall assessment of how pleasurable it was to watch the clips. The researchers correlated the general assessments with the specific ratings to find out how immediate experiences of pleasure relate to people's subsequent recollections of how much enjoyment they had.

This study and others like it have documented three factors that determine recollections of pleasure. First, the *peak moment* of pleasure at the start of an event—like the exquisite first taste of chocolate sauce and vanilla ice cream in a sundae—strongly predicts how much pleasure you'll remember later. Second, how you feel at the *end* of the event also strongly predicts your overall experience of pleasure. For instance, make sure the last few minutes of a first date you've enjoyed are especially good. Similarly, it's smart for a teacher to end a lecture with an inspiring conclusion, a provocative question, or a joke. And by all means, don't spend the last day of your vacation running around buying gifts for friends back home; take care of that earlier, and do something especially fun before heading to the airport. Third, and somewhat surprisingly, the *length* of the pleasurable experience is minimally related to the overall recollection, a bias called **duration neglect**. Whether a neck massage lasts 20 minutes or an hour, whether a first date lasts 1 hour or 10, seems to have little sway over our recollections of pleasure. What matters most is whether the peak moment and ending are good.

The same principle holds for negative experiences. Remembered pain is predicted by peak and end discomfort, not by its duration (Kahneman, 1999). In a study showing the important implications of these principles, patients reported every 60 seconds on the degree of discomfort they were experiencing during a colonoscopy, a screening procedure for colon cancer (Redelmeier, Katz, &

duration neglect Giving relative unimportance to the length of an emotional experience, whether pleasurable or unpleasant, in judging and remembering the overall experience.

BOX 6.4 **FOCUS ON *POSITIVE PSYCHOLOGY***

Nirvana in the Brain

Ever since the Buddha found enlightenment when meditating under a bo tree 2,500 years ago, billions of people have turned to meditation to find peace and happiness. There are many kinds of meditation practices, but they share certain principles. They encourage you to mindfully slow down your breathing to a healthy, steady rhythm with deep exhalations, which reduces stress-related cardiovascular arousal. Many meditation practices encourage a mindful attention to different sensations in your body. They likewise encourage a calm, nonjudgmental awareness of your thoughts and feelings. And many meditation practices, such as those popularized by the Dalai Lama, encourage training the mind in loving kindness and compassion. Here the meditator extends warm feelings of compassion to family members, friends, loved ones, strangers, the self,

and ultimately adversaries, to encourage a more compassionate stance toward fellow human beings.

Does meditation work? Neuroscientist Richard Davidson has been seeking a rigorous answer to that question (Davidson & Begley, 2012). In one line of work, he has studied Tibetan monks, who spend as much as 4 or 5 hours a day quietly and devotedly meditating. Upon scanning the brain of a Tibetan monk, he found that his resting brain showed levels of activation in the left frontal lobes— regions of the brain involved in positive emotion—to be literally off the charts. In another observation, Davidson blasted the monk with a loud burst of white noise to assess his startle response. For most people, this kind of stimulus activates an ancient and powerful startle response, the strength of which is a good indicator of how stressed out the person is. The monk didn't even blink.

These benefits are enjoyed not only by monks who have devoted their lives to meditation. Davidson, Jon Kabat Zinn, and their colleagues had software engineers train in the techniques of mindfulness meditation, developing the ability to accept without judgment their thoughts and feelings and practicing loving kindness toward others (Davidson et al., 2003). Six weeks later, the participants showed increased activation in the left frontal lobes. They also showed enhanced immune function, evident in the size of the immune response in the skin in response to a flu shot. In similarly motivated work, researchers have found that practicing mindfulness meditation, with a focus on being mindful of breathing and extending loving kindness to others, boosts happiness several weeks later (Fredrickson, Cohn, Coffey, Pek, & Finkel, 2008).

Kahneman, 2003). Those for whom the last moments of the procedure were particularly uncomfortable rated the overall experience as most aversive. Those for whom there had been just as much discomfort overall, but whose last moments weren't as bad, were more willing to have the recommended 5-year follow-up screening, and this was true even if the duration of the procedure had been been relatively long.

🔄 LOOKING BACK

Happiness combines life satisfaction and emotional well-being, the tendency to experience more positive emotions than negative ones. It's sometimes hard to predict the extent of our future happiness; we're often more resilient than we think, and we tend to focus on certain future factors while neglecting others that will influence how happy we'll be. Broad demographic factors (gender, age, income) are associated with happiness. We can cultivate happiness by practicing gratitude, by giving to others, and by focusing on experiences rather than material gain. Our recollections of previous experiences, and how much happiness we derive from looking back on them, are determined by what they were like at their peak and at the end, but not by the overall duration of pleasure or pain.

Chapter Review

SUMMARY

Characterizing Emotion

- The experience of emotion is generally brief, lasting only seconds or minutes; moods often last for hours or days.
- The five components of emotion are an appraisal process, physiological responses, expressive behavior, subjective feelings, and action tendencies.
- The *appraisal process* consists of patterns of construal for evaluating events and objects in the environment based on their relation to current goals.
- *Physiological responses* include cardiovascular changes, such as sweating and blushing, and activation of parts of the brain.
- *Expressive behavior* enables people to communicate feelings and reactions through facial expression, touch, and the voice.
- *Subjective feelings* are the felt qualities of an emotion, typically described with words.
- Emotions involve *action tendencies,* or motivation to behave in certain ways. Anger, for example, can lead to positive behaviors, such as helping restore justice.

Emotional Expression: Universal and Culturally Specific

- Universal aspects to emotion are based on evolutionary factors; emotions enable people to respond quickly and effectively to threats and opportunities related to survival.

- People in different cultures facially express happiness, surprise, sadness, anger, disgust, and fear in similar ways.
- People in certain cultures develop specific ways of expressing a particular emotion, known as *emotion accents*. Cultures vary in *focal emotions*, which are common in everyday experience.
- There are cultural differences in which emotions are highly valued, and in the *display rules* that govern how emotions are expressed.

Emotions and Social Relationships

- Emotions help solve the commitment problem, enabling people to express sincere commitment and to behave in ways that benefit others' well-being, thus strengthening social relationships. The chemical oxytocin, circulating throughout the blood, contributes to building commitment and trust.
- Emotional expressions in the face, voice, and touch trigger reactions in others, thus coordinating interactions like flirtation or attachments between parents and children.
- The experience and expression of certain emotions, like anger and pride, enable people to know their status within social groups.
- Emotional intelligence, including the four skills for using emotions wisely, predicts healthier social relationships of every kind.

Emotions and Social Cognition

- Emotions influence how people perceive information in ways that are consistent with the appraisal process for each emotion. Fear, for instance, makes people more attuned to threats in the environment.
- The *broaden-and-build hypothesis* holds that positive emotions broaden thoughts and actions, prompting people to see greater similarities between themselves and others, thereby building stronger relationships.
- According to the *social intuitionist model of moral judgment*, people have fast, emotional intuitions about right or wrong, then rely on reason to make moral judgments. *Moral foundations theory* offers five evolved, universal moral domains in which specific emotions guide moral judgments.

Happiness

- Happiness is described as the combination of life satisfaction and emotional well-being, the tendency to experience more positive emotions than negative emotions. Happiness is associated with stronger relationships, increased creativity, and better health.
- *Affective forecasting* involves predictions about how life events will influence happiness. People often fail to predict

how much an emotional experience, such as breaking up from a romantic relationship, will affect them.

- *Immune neglect* is the tendency to underestimate the resilience with which people will respond to difficult life events in the future. *Focalism* is narrowly focusing on how a single event will influence future happiness, while not considering other events.

- Older people are happier than younger people. Beyond providing a comfortable income, money does not necessarily make people happy. Relationships, including marriage, have a positive effect on people's happiness. Religious people are happier than less religious people.

- People can cultivate happiness by being grateful, practicing generosity, and focusing on experiences rather than purchasing material goods.

- A person's overall assessment of pleasure is determined by the peak and end of a pleasurable event and has little to do with its duration. The same is true of assessments of pain.

THINK ABOUT IT

1. Humans appear to have a coordinated display of embarrassment that resembles appeasement signals in other species. What does this tell us about the function of embarrassment? Why do you feel embarrassed when you trip and fall in a full lecture hall? What effects should your resultant experience and display of embarrassment have on your classmates?

2. The relationship between culture and emotion is complex. Say you're seated at a wedding reception with an older European American man, who tells you that East Asians never get excited. How would you explain to him that he's mistaken, by drawing on the concepts of ideal emotions and display rules?

3. Much communication today occurs distantly via electronic text, rather than face-to-face, whether in an online chat or text message, an e-mail, or a post on a social media site. Given what you know about the importance of emotions for social relationships, why do you think people frequently use emoticons and emojis in these communications? What social functions do they perform?

4. Suppose you just got into a huge fight with your parents on the phone, and are feeling angry. You call up your romantic partner to talk about the fight, but just end up fighting with your partner. Using what you know about emotion's effects on perception, how would you explain this second fight, and perpetuated mood states more generally?

5. If you were working as a canvasser collecting signatures for a petition to ban same-sex marriage, what strategies could you use to increase your signature count, given what you know about moral foundations theory and the effects of disgust on moral judgment?

6. Would winning several million dollars in the lottery make you happier? What would research on affective forecasting predict? What does the research on money and happiness have to say? How should you spend your winnings to maximize happiness?

THE ANSWER GUIDELINES FOR THE THINK ABOUT IT QUESTIONS CAN BE FOUND AT THE BACK OF THE BOOK . . .

Attitudes, Behavior, and Rationalization

Throughout America's long and painful military involvement in Vietnam—a conflict that split the nation into "hawks" and "doves," consumed the energies of three administrations, and ultimately cost the lives of 58,000 U.S. soldiers—the government put a positive spin on the enterprise. It maintained that there was "light at the end of the tunnel," that Communist North Vietnam would soon be vanquished, that a satisfactory peace agreement would soon be struck, and that the South Vietnamese regime the United States was supporting would soon be able to defend itself. But despite repeated positive pronouncements of this sort, many government officials had doubts about America's efforts in Vietnam and the prospects for success. Their reservations often surfaced when key decisions needed to be made, such as whether to increase the number of U.S. soldiers stationed in South Vietnam, or whether to initiate a bombing campaign against North Vietnam.

Lyndon Johnson, the U.S. president responsible for the largest buildup of American troops in Vietnam, employed an interesting tactic to deal with those in his administration who had begun privately to express such doubts, and to waver from the administration's policy on the war (Halberstam, 1969). Johnson would send the doubters on a "fact-finding" mission to Vietnam, nearly always accompanied by a group of reporters. This might seem like a risky move on Johnson's part, because if any of these less-than-staunch supporters expressed their concerns to the press, the administration's policies would be undermined. Johnson knew, however, that they would not publicly dissent, and would instead try to influence policy from the inside. Unwilling to reveal their qualms to the public and confronted by criticism of the war effort by reporters, the doubters would be thrust into

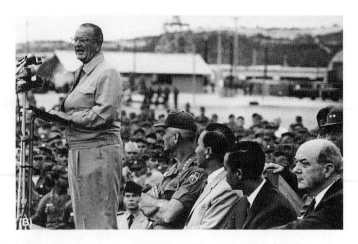

Public Advocacy and Private Acceptance

Despite continuing problems in fighting the Vietnam War, U.S. President Lyndon Johnson publicly declared that things were going well, and insisted that his advisers and cabinet members publicly express their support and confidence. (A) U.S. Secretary of Defense Robert McNamara had reservations about the war that may have been alleviated by the constant necessity of defending it. Here he is shown briefing the press on U.S. air attacks. (B) To bolster morale, Johnson himself spoke to American troops in South Vietnam, while U.S. General William Westmoreland, South Vietnamese General Nguyen Van Thieu, South Vietnamese Premier Nguyen Coo Ky, and U.S. Secretary of State Dean Rusk looked on.

the position of publicly *defending* administration policy. This public endorsement, Johnson reasoned, would serve to lessen their doubts and help turn the skeptics in his administration into advocates. Known as an unusually savvy politician, President Johnson was using some very clever psychology—psychology we'll explore in this chapter—to win support for his Vietnam policy.

Johnson's strategy highlights some important questions about the consistency between attitudes and behavior, especially whether the consistency between the two is the result of attitudes influencing behavior or behavior influencing attitudes. Both types of influence occur. Those with strong pro-environment attitudes are more likely to vote Green or Democratic than Republican. Thus, attitudes influence behavior. But everyone knows that people rationalize, so behavior influences attitudes as well. Environmentally minded individuals who drive gas-guzzling cars tend to convince themselves that automobile exhaust contributes very little to air pollution or global warming—or that they don't drive that much anyway.

Behavior Can Influence Attitudes

Many people who consider themselves environmentalists nonetheless drive gas-guzzling SUVs. Driving a vehicle that is not fuel-efficient can lead those who are concerned about the environment to convince themselves that there is not much connection between fuel efficiency and air pollution or climate change.

Which is stronger: the effect of attitudes on behavior or the effect of behavior on attitudes? It's a difficult question to answer, but decades of research on the topic have shown that the influence of attitudes on behavior is a bit weaker than most people suspect, and the influence of behavior on attitudes is much stronger than most suspect. So President Johnson was right: get skeptics to publicly endorse the policy, and they will be skeptics no longer. Or as Johnson might have put it: "Get people to say they believe something and their hearts and minds will follow."

This chapter examines what social psychologists have learned about the consistency between attitudes and behavior. Research shows that attitudes are often surprisingly poor predictors of behavior, but it also specifies the circumstances in which they predict behavior rather well. The chapter also examines two "consistency theories" that explain why people tend to maintain consistency among their attitudes and between their attitudes and behavior.

Components and Measurement of Attitudes

Let's start with the basics: What are attitudes, and how are they measured? Attitudes can have multiple components, and researchers use a variety of different methods to measure them.

Three Components of Attitudes

An **attitude** is an evaluation of an object along a positive-negative dimension. At their core, then, attitudes involve *affect* (or emotion)—how much someone likes or dislikes an object, be it a politician, a landscape, an athletic shoe, a dessert, or himself. Nearly every object triggers some degree of positive or negative emotion, which constitutes the affective component of the attitude somebody has toward it (Bargh, Chaiken, Raymond, & Hymes, 1996; Breckler, 1984; Cacioppo & Berntson, 1994; Fazio, Jackson, Dunton, & Williams, 1995; Fazio, Sanbonmatsu, Powell, & Kardes, 1986; Zanna & Rempel, 1988).

Most attitude theorists maintain that attitudes involve more than affect (Breckler, 1984; Eagly & Chaiken, 1998; Zimbardo & Leippe, 1991). Attitudes also involve *cognitions*—thoughts that typically reinforce a person's feelings. These include knowledge and beliefs about the object, as well as associated memories and images. Your attitude about a favorite city, for example, includes knowledge about its history and its most appealing neighborhoods and landmarks, as well as special times you've spent there.

Finally, attitudes are associated with specific *behaviors* (Fishbein & Ajzen, 1975). Most generally, the affective evaluation of good versus bad is connected to a behavioral tendency to either approach or avoid. In other words, attitudes alert us to rewarding objects we should approach and to costly or punishing objects we should avoid (Ferguson & Bargh, 2008; Ferguson & Zayas, 2009). When specific attitudes are primed—brought to mind, even unconsciously— people are more likely to act in ways consistent with the attitude (Chen & Bargh, 1999). Neuroscientific studies indicate that our attitudes activate particular brain regions, areas of the motor cortex, that support specific actions (Preston & de Waal, 2002). When you see a young child crying or a scrumptious hot fudge sundae, your mind prepares your body for the action of caretaking or consumption.

Measuring Attitudes

Attitudes are most commonly determined through simple self-report measures, such as survey questions. When researchers want to know how participants feel about members of other groups, their romantic partners, themselves, a public figure, and so on, they usually just ask them. More specifically, researchers typically

Likert scale A numerical scale used to assess attitudes; includes a set of possible answers with labeled anchors on each extreme.

response latency The amount of time it takes to respond to a stimulus, such as an attitude question.

implicit attitude measure An indirect measure of attitudes that does not involve a self-report.

ask their participants to rate an attitude object on a Likert scale, named after psychologist Rensis Likert, its inventor. The **Likert scale** lists a set of possible answers with anchors on each extreme—for example, 1 = strongly disagree, 7 = strongly agree. To determine attitudes toward the use of cell phones while driving, for example, researchers might have participants respond on a scale of 1 to 7, where 1 is the least favorable answer ("It's never acceptable") and 7 is the most favorable ("It's always acceptable"). You've probably responded to many of these kinds of queries yourself. Yet when it comes to many complex attitudes—such as your attitude toward capital punishment, environmentalism, or hedge fund managers—responses to these sorts of simple scales are likely to miss some important elements.

To understand why, consider the following questions: How much do you value freedom? How strongly do you feel about the need to reduce discrimination? How important is a less polluted environment? If an investigator asked these questions of a random selection of individuals, chances are most responses on a Likert scale would be very positive. But surely people differ in the strength and depth of their attitudes toward these issues. How can social psychologists better capture these other dimensions of attitudes?

One approach, developed by Russell Fazio and his team, is to measure the *accessibility* of the attitude—how readily it comes to mind (Fazio, 1995; Fazio & Williams, 1986). These researchers examined the time it takes a person to respond to an attitude question—a measure known as **response latency**. Someone who takes 750 milliseconds to respond affirmatively to a question such as "Do you approve how the president is handling the economy?" is likely to have a stronger attitude on this topic than somebody who takes several seconds. In a study conducted 5 months before Ronald Reagan and Walter Mondale squared off in the 1984 U.S. presidential election, for example, Fazio and Williams (1986) measured how long it took participants to say how good a president each of the opposing candidates would make. The response time was a strong predictor of who they believed won the first televised debate and, more importantly, which candidate they voted for 6 months later.

A second way to assess the strength and importance of someone's attitude is to determine the *centrality* of the attitude to the person's belief system (Krosnick & Petty, 1995). To evaluate attitude centrality, researchers measure a variety of attitudes within a domain and calculate how strongly each one is linked to the others. For example, to examine social and political attitudes, a researcher might ask you your opinions about abortion, stem cell research, fracking, same-sex marriage, sex education in high school, drug legalization, and taxation. If your point of view on a specific topic is very important to you, it should highly correlate with your attitudes about certain other issues. For example, if abortion is a defining issue for you, then your view on abortion is likely to be strongly correlated with your attitudes about stem cell research and sex education, and perhaps even with your attitudes about same-sex marriage and taxation.

Other ways of measuring attitudes do not rely on explicit self-reports. Investigators often use **implicit attitude measures** when there is reason to believe people may be unwilling or unable to report their true feelings or opinions. Chapter 11, on stereotypes and prejudice, discusses in some detail two widely used implicit measures: affective priming and the implicit association test (IAT). In the case of both of these measures, people don't realize their attitudes are being examined. Implicit measures let researchers tap *nonconscious attitudes*—that is, people's immediate evaluative reactions they may not be aware of, or that may conflict

BOX 7.1 **FOCUS ON *NEUROSCIENCE***

Is the Bad Stronger Than the Good?

At the core of our attitudes is a positive or negative response to an attitude object—an old friend's voice, a roommate's messy pile of dishes, the smell of freshly cut grass. Pioneering research by neuroscientist Joseph LeDoux has found that one part of the brain, the amygdala, is central to this initial, core component of our attitudes (LeDoux, 1989, 1993, 1996). After receiving sensory information about a stimulus from the thalamus, the almond-shaped amygdala then provides information about the positive or negative valence, or value, of the object. This evaluation occurs, remarkably, before the mind has categorized the object in question. Thus, even before we fully know what an object is, we have a gut feeling about it. When the amygdala is damaged, animals no longer have appropriate evaluations of objects: they eat feces, attempt to copulate with members of other species, and show no fear of threatening stimuli such as snakes or dominant animals.

LeDoux's research raises an interesting question: Are our quick positive and negative evaluations of stimuli comparable with respect to their strength? Reviews by Shelley Taylor (1991), Paul Rozin and Edward Royzman (2001), Roy Baumeister and his colleagues (Baumeister, Bratslavsky, Finkenauer, & Vohs, 2001), and John Cacioppo and Wendi Gardner (1999) have all yielded the same answer: negative evaluations are stronger than positive evaluations.

It would certainly make evolutionary sense for an organism to be more vigilant about avoiding harm than seeking pleasure, to be more watchful for danger signs than for cues to opportunity. Food or mating opportunities not pursued today might be realized tomorrow; if a predator is not avoided today, there is no tomorrow. A pronounced negativity bias might therefore increase the chances of survival.

Consider a few generalizations supporting the conclusion that the bad is stronger than the good. Negative stimuli, such as frightening sounds or noxious smells, elicit more rapid and stronger physiological responses than positive stimuli, such as delicious tastes. Losing $20 is more painful than winning $20 is pleasurable. Negative trauma, such as the death of a loved one or sexual abuse, can change a person for a lifetime; positive events don't appear to have equivalent effects. Or consider Rozin's observation about contamination: the briefest contact with a cockroach will spoil a delicious meal, but the inverse—making a pile of cockroaches delicious by spicing it up

Contamination
The presence of cockroaches on food spoils a delicious meal. (Note that the meal does not make the cockroaches suddenly seem appetizing.)

with your favorite foods—is unimaginable (Rozin & Royzman, 2001).

In related work, Tiffany Ito, John Cacioppo, and their colleagues presented participants with positively valenced pictures—pizza or a bowl of chocolate ice cream, for instance; and negatively valenced slides—such as photos of a mutilated face or a dead cat (Ito, Larsen, Smith, & Cacioppo, 1998). As they did so, they recorded the participants' brain activity on the scalp and studied brain regions known to be involved in evaluative responses to stimuli. They discovered a clear negativity bias in evaluation: the negative stimuli generated greater brain activity than the positive or neutral stimuli. In this context, it seems that the bad is indeed stronger than the good.

---

with their consciously endorsed attitudes. Researchers also sometimes use nonverbal measures, including smiling behavior and degree of physical closeness, as indices or signals of positive attitudes toward others.

Finally, physiological indicators, such as the increased heart rate and sweaty palms associated with fear, can capture people's attitudes. **Box 7.1**, for example, describes how patterns of brain activity recorded from the surface of the scalp reveal the relative strength of positive and negative attitudes.

"The evil that men do lives after them; the good is oft interrèd with their bones."

—SHAKESPEARE, ANTHONY'S FUNERAL ORATION FOR THE TITLE CHARACTER IN *JULIUS CAESAR*

Predicting Behavior from Attitudes

Most academic discussions of how well attitudes predict behavior begin with a remarkable study conducted by the sociologist Richard LaPiere in the early 1930s (LaPiere, 1934). LaPiere spent two years touring the United States with a young Chinese couple, visiting numerous hotels, auto camps, restaurants, and cafés. Although prejudice and discrimination against Chinese individuals were common at the time, LaPiere and his traveling companions were denied service by only one of the 250 establishments they visited. Maybe anti-Chinese prejudice wasn't so strong after all.

To find out, LaPiere wrote to all of the establishments they had visited and asked whether their policy was to serve "Orientals." Approximately 90 percent of those who responded said they would not, a response rate that was stunningly inconsistent with what LaPiere actually observed during his earlier tour of the country. This result was unfortunate in human terms because it indicated that anti-Chinese prejudice was indeed rather robust. And it was unfortunate from the perspective of psychological science because it suggested that attitudes don't predict behavior very well. To a scientific discipline that had treated attitudes as powerful determinants of people's behavior, this news was surprising—and rather unsettling.

Note that this inconsistency was not some fluke associated with the particulars of LaPiere's study. Many experiments conducted over the next several decades yielded similar results. As a much-cited review in the 1960s of the existing literature on attitudes and behavior concluded: "The present review provides little evidence to support the postulated existence of stable, underlying attitudes within the individual which influence both his verbal expressions and his actions" (Wicker, 1969, p. 75).

Most people find this result surprising. Why? Why do we think attitudes are strong predictors of behavior when careful empirical studies reveal this isn't true? Part of the reason is that every day, ample evidence demonstrates that attitudes and behavior do go together. People who picket abortion clinics have attitudes opposed to abortion. People who show up at the local bowling alley have positive attitudes toward the sport. Families with lots of kids (usually) have positive attitudes about children. Evidence of a tight connection between attitudes and behavior is all around us. However, such evidence only indicates that if people behave a certain way, they're likely to have positive feelings about that behavior. It does not mean, though, that those with a positive attitude toward a given behavior are inclined to behave in a manner

Attitudes Don't Always Predict Behavior

This bar in Pattaya Beach, Thailand, displays a sign declaring "No Arab to sit down here." The bar owners may indeed intend to block Arabs from their establishment, but if an Arab walked into the bar with some friends, would they really forbid the person from sitting down?

consistent with their attitude. What is not so obvious in everyday life are the many instances of people with positive attitudes about bowling who don't bowl, or people with positive attitudes about kids who don't have children.

After all, there are many reasons for failing to act on our attitudes. And once we're aware of all these reasons, the finding that attitudes so often fail to predict behavior may no longer seem so surprising. Even more important is to gain an understanding of *when* attitudes are likely to be highly predictive of behavior and when they are not (Glasman & Albarracín, 2006).

Attitudes Can Conflict with Other Powerful Determinants of Behavior

Suppose you're asked to predict the strength of the relationship between attitudes about dieting and success in dieting. Would you expect a strong relationship? Probably not. Eating less is determined by too many things other than a person's attitude about dieting, including eating habits, individual physiology, and whether a roommate happens to be pigging out at the moment—as well as the person's feelings about other things, such as ice cream, donuts, and french fries.

What's true about attitudes toward dieting is also true about attitudes in general. They all compete with other determinants of behavior. The situationist message of social psychology (and of this book) suggests that attitudes don't always win out over these other determinants, and hence attitudes are not always tightly connected to behavior.

One potent determinant of a person's actions that can weaken the relationship between attitudes and behavior is that person's understanding of the prevailing norms of appropriate behavior. You might relish the idea of talking excitedly with the guy next to you in the movie theater or lecture hall, but let's hope you refrain from doing so because you recognize it just isn't done. Others would disapprove. Similarly, the hotel and restaurant owners in LaPiere's study may have wanted to turn away the Chinese couple, but refrained from doing so out of concern for how it would look and the scene it might cause.

Attitudes Can Be Inconsistent

Many people report having a hard time pinning down their attitude toward the actor Russell Crowe. They acknowledge great admiration for his skill as an actor, but they just don't like him. This highlights two important facts about attitudes. First, attitudes may conflict with one another. We might like great acting but dislike arrogance. Second, the different components of an attitude may not always align. In particular, there can be a rift between the affective component (what we feel about Russell Crowe) and the cognitive component (what we think about him). When the affective and cognitive components are inconsistent, it's no surprise that the attitude may not predict behavior very well. The cognitive component might determine the attitude we express, but the affective component might determine our behavior (or vice versa). The restaurant and hotel owners from LaPiere's study, for example, might have thought it was bad for their business to serve Chinese individuals; but the feelings aroused by a living, breathing Chinese couple may have made it hard to deny them service.

"I do not like thee, Dr. Fell.
The reason why I cannot tell.
But this I know and know full well.
I do not like thee, Dr. Fell."
—NURSERY RHYME WRITTEN IN 1680 BY SATIRIC POET TOM BROWN AFTER BEING THREATENED WITH DISMISSAL BY THE DEAN OF HIS COLLEGE, DR. FELL OF CHRISTCHURCH, UNIVERSITY OF OXFORD

Introspecting about the Reasons for Our Attitudes

Consider your attitude toward someone you're attracted to. Why are you attracted to that person? If you ask yourself this question, a number of factors are likely to spring to mind: "She's cute." "She's ambitious." "She's fun to be with."

Sometimes, however, it's not so easy to know exactly why we like someone. It may not be because of specific, readily identifiable attributes; we may simply share some indescribable chemistry. Suppose this is the case and you're asked to come up with reasons why you like your romantic partner. Like most people, you'll probably focus on what is easy to identify, easy to justify, and easy to capture in words—and thus miss the real, but hard-to-articulate, reasons for your attraction. Why does this matter? It turns out that coming up with the (wrong) reasons for an attitude you hold can mislead you about what your attitude actually is. When this happens, no wonder the attitude you report after generating reasons doesn't end up predicting your behavior very well.

In one study testing this phenomenon, Timothy Wilson and his colleagues asked students about the person they were dating. Participants in one group simply gave an overall evaluation of their relationship. Those in another group listed the reasons they felt the way they did and then gave an overall relationship evaluation. The researchers contacted the participants again 9 months later and asked about the status of their relationship. The attitudes of participants in the first group, who evaluated the relationship without considering the reasons, were much more accurate predictors of the current relationship status than the attitudes of participants who had introspected about their reasons for liking their partners (Wilson, Dunn, Bybee, Hyman, & Rotondo, 1984). Thinking about why we like someone can mislead us in terms of our true, full attitude toward that person, thereby weakening the link between the attitude we report after generating reasons and our subsequent behavior.

Wilson has shown that this effect applies far beyond our attitudes toward romantic partners, and that introspecting about the reasons for our attitudes about all sorts of things can undermine how well they guide our behavior. The cause in all cases is the same: introspection may lead us to focus on the easiest-to-identify reasons for liking or disliking something at the expense of the *real* reasons for our likes and dislikes. Research has shown that when people are induced to think carefully about the reasons they prefer one product over another (as opposed to simply stating a preference), they are more likely to regret their choice later (Wilson et al., 1993), and their choices are less likely to correspond to the "true" value of the product as determined by experts (Wilson & Schooler, 1991).

Does this mean introspection is always (or even typically) harmful, and that we should forgo careful examination and always go with our gut? Not at all. In deciding whether to launch a military campaign, for example, it is imperative for analysts to leave no stone unturned and to exhaustively consider the reasons for and against the idea from all angles. In addition, often the real reasons for our attitudes are perfectly easy to identify and articulate, and in those cases

Inconsistent Attitudes

Attitudes may not be good predictors of behavior because people often have attitudes that conflict with one another. Elliot Spitzer, disgraced former governor of New York, had campaigned on the importance of high ethical standards among public officials and vowed to "change the ethics of Albany." Following reports that he was a frequent customer in a high-priced prostitution operation, he resigned. Did he think his involvement with prostitutes was wrong but did it anyway, or did he view participation in the sex trade as ethically acceptable?

introspection produces no rift between the variables we *think* are guiding us and those that actually are. The contaminating effect of introspection is limited to those times when the true source of our attitude is hard to pin down, such as when the basis of an attitude is largely affective. In such cases, a cognitive analysis is likely to seize on seemingly plausible but misleading cognitive reasons. When the basis is primarily cognitive, however, the search for reasons tends to yield the real reasons, and introspection isn't therefore likely to mislead us about our true attitude, or diminish the relationship between attitude and behavior (Millar & Tesser, 1986; Wilson & Dunn, 1986). Thus, examining your reasons for enjoying a certain artist's work may cause a rift between your expressed attitude and your subsequent behavior, but analyzing why you would prefer one digital camera over another probably won't create such a gap.

The Mismatch between General Attitudes and Specific Targets

Typically, the attitudes people express are about general categories, such as the environment, pushy people, French cuisine, or global trade. But the attitude-relevant behavior researchers typically assess has a more specific focus: donating to Greenpeace, reacting to a specific pushy individual, ordering foie gras, or picketing a meeting of the World Trade Organization. Given this mismatch between general attitudes and specific behaviors, no wonder attitudes don't always predict behavior particularly well.

Several studies have shown that consistency between attitudes and behavior is higher when they are both at the same level of specificity. Highly specific attitudes typically do a better job of predicting specific behaviors, and general attitudes typically do a better job of predicting how a person behaves "in general" across a number of different instances of, say, environmentalism, political activism, or xenophobia (Ajzen, 1987). In LaPiere's study, for example, the attitudes expressed by the various merchants were rather general: whether they would serve Orientals. But the behavior, of course, involved one specific Chinese couple with a specific demeanor and dressed in a specific fashion. Perhaps the results would have been different if LaPiere had asked the merchants whether they would serve a well-dressed Chinese couple who seemed pleasant and agreeable. If you want to predict a specific type of behavior accurately, you have to measure people's attitudes toward that specific type of behavior.

The broader point here is that what most people usually think of as attitudes about different classes of people, places, things, and events are often expressions of attitudes about a prototype of a given category. Therefore, if we encounter a specific situation or person who doesn't fit the prototype, our behavior probably won't reflect our stated attitude. Our general attitude doesn't apply to *that* particular person. Consider a study in which male college students expressed their attitudes about gay men (Lord, Lepper, & Mackie, 1984). The researchers also elicited from each student his stereotype of the "typical" gay man. Two months later, a different experimenter asked the participants if they would be willing to show some visiting students around campus. One of the visitors, "John B.," was described in such a way that the participants would think he was gay. For half the participants, the rest of the description of John B. was

General Attitudes and Specific Targets

A person with a general attitude about democracy may not have participated in the 2014 Hong Kong protests known collectively as the Umbrella Movement. But a person with more specific attitudes about the democratic election of leaders was probably more likely to join the protest movement.

crafted to fit their own individualized stereotype of a gay man; for the other half, it was not. The investigators found that the students' willingness to show John B. around campus—their behavior—was strongly predicted by their attitudes about gay men (those with positive attitudes said they were willing; those with negative attitudes said they were not), but only if John B. matched their prototype of a gay individual. If John B. did not fit their image, their attitudes about gay people did not predict their behavior (their willingness to show him around campus). (See also Lord, Desforges, Ramsey, Trezza, & Lepper, 1991.)

Automatic Behavior That Bypasses Conscious Attitudes

The influence of an attitude on behavior is sometimes conscious and deliberate: we reflect on our attitudes and then decide how to behave. But often our behavior is more reflexive than reflective, and the surrounding context elicits the behavior automatically.

To be sure, sometimes our automatic behavior is consistent with—indeed, caused by—our attitudes. In fact, one of the purposes of attitudes is to enable us to respond quickly, without having to do much weighing of pros and cons. We go with our gut feeling. But some types of automatic behavior bypass our attitudes altogether, as when we jump away from something that looks like a snake in the grass. When such actions are elicited directly from the surrounding context, the connection between our conscious attitudes and our behavior is necessarily weak. As noted in Chapter 4, one of the strongest and most influential research trends in social psychology over the past two decades has been the uncovering of more and more instances in which our behavior is automatically elicited by stimuli present in the environment. Recall, for example, the experiment in which people primed with the concept of elderly individuals walked more slowly down a hallway without being aware they were doing so (Bargh, Chen, & Burrows, 1996). Such findings highlight another limitation to how well attitudes predict behavior: automatic behavior that bypasses our conscious attitudes can conflict with those attitudes without our knowing it.

> ### ⬆ LOOKING BACK
>
> Attitudes can be surprisingly weak predictors of behavior. The reasons are that attitudes sometimes conflict with social norms about appropriate behavior; different attitudes can conflict with one another, or there might be a rift between affective and cognitive attitude components; examining the reasons for attitudes can cause confusion about our true feelings; general attitudes sometimes don't correspond to the specific action required in a given situation; and some types of automatic behavior bypass conscious thought altogether.

Predicting Attitudes from Behavior

Many young people resent being sent to church, temple, or mosque, and often have the complaint, "Why do I have to go? I don't believe any of this stuff." Many of them are told, "It doesn't matter if you believe it. What's important is that you continue with your studies and your prayers." Some resist to the very end and abandon all religious rituals and practices the minute their parents give them permission to opt out. But a remarkable number stick with it and eventually find themselves genuinely holding some of the very religious convictions and sentiments they once resisted. Over time, mere outward behavior can give way to genuine inner conviction.

The previous section presented the first part of the story about the connection between attitudes and behavior: attitudes can predict behavior, but not as strongly as most people would suspect. The second part of the story, as illustrated by the religion example just described, is that behavior can powerfully influence attitudes. Social psychology research over the past half-century has repeatedly documented the surprising extent to which people tend to bring their attitudes in line with their actions. Why does our behavior so powerfully influence our attitudes? A number of influential theories have been proposed to explain this relationship. Referred to collectively as *cognitive consistency theories*, they maintain that the impact of behavior on attitudes reflects the powerful tendency we have to justify or rationalize our behavior and to minimize any inconsistencies between our attitudes and actions. We focus here on the most influential of these theories: cognitive dissonance theory.

Cognitive Dissonance Theory

Leon Festinger's **cognitive dissonance theory** is one of the most influential theories in the history of social psychology (Festinger, 1957). Festinger maintained that people are troubled by inconsistency among their thoughts, sentiments, and actions, and that they will expend psychological energy to restore consistency. More specifically, he thought that an aversive emotional state—dissonance—is aroused whenever people experience inconsistency between two cognitions. And when the cognitions are about our own behavior (for example, "I just failed to live up to my vow"), we are troubled by the inconsistency between our cognitions and our behavior as well. This unpleasant emotional state motivates efforts to restore consistency. According to Festinger, people try to do so by changing the cognition to make it more consistent with the behavior.

What constitutes cognitive inconsistency, and in what circumstances does it arise? What are the different ways that people try to get rid of the inconsistency when it does occur? The tremendous amount of research Festinger's theory inspired has attempted to answer these questions, leading to a greater understanding of psychological conflict and rationalization. To develop a sense of the kinds of inconsistency people find troubling, and to get a flavor for the diverse phenomena the theory of cognitive dissonance can explain, let's look at some of the classic experiments on the subject—experiments that have inspired generations of social psychologists.

Decisions and Dissonance A mere moment's reflection tells us that all hard decisions cause some feelings of dissonance. Because the decision is hard, the rejected alternative must have some desirable features, the chosen alternative must have some undesirable features—or both. Because these

> **cognitive dissonance theory** The theory that inconsistencies among a person's thoughts, sentiments, and actions cause an aversive emotional state (dissonance) that leads to efforts to restore consistency.

elements are inconsistent with the decision made, the result is dissonance (Brehm, 1956). If you move to Los Angeles from a small town in the Midwest in pursuit of good weather, you'll enjoy the sun, but the cost of living and hours spent in traffic will probably produce dissonance. According to Festinger, once you've made an irrevocable decision to move to L.A., you'll exert mental effort to reduce this dissonance. You'll rationalize. You'll maintain that you never wanted to own a home ("Who wants all those chores?"), and you'll tell your friends how much you've learned from the audiobooks you play in your car during your long commute.

Numerous experiments have documented this tendency for people to rationalize their decisions. In one study, researchers interviewed bettors at a racetrack, some just before and some just after placing their bets (Knox & Inkster, 1968). The investigators reasoned that the act of placing a bet and irrevocably choosing a particular horse would cause the bettors to reduce the dissonance associated with the chosen horse's negative features (doesn't do well on a wet track) and the positive features of the competing horses (the perfect distance for one horse, the best jockey on another). Dissonance reduction should be reflected in greater confidence on the part of those interviewed right *after* placing their bets. Consistent with these predictions, bettors who were interviewed as they waited in line to place their bets gave their horses, on average, a "fair" chance of winning the race; those interviewed after they had placed their bets and were leaving the ticket window gave their horses, on average, a "good" chance to win. One participant provided some extra commentary that sheds light on the process of dissonance reduction. Having been interviewed while waiting in line (before placing his bet), after emerging from the ticket window, he approached another member of the research team and said, "Are you working with that other fellow there?

Well, I just told him that my horse had a fair chance of winning. Will you have him change that to a good chance? No, by God, make that an excellent chance."

Making hard decisions triggers dissonance, which in turn triggers processes of rationalization that make us more comfortable with our choices. Similar findings have been observed in elections: voters express greater confidence in their candidates when interviewed after they've voted than when interviewed right beforehand (Frenkel & Doob, 1976; Regan & Kilduff, 1988).

Festinger argued that dissonance reduction takes place only after an irrevocable decision has been made. He maintained, for example, that

Rationalizing Decisions, Reducing Dissonance

After placing a bet at the track, as here at the Kentucky Derby, people are likely to concentrate on the positive features of the horse they bet on and downplay any negatives. This rationalization process gives them greater confidence in the choice they made.

there is a clear and undeniable difference between the cognitive processes that occur during the period of making a decision and those that occur after the decision has been made. Reevaluation of alternatives in the direction of favoring the chosen or disfavoring the rejected alternative . . . is a post-decision phenomenon. (Festinger, 1964, p. 30)

The evidence from the betting and election studies seems to support Festinger's contention. However, his claim is at odds with other things we know about people. One of humankind's distinguishing characteristics is the ability to anticipate the future. If, in the process of making a decision, we see blemishes associated with what is emerging as our favorite option, why not start the process of rationalization beforehand, to minimize or eliminate dissonance altogether (Wilson, Wheatley, Kurtz, Dunn, & Gilbert, 2004)?

Indeed, more recent research has established that the same sorts of rationalization and distortion that occur after people make a decision also subconsciously take place *before* they make the decision. Research has shown that whether choosing restaurants, vacation spots, consumer goods, or political candidates, once people develop a slight preference for one option over the others, they distort subsequent information to support their initial preference (Brownstein, 2003; Brownstein, Read, & Simon, 2004; Russo, Medvec, & Meloy, 1996; Russo, Meloy, & Medvec, 1998; Simon, Krawczyk, & Holyoak, 2004; Simon, Pham, Le, & Holyoak, 2001). Thus, the small size of a particular Italian restaurant tends to be rated as a plus by those leaning toward Italian food ("It's nice and intimate"), but as a minus by those leaning toward a big burger joint ("We won't be able to talk without everyone overhearing us"). Festinger appears to have been right in maintaining that decisions evoke dissonance and dissonance reduction, yet these processes occur more often and more broadly than he anticipated; they take place both before and after decisions are made.

At this point, maybe you're convinced that people (including yourself) often reduce post-decision dissonance by changing their attitudes to be more favorable toward the chosen alternative and less favorable toward the rejected alternative. But how long-lasting are these changes in our attitudes? Maybe as time passes, our attitudes revert to where they were originally. Indeed, nearly all research on post-decision dissonance has assessed attitude change shortly after participants make their decisions. But Tali Sharot and her colleagues set out to test the durability of attitude changes that occur as a result of post-decision dissonance (Sharot, Fleming, Yu, Koster, & Dolan, 2012). They had participants evaluate a list of products—in this case, vacation destinations. Then the participants chose between two products they had rated fairly equally, and provided their evaluations of all the vacation destinations once more. The twist in this study was that they followed up with participants 3 years later, and obtained their evaluations of the same set of vacation destinations again. Immediately after making a decision, participants showed the typical reevaluation of the alternatives, rating their chosen vacation more favorably and their unchosen one less favorably, relative to their initial evaluations. These shifts in participants' evaluations remained 3 years later, suggesting that post-decision efforts to reduce dissonance can have very long-lasting effects.

Effort Justification The element of dissonance theory that rings most true to many people is the idea that if you pay a high price for something—in dollars, time, or effort—and it turns out to be disappointing, you'll probably experience dissonance. As a result, you're likely to devote mental energy to justifying what you've done; this tendency is known as **effort justification**. This sort of *sweet lemons rationalization* ("It's really not so bad") can be seen in many contexts. Those who don't have pets often suspect that pet lovers exaggerate the pleasure they get from their animals to offset all the early morning walking, poop scooping, and furniture wrecking. And those who choose not to have children suspect that homebound, sleep-deprived, overtaxed parents are fooling themselves when they say that nothing in life brings greater pleasure (Eibach & Mock, 2011).

Leon Festinger
In studying how people bring their attitudes in line with their behavior, Leon Festinger developed cognitive dissonance theory.

effort justification The tendency to reduce dissonance by justifying the time, effort, or money devoted to something that turned out to be unpleasant or disappointing.

induced (forced) compliance Subtly compelling people to behave in a manner that is inconsistent with their beliefs, attitudes, or values, in order to elicit dissonance, and therefore a change in their original views.

Researchers explored the role of dissonance reduction in such situations in an early study in which female undergraduates signed up for an experiment thinking it involved joining an ongoing discussion group about sex (Aronson & Mills, 1959). When they arrived, however, the students were told that not everyone can speak freely and comfortably about such a topic, so potential participants had to pass a screening test to join the group. Those assigned to a control condition simply read aloud a list of innocuous words to the male experimenter. Those assigned to a "mild" initiation condition read aloud a list of mildly embarrassing words, such as *prostitute*, *petting*, and *virgin*. Finally, those in a "severe" initiation group read aloud a list of obscene words and a passage from a novel describing sexual intercourse.

All participants were then told they had passed their screening test and could join the discussion group. The group was meeting that very day, but because everyone else in the discussion group had been given a reading assignment beforehand, participants were told it was best if they just listened in on the discussion. Then, through headphones in a nearby cubicle, they heard a very boring discussion of the sex life of invertebrates. Not only was the topic not what they had in mind when they signed up for a discussion group about sex, but the discussion group members "contradicted themselves and one another, mumbled several non sequiturs, started sentences that they never finished, hemmed, hawed, and in general conducted one of the most worthless and uninteresting discussions imaginable" (Aronson & Mills, 1959, p. 179).

The investigators predicted that the discussion would be boring and disappointing to all the participants, but that it would produce dissonance only for those who had undergone a severe initiation to join the group. The cognition "I suffered to get into this group" is inconsistent with the realization that "This group is worthless and boring." One way for the participants in the severe initiation condition to reduce dissonance would be to convince themselves that the group and the discussion were not so boring after all. And that's just what they did. When the experimenters asked participants at the end of the study to rate the quality of the discussion they listened to on a number of scales, those in the severe initiation condition rated it more favorably than those in the other two conditions (**Figure 7.1**).

Induced Compliance and Attitude Change Cognitive dissonance theory can also explain what often happens as a result of **induced (forced) compliance**—the compelling of people to behave in a manner that is inconsistent with their beliefs, attitudes, or values. Most people will feel some discomfort with the mismatch between their behavior and their attitudes. One way to deal with the inconsistency—the easiest and most likely way, given that the behavior can't be taken back—is for people to change their original attitudes or values. This was the core idea behind President Johnson's strategy, described in the chapter opening: when skeptics publicly defended the administration's position, the inconsistency between their private reservations

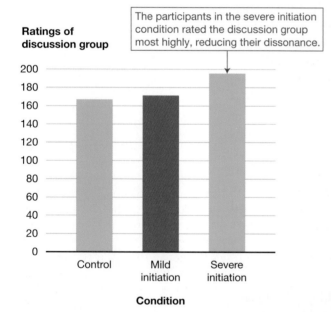

Ratings of discussion group

The participants in the severe initiation condition rated the discussion group most highly, reducing their dissonance.

Figure 7.1

Group Initiation and Liking for the Group

This graph shows the different ratings of a discussion group by participants who experienced no initiation (the control condition), a mild initiation, or a severe initiation to join the group.

SOURCE: Adapted from Aronson & Mills, 1959.

BOX 7.2

Not So Fast:
Critical Thinking about Surveys vs. Experiments

Chun Hsien "Michael" Deng, a 19-year-old student at Baruch College in New York City, was excited about having been accepted into the school's Pi Delta Psi fraternity, and the prospect of getting to know his new brothers. Like everyone else in the 2014 pledge class, he went on a weekend retreat to the Pocono Mountains, in Pennsylvania, with the more senior members of the fraternity. While there, he and his fellow pledges were subjected to a "gauntlet"-like hazing ritual in which he was blindfolded and required to negotiate a path while being knocked repeatedly to the ground. Tragically, Michael suffered a major brain trauma from this hazing ritual, and because his fraternity brothers were slow in seeking medical help, he died shortly after his eventual arrival at a nearby hospital.

Why would a fraternity do such a thing? To be sure, Michael Deng's death was anything but intentional, and representatives of the national Pi Delta Psi organization condemned the actions of the Baruch College chapter in no uncertain terms. Such condemnations notwithstanding, hazing rituals like the one that claimed Michael's life remain common. More than 60 students are known to have died in incidents like this in the United States since 2005, at least 10 of them in initiations by a single national fraternity. Why do fraternities continue to engage in such practices?

Cognitive dissonance theory provides an obvious answer. Having pledges undergo a painful initiation ritual may make them, once they've gone through it, more dedicated to the fraternity. After all, it may be hard for someone to walk away from an organization after paying such a stiff price to become a member. Doing so would likely cause a lot of dissonance, which could be reduced by deciding the fraternity is a wonderful organization, and sure to make college a golden time.

Fraternity Hazing and Commitment Fraternities try to increase the commitment of members by having them undergo difficult and embarrassing initiation rituals like the one shown here.

How can we establish that dissonance reduction really does lie at the heart of fraternity hazing? Stated differently, how can we determine whether fraternities that have more severe initiations do indeed cultivate more loyalty and enthusiasm among their members? One approach would be to survey various fraternities and evaluate membership commitment. We could also find out about the initiation practices and have judges, unaware of the purpose of the study, rate them for severity. Do the fraternities with the most severe initiations have the most committed members?

Unfortunately (and we hope you've anticipated this), such a survey-based finding would not be informative. It might mean, as dissonance theorists would expect, that undergoing a difficult initiation makes a person feel compelled to embrace the fraternity's virtues. But the finding might instead be the result of the best, most desirable fraternities having the "luxury" of subjecting its pledges to severe initiations. Maybe it's just that people wouldn't put up with a severe initiation to get into a less attractive fraternity. This is the correlation-cause problem; it plagues many empirical studies, and savvy consumers of research findings know to anticipate it (see Chapter 2). Only a true experiment—wherein people are randomly assigned to either, say, a "mild initiation" versus "severe initiation" condition—could tell us with great confidence whether more painful initiations lead to greater group loyalty than less painful ones.

and their public comments led them to dispel their doubts. Or so Johnson, in company with social psychologists, believed.

Numerous experiments have demonstrated the power of induced compliance to shift a person's original attitudes. In the very first experiment that demonstrated such an effect, Leon Festinger and Merrill Carlsmith (1959) had participants engage in what can only be described as experimental drudgery for an hour (loading spools on a tray over and over, turning pegs on a pegboard one-quarter turn at a time). Participants in the control condition were interviewed immediately afterward by someone from the psychology department, who asked them how much they enjoyed the experiment. They gave quite low ratings. No surprise there.

The researchers told participants in two other conditions that the experiment involved how performance on a task is influenced by expectations about it beforehand. These participants were led to believe they were in a control, "no expectation," condition, but that other subjects were told beforehand the study was either very interesting or boring. Looking rather sheepish, the experimenter explained that the next participant was about to show up and needed to be told the study was interesting. This was usually done, the experimenter explained, by a confederate posing as a participant. But the confederate was absent, putting the experimenter in a bit of a jam. Would you, the experimenter asked, play the role usually performed by the confederate and tell the next participant that the experiment is interesting? The experimenter offered the participant either $1 or $20 for doing so.

In this "play within a play," the true participants think they are confederates. What is most important to the experiment, and what is readily apparent to the participants, is that they have just lied (nearly every participant agreed to the request) by saying that a mind-numbingly boring study is interesting. Festinger and Carlsmith predicted this act would produce dissonance for those participants paid only $1 for the assignment. Their words were inconsistent with their beliefs, and $1 was not enough to justify the lie. To reduce their dissonance, participants in the $1 condition would rationalize their behavior by changing their attitude about the task they had performed. If they convinced themselves the task was not uninteresting after all, their lie would not really be a lie. In contrast, those paid $20 would not have any need to rationalize because the reward was good and the lie was of little consequence. Consistent with these predictions, when participants in the $1 condition later had to evaluate their experience, they rated the task more favorably than those in the other conditions. Only the participants in the $1 condition rated the activities above the neutral point (**Figure 7.2**).

There's a valuable lesson here about the best way to influence someone else's attitudes, a lesson that has important implications for child rearing, among other things. If you want to persuade people to do something (such as take school seriously, protect the environment, or refrain from using foul language) and you want them to internalize the broader message behind the behavior, you should use the smallest amount of incentive or coercion necessary to get them to do it. In other words, don't go overboard with the incentives. If the inducements are too substantial, people will justify their behavior accordingly (like participants in the $20 condition of Festinger and Carlsmith's study), and they will not have to rationalize their behavior by coming to believe in the broader purpose or

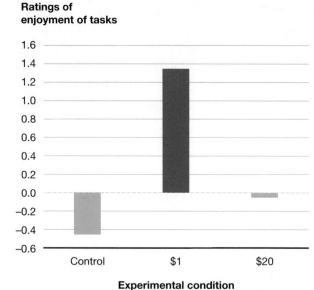

Ratings of enjoyment of tasks

Experimental condition

Figure 7.2

Induced Compliance and Attitude Change

Saying something we don't believe, and doing so with little justification ($1 instead of $20), produces dissonance. To reduce this dissonance, in this study the participants in the $1 condition rated the boring task more favorably than participants in the other two conditions, thereby providing some justification for their behavior (they did really lie).

SOURCE: Adapted from Festinger & Carlsmith, 1959.

BOX 7.3 **FOCUS ON *INTELLECTUAL HISTORY***

Pascal's Wager: The Birth of Cost-Benefit Analysis and Cognitive Consistency Theory

In a single stroke Blaise Pascal, the seventeenth-century French mathematician and Catholic philosopher, gave an impetus to both modern cost-benefit analysis (comparing the total expected costs and benefits of different options and choosing accordingly) and cognitive consistency theory. Why should people believe in God? *Benefit*: If God exists and we believe in God, we'll probably behave in such a way to guarantee eternal life. *Cost*: Not much, just forgoing a few guilty pleasures and avoiding some sins. Why should people *not* believe in God? *Benefit*: Not much, just going ahead and indulging in those pleasures and sins. *Cost*: Eternal damnation.

Anyone who accepts the logic of these arguments would agree it would be foolhardy not to wager that God exists and choose to believe in God. The benefits clearly outweigh the costs.

Payoff Matrix for Pascal's Wager

	God exists	God does not exist
Belief in God	+∞ (infinite gain)	−1 (finite loss)
Disbelief in God	−∞ (infinite loss)	+1 (finite gain)

The problem, however, is that logically concluding that it pays to believe in God may not be enough to make a person truly believe. Pascal recognized some people will say, "Try as I might, I simply cannot believe. What can I do?" As a solution, Pascal appealed to a version of what we would now call cognitive consistency theory, advising nonbelievers to behave as believers do: pray, light candles, attend church. If they behaved in such a way, Pascal reasoned, their beliefs would change to be

Blaise Pascal

consistent with the behavior. Problem solved. (But note that although Pascal was on to something very important about people's need for cognitive consistency, scholars such as Voltaire and Diderot had no difficulty spotting and articulating logical flaws in Pascal's argument for believing in God.)

---

philosophy behind it. But if the inducements are just barely sufficient (as in the $1 condition), their need to rationalize will tend to produce a deep-seated attitude change in line with their behavior. So if you're going to pay your children for doing their homework, do it on the cheap.

Induced Compliance and Extinguishing Undesired Behavior The flip side of this idea involves the use of mild versus severe punishments; this is illustrated by experiments using what is known as the "forbidden toy" paradigm (Aronson & Carlsmith, 1963; Freedman, 1965; Lepper, 1973). In one such study, a researcher showed children at a nursery school a set of five toys and asked them to say how much they liked each one. He then said he would have to leave the room for a while, but he'd be back soon. In the meantime, each child was free to play with any of the toys except for his or her second-favorite. Half the children were instructed not to play with the forbidden toy, because the experimenter would "be annoyed" if they did. This was the "mild threat" condition. In the "severe threat" condition, if the children played with the forbidden toy, the experimenter "would be very angry" and "would have to take all the toys and go home and never come back again."

While the experimenter was gone, each child was covertly observed, and none played with the forbidden toy. The investigators predicted that not playing with the forbidden toy would produce dissonance, but only for the children in the mild threat condition. For them, not playing with the toy would be inconsistent with the fact that it was highly desirable, an inconsistency they would likely resolve by devaluing the toy, convincing themselves it wasn't so great after all. Those who received the severe threat should experience no such dissonance, because not playing with it was justified by the threat they received. Thus, there was nothing to cause them to belittle the toy.

To find out whether these predictions were correct, the children had to reevaluate all five toys when the experimenter returned. As expected, those in the severe threat condition either did not change their opinion of the forbidden toy or liked it even more than before (**Figure 7.3**). In contrast, many of those in the mild threat condition viewed the toy less favorably. Thus, the threat of severe punishment will keep children from doing something you don't want them to do; but they will still, later on, want to do it. The threat of mild punishment—if it's just enough of a threat to keep them from doing it—can bring about psychological change, such that they'll no longer be tempted to do what you don't want them to do. Contrary to the old adage, you should spare the rod.

When Does Inconsistency Produce Dissonance?

Festinger's original statement describing when people will experience dissonance has some problems. Festinger thought holding two inconsistent cognitions triggered dissonance. But what constitutes inconsistency? Is it really inconsistent to refrain from playing with an attractive toy if an authority figure asks you not to? Apparently it is, given the results obtained in the forbidden toy studies. But what's so jarringly unpleasant about such inconsistency? We often refrain

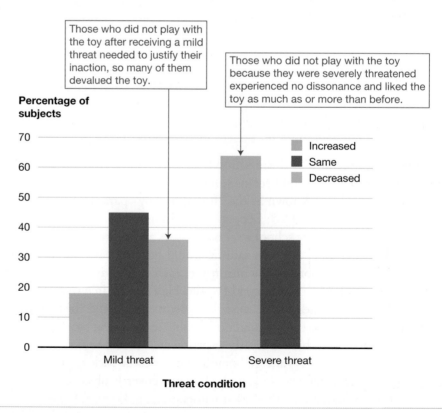

Figure 7.3

Devaluing the Forbidden Toy

For this study, the graphs show the percentages of children in the mild and severe threat conditions whose opinion of the forbidden toy increased, stayed the same, or decreased.

SOURCE: Adapted from Aronson & Carlsmith, 1963.

from doing things we know we would find enjoyable, even when we have no compelling reason (like a severe threat). Which situations are likely to cause dissonance and which ones aren't?

Eliot Aronson, a prominent dissonance researcher, offered a solution to this question. A particular inconsistency will arouse dissonance, Aronson argued, if it implicates our core sense of self (Aronson, 1969; Sherman & Gorkin, 1980). People like to think of themselves as rational, morally upright, worthy individuals, and anything that challenges such assessments tends to produce dissonance. For example, expending great effort to join a boring group calls into question our wisdom and rationality; telling another student that a tedious task is interesting challenges our integrity.

To understand the sorts of cognitions that might challenge our sense of judgment and personal character, it's useful to think about when *someone else's* actions make us question *that person's* character—or better still, to think of the justifications someone else could offer that would *prevent* us from questioning his or her judgment or moral fiber. Suppose you ask a tech-savvy friend to help you with a computer problem, but he says no. How harshly would you judge him? The answer probably depends on several factors. First, you wouldn't blame him if he could not have acted otherwise—for example, if he was at work and his boss wouldn't let him leave. He had no choice. Second, you probably wouldn't blame him much if he could justify his actions (see Chapter 5); perhaps he had to console a distraught roommate or study for an important exam. He *could* have helped out—he had some choice in the matter—but it's clear that doing so would not have been the best course of action, and you acknowledge that. Third, you would probably judge him more harshly in rough proportion to how much harm resulted from his failure to help. You would (understandably) think worse of him if you ended up failing a course because of it than if you were simply prevented from checking Facebook or surfing the Internet. Finally, you wouldn't blame him much if you'd never told him just how badly you needed his help, so he had no way to foresee the harm his refusal might cause.

This analysis of when we hold other people responsible for their actions helps us understand when we will hold *ourselves* responsible for our behavior and experience dissonance as a result. The line of reasoning suggests, in other words, that we ought to experience dissonance whenever we act in ways that are inconsistent with our core values and beliefs, and (1) the behavior was freely chosen, (2) the behavior was not sufficiently justified, (3) the behavior had negative consequences, and (4) the negative consequences were foreseeable.

Free Choice The critical role of freedom of choice was first demonstrated (and replicated many times) in a study in which college students were offered either $0.50 or $2.50 to write an essay in favor of a state law banning Communists from speaking on college campuses (Linder, Cooper, & Jones, 1967). (Since the original experiment was done in the mid-1960s, both payments seem low now; for comparable amounts today, it would be reasonable to multiply by a factor of 8: $4 and $20, respectively.) Because the law was at variance with the U.S. Constitution's guarantee of freedom of speech, nearly all students were opposed to it, and their essays thus conflicted with their true beliefs. For half the participants, their freedom to agree (or decline) to write such an essay was emphasized. For the other half, it was not. There was no dissonance effect among these latter participants. Indeed, those paid $2.50 later expressed attitudes more in favor of the ban than those paid $0.50 (presumably because writing the essay was associated with the good feelings that accompany the larger reward). In the free-choice group, however, the standard dissonance effect was obtained: those paid $0.50 changed their attitude more than those paid $2.50.

Insufficient Justification This last experiment, like all the induced-compliance studies (including Festinger and Carlsmith's original study), also demonstrates the importance of insufficient justification in arousing dissonance. If a person's behavior is justified by the existing incentives, even behavior that is dramatically in conflict with the person's beliefs and values will not produce dissonance—or the rationalizations that arise to combat it. Those paid $2.50 (about $20 today) for writing an essay that was inconsistent with their true beliefs felt no pressure to change their attitudes because their behavior was psychologically justified by the large cash payment. Those paid only $0.50 (about $4 today) had no such justification and thus felt the full weight of their behavioral inconsistency. So it appears that most of us are willing to sell our souls for money. And if the money is good enough, we don't even bother to justify the sale!

Negative Consequences If nothing of consequence results from actions that are at variance with our attitudes and values, it's easy to dismiss them as trivial. Indeed, a number of experiments have demonstrated that people experience dissonance only when their behavior results in harm of some sort. One such study, using Festinger and Carlsmith's paradigm (described earlier), had participants tell someone that a boring experiment was very interesting, by receiving either a small or a large incentive for doing so (Cooper & Worchel, 1970). Half the time, the confederate seemed convinced that the boring task was going to be interesting, and half the time the confederate clearly remained unconvinced: "Well, you're entitled to your own opinion, but I don't think I've ever enjoyed an experiment, and I don't think I'll find this one much fun." Note that there were no negative consequences when the person appeared unconvinced: no one was deceived. Thus, if negative consequences are necessary for the arousal of cognitive dissonance, the standard dissonance effect should occur only when the person is convinced. That was exactly what happened: the boring task was rated more favorably only by participants who were offered little incentive to lie to another person and the person appeared to believe the lie.

Foreseeability We typically don't hold people responsible for harm they've done if the harm wasn't foreseeable. If a dinner guest who is allergic to peanuts becomes ill after eating a dish with peanut sauce, we don't hold the host responsible if the guest never informed the host of the allergy. As this example suggests, it may be the foreseeability of the negative consequences of our actions that generates cognitive dissonance. Negative consequences that are not foreseeable don't threaten a person's self-image as a moral and decent person, so they shouldn't arouse dissonance.

This hypothesis has been verified in experiments that induced participants to write an essay in favor of a position with which they disagreed (that the size of the freshman class at their university should be doubled, for instance). If any negative consequences of such an action (the essays will be shown to a university committee charged with deciding whether to implement the policy) are made known to the participants after the fact, there is no dissonance and hence no attitude change in the direction of the essay they wrote. But if the negative consequences were either foreseen (participants knew beforehand their letters would be shown to the committee) or foreseeable (they knew ahead of time their letters *might* be shown to such a committee), the standard dissonance effect was obtained (Cooper, 1971; Goethals, Cooper, & Naficy, 1979).

Self-Affirmation and Dissonance

If dissonance results from challenges or threats to people's sense of themselves as rational, competent, and moral, it follows that they can ward off dissonance not only by dealing directly with the specific threat itself, but also indirectly by taking stock of their other qualities and core values. As we learned in Chapter 3, Claude Steele and his colleagues have argued that this sort of self-affirmation is a common way for people to cope with threats to their self-esteem (Cohen, Aronson, & Steele, 2000; Correll, Spencer, & Zanna, 2004; McQueen & Klein, 2006; Schmeichel & Martens, 2005; Sherman & Cohen, 2002, 2006; Steele, 1988; Steele, Spencer, & Lynch, 1993). "Sure, I might have violated a friend's confidence, but I am very empathetic when other people are having difficulties." "I know I drive an SUV, but no one attends church services more regularly than I do." By bolstering themselves in one area, people can tolerate a bigger hit in another.

In one of the cleverest demonstrations of the effects of self-affirmation, Steele (1988) had undergraduates majoring in science and business participate in an experiment using the post-decision dissonance paradigm (described earlier), in which participants have to choose between two objects of similar value. In a control condition, both groups of students showed the usual dissonance effect: finding hidden attractions in the chosen alternative and hidden flaws in the unchosen alternative. But in another condition, the experimenters had the business and science majors put on white lab coats before rendering their final evaluations. Steele predicted that wearing a lab coat would affirm an important identity for the science majors, but not for the business majors. The results supported his predictions. The business majors who wore lab coats reduced dissonance just as much as participants in the control condition; the science majors did not. If you feel good about yourself, you don't sweat the small stuff like minor decisions.

More recent research has examined how self-affirmation can assuage the need to reduce dissonance in a situation that will be familiar to many of us. Imagine you're having a conversation with someone—a coworker, friend, family member—and in the course of the conversation the person makes a prejudicial remark with which you strongly disagree. Do you confront the person, or let the remark pass? Let's be honest: we often let remarks like this slide because confrontation is uncomfortable and can have interpersonal costs (Czopp & Ashburn-Nardo, 2012). But for those of us who think it's important to confront prejudice, not doing so arouses dissonance, and we start rationalizing our failure to act. And that's exactly what researchers have shown: people who value confronting prejudice but fail to do so end up evaluating the person making the preducial remark more favorably, and even reducing the importance they place on confronting prejudice in the first place (Rasinski, Geers, & Czopp, 2013). There's good news though. These researchers also showed that a simple self-affirmation intervention—giving nonconfronters a few minutes to make a list of their positive characteristics—eliminated the need to reduce the dissonance arising from their failure to confront.

Is Dissonance Universal?

We have discussed cognitive dissonance as if it were a cross-culturally universal phenomenon. Is it? Substantial evidence addresses the question and yields some interesting answers. Using the free-choice, self-affirmation paradigm, researchers asked all the participants in a study to choose between two objects (CDs, in this case), but first gave some of them self-affirmation in the form of positive feedback on a personality test (Heine & Lehman, 1997). The participants were Japanese and Canadian, and the researchers wanted to see if the dissonance effect was the same in people from these two different cultures. The results for the Canadians were similar to those in earlier studies: participants exhibited a substantial dissonance effect in the control condition, finding previously unnoticed attractions in the chosen CD and previously unnoticed flaws in the unchosen one, but no dissonance effect if they had received positive feedback about their personalities. The Japanese participants, in contrast, were unaffected by the self-affirmation manipulation. More striking still, they showed no dissonance effect in *either* condition, which led the researchers to conclude that cognitive dissonance might be a phenomenon unique to Westerners. But using an induced-compliance paradigm, researchers in another study persuaded participants to do something they didn't want to do, and found dissonance effects for Japanese participants—if they were led to think that other students were observing their behavior (Sakai, 1981).

Do these findings imply that East Asians may experience dissonance in the induced-compliance paradigm but not in the free-choice paradigm? That would be messy. Fortunately, there's another way to reconcile the two sets of results. As we have emphasized throughout this book, East Asians, along with many other people in the world, are more attuned than Westerners are to other people and their reactions. If East Asians exhibit dissonance effects in the induced-compliance paradigm because they question their actions when others are observing them, then they should also show dissonance effects in the free-choice paradigm if they are led to think about other people's possible reactions to their choice.

This outcome was demonstrated in a study in which investigators had participants choose between two CDs under one of two circumstances (Kitayama, Snibbe, Markus, & Suzuki, 2004). For some participants, hanging right in front of them at eye level was the poster shown in **Figure 7.4**. The poster was allegedly a figure from an unrelated experiment, and the researchers wanted to see whether

BOX 8.3 **FOCUS ON THE *MEDIA***

The Hostile Media Phenomenon

On July 23, 2008, with the U.S. presidential race heating up and the gap between John McCain and Barack Obama narrowing, McCain sat down to talk with Sean Hannity of Fox News. Along with a discussion of the war in Iraq, the central topic they covered was media bias. McCain and Hannity claimed the media were treating Obama uncritically, in biased fashion, reacting to him as if he were a rock star rather than looking critically at his political agenda. This allegation of media bias was in part a political ploy, but it undoubtedly also reflected a genuine belief that their side was being mistreated by the media.

McCain's running mate, Sarah Palin, derided the "lame-stream media" for having what she perceived as a consistent "liberal bias." Years earlier, Richard Nixon felt the media were run by an elite Jewish clique. More recently,

in an interview in early 2013, President Obama suggested that the media, out of a desire to appear objective, blame political stalemates on the inability of Democrats and Republicans to agree, rather than acknowledging that the main obstacle to compromise is the Republican party.

The thesis that the media are ideologically biased regularly leads to the publication of best-selling books that appeal to liberals and conservatives alike. An entire organization, Fairness and Accuracy in Reporting (FAIR; www .fair.org), is devoted to documenting bias in the media (showing, for instance, that conservatives are more likely to appear as experts on such news shows as *Nightline*).

Research by Robert Vallone, Lee Ross, and Mark Lepper (1985) suggests that we all tend to believe the media are biased against our preferred causes.

According to these researchers, most people believe they see the world in a reasonable, objective fashion—a fallacy known as naïve realism (see Chapter 1). Thus, any media presentation that attempts to present both sides of an issue is going to be perceived as biased by both sides of any controversy. This basic tendency to perceive the media as hostile is a regularity in the political theater of presidential politics, as well as a common feature of our perception of the media. In one telephone survey conducted three days before the 1980 U.S. presidential election, among Jimmy Carter supporters who felt the media had favored one candidate in its coverage, 83 percent thought it favored Reagan. In contrast, for Reagan supporters who felt the media had been biased, 96 percent felt the media had favored Carter. One thing we can all agree on: the media are biased!

Resistance to Persuasion

Why don't the media have a stronger effect on what we buy, who we vote for, or whether we adopt healthier habits? Part of the answer lies in the fact that many of the important principles of social psychology—the influence of our perceptual biases, previous commitments, and prior knowledge—serve as sources of independent thought and significant forces of resistance in the face of persuasive attempts.

Attentional Biases and Resistance

The U.S. Office of the Surgeon General issued a report in 1964 linking smoking to lung cancer. This presumably incontrovertible evidence about the related health risks would logically have both smokers and nonsmokers shifting their attitude about smoking. And yet, following the release of the report, 40 percent of smokers found the document to be flawed, compared with 10 percent of nonsmokers. We all like to think we absorb data and information in relatively unbiased fashion (Pronin, Gilovich, & Ross, 2004). If we learn a particular practice

or habit is dangerous to our health, we should alter our attitude accordingly. But our minds sometimes respond selectively to information in a way that maintains our initial point of view.

Let's break this down into two concepts: selective attention and selective evaluation. Several studies indicate that people are inclined to *attend selectively* to information that confirms their original attitudes (Eagly & Chaiken, 1998; Sweeney & Gruber, 1984). We tune in to information that reinforces our attitudes, and we tune out information that contradicts them. In one study, students who either supported or opposed the legalization of marijuana listened to a message that advocated legalization (Kleinhesselink & Edwards, 1975). The message contained 14 arguments: 7 were strong and difficult to refute (and thus clearly appealing to the pro-legalization students), and 7 were silly and easy to refute (and thus very attractive to the anti-legalization students). The students heard the message through earphones accompanied by a continual static buzz. To combat this problem, students could press a button to eliminate the buzz for 5 seconds.

As you might have anticipated, the pro-legalization students pushed the button more often when the speaker was delivering the strong arguments in favor of legalization. They wanted to hear the information that would reinforce their own viewpoint. The anti-legalization students, in contrast, were more likely to push the button while the speaker was offering up the easy-to-refute arguments in favor of legalization. They wanted to hear the weakness of the pro arguments, thereby reinforcing their anti-legalization position. In a similar study, students wrote essays about federal funding for abortion or the use of nuclear energy; they tended to select reference material from magazine articles that supported their opinion (McPherson, 1983). During presidential elections, people are more inclined to read newspapers, blogs, and websites that support their preferred candidate and avoid those that support the opposition.

We not only seek out and pay disproportionate attention to information that supports our attitudes; we also *selectively evaluate* the information we find, looking favorably on material that agrees with our point of view and critically on information that contradicts it. For example, Ziva Kunda (1990) had female and male students read a story presented as a *New York Times* article describing how caffeine consumption in females is associated with an increased risk of fibrocystic disease. Half the participants were high-caffeine users (fans of lattes and diet sodas) and the other half were low-caffeine users. The female high-caffeine users, of course, should have considered the article threatening and thus should have been skeptical. As you can see in **Figure 8.6**, this expectation was confirmed. Independent of caffeine use, the male participants found the article fairly convincing, as did the females who used little caffeine. Only the high-caffeine-using females were less convinced by the article and more critical of it.

In related research, Peter Ditto and his colleagues have shown that people are more critical of evidence that violates cherished beliefs about their personal health. Patients who receive unhealthy diagnoses are more likely to downplay both the seriousness of the diagnosis and the validity of the test that produced it (Ditto, Jemmott, & Darley, 1988). In a clever extension of this work, Ditto and Lopez (1992) gave undergraduates a test of a fictitious medical condition, a

"The human understanding when it has once adopted an opinion draws all things else to support and agree with it. And though there be a greater number or weight of instances to be found on the other side, yet these it either neglects and despises, or else by some distinction sets aside and rejects, in order that by this great and pernicious predetermination the authority of its former conclusion may remain inviolate."

—FRANCIS BACON

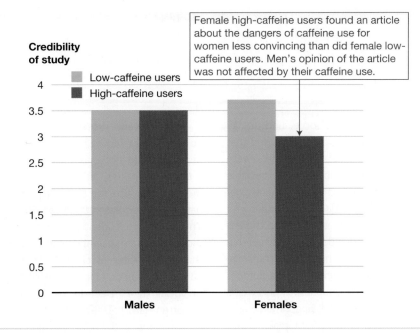

Credibility of study

Female high-caffeine users found an article about the dangers of caffeine use for women less convincing than did female low-caffeine users. Men's opinion of the article was not affected by their caffeine use.

Low-caffeine users
High-caffeine users

SOURCE: Adapted from Kunda, 1990.

Figure 8.6
Selective Evaluation
People who are personally motivated will derogate information that challenges cherished beliefs.

deficiency that was supposedly associated with pancreatic disorders later in life. The test was simple: put saliva on a piece of yellow paper and observe whether it would change color in the next 20 seconds. In the deficiency condition, participants were told that if the paper remained the same color (yellow), they had the medical condition; in the no-deficiency condition, participants were told that if the paper changed to a dark green, they had the medical condition. The paper remained yellow throughout the study.

Clearly, participants in the deficiency condition would be motivated to see the paper change color, and they should be disturbed by the evidence confronting them—the paper remaining yellow. And indeed, these participants took almost 30 seconds longer than those who got more favorable evidence to decide that their test was finished, repeatedly dipping it in saliva to give the paper every possible opportunity to turn green. Given our tendency to selectively attend to and evaluate incoming messages in ways that confirm our preexisting attitudes, it's no surprise that media effects are weak in producing attitude change. Most messages, it would seem, end up mainly preaching to the choir.

Previous Commitments and Resistance

Many persuasive messages fail because they can't overcome the target audience's previous commitments. Antidrug campaigns are aimed at decreasing habitual drug-taking behavior, which is embedded in a way of life and a community of friends centered around drugs. Some forces of resistance to change may be even more formidable than habits, one of which is genetics. Research reveals that our political allegiances are passed from parent to child to a degree and seem to be part of our DNA **(Box 8.4)**. Ads that try to get people to shift their political allegiances must, in effect, convince voters to abandon these deep commitments.

There's also evidence that public commitments make people resist attitude change. (In addition, they might make people resistant to conformity; see Asch's line judgment studies in Chapter 9.) In some studies, when participants made

BOX 8.4 **FOCUS ON *BIOLOGY***

The Genetic Basis of Attitudes

One of the deepest sources of our commitment to strong attitudes and resistance to persuasive messages is our genes. Work by Abraham Tesser (1993) indicates that our opinions and beliefs are in part inherited. He examined the attitudes of monozygotic (identical) twins, who share 100 percent of their genes, and those of dizygotic (fraternal) twins, who share 50 percent of their genes. For most of the viewpoints surveyed, the identical twins' attitudes were more similar than those of fraternal twins. This was true, for example, for opinions about the death penalty,

jazz, censorship, divorce, and socialism. Moreover, researchers found that the more heritable attitudes were also more accessible, less susceptible to persuasion, and more predictive of feelings of attraction to a stranger who had similar attitudes. Of course, there is no gene for attitudes about censorship or socialism; the hereditary transmission must occur through some element of temperament, such as impulsivity, a preference for risk taking, or a distaste for novelty (which might make a person dislike jazz but be more tolerant of censorship).

More recent research by James Fowler and his colleagues found that genes account not only for politically relevant attitudes, as Tesser documented, but also for political participation (Fowler, Baker, & Dawes, 2008). They found that identical twins were more likely to resemble each other than were fraternal twins in sharing party affiliations, and in their likelihood of voting in an election. No wonder it's often hard to shift people's political opinions and voting preferences and behavior; doing so would require changing a basic part of who they are.

---

public commitments to their attitudes—as people do every day when discussing politics and social issues with their friends—they were more resistant to subsequent counterattitudinal messages than control participants (Kiesler, 1971; Pallak, Mueller, Dollar, & Pallak, 1972).

Why do public commitments increase resistance to persuasion? One basic reason is that it's hard to back down from such endorsements without losing face, even when evidence is presented against the position we publicly embraced. A less obvious reason is that public commitments engage us in more extensive thoughts about a particular issue, which tends to produce more extreme, entrenched attitudes. Abraham Tesser labeled this idea the **thought polarization hypothesis**. To test his hypothesis, Tesser measured participants' attitudes about social issues, such as legalizing prostitution (Tesser & Conlee, 1975). He then had them think for a few moments about the issue. When they stated their opinions about the same issue a second time, they routinely gave stronger ratings; both opponents and proponents became polarized.

Similarly, the repeated expression of attitudes has been shown to lead to more extreme positions in a variety of domains, including viewpoints about particular people, artwork, fashions, and football strategies (Downing, Judd, & Brauer, 1992; Judd, Drake, Downing, & Krosnick, 1991; Tesser, Martin, & Mendolia, 1995). But a caveat is in order here. Increased thought about an attitude object can lead to more moderate attitudes for people who previously had little motivation to think about the issue or little preexisting knowledge about it (Judd & Lusk, 1984).

thought polarization hypothesis The hypothesis that more extended thought about a particular issue tends to produce a more extreme, entrenched attitude.

Knowledge and Resistance

According to the ELM approach to persuasion, prior knowledge makes people engage with persuasive messages through the central route, thereby leading them to scrutinize those messages carefully. People with a great deal of knowledge are more resistant to persuasion; their beliefs and habits (and sometimes emotions) are tied up with their attitudes, and thus their point of view tends to be fixed. This intuition has been repeatedly borne out in the experimental literature (Haugtvedt & Petty, 1992; Krosnick, 1988; Lydon, Zanna, & Ross, 1988; Zuwerink & Devine, 1996).

In a study of attitudes about environmental preservation, Wendy Wood (1982) divided students into two groups: those who were pro-preservation and knew a lot about the issue, and those who were pro-preservation but knew less about the subject. In a second session, she exposed these two groups to a message opposed to environmental preservation. Those with a great deal of knowledge about the environment changed their stance only a little bit, as they counterargued a great deal in response to the message, relying on what they already knew and strongly believed about the issue. In contrast, the less knowledgeable students shifted their attitudes considerably in the direction of the anti-preservation message.

Attitude Inoculation

Thus far, we've looked at how people's belief systems—their preexisting knowledge, commitments, and biases—make them resistant to persuasion and attitude change. Social psychologists have discovered some techniques that can be used to strengthen these tendencies.

McGuire developed one such technique, which found inspiration in a rather unusual source: inoculation against viruses. When we receive an inoculation, we're exposed to a weak dose of the virus. This small exposure stimulates our immune system, which is thus prepared to defend against larger doses of the virus. McGuire believed that resistance to persuasion could be encouraged in a similar fashion, by **attitude inoculation**—small attacks on our beliefs that would engage our preexisting attitudes, prior commitments, and background knowledge and thereby counteract the larger attack (McGuire & Papageorgis, 1961).

In his studies on attitude inoculation, McGuire first assessed participants' endorsements of different cultural truisms, such as "It's a good idea to brush your teeth after every meal if at all possible" or "The effects of penicillin have been, almost without exception, of great benefit to mankind" (McGuire & Papageorgis, 1961). More than 75 percent of the participants checked 15 on a 15-point scale to indicate their agreement with truisms like these.

Then came the intervention. McGuire and Papageorgis exposed participants to a small attack on their belief in the truism. In the toothbrushing case, they might read, "Too frequent brushing tends to damage the gums and expose the vulnerable parts of the teeth to decay." In some conditions, the researchers had the participants refute that attack by offering arguments against it; this was the attitude inoculation. In other conditions, the researchers had participants consider arguments in support of the truism. Then, at some time between 1 hour and 7 days later, the participants read a three-paragraph, full-scale attack on the truism. **Figure 8.7** presents data that attest to the immunizing effectiveness of attitude inoculation.

Applied to a real-life situation, like a smoking prevention program, the idea would be to present people with pro-smoking arguments from peers and advertisements, such as "Smoking is about freedom and maturity," then encourage

attitude inoculation Small attacks on people's beliefs that engage their preexisting attitudes, prior commitments, and background knowledge, enabling them to counteract a subsequent larger attack and thus resist persuasion.

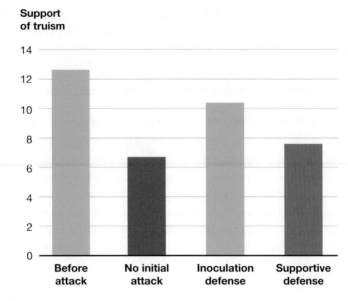

Figure 8.7

Attitude Inoculation

This study showed that using preexisting attitudes, commitments, and knowledge to come up with counter-arguments against an initial attack on an attitude makes people more resistant to persuasion in the face of a subsequent attack (third bar) compared to when there was no initial attack (second bar), or when they initially generated supportive arguments in favor of their attitude (fourth bar).

SOURCE: Adapted from McGuire & Papageorgis, 1961.

them to make counterarguments. The hope would be that counterarguing in response to an initial attack would inoculate them, thereby making them more resistant to future inducements to smoke.

Changes in Attitude Certainty

As we've discussed, if people resist a persuasive appeal, their attitude toward the target object has not changed; the direction and strength of their attitude have essentially remained the same. Is it possible, though, that other factors have been altered, while the attitude remains, say, moderately negative?

A growing body of research by Tormala, Petty, and their colleagues suggests that the conviction or certainty with which an attitude is held may change in response to a persuasive message, even if the direction and strength do not (Tormala, Clarkson, & Petty, 2006; Tormala & Petty, 2002). If people feel they're able to combat the message effectively, generating convincing counter-arguments, their original view may become more entrenched. That's important because more certain attitudes better predict behavior (Fazio & Zanna, 1978), stand up more firmly to persuasive appeals (Wu & Shaffer, 1987), and persist longer over time (Bassilli, 1996).

Thus, a good way to get people to dig in their heels and become more confident about their position on an issue is to present them with lousy counterarguments. They might rebut the arguments with ease, and their certainty about their position may increase—even if their position hasn't changed (Tormala, Clarkson, & Petty, 2006). By contrast, when people don't feel they have good arguments against a persuasive message, their confidence in their prior attitude may weaken, even if the direction and strength of their attitude haven't changed. The foundation of their view has been undermined, even if it seems the same on the surface.

🕐 LOOKING BACK

People can resist persuasive messages by selectively attending to and evaluating information that confirms their original attitudes and beliefs, and ignoring or criticizing contradictory information. Previous commitments to political ideologies or values also increase resistance to persuasion. Attitude inoculation can make people resist attitude change, because the small attacks give them the chance to muster arguments to use when faced with stronger attacks on their beliefs and attitudes. Resistance to persuasion may involve changes in the conviction with which an attitude is held, even as the direction and strength of the attitude remain intact.

Chapter Review

SUMMARY

Dual-Process Approaches to Persuasion

- Both the *elaboration likelihood model* and the *heuristic-systematic model* of persuasion hypothesize that there are two routes to persuasion. A person's motivation and ability to think carefully and systematically about the content of a persuasive message determine which route is used.
- When using the *central (systematic) route* to persuasion, people attend carefully to the message, and they consider relevant evidence and underlying logic in detail. People are especially likely to go through this route when motivation is high (the issue has personal consequences) and ability is high (they have a lot of knowledge in the domain). With the central route, people are sensitive to the quality of the persuasive arguments, leading them to be more persuaded when the arguments are strong but not when they are weak.
- In the *peripheral (heuristic) route* to persuasion, people pay attention to superficial aspects of the message. They use this route when they have little motivation (the issue has no bearing on their outcomes) or ability to attend to its deeper meaning (they have little knowledge or are distracted). With this route, people are persuaded by easy-to-process cues, such as the attractiveness and credibility of the message source, or the mere length of the persuasive message.

The Elements of Persuasion

- The elements of a persuasive attempt are the source of the message ("who"), the content of the message ("what"), and the audience of the message ("to whom").
- Sources that are attractive, credible, and confident tend to be persuasive. Although a noncredible source is unlikely to induce immediate attitude change, a *sleeper effect* may occur, in which attitude change happens gradually and the message has become dissociated from its source.
- Vivid messages are usually more persuasive than matter-of-fact ones. An example is the *identifiable victim effect*, whereby messages with a single identifiable victim are more compelling than those without such vivid imagery. Messages that instill fear in the audience can also be effective, as long as they include information about the courses of action one can take to avoid the feared outcome.
- Advertisements in independent cultures emphasize the individual, and those in interdependent societies emphasize the collective.
- Characteristics of a message's audience affect whether it is persuasive; they include the need for cognition (how deeply people like to think about issues), mood, age, and the size and diversity of the audience.

Metacognition and Persuasion

- *Metacognitions*, people's thoughts about their thinking, can play a powerful role in persuasion.
- The *self-validation hypothesis* states that when people have greater thought confidence, they are more persuaded in the (favorable or unfavorable) direction of their thoughts.
- Bodily movements, such as head nodding or shaking, can indicate the level of confidence people have in their thoughts about an attitude issue or object.

The Media and Persuasion

- According to the *third-person effect*, most people believe other people are more influenced by the media than they are. But the media have weaker effects than is generally assumed, including consumer advertising, political advertising, and public service announcements.
- The media are most effective in *agenda control*, in shaping what people think about, such as the number of stories and discussions presented on various issues.

Resistance to Persuasion

- People can be resistant to persuasion because of preexisting biases, commitments, and knowledge. They selectively attend to and evaluate information according to their original attitudes, tuning into what supports their prior attitudes and beliefs and tuning out whatever contradicts them.

- Public commitment to a position helps people resist persuasion. Just thinking about an attitude object can produce *thought polarization*, or movement toward extreme views that can be hard to change.

- People with more knowledge are more resistant to persuasion because they can counterargue against messages that take an opposite position to what they know and believe.

- Resistance to persuasion can be encouraged through *attitude inoculation*, exposing people to weak arguments against their position and allowing them to generate arguments against it.

- Even if the direction and strength of an attitude remain intact, resistance to persuasion may change the certainty with which the person holds the attitude.

THINK ABOUT IT

1. A new boutique coffeehouse just opened in your neighborhood featuring coffee sustainably sourced from small organic farms around the world. Design two ads for the coffeehouse, one using the central (systematic) route to persuasion and one using the peripheral (heuristic) route. How do your ads differ?

2. Describe the three elements of a persuasive appeal, and give two examples of each element that influence persuasiveness.

3. Suppose you are part of a global advertising team responsible for creating ads for oatmeal in both South Korea and the United States. Design an ad for each country, and explain why you designed the ads the way you did.

4. What is the self-validation hypothesis? What aspects about our thoughts, besides the valence and number of thoughts we have on a topic, influence whether or not we are persuaded by them?

5. Although your Uncle Ted watches hours of local news programming each night, he argues that "you young people" are way more susceptible to media messages than he is. Describe the phenomenon that Uncle Ted is exhibiting, and give an example of a study that scientifically supports the existence of such a phenomenon.

6. Tyrell and his girlfriend, Shea, have very different views on capital punishment: he opposes it, while she supports it. Even after Tyrell presents evidence that capital punishment is both financially wasteful and ineffective at preventing crime, Shea does not change her views. Using what you know about resistance to persuasion, how might Shea be staving off Tyrell's attempts to persuade her?

THE ANSWER GUIDELINES FOR THE THINK ABOUT IT QUESTIONS CAN BE FOUND AT THE BACK OF THE BOOK . . .

Social Influence

I n 1980, you'd have been more likely to see a woman smoking a cigar than sporting a tattoo. Back then, tattoos were rarely seen on anyone besides sailors and prison inmates. Now architects, teachers, doctors, professors, and judges have tattoos. According to a 2007 study, 40 percent of Americans under 40 have at least one tattoo, and 10 percent *over* 40 have one (Pew Research Center, 2007).

The growing popularity of tattoos over the past few decades reflects the power of social influence. The many who paid for a permanent tattoo on their body didn't suddenly sense the virtues of body art on their own; they influenced one another. The influence was sometimes implicit ("Look at that cool butterfly Jill has on her ankle"), and sometimes explicit ("Check out our fraternity letters on my triceps; you should get them too").

Social influence contributes to prison guards abusing inmates (see Chapter 1), schoolchildren failing to stop a bully, and soldiers suppressing their fear and charging into battle. Other times people consciously decide to copy others or agree to requests; sometimes they just comply, unaware they're being influenced. This chapter explores the different types of social influence that operate every day in the behavior we see around us.

The power of social influence can be seen in studies of how much people in different social networks influence each other. You are 40 percent more likely to suffer from obesity if a family member or friend is obese. You're also 20 percent more likely to be obese if a *friend* of your friend is obese, and 10 percent more likely if a friend of a friend of a friend is obese. This pattern seems to hold through three

A Social Influence Network

This visualization shows how happiness clusters among friends, spouses, and siblings in a sample of participants in Framingham, Massachusetts. Each point represents a participant (circles for women, squares for men), and the lines between each point represent their relationship (black for siblings, red for friends and spouses). The color of each point represents that person's happiness level: blue for the least happy participants, yellow for the most happy, and green for those in between. You can readily see that the most and least happy people cluster together.

SOURCE: Christakis & Fowler, 2013.

degrees of connection in social networks, and has been demonstrated in studies of drinking behavior, smoking, and general levels of happiness. If a friend of your friend is happy, you're more likely to be happy too (Christakis & Fowler, 2013).

Part of these effects is due to shared genes, and some is due to the tendency for people to associate disproportionately with people who are like them (see Chapter 10). Psychologists call the latter tendency homophily. However, not all these social network effects result from homophily and genetics. Some are the result of people influencing one another.

In one telling experiment, someone canvassed residents and encouraged them to vote; this influenced not just the person at the door, but other household members as well (Nickerson, 2008). Another study examined whether participants in a game involving real money cooperated with one another or focused on their narrow self-interest (Fowler & Christakis, 2010). Everyone played many rounds of the game, with each participant randomly assigned to a different four-person group each round. The investigators found that whether a person was altruistic on, say, round 3 was influenced (not surprisingly) by how selfish or altruistic that person's groupmates were on round 2. But that person was also influenced by what her round 2 groupmates had experienced with *their* groupmates on round 1. Because the participants were strangers randomly assigned to different groups, the results must have been due to social influence, not homophily or genetics. Thus, some types of behavior truly are contagious.

The topic of social influence highlights an important theme first raised in Chapter 1: many seemingly minor, subtle details in a situation can profoundly affect behavior. As a result, the study of social psychology changes forever the way we view human behavior—whether it's the actions of bona fide heroes, like

Social Influence and Fashion

Social influence affects what we do and say and how we present ourselves to others. (A) In the 1940s, tattoos were rarely seen on anyone other than sailors and soldiers. (B, C) Today, tattoos are common, on both men and women.

the New York City firefighters who charged into the burning World Trade Center to rescue victims trapped inside, or, at the other end of the spectrum, the behavior of those who become suicide bombers or participate in acts of genocide, such as the Holocaust in Europe or, more recently, the massacres in the Darfur region of Sudan.

In examining social influence, this chapter discusses a number of "situationist classics" in social psychology—experiments that have become well known, in both the field of psychology and the broader culture, for revealing how seemingly inconsequential elements of a social situation can have powerful effects on behavior. The results of these experiments have surprised and intrigued generations of students, forcing them to rethink some of their basic assumptions about human nature.

What Is Social Influence?

Social influence, broadly speaking, refers to the many ways people affect one another. It involves changes in behavior and/or attitudes that result from the comments, actions, or even the mere presence of others. Social influence is a subject to which everyone can relate. Other people routinely try to influence us—a friend's pressure to go out drinking, an advertiser's efforts to get us to adopt the latest fashion, a UNICEF plea for money, or the attempts of a parent, politician, or priest to shape our moral, political, or religious values. And we ourselves often try to influence others, as when we unconsciously smile at someone for actions we like, frown at someone for behavior we dislike, or deliberately try to coax a friend into doing us a favor. Effective dealings with others require knowing when to yield to their attempts to influence us and when—and how—to resist. Being effective also demands that we exercise some skill in our attempts to influence others.

Social psychologists distinguish among several types of social influence. The one most familiar to the average person is **conformity**, defined as changing one's behavior or beliefs in response to some real (or imagined) pressure from others. As noted earlier, the pressure to conform can be implicit, as when you decide to toss out your loose-fitting jeans in favor of those with a tighter cut (or vice versa) simply because other people are doing so. But conformity pressure can also be explicit, as when members of a peer group pointedly encourage one another to smoke cigarettes, try new drugs, or push the envelope on the latest extreme sport.

When conformity pressure is sufficiently explicit, it blends into another type of social influence called **compliance**, which social psychologists define as responding favorably to an explicit request by another person. Compliance attempts can come from people with some power over you, as when your boss or professor asks you to run an errand; or they can come from peers, as when a classmate asks to borrow your notes. Compliance attempts from powerful people often aren't as nuanced and sophisticated as those from peers, because they don't have to be. (Think how much easier it would be for your professor to persuade you to loan her $20 than it would be for a stranger sitting next to you in the classroom.) Another type of social influence, **obedience**, occurs when the power relationship is unequal and the more powerful person, the authority figure, issues a demand rather than a request, to which the less powerful person submits.

social influence The many ways people affect one another, including changes in attitudes, beliefs, feelings, and behavior resulting from the comments, actions, or even the mere presence of others.

conformity Changing one's behavior or beliefs in response to explicit or implicit pressure (real or imagined) from others.

compliance Responding favorably to an explicit request by another person.

obedience In an unequal power relationship, submitting to the demands of the person in authority.

Conformity

If you went back in time to the 1930s and visited any commuter train station, you would notice a number of similarities to today's commuting scene, as well as a few obvious differences. One important similarity is that most people would keep to the right, so that collisions and inconvenience are kept to a minimum. But two important differences would stand out: nearly all the commuters in the 1930s were men, and nearly all of them wore hats. The transition from a predominantly male workforce in the 1930s to today's more gender-egalitarian workplace was the product of all sorts of social influences, large and small, many of them brought to fruition intentionally and at great cost to the individuals involved. But what about the hats? Was their disappearance over the years deliberate? If so, who did the deliberating? It's hard to resist the conclusion that this trend was much more mindless—that most people simply copied the clothing choices of everyone else.

Is a tendency to go along with others a good thing or a bad thing? In today's Western society, which prizes autonomy and uniqueness, the word *conformity* connotes something negative to most people. If someone called you a conformist, for instance, you probably wouldn't take it as a compliment. And some types of social influence *are* bad. Going along with a crowd to pull a harmful prank, try a dangerous new drug, or drive a vehicle while intoxicated are good examples. Other types of conformity are neither good nor bad, such as conforming to the norm of wearing athletic pants very short (as in the 1970s) or very long (as in the 1990s).

Still other types of conformity are clearly beneficial, both to ourselves (because we don't have to think hard about every possible action) and to others (because conformity eliminates potential conflict and makes human interaction so much smoother). Conformity plays a big part, for example, in getting people to suppress anger; to pay taxes; to form lines at the theater, museum, and grocery store; and to stay to the right side of the sidewalk or roadway. Would any of us really want to do away with those conformist tendencies? Indeed, evolutionary psychologists and anthropologists have argued that a tendency to conform is

> *"Be regular and orderly in your life like a bourgeois, so that you may be violent and original in your work."*
>
> —GUSTAVE FLAUBERT, NINETEENTH-CENTURY FRENCH NOVELIST

Conformity Pressures in Daily Life
Conformity to what others are doing can be seen in these comparative images of commuters during the 1930s and commuters today. Nearly all the earlier commuters wore hats on their way to work, but very few do so now.

generally beneficial. We are often well served by doing what others are doing, unless we have a good reason not to (Boyd & Richerson, 1985; Henrich & Boyd, 1998).

Automatic Mimicry

As the cartoon on this page illustrates, sometimes we mindlessly imitate other people's behavior. It's often said that yawning and laughter are contagious, but a great deal of other behavior is as well. Like it or not, we're all nonconscious copycats; we all engage in mimicry.

The tendency to reflexively mimic the posture, mannerisms, facial expressions, and other actions of those around us has been examined experimentally. In one study, undergraduates took part in two 10-minute sessions in which each of them, along with another participant, described various photographs from popular magazines, such as *Newsweek* and *Time* (Chartrand & Bargh, 1999). The other participant was, in reality, a confederate of the experimenter, and there was a different confederate in each of the two sessions. The confederate in one session frequently rubbed his or her face, whereas the confederate in the other session continuously shook his or her foot. As the participant and confederate went about their business of describing the various photographs, the participant was surreptitiously videotaped. Doing so allowed the investigators to determine whether participants tended to rub their faces in the presence of the face-rubbing confederate and shake their feet in the presence of the foot-shaking confederate. The videotapes were taken of the participants only—the confederates were not visible on the tape—so the judges who were timing how long participants rubbed their faces or shook their feet were unaffected by knowledge of what the confederates were doing.

"I don't know why. I just suddenly felt like calling."

As predicted, the participants tended to mimic (conform to) the behavior exhibited by the confederate. They shook their feet more often in the presence of a foot-shaking confederate and rubbed their faces more often when next to a face-rubbing confederate (**Figure 9.1**). Follow-up studies have shown that this tendency to mimic others is particularly strong when people have a need to affiliate with others and when the others in question are well liked (Chartrand & Bargh, 1999; Lakin & Chartrand, 2003; Leighton, Bird, Orsini, & Heyes, 2010; Stel et al., 2010).

Reasons for Mimicry Why do we mindlessly copy the behavior of other people? There appear to be two reasons. William James (1890) provided the first explanation by proposing his principle of **ideomotor action**, whereby merely thinking about a behavior makes its actual performance more likely. Simply thinking about eating a bowl of gourmet ice cream, for example, makes us more apt to open the freezer, take out the carton, and dig in. The thought that we might type the wrong letter on the keyboard makes us more prone to typing that very letter (Wegner, 1994; Wegner, Ansfield, & Pilloff, 1998). The principle of ideomotor action is based on the fact that the brain regions responsible for perception overlap with those responsible for action. When this principle is applied to mimicry, it means that when we see others behave in a particular way, the idea of that

ideomotor action The phenomenon whereby merely thinking about a behavior makes performing it more likely.

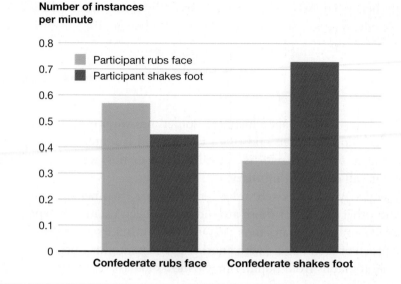

Number of instances per minute

Figure 9.1

Unconscious Mimicry

This graph shows the average number of times per minute participants performed an action (face rubbing, foot shaking) while in the presence of someone performing that action or not, demonstrating that people tend to mindlessly mimic the behavior of those around them.

SOURCE: Adapted from Chartrand & Bargh, 1999.

behavior is brought to mind (consciously or otherwise) and makes us more likely to behave that way ourselves.

The second reason we reflexively mimic others is to prepare for interacting with them, interaction that will tend to go more smoothly if we establish some rapport. Recall the study in Chapter 4 in which participants who were led to think about elderly people acted more like older people themselves, taking longer to walk down the hallway to the elevator (Bargh, Chen, & Burrows, 1996). It's as if the very idea of old people made them mindlessly prepare for being around them by slowing down their own movements. This idea has received support from follow-up studies showing that the tendency to automatically adopt the behavior of members of different social categories holds true only for those with a positive attitude toward the group in question—that is, those who might be expected to want to interact with members of that group and have the interaction go well. Individuals with positive attitudes toward older adults tended to walk more slowly when the category "elderly" was primed, but those with negative attitudes toward older adults tended to walk faster (Cesario, Plaks, & Higgins, 2006).

It appears, then, that we tend to mimic others as a way of laying the groundwork for smooth, gratifying interaction. And it works! Studies have found that people tend to like those who mimic them more than those who do not, even when they're unaware of being mimicked (Chartrand & Bargh, 1999). What's more, people who have been mimicked tend to engage in more prosocial behavior immediately afterward, such as donating money to a good cause, or leaving a larger tip for the person who mimicked them (van Baaren, Holland, Kawakami, & van Knippenberg, 2004; van Baaren, Holland, Steenaert, & van Knippenberg, 2003). Mimicry seems to be a helpful first step toward harmonious interaction and goodwill.

Cultural Differences in Mimicry People of various cultures differ in their tendencies to mimic others, and in how much mimicry they expect in social interactions. This means they also differ in the degree to which they are thrown off when the people they interact with fail to mimic them. In one study, the

Ideomotor Action and Conformity

Seeing others behave in a particular way sometimes makes us nonconsciously mimic their postures, facial expressions, and behavior. (A) Before the signing of the 1995 Middle East Peace Accord, U.S. President Bill Clinton, Israeli Prime Minister Yitzhak Rabin, Egyptian President Hosni Mubarak, and King Hussein of Jordan all adjusted their ties, as Yasser Arafat, who was not wearing a tie, looked on. (B) The tendency to mimic others begins quite early in life.

researchers interviewed both Anglo-American and Hispanic-American middle managers in a large corporation (Sanchez-Burks, Bartel, and Blount, 2009). The interview resembled a job interview, and participants had a chance to win a large amount of money if they performed well. In some of the sessions, the interviewer deliberately mirrored the interviewee's behavior—crossing his legs when the interviewee crossed his, resting his chin on his hand when the interviewee did so, and so on. In other sessions, the interviewer was careful to avoid mirroring the interviewee.

Being attuned to the emotions and behavior of others is more characteristic of Hispanic cultures than of Anglo-American cultures (reflecting a value called *sympatia*). Sanchez-Burks and his colleagues believed that such attunement includes sympathetically mirroring the behavior of others. The researchers therefore anticipated that the Hispanic participants would perform better when the interviewer mirrored their behavior, and their findings confirmed their expectation. When the interviewer mirrored a Hispanic participant, the participant reported less anxiety and was rated more highly by observers than when there was no mirroring. For Anglo-American participants, it made no difference whether the interviewer mirrored their behavior or not.

Informational Social Influence and Sherif's Conformity Experiment

Sometimes people conform to one another in a bit more conscious manner, as illustrated by an early conformity experiment by Muzafer Sherif (1936). Sherif was interested in how groups influence the behavior of individuals by shaping how reality is perceived. He noted that even our most basic perceptions are influenced by frames of reference. In the well-known Müller-Lyer illusion shown in

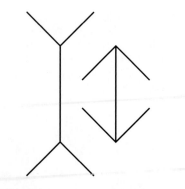

Figure 9.2
The Müller-Lyer Illusion
The framing of the vertical lines by the arrows affects how the viewer perceives their lengths. Even though the two vertical lines are exactly the same length, the one on the left appears longer than the one on the right because of its outward-pointing "fins" at the top and bottom, as opposed to the inward-pointing fins at the top and bottom of the line on the right.

Figure 9.2, for example, one vertical line appears longer than the other because of how the lines are "framed" by the two sets of arrows. Sherif designed his study to examine the circumstances in which other people serve as a *social* frame of reference.

Sherif's experiment was built around the autokinetic illusion—the sense that a stationary point of light in a completely darkened environment is moving. Ancient astronomers first noted this phenomenon, which occurs because in complete darkness there are no other stimuli to help the viewer discern where the light is located. Perhaps, Sherif thought, other people would fill the void and serve as a frame of reference that would influence the viewer's perceptions of the light's movement. To start off, Sherif put individual participants in a darkened room, presented them with a stationary point of light on trial after trial, and had them estimate how far it "moved" each time. Some people thought, on average, that the light moved very little on each trial (say, 2 inches), and others thought it moved a good deal more (say, 8 inches).

Sherif's next step was to bring several participants into the room together and have them call out their estimates. He found that people's estimates tended to converge over time. Those who individually had thought the light had moved a fair amount soon lowered their estimates; those who individually had thought it had moved very little soon raised theirs (**Figure 9.3**). Sherif argued that everyone's individual judgments quickly fused into a group norm, and the norm influenced how far the light was seen to move. A follow-up experiment reinforced his interpretation; when participants came back for individual testing up to 1 year later, their judgments still showed the influence of their group's earlier responses (Rohrer, Baron, Hoffman, & Swander, 1954).

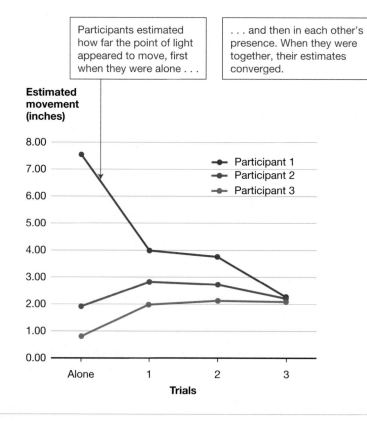

Figure 9.3
Informational Social Influence
Sherif's conformity experiment used the autokinetic illusion to assess group influence. Participants' estimates tended to become more similar over time.

SOURCE: Adapted from Sherif, 1936.

informational social
influence The influence of other
people that results from taking their
comments or actions as a source of
information about what is correct,
proper, or effective.

Social psychologists typically interpret the behavior of Sherif's participants to be the result of **informational social influence**—the reliance on other people's comments and actions as an indication of what's likely to be correct, proper, or effective (Deutsch & Gerard, 1955). We want to be right, and the opinions of other people are a useful source of information we can draw on to "get it right." This tendency is most pronounced when we're uncertain about how to behave or what is factually correct. We're more likely to conform to what others are doing in a foreign country than our own, for example. We're more likely to conform to others' views on subjects we have only vague ideas about, such as macroeconomic policy, than on familiar topics, such as how much fun it would be to vacation in Vladivostok versus Bali.

Note that the task Sherif asked his participants to perform was about as ambiguous as it gets, so informational social influence was strong. The light, in fact, didn't move at all; it just appeared to move. The uncertainty of the light's movement left the participants open to the influence of others. (See also Baron, Vandello, & Brunsman, 1996; Levine, Higgins, & Choi, 2000; Tesser, Campbell, & Mickler, 1983.)

Normative Social Influence and Asch's Conformity Experiment

You might be wondering: What's the big deal here? Why *wouldn't* participants conform to one another's judgments? After all, the task was impossible, and participants couldn't have felt confident in their own estimates. Why *not* rely on others? If you felt this way, you were thinking just like another pioneer of conformity research, psychologist Solomon Asch. Asch thought Sherif's experiment, although informative about a certain type of conformity, didn't address situations in which there is a clear conflict between an individual's own judgment and that of the group. It does not apply, for example, to the experience of knowing you've consumed too much alcohol to drive safely while your peers are urging you to get behind the wheel ("Come on. Don't be a wimp, you'll be fine"). Asch predicted that in a case of clear conflict between a person's own position and the viewpoint of the group, there will be far less conformity than that observed by Sherif. He was right. The reduced rate of conformity, however, was not what made Asch's experiment one of the most famous in the history of psychology. What made his study so well known was how often participants actually *did* conform, even when they thought the group was out of its collective mind.

You may already be familiar with Asch's experiment (Asch, 1956). Eight participants were gathered together to perform a simple perceptual task: determining which of three lines was the same length as a target line (**Figure 9.4**). Each person called out his judgment publicly, one at a time. The task was so easy that the experience was uneventful, boring even—at first.

On the third trial, however, one participant found that his private judgment was at odds with the expressed opinions of everyone else in the group. He was the only true participant in the experiment; the seven others were confederates instructed by Asch to respond incorrectly. The confederates responded incorrectly on 11 more occasions before the experiment was over. The question was: How often would the participant forsake what he knew to be the correct answer and conform to the incorrect judgment given by everyone else? Here there was no ambiguity, as there was in Sherif's experiment; the right answer was clear to

Solomon Asch
A pioneer of conformity research, Asch studied the effect of normative social influence.

Figure 9.4
Normative Social Influence
Participants in Asch's conformity study had a difficult time understanding why everyone appeared to be seeing things incorrectly. Even though it was clear to them what the right answer was, they ended up going along with the erroneous majority a third of the time.

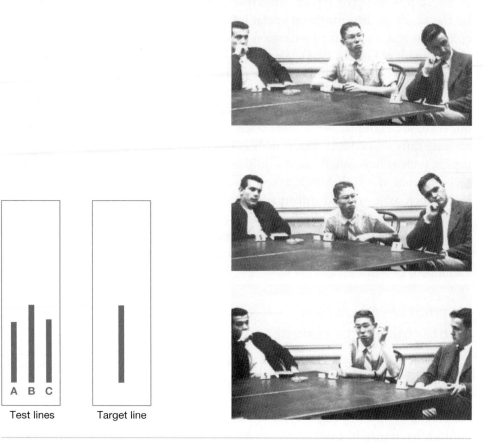

Test lines   Target line

SOURCE: Adapted from Asch, 1956.

participants. (When participants in a control group made these judgments by themselves, with no social pressure, they almost never made a mistake).

As Asch predicted, there was less conformity in his study than in Sherif's, but the rate of caving in to the group was still surprisingly high. Three-quarters of the participants conformed to the erroneous majority at least once. Overall, participants conformed on a third of the critical trials. The reason Asch's experiment has had such impact is not simply that the results are surprising; they are disturbing to many people as well. We like to think of people, ourselves especially, as sticking to what we think is right rather than following the herd (Pronin, Berger, & Molouki, 2007). In addition, we worry about people abandoning the dictates of their own conscience to follow others into wrongheaded or potentially destructive behavior.

As this discussion implies, informational social influence doesn't seem to be the main source of conformity pressure in Asch's experiment. There is undoubtedly some informational social influence at work here; the erroneous judgments called out by the majority were for lines that were between one-half and three-fourths inch off the correct answer. Some participants may therefore have questioned their own judgment and regarded the confederates' responses as informative. But again, in the absence of social pressure, control participants got the answer right nearly 100 percent of the time, so the primary reason people conformed was to avoid standing out, negatively, in the eyes of the group. Social psychologists refer to this as **normative social influence**—the desire to avoid being criticized, disapproved of, or shunned (Deutsch & Gerard, 1955).

normative social influence The influence of other people that comes from the desire to avoid their disapproval and other social sanctions (ridicule, barbs, ostracism).

BOX 9.1 **FOCUS ON *HEALTH***

Bulimia and Social Influence

Why do young women engage in binge eating and then purging by vomiting or using laxatives? The phenomenon is relatively new. This sort of behavior, an eating disorder known as bulimia, was virtually unheard of until about 45 years ago. Has it become more common because the fashion industry and media have persuaded women to want to be thinner than is natural or healthy (see Chapter 10)? Is it because depression and anxiety have increased in recent decades? Is it because body image and self-esteem have worsened?

All these factors may play a role in the current epidemic of bulimia, but another factor is simple social influence. Christian Crandall (1988) studied sorority women at a large university and found that the more bulimic a woman's friends were, the more bulimic she was likely to be. As Crandall learned, this relationship was not because bulimic women discovered each other and became friends, while nonbulimic women preferred to associate with other nonbulimics. Early in the school year, when women had known one another for only a short time, there was no association between the level of a woman's bulimia and that of her friends. But over the course of the

year, women in established friendship groups (not different, newly formed groups) came to have similar levels of bulimia.

Crandall studied two sororities and found two slightly different patterns of influence. In one sorority, women who differed in their level of bulimic activity from the average level in their sorority were less likely to be popular. Crandall inferred from this that there was an

"appropriate" or normative level of bulimia in that sorority, and deviations from it *in either direction* were punished by rejection. In the other sorority, more binge eating (up to quite a large amount) was associated with more popularity. In that sorority, Crandall concluded, there was pressure toward considerable binge eating, and those most inclined to binge were rewarded with acceptance and popularity.

Thinness and Social Influence
When some members of a sorority engage in binge eating and purging to stay thin, pressures on other members of the sorority to do likewise can be intense.

People are often reluctant to depart from the norms of society, or at least the norms of those subgroups they care most about, because they fear the social consequences (Cialdini, Kallgren, & Reno, 1991). The normative social pressures in Asch's experiment were sufficiently intense that the participants found themselves in a wrenching dilemma: "Should I say what I truly think it is? But what would everyone else think? They all agree, and they all seem so confident. Will they think I'm nuts? Will they interpret my disagreement as a slap in the face? But what kind of person am I if I go along with them? What the #@!$% should I do?"

To get an idea of the intensity of the participants' dilemma, imagine the following scenario. As part of a discussion of Asch's experiment, your social psychology professor shows an overhead of the target line and the three test lines and reports that although the right answer is line B, the confederates all say it's C. As your professor begins to move on, one student raises his hand and announces with conviction, "But the right answer *is* C!"

What would happen? Doubtless everyone would chuckle, making the charitable assumption that the student was trying to be funny. But if the student insisted that the confederates' answer was correct, the chuckles would turn to awkward, nervous laughter, and everyone would turn toward the professor in an implicit plea to "make this awkward situation go away." In subsequent lectures, most people would avoid sitting by the individual in question, and a buffer of empty seats would surround him. (And, of course, lunch invitations, dating opportunities, and offers to join a fraternity would diminish as well.) *That* was the fate Asch's participants felt they risked if they departed from the majority's response. Perhaps it's no surprise, then, that participants so often chose not to take the risk and conformed to the majority response (Janes & Olson, 2000; Kruglanski & Webster, 1991; Levine, 1989; Schachter, 1951). Next we'll consider when and why these conformity pressures are likely to be especially potent.

Factors Affecting Conformity Pressure

Several generations of researchers have examined the characteristics of the group, the surrounding context, and the task or issue at hand that influence the tendency to conform. This research has provided a clearer understanding of when people are especially likely to conform and when they're not. Both informational and normative social influences are powerful forces; as either one intensifies, so does the rate of conformity.

Group Size It's no surprise that conformity increases as the size of the group increases. Larger groups exert both more normative social influence and more informational social influence than smaller groups. What *is* surprising, perhaps, is that the effect of group size levels off pretty quickly (**Figure 9.5**). Research using Asch's paradigm, for example, has shown an increase in conformity as the size of the group increases, but only to a group size of three or four; after that, the amount of conformity levels off (Campbell & Fairey, 1989; Gerard, Wilhelmy, & Conolley, 1968; Insko, Smith, Alicke, Wade, & Taylor, 1985; Rosenberg, 1961).

The effect of group size makes sense, of course, from the standpoint of both informational and normative social influences. The larger the number of people who express a particular opinion, the more likely it has merit—but only to a certain point. The validity of a consensus opinion increases only if the opinions are independent of one another. And the more people there are, the less likely it is that their views are independent, so additional consenting opinions don't offer any additional real information. Also, the larger the group, the more people one stands to displease. But here, too, the impact of group size goes up only to a certain point. A person can feel only so much embarrassment, and the difference between being viewed as odd, foolish, or difficult by 2 versus 4 people is psychologically much more powerful than the difference between being viewed that way by 6 versus 8 or by 12 versus 14.

Group Unanimity A striking effect was observed in Asch's original studies when the unanimity of the group was broken. Recall that in the basic paradigm, the participant went along and reported the wrong answer a third of the time. That figure dropped to 5 percent when the true participant had an ally—that is, when just one other member of the group deviated from the majority (**Figure 9.6**). This

"'The way to get along,' I was told when I entered Congress, 'is to go along.'"

—JOHN F. KENNEDY

"It takes a great deal of bravery to stand up to our enemies, but just as much to stand up to our friends."

—ALBUS DUMBLEDORE, IN *HARRY POTTER AND THE SORCERER'S STONE*

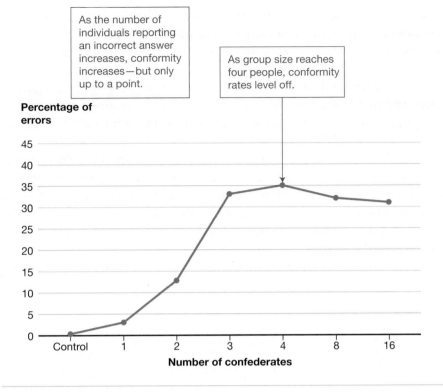

As the number of individuals reporting an incorrect answer increases, conformity increases—but only up to a point.

As group size reaches four people, conformity rates level off.

Percentage of errors

Number of confederates

SOURCE: Adapted from Asch, 1951.

Figure 9.5
The Effect of Group Size on Conformity

As the number of people in a majority increases, so does the tendency to conform, but only up to a unanimous majority of three or four. After that, conformity levels off.

effect occurs because the presence of an ally weakens both informational social influence ("Maybe I'm not crazy after all") and normative social influence ("At least I've got someone to stand by me"). This suggests a powerful tool for protecting independence of thought and action: if you expect to be pressured to conform and want to remain true to your beliefs, bring an ally along. Indeed, an important subtext of Asch's research is just how hard it can be to go it alone. People can stand up to misguided peers, but they usually need some help. Being the lone dissenter is agonizingly difficult.

Note that the other person who breaks the group's unanimity doesn't need to offer the correct answer—just one that departs from the group's answer. Suppose the right answer is the shortest of the three lines, and the majority claims it's the longest. If the fellow dissenter states that it's the middle line, it reduces the rate of conformity even though the participant's own view hasn't been reinforced. What matters is the break in unanimity. This fact has important implications for free speech. It suggests that we might want to tolerate loathsome and obviously false statements ("The Holocaust never happened"; "The president wasn't born in the United States"; "The World Trade Center attacks were a government hoax") not because what is said has any value, but because it liberates *other people* to say things that *are* of value. The presence of voices, even bizarre voices, that depart from conventional opinion frees the body politic to speak out and thus can foster productive political discourse.

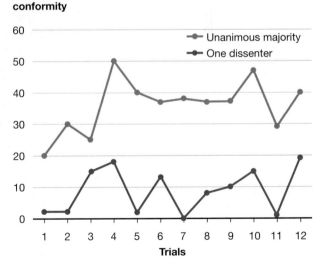

Percent conformity

- Unanimous majority
- One dissenter

Trials

Figure 9.6
The Effect of Group Unanimity on Conformity

The tendency for people to go along with a misguided majority drops precipitously once there's a break in the majority, when there is just one other person willing to dissent.

SOURCE: Adapted from Asch, 1956.

Anonymity If standing up to a misguided majority is hard, what happens when a person can register dissent without having to stand? In other words, what happens when a person can respond anonymously? Anonymity eliminates normative social influence and therefore should substantially reduce conformity. Indeed, when the true participant in Asch's paradigm is allowed to write his judgments on a piece of paper instead of saying them aloud for the group to hear, conformity drops dramatically. When nobody else is aware of his judgment, he has no need to fear the group's disapproval.

This highlights an important distinction between the impact of informational and normative social influence. Informational social influence, by guiding how we come to see the issues or stimuli before us, leads to **internalization**—our private acceptance of the position advanced by the majority (Kelman, 1958). We don't just mimic a particular response; we adopt the group's perspective. Normative social influence, in contrast, often has a greater impact on public compliance than on private acceptance. To avoid disapproval, we sometimes do or say one thing but continue to believe another. (Another name for that practice, of course, is *hypocrisy*.)

Expertise and Status Suppose you were a participant in Asch's experiment, and the other participants who were inexplicably stating what you thought was the wrong answer were all former major-league batting champions. If you proceeded on the assumption that a player can't lead the league in hitting without exceptional eyesight, you'd probably grant the group considerable authority and go along with their opinion. In contrast, if the rest of the group were all wearing thick eyeglasses, you'd be less apt to take their opinions seriously.

As this thought experiment illustrates, the expertise and status of the group members powerfully influence the rate of conformity. The two often go together, because we grant greater status to those with expertise, and we often assume (not always correctly) that those with high status are experts (Koslowsky & Schwarzwald, 2001). To the extent that these characteristics can be separated, however, expertise primarily affects informational social influence. Experts are more likely to be right, so we take their opinions more seriously. Status, in contrast, mainly affects normative social influence. The disapproval of high-status individuals can hurt more than the disapproval of people we care less about.

Many researchers have examined the effect of expertise and status on conformity (Cialdini & Trost, 1998; Crano, 1970; Ettinger, Marino, Endler, Geller, & Natziuk, 1971). One of the most intriguing studies used a paradigm quite different from Asch's. Torrance (1955) gave the members of navy bombing crews—pilot, navigator, and gunner—a number of reasoning problems, such as this horse-trading problem:

> A man bought a horse for $60 and then sold it for $70. He later repurchased the horse for $80 and then, changing his mind yet again, sold it for $90. How much money did he make on his series of transactions? (To get the correct answer, see the next page.)

The crews then had to report one answer for the whole group. Torrance monitored the group's deliberations and found that if the pilot (who generally held the highest status) originally came up with the correct solution, the group eventually reported it as their answer 91 percent of the time. If the navigator offered the correct answer, the group reported it 80 percent of the time. But if the lowly gunner offered the correct answer, the group offered it up only 63 percent of the time.

internalization Private acceptance of a proposition, orientation, or ideology.

The opinions of higher-status individuals thus tend to carry more weight with the group as a whole (Foushee, 1984).

Culture As we emphasize throughout this book, people from interdependent cultures are much more concerned about their relationships with others and about fitting into the broader social context than are people from independent cultures. People reared in interdependent cultures are therefore likely to be more susceptible to both informational social influence (they consider the actions and opinions of others more telling) and normative social influence (they consider the high regard of others more important). Thus, people from interdependent cultures might be expected to conform more than those from independent cultures.

Evidence supports this contention. In one early test of cross-cultural differences in conformity, Stanley Milgram conducted experiments using Asch's paradigm in Norway and France (Milgram, 1961). He maintained that Norwegians emphasize group cohesiveness and politeness, whereas the French enjoy conversational combat and don't shrink from disagreements. (*"Vous êtes capitaliste? Seulement idiots sont capitaliste!"*) Just as he expected, Milgram found that the Norwegian participants conformed more than the French participants.

Aside from the fact that both are delightful places to visit and conduct research, why study Norway and France? In the examination of independent versus interdependent cultures throughout this book, France and Norway have not loomed large in the discussion. What about the greater independent-interdependent divide that exists between a broader sample of the world's regions? A more systematic analysis of the results of 133 experiments using the Asch paradigm in 17 countries found that conformity does indeed tend to be greater in interdependent countries (Bond & Smith, 1996). The individualism that is highly valued in American and Western European societies has given individuals in those independent cultures a greater willingness to stand apart from the majority. And the willingness to resist the influence of the majority may be increasing. More recent conformity experiments in the United States and the United Kingdom using Asch's procedure have tended to find somewhat lower rates of conformity (Bond & Smith, 1996; Perrin & Spencer, 1981).

Tight and Loose Cultures Michele Gelfand and her colleagues have pursued a distinction between cultures that overlaps somewhat with the independence-interdependence dimension but differs enough that it deserves a name of its own: tightness versus looseness (Gelfand et al., 2011). Conformity to social norms lies at the heart of this construct. Some cultures, which Gelfand calls "tight," have strong norms regarding how people should behave and do not tolerate departure from those norms. Other cultures are "loose"; their norms are not as strong, and their members tolerate more deviance.

In a highly ambitious study, the Gelfand team examined a number of variables in 33 nations (Gelfand et al., 2011). They found that compared with loose nations, tight nations are more likely to have governments that are autocratic or dictatorial, to punish dissent, to have sharp controls on what can be said in the media, to have more laws and higher monitoring to ensure that the laws are

Expertise, Status, and Social Influence

When the United States was preparing to invade Iraq to unseat Saddam Hussein and secure his putative weapons of mass destruction in March 2003, the government sent Secretary of State Colin Powell to speak to the delegates of the United Nations because he had great credibility. Powell presented the case for the U.S. government's contention that Iraq had weapons of mass destruction, hoping to convince the delegates of the need to invade Iraq.

Answer to Horse Problem on p. 316

$20.
Amount paid = $140 ($60 + $80).
Amount received = $160 ($70 + $90).

Tight vs. Loose Cultures
(A) As this picture of Chinese girls lined up for school illustrates, some cultures are relatively tight; they have strong norms about how people should behave and tolerate very little leeway in deviating from those norms. (B) Other cultures are relatively loose; their norms are not as stringent, as this more chaotic line indicates.

obeyed, and to inflict more punishment for disobedience. If a nation was tight on one of these dimensions, it tended to be tight on all; if it was loose on one of the dimensions, it tended to be loose on all. Tight countries include India, Germany, People's Republic of China, South Korea, Japan, Austria, Portugal, Britain, Turkey, and Italy. Loose countries include Greece, Hungary, Israel, the Netherlands, Ukraine, New Zealand, and Brazil.

Gelfand and her colleagues surveyed people in each of the 33 countries, asking them about the appropriateness of arguing, crying, laughing, singing, flirting, reading a newspaper, and several other behaviors in each of 15 different situations or places, including a bank, doctor's office, restaurant, funeral, library, elevator, and movie theater (Gelfand, 2011). The tighter the nation's laws and norms, the fewer behaviors were allowed in these various situations. The researchers also asked people if their country had many social norms, whether others would strongly disapprove if someone acted inappropriately, and so forth. Again, the tighter the nation, the more its citizens pointed to tight constraints.

Why are some nations tight and some loose? The Gelfand team found that tighter nations tend to have higher population densities, fewer natural resources, unreliable food supplies, less access to safe water, more risk of natural disasters, more territorial threats from neighbors, and a higher prevalence of pathogens (Gelfand, 2011). It appears, then, that behavioral constraints are associated with, and perhaps partly caused by, ecological constraints.

Gender There are significant differences in how various cultures socialize boys and girls, but they have one thing in common: they all sex type to some degree. If there are cultural differences in conformity behavior, should we expect gender differences as well? Perhaps. Women are raised to value interdependence and to nurture important social relationships more than men are, whereas men are raised to value and strive for autonomy and independence more than women are. So we might expect women to be more subject to social influence and thus to conform more than men do.

However, people tend to conform when they're confused by the events unfolding around them. And if women are taught to nurture relationships, and thus are more likely to be the "experts" in that area, they might have the confidence

BOX 9.2

Not So Fast:
Critical Thinking about the Interpretive Context of Conformity and Disagreement

Like everyone else, participants in experiments respond to how they subjectively interpret their situation, not to the objective situation itself. A common reaction upon learning about Asch's experiment is to think, "Wow, if people conform that much to a group of strangers, imagine how much they'd conform to the judgments of those they care about and have to deal with in the future!" There is clearly some merit to that reaction, as normative social influence is diminished in situations, like Asch's, in which everyone is a stranger and they all assume they'll never see one another again (Lott & Lott, 1961; Wolf, 1985).

Yet there are other, more subtle aspects of Asch's procedure that can lead to *more* conformity than usually occurs in daily life. Participants in Asch's experiment faced a double whammy. First, they had to confront the fact that everyone else saw things differently than they did. Second, they had no basis for understanding *why* everyone else saw things differently. ("Could I be mistaken? No, it's as plain as day. Could they be mistaken? I don't see how, because they're not any farther away than I am and it's so clear. Are they

unusual? No, they don't look much different from me or anyone else.")

Knowing why our opinions are different ("They don't see things the way I do because they're wearing distorting glasses") lessens both informational and normative social influence. Informational social influence is reduced because the explanation can diminish the group's impact as a source of information ("They're biased"). Normative social influence is reduced because we can assume those in the majority are aware of why we differ from them. For instance, if we have different views on some burning political issue of the day, those we disagree with might think we're biased, selfish, or have different values, but at least they won't think we're crazy. In Asch's situation, in contrast, the participants faced the reasonable fear that if they departed from everyone else's judgment, their behavior would look truly bizarre, and everyone would think they were nuts.

The broader lesson here is about the importance of construal, even in the context of experiments. As we have stressed throughout this book, people respond

not to the objective situations they face, but to their subjective interpretations of those situations. Participants in Asch's study were in a situation in which it was unusually hard to develop a compelling interpretation of what was going on. It's hard to act independently and decisively when things have stopped making sense, so it may be a mistake to assume that Asch's participants would conform even more outside the psychology lab (Ross, Bierbrauer, & Hoffman, 1976).

To understand the real meaning of any experiment, it's important to pay attention to how the participants might have interpreted the instructions, procedures, and stimuli they faced. The same is true for experimenters. They must pay attention to the meaning the participants are apt to give their experience in the lab, in order to design studies that constitute truly informative tests of their hypotheses. Running participants in experiments is not the same as running rats in mazes: people don't passively record and respond to the surrounding context; they actively construe it and respond to what they've construed.

necessary to resist the influence of the majority. The research findings are what we might expect, given these two opposing considerations.

Reviews of the literature on gender differences in conformity have shown that women tend to conform more than men—but only a bit (Bond & Smith, 1996; Eagly, 1987; Eagly & Carli, 1981; Eagly & Chrvala, 2006). The difference tends to be greatest when the situation involves face-to-face contact, as in Asch's original study. However, the difference also seems to be strongly influenced by the specific content of the issue at hand. For instance, would you be more likely to conform to other people when they assert that the atomic number of beryllium is 62, or when they assert that the most important ingredient in a good sandwich is horseradish? If you're like most people, you know more about sandwiches than the periodic table, so you would be more likely to stand your ground when discussing lunchtime meals. Analyses of the specific contexts in which men and women differ in the tendency to conform reveal just this effect (Sistrunk & McDavid, 1971). Thus, women tend to conform more in stereotypically male domains (on questions about geography or deer hunting, for instance), whereas men tend to conform more in stereotypically female domains (such as questions about child rearing or cosmetics). It should be no surprise, then, that overall, women and men tend to differ in conformity, but only slightly.

The Influence of Minority Opinion on the Majority

There was a time in the United States when people owned slaves, when women were not allowed to vote, and when children worked long hours for scandalously low pay in unhealthy conditions. Small groups of abolitionists, suffragettes, and child welfare advocates saw things differently than their peers, however. They worked tirelessly to change public opinion about each of these issues—and they succeeded. In each case the broader public changed its views, and important legislation was passed. Minority opinion became the majority opinion. One of the most dramatic examples of minority influence in the West is quite recent. Over the past 20 years, the acceptance of same-sex marriage has gone from a small minority to a majority today.

Examples like these are reminders that although conformity pressures can be powerful, majority opinion doesn't always prevail. It's possible to resist conformity pressure, and minority voices are sometimes loud enough to change the prevailing norms. How do minority opinions come to influence the majority? Are the sources of influence the same as those that majorities bring to bear on minorities?

In the first experimental examination of these questions, Serge Moscovici and his colleagues had participants in a group setting call out whether a color was green or blue (Moscovici, Lage, & Naffrechoux, 1969). The border between blue and green is not always clear, but the critical stimuli the participants saw were ones that, when tested alone, they nearly always thought were blue. The

"Give me a firm place to stand and I will move the world."

—ARCHIMEDES OF SYRACUSE

Minority Influence on the Majority

Minority opinions can influence the majority through consistent and clear messages that persuade the majority to systematically examine and reevaluate its opinions. (A) British suffragette Emmeline Pankhurst presented her views in favor of women's right to vote to an American crowd in 1918. (B) Rosa Parks refused to give up her seat at the front of a bus in Montgomery, Alabama, in December 1955. Her actions resulted in a citywide bus boycott that eventually led the U.S. Supreme Court to declare that segregation was illegal on the city bus system. (C) Harvey Milk was the first openly gay person to be elected to public office in California. His activism contributed to the much greater support for the civil rights of gay and lesbian individuals that we see today.

experimenter showed participants these stimuli in the presence of a minority of respondents (confederates in the study) who responded "green"; the experimenter then recorded how the true participants responded.

When the minority varied their responses randomly between "green" and "blue," the participants said "green" after the others did so only 1 percent of the time, about the same as when they responded alone. But when the minority responded with "green" consistently, the true participants responded likewise 8 percent of the time. The influence of the consistent minority showed up in other ways as well. When the participants thought the study was over, the experimenter introduced them to a second investigator who was also interested in color vision. This second person showed participants a series of blue-green colors and recorded where each participant, individually, thought blue left off and green began. Those who had earlier been exposed to a consistent minority now identified more of these stimuli as green; their sense of the border between blue and green had shifted. Thus, when the minority opinion was consistent, it had both a direct effect on participants' responses in the public setting and a latent effect on their subsequent, private judgments.

Further investigations of minority influence using similar paradigms have shown that minorities have their effect primarily through informational social influence (Moscovici, 1985; Nemeth, 1986; Wood, Lundgren, Ouellette, Busceme, & Blackstone, 1994). People in the majority are typically not terribly concerned about the social costs of stating their opinion out loud—they have the majority on their side and normative social influence is minimized. But they might wonder why the minority keeps stating its divergent opinion. This can lead the majority to consider the stimulus more carefully, resulting in a level of scrutiny and systematic thought that can produce genuine change in attitudes and beliefs. Thus, majorities typically elicit more conformity, but it is often of the public compliance sort. In contrast, minorities typically influence fewer people, but the nature of the influence is often deeper and results in true private acceptance (Maass & Clark, 1983).

⟲ LOOKING BACK

Conformity can be a response to implicit or explicit social pressures, and it can be the result of automatic mimicry, informational social influence, or normative social influence. Group size influences conformity, but it appears to reach maximum effect at around four people. Unanimity is also crucial in conformity, and a single ally can help an individual hold out against the group. People conform more to those with high status or expertise, and when they must express their opinions publicly rather than register them in private. People from interdependent cultures conform more than people from independent cultures, and women conform slightly more than men. Conformity pressures notwithstanding, minorities often make an impact, primarily through informational social influence.

Compliance

You need a favor from a friend. How should you ask? You're volunteering to raise funds for a favorite charity. How should you go about getting people to donate their hard-earned money? Your first job out of college is in sales. How do you

norm of reciprocity A norm dictating that people should provide benefits to those who benefit them.

get people to sign on the dotted line? These are all questions about compliance: getting people to comply with something you want. Coming from the other direction, how can you avoid being influenced by the compliance attempts of others? What techniques should you watch out for? Social psychologists have studied different strategies for eliciting compliance, and their research findings help explain how (and how effectively) these strategies work.

There are three basic types of compliance approaches: those directed at the mind, those directed at the heart, and those based on the power of norms (which, given the impact of informational and normative influences, appeal to both the mind and the heart). People can be led to comply with requests because they see good reasons for doing so, because their emotions compel them to do so, or because everyone else is doing so. Of course, these types of influence are not always neatly separable, and many compliance efforts are a blend of the three approaches.

Reason-Based Approaches

When someone does something for us, we usually feel compelled to do something in return. Indeed, all societies that have ever been studied possess a powerful **norm of reciprocity**, according to which people are expected to benefit those who benefit them (Fiske, 1991; Gouldner, 1960). This norm also exists in many bird and mammal species. When one monkey removes parasites from another's back, the latter typically returns the favor, thus helping cement the social bond between them.

When someone does you a favor, you have an obligation to agree to any reasonable request that person might make in turn. To fail to respond is to violate a powerful social norm and run the risk of social sanction (Cotterell, Eisenberger, & Speicher, 1992). Indeed, the English language is rich in derogatory terms for those who don't uphold their end of the bargain: *sponge, moocher, deadbeat, ingrate, parasite, bloodsucker, leech.* If you do a favor for someone, that person will probably agree to a reasonable request you subsequently make, to avoid being seen as a sponge or a moocher. This may be why restaurant customers often leave larger tips when the server gives them a piece of candy (Strohmetz, Rind, Fisher, & Lynn, 2002).

The influence of the norm of reciprocity in eliciting compliance was demonstrated with particular clarity in a simple experiment in which two people were asked to rate a number of paintings, supposedly as part of a study of aesthetics (Regan, 1971; see also Whatley, Webster, Smith, & Rhodes, 1999). One was a real participant; the other was a confederate of the experimenter. In one condition, the confederate returned from a break with two sodas and offered one to the participant. "I asked (the experimenter) if I could get myself a Coke, and he said it was OK, so I bought one for you, too." In another condition, the confederate returned empty-handed. Later, the confederate asked the participant for a favor. He explained that he was selling raffle tickets; the prize was a new car, and he'd win $50 if he sold the most raffle tickets. He then proceeded to ask if the participant was willing to buy any tickets, for 25 cents apiece: "Any would help, the more the better."

Reciprocity and Grooming among Mammals
Reciprocity helps promote group living and reduce aggression, as evidenced by grooming in macaques. They abide by the rule "You scratch my back and I'll scratch yours." Macaque A is more likely to groom Macaque B than a random other macaque if Macaque B has previously groomed Macaque A.

(To make sure all participants had the means to purchase some tickets, they had already been paid—in quarters—for participating in the study.)

In a testament to the power of the norm of reciprocity, participants who were earlier given a soda by the confederate bought twice as many raffle tickets as those who were not (or those who were given a soda by the experimenter, to control for the possibility that simply receiving a soda, and perhaps being in a good mood, is what had increased compliance).

Thus, doing a favor for someone creates an uninvited debt that the recipient is obligated to repay. Businesses and other organizations often try to take advantage of this pressure by preceding their request with a small gift. Insurance agents give out calendars or return-address labels. Pollsters who want us to complete a survey send it along with a dollar. Cult members offer a flower before giving their pitch. Our hearts sink when we see these gifts coming, and we often go to great lengths to avoid them—and the obligations they bring.

The Reciprocal Concessions (Door-in-the-Face) Technique Robert Cialdini, social psychology's most innovative contributor to the literature on compliance, has explored a novel application of the norm of reciprocity. The inspiration for his research on the subject is best introduced in his own words:

> I was walking down the street when I was approached by an eleven- or twelve-year-old boy. He introduced himself and said that he was selling tickets to the annual Boy Scouts circus to be held on the upcoming Saturday night. He asked if I wished to buy any at five dollars apiece. Since one of the last places I wanted to spend Saturday evening was with the Boy Scouts, I declined. "Well," he said, "if you don't want to buy any tickets, how about buying some of our big chocolate bars? They're only a dollar each." I bought a couple and, right away, realized that something noteworthy had happened. I knew that to be the case because: (a) I do not like chocolate bars; (b) I do like dollars; (c) I was standing there with two of his chocolate bars; and (d) he was walking away with two of my dollars.
>
> (*Cialdini, 1984, p. 47*)

Cialdini's experience with the Boy Scout led him to articulate a general compliance technique whereby people feel compelled to respond to a concession with one of their own (Cialdini et al., 1975; O'Keefe & Hale, 1998, 2001; Reeves, Baker, Boyd, & Cialdini, 1991). First, you ask someone for a very large favor that he or she will certainly refuse, and then you follow that request with one for a more modest favor that you are really interested in receiving. The idea is that the drop in the size of the request will be seen as a concession, which you must match to honor the norm of reciprocity. The most available concession is to comply with the second request.

Another way of looking at this **reciprocal concessions technique** is that the first favor is so large and unreasonable that the target inevitably refuses, slamming the door in the face of that request but then keeping it open just a crack for the subsequent, smaller request. Accordingly, it's also known as the *door-in-the-face technique*.

Cialdini demonstrated the power of this technique in a field study in which members of his research team posed as representatives of the "County Youth Counseling Program" and approached students around campus. They asked individual students if they would be willing to chaperone a group of juvenile delinquents on a trip to the zoo. Not surprisingly, the overwhelming majority, 83 percent, refused. But the response rate was much different for a second group

"All contacts among men rest on the schema of giving and returning the equivalent."
—GEORG SIMMEL, GERMAN SOCIOLOGIST

"There is no duty more indispensable than that of returning a kindness."
—CICERO

reciprocal concessions technique A compliance approach that involves asking someone for a very large favor that he or she will certainly refuse and then following that request with one for a smaller favor (which tends to be seen as a concession the target feels compelled to honor); also called *door-in-the-face technique*.

of students who had first encountered a much larger request. They were first asked whether they would be willing to counsel juvenile delinquents for 2 hours a week for the next 2 years! Not surprisingly, all of them refused, at which point they were asked about chaperoning the trip to the zoo. Fifty percent of these students agreed to chaperone—triple the rate of the other group (Cialdini et al., 1975). A series of carefully crafted follow-up studies revealed that the pressure to respond to what was perceived as a concession was responsible for the dramatic increase in compliance. For example, this technique doesn't work when the two requests are made by different individuals. In that case, the second, smaller request is not seen as a concession, so it doesn't create the same felt obligation.

The That's-Not-All Technique Another technique that uses the norm of reciprocity may be more familiar to you. Suppose you're at an electronics store and you ask about a plasma TV. The salesperson says it costs $1,299 and comes with a three-year warranty. After a moment in which you say nothing, the salesperson says, "And that's not all; it also comes with a free DVD player!" An add-on like this may strike you as a gift from the store or the salesperson, and therefore may create some pressure to reciprocate. This sort of pressure can result in increased sales.

Jerry Burger demonstrated the effectiveness of this approach, the **that's-not-all technique**, at an arts fair on a college campus (Burger, 1986). Some people who approached the booth of the Psychology Club bake sale were told one cupcake and two medium-sized cookies cost a total of 75 cents. Others were initially told that each cupcake cost 75 cents, and then, before they said whether they wanted one or not, they were told the price included two medium-sized cookies. Seventy-three percent of those in the latter, "that's-not-all" condition purchased the snacks, compared with only 40 percent in the control "all-at-once" condition (Burger, 1986; see also Burger, Reed, DeCesare, Rauner, & Rozolis, 1999; Pollock, Smith, Knowles, & Bruce, 1998).

The Foot-in-the-Door Technique All of us perform certain actions because they're consistent with our self-image. Environmentalists take the time to recycle, even when sorely tempted to toss a bottle or can into the trash, because that's part of what it means to be an environmentalist. Skiers rise early to tackle fresh snow, even when they really want to hit the snooze button on the alarm clock, because that's what real skiing enthusiasts do. It's logical, therefore, that if requests are crafted to appeal to a person's self-image, the likelihood of compliance is increased.

One way to pull this off is to employ what's known as the **foot-in-the-door technique**, which in a sense is the opposite of the door-in-the-face technique. It starts with a small request to which nearly everyone complies, thereby allowing the person making the request to get a foot in the door. She then follows up with a larger request involving the real behavior of interest. The idea is that the initial agreement to the small request will lead to a change in the target person's self-image as someone who does this sort of thing or who contributes to such causes. That person then has a reason for agreeing to the subsequent, larger request: "It's just who I am."

In an early test of the foot-in-the-door technique, the investigators knocked on doors in a residential neighborhood and asked homeowners whether they would be willing to have a large billboard sign bearing the slogan "Drive Carefully" installed in their front yard for one week (Freedman & Fraser, 1966).

that's-not-all technique A compliance approach that involves adding something to an original offer, thus creating some pressure to reciprocate.

foot-in-the-door technique A compliance approach that involves making an initial small request with which nearly everyone complies, followed by a larger request involving the real behavior of interest.

One group saw a picture of the sign; it was large and unattractive, so not surprisingly only 17 percent agreed to the request. Another group of residents was approached with a much smaller request—to display in a window of their home a 3-inch-square sign bearing the phrase "Be a Safe Driver." Virtually all of them agreed with the request. Two weeks later, when this group was asked to display the billboard in their yard, a staggering 76 percent of them agreed to do so.

You've probably heard politicians oppose a piece of legislation—not because there's anything wrong with the legislation itself, but because they think it might create a "slippery slope" leading to the passage of more questionable legislation later on. Research on the foot-in-the-door technique suggests that there is merit to this concern. Human behavior, like a ball rolling down a sloping plane, is subject to momentum. Getting people started on something small often makes it easier to get them to do much bigger things down the road. We'll see just how powerful these slippery slopes can be when we discuss the most famous studies in the history of social psychology later in this chapter.

The Foot-in-the-Door Technique
After getting the customer to agree to a test drive, it may be easier for the salesperson to close the deal and have her buy the car.

Emotion-Based Approaches

Cognitive, or reason-based, approaches aim at the head and, as we have seen, can be very effective in obtaining compliance. Affective, or emotion-based, approaches aim at the heart, and they too are powerful tools for eliciting compliance.

Positive Mood Suppose you want to ask your dad for a new computer, a new amplifier for your guitar, or simply to borrow the family car for a road trip. When would you ask? When he's just come home from work in a foul mood, cursing his boss and his suffocating job? Or after he's just landed a promotion and a big raise? It doesn't take an advanced degree in psychology to know that it's better to request a favor when the person's in a good mood (Andrade & Ho, 2007). A positive mood makes people feel expansive and charitable, so they're more likely to agree to reasonable requests. Even little children know to wait before asking someone for a favor until that person seems cheerful.

The wisdom of this approach has been verified in countless experiments. In one study, participants received a telephone call from someone who claimed to have spent her last dime on this very ("misdialed") call; she asked if they would dial a specified number and relay a message (Isen, Clark, & Schwartz, 1976). In one condition, no more than 20 minutes before receiving the call, participants were given a free sample of stationery to put them in a positive mood. In another condition, participants did not receive a free sample before the call. When the request was made of those without the free sample, only 10 percent complied. But the compliance rate shot up dramatically among participants who received the request a few minutes after receiving the gift, and then declined gradually as the delay between the gift and the request increased (**Figure 9.7**).

Feeling good clearly makes people more likely to agree to requests and, more generally, to help others. This effect has been shown in experiments that have lifted participants' moods by telling them they did well on a test, having them

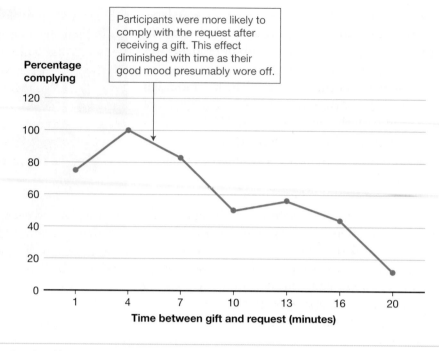

Percentage complying

Participants were more likely to comply with the request after receiving a gift. This effect diminished with time as their good mood presumably wore off.

Time between gift and request (minutes)

Figure 9.7
Positive Mood and Compliance

In this study, being in a good mood boosted participant compliance, with the effect slowly wearing off with the passage of time.

SOURCE: Adapted from Isen, Clark, & Schwartz, 1976.

think happy thoughts, giving them cookies, or playing cheerful music. Participants have been shown to respond favorably to requests to make change, donate to charity, help with experiments, give blood, and tutor students (Carlson, Charlin, & Miller, 1988; Isen, 1999).

A positive mood tends to increase compliance for two main reasons. First, our mood colors how we interpret events. We are more likely to view requests for favors as less intrusive and less threatening when we're in a good mood. We give others the benefit of the doubt. For instance, you might consider someone who asks to borrow your class notes to be a victim of circumstance who could get back on track with a little help, not an irresponsible or lazy person who doesn't deserve to be bailed out (Carlson et al., 1988; Forgas, 1998a, 1998b; Forgas & Bower, 1987).

The second reason a good mood increases compliance involves what's known as mood maintenance. Pardon the tautology, but it feels good to feel good, and we typically want the feeling to last as long as possible (Clark & Isen, 1982; Wegener & Petty, 1994). One way to sustain a good mood is to do something for another person (Dunn, Aknin, & Norton, 2008). Stated differently, one way to wreck a good mood is to turn down a request and invite all sorts of self-recrimination: "What kind of heartless person am I?" That negative feeling obviously erodes a positive mental state.

Several studies have shown that mood maintenance is an important component of the impact of a positive mood on compliance. In one experiment, some

Positive Mood and Requests

When people are in a good mood, they are more likely to agree to requests. Those attending this benefit for UNICEF are therefore more likely to donate money to UNICEF's humanitarian relief efforts.

of the participants were first given cookies, which put them in a good mood; the others were not given cookies. All of them were then asked (by someone other than the person who provided the cookies) if they would be willing to assist with an experiment by serving as a confederate. Half the participants were told the job of confederate would involve *helping* the "true" participant in the experiment; the other half were told it would involve *hindering* the participant. Having received a cookie (and being in a good mood) increased the compliance rate when the task involved helping the participant, but not when it involved hindering the participant. Helping another person promotes feeling good; hurting someone does not.

Negative Mood If a good mood increases compliance, does a bad mood decrease it? It surely can, but even the slightest introspection reveals that certain types of bad moods are likely to *increase* compliance, not decrease it. Some people know this and use it to their advantage. Suppose, for example, your girlfriend was flirting too much with someone (alas, not you, or it wouldn't be too much), and you point out the offense. Would that be a good time to ask her for something? You bet it would! When people feel guilty, they're often motivated to do whatever they can to get rid of that awful feeling. So at least one type of bad mood, centered around feelings of guilt, should increase compliance.

Social psychologists have demonstrated a strong, positive association between guilt and compliance in many experiments. Participants have been led to feel guilty by being induced to lie, tricked into thinking they've broken a camera, maneuvered into knocking over stacks of carefully arranged index cards, or convinced they've injured an adorable laboratory rat (Carlsmith & Gross, 1969; Darlington & Macker, 1966; O'Keefe & Figgé, 1997; J. Regan, 1971; D. T. Regan, Williams, & Sparling, 1972). In a particularly clever test of the effect of guilt on compliance, researchers asked Catholics to donate to the March of Dimes when they were either on their way into church for confession or on their way out (Harris, Benson, & Hall, 1975). The presumption was that those on their way in were rehearsing their sins and thus feeling guilty; those on their way out had done penance for their sins and were no longer plagued by guilt. As predicted, those solicited on the way in gave more money than those solicited on the way out.

Other types of bad moods, not just those produced by guilt, can also increase compliance. In one study, watching an adorable lab rat get "accidentally" jolted with an intense shock led participants to donate more money to a charitable cause than those who hadn't seen the unfortunate event (J. Regan, 1971). And in general it seems that bad moods sometimes increase compliance, in part because we don't want to feel bad, so we jump at the chance to do something to brighten our mood. According to the **negative state relief hypothesis**, taking an action to benefit someone else, especially when it's for a good cause, is one way to make ourselves feel better (Cialdini, Darby, & Vincent, 1973; Cialdini & Fultz, 1990; Cialdini et al., 1987). We often help others, in other words, to help ourselves.

negative state relief hypothesis The idea that people engage in certain actions, such as agreeing to a request, to relieve their negative feelings and feel better about themselves.

Negative State Relief
Oskar Schindler (in the center) saved the lives of 1,200 Polish Jews during the Holocaust. Initially driven by the desire for easy profits, he took over a Jewish factory and ran it with cheap Jewish labor. Perhaps in a desire for negative state relief or from sheer humanitarianism, he used the millions he made from the cheap labor to bribe officials to save those who were slated for death. He is pictured here in Tel Aviv with some of those he saved and their descendants.

A final word about the impact of moods, good and bad, on compliance. Investigators in Israel have found that if parole judges had just finished a meal before hearing a prisoner's plea for release from prison, there was a two-thirds chance they would vote for parole (Danziger, Levav, & Avnaim-Pesso, 2011). Cases that came up just before lunch, however, when the judges were hungry and presumably crankier, had precisely a zero chance for parole. A full stomach counts, so hit your dad up for the car keys after dinner, not before.

Norm-Based Approaches

Adolescent girls exposed to pregnant teenagers are more likely to become pregnant themselves (Akerlof, Yellen, & Katz, 1996); planning for retirement is greatly influenced by coworkers' plans (Duflo & Saez, 2003); and student drinking is connected to student perceptions of how much other students drink (Lewis & Neighbors, 2004). Clearly, people conform to the behavior of those around them, and this tendency can be harnessed to achieve compliance with explicit requests or implicit suggestions. Norm-based approaches to compliance are based on the power of social norms. They appeal to both the mind and the heart.

Effective Norm-Based Appeals Letting people know what others are doing can be used to advance the public good. Consider a norm-based approach to energy use that was instituted in California (Schultz, Nolan, Cialdini, Goldstein, & Griskevicius, 2007). Researchers left hang-tags on people's doors indicating their average daily residential energy use (in kilowatt-hours), as well as that of their neighbors. The effect of this simple intervention was clear-cut and immediate: those who consumed more energy than average altered their habits to significantly reduce their energy use.

What about the households that used *less* energy than average? Did telling them that their neighbors tended to be less conscientious make them more wasteful? Yes, it did. But the investigators had a simple remedy at hand that preserved the gains among above-average energy users while avoiding increased energy use by below-average users. The usage information given to half the households was accompanied by a small sign of approval or disapproval: a happy face for those who had used relatively little energy and a sad face for those who had used more than average. The signal of approval to the former was enough to maintain the superior conservation efforts of those who might otherwise have slacked off (**Figure 9.8**). Used wisely, providing information about norms can be a powerful tool to promote energy conservation. Interventions like these have saved customers in the United States over half a billion dollars in utility costs and kept 7.6 billion pounds of CO_2 out of the atmosphere.

Another ecologically minded norm-based approach was directed at persuading hotel guests to reuse their towels and thus conserve water and energy. The investigators in one study found that when the small card urging guests to reuse their towels included a statement that a majority of past hotel guests had chosen to reuse their towels, a significantly higher percentage complied (Goldstein, Cialdini, & Griskevicius, 2008). Interestingly, the rate of compliance increased even further when the card stated that a majority of guests who "stayed in this room" reused their towels.

Telling people about social norms is likely to be most effective when the norm is misunderstood, such as when people overestimate the popularity of

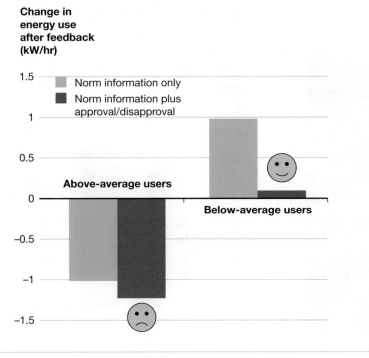

SOURCE: Adapted from Schultz et al., 2007.

Figure 9.8
Using Norms to Conserve Energy
In this study, telling above-average energy consumers how much energy they use and how much the average household uses significantly reduced energy consumption (bars on the left). Providing this information to below-average energy consumers led to significantly greater energy consumption, unless it was accompanied by a simple symbol of approval (bars on the right).

destructive behavior or underestimate the popularity of constructive behavior. Student drinking is a case in point. On campuses across the United States, students think that binge drinking is much more common than it actually is, and that "teetotaling" or moderate drinking is much less common than it is (Perkins, Haines, & Rice, 2005). These are instances of the phenomenon of pluralistic ignorance (discussed in Chapter 4). In one study, Deborah Prentice and Dale Miller (1993) examined the discrepancy between private attitudes and public norms about alcohol use at Princeton University. They thought the discrepancy might be due to the following reasons:

> The alcohol situation at Princeton is exacerbated by the central role of alcohol in many of the university's institutions and traditions. For example, at the eating clubs, the center of social life on campus, alcohol is on tap 24 hours a day, 7 days a week. Princeton reunions boast the second highest level of alcohol consumption for any event in the country after the Indianapolis 500. The social norms for drinking at the university are clear: students must be comfortable with alcohol use to partake of Princeton social life.
>
> (Prentice & Miller, 1993, p. 244)

Prentice and Miller asked Princeton undergraduates how comfortable they felt about campus drinking habits, as well as the comfort level of both their *friends* and the *average undergraduate* with alcohol. If the students were suffering from pluralistic ignorance on this issue, they would indicate that they were less at ease with drinking than they supposed most students were. The results, shown in **Figure 9.9**, indicate that this is exactly what happened. Hidden discomfort with alcohol existed side by side with perceived popular support.

Efforts to stem excessive alcohol consumption by providing students with accurate information about their peers' drinking habits have proved to be quite effective (Neighbors, Larimer, & Lewis, 2004; Perkins & Craig, 2006; Schroeder

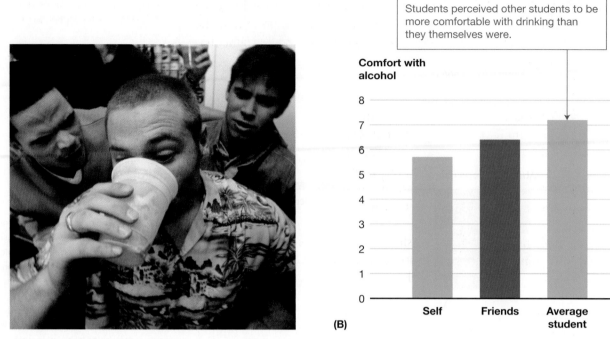

(A)

(B)

Students perceived other students to be more comfortable with drinking than they themselves were.

Comfort with alcohol

Figure 9.9

Pluralistic Ignorance

(A) University students believe drinking alcohol is more popular among their peers than it really is. Because of this belief, they censor their own reservations about drinking, thus furthering the illusion that alcohol is so popular. (B) These study results show student ratings of their own and others' comfort with campus drinking habits at Princeton University.

SOURCE: Part B, adapted from Prentice & Miller, 1993.

and Prentice, 1998). In one study, students attending regularly scheduled club or organizational meetings typed into wireless keypads information about their own drinking behavior and their beliefs about the drinking habits of their peers (LaBrie, Hummer, Neighbors, & Pedersen, 2008). Their aggregate responses were immediately projected for all to see, giving everyone telling information about actual drinking behavior on campus—and correcting widespread misunderstandings of how much and how often other students drink. Follow-up online surveys conducted 1 and 2 months later revealed that students who received this information reported drinking significantly less than they had previously, and less than students in a control group.

Drinking in college has numerous consequences, some of them quite serious, and many are the result of unfortunate social influence. (You've surely heard of alcohol-fueled fraternity initiations that result in death.) Economists Michael Kremer and Dan Levy examined the GPAs of students whose freshman roommate had been assigned to them at random (Kremer & Levy, 2003). The investigators found out the approximate amount of alcohol each student had consumed in high school. Students with a roommate who came to college with a history of substantial drinking got grades a quarter-point lower than students assigned a teetotaler. That can easily mean a GPA of B+ versus A- or C+ versus B-. If the student himself had been a drinker prior to college, he got grades a full point lower if his roommate had been a drinker than if he had not! That can mean the difference between getting into a good medical school and not getting into medical school at all. (We use the masculine pronoun deliberately; there was no effect on females of having a drinking roommate.) It seems likely that the heavy drinker influenced the alcohol consumption of his roommate, especially if the roommate was already inclined to drink, and the alcohol led to behavior that undermined study habits.

Descriptive and Prescriptive Norms In constructing norm-based compliance appeals, it's important to be aware that there are two kinds of norms. **Descriptive norms** are simply descriptions of what is typically done. **Prescriptive norms**, often called *injunctive norms*, are what one is supposed to do. Descriptive norms correspond to what *is*; prescriptive norms correspond to what *ought to be*. University administrators often say that students should get 8–9 hours of sleep each night (prescriptive norm), but most students sleep much less (descriptive norm).

To increase compliance, the two norms should not be placed in conflict with each other. A common mistake is to try to strengthen the pull of the prescriptive norm by stating how infrequently it is followed. "Isn't it a shame that so few people . . ." vote in elections, eat a healthy diet, get screened for cancer—you name it. Making such an appeal is understandable, but note that it inadvertently pits a descriptive norm against the prescriptive norm it is trying to highlight (Sieverding, Decker, & Zimmerman, 2010). By saying what a shame it is that so few people vote, you're actually informing them that few people vote. Given the power of descriptive norms, such information can make people *less* likely to vote, not more likely. Indeed, those involved in get-out-the-vote campaigns now realize, thanks to social psychological research, that it's more effective to emphasize how many people vote, not how few (Gerber & Rogers, 2009).

Researchers conducted an ingenious investigation of this approach in the Petrified Forest National Park in Arizona, where visitors sometimes take samples of petrified wood home with them as souvenirs (Cialdini, Demaine, Sagarin, Barrett, Rhoads, & Winters, 2006). If everyone took samples, of course, there would soon be no Petrified Forest to visit. To examine the most effective ways to deal with the problem, the investigators rotated different warning signs at various locations in the park. One sign included the usual emphasis on the severity of the problem, stating, "Many past visitors have removed petrified wood from the park, changing the state of the Petrified Forest," accompanied by photographs of visitors taking wood. An alternative sign was framed positively: "The vast majority of past visitors have left the petrified wood in the park, preserving the natural state of the Petrified Forest," with accompanying pictures of visitors admiring and photographing a piece of petrified wood. The investigators placed specially marked pieces of wood along trails near these signs and monitored how many of them were stolen over the course of the experiment. In a remarkable demonstration of the importance of aligning prescriptive and descriptive norms, the theft rate was over four times lower when the signs emphasized how few people take wood samples away from the park.

descriptive norm The behavior exhibited by most people in a given context.

prescriptive norm The way a person is supposed to behave in a given context; also called *injunctive norm*.

Descriptive and Prescriptive Norms in Conflict

By telling people they shouldn't remove petrified wood from the Petrified National Forest (prescriptive norm), park officials are communicating that stealing wood is something people do (descriptive norm). This can increase the very action—theft—the authorities want to prevent.

BOX 9.3 **FOCUS ON *POSITIVE PSYCHOLOGY***

Resisting Social Influence

People don't always conform, comply, and obey. They sometimes engage in heartening, even heroic, acts of independence—refusing to go along with misguided peers, defying the illegitimate demands of a commanding officer, or blowing the whistle on unethical business practices. What enables people to hold their ground, follow their conscience, and resist being influenced by others?

The pressure to give in to others can be offset by the tendency to resist attempts to restrict freedom of action or thought. According to **reactance theory**, people experience an unpleasant state of arousal when they believe their free will is threatened, and they often act to reduce this discomfort by reasserting their prerogatives (Brehm, 1956). If your parents tell you you mustn't dye your hair, does your desire to have it dyed diminish or increase? Reactance theory predicts that the moment you feel your freedom is being taken away, it becomes more precious and your desire to maintain it increases.

Once motivated to resist, what factors might increase your ability to stand firm? One important variable is practice. In Milgram's obedience studies (see below), many participants wanted to disobey and even tried to do so, but they weren't very good at it (Milgram, 1963, 1974). Maybe if they had been trained to disobey when the situation called for it, they would have done a better job. There is evidence that the Christians who tried to save Jews during the Holocaust tended to be people who had a history of helping others, either as part of their job or as volunteers. Those who helped the most often did not have any higher regard for their Jewish neighbors than those who helped less; they were simply more practiced in reaching out and providing aid.

Another way to increase the ability to resist social influence is to have an ally. In Asch's conformity experiment, having just one additional person who departed from the majority was enough to drastically reduce conformity (Asch, 1956). Indeed, the most important lesson of Asch's research is just how difficult it can be to be the *lone* holdout. People also need to be wary of potentially slippery slopes. The stepwise procedure in Milgram's experiments may have played an important role in the surprising levels of obedience observed in those studies. It's often easiest to resist influence from the start, rather than giving in and hoping to put a stop to things later on. As the Catholic Church teaches, "Avoid the near occasion of sin."

It's important to keep in mind, too, that many social influence attempts are based on appeals to emotion, as we discussed earlier. A particularly effective strategy for dealing with emotion-based approaches is simply to put off a response. If there is a "first law" of emotional experience, it is that emotions fade and moods change. Therefore, the compulsion to give in because you are caught up in a particular emotion can be diminished simply by waiting to respond. After the initial feelings dissipate, you can then decide whether to comply with a request on the merits of the idea, not on the basis of a bad mood or an intense emotional state.

"I'd rather be a free man in my grave / Than living as a puppet or a slave."

—REGGAE LEGEND JIMMY CLIFF

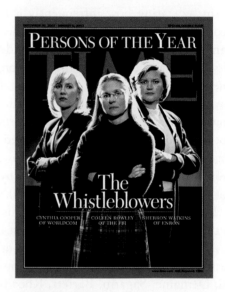

Resisting Social Influence
The women pictured on this magazine cover all refused to go along with those who were knowingly covering up wrongdoing. Cynthia Cooper (left), a vice president of the internal audit department of WorldCom, discovered an accounting fraud and confronted the company's controller with her findings. Coleen Rowley (center), an FBI agent, told her superiors before 9/11 that the flight training of known suspects may have constituted a terrorist threat. Sherron Watkins (right), a vice president of corporate development at Enron, identified fraud at the company and wrote a letter to her boss detailing her suspicions, rather than pretending nothing was wrong.

➊ LOOKING BACK

Reason-based approaches induce compliance by providing good reasons for people to agree to a request. The norm of reciprocity compels people to benefit those who have benefited them. In the reciprocal concessions (door-in-the-face) technique, people who have refused a large request are then induced to agree to a smaller request. In the that's-not-all technique, people are induced to buy an expensive product because a gift has been added to the deal. In the foot-in-the-door technique, people comply with a small request and then are induced to grant a larger request. Emotion-based approaches also can lead to compliance. People who are in a positive mood are more likely to comply with a request in order to maintain their good mood. In contrast, according to the negative state relief hypothesis, people who feel guilty or sad are also likely to comply with a request in order to feel better. Norm-based approaches capitalize on people's tendencies to look to others for guidance. People are responsive to both descriptive and prescriptive norms, but it is important that norm-based appeals do not pit the two against each other.

Obedience to Authority

The study of when and why people obey the commands or instructions of someone in authority has been dominated by the most famous set of social psychological experiments ever conducted—those of Stanley Milgram (previously discussed in Chapters 1 and 5). Milgram's experiments are so well known, in fact, that the social psychologist Lee Ross says they "have become part of our society's shared intellectual legacy—that small body of historical incidents, biblical parables, and classic literature that serious thinkers feel free to draw on when they debate about human nature or contemplate human history" (Ross, 1988, p. 101).

The Setup of the Milgram Experiments

Milgram's research on obedience began as an investigation of conformity. Milgram was interested in whether the kind of pressures observed in Asch's conformity experiment were powerful enough to lead people to do something far more significant than report an incorrect line length. He wondered what would happen if he asked participants to deliver electric shocks whenever a subject performing a task (in reality the experimenter's confederate) responded incorrectly. Would participants conform, when doing so involved hurting another human being?

This is an interesting question, but Milgram never pursued it. The reason is that he first needed to obtain data from a control group to determine the willingness of participants to deliver electric shocks when there was no pressure to conform (Evans, 1980). And that's where he got his surprising result—one that entirely changed his research agenda. A large percentage of participants were willing to do something they thought was hurting another person, even when there was no group of other participants leading the way.

Recall from Chapter 1 the basic procedure of Milgram's experiments. After responding to a newspaper ad, participants reported for an experiment on learning. A "random" draw was rigged so the participants always became the

Stanley Milgram
Using a shock generator that looked real but was actually just a prop, Milgram studied whether participants would continue to obey instructions and deliver electric shocks to a learner, even when they thought the learner was in grave distress.

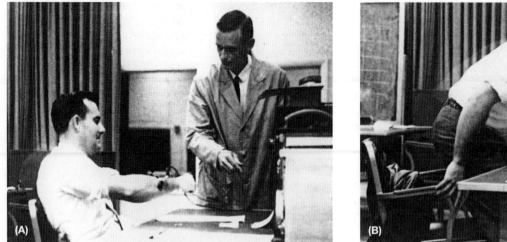
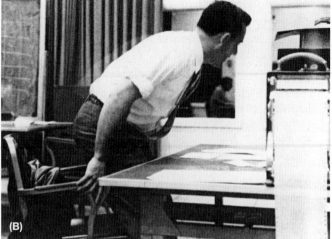

The Milgram Experiment

Participants were led to believe that the shock generator had 30 levels of shock, ranging from "slight shock" to "danger: severe shock" to "XXX." (A) A participant being given a sample shock of 45 volts (this was the only real shock in the experiment). (B) A participant standing up to ask the experimenter if he could stop the experiment.

"teacher" and the confederate always became the "learner." The teacher's job was to administer an electric shock every time the learner—a genial, middle-aged man who was strapped into a chair with his arm attached to a pretend shock generator—made a mistake by reporting the wrong word from a list of word pairs (for example, *glove/book, grill/detergent, anvil/pope*). Teachers were briefly strapped to the chair themselves and given a 45-volt shock so they would know the shocks were painful. The teacher started off by delivering 15 volts after the learner's first mistake, then increased the shock in 15-volt increments after each subsequent mistake. As the mistakes accumulated, participants found themselves required to deliver 255, 300, and 330 volts of electricity—all the way up to 450 volts. (In reality, no electric shock was delivered to the learner.) If a participant expressed reservations or tried to terminate the experiment, the experimenter would respond with a carefully scripted set of responses: "Please continue," "The experiment requires that you continue," "It is absolutely essential that you continue," "You have no other choice; you must go on."

The great surprise in these studies was how many participants continued to obey the experimenter's orders and deliver the maximum level of shock to the confederate. In the remote-feedback version of the experiment, in which the learner was in an adjoining room and could not be heard except when he vigorously pounded on the wall after a shock of 300 volts, 66 percent of the participants continued the learning experiment and delivered the maximum shock of 450 volts. In the voice-feedback version, the participants could hear a series of increasingly desperate pleas by the learner—including screaming that he had a heart condition—until finally, ominously, he became silent. Despite these cues that the learner was suffering, 62.5 percent of the participants delivered the maximum shock (Milgram, 1965, 1974).

Opposing Forces

Milgram's participants were caught in an agonizing conflict. On the one hand were forces compelling them to complete the experiment and continue delivering shock (Reeder, Monroe, & Pryor, 2008). Among these forces was a sense of fair play; they had agreed to serve as participants, they had already received payment for doing so, and they felt they now had to fulfill their part of the bargain. Some were probably also motivated by the reason they'd agreed to participate in the first place: to advance science and the understanding of human behavior. Another important motivating factor was normative social influence—in this case, the desire to avoid the disapproval of the experimenter or anyone else associated with the study. Closely related to this concern was the very human desire to avoid "making a scene" and upsetting others (Goffman, 1966; Miller, 1996).

On the other hand, several powerful forces compelled the participants to want to terminate the experiment. Foremost among these was the moral imperative to stop the suffering of the learner (Burger, Girgis, & Manning, 2011). Participants may have felt a specific desire not to hurt the genial man they had met earlier, as well as a more abstract reluctance to hurt others. Some were also probably concerned about what would happen if something went wrong. "What if he dies or is permanently injured?" "Will there be a lawsuit?" Still others may have wondered about the prospect of having to walk out with the learner after everything was over, and the resulting embarrassment (even retaliation).

Understanding these opposing forces leads to a better understanding of why participants responded the way they did, and why the whole experience was so stressful. How might the rate of obedience change if the strength of these opposing forces were modified (Blass, 2000, 2004; Miller, 1986)? This is exactly the question Milgram tried to answer through a comprehensive series of studies in which he conducted important variations on the original.

Tuning in the Learner Milgram directed his initial efforts at increasing the forces that compelled people to want to terminate the experiment. These forces were all triggered by an awareness of the learner's suffering, so Milgram tried to increase them by making the learner more prominent—or, in his words, by "tuning in the learner." (Participants spontaneously tried to do the opposite—that is, to deal with their own discomfort by tuning *out* the learner, sometimes literally turning away from him in their chair.) In the *remote-feedback* version of the experiment, the teacher could neither see nor hear the learner (except for one episode of vigorous pounding). In the *voice-feedback* version, the learner was still not in view, but he and his vigorous protests were clearly audible, and the teacher was constantly aware of him. In a *proximity* version, the learner received his shock in the same room where the participant delivered it, from only 1.5 feet away. Finally, in the *touch-proximity* version, the participant was required to force the learner's hand onto the shock plate (a sheet of insulation supposedly kept the participant from being shocked, too). **Figure 9.10** shows the effect of these manipulations. As the learner became more and more present and "real," the teachers found it increasingly difficult to deliver the shocks, and obedience rates diminished.

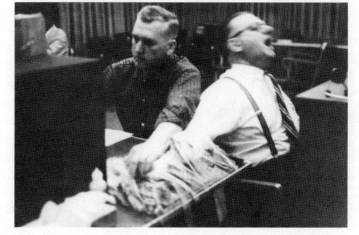

In Touch with the Learner
In a "touch-proximity" version of Milgram's original experiment, participants were required to force the learner's hand onto the shock plate, which reduced the participants' obedience rates.

One lesson to be drawn from this experiment is chilling: the more removed we are from others, the easier it is to hurt them. Consider, for example, the military technologies that allow individuals to inflict harm on others from a great distance. Combat is often no longer hand to hand. A mere push of a button can

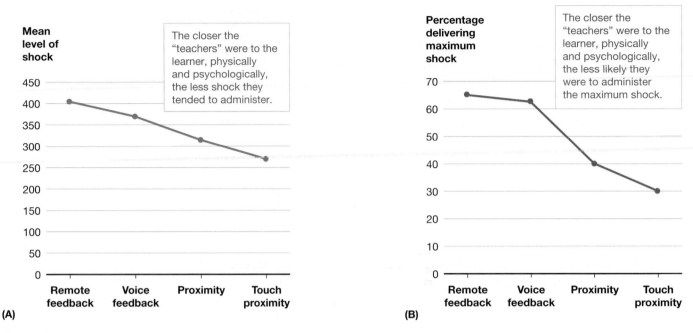

Mean level of shock

> The closer the "teachers" were to the learner, physically and psychologically, the less shock they tended to administer.

(A)
Remote feedback · Voice feedback · Proximity · Touch proximity

Percentage delivering maximum shock

> The closer the "teachers" were to the learner, physically and psychologically, the less likely they were to administer the maximum shock.

(B)
Remote feedback · Voice feedback · Proximity · Touch proximity

Figure 9.10

Tuning in the Learner

The effect of Milgram's experimental manipulations that made the learner more and more salient on (A) the mean level of shock participants delivered and (B) the percentage of participants who delivered the maximum amount of shock. As the "signal" coming from the learner got stronger, obedience declined.

SOURCE: Adapted from Milgram, 1965.

guide a Predator drone to a target or fire a missile from an underground silo a continent away. The remoteness of the victims in such cases makes the harm done to them abstract, so the emotional brakes on aggression are weakened dramatically.

Tuning Out the Experimenter Another way Milgram influenced the rate of obedience was to strengthen or weaken the "signal" coming from the experimenter, thereby strengthening or weakening the forces acting on participants to complete the experiment. Milgram conducted several variations on this theme as well. In the standard version of the study, the experimenter was present in the same room, right next to the participant. In an *experimenter-absent* version, the experimenter gave the initial instructions alongside the participant, but then left the room and issued his orders over the telephone. By physically removing himself from the scene, the experimenter lost much of his influence.

Another way to diminish the experimenter's power is to alter his authority. In one version, for example, an "ordinary person" (seemingly another participant, but in reality a confederate) was the one who delivered the orders to increase the shock level each time the learner made a mistake. In still another version, two experimenters initially instructed the participant to shock the learner. At one point, however, one of the two experimenters announced that he found the proceedings objectionable and argued with the other experimenter, who continued to urge the participant to complete the experiment.

Tuning Out the Victim

Missiles can be fired from drone (pilotless) aircraft by a person located thousands of miles away. This distance can make the harm more abstract, and therefore orders to fire less likely to be questioned.

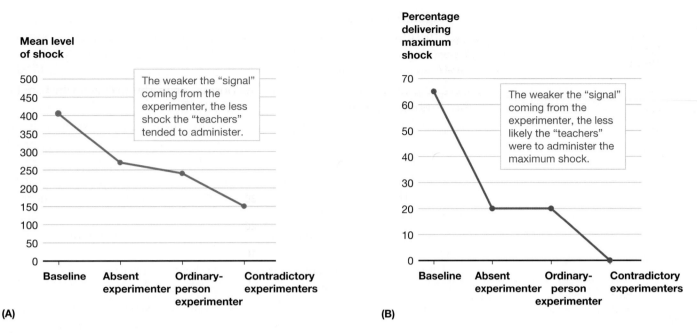

Mean level of shock (A)

The weaker the "signal" coming from the experimenter, the less shock the "teachers" tended to administer.

500
450
400
350
300
250
200
150
100
50
0

Baseline   Absent experimenter   Ordinary-person experimenter   Contradictory experimenters

Percentage delivering maximum shock (B)

The weaker the "signal" coming from the experimenter, the less likely the "teachers" were to administer the maximum shock.

70
60
50
40
30
20
10
0

Baseline   Absent experimenter   Ordinary-person experimenter   Contradictory experimenters

Figure 9.11
Tuning Out the Experimenter
The effect of Milgram's experimental manipulations that made the experimenter less and less salient on (A) the mean level of shock participants delivered and (B) the percentage of participants who delivered the maximum amount of shock. As the "signal" coming from the experimenter got weaker, obedience declined.

SOURCE: Adapted from Milgram, 1965.

Figure 9.11 shows the results of these manipulations. As the experimenter became less salient and less of an authority in the participant's mind, it became easier for the participant to defy him, so the rate of obedience declined. Notice that this series of experimental variations had a more pronounced effect than the "tuning in the learner" series (compare **Figures 9.10** and **9.11**). Making it *easier* for participants to disobey thus seems to be more effective than increasing their *desire* to disobey. This distinction provides an important clue to understanding the surprising levels of obedience observed in Milgram's experiments.

Would You Have Obeyed?

Nobody anticipated the widespread obedience Milgram found. A group of psychiatrists predicted that fewer than 1 percent of all participants—a pathological fringe—would continue until they delivered the maximum amount of shock. This failure of prediction is matched by an equally noteworthy failure of after-the-fact insight: almost no one believes, even after hearing the basic results and all the experimental variations, that he or she would deliver very high levels of shock. Thus, although Milgram's experimental variations shed light on when and why people engage in such surprising behavior, they don't provide a fully satisfying explanation. As Ross put it, the experiments do not pass a critical "empathy test" (Ross, 1988). They don't lead us to empathize fully with the obedient participants and take seriously the possibility that *we* would also obey to the end—as most participants did. A truly satisfying explanation might not convince us that we would *surely* do so, but it should at least convince us that we *might* act that way.

Milgram's work is often mentioned in discussions of how people sometimes obey the directives of malevolent government officials and engage in sadistic, demeaning torture, such as that observed at Abu Ghraib, or commit hideous crimes against humanity, such as those witnessed during the Holocaust in Nazi Germany, in the "ethnic cleansing" in Bosnia, or in the massacres in Cambodia, Rwanda, or Darfur. Explanations of such incomprehensible cruelties vary along an "exceptionalist-normalist" continuum. The exceptionalist thesis is that such crimes are perpetrated only by "exceptional" people—that is, exceptionally sadistic, desperate, or ethnocentric people. Many Germans were virulent anti-Semites. The Serbs harbored long-standing hatred and resentment against the Bosnians. The Rwandan Hutus had a score to settle with the Tutsis. The normalist thesis, in contrast, is that most people are capable of such destructive obedience, and given the right circumstances, almost anyone would commit such acts (**Box 9.4**).

Milgram's research, of course, is typically taken to support the normalist position. Milgram himself certainly took this position. When Morley Safer on the CBS TV show *60 Minutes* asked whether he thought something like the Holocaust could happen in the United States, Milgram offered this opinion:

> I would say, on the basis of having observed a thousand people in the experiment and having my own intuition shaped and informed by these experiments, that if a system of death camps were set up in the United States of the sort we had seen in Nazi Germany, one would be able to find sufficient personnel for those camps in any medium-sized American town. (Quoted in Blass, 1999, p. 955)

Let's take a closer look.

They Tried but Failed One of the reasons people think they would never behave like the average participant in Milgram's studies behaved is that they misunderstand exactly how the average participant acted (Ross, 1988). People conjure up images of participants blithely going along with the experimenter's commands, increasing the shock level from trial to trial, being relatively inattentive to the learner's situation. Indeed, Milgram's experiments have often been described as demonstrations of "blind" obedience.

But that's not what happened. Participants did not mindlessly obey. Nearly all tried to disobey in one form or another. Nearly everyone called the experimenter's attention to the learner's suffering in an implicit plea to stop the proceedings. Many stated explicitly that they refused to continue (but nonetheless went on with the experiment). Some got out of their chair in defiance, only to sit back down moments later. The participants tried to disobey, but they weren't particularly good at it. As Ross pointed out, "the Milgram experiments have less to say about 'destructive obedience' than about ineffective and indecisive *disobedience*" (Ross, 1988, p. 103).

This distinction is critical. Most of us have had the experience of having good intentions without being able to translate those intentions into effective action. For instance, maybe you've *wanted* to speak up more forcefully and effectively against racist or sexist remarks, but were too slow to respond or the words didn't come out as forthrightly as you intended. Or maybe you've *wanted* to reach out to someone who was being ignored at a party, but you were distracted by your own social needs. Most of us can relate to being good-hearted but ineffective, but not to being uncaring.

BOX 9.4 **FOCUS ON *TODAY***

Would Milgram Get the Same Results Now?

Milgram's studies were done in the early 1960s. But that was then, this is now. If you conducted Milgram's experiments today, would you get the same results? Some argue that today's more intense media coverage of such events as domestic spying by the U.S. National Security Agency, and the dubious intelligence reports about weapons of mass destruction before the 2003 invasion of Iraq, have made people less trusting of authority and thus less likely to obey instructions to harm another individual. Perhaps, but that's a difficult idea to test because ethical concerns make it impossible to replicate Milgram's experiments today. All psychological research must now be approved by an institutional review board, whose responsibility is to make sure any proposed research would not cause undue stress to the participants or harm them in any way (see Chapter 2). Few, if any, IRBs would approve a direct replication of Milgram's experiments.

Jerry Burger, at Santa Clara University in California, did the next best thing, by conducting a near-replication of Milgram's basic experiment to investigate whether the tendency to obey authority has changed since Milgram's time (Burger, 2009; Burger, Girgis, & Manning, 2011). Burger identified a critical moment in the original proceedings when disobedience was most likely: right after the participant had (supposedly) delivered 150 volts of electric shock, and the learner protested and demanded to be released. It was something of a now-or-never moment: four out of five of Milgram's participants who did not stop at this point never stopped at all.

Burger saw an opportunity. It would be ethically unacceptable to put people through the stress of deciding between disobeying the experimenter and administering 300 or 400 volts of electricity. But the procedure is not so stressful—and thus more ethically acceptable—up to the 150-volt level. Until that point Milgram's learner hadn't protested, and the pain caused by the shocks, the participants would

presume, can't be that bad. Burger therefore sought and received permission from Santa Clara's IRB to replicate Milgram's basic experiment up to that point only.

Burger also took steps to safeguard the welfare of his participants. First, his team asked people who were interested in participating whether they had ever been diagnosed with a psychiatric disorder, were currently in psychotherapy or taking medication for anxiety or depression, or had ever experienced any serious trauma. Anyone who answered yes to any of these questions was not allowed to participate. Second, those who passed this initial screening were told they would receive $50 for two 45-minute sessions. In the first session, participants filled out a number of psychological scales, such as the Beck Depression Inventory, and then were interviewed by a licensed clinical psychologist. If the psychologist detected any sign in the questionnaire responses or in the face-to-face interview that a potential participant might not be up

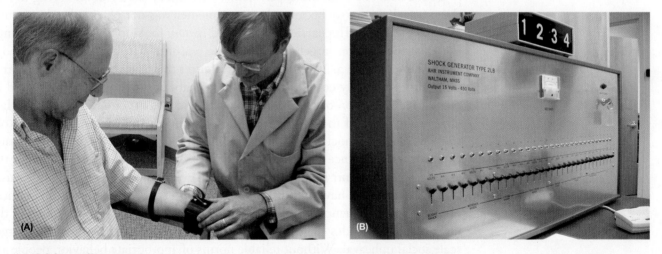

Revisiting Milgram

(A) In Burger's 2009 near-replication of the original Milgram experiments from the 1960s, participants faced the same conflict over whether to administer increasing levels of shock (up to 165 volts) to the learner, or to call a halt to his suffering by refusing to continue. (B) Burger used the same type of bogus shock generator as Milgram.

to the challenge of being in the study, that person was paid $50 right then and excluded from the second session.

Those who made it past both screenings were run through a replication of the voice-feedback version of Milgram's experiment. The results were essentially the same as those obtained by Milgram himself. In Burger's study, 70 percent of the participants were willing to administer the next level of shock (165 volts) after hearing the learner's protest. This compares with 82 percent of Milgram's participants—not a statistically significant difference. Men and women were equally likely to continue past the critical 150-volt level. In addition, whether participants obeyed the experimenter was unrelated to how they scored on personality scales measuring empathy or their desire to control events in their lives. Today, people seem to react to pressure to obey the same way they did more than 50 years ago.

A chilling parallel to the behavior of Milgram's participants is the behavior of some (and only some) of the German soldiers called on to execute Polish Jews during World War II (Browning, 1992). Members of German Reserve Police Battalion 101 were mostly men who hoped to avoid the inevitable violence of the war by volunteering for police duty in Hamburg. After the invasion of Poland, however, they were reassigned to serve as military police in occupied Poland. Most of their duties consisted of routine police work. But on July 13, 1942, the men were roused from their barracks before dawn and taken to the outskirts of the village of Józéfow, where they were given gruesome orders: to round up all the Jewish men, women, and children from the village, send all able-bodied young men to a work camp, and shoot the rest.

Most were shocked and repelled by their orders. Many resisted. But their resistance, like that of Milgram's participants, was feeble. Some kept busy with petty errands or moved to the back of the battalion, hoping to avoid being called on. Others took part in the roundup but then refrained from shooting if no one was watching. Still others fired but missed intentionally. What they *didn't* do was state assertively that they wouldn't participate, that what they were being asked to do was wrong. They tried to find an easy way to disobey, but there was no easy way.

In the case of Milgram's experiments, participants had trouble trying to halt the proceedings partly because the experimenter was not playing by the normal rules of social life. The participants offered *reasons* for stopping the experiments, but the experimenter largely ignored those reasons, making minimally responsive statements such as "The experiment requires that you continue." Participants were understandably confused and uncertain about how to act. As we noted in our earlier discussion of conformity, people tend not to act decisively when they lack a solid grasp of the events happening around them. What to do when told to deliver electric shock to "teach" someone who's no longer trying to learn anything, at the insistence of an authority figure who seems unconcerned about the learner's predicament? How to respond when events have stopped making sense?

These questions have important implications for those real-world instances of destructive obedience with which we should be most concerned. Many of the most hideous episodes of genocide, for example, have occurred right after large-scale social upheaval. Without reliable norms of appropriate behavior, people are less able to muster the confidence necessary to take decisive action to stop such atrocities.

Release from Responsibility The inability of Milgram's participants to stop the experiment meant they were trapped in a situation of terrible conflict and stress.

Although they knew what was happening should not continue, they couldn't bring it to an end. They were therefore desperate for anything that would reduce their stress. Fortunately for the participants (but unfortunately for the learner, if he really had been receiving electric shock), the experimenter provided something to reduce their stress by taking responsibility for what was happening. When participants asked, as many did, "Who is responsible for what happens here?" the experimenter responded, "I am responsible." Participants seized on this as a justification for their actions, and the stress they were experiencing was significantly reduced.

We have all been in stressful, confusing situations when we wanted the discomfort and confusion to end. "My friends are making me uncomfortable by savagely teasing that guy in our English class, but they'll think I'm a jerk if I speak out." "Everyone's popping those pills as if they weren't harmful, and they'll think I'm a wimp if I don't too." It is always tempting in such situations to grab at anything that would make the dilemma go away. "Maybe the guy in our class really does deserve it, and I'm being too sensitive." "Maybe the pills really are harmless, and I'm blowing things out of proportion."

Of course, the cover, or "out," the experimenter provided in Milgram's experiments worked only because participants viewed the person taking responsibility as a legitimate authority. People generally won't let just anyone take responsibility and then assume everything is okay. Suppose you're approached by a strange character on campus who says, "Quick, help me set fire to the psychology building; I'll take full responsibility"—you certainly would refuse to pitch in. In Milgram's experiments, however, participants believed they could legitimately transfer responsibility to the experimenter because he was a representative of science; in nearly all the variations, he was affiliated with Yale University, a respected institution (although obedience was still high when the experimenter operated out of a storefront in downtown Bridgeport, Connecticut). These aspects of the situation made it easier for participants to reduce their own stress over what was happening by assuming the experimenter knew better and was ultimately responsible for what happened.

Legitimizing the Experiment

To see how participants would react if the experiment were not conducted at Yale and the authority seemed less legitimate, Milgram had them report to (A) a fictitious business called Research Associates of Bridgeport, located above a storefront in downtown Bridgeport, and (B) inside a seedy office. Obedience rates declined somewhat but remained high even under these conditions.

The cover provided by authorities has implications for some of the worst acts of destructive obedience in history. In Nazi Germany, in Rwanda, and at Abu Ghraib, the demands to obey were issued by authority figures who either explicitly took responsibility or whose position supported an assumption of responsibility. And such claims of responsibility have nearly always been legitimized by some overarching ideology. Whether based on nationalism, religious ideology, or ethnic identity, every example of such organized aggression has been draped in a legitimizing ideology that seeks to present otherwise hideous actions in a way that makes them seem like morally appropriate behavior (Staub, 1989; Zajonc, 2002).

Step-by-Step Involvement It's important to remember as well that the participants in Milgram's experiments did not deliver 450 volts of electric shock right away. Instead, each participant first administered only 15 volts to the learner. Who wouldn't do that? That's feedback, not punishment. Then 30 volts. No problem there either. Then 45, 60, 75—each step a small one. Once participants started down this path, though, it was hard to stop, and they administered more and more shock. Indeed, the increments were so small that if a certain level of shock seemed like too much, why wouldn't the previous level also have been too much (Gilbert, 1981)?

The step-by-step nature of participants' obedience in these experiments is a powerful reason why so many administered as much electric shock as they did. Most of us have had the experience of gradually getting in over our heads in this way. We may tell a "little white lie"—one that sets in motion a cascade of events that requires more and more deception. (Many a TV sitcom plot rests on this very sequence.) Or we may dig in our heels over a small matter in a dispute—and later find it hard to back down because of our initial stubbornness. Our behavior often creates its own momentum, and it's hard to know in advance where it will lead. Milgram's participants can certainly be forgiven for not foreseeing how everything would unfold. Would any of us have seen it any more clearly?

The parallels between this element of Milgram's procedure and what happened in Nazi Germany are striking (**Box 9.5**). German citizens were not asked, out of the blue, to assist with or condone the deportation of Jews, Gypsies, homosexuals, and communists to the death camps. Instead, the rights of these groups were gradually stripped away. Certain business practices were restricted, then travel constraints were imposed, and then citizenship was narrowed; only later were people loaded into boxcars and sent to the death camps. The Nazis would doubtless have had a much harder time if they had started with the last step. Their own citizens would probably have been less cooperative; more of their victims would probably have resisted more violently. In this context, it's significant that the most vigorous defiance of the Nazis' genocide plans took place not in Germany, but in the countries Germany overran. Among the many reasons for this difference may well have been that Germany carried out the "final solution" much faster in the conquered countries than in Germany itself.

BOX 9.5 **FOCUS ON *HISTORY***

Step-by-Step to Genocide

Anti-Jewish laws and policies of the German government before and during World War II are listed below. Notice the gradual nature of their severity.

1. April 1, 1933
Boycott of Jewish businesses is declared.

2. April 7, 1933
Law for the Restoration of the Professional Civil Service authorizes the dismissal of most non-Aryan civil servants (especially those with Jewish parents or grandparents).

3. September 22, 1933
Reestablishment of the Reich Chamber of Culture leads to the removal of non-Aryans from organizations and enterprises related to literature, the press, broadcasting, music, and art.

4. September 15, 1935
The Reich Citizenship Law defines citizens of the Reich as only those who are of German or kindred blood.

5. September 16, 1935
The Law for the Protection of German Blood and German Honor forbids marriage between Jews and nationals of German or kindred blood and declares marriages conducted in defiance of this law void, forbids relations outside of marriage between Jews and nationals of German or kindred blood, and forbids Jews from employing in their household female nationals of German or kindred blood who are under age 45.

6. November 16, 1936
Jews are prohibited from obtaining passports or traveling abroad, except in special cases.

7. April 1938
Jews are forced to register with the government all property valued at 5,000 marks or more.

8. July 25, 1938
The Fourth Decree of the Reich Citizenship Law terminates the licenses of Jewish physicians as of September 30, 1938.

9. September 27, 1938
The Fifth Decree of the Reich Citizenship Law allows Jewish legal advisers to attend professionally only to the legal affairs of Jews.

10. October 5, 1938
Jewish passports and ration cards are marked with a *J*.

11. January 1, 1939
All Jews are required to carry a special ID card.

12. July 1940
Purchases by Jews are restricted to certain hours and stores; telephones are taken away from Jews.

13. September 19, 1941
Jews are forced to display the Jewish badge prominently on their clothing and with few exceptions are not allowed to use public transportation.

14. October 14, 1941
Massive deportation of German Jews to concentration camps begins.

15. October 23, 1941
Jewish emigration is prohibited.

16. January 20, 1942 (the Wansee Conference)
Nazi leaders decide that 11 million Jews (every Jew in Europe) are to be killed.

⟳ LOOKING BACK

Many factors contribute to people's willingness to obey leaders who demand immoral behavior. Several elements of the situation may make obedience easier to understand: a person's attempts to disobey are often blocked; the person in authority often takes responsibility for what happens; and once the obedience begins, there is typically no obvious stopping point. But when circumstances lead the individual to be tuned in to the victim, obedience decreases substantially. When circumstances lead the individual to tune out the person in authority, obedience is also greatly reduced.

SUMMARY

What Is Social Influence?

- There are three types of *social influence*. *Conformity* involves a change in a person's attitudes or behavior in response to explicit or implicit pressure from others. *Compliance* involves going along with explicit requests made by others. *Obedience* is submitting to the demands of a person in authority.

Conformity

- Mimicry is the conscious or nonconscious imitation of someone else's behavior. People sometimes conform because of *informational social influence*; they view the actions of others as informative about proper behavior. People also conform because of *normative social influence*, out of a concern for the social consequences of their actions.
- Conformity pressure depends on group characteristics. The larger the size, the greater the group's influence, but only up to about four people. Unanimous groups exert more pressure to conform than those with even a single dissenter. The greater the expertise *and* status of the group members, the greater their influence.
- People from interdependent cultures are more likely to conform than people from independent cultures. Women tend to conform more than men, and both women and men conform more in domains in which they have less knowledge.
- The direction of influence is not always from the majority to the minority. Sometimes minority influence can be substantial, especially when the minority expresses consistent views.

Compliance

- Reason-based approaches to compliance include invoking the *norm of reciprocity* by doing a favor for someone, making a concession and using the *reciprocal concessions technique*, or adding things to an original offer and using the *that's-not-all technique*. With the *foot-in-the-door technique*, a person first gets someone to agree to a small request before making a more substantial request.
- Emotion-based approaches to compliance include getting the targeted person in a good mood, which is likely to increase compliance because of *mood maintenance* and because of the influence of the good mood on how the request is interpreted.
- Compliance may also result from a desire for *negative state relief* because an act of compliance may reduce guilt or sadness.
- Norm-based approaches to compliance take advantage of the tendency to look to others for guidance about how to behave. People are generally reluctant to stray too far from the mainstream, and *descriptive norms* indicate how people actually behave in specific contexts. *Prescriptive norms* indicate how people should behave in various situations.

Obedience to Authority

- The study of obedience has been dominated by the Milgram experiments, which demonstrated the surprising willingness of most people to go along with the seemingly harmful demands of an authority.
- Participants in obedience studies are caught in a conflict between two opposing forces: normative social influence and moral imperatives. The balance between these forces shifts toward the former when participants tune out the learner and tune in the experimenter. It shifts toward the latter when participants tune out the experimenter and tune in the learner.
- Although Milgram's results strike nearly everyone as wildly counterintuitive, they can be rendered less surprising by considering the stepwise nature of the demands, the (mostly ineffective) attempts to terminate the experiment made by most participants, and the ability of participants to place the burden of responsibility on the experimenter, not themselves.

THINK ABOUT IT

1. What two reasons appear to explain why people so often mimic one another? How might each of these processes function differently in Hispanic versus Anglo-American cultures?

2. Suppose your dining hall is having a contest, and you have to guess how many gumballs are in a giant jar (the closest guess wins). You and a few friends walk up to the gumball jar and tell your guesses to the volunteer running the contest. Your friends all say their guesses out loud, and you go last. You find yourself increasing your gumball estimate to be closer to those of your friends. How could each type of social influence (normative and informational) have affected your guess? How could you reduce the normative social influence in this situation?

3. In the battle for LGBT rights, what kind of social influence can minority LGBT groups exert on the majority?

Should their goal be to engage public support or private internalization and acceptance of their arguments among members of the majority?

4. Although they are distinct compliance strategies, the that's-not-all and door-in-the-face techniques share a common mechanism. What is it, and how does it work in each case?

5. Suppose you want to increase voting rates among millennials (people born in the 1980s and 1990s). Describe one reason-based approach, one emotion-based approach, and one norm-based approach you could use to do so.

6. In the context of the Milgram experiment, give an example of "tuning in the learner" and an example of "tuning out the experimenter," and explain how each one affects obedience rates.

THE ANSWER GUIDELINES FOR THE THINK ABOUT IT QUESTIONS CAN BE FOUND AT THE BACK OF THE BOOK . . .

Relationships and Attraction

In the pilot episode of the popular television series *Modern Family*, viewers meet Claire and Phil, parents in a household that—although modern in terms of clothing, language, and technology—is not really different from the conventional TV families of several decades ago, such as those in *Leave It to Beaver, Father Knows Best*, and *I Love Lucy*. Claire and Phil are both white, have been married for 16 years, and have three biological children. Phil is the sole breadwinner. Chaos ensues as the oldest daughter, Hayley, brings home her first boyfriend.

We then meet Jay, a gruff 50-something-year-old with a well-concealed heart of gold; his beautiful young Colombian wife of 6 months, Gloria; and her son from a previous marriage, Manny. More chaos ensues as people keep assuming Jay is Gloria's father and Manny declares his love for a girl out of his league.

Next we meet Cam and Mitchell, a gay couple, as they return to Los Angeles with their newly adopted Vietnamese infant daughter, Lily. Still more chaos, this time centered on which of the two men is best suited for the more feminine sides of raising a child, and how they should break the news of the adoption to Mitchell's apparently not-so-accepting family.

When Cam and Mitchell arrive at a family gathering, we discover Mitchell's family consists of all the other characters we met earlier. Jay is his dad—and Claire's. This makes Claire's three kids and Lily cousins; Manny, Claire's stepbrother; and Gloria, although younger, Claire's stepmother. Modern indeed.

The series captures the complications that can arise in the superextended families of varying compositions so common in today's world. And despite the chaos—in this show at least, and often in real life—it all works. The show was a hit from the first episode because viewers, whatever their own family circumstances, found

Modern Family

As this hit TV show illustrates, families can be quite diverse, and people form all sorts of romantic bonds.

it easy to imagine being a part of this particular extended family—and liking what they imagined.

What can *Modern Family* tell us about relationships and attraction? For one thing, it shows that human beings can find themselves romantically attracted to all kinds of people: people of the same or different sex, people from different cultures, and people spanning a considerable age range. It also shows us that various types of relationships, even those within an extended family, can work. They work in the sense of helping meet the needs of the individuals involved.

This chapter explores a broad range of enduring relationships—with parents, friends, and romantic partners, and with members of the same and opposite sex. We focus mainly on interpersonal relationships, attachments in which bonds of family or friendship, or love or respect or hierarchy, tie together two or more individuals over an extended period of time. In such relationships, the people involved generally engage in activities together and have joint memories of shared experiences. Research has shown that these relationships are central to everyday human functioning.

Characterizing Relationships

In studying relationships, researchers face certain challenges that are not as common in other areas of social psychology (Bradbury & Karney, 1993; Finkel & Eastwick, 2008; Gonzalez & Griffin, 1997; Karney & Bradbury, 1995). For example, many studies of relationships are not true experiments with random assignment of participants to different conditions. Instead, researchers use longitudinal methods to examine the dynamics that unfold over time in preexisting relationships. They attempt to understand, for example, what factors early in a relationship make for happier or more problematic bonds. This kind of research involves the challenging methodological problem of self-selection, which occurs whenever investigators are unable to assign participants to the conditions being compared (see Chapter 2). When participants "select" their own condition, researchers can't know whether an observed difference between two conditions is a reflection of the different experiences of the people in those conditions, or simply a result of different types of people tending to gravitate to each of the two conditions.

Here's a specific example. Couples who make a special effort to celebrate their wedding anniversary may be less likely to get divorced than couples who don't. But is the failure to celebrate an anniversary a cause of discord, or is it that people who aren't getting along don't do it? Despite these methodological challenges, the social psychological literature on relationships is flourishing, revealing fundamental truths about the bonds people the world over form with one another.

The Importance of Relationships

Many people from Western cultures define themselves in independent, individualistic terms, focusing on how they are different and separate from others. Nevertheless, human nature is profoundly social, and a person's identity and sense of self are shaped by social relationships (see Chapter 3). Indeed, human beings (and many other kinds of animals) have what appears to be a biological need for belonging in relationships.

It's self-evident that humans have biologically based needs for food, oxygen, warmth, and safety. Without food, air, or water, we die. Roy Baumeister and Mark Leary claim that the same is true of relationships: we have a need to be embedded in healthy relationships (Baumeister & Leary, 1995). These researchers offer a number of arguments to support their claim that we all have a need—not just a desire—to belong.

Arguments for the Need to Belong Baumeister and Leary point out the likely evolutionary basis of our tendency to seek out relationships. There's a great deal of consensus that relationships help individuals and offspring survive, thus increasing the likelihood of passing on one's genes. Long-term romantic bonds evolved to facilitate reproduction and to raise offspring, who are vulnerable and dependent for many years (Diamond, 2003; Ellis, 1992). Parent-offspring attachments help ensure that infants and children are protected and will survive until they can function independently (Bowlby, 1982). Friendship evolved as a means for non-kin to cooperate, thereby avoiding the costs and perils of competition and aggression (Trivers, 1971).

If relationships have an evolutionary basis, then they could be expected to have many universal features. Similar kinds of dynamics should exist between romantic partners, between parents and children, between siblings, and between friends in different cultures around the world. Pioneers in the field of human ethology, who studied hunter-gatherer groups in their natural environments, documented patterns of social behavior that appear to be universal—caregiving between mother and child, wrestling between siblings, flirtation by young people who are courting, affection between romantic partners, dominance displays between adolescent males (Eibl-Eibesfeldt, 1989).

Baumeister and Leary also note that if the need to belong is truly a need, it should be satiable. When we are thirsty or hungry, we drink or eat—but only

> "We are all in this together, by ourselves."
> —LILY TOMLIN

> "No more fiendish punishment could be devised, were such a thing physically possible, than that one should be turned loose in society and remain absolutely unnoticed by all the members thereof."
> —WILLIAM JAMES

to a point. The same appears to be true of our social lives. Consider friendship. In Western European cultures, college students tend to restrict their meaningful interactions to, on average, about six friends (Wheeler & Nezlek, 1977). It seems that we satisfy our need for friendship with a limited number of close friends, and once that need is satisfied, we don't continue to seek other relationships. But if the need to belong isn't satisfied in existing relationships, we'll seek to satisfy it in other relationships. Observational studies in prisons, for example, find that prisoners suffer great anguish at the loss of contact with their family. As a result, they often form substitute families based on kinship-like ties with other prisoners (Burkhart, 1973).

Evidence for the Need to Belong When the need to belong is not met over a long period of time, people tend to suffer profoundly negative consequences. In a classic series of experiments, Harry Harlow (1958) raised baby rhesus monkeys without contact with other rhesus monkeys but with access to two "mother surrogates"—props vaguely resembling monkeys. One prop was covered in cloth, where the monkeys could go for comfort when feeling threatened; the other was made out of wire that could provide milk when the monkeys were hungry (**Figure 10.1**). The monkeys preferred the mother that could provide comfort to the one that could provide food. Those raised with these mothers, but otherwise in isolation, were in no way normal when they reached adolescence. As adolescents, they were highly fearful, could not interact with their peers, and engaged in inappropriate sexual behaviors—for example, attacking potential mates or failing to display typical sexual positions during copulation.

A natural experiment with elephants makes a similar point. A natural experiment involves an accidentally produced set of conditions (rather than conditions created by an experimenter) that largely avoids self-selection problems. Elephants in some areas of Africa have been slaughtered for the ivory in their tusks, leaving young elephants to grow up on their own. These adolescent elephants prove to be quite antisocial and aggressive toward members of their own species as well as others; they kill rhinoceroses for sport, for example. African gamekeepers have solved the problem of the wild elephants by importing adult elephants to show the adolescents how to be elephants.

Figure 10.1
Social Isolation Leads to Social Impairments
The rhesus monkeys in Harlow's classic experiments, provided with mother surrogates in the form of props resembling monkeys but otherwise reared in isolation, showed significant social deficiencies in adolescence.

The Universality of Relationships

(A, B) Siblings in different cultures all play, support, and fight with each other, although the specific kinds of play, support, and conflict may vary according to the culture. (C) Parents in different cultures show similar kinds of attachment behaviors, including patterns of touch and eye contact.

There's ample evidence for the need to belong in humans as well. Mortality rates are higher for divorced, unmarried, and widowed individuals (Lynch, 1979). Admissions to hospitals for psychological problems are 3 to 23 times higher for divorced than married people, depending on the study and nature of the psychological problems in question (Bloom, White, & Asher, 1979; Hughes & Waite, 2009). Suicide rates are higher for single and divorced individuals (Rothberg & Jones, 1987), as are crime rates (Baumeister & Leary, 1995). According to the so-called marriage benefit, married people fare better than unmarried ones on various indices of well-being (Gove, Style, & Hughes, 1990; Ross, Mirowsky, & Goldsteen, 1990). This appears to extend to gay and lesbian relationships, as seen in a recent survey in which partnered gay men and lesbians scored higher on well-being than their non-partnered counterparts (Wienke & Hill, 2009). Having support from others also contributes to good health, by strengthening the cardiovascular, immune, and endocrine systems (Oxman & Hull, 1997; Uchino, Cacioppo, & Kiecolt-Glaser, 1996).

The Need to Belong

There is an evolutionary basis for the need to belong. Not only do elephant parents feed and protect young elephants, but they teach them appropriate social behavior that enables them to live in groups. If the young elephants grow up without adults, they are likely to become antisocial and aggressive and have difficulty living in groups.

communal relationship A relationship in which the individuals feel a special responsibility for one another and give and receive according to the principle of need; such relationships are often long term.

exchange relationship A relationship in which individuals feel little responsibility toward one another; giving and receiving are governed by concerns about equity and reciprocity; such relationships are usually short term.

"Sticks in a bundle are unbreakable."

—KENYAN PROVERB

Different Ways of Relating to Others

Although many types of relationships contribute to our well-being, we obviously behave in very different ways with a new romantic partner, with friends from our ultimate Frisbee team, with a minister or rabbi, or with our supervisors at work (Fiske, 1992; Moskowitz, 1994). Although this chapter focuses on interpersonal relationships such as those among friends or romantic partners, it's necessary to understand some important distinctions among different types of relationships.

Communal and Exchange Relationships In the incredible economic growth China and India have witnessed in the past decade, millions of young people have left their villages and moved to the large cities that have mushroomed in these new economic superpowers. A quiet village life of friends and family has been replaced by one of interacting mostly with strangers and bosses with whom they have no personal connection. How best to think about these changes in psychological terms?

Margaret Clark and Judson Mills argue that two fundamentally different types of relationships—communal relationships and exchange relationships—arise in different contexts and are governed by different norms (Clark, 1992; Clark & Mills, 1979, 1993). In a **communal relationship**, the individuals feel a special responsibility for one another and often expect their relationship to be long term. Communal relationships are based on a sense of "oneness" and family-like sharing of common identity (Fiske, 1992). People in communal relationships, such as close friends, come to resemble one another in the timing of their laughter and their specific emotional experiences. In communal relationships, individuals give and receive according to the principle of need—that is, according to who has the most pressing need at any given time. Prototypical examples of communal relationships are ones between family members and between close friends—the kinds of relationships that are the social fabric of communal life in small villages.

An **exchange relationship**, in contrast, is trade-based, often short term, and the individuals feel no special responsibility toward one another. In exchange relationships, giving and receiving are governed by concerns about equity (you get what you put into the relationship) and reciprocity (what you receive is returned in proportion to what you give). Examples of exchange relationships are interactions with salespeople and bureaucrats, or with workers and supervisors in a business organization.

The distinction between communal and exchange relationships highlights notable cultural differences. Societies differ widely in which approach they generally prefer. People in East Asian and Latin American societies are inclined to take a communal approach to many situations in which people in European and Commonwealth countries would be inclined to take an exchange approach. Consider the question, raised in Chapter 1, of how businesspeople would treat an employee who had put in 15 good years of service, but over the past year had fallen down on the job and showed little chance of getting back on track. East Asians tended to feel the company had an obligation to treat the employee as family and keep him on the payroll. Western businesspeople were more likely to feel the relationship was purely contractual, or exchange-based, and that the employee should be

"O.K., who else has experienced the best-friend relationship as inadequate?"

let go. There are differences among Western nations, however: people from Catholic countries are more likely to take a communal stance than people from Protestant countries. Indeed, even within the United States, Catholics are more likely than Protestants to take a communal stance in relationship matters (Sanchez-Burks, 2002, 2004).

Rewards and the Social Exchange Theory of Interpersonal Relationships

The important distinction between communal and exchange relationships notwithstanding, many social psychologists believe that even the most intimate relationships are based, to a certain extent, on rewards of some sort. Indeed, one of the most widely accepted principles of interpersonal relationships has the virtue of simplicity: people tend to like and gravitate toward those who provide them with rewards. The rewards don't have to be tangible or immediate, and they don't have to come from direct interaction. But according to this reward framework, people tend to like those who make them feel good (Clore & Byrne, 1974; Lott & Lott, 1974).

Here's how you can test the reward principle yourself. Think of all your friends, and ask yourself whether this principle helps explain why you like each of them. Some of the rewards are easy to identify. You may like one friend because you can count on her to share your setbacks and heartaches as well as your achievements and joys. You may like another person because she's hilarious and you have fun when you hang out together. One interesting illustration of this idea comes from research on friendships between heterosexual women and gay men. These relationships are often mutually rewarding because they enable each party to get the perspective of the sex to which they are attracted from a friend who they know doesn't have a romantic or sexual agenda (Russell, DelPriore, Butterfield, & Hill, 2013).

Note that the reward framework helps answer one of the most basic and practical of questions: What can you do to get others to like you? Reward them. Make other people feel good when they are around you. This approach is similar to the advice given by Dale Carnegie in his book *How to Win Friends and Influence People* (which has sold 15 million copies since its first printing in 1937): to win friends, "Dole out praise lavishly." It might seem that such a strategy would backfire. People surely see through most efforts to gain favor and resent the attempt to influence them. Wealthy individuals, for example, are surely alert to the existence of "gold diggers" who fake affection in an effort to part them from their money. But the term *gold digger* probably wouldn't even exist if a great many of them were not successful in their quest. Their success suggests that ingratiation may be more effective than it "should" be. Flattery may get you pretty far after all (Jones, 1964; Vonk, 2002).

The notion that relationships involve rewards lies at the heart of a theory that views much of human interaction as social exchange (Kelley & Thibaut, 1978; Rusbult, 1983). **Social exchange theory** starts with the assumption that people are motivated to maximize their own feelings of satisfaction. People seek out rewards in their interactions with others, and they are willing to pay certain costs to obtain them. Typically, people prefer interactions or relationships in which the rewards exceed the costs. If rewarding interactions are not available, however, an individual is likely to seek out those interactions in which the costs exceed the rewards by the smallest amount.

People have certain standards that influence their evaluations of the rewards and costs in their relationships. One is known as the **comparison level**, which

> "Love is often nothing but a favorable exchange between two people who get the most of what they can expect, considering their value on the . . . market."
>
> —ERICH FROMM

> "A proposal of marriage in our society tends to be a way in which a man sums up his social attributes and suggests to a woman that hers are not so much better as to preclude a merger or a partnership in these matters."
>
> —ERVING GOFFMAN

> "We always do believe in praise of ourselves. Even when we know it is not disinterested, we think it is deserved."
>
> —DAVID LODGE, AUTHOR OF *THINKS*

social exchange theory A theory based on the idea that how people feel about a relationship depends on their assessments of its costs and rewards.

comparison level Expectations about what people think they deserve or expect to get out of a relationship.

comparison level for alternatives Expectations about what people think they can get out of alternative relationships.

equity theory The idea that people are motivated to pursue fairness, or equity, in their relationships; a relationship is considered equitable when the benefits are proportionate to the effort both people put into it.

attachment theory The idea that early attachments with parents and other caregivers can shape relationships for a person's whole life.

reflects the outcomes people think they deserve, or expect to get, out of a relationship. People who have a high comparison level expect a lot from their relationships. Another is the **comparison level for alternatives**, which reflects the outcomes people think they can get out of alternative relationships (Broemer & Diehl, 2003; Thibaut & Kelley, 1959). If you have plenty of attractive suitors knocking at your door, you're likely to have a pretty high comparison level for alternatives. Both of these standards are subjective, and they vary from person to person. Such variations help explain why, for example, a person chooses to stay in an abusive relationship that most people would have ended long ago (the person has a very low comparison level), or why an individual never seems to be able to stay in a relationship for more than a few months (the person has a high comparison level for alternatives).

Another nuance in evaluating the rewards and costs of a relationship is that sometimes the combination of too many rewards and too few costs can be unattractive because it feels unfair. Indeed, **equity theory** maintains that people are also motivated to pursue fairness, or equity, in their relationships, such that the ratio of rewards to costs is similar for both partners (Walster, Walster, & Berscheid, 1978). In other words, both partners ought to receive roughly what they put into a relationship. Thus, for instance, a relationship can feel equitable even if one person gets more out of it than the other, as long as that person tends to put in more effort.

It should be noted that some aspects of social exchange theory apply mostly to people who live in individualistic, egalitarian cultures. There are good reasons to suspect that equity is not always the goal in more collectivist cultures, and that hierarchy and imbalance are more acceptable, sometimes actually more desirable, in such cultures.

Attachment Styles

Attachment theory was first advanced by John Bowlby, an early advocate of an evolutionary approach to human behavior (Bowlby, 1982; Hazan & Shaver, 1994; Mikulincer & Shaver, 2003; Simpson & Rholes, 1998). The central thesis of Bowlby's theory is that our early attachments with our parents and other caregivers shape our relationships for the rest of our lives.

Bowlby noted that, unlike many mammals, human infants are born with few survival skills. Being extremely vulnerable, babies require several years to reach even a limited amount of independence, and they survive by forming intensely close attachments to parents or parental figures. Evolution has given infants a variety of traits that promote parent-offspring attachments, including the heart-warming smiles, laughs and coos, and facial features that evoke love and devotion (Berry & McArthur, 1986; McArthur & Baron, 1983). Likewise, evolution has led to a variety of parental traits that promote attachment—most notably, strong feelings of parental love and protective instincts toward their offspring (Fehr, 1994; Fehr & Russell, 1991; Hazan & Shaver, 1987, 1994; Hrdy, 1999).

Early in development, children rely on their parents for a sense of security, which allows them to explore the environment and to learn. A child's confidence in the secure base the parents provide stems in part from the parents' availability and responsiveness to the child's ever-shifting emotions. Over time, children develop internal "working models" of themselves and of how relationships function based on their parents' availability and responsiveness to them (Baldwin,

Keelan, Fehr, Enns, & Koh-Rangarajoo, 1996; Bowlby, 1969, 1973, 1980; Collins & Read, 1994; Pietromonaco & Feldman-Barrett, 2000). Internal working models of the self reflect individuals' beliefs about their lovability and competence. Internal working models of how relationships work reflect individuals' beliefs about other people's availability, warmth, and ability to provide security. These working models, Bowlby claimed, originate early in life and shape our relationships from cradle to grave, giving rise to distinct styles of attachment.

Inspired by Bowlby's ideas, Mary Ainsworth classified the attachment patterns of infants according to how they responded to separations and reunions with their caregivers, both in the laboratory and in the home (Ainsworth, 1993; Ainsworth, Blehar, Waters, & Wall, 1978). Using an experimental procedure that came to be known as the strange situation, Ainsworth had infants and their caregivers enter an unfamiliar room containing many interesting toys. As the infant explored the room and began to play with some of the toys, a stranger walked in. The stranger remained in the room, and the caregiver quietly left. Returning after 3 minutes, the caregiver greeted and comforted the infant if he or she was upset. The separation typically caused infants to be distressed. Infants whose caregivers responded quickly and reliably to their distress cries, as assessed by outside observers, tended to be securely attached. They were comfortable in moving away from their caregivers to explore a novel environment—with the occasional glance back at the caregiver to make sure things were okay. These children felt safe even though they weren't in contact with their caregiver.

Caregivers who were not as reliable in their responses to their infants—sometimes intruding on the child's activities and sometimes not, in an unpredictable fashion—tended to have infants who showed anxious attachment; they were generally distressed when placed in novel environments, and were less comforted by contact with their caregiver when it occurred. Caregivers who rejected

"Ezra, I'm not inviting you to my birthday party, because our relationship is no longer satisfying to my needs."

The Strange Situation

In Ainsworth's experimental situation, she was able to measure infants' attachment styles to their caregivers. (A) A mother and child enter an unfamiliar room with interesting toys. While the infant explores the room and plays with the toys, a stranger enters and the mother leaves. (B) When the mother returns to the room, she picks up the infant and comforts him if he is upset that she has left the room. (C) The mother then puts the infant down, and he is free to return to playing with the toys, or he might react by crying and protesting the separation.

their infants frequently tended to produce children with an avoidant attachment style. In a strange situation, the avoidant child tended to be the least inclined to seek out the caregiver and might even reject attention when it was offered.

Attachment Types or Dimensions? In the late 1980s, Cindy Hazan and Phillip Shaver published a paper that changed the landscape of social psychology research on relationships (Hazan & Shaver, 1987). They had the insight that the theoretical ideas about attachment being used to understand the infant-caregiver relationship could shed light on the dynamics of relationships between adults. In other words, adult relationships may work in a lot of the same ways that relationships between an infant and caregiver work.

That idea seems plausible. It's common for adults to protest separations from family, friends, and romantic partners, just as infants often protest being separated from a caregiver. Adults also seek comfort and support from relationship partners, and find the security in their relationships to venture forth in the world. Building on this key insight, Hazan and Shaver developed three short paragraphs, each describing an adult analogue of one of the three attachment types Ainsworth had identified in her work with infants: secure, avoidant, and anxious-ambivalent (**Figure 10.2**).

Over the years, countless research participants have been presented with the three paragraphs shown in Figure 10.2 and asked to choose the one that best describes their relationships. By virtue of their choice, respondents are assumed to be a certain type of person: securely attached, avoidantly attached, or anxious-ambivalently attached. Research taking this "attachment types" approach has yielded numerous findings in support of the basic idea that there are parallels in the relationships adults form with one another and the bonds infants form with their caregivers. For example, secure people report trusting their romantic partners more than either anxious-ambivalent or avoidant people, can more readily retrieve trust-related, positive relationship memories, and deal with trust violations of their partners in a more constructive manner (Mikulincer, 1998).

Before long, however, adult attachment researchers began to question whether thinking about attachment in terms of types or categories overlooks important variations within categories (Bartholomew & Horowitz, 1991; Brennan, Clark, & Shaver, 1998; Collins & Read, 1990). These days, although some researchers continue to rely on categorical measures of attachment, or find it convenient to refer

Figure 10.2
Three Attachment Types
The three adult attachment types were inspired by the identification of three different types of attachment in infants: secure, avoidant, and anxious-ambivalent.

Secure
I find it relatively easy to get close to others and am comfortable depending on them and having them depend on me. I don't often worry about being abandoned or about someone getting too close.

Avoidant
I am somewhat uncomfortable being close; I find it difficult to trust them completely, difficult to allow myself to depend on them. I am nervous when anyone gets close, and often, love partners want me to be more intimate than I feel comfortable being.

Anxious-ambivalent
I find that others are reluctant to get as close as I would like. I often worry that my partner doesn't really love me or won't stay with me, I want to merge completely with another person, and this desire sometimes scares people away.

SOURCE: Adapted from Hazan & Shaver, 1987.

to people as being of a certain attachment type, the emerging consensus is that the distribution of attachment variations among people is more accurately represented in terms of dimensions instead of types (Fraley, Hudson, Hefferman, & Segal, 2015).

The two dimensions that have been shown to capture most of the variation in attachment are referred to as anxiety and avoidance (Fraley, Waller, & Brennan, 2000). The **anxiety dimension of attachment** refers to the amount of fear a person feels about rejection and abandonment within close relationships. The **avoidance dimension of attachment** refers to whether a person is comfortable with intimacy and dependence in primary adult relationships, or finds them aversive to a degree. The individual who scores low on both of these dimensions is, in the parlance of attachment types, the prototypical securely attached person—someone who is not anxious about rejection or abandonment, who is comfortable with intimacy, and who seeks closeness to and support from relationship partners. By conceptualizing attachment along dimensions, researchers can capture variation in, say, the degree of anxiety between two people who would both be categorized as anxious-ambivalent from an attachment types approach—variation that corresponds to meaningful differences in how the two of them think, feel, and behave in their close relationships.

Stability of Attachment Styles Regardless of whether we think of attachment in terms of types or dimensions, a central principle of attachment theory is that internal working models of attachment are established early and are relatively stable throughout a person's life. The attachments you form as a child shape the way you relate as an adult to your romantic partners, your children, and your friends. Evidence supports this provocative thesis: important early life events are associated with later attachment styles. Brennan and Shaver (1993) found that anxious individuals were more likely to have experienced the death of a parent, abuse during childhood, or the divorce of their parents. In a 40-year longitudinal study of women who graduated from college in 1960, Klohnen and Bera (1998) found that those who classified themselves as avoidant at age 52 had also reported greater conflict in the home 31 years earlier at age 21. What's more, individuals classified as secure, avoidant, or anxious at age 1 tend to be similarly classified in early adulthood (Fraley & Spieker, 2003).

You might expect that a secure attachment style would predict more positive life outcomes. You would be right (Cooper, Shaver, & Collins, 1998). Securely attached people report the greatest relationship satisfaction (Shaver & Brennan, 1992). In a 4-year longitudinal study, secure participants were less likely to have experienced a romantic breakup (25.6 percent) over the period under study than avoidant ones (52.2 percent) or anxious ones (43.6 percent). In the Klohen and Bera study, secure women were more likely to be married at age 52 than avoidant women (82 percent versus 50 percent) and to report fewer marital problems. Moreover, several studies have documented especially high rates of depression, eating disorders, alcohol abuse, and substance abuse in those with an anxious attachment style (Mikulincer & Shaver, 2003). Recent research suggests that, by and large, such attachment-related processes and outcomes, mostly documented in heterosexual relationships, operate in a similar manner in same-sex romantic relationships (Mohr, Selterman, & Fassinger, 2013).

If you've become concerned while reading this that your future relationships are doomed because you've had some negative relationship experiences that have

anxiety dimension of attachment A facet of attachment that captures the degree to which a person is worried about rejection and abandonment by relationship partners.

avoidance dimension of attachment A facet of attachment that captures the degree to which a person is comfortable with intimacy and dependence on relationship partners.

BOX 10.1 **FOCUS ON *CULTURE***

Building an Independent Baby in the Bedroom

If you are a white, middle-class North American, odds are you slept by yourself in your own bedroom from infancy on. And that probably seems perfectly normal to you. Normal, maybe; common, definitely not. There are few cultures in the world where such a sleeping arrangement is customary. In an article titled "Who Sleeps with Whom Revisited," Shweder, Jensen, and Goldstein (1995) describe the sleeping arrangements of people in many of the world's cultures. The sleeping arrangements predict fairly well how independent and individualistic a given culture is. In Japan, most children sleep with their parents until they are adolescents. In

the non-Western, developing world, it is virtually unheard of for a very young child *not to* sleep with his or her parents, and such a practice would be regarded as a form of child abuse. Even in the United States, 55 percent of African-American children less than 1 year of age sleep with a parent every night, and 25 percent of African-American children ages 1–5 sleep with a parent. In a white, predominantly blue-collar community in Appalachian Kentucky, 71 percent of children between the ages of 2 months and 2 years were found to sleep with their parents, as well as 47 percent of children between 2 and 4 years of age.

This study reveals the extent to which interdependent and independent self-construals permeate social behavior. In more interdependent cultures, young children are much more likely to sleep side by side with their parents than in independent cultures. While psychologists can only speculate about the effects these patterns of sleep have on attachment patterns, we might expect secure attachments in the independent cultures to be characterized by greater independence and autonomy than secure patterns in interdependent cultures.

left you feeling insecurely attached, don't despair. Although attachment theorists assume people's early experiences shape their relationships throughout life, and there is evidence pointing to some degree of stability in attachment styles, the amount and nature of the stability to be expected is rather complex.

First, there's the question of whether people tend to have the same attachment style across all their relationships—with parents, friends, siblings, and romantic partners. Mark Baldwin and his colleagues asked undergraduates to list ten important relationships in their lives and then had them indicate the attachment style (secure, anxious-ambivalent, or avoidant) that best characterized them in each relationship (Baldwin, Keelan, Fehr, Enns, & Koh-Rangarajoo, 1996). Did they see themselves as having the same attachment style across all, or even most, of their relationships? On the contrary, more than 50 percent of participants characterized themselves as having all three attachment styles across their ten relationships. In other words, people often develop working models of attachment that are specific to a particular close other (Chen, Boucher, & Tapias, 2006). Moreover, consistent with the idea that people have multiple kinds of attachment working models stored in their memories, the Baldwin team found that different attachment styles can be momentarily primed or activated—in effect, leading a person to respond in, for example, a securely attached manner even if she is avoidant in most of her relationships.

A second question is whether a person's attachment style within a given relationship is stable across time. The evidence described earlier points to some degree of stability, but it's a moderate degree at most (Fraley, Vicary, Brumbaugh, & Roisman, 2011). Overall, given that most people appear to have different attachment styles with different relationship partners, and given that the stability of attachment style within any particular relationship is a matter of degree, it would seem likely that there's room for change in a person's attachment style even within a specific relationship.

Finally, it's worth noting that the findings described here about attachment apply most readily to modern Western cultures (Morelli & Rothbaum, 2007). In cultures that place less value on autonomy, infants who are left in a room without their mothers may be more fearful about exploring the environment, and the reunion with their mother may be much more turbulent. This observation does not imply that such children are "insecurely attached." Instead, it means they've been socialized to be interdependent with others, especially family members.

↑ LOOKING BACK

Relationships are essential to daily social functioning. The need to belong is an evolved, universal motive that shapes our thoughts and actions; if not satisfied, that need can have highly negative consequences for our well-being. In communal relationships, generally long term, people are concerned with each other's needs; in contrast, exchange relationships, generally short term, are governed by concerns over equity and reciprocity. According to social exchange theory, people want interactions in which rewards exceed costs; satisfaction with rewards and costs also depends on what people expect to get out of a current relationship or an alternative one. Equity theory maintains that people are most satisfied when the ratio of rewards to costs is about equal for both partners in a relationship. The way people interrelate has origins in early bonds with parents; childhood attachments influence adult relationships, including how people act toward others and appraise events within a relationship, as well as personal well-being. Although people are often viewed as being a certain attachment type, attachment is more accurately described in terms of dimensions, with room for variation.

Attraction

Forming relationships is instinctive, and clearly necessary to our health and well-being. But why are we drawn to some people and not to others? Although we generally know *whether* we like someone, we are often at a loss to explain *why*. To be sure, we know we like people who are nice to us, make us laugh, share our values, and so on. But these obvious influences notwithstanding, sometimes we're drawn to certain people and mildly put off by others for reasons we can't explain.

What are the most powerful determinants of whether you will like someone? What is the underlying basis of good or bad "chemistry"? And, in particular, what leads two people to be romantically attracted to each other? In this section we'll consider several answers to these questions. Many of the variables that you might expect to influence attraction do indeed have an effect, sometimes a more powerful effect than you would have guessed.

Proximity

Who are your best friends on campus? Are they the people who were on your hall freshman year? Are they the ones you encountered most often in class? Are they your peers on the track team, drama club, or debate society? Something that *has* to influence whether people become friends or lovers is simple physical proximity. And, in fact, the most enduring friendships are forged between people whose paths cross frequently.

"Despite the fact that a person can pick and choose from a vast number of people to make friends with, such things as the placement of a stoop or the direction of a street often have more to do with determining who is friends with whom."

—WILLIAM WHYTE, *THE ORGANIZATION MAN*

Studies of Proximity and Attraction A number of studies have demonstrated the effects of proximity on who become friends and romantic partners. One was conducted at MIT in the 1940s, in a married student housing project known as Westgate West, for returning American servicemen and their families after World War II (Festinger, Schachter, & Back, 1950). It consisted of 17 ten-unit apartment buildings that were isolated from other residential areas of the city. The incoming students were randomly assigned to their residences, and few of them knew one another beforehand. **Figure 10.3** shows the layout of the Westgate West apartment houses.

The investigators asked each resident to name the three people in the housing project with whom they socialized most often. The effect of proximity was striking: two-thirds of those listed as friends lived in the same building as the respondent, even though those in the same building represented only 5 percent of the residents of Westgate West. More striking still was the pattern of friendships *within* each building. Even though the physical distance between apartments was quite small—19 feet between the doorways of adjacent apartments and 89 feet between those at the ends of each hallway—41 percent of those living in adjacent apartments listed each other as friends, compared with only 10 percent of those living at opposite ends of the hallway.

Proximity presumably leads to friendship because it facilitates chance encounters. If so, then pure physical distance should matter less than **functional distance**—the influence of an architectural layout to encourage or discourage contact between people. The MIT study shows just how important functional distance is. As Figure 10.3 indicates, the stairs are positioned such that upstairs residents will encounter the occupants of apartments 1 and 5 much more often than the occupants of the middle apartments. And in fact, the residents of apartments 1 and 5 formed

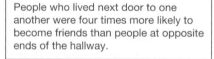

People who lived next door to one another were four times more likely to become friends than people at opposite ends of the hallway.

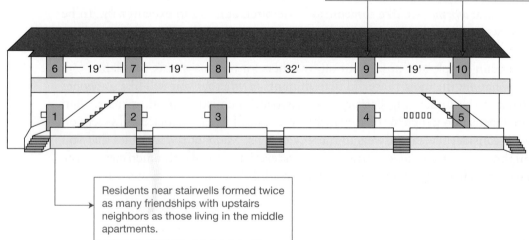

Residents near stairwells formed twice as many friendships with upstairs neighbors as those living in the middle apartments.

Figure 10.3
The Effect of Physical Proximity on Forming Friendships
The location and layout of the married student apartments influenced the extent to which residents formed friendships with one another.

SOURCE: Adapted from Festinger, Schachter, & Back, 1950.

twice as many friendships with their upstairs neighbors as those living in the middle apartments. Notice also that the residents of apartments 1 and 6 and apartments 2 and 7 are equidistant apart and reside directly above one another. But the stairs that pass the door of apartment 1 make it and apartment 6 vastly closer from a functional perspective. No wonder residents of apartments 1 and 6 were 2.5 times more likely to become friends than the residents of apartments 2 and 7. Thus, it's functional distance more than physical distance that is decisive. Proximity promotes friendship because it (literally) brings people together.

But are any cautions in order? You may be wondering about the diversity of the residents in the MIT study. Perhaps proximity has a powerful effect on friendship formation in homogeneous groups, but not in heterogeneous groups, where other factors—such as similarity of age, race, class, or religion—are also involved. Actually, in studies involving more diverse populations, the largest effects of proximity on friendship formation have been found between people of *different* races, ages, or social classes. One study, for example, examined the patterns of friendships in a Manhattan housing project in which half the residents were black, one-third were white, and the rest were Puerto Rican (Nahemow & Lawton, 1975). Each ethnic group included people of all ages. Both proximity and similarity had strong effects on who befriended whom. Eighty-eight percent of those designated as a "best friend" lived in the same building as the respondent, and nearly half lived on the same floor. Yet the effect of proximity was especially pronounced in friendships that developed *across* age and racial groups. Seventy percent of the friendships between people of different ages and races involved people who lived on the same floor as each other, compared with only 40 percent of the same-age and same-race friendships. It appears that people are willing to look beyond the immediate environment to find friends of their own age and race. Their friendships with people of a different age or race, on the other hand, tended to be those that fell in their laps.

The Mere Exposure Effect Part of the reason proximity has such a big influence on friendship is simply that it makes contact more likely: you're not going to become friends with someone you haven't met. But simple contact is not the whole story. Robert Zajonc has offered compelling evidence for another reason that proximity leads to liking: the **mere exposure effect**—the notion that the more you are exposed to something, the more you tend to like it (Zajonc, 1968). This may strike you as implausible. After all, what about all those pop tunes on the radio that seem to become more irritating each time you hear them? And why are there sayings like "Familiarity breeds contempt"? Upon reflection, however, Zajonc's claim makes more sense. You probably recall hating a song that played all the time on the radio when you were younger, only to discover some nostalgic virtue in it when you hear it now. All that early exposure led to a later fondness you didn't want to have.

Researchers have generated a great deal of evidence for the mere exposure effect (Bornstein, 1989; Moreland & Beach, 1992; Zajonc, 1968). Some of the most striking (though less convincing) evidence is correlational. There is a remarkably strong correlation between how frequently people are exposed to various items (words, fruits, cities, chemical elements) and how much they like those items. For example, there is a strong correlation between people's preference for various letters in the English alphabet and how often they appear in the language (Alluisi & Adams, 1962). It's hard to imagine the English language contains so

mere exposure effect The idea that repeated exposure to a stimulus, such as an object or a person, leads to greater liking of the stimulus.

The Influence of Mere Exposure on Liking

Many famous landmarks that are beloved and respected today initially elicited anything but reverence. (A) When the Eiffel Tower was completed in Paris in 1889, to commemorate the French Revolution's centennial, a group of artists and intellectuals, including Alexandre Dumas, Guy de Maupassant, and Emile Zola, signed a petition calling it "useless and monstrous" and "a disgraceful column of bolts." (B) Likewise, San Francisco's TransAmerica building, completed in 1972, received negative reactions at first; renowned *San Francisco Chronicle* columnist Herb Caen angrily suggested knitting a giant tea cozy to cover the spire.

"I don't like that man. I must get to know him better."

—ABRAHAM LINCOLN

many *e*'s or *r*'s just because people like those letters; it's more plausible that people like them because they are exposed to them so often.

To test the mere exposure effect in an experimental setting, Zajonc (1968) created a stimulus set of Turkish words that were unfamiliar to his participants, such as *kadirga, afworbu*, and *lokanta*. Different words within this set were then shown to participants 0, 1, 2, 5, 10, or 25 times. Afterward, the participants were asked to indicate the extent to which they thought each word referred to something good or bad. The more times participants saw a given word, the more they assumed it referred to something good. Zajonc replicated this experiment using Chinese pictographs (symbols used in Chinese writing) and college yearbook photos as stimuli (in the latter case, subjects judged how much they thought they would like the person). The mere exposure effect was supported each time. More recent studies have found that in face-to-face and online social interactions, people become more attracted to strangers as they interact with them more frequently (Reis, Maniaci, Caprariello, Eastwick, & Finkel, 2011).

Further evidence for the mere exposure effect is based on the observation that the image each of us has of our own face is not the same as the image our friends have of us. Because we typically see ourselves in the mirror, the image we have of ourselves is in reverse, a mirror image, whereas our friends typically see our "true" image. Thus, if simple exposure induces liking, we should prefer our mirror image, and our friends should prefer our true image. And when an experiment showing participants' mirror-image and true-image photographs was conducted, that's exactly what happened (Mita, Dermer, & Knight, 1977). Try this out by looking at the two photographs of President Obama in **Figure 10.4**.

Perhaps the most intriguing test of the mere exposure effect was done with albino rats (Cross, Halcomb, & Matter, 1967). One group of rats was raised in an environment where selections of Mozart's music were played for 12 hours

FIGURE 10.4 You Be the Subject: The Mere Exposure Effect

Which image do you prefer, the one on the left or the one on the right?

Results: People prefer true photos of others, but mirror-image photos of themselves. (The one on the left is the true image.)

Explanation: People see themselves when they look in the mirror, which means that they are familiar with a reverse image of themselves—and this is the image they generally prefer. They see others, however, as they truly are and usually prefer this true image to a mirror image.

each day. A second group was exposed to an analogous schedule of music by Schoenberg. The rats were then placed individually in a test cage that was rigged so the rat's presence on one side of the cage would trip a switch that caused previously unheard selections of Mozart to be played, whereas the rat's presence on the other side would generate new selections of Schoenberg. The rats were thus able to "vote with their feet" and express a preference for the quintessentially classical music of Mozart or the modern, atonal compositions of Schoenberg. The results support the mere exposure effect: rats raised on a musical diet of Mozart moved significantly more often to the side of the cage that caused Mozart to be played, whereas those raised on a diet of Schoenberg moved to the side that caused Schoenberg's music to be played (**Figure 10.5**). (Rats in a control condition with no initial exposure to music later exhibited a preference for—you guessed it, Mozart; maybe twenty-first century rats will have developed a taste for Schoenberg.)

But *why* does mere repeated exposure lead to liking? One explanation is that people find it easier to perceive and cognitively process familiar stimuli—the processing of familiar stimuli is more "fluent." And because people find the experience of fluency inherently pleasurable, those positive feelings make the stimuli more appealing (Reber, Schwarz, & Winkielman, 2004; Winkielman & Cacioppo, 2001; see also Chapter 4).

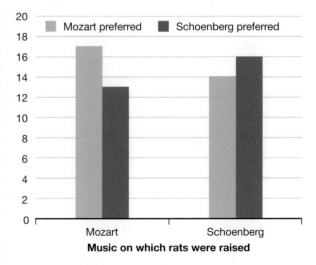

Average amount of time rats spent on Mozart and Schoenberg sides of the cage (minutes)

Music on which rats were raised

Figure 10.5
Repeated Exposure and Musical Preference
Exposure leads to liking. In this study, exposure to Mozart's music led to a preference for Mozart, and likewise for Schoenberg.

SOURCE: Adapted from Cross, Halcomb, & Matter, 1967.

BOX 10.2 **FOCUS ON *AESTHETICS***

The Basis of Beauty

What makes the Golden Gate Bridge so aesthetically pleasing? Why do mathematicians describe certain proofs as beautiful or elegant? And why are pandas and harp seals considered more adorable than mollusks and vultures? Thinkers throughout the ages have pondered and argued about the nature of aesthetic beauty. Those who have taken the *objectivist view*, the ancient Greeks especially, argue that beauty is inherent in the properties of objects that produce pleasant sensations in the perceiver. Their goal has been to identify the stimulus features that have such effects—balance, proportion, symmetry, contrast. All of these, and others, have been put forward as important elements of beauty. Other scholars, those who subscribe to the *subjectivist view*, argue that "beauty is in the eye of the beholder," and therefore the search for general laws of beauty is futile.

Psychologists have recently offered a different view, one that attributes aesthetic pleasure to perceptual and cognitive fluency, or how easily information can be processed (Reber, Schwarz, & Winkielman, 2004). Some objects are more easily identified than others (perceptual fluency), and some are more easily interpreted, defined, and integrated into existing knowledge (cognitive fluency). The core idea is that the more fluently an object is processed, the more positive the aesthetic experience. An important part of this argument is that people experience pleasure when processing fluent stimuli. Electromyography (EMG) recordings of people's faces reveal more activation of the so-called smiling muscle (zygomaticus major) when they are exposed to fluent stimuli rather than disfluent stimuli (Winkielman &

Cacioppo, 2001). Another critical part of the argument is that all the features that objectivists regard as inherently pleasing—symmetry, contrast, and so on—tend to increase perceptual fluency.

Symmetrical patterns are processed efficiently, and symmetrical faces are considered particularly good looking—as are symmetrical structures like the Eiffel Tower, the Chrysler Building, and the Golden Gate Bridge. Objects characterized by high contrast can be recognized quickly, and studies have found that such stimuli are judged to be particularly attractive—as are flowers, goldfinches, and photographs taken by Ansel Adams (Reber, Winkielman, & Schwarz, 1998). Aside from the impact of these classic features, the fluency perspective maintains that anything that increases the fluent processing of an object ought to increase its aesthetic appeal. Previous exposure to a stimulus makes it easier to process, and mere repeated exposure leads to greater liking. Prototypical members of a category are processed fluently, and people find "average" faces attractive—as well as average automobiles, birds, and fish (Halberstadt & Rhodes, 2000, 2003).

But how does this explain people's aesthetic appreciation of complicated stimuli, such as Beethoven's Symphony No. 9, the Guggenheim Museum in Bilbao, Spain, or the ceiling of the Sistine Chapel? Simple stimuli are surely processed more fluently than complex

Aesthetic Assessments
Symmetrical stimuli are easy to process (they're fluent), and, like fluent stimuli in general, tend to be experienced as aesthetically pleasing. The symmetry of the Golden Gate Bridge may be one reason it's regarded as one of the most beautiful bridges in the world.

stimuli, but the simplest things are not always the most pleasing. True enough. What seems to be particularly appealing is "simplicity in complexity." People seem to like those things that are processed more easily than one might expect given their overall complexity. Processing a simple image fluently is often unsatisfying, but a complex image or sound pattern made accessible by some underlying structure often yields the greatest sensation of aesthetic pleasure.

The fluency perspective on aesthetic beauty thus occupies a middle ground between the objectivist and subjectivist views. Beauty is indeed in the eye of the beholder, but not in the sense that it is completely arbitrary and variable from person to person. Rather, beauty lies in the processing experience of the beholder, an experience that is strongly determined by how objective stimulus properties influence perceptual and cognitive fluency.

Zajonc offered a second interpretation that draws on the psychological processes involved in classical conditioning. Upon repeated exposure to a stimulus without any negative consequences resulting from the encounter, we learn to associate the stimulus with the absence of anything negative and thus form a comfortable, pleasant attachment to it. Mere repeated exposure leads to attraction, in other words, because it is reinforcing. This conditioning process helps organisms distinguish stimuli that are "safe" from those that are not (Zajonc, 2001). Thus, the more often people are exposed to something, the more they tend to like it.

Similarity

Another important determinant of attraction is similarity: people tend to like other people who are similar to themselves (Berscheid & Reis, 1998; Byrne, 1961; Byrne, Clore, & Smeaton, 1986; Caspi & Herbener, 1990; Locke & Horowitz, 1990; Ptacek & Dodge, 1995; Rosenblatt & Greenberg, 1988). After all, "Birds of a feather flock together." Not that friends agree about everything, of course. Agreement on core political values is likely to have more of an impact on whether you like someone than whether you root for the same baseball team or agree on the best musical artists from the past decade.

Studies of Similarity and Attraction The impact of similarity on attraction has been documented in many ways. Couples who intend to marry are quite similar to each other on a wide range of characteristics. In one study, the members of 1,000 engaged couples—850 of whom eventually married—were asked to provide information about themselves on 88 characteristics (Burgess & Wallin, 1953). The investigators then compared the average similarity of the couples with the similarity of "random couples" created by pairing individual members of one couple with individual members of another couple. This analysis revealed that members of engaged couples were more similar to one another than members of random couples on 66 of the 88 characteristics. Furthermore, for none of the characteristics were the members of engaged couples more *dissimilar* than the "random couples." The similarity of engaged couples was strongest for demographic characteristics (such as social class and religion) and physical characteristics (such as health and physical attractiveness; **Box 10.3**). Similarity was less strong—but still present—for personality characteristics (such as leadership and sensitivity). Subsequent research has shown that married couples exhibit considerable similarity in the behaviors indicative of such core personality characteristics as extraversion and genuineness (Buss, 1984). Moreover, interracial and inter-ethnic couples tend to be more similar to each other in terms of their personality traits than are couples of the same race and ethnicity. People may compensate for dissimilarity on one dimension by seeking out greater similarity on others (Rushton & Bons, 2005).

A second type of evidence that supports the link between similarity and attraction comes from studies in which individuals are thrown together for an extended period of time. In one study, Theodore Newcomb recruited male college transfer students to live for a year, rent free, in a large house in exchange for filling out surveys a few hours each week (Newcomb, 1956, 1961). The

"We are so in sync. I was just about to ask you for a divorce."

BOX 10.3 **FOCUS ON *DAILY LIFE***

Do Couples Look More Alike over Time?

Many people claim that not only do the two people in a couple tend to look like each other, but they look more alike the longer they've been together. There are many reasons why this might be so. People who live together may adopt similar styles of dress and grooming. They might have similar diets, which could contribute to making them look more alike over time, influencing skin tone, for example, or the health of their teeth. They obviously live in the same region of the country, and because of climatic factors, they may acquire the same suntan and a similar pattern of wrinkles.

Perhaps most interesting from a psychological perspective, couples also experience many of the same emotions. The death of a child devastates both parents; winning the lottery brings elation to both. More generally, a downbeat household is typically one in which both members are unhappy; an upbeat household is one in which both are happy. Eventually, a lifetime of experiencing the same emotions may have similar effects on the face and physical bearing of each member of the couple. As someone once said,

"After age 40, we all have the faces we deserve." A happy lifetime tends to produce crow's feet around the eyes; an unhappy one tends to leave creases around the outside of the mouth. Thus people who live together and experience the same emotions may converge in facial appearance.

Zajonc and his colleagues collected evidence indicating that there is truth to this idea, by enlisting the help of 12 married couples to see whether they came to look more alike over time (Zajonc, Adelmann, Murphy, & Niedenthal, 1987). The couples provided both current photos of themselves, at age 50–60, and photos taken during their first year of marriage, about 25 years earlier. The photos were cropped to remove extraneous identifying information, leaving just the head and shoulders. Judges who were unaware of who was married to whom were then asked to assess how much each of the men resembled each of the women (for both the current and the older photos).

To check for the possibility that older people as a whole are simply more alike, the Zajonc team established a set of control couples by pairing

Physical Similarity
Over time, the members of a couple tend to look like each other, perhaps because of initial physical similarities, but also because of shared living conditions, diet, and emotional experiences.

members of different couples with one another and then assessing the similarity of these "random couples." Contrary to the notion that older people are generally more homogeneous in appearance, there was no tendency for the random couples to converge in appearance over time. This set them apart from the actual couples, who looked significantly more alike roughly 25 years into their marriages than they did as newlyweds. Thus, not only do we seek mates who are similar to ourselves, we become even more similar in appearance over time.

participating students didn't know each other beforehand. In response to one of the survey questions, they indicated how much they liked each of their housemates. To an increasing degree over the course of the 15-week study, as students got to know one another better and better, their mutual liking was predictable from how similar they were (see also Griffitt & Veitch, 1974).

Another type of evidence supporting the proposition that people are attracted to those who are similar to themselves comes from the "bogus stranger" paradigm (Byrne, 1961; Byrne et al., 1986; Byrne, Griffitt, & Stefaniak, 1967; Byrne & Nelson, 1965; Griffitt & Veitch, 1971; Tan & Singh, 1995). In these experiments, participants are given the responses to attitude or personality questionnaires supposedly filled out by someone else (but really created by the experimenter to show a given level of similarity to the participants' own responses). After reading the responses of the bogus stranger, the participants rate him or her on several dimensions, including their liking of the person in question. In study after study of this type, the more similar the stranger is to the participant, the more the participant likes him or her.

Don't Opposites Attract? Although most people accept the idea that similarity fosters attraction, they also endorse the theory of **complementarity**—the idea that opposites attract; that individuals with different characteristics should complement each other and thus get along well. It does seem that a dependent person might profit from being with someone who is nurturing, or that a person who is quiet might get along with someone who likes to talk. The yin and yang of two divergent personalities *ought* to create a successful unity.

It's important to note, however, that the effect of complementarity on attraction is likely to be more limited than that of similarity. Unlike similarity, there is no reason to expect that complementary attitudes, beliefs, or physical characteristics will lead to attraction. The complementarity hypothesis really makes sense only for those traits for which one person's needs can be met by the other (Levinger, 1964). Someone who is dependent can have his or her needs taken care of by a partner who is nurturing. But someone who is a hard worker probably won't want to be with someone who is lazy, and someone who values honesty is not likely to associate with a habitual liar. Thus, we might expect to find complementarity in such traits as dependence-nurturance or introversion-extraversion, but not in such traits as honesty, optimism, or conscientiousness.

A few studies have provided evidence supporting the complementarity hypothesis (Wagner, 1975; Winch, 1955; Winch, Ktanes, & Ktanes, 1954, 1955). But many of them have been criticized for their methodological problems (Katz, Glucksberg, & Krauss, 1960). In addition, many more studies have failed to provide evidence for the hypothesis (Antill, 1983; Boyden, Carroll, & Maier, 1984; Levinger, Senn, & Jorgensen, 1970; Meyer & Pepper, 1977; Neimeyer & Mitchell, 1988).

Thus, similarity appears to be the rule and complementarity the exception. Even when two people seem to represent a perfect example of complementarity, they are likely to complement each other on only one or two features of their personalities. Their other characteristics are likely to be similar or unrelated.

Physical Attractiveness

Not surprisingly, one of the most powerful determinants of interpersonal attraction is physical attractiveness. Who are the ones who get the most attention at parties, the gym, or the checkout line at the campus bookstore? Attractive people have an advantage in winning other people's attention and affection. Because a person's physical appearance is so visible—and visible so *immediately*—it affects our instantaneous, gut reaction to someone we meet for the first time. Although someone's keen intelligence and strong moral fiber can be demonstrated, that usually takes some time. Beauty is obvious right away. Partly for this reason, empirical research indicates that a person's looks play an even more important role in interpersonal attraction than intuition might suggest.

Before considering the relevant findings, it's worthwhile—and bracing, for those of us who aren't so attractive—to keep in mind some important caveats. First, although certain features are deemed attractive by most people, there's considerable variability in what individuals find attractive. Social psychologist Elaine Walster, a pioneer in the study of attraction, conducted an informal study in which she asked people on her campus if anyone had ever told them they were

complementarity The tendency for people to seek out others with characteristics that are different from, and complement, their own.

"Jack Sprat could eat no fat. His wife could eat no lean. And so between them both you see, they licked the platter clean."
—MOTHER GOOSE NURSERY RHYME

"There are many more obscure, miserable, and impoverished geniuses in the world than underappreciated beauties."
—JERRY ADLER, NEWSWEEK

good-looking or told them they were not. The researchers deliberately surveyed the least attractive and most attractive people they encountered. All of the most unattractive people said there were people who thought they were good-looking, and all of the most attractive people said there were people who considered them ugly.

Second, although people like people who are physically attractive, the reverse is also true. People find those they like more attractive than those they don't like (Kniffin & Wilson, 2004). Third, happy couples tend to perceive each other as physically attractive even if other people don't see them that way (Murray & Holmes, 1997; Murray, Holmes, & Griffin, 1996). Fourth, although some people are considered good-looking throughout their lives, physical attractiveness is less stable than most of us think (Zebrowitz, 1997; Zebrowitz, Olson, & Hoffman, 1993). People who are unattractive in their teens sometimes bloom in young adulthood, while the looks of the kings and queens of the high school prom often fade. The 98-pound weakling may turn into the lean but well-built man. The dashing (pun intended) quarterback may lose his youthful, athletic form.

Benefits of Being Attractive The most frequently documented finding about the impact of physical attractiveness in everyday life—and the least surprising—is that attractive individuals are much more popular as friends and potential romantic partners than their less attractive counterparts. This effect has been shown in studies that correlate various indices of popularity, such as dating frequency and friendship ratings, with physical attractiveness (Berscheid, Dion, Walster, & Walster, 1971; Curran & Lippold, 1975; Feingold, 1984; Reis, Nezlek, & Wheeler, 1980); in investigations where blind dates are later asked how attracted they are to their partners (Brislin & Lewis, 1968; Curran & Lippold, 1975; Walster, Aronson, Abrahams, & Rottman, 1966); and in studies of online and speed dating in which participants indicate how attracted they are to people they can see in photographs or in brief face-to-face encounters (Alterovitz & Mendelsohn, 2009; Asendorpf, Penke, & Back, 2011; Eastwick & Finkel, 2008; Luo & Zhang, 2009; Riggio & Woll, 1984; Woll, 1986).

But attractive folks benefit in other areas as well. An essay supposedly written by an attractive author is typically evaluated more favorably than one attributed to an unattractive author (Anderson & Nida, 1978; Cash & Trimer, 1984; Landy & Sigall, 1974; Maruyama & Miller, 1980). Men are more likely to come to the aid of an injured female if she is good-looking (West & Brown, 1975). Other studies have shown that each 1-point increase (on a 5-point scale) in physical attractiveness is worth about $2,000 in additional annual salary—closer to $3,500 in current inflation-adjusted dollars (Frieze, Olson, & Russell, 1991; Hamermesh & Biddle, 1994; Roszell, Kennedy, & Grabb, 1989; see also Cash & Kilcullen, 1985). Stated another way, men who are better-than-average looking can expect to earn nearly a quarter of a million dollars more during their careers than their less attractive counterparts (Hamermesh, 2011).

In addition, jurors often give attractive defendants a break (Efran, 1974); even when convicted, attractive criminals receive lighter sentences from judges (Gunnell & Ceci, 2010; Sigall & Ostrove, 1975; Stewart, 1980). In one study, for example, participants recommended prison sentences that were 86 percent longer for unattractive defendants than for attractive ones (Sigall & Ostrove, 1975). Crime may not pay, but the wages are clearly better for those who are good-looking.

"Beauty is life's E-Z Pass."

The Halo Effect Attractive individuals benefit from a **halo effect**, the common belief (accurate or not) that people who are appealing to look at have a host of positive qualities beyond their physical appearance. Thus, people may try to date, mate, and affiliate with those who are physically attractive not only because of their looks but also because of many other attributes they're thought to have. In experiments that require people to make inferences about individuals depicted in photographs, good-looking men and women were judged to be happier, more intelligent, and more popular, and to have more desirable personalities, higher incomes, and more professional success (Bar-Tal & Saxe, 1976; Dion, Berscheid, & Walster, 1972; Eagly, Ashmore, Makhijani, & Longo, 1991; Feingold, 1992b; Jackson, Hunter, & Hodge, 1995; Moore, Graziano, & Millar, 1987). The only consistently negative inferences about physically attractive individuals are that they are immodest and less likely to be good parents (Bar-Tal & Saxe, 1976; Dion et al., 1972; Wheeler & Kim, 1997). Attractive women are sometimes also seen as vain and materialistic (Cash & Duncan, 1984; Dermer & Theil, 1975; Podratz, Halverson, & Dipboye, 2004).

halo effect The common belief (accurate or not) that attractive individuals possess a host of positive qualities beyond their physical appearance.

This halo effect appears to vary in predictable ways across different cultures. In independent cultures such as the United States, physically attractive people are assumed to be more dominant and assertive. In interdependent cultures such as Korea, attractive people are thought to be more generous, sensitive, and empathic than unattractive individuals (Wheeler & Kim, 1997).

Is there any validity to these beliefs? Given the preferential treatment good-looking people often receive, it would be surprising if there were not some impact on their behavior and their sense of themselves. Indeed, physically attractive people seem to be somewhat happier, less stressed, and more satisfied with their lives, and they perceive themselves as having greater control over what happens to them (Diener, Wolsic, & Fujita, 1995; Umberson & Hughes, 1987).

Physically attractive people also behave differently in social interactions, and in ways that generate more favorable impressions in others. In one study, participants had 5-minute telephone conversations with members of the opposite sex (Goldman & Lewis, 1977). The experimenters rated all participants for physical attractiveness. Because the conversations took place over the phone, however, the participants themselves did not know what the person they were talking to looked like. Still, when the participants rated their partners afterward, those who had been deemed attractive by the experimenters were rated as more likable and socially skilled than their less attractive counterparts. A history of easier, rewarding social encounters appears to instill in good-looking people the confidence and social skills that bring about more rewarding interactions in the future (Langlois et al., 2000; Reis et al., 1982).

What happens, though, when the attractiveness of the conversation partner is known? Because those who are good-looking are thought to possess a host of desirable characteristics, people may listen better and be more responsive, more energetic, and more willing to express agreement with an attractive person. The net result is that attractive people may have an easier time coming across as socially skilled, even when they aren't. In other words, the physical attractiveness stereotype may give rise to a self-fulfilling prophecy—people behaving in ways that bring about the very thing they expect to happen (see Chapters 4 and 11).

This phenomenon was demonstrated in an experiment in which male participants had a get-acquainted conversation with a woman over the phone (Snyder, Tanke, & Berscheid, 1977). Each man had a photograph supposedly taken of his

"Not to worry—I'm going to put our best-looking people on the job."

conversation partner. In reality, the females in the chosen photos were quite attractive for half the participants and unattractive for the others. The conversations were recorded, and when just the woman's comments—and *only* the woman's comments—were played to other participants who were not shown the woman's photo, and thus had no preconceptions about her appearance, a rather stunning result emerged. They rated the woman who had talked to someone who thought she was attractive as being warmer and more socially poised than the woman who had talked to someone who thought she was unattractive. Once again, the deck is stacked in favor of the physically attractive: people talk to them in ways that bring out their warmth and confidence, thereby confirming the stereotype that they are socially skilled.

The Role of Gender Attractiveness is more important in determining women's life outcomes than men's. Obesity, for example, negatively affects the social mobility of women but not men. Women deemed unattractive at work have more negative experiences than similarly unattractive men (Bar-Tal & Saxe, 1976). And physical attractiveness matters more for women, and for gay men, than it does for heterosexual men when it comes to popularity, dating prospects, and even marriage opportunities and enduring satisfaction in marriage (Margolin & White, 1987; Meltzer, McNulty, Jackson, & Karney, 2014; Peplau, Frederick, Yee, Maisel, Lever, & Ghavami, 2009). A study showed that simply growing up in an area that has fluoridated water, which improves the look and quality of one's teeth, is associated with a 4 percent average increase in a woman's annual earnings in adulthood, but has no effect on a man's earnings (Glied & Neidell, 2008).

Beauty, therefore, can translate into power for women. It functions as a kind of currency women can use in obtaining financial and social resources. Barbara Fredrickson and Tomi-Ann Roberts (1997) have argued that these kinds of external rewards encourage women's preoccupation with their own attractiveness, even coaxing them to adopt a kind of outsider's perspective on their physical selves. This can be costly in terms of their satisfaction with who they are and even how well they do academically and professionally.

The Universality of Physical Attractiveness What exactly is it that people find appealing about good-looking individuals? What do people who are considered attractive look like? What features set them apart from everyone else?

These questions might seem impossible to answer. After all, doesn't it depend on who's doing the evaluating, and on the unique preference of each person as well as the more general tastes of the prevailing culture or historical era? In short, doesn't the assessment of what constitutes physical attractiveness vary enormously from person to person, culture to culture, and era to era?

Yes, of course, there is considerable variation from one person to the next in terms of specific preferences (Beck, Ward-Hull, & McLear, 1976; Wiggins, Wiggins, & Conger, 1968). There's also substantial variation in preferences between cultures and subcultures and across historical periods (Darwin, 1871; Fallon, 1990; Ford & Beach, 1951; Hebl & Heatherton, 1997; see **Box 10.4**). But such variations don't mean all determinants of physical attractiveness are arbitrary or subject to the whims of fashion. People in Western cultures widely agree on who is attractive and who is not (Cross & Cross, 1971; Iliffe, 1960; Langlois et al.,

BOX 10.4 **FOCUS ON *HEALTH***

The Flight to Thinness

Anyone who has seen the paintings of Renoir or Rubens is aware of how times have changed when it comes to the ideal weight for women. This shift has received a great deal of media attention in recent years because much of the world—particularly the United States—is obsessed with thinness. It's an unhealthy obsession, and has been blamed for the alarming increase in such eating disorders as bulimia and anorexia nervosa in young women (Brumberg, 1997). Society's current preference for thin women is something of an anomaly, given the historical preference for a heavier figure. Heaviness was not always viewed as negatively as it is now. Just consider this claim by the eighteenth-century French gourmand Brillat-Savarin: "To acquire a perfect degree of plumpness . . . is the life study of every woman in the world" (Shapin, 2006).

The modern trend toward thinness has been documented in a number of ways. Researchers examined photographs of women appearing in *Vogue* and *Ladies' Home Journal* over the course of the twentieth century, computing the relative size of the women's busts and waists. The bust-to-waist ratio declined markedly across this time span, indicating a turning away from a more voluptuous standard of female beauty (Silverstein, Perdue, Peterson, & Kelly, 1986). Analyses of *Playboy* centerfolds and Miss America contestants over the latter half of the twentieth century have revealed a similar trend toward slenderness (Garner, Garfinkel, Schwartz, & Thompson, 1980; Wiseman, Gray, Mosimann, & Ahrens, 1992).

To try to make sense both of the historical norm and the current norm, Judith Anderson examined the preferred female body type in 54 cultures (Anderson, Crawford, Nadeau, & Lindberg, 1992). She and her colleagues found a relationship between body-weight preferences and the reliability of the food supply across cultures. In cultures with a relatively uncertain food supply, moderate-weight to heavyset women were considered more desirable. But in cultures with very reliable supplies of food, a thin body type was generally preferred. And it's hard to imagine a culture with a more stable food supply and a more pronounced infatuation with slender bodies than that of the United States today.

The ongoing obsession with thinness also appears to be characterized by some misperceptions. In one telling study, male and female undergraduates were shown a series of nine drawings of body types ranging from very thin to very heavy (Fallon & Rozin, 1985). The participants had to identify the body types along a continuum that represented (1) their own current body type, (2) the body type they would most want to have, (3) the body type they thought would be most attractive to the opposite sex, and (4) the body type of the opposite sex that they personally found most attractive (this time, of course, on a set of drawings of the opposite sex). The male students, on average, thought their current body type was precisely as heavy as the ideal body type. Moreover, they also believed their body type was most attractive to female students (although

Preferred Body Types
Although most modern American women wish to be thin, for centuries the standard of female beauty was a heavier figure with more curves. (A) Rubens' *Venus before a Mirror* (1614–1615). (B) Renoir's *Blond Bather* (1919). (C) Marilyn Monroe (1950s). (D) Keira Knightley (today).

(continued)

(continued)

the women actually preferred a more slender male physique than the men anticipated). The results were different for the female students. The women judged themselves to be heavier than their own ideal and also heavier than what they thought would be most attractive to men. The most disturbing finding is that the women believed the most attractive body type to men was much more slender than the ideal the men actually preferred. An unfortunate pair of "thought bubbles" spring immediately to mind: a women standing next to a man worrying that "I'd feel more comfortable around him if only I lost a few pounds," while the man is simultaneously thinking, "She looks great, but

she would look even better if she'd gain a few pounds."

Why would women think men are more attracted to slender female figures than they actually are? Most images come from the mass media, flooded with images of slim actresses, newscasters, and pop stars, not to mention rail-thin supermodels. While there may be truth to the claim, it raises a further question: Why would the media perpetuate an image of an ideal body type that neither men nor women truly think is ideal? One explanation places the blame on the fashion industry. Designers want their clothes to take center stage, not the models wearing them, and a curvaceous figure

"spoils the line." Stated differently, many clothes look better on lanky women (at least top fashion designers think so). The net result, according to this interpretation, is a society that is literally making itself sick (through excessive dieting, anorexia, or bulimia) in the service of the narrow interests of the fashion industry. Fortunately, there are now many approaches girls and young women can take for combatting the pernicious effects of society's expectations about body image. The recent plus-size movement of clothing and models suggests that fashion trends are changing as well.

2000). They aren't alone; people from different cultures and subcultures tend to share their assessments as well (Cunningham, Roberts, Barbee, Druen, & Wu, 1995; Langlois et al., 2000; Rhodes et al., 2001). Asians, blacks, and whites, for example, share roughly the same opinions of which Asian, black, and white faces they find attractive (Bernstein, Lin, & McClellan, 1982; Maret, 1983; Maret & Harling, 1985; Perrett, May, & Yoshikawa, 1994; Thakerar & Iwawaki, 1979).

Moreover, infants prefer to look at attractive faces. Experimenters have shown infants as young as 3 months slides of two human faces side by side. Adults had previously judged one of the faces as attractive and the other as unattractive. The slides were typically shown to the infant for 10 seconds, and the time the infant spent looking at each one was recorded and interpreted as an index of the infant's preference. Infants showed a clear preference for attractive over unattractive faces (Langlois et al., 1987; Langlois, Ritter, Roggman, & Vaughn, 1991; Samuels & Ewy, 1985; Slater et al., 1998). By the end of the first year, when infants' behavioral repertoires are more advanced, they are more inclined to play contentedly with an adult stranger who is attractive than one who is unattractive.

Evolution and Attraction What are the features that adults and children, across cultures, find physically attractive? Most attempts to address this question have been guided by evolutionary theorizing and have focused on romantic or sexual attraction. The central idea is that we've evolved to prefer people whose physical features signify health or, more generally, **reproductive fitness**—the capacity to pass one's genes to subsequent generations. By mating with reproductively fit individuals, people maximize the chances of their own genes being passed on.

Following the evolutionary thesis, we should be attracted to people whose features signify reproductive fitness and not to people whose physical characteristics might indicate disease or reproductive problems. Thus, we might steer clear of people with facial features that are too unusual—for example, eyes placed so close together that the person looks like a cyclops, or so far apart that the person looks like an extraterrestrial. At the extremes, such features could reflect genetic

reproductive fitness The capacity to pass one's genes on to subsequent generations.

problems or indicate that something has gone wrong during early development—both of which could make the person's offspring poor evolutionary prospects.

There's evidence that people do indeed find unusual facial features unattractive and that they are drawn to "average" faces (**Figure 10.6**). Photographic and computer technology can be used to create a composite (or average) face out of any number of individual faces (Galton, 1878; Langlois & Roggman, 1990; Said & Todorov, 2011). People typically consider such composite faces of both men and women as more attractive than the average individual face in the set of faces from which they were constructed, and this effect is stronger as more individual faces are put into the composite. To a significant extent, then, the more average, or typical, a face is, the more attractive it is.

This doesn't mean that averageness is all there is to attractiveness, however (Rhodes, 2006; Said & Todorov, 2011). Many people are attractive precisely because of something extreme in their appearance. The "bee stung" lips or severe cheekbones of many supermodels depart from the norm, and people with strikingly colored eyes are considered especially attractive by most people.

To explore the attraction to exaggerated features, researchers in one study used three types of composite faces: an *average* composite from averaging all the faces from a pool of 60 photographs, an *attractive* composite from averaging only the photos of the 15 faces previously judged to be most attractive, and an *attractive + 50 percent* composite from calculating the point-by-point differences between the average and attractive composites and then exaggerating these differences by 50 percent (Perrett, May, & Yoshikawa, 1994).

Preferred Facial Features
(A) Queen Nefertiti, of prebiblical times, was considered physically attractive in her time—and is in ours. Her clear skin, widely spaced and large eyes, small nose and chin, full lips, and high eyebrows are features deemed attractive in all eras. (B) These same features can be found in many people considered very attractive today, such as Angelina Jolie.

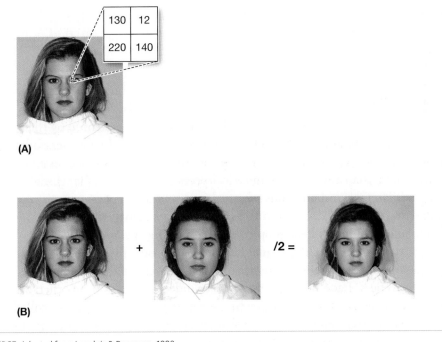

(A)

(B)

SOURCE: Adapted from Langlois & Roggman, 1990.

Figure 10.6
Attraction to Average Faces
In this study, the researchers created average faces by dividing an individual face into small squares. (A) Each square's number was on a shade of gray. (B) They averaged the shades of gray across two photos to create an averaged configuration of two faces, and continued averaging even more individual faces with the newly created face. Faces that are closest to average are judged to be more attractive.

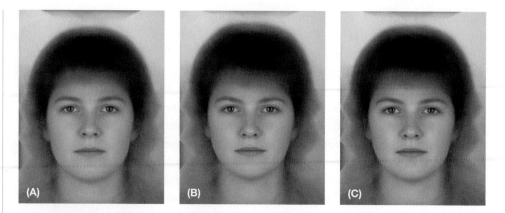

Attraction to Exaggerated Features

In this study, the researchers made three different kinds of composite faces: (A) a face created by averaging 60 faces, (B) a face created by averaging only the 15 most attractive of these faces, and (C) a face created by calculating the differences between the first two composites and then exaggerating these differences by 50 percent. Participants found the exaggerated face to be the most attractive.

SOURCE: Adapted from Perrett et al., 1994.

If averageness were all there was to attractiveness, then the average composite should be the most attractive because it was created by averaging a greater number of faces. In addition, any composite that is exaggerated away from the average should be perceived as less attractive than an average face. Yet neither of these results was obtained. Instead, participants judged the attractive composite to be significantly more attractive than the average composite, and the attractive + 50 percent composite was judged to be even more attractive than either of the simple composites.

Another factor that plays an important role in judgments of physical attractiveness is bilateral symmetry. Bilaterally symmetrical individuals in a variety of animal species have been shown to have an advantage in sexual competition (Manning & Hartley, 1991; Markow & Ricker, 1992; Moller, 1992a). In humans, facial attractiveness is correlated with the degree of bilateral symmetry (Scheib, Gangestad, & Thornhill, 1999; Thornhill & Gangestad, 1993).

Biologists believe that departures from symmetry typically result from injuries to an organism in utero (before birth), particularly injuries caused by exposure to parasites (Hubschman & Stack, 1992; Moller, 1992b; Polak, 1993) and by infectious diseases experienced by the mother during pregnancy (Livshits & Kobyliansky, 1991). In addition, bilaterally symmetrical adults tend to have fewer respiratory and intestinal infections than their less symmetrical peers (Thornhill & Gangestad, 2005). Bilateral symmetry thus seems to serve as a signal of an organism's ability to resist disease. According to evolutionary theory, then, bilaterally symmetrical individuals should be sought out by potential mates.

Two features that signal health and reproductive fitness—averageness and bilateral symmetry—are important determinants of perceived attractiveness. Each of these effects exists independently of the other: averageness affects attractiveness ratings when symmetry is statistically controlled, and vice versa. This is important to establish because a face that is "average" in configuration will also be highly symmetrical.

Aggregated Faces

In an increasingly multicultural society, the typical face in many countries will mix the attributes of many ethnicities.

Gender Differences in Mate Preferences

Any discussion of the evolutionary basis of attraction leads inevitably to the question: Do men and women look for different things in a mate? Evidence indicates that they do. Do gender differences arise because of evolutionary processes, or are they the result of social and cultural influences? Let's explore the core ideas laid out by evolutionary psychologists and some of the evidence they offer to advance their claims, along with a critique of the evolutionary approach from an alternative, sociocultural perspective.

Investment in Offspring Evolutionary psychologists claim that evolution favors fundamentally different preferences in women and men because of the different investments each gender typically makes in offspring. Women tend to invest much more, even before the child's conception. Men contribute infinitesimally small sperm, which contain little more than genetic material; women provide a much larger egg, which contains both genetic material and nutrients the developing embryo needs in the initial stages of life. Because of this difference, eggs are much more "expensive" to produce, and the average woman produces only 200–250 mature eggs in her lifetime, compared with the millions of sperm the average man produces each *day*. After conception, of course, in utero development takes place entirely within the woman, taxing her physiologically and preventing her from conceiving another child for at least 9 months. During that time her male partner is able—biologically—to conceive a large army. (It's estimated that 1 in 200 men alive today are descendants of the twelfth-century Mongol leader Genghis Khan, who conquered 12 million square miles of Asia and Europe and impregnated tens of thousands of women along the way.)

After the child is born, an extended period of nursing further taxes the woman and drastically reduces her fertility, thus increasing the time until she's capable of producing additional offspring. Biologists have observed throughout the animal kingdom that the sex that invests the most in the offspring is almost always more "selective" in choosing a mate than the sex that invests less. Males typically must compete more vigorously among themselves (*intrasex competition*) for the attention and affection of females (*intersex attraction*). Because of their direct competition with one another, evolution has favored males with greater size. Due to the pressures of intersex attraction, the male is typically the louder, gaudier member of the species. (Of course, humans are something of an exception in this regard: more effort goes into managing and accentuating women's appearance, although in some societies men are the more extensively adorned sex.)

Consider, too, species in which the *male* invests more in the offspring. Male Panamanian poison-arrow frogs, for example, lure females to nesting sites where they lay their eggs. The male then fertilizes them and feeds, protects, and cares for the young until adulthood. Is the typical pattern of behavioral sex differences found so widely in the animal kingdom reversed in species like this? Absolutely. The females are larger than the males, and they compete with one another more fiercely for the favors of the relatively choosy males (Trivers, 1985).

Thus, one of the most straightforward predictions from evolutionary psychology is that women ought to be more selective in their choice of mates; or, stated the other way, men should be more indiscriminate than women. This hypothesis conforms to both the historical record and to everyday observation: in virtually all societies in which this issue has been systematically studied, the average man

appears ready to jump into bed much more quickly and with a much wider range of potential partners than the average female. (Note that in the world's oldest profession, prostitution, it's nearly always a man making the payment.)

Several studies make this point empirically, the most ambitious being a cross-cultural study with over 16,000 participants from societies all over the globe. Men and women were asked, "Ideally, how many different sexual partners would you like to have?"—over various time intervals, ranging from 1 month to the rest of their lives. For every time interval and in all regions of the world, men expressed a desire for a greater number of sexual partners (Schmitt, 2003). Similar trends are observed in studies of the sexual inclinations of gay men, who express a greater interest in more partners than lesbians or heterosexual women, and less interest in monogamy (Peplau & Fingerhut, 2007).

What Do Men Want? What Do Women Want? In heterosexual relations, what do men find attractive in a mate? And if women are indeed more discriminating than men, what do women find attractive in a potential mate? From an evolutionary perspective, if men are to reproduce successfully, they need to find mates who are fertile. But how does one spot a fertile woman? There are no direct cues, but because women experience a relatively narrow window of lifetime fertility (the biological clock), there's at least one reasonably good indirect cue—youth. Men should thus be drawn to younger women and the cues associated with youth: smooth skin, lustrous hair, full lips, and a figure in which the waist is much narrower than the hips (Singh, 1993).

The key reproductive facts for women are much different. Although the quality of a man's sperm tends to decline a bit in older age, men typically continue to be fertile throughout life, so there is less evolutionary pressure for women to be attracted to youthful men. Instead, given the demands of 9 months of pregnancy and years of breast-feeding, a critical task for women in our ancestral past was to acquire a mate who had resources and who could be counted on to invest them in their children. According to evolutionary psychologists, then, women should be attracted to men who either possess material resources or the characteristics associated with acquiring them: physical strength, industriousness, and social status.

This proposed asymmetry in mate selection has been examined systematically in studies of personal ads and online dating sites in the United States, Canada, India, and Brazil (Alterovitz & Mendelsohn, 2009; Camposa, Ottab, & Siquiera, 2002; Gustavsson, Johnsson, & Uller, 2008; Harrison & Saeed, 1977; Kenrick & Keefe, 1992; Rajecki, Bledsoe, & Rasmussen, 1991). These studies reveal an overwhelming tendency for men to seek youth and beauty and to offer material resources, and for women to seek resources and accomplishment and to offer youth and beauty. (For more extensive evidence, see Feingold, 1990, 1992a.)

"It is a truth universally acknowledged, that a single man in possession of a good fortune, must be in want of a wife."

—JANE AUSTEN, *PRIDE AND PREJUDICE*

"Will he ever be able to produce revenue again?"

It's noteworthy that similar patterns are observed in the ads of gay men, who seek attractive partners more than lesbians do (Hatala & Prehodka, 1996).

This trend also emerged in a survey of over 10,000 participants from 37 different cultures (Buss, 1989, 1994). Respondents were from the West (Germany and the Netherlands); industrialized regions in non-Western countries (Shanghai, China, and Tehran, Iran); and more rural societies (the Gujarati Indians and South African Zulus). Notably, when asked what they desire in a mate, both men and women in *all* cultures rated kindness and intelligence more highly than either physical attractiveness or earning potential, as do gay men and lesbians (Lippa, 2007). Nevertheless, just as evolutionary psychologists would predict, men in nearly every culture rated physical attractiveness as more desirable in a mate than women did (**Figure 10.7A**). And in *every* culture, men preferred marriage partners who were younger than they were (**Figure 10.7B**). Women consistently preferred partners who were older than they were and consistently assigned greater importance than men did to various indices of a potential mate's ability to provide material resources, such as having "good financial prospects," "social status," and "ambition-industriousness" (**Figure 10.7C**).

Similar evidence exists in the folk tales of traditional people, living in preindustrial conditions. One research team coded the mate preferences expressed by male and female characters in over 600 folk tales from 48 traditional cultures around the world (Gottschalk, Martin, Quish, & Rea, 2004). The male characters were 2.5 times more likely than female characters to express an interest in a physically attractive mate, and the female characters were much more likely to express an interest in a mate with status and wealth.

Critique of Evolutionary Theorizing on Gender Differences in Mate Preferences The empirical evidence on human gender differences in mate preferences converges with everyday observation. But to what extent is the evolutionary perspective supported?

This is not an easy question. Consistency with the available data is certainly one criterion by which theories are judged, yet nearly all the research results can be explained without reference to reproductive fitness or any inherited male/female differences. One alternative account, from Alice Eagly and Wendy Wood, maintains that because men have, on average, greater physical size and strength and don't experience the restrictions of pregnancy and nursing, a division of labor has emerged in which men are usually engaged in work outside the home and women are the primary caretakers of children (Eagly & Wood, 1999; Wood & Eagly, 2002). This division of labor has allowed men to have disproportionate control over material resources in virtually all cultures. Being relatively vulnerable economically, women might be more concerned with material needs, and finding mates with resources is one way of meeting those needs.

One implication of this difference in material resources is that in societies where the two genders have relatively equal power, the greater female emphasis on finding a mate with status and economic resources should be lessened. In a reanalysis of the data from the 37-nation study of mate preferences, Wood and Eagly (2002) found just this pattern. The greater the gender equality in a society (as indicated by United Nations data on income differential, the proportion of women in the national legislature, and so on), the less importance women placed on earning capacity in a potential mate. Gender equality did not affect how much importance men placed on women's attractiveness, however. More

"I love a cute guy walking down the street checking me out. . . . I have blonde shoulder-length hair, a nice toushie [sic], and brown bedroom eyes."

"I am looking for someone to spoil. To be blunt I work for an investment firm and I make quite a bit of money. I am looking for a sweet, cute girl/woman to take care of financially."

—PERSONAL ADS FROM CRAIGSLIST

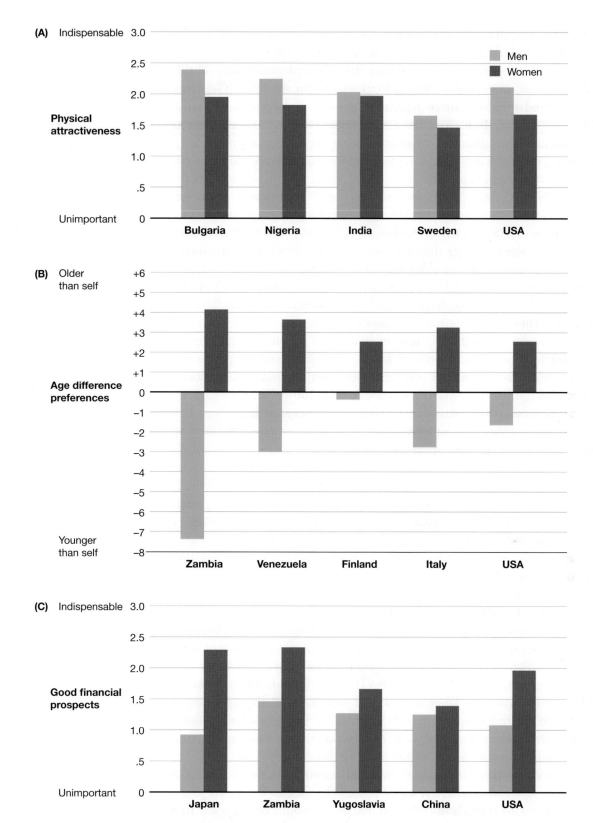

Figure 10.7

Differences in Male and Female Mating Preferences

The bars show representative findings from a cross-cultural survey of mating preferences. The importance of physical attractiveness and good financial prospects was rated on a 4-point scale ranging from "indispensable" to "unimportant." Age difference preferences are simply the respondents' average preferred age difference between self and spouse.

SOURCE: Adapted from Buss, 1989.

recently, Zentner and Mitura (2012) found that in cultures with greater gender equality, such as the U.S., Finland, and Republic of the Philippines, the usual pattern of men seeking beautiful mates and women seeking mates with resources was small; but in cultures with greater gender inequality, such as Turkey and Mexico, these differences were more pronounced.

Evolution or Culture? If the most frequently cited evidence in support of the evolutionary approach to gender differences in mate preferences can so easily be questioned, how much stock should we put in it? Stated differently, which account should we believe, the evolutionary view or a more cultural, role-based theory like Eagly and Wood's? Most psychologists would say that the best way to respond to this interpretive problem is the way it's always handled in science— by examining what happens across a range of conditions, and seeing which theory provides the best explanation of the full range of different results.

Observing a broad range of conditions, of course, was precisely the point of the ambitious cross-cultural studies that evolutionary psychologists cite as support for their perspective (Buss, 1989; Schmitt, 2003). The guiding logic has appeal: if the predicted gender differences show up in culture after culture, they are unlikely to result from socialization practices (which vary widely among cultures). But as just discussed, the strength of the argument in this case can be questioned. Cross-cultural uniformity may be the indirect result of simple differences between men and women in physical size and strength, and in pregnancy and breast-feeding, leading to divisions of labor and power imbalances that explain gender differences in mate preferences observed in country after country. In the end, cross-cultural studies cannot deliver all that their advocates would like to claim. Ultimately, these studies never overcome the problem of resting on a sample size of one—the human species.

Even so, we must bear in mind that the broader theory of evolution is unsurpassed in its ability to explain many of the complicated behavioral patterns observed throughout the animal kingdom. It would be hard to maintain that evolution has shaped the behavioral tendencies of every plant and animal on Earth—but not those of humans.

What, then, would qualify as clearer support for the evolutionary perspective on attraction and mate preferences? The answer is simple: any empirical result that would not be discovered without the guidance of evolutionary theory, and that all other accounts would have difficulty explaining. As it turns out, there are some findings that fit the bill. Recall our earlier discussion of bilateral symmetry. We're attracted to symmetrical faces because symmetry is a sign of good genes, and combining a sexual partner's good genes with our own increases the chances that our genes will be passed on to our children and future generations. This logic has led investigators to propose that symmetry ought to be especially preferred in potential mates when the probability of conception is relatively high (the only time, after all, when genetic transmission is relevant).

Thus, in one study the researchers had women during various phases of their menstrual cycles sniff (no kidding) a number of T-shirts that had earlier been worn by a group of men whose degrees of facial bilateral symmetry varied (Gangestad & Thornhill, 1998; Thornhill & Gangestad, 1999; Thornhill et al., 2003). As the investigators anticipated, the T-shirts of the facially symmetrical men were judged to have a better aroma than those of less symmetrical men—but only by those women who were close to the ovulation phase of their menstrual

cycle. It's unlikely that anyone, without the help of evolutionary theory, would ever have predicted or sought to test such an association.

Evidence also shows that women's preferences may change in other ways at different points in their menstrual cycle. For example, it has been argued that the strong jaw of particularly masculine-looking male faces is also a sign of good genes. But women generally rate slightly *feminized* male faces as most attractive (Perrett et al., 1998)—*except* when they are ovulating and the chances of conception are highest. Near ovulation, their preferences tend to shift toward more masculinized faces (Penton-Voak et al., 1999; **Figure 10.8**).

Additional studies along these lines have shown that during the ovulatory phase of their menstrual cycle, women (1) can more quickly recognize male faces as male (but not female faces as female) than during other times of the month; (2) would prefer to have a fling with a man with a lower, more masculine voice (Puts, 2005); and (3) prefer men who pursue more confident, assertive, and competitive tactics of self-presentation (Gangestad, Simpson, Cousins, Garver-Apgar, & Christensen, 2004; Macrae, Alnwick, Milne, & Schloerscheidt, 2002).

Where a woman is in her menstrual cycle also appears to influence the behavior of the men around her. In one study, men were asked to smell the T-shirts worn by women at different points in their cycles (Miller & Maner, 2010). Those exposed to the scent of a woman near ovulation had higher levels of testosterone

50% more feminized ← Original   Original → 50% more masculinized

Figure 10.8

Male Attractiveness to Women during the Menstrual Cycle

In this study, women selected the one face they thought was most attractive from photos varying from 50-percent masculinized to 50-percent feminized. The graph shows that the women tended to select somewhat feminized faces overall, but the mean degree of feminization of the selected face was less for women who were at a stage in their cycle when the chance of pregnancy was high.

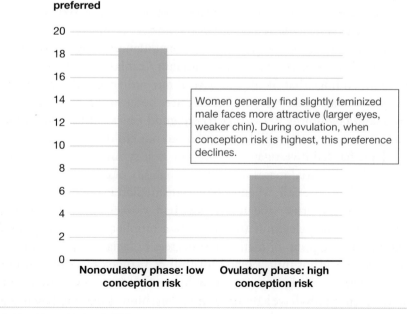

Mean feminization preferred

Women generally find slightly feminized male faces more attractive (larger eyes, weaker chin). During ovulation, when conception risk is highest, this preference declines.

Nonovulatory phase: low conception risk   Ovulatory phase: high conception risk

SOURCE: Adapted from Penton-Voak et al., 1999.

than those exposed at other times. In another study, men who interacted with a female confederate who was near the ovulatory phase of her cycle were both more likely to mimic her nonverbal behavior and more likely to take risks in a decision-making task in her presence, presumably in an effort to make a favorable impression (Miller & Maner, 2011).

Studies like these, that assess changes in judgments of attractiveness across biologically meaningful conditions, provide the strongest evidence to date for the evolutionary approach to human attraction. They take us far beyond simple empirical demonstrations of male and female differences that most people have already observed in their daily lives.

🕐 LOOKING BACK

Proximity causes people to have direct encounters, and mere exposure leads to liking. When people know they will interact frequently, they do their best to make sure their interactions go smoothly. People are also more inclined to be attracted to those who are similar to themselves, because they validate one's beliefs and values. Physically attractive individuals are more popular with members of the opposite sex, are evaluated more positively, and tend to have better social skills. The effects of physical attractiveness appear to be based in part on biological predispositions: certain elements of physical attractiveness may indicate reproductive fitness.

Romantic Relationships

Throughout history and across many different cultures, the reasons for marrying have varied dramatically (Coontz, 2005). In hunter-gatherer societies, parents married their children off to members of neighboring tribes. This practice had the effect, whether intended or not, of ensuring more cooperative trading relationships between groups; it also reduced the likelihood of genetic problems that can stem from inbreeding. For much of Western European history as well, marriages were arranged, by parents, to consolidate ties with other families, thereby ensuring that property and wealth stayed within the families. In some cultures, arranged marriages are still common today.

But for most of the roughly 2.3 million couples who get married each year in the United States (the vast majority of all North Americans marry), marriage is about romance—about love. So what is this thing we call love? How does love change over the course of a long-term relationship? And what determines which way a relationship will go—toward contentedness and happiness, or toward dissatisfaction and breakup?

What Is Love?

Ask some friends this question, and you'll probably get as many different answers as the number of people you ask. Sure, there will be some overlapping sentiments in the responses, but there'll be a lot less overlap than you would have thought. When researchers Beverley Fehr and James Russell (1991) asked undergraduates to list as many different types of love as they could, the students came up with 216 different kinds—and almost half of these were mentioned by more than one person!

Marriage across Cultures

Wedding ceremonies vary in their specific styles and formats according to cultural practices, but they are held throughout the world. Here are ceremonies in (A) Lapland, Scandinavia; (B) Gondar, Ethiopia; and (C) Shanghai, China.

Most social psychology studies account for multiple varieties of love, but researchers organize them into broad categories, such as companionate love, compassionate love, and romantic love (Berscheid, 2010; Sternberg, 1986). *Companionate love* is the love we typically experience with friends and family members; these are people we generally trust, share activities and interests with, and usually like to be around. *Compassionate love* is akin to a communal relationship, with bonds that focus on monitoring and responding to another person's needs, such as how a mother looks out for her child's well-being. But it's *romantic love* we're referring to when we say we're "in love" with someone. This is the love that we're moved by in poetry and epic romance novels, that we laugh about in romantic comedies, and that we search for on dating websites. Romantic love is the love associated with intense emotion and sexual desire, which is why it's sometimes referred to as *passionate love*. What do we know about this kind of love?

One prominent feature of romantic love is its time course. Early in romantic love relationships, partners experience powerful, at times all-consuming, feelings of passion, or sexual arousal, for each other. The intensity of romantic passion is expressed in a host of metaphors that capture its single-mindedness and loss of control: lovers feel "knocked off their feet," "hungry" for each other, and "mad" or "crazy" with desire (Lakoff & Johnson, 1980). These feelings of passion are registered in specific patterns of touch, cuddling, and sexual behavior and fluctuate for women with rising levels of certain sex hormones, especially estrogen (Konner, 2003).

It's important to note that people feel this early passion uniquely—and only—for one preferred romantic partner. Eli Finkel and Paul Eastwick have pioneered the speed-dating approach to the study of early desire (Finkel & Eastwick, 2008). In this research, a dozen or so young women and a dozen or so young men arrive at the lab and engage in a series of rapid-fire, 2-minute get-acquainted conversations with all the members of the opposite sex. After each supercharged interaction, the participants rate their sexual desire and feelings of chemistry for one another. The researchers found that when one person feels unique desire and chemistry for another, those feelings are reciprocated (Eastwick, Finkel, Mochon, & Ariely, 2007). Speed-daters who felt chemistry for many other people actually generated little desire or chemistry in others. Apparently, people can detect whether interest is targeted or promiscuous.

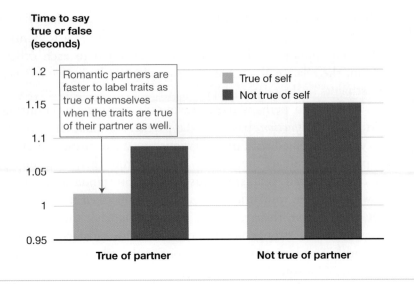

Time to say true or false (seconds)

Romantic partners are faster to label traits as true of themselves when the traits are true of their partner as well.

☐ True of self
■ Not true of self

True of partner   Not true of partner

SOURCE: Adapted from Aron et al., 1991.

Figure 10.9
Construing Close Others as We Construe Ourselves
When we fall in love, does our identity merge with that of our partner? In exploring this question, the researchers in this study had romantic partners label traits as true or not true of the self. Some traits were also true of the partner; others were not.

Surveys indicate that when two people spend increasing amounts of time together, early passion ebbs and a second element of the romantic relationship becomes more prominent—a deep sense of intimacy (Acevedo & Aron, 2009; Sprecher & Regan, 1998). Couples feel increased comfort and security from the sense of being close and knowing each other better. With increasing intimacy, romantic partners include their partner's perspectives, experiences, and characteristics more and more into their own self-concept (Aron & Aron, 1997; Aron, Aron, & Allen, 1989; Aron & Fraley, 1999). In one study of this second phase, married couples first rated 90 trait adjectives for how accurately they described themselves and their spouse (Aron, Aron, Tudor, & Nelson, 1991). After a brief distracter task, participants viewed each trait on a computer screen and indicated as quickly as possible whether the trait was "like me" or "not like me." As you can see in **Figure 10.9**, participants were faster to identify traits on which they were similar to their spouse and slower to ascribe traits to themselves that their partner did not also possess. With increasing intimacy, it's almost as if the two partners become one.

Romantic love is thought to promote commitment in part by provoking verbal and nonverbal communication of one's devotion to a partner (Gonzaga, Keltner, Londahl, & Smith, 2001). No wonder people place so much importance on whether or not romantic partners have uttered the words "I love you" yet—the magical three-word phrase that signals one's commitment to the relationship (Ackerman, Griskevicius, & Li, 2011). Long-term, committed relationships involve many sacrifices—forgoing other flirtations, relationships, and reproductive opportunities; committing resources to each other; and pragmatic demands of coordinating two sets of interests, values, friends, and career aspirations (Frank, 1988). Why do some romantic partners commit to the relationship, whereas others don't?

An Investment Model of Commitment

One approach to understanding why some romantic partners remain committed to their relationships, whereas others don't, is provided by Caryl Rusbult's **investment model of commitment** (Rusbult, 1980, 1983). This model represents

investment model of commitment A model of interpersonal relationships maintaining that three determinants make partners more committed to each other: relationship satisfaction, few alternative partners, and investments in the relationship.

The Investment Model of Commitment

This model maintains that commitment to a relationship depends on satisfaction with the relationship, presence and quality of alternatives to the relationship, and investments in the relationship.

an integration of many of the features of social exchange theory (described earlier). According to the model, once partners have a romantic bond, three determinants make them more committed to each other: satisfaction, the relative absence or poor quality of alternative partners, and investments in the relationship.

The first and perhaps most obvious determinant of enduring commitment is *satisfaction*, based on the partners' evaluation of the rewards and costs associated with their relationship. We've already discussed how people often evaluate the rewards they get from their relationships, and the costs incurred, against various comparison standards. Still, evidence shows that when romantic partners are simply asked to rate the rewards they receive from their relationship as well as what they provide to the other, one of the strongest correlates of romantic satisfaction in long-term relationships is how much they get out of the relationship (Cate, Lloyd, Henton, & Larson, 1982).

Satisfaction based on a favorable assessment of rewards relative to costs, however, doesn't tell the whole commitment story. Whether or not *alternative partners* are available is another strong contributor to the enduring commitment a partner feels. The fewer options a romantic partner has outside the relationship, the more committed he or she tends to feel, and the more likely the partner is to remain in the relationship. For example, in questionnaire studies, romantic partners who report few potential alternative partners are less likely to break up later (White & Booth, 1991).

The third determinant of commitment is the magnitude of the *investments* the couple puts into the relationship. A person is more likely to remain in a relationship if he or she has invested heavily in it. Investments can include the time, effort, caring, and love expended, as well as the shared memories, mutual friends, and shared possessions that are part of having a life together. Just as it's hard to walk away from a business venture into which one has invested substantial time and money, it's difficult to end a relationship into which one has poured a lot of time and energy. Indeed, for committed romantic partners, the self is literally invested in the relationship in the sense that both people come to mentally view themselves as a single unit with their partners, using the plural pronoun *we* to refer to themselves (Agnew, Van Lange, Rusbult, & Langston, 1998).

Recent findings suggest that investing in a relationship not only increases one's own commitment to the relationship, but also increases one's partner's investment to the relationship. In one experiment, participants listed various ways their romantic partner invested in their relationship, including a specific example that was particularly meaningful and important; they subsequently reported greater commitment to the relationship relative to control participants, who listed their own investments or did not list any at all (Joel, Gordon, Impett, MacDonald, & Keltner, 2013). They also reported more gratitude and this gratitude accounted for the link between thinking about their partners' investments and their higher commitment to the relationship.

In empirical tests of Rusbult's investment model, romantic partners typically report on the three determinants of their commitment (satisfaction, alternative partners, and investments), and the level of their commitment every 6 months or so for a couple of years (Berg & McQuinn, 1986; Rusbult, 1983; Simpson, 1987). More concretely, participants indicate their level of agreement with statements tapping commitment, as well as ones capturing the three

TABLE 10.1 MEASURING THE COMMITMENT DETERMINANTS IN ROMANTIC RELATIONSHIPS

DETERMINANT	SAMPLE ITEM
Satisfaction	"Our relationship does a good job of fulfilling my needs for intimacy."
Alternative partners	"People other than my partner are appealing."
Investments	"I feel very involved in our relationship, like I've put a great deal into it."
Commitment level	"I am committed to maintaining my relationship with my partner."

SOURCE: Adapted from Rusbult, Martz, & Agnew, 1998.

determinants of commitment: satisfaction, alternative partners, and investments (Rusbult, Martz, & Agnew, 1998). Examples of these statements are shown in **Table 10.1**. The level of partner agreement for each of the three determinants of commitment early on predicted whether a couple stayed together or broke up down the road.

How exactly, then, does commitment promote relationship longevity? Is it enough to simply be committed? If only it were that easy. Research shows that commitment is linked to longer-lasting relationships because it encourages behaviors that are good for the relationship, such as forgiveness. For example, Finkel and his colleagues have shown that higher commitment is associated with forgiving in response to a romantic partner's mistakes (Finkel, Rusbult, Kumashiro, & Hannon, 2002). Other researchers have found that commitment is also linked to greater self-sacrifice in couples, as when one partner agrees to move to an undesirable city for the sake of his partner's job, or when one gives up meat because it offends her vegan spouse (Van Lange, Agnew Harinck, & Steemers, 1997).

Marital Dissatisfaction

It's widely known that roughly half of first marriages in the United States end in separation or divorce, although this trend has been on the decline recently (Martin & Bumpass, 1989; Myers, 2000a). Less widely known is the finding that marriages are less satisfying today than they were 30 years ago (Glenn, 1991; Myers, 2000a). Marital conflict stimulates adrenal and pituitary stress responses, which are known to cause cardiac problems and inhibit immune system protections (Kiecolt-Glaser, Malarkey, Cacioppo, & Glaser, 1994). In addition, unhappy marriages can leave a disturbing legacy: children of divorced parents are more likely to experience greater personal, academic, and romantic difficulties, both during childhood and later in adulthood (Amato & Keith, 1991; Wallerstein, Lewis, & Blakeslee, 2000). Given that romantic dissatisfaction is so widespread and has such far-reaching effects, learning about what predicts romantic dissatisfaction and divorce is important.

Predictors of Dissatisfaction and Divorce One way to understand unhappy romantic relationships is to ask whether certain kinds of people or specific circumstances make marital dissatisfaction or divorce more likely. Does the kind of person you marry matter? What about the social class or age of the two people?

To answer these questions, researchers relate measures of marital satisfaction to measures of personality and background. They have learned, first, that personality matters. Neurotic people, who tend to be anxious, tense, emotionally volatile, and plaintive, have less happy romantic relationships and are more likely to divorce (Karney & Bradbury, 1997; Karney, Bradbury, Fincham, & Sullivan, 1994; Kurdek, 1993). For similar reasons, people who are highly sensitive to rejection have greater difficulties in intimate relationships (Downey & Feldman, 1996; Downey, Freitas, Michaelis, & Khouri, 1998; see also Murray, Holmes, MacDonald, & Ellsworth, 1998). Moreover, romantic partners and friends who are sensitive to rejection respond with greater hostility when feeling rejected by intimate others (Ayduk, Downey, Testa, Yen, & Shoda, 1999; Downey, Feldman, & Ayduk, 2000; Downey et al., 1998).

Certain demographic factors also predict problems in romantic relationships. Most notably, individuals from lower socioeconomic backgrounds are more likely to divorce (Williams & Collins, 1995). Socioeconomic status (SES) refers to the combination of educational background, income, and occupational prestige of a person and his or her family (see Chapters 3 and 5). Lower SES is apt to introduce into the relationship financial difficulties and the burdens of finding gratifying and stable work, some of the primary reasons that marriages break up (Berscheid & Reis, 1998).

In terms of the age of couples, people who marry at a younger age are more likely to divorce. Of several possible explanations for this finding, here are two: younger people may not be as effective at being long-term committed partners, and people who marry young may not be as effective at choosing the right partners.

The Four Horsemen of the Apocalypse As romantic partnerships mature, they revolve more and more around conversations and emotional exchanges about parenting, children, finances, and intimacy. Are there telltale signs in couples' patterns of communication that indicate a relationship is in trouble? To answer this question, John Gottman and Robert Levenson have pioneered the interaction dynamics approach to studying gay, lesbian, and heterosexual relationships. This approach identifies the specific emotions and patterns of communication that predict dissatisfaction and, ultimately, dissolution (Gottman & Levenson, 1992, 1999; Levenson & Gottman, 1983).

Gottman and Levenson videotape married couples engaged in intense conversations in the laboratory, and then study the videos carefully for clues to romantic dissatisfaction. In a conflict discussion task, partners talk for 15 minutes about an issue they both recognize as a source of intense conflict in their relationship, and they try their best to resolve it. The researchers then code the interactions for anger, criticism, defensiveness, stonewalling, contempt, sadness, and fear, as well as several positive behaviors, including affection, enthusiasm, interest, and humor.

"I hope when I grow up I'll have an amicable divorce."

BOX 10.5

Not So Fast
Critical Thinking about the Variable Being Measured

Most newlyweds are happy with each other; however, as the harsh reality of a 50-percent divorce rate shows, many don't stay that way. Is there any way to predict which couples are likely to thrive over the long term and which ones are headed for trouble? Would it be better to ask the newlyweds directly what they think of each other, or would an indirect, implicit measure be better?

To find out, a group of investigators asked 135 newlywed couples to rate their relationship on a number of scales, such as good/bad and satisfied/dissatisfied (McNulty, Olson, Meltzer, & Shaffer, 2013). They also administered an implicit measure of how much they liked each other, by flashing a picture of their partner very briefly (a third of a second) before showing them pictures of positive and negative items (such as flowers and spiders). The participants indicated, as quickly as possible, whether the latter pictures were positive or negative, and the investigators used the extent to which the partner's photo speeded up participants' responses to the positive words and slowed down their responses to the negative words

as an indirect measure of how much they liked their partner. The investigators then checked in with the newlyweds every 6 months for the next 4 years and asked how satisfied they were with their relationship.

The indirect measure did a very good job of predicting relationship satisfaction down the road. The more positive they felt about each other as newlyweds by that measure, the more satisfied they were 4 years later. The explicit measure was worthless. Participants' conscious assessments of how good/bad or satisfied/unsatisfied they felt about their relationship as newlyweds was not related to how they felt down the road. It seems that people's automatic, nonconscious attitudes can reveal a lot about what's really going on inside, but explicit assessments don't really reveal anything. As the investigators put it in the title of their paper, "Though they may be unaware, newlyweds implicitly know whether their marriage will be satisfying" (McNulty et al., 2013).

Not so fast. Things aren't always as they seem, and the phrase "may be unaware" is a telling hedge. What this study shows is

that this particular *measure* of the newlyweds' explicit attitudes are a poor predictor of the course of their relationship. It doesn't mean their explicit attitudes are a poor predictor. Maybe this measure doesn't really capture their explicit attitudes. After all, if you had concerns about the person with whom you'd just tied the knot—"I worry about his drinking"; "Is she going to end up looking like her mother?"—you might be unwilling to express that in a survey. And maybe that's why the explicit measure did not predict subsequent relationship satisfaction.

The broader point here is that we are fundamentally interested in the relationship between *variables* (sexual orientation, intelligence, self-esteem, for instance), but we are restricted to working with *measures* of those variables (what someone says about their sexual orientation, a score on an intelligence test, the size of a person's signature). We can get into trouble and draw the wrong conclusion when we confuse the two—as the title of this particular paper ("Though they may be unaware . . .") encourages us to do.

In one long-term study using these techniques, Gottman and Levenson (1999) followed the marriages of 79 couples, from one city, over many years. Based on their observations, they identified "the Four Horsemen of the Apocalypse"—that is, the four negative behaviors that are most harmful to relationships: criticism, defensiveness, stonewalling, and contempt.

The researchers found, just as you would expect, that married individuals who continually carp and find fault with their partners have less satisfying marriages. The same is true of people who are prone to defensiveness and stonewalling (resisting dealing with problems). When romantic partners are unable to talk openly and freely about their difficulties without being defensive—refusing to consider the possibility that something they are doing might contribute to the conflict—they are in trouble. This is especially true of men. To the extent that the male partner stonewalls, withdraws, and denies the issues his partner brings

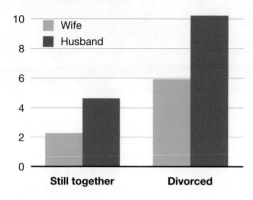

Frequency of contempt expressions shown in a 15-minute conversation

Wife
Husband

Still together   Divorced

Figure 10.10

Contempt and Marital Dissatisfaction
In this study, married partners who expressed contempt in a brief conversation about a source of conflict were more likely to be divorced 14 years later, compared to couples who exhibited less contempt. Feeling contempt is clearly toxic for a relationship.

SOURCE: Adapted from Gottman & Levenson, 1999.

up, there is often great dissatisfaction in the relationship. In contrast, the more couples disclose to each other, the more they tend to like each other (Collins & Miller, 1994).

Contempt, the emotion felt by one person looking down on another, is particularly toxic to maintaining romantic bonds. **Figure 10.10** shows how frequently couples who did or did not eventually divorce were observed to express contempt (Gottman & Levenson, 1999). The couples who eventually divorced expressed more than twice as much contempt as the couples who stayed together.

Gottman and Levenson's studies are susceptible to the problem of self-selection mentioned earlier. Do married couples get divorced because they express contempt and other negative emotions, or do they express these emotions because their relationship is on rocky ground? Additional findings by Gottman and Levenson indicate that negative communication patterns may in fact contribute directly to divorce. In another study of the 79 couples mentioned above, they used measures of the four toxic behaviors (criticism, defensiveness, stonewalling, and contempt) early in the relationship to predict who would stay together and who would be divorced 14 years later. Remarkably, based on these four measures gathered from a 15-minute conversation, they could predict with 93 percent accuracy who would get divorced (Gottman & Levenson, 2000).

Dangerous Attributions Certain construal tendencies are also related to the maintenance of romantic bonds. One construal tendency associated with dissatisfaction is blame. Bradbury, Karney, and their colleagues have looked at the relationship between romantic partners' causal attributions and their relationship satisfaction (Bradbury & Fincham, 1990; Karney & Bradbury, 2000; McNulty & Karney, 2001). Across multiple investigators, these researchers have found that dissatisfied, distressed couples make attributions that cast their partner and their relationship in a negative light; that is, they attribute rewarding, positive events in their relationships to unstable causes that are specific, unintended, and selfish. For example, a distressed partner might interpret a partner's unexpected gift of flowers as the result of a whim, particular to that day, and anticipate the gift to be followed by some selfish request. Happier couples, on the other hand, tend to attribute the same positive events to stable causes that are general, intended, and selfless. A satisfied romantic partner thus might attribute a gift of flowers to his or her partner's enduring kindness. Similarly, happier partners attribute negative events—the forgotten anniversary or sarcastic comment—to specific and unintended causes, whereas distressed partners attribute the same kinds of negative events to stable and global causes and see their partners as blameworthy and selfish.

Creating Stronger Romantic Bonds

Now that we've identified some of the most common trouble spots in relationships, let's turn to the kinds of things you might do to build healthier romantic bonds. You might be wise to marry when you're a bit older; to avoid highly anxious, rejection-sensitive, neurotic individuals when choosing a partner; to minimize criticism, defensiveness, stonewalling, and contempt in your interactions; and to try to interpret your partner's actions in a praiseworthy fashion. Social

psychologists have begun to make progress in identifying other things that may contribute to healthier romantic relationships.

Capitalizing on the Good Are there healthy patterns of conversation that foster more satisfying bonds? Shelly Gable and her colleagues believe it's particularly important to capitalize on the good—to share what's good in your life with your partner, and vice versa (Gable, Gonzaga, & Strachman, 2006; Gable, Reis, Impett, & Asher, 2004). In their research, these investigators found that individuals who received active, constructive "capitalization" from their significant others reported greater relationship satisfaction (Gable et al., 2004). Such responses are evident when one partner responds to the other's good news with engaged enthusiasm. For example, at the news of a partner's forthcoming art show, the actively constructive partner might ask questions about what pieces to show and whom to invite—questions that reveal an active engagement in such an important development in the partner's life.

Being Playful Courtship and the early phases of a relationship involve unusual levels of fun: late-night dancing, candlelit exchanges of poetry, weekend getaways, summer trips, and other exhilarating activities. The later stages, especially when children are involved, become focused on less inherently enjoyable activities—diaper changing, house cleaning, bill paying, and chauffeuring children to soccer practice and piano lessons. It's not surprising that having children, while bringing many joys, typically leads to a drop in romantic satisfaction (Myers, 2000a). In fact, married partners typically do not return to their previous level of satisfaction until the children leave home. (This point is nicely made in an exchange between a priest, a rabbi, and a minister on when life begins: the priest says at conception, the rabbi says at birth, and the minister says when the dog dies and the last child goes away to college.)

Being playful can help. Experimental work by Art Aron and his colleagues attests to the benefits of a bit of exhilarating silliness in a marriage (Aron, Norman, Aron, McKenna, & Heyman, 2000). In their study, spouses who had been married for several years engaged in one of two tasks. In a playfully arousing condition, partners were tied together at the knees and wrists with Velcro straps, and they were required to move a soft ball positioned between their heads across

> *"A baby is an inestimable blessing and bother."*
>
> —MARK TWAIN

Keys to Good Relationships
(A) Shared laughter and play are vital to healthy relationships. (B) Open communication and disclosure during conflicts are more helpful than stonewalling.

a long mat. In the other condition, each partner had to push a ball on his or her own to the middle of the mat with a stick. Spouses reported significantly higher marital satisfaction after engaging in the novel, amusing joint task, compared with participants in the other condition and with a baseline assessed earlier. Unusual, playful activities are arousing—and spouses often misattribute their arousal to their feelings about their partner, thereby enhancing both partners' satisfaction with the relationship.

Looking on the Bright Side Sandra Murray and her colleagues suggest that a tendency to idealize one's romantic partner is another important ingredient in a satisfying intimate bond (Murray & Holmes, 1993, 1997; Murray, Holmes, Dolderman, & Griffin, 2000; Neff & Karney, 2002). In one study, married couples and dating partners rated themselves and their partners on 21 traits related to virtues (such as understanding and patience), desirable attributes within romantic relationships (such as easygoing, witty), and faults (such as complaining or distant) (Murray, Holmes, & Griffin, 1996). The researchers compared the participants' ratings of their partners' virtues and faults to their ratings of their satisfaction in the relationship. Those who idealized their romantic partners—that is, rated the partner higher on these traits than the partner did himself or herself—were more satisfied with their relationships. Individuals also reported greater relationship satisfaction when their partners idealized them.

The relationship benefits of perceiving one's romantic partner through rose-colored glasses appear to hold for different sexual orientations. A research team examined lesbian, gay, heterosexual married, and heterosexual cohabiting couples and found that for all four types of couples, viewing one's romantic partner in an idealized fashion was linked to greater satisfaction with the relationship (Conley, Roesch, Peplau, & Gold, 2009).

In other studies, investigators have explored precisely how people idealize their romantic partners. In one case, people were asked to write about their partners' greatest fault (Murray & Holmes, 1999). Satisfied partners engaged in two forms of idealization. First, they saw virtue in their partners' faults. For example, an individual might write that his or her partner was melancholy, but that melancholy quality gave the partner a depth of character that was incomparably rewarding. Second, satisfied partners were more likely to offer "yes, but" refutations of the fault. For instance, a satisfied partner might write that her husband did not like to hold down a steady job, but at least that gave him more time to help out at home. (For a possible neuroscientific explanation, see **Box 10.6**.)

Love and Marriage across Cultures

To a degree that's hard for modern Westerners to comprehend, some of our generalizations about love and marriage do not apply to most of the world's cultures, nor even to most Western cultures until relatively recently. Although romantic love seems to exist in almost every culture, it has generally not been regarded as a prerequisite to marriage (Dion & Dion, 1993). The more typical pattern is a marriage arranged by parents. A young man's parents and a young woman's parents come to an agreement about the suitability of the pair for each other, and they announce the marriage transaction to their children. The term *transaction* often applies in a very economic sense: the prospective bride's parents provide a dowry, or, somewhat less often, the groom's parents pay a "bride price." These

"Love to faults is always blind, Always is to joy inclined, Lawless, winged, and unconfined, And breaks all chains from every mind."

—WILLIAM BLAKE

BOX 10.6 **FOCUS ON *NEUROSCIENCE***

This Is Your Brain in Love

As the work of Murray and her colleagues suggests, the mind does amazing things when in love, turning faults into charming idiosyncrasies (Murray & Holmes, 1999). What does your brain do during love? Recently, neuroscientists and relationship researchers have joined forces to answer this question, and their answers are both intuitive and surprising. In these studies, fMRI images record the brain's pattern of activation while a person looks at a picture of a romantic partner or is in the throes of feeling intense love (Fisher, Aron, & Brown, 2006). Not surprisingly, these neuroimaging methods reveal that romantic love is associated with activation in reward regions of the brain (the ventral striatum)—regions rich with receptors for oxytocin (which promotes trust and love; see Chapter 6) and dopamine (which promotes approach-related behavior).

What may surprise you, though, is that romantic love also deactivates the amygdala, a region of the brain associated with the perception of threat. It appears that in the throes of love, the brain disables your ability to see what is threatening or dangerous about the new love. This finding may help your parents understand why you might fall in love with someone who does not quite live up to their standards. Your brain simply isn't reacting to potential signs of risk in your new love—the fondness for motorcycles, the odd tattoos, the disregard for conventional society. These findings also shed light on what the brain might be doing as you turn your partner's faults and flaws (which in others might activate the amygdala) into pleasing virtues, as the Murray team found.

Love, even if not in the romantic sense, frequently follows marriage; and many cultures have an expression for this development, such as "Loves comes in the pillow." In other words, the post-romantic feelings of companionability, affection, and commitment are expected to follow rather than precede marriage. Some historians believe that the idea that romantic love should precede marriage is relatively recent, emerging only in the past 500 years or so. You might be intrigued to learn that the first Americans to hold to the rule that love should precede marriage were the Puritans of early New England. Their young people were encouraged to get acquainted with possible marriage partners. In the cold season, young people who were mutually interested got into a bed together, to get to know each other better and perhaps develop romantic feelings. They would be separated by what was called a "bundling board" to keep affection from getting out of hand.

sorts of transaction are common today in much of South, East, and Southeast Asia and in much of Africa.

Arranged marriages avoid some of the pitfalls of marrying for romantic love, including mismatches between the couple's socioeconomic status and religion, two factors associated with relatively high rates of divorce. In an arranged marriage, the in-laws are more apt to be respectful of one another—a stance perhaps less common when the in-laws are dragged together for reasons having nothing to do with mutual regard. The lack of expectation that there should be romantic love also makes it less likely that the natural, gradual transformation from romantic to a more companionate form of love will be a source of disappointment and discontent.

⬅ LOOKING BACK

Romantic relationships are a human universal, essential to our well-being, but in today's world they can be a difficult enterprise. Personality and demographic factors predict unhappiness in marriage, as do toxic behaviors like criticism, defensiveness, stonewalling, contempt, and blame. Research on relationships by social psychologists is yielding important insights about successful and rewarding relationships, in which partners capitalize on the good, choose to be playful, and see each other in a flattering light.

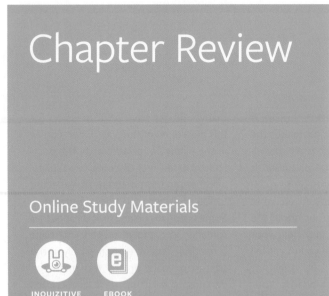

Chapter Review

Online Study Materials

INQUIZITIVE   EBOOK

SUMMARY

Characterizing Relationships

- The need to belong is biologically based, as evident in the evolutionary benefits and universality of human relationships and the negative consequences that result from their absence.
- In long-term *communal relationships*, people feel responsible for each other; in short-term *exchange relationships*, people are concerned with equity and reciprocity.
- *Social exchange theory* is based on the idea that how people feel about a relationship depends on their assessments of its costs and rewards, and what they believe alternative relationships can offer.
- According to *attachment theory*, early attachments with parents and other caregivers shape relationships for a person's whole life. The two dimensions of attachment are anxiety (fear of rejection) and avoidance (discomfort with intimacy). Attachment style is relatively stable and has wide-ranging effects on a person's well-being throughout life.

Attraction

- Proximity, the sheer closeness of contact, leads to attraction and liking. Liking can be influenced by the *functional distance* created by the architectural layout of a living arrangement that encourages social contact. This is partly explained by the *mere exposure effect,* the tendency to like a stimulus the more frequently it is encountered.
- Similarity determines attraction because people like others who resemble them. There is little evidence that opposites attract.
- Physically attractive people are more popular with the opposite sex, earn more money, and receive lighter sentences for crimes. Because of the *halo effect,* they are believed to have many positive qualities that go beyond their physical appearance. Physical appearance affects the lives of women more than men.
- *Reproductive fitness* is the capacity to pass one's genes on to future generations, and people seek mates with characteristics, such as the ability to resist disease, that enhance the likelihood of reproductive success.
- Intrasex competition occurs in species where parental investment is greater for the female, and the males must compete; in intersex attraction, males also must compete for the females' attention and thus are typically the louder and physically showier.
- Evolutionary psychologists believe that parental investment by men and women leads men to prefer women whose physical appearance indicates they will be fertile. Women are attracted to men who can provide for them and their children.

Romantic Relationships

- Romantic relationships, an important part of social life, are essential for well-being and physical health.
- There are many kinds of love, including companionate love, compassionate love, and romantic love.
- According to the investment model of commitment, three determinants make partners more committed to each other: satisfaction, few alternative partners, and investments in the relationship.
- Commitment is linked to longer-lasting relationships because it increases relationship-promoting behaviors such as forgiveness and self-sacrifice.
- Predictors of marital dissatisfaction and divorce include disparities in personality and socioeconomic status, marrying too young, communication issues, and behavioral problems, such as criticism, defensiveness, stonewalling, contempt, and blame.
- In healthy relationships, couples work on strengthening their bond by capitalizing on the good events in their lives, being playful, and looking on the bright side by seeing each other's positive attributes.
- In many cultures around the world, marriages are arranged by the parents, and love between the two partners is expected to follow marriage, even if it's not romantic love.

THINK ABOUT IT

1. The need to belong is thought to be a fundamental human drive. Similar to physical drives like hunger, when people have their need to belong satisfied, they are unlikely to pursue this drive further. Based on this idea of drive satiation, who should be more likely to call up a friend to make plans: Betty, who's been spending lots of quality time with her children lately, or Blanche, who tends to stay home by herself?

2. Sean and Mitch are just starting a relationship, but they seem to have different expectations about what each one deserves from a romantic partner. Sean thinks if his partner doesn't treat him extremely well, he's just not worth his time because there are better guys out there. Mitch, on the other hand, has been in several bad relationships and puts up with just about anything from a partner because he's deeply afraid of being alone. How would you describe Sean and Mitch's respective comparison levels and comparison levels for alternatives? What might the consequences of these levels be?

3. If Jenny feels comfortable relying on and being close to her immediate family members, and she seeks extremely intimate, clingy romantic relationships but keeps her distance from her friends, not disclosing much to them or counting on them, how would you analyze her attachment styles? How would you describe her working models?

4. Robert has a crush on Marilyn, but she doesn't seem to know he's alive. What could Robert do to make himself more attractive to Marilyn, based on the principles of proximity and similarity in terms of liking and attraction?

5. Suppose Alice wants to try an experiment about the halo effect of physical attractiveness on an online dating website. She sets up two profiles for herself, making the content of the profiles identical except for her picture. On one profile, she uses a beautiful photo of herself as her profile photo, but on the other profile, she uses a horrible photo of herself. How might men respond to these two profiles, and how might Alice respond to them in turn?

6. How can the investment model of commitment help explain why people stay in long-term abusive relationships? How might an abusive partner manipulate the factors that contribute to commitment, to make an abuse victim stay in the relationship?

THE ANSWER GUIDELINES FOR THE THINK ABOUT IT QUESTIONS
CAN BE FOUND AT THE BACK OF THE BOOK . . .

I AM GAY

AND THIS IS WHERE I PLAY

We have always been a part of this community.

Gay and straight, we play ball together, and see each other at the
barbershop and church. It's time to treat us with the love we deserve.

We Are Part Of You.org

Campaign for
Black Gay
Men's Lives
Funded by DOHMH
Design by Better World Advertising [www.socialmarketing.com]

Stereotyping, Prejudice, and Discrimination

Cristóbal Colón, better known as Christopher Columbus, was surely in a good mood on the morning of October 12, 1492, when he went ashore in the Bahamas on Guanahani Island, which he renamed San Salvador. Eleven weeks at sea since departing from Spain, he was trying to find a western route to Japan, China, and the East Indies. Now that he had spotted land, his glory was ensured, along with his appointment as viceroy and governor-general of all territories he might discover.

It is understandable, then, that Colón was expansive in his journal that day. His good mood was reflected in his description of the inhabitants of San Salvador (Columbus, 1492/1990):

> They swam out to the ships' boats where we were and brought parrots and balls of cotton thread and spears and many other things, and they bartered with us for other things which we gave them, like glass beads and hawks' bells. In fact they took and gave everything they had with good will. . . . They were well built, with handsome bodies and fine features. Their hair is thick, almost like a horse's tail. . . . They are all fairly tall, good looking and well proportioned.
>   They ought to make good slaves. (p. 1)

Colón's journal entry touches on the main ideas in this chapter. He was starting to develop a favorable stereotype of the islanders, characterizing them in general, based on the ones he happened to meet that day. Nevertheless, he was immediately prejudiced against them because their appearance and customs differed from those of his own people. He felt no need to treat them like his crew or other Europeans, as his chilling statement "They ought to make good slaves" makes clear.

Stereotyping Outgroups
Upon landing on an island in the Bahamas, Christopher Columbus was greeted by the natives and offered gifts of welcome, as shown in this German engraving. Yet Columbus was prejudiced against the indigenous people because they differed from Europeans; he stereotyped them as a group that would make good slaves, and he treated them as such.

We may be tempted to dismiss Colón's reactions as outdated, believing that people are more enlightened today. In many ways, they are. Slavery still exists but no longer as a sanctioned, state-sponsored enterprise. The world is now more multicultural than ever, with members of different races, ethnicities, and religions living and working alongside one another more peacefully and productively than ever before. In 2008, and again in 2012, the United States elected its first African-American president, a triumph that nearly all pioneers of the Civil Rights Movement said they never thought they'd see in their lifetime. As Martin Luther King, Jr., famously noted in 1965, "The arc of the moral universe is long, but it bends toward justice."

Despite such progress, however, it's abundantly clear that the human tendencies to stereotype, harbor prejudice, and engage in discrimination are still with us. Sunni and Shia Muslims are at each other's throats in numerous hotspots in the Middle East, and the prospects for peace between Israelis and Palestinians seem as remote as ever. The conflicts in Bosnia, Darfur, Rwanda, Somalia, and Ukraine show that intergroup enmity continues to be a distressingly common component of the human condition.

Stereotyping, prejudice, and discrimination prevail in the United States as well, as evidenced by videotapes of police officers brutalizing members of minority groups. In addition, there have been countless instances of minority drivers being pulled over by the police for no reason, and minorities being passed over by potential employers. Describing his earlier experience as a young black man, U.S. Senator Cory Booker recalled: "In the jewelry store, they lock the case when I walk in. In the shoe store, they help the white man who walks in after me. In the shopping mall, they follow me" (Kristoff, 2014, p. 9). The consequences are sometimes dire. As we write this, demonstrators across the country are protesting the failure to indict the white police officers who, in Ferguson, Missouri, and Staten Island, New York, killed African-Americans Michael Brown and Eric Garner. And although the legalization of same-sex marriage in many European countries and the United States is a sign of genuine improvement in civil rights, gays and lesbians continue to face discrimination—daily and worldwide. Women in nearly all countries continue to earn less than men doing comparable work, even the most active and vital elderly people are often dismissed as incompetent, and people who are not good-looking have challenges that their more attractive peers never face. Stereotyping, prejudice, and discrimination are still all around us.

Theoretical Perspectives

The pervasiveness of stereotypes and the persistence of ethnic, religious, and racial animosity challenge us to understand the underlying causes of intergroup tension. Where do stereotypes, prejudice, and discrimination come from? Why do they persist? What can be done to eliminate or reduce their impact?

Any serious attempt to address these questions must begin with the recognition that there will likely never be a single, comprehensive theory of stereotyping, prejudice, or discrimination. The causes of each of them are many and varied, and any satisfactory account of these intertwined phenomena must incorporate numerous elements. This chapter focuses on three general perspectives that shed light on these issues. The *economic perspective* identifies the roots of much intergroup hostility in competing interests that can set groups apart from one another. The *motivational perspective* emphasizes the psychological needs that lead to intergroup conflict. The *cognitive perspective* traces the origin of stereotyping to the same cognitive processes that enable people to categorize, say, items of furniture into distinct classes of chairs, couches, and tables. This perspective takes into account the frequent conflict between people's consciously held beliefs and values and their quick, reflexive reactions to members of specific racial, ethnic, occupational, sexual orientation, or other demographic groups.

Note that these three perspectives are exactly that—perspectives, not sharply defined categories. In addition, they're not competing accounts, but complementary elements of a more complete analysis. Sometimes the same phenomenon or the same empirical finding can be considered an example of both an economic and motivational influence. Furthermore, the three elements influence one another. Jews, expatriate Chinese, and Armenians have all been the victims of genocides. The reasons in each case were partly economic. These groups were richer than many others in their countries. The economic element drove the cognitive element—causing people to perceive these minority groups as fundamentally different from themselves. The cognitive element in turn fed into the motivational element of anger over the wealth of the minority groups. Nevertheless, the distinctions are useful for the purpose of organizing and thinking clearly about the varied causes of stereotyping, prejudice, and discrimination—as well as the ways intergroup conflict can be reduced.

Characterizing Intergroup Bias

Do you believe that Asians are industrious, Italians are temperamental, Muslims are fanatical, or that Californians are "laid back"? Such beliefs are examples of **stereotypes**—beliefs that certain attributes are characteristic of members of particular groups. A stereotype can be positive or negative, true or false. And whether valid or not, stereotyping is a way of categorizing people (Lee, Jussim, & McCauley, 1995). It involves thinking about a person not as an individual, but as a member of a group, and projecting what (you think) you know about the group onto your expectations about that person.

Certain stereotypes have some truth to them and others don't. Consider the old joke that heaven is a place where you have an American house, a German car, French food, British police, an Italian lover, and everything is run by the Swiss. Hell, on the other hand, is a place where you have a Japanese house, a French car, British food, German police, a Swiss lover, and everything is run by the Italians. The Swiss bureaucracy is indeed more widely praised than the Italian, and automobile magazines rave more about what's rolling off the assembly lines at BMW and Audi than at Peugeot and Renault. Some stereotypes are accurate.

stereotype The belief that certain attributes are characteristic of members of a particular group.

"I speak French to my ambassadors, English to my accountant, Italian to my mistress, Latin to my God and German to my horse."

—FREDERICK
THE GREAT OF PRUSSIA

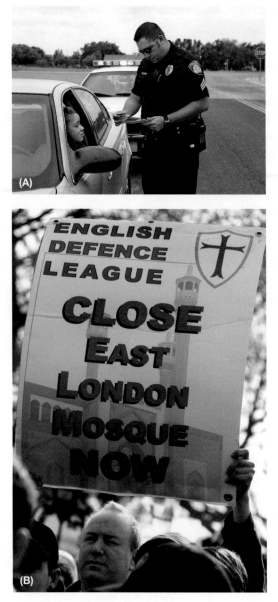

But is there really any reason to be especially wary of German police? There certainly was during the 1930s and 1940s, but has German law enforcement been unusually prone to encroach on civil liberties since then? Maybe, maybe not. Are Italian lovers preferable to Swiss? You make the call.

Stereotypes about Swiss administrators, German police, or Italian lovers (valid or not) are not what concern most social psychologists (Judd & Park, 1993). They have focused instead on those stereotypes considered most questionable, and those most likely to lead to pernicious forms of prejudice and discrimination.

Prejudice refers to an attitudinal and affective response toward a group and its individual members. Negative attitudes generally get the most attention, but it's also possible to be positively prejudiced toward a particular group. Prejudice involves *prejudging* others because they belong to a specific category. **Discrimination** refers to negative or harmful behavior directed toward members of a particular group. It involves unfair treatment of others, based not on their individual character or abilities, but strictly on their membership in a specific group.

Roughly speaking, stereotyping, prejudice, and discrimination refer to the belief, attitudinal, and behavioral components, respectively, of negative intergroup relationships. Stereotyping, prejudice, and discrimination often go together. People are more inclined to injure those they hold in low regard. But the components of intergroup bias don't have to occur together. A person can discriminate without prejudice, for example. Jewish parents sometimes say they don't want their children to marry outside the faith, not because they have a low opinion of other groups, but because they're concerned about assimilation and its implications for the future of Judaism. Members of nearly all ethnic groups have harbored similar sentiments out of the same concern about preserving a cultural identity or way of life. Thus, ingroup favoritism can arise in the absence of outgroup enmity. Sometimes, of course, statements such as "I have nothing against them, but . . ." are merely cover-ups of underlying bigotry. At other times, they are doubtless sincere (Gaertner, Iuzzini, Witt, & Orina, 2006; Lowery, Unzueta, Knowles, & Goff, 2006).

It's also possible to be prejudiced and yet not discriminate, particularly when a culture frowns on discrimination. Civil rights laws in the United States are specifically designed to uncouple prejudicial attitudes and discriminatory actions. The threat of punishment is intended to keep people's discriminatory impulses in check.

Modern Racism

Throughout much of the world, norms about how different groups of people are viewed and treated have changed. In Western countries in particular, it's illegal to engage in many forms of discrimination that were common half a century ago, and it is not socially acceptable to express the sorts of prejudices and stereotypes that were common until relatively recently. These changes have caused some people to be conflicted—between what they truly think and feel, and what they think they *should* think and feel (or what they believe is prudent to say or do publicly). For many, the changes have also created a conflict between

Seeds of Intergroup Bias
(A) The stereotype of African-Americans being more likely than other groups to break the law, combined with anti-black sentiment, can lead to discriminatory behavior, such as police officers pulling over African-American drivers in wildly disproportionate numbers. (B) The stereotype linking Islam with extremism can lead to negative reactions toward Muslims and Islamic institutions.

prejudice A negative attitude or affective response toward a group and its individual members.

discrimination Unfair treatment of individuals based on their membership in a particular group.

competing beliefs and values (such as a belief in equal treatment versus a desire to make up for past injustice through affirmative action), or between competing abstract beliefs and gut-level reactions (such as a belief that one should feel the same toward members of all groups versus some hard-to-shake resistance to that belief). In addition, as research has shown, some people's reactions to other groups are unconscious and automatic, and these responses may differ greatly from their more thoughtful beliefs and attitudes. These kinds of conflicts have inspired social psychologists to develop new theories to explain this modern, more constrained, more conflicted sort of prejudice.

This shift in theoretical approaches is particularly noteworthy with respect to race relations in the United States. Some have argued that old-fashioned racism has largely disappeared in the United States but has been supplanted by a subtler, more modern counterpart (Kinder & Sears, 1981; McConahay, 1986; Sears, 1988; Sears & Henry, 2005; Sears & Kinder, 1985; see also Haddock, Zanna, & Esses, 1993 on homophobia; and Swim, Aiken, Hall, & Hunter, 1995 on sexism). In one example of this theoretical shift, **modern racism** is defined as a rejection of explicitly racist beliefs—blacks being morally inferior to whites, for instance—while nevertheless feeling animosity toward African-Americans or being highly suspicious of them and being uncomfortable dealing with them.

Sam Gaertner and Jack Dovidio (1986; Dovidio & Gaertner, 2004) have explored the conflicts and inconsistencies that often accompany modern racism. They note that many people hold strong egalitarian values that lead them to reject prejudice and discrimination, yet they also harbor unacknowledged negative feelings and attitudes toward minority groups that stem from ingroup favoritism and a desire to defend the status quo (Kteily, Sidanius, & Levin, 2011; Sidanius & Pratto, 1999). Whether these individuals will act in a prejudiced or discriminatory manner depends on the details of the situation. If the situation offers no justification or "disguise" for discriminatory action, their responses will conform to their egalitarian values. But if a suitable rationalization is available, the modern racist's prejudices will emerge.

In an early test of this idea, participants were in a position to aid a white or black person in need of medical assistance (Gaertner & Dovidio, 1977; see also Dovidio, Smith, Donella, & Gaertner, 1997; Saucier, Miller, & Doucet, 2005). If the participants thought they were the only one who could help, they came to the aid of the black person somewhat more often (94 percent of the time) than for the white person (81 percent). But when they thought other people were present and their own inaction could be justified on nonracial grounds ("I thought somebody else with more expertise would intervene"), they helped the black person much less often than the white person (38 percent versus 75 percent). In situations such as this, the prejudice or discrimination is "masked," and the individual remains comfortably unaware of being racist. Thus, modern racism shows itself in subtle ways. The modern racist would never join the Ku Klux Klan but might consistently give black passersby a wider berth. Such a person might never utter a racist word, but might insist that "discrimination against blacks is no longer a problem in the United States" (the latter an item on the Modern Racism Scale; McConahay, 1986).

In another telling study, white participants evaluated black and white applicants to college (Hodson, Dovidio, & Gaertner, 2002). Participants whose scores on the Attitudes toward Blacks Scale indicated they were high or low in explicit prejudice toward blacks rated white and black applicants the same

modern racism Prejudice directed at racial groups that exists alongside the rejection of explicitly racist beliefs.

when the applicants excelled on all pertinent dimensions (SAT scores and high-school grades), or were below average on all dimensions. But when the applicants excelled on certain dimensions (e.g., high SAT scores) and were below average on others (e.g., low GPA), the ratings of prejudiced and unprejudiced participants diverged: the prejudiced participants rated the black applicants less favorably than did the unprejudiced participants. In these latter cases, prejudiced participants' discriminatory responses could be defended as nondiscriminatory—that is, they could be hidden—by claiming that the dimensions on which the black applicants fell short were more important than those on which they excelled.

Benevolent Racism and Sexism

Statements like "Some of my best friends are _____" (fill in the blank) or "I'm not sexist; I love women!" illustrate a common conviction that stereotypes must be negative to be harmful. In fact, however, many of our "isms"—racism, sexism, ageism, heterosexism—are ambivalent, containing both negative and positive features (Czopp & Monteith, 2006; Devine & Elliot, 1995; Ho & Jackson, 2001). Someone might believe, for example, that Asians are colder and more rigid than whites—and at the same time believe they are more intellectually gifted. Similarly, someone might believe that women are less competent and intelligent than men—and at the same time believe women are warmer and have better social skills.

In their work on ambivalent sexism, Peter Glick and Susan Fiske (2001a, 2001b) interviewed 15,000 men and women in 19 nations and found that benevolent sexism (a chivalrous ideology marked by protectiveness and affection toward women who embrace conventional roles) often coexists with hostile sexism (dislike of nontraditional women and those viewed as usurping men's power). Glick and Fiske argue that even these partly positive stereotypes aren't necessarily benign. Ambivalent sexist or racist attitudes may be particularly resistant to change. The favorable features of such beliefs enable the stereotype holder to deny any prejudice. (Think of the trucker who romanticizes women so much he decorates his mud flaps with their likeness.)

By rewarding women and minorities for conforming to the status quo, benevolent sexism and racism inhibit progress toward equality. In other words, those who hold ambivalent attitudes tend to act positively toward members of out-groups only if they fulfill their idealized image of what such people should be like—say, the happy housewife or the dutiful staffer bringing coffee. Those who deviate tend to be treated with hostility (Lau, Kay, & Spencer, 2008). Furthermore, benevolent sexism can be as injurious as hostile sexism. In one study, for example, women treated in a paternalistic, sexist manner performed less well on a series of intellectual tests because of the self-doubts aroused by the treatment they received (Dardenne, Dumont, & Bollier, 2007).

Measuring Attitudes about Groups

The most straightforward way to assess how people feel about various groups is, of course, to ask them. Researchers have developed various attitude scales for this purpose, including the Attitudes toward Blacks Scale (Brigham, 1993), the Modern Racism Scale (McConahay, Hardee, & Batts, 1981), the Internal Motivation to Respond without Prejudice Scale (Plant & Devine, 1998), and the Sexual Prejudice Scale (Chonody, 2013). But surveys of people's attitudes toward

artifact A spurious research result arising from a faulty method of investigation.

Suppose you want to see whether gender stereotypes bias a teacher's judgments of student work. How would you find out? Researchers have generally used a straightforward approach: They've given essays to groups of participants, telling some of them the essay was written by, say, John, and others that it was written by Jane. They have then had participants assess its quality. Of course, it's important for the researchers to choose the names assigned to the essay carefully. Comparing the ratings of an essay supposedly written by Adolf with those of an essay written by Jennifer wouldn't work, because there's too much baggage associated with the name Adolf. How do researchers ensure the names are comparable? One way is to choose pairs of male and female names that are as similar as possible—Michael and Michelle, Paul and Paula, Robert and Roberta, and so on. This is precisely what researchers interested in gender bias have done, and what they have found is abundant evidence of sexism. The very same essay tends to be rated more favorably when it's attributed to a male student than a female student (Goldberg, 1968). What could be more straightforward and telling?

It turns out that these studies are not so straightforward and informative after all. In fact, when you try to create pairs of male and female names that are as similar as possible, you can easily end up with a set of male names that people tend to like more than the female names. The higher ratings given to essays purportedly written by Michael or Paul may not be due to the fact that they're thought to be written

by men, but because they're thought to be written by people with more desirable names. These studies, in other words, may showcase *nameism* rather than sexism. In fact, when the male and female names are equated in terms of how much participants like them as names, and not by how similar they are in other ways (length, phonemic overlap, and so on), there is no effect of the gender of the purported author on how favorably an essay is evaluated (Kasof, 1993). Sexism in the evaluation of essays disappears. The finding that gender made a difference was spurious, due to an error by the experimenters.

Does this mean there's no sexism when it comes to evaluating a person's performance? Of course not. It just means there may be no sexism when it comes to the evaluation of essays. And that shouldn't be surprising. Girls are known to perform better than boys in school, especially when it comes to reading and writing, and how their work is judged is more likely to benefit from stereotyping than suffer from it. But there are other areas in which sexist stereotypes might undermine the evaluation of a woman's performance. Historically, for example, it was thought that women didn't have the same musical talent as men, and their performance during auditions for premier orchestras appeared to validate that assessment. But when orchestra directors had musicians audition behind a screen so they couldn't be seen, there was a sharp rise in the percentage of women deemed worthy of positions in the world's most esteemed orchestras (Goldin & Rouse, 2000).

Moreover, although there may not be any sexism on the part of *individuals* evaluating essays written by men and women, there might nevertheless be *societal* sexism when it comes to how names are created. Nearly all pairs of very similar male and female names—Paul and Pauline, Donald and Donna—result from the female name being derived from the male name. Society is apparently more tolerant of derivative female names than derivative male names. That's a different kind of sexism, but it's sexism nonetheless.

What's especially noteworthy about the research in this area is that the very strategy the investigators used to rule out an alternative interpretation of their results opened the door to an alternative interpretation! What could be more sensible—more seemingly scientific—than to choose male and female names that were as alike as possible? Who would have thought that doing so would introduce a powerful **artifact**? Research like this serves as a reminder that knowledge is hard won. It also serves as a reminder that selecting the proper comparison is not always as easy as it seems. Should I pair Jack's essay with one supposedly written by Jane or by Joan? Or, in other studies, should I have participants in the control group complete their questionnaires right after they've finished reading the instructions, as those in the experimental group did, or, since the experimental group had more to read, after the same amount of time has passed? Making the right call can be the difference between an experiment that's informative and one that's misleading.

implicit association test (IAT) A technique for revealing nonconscious attitudes toward different stimuli, particularly groups of people.

certain groups can't always be trusted because respondents may not think it's acceptable to express what they really feel, or because what people report verbally is only a part of their stance toward members of other groups. Given that so many forms of prejudice are ambivalent, uncertain, or hidden—even from the self—they're not likely to be revealed through self-report (Crandall & Eshleman, 2003). Social psychologists have therefore used a number of indirect measures of prejudice and stereotyping, two of which we discuss here. (For overviews of a wider set of implicit measurement procedures, see Gawronski & Payne, 2010; Wittenbrink & Schwarz, 2007.)

The Implicit Association Test (IAT) Anthony Greenwald and Mazarin Banaji (1995) have pioneered a technique called the **implicit association test (IAT)** for revealing subtle, nonconscious prejudices, even among those who sincerely believe they are bias-free. Here's how the technique works. A series of words or pictures are presented on a computer screen, and the respondent presses a key with the left hand if the picture or word conforms to one rule and another key with the right hand if it conforms to another rule. You can try a noncomputerized version in **Figure 11.1**. Or you can see whether you hold any implicit

FIGURE 11.1 **You Be the Subject: The Implicit Association Test (IAT)**

First, as you read each word in the column below, tap your left index finger if it is either a female name or a "weak" word, and tap your right index finger if it is either a male name or a "strong" word.

Martha
Vigorous
Jason
Small
David
Powerful
Karen
Delicate
Gloria
Feather
Tony
Mighty
Matthew
Wispy
Rachel
Robust
Amy
Fine
George
Flower
Betsy
Stout
Charlene
Iron

Now repeat the procedure, but as you read each word, tap your left index finger if it is either a female name or a "strong" word, and tap your right index finger if it is either a male name or a "weak" word.

Did you find yourself tapping faster as you read the words the first time or the second?

stereotypes or prejudice toward a variety of groups by taking some of the IATs online at https://implicit.harvard.edu/implicit/research/.

Greenwald and Banaji argued that respondents would be faster to press one key for members of a particular group and words stereotypically associated with that group than to press the same key for members of that group and words that contradict the stereotype associated with that group. It's easy to respond quickly when the category members and the attributes associated with the group are signaled with the same hand rather than different hands.

The same general procedure is used to assess implicit prejudice (rather than stereotyping). In this case, participants press one key for both positive words and photos of people in one group, and another key for both negative words and people in another group. People prejudiced against older adults, for example, should be faster to press the appropriate key when the same key is used for old faces and negative words (because older people are viewed negatively) and slower when the same key is used for old faces and positive words. Participants then repeat the procedure with the pairings of the two groups and positive/negative words switched. A nonconscious prejudice toward older people would be captured by the difference between the average time it takes to respond to old faces/positive words and the average time it takes to respond to old faces/negative words (Nosek, Greenwald, & Banaji, 2005).

Millions of people have taken the IAT online. Among other results, researchers have found that both young and older individuals show a pronounced prejudice in favor of the young over the old, and about two-thirds of white respondents show a strong or moderate prejudice for white over black (Nosek, Banaji, & Greenwald, 2002). In addition, about half of all black respondents also show some prejudice in favor of white faces.

An important question, however, is whether a person's responses on the IAT are predictive of behavior that is more significant than pressing computer keys (Amodio & Devine, 2006; Brendl, Markman, & Messner, 2001; Karpinski & Hilton, 2001). Although the test has its critics (Blanton & Jaccard, 2008; Blanton et al., 2009), there's evidence that IAT responses do correlate with other measures of prejudice (Lane, Banaji, Nosek, & Greenwald, 2007; Rudman & Ashmore, 2007). In one study, participants in a brain-imaging machine viewed pictures of black and white faces. The participants' earlier IAT responses were significantly correlated with heightened neural activity in the amygdala (a brain center associated with fear and with emotional learning) in response to the black faces. Their scores on a more traditional, conscious measure of prejudice, the Modern Racism Scale, were not correlated with this difference in neural activity, suggesting that the IAT assessed an important component of attitudes that participants were unable or unwilling to articulate (Phelps et al., 2000).

In another study, participants interacted with a white experimenter, took the IAT, and then interacted with a black experimenter. The participants' IAT scores, it turns out, predicted the discrepancy between how much they spoke to the white versus the black experimenter, how often they smiled at the white versus the black experimenter, and the number of speech errors and hesitations they exhibited when interacting with the white versus the black experimenter (McConnell & Leibold, 2001).

Priming and Implicit Prejudice Social psychologists have also measured prejudices that individuals might not know they have, or that they may wish to deny,

PRIME

TARGET

dangerous

REAL WORD?

malk

REAL WORD?

Figure 11.2

An Affective Priming Paradigm

If people are faster to identify negative words than positive words after pictures of members of a given group are presented, it would be evidence that they have at least some negative associations to that group.

priming The presentation of information designed to activate a concept (such as a stereotype) and hence make it accessible. A prime is the stimulus presented to activate the concept in question.

by using a number of **priming** (mental activation) procedures (see Chapter 4). The logic is simple. If I show you the word *butter* and then ask you to tell me, as quickly as you can, whether a subsequent string of letters is a word, you'll recognize that *bread* is a word more quickly than you'll recognize that *car* is a word because of your preexisting association between bread and butter. Similarly, if you associate nuns with virtue and charity, you're likely to respond quickly to positive terms (*good, benevolent, trustworthy*) after seeing a picture of a nun. But if you have negative associations to nuns as, say, strict, rigid, or cold, you are likely to respond more quickly to negative terms (*mean, unhappy, unbending*) after seeing a picture of a nun.

As shown in **Figure 11.2**, an implicit measure of prejudice can thus be derived by comparing a person's average reaction time to real and made-up words preceded by faces of members of the target category (compared with "control" trials, in which positive and negative words are preceded by faces of noncategory members). As discussed later in this chapter, numerous studies using these priming methods have shown that people who are sure they aren't prejudiced against blacks nonetheless respond more quickly to negative words preceded by pictures of black faces, and more slowly to positive words preceded by pictures of black faces (Banaji, Hardin, & Rothman, 1993; Bessenoff & Sherman, 2000; Dijksterhuis, Aarts, Bargh, & van Knippenberg, 2000; Dovidio, Kawakami, & Gaertner, 2002; Fazio & Hilden, 2001; Friese, Hofmann, & Schmitt, 2008; Gawronski, Cunningham, LeBel, & Deutsch, 2010). And there's no reason to assume that people are lying when they deny such prejudices: they simply may not have conscious access to many of their attitudes and beliefs.

🔄 LOOKING BACK

In much of today's Western world, prejudice and discrimination are frowned upon. This trend has led to an explicit rejection of prejudiced attitudes that nonetheless is sometimes accompanied by subtle and often nonconscious discriminatory behavior. The schism between what people consciously maintain and how they sometimes feel or act has led to the development of various indirect measures of attitudes toward different groups. These include the implicit association test and priming procedures, which measure the degree to which different groups trigger positive or negative associations.

The Economic Perspective

Not surprisingly, some of the most intense intergroup tensions arise between groups that vie for the same limited resource. Israelis and Palestinians claim ownership of much of the same small strip of land, and, to put it mildly, they have difficulty getting along. Immigrants from Mexico and Central America face some of the harshest discrimination from those U.S. citizens who see them as threats to their own jobs. Philippino, Sri Lankan, and African guest workers in rich Gulf countries like Qatar and the United Arab Emirates have been known to quarrel with one another and to "stick to their own kind."

These observations highlight the core tenets of the economic perspective on prejudice and discrimination. Groups develop prejudices about each other and discriminate against one another when they compete for material resources. Religious groups, racial groups, and cultural groups all stand ready to protect and promote their own interests by lashing out at those they perceive to be threatening them.

Realistic Group Conflict Theory

One version of the economic perspective has been called **realistic group conflict theory** because it acknowledges that groups sometimes confront real conflict over what are essentially economic issues (LeVine & Campbell, 1972). According to this theory, prejudice and discrimination often arise from competition over limited resources. The theory predicts, correctly, that prejudice and discrimination should increase under conditions of economic difficulty, such as recessions and periods of high unemployment (King, Knight, & Hebl, 2010; Krosch & Amodio, 2014; Rodeheffer, Hill, & Lord, 2012). When there is less to go around or when people are afraid of losing what they have, competition intensifies.

The theory also predicts that prejudice and discrimination should be strongest among groups that stand to lose the most from another group's economic advance. For example, working-class white Americans exhibited the most anti-black prejudice in the wake of the Civil Rights Movement (Simpson & Yinger, 1985; Vanneman & Pettigrew, 1972). Blue-collar jobs were most at risk once millions of black Americans were allowed to compete more freely for entry-level manufacturing jobs in companies from which they had previously been excluded.

Realistic group conflict theory also specifies some of the ways group conflict plays out. First of all, a pronounced **ethnocentrism** develops—that is, the other group is vilified and one's own group is glorified. Anyone who has ever played pickup basketball knows this phenomenon well. An opponent whose antics seem intolerable instantly becomes more likable once that person becomes a teammate. More generally, people in the outgroup are often thought of in stereotyped ways and are treated in a manner normally forbidden by one's moral code. At the same time, loyalty to the ingroup intensifies, and a "circle the wagons" mentality develops. For example, in the wake of the 9/11 attacks on the World Trade Center, many people reported that different ethnic and racial groups in the United States seemed to pull together more than they had beforehand. In an experimental investigation of this tendency, telling white students that the attacks were directed at all Americans, regardless of race and class, served to reduce prejudice toward African-Americans (Dovidio et al., 2004).

The Robbers Cave Experiment

A group of researchers explored the ethnocentrism that results from intergroup competition in one of social psychology's classic studies. In 1954, Muzafer Sherif and his colleagues carried out an ambitious experiment far from the confines of the psychology laboratory (Sherif, Harvey, White, Hood, & Sherif, 1961). Twenty-two fifth-grade boys were taken to Robbers Cave State Park in southeastern Oklahoma (so named because the outlaws Belle Starr and Jesse James supposedly hid there). The boys had signed up for a two-and-a-half-week

realistic group conflict theory A theory that group conflict, prejudice, and discrimination are likely to arise over competition between groups for limited resources.

ethnocentrism Glorifying one's own group while vilifying other groups.

summer camp experience that, unbeknownst to them, was also a study of intergroup relationships. The research team spent over 300 hours screening boys from the Oklahoma City area to find 22 who were unexceptional in nearly every respect: none had problems in school, all were from intact, middle-class families, and there were no notable ethnic group differences among them. The boys, none of whom knew each other beforehand, were divided into two groups of 11 and taken to separate areas of the park. Neither group even knew of the other's existence—initially.

Competition and Intergroup Conflict In the first phase of the experiment, the two groups independently engaged in activities designed to foster group unity (pitching tents, preparing meals) and took part in such common camp activities as playing baseball, swimming, and putting on skits. Cohesion developed within each group, and the boys came up with names for their groups: the Eagles and the Rattlers. A consistent hierarchical structure also emerged within each group: the "effective initiators"—those who made the most suggestions the others accepted—were rated most popular.

In the second phase, the Eagles and Rattlers were brought together for a tournament. Each member of the winning team would receive a medal and a highly coveted pocket knife (a reward researchers would certainly not hand out to young boys today). Members of the losing team would get nothing. The tournament lasted 5 days and consisted of such activities as baseball, touch football, tug-of-war, cabin inspections, and a treasure hunt. The competitive nature of the tournament was designed to encourage each group to see the other as an impediment to the fulfillment of its own goals and hence as a foe. And that's exactly what happened.

From the very first competitive encounter, and with steadily increasing frequency throughout the tournament, the two groups hurled insults at each other, calling those in the other group "bums," "cowards," "stinkers," and so on. Although such terms may be tame by today's trash-talking standards, they are clearly not terms of endearment, and they differ markedly from the self-glorifying and congratulatory comments the boys made about members of their own group. Expressions of intergroup hostility, moreover, weren't limited to

Competition in the Robbers Cave Experiment
Two groups of fifth-graders participated in a study that demonstrated intergroup competition and cooperation. (A) During an early phase of the study, the two groups competed against one another, like here in this tug-of-war contest. (B) This competition led to numerous acts of aggression—they raided each other's cabins, called one another names, and stole things from one another, as shown here with the Rattlers showing off a pair of pants they stole from a member of the Eagles.

SOURCE: Adapted from Sherif et al., 1961.

Cooperation in the Robbers Cave Experiment
To study ways of diminishing intergroup conflict, Sherif and his research team engineered a number of crises that could be overcome only if the two groups worked together. (A) Here the boys pulled a stalled truck, something that could be done only if everyone pitched in. (B) Working together on these superordinate goals led the two groups of boys to set aside their differences and become friends.

SOURCE: Adapted from Sherif et al., 1961.

words. The Eagles captured and burned the Rattlers' flag, which naturally led to a retaliatory theft of the Eagles' flag. Food fights broke out in the dining area, they raided each other's cabins, and issued challenges to engage in physical fights.

It's particularly interesting to note how the internal dynamics of the two groups changed as they became locked into this competitive struggle. Boys who were either athletically gifted or who advocated a more aggressive stance toward the other group tended to gain in popularity. The initial leader of the Eagles, for example, had neither of these characteristics, and he was essentially deposed by someone who was more athletic and more of a firebrand.

More contemporary research has provided additional evidence that people tend to value toughness in a leader during periods of conflict with other groups. In one study, a composite image of a face constructed by averaging the photos of several individuals was then morphed to make it more masculine or more feminine. When asked which person depicted in the two morphed images they'd prefer as a leader "in a time of peace," the majority opted for the feminized face. But when asked who they'd prefer "in a time of war," their preferences shifted to the masculinized face (Little, Burris, Jones, & Roberts, 2007). In another study, participants expressed a preference for female leaders when experiencing conflict within their group, but preferred male leaders when experiencing conflict with another group (Van Vugt & Spisak, 2008).

Reducing Intergroup Conflict through Superordinate Goals The third and final part of the experiment is in many respects the most important, because it addressed ways to reduce the conflict between the two groups. On seven occasions over the next 2 days, the two groups were simply brought together in various noncompetitive settings to see whether their hostility would dissipate. It did not. Simple contact between the two groups just led to more name calling, jeering, food fights, and insults.

Given that simple noncompetitive contact failed to reduce intergroup friction, the investigators contrived to confront the boys with a number of crises that

superordinate goal A goal that transcends the interests of any one group and can be achieved more readily by two or more groups working together.

could be resolved only through the cooperative efforts of both groups. For example, the water supply to the camp was disrupted, and the entire length of pipe from the reservoir to the campgrounds had to be inspected to find the source of the problem—a task made much more manageable if the boys in both groups were assigned to inspect different segments of the line. Also, a truck carrying supplies for a campout at a distant area of the park mysteriously "broke down." How to get it running again? The investigators left a large section of rope near the truck, hoping the boys might try to pull the truck to get it started. One of the boys said, "Let's get our tug-of-war rope and have a tug-of-war against the truck." In doing so, members of both groups intermingled throughout the length of rope and pulled it together.

Relations between the two groups quickly showed the effects of these **superordinate goals**—goals that could not be achieved by either group alone but could be accomplished by both working together. Name calling abruptly dropped off and friendships between members of the two groups developed. When the study was completed, the boys insisted that everyone return to Oklahoma City on the same bus rather than on the separate buses by which they had arrived. And when the bus pulled over at a roadside diner, the group that had won $5 in the tournament competition—the Rattlers—decided to spend their money on malted milks for everyone, Eagles included. The hostility produced by 5 days of competition was erased by the joint pursuit of common goals. In short, a happy ending.

The Robbers Cave experiment offers several important lessons. One is that neither differences in background nor differences in appearance nor prior histories of conflict are necessary for intergroup hostility to develop. All that's required is that two groups enter into competition for goals that only one can achieve. Another lesson is that competition against outsiders often increases group cohesion. This tendency is often exploited by political demagogues who invoke the specter of outside enemies to try to stamp out dissension or deflect attention from problems or conflict within the group itself. The final lesson points to how intergroup conflict can be diminished. To reduce the hostility that exists between certain groups, policy makers should think of ways to get them to work together to fulfill common goals. Simply putting adversaries together "to get to know one another better" is usually not enough (Bettencourt, Brewer, Croak, & Miller, 1992; Brewer & Miller, 1988; Stephan & Stephan, 1996; Wilder, 1986). It's the pursuit of superordinate goals that keeps everyone's eyes on the prize and away from troublesome subgroup distinctions.

Evaluating the Economic Perspective

The economic perspective on stereotyping, prejudice, and discrimination "works" in the sense that it fits nicely with what we see around us as the successes and failures of intergroup relationships. Consider race and ethnic relations in the United States and the effort to build harmonious relationships between groups with long histories of conflict and suspicion. Where have efforts toward integration been most successful? Many analysts cite the integration of African-Americans, Hispanic-Americans, Native Americans, and whites in the military (as well as many white subgroups that have not always looked on one another favorably, such as Irish, Italians, Slavs, Jews, and Catholics).

The success of integration in the military makes perfect sense in light of the lessons learned from the Robbers Cave experiment. Different ethnic and

religious groups in the military are in the equivalent of phase 3 of the Robbers Cave experiment. Their whole purpose is to be ready to defend the United States against a common outside enemy. They have to engage in cooperative, interdependent action to accomplish shared goals—precisely the set of circumstances that brought about healthy intergroup functioning in the Robbers Cave experiment. In such circumstances, the group or category to which a person belongs recedes in importance, and what the person can contribute to the joint effort becomes more prominent (Gaertner, Mann, Dovidio, Murrell, & Pomare, 1990; Gaertner, Murrell, & Dovidio, 1989; Miller & Brewer, 1986).

What are the implications for race and ethnic relations on college campuses? For many students, minorities and majority alike, the college years are the first time they've had close and sustained contact with members of other ethnic groups. How well does it work? The first thing to note is that the conditions of intergroup contact are not as favorable in the classroom as they are on the battlefield. Although students will assist their close friends to help them achieve higher grades, rarely do students feel a strong cooperative bond with their classmates in general. Few students ask themselves, "Is there anything I can do to increase the mean grade of everyone else in the class?" Rather, the common reliance on curved grading can encourage a competitive struggle of "all against all," in which another student's triumph is seen as a threat to one's own grade.

Moreover, it's quite common to see college students segregate themselves almost exclusively with other members of their own race or ethnic group in their choice of residence, dining hall, and even fields of study. Countless undergraduates, faculty members, and administrators have struggled with efforts to curtail this tendency for students of different races or ethnic origins to inhabit different niches in the university and instead to develop more connections across ethnic and racial lines. To be sure, many students—perhaps most—from different ethnic groups do mix on college campuses, and integration attempts have generally been a great success. Nevertheless, integration efforts at universities may have lagged behind those in the military—a result that a close look at the Robbers Cave experiment would lead us to expect (**Box 11.2**).

BOX 11.2 **FOCUS ON *EDUCATION***

The "Jigsaw" Classroom

If the competitive atmosphere of most classrooms can increase racial and ethnic tensions in integrated schools, what would happen if the classroom were made less competitive? Might a more cooperative learning environment improve academic performance and intergroup relations in integrated settings?

Social psychologist Elliot Aronson developed a cooperative learning procedure to find out. When the public school system in Austin, Texas, was integrated in 1971, the transition was not smooth. A disturbing number of physical confrontations took place between black, Hispanic, and white children, and the atmosphere in the classrooms was not what proponents of integration had hoped it would be. The superintendent of schools invited Aronson to do something to improve matters. Mindful of the lessons of the Robbers Cave experiment, Aronson wanted to institute procedures that would unite students in the common goal of mastering a body of material, rather than competing for the highest grades and the teachers' attention. He and his colleagues came up with something called the "jigsaw" classroom

(Aronson, Stephan, Sikes, Blaney, & Snapp, 1978; Aronson & Thibodeau, 1992).

In the jigsaw classroom, students are divided into small groups of about six each. Every effort is made to balance the groups in terms of ethnicity, gender, ability level, leadership, and so on. The material on a given topic is then divided into six parts, and each student is required to master one part (and only one part) and teach it to the others. For a lesson on Barack Obama, for example, one student might be responsible for Obama's early years in Hawaii and Indonesia, another for his time as a law professor at the University of Chicago, a third for his accomplishments in the Illinois state legislature, a fourth for his historic presidential election campaign, and a fifth for his White House years. By dividing the material in this way, Aronson ensured that no student could learn the entire lesson without help from peers. Each student's material must, like the pieces of a jigsaw puzzle, fit together with all the others for everyone in the group to learn the whole lesson.

The students' dependence on one another dampens the usual competitive

atmosphere and encourages them to work cooperatively toward a common goal. To the extent that the groups are ethnically heterogeneous, members of different ethnic groups gain the experience of working together as individuals rather than as representatives of particular ethnic groups.

The effectiveness of this approach has been assessed in field experiments comparing students in jigsaw classrooms with those in classrooms that teach the same material in the usual fashion. These studies have typically found that students in the jigsaw classrooms like school more and develop more positive attitudes toward different ethnic groups than students in traditional classrooms (Slavin, 1995).

Thus, the lessons learned from the Robbers Cave experiment—that intergroup hostility can be diminished by cooperative activity directed at a superordinate goal—have profound practical significance. A simple classroom procedure derived from these lessons— one that can be used in conjunction with traditional, more individualistic classroom exercises—can both boost academic performance and facilitate positive racial and ethnic relationships.

🔄 LOOKING BACK

Consistent with the economic perspective, prejudice can arise from realistic conflict between groups over limited resources. The Robbers Cave experiment serves as an instructive model of this sort of conflict, showing how otherwise friendly boys could turn into enemies when placed in groups competing for limited resources. The hostility between the groups evaporated when they had to cooperate to achieve superordinate goals of value to both groups. This result has considerable implications for managing potentially troublesome intergroup relationships worldwide.

The Motivational Perspective

minimal group paradigm An experimental paradigm in which researchers create groups based on arbitrary and seemingly meaningless criteria and then examine how the members of these "minimal groups" are inclined to behave toward one another.

Hostility between groups, it turns out, can develop even in the absence of competition. In the Robbers Cave experiment, there were signs of increased ingroup solidarity when the two groups first learned of each others' existence—*before* they were engaged in, or even knew about, the organized competition. Midway through phase 1 of the experiment, when the two groups were still being kept apart, they were allowed to get within earshot of one another. The mere fact that another group existed made each set of boys take their group membership much more seriously. Both groups quickly became territorial, referring to the baseball field as "*our* diamond" rather than "the diamond" and a favorite swimming spot as "*our* swimming hole." The Eagles, who beforehand had not found it necessary to have a group name, quickly settled on the name Eagles once they learned there was another group of boys in the park. Furthermore, when the two groups learned about each other's existence, both wanted to "run them off" and "challenge them."

The fact that these developments took place before any competition had been arranged indicates that intergroup hostility can develop merely because another group exists. The existence of group boundaries among any collection of individuals, then, can be sufficient to initiate group discrimination. The motivational processes that lead to this sort of hostility have been explored in a telling research paradigm.

The Minimal Group Paradigm

People's readiness to adopt an "us versus them" mentality has been extensively documented in experiments using the **minimal group paradigm** pioneered by Henri Tajfel (Tajfel & Billig, 1974; Tajfel, Billig, Bundy, & Flament, 1971; see also Ashburn-Nardo, Voils, & Monteith, 2001; Brewer, 1979; Yamagishi, Mifune, Liu, & Pauling, 2008). Tajfel's lifelong interest in intergroup dynamics can be traced to his own experiences as a young man. Because of restrictions on Jewish higher education in Poland, he emigrated to France to study at the Sorbonne. When World War II broke out, he volunteered to serve in the French Army, which he did for a year before being taken prisoner. He spent the rest of the war in a German prisoner of war camp, fully aware that if his captors had thought of him as Jewish rather than French he would have shared the same fate as everyone else in his immediate family, none of whom survived the war.

Tajfel created groups based on arbitrary and seemingly meaningless criteria and then examined how the members of these "minimal groups" behave toward one another. The participants first perform a rather trivial task and are then divided into two groups, ostensibly on the basis of their responses. In one such task, for example, participants estimate the number of dots projected briefly on a screen. Some participants are told they belong to a group of "overestimators," and others that they belong to a group of "underestimators." In reality, the participants are randomly assigned to the groups, and they learn only that they are assigned to a particular group; they never learn who else is in their group or who is in the other group. Thus, what it means to be part of a "group" is boiled down to the bare minimum.

After learning their group membership, the participants are taken to separate cubicles and asked to assign points, redeemable for money, to successive pairs of their fellow participants. They don't know the individual identity of those to whom they're awarding points; they know only a participant's "code number" and group membership. Participants assign points to, say, "Number 4 of the

TABLE 11.1	AWARDING POINTS IN THE MINIMAL GROUP PARADIGM									
Ingroup	18	17	16	15	14	13	21	11	10	9
Outgroup	3	5	7	9	11	13	15	17	19	21

overestimator group" and "Number 2 of the underestimator group." The options from which participants can choose allow the investigators to determine whether participants seem most interested in assigning points equally to ingroup and outgroup members, in maximizing the total payout regardless of group membership, or in maximizing the relative advantage of what's given to the ingroup.

Table 11.1 provides an example. In some minimal group experiments, participants can choose from an array of the number of points for two participants, one from the ingroup and one from the outgroup. Someone who chooses 13 and 13 would appear to be interested in equality; someone who chooses 9 for the ingroup member and 21 for the outgroup member would appear to be interested in handing out the greatest number of points overall; someone who chooses 18 for the ingroup member and 3 for the outgroup member would appear to be interested in maximizing the relative advantage of the ingroup.

Numerous experiments have shown that a majority of participants are interested more in maximizing the *relative* gain for members of their ingroup than in maximizing the absolute gain for their ingroup. A moment's reflection reveals just how extraordinary this is. The participants don't know who the ingroup and outgroup members are; the points awarded are never for themselves; and, of course, the basis for establishing the two groups is utterly trivial. Yet participants still exhibit a tendency to favor their minimal ingroup. In fact, they're willing to do so at a cost to the ingroup, which earns fewer points than if the focus were on absolute gain rather than "beating" the other group. The ingroup favoritism that emerges in this context demonstrates how easily we slip into thinking in terms of *us* versus *them* (Brewer & Brown, 1998). And if history has taught us anything, it is that the us/them distinction, once formed, can have enormous—and enormously unfortunate—implications.

Social Identity Theory

Studies using the minimal group paradigm have shown the pervasiveness and tenacity of ingroup favoritism, but what does it have to do with the motivational perspective on prejudice? Might it not reflect a purely cognitive tendency to divide the world into categories of *us* and *them*? Just as all children quickly learn to distinguish the self from all others, might we not all learn to distinguish "my side" from the "other side"?

Much of the psychology behind ingroup favoritism might very well reflect cognitive influences. The us/them distinction may be one of the basic cuts people make in dividing up and organizing the world. Still, the ingroup favoritism observed in the minimal group situation can't be the product of cognition alone. For that we need a motivational theory—a theory to explain why, once the us/them distinction is made, *we* are treated better than *they*. Some divisions into *us* and *them* have the kind of material or economic implications discussed earlier, and those implications often provide motivation enough for people to treat ingroup members better than outgroup members. But not all motivations are economic, and certainly no meaningful economic implications are riding on the

"Cruelty and intolerance to those who do not belong to it are natural to every religion."
—SIGMUND FREUD

Social Identity Theory

People derive their sense of identity not only from their individual accomplishments but also from those of the groups to which they belong. (A) These delegates at the U.S. Republican National Convention identify with the Republican Party. (B) These individuals derive part of their identity from belonging to the community of surfers.

ingroup/outgroup partition in the minimal group paradigm. To explain that sort of ingroup favoritism, a much broader motivational perspective is needed.

The most widely recognized theory that attempts to explain the ubiquity of ingroup favoritism, even when the ingroups and outgroups do not differ in any significant way, is **social identity theory**, which is based on the fact that people's self-esteem derives not only from their personal identity and accomplishments, but also from the status and accomplishments of the various groups to which they belong (Tajfel & Turner, 1979; see also Spears, 2011; Stroebe, Spears, & Lodewijkx, 2007). Being "an American" is an element of the self-concept of most Americans, and with it comes the pride associated with, say, the Bill of Rights, U.S. economic and military clout, and the accomplishments of American scientists, industrialists, athletes, and entertainers. With it, too, comes the shame associated with slavery in the United States and the treatment of Native Americans. Similarly, being a gang member, a professor, a film buff, or a surfer means that our identity and esteem are intimately tied up with the triumphs and shortcomings of our fellow gang members, academics, film buffs, and surfers.

Boosting the Status of the Ingroup Because our self-esteem is based in part on the status of the various groups to which we belong, we may be tempted to boost the status and fortunes of those groups and their members. Therein lies a powerful cause of ingroup favoritism: doing whatever we can to feel better about the ingroup leads us to feel better about ourselves. Evidence supporting this idea comes from studies that have assessed participants' self-esteem after they've had an opportunity to exhibit ingroup favoritism in the minimal group situation. As expected, those who had been allowed to do this had higher self-esteem than those who hadn't had a chance to boost their own group at the expense of another (Lemyre & Smith, 1985; Oakes & Turner, 1980). Other research has shown that people who take particularly strong pride in their group affiliations are more prone to ingroup favoritism when placed in a minimal group situation (Crocker & Luhtanen, 1990). And people who are highly identified with a particular group react to criticism of the group as if it were criticism of the self (McCoy & Major, 2003).

Basking in Reflected Glory Social identity theory also receives support from the everyday observation that people go to great lengths to announce their affiliation

social identity theory The idea that a person's self-concept and self-esteem derive not only from personal identity and accomplishments, but also from the status and accomplishments of the various groups to which the person belongs.

Basking in Reflected Glory
Sports fans, like these Ohio State students, passionately identify with their team and feel joyous when the team wins and dejected when it loses. To connect themselves to the team, fans often wear team jerseys to the game, and even to class or work the next day if the team wins.

"Victory finds a hundred fathers but defeat is an orphan."

—COUNT GALEAZZO CIANO,
THE CIANO DIARIES (1945)

basking in reflected glory Taking pride in the accomplishments of other people in one's group, such as when sports fans identify with a winning team.

with a certain group when that group is doing well. Sports fans, for example, often chant, "We're number 1!" after a team victory. But what does "*We're* number 1" mean? It's a rare fan indeed who does anything other than cheer their team or heckle referees and opposing players. Yet countless fans want to be connected to the effort when the outcome is a victory. After a loss, not so much.

Robert Cialdini refers to this tendency to identify with a winning team as **basking in reflected glory**. He investigated the tendency by recording how often students wore their school sweatshirts and T-shirts to class after their football team had just won or lost a game. As expected, students wore the school colors significantly more often following victory than after defeat. Cialdini and his colleagues also tabulated students' use of first-person versus third-person references. It's no surprise to learn that, as a general rule, "we" won, whereas "they" lost (Cialdini et al., 1976). As social identity theory predicts, the triumphs and failings of the groups with which we affiliate affect our self-esteem—even when the group is simply a favorite sports team (Hirt, Zillman, Erikson, & Kennedy, 1992). We therefore have an incentive to identify with such groups when they do well but to distance ourselves from them when they lose.

Denigrating Outgroups to Bolster Self-Esteem To bask in reflected glory is to use ingroup identity to enhance self-esteem. But does denigrating outgroups boost self-esteem? Does criticizing another group make people feel better about their own group—and hence themselves? Alas, it can have this effect. Several studies have shown how stereotyping and prejudice can strengthen or maintain self-esteem in this way.

In one study, researchers threatened the self-esteem of half the participants by telling them they had just performed poorly on an intelligence test; the other half were told they had done well (Fein & Spencer, 1997). The participants then watched a videotaped interview of a job applicant. The video made it clear to half the participants (none of whom was Jewish) that the candidate was Jewish, but not to the other half. Participants later rated the job candidate (**Figure 11.3**). Participants whose self-esteem had been threatened rated the candidate negatively

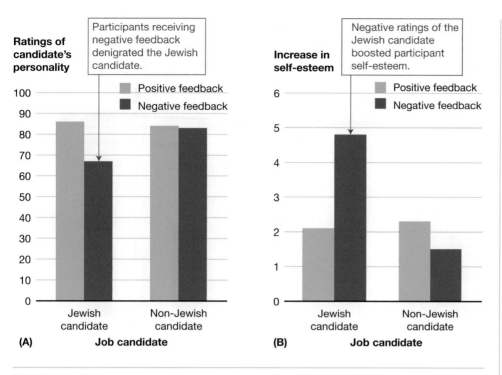

Ratings of candidate's personality

Participants receiving negative feedback denigrated the Jewish candidate.

- Positive feedback
- Negative feedback

(A) Job candidate

Increase in self-esteem

Negative ratings of the Jewish candidate boosted participant self-esteem.

- Positive feedback
- Negative feedback

(B) Job candidate

SOURCE: Adapted from Fein & Spencer, 1997.

Figure 11.3
Bolstering Self-Esteem
This graph shows the average ratings of a job candidate's personality and the increase in raters' self-esteem, depending on whether or not the candidate was identified as Jewish and whether the rater had earlier received positive or negative feedback. The results demonstrate that feeling down on oneself can make a person more likely to denigrate outgroups, and receive a boost in self-esteem from doing so.

if they thought she was Jewish; participants whose self-esteem was not threatened did not (Figure 11.3A). In addition, the participants whose self-esteem had been threatened and had "taken it out" on the Jewish candidate experienced an increase in their self-esteem from the time they received feedback on the IQ test to the end of the experiment (Figure 11.3B). It appears that denigrating members of outgroups can indeed bolster self-esteem.

Lisa Sinclair and Ziva Kunda explored a related way that outgroups are strategically used to bolster or enhance self-esteem. In this study, (non-black) participants were either praised or criticized by a white or black doctor (Sinclair & Kunda, 1999). The investigators predicted that the participants would be motivated to cling to the praise they received but to challenge the criticism, and that they'd use the race of their evaluator to help them do so. In particular, they thought participants who received praise from a black doctor would tend to think of him more as a doctor (a prestigious occupation) than as a black man, whereas those who were criticized by a black doctor would tend to think of him more as a black man than as a doctor.

The participants performed a lexical decision task right after getting feedback from the doctor (Sinclar & Kunda, 1999). The researchers flashed a series of words and nonwords on a computer screen and had the participants indicate, as fast as they could, whether each string of letters was a word. Some of the words were related to the medical profession (for example, *hospital, prescription*) and some were associated with common stereotypes of blacks (*rap, jazz*). Sinclair and Kunda reasoned that if the participants were thinking of their evaluator primarily as a doctor, they would recognize the medical words faster; if they were thinking of their evaluator primarily as a black man, they would recognize the words related to the black stereotype faster.

As **Figure 11.4** shows, that's exactly what happened. Participants were particularly fast at recognizing words associated with the black stereotype when they'd been criticized by the black doctor, and slow to recognize those words when

Alternative Construals
Do you see this person mainly as a man? A doctor? A black man? A black doctor? How you see him may depend on how each construal contributes to your self-esteem.

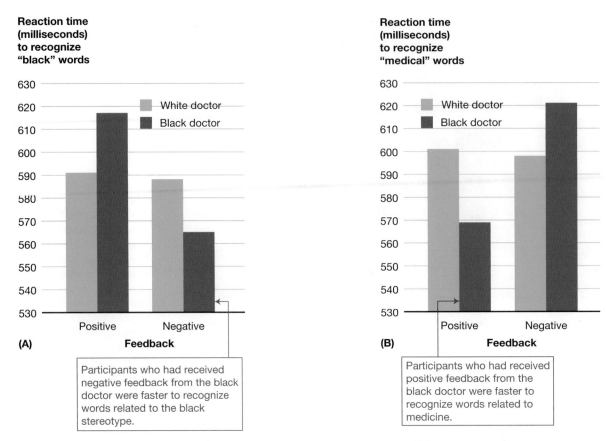

Reaction time (milliseconds) to recognize "black" words

630
620 — White doctor
610 — Black doctor
600
590
580
570
560
550
540
530

Positive | Negative

(A) | **Feedback**

Participants who had received negative feedback from the black doctor were faster to recognize words related to the black stereotype.

Reaction time (milliseconds) to recognize "medical" words

630
620 — White doctor
610 — Black doctor
600
590
580
570
560
550
540
530

Positive | Negative

(B) | **Feedback**

Participants who had received positive feedback from the black doctor were faster to recognize words related to medicine.

Figure 11.4
Self-Esteem and Racial Prejudice

Participants were either praised or criticized by a white or black doctor. Reaction times to "black" words and "medical" words after criticism or praise by white doctors were virtually the same, but this was not true for reaction times after criticism or praise by black doctors.

SOURCE: Adapted from Sinclair & Kunda, 1999.

praised by the black doctor (Figure 11.4A). When he criticized them, in other words, participants saw him as a black man—something they didn't do as readily when he praised them. The reverse was true for the medical words (Figure 11.4B). Participants were fast at recognizing medical words when they'd been praised by the black doctor, and slow to do so when criticized by the black doctor.

Evaluating the Motivational Perspective

According to the motivational perspective, stereotyping, prejudice, and discrimination serve motivational purposes, like helping people boost or maintain their self-esteem. The perspective builds on two important elements of the human condition. First, people readily draw the "us versus them" distinction. Second, people's identities are intimately connected to the groups to which they belong, so they tend to favor their own groups at the expense of all sorts of outgroups. Social psychologist Roger Brown once likened conflict between groups to "a sturdy three-legged stool" because it rests on the pervasive human tendencies to glorify the ingroup, to form societies in which there are unequal distributions of resources, and to stereotype members of different groups (Brown, 1986, p. 533). Both the motivational and the economic perspectives have shown how readily people will reward their own and penalize outsiders—leg number 1. Both perspectives also speak to how an unequal distribution of resources can sow the seeds of intergroup hostility—leg number 2. We now consider the cognitive perspective to better understand stereotyping—leg number 3.

⊙ LOOKING BACK

Consistent with the motivational perspective on stereotyping, prejudice, and discrimination, people are inclined to favor ingroups over outgroups, even when the basis of group membership is trivial. Part of the reason is that people identify with their groups and feel good about themselves when they feel good about their groups. Threats to self-esteem also result in the denigration of outgroup members.

The Cognitive Perspective

From the cognitive perspective, stereotyping is inevitable. It stems from the ubiquity and necessity of categorization. People categorize nearly everything, both natural (bodies of water—creek, stream, river) and artificial (cars—sports car, sedan, SUV). Even color, which arises from continuous variation in electromagnetic wavelength, is perceived as distinct categories. Moreover, all of this categorizing comes easily; it's what our schemas about bodies of water, cars, and colors allow us to do rather effortlessly (see Chapter 4).

Categorizing, in other words, has a purpose: it simplifies the task of taking in and processing the incredible volume of stimuli surrounding us. The American journalist Walter Lippmann, who is credited with coining the term *stereotype*, stated:

> The real environment is altogether too big, too complex, and too fleeting, for direct acquaintance. We are not equipped to deal with so much subtlety, so much variety, so many permutations and combinations. . . . We have to reconstruct it on a simpler model before we can manage with it. (Lippmann, 1922, p. 16)

Stereotypes provide us with those simpler models that allow us to deal with the "great blooming, buzzing confusion of reality" (Lippmann, 1922, p. 96). More generally, according to the cognitive perspective, stereotypes are a natural result of the way our brains are wired to store and process information.

Stereotypes and the Conservation of Cognitive Resources

If stereotypes are useful schemas that enable people to process information efficiently, we should be inclined to use them when we're overloaded, tired, or mentally taxed in some way—in other words, when we're in need of a shortcut. Several experiments have demonstrated exactly that (Kim & Baron, 1988; Macrae & Bodenhausen, 2000; Macrae, Hewstone, & Griffiths, 1993; Pratto & Bargh, 1991; Stangor & Duan, 1991; Wigboldus, Sherman, Franzese, & van Knippenberg, 2004).

In one intriguing study, participants were more likely to invoke stereotypes when tested at the low point of their circadian rhythm. "Morning people," when tested at night, tended to invoke a common stereotype and conclude, for example, that a person charged with cheating on an exam was guilty if he was an athlete. "Night people," when tested in the morning, were more inclined to conclude that a person charged with dealing drugs was guilty if he was black (Bodenhausen, 1990). Thus, people are more likely to fall back on stereotypes when they lack mental energy.

If the use of stereotypes conserves intellectual energy, then encoding information using stereotypes should furnish extra cognitive resources that can be applied to other mental tasks. In one test of this idea, participants performed two tasks simultaneously (Macrae, Milne, & Bodenhausen, 1994). On one task, they formed an impression of a (hypothetical) person described by a number of trait terms presented on a computer screen (for example, *rebellious, dangerous, aggressive*). The other task involved monitoring a tape-recorded lecture on the economy and geography of Indonesia. For half the participants, the trait terms were accompanied by an applicable stereotype (such as skinhead); for the other half, the trait terms were presented alone. The key questions were whether the applicable stereotype would facilitate participants' later recall of the trait terms they'd seen, and, more importantly, whether it would also release extra cognitive resources that could be devoted to the lecture on Indonesia. The participants were given a brief quiz on the contents of the lecture ("What is Indonesia's official religion?" "Jakarta is found on which coast of Java?").

As the experimenters anticipated, the use of stereotypes eased the participants' burden in the first task and thereby facilitated their performance on the second (**Figure 11.5**). Those given a stereotype not only remembered the relevant trait information better but also performed better on the surprise multiple-choice test on Indonesia (Macrae, Milne, & Bodenhausen, 1994).

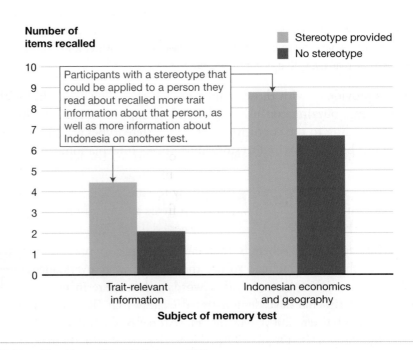

Figure 11.5
Conserving Cognitive Resources
Invoking stereotypes facilitates the recall of stereotypically consistent information, thereby conserving mental energy for use in performing other tasks.

SOURCE: Adapted from Macrae, Milne, & Bodenhausen, 1994.

Construal Processes and Biased Assessments

Relying on stereotypes can save time and effort, but it can also lead to mistaken impressions and unfair judgments about individuals. After all, not every member of a given category conforms to the stereotype.

Social psychologists have produced countless demonstrations of this point. A simple and particularly unsettling example comes from an early study by John Darley and P. H. Gross (1983). They had students watch a videotape of a fourth-grader named Hannah. One version of the video reported that Hannah's parents were professionals and showed her playing in an obviously upper-middle-class area. Another version reported that Hannah's parents were working-class and showed her playing in a rundown environment.

The next part of the video showed Hannah answering academic achievement questions involving math, science, and reading. Her performance was ambiguous; she answered some difficult questions well but also seemed distracted and flubbed easier questions. The researchers asked the students how well they thought Hannah would perform in relation to her classmates. Those who saw an upper-middle-class Hannah estimated she would perform better than average, while those who saw working-class Hannah assumed she would perform worse than average.

It's sad but true that predictions about Hannah will be more accurate if her social class is known. The reason is that on average, upper-middle-class children perform better in school than working-class children. Therefore, given an ambiguous performance by a child, we might reasonably anticipate her long-term academic success would be greater if she's upper-middle-class than if she's working-class. Whenever the direct evidence about a person or object is unclear or ambiguous, background knowledge in the form of a schema or stereotype can increase the accuracy of judgments to the extent that the stereotype has some genuine basis in reality.

The much sadder fact is that working-class Hannah starts life with two strikes against her. People will expect and demand less of her, and will perceive a given performance as worse than if she were upper-middle-class. Moreover, the mistaken impression about Hannah will tend to reinforce the stereotype that working-class people are less academically able than middle-class children.

Biased information processing is especially pernicious when the stereotypes on which it's based are completely lacking in validity. If people suspect—because of something they've been told, or the implications of a joke they heard, or a misinterpreted statistic—that a particular group of people might differ from other groups in some way, it's shockingly easy to construe information about an individual in a way that confirms and solidifies the suspicion. The stereotype is then strengthened due to "confirmation" by the biased observations. A vicious cycle indeed.

The cognitive perspective on stereotyping does more than demonstrate that stereotypes can bias our perceptions of others. Cognitively oriented social psychologists also seek to identify the precise construal processes that give rise to such distortions. What kind of faulty reasoning leads to inaccurate stereotypes? How, in other words, might a well-meaning person, lacking any

"Why is it we never focus on the things that unite us, like falafel?"

malice, nonetheless come to hold the kind of troublesome and inaccurate convictions that are at the heart of some of the most troubling stereotypes? How might such beliefs arise from cognitive processing alone? To answer these questions, we need to consider the kinds of construal processes that are invoked once individuals are known to belong to particular groups.

Accentuation of Ingroup Similarity and Outgroup Difference There is an apocryphal story about a man who owned a farm near the Russian–Polish border. Over the course of European history, the farm had gone back and forth under the rule of each country many times. Indeed, after the most recent boundary was drawn, the farmer was uncertain whether he lived in Poland or Russia. To settle the issue, the farmer saved up to have a proper survey conducted and his national identity established. When the survey was finished, the farmer, scarcely able to contain his anticipation, asked, "Well, do I live in Russia or Poland?" The surveyor replied that although remarkably near the border, the entire farm was located in Poland. "Good," the farmer stated, "I don't think I could take those harsh Russian winters."

The point of the story, of course, is that although an arbitrary national border can't affect the weather at a fixed location, arbitrary categorical boundaries can have significant effects on the way we perceive things. Indeed, research has shown that merely dividing a continuous distribution into two groups leads people to see less variability within each group and more variability between the two groups. In one study, participants were divided into two "minimal" groups. They then filled out an attitude questionnaire twice—once to record their own attitudes and once to record how they thought another ingroup or outgroup member might respond. Participants consistently assumed their beliefs were more similar to those of another ingroup member than to those of an outgroup member, even though the basis of group membership was arbitrary (Allen & Wilder, 1979; Wilder, 1984).

The remarkable thing about this result is *not* that people assume more similarity between members within a group than across groups. That only makes sense. After all, why categorize members into groups in the first place if the members of each group are not, on average, more similar to one another than they are to the members of the other group? What *is* remarkable, and potentially troubling, is that people make such assumptions even when the groups are formed arbitrarily, or on the basis of a dimension (such as skin color, age, or body weight) that may have no bearing on the attitude or behavior under consideration. In these circumstances, the pure act of categorization distorts judgment. Also, the more people think of outgroup members as homogeneous, the more likely they are to spout prejudices about them and discriminate against them (Brauer & Er-rafiy, 2011).

The Outgroup Homogeneity Effect Think of a group to which you do not belong: Islamic fundamentalists, reality TV participants, heroin addicts, Hummer owners. It's tempting to think of such groups as a unitary *they*. We tend to call to mind an image of such groups in which all members think alike, act alike, even look alike. We also tend to assume that an outgroup's within-group similarity is much stronger than that of our ingroup. *They* all think, act, and look alike. *We*, on the other hand, are a remarkably varied lot. This tendency is called the **outgroup homogeneity effect**.

***They* Are All Alike (Unlike Us)**
We often think of outgroups as having members who all think, dress, and act alike. We expect to see older adults in a lounge chair or playing golf, cards, or bingo—not riding a skateboard like Doc Ball. This legendary surfer from Southern California surfed and skateboarded regularly until his death at age 94 in 2001.

One study examined the outgroup homogeneity effect by showing Princeton and Rutgers students a series of videos of other students making decisions, such as whether to listen to rock or classical music, or whether to wait alone or with other participants during a break in an experiment (Quattrone & Jones, 1980). Half the participants were told the students on the video were from Princeton; half were told they were from Rutgers. Afterwards, the participants estimated the percentage of students at the same university who would make the same choices as those they had seen on the video. The results indicated that the participants assumed more similarity among outgroup members than among ingroup members. Princeton students who thought they had witnessed the behavior of a Rutgers student were willing to generalize that behavior to other Rutgers students. In contrast, Princeton students who thought they had witnessed the behavior of a Princeton student were less willing to generalize. The opposite was true for Rutgers students. People see more variability of habit and opinion among members of the ingroup than they do among members of the outgroup (Quattrone & Jones, 1980; see also Bartsch, Judd, Louw, Park, & Ryan, 1997; Linville, 1982; Linville, Fischer, & Salovey, 1989; Ostrom & Sedikides, 1992; Park & Judd, 1990; Park & Rothbart, 1982; Read & Urada, 2003; Simon et al., 1990).

It's easy to understand why the outgroup homogeneity effect occurs. For one thing, we typically have much more contact with fellow members of an ingroup than with outgroup members, so we have more opportunity to encounter evidence of divergent opinions and habits among ingroup members. Indeed, sometimes *all* we know about outgroup members is what their stereotypical characteristics are reputed to be. But differences in the number of interactions make up only half the story. The nature of the interactions we have with ingroup and outgroup members is likely to be different as well. Because we share the same group membership, we don't treat an ingroup member as a representative of a group. It's the person's idiosyncratic likes, dislikes, talents, and shortcomings that are front and center. Not so with outgroup members. We often treat an outgroup member merely as a representative of a group, so the person's unique characteristics recede into the background. If we think they're all alike, we're more inclined to behave toward all of them in the same way—thereby eliciting the same kind of behavior from them all!

Distinctiveness and Illusory Correlations Although the cognitive perspective emphasizes the role of pure cognition in the formation and maintenance of stereotypes, it's not always clear where impartial information processing leaves off and passions, motives, and self-interest begin. The tendency to see outgroups as more homogeneous than ingroups, for example, may be largely due to the cognitive processes just described, but the effect is sometimes accentuated by the wish to think of an ingroup as more diverse, multifaceted, and nonconformist than other groups.

At least one type of stereotyping bias does arise from cognitive processes alone. People sometimes "see" correlations (relationships) between events, characteristics, or categories that are not actually related—a phenomenon referred to as illusory correlation in Chapter 4 (Fiedler, 2000; Fiedler & Freytag 2004; Garcia-Marques & Hamilton, 1996; Hamilton & Sherman, 1989; Hamilton, Stroessner, & Mackie, 1993; Klauer & Meiser, 2000; Shavitt, Sanbonmatsu, Smittipatana, & Posavac, 1999; Stangor & Lange, 1994). Some illusory correlations result simply from the way we process unusual or distinctive events.

paired distinctiveness The pairing of two distinctive events that stand out even more because they occur together.

Distinctive events capture our attention. We would notice if a student came to a lecture wearing a clown outfit—or nothing at all. Because we attend more closely to distinctive events, we're also likely to remember them better, and as a result they may become overrepresented in our memory. These processes have important implications for the kinds of stereotypes that are commonly associated with minority groups. By definition, minority groups are distinctive to most members of the majority, so minority group members stand out. In addition, negative behaviors, such as robbing, assaulting, and murdering, are (fortunately) much less common than positive behaviors, such as saying thank you and obeying traffic signs, so negative behaviors are distinctive as well. Negative behavior on the part of minority group members is therefore doubly distinctive and doubly memorable. And because negative behavior by the majority or positive behavior by the minority is not as memorable, negative actions by the minority are likely to seem more common than they really are. Minority groups are therefore often thought to be responsible for more instances of problematic behavior than is actually the case.

An experiment by David Hamilton and Robert Gifford (1976) demonstrates the impact of **paired distinctiveness**—the pairing of two distinctive events that stand out even more because they occur together. Participants viewed a series of 39 slides, each one describing a positive or negative action initiated by a member of "group A" or "group B." ("John, a member of group A, visited a sick friend in the hospital." "Bill, a member of group B, always talks about himself and his problems.") The groups were fictional, so any judgments made about them couldn't be the result of participants' preexisting knowledge or experience. Two-thirds of the actions were attributed to group A, thus making A the majority group. Most of the actions attributed to each group were positive, and they were distributed equally: 9 of 13, or 69 percent, of the actions attributed to group B were positive, as were 18 of 26, or 69 percent, of the actions attributed to group A. There was thus no correlation between group membership and the likelihood of positive or negative behavior.

After viewing the entire series of slides, participants then saw only the behaviors they had seen earlier, with no names or groups attached, and indicated the group membership of the person who had performed each one (Hamilton & Gifford, 1976). They also rated the members of the two groups on a variety of trait scales. Both measures indicated that the participants had formed a distinctiveness-based illusory correlation (**Figure 11.6**). They overestimated how often a negative behavior was performed by a member of group B (the smaller group), and they underestimated how often such a behavior was performed by a member of group A (the larger group). As a result, they also rated members of the larger group more favorably.

To show that paired distinctiveness, rather than something about negative behavior, had produced their results, Hamilton and Gifford showed that an illusory correlation was also obtained when positive behaviors were less common. Under these circumstances, participants overestimated how often a *positive* behavior was associated with the smaller group.

In generalizing these findings to the types of firmly held stereotypes common everywhere around the world, it's important to keep two important points in mind. The first is that these results are particularly

Over- and under-attribution

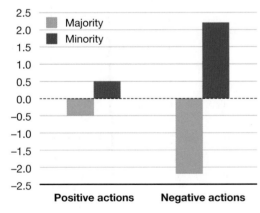

Figure 11.6

Distinctiveness and Illusory Correlation

Distinctive events, such as negative actions by members of minority groups, tend to stand out and exert a disproportionate influence on judgments. In this study, participants attributed more of the negative behaviors to the minority group than they were actually responsible for.

SOURCE: Adapted from Hamilton & Gifford, 1976.

impressive because they were obtained in a laboratory context, thereby excluding a number of factors that might encourage illusory correlations in everyday life. When members of different ethnic groups come together, they're often acutely aware of one another's ethnicity. If you're conscious of a person's ethnicity and he proceeds to do something unusual, ethnicity might immediately come to mind to explain the behavior. If you've seen few Polynesians in your life, for instance, but you see a Polynesian curse at the bank teller serving your line, you might be tempted to conclude that something about being Polynesian was at least part of the reason. ("I guess that's just the way they are.") Of course, if a member of your own ethnic group behaved that way, you probably wouldn't consider her ethnicity as a possible explanation ("Every group has some jerks") (Risen, Gilovich, & Dunning, 2007). Members of your group do plenty of obnoxious things as well as wonderful things, but being a member of your own group doesn't normally count as an explanation for any specific behavior.

The second point to keep in mind is that illusory correlations are also fueled by media depictions. The media generally focus on more extreme members of different minority groups, such as gay men in high heels or feather boas at a gay pride parade, anarchists at an environmental rally, or the most provocative Muslim imams.

One aspect of Hamilton and Gifford's work doesn't fit real-world stereotyping that well. Their analysis predicts that people should be prone to develop illusory correlations between *any* two variables that are jointly distinctive, but people don't always do so. Being left-handed and being a vegetarian are both relatively uncommon, but our culture has no stereotype of southpaws being particularly averse to eating meat. Latinos are not seen as unusually likely to be

Paired Distinctiveness
(A) When we see unusual actions performed by people we rarely encounter (such as, for westerners, these Vietnamese children), we tend to wonder whether "those people" are fond of that type of activity, and a link between the two is often formed. (B) When the same actions are performed by types of people we encounter frequently (such as a child from the United States), we don't draw any conclusions about "those people."

gay, and Asians aren't thought to be especially fond of snowboarding. Thus, although Hamilton and Gifford's provocative analysis captures something real and important about certain illusory correlations, it predicts more illusory correlations than people actually endorse. More research is needed to specify *which* jointly distinctive pairings are likely to form the core of commonly held stereotypes, and which are not.

Expectations and Biased Information Processing Because of the outgroup homogeneity effect, people are more likely to assume a single action is typical of a group if the group is not their own. But regardless of whether it's an ingroup or outgroup under consideration, people don't generalize equally from everything they see. Some acts (an epileptic seizure, for example) discourage generalization from the individual to the group no matter who the actor is; other behaviors (such as rudeness) invite it. In general, people are more likely to generalize behaviors and traits they already suspect may be typical of the group's members. This is another way in which stereotypes can be self-reinforcing. Actions that are consistent with an existing stereotype are noticed, deemed significant, and remembered, whereas those at variance with the stereotype may be ignored, dismissed, or quickly forgotten (Bodenhausen, 1988; Kunda & Thagard, 1996; von Hippel, Sekaquaptewa, & Vargas, 1995).

Stereotypes also influence how the details of events are interpreted. In a striking demonstration of this effect, white participants watched a videotape of a heated discussion between two men, one black and one white, and were asked to code the behavior they were watching into one of several categories, such as "Gives information," "Playing around," or "Aggressive behavior" (Duncan, 1976; see also Dunning & Sherman, 1997; Kunda & Sherman-Williams, 1993; Plant, Kling, & Smith, 2004; Sagar & Schofield, 1980). At one point in the video, one of the men shoved the other. For half the participants, a black man shoved the other man; for the other half, a white man did the shoving. The race of the person made a difference in how the action was interpreted. When perpetrated by a white man, the incident tended to be coded as more benign (as "Playing around," for example). When perpetrated by a black man, it was coded as a more serious action (such as "Aggressive behavior").

The results of this study are remarkable because the participants saw the shove with their own eyes. The influence of stereotypes can be even greater when the episode is presented to people secondhand and is therefore more open to being construed in different ways. In one study, for instance, participants listened to a play-by-play account of a college basketball game and were told to focus on the exploits of one player in particular, Mark Flick (Stone, Perry, & Darley, 1997). Half the participants saw a photo of Mark that made it clear he was African-American and half saw a photo that made it clear he was white. When participants rated Mark's performance, their assessments reflected commonly held stereotypes about black and white basketball players. Those who thought Mark was African-American rated him as more athletic and as having played better; those who thought he was white rated him as having hustled more and as having played a more savvy game.

Studies like these demonstrate that people don't evaluate information even-handedly. Instead, information that's consistent with a group stereotype typically has more impact than information that's inconsistent with it. This is yet another way that even inaccurate stereotypes can stay alive and even grow in strength.

"Stereotypic beliefs about women's roles, for example, may enable one to see correctly that a woman in a dark room is threading a needle rather than tying a fishing lure, but they may also cause one to mistakenly assume that her goal is embroidery rather than cardiac surgery."

—DAN GILBERT, HARVARD SOCIAL PSYCHOLOGIST

Self-Fulfilling Prophecies Stereotypes can also endure because they "benefit" from self-fulfilling prophecies: that is, people act toward members of certain groups in ways that encourage the very behavior they expect. Thinking that members of a particular group are hostile, a person might act toward them in a guarded manner, thereby eliciting a coldness that's seen as proof of their hostility (Shelton & Richeson, 2005). A teacher who believes members of a specific group lack intellectual ability may give them less attention in class, thereby increasing the chances that they'll fall behind their classmates. As Robert Merton, who coined the term *self-fulfilling prophecy*, once said, "The specious validity of the self-fulfilling prophecy perpetuates a reign of error. For the prophet will cite the actual course of events as proof that he was right from the very beginning" (Merton, 1957, p. 423).

The trap that's sprung by certain types of self-fulfilling prophecies was powerfully illustrated in an experiment in which white undergraduates interviewed both black and white men pretending to be job applicants (Word, Zanna, & Cooper, 1974). The interviews were monitored, and the researchers discovered that the students (the white interviewers) unwittingly treated black and white applicants differently. When the applicant was black, the interviewer tended to sit farther away, to hem and haw throughout the session, and to terminate the proceedings earlier than when the applicant was white. That is not the type of environment that inspires self-possession and smooth interview performance.

Sure enough, the second phase of the experiment showed just how difficult it had been for the black applicants. Interviewers were trained to treat *new* applicants, all of whom were white, the way that either the white or the black applicants had been treated earlier. These interviews were tape-recorded and later rated by independent judges. Applicants who had been interviewed in the way the black applicants had been interviewed earlier were evaluated more negatively than those who'd been interviewed the way the white applicants had been interviewed. In other words, by placing black applicants at a disadvantage, the white interviewers confirmed their negative stereotypes of blacks. Similar results have been obtained in interview studies of gay and lesbian job applicants (Hebl, Foster, Mannix, & Dovidio, 2002).

> "Oppression has no logic—just a self-fulfilling prophecy, justified by a self-perpetuating system."
>
> —GLORIA STEINEM

Explaining Away Exceptions

If every rule has an exception, the same is true for stereotypes. Groups known for their intellectual talents nonetheless include a few dolts. Groups renowned for their athletic abilities are sure to include a klutz or two. Even if a stereotype is largely accurate, there is almost certain to be some contradictory evidence. Of course, if the stereotype is invalid, the amount of disconfirmatory evidence will be much greater. What happens when people discover evidence that disagrees with their view? Do they abandon their stereotypes or hold them less confidently?

The way people respond to stereotype disconfirmation varies according to their emotional investment in the stereotype, whether the stereotype is idiosyncratic or widely shared, and numerous other factors. One thing is clear, however: people do not give up their stereotypes easily. As numerous studies have demonstrated, people evaluate disconfirming evidence in a variety of ways that have the effect of dampening its impact. An understanding of these processes provides some insight into one of the most vexing questions about stereotypes—namely, why they so often persist in the face of evidence that would seem to contradict them.

subtyping Explaining away exceptions to a given stereotype by creating a subcategory of the stereotyped group that can be expected to differ from the group as a whole.

Subtyping No stereotype contains an expectation of perfectly consistent behavior. Groups thought to be dishonest, lazy, or carefree are thought to be dishonest, lazy, or carefree *on average*, or at least more dishonest, lazy, or carefree than other groups; not all members are expected to behave in those ways all the time. This loophole lets people remain unmoved by apparent disconfirmations of their stereotypes, because anyone who acts at variance with the stereotype is simply walled off into a category of "exceptions." Psychologists refer to this tendency as **subtyping** (Queller & Smith, 2002; Richards & Hewstone, 2001; Weber & Crocker, 1983). Sexists who believe women are passive and dependent and should stay home to raise children are likely to subtype assertive, independent women who choose not to have children as "militant" or "strident" feminists, thereby leaving their stereotype of women largely intact. Similarly, racists who maintain that African-Americans can't excel outside of sports and entertainment are likely to remain untroubled by the likes of, say, President Barack Obama ("He's half white") or Attorney General Eric Holder ("His parents were immigrants from Barbados"). To the racist mind, they are merely the "exceptions that prove the rule." (Incidentally, if you've ever wondered how an exception can prove a rule—it can't. The expression uses the word *prove* in its less common meaning: to test.)

Subtyping reflects a more general truth: people treat evidence that supports a stereotype differently from evidence that refutes it. People tend to accept supportive evidence at face value, whereas they often critically analyze and discount contradictory evidence. One way they do this, in keeping with the self-serving attributional bias (see Chapter 5), is by attributing behavior consistent with a stereotype to the dispositions of the people involved and attributing inconsistent behavior to external causes (Crocker, Hannah, & Weber, 1983; Deaux & Emswiller, 1974; Kulik, 1983; Swim & Sanna, 1996; Taylor & Jaggi, 1974). An anti-Semite who believes that Jews are "cheap" is likely to dismiss a Jewish person's acts of philanthropy as reflecting a desire for social acceptance, but to interpret any pursuit of self-interest as being a reflection of some "true" Jewish character. Thus, episodes consistent with a stereotype reinforce its perceived validity; those that are inconsistent with it are deemed insignificant (Pettigrew, 1979).

Concrete vs. Abstract Construal Another way we differentially process supportive and contradictory information is by varying how concretely or abstractly we encode the actions of people from different groups. Almost any action can be construed at different levels of abstraction (Vallacher & Wegner, 1987; see Chapters 5 and 8). If you see someone lifting someone who has fallen, you could describe the action concretely as exactly that—an act of lifting. Alternatively, you could say, more abstractly, that the person was "helping"

Explaining Away Exceptions
People who hold stereotypes of ethnic groups sometimes dismiss examples of individuals who don't conform to the stereotype as exceptions or members of relatively rare subtypes.

the fallen individual. More broadly still, you might say the person was being "helpful" or "altruistic." These different levels of abstraction carry different connotations. The more concrete the description, the less it says about the person involved.

The implications of these differences in concrete versus abstract construal were examined in a study that took place during the annual *palio* competition in

Concrete and Abstract Construals during the Palio Competition
Fans of the Palio Competition in Ferrara, Italy, tended to see positive actions by members of their team in abstract, meaningful terms and negative actions in concrete, less meaningful terms. They did just the opposite for the positive and negative actions of members of the opposing team, making it easier for them to continue to think more positively of their own team than their opponents.

Ferrara, Italy (Maass, Salvi, Arcuri, & Semin, 1989). The *palio* are horse-racing competitions that have taken place in various Italian towns since the thirteenth century (with a brief interruption during the time of the Black Plague). Pitting teams from different districts, or *contrade*, against one another, the races take place in the context of an elaborate festival in which residents of each *contrada* root for their team. In the weeks leading up to the *palio*, feelings of intergroup competition run high.

Before one such *palio* competition, the researchers showed the residents of two *contrade*, San Giorgio and San Giacomo, a number of sketches depicting a member of their own team or of the rival team engaged in an action. The *contrada* membership of the person depicted was established simply by having the color of the protagonist's shirt match that of one *contrada* or another. Some of the sketches portrayed desirable actions (such as helping someone), and some portrayed undesirable actions (such as littering). After inspecting each sketch, the participants described what it depicted, and their responses were scored for level of abstraction.

The results revealed a clear bias (**Figure 11.7**). Participants maintained positive views of their own group by describing negative actions at a low level of abstraction, and maintained their less favorable views of the other group by describing negative actions at a high level of abstraction. ("The guy from my *contrada* dropped a piece of paper. The guy from your *contrada* is a litterbug.") They did precisely the opposite for positive actions. ("The guy from my *contrada* is very kind. The guy from your *contrada* lifted the little kid on his shoulders.") This asymmetry feeds the tendency to perceive the ingroup in a favorable light. Abstractly encoding events that fit one's stereotypes lends them greater import; concretely encoding events that violate one's preferences or expectations renders them less consequential.

Automatic and Controlled Processing

Some of the cognitive processes that give rise to stereotyping and prejudice are deliberate, elaborate, and mindful—in other words, conscious. Subtyping, for

Figure 11.7
Stereotypes and the Encoding of Behavior

People encode events consistent with their preexisting stereotypes at a more abstract, and therefore more meaningful, level than events that are inconsistent with preexisting stereotypes. This graph shows the percentage of abstract versus concrete terms used to describe desirable and undesirable actions by members of the ingroup and outgroup. Abstract terms consist of state verbs or trait terms (*hates, hateful*), and concrete terms consist of descriptive and interpretive action verbs (*hits, hurts*).

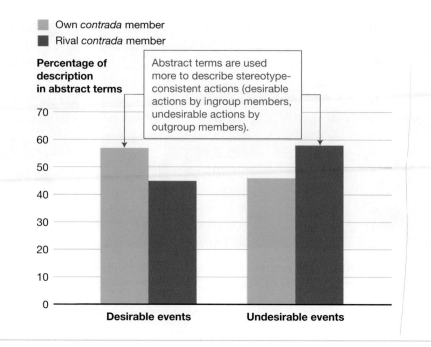

SOURCE: Adapted from Maass et al., 1989.

example, is often a conscious process (Devine & Baker, 1991; Kunda & Oleson, 1995; Weber & Crocker, 1983). Other cognitive processes, in contrast, give rise to stereotyping and prejudice rapidly and automatically, without much conscious attention and elaboration. This is likely to be the case for distinctiveness-based illusory correlations and the outgroup homogeneity effect.

In the past 25 years, researchers have explored the interplay of automatic and controlled processes and how they collectively influence the way people react to members of different groups (Bodenhausen, Macrae, & Sherman, 1999; Devine & Monteith, 1999; Fazio & Olson, 2003; Sherman et al., 2008; Sritharan & Gawronski, 2010; Wittenbrink, 2004). This research has shown that our reactions to different groups of people are, to a surprising degree, guided by quick and automatic mental processes that we can override but not eliminate. The findings also highlight the common discrepancy between our immediate, reflexive reactions to outgroup members and our more reflective responses.

Patricia Devine (1989b) examined the joint operation of automatic and controlled processes by investigating the schism that exists for many people between their knowledge of racial stereotypes and their own beliefs and attitudes toward those same groups. More specifically, Devine sought to demonstrate that what separates prejudiced and nonprejudiced people is not their knowledge of derogatory stereotypes, but whether they resist the stereotypes. To do so, she relied on the distinction between automatic processes, which we do not consciously control (such as the use of binocular disparity to judge distance), and controlled processes, which we direct more consciously. The activation of stereotypes is typically an automatic process; thus, stereotypes can be triggered even if we don't want them to be. Even a nonprejudiced person will, under the right circumstances, access an association between Muslims and fanaticism, blacks and criminality, and WASPs and emotional repression, because those associations are present in our culture. Whereas a bigot will endorse or employ such stereotypes, a nonprejudiced person will employ more controlled cognitive processes to suppress them—or at least try to.

To test these ideas, Devine selected groups of high- and low-prejudiced participants on the basis of their scores on the Modern Racism Scale (Devine, 1989b). To show that these two groups don't differ in their automatic processing of stereotypical information, she presented each participant with a set of words, one at a time, so briefly that they could not be consciously identified. Some of them saw neutral words (*number, plant, remember*) and others saw words stereotypically associated with blacks (*welfare, jazz, busing*). Devine hypothesized that although the stereotypical words were presented too briefly to be consciously recognized, they would nonetheless prime the participants' stereotypes of blacks. To test this hypothesis, she presented the participants with a written description of an individual who acted in an ambiguously hostile manner (to bring to mind hostility, a feature of the African-American stereotype). In one incident, for example, the target person refused to pay his rent until his apartment was repaired. Was he being needlessly belligerent or appropriately assertive? The results indicated

Shared Stereotypes
Nearly everyone, prejudiced or not, shares common stereotypes (that they may or may not try to suppress). In these photos, you may have associated the basketball with the black man, the computer with the Asian student, and the explosion with the Muslim, even though they weren't aligned in this presentation.

that he was seen as more hostile—and more negative overall—by participants who had earlier been primed by words designed to activate stereotypes of blacks (words such as *jazz*, it's important to note, that are not otherwise connected to the concept of hostility). Most importantly, this result was found equally for prejudiced and nonprejudiced participants. Because the stimulus words unconsciously activated their stereotypes, the nonprejudiced participants were caught off guard and were unable to suppress the automatic processing of stereotypical information.

To demonstrate that prejudiced and nonprejudiced people differ primarily in their *controlled* cognitive processes, Devine next asked her participants to list characteristics of black Americans (Devine, 1989b). As predicted, the two groups differed substantially in the output of this consciously controlled procedure: prejudiced participants listed many more negative characteristics stereotypically associated with blacks than did nonprejudiced participants. Thus, even though both prejudiced and nonprejudiced people may know the same negative stereotypes of black Americans (as shown in the first part of Devine's study), those who are prejudiced believe them and are sometimes willing to voice those beliefs, whereas those who are not prejudiced reject them.

Subsequent investigations have further explored the frequent rift between the beliefs and sentiments elicited by automatic processes and those elicited by more controlled processes. In one study, the investigators first used a priming procedure to assess white participants' implicit prejudice toward blacks (Dovidio, Kawakami, and Gaertner, 2002). They also measured their explicit attitudes with the Attitudes toward Blacks Scale (Brigham, 1993). They then had the participants engage in two 3-minute conversations, one with a white student and one with a black student. They videotaped and later scored these conversations, once with the sound removed and once with all channels included, for the amount of friendliness exhibited by the participant.

The researchers anticipated that the explicit measure of prejudice (the attitude scale) would predict ratings of the participants' friendliness made from the full videotape because those ratings would be determined primarily by what participants said, and people can readily control what they say. But they expected the implicit measure of prejudice to predict participants' nonverbal friendliness— that is, the ratings of participant friendliness made from the video channel only—because nonverbal behavior is harder to control. And that's precisely what happened. Participants' scores on the Attitudes toward Blacks Scale predicted how differentially friendly they were to the white and black students as assessed from the full videotape. But their scores on the implicit measure of prejudice (their reaction times) predicted how differentially friendly they were to the white and black students as assessed from the video-only ratings. Explicit measures of prejudice, it seems, can predict controlled behavior, but implicit measures sometimes do a better job of predicting automatic behavior (see also Fazio, Jackson, Dunton, & Williams, 1995).

The results of another study of people's automatic reactions to members of stigmatized groups are rather disturbing. Researchers had participants decide as quickly as possible whether an object depicted in a photo was a handgun or a hand tool, such as pliers (Payne, 2001). Each photograph was immediately preceded by a picture of either an African-American or a white face. The participants (all of whom were white) were faster to identify a weapon as a weapon

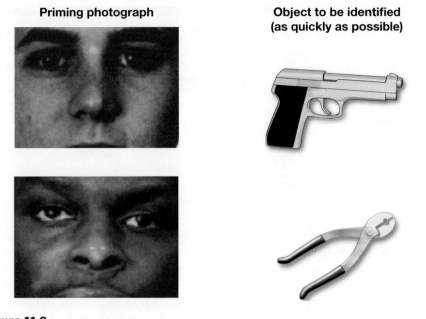

Priming photograph

Object to be identified (as quickly as possible)

Figure 11.8
Stereotypes and Categorization
In this study, culturally shared stereotypes of African-Americans led white participants to identify handguns more quickly if they had been primed by an African-American face than a white face.

SOURCE: Adapted from Payne, 2001.

when it was preceded by an African-American face and faster to identify a hand tool as a hand tool when it was preceded by a white face (**Figure 11.8**).

Is this the result of automatic prejudice toward African-Americans on the part of white participants? In other words, is the recognition of handguns facilitated by African-American faces because both handguns and African-Americans are evaluated negatively by white participants? Or is this effect due to automatic stereotyping? In other words, is the facilitation caused by a stereotypical association between handguns and African-Americans that exerts its effect even for people who aren't prejudiced?

The good news (limited, perhaps, but good news nonetheless) is that it appears to be the latter. Charles Judd, Irene Blair, and Kristine Chapleau (2004) replicated Payne's experiment with four types of target stimuli that varied in whether they were viewed positively or negatively and whether they were stereotypically associated with African-Americans. Specifically, the stimuli associated with African-Americans consisted of pictures of handguns (negative) and sports equipment (positive), and the stimuli not associated with African-Americans consisted of pictures of insects (negative) and fruit (positive). Judd and his colleagues found that African-American faces facilitated the recognition of both positive and negative stereotypical items (handguns and sports equipment), but not the nonstereotypical items (insects and fruits), regardless of whether they were positive or negative.

A similar conclusion emerges from studies with even more chilling implications for the everyday lives of African-Americans (**Box 11.3**). This research was inspired by the tragic death of Amadou Diallo, a black West African immigrant who in 1999 was riddled with 19 bullets by policemen who said later they

BOX 11.3 **FOCUS ON *THE LAW***

Stereotypical Facial Features and the Death Penalty

The election of Barack Obama as the 44th president of the United States highlights the often ambiguous nature of race. Although the child of a white mother and black father, Obama is almost always referred to as the first African-American president, not the first biracial president. This is no doubt a legacy of the "one-drop rule": historically, individuals were considered black if they had any trace of black ancestry at all. Various Southern states used this standard to back the notorious Jim Crow laws that enforced racial segregation and restricted the rights of blacks. But now that society has moved beyond the ridiculous one-drop rule, we are left with the difficult issue of "who counts" as black, white, Asian, Hispanic, and so on. Indeed, many biologists question whether racial categories make any sense at all—that is, whether race really exists (Bamshad & Olson, 2003).

The psychology behind the one-drop rule notwithstanding, race-based judgments about others often differ in intensity depending on how much a person's physical features conform to a stereotype. African-American faces with more stereotypically African features (darker skin, fuller lips, more flared nostrils) elicit prejudiced reactions more readily than faces with less stereotypical features (Livingston & Brewer, 2002; Ma & Correll, 2011). Furthermore, both black and white individuals with more stereotypically African features are assumed to have traits associated with common stereotypes of African-Americans (Blair, Judd, Sadler, & Jenkins, 2002). In the most consequential manifestation of this tendency, people with stereotypically African features tend to receive harsher sentences than those with less stereotypically African features (Blair, Judd, & Chapleau, 2004), and blacks accused of capital crimes are more likely to end up on death row if they have stereotypically African features (Eberhardt, Davies, Purdie-Vaughns, & Johnson, 2006). Moreover, testifying to the utility of the motivational perspective on stereotyping and prejudice, people are more likely to categorize ambiguous faces as black when they are primed with thoughts of economic scarcity (Krosch & Amodio, 2014; Rodeheffer, Hill, & Lord, 2012).

thought, incorrectly, that he was reaching for a gun. In these studies, participants watched a video game in which, at unpredictable moments, a target individual—sometimes white, sometimes African-American—popped up out of nowhere holding either a gun or some other object (Correll, Park, Judd, & Wittenbrink, 2002; Correll, Urland, & Ito, 2006; Ma & Correll, 2011; Payne, 2006). Participants were instructed to "shoot" if the person was holding a gun and to press a different response key if he was not. Because participants were instructed to respond as quickly as possible, they were bound to make occasional mistakes, and as **Figure 11.9** shows, they clearly treated African-American and white targets differently. They made both types of mistakes—shooting an unarmed target and not shooting an armed target—equally often when the target individual was white. But for African-American targets, participants were much more likely to make the mistake of shooting if the target was unarmed than failing to shoot if the target was armed.

Notably, the same effect was obtained in a follow-up experiment with African-American participants. Prolonged experience with these sorts of shoot/don't shoot decisions, either through laboratory exposure or real-world police work, seems to diminish the tendency to shoot unarmed blacks more than unarmed whites, but the reaction time differences (faster to decide to shoot an armed black and not to shoot an unarmed white) tend to persist (Correll, Park, Judd, Wittenbrink, Sadler, & Keesee, 2007; Glaser, 2015; Payne, 2006; Plant & Peruche, 2005; Plant, Peruche, & Butz, 2005).

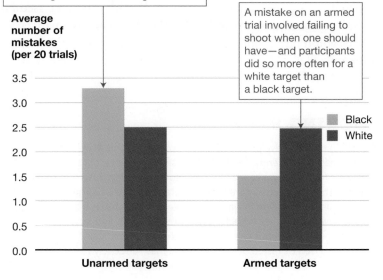

A mistake on an unarmed trial involved shooting when one should not have—and participants did so more often for a black target than a white target.

A mistake on an armed trial involved failing to shoot when one should have—and participants did so more often for a white target than a black target.

Average number of mistakes (per 20 trials)

■ Black
■ White

Unarmed targets   Armed targets

SOURCE: Adapted from Correll et al., 2002.

Figure 11.9
Automatic Stereotyping and Prejudice
Participants were shown images of an armed or unarmed individual who appeared suddenly on a computer screen. They were told to respond as quickly as possible by pressing one button to "shoot" an armed individual and another button if the individual was unarmed.

Evaluating the Cognitive Perspective

Critics of the cognitive perspective have said that although the approach has made strides in advancing psychologists' understanding of intergroup conflict, the recent emphasis on reaction-time methods and brief, reflexive phenomena may lead us to lose sight of the causes of the disturbing manifestations of stereotyping, prejudice, and discrimination that are all-too-common elements of real-world experience. Indeed, when ethnic groups in Africa, the Middle East, and around the world are bent on subjugating or exterminating one another, and when police officers in countless countries brutalize minorities with alarming frequency, reaction-time assessments of subtle prejudices can seem rather removed from the heart of the matter. Critics have also noted that many of the documented effects are very short-lived. Seeing someone who belongs to a particular ethnic group may automatically activate our stereotypical associations to that group, but the activation is often brief, and often replaced by thoughts and feelings about the individual involved, not that person's group. We may think of someone primarily as black, a Scientologist, a priest, or a Texan only until he tells us he's a vegetarian, a libertarian, or a Rotarian.

Nevertheless, it's important to note that a great deal of damage can be done on the basis of people's initial, quick responses, as the shooting studies described above make abundantly clear. It is surely no consolation to Diallo's family to know that the cognitive operations that made the policemen think Diallo was reaching for a gun rather than a wallet would have soon been overridden by more level-headed processes. And however brief these initial, automatic processes might be, they can get the ball rolling in an unfortunate direction. They can be the seeds from which deeper sorts of prejudice and discrimination are sown.

The Dire Cost of Stereotyping and Reacting Automatically
White police officers in New York City attempted to question Amadou Diallo, a black West African immigrant who had gone outside his apartment building to get some air and who seemed to fit the description of the serial rapist they were looking for. Diallo ran up the steps of his building and then reached inside his jacket for what police believed was a gun but was actually his wallet. Reacting out of fear that Diallo was about to start firing a weapon, the four policemen fired 41 shots, striking the innocent Diallo 19 times and killing him.

Furthermore, social psychologists working from the cognitive perspective have clarified the fact that we all tend to stereotype, and we all have the capacity to harbor troubling prejudices—prejudices we're often unaware we have. Subjecting yourself to implicit measures of prejudice like the IAT (see Figure 11.1) can yield undeniable evidence that you have certain negative associations to particular groups you'd rather not have. That knowledge can be the first step toward overcoming prejudice.

↻ LOOKING BACK

Consistent with the cognitive perspective, stereotypes help us make sense of the world and process information efficiently, freeing us to use cognitive resources for other work. But they can also cause us to make many errors, such as seeing outgroup members as more homogeneous than they actually are. Our expectations of what a group of people is like can lead us to process information in ways that make stereotypes resistant to disconfirmation, as we explain away information that violates a stereotype and subtype those who don't fit the stereotype. Stereotypes can result from both automatic and controlled processing. Even people who don't express prejudicial views may reflexively respond to individuals on the basis of their unconscious stereotypes and prejudices.

Being a Member of a Stigmatized Group

So far, this chapter has focused on the perpetrators of prejudice—who, it should be clear by now, can include all of us. But what about the victims of prejudice? They, of course, pay an unfair price in terms of numerous indicators of material and psychological well-being—health, wealth, employment prospects, and longevity, among others. What's more, members of stereotyped or stigmatized groups are usually aware of the stereotypes others hold, and this awareness can have negative effects on them as well (Crocker, Major, & Steele, 1998; Herek, 1998; Inzlicht, Aronson, & Mendoza-Denton, 2009; Jones et al., 1984; Pinel, 1999; Shelton, Alegre, & Son, 2010; Shelton, Richeson, & Salvatore, 2005). Social psychologists have focused on three burdens that come with knowing others might be prejudiced against one's group: attributional ambiguity, stereotype threat, and the psychological costs of concealing one's identity.

Attributional Ambiguity

To function effectively, people need to understand the causes of events happening around them. But this understanding is threatened for members of stigmatized groups because they can't always tell whether their experiences have the same causes as those of everyone else, or whether they're the result of prejudice. "Did my officemate get the promotion instead of me because I'm so overweight?" "Would the state trooper have pulled me over if I were white?" "Did I get that fellowship because I'm Latino?" Questions like these may be vexing with respect to negative outcomes, but they are also disconcerting in the context of positive outcomes. When someone has to wonder whether an accomplishment is the product of an affirmative action policy, it can be difficult to completely "own" it and reap the full measure of pride it would ordinarily afford.

In one study that examined this type of attributional predicament, African-American and white students received flattering or unflattering feedback from a white student in an adjacent room (Crocker, Voelkl, Testa, & Major, 1991). Half the participants were led to assume the white student could see them through a one-way mirror, and half thought they couldn't be seen, because a blind covered the mirror. Whether or not they could be seen had no effect on how white students reacted to the feedback, but it did affect how black students reacted. When black students thought the other person could not see them—and therefore didn't know their race—their self-esteem went down from the unflattering feedback and was boosted by the positive feedback. When they thought the other person could see them, in contrast, their self-esteem was not injured by the bad news, nor was it enhanced by the good news. Thus, this study indicates that members of stigmatized groups live in a less certain world, not knowing whether to attribute positive feedback to their own skill or to others' condescension and not knowing whether to attribute negative feedback to their own error or to others' prejudice.

stereotype threat The fear of confirming the stereotypes others have about one's group.

Stereotype Threat

An extensive program of research initiated by Claude Steele and his colleagues highlights a second difficulty for members of stigmatized groups (Steele, 1997; Steele, Spencer, & Aronson, 2002). Their performance can be impaired by **stereotype threat**, the fear that they will confirm the stereotypes others have about their own group. In one study, researchers examined the effect on women's math test scores of making salient the stereotype that women don't perform well in mathematics (Spencer, Steele, & Quinn, 1999). In one condition, participants were told there was no gender difference on a particular test they were about to take. Other participants were told that there was a gender difference in favor of men. As **Figure 11.10** shows, men and women performed equivalently when they

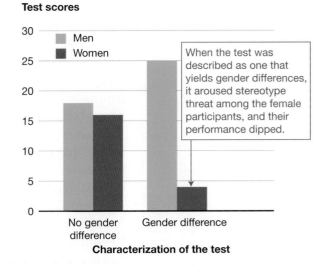

Test scores

When the test was described as one that yields gender differences, it aroused stereotype threat among the female participants, and their performance dipped.

Figure 11.10
Stereotype Threat and Performance
This study shows the performance of men and women on a math test when they thought the test tapped gender differences, and when they did not.

SOURCE: Adapted from Spencer et al., 1999.

thought there was no gender difference on the test, but women performed worse than men when they thought there was a gender difference.

It's not necessary to be so blatant in the manipulation of stereotype threat for it to have an effect. Michael Inzlicht and Talia Ben-Zeev (2000) had female undergraduates take a math test in the company of either two other women or two men. Those who took the test with other women got 70 percent of the problems right on average. Those who took the test with men got 55 percent right on average.

In another study, Claude Steele and Joshua Aronson examined the sensitivity to stereotype threat on the part of African-American students (Steele & Aronson, 1995). Playing on a stereotype that questions blacks' intellectual ability, they gave black and white college students a difficult verbal test taken from the Graduate Record Exam. Half the students were led to believe the test could measure their intellectual ability, and half were told the investigators were in the early stages of developing the test, and that nothing could be learned about intellectual ability from their scores. This manipulation had no effect on the performance of white students. In contrast, the African-American students did as well as the white students when they thought it was the test that was being tested, but they performed much worse than the white students when they thought their intellectual ability was being tested. Again, a blatant manipulation was not required to produce a significant effect on the performance of African-Americans. In a follow-up study, it was enough simply to have participants indicate their race at the top of the page to cause African-American students' performance to be worse than in a control condition in which they did not indicate their race (Steele & Aronson, 1995).

It seems that no one is safe from stereotype threat. Another research team showed that the math performance of white males deteriorated when they were reminded of Asian proficiency in math (Aronson et al., 1999). And in a particularly clever experiment, Jeff Stone and his colleagues had college students perform a laboratory golf task described as a measure of "natural athletic ability," "sports intelligence," or "sports psychology" (Stone, Lynch, Sjomeling, & Darley, 1999). White and black students performed equally well in the "sports psychology" condition. But black students performed significantly worse when it was described as a test of "sports intelligence," and white students performed worse when it was described as a test of "natural athletic ability." In still another telling study, Asian-American women did worse on a math test than control participants when their gender was made salient, but better than control participants when their race was highlighted (Shi, Pittinsky, & Ambady, 1999).

Stereotype threat appears to undermine performance in a number of ways. Stereotype threat leads to increased arousal, which can directly interfere with performance on complex tasks (Ben-Zeev, Fein, & Inzlicht, 2005) and serve as a source of distraction that interferes with concentration on the task at hand (Cheryan & Bodenhausen, 2000). Furthermore, knowing that one's group is "suspect" in the eyes of others tends to elicit negative thinking (Cadinu, Maass, Rosabianca, & Kiesner, 2005). This can both directly undermine performance and lead individuals to "play it safe" by being more obsessed with avoiding failure than reaching for success (Seibt & Forster, 2004).

Although all people are vulnerable to some type of stereotype threat based on their group memberships, Steele (1997) maintains that the vulnerability of

African-Americans has particular potential for damage. Stereotype threat can result in poorer overall academic performance, which undermines confidence, rendering the individual still more susceptible to stereotype threat. This vicious cycle can result in "disidentification" from academic pursuits, as students who feel the threat most acutely opt out of academics altogether and identify other areas in which to invest their talent and energy and from which to derive their self-esteem. Fortunately, social psychologists have developed a number of low-cost, highly effective interventions for dealing with the debilitating effects of stereotype threat in schools (see Application Module 3).

The Cost of Concealment

Australia is known for its powerhouse Olympic swimming teams, but no Aussie swimmer has had a bigger hold on the country's imagination than Ian Thorpe. Nicknamed "the Thorpedo" for the speed and grace with which he cut through the water, Thorpe won five Olympic gold medals in his career and anchored Australia's 4x100 freestyle relay team in its upset of the powerhouse U.S. squad during the 2000 Olympics in Sydney—the first time the Americans had ever lost that race. Throughout his career, Thorpe was dogged by rumors that he was gay, rumors he steadfastly denied. "You know, I'm a little bit different to what most people would consider being an Australian male. That doesn't make me gay. I mean I'm straight, so people want to claim me as part of a minority group and put labels on you and that's not what I'm about, and I don't understand why people are like that" (Magnay, 2002). After retiring from swimming, however, Thorpe announced during a television interview that he was in fact gay.

Sadly, Ian Thorpe's experience is not unusual. Members of stigmatized groups throughout history have often felt compelled to hide their true identity. Gay and lesbian individuals have often chosen to remain "in the closet," light-skinned blacks have sometimes tried to "pass" as white, and many older adults get plastic surgery, tummy tucks, and toupees. The ubiquity of such underground experiences makes one wonder what they're like, and what sort of toll they exact.

A big one, it turns out. Physically, the concealment of sexual orientation is associated with cardiovascular stress, and gay men who conceal their sexual orientation show more rapid progression of HIV symptoms (Cole, Kemeny, Taylor, & Visscher, 1996; Pérez-Benítez, O'Brien, Carels, Gordon, & Chiros, 2007). Psychologically, being out of the closet is associated with a variety of indicators of better mental health, including reduced depression, less anger, and higher self-esteem (Legate, Ryan, & Weinstein, 2012; Miranda & Storms, 1989; Ross, 1990; Szymanski, Chung, & Balsam, 2001).

Concealment can also take a cognitive toll. In one study, researchers Clayton Critcher and Melissa Ferguson instructed half the participants to conceal their sexual orientation during a mock interview while the control participants were free to say whatever they wanted (Critcher & Ferguson, 2013). The investigators predicted that the act of concealment would be mentally taxing, making them less able to perform well on subsequent tasks. Indeed, across several experiments, they found that those asked to conceal their sexual orientation did less well on tests of spatial ability, self-control, and physical stamina. Concealing an important part of oneself is demanding, and meeting those demands can have unfortunate consequences later on.

🔄 LOOKING BACK

Victims of stereotyping can suffer attributional ambiguity, not knowing whether performance feedback is genuine or based on their group membership. They can suffer from stereotype threat, performing worse because they are afraid of confirming a stereotype that exists about their group. Members of some minority groups feel compelled to try to cover up their minority status, an effort that can exact a physical and psychological toll.

Reducing Stereotypes, Prejudice, and Discrimination

This chapter began with a discussion of the progress that has been made in intergroup relations in the United States and across much of the globe—and how much farther we must go to achieve true equality of opportunity for everyone. What has contributed to the improvements we've witnessed thus far, and what principles can we draw on to advance even more?

Many factors, including specific legal interventions and broad economic developments, have brought about improved relations between gays and straights, blacks and whites, Latinos and Anglos, and numerous other groups. One factor that is both cause and consequence of these developments is the increased daily interactions among members of different groups. When people interact frequently, it becomes easier to see people as individuals, rather than representatives of particular groups. As President Obama said in his 2008 inaugural address, "As the world grows smaller, our common humanity shall reveal itself."

Simple contact between broad cross-sections of different groups is not a magic solution for harmonious relationships, however, and some types of contact are more helpful than others. Numerous studies have assessed the effect of the U.S. Supreme Court's desegregation decision in *Brown v. the Board of Education of Topeka* (1954) on race relations in American schools. The initial studies did not provide strong support for what came to be known as the contact hypothesis—the straightforward idea that bringing together students of different races and ethnicities would reduce prejudice and discrimination. One review of the literature found that in a majority of the studies examining the effect of integration on interracial attitudes, an *increase* in prejudice was observed (Stephan, 1986).

This was not an encouraging finding, to be sure, but in many ways, it's not surprising either. After all, simply bringing the Rattlers and Eagles together did not reduce the animosity between the two groups at Robbers Cave. Contact between different groups is likely to be more positive and more productive if certain conditions are met. First, the groups need to have equal status. If one group feels superior and the other resentful, then harmonious, productive interactions are not likely to be the norm. Second, as in the Robbers Cave study, productive intergroup interactions are facilitated if the different groups have a shared goal that requires mutual cooperation, thereby promoting a common ingroup identity (Gaertner & Dovidio, 2000, 2009; Nier, Gaertner, Dovidio, Banker, & Ward, 2001; West, Pearson, Dovidio, Shelton, & Trail, 2009).

Third, a community's broader social norms must support intergroup contact. If children of different races, religions, and ethnicities go to school with one another but their parents send them begrudgingly and rarely miss an opportunity to speak ill of the "other" children, the students themselves are unlikely to reach out across group boundaries. On the other hand, merely knowing that someone in one's group is friends with a member of an outgroup—and what that implies about perceived social support for contact with the outgroup—is sufficient to reduce stereotyping and outgroup denigration (Wright, Aron, McLaughlin-Volpe, & Ropp, 1997). Finally, the contact should encourage one-on-one interactions between members of the different groups. Doing so puts each person's identity as an individual in the foreground and downplays a person's group membership.

An analysis of numerous studies on the effect of desegregation, involving tens of thousands of students in over 25 countries, found that when most of these conditions are met, contact between members of different groups does indeed tend to be effective in reducing prejudice (Pettigrew & Tropp, 2000, 2006, 2008). And university students who are assigned roommates of a different race report reduced anxiety about cross-race interactions and register a significant improvement on implicit measures of attitudes toward the other group (Shook & Fazio, 2008).

Reducing Prejudice Advocates of the contact hypothesis maintain that greater familiarity with members of stigmatized groups can reduce prejudice directed toward those groups, especially when the increased contact takes place under certain favorable conditions. Many have noted that more exposure to individual gay and lesbian people, and gay couples in particular, has contributed to additional support for gay rights over the past few decades.

It's important to note, however, that even if increased intergroup contact were entirely effective in eliminating prejudice, the ideas discussed in this chapter make it clear that other prejudices and animosities are at risk of arising anew. Powerful elements of human nature encourage stereotyping, prejudice, and discrimination—forces that require constant attention if relations between different groups are to remain harmonious. Resources are finite, and realistic conflict over who should get them guarantees that there will always be conflict between groups (the economic perspective). Also, people need to feel valued and have a sense of self-worth, a sense that stems in part from the groups to which they belong. Thus, even when conflict over limited resources is diminished, these motivational concerns can sour intergroup relationships (the motivational perspective). And what psychologists have learned about how the mind works makes it clear that people categorize and make inferences in a way that sharpens distinctions between groups and can serve to exacerbate intergroup conflict (the cognitive perspective).

Thus, the capacity to stereotype, harbor prejudice, and act in a discriminatory fashion is present in all of us, and the responsibility for reducing intergroup hostility and conflict lies with each of us as well. We must all do our part as citizens to make sure, at a societal level, that civil rights laws are honored and

BOX 11.4 **FOCUS ON *APPLIED SOCIAL PSYCHOLOGY***

Conflict Remediation

Research by social psychologists on the contact hypothesis has inspired numerous efforts to dampen intergroup hostility by bringing together people from groups with a history of conflict. For example, programs have been designed to improve relations between Israelis and Palestinians, such as Seeds of Peace. This program brings groups of Israeli and Palestinian teenagers to the United States for a 3-week summer camp experience, in which they (like the Robbers Cave participants) tackle a variety of challenges that can only be met if everyone cooperates. Campers are also encouraged to "make one friend" with someone from the other group of kids.

Do these types of coexistence programs work? To find out, Juliana Schroeder and Jane Risen surveyed four sets of Seeds of Peace campers, 279 in all, before camp began, as it ended, and more than 9 months later (Schroeder & Risen, 2014). The participants described their attitudes toward the Israelis and Palestinians they met at camp, toward Israelis and Palestinians in general, and indicated whether they had made any friends from the other group at camp. They found that living together for 3 weeks led to attitudes at the end of the camp that were more mutually favorable, and more favorable toward each other's ethnic group, than they were at the beginning.

Some of this positive feeling ebbed when the Israeli and Palestinian teenagers returned to their homes in the Middle East. But not all of it: attitudes more than 9 months later were still more favorable than they had been at the beginning of camp. The investigators also found that forming a friendship with someone from the other group was a significant predictor of mutual attitudes after they had gone back to their normal lives.

Seeds of Peace

When Israeli and Palestinian teenagers are brought together for a 3-week residential summer camp experience in which they complete a variety of interdependent tasks, their attitudes toward each other, and toward Israelis and Palestinians in general, tend to improve.

enforced, that media depictions of different groups are not biased, and that different groups are given more opportunities to work together to achieve common goals, rather than compete for resources. Moreover, on an individual level, we can all try harder to overcome our fear that members of other groups don't really want to interact with us (Shelton & Richeson, 2005; Trawalter, Richeson, &

Shelton, 2009). Only when we reach out and interact with members of other groups as individuals will group boundaries begin to lose their significance.

⟳ LOOKING BACK

Contact between members of different groups can go a long way toward reducing group stereotypes and intergroup hostility. Intergroup contact is especially beneficial when members of different groups interact as equals, work together to try to accomplish common goals, and come together on a one-on-one basis, as well as when these interactions are supported by broader societal norms.

Chapter Review

SUMMARY

Theoretical Perspectives

- Three approaches to studying stereotyping, prejudice, and discrimination are the economic perspective, the motivational perspective, and the cognitive perspective.

Characterizing Intergroup Bias

- *Stereotypes* are generalizations about groups that are often applied to individual group members. *Prejudice* involves a negative attitude and emotional response to members of a group. *Discrimination* is unfair treatment of an individual because of the person's membership in a specific group.

- Blatant, explicit racism in much of the world is now relatively rare. But *modern racism*, whereby people consciously hold egalitarian attitudes while unconsciously having negative attitudes and exhibiting more subtle forms of prejudice, still exists.

- Benevolent racism and sexism consist of attitudes the individual thinks of as favorable toward a group but that have the effect of supporting traditional, subservient roles for members of disadvantaged groups.

- The *implicit association test (IAT)* measures nonconscious attitudes by comparing reaction times when outgroup pictures (or words) and positive items are in the same response category versus when outgroup pictures (or words) and negative items are in the same category. Another implicit measure involves *priming* with a picture of a member of some group right before the participant must identify different words; speeded response times to negative words and delayed response times to positive words reveal negative prejudice.

The Economic Perspective

- One version of the economic perspective is *realistic group conflict theory*, the theory that group conflict, prejudice, and discrimination are likely to arise over competition between groups for limited resources.

- The classic Robbers Cave experiment put two groups of boys in competition at a camp, and soon they were expressing open hostility toward each other. When the groups were brought together in noncompetitive situations where they had to cooperate to achieve shared *superordinate goals*, the hostility dissipated.

The Motivational Perspective

- According to the *motivational perspective*, poor intergroup relations can result simply because there *are* two groups, and an us/them opposition results. This occurs in the *minimal group paradigm*, where members of arbitrarily defined groups favor their fellow group members over members of the other group.

- *Social identity theory* attempts to explain ingroup favoritism, maintaining that self-esteem is derived in part from group membership and group success.

The Cognitive Perspective

- The *cognitive perspective* focuses on stereotypes, which are a form of categorization. People rely on them all the time, but especially when they are tired or overburdened.

- Several construal processes lead to inaccurate stereotypes. People tend to assume outgroups are more homogeneous than ingroups, leading to the *outgroup homogeneity effect*. People engage in biased information processing, seeing aspects of other groups that confirm their own stereotypes and failing to see facts that are inconsistent with them.

- Erroneous stereotypes can also be unknowingly maintained through self-fulfilling prophecies, when a person acts toward members of certain groups in ways that encourage the very behavior they expect.

- Distinctive groups (because they are in the minority) are often associated with distinctive (rare) behaviors. This *paired distinctiveness* results in attributing illusory properties to such groups, creating illusory correlations.

- Contradictory evidence about group members may not change people's ideas about a group because people often consider such evidence an exception that proves the rule. Behavior consistent with a stereotype tends to be attributed to the dispositions of the group members, whereas behavior that is inconsistent with a stereotype is often attributed to the situation.

- People tend to code favorable evidence about ingroup members more abstractly and the same sort of evidence about outgroup members less abstractly. The reverse is true for unfavorable evidence.

- People sometimes respond to outgroup members reflexively, relying on automatic processes whereby prejudice is unleashed outside of awareness. Often these automatic reactions can be corrected by conscious, controlled processes.

Being a Member of a Stigmatized Group

- Members of stigmatized groups suffer from attributional ambiguity. They have to ask whether others' negative or positive behavior toward them is due to prejudice or to some factor unrelated to their group membership.

- The performance of members of stigmatized groups can be impaired by *stereotype threat*, the fear that they will confirm others' stereotypes.

- Members of minority groups are sometimes tempted to try to hide their minority group status, an effort that is associated with physical and psychological costs.

Reducing Stereotypes, Prejudice, and Discrimination

- Contact between members of different groups can reduce intergroup hostility, especially if the contact involves one-on-one interactions between individuals of equal status, if it encourages the cooperative pursuit of superordinate goals, and if it is supported by the prevailing norms in each group.

THINK ABOUT IT

1. Is it possible for people to be prejudiced without being aware of it? How have researchers addressed this question, and what evidence have they found?

2. Suppose every year, the male CEO of a small company always asks a female employee to take care of organizing the company's holiday party. When one female employee asks the CEO why he always gives this task to women, he says that women are better party planners than men. Is this an example of sexism? Why or why not? What adverse effects might the CEO's positive stereotype regarding women's party planning ability have on the female employees?

3. Describe the Robbers Cave experiment, and outline three important points this study revealed about intergroup relations.

4. Imagine that a conversation about race relations in the United States develops during a family dinner. One of your relatives argues that given how ubiquitous stereotypes are, prejudice and discrimination are inevitable.

Using research from the cognitive perspective, in particular automatic and controlling processing, how would you respond to this assertion? Are prejudice and discrimination inevitable? Under which conditions are they more likely to emerge?

5. Suppose a woman named Taylor was applying for a job at an accounting firm, and applicants had to complete a math test as part of the onsite interview process. If Taylor met her older male interviewer just prior to taking the math test and he (inappropriately) exclaimed, "You're Taylor? I was expecting, well, a man . . ." what impact might that have on Taylor's test performance, interview performance, and eventual likelihood of getting the job?

6. Suppose you are a social psychologist and have been hired to help reduce prejudice and discrimination among students of different races, classes, cultures, and sexual orientations in a school system. What might you evaluate or implement in addressing this concern?

THE ANSWER GUIDELINES FOR THE THINK ABOUT IT QUESTIONS
CAN BE FOUND AT THE BACK OF THE BOOK . . . 👉

Groups

On March 16, 1985, a beautiful sunny morning in Beirut, Lebanon, Terry Anderson, the Middle East bureau chief for the Associated Press, was returning from a tennis game, eager to see his pregnant fiancée. As he was dropping off his tennis opponent, a young AP photographer, a green Mercedes pulled up and three men brandishing 9-mm pistols jumped out and forced Anderson into the car. They put a blanket over his head and sped off to an unknown location in the city.

Thus began his six-and-a-half-year ordeal as a hostage in the hands of the group Islamic Jihad. He was transferred many times to different locations throughout Lebanon, sometimes with other hostages, sometimes alone. He was not tortured in the sense of being subjected to intense physical pain in an effort to extract information. But he was frequently slapped or beaten as a result of perceived offenses; he was chained to a cot and unable to move for long periods of time, and most places he was kept were dark and filthy, and permitted very little movement.

What he dreaded most, however, were the long periods when he was held somewhere alone, without other prisoners. In his 1993 memoir, he wrote:

> This solitary confinement is killing me . . . There is nothing to hold on to, no way to anchor my mind . . . there's nothing there, just a blankness. . . . I never realized how dependent I was on other people, how much I needed to be around others, to feed off them mentally. Do I have anything of my own inside me? Is there any core there? (pp. 187–188)

Three years into his ordeal, he snapped. "My mind started spinning out of control, thoughts just spinning and spinning. I couldn't stop it. I walked over to the wall and began beating my forehead against it, hard, harder, trying to make it all

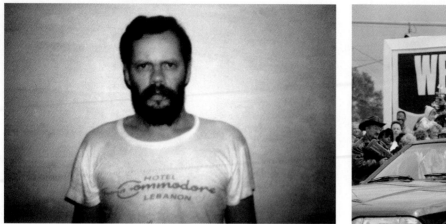

The Importance of Group Life
Terry Anderson suffered in many ways during the years he was held hostage, but he said the worst parts were the periods when he was kept in isolation. His experience, and that of many other prisoners, highlights our fundamentally social nature.

stop" (Anderson, 1993, p. 233). Although he often fought with the other hostages when they were together (no surprise, given their physical and mental state and the conditions in which they were kept), Anderson was clear that he would rather have any companionship, even that of his most brutal guards, than no companionship at all.

The Nature and Purpose of Group Living

"No man is an island, entire of itself; every man is a piece of the continent, a part of the main."

—JOHN DONNE, ENGLISH POET

Anderson's experience speaks to our fundamentally social nature. Humans and all large primates (except orangutans) live in groups, so group life must provide some advantages in the struggle for survival. These advantages, however, are not well understood, because different mammalian species have successfully pursued both solitary and group lifestyles. Wolves live in groups but bears do not, and neither of these species appears any worse off for the particular lifestyle it has pursued.

Still, it's generally maintained that life with others gave our ancestors protection from predators, efficiency in acquiring food, assistance with rearing children, and defense against aggressors—benefits that humans are less equipped to do without than bears or orangutans. It's also generally maintained that these benefits are so crucial to survival that we have a psychological need to be with others and belong to groups (Baumeister & Leary, 1995; Correll & Park, 2005).

What, exactly, is a group? This is not an easy question to answer, since there are so many different types of groups, and they don't always share many features. The members of a baseball team are clearly a group, but most people wouldn't consider the members of a large lecture course to be a group. Similarly, most people would say the individuals riding together in an elevator are not a group. But suppose the elevator breaks down, and those inside must figure out how to escape or summon help. Most would say the people in the elevator now seem more like a real group. Why?

A group has been described as "a collection of individuals who have relations to one another that make them interdependent to some significant degree" (Cartwright & Zander, 1968, p. 46). Thus, the people in the functioning elevator don't make up a group because they're not very interdependent. But once the elevator breaks down and they must decide on joint action (or whether to take joint action), they become interdependent and hence more of a group. There are degrees of interdependence, of course, and therefore degrees of "groupness" (McGrath, 1984). The members of a family are more of a "real" group than are participants in a seminar, and seminar attendees, in turn, are more of a group than are students in a large lecture course. By this reasoning, a nation's citizens make up something of a group, but they are less of a group than the members of a tribe or band, who interact more often and are more directly dependent on one another.

This chapter explores how groups function, how they make decisions, and how group decision making can go wrong. It also examines how people achieve positions of leadership within a group, as well as the effects of power on people with authority. Finally, the chapter explores how orderly groups can devolve into unruly mobs when its members' personal identities are diminished.

Social Facilitation

Let's begin by considering one of the simplest, most basic questions about social life: What effect does the presence of other people have on human performance? Does the presence of others typically help or hinder performance, or does it have no effect at all? To address these questions, let's consider them in more personal and vivid terms. Suppose you're by yourself trying to perfect a skill—practicing the piano, developing a topspin lob for your tennis game, or working through the intricacies of conjugating Latin verbs. You feel you're making progress when someone takes a seat nearby and proceeds to observe—a perfect stranger, your mother, or even, say, Meryl Streep or Benedict Cumberbatch. What does this other person's presence do to your performance? Does it give you the energy and focus necessary to bring your performance to new heights? Or do you become so nervous and distracted that your performance suffers?

Initial Research

Norman Triplett (1898) is often credited with being the first person to experimentally examine the effect of other people's presence on human performance. Triplett was something of a bicycling enthusiast (or "wheelman," as they were known at the time). After reviewing speed records put out by the Racing Board of the League of American Wheelmen, Triplett noticed that the fastest times were recorded when cyclists competed directly against one another on the same track at the same time. Much slower speed records were obtained when cyclists raced alone against the clock. Thus, Triplett believed that the presence of others tended to facilitate human performance.

Triplett realized, however, that cycling records did not offer the best test of his hypothesis, so he conducted what is widely referred to as social psychology's first experiment (Triplett, 1898). He invited a group of 40 children to his laboratory

Social Facilitation and Competition
Performance is typically enhanced in the presence of others when the activity is well learned, as cycling is for Vincenzo Nibali of Italy, shown here entering Paris as the winner of Le Tour de France 2014.

and had them turn a fishing reel as fast as they could. Each child did so on six trials with rest periods in between. On three of the trials the child was alone, and on three trials another child was alongside doing the same thing. Under these more controlled conditions, Triplett found that the children tended to turn the reel faster when in the presence of another child engaged in the same activity. The presence of others appeared to facilitate their performance. Research on this subject thus came to be known as **social facilitation** research.

A number of subsequent experiments reinforced Triplett's findings and extended them in two important ways. First, the same effects were obtained when the others were not doing the same thing (that is, not "coacting"), but were merely present as an audience of passive observers (Gates, 1924; Travis, 1925). Second, the same effect was also observed in a vast number of animal species, indicating that the phenomenon is quite general and fundamental. For example, animals as diverse as dogs, fish, armadillos, opossums, and frogs have been shown to eat more when in the presence of other members of the same species than when alone (Boice, Quanty, & Williams, 1974; Platt & James, 1966; Platt, Yaksh, & Darby, 1967; Ross & Ross, 1949; Uematsu, 1970). Other studies have shown that ants dig more earth (Chen, 1937), fruit flies do more preening (Connolly, 1968), and centipedes run faster through mazes (Hosey, Wood, Thompson, & Druck, 1985) when together than when alone. For both humans and other animals, then, much of the research on this topic indicates that the presence of others facilitates performance.

Unfortunately, however, numerous exceptions emerged soon after Triplett's original findings. Floyd Allport (1920), for example, asked undergraduate students to refute philosophical arguments as best they could in a 5-minute period. The students provided higher-quality refutations when working alone than when working in the presence of another student. The presence of others has also been shown to inhibit performance on arithmetic problems, memory tasks, and maze learning (Dashiell, 1930; Pessin, 1933; Pessin & Husband, 1933). And the presence of other members of the same species has sometimes been found to inhibit the performance of animals (Allee & Masure, 1936; Shelley, 1965; Strobel, 1972).

Resolving the Contradictions

For a time, then, it seemed that the best answer to the question of what is the effect of the presence of others on performance was that it sometimes helps and sometimes hurts. That's not a terribly satisfying answer. It's about as helpful as a political pundit saying that the Democrats will regain a Senate majority in the next election, but then again they might not. Although that may be all you'd expect from a political forecaster, you probably want more from research psychologists who study social facilitation.

Zajonc's Theory Fortunately, a more satisfying understanding eventually emerged when social psychologist Robert Zajonc proposed an elegant theory to account for all the divergent findings on this topic. Zajonc (1965) argued that the presence of others, indeed the *mere* presence of others, tends to facilitate

"The bodily presence of another contestant participating in the race serves to liberate latent energy not ordinarily available."

—NORMAN TRIPLETT

social facilitation Initially a term for enhanced performance in the presence of others; now a broader term for the effect, positive or negative, of the presence of others on performance.

performance on simple or well-learned tasks, but it hinders performance on difficult or novel tasks. Even more importantly, Zajonc's theory explained *why* the presence of others has these effects.

Zajonc's theory has three components (**Figure 12.1**). First, the mere presence of others makes a person more aroused. (More generally, the mere presence of another member of the same species tends to arouse most organisms.) Other people are dynamic and unpredictable stimuli, capable of doing almost anything at any time. We therefore need to be alert, or aroused, in their presence so we can react to what they might do.

Second, arousal tends to make a person more rigid, in the sense that she becomes even more inclined to do what she's already automatically inclined to do. In the language Zajonc used, arousal makes a person more likely to make a **dominant response**. Think of it like this: in any situation, you can respond in a variety of ways, arranged in a hierarchy according to their likelihood of occurrence. Whatever you are most inclined to do in that situation is at the top of the hierarchy and is thus the dominant response. When aroused, Zajonc argued, people are even more inclined to make that dominant response.

The third component of Zajonc's theory links the increase in dominant response tendencies to the facilitation of simple tasks and the inhibition of complex tasks. For easy or well-learned tasks, the dominant response is likely to be the correct response. In fact, that's tantamount to what it means for a task to be easy or well learned. Thus, the presence of other people, by facilitating the dominant response, facilitates the correct response and improves performance. In contrast, for difficult or novel tasks, the dominant response is not likely to be the correct response. Again, that's what it means for a task to be difficult or novel. Thus, the presence of others facilitates an *incorrect* response and hinders performance.

Robert B. Zajonc

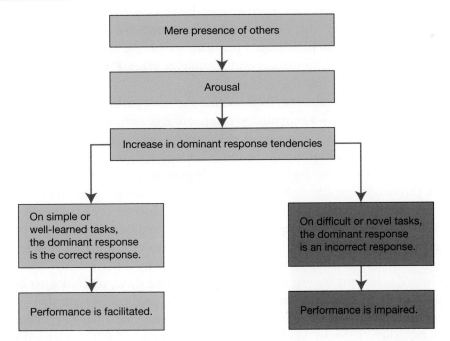

Figure 12.1

Zajonc's Model of Social Facilitation

The presence of others (indeed, their mere presence) increases arousal and facilitates dominant response tendencies. This improves performance on easy or well-learned tasks but hinders performance on difficult or novel tasks.

dominant response In a person's hierarchy of possible responses in any context, the response he or she is most likely to make.

Testing the Theory Zajonc's theory provided a remarkably accurate summary of the diverse findings that existed at the time. Like any theory, however, it had to be subjected to more stringent challenges in order to be validated. The available results didn't provide a sufficiently rigorous test; after all, the theory was based on the existing findings and therefore *had* to be consistent with them. Thus, since its publication, Zajonc's theory has been tested in a variety of ways on numerous occasions, and it has held up extremely well.

For example, Zajonc and his colleagues placed cockroaches in the start box of one of two mazes and then shone a light at the start box (Zajonc, Heingartner, & Herman, 1969). Cockroaches instinctively flee from light and head toward a dark area; in this case, the cockroaches would try to reach the dark goal box. In the simple maze (a "runway"), getting to the darkened chamber was easy. The cockroach needed only to do what it does instinctively: run directly away from the light (its dominant response). In contrast, getting to the darkened chamber in the complex maze was more of a challenge: the cockroach had to do more than follow its instincts and flee from the light; it had to execute a turn. Two features of this setup were especially important. First, because cockroaches invariably run from light, doing so is clearly their dominant response. Second, Zajonc created two different conditions: in one, the dominant response led to the goal (the simple maze); in the other, it did not (the complex maze).

RUBES®　　　　**By Leigh Rubin**

OK, EVERYBODY, STAY QUIET... I HEAR BOB COMING!

HAPPY BIRTHDAY

CLICK

ZIP! ZIP! ZIP!

Why cockroaches give lousy surprise parties.

Zajonc had the cockroaches run one of these two mazes either alone or with another cockroach. He predicted that cockroaches running the simple maze would get to the goal box more quickly when together than when alone, but that those running the complex maze together would take longer to reach the chamber. Indeed, that's exactly what happened: the presence of another cockroach facilitated performance on the simple maze but hindered performance on the complex maze (**Figure 12.2**).

Coacting vs. Mere Presence To show that the *mere* presence of another cockroach has these effects—as opposed to competition or some other, more complex factor than the presence of others of the same species—Zajonc added a condition in which the cockroach ran the maze not with another cockroach running alongside, but with other cockroaches merely present as a passive "audience." To create this condition, Zajonc built a set of Plexiglas boxes, or "grandstands," that flanked the two mazes and then filled them with observer cockroaches. Again, as Figure 12.2 indicates, the results were exactly as predicted: the presence of the observing cockroaches facilitated performance on the simple maze but inhibited performance on the complex maze.

Once Zajonc's theory was validated in studies like these, psychologists could apply it to the real world by making more precise predictions than they could beforehand about what ought to happen in everyday life (Ben-Zeev, Fein, & Inzlicht, 2005; Thomas, Skitka, Christen, & Jurgena, 2002). An experiment conducted in a university pool hall is a good example of such a real-world extension (Michaels, Blommel, Brocato, Linkous, & Rowe, 1982). Students playing recreational pool were unobtrusively observed and deemed skilled or unskilled based on their performance. Zajonc's theory predicts that the presence of an

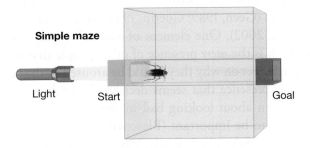

Simple maze

Light   Start   Goal

In the **simple maze**, the cockroach need only follow its dominant response and run directly away from the light to get to the goal.

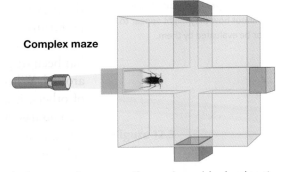

Complex maze

In the **complex maze**, the cockroach's dominant response does not easily lead it to the goal. The cockroach must execute a turn.

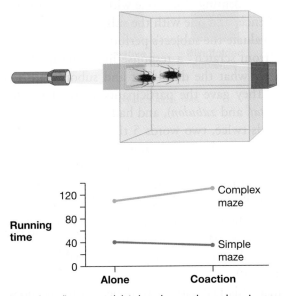

Average time (in seconds) taken by cockroaches to negotiate simple or complex mazes when alone or alongside another cockroach.

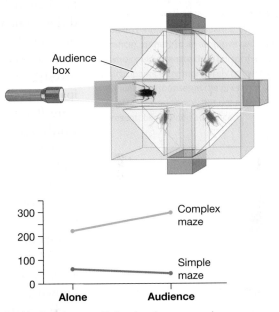

Audience box

Average time to negotiate simple or complex mazes when alone or in the presence of an audience.

Figure 12.2

Social Facilitation in Another Species

For cockroaches, as for humans, the presence of others increases dominant response tendencies, leading to better performance on easy tasks and worse performance on difficult tasks.

SOURCE: Adapted from Zajonc et al., 1969.

audience should make the skilled players perform better (for them, the task is easy) and the unskilled players perform worse (for them, the task is difficult). To test this prediction, the experimenters walked up to the pool tables and watched. As expected, the good players did even better than before, and the poor players did even worse.

Mere Presence or Evaluation Apprehension?

Zajonc's theory remains the most compelling and widely accepted account of social facilitation. Few social psychologists question his contention that the presence of others increases arousal, and virtually no one disputes the claim that

TABLE 12.1 SOCIAL FACILITATION AND THE EFFECT OF AN AUDIENCE

	ALONE	MERELY PRESENT AUDIENCE	ATTENTIVE AUDIENCE
WELL-LEARNED TASKS (OWN SHOES)	16.5 sec	13.5 sec	11.7 sec
NOVEL TASKS (LAB SHOES, SOCKS, AND COAT)	28.8 sec	32.7 sec	33.9 sec

SOURCE: Adapted from Markus, 1978.

to worry about being observed or evaluated. From the participant's perspective, the experiment has yet to begin, and therefore there is no cause for evaluation apprehension. The subject believes that he or she is both physically and psychologically alone.

Even though the participants did not think they were "performing," Zajonc's theory predicts that they should change their own clothes faster and the novel clothes more slowly when in the mere presence of another person. As shown in **Table 12.1**, that's exactly what happened. Participants took off and put on their own shoes more quickly, and the experimenter's shoes, socks, and coat more slowly, when in the presence of another person—even when the other person had his back turned and was unable to observe. Thus, when a true alone condition is included, an effect of the mere presence of someone else can be observed. Note again that the effects were stronger for an attentive audience than for a merely present audience, but that is not a problem for the theory. It just means evaluation apprehension can add to a person's arousal and thus compound the effect of mere presence. Overall, these results and those of similar investigations strongly support Zajonc's theory (Cottrell et al., 1968; Platania & Moran, 2001; Rajecki, Ickes, Corcoran, & Lenerz, 1977; Schmitt, Gilovich, Goore, & Joseph, 1986).

In light of the research by Zajonc and Markus, it seems safe to say that the mere presence of others is sufficient to increase arousal and thus facilitate performance on well-learned tasks and inhibit performance on novel tasks. At the same time, an interesting and healthy debate continues about *why* the mere presence of others has such effects. Some social psychologists have argued, in fact, that it is not the mere presence of another person that has these effects, but something that always accompanies the awareness of the mere presence of another. They have put forward a **distraction-conflict theory** of social facilitation based on the idea that being aware of another person's presence creates a conflict between attending to that person and attending to the task at hand. They believe that this attentional conflict is arousing, and that *this* arousal underlies the standard social facilitation effects (Baron, 1986; Baron, Moore, & Sanders, 1978; Groff, Baron, & Moore, 1983; Huguet, Galvaing, Monteil, & Dumas, 1999; Sanders, 1981). Thus far, not enough data in support of this claim have been collected to settle the issue (Guerin, 1993). However, researchers have shown, intriguingly, that nonsocial distractions (such as being required to perform two tasks simultaneously) can generate effects just like the standard social facilitation effects (Sanders & Baron, 1975).

distraction-conflict theory A theory based on the idea that being aware of another person's presence creates a conflict between paying attention to that person and paying attention to the task at hand, and that this attentional conflict is arousing and produces social facilitation effects.

Practical Applications

The basic pattern of facilitation of simple tasks and inhibition of complex tasks is reliable enough to warrant some practical advice. Of greatest relevance to student life, perhaps, is the obvious recommendation for how to study. Study alone. When the material is unfamiliar and must be committed to memory, it's best to do so without the arousal and distraction brought on by the presence of others. Study groups may be helpful for reviewing or for dividing up and summarizing vast amounts of material, and groups can be invaluable when some members have information or approaches that the others do not, but the hard work of absorbing and integrating new ideas should be done alone. Then, once the material is assimilated, sitting cheek by jowl with the other students in the examination room will often aid performance.

Another potentially important practical application involves the way workspaces might be designed. If the tasks to be accomplished are simple or repetitive, then the setting should be designed so that people are in contact with one another. Such a design reaps the benefits of social facilitation of simple tasks. But if the tasks to be performed are challenging and ever-changing, it may be wise to give everyone the luxury of privacy.

Dominant Responses and Social Facilitation
People tend to do better on well-learned tasks but worse on difficult or poorly mastered tasks in the presence of others. Presumably, the children who know the material well will do better on these standardized tests in the presence of other test takers because their dominant responses will be correct. But children who don't know the material well will be more likely to give incorrect answers in the presence of others.

Beyond Social Facilitation

One hundred years of research on social facilitation has made it clear that the mere presence of others is sufficient to increase arousal and thus facilitate performance on well-learned tasks and inhibit performance on novel tasks. It's also clear, however, that people are complex stimuli and that their presence can have a variety of effects that overlay the influence of mere presence examined here. People are often very concerned about making a good impression, and their evaluation apprehension can intensify arousal and lead to more pronounced social facilitation effects.

At times, however, the presence of others can mask the typical social facilitation effects. If those who are present belittle effort and devalue accomplishment, then performance will be inhibited even on simple tasks. In many work settings, for example, employees have powerful norms against working too hard, and "rate busters" are made to feel the wrath of the group, so that output suffers on even the simplest tasks (Homans, 1965). Similarly, African-American students sometimes put out less effort—and hence don't perform as well—in the presence of other African-Americans in order to avoid "acting white" (Ogbu, 1991; Ogbu & Davis, 2003). And consider Erving Goffman's rather charming example of adolescent boys riding a carousel. When others are present, the boys engage in a variety of behaviors designed to convey "role distance," or lack of interest in the carousel (Goffman, 1961). If such a desire to maintain role distance were to emerge in a performance setting, it would surely impede output, regardless of how energizing the presence of others might be.

Perhaps the most common pattern of responses that runs counter to the standard social facilitation effects is what social psychologists call **social loafing**, or the tendency to exert less effort when working on a group task in

social loafing The tendency to exert less effort when working on a group task in which individual contributions cannot be monitored.

which individual contributions cannot be monitored (Hoeksema-van Orden, Gaillard, & Buunk, 1998; Karau & Williams, 1995; Latané, Williams, & Harkins, 1979; Plaks & Higgins, 2000; Price, Harrison, & Gavin, 2006; Sanna, 1992; Shepperd, 1995; Shepperd & Taylor, 1999; Williams, Harkins, & Latané, 1981). If you and your friends have to move a couch up a flight of stairs, for example, you might be tempted to coast a bit and hope your friends' more vigorous efforts will get the job done. In these situations, people often loaf because their contributions are not seen as crucial to the success of the effort, and because their individual contributions—and hence they themselves—can't be assessed.

Social Loafing
When their contributions cannot be individually monitored, people have a tendency to loaf, working less hard than they would otherwise and relying on the efforts of others to get the job done.

🕙 LOOKING BACK

Even the most minimal group situation—the mere presence of a single other person—can influence performance. The presence of others is arousing, and arousal accentuates a person's existing performance tendencies. Easy tasks are made easier, and difficult tasks are made more difficult.

Group Decision Making

When people come together in groups, one of the most important things they do is make decisions. Groups that can't decide what to do or how to act don't function well. They bicker, wallow, and often split apart. It should come as no surprise, then, that social psychologists have spent considerable energy studying how—and how well—groups make decisions (Hinsz, Tindale, & Vollrath, 1997; Kerr, MacCoun, & Kramer, 1996; Laughlin, Hatch, Silver, & Boh, 2006; Levine & Moreland, 1990, 1998; Sommers, 2006).

Much of the research on group decision making has been guided by the assumption that decisions made by groups are typically better than those made by individuals. Many heads are better than one. And indeed, when groups and individuals are presented with problems for which there are precise, factual answers (such as the horse-trading problem discussed in Chapter 9), groups are more likely than the average individual to come up with the correct solution (Laughlin, 1988; Laughlin & Ellis, 1986).

Yet in many contexts, group decisions are no better than those rendered by individuals. The key to understanding such contexts is to recognize that although arriving at a best possible solution to a problem may be the *group's* most important goal, it may not be the most important goal for any of the individual group members. Individuals may be more concerned with how they will be judged by everyone else, how they can avoid hurting someone's feelings, how they can dodge responsibility if things go wrong, and so on. When people get together to make group decisions, some predictable social psychological processes unfold that can subvert the stated goal of arriving at the best possible choice.

"[When people] come together . . . they may surpass, collectively and as a body, the quality of the few best. . . . When there are many who contribute to the process of deliberation, each can bring his share of goodness and moral prudence."

—ARISTOTLE

Groupthink

In informal settings where social harmony is all-important and the costs of making an incorrect decision are not great, it's hardly surprising that group pressure to be agreeable and arrive at a unanimous decision can lead to defective decision making. But what happens when life and death are literally at stake, and the incentives to "get it right" are high? In those contexts, surely people wouldn't go along with faulty reasoning merely to preserve group harmony or to avoid embarrassment, would they? Yes, they would—and they do.

Irving Janis carefully analyzed a number of decisions made at the very highest levels of the U.S. government and found evidence of just this sort of calamitous group decision making (Janis, 1972, 1982; see also Esser, 1998). Here are a few of the fiascos Janis looked at:

- The Kennedy administration's attempt to foster the overthrow of Fidel Castro's regime by depositing a group of CIA-trained Cuban refugees on the beaches of Cuba's Bay of Pigs but failing to provide air cover. (The refugees were captured in short order, thus humiliating the United States internationally, both for its role in trying to undermine a sovereign nation and for initially denying its involvement in the affair.)

- The Johnson administration's decision to increase the number of American soldiers fighting in Vietnam. (This policy failed to advance U.S. objectives in the region and substantially increased the number of lives lost.)

- The conclusion by the U.S. naval high command that extra precautions were not needed at Pearl Harbor despite warnings of an imminent attack by the Japanese. (This had severe repercussions on December 7, 1941, the "day of infamy," when the Japanese destroyed a large part of the U.S. Pacific Fleet at the Pearl Harbor naval base in a surprise attack.)

Janis maintained that these calamitous decisions were made because of **groupthink**, a kind of faulty thinking by highly cohesive groups in which the critical scrutiny that should be devoted to the issues at hand is subverted by social pressures to reach consensus. Other investigators have made the same claim about other disasters, such as the ill-fated launches of the space shuttles *Challenger* and *Columbia*, and more recent consequential government decisions (Esser & Lindoerfer, 1989; Glanz & Schwartz, 2003; see **Box 12.1**).

Symptoms and Sources of Groupthink According to Janis, groupthink is a sort of psychological diminishment characterized by a shallow examination of information, a narrow consideration of alternatives, and a sense of invulnerability and moral superiority (Janis, 1972). Especially under the direction of a strong leader, groups may ignore or reject alternative viewpoints, discourage others from coming forward with alternative ideas and assessments, and end up overly confident about the wisdom and moral correctness of their proposed solutions. Thus, the very source of a group's potentially superior decision making—the airing of differing opinions and the presentation of varied facts and perspectives—never comes into play (**Figure 12.4**).

The historical record shows that social psychological forces have had a hand in numerous instances of faulty decision making, sometimes with disastrous consequences. Less clear, however, is whether these psychological processes cluster together to produce a recognizable condition of groupthink (Choi & Kim, 1999;

groupthink Faulty thinking by members of highly cohesive groups in which the critical scrutiny that should be devoted to the issues at hand is subverted by social pressures to reach consensus.

BOX 12.1 **FOCUS ON *GOVERNMENT***

Groupthink in the Bush Administration

Groupthink seems to have played a role in the miscalculations that plagued the Bush administration's decision to invade Iraq in 2003. A report by the U.S. Senate Intelligence Committee identified groupthink as one factor that led the principal decision makers to err so badly in their claim that Iraq possessed weapons of mass destruction (WMDs). Specifically, the report concluded that many of the groups involved in assessing the threat posed by Iraq "demonstrated several aspects of groupthink: examining few alternatives, selective gathering of information, pressure to conform within the group or withhold criticism, and collective rationalization" (Select Committee on Intelligence, 2004). The committee also found fault with administration analysts for failing to put in place common safeguards against groupthink, "such as . . . 'devil's advocacy,' and other types of alternative or competitive analysis."

Unfortunately, this tendency by policy-making groups to seek support

The Dangers of Groupthink
Post-mortem analyses of the decision to invade Iraq in 2003 identified examples of apparent groupthink on the part of those responsible for the decision.

for existing views rather than subject them to critical scrutiny is sufficiently common that the U.S. military has its own name for the phenomenon—incestuous amplification, which *Jane's* *Defense Weekly* defines as "a condition in warfare where one only listens to those who are already in lock-step agreement, reinforcing set beliefs and creating a situation ripe for miscalculation."

Henningsen, Henningsen, Eden, & Cruz, 2006; Turner & Pratkanis, 1998). Do such conditions as cohesiveness, insularity, and high stress tend to occur together, or are they separate variables that might inhibit effective decision making? And are the various sources and symptoms of groupthink *essential* ingredients of this sort of faulty decision making? Questions like these have not been adequately resolved, and the evidence gathered to test Janis's thesis has been mixed at best (Aldag & Fuller, 1993; Longley & Pruitt, 1980; McCauley, 1989; Tetlock, Peterson, McGuire, Chang, & Feld, 1992). Nonetheless, his observations have been useful in identifying social factors that can lead to calamitous decisions, as well as factors that can improve group decision making.

For example, strong, directive leaders who make their preferences known sometimes intimidate even the most accomplished group members and stifle vigorous discussion (McCauley, 1998). Also, just as Janis contends, at times the issue that must be decided is so stressful that groups seek the reassurance and comfort of premature or illusory consensus. In addition, both strong leaders and the drive to find consensus breed **self-censorship**, or the decision to withhold information or opinions. Janis reports that Arthur Schlesinger, a member of

self-censorship Withholding information or opinions in group discussions.

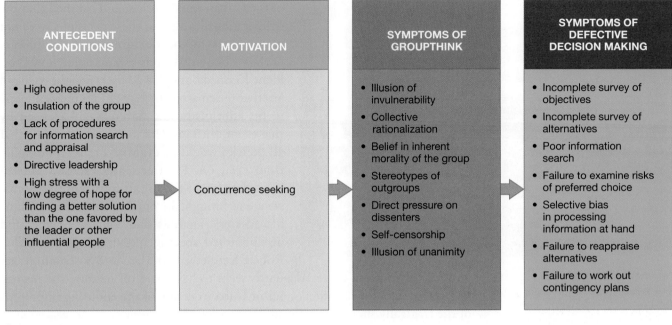

ANTECEDENT CONDITIONS	MOTIVATION	SYMPTOMS OF GROUPTHINK	SYMPTOMS OF DEFECTIVE DECISION MAKING
• High cohesiveness • Insulation of the group • Lack of procedures for information search and appraisal • Directive leadership • High stress with a low degree of hope for finding a better solution than the one favored by the leader or other influential people	Concurrence seeking	• Illusion of invulnerability • Collective rationalization • Belief in inherent morality of the group • Stereotypes of outgroups • Direct pressure on dissenters • Self-censorship • Illusion of unanimity	• Incomplete survey of objectives • Incomplete survey of alternatives • Poor information search • Failure to examine risks of preferred choice • Selective bias in processing information at hand • Failure to reappraise alternatives • Failure to work out contingency plans

Figure 12.4
Elements of Janis's Groupthink Hypothesis
Certain conditions lead decision-making groups to be excessively concerned with seeking consensus, which detracts from a full, rational analysis of the existing problem.

SOURCE: Adapted from Janis & Mann, 1977, p. 132.

President Kennedy's inner circle during the Bay of Pigs deliberations, was ever afterward haunted

> for having kept so silent during those crucial discussions in the Cabinet Room. . . . I can only explain my failure to do more than raise a few timid questions by reporting that one's impulse to blow the whistle on this nonsense was simply undone by the circumstances of the discussion. (Quoted in Janis, 1982, p. 39)

Some of the participants in that fiasco have written that the pressures to agree with the unsound plan were so great because the group was newly created, and the participants were reluctant to step on each other's toes. In contrast, by the time they came together to deliberate over subsequent crises, they had been around the block with one another and were more willing to offer and accept criticism without worrying so much about threatening their relationship with the group.

Preventing Groupthink Even though the theory may be less than precise, Janis's suggestions for how to improve group deliberations have been shown to have merit. Freer, more vigorous discussion is likely to take place, for example, if the leader refrains from making his or her opinions or preferences known at the beginning. Groups can also avoid the tunnel vision and illusion of consensus that Janis describes by making sure the group isn't cut off from outside input. Individuals who haven't been privy to the early stages of a discussion can provide a fresh perspective as well as put the brakes on any rash actions that might otherwise develop. Finally, a similar safeguard against rash action and unsound argumentation is to designate one person in the group to play devil's advocate—to be given every incentive to name any and all weaknesses in the group's proposed plan of action.

In addition to his analysis of foreign policy fiascos, Janis examined a number of highly successful decisions, including the Kennedy administration's handling

Preventing Groupthink
John F. Kennedy's cabinet met during the Cuban missile crisis to try to resolve the impasse with the Soviets over Soviet missiles in Cuba. They took steps to avoid groupthink by encouraging vigorous debate and making recommendations based on unbiased analysis.

of the Cuban missile crisis, and claimed that the deliberations leading to these decisions were not marked by symptoms of groupthink. In the case of the Cuban missile crisis, Janis noted how President Kennedy and his advisers sought to avoid another fiasco after the Bay of Pigs incident early in his administration. Severely embarrassed by that event, the president took steps to ensure that all policies would be evaluated more thoroughly from then on. He frequently excused himself from the group so as not to constrain the discussion. He brought in outside experts to critique his advisers' analysis and tentative plans, and he appointed specific individuals (his brother, Robert Kennedy, and Theodore Sorensen) to act as devil's advocates. These safeguards seem to have paid off because the negotiations that kept Soviet missiles out of Cuba were one of the enduring highlights of the tragically short Kennedy administration.

Groupthink in Other Cultures Groupthink can take different forms in non-Western cultures. The drive toward harmony is greater, for example, in East Asian cultures such as Japan than in Western cultures such as the United States (Nisbett, 2003). Groupthink in places like Japan can be so great, in fact, that even at scientific meetings there is rarely true debate or any other exchange that might appear confrontational or cause anyone to lose face. Japanese scientists who are familiar with Western norms of scientific discourse believe their own science suffers from not giving ideas a public airing. In fact, Japanese science seems to be underperforming, given the amount of money spent on scientific research in that country (French, 2001).

Still, Japanese corporations are in general highly effective, and in some industries they are the most competitive in the world. How is this possible if open and free debate does not take place? Japanese managers have meetings where they discuss policy issues, but these discussions may only appear to be like Western meetings. Nothing is really debated; instead, participants simply nod their approval of the proposal brought to them. This sounds like a recipe for disaster, but it turns out that managers typically discuss matters with everyone individually before the meeting to find out their views. The frank exchange goes on before the meeting, consensus is achieved as a result of these individual encounters, and the larger meeting is then little more than a rubber stamp. Although this procedure of one-on-one discussion and establishing consensus may be different from procedures to improve group decision making in Western organizations, it seems likely that it's helpful in preventing groupthink.

Group Decisions: Risky or Conservative?

Implicit in all the concern over avoiding groupthink is the suspicion that groups are often too rash—that decisions made by groups are often riskier and less thoroughly thought out than those made by individuals. But popular culture tends to hold precisely the opposite belief—namely, that groups abhor risk and tend to adopt middle-of-the-road solutions. Thus, in the United States at least, we tend to celebrate the swashbuckling CEO or politician who breaks free of institutional inertia and "takes chances" and "gets things done." So which is it? Do groups tend to make riskier or more cautious decisions than individuals? What type of error do we invite—risky or conservative—when we turn over a difficult decision to a group?

James Stoner put this very question to the test in 1961 by conducting a study in which participants made decisions about various choice dilemmas. They had to render advice to a set of hypothetical individuals considering various risky courses of action. In one scenario, an engineer had to decide whether to stay in his current job, which paid a moderate salary, or take a position with a new firm in which, if successful, he could earn a great deal more money. Should he stick with the security of his current firm or take a gamble on the new job? Here is the dilemma in full (adapted from Stoner, 1961):

> Mr. A., an electrical engineer who is married and has one child, has been working for a large electronics corporation since graduating from college five years ago. He is assured of a lifetime job with a modest, though adequate, salary, and liberal pension benefits upon retirement. On the other hand, it is very unlikely that his salary will increase much before he retires. While attending a convention, Mr. A. is offered a job with a small, newly founded company that has a highly uncertain future. The new job would pay more to start and would offer the possibility of a share in the ownership if the company survived the competition of the larger firms.
>
> Imagine that you are advising Mr. A. Listed below are several probabilities or odds of the new company's proving financially sound.
>
> Please check the lowest probability that you would consider acceptable to make it worthwhile for Mr. A to take the new job.
>
> ___ The chances are 1 in 10 that the company will prove financially sound.
> ___ The chances are 3 in 10 that the company will prove financially sound.
> ___ The chances are 5 in 10 that the company will prove financially sound.
> ___ The chances are 7 in 10 that the company will prove financially sound.
> ___ The chances are 9 in 10 that the company will prove financially sound.
> ___ Place a check here if you think Mr. A should not take the new job no matter what the probability.

As you can see, participants were asked to give their advice by specifying the likelihood of success necessary for the engineer to take the job with the new company. If the new company was sure to succeed, clearly the engineer should take it because it would pay more money; if it was sure to fail, the engineer should stay put. Participants had to decide what the new firm's chances had to be to make the switch worthwhile.

Stoner's participants rendered 12 such decisions. First they did so individually, and then after meeting with other participants and arriving at a consensus. Stoner then compared the group odds with the average odds specified by each individual. He expected the group to insist on higher odds of success (that is, to make more conservative recommendations) than the average odds specified individually by each group member. He found just the opposite. The groups tended to recommend riskier courses of action than did the individual group members.

Stoner, and many after him, concluded that groups tend to make riskier decisions than individuals, a pattern that came to be known as the **risky shift** (Stoner, 1961; Wallach, Kogan, & Bem, 1962). And the group members weren't

risky shift The tendency for groups to make riskier decisions than individuals would.

"It's agreed, then, that we move forward on the philodendron."

just feigning boldness to appear courageous to everyone else. When participants were subsequently asked to render new *individual* decisions, the group discussion had left its mark. These later individual recommendations tended to be riskier than what these same people had recommended originally.

As with the findings on social facilitation, however, the initial, clear picture of whether groups make riskier decisions than individuals soon became murky. Several follow-ups to Stoner's work found that decisions made by groups were sometimes more cautious or "risk averse" than those made by individuals; that is, groups sometimes insist on greater odds of success before they're willing to recommend a risky course of action. Indeed, such a result was even found on two of Stoner's 12 original choice dilemmas. But the notion that groups sometimes make riskier decisions than individuals and sometimes make less risky decisions is hardly satisfying. Can't social psychologists tell us when groups tend to be risky and when they tend to be more cautious?

They can, and the key to discovering the higher-order pattern is to examine, in detail, the kind of issues that elicit conservative group decisions and the kind that tend to induce risky decisions. You've already seen an example of an issue for which group discussion tends to make everyone riskier. Now consider a choice dilemma for which group discussion tends to make everyone more cautious (adapted from Stoner, 1961):

> Mr. C., a married man with a 7-year-old son, can provide his family with all the necessities of life, but few of the luxuries. Mr. C.'s mother recently died, leaving his son (that is, her grandson) a small inheritance she had accumulated by scrimping and saving, making regular donations to a savings account at her local bank. Mr. C. would like to invest his son's inheritance in the stock market. He is thinking about investing in a group of "blue-chip" stocks and bonds that should earn a 6 percent return on investment with reasonable certainty. However, he recently received a reliable tip about a new biotech company that has excited all the venture capitalists. If things go as well as predicted, he could more than quadruple his son's investment in the company within the first year; if things do not go well, however, he could lose the money and join the long list of those who have been burned by investing in high-tech start-ups.

How does this example differ from the earlier one? Many people report that their first reaction to the two scenarios is very different. In the first, stay-or-switch-jobs dilemma, they find themselves thinking, "Go for it. Don't be stuck in a dead-end job all your life; you'll regret it later." In contrast, when reading the second scenario, they find themselves thinking, "Not so fast! You shouldn't put your son's (and his grandmother's) legacy at risk."

Group Polarization

After examining responses to a number of dilemmas like these, researchers hypothesized that group discussion tends to make people more inclined to go in the direction they are already inclined to go. If the issue prompts most people to be inclined toward risk, talking it over with other members of a group may make everyone even more risk seeking. If the issue prompts most people to be reluctant to take a chance, talking it over may make everyone even more conservative. Rather than an overall risky shift, in other words, there is a **group polarization** effect; that is, group decisions tend to be more *extreme* than those made by individuals. Whatever way the majority of the individuals are leaning, group discussion tends to make them lean further in that direction (Moscovici & Zavalloni, 1969; Myers & Bishop, 1971; Zuber, Crott, & Werner, 1992).

The same result holds true even when groups discuss issues that have nothing to do with risk. In one study, for example, French students expressed their opinions about General Charles de Gaulle and about Americans, first individually and then again after having discussed them in groups. The results? Their initially positive sentiments toward de Gaulle became even more positive, and their initially negative sentiments toward Americans became even more negative (Moscovici & Zavalloni, 1969). It appears that we are more likely to hear "ugly American" from a group of foreigners than from a collection of individual foreigners.

Why does group discussion lead to more extreme inclinations by group members? Why don't those in the group simply conform to the group average, with the result that group discussion doesn't tend to move the group in one direction or the other? Research indicates that two causes work in concert to produce group polarization. One involves the persuasiveness of the information brought up during group discussion; the other involves people's tendency to try to claim the "right" position in the distribution of opinions within the group. Let's consider each explanation in turn.

The "Persuasive Arguments" Account When trying to decide whether to pursue a risky or conservative course of action, people consider the different arguments in favor of each course. It stands to reason that when people are predisposed to take chances in a given situation, they can think of more and better arguments in favor of risk. When people are predisposed to play it safe, in contrast, they can think of more and better arguments that favor caution. But any one person is unlikely to think of *all* the arguments in favor of one alternative or the other. Thus, when the issue is discussed by the group, each person is likely to be exposed to new arguments. This expanded pool of arguments, in turn, is likely to be skewed in favor of risk when the people are already predisposed toward risk but skewed in favor of caution when people are already predisposed to play it safe.

The net result, then, is that group discussion tends to expose the average person to even more arguments in favor of the position that the average person was already inclined to take. This exposure only serves to strengthen those initial inclinations, and group polarization is the inevitable result. This explanation suggests that personal, face-to-face discussion is not necessary to produce group polarization. All that's needed is exposure to the pool of arguments that true group discussion tends to elicit. Several studies have tested this idea by having participants read the arguments of other group members in private so that they are exposed to the arguments without knowing who in the group might have advanced them. In support of the persuasive arguments interpretation, these studies have shown that reading others' arguments is sufficient to produce group polarization (Burnstein & Vinokur, 1973; Burnstein, Vinokur, & Trope, 1973; Clark, Crockett, & Archer, 1971).

The "Social Comparison" Interpretation Although exposure to the full pool of arguments is sufficient to induce group polarization, other social psychological

group polarization The tendency for group decisions to be more extreme than those made by individuals; whatever way the group as a whole is leaning, group discussion tends to make it lean further in that direction.

processes also encourage polarization. Foremost among them is the very human tendency to compare ourselves with everyone else. "Am I as smart as most people here?" "Do my neighbors all drive better cars than I do?" "Am I getting as much out of life as everyone else?" Consider how these sorts of comparisons might lead to group polarization. When evaluating an issue for which people are inclined to take risks (a career choice early in life), people are likely to think they're more tolerant of risk than the average person. In this case, riskiness is valued, and people like to think of themselves as having more than an average amount of a valued trait. When considering an issue for which people are inclined to be cautious (investing money that belongs to a beloved relative), however, most people are likely to think they are more prudent or risk averse than the average person. People tend to think, in other words, that they are farther out on the correct side of the opinion distribution on most issues.

What happens when everyone in a group is inclined to make the same choice—say, a risky choice—and are also inclined to think of themselves as more likely than average to take risks? Many of them will find, inevitably, that their tolerance of risk is closer to average than they thought—perhaps even below average. This realization leads some individuals to attempt to show that they are in fact more risk-tolerant than average. The group as a whole, then, becomes a bit riskier on those issues for which a somewhat risky approach initially seemed warranted. Similarly, the group would become a bit more conservative on those issues for which a somewhat cautious approach seemed warranted. In other words, the desire to distinguish oneself from others by expressing a more extreme opinion in the "right" direction leads predictably to the group polarization effect. As one journalist put it, "People are always trying to outdo one another; if everyone in a group agrees that men are jerks, then someone in the group is bound to argue that they're assholes" (Kolbert, 2009, p. 112).

This interpretation can be tested by doing just the opposite of what was done to test the persuasive arguments account: expose people to everyone else's positions without conveying the content of any of the arguments for or against one position or another. As predicted, when people are told only about others' positions and not the basis of those positions, the group polarization effect is observed (Teger & Pruitt, 1967). Notably, the group polarization effect in this experiment was weaker than usual, as would be expected if both persuasive arguments and social comparison contribute to the effect.

Valuing Risk There's one more piece to the puzzle. Social psychologists have provided satisfactory accounts of why group discussion tends to intensify group members' initial leanings. But why do group members tend to lean so often in the risky direction? Recall that in Stoner's original investigation, a shift toward greater risk was observed on 10 of the 12 scenarios, a predisposition toward risk that has been replicated in subsequent studies.

The logic of both the persuasive arguments and social comparison interpretations leads to the inescapable inference that people—or, at least, the American college students who have made up the bulk of the participants in these studies—must typically value risk taking over caution. It's not hard to show that this is the case. When American participants read descriptions of people, some described as risk takers and others not, they assume that the risk takers possess a variety of favorable traits such as intelligence, confidence, and creativity as well (Jellison & Riskind, 1970). Also, when participants are asked to specify

Risk Takers
The value placed on risk taking is reflected in the widespread admiration of bold entrepreneurs who took big chances and ended up reshaping entire industries. Ted Turner altered the landscape of television news and Steve Jobs transformed the world of computers, music, and communications.

the level of risk the average person is comfortable with and the person they *most admire* is comfortable with, the latter is assumed to be comfortable with more risk (Levinger & Schneider, 1969).

The high value Americans place on risk is typically attributed to the broader culture of the country. The hard-edged capitalism that is such an integral feature of U.S. life requires an active encouragement of risk and a willingness to take on the possibility of failure. (Note that two-thirds of all new businesses in the United States go under within a year.) Thus, Americans celebrate the stories of people like J. C. Penney, who went bankrupt twice before making his fortune, or Ted Turner, who bet the ranch on his vision of a global, 24-hour television news service (CNN). Some have even argued (in what may be a shaky contention) that the American love affair with risk is part of our biological makeup. Because America is a nation of immigrants, the argument goes, we inherited the genes of those who took a chance on life in the New World—a gamble not taken by those who had a cautious outlook (Farley, 1986).

By this logic, a risky shift after group discussion should occur more often among U.S. participants than among participants in other cultures that do not value risk as highly. That is indeed the case. In studies conducted in Uganda and Liberia, the recommendations made by participants in response to choice dilemmas tended to be more cautious than those made by U.S. participants, and the recommendations did not become riskier after group discussion (Carlson & Davis, 1971; Gologor, 1977).

⬆ LOOKING BACK

Groupthink can lead to defective decision making as people in highly cohesive groups censor their reservations, reject alternative viewpoints, and succumb to ingroup pressures. To avoid this problem, the group should encourage the airing of all viewpoints, leaders should refrain from stating their opinions at the outset, and someone should be designated to play devil's advocate. Group decision making can also lead to group polarization, in which group decisions tend to be more extreme than those made by individuals due to the force of persuasive arguments and social comparison.

Leadership and Power

Social hierarchies are a natural part of group life. So are leaders and people who are led. When children as young as 2 join their first groups—their packs of friends in preschool—some quickly rise to the top rungs of status. When middle-school children form groups of friends at summer camp, they quickly identify the leaders and those who are more likely to follow (Savin-Williams, 1977). Even in the college dorm, one of the most egalitarian environments there is, hallmates within the first week of living together agree on who are the floor leaders and who are not (Anderson, John, Keltner, & Kring, 2001).

Groups quickly evolve into hierarchies because having leaders helps solve some of the problems inherent in group living (Anderson & Brown, 2010). The allocation of resources can give rise to intense conflict between group members, and a social hierarchy provides rules for dividing up resources that, although often unfair (those on top get more), can dampen or avoid that strife. Group decision making can sometimes be unmanageably complex, and hierarchies provide a shared notion of who guides group discussion and how decisions are made. The collective actions in which groups engage demand that individual behaviors be coordinated, and having leaders helps get the group going and provides needed order. Finally, group life often requires that individuals sacrifice their own interests to benefit the group, and leaders (especially charismatic leaders) can help motivate selfless action.

Leaders and hierarchies are an inevitable part of group life, and this leads to two important questions: Who rises to positions of leadership? And what happens to leaders once they're in positions of power?

Characteristics of Leaders

How do people become leaders within social hierarchies? This question interests everyone, in light of the many advantages people in the upper echelons enjoy. The influential Italian philosopher Niccolò Machiavelli offered his hypotheses in *The Prince*, the most influential book ever written on the nature of leadership. His thesis was that people rise to positions of leadership by being deceptive, by pitting competitors against one another, and by coercion, fear, and manipulation rather than directness, honesty, and inspiration (Machiavelli, 1532/2003).

Fortunately, social psychological studies of how people rise through the ranks have proved Machiavelli wrong. One of the most important determinants of leadership is expertise and skill relevant to the goals of the group; there is no substitute for having specific talents that enable groups to achieve their goals (Anderson & Brown, 2010; French & Raven, 1959). The officer with new insights about how to best employ high-tech weaponry is likely to rise in the military; the basketball player who has mastered all the subtle skills that make teams better—the timely pass, the well-positioned screen, defensive help, or clutch shot—is more likely to become captain. Cameron Anderson and Gavin Kilduff have found that groups tend to quickly choose as leaders those individuals who demonstrate knowledge and skill in tasks central to the group's identity and goals (Anderson & Kilduff, 2009). When leaders have the knowledge and skill that enable better group performance, everyone benefits.

Of course, leadership is not based on expertise, knowledge, and technical skill alone. Groups are more likely to be effective if they're cohesive—when they function smoothly together and the whole is greater than the sum of the parts. Thus, individuals who have the social skills to build strong, cooperative relations among group members also increase their chances of rising to positions of leadership. In summer camps, the more socially dynamic, outgoing children

Leadership Characteristics
Influential Italian statesman Niccolò Machiavelli.

tend to become leaders (Savin-Williams, 1977). In fraternities, the more humorous, playful members who are adept at telling stories assume leadership roles (Keltner, Young, Heerey, Oemig, & Monarch, 1998). In college dorms and in the workplace, extraverted individuals, who are socially engaged and adept at building and maintaining relationships, are more likely to achieve status and reach positions of leadership (Anderson et al., 2001; Judge, Bono, Hies, & Gerhardt, 2002). And emotionally intelligent people, who can read the moods and needs of others, tend to be effective managers (Côté & Miners, 2006). Even in our close primate relatives, the socially skilled chimpanzees and bonobos who build strong alliances, negotiate conflicts between subordinates, and ensure just allocations of resources are the ones who acquire and maintain elevated positions of rank in their primate hierarchies (de Waal, 1986).

Finally, alongside expertise and social skills, someone who can provide rewards to the group is more likely to rise to a leadership role. Empirical studies find that individuals who selflessly share resources with others are more likely to rank highly in social hierarchies (Anderson & Brown, 2010; Willer, 2009). This tendency to grant authority to the more generous group members is another example of how leadership often comes to those whose traits and talents promise to benefit the group as a whole.

The Elements of Power

When people assume leadership positions, they experience many things: more responsibility, of course, and the challenge of managing people with diverse needs and interests, but also increased wealth and prestige, the respect of colleagues, and that great intangible that so many in history have lusted after—power. And with power, a person's behavior is likely to change in many ways, some of them not at all obvious.

To understand the influence of power on social behavior, it's important to describe it more carefully. **Power** is usually defined as the ability to control one's own outcomes and those of others; it's also described as the freedom to act (Fiske, 1993; Kelley & Thibaut, 1978). Power is related to three other kinds of social

power The ability to control one's own outcomes and those of others; the freedom to act.

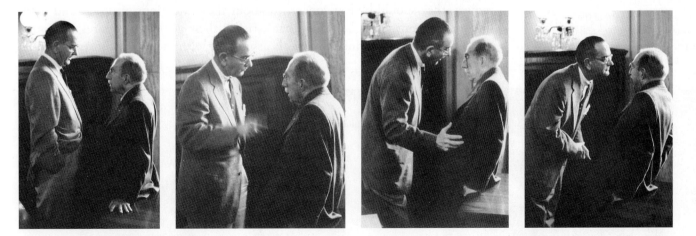

Power and Intimidation

High-power people often feel less constrained by social rules about appropriate behavior than people of lower rank. President Lyndon Johnson approaches Senator Theodore Green more closely than is generally socially acceptable, touches his arm, and leans in close to his face as he seeks to intimidate him into voting the way Johnson wants him to.

status The outcome of an evaluation of attributes that produces differences in respect and prominence, and which contributes to determining a person's power within a group.

authority Power that derives from institutionalized roles or arrangements.

dominance Behavior enacted with the goal of acquiring or demonstrating power.

approach/inhibition theory A theory maintaining that high-power individuals are inclined to go after their goals and make quick (and sometimes rash) judgments, whereas low-power people are more likely to constrain their behavior and pay careful attention to others.

Abuses of Power
As the approach/inhibition theory of power maintains, being in a position of power can lead people, such as the powerful men shown here (former U.S. president Bill Clinton, former New York congressman Anthony Weiner, and former director of the International Monetary Fund Dominique Strauss-Kahn), to ignore many of the usual constraints on behavior and to act in ways that promote their desires.

rank—status, authority, and dominance—but it is not synonymous with them. **Status** is the result of an evaluation of attributes that produces differences in respect and prominence, which contributes to determining a person's leadership position and power within a group (French & Raven, 1959; Kemper, 1991). It's possible to have power without status (think of a dictator or a corrupt politician) and status without relative power (think of a religious leader in a slow-moving line at the Department of Motor Vehicles). **Authority** is power that derives from institutionalized roles or formalized positions within a hierarchy (Weber, 1947). But power, of course, can exist in the absence of formal roles (such as within informal social groups). **Dominance** is behavior enacted with the goal of acquiring or demonstrating power. Yet power can be attained without any attempt to establish dominance (as with leaders who attain their positions through their efforts to instill goodwill in the group and to benefit the group).

The Influence of Power on Behavior

Throughout human history, the world has seen astonishing abuses of power. Consider the horrifying genocides perpetrated by despotic leaders—the likes of Hitler, Stalin, Mao Zedong, Pol-Pot, Idi Amin, Saddam Hussein, and Bashar al-Assad. Consider also the much less horrifying but still troublesome impulsive actions of so many leaders—Bill Clinton's reputation-ruining affair with intern Monica Lewinsky, Dominique Strauss-Kahn's boorish behavior toward so many women, Bill Cosby's beyond-boorish behavior toward even more women, and famed basketball coach Bobby Knight's tendency to abuse his players (and members of the press). And then there are the outrageous excesses of Hollywood celebrities and record-industry stars covered so assiduously by the tabloid press. This impulsive, often immoral side to power is reflected in such time-honored sayings as "Power corrupts" and "Money [a source of power] is the root of all evil." And it begs for a social psychological explanation.

The **approach/inhibition theory** of power offers one account of how power can lead to this sort of behavior (Keltner, Gruenfeld, & Anderson, 2003; Keltner, Van Kleef, Chen, & Kraus, 2008). If, as noted earlier, power involves a lack of constraint and the freedom to act as one wishes, when people experience elevated power, they should be less concerned about the evaluations of others and more inclined to engage in behavior that satisfies their goals and desires (Guinote, 2007). In contrast, reduced power is associated with increased constraint and a

vulnerability to the actions of others. As a result, the experience of diminished power should make a person more vigilant and careful in making judgments and decisions and more inhibited with respect to taking action. In effect, power gives the green light to the pursuit of an individual's goals and desires. Reduced power is more like a yellow light: caution is in order.

The approach/inhibition theory of power has two core elements. The first concerns the influence of power on how people perceive others. High-power individuals, inclined to go after their own goals, are predicted to be less careful and systematic in how they assess others (Brauer, Chambres, Niedenthal, & Chatard-Pannetier, 2004; Vescio, Snyder, & Butz, 2003). Consistent with this hypothesis, high-power individuals are more likely to stereotype others rather than carefully attending to individuating information (Fiske, 1993; Goodwin, Gubin, Fiske, & Yzerbyt, 2000; Neuberg & Fiske, 1987; see also Vescio, Snyder, & Butz, 2003). They are also less accurate judges of others' emotions (Gonzaga, Keltner, & Ward, 2008). This may be one reason that males, who on average have disproportionate power in the world, tend to be a bit less accurate than females in judging expressive behavior (Henley & LaFrance, 1984; LaFrance, Henley, Hall, & Halberstadt, 1997; see also Hall, 1984).

Perhaps the most dramatic demonstration of the empathy failures associated with elevated power was provided by Joseph Magee and his colleagues (Magee, Galinsky, Inesi, & Gruenfeld, 2006). These investigators first induced people to feel relatively powerful or powerless by having them recall a time when they exerted control over another person or when they were controlled by someone else. Participants then performed a simple perspective-taking task: drawing the letter *E* on their forehead so that someone across from them could read it. This task requires the participant to take the other person's perspective and draw the *E* in reverse. As you can see in **Figure 12.5**, participants feeling a surge of power were much less likely to spontaneously draw the *E* in a way that took the other

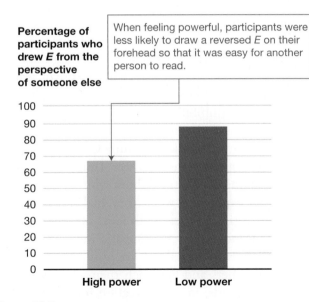

Percentage of participants who drew *E* from the perspective of someone else

When feeling powerful, participants were less likely to draw a reversed *E* on their forehead so that it was easy for another person to read.

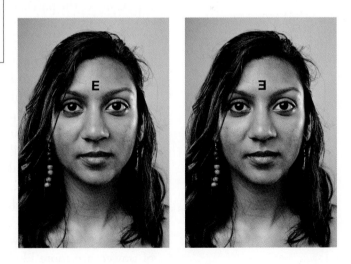

Figure 12.5
Power and Empathy Failures
This study showed how power diminishes one's capacity to consider the perspective of others.

SOURCE: Magee et al., 2006.

person's perspective into account. Power reduces the ability to empathize with others and acknowledge their point of view.

The influence of power on social perception can have unfortunate consequences. Theresa Vescio and her colleagues have found that powerful men who stereotype female employees by focusing exclusively on their weaknesses tend to grant female employees fewer resources (Vescio, Gervais, Snyder, & Hoover, 2005), evaluate them more negatively in masculine contexts, and anticipate less success by female employees than by male employees (Vescio, Snyder, & Butz, 2003). In a similar vein, feeling powerful leads prejudiced whites to focus to a greater extent on the weaknesses of black employees relative to other employees (Vescio, Gervais, Heidenreich, & Snyder, 2006).

These findings no doubt resonate with things you've seen in your own life. People with lots of power are often inattentive to those around them, whereas the powerless are often vigilant toward others, especially toward those with power. Powerful individuals will therefore sometimes appear somewhat clueless socially, whereas the powerless seem clued in. But are there costs to the heightened vigilance low-power individuals maintain as they carefully attend to others? There are indeed. The experience of diminished power makes people less flexible in their thoughts and less able to shift their attention to meet the varied demands of the task at hand (Smith & Trope, 2006). For example, Pamela Smith and her colleagues induced people to feel elevated power or diminished power by priming them with low- or high-power words (*obey, dominate*) or having them recall an experience of low or high power (Smith, Jostmann, Galinsky, & van Dijk, 2008). Participants then worked on a variety of cognitive tasks. In one task, words were flashed one at a time on a computer screen, and participants indicated whether a current word on the screen matched the word presented two trials earlier. In another, the Stroop task, participants had to name the color of the ink in which a word was written (*sedan*)—a task made more difficult on trials in which the word itself referred to a different color (*blue*). Performance on these tasks requires considerable cognitive flexibility and control. In the Stroop task, for example, the participant must ignore the meaning of the word when naming the color of the ink in which it is written. As predicted, participants randomly assigned to feel relatively powerless proved less effective in performing these cognitive tasks. The vigilant and narrowed focus that comes with a sense of reduced power can diminish an individual's ability to think flexibly and creatively.

The second core element of approach/inhibition theory is the prediction that power should make people behave in less constrained and at times more inappropriate ways. Take sex, for example. Do you think it's mainly CEOs, politicians, and rock stars who exhibit sexually inappropriate behavior? Think again. Social psychologists have found that just giving people the faintest whiff of power—for example, by having them recall an experience when they had power or having them read power-related words (priming them with ideas of power)—leads them to act in sexually assertive and potentially problematic ways. People who have a good deal of power, as well as individuals who are primed with feelings of power, are more likely to touch others and approach them closely, to have sexual ideas running through their minds, to feel attraction for a stranger, to overestimate another's sexual interest in them, and to flirt in an overly forward fashion (Bargh, Raymond, Pryor, & Strack, 1995; Kuntsman & Maner, 2011; Rudman & Borgida, 1995). In one survey of 1,261 employees, the higher an individual's rank in the organization, the more likely he or she was to report having

"Power is the ultimate aphrodisiac."

—HENRY KISSINGER,
FORMER U.S. SECRETARY OF STATE

BOX 12.2 **FOCUS ON *BUSINESS***

Power, Profligacy, and Accountability

In 2001 and 2002, Enron, an energy-trading company based in Houston, Texas, collapsed in spectacular fashion. Once one of the most lauded companies in the world, it proceeded to lose billions of dollars in stockholders' assets and had to lay off thousands of workers, largely due to fraudulent accounting practices. Most emblematic of the Enron managers who exhibited corruption, greed, and immorality was the CEO, Jeffrey Skilling.

Fresh from earning an MBA from Harvard University, Skilling was hired at Enron and saw himself as the company visionary, specializing in creating new energy markets. He was aggressive, brash, and, soon, out of control. He shouted profanities at financial analysts who questioned his proposals. He took his favorite employees on outrageous vacations—in one, he and his friends trashed expensive SUVs in the Australian outback. He frequented Enron parties with strippers and eventually divorced his wife to marry his secretary, whom he quickly promoted to a new job with an annual salary of $600,000. He had difficulties with alcohol. Eventually, his reckless, deceptive business practices took their toll and helped fuel the Enron demise.

One way to understand the Enron collapse is to consider the context and culture of the firm and how it encouraged the reckless and illegal practices that led to the company's downfall. A similar culture was said to exist in many

Former Enron CEO Jeffrey Skilling

of the multinational banks and Wall Street investment firms whose actions led to the severe recession of 2008. It's a culture that feeds the sense of power and the feeling of being a "master of the universe" (Wolfe, 1987). Institutions that encourage such feelings offer a valuable lesson about the perils of unchecked power and its disinhibiting effects.

A different approach to trying to understand the actions of Skilling, his colleagues at Enron, and some of their peers in the banking industry is to think about the kinds of people who actively pursue positions of power and how their drive for power might make them more likely to act in so greedy or reckless a fashion. David Winter and his colleagues have taken this approach. They used college students' interpretations of the ambiguous social situations portrayed in Thematic Apperception Test scenes to measure the students' need

for power (Winter, 1973, 1988; Winter & Barenbaum, 1985). They found that the students with a high need for power were more likely to become officers in their dorms, fraternities, and university organizations, and to seek high-power careers, such as the law. These students were also more inclined to engage in profligate, disinhibited behaviors reminiscent of Jeffrey Skilling's reckless actions: they tended to gamble, drink, and seek one-night stands.

Winter and his colleagues also documented an important factor that constrains the disinhibiting effects of power: accountability. Accountability refers to the condition in which one person feels responsible to others. When people with a high need for power experience life events that enhance accountability, such as having children, they are less likely to engage in profligate behaviors like gambling or drinking.

had sexual affairs when married (Lammers, Stapel, & Galinsky, 2011). Power is indeed the ultimate aphrodisiac (**Box 12.2**).

In contrast, low-power individuals tend to inhibit themselves in a variety of ways (Guinote, Judd, & Brauer, 2002). Those with little power often constrict their posture and dampen their expressive behavior (Ellyson & Dovidio, 1985). Low-power people tend to refrain from speaking up: they inhibit their speech and clam up and withdraw during group interactions, thus depriving the group

FIGURE 12.6 You Be the Subject: Strike the Pose of Power

Primates at your local zoo are well known for their power displays—chest pounding and physical expansion to show greater power; cowering and postural contraction to show submissiveness. Using the body to signal leadership and rank within social hierarchies is not restricted to our primate relatives; it's seen regularly in human life, too. We express leadership and power through displays of increased physical size, including expanding the chest and shoulders and raising the arms over the head. And we express weakness and low rank by shrinking—caving in our chests and constricting our shoulders to make our bodies small.

Can you become more powerful by striking a pose? Dana Carney and her colleagues think so (Carney, Cuddy, & Yap, 2010). Carney and her colleagues asked whether participants who assumed high- or low-power poses would experience some of the qualities of power discussed so far. In one study, participants were hooked up to physiological recording devices on their arm and leg and were directed to assume either two high-power postures or two low-power postures for 1 minute each. (They were told to hold these postures to eliminate error in the physiological measurements.) Holding the body in the high-power postures led to increases in testosterone levels, a hormone known to increase dominant behaviors and aggression. Holding the body in the low-power postures, in contrast, increased levels of cortisol in participants, a stress hormone that increases vigilant and inhibited behavior and is known to be activated in submissive individuals. It also changed their approach to risk: participants who held their bodies in a high-power posture were much more likely to take a chance on gambling away money.

Try adopting one of the power displays depicted in these photos. After holding the posture on the left for a while, do you feel slightly more powerful and authoritative?

of potentially important information and alternative perspectives (Holtgraves & Lasky, 1999; Hosman, 1989; Moreland & Levine, 1989) (**Figure 12.6**).

Perhaps most unsettling are studies showing that elevated power is associated with increased antisocial behavior. People in positions of power, for instance, have a tendency to violate politeness-related communication norms, such as interrupting, speaking out of turn, and acting rudely at work (DePaulo & Friedman, 1998; Pearson & Porath, 1999). Another study had two low-power fraternity members and two high-power members tease each other by making up nicknames and telling amusing stories about one another (Keltner, Young, Heerey, Oemig, & Monarch, 1998). Although teasing can be a harmless way for friends to pass the time, in this study high-power participants teased low-power participants in more aggressive and humiliating ways, whereas low-power participants were quite restrained in how they teased their high-power fraternity brothers (**Figure 12.7**). Across a wide variety of contexts—school playgrounds,

"Nearly all men can stand adversity, but if you want to test a man's character, give him power."

—ABRAHAM LINCOLN

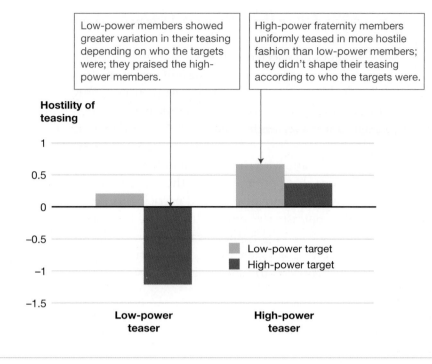

Low-power members showed greater variation in their teasing depending on who the targets were; they praised the high-power members.

High-power fraternity members uniformly teased in more hostile fashion than low-power members; they didn't shape their teasing according to who the targets were.

SOURCE: Adapted from Keltner et al., 1998.

Figure 12.7

An Approach/Inhibition Theory of Power and the Dynamics of Teasing

High-power people are more impulsive in their behavior, whereas low-power people are more likely to inhibit their behavior and shift it according to social context. In this study, high- and low-power fraternity members teased each other in groups of four by making up nicknames.

hospital settings, the workplace—high-power individuals are more likely to tease in a hostile fashion (Keltner, Capps, Kring, Young, & Heerey, 2001).

Power sometimes disinhibits, or encourages, more harmful aggressive impulses as well, leading to violent behavior against the relatively powerless. For example, power asymmetries between coworkers increase the likelihood of sexual harassment (Studd, 1996). The prevalence of rape rises with a culture's acceptance of male dominance and the subordination of women (Reeves-Sanday, 1997). The incidence of hate crimes against minority groups rises in direct proportion to the numerical advantage the majority enjoys in the local environment (Green, Wong, & Strolovitch, 1996).

On the whole, the research on power does not cast it in a flattering light. High-power individuals tend to act in an overly direct, impulsive, and even aggressive fashion. They are more likely to engage in unethical behavior and to be more critical of others than they are of themselves for the same behavior, thus revealing blindness to their own moral failings (Lammers et al., 2011). Research on power provides considerable insights about a number of disturbing trends in society—the child abuse perpetrated by some Catholic priests, the excessive bonuses CEOs permit themselves to take while their companies are performing poorly, or the senator who uses public funds to finance his out-of-town trysts. These tendencies are all the more alarming when we consider the influence powerful people have over our lives.

It's important to bear in mind that the consistent effect of power is that it disinhibits. It encourages people to express their underlying inclinations, both good and bad. If the person is inclined toward competitive, aggressive, or boorish behavior, having power will make such behavior more likely. But, if the

"The fundamental concept in social science is Power, in the same sense that Energy is the fundamental concept in physics. . . . The laws of social dynamics are laws which can only be stated in terms of power."

—BERTRAND RUSSELL

"I'm not a machine, Deborah. I can't just turn my greed on and off."

person is more concerned about the public good, increased power is likely to have more socially beneficial effects. In one study that illustrates this tendency, Serena Chen and her colleagues preselected participants who were either self-interested and exchange-oriented or more compassionate and communally oriented (Chen, Lee-Chai, & Bargh, 2001). Each participant was then randomly assigned to a high-power or low-power position in a clever, subtle manner: high-power participants were seated in a snazzy leather professorial chair during the experiment; low-power people were seated in a plain chair. Participants were then asked to complete a long questionnaire with the help of another participant, who was late. Consistent with the idea that power amplifies the expression of preexisting tendencies, the high-power communally oriented participants performed the lion's share of the task. In contrast, the more self-interested participants with high power acted in a more self-serving fashion, leaving more of the task for the other participant (see also Gordon & Chen, 2013). The effects of power, then, depend on who holds it. Power corrupts the corruptible.

> ### ⬑ LOOKING BACK
>
> Individuals are more likely to become leaders if they have knowledge and skills that help a group get along and reach its goals. Power is the freedom to act and the ability to control one's own outcomes and those of others. Knowledgeable, outgoing, and socially adept people tend to assume positions of leadership within a group. Power tends to make people less careful in their thoughts about others and more impulsive in their behavior.

Deindividuation and the Psychology of Mobs

Consider the following quite similar reactions to two very different events in San Francisco. The first involved the tragic circumstances surrounding the murders of Mayor George Moscone and Supervisor Harvey Milk in 1978. On November 27 of that year, Milk's political rival Dan White shot and killed both Moscone and Milk, San Francisco's first openly gay supervisor, in City Hall. In a rather swift trial, White's lawyers argued that he was minimally responsible for his deeds because of severe depression. His lawyers claimed that his depression led him to subsist on a junk-food diet, which further "diminished his capacity" to distinguish right from wrong. These tactics, ridiculed in the press as the "Twinkie defense," were nonetheless effective. Instead of a first-degree murder conviction, White was found guilty of the lesser charge of voluntary manslaughter and faced a maximum sentence of 8 years in prison. With good behavior, he would be eligible for parole in less than 5 years. (White ended up serving a little over 5 years, but 22 months after his release from prison, he committed suicide.)

The verdict infuriated members of San Francisco's gay community. Many thought the verdict would have been more severe if a supervisor other than Harvey Milk had been slain. The evening of the verdict, gay activists organized a peaceful protest march, but events quickly got out of hand. It began with several demonstrators smashing the glass windows and doors of city hall. Over the pleas of rally organizers urging calm, the crowd began to chant, "Kill Dan White! Get Dan White!" Vandalism and violence soon intensified. When police moved in to quell the disturbance, a battle ensued. The demonstrators threw rocks and bottles at police, set fire to numerous police cars, and looted nearby stores. In the end, 12 police cars were gutted by fire, 20 police officers were injured, and 70 demonstrators needed medical attention. Eight people were arrested. As unfortunate and destructive as the rioting was, it nevertheless strikes most people as understandable. However much they might disapprove, most observers would not think of the rioters' actions as bizarre: the rioters were lashing out against a justice system they thought had failed.

Now consider the striking similarity to events that erupted in the same city 3 years later in response to a much less understandable cause: the San Francisco 49ers' *victory* over the Cincinnati Bengals in Super Bowl XVI, a victory that earned the city its first professional championship in any sport. Within minutes of the game's conclusion, giddy fans poured out of homes and bars and into the streets to celebrate. At first it was all harmless, celebratory stuff—horns blared, beer was chugged, champagne was sprayed. As the evening wore on, however, events took a more sinister turn, eventually echoing what had transpired in the aftermath of the Dan White verdict. Bonfires were started in an intersection and atop a car. When police tried to restore order, they were met with a barrage of stones, bricks, and bottles. Before the streets were cleared, 8 police officers and 100 others were treated for injuries, and 70 arrests were made.

Deindividuation and the Group Mind

These two events in San Francisco's history, as well as a great many similar events around the world, challenge us to understand how large groups of people are sometimes transformed into unruly mobs. How do peaceful gatherings spin out of control and become violent? Why do law-abiding citizens, when immersed in a crowd, engage in acts of destruction they would never commit alone? How can we understand the psychology of "the mob"?

The Psychology of Mobs
(A) Upon learning of the killing of Harvey Milk and George Moscone by Dan White, a mob of demonstrators gathered to mourn their passing. (B) When Dan White was given a light sentence in his trial for the murder, demonstrators again took to the streets, rioting and setting cars on fire in protest of what they saw as a travesty of justice.

Emergent Properties of Groups

Some behaviors surface only when people are part of a group and submerge their individual identities into the group. The people in this flash mob converged at this store after receiving e-mails telling them when and where to gather. Their actions reflect the fact that they are in a group—behavior that would be highly unlikely if each of them were there alone.

"Whoever be the individuals that compose it, however like or unlike be their mode of life, . . . their character, or their intelligence, the fact that they have been transformed into a crowd puts them in possession of a sort of collective mind."

—GUSTAV LE BON

deindividuation A reduced sense of individual identity accompanied by diminished self-regulation that can come over people when they are in a large group.

Social psychologists have addressed these questions in the context of examining the *emergent properties of groups*—behaviors that emerge only when people are in groups. People do things in groups that they would never do alone. Indeed, we often hear people say that a group has "a mind of its own." As a result, the behavior of large groups of people is more than the sum of the behavioral tendencies of its individual members. You might dance, sing, and play air guitar at a rock concert with all your friends, but you'd be much less likely to do so if the band were playing a private concert just for you.

One of the first people to offer an extensive analysis of the psychology of the mob was a nineteenth-century French sociologist, Gustav Le Bon. Le Bon thought people tended to lose their higher mental faculties of reason and deliberation when they were in large groups: "By the mere fact that he forms part of an organised crowd, a man descends several rungs in the ladder of civilization" (1895, p. 52). For Le Bon, this descent stems from the collection of individual, rational minds giving way to a less reflective "group mind."

Social psychologists have expanded on Le Bon's ideas by examining how the thought patterns of individuals change when they come together in large groups and how these changes make them more susceptible to group influence. Most of the time, we feel individuated—that is, we feel individually identifiable by others, we consider ourselves individually responsible for our actions, and we are concerned with the propriety and future consequences of our behavior. But as a number of social psychologists have noted, we often experience a loss of individual identity—a sense of **deindividuation**—when we're in a large group (Diener, 1980; Festinger, Pepitone, & Newcomb, 1952; Prentice-Dunn & Rogers, 1989; Singer, Brush, & Lublin, 1965; Zimbardo, 1970). When in large crowds, we sometimes feel "lost in the crowd," caught up in what is happening in the moment, with a diminished sense of responsibility for our actions.

A Model of Deindividuation

Philip Zimbardo (1970) proposed a theoretical model of deindividuation that specifies how certain conditions create the kind of psychological state that promotes the impulsive and often destructive behaviors observed in mobs (**Figure 12.8**). Perhaps the most important of these conditions are the anonymity individuals enjoy by blending in with a large group, and the diffusion of responsibility that occurs when there are many people to share the blame. These conditions, along with the arousal, heightened activity, and sensory overload that often accompany immersion in a large group, lead to the internal state of deindividuation. The deindividuated state is characterized by diminished self-observation and self-evaluation, and a lessened concern with how others evaluate us.

Thus, a deindividuated person is less aware of the self, more focused on others and the immediate environment, and hence more responsive to behavioral cues—for good or for bad. Being in a deindividuated state lowers the threshold for exhibiting actions that are typically inhibited. People are more likely to engage in a host of impulsive behaviors, both because there is more of a "push"

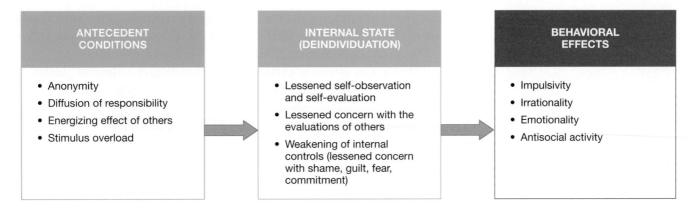

ANTECEDENT CONDITIONS	INTERNAL STATE (DEINDIVIDUATION)	BEHAVIORAL EFFECTS
• Anonymity • Diffusion of responsibility • Energizing effect of others • Stimulus overload	• Lessened self-observation and self-evaluation • Lessened concern with the evaluations of others • Weakening of internal controls (lessened concern with shame, guilt, fear, commitment)	• Impulsivity • Irrationality • Emotionality • Antisocial activity

Figure 12.8
A Theoretical Model of Deindividuation
Certain antecedent conditions lead to an internal state of deindividuation, which in turn leads to behavioral effects that in other situations would be kept under control.

SOURCE: Adapted from Zimbardo, 1970.

to do so (because of increased arousal and many impulsive others to imitate) and because the constraints that usually "pull" them back from such actions are weakened (because of a lessened sense of evaluation and responsibility).

What emerges is the kind of impulsive, irrational, emotional, and occasionally destructive behavior characteristic of mobs. This kind of behavior often creates its own momentum and is less responsive to stimuli that might, if a person were alone, bring it under control, thereby leading to behavior that's difficult to stop. Thus, Zimbardo's model of deindividuation is not an account of mob violence per se. Instead, it is a theoretical analysis of crowd-induced *impulsive* behavior—behavior that because of its very impulsivity often turns violent (Spivey & Prentice-Dunn, 1990).

One implicit element in the model is that people often find the impulsivity that accompanies deindividuation to be liberating. Zimbardo argues that people go through much of their lives in a straitjacket of cognitive control. Living under such constraints can be tiresome and stifling, so people sometimes yearn to break free and act more impulsively. In support of this idea, Zimbardo notes that virtually all societies try to safely channel the expression of this yearning by scheduling occasions when people are encouraged to "let loose." We see this in harvest rites in agrarian cultures, carnivals in religious societies, galas and festivals throughout history, and, perhaps, in the mosh pits and use of intoxicants at modern rock concerts.

Testing the Model

It should be noted at the outset that the psychology of the mob and other emergent properties are extremely difficult to study. People are on their best behavior when they enter a scientific laboratory, and it's difficult to create a situation where they will act impulsively and destructively. Also, there are ethical constraints against putting people in situations where aggressiveness and acts of destruction

Deindividuation and Rioting
When people are in a group and angry, they may let go of self-control and give in to impulses to wreak havoc. Normally law-abiding citizens merge into this crowd and break windows and smash cars with little thought to personal responsibility or the law.

are likely. Therefore, some of the most informative research on the subject takes place out in the world and not in the lab (for exceptions, see Lea, Spears, & de Groot, 2001; Postmes & Spears, 1998).

This research also involves relatively few controlled experiments. Instead, it often involves the examination of archives—data originally gathered with no thought to its relevance to deindividuation. Investigators use these records to search for predicted correlations between the various antecedent conditions and resultant behaviors.

Because these empirical tests are not controlled experiments, they don't control for, or rule out, various alternative interpretations of the results. Indeed, you might think of explanations having nothing to do with deindividuation for some of the empirical results reported here. Even so, it's important to ask whether any one alternative interpretation can account for *all* of the relevant findings. If each finding requires a *different* alternative explanation, but all fit the model of deindividuation, the deindividuation account becomes the most likely and most parsimonious interpretation.

Suicide Baiting Imagine you're on your way to class when you notice a disturbance up ahead. When you get closer, you find that everyone is looking up at the top floor of a high-rise dormitory. Apparently a student is halfway out an open window and threatening to jump. What do you do? Try to stop the poor soul from jumping? Call for help?

Hard as it may be to believe, people occasionally do just the opposite—they engage in suicide baiting, urging the person to jump. Is suicide baiting more likely when many people are gathered below? In other words, are people more likely to engage in suicide baiting when they feel deindividuated?

To answer these questions, researchers examined 15 years of newspaper accounts of suicidal jumps and averted jumps (Mann, 1981). They found 21 instances of attempted suicide, and suicide baiting occurred in 10 of them. They then analyzed the data to determine whether two variables associated with deindividuation—the cover of darkness and the presence of a large group of onlookers—are related to whether suicide baiting occurred. As shown in **Figure 12.9**, suicide baiting was more than twice as likely when the crowd size exceeded 300. Also, suicide baiting was more than four times as likely if the episode took place after 6 p.m. As people feel more anonymous, either by being lost in a large crowd or under the cloak of darkness, they are more inclined to egg on a potential suicide.

It's possible to question some of the details of these analyses—for example, why the cutoffs were set at 300 people and 6 p.m. It's also possible to suggest alternative interpretations: for example, the larger the group, the more likely it is to contain a psychopath who starts the baiting. However, the data are nevertheless consistent with the idea that variables leading to deindividuation also lead to antisocial behavior.

Deindividuation and Impulsive Behavior

During carnivals and festivals, people tend to "let loose" and relax their usual control over their behavior. Here, a woman lets go of her inhibitions during a Mardi Gras parade in New Orleans.

The Conduct of War Wars have always been a part of what English novelist and scientist C. P. Snow calls the "long and gloomy history of man." The conduct of warfare, however, has varied enormously from culture to culture and epoch to epoch. Warfare practices vary in their ferocity, for example. At the high end of the ferocity scale are beheadings, ritualistic torture, and the systematic slaughter of civilian noncombatants. At the very low end would be what Tom Wolfe (1979) has described as

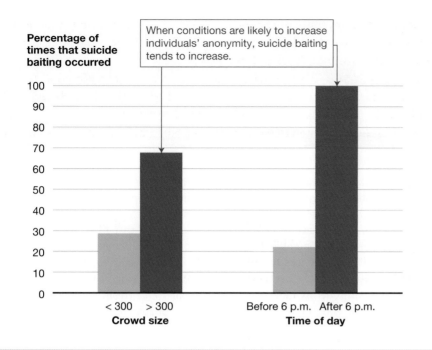

Percentage of times that suicide baiting occurred

When conditions are likely to increase individuals' anonymity, suicide baiting tends to increase.

Crowd size: < 300, > 300
Time of day: Before 6 p.m., After 6 p.m.

SOURCE: Adapted from Mann, 1981.

Figure 12.9
Deindividuation and Suicide Baiting
Conditions that promote a sense of deindividuation can also promote impulsive, antisocial behavior. In this study, people were found to be more likely to bait someone to commit suicide when they were part of a large crowd or during the evening.

single-combat warfare: the David and Goliath battles in which the warring parties select a single warrior to do battle with each other. The losing side pays a price in territory or some other form of wealth, but less damage is done to both groups.

Is the brutality of warfare related to deindividuation? The theory predicts that it should be. It should be easier for people to let go of the usual prohibitions against barbarity when they feel anonymous and unaccountable for their actions. To determine whether such a relationship exists, the warfare practices of 23 non-Western cultures were investigated (Watson, 1973). The researchers examined each culture to see whether its warriors were deindividuated before battle (whether they wore masks or war paint) and how aggressively they waged war (whether they tortured the enemy, whether they fought to the death in all battles, and so on). As predicted, there was a strong correlation between deindividuation and aggressiveness in warfare. Among those cultures whose warriors changed their appearance before battle, 80 percent were deemed particularly aggressive; among those cultures whose warriors did not change their appearance, only 13 percent were deemed especially aggressive. When warriors are disguised in battle, they fight more ferociously. (On the other hand, the ancient Celts were in the habit of fighting naked, and they were ferocious fighters the Romans were terrified to face. Of course, whether to consider nakedness an increase in individuation or a decrease isn't clear.)

Halloween Mayhem For Americans, one of the most familiar occasions for uninhibited and impulsive behavior is Halloween night. The destructive acts that occur on that holiday range from mild episodes of egg throwing to much more serious hooliganism. One group of social psychologists decided to take advantage of the Halloween atmosphere to conduct an ambitious test of the role of deindividuation in antisocial behavior

Warfare and Deindividuation
Warriors in tribes that deindividuate themselves before battle by wearing war paint and war masks tend to engage in more brutal warfare practices.

BOX 12.3

Not So Fast
Critical Thinking about Correlated Trends

If you look up statistics on the number of people regularly attending their church, temple, or mosque each year over the past quarter century and tally up instances of especially brutal episodes of violence each year over that same time span (beheadings, suicide bombings, torture), you'll observe a high correlation. Why? Has increased religious fervor encouraged a dehumanization of religious outgroups? Has exposure to gruesome images of this sort of violence led people to seek solace in religion?

Perhaps both are true, and by this point in the book we hope you've learned not to jump to any one conclusion on the basis of a simple correlation. But there's another possibility: the two may have absolutely nothing to do with each other, and their correlation reflects the basic fact that both have increased over this time period. The number of people attending religious services has gone up over this period simply because world population has gone up. Beheadings and bombings have gone up for all sorts of geopolitical reasons. The broader point is that whenever *any* two variables have increased over time there will be a substantial year-to-year correlation between them. Thus, if you look up the number of search requests for, say, Ryan Gosling or Kate Upton over the past 5 years and the number of search requests for jihad (or the number of suicide bombings for that matter), you'll find a positive correlation between the two. Both have been going up during that time, so they *have* to be correlated.

Statisticians refer to any systematic increase or decrease over time as a *secular trend* (from the late Latin word for age or span of time), and the lesson here is that it's important to be especially cautious about interpreting a significant correlation involving two such trends. It may have no more meaning than the correlation between the yearly sales of salted caramel ice cream and legalized marijuana (both of which have been growing substantially in recent years).

(Diener, Fraser, Beaman, & Kelem, 1976). They set up research stations in 27 homes throughout the city of Seattle and monitored the behavior of over 1,000 trick-or-treaters. At each participating house, the children were told they could take one piece of candy from a large bowl sitting on a table in the entrance to the house. Next to the bowl of candy was a bowl filled with coins. The experimenter then excused herself from the scene and covertly monitored the children's actions from afar. Would the children take just their allotted single piece of candy, or would they take more—perhaps even some coins?

The investigators examined the influence of two variables connected to deindividuation. First, the children arrived either individually or in groups, and the investigators expected those in groups to feel more anonymous and therefore be more likely to transgress. Second, the experimenter purposely "individuated" a random sample of children arriving both alone and in groups; before departing, she asked each child his or her name and address and then repeated this information aloud for emphasis. Individuating the children—that is, identifying them by name so they'd no longer feel anonymous—was predicted to inhibit any temptation to transgress.

As **Figure 12.10** shows, both variables had the anticipated effect. The children who arrived in groups were much more likely to transgress than those who were alone, regardless of whether they were anonymous or not. Children who were anonymous were much more likely to transgress than those who were individuated, regardless of whether they were alone or in groups. Putting these two findings together, the children in anonymous groups were the most likely to transgress.

Self-Awareness and Individuation

If "losing ourselves" in a crowd and becoming deindividuated makes us more likely to behave impulsively, it stands to reason that being especially self-conscious would have the opposite effect. Anything that focuses attention on the self, such as being in front of a camera, seeing ourselves in a mirror, or wearing a name tag, may lead to **individuation** and make us particularly inclined to act carefully and in accordance with our sense of propriety. This is just what **self-awareness theory** predicts. When people focus their attention inward on themselves, they become concerned with self-evaluation and how their current behavior conforms to their internal standards and values (Duval & Wicklund, 1972).

Studies of Self-Awareness Many experiments have shown that people do indeed act in ways that are more consistent with their enduring attitudes and values when they've been made self-conscious by being placed in front of a mirror or an attentive audience (Beaman, Klentz, Diener, & Svanum, 1979; Carver, 1974; Carver & Scheier, 1981; Duval & Lalwani, 1999; Froming, Walker, & Lopyan, 1982; Gibbons, 1978; Scheier, Fenigstein, & Buss, 1974). In one study, college students were asked to solve a series of anagrams and told to stop when a bell sounded. In a control condition, nearly three-quarters of them fudged a bit by continuing to work beyond the bell. But in a condition that caused participants to be made self-aware by working in

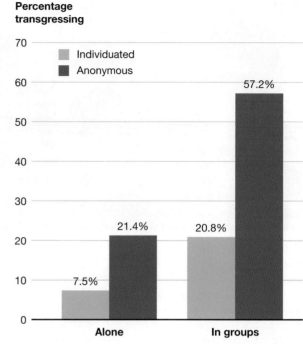

Figure 12.10
Deindividuation and Transgression
In this study, the percentage of trick-or-treaters who transgressed was affected by whether they had been asked to give their name (individuated condition) or not (anonymous condition) and whether they were alone or in a group.

SOURCE: Adapted from Diener et al., 1976.

Coconuts and White-Collar Crime, or a Coconut Is Watching You
In many offices it's common to have a coffee urn with an "honest box" next to it. Someone who gets a cup of coffee is supposed to put some money in the box. If you want to increase donations to the honest box, place nearby a coconut like the one on the left. That would likely cause people to behave more honestly. An inverted coconut like the one on the right would likely net you nothing. The coconut on the left resembles a human face and people subconsciously sense their behavior is being monitored. (Tacitly, of course; people who literally thought they were looking at a human face would be in dire need of an optometrist or psychiatrist, possibly both.) Actually, it's sufficient to just have a picture of three dots in the orientation of the coconut on the left to get more contributions.

SOURCE: Rigdon, Ishii, Watabe, & Kitayama, 2009.

individuation An enhanced sense of individual identity produced by focusing attention on the self, which generally leads people to act carefully and deliberately and in accordance with their sense of propriety and values.

self-awareness theory A theory maintaining that when people focus their attention inward on themselves, they become concerned with self-evaluation and how their current behavior conforms to their internal standards and values.

Individuation and Self-Awareness

Anything that focuses attention on the self and individual identity is likely to lead to heightened concern with self-control and propriety. Name tags on these people at a business conference can encourage a sense of individuation and, most likely, restrained behavior.

front of a mirror, fewer than 10 percent cheated (Diener & Wallbom, 1976). Although most students *say* that cheating is a bad thing, it appears to take some self-awareness to get them to act on that belief. Note that because being in a state of self-awareness is the flip side of feeling deindividuated, all of these experiments that support self-awareness theory also provide indirect support for the model of deindividuation.

Self-Consciousness and the Spotlight Effect The negative relationship between self-consciousness and deindividuation raises the question of how self-conscious people typically are in the normal course of events. There are pronounced individual differences, of course, in how focused people are on themselves and in how much they believe others are focused on them as well (Fenigstein, Scheier, & Buss, 1975). But there is also reason to believe that the typical level of self-consciousness is fairly high, particularly when others are around. People begin to feel deindividuated only in the presence of a large crowd. This is why, as noted earlier, it has been assumed that people enjoy feeling deindividuated; it's a welcome break from the usual self-conscious state.

Evidence that people are indeed prone to a high level of self-consciousness comes from research on the **spotlight effect**—people's conviction that other people are paying attention to their appearance and behavior more than is actually the case (**Figure 12.11**). People who make an insightful comment in a group discussion, for example, believe others will notice their comment and remember it better than others actually do. People who suffer an embarrassing mishap, such as triggering an alarm in a public building, or stumbling and falling down while entering a lecture hall, think others are judging them more harshly than they actually are (Epley, Savitsky, & Gilovich, 2002; Fortune & Newby-Clark, 2008; Gilovich, Kruger, & Medvec, 2002; Gilovich, Medvec, & Savitsky, 2000; Savitsky, Epley, & Gilovich, 2001).

In one of the clearest demonstrations of the spotlight effect, participants who arrived individually for an experiment were asked to put on a T-shirt sporting a

spotlight effect People's conviction that other people are paying attention to them (to their appearance and behavior) more than they actually are.

FIGURE 12.11 **You Be the Subject: The Spotlight Effect**

Imagine that you go to a dinner party and discover that everyone except you brought a gift for the host.

1. Rate how harshly you would be judged by the host for this omission:

Totally fine   0   1   2   3   4   5   6   7   8   9   10   **Unforgivable**

2. Rate how harshly you would judge a guest who failed to bring a gift:

Totally fine   0   1   2   3   4   5   6   7   8   9   10   **Unforgivable**

Which ratings are lower?

Result: Did you assign a higher number for rating 1 than rating 2? In part because of the spotlight effect, most people think that their own actions (the social blunder, in this case) stand out more than they acually do.

picture of the pop singer Barry Manilow. Despite obvious signs of displeasure, everyone did so. They then reported to another room down the hall where, upon entering, they found a group of fellow students filling out questionnaires. After leaving the room moments later, the participants had to estimate the percentage of those other students who would be able to recall the person pictured on the T-shirt. As predicted, the participants overestimated how much they had stood out in their new shirt. They estimated that roughly half the other students would be able to identify that it was Barry Manilow pictured on their shirt, when in fact only about one-quarter were able to do so (Gilovich et al., 2000).

🔁 LOOKING BACK

Social psychologists have examined the relationship between self-consciousness and behavior from two directions. Research on deindividuation has shown that the diminished sense of self-awareness that sometimes occurs when we are immersed in large groups makes us get caught up in ongoing events and encourages impulsive, and sometimes destructive, actions. Research on self-awareness and the spotlight effect has shown how carefully we typically monitor our own behavior with an eye toward what others might think, and how our awareness of self encourages us to act with a greater sense of propriety.

Chapter Review

Online Study Materials

INQUIZITIVE   EBOOK

SUMMARY

The Nature and Purpose of Group Living

- Human beings, like all large primates except the orangutan, are group-living animals who influence, and must get along with, others.

Social Facilitation

- *Social facilitation* refers to the positive or negative effect on performance due to the presence of others. Arousal from the presence of others increases people's tendency to do what comes naturally. On easy tasks, they are predisposed to respond correctly, so increasing this tendency facilitates performance; on new or hard tasks when they're not predisposed to respond correctly, arousal hinders performance by making them more likely to respond incorrectly.
- The mere presence of others leads to social facilitation effects, and other factors, including *evaluation apprehension*, can intensify them. According to *distraction-conflict theory*, awareness of another person can create a conflict between focusing on that person and the task at hand, a conflict that is itself arousing.
- *Social loafing* is the tendency to exert less effort on a group task when individual contributions cannot be monitored.

Group Decision Making

- *Groupthink* refers to the faulty thinking by members of cohesive groups, in which critical decision-making scrutiny is subverted by social pressures to reach consensus. Groupthink has been implicated in the faulty decision making that has led to various policy fiascos.
- Group decision making is affected by how cohesive a group is, how directive its leader is, and by ingroup pressures that can lead to the rejection of alternative viewpoints and to *self-censorship*, the tendency to refrain from expressing reservations in the face of apparent group consensus.
- Group discussion can create *group polarization*; initial leanings in a risky direction tend to be made riskier by group discussion, and initial leanings in a conservative direction tend to be made more conservative.
- Group polarization can result when group discussion exposes members to more persuasive arguments in favor of a consensus opinion than they would have thought of themselves, and through social comparison, when people compare their opinions with those of others.
- People from cultures that place a high value on risk are more likely to make risky decisions after group discussion than people from cultures that do not value risk as highly.

Leadership and Power

- Power involves control and the freedom to act. It derives from interpersonal sources, such as a person's position of authority or expertise, as well as individual factors, such as the ability to engage with others socially and build strong alliances.
- According to the *approach/inhibition theory*, people in positions of elevated power look at things more simplistically and act in more disinhibited ways, sometimes leading to excesses and abuse.
- People with knowledge and skills that help group members get along and help the group reach its goals are generally most likely to become leaders.

Deindividuation and the Psychology of Mobs

- Large groups sometimes transform into unruly mobs; the anonymity and diffusion of responsibility people feel in large groups can lead to a mental state of *deindividuation* in which they are less concerned with the future, with normal societal constraints on behavior, and with the consequences of their actions.
- The deindividuated state of getting lost in the crowd contrasts with how people normally feel, which is individually

identifiable. *Self-awareness theory* maintains that focusing attention on the self leads people to a state of *individuation*, marked by careful deliberation and concern with how well their actions conform to their moral standards.

• People tend to overestimate how much they personally stand out and are identifiable to others, a phenomenon known as the *spotlight effect*.

THINK ABOUT IT

1. Open-plan offices, where large communal desks are used in place of private rooms or cubicles, are becoming increasingly popular. From the perspective of Zajonc's social facilitation theory, do you think open-plan offices are likely to facilitate or hinder performance and productivity? Why or why not? How might it depend on the type of work being conducted?

2. Can you think of any examples in your own life where groupthink has taken place? What factors contributed to groupthink in these situations? What kinds of safeguards could you put in place in similar future situations to promote better decision making?

3. Suppose your company is trying to decide whether to make a risky new hire. Individually, most of the members of the hiring team lean toward hiring the candidate, as it could substantially increase revenues if it works out. When the hiring team gets together to discuss the potential hire, how might you predict that the attitudes of the individuals in the group will shift? What decision is likely to be made?

4. In *The Prince*, Machiavelli argued that people gain power through deception, manipulation, coercion, and the use of fear tactics. How does this perspective compare with research findings about who rises to power?

5. Do you think it's accurate to say that power corrupts? Why or why not? What factors influence the extent to which power leads to prosocial versus antisocial behavior?

6. What does research on deindividuation show about why crime rates are so high on Halloween?

7. How could you use your knowledge of self-awareness theory to reduce cheating behavior on a test that relies on the honor system?

THE ANSWER GUIDELINES FOR THE THINK ABOUT IT QUESTIONS CAN BE FOUND AT THE BACK OF THE BOOK . . . ☞

Aggression

O n the evening of April 6, 1994, Odette and Jean-Baptiste, Rwandan husband-and-wife physicians, were enjoying a drink with a friend while listening to the radio. Just after 8 p.m., they heard that the plane carrying President Juvenal Habyarimana of Rwanda, a Hutu, had been shot down near Kigali, Rwanda's capital. Odette knew there was going to be trouble. Unlike the Hutu president or her husband, Odette was a Tutsi, and she had witnessed several massacres of her people at the hands of the Hutus, with whom they shared language, religion, and a history of living together. She was worried that the incident would fuel anti-Tutsi sentiment among the majority Hutus.

Tragically, she proved to be right. In the 100 days that followed, Hutus would massacre approximately 800,000 Tutsis and moderate Hutus (Gourevitch, 1998). Many of the massacres were carried out by militiamen known as the *interahamwe*. They set up roadblocks throughout Rwanda, pulled Tutsis from their cars, and killed them. In small Rwandan towns, Hutus turned on their Tutsi neighbors, brutally killing them with machetes. Hutu schoolteachers massacred their Tutsi students. Even Tutsis taking sanctuary in churches were slaughtered. Throughout the rolling hills of Rwanda, flocks of crows and buzzards flew above the sites where massacres had taken place.

Regrettably, massacres like the Rwandan genocide are a recurring part of history. In 2003 in Darfur, Sudan, several groups, desperate because of drought and starvation, attacked the Sudanese government. The government's response resembled the one in Rwanda. Government-sponsored militias pursued a scorched-earth strategy in combating the rebels: they burned villages, raped women, and slaughtered tens of thousands of people.

OUTLINE

Situational Determinants of Aggression

Construal Processes and Aggression

Culture and Aggression

Evolution and Aggression

Conflict and Peacemaking

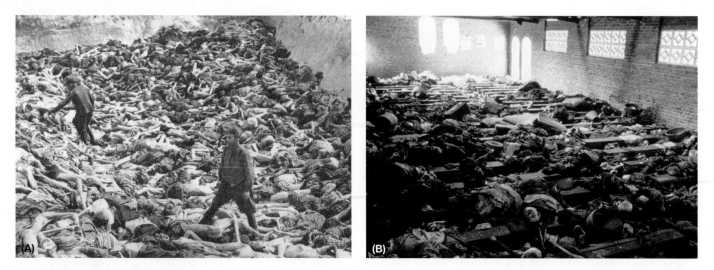

Genocide

In addition to the mass murders by the Nazis, genocide has also occurred in the former Yugoslavia, in Cambodia, in Rwanda, and in Sudan, among other places. (A) An open grave of 10,000 naked bodies was found at the Bergen-Belsen concentration camp when the British liberated the camp in April 1945. (B) A church in Nitarama, Rwanda, holding the remains of 400 Tutsis killed by the Hutu *interahamwe* was discovered by a United Nations team in September 1994.

Based on the sheer number of people killed by their fellow human beings, the twentieth century was the most violent in history. How do social psychologists make sense of such genocides, and of other forms of violence considered in this chapter—school shootings, homicide, rape, and the violence in families? How do situational factors produce aggression, and how does a person's construal of complex situations give rise to violence? What factors promote group conflict—and, more importantly, what factors can pave the way for more enduring peace?

Situational Determinants of Aggression

In considering the massacres of Rwanda and Darfur, it's striking how quickly peaceful, stable relations between groups can turn to aggression. Just as the right ecological conditions can transform a healthy forest into a roaring inferno, the right mix of situational factors can give rise to violence, whether between different ethnic or religious groups, teenage boys encountering each other on a Friday night, or children on grade-school playgrounds.

Explanations of aggression vary according to whether the behavior is hostile or instrumental. **Hostile aggression** refers to behavior motivated by feelings of anger and hostility and whose primary aim is to harm another, either physically or psychologically. Clearly, the genocide in Rwanda emerged in part for purely hostile reasons: Hutus seeking revenge on Tutsis out of anger about past grievances. **Instrumental aggression**, in contrast, refers to behavior that is intended to harm another in the service of motives other than pure hostility. People harm others, for example, to gain status, to attract attention, to acquire wealth, and to advance political and ideological causes. The genocide in Rwanda was committed partly in pursuit of political purposes: the Hutus were seeking to displace the more powerful Tutsis. Many acts of aggression involve a mix of hostile and instrumental motives. A football player who intentionally harms another might do so out of aggressive emotion (hostile aggression) or for a variety of

hostile aggression Behavior intended to harm another, either physically or psychologically, and motivated by feelings of anger and hostility.

instrumental aggression Behavior intended to harm another in the service of motives other than pure hostility (such as attracting attention, acquiring wealth, or advancing political or ideological causes).

BOX 13.1 **FOCUS ON *GENES AND ENVIRONMENT***

Nature or Nurture? It's Both

Many biological factors predispose people to act aggressively, ranging from the levels of testosterone in the blood to the density of neural connections in the frontal lobes (White, 1997; Yudko, Blanchard, Henne, & Blanchard, 1997). Research by Avshalom Caspi, Terrie Moffitt, and their colleagues indicates that aggression might best be thought of as the interaction of situational factors and genetically based individual differences (Caspi et al., 2002). They tested for the two forms of the monoamine oxidase A (MAOA) gene. Monoamine oxidase is an enzyme that metabolizes certain neurotransmitters in the synapses in the brain, allowing for smooth communication between neurons. In nonhuman species, individuals with a defective, short form of the MAOA gene have been shown to be more aggressive,

suggesting that this gene might also predict aggressive behavior in humans. Caspi and his colleagues identified men with this defective short form of the gene (37 percent of their sample) and those with the long form of the gene. To examine the influence of situational factors, they also identified men who had or had not been mistreated by their parents as children—one of the most potent factors in a person's childhood that can lead to violent behavior in adulthood.

Overall, the defective MAOA gene alone didn't affect whether the boys committed violent crimes (rape, assault, robbery) by age 26. This finding suggests that by itself, a genetic predisposition does not determine whether an individual will engage in aggression. The twin catalysts of aggressive behavior proved to be the

combination of the short form of the MAOA gene and a family environment of physical abuse. Boys who had the defective gene *and* were mistreated as children were three times more likely to have been convicted of a violent crime by age 26 than the boys who had the defective gene but had *not* been mistreated. Although those with the gene for low MAOA activity who had also suffered mistreatment were only 12 percent of the population in the study, they were responsible for 44 percent of the group's convictions for violent crime. Another way of putting it is that some 85 percent of the boys with the short form of the MAOA gene who were severely mistreated engaged in some form of antisocial behavior. The important lesson of this telling study is that nature typically requires nurture to shape behavior.

---

instrumental reasons, such as to foster a reputation for fearlessness, to help his team win, or to make the kind of plays that secure a place on the team or that earn a lucrative contract.

It's tempting to believe that aggression is largely the province of aggressive people—the bullies, sociopaths, and criminal personalities among us. There's certainly a grain of truth to this belief; but once again, social psychology research makes it clear that a situational perspective is crucial to an adequate understanding of aggression. For example, scientists have discovered that certain genes may predispose people to aggression, but these genes increase the likelihood of aggressive action only in certain circumstances (**Box 13.1**). The important point is that situations give rise to or release people's aggressive tendencies. Let's take on social psychology's challenge and explore some of the situational factors that might lead to violence.

Hot Weather

The first line of Spike Lee's classic movie *Do the Right Thing* comes from a radio newscaster who says, "It's hot out there, folks." It's early in the morning, and the main characters, wearing T-shirts and shorts, are already uncomfortable and sweating profusely. By the end of the day, tensions between African-Americans and Italian-Americans escalate, and a race riot ensues.

Heat and Aggressive Action

In Spike Lee's movie *Do the Right Thing*, a confrontation between whites and blacks begins on a very hot day in this restaurant and escalates into a race riot.

People have long believed that moods and actions are closely tied to the weather. Perhaps the most widely assumed connection is between heat and aggression. We think of angry people as "boiling over," "steamed," or "hot under the collar." Indeed, anger literally raises the temperature of the body because of accelerated heart rate and increased distribution of blood to certain areas, such as the hands. But the connection between aggressive behavior and heat may also be associated with what the ambient temperature does to people's emotions.

Are people more aggressive when it's hot outside? As early as the nineteenth century, people noted that violent crime rates were higher in southern France and southern Italy, where the temperatures are hotter, than in northern France and northern Italy. Of course, other factors—such as levels of unemployment, per capita income, ethnic composition, the proportion of young men in the population, or average age—might also have produced these regional differences.

Craig Anderson has provided evidence that higher-than-normal temperatures per se are associated with increased aggression (Anderson, 1987, 1989). There are higher rates of violent crimes in hotter regions. Anderson examined the crime rates of 260 cities throughout the United States. For each city, he identified the number of days when the temperature exceeded 90 degrees Fahrenheit. The number of hot days (above 90 degrees) was a strong predictor of elevated violent crime rates but not nonviolent crime rates. This was true even when Anderson controlled for the city's level of unemployment, per capita income, and average age of its citizens (Anderson, 1987).

People are also more violent in the U.S. during hot months, such as July and August, than during cooler months, such as January and February. (The one exception is December, when violent crime rates also rise—so much for holiday good cheer.) In **Figure 13.1** you can see that murder and rape increase during the summer months. Moreover, one of the cleverest studies of heat and aggression found that major league baseball pitchers are more likely to hit batters with a pitch as the weather gets hotter (Reifman, Larrick, & Fein, 1991). This is especially true when the pitcher's teammates have been hit by the opposing pitcher earlier in the game (Larrick, Timmerman, Carton, & Abrevaya, 2011). This effect can't be attributed to reduced competence; neither wild pitches nor walks go up with the temperature (Kenrick & MacFarlane, 1984).

These findings point to a potentially unsettling consequence of climate change: as Earth's temperature rises, we might expect to see increases in violence throughout the world. Recently, scientists have addressed this possibility, and the results provide one more reason to be concerned about climate change. Solomon Hsiang and his colleagues looked at data for the past 50 years and found that during what are known as El Niño years in tropical countries, when the weather is especially hot and dry, the likelihood of civil conflict rises dramatically (Hsiang, Meng, & Cane, 2011).

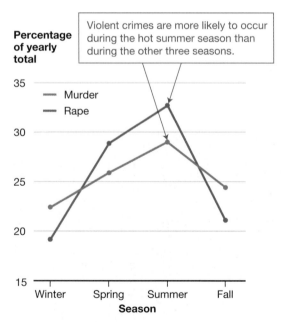

Figure 13.1

Seasonal Effects on Violent Behavior

Do the hot months of summer make people more aggressive? Various studies of aggressive behaviors throughout different months of the year indicate that they do.

SOURCE: Adapted from Anderson, 1989, p. 82.

What is it about hot weather that makes people more aggressive? One explanation assigns a prominent role to attributional processes (see Chapter 5). People are aroused by the heat, but they are often unaware of the extent to which hot weather is the source of their arousal. When they encounter circumstances that prompt anger—say, a frustrating driver or an irritating romantic partner—they attribute their arousal to that person, and this misplaced annoyance gives rise to amplified feelings of anger, which can lead to aggression.

Media Violence

Visual media are saturated with images of aggression. The average American child watches 3–4 hours of television a day, and about 90 percent of those programs portray at least some form of violence (Gerbner, Gross, Morgan, & Signorelli, 1986). By age 12, the average viewer of American TV has seen about 100,000 acts of violence—from car crashes on reality police shows, to murders and beatings on weekly crime or courtroom dramas, to dead bodies on the nightly news. This estimate doesn't include the violence they see in movies, in video games, and on websites.

Does the violence portrayed in the media make people more aggressive? Every year, concerned citizens urge the entertainment industry to stop depicting so much violence. Journalists routinely decry the violence on television and in the movies. Are their concerns warranted? Does scientific research unambiguously link violent media depictions to real-life aggressive behavior?

Several strands of evidence indicate that people who campaign against media violence may be justified in their basic assumption: that exposure to media violence increases aggressive behavior. Let's start with copycat violence, the imitation of specific violent acts depicted in the media. In March 1981, John Hinckley, Jr., attempted to assassinate President Ronald Reagan, shooting him in the chest and, by many accounts, impairing Reagan's ability to lead the country in the months afterward. What investigators soon discovered was disturbing evidence about the nature of copycat violence. Hinckley had seen Martin Scorsese's

*"I pray thee good Mercutio, let's retire;
The day is hot, the Capulets abroad.
And, if we meet, we shall not 'scape a brawl,
For now, these hot days, is the mad blood stirring."*

—SHAKESPEARE, *ROMEO AND JULIET*

Copycat Violence
Violence in the media is sometimes imitated in real life. (A) In *Taxi Driver*, De Niro's character tries to assassinate a politician. (B) Hinckley attempted to assassinate President Reagan after seeing the film.

BOX 13.2 **FOCUS ON *THE MEDIA***

Copycat Violence

David Phillips (1986) has gathered evidence indicating that one type of copycat violence, suicide—the ultimate form of violence against the self—is a very real phenomenon. In one study, Phillips identified 35 suicides reported in the U.S. media from 1947 to 1968 and examined the suicide rates in the following months. He compared the suicide rates during those months with those during the same months in the years before and after each suicide. This comparison allowed him to control for the effects of weather and season on aggressive behavior.

In 26 of the 35 widely reported suicides, the suicide rate rose substantially more in the month following the suicide than in the two comparison months. For example, Marilyn Monroe's widely publicized death from an overdose of prescription medication in August 1962 was followed by a 12-percent increase in suicides in the United States and a 10-percent increase in Great Britain. Phillips also observed a strong positive correlation between the amount of media coverage the suicide received and the increased suicide rate: the more newspaper space devoted to a suicide, the greater the increase in copycat suicides. More detailed analyses suggested that people weren't killing themselves out of grief over the death of beloved celebrities; people even imitated the suicides of despised individuals, such as a leader of the Ku Klux Klan.

Of course, Phillips could not measure a number of variables that might have affected suicide rates. For example, were particularly depressive or aggressive people—those more inclined initially to harm themselves or others—most likely to imitate the publicized acts of violence and commit suicide? Phillips' data don't answer that question. But even if depressed or aggressive people are more likely to commit copycat suicide, the claim about imitative suicide still holds. It may simply be that the effect is especially pronounced in certain segments of the population.

movie *Taxi Driver*, in which Robert De Niro portrayed a violent sociopath who attempts to kill a politician to win the love of a young prostitute played by Jodie Foster. A letter addressed to Jodie Foster was found in Hinckley's hotel room, in which he declared he was going to kill President Reagan for her.

How prevalent is copycat violence? Researchers have explored this question by examining the effects of exposure to media violence on aggression immediately afterward (Anderson et al., 2003; Geen, 1998). In these studies, participants typically view aggressive films and then have an opportunity to act in an aggressive fashion, such as by shocking a confrontational confederate (for a review, see Berkowitz, 1993). Researchers have found that watching aggressive films does indeed make people more aggressive. For example, one study showed that watching aggressive films made juvenile delinquents confined in a minimum-security prison more aggressive (Leyens, Camino, Parke, & Berkowitz, 1975). In another study, male college students applied more intense shocks to a female confederate when they were angered and had been exposed to violent media imagery (Donnerstein, 1980; Donnerstein & Berkowitz, 1981). Exposure to violent pornography increases the endorsement of aggression against women (Allen, Emmers-Sommer, Gebhardt, & Giery, 1995).

Experiments have identified the specific sorts of media violence that most likely lead to aggression. People tend to be more aggressive, for example, after seeing films in which they identify with the perpetrator of the violent act (Leyens & Picus, 1973). People are also more inclined to be aggressive after watching violent films that portray justified violence—that is, violence perpetrated against "bad people" (Berkowitz, 1965). However, when participants are led to direct their attention away from the aggressive content of the violent film—by focusing on the aesthetic features of the film, for instance—they are less likely to behave aggressively later (Leyens, Cisneros, & Hossay, 1976).

Before concluding that media violence causes aggression, let's consider a couple of limitations of these lab studies. First, the measures of aggression, such as applying electric shock to a confederate, may have little to do with real-world violence: murder, rape, assault, genocide, and hate crimes. Another limitation is whether exposure to violent media has more enduring effects on aggression than the short-term effects found in the studies reviewed.

Several studies have addressed these concerns by examining whether watching violent TV programs early in life is associated with increased real-world aggression later. Researchers surveyed more than 500 youngsters in the Chicago area, ages 6–9; they collected measures of the children's TV viewing habits, their aggressiveness (as rated by their friends), and various control variables (Huesmann, Moise-Titus, Podolski, & Eron, 2003). Fifteen years later, the researchers gathered measures of participants' self-reported aggressiveness (getting into fights) and whether they had been convicted of a crime. Paralleling the results of the lab studies, boys and girls who watched a lot of violent TV as children were more aggressive as adults, and more likely to have been convicted of a crime. This effect held even when controlling for how aggressive and intelligent the participants were as children, as well as their parents' aggressiveness and social class.

Violent Video Games

The enormous popularity and use of online social media, search engines, and video games provide vast exposure to violent imagery. Research shows that about 85 percent of American teenagers play video games regularly (Anderson & Bushman, 2001). A nationally representative sample found that the average American between the ages of 8 and 18 spends about 13 hours a week playing video games (Gentile, 2009). Boys spend more time playing on average (just over 16 hours) than girls (about 9 hours). According to this survey, some 8 percent of all American children spend an average of 24 hours a week with video games; kids who do this obsessively show symptoms of addiction—playing gives them a high, and they feel withdrawal symptoms when they don't play. In addition, such constant attention to video games creates conflicts within the family.

Two aficionados of video games—specifically, violent games—were Eric Harris and Dylan Klebold. They played hour after hour, and their favorite game was *Doom*. Harris, in fact, created a custom version of *Doom* in which two shooters, armed with extra weapons and unlimited ammunition, would gun down an array of helpless victims. Tragically, on April 20, 1999, Harris and Klebold's real-life actions mirrored their video game world. The two teenagers took several guns and massive amounts of ammunition to their own school, Columbine High School, in Littleton, Colorado. There they killed 12 of their classmates and a teacher, as well as injuring another 23 students, before killing themselves.

Are violent video games the cause of this kind of violence? Certainly it's not the only cause, and many in the video game industry vehemently deny any relationship between playing video games and violent behavior. In a May 12, 2000, interview on CNN, Doug Lowenstein, then president of the Interactive Digital Software Association, stated, "There is absolutely no evidence, none, that playing a violent video game leads to aggressive behavior." Yet research by

Violent Video Games and the Columbine Massacre

(A) This is an image from a violent video game. The correlation between playing such games and aggressive thoughts and behavior documented in lab studies may play out in real life. (B) Harris and Klebold obsessively played the violent video game *Doom*, and some speculate that may have contributed to the boys' decision to plant bombs and shoot their classmates at Columbine High School in Littleton, Colorado. Here, cameras in the school cafeteria on April 20, 1999, showed Harris and Klebold armed with guns, getting ready to shoot their fellow students, huddled beneath the tables.

Craig Anderson and Brad Bushman and their colleagues indicates otherwise (Anderson & Bushman, 2001; Anderson & Dill, 2000).

In one illustrative study, 43 undergraduate women and men with an average amount of experience playing video games were randomly assigned to play one of two games (Bartholow & Anderson, 2002). Some played *Mortal Kombat*, in which the player chooses a character and attempts to kill six other characters, winning points for each violent death. Others played *PGA Tournament Golf*, in which players complete 18 holes of simulated golf, choosing appropriate clubs and shots best suited to the simulated wind conditions, sand traps, and trees. All participants played several rounds of one of these games against a confederate. When participants lost, they were punished by the confederate with a burst of white noise. When participants won, they returned the favor, punishing the confederate with white noise. Participants who had played *Mortal Kombat* gave longer and more intense bursts of white noise to their competitor than those who had played the golf game.

There have been over 100 studies of the effects of playing violent video games. Some were experiments, like the one described above. Others were longitudinal studies examining whether the amount of violent video games a child plays predicts levels of aggression months later (Anderson et al., 2008). Anderson and his colleagues have documented five unsettling reactions associated with playing violent video games (Anderson et al., 2010; Anderson & Bushman, 2001). Playing these games appears to (1) increase aggressive behavior; (2) reduce prosocial behavior, such as helping or altruism; (3) increase aggressive thoughts; (4) increase aggressive emotions, especially anger; and (5) increase blood pressure and heart rate, physiological responses associated with fighting. These effects were observed in children and adult women as well as men, in the United States, several European countries, and Japan.

Social Rejection and Aggression

The Columbine massacre prompted considerable reflection in the United States. Many hypotheses about the origins of the shooting spree were proposed, including the one just discussed—that playing violent video games increases aggressive

BOX 13.3

Not So Fast
Critical Thinking about Third Variables and Spurious Associations

In light of extensive research showing the increased numbers of young people watching violent TV shows and movies and playing violent video games, you might be tempted to make a gloomy prediction: violent behavior should be rising dramatically among young people. Not so. While it's clear that kids are exposed to more violence in the media and are playing more violent video games than in the past, empirical analyses find that rates of violent behavior by young people are actually declining.

What's going on? How can the association between exposure to violence and aggression observed in society be the opposite of what's been documented in the lab? Critics of the longitudinal studies linking media and violent video game exposure to aggression later in life have brought into focus what they call the third variable critique. Recall from Chapter 2 that in correlational research, such as the studies of media and violence, researchers must be concerned about variables that were not measured but which might be responsible for the observed association between two variables. For example,

if you find the amount of ice cream people eat is associated with the likelihood of violent behavior, you'd wisely attribute such an association to a third variable described in this chapter: hot weather. People eat more ice cream and engage in more violent behavior when it's hot (the third variable), so the apparent relationship between eating ice cream and violence is spurious—produced by some other cause.

What unmeasured variables, then, might produce the association between media exposure to violence in childhood and later aggressive behavior? Chris Ferguson and his colleagues have noted a few (Ferguson & Kilburn, 2010). In the studies of interest, researchers rarely if ever control for how depressed the child is, and depression is known to predict both aggressive behavior and the consumption of media violence. Rarely do studies measure aggressive behavior in the child's peer group, yet kids who hang around aggressive peers are almost certainly more likely to play violent video games and to engage in aggressive behavior. When these unmeasured variables—the

depression of the child and the aggression of his peer group—are controlled for, the association between playing the games and subsequent aggression is reduced significantly (Ferguson, San Miguel, & Hartley, 2009).

Let's consider another unmeasured variable that's typically not assessed: the level of violence in the family. It's well established that a violent family atmosphere—where cruel comments, harsh punishment, and physical and emotional abuse are daily occurrences—is one of the strongest predictors of children acting out in aggressive ways. And a violent family environment is also associated with the tendency to consume violent media. Yet few, if any, studies have measured the degree to which the family environment is hostile, leaving open the possibility that this might be responsible for the observed association between playing violent video games and later aggression. (The same point can be made, of course, about violent TV shows and movies.) As always, controversy and criticism pave the way for more rigorous science and sharper answers to the questions that matter.

behavior. Another hypothesis was that social rejection contributed to the violence: Harris and Klebold felt rejected by the more popular students at school, and their shooting rampage was viewed by many as a reaction to being ostracized. Following the massacre, the U.S. Department of Education issued a report endorsing this hypothesis, concluding that school shooters like Harris and Klebold tend to feel rejected by their peers. Of course, it's clear that social rejection by itself was not a sufficient cause of their behavior. Cullen (2009) emphasizes the underlying pathologies of both boys.

How might social rejection trigger aggression on the scale of the Columbine massacre? Geoff MacDonald and Mark Leary have proposed an answer (MacDonald & Leary, 2005). Throughout the long course of human evolution, MacDonald and Leary reason, being socially rejected from the group was akin to a death warrant, given our profound dependence on others for food, shelter, defense, and affection. Because of the many evolutionary advantages to being

Social Isolation and Aggressive Behavior
Newtown shooter Adam Lanza fatally shot 20 first-graders at Sandy Hook Elementary School, 6 teachers, his mother, and himself in Connecticut in 2012. His social circumstances echo those of Harris and Klebold, perpetrators of the Columbine massacre. Lanza immersed himself in violent chat rooms and video games on the Internet. Throughout his life he experienced profound rejection and isolation, remaining holed up in his room for three continuous months before the shooting took place.

integrated into groups, social rejection came to activate a threat defense system, involving stress-related cardiovascular arousal; the release of the stress hormone cortisol; feelings of distress and pain; and, most relevant to the current discussion, defensive aggressive tendencies. Early in primate evolution, this threat defense system was attuned to cues of physical aggression, such as a predator's attack, and it enabled our ancestors to fare well in aggressive encounters. As humans evolved, social cues—hearing someone's gossip, seeing a sneer or contemptuous eye roll, hearing a superior's critical tone of voice—acquired the power to trigger this threat defense system.

Dozens of studies have clarified how social rejection sets in motion feelings that can lead to aggression. For example, people who feel rejected report higher levels of chronic physical pain and physical ailments (MacDonald & Leary, 2005). To study experimentally the painful consequences of rejection, Kip Williams developed an ingenious ball-tossing paradigm, which may remind you of the politics of playing four square on your grade-school playground. One participant plays a ball-tossing game with two confederates. At a predetermined time in the experiment, the two confederates stop throwing the ball to the participant and throw it back and forth to each other for 5 minutes. Sure enough, the participant's being rejected in this game triggers feelings of distress, shame, self-doubt, and a submissive, slouched posture (Williams, 2007).

In a neuroimaging study conducted by Williams and his colleagues, participants thought they were playing a computerized version of the ball-tossing game with two other people. In actuality, the actions of the other two "people" had been programmed by the experimenter (Eisenberger, Lieberman, & Williams, 2003). When the participant experienced this virtual form of rejection, fMRI images revealed that a region of the brain (the anterior cingulate) that processes physically painful stimuli lit up. Supporting the idea that social pain is similar in nature to physical pain, C. Nathan DeWall and his colleagues have found that acetaminophen, the active ingredient in common painkillers, diminishes social pain just as it does physical pain (DeWall et al., 2010).

Social rejection also increases the likelihood of aggression. People who report a chronic sense of rejection are more likely to act aggressively in their romantic relationships, even resorting to physical abuse (Dutton, 2002). In experimental work, Jean Twenge and her colleagues have found that people who were led to imagine a lonely, socially rejected future were more likely than control participants to administer unpleasant noise blasts to strangers who had nothing to do with the participant's rejection (Twenge, Baumeister, Tice, & Stucke, 2001). Putting these findings together, MacDonald and Leary have argued that social rejection is a root cause of school shootings, like those at Columbine and Sandy Hook, that are tragically an all too common feature of the contemporary landscape in the United States and other countries, such as Scotland, Germany, and Norway (Leary, Kowalski, Smith, & Phillips, 2003).

Income Inequality

We've seen that short-term factors, such as hot weather and exposure to violent media, can lead to higher levels of aggression, and social conditions such as an individual's experience of social rejection or family violence can as well. Social psychologists are also interested in whether more enduring conditions in a person's life influence levels of aggression, such as the presence of parks and green spaces in the neighborhood and the prevailing economic conditions. Let's consider one such economic factor: the level of income inequality, or the degree to which the wealthy differ from the poor in their yearly income and net wealth. Some countries are characterized by high economic inequality: the highest-paid professionals—CEOs, lawyers, and financial managers—have vastly more annual income than the average worker. The United States is characterized by fairly extreme inequality. As you can see in **Figure 13.2**, income inequality in the United States is higher than every European country and is exceeded on this measure only by less wealthy and less developed countries, such as the Philippines, Venezuela, and South Africa.

Does economic inequality increase violence? To explore this question, researchers measured the degree of inequality, indicated by differences between the relatively wealthy in a society (usually the top 20 percent) and the relatively poor (usually the bottom 20 percent) (Wilkinson & Pickett, 2009). They then looked at whether regional inequality—by country, state, or county—correlates with the prevalence of different kinds of violence. Indeed it does. In countries characterized by high economic inequality, such as Bolivia, Iran, Kenya, and the United States, the average citizen is much more likely to be murdered, assaulted, or raped than in countries with less economic inequality, such as Germany, Taiwan, Ireland, and Norway (see Figure 13.2 for the relationship between inequality and homicide rate). In addition, children in countries with greater income inequality are more likely to experience conflict with their peers and to report being victims of bullying.

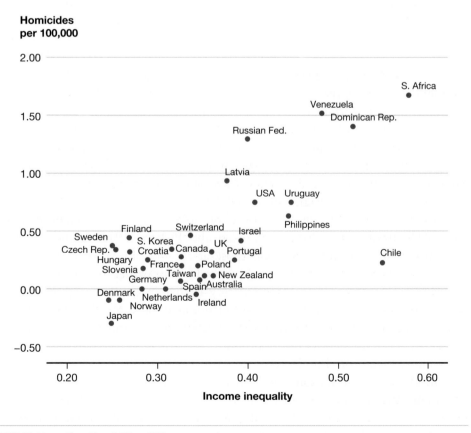

Figure 13.2

Income Inequality and Homicide Rates in Several Industrialized Countries

Homicides are more likely in countries where there is greater income inequality between the rich and the poor.

SOURCE: Adapted from Elgar & Aitken, 2011.

BOX 13.4 **FOCUS ON *THE ENVIRONMENT***

Green Neighborhoods Make More Peaceful Citizens

The current environmental movement was inspired by philosophers Henry David Thoreau and Ralph Waldo Emerson, who were known as the transcendentalists. These writers found great calm and peace in being out in the woods. Their writings inspired a young naturalist, John Muir, whose experiences as a young man in the Sierra Nevada mountains of California led him to found the Sierra Club and lobby on behalf of state and national parks, which he helped create.

Social psychologists have recently begun to examine how easy access to nature and green spaces influences our psychological health. Recent experiments have found, for example, that a walk in the woods (as opposed to a walk through a town) enables adults to perform better on a measure of concentrated attention (Berman, Jonides, & Kaplan, 2008), and that reports of experiences in nature are the best predictor, compared with other recreational activities, of calming down from the stress of work (Korpela & Kinnunen, 2009).

These findings raise a question: Might green spaces decrease neighborhood violence? Social psychologist Frances Kuo thinks so. In one line of research, Kuo studied police reports of violence occurring near 98 low-rise buildings that are part of the Ida Wells housing project in Chicago (Kuo & Sullivan, 2001). Some of the buildings were surrounded by trees and lawns, others by asphalt and a lack of greenery. The residents in these 98 buildings came from similar backgrounds, were enduring similar levels of unemployment and economic hardship, and had been randomly assigned to the buildings they lived in. Kuo discovered that the likelihood of violent crime was lower near apartments surrounded by green spaces. In experimental research, Kuo has allowed children with attention deficit disorder, who are more prone to aggressive acts, to go for a walk of comparable length and physical exertion in one of three places: a green park, a quiet neighborhood, or in noisy downtown Chicago (Taylor & Kuo, 2009). She found that children scored better on a measure of concentration only after the walk in the park. Green spaces seem to calm people's minds, enabling them to concentrate more effectively and better handle the frustrations of daily living.

When states within the United States are classified according to their levels of economic inequality, the pattern repeats itself. Rates of homicide, for example, are higher in states with relatively high inequality (such as Louisiana and California) than in those with low inequality (such as Utah and Wisconsin). Inequality also seems to play a role in determining which neighborhoods are more violent. Robert Sampson and his colleagues have found that there are higher rates of violence in urban neighborhoods in the United States with high income inequality (Morenoff, Sampson, & Raudenbush, 2001).

Why does income inequality give rise to violence? Social psychologists have provided several explanations. Wilkinson and Pickett (2009) found that the powerful feelings of social rejection those at the bottom in unequal societies have might trigger violence, a claim supported by our earlier discussion of social isolation and rejection. Another possibility is that inequality undermines the cohesiveness of a neighborhood, state, or country—the feelings of trust and goodwill among people. Sampson and his colleagues found that more violent crimes occur in less cohesive neighborhoods, where neighbors report less trust for one another (Sampson, Raudenbush, & Earls, 1997). Evolutionary psychologists Martin Daly, Margot Wilson, and Shawn Vasdev (2001) propose another possibility, contending that inequality throws males into more extreme competition for economic resources and access to mates, two sources of conflict that often motivate murder and other crimes.

↑ LOOKING BACK

Many situational factors contribute to the likelihood of aggressive behavior. These include hot weather, violence in the media, violent video games, social rejection, and economic inequality.

Construal Processes and Aggression

Thus far, we've considered various situational determinants of aggression. Situations, however, do nothing by themselves; their influence is channeled through construal processes. Most people who live in extremely hot environments, see lots of violent images in movies or in video games, and encounter social rejection and income inequality do so without acting aggressively. Let's explore what particular construals of such states as feeling excessively hot and being socially isolated might lead to aggressive behavior.

Anger

For centuries, social theorists have known that anger is a potent construal that leads to aggressive behavior. Leonard Berkowitz has offered a theoretical account that suggests this focus is justified. He argues that any unpleasant stimulus triggers a fight-or-flight response of anger. This is true of more obvious causes of aggression, such as being exposed to violent images in the media, living in a neighborhood defined by income inequality and poverty, and being insulted, as well as such factors as physical discomfort, hunger, and feelings of shame and depression (Berkowitz, 1989, 1993). Once angry, people tend to think things are unfair, to perceive others has having more adversarial intentions, and to imagine ways of inflicting harm (DeSteno, Petty, Wegener, & Rucker, 2000; Keltner, Ellsworth, & Edwards, 1993). This line of thinking helps clarify when aspects of a situation will lead to aggression—when they trigger anger. For instance, sometimes extreme hot weather doesn't trigger anger (it might prompt relaxation), and thus won't lead to aggressive behavior. Other times, though, the discomfort of extreme heat will stimulate anger, thereby making people more prone to acting aggressively.

In one test of this theory, Berkowitz examined how anger and the presence of weapons combine to make people more aggressive. Today weapons are everywhere, and a source of intense political debate. Worldwide, roughly 650 million guns are in the hands of civilians (Small Arms Survey, 2011). The same survey found that in the United States there are nearly 89 guns for every 100 citizens. According to Berkowitz, though, the presence of guns will only lead to aggression when combined with experiences of anger. To test his hypothesis, Berkowitz had male participants work on a series of problems with a male confederate, taking turns "evaluating each other's performance" by delivering shocks for performances that needed improvement (Berkowitz & LePage, 1967). The participants worked on the problems first, and were shocked by the confederate. Unknown to the participants, the confederate delivered shocks based on whether the participants had been assigned to a neutral or anger condition (not based on

"Anybody can become angry— that is easy, but to be angry with the right person and to the right degree and at the right time and for the right purpose, and in the right way—that is not within everybody's power and is not easy."

—ARISTOTLE

BOX 13.5 **FOCUS ON *SPORTS***

The Effect of Uniform Color on Aggression

The tendency to act more aggressively when a weapon is nearby reinforces a core lesson of social psychology—the situationist message that seemingly small changes in the environment can have a substantial impact on behavior. This tendency also raises the question whether other environmental cues might foster or inhibit aggression. For example, might the clothes people wear influence how they behave, including whether they behave aggressively? Might the menacing black shirts worn by Hitler's S.S. (*Schutzstaffel*) have made it easier for them to brutalize the populace of conquered lands?

Support for such a possibility comes from research on the effect of uniform color on aggressiveness in professional sports (Frank & Gilovich, 1988). The investigators began by examining the penalty records of all teams in American professional football (the NFL) and ice hockey (the NHL) from 1970 to 1985. As shown in **Figure 13.3**, the black-uniformed teams consistently ranked near the top in penalties every year.

As pronounced as this tendency might be, however, it can't predict whether wearing black actually causes players to be more aggressive. There are two other possibilities. First, because of some negative stereotypes involving the color black (such as the typical dress of movie villains), players in black uniforms may look more intimidating even if they play no differently than players on other teams who aren't wearing black. Thus, players in black uniforms may be more likely than others to be penalized for marginal infractions. Second, the finding may simply be a selection effect; that is, the general managers of certain teams, believing that aggressiveness pays off in victories, may both recruit particularly aggressive players and, incidentally, give them black uniforms to foster an aggressive image.

The latter interpretation can be ruled out. By a convenient twist of fate, several teams switched uniforms from non-black to black during the period under investigation, and all experienced a corresponding increase in penalties. One team, the NHL's Pittsburgh Penguins, changed uniform colors in the middle of a season, so the switch was not accompanied by any changes in players, coaches, or front-office personnel. Nevertheless, the Penguins averaged 8 penalty minutes in the blue uniforms they wore before the switch and 12 penalty minutes in the black uniforms they wore after—a 50-percent increase.

Follow-up laboratory experiments have provided support for both perceptions of aggressiveness and actual aggressiveness of players in black. Thus, the tendency for black-uniformed teams to draw so many penalties appears to be the joint effect of a bias on the part of referees and a tendency for players wearing black to act more aggressively (Frank & Gilovich, 1988).

But does wearing black always make people more aggressive? Probably not. The effect seems to be limited to contexts that are already associated with confrontation and aggression. The black clothing worn by Catholic clerics and Hasidic Jews may not make them any more aggressive, but the black shirts worn by Hitler's S.S. might very well have contributed to their brutality.

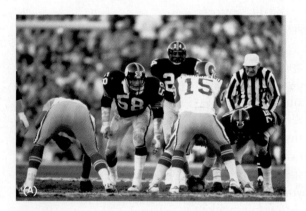

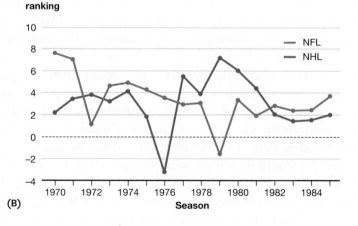

Figure 13.3

Uniform Color and Aggression

(A) The Pittsburgh Steelers, wearing black uniforms, were known for their aggressive play. (B) Points on the graph of penalty records represent the difference between the average ranking of the black-uniformed teams and the average to be expected based on chance alone (dotted horizontal line at 0).

SOURCE: Adapted from Frank & Gilovich, 1988.

their actual performance). The confederate shocked those assigned to the neutral condition 1 time and those assigned to the anger condition 7 times. The participant then watched the confederate work on the problems and provided his feedback on the confederate's performance in the form of shocks. The participant did so under one of three conditions. In a "no object" condition, no objects were near the shock machine. In a "neutral object" condition, badminton rackets and shuttlecocks were nearby the shock machine. In a "gun" condition, a revolver and a shotgun lay near the shock machine—rather unusual experimental props, to say the least.

The results from this study are shown in **Figure 13.4**. Most noteworthy is that the presence of guns alone did not make participants more aggressive. Instead, guns made them more aggressive when they were also angered by the confederate's actions (see also Frodi, 1975; Turner & Leyens, 1992). In further support of this point, a more recent study found that hunters do not become more aggressive when presented with images of guns, because they construe guns as objects for recreation and fun rather than for violence (Bartholow, Anderson, Carnagey, & Benjamin, 2005).

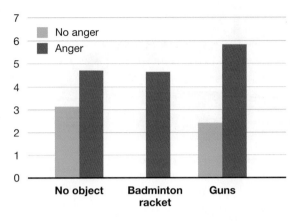

Figure 13.4
Anger, Weapons, and Aggression
When people are angry and in the presence of weapons, they behave more aggressively.

SOURCE: Adapted from Berkowitz & LePage, 1967.

Dehumanization

Acts of aggression often go hand-in-hand with a particularly disastrous construal process known as **dehumanization**, the attribution of negative, nonhuman characteristics to other people. Studies of escalating conflict and genocide regularly find that dehumanization fuels extreme violence. During the Rwandan genocide, the Hutus referred to the Tutsis as "cockroaches." The Nazis described the Jews as "lice." During the eighteenth-century slave trade, Europeans referred to the Africans they captured, sold, and killed as "brutes" and "beasts." Hate crimes against gay men often are justified with dehumanizing rhetoric. Even in more peaceful times, dehumanization arises in more subtle forms. You might hear a political pundit refer to an "infestation" of illegal aliens when talking about immigration, or a candidate he doesn't like as a "robot."

Nick Haslam and Steve Loughnan propose two varieties of dehumanization (Haslam & Loughnan, 2014). First, a person can be denied *human nature*, that is, the qualities that distinguish us from inanimate entities, such as computers and robots. These include our capacity for emotion, for feeling pain, and for expressing warmth towards others. A second kind of dehumanization involves denying a person *human uniqueness*, that is, the attributes that distinguish humans from other species. These attributes include our capacity for civility, refinement, and our complex cognitive capacities—for symbolic language or mathematics, for example. In the nineteenth century, when Western Europeans referred to people from other cultures as "savages," their minds fell prey to this second kind of dehumanization. This kind is regrettably common today: people are more likely to associate apelike qualities (and not other animal qualities) with the

dehumanization The attribution of nonhuman characteristics and denial of human qualities to groups other than one's own.

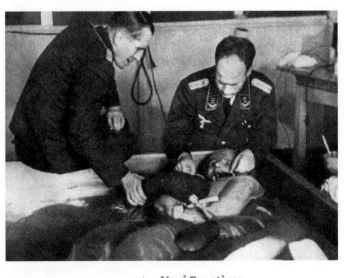

Nazi Practices
The pain experiments Nazis performed on Jews during the Holocaust were an extreme example of dehumanization.

Negative Characterizations
During wartime, dehumanization can be found in all kinds of publications. This is a page from a 1938 Nazi children's book. The translated caption says: "Just look at these guys! The louse-infested beards! The filthy, protruding ears, Those stained, fatty clothes . . . Jews often have an unpleasant sweetish odor. If you have a good nose, you can smell the Jews."

category "Black Americans" than the category "White Americans" (Goff, Eberhardt, Williams, & Jackson, 2008).

Dehumanization can unleash aggression for the simple reason that it's easier to harm others who seem less human, less like ourselves. For example, dehumanizing others has been found to play a role in bullying behavior (Haslam & Loughnan, 2014) and in condoning police violence against African-Americans (Goff et al., 2008). In a study of sexual violence, Rudman and Mescher identified men who were more likely to dehumanize women as animals according to how quickly they paired the concept of "woman" with concepts such as "animal" and "instinct" (Rudman & Mescher, 2012). Men who were more likely to dehumanize women in such fashion reported that they themselves would be more likely to harass women sexually, that if no one would ever find out about it they would force a woman to have sex, and that women on occasion deserve to be raped.

One factor that increases the likelihood of dehumanization might sound surprising: loyalty to valued social groups. When we feel strongly committed to a group, whether a political party, an ethnic group, or a sports team, we are more disposed to dehumanize others. In one survey of over 180 groups in developing countries, tribes characterized by powerful ingroup loyalty and a strong sense of "we feeling" were more likely to dehumanize other tribes and act in violent fashion against them (Cohen, Montoya, & Insko, 2006).

Shockingly, even rather benign feelings of social connection increase the likelihood of dehumanization. Here the thinking is that although feeling socially connected brings us closer to people within our group, it creates greater distance from those who are different from us, making dehumanization more likely. In one study guided by this idea, students who were asked to recall a time of feeling connected to another person attributed less human-like mental states, such as empathy and moral concern, to outgroups such as the wealthy and poor (Waytz & Epley, 2012). In a clever extension of this work, when participants reported their attitudes while sitting next to a friend (thus feeling socially connected) as opposed to sitting next to a stranger, they were more likely to dehumanize non-U.S. citizens who were detained for security reasons, and to more strongly endorse forms of torture such as waterboarding and the application of electric shock (Waytz & Epley, 2012).

Cognitive Control of Anger

Anger, aggression, and dehumanization are things we'd like to avoid as much as possible. How might we combat these tendencies? Social psychology offers some important suggestions. **Catharsis** is the release of a strong emotion, such as anger, to purge oneself of the impulse to behave inappropriately. The belief in the efficacy of catharsis has led therapists to have struggling couples strike each other with foam bats, parents to direct their children to bite pillows instead of siblings, and jilted romantic partners to throw darts at photos of their exes.

However, there's not a shred of scientific evidence in support of the idea that catharsis is a healthy way of handling anger, and some evidence that it is ill-advised (Berkowitz, 1993). For example, participants in one study were insulted by a confederate who harshly criticized their personal writing (Bushman, 2002). Participants then either relaxed, hit a punching bag while keeping the image of another undergrad in their mind, or they hit a punching bag while keeping

catharsis The release of a strong emotion, such as anger, by expressing it directly.

the image of the insulting confederate in mind (the catharsis condition). When given the chance to punish the confederate in a later part of the study, it was the participants in the catharsis condition who applied the most intense shocks. The would-be cathartic exercise did not diminish aggression, it increased it.

A better strategy is to take a step back from our anger. Ozlem Ayduk and Ethan Kross have proposed that any experience of anger can be viewed from a distance or up close (Ayduk & Kross, 2008). To view our anger from a distance, we might think of the frustrating event as just one moment in time, or as a single episode of a much longer relationship, or the current situation as if it was part of a movie or novel. Construed each of these ways, we can find some distance from anger, and research suggests this is a good thing. In one study, participants were asked to think about a time that had made them angry (Ayduk & Kross, 2008). Half of them were told to immerse themselves in the experience, and vividly feel it in the present moment. The other half, those in the distance condition, were told to look at it from a distance, as if they were watching themselves in a movie. Those participants who distanced themselves from their anger showed less fight-or-flight increases in blood pressure, and reported a greater sense of calm.

Remarkably, Grossman and Kross (2014) have shown that when you ask a person to think about why "Jennifer"—using the first name—is worked up about something, there is less negative emotion than when you ask the person why "she" is upset. Both common experience and research indicate it's easier for people to reason calmly about other people's problems than their own (Grossmann & Kross, 2014). When people use their own names to think about the self, it leads them to think about themselves as though they were someone else (albeit another person whose inner thoughts and feelings they have privileged access to), providing them with the psychological distance needed to calmly reason though stressful situations.

⟲ LOOKING BACK

People's construals of situations can be crucial in determining whether they act aggressively. When any kind of stimulus triggers anger, we're more likely to act aggressively. Our tendency to dehumanize others, to deny them basic human nature and human uniqueness, can fuel aggression. We are not prisoners of such hostile construals. When we step back from them, and look at what's making us angry from a distance, we become less hostile and more calm.

Culture and Aggression

Anthropologists have long noted dramatic cultural variations in the expression of aggression. People in certain cultures have been observed to be kind, peaceful, and cooperative. Alaskan Inuits, for example, have been described as rarely expressing anger or aggression, and as remarkably kind in their actions with others. People in other cultures have been portrayed as violent, belligerent, and aggressive. Among the Yanomami, who live in the Amazon region, aggression is encouraged in children, intratribal fighting with spears and knives is a weekly source of injury and death, and rape and war are considered an intrinsic part of human nature (Chagnon, 1997). Their fitting name for themselves is "the fierce people."

Cultural Differences in Aggressive Expression
(A) The Alaskan Inuits rarely express anger or aggression. (B) The Yanomami encourage aggression in their children and are known for their violent raids against their enemies.

The cultural perspective on aggression holds that certain values, as well as habitual ways of construing the self and others, make members of one culture more aggressive and violent than others. Social psychologists have developed ways of bringing notable and puzzling human tendencies, including cultural differences in aggressive behavior, into the laboratory to find explanations for them.

The Culture of Honor

As you'll recall from Chapter 2, Richard Nisbett and Dov Cohen have explored regional differences in violence in the United States (Cohen & Nisbett, 1997; Cohen, Nisbett, Bowdle, & Schwarz, 1996; Nisbett, 1993; Nisbett & Cohen, 1996). They argue that a **culture of honor** is prevalent in the U.S. South. Men in such cultures tend to be concerned about their reputation for toughness, machismo, and their willingness and ability to avenge a wrong or insult. These concerns give rise to firm rules of politeness, as well as additional ways people recognize the honor of others, thus lending stability to social relationships and reducing the risk of violence. The downside of the concern with honor is that it makes people particularly sensitive to slights and insults, thereby leading them to feel obligated to respond with violence to protect or reestablish their honor.

Using a variety of methods, the investigators present several lines of evidence indicating that when their honor is slighted, Southerners are more likely than Northerners to respond with aggression (Nisbett & Cohen, 1996). In archival research, Nisbett and his colleagues found that murders in the context of a felony were about equally common in the North, South, and Southwest; but murders that occurred as a result of an argument or perceived insult were far more common in the South and Southwest than the North (**Figure 13.5**).

To examine participants' sensitivity to slights and insults, Cohen and his colleagues exposed Southerners and Northerners to an insult in the context of a laboratory study. An accomplice of the experimenter bumped into the subject and called him an "asshole" (Cohen et al., 1996). Insulted participants from Southern states showed more anger in their facial expressions than insulted Northerners. The insulted Southerners' testosterone and cortisone levels increased significantly

culture of honor A culture defined by its members' strong concerns about their own and others' reputations, leading to sensitivity to insults and a willingness to use violence to avenge any perceived wrong.

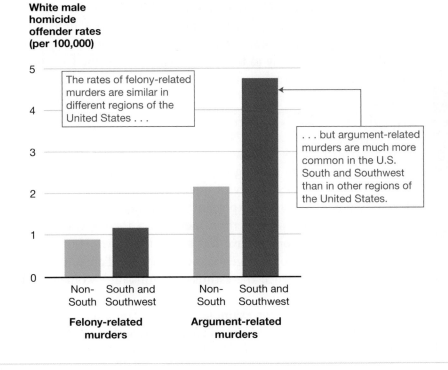

White male homicide offender rates (per 100,000)

The rates of felony-related murders are similar in different regions of the United States . . .

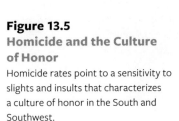

. . . but argument-related murders are much more common in the U.S. South and Southwest than in other regions of the United States.

	Felony-related murders	Argument-related murders
Non-South / South and Southwest		

SOURCE: Adapted from Nisbett & Cohen, 1996, p. 21; based on data from Fox & Pierce, 1987.

Figure 13.5
Homicide and the Culture of Honor
Homicide rates point to a sensitivity to slights and insults that characterizes a culture of honor in the South and Southwest.

more than those of insulted Northerners. Following the insult, the insulted Southerners shook another person's hand more firmly, and refused to move out of the way of an imposing confederate walking toward them in a narrow hallway. In a field experiment, Cohen and Nisbett (1997) found that some Southern employers actually expressed a good deal of warmth toward a potential job applicant who confessed to having been convicted of manslaughter after defending his honor.

Where did this regional difference in the importance attached to honor come from? Why is honor-related homicide more common in the South? Could it just be the hot weather? It's not likely, because honor-related homicides are more common in the relatively cool mountain regions of the South (Kentucky, Arkansas) than in the relatively hot agricultural lowlands (Mississippi, Alabama). Could it be the brutal history of slavery? Again, it's not likely, and for the same geographical reason. Homicide is more common in the highlands, where slavery was relatively uncommon, than in the lowlands, where slavery was ubiquitous.

Nisbett and Cohen (1996) argue that the culture of honor in the South is a variant of a cultural perspective found worldwide among people who earn their living by herding animals. Herders are susceptible to losing their entire wealth in an instant if someone steals their cows, pigs, or sheep. Farmers, in contrast, are susceptible to no such rapid and catastrophic loss, at least not at the hands of another person. The vulnerability of the herder means he has to develop a tough exterior and make it clear he's willing to take a stand against the slightest threat, even an insult or a joke at his expense. This difference fits the pattern of violence in the United States because the North was founded primarily by farmers from England, Germany, and the Netherlands, whereas the South was founded primarily by Scottish and Irish settlers (and especially the Scotch-Irish

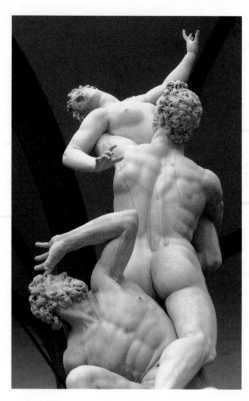

The Rape of the Sabine Women

Rape is a disturbingly common form of violence, especially during periods of war and in contexts where women occupy positions of low power. Such was the case in the legend of the rape of Sabine women, who were forced, in 750 BC, to marry the Romans who conquered their town and raped them. This famous statue by the sculptor Giambologna is in Florence, Italy.

of Northern Ireland, Celtic peoples who had herded, rather than farmed, since prehistoric times). Thus, the people in the Southern highlands, where the herding culture continued to be a major economic activity until quite recently, were more likely to be violent than those in the lowlands, where settlers had taken advantage of the rich soil to become farmers.

Culture and Sexual Violence

In 1990, Nobel Prize–winning economist Amartya Sen estimated that there were 100 million missing women in the world (Sen, 1990). Women, holding constant their country of origin and class background, are more likely to enjoy a longer life expectancy than men, so a given population should include more women than men. But in some countries, particularly those where women have less status than men, women are more vulnerable to patterns of negligence and violence and are underrepresented in the population—hence the estimate of "missing" women (Kristof & WuDunn, 2009).

In certain countries, for example, female infanticide is practiced, parents are less likely to immunize their daughters than their sons or take daughters to the hospital, and as a result girls are more likely to die early deaths due to preventable or curable sicknesses. Bride burning, the practice of punishing a young woman for her family's failure to confer a sufficient dowry on the groom's family in marriage, claims the lives of thousands of young women in India every year. And the sexual trafficking of young girls into prostitution, widespread throughout the world, claims the lives of thousands of girls each year as young as age 8, some of whom are sold by their own families.

Less deadly forms of sexual violence are common in virtually every country. For example, in the United States, 50–80 percent of women have been sexually harassed, having been stalked, catcalled, or made the target of obscene comments at work or over the phone (Fairchild & Rudman, 2008). Twenty-percent of female American teenagers have been sexually assaulted by someone they are dating.

One of the most disturbing and common acts of violence against women is rape, the coercive forcing of sex by one person (usually male) upon another (typically female). Rape is often used as an instrument of terror during war, as it was in the genocides in Bosnia, Rwanda, and Darfur. But acts of rape are not limited to the madness of war. The latest estimates from the organization UN Women (2011) are that sexual violence and rape are disturbingly common in marriages around the world. A survey of 86 countries found that, on average, about 20 percent of women experience sexual violence or rape in a romantic relationship at some time in their lives. In some countries, this rarely happens; for example, only 2.7 percent of women in Cambodia reported such an experience. In other countries, the statistics are staggering: in Ethiopia, 58.6 percent of women reported experiencing at least one episode of sexual violence in an intimate relationship.

What makes rape more prevalent in certain cultures than in others? And how can such a question be tackled empirically? Peggy Reeves Sanday (1981, 1997) relied on archival records to study the cultural determinants of rape. She read descriptions provided by historians and anthropologists of 156 cultures dating back to 1750 BCE and continuing to the 1960s. Looking carefully for references to rape in these accounts, Sanday identified what she called **rape-prone cultures**. She defined such cultures according to whether they used rape as an act of war against enemy women, a ritual act, such as part of a wedding ceremony or an adolescent male's rite of passage to adulthood, or a threat against women to keep them subservient to men.

Of the 156 cultures Sanday studied, 47 percent were classified as rape-free, in that there were no reports of rape in the accounts of the culture; 18 percent as rape-prone by her definition; and 35 percent as rape-present, where rape occurs but not as a ritual, threat, or act of war. It would be no surprise, however, if these figures underestimated the prevalence of rape-proneness across cultures. They are based largely on anthropologists' observations, and rape is one of the most difficult acts to observe, as well as being a taboo subject in many cultures.

Putting these concerns aside, let's look at some of Sanday's specific findings. One question she addressed was the type of sexual attitudes that predicted the prevalence of rape across the 156 cultures. For example, is there more rape in more sexually repressed cultures, because individuals resort to rape to gratify their sexual desire? She assessed the extent of each culture's sexual repressiveness according to the prevalence of postpartum (following child delivery) taboos and premarital sex taboos. Sanday found that the prevalence of rape was unrelated to a culture's sexually restrictive beliefs or practices.

What about the general level of violence in the culture? If rape at its core is an act of violence, then it should be more prevalent in more aggressive, violent cultures. This prediction would fit with what we learned earlier—that people in hostile cultures, where anger is in the air, so to speak, should be more prone to committing aggressive acts, including rape. This indeed proved to be the case. Rape-prone cultures were more likely to have high levels of violence, a history of frequent warfare, and an emphasis on machismo and male toughness.

Finally, many scholars have treated rape as an act of dominance, a means of subordinating women. This suggests that rape may be more prevalent in cultures whose women have lower status, and it's a prediction that has received support. Women in rape-prone cultures are less likely to participate in education and political decision-making than women in rape-free cultures. Women in rape-free cultures are more empowered and more likely to be granted equal status with men. Consider the Mbuti Pygmies as an illustration of these findings (Turnbull, 1965). In this (reportedly) nearly rape-free society, there is minimal interpersonal violence and fighting. Great prestige is attached to the raising of children, and women's contribution to group well-being is valued. Women and men assume different duties, but they have equal standing. And women and men participate equally in political decision making. This pattern of gender egalitarianism is typical of contemporary hunter-gatherers, whose style of life is presumed to be much like those of humans before the development of agriculture.

Sexual Violence on Campus
The continuing prevalence of sexual violence prompted a new federal investigation of 55 American universities and colleges for failing to take appropriate measures in responding to sexual attacks on campus.

rape-prone culture A culture in which rape tends to be used as an act of war against enemy women, as a ritual act, or as a threat against women to keep them subservient to men.

Gender Equality in a Rape-Free Culture
The Mbuti Pygmies, in the Congo region of Africa, are known for their low levels of violence against women.

↰ LOOKING BACK

Cultures differ greatly in their propensity toward aggression of various kinds. Members of cultures of honor, which frequently were herding cultures in the past, are more inclined to commit violence when insulted. Cultures that are prone to rape are characteristically those that devalue women and have extreme gender inequality.

Evolution and Aggression

For many people, the word *evolution* brings to mind a violent struggle for survival and the opportunity to reproduce—the "nature red in tooth and claw" in Tennyson's poem. As we've emphasized at several points in this book, evolutionary theory is more than just a theory of competition and violence; it's helped illuminate all manner of social behaviors, from romantic attraction to empathy. And evolutionary psychologists have indeed offered new insights about the origins of aggression.

Violence in Stepfamilies

World literature is full of tales of wicked stepparents who abuse their children. In the animal kingdom, "step-relations" seem similarly prone to violence. To take one example, when male lions acquire a new mate, they routinely kill all the female's cubs from prior matings. Evolutionary psychologists Margo Wilson and Martin Daly argue that these tendencies in our mammalian forebears have left their trace in human nature (Daly & Wilson, 1996; Wilson, Daly, & Weghorst, 1980).

Natural selection, Daly and Wilson maintain, rewards those parents who devote resources to their own offspring. All the behaviors related to parental care, from filial love to breast-feeding, assist the survival of our own offspring, thereby increasing **inclusive fitness**—our own survival plus that of children carrying our genes. But parental care is costly, as any parent of a newborn knows; it requires time, effort, and material resources. It's been estimated that hunter-gatherers typically don't become net contributors of food and other resources until around the age of 21. (Your parents should be so lucky!) In evolutionary terms, parental expenditures are offset by the gains of having offspring—namely, the survival of their genes. Stepparents, in contrast, incur the same costs with no enhancement of their inclusive fitness, since they don't share genes with their stepchildren.

Survey results consistently indicate that relationships between stepparents and stepchildren tend to be more distant and conflicted, as well as less committed and satisfying, than between parents and their genetic offspring (Hobart, 1991). The archival evidence is even more sobering. Daly and Wilson (1996) found that in the United States, children who are younger than age 2 are 100 times more likely to be abused to the point of death by stepparents than genetic parents, and in Canada, they are 70 times more likely to be killed by stepparents than genetic parents. These findings hold, it's important to note, even when researchers control for a variety of contributing causes, such as poverty, age of the mother, length of time the couple has lived together, and number of children in the

inclusive fitness According to evolutionary theory, the fitness of an individual based on reproductive success and the passing on of genes to future generations.

Mistreated Stepchildren

Literature and fairy tales abound with tales of stepchildren treated badly by their stepmothers. (A) Cinderella becomes the scullery maid for her stepmother and stepsisters. (B) Hansel and Gretel are sent out to die in the forest at the urging of their stepmother.

home. In a study of a South American hunter-gatherer people, 43 percent of children raised by a mother and stepfather died before their fifteenth birthday; that's more than twice the rate of death (19 percent) of children raised by two genetic parents. (This statistic doesn't imply that the stepchildren were killed; but at the very least, they were more likely to have been denied resources, such as food and physical care, that were made available to genetic offspring.)

Gender and Aggression

When we hear about school shootings or think about teen violence, or when we read about rape or the genocides in Rwanda and Darfur, these acts of aggression are almost always committed by young men. Physical aggression is, in fact, from early childhood to old age, among the most marked gender differences in behavior. In the United States, 99 percent of all people arrested for rape, 88 percent of all those arrested for murder, 92 percent arrested for robbery, and 87 percent arrested for aggravated assault are men (Kimmel, 2004). As early as age 2, boys are more physically aggressive than girls (Archer, 2009). Men are also overwhelmingly the victims of violence. For example, men are 20 times as likely to kill other men as women are to kill other women (Daly & Wilson, 1988).

Women, of course, are also aggressive, but in different ways. Women seem to exceed men in what's known as relational aggression or emotional aggression; they gossip, form alliances, and practice the fine art of social rejection to hurt others (Coie et al., 1999; Dodge & Schwartz, 1997; McFayden-Ketchum, Bates, Dodge, & Pettit, 1996). Many female readers will remember with a wince the vicious ways girls can behave toward one another in

A Scene from the Movie *Mean Girls*

Although men commit most of the acts of physical aggression, women are more likely to engage in relational or emotional aggression.

middle school: talking behind people's backs and tarnishing reputations. Obviously, this kind of aggression can be extremely hurtful emotionally. Alas, it's not just sticks and stones: names actually will hurt you.

Most striking and well documented is the tendency for men to engage in more physical violence than women. Both evolutionary and cultural theorists have proposed explanations of men's greater levels of physical aggression. Let's first look at an evolutionary approach to this pronounced gender difference.

Evolutionary psychologists, including John Archer, have sought to understand the striking gender differences in aggression in terms of access to reproductive opportunities (Archer, 2009; Daly & Wilson, 1988). This theorizing builds on the concept of parental investment (see Chapter 1). According to this thinking, women invest more in their offspring than men, and thus are less likely to desert their offspring and seek other reproductive opportunities. Men, in contrast, are freer to go outside the primary relationship and compete with other men for access to mates. Within this competition, high-status men are much more successful than low-status men in terms of reproductive success, or number of offspring. Thus, some men have children with many women, whereas other men's chances for reproduction are much more uncertain, making the competition for mates more difficult. By contrast, reproductively healthy women who want to pass on their genes are, almost without exception, able to do so.

Throughout evolutionary history, this basic difference in reproductive opportunities led males to evolve characteristics and strategies for outcompeting other males for mates. Physical aggression is one such strategy, and it accounts for the evolution of certain traits that would serve males well in competing with other males. For example, surveys from cultures around the world reveal that men are 7.6 percent taller than women, 25 percent heavier, and 1.5 times physically stronger (Archer, 2009). Male physical prowess evolved for aggressive encounters with other men, and indeed, today bigger men tend to engage in more aggressive behaviors (DeWall, Bushman, Giancola, & Webster, 2010). Another advantage of male size and strength is for protecting offspring against animal predators and other humans.

According to the evolutionary psychologists, nonverbal signals of size and strength evolved in males so they could negotiate their rank in status hierarchies, to gain privileged access to mates. Cues of physical strength include a broader chin, a deeper voice (which correlates with physical size), and even facial hair—all of which have evolved, the thinking goes, for men to signal strength to other males, and enjoy elevated status (Archer, 2009).

The evolutionary approach helps explain the increases in muscle mass, facial hair, and other signs of physical development during puberty in young men. Initial studies found that testosterone was associated with higher levels of aggression. For example, delinquents have higher levels of testosterone than college students (Banks & Dabbs, 1996). Members of rowdier fraternities have higher testosterone levels than members of more responsible fraternities (Dabbs, 2000). Social psychologists have also found that testosterone promotes status-related behaviors in competitive settings (Mehta & Josephs, 2010). Two general patterns of results suggest that testosterone probably served men well in the competition for mates (Schultheiss, 2013). First, men who have higher levels of testosterone tend to exhibit more dominant, assertive behaviors that presumably help them to achieve higher status. (In women, the hormone estradiol, which converts to testosterone in the body, has a similar effect.) Second, men who care a lot about

Evolutionary Theory and Physical Appearance
According to evolutionary theorists, someone like Don Draper in the TV series *Mad Men* could be expected, on the basis of his physical appearance, to have many mates.

power and status show increased testosterone (in women, increased estradiol) after winning competitions.

Cultural theorists have a very different take on these striking gender differences in aggressive behavior, noting that men are socialized into roles that encourage physical aggressiveness. Parents, teachers, media sources, and social institutions systematically, and often unwittingly, cultivate more aggressive tendencies in men. Consider, for example, how young boys are treated from the earliest stages. When parents see a video of an infant looking startled, the parents are likely to say the infant is angry if it's a boy. If the same infant is described as a girl, the parents say the infant is fearful (Condry & Condry, 1976). Mothers talk more about emotions with their daughters than with their sons, and such conversations may cultivate greater empathy in women (Fivush, 1991). The one exception to the generalization that mothers talk more about emotions with their daughter is anger, which mothers are more likely to mention in labeling the emotions of their sons. Thus, starting very early in life, anger and aggressive reactions are made more salient to young boys than to young girls. Given that anger is a primary determinant of aggression, this socialization process might account for at least some of the gender differences we're discussing.

Combining the evolutionary and cultural approaches to male aggression, Jennifer Bosson and Joseph Vandello have proposed that as a consequence of both evolutionary and socialization processes, a man's gender identity is significantly tied up in his physical strength, toughness, and fierceness. However, according to their **precarious manhood hypothesis**, many factors—competition, status contests, being the target of male violence, shifting economic conditions—can render a man's gender identity relatively uncertain (Bosson & Vandello, 2011). It's more vulnerable than the gender identity of women, and as a result, men need to resort to risky, and often aggressive, actions to continually prove their manhood.

Empirical studies show that people do indeed believe that manhood is precarious (Bosson & Vandello, 2011). For example, in one study participants read proverbs that portrayed the insecure nature of manhood ("manhood is hard won and easily lost") or the same proverbs phrased to focus on the uncertain nature of womanhood ("womanhood is hard won but easily lost"). Participants endorsed the proverbs portraying precarious manhood significantly more.

Aware of their more vulnerable gender identity, men should be more sensitive to threats to their manhood and thus more likely to resort to risky and often aggressive behaviors to prove themselves. For some readers this may be reminiscent of high school derring-do—the dangerous acts young men routinely engage in, challenging each other physically, provoking fights, climbing water towers, driving recklessly. (We've been told by physicians in the Southwest that the only people who show up in hospitals with rattlesnake bites are inebriated young men!) In one study, men first either braided a bunch of ropes, or braided the hair of a wig, the latter being a more feminine task and a threat to stereotypical notions of masculinity (Bosson & Vandello, 2011). All participants then put on boxing gloves and struck a punching bag. Men who had braided hair hit the bag much harder than those who had braided ropes. These findings suggest a link between precarious manhood and violence against gays (here too almost exclusively perpetrated by men). In laboratory studies, men whose manhood has been threatened express more distance from gays and greater aggression toward them (Bosson & Vandello, 2011).

precarious manhood hypothesis The idea that a man's gender identity of strength and toughness is more easily lost in competition, and that such a loss can trigger aggressive behavior.

BOX 13.6 **FOCUS ON *MENTAL HEALTH***

The Cold-Hearted Psychopath

Cold-hearted killers, such as Anton Chigurh in the movie *No Country for Old Men*, are stock figures in violent films. The inspiration for these characters is a clinical category known as Antisocial Personality Disorder, or psychopaths—people, usually male, who are prone to extreme patterns of violence and who make up a significant number of individuals in prisons who have been convicted of violent crimes (Hare, 1991). A long-standing assumption is that psychopaths have profound empathy deficits, lacking any feeling for those they harm.

Research reveals a more nuanced picture, suggesting that while psychopaths are as adept as the average person in *understanding* the emotions of others, they have deficits in *responding* emotionally to the suffering of others. The most systematic study of psychopaths has been conducted by James Blair and his colleagues (Blair, Mitchell, & Blair, 2005). These researchers find that psychopaths

cognitively understand the emotions of others quite well. For example, when shown photos of facial expressions of emotion, psychopaths do as well as appropriate comparison participants in identifying emotions from the face. They also prove to be quite capable at assessing the mental states of other people; they can reliably infer what other people are thinking. They do show empathic deficits in their responses to others' sadness, however. Show a photo of a sad face to the average adult, and that person will respond with a galvanic skin response, a measure of the sweat response in the palms that indicates a physiological reaction to the other person's suffering. By contrast, psychopaths show no such physiological response to the

The Psychopath in Movies

In *No Country for Old Men*, Javier Bardem plays the psychopathic hitman Anton Chigurh, whose lack of emotion in causing pain illustrates the finding that psychopaths often respond with little empathy to the suffering of others.

sadness of others, but they do show such galvanic skin responses to other emotionally evocative images, such as images of guns. The results of the Blair research indicate that psychopaths understand quite well the emotions and mental states of others, but they lack any feeling for them, most notably their suffering.

🔄 LOOKING BACK

Evolutionary theory leads social psychologists to expect that stepparents are more likely than genetic parents to behave in violent ways toward children. Males will be more aggressive than females partly because such behavior can help them attain status and gain access to females. Males are generally more physically assertive than females, and females are generally more relationally or emotionally aggressive. Cultural theorists believe evolutionary arguments are unnecessary to explain gender differences, and that socialization processes are explanation enough. Recent studies on precarious manhood bring these two lines of theorizing together, helping explain why threats to a sense of manhood can trigger violence in men.

Conflict and Peacemaking

This chapter began with an account of the Rwandan genocide, a story that seems to repeat itself with discouraging regularity in human history. In the aftermath of that genocide, Rwandans went through a process of reconciliation, following principles similar to those used in post-apartheid South Africa to help blacks and whites move beyond a history of violence and oppression to a more just, peaceful society. In Rwanda, formal court proceedings convicted several leaders of the genocide. In informal "truth and reconciliation" gatherings in Rwandan villages, Hutu perpetrators apologized to the relatives of their victims, who were given a public arena to air their rage. Today, by most accounts, Rwanda is a stable and peaceful society. Although tensions and bitterness persist, levels of aggression and conflict between the Hutus and Tutsis are low.

What does social psychology have to say about transitions between adversarial relationships and reconciliation? Some empirically tested insights point to the power of construal as a source of both conflict and peacemaking.

Misperception

The frenzied rush toward genocide in Rwanda was stirred by a manifesto known as the Hutu Ten Commandments, which was published in a widely read newspaper, the *Kangura*, and broadcast by local radio stations. The Hutu Ten Commandments warned of the threat posed by the Tutsis, insisting that Tutsi women were secret agents bent on Hutu demise, that Hutu men who married or employed Tutsi women were traitors, and that Hutus who did business with a Tutsi were enemies of the Hutu people. These and other rumors and fears led Hutus to form deadly misperceptions about the Tutsis that helped fuel the genocide. Such misperceptions are commonly promoted in wartime propaganda and the rhetoric that accompanies international crises. As conflicts escalate between groups, adversaries misperceive one another in several ways, forming "mirror images" of each other (Bar-Tal, 1990). It's common for both sides in escalating conflicts to attribute inhuman qualities to the other group, and these images of the enemy serve as ready justification for aggression.

Alongside this tendency to misperceive and dehumanize, the parties in conflict often consider their strife as a fight between good and evil (Bar-Tal, 1990). Group members have a powerful tendency to think of their own group as moral and good, and the other side as immoral and evil (Brewer & Kramer, 1985). Conflicts between groups over practical matters—trade routes, levels of compensation, territory, peace treaties—are quickly seen in moral terms.

Besides justifying aggression, these kinds of construals can amplify social conflict and make peacemaking difficult or impossible. For one thing, they can lead opponents to overlook areas of agreement with each other. In survey studies, for example, Lee Ross and his colleagues recruited opponents in ideological conflicts over such issues as abortion and the death penalty, as well as enemies embroiled in geopolitical conflicts like those in Northern Ireland and the Middle East (Ross & Ward, 1995). The researchers had members of both sides report on their own attitudes and estimate the attitudes of their opponents (Robinson, Keltner, Ward, & Ross, 1995). These data revealed that group members systematically overestimate the extremity of their opponents' attitudes; that is, they assume the other side is made up of fanatical extremists, when in fact many people on the other side are more moderate in their convictions. As a result of their errant assumptions, group members sometimes overestimate the differences between the two groups. Whereas the attitudes of opponents in social conflicts typically share a fair amount of common ground, group members assume there is little or none. Studies of negotiations reveal a similar tendency. Negotiators

BOX 13.7 **FOCUS ON *CULTURE***

Moral Murders?

Alan Fiske and Tage Rai, in their book *Virtuous Violence,* have gone so far as to say that most murders are committed by people who feel they're acting morally (Fiske & Rai, 2014). The perpetrators feel that what they're doing is just and right. Hundreds of thousands of European Protestants were killed by Catholics to end a heresy that presented a mortal challenge to the true faith. Hundreds of thousands of Catholics were murdered by Protestants to rid the world of people who willingly supported a manifestly evil institution. The Nazis' killing of Jews was carried out in service to a moral obligation to rid the country of "vermin" who had been deliberately undermining the fatherland for decades. Stalin killed millions of Russians because they were evil capitalists blocking the path to a communist Utopia. Mao Tse-tung and Pol Pot killed untold numbers of their countrymen for the same reason.

Most family feuds and tribal conflicts are seen by their participants as having moral motives: "We must defend the family honor." "They killed one of ours, it would be cowardly and wrong not to kill one of theirs." Many more soldiers have fought for love of tribe or country than for blood lust. Loyalists of ISIS (Islamic State of Iraq and Syria) behead enemies in service to the moral obligation to hasten the coming of the world caliphate.

Even the murder of one person by another over a quarrel or a perceived

Mass Killings through History
Queen Mary of England, who earned the nickname "Bloody Mary," restored Catholicism in England and during her reign executed numerous Protestants, including these ten Protestant martyrs portrayed in this etching.

injustice can be rationalized by a spirit of self-righteousness: "The victim deserved to die because of the evil thing he did to me." Members of a group will sometimes kill one of their own because of transgressions against the group's moral code, as in stonings for adultery or stranglings for slander.

None of this implies such actions are objectively moral, but rather that the actors' subjectively feel their behavior will make the world a better place. Fiske and Rai (2014) maintain that if we fail to recognize the self-perceived morality of people who

are willing to kill on a massive scale, we're likely to misunderstand their motives and make serious mistakes in our conduct toward them. For example, governments often assume that if they simply build a strong enough war machine, they'll defeat insurgents fighting in what they believe is a sacred cause. Such insurgent groups have been known to shock their enemies by winning the day against a force ten times larger than their own, something they're able to pull off because of the great moral commitment and fervor they have for their cause.

may underestimate the amount of common ground with their counterparts, thereby settling for less desirable outcomes than might actually be available (Thompson & Hrebec, 1996).

A closely related tendency, and another barrier to more peaceful relations, arises when group members assume their opponents' interests are the exact opposite of their own; any gain for one side means a loss to the other (Plous, 1985). In the context of negotiation, this situation leads to **reactive devaluation**, attaching less value to an offer in a negotiation; the mere fact that the other side makes a concession is enough to reduce its attractiveness (Ross & Stillinger, 1991). In other words, "You're my enemy, so if you made this proposal it must not be in my interests or morally sound."

reactive devaluation Attaching less value to an offer in a negotiation once the opposing group makes it.

To explore this tendency, researchers measured student protestors' attitudes toward their university's proposal about its investments in companies doing business in South Africa during the height of student protests against apartheid in the 1980s (Ross & Stillinger, 1991). Before the university adopted the plan, when students were considering its merits in the abstract, they felt it was a significant and positive move. But after the plan was adopted and it was no longer an abstract proposal, students evaluated it much less favorably. The mere fact that "the other side" (the university administration) was known to have adopted the plan was enough to make students regard it as less acceptable. When parties to a conflict react in this way, it can be difficult indeed to reach a satisfactory resolution.

Simplistic Reasoning and Rhetoric

In the heat of conflict, group members are prone to misperceive their opponents' intentions, and distrust their actions and proposed resolutions rather than think about them in a nuanced way. Psychologist Phil Tetlock (1981) has found that this kind of simplistic reasoning can lead to simplistic rhetoric as well, which in turn can also contribute to escalating conflicts.

Tetlock notes that adversaries can reason and speak to each other in relatively complex or simple fashion. The complexity (or simplicity) of a position in a conflict is defined by two qualities: (1) the level of differentiation, or number of principles and arguments in the position; and (2) the level of integration, or connections drawn between the different principles and arguments. Those taking complex positions in conflicts consider many arguments and principles, even opposing ones, and draw many connections between them. Simpler positions involve fewer arguments: very few arguments from the other side especially, and few connections between the arguments and information being considered. For example, a complex position on marriage equality would involve many principles (ideas about individual rights, views on the nature of marriage, legal precedents) and factual arguments (economic consequences and policy implications of legalizing same-sex marriage, data related to family outcomes in gay and straight families), as well as various connections between them (how legal precedent might influence tax-related benefits for gay citizens when they are allowed to marry). A simple position on same-sex marriage might be that it should be accepted in order to honor the principle of equality, or that it is unacceptable because marriages involve only partnerships between women and men.

How does the complexity or simplicity of reasoning influence group conflict? To answer this question, Tetlock and his colleagues have coded the complexity of politicians' reasoning from their speeches and interviews (Tetlock, 1981). They found that politicians are more simplistic and extreme while combating opponents and wooing potential voters on the campaign trail, and more complex as elected officials, when dealing with the give-and-take of policy making.

Tetlock and his colleagues have also found that the complexity of reasoning and rhetoric can pave the way for more effective peacemaking. In a study of British politicians, more complex politicians on both the right and the left

"You campaign in poetry. You govern in prose."
—MARIO CUOMO, FORMER GOVERNOR OF NEW YORK

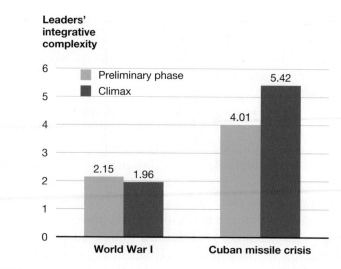

Figure 13.6

Conflict and the Complexity of Rhetoric

In international crises, leaders who speak in ways that are more complex, taking into consideration the other side's views, are more likely to avoid escalating conflicts.

SOURCE: Adapted from Suedfeld & Tetlock, 1977.

deemphasized differences between the two parties, expressed tolerance of their opponents' views, and resisted blaming their opponents for England's woes at that time; they avoided the misperceptions and polarization we've discussed (Tetlock, 1984).

In another study, researchers examined the complexity of political leaders' rhetoric during two crises: the buildup to World War I in 1914 and the 1962 Cuban missile crisis, in which U.S. President John F. Kennedy and Soviet Premier Nikita Khrushchev averted a nuclear encounter (Suedfeld & Tetlock, 1977). **Figure 13.6** shows that between the preliminary phase of the conflict and the climax that led to World War I, the complexity of the political leaders' rhetoric decreased. In the Cuban missile crisis that was successfully resolved, the complexity of the leaders' rhetoric increased between the preliminary phase of the conflict and the climax.

Who do you think is a more complex group, liberals or conservatives? (Your answer, of course, probably depends on your own political affiliation.) It turns out that extremists on both sides are less complex in their public rhetoric than moderate liberals and moderate conservatives. In a study, Tetlock coded the interviews of 89 members of the British House of Commons and found that extreme socialists and extreme conservatives were less complex than moderate socialists or moderate conservatives (Tetlock, 1984).

Communication and Reconciliation

Often in the heat of conflict, or in the aftermath of aggression, the adversaries tend to stop communicating, to separate themselves from one another. Politicians fighting over a budget deal hunker down with their own party, formulating strategy intended to cut their opponents out of the deal. Warring nations expel diplomats and end formal communication. In divorce proceedings, the husband and wife are told not to communicate with each other, no matter how benign their intentions.

The Camp David Peace Accords
Although the communication in 1978 was painful and filled with conflict, it led to a lasting peace between Israel and Egypt. Shown here are U.S. President Jimmy Carter (in center), Israeli Prime Minister Menachem Begin, and Egyptian President Anwar Sadat.

This tendency of avoiding adversaries flies in the face of one of the most potent tools for reducing conflict: face-to-face communication (Frank, 1988). Numerous empirical studies find that simply allowing adversaries to communicate reduces levels of competition and aggression and increases the chances of finding satisfying resolutions to many kinds of conflict (Thompson, 2005). Communication helps reduce the misperceptions of opponents and paves the way for peacemaking and cooperation.

As adversaries communicate, they often show a powerful tendency to reconcile, to make amends for hurtful words and harmful acts, and to return to more peaceful relations. Our primate relatives exhibit instinctual tendencies toward reconciliation (de Waal, 1996). For example, in the heat of conflict, chimpanzees display submissive postures and vocalizations, actions that trigger conciliation behaviors such as grooming, open-handed gestures, and even embraces. Humans resort to more complex reconciliation behaviors—confessions, apologies, signs of remorse—that may trigger forgiveness, leading to reduced feelings of revenge and increased acceptance of the other person (McCullough, 2008).

This process of reconciliation is a powerful tool for reducing conflict and aggression. In Rwanda, face-to-face reconciliation, as in South Africa at the end of apartheid, was critical to the successful peacemaking efforts after the genocide. Families fare better over time if the parents actively pursue strategies that encourage forgiveness during family conflicts (McCullough, Fincham, & Tsang, 2003). Merely imagining the act of forgiving a perpetrator of harm can reduce the fight-or-flight response of anger, which is a trigger of aggression (Lawler et al., 2003).

Studies of reconciliation by social psychologists have led to an innovative approach adopted by the criminal justice system in the United States, Australia, and other countries (McCullough, 2008). In many jurisdictions, the perpetrator and victim of violent crimes are usually separated (often for very good

A Picture of Reconciliation
This conciliatory photograph shows Jean Pierre Karenzi, a perpetrator, and Viviane Nyiramana, a survivor of the Rwandan genocide, 20 years later. They express their feelings in the following statements. *Karenzi*: "My conscience was not quiet, and when I would see her I was very ashamed. After being trained about unity and reconciliation, I went to her house and asked for forgiveness. Then I shook her hand. So far, we are on good terms." *Nyiramana*: "He killed my father and three brothers. He did these killings with other people, but he came alone to me and asked for pardon. He and a group of other offenders who had been in prison helped me build a house with a covered roof. I was afraid of him—now I have granted him pardon, things have become normal, and in my mind I feel clear." (Quoted in Hugo & Dominus, 2014.)

reason) and denied any opportunity to communicate and reconcile. As an alternative to this approach, in programs focused on restorative justice, professionals who are trained in both counseling and the law mediate conversations between perpetrators and victims. These conversations are based on several principles. The offender takes responsibility for the crime (in a courtroom, offenders often resist making such confessions). The offender tries to "undo" the crime through apology or acts of reparation, and the offender and victim are encouraged to engage in a respectful dialogue. As difficult as these conversations may sound, they are often highly effective. Victims of crime who participate in restorative justice programs report many fewer thoughts of revenge than comparison individuals do, and they're more than twice as likely to forgive the offender and say that the criminal justice system is fair (Sherman & Strang, 2007).

Moving toward a Less Violent World?

People the world over have witnessed horrific levels of violence in the past 100 years, in the form of wars and genocides. But despite the dispiriting news we hear daily, psychologist Steven Pinker has offered a very different perspective on our current times (Pinker, 2007, 2011). He argues that we are enjoying one of the least aggressive, most cooperative periods in human history. The data he draws on to make his claim are broad in scope. For example, people are dramatically less likely to die in today's wars as opposed to those in the past. Gone are the days in Europe when soldiers marched to their death in orderly rows, stepping over the bodies of comrades in previous rows mowed down by musket and cannon fire.

Murder rates have also fallen precipitously in every European culture that has been analyzed, including former European colonies in the Western and Southern hemispheres. In fifteenth-century England the annual murder rate was 24 per 100,000 people; in 1960 England, it was 0.6 per 100,000. The "enhanced interrogation" techniques used by the United States at various times since the World Trade Center attacks in 2001 have drawn criticism from many quarters; but several hundred years ago, much more brutal torture was the norm, and it was often a form of public entertainment. Enhanced interrogation in the Spanish Inquisition often meant breaking every bone in the suspected heretic's body with iron bars, or roasting him slowly in an oven in the shape of a bull. It is also notable (and likely underappreciated) that there have been no armed conflicts between the great powers in 70 years.

How do we explain such broad cultural shifts in violence and today's more humane treatment of our foes? Pinker believes that the printing press and video-camera have played a role. If everyone can read, everyone can be exposed to arguments against war and violence. Images of the horrors of genocide and the devastation wrought by modern weaponry lead to a revulsion that can chill the march to war. In addition, armed conflict has become an obviously terrible solution to any problem.

The world has become substantially more interconnected: our interests are more intertwined with those of people from other communities and nations.

Globalization has made businesses multinational. Solutions to global warming and many other environmental problems will require treaties that involve many countries. Many college campuses in the United States and Canada draw students from all over the world. People communicate with others in distant lands over the Internet, on Facebook, on Twitter, and through Skype. People are much more likely to marry and form friendships with people from different backgrounds. This expanding interdependence has given rise to greater cooperation among nations, states, and communities (Wright, 2000). Cooperation, Pinker argues, has short-circuited our more aggressive tendencies, thereby leading to behavior that is more prosocial.

⬆ LOOKING BACK

Several construal biases, including dehumanization, misperceiving common ground, and simplistic reasoning and rhetoric, can escalate group conflict. Reconciliation processes can be a powerful tool for increasing peacemaking tendencies during, and in the aftermath of, conflict.

Chapter Review

SUMMARY

Situational Determinants of Aggression

- *Hostile aggression* is motivated by anger and hostility, and has the primary aim of harming others, either physically or psychologically. *Instrumental aggression* is behavior intended to harm others in order to achieve a goal.
- Hot weather affects levels of aggressive behavior and violence. Hotter cities have higher rates of violent crime, and more violence occurs during hot months than during cool months.
- Media violence has been shown to promote aggressive acts in real life. When a highly publicized suicide occurs, copycat suicides follow. Children who watch violence on TV tend to commit serious crimes as adults, compared to kids who don't. Watching violent TV shows can also lead to more aggressive behavior in the short run, as can playing violent video games.
- Social rejection and isolation are powerful triggers of aggressive tendencies.
- Income inequality at the level of nation, state, county, and neighborhood strongly predicts aggression of just about every kind.

Construal Processes and Aggression

- Anger-related thoughts of blame and revenge, as well as patterns of fight-or-flight responses, make people more likely to respond aggressively when prompted by cues, such as the presence of weapons.

- Extreme forms of violence, such as genocide and rape, are often accompanied by *dehumanization*, when people deny others their basic human nature and the unique attributes that differentiate humans from other things. Group loyalty predicts increases in dehumanization.
- People can modify their tendencies toward anger, dehumanization, and aggression through certain kinds of cognitive control. Looking upon frustrating things from a distance makes people more peaceful.

Culture and Aggression

- People in some cultures, including the U.S. South, are especially likely to adhere to a *culture of honor*; they are inclined to respond to insults and actions that convey malicious intent with violence or threats of violence. Such cultures exist where there is a history of herding, with the associated risks of losing all wealth.
- In *rape-prone cultures*, levels of violence tend to be high in general, and rape is used as a weapon in battle. Rape is used as a ritual act and as a threat to keep women subservient to men. Relatively rape-free cultures tend to grant women equal status.

Evolution and Aggression

- Evolutionary theory provides a perspective on family violence, such as stepchildren being more subject to abuse than genetic offspring, who can carry on the genetic line.
- Violent and aggressive acts are generally committed by men more than by women. Women are usually aggressive in different ways than men, using relational aggression such as gossip and ostracism to hurt others emotionally.
- The evolutionary perspective explains that men are more likely to harm other men than women harm women because they face a fiercer competition for mates.
- In a recent synthesis of evolutionary and cultural approaches to male violence, researchers have proposed the *precarious manhood hypothesis*: a man's gender identity is variable and vulnerable. This makes men more reactive to threats to their identity, and more likely to behave aggressively to prove their manhood.

Conflict and Peacemaking

- Groups in conflict tend to misperceive the other side as extremist and overestimate their differences, dehumanize the opponent, assume the other side's actions are motivated by hostility, and reactively devalue any offers or concessions.
- Complex reasoning involving more evidence and integration of ideas promotes peacemaking in international conflicts.
- Communication is a powerful way to reduce conflict.

THINK ABOUT IT

1. Describe the culture of honor, and provide two pieces of evidence that support this characterization. What might be the origin of these cultural tendencies?

2. According to the research described in this chapter, what kinds of attitudes and behaviors are more likely among men who dehumanize women as animals? Is this form of dehumanization a denial of human nature or a denial of human uniqueness?

3. Suppose you're the warden at a prison and can select the temperature setting for the master prison thermostat, but the thermostat didn't have enough settings, forcing you to choose between an uncomfortably cold setting and an uncomfortably hot setting. Which should you choose and why?

4. Sometimes people respond to social rejection with physical aggression. How does the fundamental nature of our need for social connectedness help explain this tendency?

5. Suppose a friend said to you, "Well, men are just biologically hard-wired to be more aggressive than women." How would you respond? What nuances might this perspective miss?

6. What kinds of strategies have been shown to be most effective for reducing conflict and promoting peace, and why?

THE ANSWER GUIDELINES FOR THE THINK ABOUT IT QUESTIONS CAN BE FOUND AT THE BACK OF THE BOOK . . .

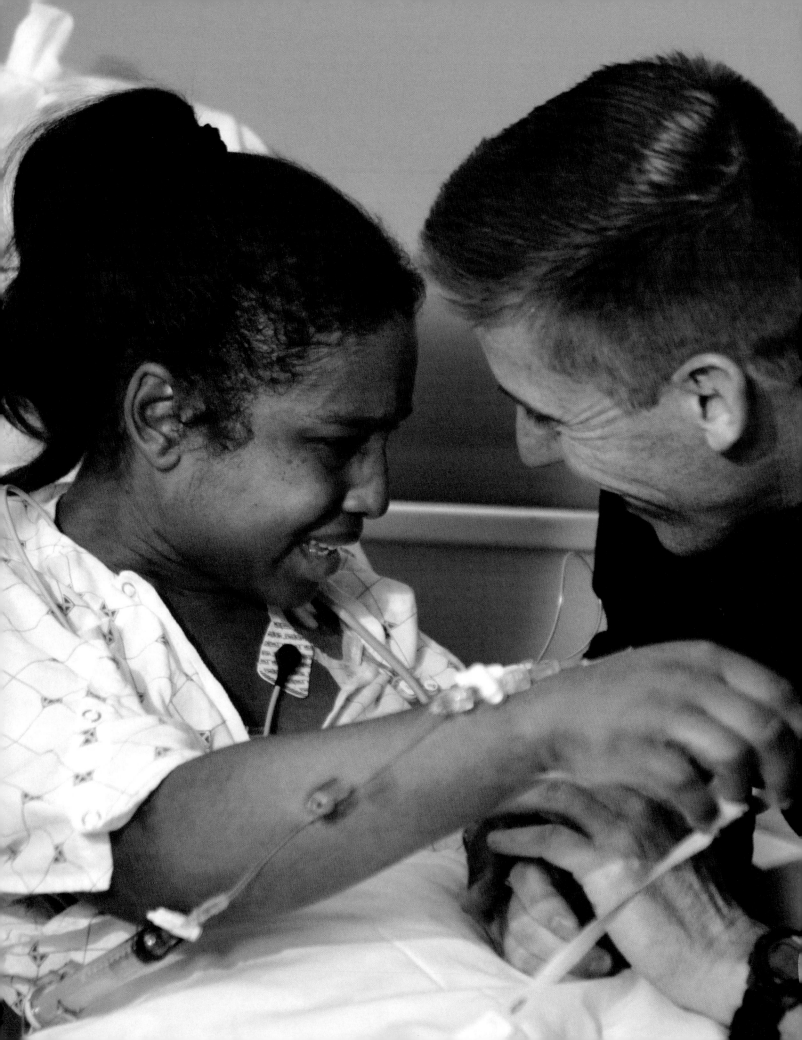

Altruism and Cooperation

I n a few seconds on January 2nd, 2007, Wesley Autrey became a national hero. The 50-year-old construction worker was waiting with his two young daughters to catch a subway train at the 137th and Broadway station in New York City. As they waited, a young film student, Cameron Hollopeter, collapsed to the ground, suffering from what appeared to be a seizure. Autrey and two women rushed to help the young student, who was twisting and convulsing on the ground. With a borrowed pen, Autrey managed to pry Hollopeter's mouth open and clear his respiratory passages so he could recover his breath and strength.

Autrey's heroics were just beginning. Hollopeter stood up, staggered to the platform's edge, and then fell onto the tracks, landing face down between two rails. The lights of an oncoming train appeared. Autrey had to make a split-second decision: jump onto the tracks with his daughters waiting nearby, or let the train run over Hollopeter. Autrey chose to jump. He landed on the tracks and lay on top of Hollopeter. The train's brakes screeched, but it could not stop in time: five cars of the train rolled over Autrey and Hollopeter. As the crowd screamed and cried, Autrey called out, asking those nearby to tell his two young daughters that their father was okay. The train had missed Autrey by one inch, leaving grease smears on his blue cap.

In the aftermath of the event, Autrey was celebrated as a hero. He appeared on the daily television shows, was named one of *TIME Magazine*'s 100 most influential people, received a standing ovation at President George W. Bush's State of the Union address, and was awarded the Bronze Medallion, New York City's highest award for excellence in citizenship. Autrey modestly remarked: "I don't feel like I did something spectacular; I just saw someone who needed help. I did what I felt was right."

Extraordinary Altruism
Wesley Autrey jumped on the New York subway tracks to save a fallen man in the face of an oncoming train. He is pictured here (A) with his children and (B) at President Bush's State of the Union address.

Altruism in Rwanda
Paul Rusesabagina, acting manager of the Mille Collines Hotel in Kigali, Rwanda, saved over a thousand people from massacre by sheltering them at the hotel, bribing the local militia, and appealing to influential contacts.

altruism Unselfish behavior that benefits others without regard to consequences for oneself.

Altruism

Reports of people risking their lives for strangers in need, as Autrey did, are not rare. Even during the unspeakable violence of the Rwandan genocide, discussed in Chapter 13, individuals engaged in inspiring acts of concern for others. Paul Rusesabagina, a Hutu, was the acting manager of the Mille Collines, the most prestigious hotel in the capital city of Kigali. As the massacres unfolded, he hid over a thousand people (both Tutsis and moderate Hutus) at the hotel. Each day, the Hutu *interahamwe* (militia) would arrive and demand to take some of the Tutsis away. And each day Rusesabagina would plead and ply them with beer and money to prevent further massacres. Around the clock he frantically called and faxed influential contacts, appealing for their help. Often risking his own life and those of his children and wife, he pleaded and schemed tirelessly for the survival of his guests.

Autrey's and Rusesabagina's actions are clear examples of **altruism**—unselfish behavior that benefits others without regard to consequences for oneself. Humans are prone to feelings of compassion that lead us to behave in ways that benefit others who are suffering, often at a cost to ourselves. At the same time, we don't always act on such prosocial feelings. Many forces can inhibit altruistic action, including basic tendencies toward self-preservation and fear of embarrassment (like misinterpreting a mundane situation as an emergency). When do we act altruistically, and when don't we?

Empathic Concern: A Case of Pure Altruism?

During the Los Angeles riots of 1992, Reginald Denny, a white truck driver, was being beaten severely by four black youths. Several black residents who lived near the area saw the beating live on television and rushed to the scene to save Denny's life, risking their own lives in the process. What motivates this kind of action?

Compassion from Strangers

Strangers will often respond to an individual's distress and offer aid without thought of danger or reward. (A) During the riots in Los Angeles in 1992, Reginald Denny was pulled from his truck and severely beaten. (B) Upon seeing the incident on TV, Bobby Green (pictured here) and several other local residents rushed to the scene to rescue Denny.

In an important line of research, Daniel Batson has made a persuasive case for a selfless, other-oriented state that motivates altruistic behavior like that displayed by Autrey, Rusesabagina, and Denny's saviors (Batson & Shaw, 1991). Batson begins by proposing that in any altruistic action, several motives are likely to be in play. Two of these motives are essentially selfish (egoistic); a third is more purely oriented toward unselfishly benefiting another person.

The first selfish motive is **social reward**—being esteemed and valued by others, in the form of praise, an award, or acknowledgement in the mass media or social media, such as Facebook and Instagram. Those motivated by social rewards act altruistically to enjoy the positive regard of others (Campbell, 1975; Nowak, Page, & Sigmund, 2000). Recent neuroscientific studies find that being esteemed by others activates circuits in the brain associated with rewards and personal safety (Inagaki & Eisenberger, 2013). In fact, social rewards can be so potent that they can trigger arms races of altruism, referred to as competitive altruism (Hardy & van Vugt, 2006). People will try to outdo one another in their altruistic acts, all in the service of being the most highly esteemed. For example, in many hunter-gatherer cultures, it's the individual who gives away the most food—seal meat among the Inuit of Alaska, yams in hunter-gatherer tribes in New Guinea—who enjoys the greatest status. In laboratory studies, group members will give greater social status to other group members who act altruistically (Hardy & van Vugt, 2006; Nowak & Sigmund, 2005). Social rewards are a powerful motive for altruism, but an egoistic one.

A second selfish motive for helping is **personal distress**; people are motivated to help others in need in order to reduce their *own* distress (Cialdini & Fultz, 1990; Cialdini & Kenrick, 1976). This behavior starts very early in life. In one study, for instance, newborn infants heard a tape recording of their own crying, the crying of another day-old, or the crying of an 11-month-old (Martin & Clark, 1982). The newborns cried the most in response to the cries of another newborn.

"[Sympathy] will have increased through natural selection; for those communities which included the greatest number of the most sympathetic members, would flourish best, and rear the greatest number of offspring."

—CHARLES DARWIN, *THE DESCENT OF MAN* (1871)

social reward A benefit, such as praise, positive attention, something tangible, or gratitude, that may be gained from helping others, and serves a motive for altruistic behavior.

personal distress A motive for helping others in distress that may arise from a need to reduce one's own distress.

Empathy among Newborns
When newborn babies hear another newborn cry, they feel the distress of the other baby and will also begin to cry, as seen in this photo of infants in a hospital nursery.

empathic concern Identifying with someone in need, including feeling and understanding what that person is experiencing, accompanied by the intention to help the person.

Later in life, too, when we see someone crying, experiencing physical pain, or stuck in an embarrassing situation, we usually experience our own feelings of personal distress. Neuroscientific studies find that when we watch someone else experience pain, the pain regions of the brain are activated (Singer et al., 2004). The resulting feelings lead us to act in ways that return us to a more peaceful state. The most direct way to alleviate our own personal distress is to reduce the distress of the other person, and helping behavior is one way to do it.

The third motive is **empathic concern**, the feeling people experience when identifying with someone in need, accompanied by the intention to enhance the other person's welfare. When we encounter somebody else in need or in pain, we not only experience our own feelings of distress but also imagine what that person must be experiencing. Taking the other's perspective in this way results in an empathic state of concern, which motivates us to help that person address the needs and thus enhance his or her welfare, even at our own expense.

According to Batson's reasoning, this experience of empathic concern is fast and intuitive and produces a selfless or other-oriented altruism. It is the split-second feeling that led Autrey to help the young student on the subway tracks, and caused Rusesabagina to risk his life and the lives of his family to help the Tutsis. One recent study examined the reasons extreme altruists gave for why they risked their own lives to save others (Rand & Epstein, 2014). Most typically, they referred to an automatic, emotion-like impulse to help others in explaining their life-imperiling acts of altruism.

Empathy vs. Personal Distress Now comes the tricky part: How can researchers document that altruistic action can be motivated by empathic concern alone, independent of the desire for social rewards or to reduce personal distress? Daniel Batson and his colleagues have carried out studies in which participants encounter another person in distress for whom they feel empathic concern (Batson & Shaw, 1991). At the same time, egoistic motives are manipulated to make helping behavior less likely. Participants might be allowed to reduce their personal distress without helping. Or in the experiment there may be no social rewards for helping, which should reduce the likelihood of altruistic action. If participants still help in these circumstances, it's highly likely there's an empathy-based form of helping that's not selfishly motivated.

An initial study pitted empathic concern against the selfish motive of reducing personal distress by allowing participants to simply leave the experiment (Batson, O'Quin, Fultz, Vanderplas, & Isen, 1983). Participants were told they'd interact with another participant of the same sex, who would complete several trials of a digit-recall task and receive a shock after each mistake. In the easy-escape condition, the participant had to watch the confederate receive only two of the ten shocks, and was then free to leave the experiment while the confederate finished the study. In the difficult-to-escape condition, the participant was told it would be necessary to watch the other person take all ten shocks.

After the first two trials, the confederate, made up to look a little pale, asked for a glass of water, mentioned feelings of discomfort, and recounted a traumatic shock experience from childhood. At this point, participants reported on their current feelings, which were used to divide participants into those who were feeling egoistic distress and those who were feeling empathic concern. The experimenter then turned to the participant to ask whether he or she would be willing to take some of the confederate's shocks. If there is such a thing as altruism based on empathic concern, the researchers reasoned, then they should see substantial levels of altruism (agreeing to sit in for the confederate) on the part of participants who felt empathic concern for the confederate, even when they could simply leave the experiment and escape their empathic distress. In keeping with this reasoning, those participants who mostly felt distress and could escape the situation took few shocks on behalf of the confederate. Those participants who felt empathic concern, however, volunteered to take more shocks, even when they could simply leave the study.

Those still skeptical about the idea of pure altruism based on empathic concern might have a few reservations about this first study. First of all, empathic concern was not manipulated; instead, Batson and his colleagues identified empathic participants according to their self-reports. Perhaps there was a selection bias in this study—that is, the high-empathy participants might just be more helpful in general for reasons other than a selfless response to the confederate in need. Second, the experimenter knew how the participant acted, so a social rewards account of this study cannot be ruled out. Perhaps participants who took more shocks on behalf of the confederate hoped to impress the experimenter, or wanted to avoid embarrassing themselves by leaving a person in obvious need. It would be much more telling to show that there are substantial rates of helping when doing so is completely anonymous. That notion motivated Batson's next study.

Altruism in Animals and Humans
Taking care of others is seen in many non-human species, such as these elephants helping a younger elephant.

Anonymous Altruism In this study, Batson and his colleagues had female participants interact with another person, a communicator, seated in another cubicle (Fultz, Batson, Fortenbach, McCarthy, & Varney, 1986). The communicator, a student confederate who called herself Janet Arnold, wrote two notes to the participant, expressing supposedly honest information about herself. The task of the listener (the actual participant) was to form as accurate an impression of Janet as possible. This time, empathic concern was manipulated. In the low-empathy condition, the participant was told to be as objective as possible when reading the notes, to concentrate on the facts at hand. In the high-empathy condition, the participant was told to imagine as vividly as possible how the communicator—the other person—felt. In the first note to the participant, Janet confessed to feeling out of place at her new home at the university. In the second note, Janet expressed a strong need for a friend, and asked the participant if she'd like to hang out a bit.

After receiving the second note, the participant was told Janet had finished and left the study. The experimenter then gave the participant a form that described another "long-term relationship study" and asked whether the participant would like to spend time at some later date with Janet Arnold. In the low-social-evaluation condition, Janet's notes were delivered in sealed envelopes, and the experimenter did not read them. Similarly, the participant indicated how much time she would spend with Janet on a form enclosed in a sealed envelope to be sent to the professor conducting the study (who was never to meet the participant). Neither the experimenter nor Janet would know of the participant's response. In contrast, in the high-social-evaluation condition, both

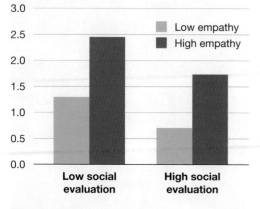

Hours participant would spend with Janet

Figure 14.1
Empathy and Altruism
This study showed that when participants empathize with someone who is in need, they engage in more altruistic action, even when their sacrifice is anonymous.

SOURCE: Adapted from Fultz et al., 1986.

"I have shewed you all things, how that so labouring ye ought to support the weak, and to remember the words of the Lord Jesus, how he said, It is more blessed to give than to receive."

—ACTS 20:35

volunteerism Assistance a person regularly provides to another person or group with no expectation of compensation.

the experimenter and the participant read Janet's notes, and Janet and the experimenter would know how much time the participant said she would be willing to spend with Janet. The critical dependent measure was the number of hours the participant volunteered to spend with Janet. As **Figure 14.1** shows, participants in the high-empathy condition volunteered to spend more time with her, even when no one would know of their action.

Physiological Indicators of Empathy One final study is especially helpful in assessing whether, as Batson supposes, some kind of selfless state motivates altruistic behavior. Strong evidence for such a motive would be a demonstration that empathic concern is associated with a distinct physiological pattern that predicts whether a person will act altruistically.

To study this question, Nancy Eisenberg and her colleagues showed a videotape of a woman and her children who had recently been in an accident to second-graders, fifth-graders, and college students (Eisenberg et al., 1989). The children in the video missed school while they recovered from their injuries in the hospital. As the participants watched this moving story, their facial expressions were recorded and continuous measures of heart rate were taken. After watching the video, the participants had the chance to help by taking homework to the recovering children during their recess (and thus sacrificing their own playtime). The researchers found that both the facial expressions of the participant children and college students who felt sympathy for the accident victims (or empathic concern, in Batson's terms) had eyebrows pulled in and upward and a concerned gaze, as well as heart rate deceleration—a physiological response the opposite of the accelerated heart rate associated with a fight-or-flight response. These participants were also more likely to help. In contrast, participants who reported distress while watching the video had a pained wince in the face and heart rate acceleration, and they were less likely to help. Thus, empathic concern produces more helping behavior than distress; it also appears to do so in part through a different pattern of physiological responses.

Empathic Concern and Volunteerism Batson's research shows that feelings of empathic concern and sympathy increase the likelihood that people will act altruistically, helping those who suffer. These feelings also appear to be a primary determinant of other prosocial behaviors. For example, Allen Omoto and Mark Snyder have studied **volunteerism**, which they define as nonmonetary assistance; people help out with no expectation of receiving any compensation (Omoto & Snyder, 1995; Penner, Dovidio, Piliavin, & Schroeder, 2005). In the United States, estimates indicate that over 61 million people—close to 30 percent of the population—volunteer, providing companionship to older adults, mentoring troubled children, feeding those in poverty, or assisting the sick and dying (Omoto, Malsch, & Barraza, 2009). As with altruism, volunteerism has many motives, including a desire for social rewards and a desire to reduce personal distress. But Omoto and his colleagues have found that self-reports of feelings of empathic concern also predict the likelihood that an individual will engage in volunteerism (Omoto et al., 2009).

Recent evidence suggests that volunteering is good for your health. Stephanie Brown and her colleagues studied a sample of 423 elderly married couples over the course of 5 years and found that volunteerism increases longevity (Brown, Nesse, Vinokur, & Smith, 2003). At the beginning of the study, the researchers

BOX 14.1 **FOCUS ON *HUMAN NATURE***

Are We Wired to Care and Share?

Batson's studies of empathic concern were some of the first to document with scientific precision that humans may act altruistically, guided by a more selfless motivational state—in his terminology, empathic concern. Since this important line of research, social psychologists have made several discoveries that further suggest we are wired to care and share (Keltner, Kogan, Piff, & Saturn, 2014). One kind of evidence comes from our primate relatives. If empathic concern is a basic motive for human action, then we might expect other primates to show rudimentary forms of altruistic behavior. Indeed, observations of chimpanzees and bonobos find that they do occasionally provide care to those in need, such as fellow primates that have lost their eyesight or who are crippled (de

Waal, 1996). They also regularly share food with non-kin in their community, a basic form of altruistic action (de Waal & Lanting, 1997).

If a selfless form of altruism is part of our evolutionary heritage, we might also expect to observe it in young children, much as children reliably show other species-defining tendencies, such as the fear of strangers, the ability to learn language, and theory of mind. Work by Felix Warneken and Michael Tomasello provides impressive evidence of the altruistic tendencies of young children (Warneken & Tomasello, 2006). In this research, 18-month-olds encountered adults in need. For example, in one situation, the toddler saw an adult drop a pen and attempt, unsuccessfully, to pick it up from the floor. In another situation,

the toddler saw an adult try to open closed doors of a cabinet, again unsuccessfully. In each situation, the toddler could readily offer assistance. In the control conditions, the 18-month-olds encountered the same stimuli—a dropped pen or doors that couldn't be opened—but the adult nearby did not express any need associated with the stimulus. Impressively, across these types of situations, 40–60 percent of the children helped the adult strangers in need, but they did not engage in the helpful actions in the control conditions. These findings suggest that beginning quite early in development, children will respond altruistically to others in need, thus providing still more evidence that we are wired to care and share.

assessed the degree to which each partner offered help to other people, by doing errands, shopping, or providing childcare for neighbors. The participants also indicated how often they received this kind of help from people other than their spouses, to capture how much they were the beneficiaries of volunteerism. Following the participants over the course of 5 years, the researchers kept track of who died (as 145 of them did during the study). Remarkably, people who gave more to others were less likely to die during the 5 years of the study, when controlling for the participant's initial health, gender, and social contacts. And how about the recipients of help? They were no less likely to die than people who did not receive help. It may indeed be better to give than to receive.

What cultivates empathic concern in people? What produces the Wesley Autreys and Paul Rusesabaginas of the world, or the good-hearted citizens who make sacrifices and volunteer for others? One answer comes from the remarkable work of the Oliners, who interviewed over 100 rescuers from World War II, individuals who risked their lives to save Jews during the Nazi Holocaust (Oliner & Oliner, 1988). (Samuel Oliner himself was saved by such a person in Poland as a young boy.) In the course of these interviews, rescuers reported that altruism

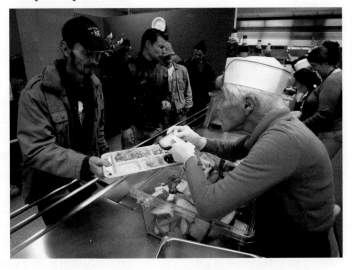

Volunteering and Better Health

Volunteering takes many forms, including serving food to the homeless in soup kitchens, which can contribute to improving the volunteer's health.

and compassion were highly valued in their homes. Rescuers reported that their parents and grandparents frequently told stories from their own lives and from their culture in which altruism was a theme. Altruism was a central theme in the books the family read and the teachings they discussed. In their dinnertime conversations about the events of the day, they discussed things through the lens of altruism and concern for other people. Altruism was explicitly invoked as an important ethical principle. Empathic concern apparently is a powerful force for good in human societies, and can be passed from parents to children.

Situational Determinants of Altruism

People don't always act on the basis of their empathic impulses. Consider the horrifying tragedy that befell Kitty Genovese on March 13, 1964, when Winston Moseley stalked her as she walked home in Queens, New York. He attacked her near her apartment and stabbed her in the chest. As she screamed for help, lights went on and several windows opened in the surrounding apartments. From his seventh-floor window, one neighbor yelled, "Let that girl alone!" Moseley left but returned soon, stalking his screaming victim to a stairwell in her building, then stabbed her eight more times and raped her. New York police got a call 30 minutes after the cries of distress first awakened neighbors. By the time they arrived, Kitty Genovese was beyond help. Thirty-eight neighbors admitted to hearing screams, and many must have felt the pangs of empathic concern. But no one intervened aside from the neighbor who yelled from afar. Not a single person intervened. Instead, investigators heard explanations such as "I was tired"; "We thought it was a lover's quarrel"; "We were afraid." One couple watched the assault from behind curtains in their dimly lit apartment.

The Genovese incident shocked the American public. Like Milgram's studies of obedience to authority (see Chapters 1, 5, and 9), the episode also raises fundamental questions about human nature. Are we really that indifferent to the suffering of others? The research findings on empathic concern, altruism, and volunteerism suggest not. Kitty Genovese's murder moved several social psychologists to attempt to understand the processes that dampen our empathic concern, inhibit altruistic action, and make people reluctant to intervene during emergencies.

Darley and Batson's Good Samaritan Study No research better reveals the powerful situational determinants of altruism than a classic study by John Darley and Daniel Batson from 1973 (discussed briefly in Chapter 1). Their study was modeled on the timeless tale of the Good Samaritan, which concerns different reactions to a man who has been robbed, stripped, and left in a ditch. In the Bible story, a busy priest first walks by. Despite being a religious leader and supposedly concerned with those in need, he fails to stop and help the man. Next a Levite, another religious functionary, arrives and also avoids the man. Finally, a resident of Samaria, a member of a group that followed different religious customs and was despised by mainstream society, sees the half-dead man. The Samaritan stops, helps the man, takes him to an inn, and provides money for clothes and food to restore his strength. Darley and Batson's study, inspired by the Good Samaritan parable, makes an even better story than the classic tale itself. The lesson is that subtle situational factors, such as whether you're on time or late, powerfully determine whether you'll help someone in need.

Failing to Intervene in an Emergency
Kitty Genovese was a young woman who was stalked and killed at her apartment in Queens, New York, as her neighbors watched from their windows and failed to intervene.

The researchers had students attending Princeton Theological Seminary give a talk to undergraduates at another location on the Princeton campus (Darley & Batson, 1973). In one condition, the seminary students were told the topic would be the jobs that seminary students typically find upon graduating. In a second condition, the topic would be the tale of the Good Samaritan. The experimenter than gave participants a map of the campus and showed them where they'd give their talk. In one condition, the no-hurry condition, participants were told they had plenty of time to get to the designated room. In the moderate-hurry condition, the students would have to hustle to be on time. In the high-hurry condition, the seminarians were told they were already a bit late for the students waiting to hear their words of wisdom.

As the seminarians crossed the Princeton campus, their path led them past a man (actually a confederate) who was slumped over and groaning in a passageway. When the students got within earshot, the man complained that he was having trouble breathing. The man was visibly and audibly in distress. The question was: What proportion of seminary students in the various conditions would stop to help the man?

The topic of the talk had no statistically significant effect on the seminary students' likelihood of helping the man in distress. The largest effect was produced by the most subtle of variables: whether or not the students were late. Those who were not in a hurry were more than six times as likely to stop and attend to the suffering man as those who were in a hurry to give a talk. Only 10 percent of the students in the high-hurry condition stopped to help (see Figure 1.1 in Chapter 1).

Like so many of the classic studies in social psychology, this one offers lasting lessons about how powerful situations can be. Being late made it unlikely that the very people expected to exhibit altruism—students studying to be spiritual leaders—would do so. The study itself has many compelling features: the use of seminary students as participants, the naturalistic setting, the assessment of real behavior as the dependent measure. Let's now look at other kinds of situational determinants of altruistic behavior.

The Presence of Other People One important factor that influences whether people will stop to offer help to others in need is the presence of other people. **Bystander intervention** refers to helping someone when people are witness to an emergency. Researchers who have studied this behavior have found that people are less likely to help when other people are around (Latané & Nida, 1981). In part, the presence of other bystanders at emergencies reduces the likelihood of helping because of a **diffusion of responsibility**; knowing others have seen the situation, each bystander tends to assume they will intervene, indeed may be better positioned to intervene, and thus each person feels less responsibility for helping out. The witnesses of the Genovese murder may have seen other apartment dwellers' lights go on, or might have seen others in the windows, thereby assuming someone else would help. The end result is a disturbing lack of action.

Diffused Responsibility
Humans often fail to help someone in obvious need, because they may not interpret the situation as an emergency or assume others will help.

One of the best-known studies on the effect of other people's presence on altruistic behavior was inspired by the Genovese tragedy (Darley & Latané, 1968). College students sat in separate cubicles discussing the problems associated with living in an urban environment. They engaged in this conversation

bystander intervention Assistance given by a witness to someone in need.

diffusion of responsibility A reduction of the sense of urgency to help someone involved in an emergency or dangerous situation, based on the assumption that others who are present will help.

over an intercom system, which allowed only one participant to talk at a time. One of them, a confederate (one of the authors of this book, as it happens), described his difficulties in adjusting to urban life and mentioned he had problems with seizures from time to time, especially when under stress. Then, after everyone else had spoken, the confederate took his second turn. As he did so, he became increasingly loud and incoherent; he choked and gasped. Before falling silent, he uttered the following words:

> If someone could help me out it would it would er er s-s-sure be sure be good . . . because er there er er a cause I er I uh I've got a a one of the er sei-er-er things coming on and and and I could really er use some help so if somebody would er give me a little h-help uh er-er-er-er-er c-could somebody er er help er uh uh uh (choking sounds) . . . I'm gonna die er er I'm gonna die er help er er seizure er (chokes, then quiet). (Darley & Latané, 1968, p. 379)

In one condition, participants were led to believe that their discussion group consisted of only two people (the participant and the victim). In another condition, the conversation was among three people (the participant, the future victim, and another person). And in a final condition, the audience was the largest: the conversation apparently involved six people (the participant, the victim, and four other people). The question, of course, was whether the other students would leave their cubicles to help the victim, who was presumably suffering from a potentially lethal epileptic seizure. The presence of others had a strong effect on helping rates. Eighty-five percent of the participants who were in the two-person condition, and hence the only witness of the victim's seizure, left their cubicles to help. In contrast, 62 percent of the participants who were in the three-person condition and 31 percent of those in the six-person condition attempted to help the victim.

Several types of studies have pursued this question: whether people are less likely to help someone out when other people are around or when they are alone (for a review, see Latané & Nida, 1981). In these studies, the participant might witness a victim in danger, or someone passed out in the subway, or a theft occurring in a store. Across these kinds of studies, 75 percent of people helped when they were alone compared with 53 percent who helped when they were in the presence of others.

These studies have focused on the presence of strangers. But what about the presence of friends? Many real-world observations would suggest that the presence of friends might boost levels of altruism. For example, soldiers readily risk their lives to save their combat buddies. Good friends in grade school often stand up to bullies on the playground when their friends are nearby.

Mario Mikulincer and Phil Shaver have collected evidence suggesting that the presence of friends may indeed increase altruistic action (Mikulincer, Shaver, Gillath, & Nitzberg, 2005). In their study, participants first completed a task in which they judged whether ten strings of letters made up actual words. In the midst of this task, they were shown the name of a casual acquaintance or another person, usually a friend, to whom they felt strongly attached. In the third condition, the investigators reasoned, the prosocial tendencies associated with a sense of a secure attachment should be activated by viewing the name of a close friend (see Chapter 10). Participants then moved on to "another study" in which they evaluated another participant, actually a confederate, who had to complete a sequence of upsetting tasks. They watched the confederate look over

BOX 14.2 **FOCUS ON *DAILY LIFE***

The Likelihood of Being Helped

A typical bystander is less likely to help in an emergency situation if other bystanders are around. But what are the chances of someone receiving help from *any* of the bystanders? When there are more bystanders, there are more people who might help. Consider the "seizure" study described in this chapter. When participants thought they were alone, they helped 85 percent of the time. When they thought there was one other person who might help, they intervened 62 percent of the time. If there really had been two bystanders, each of them with a 62-percent chance of intervening, the victim would have received help 86 percent of the time—virtually identical to the rate of receiving help with one bystander (probability of receiving help $= 1 - .38^2 = .86$). When participants thought there were four other people who might render assistance, they intervened 31 percent of the time. Again, had there really been five bystanders, each of them with a 31-percent chance of intervening, the victim would have received help 85 percent of the time (probability of receiving help $= 1 - .69^5 = .85$).

Does this mean it doesn't matter whether there are many or few people around? Not so fast. These studies have also measured how quickly people come to the aid of someone in distress, and they have consistently found that single bystanders act more quickly than the *quickest* person to react in a group of bystanders. And when somebody's in an emergency situation, a lack of speed can be deadly.

gory photos, hold a rat, hold her arm in near-freezing water, and finally handle a large, hairy tarantula. In the middle of this last task, the confederate gave up and asked whether a participant might be able to take over. Those participants who had seen their close friend's name felt more empathic concern for the confederate than the ones who saw the other names. They were also more likely to volunteer to hold the spider. Whereas groups of strangers appear to inhibit altruistic responses to emergencies, friends can evoke our nobler tendencies.

Victim Characteristics Needless to say, altruism is not blind, nor is it indiscriminate. People are most likely to help when the harm to the victim is clear and the need is unambiguous (Clark & Word, 1972; Gaertner & Dovidio, 1977). Researchers have studied altruistic intervention when a person in need either screams or remains silent. Bystanders help victims who scream and make their needs known 75–100 percent of the time, but they help silent victims only 20–40 percent of the time.

That said, one powerful determinant of helping is whether anything about the victim suggests it might be costly to render assistance. The greater the costs associated with helping, the less inclined people are to act altruistically. In one study on this theme, carried out on a subway train, a "victim" (actually a confederate) staggered across the car, collapsed to the floor, and then stared up at the ceiling (Piliavin & Piliavin, 1972). In one condition, a trickle of blood flowed from the victim's chin. In the other condition, there was no blood. When the victim was bleeding and the associated costs of helping were high, he received help 65 percent of the time; when he was not bleeding, he received help 95 percent of the time. Even though the bleeding victim's need was more apparent, the perceived costs of helping inhibited altruistic intervention.

More enduring characteristics of the victim also influence rates of helping. For example, people are more likely to help similar others (Dovidio, 1984; Dovidio & Gaertner, 1981), including those from their own racial or ethnic group

Cross-Species Helping

Altruism between different species occurs with surprising frequency. This Rhodesian ridgeback adopted a tiny piglet when it was rejected by its mother, and went so far as to feed it with milk from her own body.

(Latané & Nida, 1981). In recent work by Joan Chiao and her colleagues, African-Americans responded with greater empathy and more altruistic inclinations when viewing the suffering of African-Americans as opposed to European-Americans. Only the suffering of participants' own group members activated a brain region (the medial prefrontal cortex) that is involved in empathic response (Mathur, Harada, Lipke, & Chiao, 2011).

Other species appear to respond altruistically only to their own group as well. Several nonhuman primates will give up the opportunity to eat and partially starve themselves if their action will terminate a shock that is being administered to a member of their own species—something they will not do for members of other species (Preston & de Waal, 2002).

Construal Processes and Altruism

What would go through your mind if you encountered a person slumped over in a hallway while on your way to a talk, or if you witnessed someone passing out on the subway? What is it about being late, or hearing obvious cries of distress, or being in the presence of others that influences our inclination to help? In other words, what are the construal processes that influence whether we help or not?

In everyday life, many instances of distress are surprisingly ambiguous. A loud apparent dispute between a man and a woman overheard on the street might be careening toward violence and require intervention. But perhaps it's a non-threatening lovers' spat, or just two thespians acting out a dramatic scene from a play. A group of adolescent boys may be pummeling a smaller boy—or perhaps they're just playfully wrestling.

Pluralistic Ignorance

If someone's in trouble, bystanders may do nothing if they aren't sure what is happening and don't see anyone else responding. This crowd of children may collectively conclude the boys are just playing, when bullying might be taking place, given the ambiguous responses of other kids.

Helping in Ambiguous Situations Given the ambiguity of many emergencies, the decision to offer help means the potential helper first has to believe assistance is actually needed, based on clues from the victim's behavior. As discussed earlier, when people in need vocalize their distress with loud cries, they are much more likely to be helped (Clark & Word, 1972; Schroeder, Penner, Dovidio, & Piliavin, 1995). Similarly, another study found that people are more likely to provide assistance when they are vividly aware of the events that led to the victim's distress (Piliavin, Piliavin, & Broll, 1976). In the study, participants saw a confederate who was unconscious. In the more vivid condition, participants saw the confederate faint and slowly regain consciousness. In the less vivid condition, the participant saw only the aftermath of the incident—a confederate just regaining consciousness. Participants were much more likely to come to the individual's aid (89 percent versus 13 percent) when they saw the entire drama unfold, so that they could understand the full nature of the problem.

The surrounding social context also influences whether bystanders will think help is needed. A form of pluralistic ignorance occurs when people are unsure about what is happening and assume nothing is wrong because no one else is responding or appears concerned (see Chapter 4). Staying calm and collected in public, especially during emergencies, is dictated by established social norms.

It's embarrassing, after all, to be the one who loses composure when there is no actual danger. When everyone in a potentially dangerous situation behaves as if nothing is wrong, each person will tend to mistake the others' calm demeanor as a sign that there's no emergency (Latané & Darley, 1968).

In one study that examined the role of pluralistic ignorance in bystander intervention, researchers asked participants to fill out a stack of questionnaires (Latané & Darley, 1968). There were three conditions: alone, in a room with two passive confederates exhibiting the calm demeanor intended to produce pluralistic ignorance, or with two other genuine participants. As participants in these three conditions completed their questionnaires smoke started to filter in from beneath a door, filling the room. When participants were alone and had no input from other participants as to what was happening, 75 percent of them left the room and reported the smoke to the experimenter. (What could the other 25 percent of the participants have been thinking?) In the two other conditions, pluralistic ignorance took hold, and participants were less likely to assume that something was amiss. With three real participants, only 38 percent of the participants left to report the smoke. And remarkably, with two passive confederates showing no signs of concern, only 10 percent reported the smoke to the experimenter.

Anecdotal evidence from this study suggests that participants construed the smoke differently in the three conditions. Participants who did not report the smoke to the experimenter consistently told the experimenter they didn't believe it was dangerous. One participant ventured the hypothesis that it was truth gas! The students who did report the smoke construed it as a sign of imminent danger.

Combating Pluralistic Ignorance Bystanders are less likely to fall prey to pluralistic ignorance when they can clearly see one another's initial expressions of concern (and before their initial expressions are covered up out of the desire to seem less alarmed). This hypothesis was tested in a study in which participants were led through a construction-filled hallway to a lab (Darley, Teger, & Lewis, 1973). Along the way, they passed several stacks of wooden frames used in construction and a workman (actually a confederate) doing repairs. Once in the lab room, the participants began the ostensible task of the experiment: doing their best drawing of a model horse. Darley and his colleagues varied the degree to which participants would be able to see others' nonverbal expressions, those reliable signals of concern about a possible emergency. In the control condition, the participant was alone. In another condition, two participants were seated facing each other as they drew the model horse, and could see each other's immediate, spontaneous expressions of emotion when the emergency occurred. In a final condition, participants were seated back-to-back. Here they had no visual access to each other's immediate reactions.

As the participants labored over their drawings, they suddenly heard a loud crash and the workman crying out in obvious pain, "Oh, my leg!" The results of this study make it clear that seeing others' spontaneous emotional expressions reduces the effects of pluralistic ignorance: 90 percent of those who were alone left the room to help the workman; 80 percent of those who were seated face-to-face did so as well. But only 20 percent of the participants who were

"I said, 'I'm not on duty! I just came back to get my flip-flops.'"

a diffusion of responsibility could discourage people from helping out in urban settings. Finally, it's probable that in rural settings, people's actions are more likely to be observed by people who know them, and who can comment on their reputation to others. Later we'll learn how powerful reputational concerns are as triggers of prosocial behavior.

Social Class and Altruism In June 2010, Bill Gates of Microsoft and investment guru Warren Buffet launched the Giving Pledge, a campaign to encourage the wealthiest people in the world to make a commitment to donate most of their wealth to philanthropic causes. They asked that the richest people in the United States give at least half of their wealth to charity. Buffet, a billionaire, pledged to give away 99 percent of his fortune by the end of his life. More than 40 of America's richest individuals soon followed suit, including Larry Ellison of Oracle and Mark Zuckerburg and Sheryl Sandberg of Facebook. By some estimates, if the wealthiest Americans honored the Giving Pledge, charities would receive some $600 billion.

How does social class influence levels of altruism? Are the Gates and Buffets and Sandbergs of the world the rule, or the exception to the rule? When it comes to altruism, it turns out that those who have less give more, at least in terms of the proportion of their income they donate to charity. Nationwide surveys of charitable giving in America find that wealthy individuals give away smaller proportions of their income to charity than people who are less well-off (Greve, 2009). For example, a study by the organization Independent Sector (2002) found that people making less than $25,000 per year gave away an average of 4.2 percent of their income, whereas those making over $100,000 per year donated only 2.7 percent. It would seem that people like Gates and Buffet are exceptions.

What investigators have learned about empathic concern and altruism sheds light on why the poor may give more than the rich. Specifically, Michael Kraus, Paul Piff, and their colleagues reason that a relative scarcity of resources leads lower-class individuals to be empathically attuned to others, and they build strong relationships to help them adapt to their more unpredictable, taxing, and sometimes threatening environments (Kraus, Piff, & Keltner, 2011). Upper-class people, by contrast, enjoy more abundant resources and opportunities that enable them to be more independent. In keeping with this theorizing, lower-class people prove to be more empathetic than upper-class people in a variety of ways that assess empathy: they are better judges of the emotions of a stranger with whom they've just interacted, they are better judges of a friend's emotions, and they are more accurate in their inferences about the emotions revealed in photographs (Kraus, Côté, & Keltner, 2010).

Given these social class differences in empathy, are lower-class people more likely to act in a prosocial fashion? Indeed, Piff and his colleagues have found that they are (Piff, Kraus, Côté, Cheng, & Keltner, 2010). In one study, for example, people from different class backgrounds played the dictator game, an economic game in which they received 10 points and were asked to give some portion of those points to a stranger. The points participants had at the end of the experiment determined their chances in a lottery conducted after all participants had completed the study. On average, participants gave away 41 percent of their points, and lower-class participants gave away more of their points to a stranger than did members of the upper class.

A second study tied the tendency for lower-class people to act more prosocially to their tendency to feel more empathic concern for strangers in need (Piff et al., 2010). Participants were given the chance to help an obviously distressed confederate who had arrived late for the experiment and therefore needed the participant's assistance to complete required tasks. Before this opportunity to provide help, participants watched either a neutral film clip (a relatively uninteresting scene from the movie *All the President's Men*) or a moving portrayal of the suffering of children living in poverty. Showing the film about poor children was intended to induce upper-class participants to feel the same level of empathic concern typical of lower-class participants, which the investigators predicted would lead them to help more. The findings supported these predictions. **Figure 14.3** shows the class difference in prosocial behavior discussed earlier: after watching a neutral film clip, lower-class participants offered to do more of the other participant's tasks than upper-class participants did. When upper-class people are made to feel compassion, however, they respond in the same prosocial fashion as their lower-class counterparts.

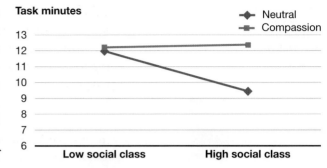

Figure 14.3
Social Class and Altruism
This study demonstrated that lower-class people help more than upper-class people, except when both groups are made to feel compassion.

SOURCE: Piff et al., 2010.

Religion, Ethics, and Altruism People throughout the world define themselves in terms of religion—Muslims, Protestants, Methodists, Unitarians, Jews, Catholics, Mormons, Buddhists, Hindus, Sikhs, and so on. Many others who don't have a religious affiliation are spiritual people who believe in forces that transcend the physical laws of nature. Like social class, religion can shape almost every facet of social life, ranging from moral beliefs to marriage partners.

The world's major religions emphasize compassion, altruism, and treating others, even strangers and adversaries, with kindness (**Table 14.1**). This conduct is seen in such religious practices as tithing and tending to those who suffer, and in moral codes such as the golden rule: treating others as we would like to be treated ourselves. It's demonstrated in the texts of the major religions, which

TABLE 14.1 THE GOLDEN RULE ACROSS CULTURES AND RELIGIONS	
Matthew 7:12	"In everything, therefore, treat people the same way you want them to treat you, for this is the Law and the Prophets." (*New American Standard Bible*, 1995)
Sextus the Pythagorean	"What you wish your neighbors to be to you, you will also be to them."
Buddhism	"Putting oneself in the place of another, one should not kill nor cause another to kill."
Tibetan Buddhism	"If you want others to be happy, practice compassion. If you want to be happy, practice compassion." (Dalai Lama)
Hinduism	"One should never do that to another which one regards as injurious to one's own self." (*Mahabharata*)
Muhammad	"Hurt no one so that no one may hurt you."
Taoism	"He is kind to the kind; he is also kind to the unkind."

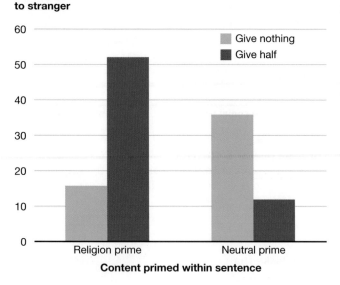

Proportion of participants making gift to stranger

Figure 14.4
Religion and Altruism
As this study showed, being primed with religious concepts leads to greater generosity.

SOURCE: Adapted from Norenzayan & Shariff, 2008.

encourage a prosocial stance toward others through fables and time-honored passages. Admittedly, many of the world's religions include stories of taking revenge, putting people to death for seemingly trivial offenses, and treating nonbelievers in cruel ways. Still, these troublesome elements aside, all religions stress compassion and the need to treat others—at least some others—well.

Does exposure to religious concepts make people more prosocial? Research by Ara Norenzayan and Azim Shariff addresses this question (Norenzayan & Shariff, 2008; Shariff & Norenzayan, 2007). In a first study, participants were shown sequences of five words, randomly arranged, and asked to generate sentences using four of those words. In a religion prime condition, the five words always included at least one word with religious meaning, such as *spirit*, *divine*, *God*, *sacred*, and *prophet*. For example, in this condition participants would read "Felt she eradicate the spirit" and create the sentence "She felt the spirit." In a neutral prime condition, participants did the same task of unscrambling sentences, but none of the words had religious meaning. Participants then received 10 Canadian dollars and were asked to give some amount away to a stranger. **Figure 14.4** shows the powerful effect of being primed by religious concepts like "divine" or "sacred." Participants in the neutral prime condition were more than twice as likely to give nothing to a stranger, compared to those in the religion prime condition (36 percent versus 16 percent). By contrast, people who were primed with religious concepts were more than four times as likely to treat a stranger as an equal by giving half of the money to the stranger (52 percent versus 12 percent).

Shariff and Norenzayan also examined whether secular, nonreligious concepts related to kindness and ethical behavior generate similar levels of generosity (Shariff & Norenzayan, 2007). In what they called a "civic" condition, participants unscrambled sentences that included words related to the secular institutions and ideas that build more cooperative societies, such as *civic*, *jury*, *court*, *police*, and *contract*. These words also generated high levels of generosity in the economic game—as much generosity, in fact, as the religious words prompted. It seems that the emphasis on fairness and cooperation and equality, seen in both religious traditions and secular treatments of ethics, can do a great deal to elicit prosocial behavior.

Shinobu Kitayama and his colleagues have gathered evidence showing that the sense of being watched, so prominent in religions of different kinds, increases altruism. In fact, so powerful is this effect, it can be achieved by simply seeing an upside-down triangle of three dots, which capture the geometric arrangement of the eyes and mouth of a human face. Seeing this arrangement of dots evokes the sense that someone is looking at you, and, the reasoning goes, triggers more cooperative behavior. In the relevant study, participants played the dictator game. They were given a sum of money and asked to write down on a sheet of paper the amount, including none at all, they wanted to give to a stranger (Rigdon, Ishii, Watabe, & Kitayama, 2009). On the paper, they saw one of two sets of dots, shown in **Figure 14.5**. In one condition, participants saw the pattern

BOX 14.3 **FOCUS ON *CULTURE***

Prosocial Behavior and the Sense of Being Watched

Common to many religions is the idea that God is watching over people as they carry on with their mundane lives on Earth. The Greeks believed their gods guided their everyday actions. The same is true for many Christians today, who refer to being watched by Jesus in the sky. And in many religions, this idea of being observed translates directly into religious iconography and architecture. For example, if you travel to Nepal and visit its temples, such as the fifth-century BCE temple Swayambhuntha, you'll have the distinct impression of being watched, because of the prominence of the eyes

on the surface. You might have a similar experience when visiting the Sistine Chapel, Michelangelo's famous painted ceiling in the Vatican in Rome. There, if you look up into the center of the ceiling, you'll see God looking down upon Adam and Eve, in one of the most well-known works of art from the Renaissance.

The Swayambhuntha Temple
The eyes painted on the surface toward the top of the temple give visitors the feeling they're being watched.

of three dots evocative of the human face (the pattern on the left). In a second condition, participants saw the same dots but configured upside-down (the pattern on the right). When presented with dots upside-down on the response sheet, 40 percent of the participants decided to keep all the money for themselves. This selfish tendency dropped to 25 percent when the dots representing the face were on the response sheet.

Evolution and Altruism

Few behaviors are more problematic to explain from an evolutionary perspective than altruism. Natural selection favors behaviors that increase the likelihood of survival and reproduction. Altruistic behavior, by its very nature, is costly; it devotes precious resources to others that could be used for ourselves or our

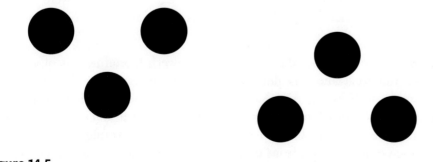

Figure 14.5
Being Watched
A simple triangular arrangement of dots is a reminder of the human face (the three dots to the left), and the associated sense of being observed can encourage cooperation.

kin selection An evolutionary strategy that favors the reproductive success of one's genetic relatives, even at a cost to one's own survival and reproduction.

"A chicken is only an egg's way of making another egg."

—SAMUEL BUTLER, *LIFE AND HABIT*

"An organism is a gene's way of making another gene."

—RICHARD DAWKINS

genetic relatives. The costs of altruism can include the ultimate sacrifice. Consider the fates of four friends who took a day off from their jobs at a summer camp to relax at a swimming hole near some scenic waterfalls. While walking down a steep path to get there, one of them slipped and fell into a whirlpool. When he was sucked down under the raging, foamy water, each of his three friends was moved by altruistic concerns and, in succession, jumped into the river to save the others. They all died. Individuals guided by unbounded altruism would not have fared well in evolutionary history. How, then, have evolutionary theorists accounted for altruistic behavior, which surely exists? Two evolutionary explanations have been offered: kin selection and reciprocity.

Kin Selection **Kin selection** is an evolutionary strategy that favors behaviors that increase the chance of survival of genetic relatives (Hamilton, 1964). Recall from Chapter 13 that inclusive fitness is the fitness of an individual based on reproductive success and the passing on of genes to future generations. Thus, from the perspective of kin selection, people should be more likely to help those who share more of their genes, helping siblings more than first cousins, first cousins more than second cousins, and so on. By helping relatives survive, people help their own genes pass to future generations.

The most obvious prediction from kin selection theory is that we should direct more of our helping behavior toward kin than toward non-kin. There is support for this hypothesis in studies of nonhuman species as well as humans. Here are two examples in the animal world. Mockingbirds have been observed to feed hungry nestlings that are not their own but that are more closely related than other hungry nestlings (Curry, 1988). Ground squirrels, when sensing a predatory coyote or weasel is in the vicinity, seem to emit an alarm call, thus putting themselves in danger by calling the predator's attention to their own location, in order to warn a genetic relative or a squirrel they have lived with, rather than warn unrelated squirrels or squirrels from other areas (Sherman, 1985).

In humans, genetic relatedness seems to influence helping behavior as well. Across many cultures, people report receiving more help from close kin than from more distant relatives or nonrelatives (Essock-Vitale & McGuire, 1985). When hypothetical situations are described to them, people report being more willing to help close relatives (especially those young enough to have children) than more distantly related people or strangers (Burnstein, Crandall, & Kitayama, 1994). In a study of kidney donations, donors were about three times as likely to engage in this altruistic act for a relative (73 percent) than for nonrelatives (27 percent) (Borgida, Conner, & Manteufel, 1992). In a puzzle task that required cooperation, identical twins, who share all their genes, were found to cooperate about twice as often (94 percent) as fraternal twins (46 percent), who share only half of their genes (Segal, 1984; see also Burnstein, 2005).

Reciprocity Genetic relatedness, then, is a powerful determinant of altruistic behavior. But what about helping those who are not our kin? We often go to great lengths to help our friends. We give them money, let them sleep at our apartment and eat out of our refrigerator, help them move, and so on. And sometimes we put our lives on the line to help them, as did the young people who died trying to save their friend from drowning. Even more compelling, perhaps, is how often we help total strangers. People will dive into icy waters to save people they've never met, donate money anonymously to charities, and engage in all sorts of more ordinary, less costly behaviors, such as giving up a seat on a bus or taking the time to help someone cross a street. Such actions can be accounted for in part by reciprocity and cooperation, which form the basis of the second major evolutionary explanation for altruism.

In traditional, preliterate societies, individuals living in groups were best able to survive when they cooperated with one another. To explain how cooperation evolved, evolutionary theorists generally use the concept of **reciprocal altruism**—helping other people with the expectation that they'll help in return at some other time (Trivers, 1971). Cooperation among non-kin provides many benefits that increase the chances of survival and reproduction for both parties. Reciprocal altruism reduces the likelihood of dangerous conflict, helps overcome problems arising from scarce resources, and offers a basis for people to form alliances and constrain more dominant individuals (Preston & de Waal, 2002).

There is some evidence for the mutual helping that is the essence of reciprocal altruism in nonhuman species. Vampire bats need blood meals to survive and may starve to death if they do not have a blood meal after 60 hours. Researchers have found that satiated bats will regurgitate blood to feed bats that have given to them in the past, but will not make a donation to a bat that has not been a donor itself (Wilkinson, 1990). In his observations of chimpanzees and bonobos, Frans de Waal (1996) has found that primates are disposed to share food with other primates who share with them, to look after each other's offspring, and to systematically groom other primates who have groomed them earlier.

In humans, the impulse to reciprocate is a powerful motive, and the tendency to return favors a likely human universal (Gouldner, 1960). In hunter-gatherer societies around the world, meat gained from hunts is carefully divided up and shared with others, on the assumption that present acts of generosity will be paid back at some later date (Flannery & Marcus, 2012). In studies using games where players can either cooperate or compete with one another, people are more likely to seek out and cooperate with individuals who have cooperated on the previous round of the game (Rand, Arbesman, & Christakis, 2011).

Perhaps an even more dramatic illustration of our tendency to reciprocate is the following experiment. Researchers mailed Christmas cards to numerous complete strangers. About 20 percent reciprocated by sending their own Christmas cards back to the senders, whom they had never met (Kunz & Woolcott, 1976). Either the participants had too few friends to accommodate the stacks of Christmas cards they bought, or they felt compelled by the norm of reciprocity to respond with a Christmas card to the sender.

Adam Grant and Francesca Gino have made the case that expressions of gratitude act as social rewards, and are a powerful trigger of subsequent cooperation, which is in keeping with the reciprocal altruism thesis (Grant & Gino, 2010). More specifically, they propose that an act of appreciation functions like a gift; the recipient feels socially valued. Feeling rewarded, the recipient should be more inclined to reciprocate, and behave altruistically. And that's exactly what Grant and Gino have found.

In one study, participants helped an experimenter edit a letter online (Grant & Gino, 2010). In the gratitude condition, participants were thanked via e-mail. In the control condition, participants received a polite message of equal length, but

Reciprocal Altruism
Vampire bats will regurgitate blood to feed starving bats that have given blood to them in the past, but they will not give blood to bats that have not helped them in the past. Thus, reciprocally altruistic behavior is observed in nonhuman species as well as humans.

reciprocal altruism Helping others with the expectation that they will probably return the favor in the future.

Food Sharing
In cultures around the world, the sharing of food is a way that people build and maintain cooperative relationships. These Masai men in Africa share beef.

without a note of thanks. When asked if they would help the experimenter edit a second letter, those who were thanked responded affirmatively 66 percent of the time compared to 32 percent in the control condition. In a similar study out in the work world, university fundraisers who were thanked directly by their supervisor, compared to individuals in a control condition, were observed to increase their fundraising calls dramatically over the course of the next week (Grant & Gino, 2010).

🔄 LOOKING BACK

Altruistic tendencies are the unselfish behaviors that benefit others. People may act altruistically for selfish motives, such as reducing distress or gaining social rewards, but some acts of altruism are based on a more selfless state of empathic concern. Situational determinants influence whether or not people help others. The presence of bystanders may lead to a diffusion of responsibility, in which everyone assumes someone else will help. Characteristics of the victim can affect whether people will help: people are more likely to help similar others. Construal processes also influence helping; pluralistic ignorance can lead people to be less likely to help. People in rural settings and those from lower-class backgrounds are more likely to help than people in urban settings or from upper-class backgrounds. Two evolutionary concepts that can account for the existence of altruism are kin selection and reciprocity.

Cooperation

Cooperating with others is part of our evolutionary heritage. The profound vulnerability and dependence of our offspring, who have a long period of complete reliance on adults for food and protection, required cooperative child care; both parents shared the burdens of raising children who were entirely dependent on them (Konner, 2003). From archaeological studies of the bones of animals our hominid predecessors killed for food, we know that early humans hunted in cooperative groups (Mithen, 1996). The inclination to cooperate for common goals is almost a defining attribute of humans.

One of the most striking aspects of human relations is how quickly adversarial relationships can become cooperative (and vice versa). In World War II, the

Cooperation between Wartime Enemies

During World War I, instances of cooperation took place between enemy soldiers, as during this informal Christmas truce in 1914. Soldiers from both sides emerged from their trenches and fraternized in no-man's-land. This lithograph was published in 1915.

mortal enemies of the United States were the Germans and Japanese. Shortly after the end of the war, the United States became strong allies with these former enemies. During the Rwandan genocide, Hutus sought to annihilate Tutsis; since then, the two groups have become more collaborative. It is an important lesson of history, how readily people shift from competition and aggression to cooperation.

The Prisoner's Dilemma

Core principles that account for how and why humans cooperate have been examined through the use of an experimental paradigm known as the **prisoner's dilemma**, also referred to as a type of economic game. Imagine being in an experiment in which you're ushered into a small cubicle; the experimenter tells you there's another participant (whom you will never meet) in a cubicle nearby. Both you and the other participant are required to make a simple decision: independently, you must choose to "cooperate" with each other (do what will benefit both of you) or "defect" (do what will disproportionately benefit yourself). You will be paid for your participation, and your compensation will depend on the choices you make. If both of you cooperate, you'll each receive $5. If both of you defect, you'll each get $2. If one cooperates and the other defects, the defector will receive $8, and the cooperator will not receive anything. The experimenter says you'll be paid as soon as each of you makes your choice, and reiterates that you and the other person will never meet. What do you do?

From the perspective of maximizing your own self-interest, the best, or "rational," choice is to defect. Whatever your partner does, you make more money by defecting than by cooperating. To see this, consult the summary of payoffs presented in **Figure 14.6**. If your partner cooperates, you receive $8 by defecting but only $5 by cooperating. If your partner defects, you receive $2 by defecting and nothing by cooperating. Defection thus "dominates" cooperation. So why not defect?

Here's the catch: the payoffs are the same for both players, so if both reason this way and choose to defect, they receive only $2 rather than the $5 that would be theirs through mutual cooperation. The "best" choice for each person (defection) is a terrible choice from the standpoint of the two people in combination.

On the surface, the prisoner's dilemma game seems to hold little promise for teaching anything significant about real human interaction. Unlike many real-world situations, the game offers no range of cooperative to competitive behaviors to choose from; instead, there are only two behaviors—cooperate or defect. In addition, participants are not allowed to discuss the choices beforehand, and they are never permitted to explain or justify them afterward. Overall it seems too limited, too artificial, to demonstrate anything significant about real-world cooperation and competition.

Looks may be deceiving, however. As simple as the prisoner's dilemma seems, it nevertheless captures the essential features of many significant situations in life (Dawes, 1980; Schelling, 1978). Let's consider a real-world analogue. India and Pakistan have been engaged in an arms race for decades. Like nearly all such struggles, the contest is ultimately futile because its structure is that of the prisoner's dilemma. Each

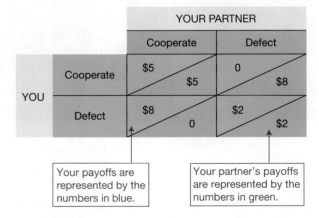

Figure 14.6
The Payoff Matrix for the Prisoner's Dilemma Game

The Cooperative Brain

Cooperation is vital to human survival, but as a social strategy it can incur certain costs. When we cooperate, we also risk being exploited by others. Often, the rewards of cooperation will be enjoyed much later, as when we cooperate with colleagues on a long-term project. James Rilling and his colleagues have found that the brain may be wired to enable cooperation in the face of these kinds of uncertainties

(Rilling et al., 2002). They have shown that during acts of cooperation, our brain fires as if we are receiving rewards.

In their study, 36 women played an online version of prisoner's dilemma with another person. Using fMRI technology, the researchers scanned the brains of the participating women when they cooperated with the online stranger—which was their most common choice. They found that

reward-related regions of the brain (the nucleus accumbens, ventral caudate, and ventromedial/orbitofrontal cortex) exhibited increased activation when the women cooperated. These brain regions are rich in dopamine receptors and are activated by all sorts of rewards, such as sweet tastes, pleasant smells, pictures of tropical vacations, and pleasing touches. Cooperation, it seems, is inherently rewarding.

country must decide whether to spend more on armaments or to stop spending money on more arms and enjoy a significant economic "peace dividend," as the United States did following the breakup of the Soviet Union. However, regardless of what the other does, it is "better" to acquire more arms. (If India freezes its acquisition of weapons, Pakistan can achieve an edge by spending more. If India builds up its arsenal, Pakistan has to spend more to avoid vulnerability.) Nonetheless, because the new weapons systems developed by one side are quickly matched by the other, the net effect is waste. The two countries pay dearly for a military balance that was attainable for less expense.

Thus, although the prisoner's dilemma may seem like a sterile and artificial paradigm on the surface, it captures many difficult real-world choices between cooperation and competition. Thousands of studies using the prisoner's dilemma game have yielded some valuable insights about how people make these difficult choices, illuminating why people or groups or countries would be likely to defect or cooperate, and suggesting what might be done to foster cooperative relations.

Developing Cooperative Relationships

Cooperation can emerge between the most violent of enemies and in the most extreme circumstances. Here, members of two rival gangs in El Salvador, MS-13 and 18th Street, stand next to each other, in a spirit of cooperation created by a truce signed a year earlier.

Situational Determinants of Cooperation

The prisoner's dilemma game sets up the simplest of situations: participants are involved in just one round with someone they don't even know. Of course, our social lives are much more complex. Very often we interact repeatedly over time with people, in our careers and our relationships. Are we more cooperative when we interact repeatedly with the same person over time, compared to a one-shot interaction? Indeed we are. David Rand and Martin Nowak have reviewed numerous studies that varied the number of rounds people played prisoner's dilemma with each other. The evidence is clear: as the likelihood of interacting with someone in the future rises, we become more cooperative (Rand & Nowak, 2013).

In daily life, we interact with people we know, and, often, whose reputations we know from others. **Reputation** refers to the collective beliefs, evaluations, and impressions about an individual's character that develop within a group or social network (Emler, 1994). Studies of people at work find that they quickly develop reputations for being good citizens (cooperators) or "bad apples" (defectors), and that these reputations spread through the organization and persist over time (Burt, Kilduff, & Tasselli, 2013). Very often, when you interact with someone, say in a dorm or at work, you are likely to know a bit about that person's reputation. Does such knowledge influence levels of cooperation?

To answer this question, some researchers have added a twist to the prisoner's dilemma game: prior to playing, participants are told about their partner's reputation, as being someone who cooperates or defects. As you would expect, participants will readily cooperate and give resources to an interaction partner whom they know to have a reputation for cooperation, but they will defect and choose not to give resources to interaction partners known to be greedy (Wedekind & Milinski, 2000).

These findings raise an intriguing question: How do we come to know each other's reputation? One idea is that reputations spread through gossiping, something most people are reluctant to admit to doing, but certainly enjoy when they do. Gossip is a communicative act in which one person comments on the reputation of another who is not present (Feinberg, Willer, Stellar, & Keltner, 2012). One of the primary reasons we gossip is to figure out the reputations of other people; through gossip, we investigate whether other group members are inclined to act in ways that strengthen the group (like by being civil, fair, and cooperative) or in ways that might create friction and ill will. This analysis yields what might strike us as a counterintuitive prediction: we might expect groups in which gossip takes place to actually be more cooperative. And indeed, that's what Matthew Feinberg and his colleagues have found.

In their study, participants played an economic game in which they could give some money to other people in their group (Feinberg, Willer, & Schultze, 2014). In one condition, they were allowed to gossip about each other's generosity (or lack thereof). In a second condition, no such opportunity to gossip was afforded. Over the course of several iterations, the groups whose members could gossip became more cooperative than the groups who were not allowed to gossip. The threat of gossip makes people aware of what might happen to their reputations should they choose to act selfishly, thus encouraging more cooperative behavior.

Construal Processes and Cooperation

Construal processes matter a great deal in shaping interactions toward more cooperative or competitive outcomes. In a compelling demonstration of the power of construal to influence levels of cooperation, Steve Neuberg (1988) had male undergraduates participate in a standard prisoner's dilemma experiment. Before doing so, however, the participants were subliminally "primed" with one of two different sets of stimulus words, ostensibly as part of another experiment. For one group, Neuberg flashed 22 hostile words (such as *competitive*, *hostile*, *unfriendly*) for 60 milliseconds—too fast for anyone to "see" them and consciously register what they were, but long enough for them to leave a subconscious impression. He showed another group a list of neutral words (*house*, *looked*, *always*) for an equally brief period. The question was whether exposure to

reputation The collective beliefs, evaluations, and impressions people hold about an individual within a social network.

"It takes many good deeds to build a good reputation, and only one bad deed to lose it."

—BENJAMIN FRANKLIN

BOX 14.5

Not So Fast
Critical Thinking about Generalizing to the Real World

Much of our discussion about cooperation thus far has come from studies using the prisoner's dilemma and related games, such as the dictator game (collectively known as economic games). Their structure captures a basic tension between cooperating and defecting in relationships of many kinds, from negotiations between adversarial nations to the daily lives of romantic partners. If you're skeptical about the external validity of these games—that is, the extent to which they generalize to cooperative behavior outside the lab—you're not alone.

Critics describe three kinds of doubts about the external validity of economic games (Levitt & List, 2007). First are the stakes involved: people are given money for cooperating or defecting, or they give away money that's been given to them in an experiment. People are dealing with "play" money and not actual money they've earned, which raises the question of whether we would observe similar patterns of cooperation when the money is real, earned, and costly to sacrifice. Second, critics suggest that being in a laboratory makes norms of cooperative behavior more salient. Therefore, simply signing up for an experiment, getting there on time, and following instructions from an experimenter are all acts guided by norms of cooperation, again suggesting that patterns of cooperation observed in the lab may diverge from those out in

the real world. Third, in lab studies people are acutely aware of being scrutinized, and scrutiny strengthens the likelihood of cooperative behavior.

The best response to concerns about the external validity of a paradigm is twofold. First, researchers can ask whether behavior observed in the lab, such as cooperation in the prisoner's dilemma game, predicts actual behavior out in the world. On this question, there is mounting evidence that a person's behavior in economic games predicts forms of charity and working to help others (Levit & List, 2007). For example, in one study, participants first played the dictator game (Franzen & Pointner, 2013). They were given 10 euros, and then they chose an amount to give to a stranger, under anonymous conditions. Some 4–5 weeks later, participants got a letter that actually was meant for another student, whom they didn't know. When they opened up the envelope, addressed to them, they discovered a letter from a grandmother to another student, Alexander, congratulating him on doing well academically. Inside the envelope were 10 euros and Alexander's correct address, which gave participants the opportunity to mail the misdirected letter to Alexander. Did the amount the participants shared in the dictator game 4 weeks earlier predict whether or not they would take time out

of their day and mail the letter to Alexander? Indeed it did. People who gave more in the dictator game were more likely to return the misdirected letter.

A second way to address concerns about the external validity of economic games is with field experiments that seek to replicate findings observed in the lab. Recall that field experiments are studies conducted outside the lab, observing real-world behavior. Here again the evidence supports the principles of cooperation that have been uncovered with economic games. In one study, the researchers wanted to encourage residents in 15 homeowners associations to agree to a more energy-efficient use of their air conditioners (Yoeli, Hoffman, Rand, & Nowak, 2013). They did so by having participants sign up on a sheet posted on a kiosk near the mailboxes for the homes or apartments. In one condition, participants wrote their names on the sheet; in a second condition, they signed up with a numerical code. When people are aware of their own reputations, they're more cooperative in economic games of different kinds. Would this effect of reputation replicate in energy-saving but costly cooperation out in the world? Yes. When participants signed up using their names, they were three times more likely to sign up for the service than when they did so anonymously.

the hostile words would lead participants to look out for their own interests, on the assumption that "it's a dog-eat-dog world out there."

Exposure to the hostile words affected the participants' actions. Eighty-four percent who were exposed to the hostile words defected on a majority of the trials in the subsequent prisoner's dilemma game; only 55 percent who saw the neutral words did so. This study raises concern about the kinds of stimuli to

BOX 14.6 **FOCUS ON *POSITIVE PSYCHOLOGY***

Is Cooperation Contagious?

Popular movies and clever advertisements have used the "pay it forward" concept: when we cooperate, we inspire others to be more cooperative in subsequent situations. Is cooperation contagious? For years, James Fowler and Nicholas Christakis have been gathering evidence on the contagious nature of human behavior, and have discovered that smoking, anxiety, happiness, and obesity, for example, spread through communities from one person to another (Christakis & Fowler, 2009). We are a mimetic species, prone to imitating the behaviors of others around us. Using an economic game, Fowler and Christakis found that cooperative acts inspire others to be more cooperative in ensuing situations (Fowler & Christakis, 2010).

In the study, participants played several rounds of an economic game in groups of four; each round involved an entirely new set of participants. In each round, the participant was given 20 money units (MUs) and allowed to give some amount, between 0 and 20, to the group. Each MU the participant gave to the group was translated to an increase of 0.4 MU for each of the four group members. This means that each gift of 1 MU would cost the giver 0.6 MU personally but benefit each other group member. If participants kept all their MUs, they would end the game with 20 MUs. If they each gave all their MUs to the group, each member would end the game with 32 MUs.

This method created the usual dilemma—that behaviors costly to the self are beneficial for the group—and allowed Fowler and Christakis to examine how cooperative gifts to other players by a player in one round might influence those other players' levels of generosity in subsequent rounds. They

Paying It Forward
The popular movie *Pay It Forward* focuses on the theme of how one person's generosity leads to other acts of generosity.

found that for every MU a player gave, his or her partners would give 0.19 MUs more on average to a *new* set of players in the next round, and 0.07 MUs on average to still other players in the round after that, two times removed from the original round.

---

which people are commonly exposed. The ideas in the air—the competitive and aggressive images we see in the media, in video games, in films—may foster a more competitive society.

Based on the results of Neuberg's study (1988), it might seem that the way we explicitly label situations could influence levels of competition and cooperation. If we think of international crises as buildups to war, diplomatic solutions may become less likely. When lawyers treat divorce settlements as adversarial, and as opportunities to get their client the best outcome at the expense of the estranged spouse, entrenched bitterness seems inevitable.

In a striking demonstration of the power of labels, Liberman, Samuels, and Ross (2002) conducted a study in which they labeled the prisoner's dilemma game in one of two ways. Half the participants were told they were going to play the "Wall Street" game, and the other half were told it was the "community" game. Everything else about the experiment was the same for the two groups. What might seem to be a trivial change of labels had a dramatic effect on the participants' behavior. Those playing the community game cooperated on the opening round twice as often as those playing the Wall Street game. Moreover, these initial differences were maintained throughout the subsequent rounds of the experiment. The Wall Street label doubtless made the participants adopt a perspective that made maximizing their own profits paramount. In contrast, the community label conjured up a different set of images and motives that increased the appeal of maximizing the participants' joint outcomes.

Culture and Cooperation

Given how labels—and therefore construals—shape levels of cooperation, you might expect cultural factors to have a similar influence on the inclination to either cooperate or defect. Let's consider the influence of a relatively specific subculture on cooperation: the discipline you choose to study in college and eventually apply in your career. One of the most popular majors at many American campuses is economics. Economic theory assumes that people are rational actors who always act in self-interested ways, attempting to maximize their own gains. Many people think this is a cynical view of the human condition; but in keeping with the ideas of eighteenth-century philosopher Adam Smith, economists have assumed that people and society are best served if individuals are allowed to selfishly pursue their own ends. The storekeeper and restaurateur will succeed to the extent that they serve their patrons well, simultaneously improving their customers' lives and doing well themselves by charging as much as a competitive market will allow.

Does training in the discipline of economics encourage people to act more selfishly? The results of several studies indicate that it does (Carter & Irons, 1991; Frank, Gilovich, & Regan, 1993; Marwell & Ames, 1981). In one study, undergraduates majoring in economics and in a variety of other disciplines participated in a single-trial prisoner's dilemma game in which researchers took great pains to ensure that each person's response remained anonymous (Frank et al., 1993). Seventy-two percent of the economics majors defected on their partners, whereas only 47 percent of those majoring in other disciplines defected. In a random sample of over 1,000 professors in 23 disciplines, participants were asked how much money they gave annually to public television, the United Way, and other charitable causes (Frank et al., 1993). The economists were twice as likely as all the others to take a free ride on the contributions of their fellow citizens; in other words, giving nothing to charity, while presumably enjoying services such as public television to the same extent as everyone else. The subculture in which people are immersed appears to powerfully influence their inclination to cooperate with others or look only after themselves.

To study the prevalence of cooperation in different cultures around the world, Joseph Henrich and his colleagues recruited individuals from 15 different small societies to play the ultimatum game, a close relative of the prisoner's dilemma game (Henrich et al., 2001). In the original version of the ultimatum game, one player, the allocator, is given a certain amount of money (say, $10); he keeps a certain amount and allocates the rest to a second participant, the responder. The responder can then choose to either accept or reject the allocator's offer. If the responder accepts, he receives what was offered and the allocator keeps the balance. If the responder rejects the offer, neither player receives anything.

In the Henrich team's version of the study, the participants were foragers, slash-and-burn farmers, nomadic herding groups, and individuals in settled, agriculturalist societies in Africa, South America, and Indonesia. What they were allowed to offer an anonymous stranger differed. In some cultures it was

Cooperation in Different Cultures

(A) The Machiguenga of Peru collaborate little with others outside their family and gave little in the ultimatum game (described in the text). (B) The Lamerala of Indonesia collaborate extensively in fishing and gave a lot.

money, in others a cherished good such as tobacco. In all cases, the researchers attempted to make rewards equal to approximately the same fraction of a daily wage in each culture.

The first finding of note was how cooperative humans are in the variety of cultures studied (Henrich et al., 2001). An economist of the rational self-interest view might argue that the sensible offer of the allocator is a small amount, such as 10 percent of the good ($1 if the allocator has been given $10). This approach would advance the material wealth of both allocator and responder. In contrast, the researchers observed a pattern of results that would puzzle Adam Smith. In the 15 cultures, allocators offered, on average, 39 percent of the good to anonymous strangers. (In other research across Western cultures, 71 percent of the allocators offered the responder 40–50 percent of the money; Fehr & Schmidt, 1999.) Of course, it's important to bear in mind that there are strategic reasons for participants making initial generous offers that have nothing to do with altruistic tendencies. Most notably, they probably anticipated that the respondent would reject unfair, trivial offers.

Henrich and his colleagues then looked closely at the 15 cultures to determine what cultural factors predict the likelihood of cooperative generosity in the ultimatum game (Henrich et al., 2001). One factor stood out: how much the individuals in a culture needed to collaborate with others to gather resources to survive. The more the members of a culture depended on one another to gather food and meet other survival needs, the more they offered to a stranger when they were allocators in the ultimatum game. For example, the Machiguenga people of Peru rarely collaborate with members outside of their family to produce food. Their average allocation in the ultimatum game was 26 percent of the resource. The Lamerala of Indonesia, by contrast, fish in highly collaborative groups of individuals from different families. Cooperation is essential to their livelihood and subsistence. Their average gift in the ultimatum game was 58 percent. Thus, interdependence increases people's cooperation and generosity with anonymous others.

"Every individual . . . endeavors as much as he can . . . to employ his capital in the support of domestic industry, and so to direct that industry that its produce may be of greatest value; every individual necessarily labours to render the annual revenue of the society as great as he can. He . . . neither intends to promote the public interest, nor knows how much he is promoting it. By . . . directing that industry in such a manner as its produce may be of greatest value, he intends only his own gain, and he is in this, as in many other cases, led by an invisible hand to promote an end which was no part of his intention."

—ADAM SMITH (1776)

Evolution and Cooperation: Tit for Tat

In *The Evolution of Cooperation* (1984), political scientist Robert Axelrod asked the following question: How might cooperation emerge in competitive environments governed by the ruthless pursuit of self-interest? In the context of human evolution, how might non-kin begin to act with an eye toward advancing the welfare of others?

Axelrod assumed that cooperation was part of our evolutionary heritage, given its universality and its emergence in even the most unlikely of social contexts. For example, in the trenches of World War I, British and French soldiers were separated from their enemies, the Germans, by a few hundred yards of no-man's-land (Axelrod, 1984). Brutal assaults by one side were typically met with equally fierce counterattacks by the other. And yet even here cooperation frequently emerged, allowing soldiers to eat meals peacefully, to enjoy long periods of nonconfrontation, and even to fraternize with one another. The two sides would fly special flags, make verbal agreements, and fire deliberately misguided shots, all to signal and maintain peaceful cooperation between episodes of attack in which each side was bent on exterminating the other.

Axelrod conducted a study that helps illuminate the evolutionary origins of cooperation. Although simple in design, this study yields profound lessons. Axelrod ran a tournament in which players—academics, prize-winning mathematicians, computer hackers, and common folk—were invited to submit computer programs that specified what choices to make on a round of the prisoner's dilemma game, given what had happened on previous rounds (Axelrod, 1984). In the first tournament, 14 strategies were submitted. Each strategy played 200 rounds of the prisoner's dilemma game with every other strategy. The points were tallied, and the most effective strategy was announced. The winner? It was a so-called tit-for-tat strategy, submitted by mathematical psychologist Anatol Rapaport.

The **tit-for-tat strategy** is disarmingly simple. It cooperates on the first round with every opponent and then reciprocates whatever the opponent did on the previous round. An opponent's cooperation was rewarded with immediate cooperation; defection was punished with immediate defection. In other words, start out cooperatively, and reciprocate your partner's previous move. Axelrod held a second tournament that attracted the submission of 62 strategies. All the entrants knew the results of the first round—that the tit-for-tat strategy had won. In the second tournament, the tit-for-tat strategy again prevailed. Note that the tit-for-tat strategy did not win every round when pitted against all the different strategies. Instead, it did better overall against the diversity of strategies. What makes the tit-for-tat strategy special, and why might it be relevant to your own life?

Axelrod contends that the tit-for-tat strategy is based on a set of valuable principles for applying when forming friendships, dealing with a difficult personality at work, negotiating with bosses, maintaining long-term romantic relationships, and raising children. Five factors make it an especially compelling strategy. (1) It is cooperative, and thus encourages mutually supportive action toward a shared goal. (2) It is not envious; a partner using this strategy can do extremely well without resorting to competitive behavior. (3) It is not exploitable, meaning it's not blindly prosocial; if you defect on the tit-for-tat, it will defect on you. (4) It is forgiving; that is, it is willing to cooperate at the first cooperative action of

tit-for-tat strategy A strategy in the prisoner's dilemma game in which the player's first move is cooperative; thereafter, the player mimics the other person's behavior, whether cooperative or competitive. This strategy fares well when interacting with other strategies.

the partner, even after long runs of defection and competition. (5) It is easy to read; it shouldn't take long for others to know that the tit-for-tat strategy is being played. Being nice, stalwart, forgiving, and clear—that's a good set of principles to live by.

⬆ LOOKING BACK

Cooperation is part of our evolutionary heritage. The prisoner's dilemma game models the many situations in everyday life when defection is the best solution for each person separately, but cooperation benefits the two together. Situational factors, such as the likelihood of repeated interactions and whether your reputation is on the line, influence levels of cooperation and competition. So, too, do construal processes: people can be primed to cooperate or defect. Studies of cultures in remote parts of the world reveal that cooperation is a human universal, and that cultures characterized by economic interdependence show greater cooperation. The tit-for-tat strategy involves initial cooperation and then reciprocation of an adversary's behavior, in order to encourage mutual cooperation.

Chapter Review

SUMMARY

Altruism

- People help others out of selfish motives, including reducing personal distress and gaining social rewards, such as praise, attention, or gratitude.
- A form of pure, undiluted altruism is based on *empathic concern*, the feeling of concern for another person after observing and being moved by that person's needs. People who help others to avoid personal distress have different physiological patterns than those who help for empathic reasons.
- Empathic concern motivates people to volunteer, to enhance the welfare of others.
- People vary dramatically in their altruistic behavior according to features of the situation, such as how much time they have, who is present, and what sort of need or suffering they encounter.
- *Bystander intervention* depends on the number of people observing an incident of someone needing help. The presence of others can lead to a *diffusion of responsibility*, in which nobody takes responsibility for helping the person in need.

- When people are unsure about an emergency situation, they might do nothing, for fear of embarrassment in case nothing is really wrong.
- Victim characteristics that increase the likelihood of being helped include whether the person is similar to potential helpers, and whether the victim makes his or her distress known.
- People who live in rural settings are more likely to help others than people who live in urban settings.
- People from lower-class backgrounds are more empathetic than people from upper-class backgrounds, and are more likely to give resources to strangers and help people in need.
- Exposure to religious concepts increases levels of altruism, perhaps through the effects of feeling watched.
- From the standpoint of evolution, people's actions should serve to increase the likelihood of survival and reproduction. The *kin selection* hypothesis explains, however, that people will help others to preserve the genes of close kin.
- In *reciprocal altruism*, people help others or grant favors in the belief that such behavior will be reciprocated in the future.

Cooperation

- Cooperation is part of human evolutionary heritage, and it is evident in almost all societies.
- The prisoner's dilemma game, used to study cooperation, tempts participants to maximize their own outcomes at the expense of another person by defecting. This strategy backfires if the other person also defects. The optimal outcome is for both to settle for something less than the maximum by cooperating.
- Interacting with people repeatedly over time increases cooperation.
- Knowing a person's reputation as cooperative or competitive influences levels of cooperation in profound ways.
- Gossip is a means of spreading information to other group members about an individual's reputation, and it can increase cooperation in groups.
- Cooperation is widespread in certain types of cultures, particularly where members are dependent on one another to gather resources.
- The *tit-for-tat strategy* in the prisoner's dilemma game is a reciprocal strategy that is cooperative, nonenvious, nonexploitable, forgiving, and easy to read. It helps maximize outcomes in potentially competitive situations that occur in real life.

THINK ABOUT IT

1. Someone might argue that as long as you're helping, your motives don't matter. Do you agree? Why or why not? In what situations might motives matter most?

2. Based on what you've learned about bystander intervention and diffusion of responsibility, what actions could you take to increase the likelihood that someone would help you in an emergency that happens in front of a large crowd?

3. Research indicates that lower-class people tend to be more empathic and giving than upper-class people. What factors might explain this difference? How might they relate to what you learned about power and prosocial behavior?

4. According to evolutionary theory, behaviors that optimize survival and reproduction are favored by natural selection and therefore more likely to persist. How, then, can we explain the evolution of altruism, which is by definition costly to the self?

5. After learning about research on gossip, have your feelings about this behavior changed? Under what circumstances might gossip serve a useful purpose?

6. In what ways could the tit-for-tat strategy be relevant in your life, such as a romantic relationship?

THE ANSWER GUIDELINES FOR THE THINK ABOUT IT QUESTIONS
CAN BE FOUND AT THE BACK OF THE BOOK . . .

Social Psychology and Health

Marie Antoinette, the notorious Queen of France during the late eighteenth century, was fond of gambling, fine clothes, behind-the-scenes political maneuvers, and extramarital affairs. She was a favorite target of the revolutionaries when they overthrew the monarchy during the French Revolution. Legend has it that after her capture, during the night before her execution by guillotine, Marie Antoinette's hair turned white.

We know it's physiologically impossible for hair to turn white during the course of a day. But excessive levels of stress—in Marie Antoinette's case, her husband's execution, the political upheaval she helped bring about, and her imminent demise—can damage the body. The stress response evolved to help us handle immediate pressures in the short run, but chronic and continuous stress can lead to myriad health problems. For example, physicians now estimate that 1–2 percent of those with the symptoms of a heart attack actually reflect a condition known as apical ballooning syndrome (ABS). ABS arises when stress hormones, such as epinephrine, flood the left ventricle of the heart, causing it to swell to dangerous levels. ABS is often triggered by excessive emotional stress—the death of a child, the loss of a spouse, or exposure to warfare and extreme violence. In 1 percent of cases, ABS can be fatal.

Stress is just one of many emotional and social factors that can affect overall health. Elements of one's culture, such as social class, influence health and well-being, leading people from lower-class backgrounds to suffer more frequently from almost every kind of health problem. Social situations, particularly the richness of social connections, can benefit health. Even certain construal processes—perceptions of control and optimism—can contribute to healthier lives.

Evolution and Health: Short-Term and Chronic Stress

Psychological stress results from the sense that our challenges and demands surpass our current capacities, resources, and energies (Lazarus, 1966; Sapolsky, 1994). Not all of them cause equal amounts of stress, however. As a review of over 200 studies reveals, the obligations and expectations that threaten social identity and our connection to others are particularly likely to contribute to our stress levels (Dickerson & Kemeny, 2004). The challenges of daily life often exceed our capacity to meet them, and stress can arise in almost any situation: pressures at work, the loss of a loved one, economic hardship, conflicts with family members, trying times in a marriage. Even positive events can be surprisingly stressful, such as graduation, a new job, planning a wedding, the early stages of marriage. And young children, while introducing incomparable joys for new parents, place new demands and create unexpected sources of stress. In any of these circumstances, we may feel we don't have the energy or skill to handle the challenges effectively; as a result, we experience psychological stress.

How does psychological stress harm physical health? The process begins in a system of the body known as the hypothalamic-pituitary-adrenal (HPA) axis and the stress hormone cortisol (**Figure A1.1**). Stressful events activate the amygdala, a region of the brain that processes information related to threat. The amygdala stimulates the hypothalamus, which sends chemical messages to the pituitary gland to produce adrenocorticotropic hormone (ACTH). ACTH stimulates the adrenal glands (near the kidneys) to release cortisol into the bloodstream.

psychological stress The sense that challenges and demands surpass one's current capacities, resources, and energies.

557

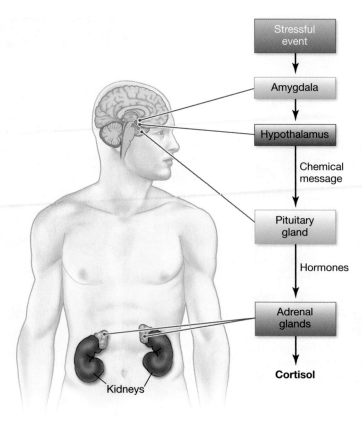

Figure A1.1
The HPA Axis and the Release of Cortisol

Cortisol has many effects on the body. Most notably, cortisol increases the heart rate and blood pressure, distributing blood to appropriate muscle groups involved in the fight-or-flight response to stress. The hands sweat—a process some think evolved to facilitate grasping. Cortisol suppresses the activity of the immune system, thus keeping resources available for metabolically demanding fight-or-flight behavior. It is also involved in forming flashbulb, stress-related memories in the hippocampus, thereby aiding the recall of sources of danger in the environment.

Activation of the HPA axis and the accompanying release of cortisol into the bloodstream help us respond to short-term stress—immediate threats to survival. During early evolution, this stress response enabled our ancestors to detect an approaching predator or an enraged rival and respond quickly with appropriate action. Today, this same stress response helps us power through lecture notes to study for an exam, avoid danger, or stay up until the wee hours of the morning taking care of a sick friend or child. Not surprisingly, researchers have observed elevated levels of cortisol in race car drivers, parachute jumpers, and students taking exams (Coriell & Adler, 2001).

The normal response to short-term stress is not usually a problem for most of us. Trouble begins when we experience chronic stress, which is frequently the result of **rumination**, the tendency to think about some stressful event over and over again (Nolen-Hoeksema, 1987). When we ruminate, we focus on a specific event, and by thinking of all its deep causes and ramifications, turn it into a continuous source of stress that touches on all facets of our life. Suppose your boss offers some criticism about how to sharpen up a proposal you've been working on. If you were to ruminate about it, you'd take the criticism and elaborate on how that event reflects more general problems you have at work, how you're never living up to expectations, how you'll let your parents down yet again.

Studies have shown that people who ruminate about a negative event experience prolonged stress compared to people who distract themselves from the event (Lyubomirsky & Nolen-Hoeksema, 1995; Morrow & Nolen-Hoeksema, 1990). Through rumination, specific stresses become chronic ones: a marital spat begins to feel like the fast road to divorce; a dip in the economy feels like a prolonged recession; a transient health problem feels like a verdict of deteriorating health.

Moreover, chronic stress can kill. Studies have found that chronic stress can lead to ulcers, heart disease, cancer, and even cell death in the hippocampus and consequent memory loss, in part because chronically high levels of cortisol damage different cells and organs in the body (Sapolsky, 1994). Feeling chronically stressed makes people more vulnerable to the common cold (Cohen et al., 2008). Chronic stress can even prematurely age the cells. Elissa Epel and her colleagues found that premenopausal women who reported elevated levels of stress showed shortened telomeres, parts of cells that normally shorten as part of the aging process (Epel et al., 2004). The telomeres of the most stressed women in this study had prematurely aged by 10 years.

rumination The tendency to think about a stressful event repeatedly.

How to Stop Ruminating

One thing you're probably ruminating about right now is how to stop ruminating and avoid the damaging effects of chronic stress. Susan Nolen-Hoeksema, the leading scholar in the study of rumination, offers several tips for reducing the tendency to ruminate (Nolen-Hoeksema, 2003). Here are a few. First, break loose from your pattern of rumination; turn your attention away from those recurring thoughts. Nolen-Hoeksema has documented how engaging in distracting activities during stressful periods—doing a crossword puzzle, knitting, reading a book, or working on a Sudoku problem—quiets the ruminative mind and calms you during stressful times.

A second tip is the stop strategy. Here Nolen-Hoeksema recommends that you simply say "Stop" to yourself, even shout it, when you find yourself ruminating. Shift your attention to other matters in your life rather than the negative thing you're dwelling on— what you need to do to prepare for grad school, where you might travel in the upcoming years, or friends you need to contact.

Finally, Nolen-Hoeksema recommends that if you're a dyed-in-the-wool ruminator, simply set aside 30 minutes of ruminating time each day, ideally when you're feeling pretty calm. Knowing you've reserved that time period will reduce your tendency to be overcome unexpectedly by rumination at random times throughout the day. Ethan Kross and his colleagues have shown that even for that deliberate period of rumination, it's helpful to engage in **self-distancing**, focusing on your feelings from the perspective of a detached observer (Kross, Ayduk, & Mischel, 2005). Revisiting a situation not from the perspective you initially had, but from the standpoint of a real or imagined observer, lets you reflect on stressful thoughts and feelings without becoming overwhelmed by negativity (Ayduk & Kross, 2008; Kross & Ayduk, 2008).

The message from the literature on stress and cortisol couldn't be clearer. Evolution has equipped us with an immediate stress response, associated with elevated HPA activation and cortisol release, that enables us to respond to pressing problems. However, short-term stresses can sometimes become chronic, triggering excessively high levels of cortisol that damage our health. Ruminating over stressful or negative events can have precisely that effect.

Culture and Health: Class, Stress, and Health Outcomes

In a celebrated but perhaps apocryphal exchange, F. Scott Fitzgerald told Ernest Hemingway, "The rich are different from you and me." Hemingway replied, "Yes, they have more money." Hemingway could have added that the rich also lead healthier and longer lives.

Social psychologists think of wealth in terms of class, or socioeconomic status (SES). We often refer to SES by using such categories as working class and upper class. Researchers measure social class in terms of three variables: family wealth and income, educational achievement (and that of the parents), and the prestige of work or career (and that of the parents) (Oakes & Rossi, 2003; Snibbe & Markus, 2005).

As you've learned throughout this book, social class is an important cultural dimension of one's identity. People of various socioeconomic backgrounds tend to prefer different kinds of music (Snibbe & Markus, 2005), they explain

self-distancing The ability to focus on one's feelings from the perspective of a detached observer.

economic and political events in different ways (see Chapter 5), and they appear to be prone to different levels of altruism (see Chapter 14).

What does social class have to do with physical health? A great deal, it turns out. Dozens of studies have explored the association between social class and indicators of physical health. Just about every health problem is more prevalent in lower-SES people—those of lesser means (Adler et al., 1994; Coriell & Adler, 2001). Lower-SES newborns are more likely to have a low birth weight, which is a major predictor of later health problems. Lower-SES children are more inclined to develop asthma, diabetes, and obesity, other early predictors of health problems later in life. In adulthood, lower-SES people are more likely to suffer from high blood pressure, cardiovascular disease, diabetes, respiratory illness, and poor metabolic functioning related to blood sugar levels. They are also more likely to experience poor health subjectively, with symptoms ranging from stomach upsets to headaches and bad backs (Adler et al., 1994; Gallo, Bogart, Vranceanu, & Matthews, 2005; Lehman, Taylor, Kiefe, & Seeman, 2005; Singh-Manoux, Adler, & Marmot, 2003).

Class, Neighborhood, and Stress

How would you explain these class-based health differences? Your first inclination might be to take a situationist view and think about how the physical environments of poorer people might contribute to health-damaging chronic stress. Situations matter, and so does a person's daily environment. For instance, if you live close to someone, you're more likely to become friends (see Chapter 10). Generous acts are more common in rural settings than in urban settings (see Chapter 14). And it's clear that people from lower-SES and upper-SES backgrounds inhabit very different social and physical environments (see Coriell & Adler, 2001).

The Influence of Neighborhood Quality on Stress
(A) Lower-SES neighborhoods have fewer green spaces and play structures than (B) higher-SES neighborhoods, which allow for more stress-reducing play and relaxation.

People living in poorer neighborhoods are more often exposed to air and water pollution, pesticides, and hazardous wastes. Toxins like these harm the nervous system directly, and they can also boost levels of stress. Lower-SES neighborhoods have fewer recreational spaces and parks, so residents have fewer opportunities to exercise, to be outdoors, to relax, or to calm down. It is well known that physical exercise reduces stress and increases general health (Lyubomirsky, 2007). Poorer neighborhoods also have a higher incidence of violent crime, and residents experience more pervasive feelings of threat (Macintyre, Maciver, & Solomon, 1993). And lower-SES neighborhoods tend to have few healthy grocery stores or health care centers, all of which would support a healthier lifestyle.

Class, Rank, and Health

Another explanation for the connection between social class and health has to do with rank, or power (Adler et al., 1994). Lower-SES individuals have fewer resources and more limited access to opportunities, and these play an important role in defining a person's rank in society. Researchers have learned that having subordinate status, in human and nonhuman groups alike, leads to chronic feelings of threat and stress, accompanied by activation of the HPA axis and elevated cortisol. Robert Sapolsky has found, for instance, that subordinate baboons have chronically higher cortisol levels, as well as a variety of health problems, including an increased risk of cardiovascular disease and lower reproductive success (Sapolsky, 1982, 1994).

Social class may influence physical health through perceptions of rank or relative status. Lower-SES people may construe their lives in terms of occupying positions of subordinate status, and it may be this construal that damages their health. To capture this idea, researchers have begun to measure construals of rank with what is known as the ladder measure. Take a look at **Figure A1.2**. Think of the ladder as representing the social class of people in the United States. At the top are those who have the most money, the most education, and the most respected jobs. At the bottom are those who have the least money, least amount of education, and the least respected job or no job. The higher up you are on this ladder, the closer you are to the people at the very top. The lower you are, the closer you are to the people at the very bottom. Where would you place yourself on this ladder?

What's interesting about this measure is that it's based on subjective construal. A fairly wealthy person living among Fortune 500 CEOs, for example, could indicate a lower rank on this scale—and that would have important health outcomes. With each jump up the ladder of the class hierarchy, people are likely to enjoy better health. In a study of employees of the British Civil Service, those in the lowest-ranked positions (such as janitors) were three times more likely to die over a 10-year period than the highest-ranked administrators (Marmot, Shipley, & Rose, 1984). The experience of subordinate rank clearly can be damaging to one's overall health. Conversely, the feeling of being empowered benefits one's sense of agency and self-esteem, and therefore, general health.

Nancy Adler and her colleagues have found that with each move up the class hierarchy, people are less likely than people just below them to die in infancy, and are less vulnerable to coronary heart disease, lung cancer, bronchitis, respiratory disease, asthma, arthritis, cervical cancer, and neurological disorders

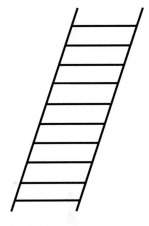

Figure A1.2
The Ladder Measure
Place a large X on the rung that best represents your socioeconomic rank.

(Adler et al., 1994). The experience of subordinate rank, even for people who have a good deal in life (those in the middle or upper-middle classes), leads to chronic activation of the HPA axis and the associated health problems.

Situational Factors and Health: Benefits of Social Connection

We are a species that has evolved to connect with other people and to enjoy many kinds of relationships. And when we connect, we are healthier. To explicitly examine the relationship between social connection and health, researchers have measured the strength of social support, using scales like the one in **Table A1.1**. This scale captures the extent to which we can count on friends and family for support and care. With measures like these, researchers have documented that social connections are vital to our physical, mental, and emotional health.

Consider some more specific findings. In one study, people who had fewer meaningful connections to others were 1.9 to 3.1 times more likely to have died 9 years later (Berkman & Syme, 1979). People who report having strong ties to others live longer (Berkman, 1995; Coriell & Adler, 2001). Janice Kiecolt-Glaser and her colleagues have found that people who report being lonely show higher levels of cortisol, suggesting that strong social connections calm HPA axis activation (Kiecolt-Glaser & Glaser, 1995).

These correlational studies raise questions about causation. Do strong relationships promote physical health? Or are physically healthy people more likely to enter into psychologically healthy relationships? Both causes are plausible.

Experimental results indicate that physiological stress is calmed by being with supportive other people. In one study, for example, women performed stressful, challenging tasks either in the presence of a friend or alone. Those accompanied

---

TABLE A1.1 A SOCIAL SUPPORT SCALE

1. There is a special person who is around when I am in need.
2. There is a special person with whom I can share my joys and sorrows.
3. My family really tries to help me.
4. I get the emotional help and support I need from my family.
5. I have a special person who is a real source of comfort for me.
6. My friends really try to help me.
7. I can count on my friends when things go wrong.
8. I can talk about my problems with my family.
9. I have friends with whom I can share my joys and sorrows.
10. There is a special person in my life who cares about my feelings.
11. My family is willing to help me make decisions.
12. I can talk about my problems with my friends.

SOURCE: Adapted from Zimet, Dalhem, Zimet, & Farley, 1988.

by a friend showed a milder stress-related cardiovascular response to the challenging tasks (Kamarck, Manuch, & Jennings, 1990). In another study, people were required to give a public speech with very little time to prepare, which no doubt caused rattled nerves and elevated cortisol. Those who had a supportive person in the audience, compared with those who did not, had lower blood pressure during the course of the speech (Lepore, Allen, & Evans, 1993). In still other work, participants made a presentation about why each of them would be a good candidate for an administrative job on campus, while two audience members looked on, expressionless, offering few signs of enthusiasm and a great deal of skepticism (Taylor et al., 2008). Before and after the speech, participants' cortisol levels were measured. Those who reported having strong connections with others, a sense of autonomy, and healthy self-esteem showed less intense cortisol responses to the stressful speech.

Perhaps the most dramatic evidence of the health benefits of social connection comes from an influential study by David Spiegel and his colleagues (Spiegel, Bloom, Kraemer, & Gottheil, 1989). Spiegel was interested in whether a sense of social connection would enable more favorable responses to breast cancer. Participants were randomly assigned to one of two conditions. In one condition, they engaged in weekly sessions of emotionally supportive group therapy with other breast cancer patients; in a second condition, participants were assigned to a nonintervention control group. As you can see in **Figure A1.3**, those in the group therapy condition survived 18 months longer (37 months) than women in the nonintervention control group (19 months).

These results support the thesis that social connections lead to positive responses to stress and better health overall. To integrate these findings, Shelley Taylor and her colleagues have offered an influential account of the benefits of a "tend-and-befriend" approach to stress (Taylor et al., 2000). Taylor argues that paying attention to the needs of others engages physiological processes that calm the stress-related HPA axis activation, thus paving the way for better health. A central player in this tend-and-befriend branch of the nervous system is the chemical oxytocin. Oxytocin floats through the brain and bloodstream and fosters feelings of trust, love, and devotion (see Chapter 6). In nonhuman

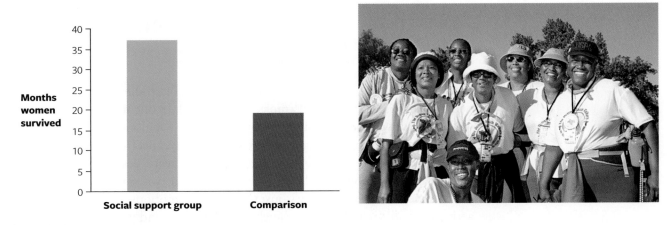

Figure A1.3
Health Benefits of Social Connection
This study demonstrated that breast cancer survivors live longer thanks to social support.

SOURCE: Adapted from Spiegel et al., 1989.

Tips for Reducing Stress

In her book *The How of Happiness,* Sonja Lyubomirsky summarizes the vast amount of published research and offers some simple recommendations for reducing the effects of stress (Lyubomirsky, 2007). None of them cost much, and all of them yield great health benefits.

1. *Focus on an adaptive coping approach.* Devise specific strategies for responding to your sources of stress, one step at a time, with concrete actions. If you're stressed about how to get into graduate school, write down the specific actions you need to take to get ready to apply—volunteering in a lab, doing extracurricular activities, forming relationships with different professors, preparing for the GREs.

2. *Exercise (the more, the better).* You can get a runner's high not only from jogging, but from many kinds of exercise—dance, pickup basketball, hiking in the mountains, a lunchtime walk with a friend, cross-country skiing. Almost any kind of exercise tends to lower stress levels.

3. *Seek out positive emotions.* Several studies suggest that the more you experience positive emotions, the less stress you'll have. People who experience positive emotions, such as gratitude, love, contentment, and awe, have lower mortality rates (Moskowitz, Epel, & Acree, 2008). When feeling stressed, take a moment to write down something for which you're grateful. If someone has done something to harm you, try to forgive. Go to the movies and see a comedy. Or just take a break and have an outing with friends. All these experiences bring different kinds of positive emotion, which will reduce your stress.

4. *Meditate.* There are many kinds of meditation: focusing on the breath, focusing on different sensations in the body, practicing a kind approach to other people, and being mindful, or aware, of ordinary everyday actions, such as eating and walking. An expanding body of scientific literature shows that meditation reduces levels of cortisol and stress.

species—from rats to primates—oxytocin increases attachment-related behavior and reduces cortisol levels. When we give, care, and connect, Taylor reasons, we activate oxytocin and this attachment system, thereby moderating our own stress. One of the most important clues to a healthy life, then, is to stay connected.

Construal and Health: Benefits of Perceived Control and Optimism

In the early 1980s, Shelley Taylor began a series of studies of how people live with serious disease (see, for example, Taylor, 1983). In one study, she interviewed women who were being treated for breast cancer. One out of seven women in the United States and Canada suffers from breast cancer during the course of her life. While the survival rates are improving every year, the psychological ramifications are complex. Upon being diagnosed, women often feel anxiety, fear, shame, and even hostility—just the kinds of emotions that trigger HPA axis activation and cortisol release, thereby causing stress and perhaps worsening the effects of the disease.

In studying the interviews, Taylor found that women with a breast cancer diagnosis did not necessarily accept their condition passively. Instead, they actively constructed narratives about this new dimension to their identity. Many of them found reasons to be grateful in surprising kinds of social comparisons. Women who were diagnosed later in life felt grateful it hadn't happened to them as young women, while they were raising children and starting a career; they appreciated having had the chance to live a full life without cancer. Younger women, by contrast, were grateful they weren't older when they got their diagnosis, for they felt they had the physical robustness to respond strongly to the disease.

One construal process that seems to benefit a person's overall health is developing a sense of control—a feeling of mastery, autonomy, and efficacy in influencing important life outcomes (Shapiro, Schwartz, & Astin, 1996). In Taylor's study of breast cancer patients, perceived control proved to be a source of good health. Taylor found that more than two-thirds of the women reported a sense of control over their situation. They assumed that through diet, exercise, and/or positive beliefs, they could influence the course of their disease. (People suffering from other conditions, such as HIV/AIDS and coronary problems, have similar feelings.) And the more the patient reported perceived control, the better she responded to the disease, as assessed by her physician (Taylor, Wood, & Lichtman, 1983; Taylor, Lichtman, & Wood, 1984).

In general, people with a more pronounced sense of control enjoy better health and well-being (Cohen & Herbert, 1996). Diseases and other health problems threaten our basic belief about the control we have over our body and our life, and a sense of losing that control is stressful in its own right. Thus, a good dose of perceived control can counter that stress and promote better health.

These findings raise an intriguing possibility: Might introducing a sense of control into the lives of people with declining health improve their health and well-being? That question motivated a striking study by Ellen Langer and Judith Rodin (1976) of nursing home residents. As people age into their later years, they often experience a pronounced loss of control in many realms: the loss of eyesight, muscular coordination, and strength makes simple physical tasks more challenging; the loss of memory can make social interactions difficult. These age-related losses are amplified, many believe, by some of the conditions of certain facilities, where older people forfeit even more control—over their schedules, their meals, and their social activities.

Langer and Rodin did something ingenious. They decided to explore the effects of increasing the sense of control in a particular nursing home (Langer & Rodin, 1976). The participants were all healthy, ambulatory residents, ages 65–90. On one floor, individuals were brought together and led in a discussion, by a young male staff member, about personal responsibility and the various ways they had personal control in their residence, ranging from planning their free time to voicing complaints to the staff. Each participant then received a small plant and was asked to take care of it. In a second condition, on a neighboring floor, participants were told about all the things in the nursing home available to them, with no mention of their personal control. They, too, all received plants but were told the staff would water and care for them.

Before these discussions and again 3 weeks later, the researchers gathered several measures of how well the elderly residents were faring (**Figure A1.4**). Sure enough, participants on the floor that emphasized personal control showed greater increases in happiness compared with those on the neighboring floor.

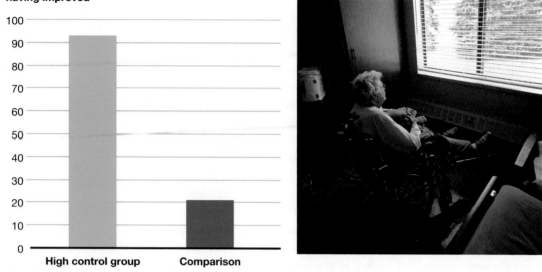

Percentage of residents rated by nurses as having improved

100
90
80
70
60
50
40
30
20
10
0

High control group   Comparison

Figure A1.4
Personal Control and Happiness
This older woman appears to be experiencing little control in her nursing home.

SOURCE: Adapted from Langer & Rodin, 1976.

They were more inclined to attend a free movie. They were ten times as likely to participate in a game proposed by the staff. And as rated by the nurses, nearly four times as many of the participants with the uplifted sense of control were judged to have improved in their overall functioning. Having a sense of personal control appears to quiet the emotions that activate the HPA axis.

A second construal that has emerged as quite important in health is optimism (see Chapter 5). Highly optimistic people have positive expectations about the future. They are likely to endorse the statement, "In uncertain times, I usually expect the best," and disagree with the statement, "If something can go wrong for me, it will." Studies have shown that people who are more optimistic tend to have greater happiness and well-being—and they enjoy better health as well. For example, Charles Carver and Michael Scheier found that individuals who report higher levels of optimism respond with greater robustness to coronary artery bypass surgery and breast cancer, and recover more quickly (Carver & Scheier, 1982). Researchers have found that self-reports of pessimism predict a more rapid weakening of the immune system (O'Donovan et al., 2009). In a study of men who graduated from college in 1945, those who reported higher levels of optimism at age 21 reported higher levels of physical health 35 years later (Peterson, Seligman, & Valliant, 1988).

Taylor and her colleagues have argued that belief in perceived control and optimism benefit health in several ways. With an increased sense of control, people generally respond to stress more effectively. Moreover, people with a heightened sense of control and an optimistic outlook tend to engage in better health practices. In one study, optimistic HIV patients had healthier habits and involvements, including building strong networks of social support (Taylor et al., 1992).

Module Review

SUMMARY

Evolution and Health: Short-Term and Chronic Stress

- *Psychological stress* is the sense that challenges and demands surpass one's capacities, resources, and energies.
- The hypothalamic-pituitary-adrenal (HPA) axis produces the stress hormone cortisol, the continuous release of which results in chronic stress.

- *Rumination*, or repeatedly thinking about some stressful event, can be reduced by *self-distancing*, focusing on feelings from the perspective of a detached observer.

Culture and Health: Class, Stress, and Health Outcomes

- People of lower socioeconomic status have poorer health than higher-SES individuals, in part because they have more stress in daily life.
- The subjective construal of lower rank or status, such as being a subordinate executive, can cause stress-related illnesses.

Situational Factors and Health: Benefits of Social Connection

- People with more meaningful relationships and connections to others are healthier.
- Being accompanied by a sympathetic person when undergoing a stressful experience significantly reduces the potentially damaging physiological and psychological effects.

Construal and Health: Benefits of Perceived Control and Optimism

- Having a sense of perceived control over one's circumstances reduces stress and yields health benefits.
- Having a sense of optimism, and a viewpoint that positive outcomes are likely in the future, is associated with better health.

THINK ABOUT IT

1. The experience of psychological stress typically triggers a host of physiological changes, including increased heart rate and blood pressure, sweating, and suppression of the immune system. When might these changes be helpful, and when are they more likely to be harmful?

2. Who is more likely to suffer from health problems, a janitor or a Fortune 500 CEO, and why? How might each person's subjective construal of their position influence their health?

3. According to the tend-and-befriend theory, why might social support improve health?

4. Research indicates that optimistic people tend to enjoy better health. Can you conclude from these findings that becoming more optimistic will improve your health? Why or why not? If you were a researcher conducting a study on this topic, what other factors might you want to control for?

THE ANSWER GUIDELINES FOR THE THINK ABOUT IT QUESTIONS CAN BE FOUND AT THE BACK OF THE BOOK . . .

Social Psychology and Personal Finance

On October 10, 2007, the Dow Jones Industrial Average, a widely cited index of the U.S. stock market and an indicator of the health of the American economy, stood at $14,164. People with heavy investments in the stock market were flush. One year later, however, the Dow closed at $8,579, wiping out 40 percent of the retirement savings and college funds of many families. Six more months and the Dow closed even lower, at $6,547—less than half the value at its peak. Unemployment at the beginning of this period was 4.6 percent; a year and a half later, it was twice as high. The United States and most of the developed world have been in an economic slump ever since. What happened?

Nothing. There was no great calamity that diminished the productivity of U.S. firms or the country's ability to produce goods and services. No new war was declared. No hurricane wiped out America's refining capacity. Oil-exporting countries did not boycott the United States. As President Franklin D. Roosevelt famously said with equal truth about the Great Depression in the 1930s, "We are stricken by no plague of locusts."

What *did* happen was the accumulation of human error in millions upon millions of economic transactions. Home owners borrowed money against their homes; since they still owned the house and had more money in their pockets, they concluded they were wealthier than they actually were. Banks approved mortgages for people with very shaky finances and then sold the mortgages on a secondary market to buyers who didn't fully know what they were getting. "Irrational exuberance" convinced people that housing and stock prices could only go up, so they had to "get in the game," with borrowed money if necessary (Greenspan, 1996; Shiller, 2000).

But housing and stock prices don't only go up. And when they went down, just a bit at first, the balance sheets of many people and institutions were in disarray. Many of those who had borrowed heavily couldn't meet their obligations. If they couldn't borrow even more money, they had to sell. The selling reduced the prices of what they owned, further weakening their balance sheets, which led to more selling, and so on. The housing market sank, pulling down large segments of the banking system and the construction industry, and these declines reverberated into every area of the economy.

> "Money is better than poverty, if only for financial reasons."
> —WOODY ALLEN

Behavioral Economics and Financial Markets

According to standard economic thinking, the cascade of human error that caused the 2008 downturn shouldn't—indeed, couldn't—happen. The field of traditional economics is based on two fundamental assumptions: people are rational and people are selfish. Economists assume, in other words, that people can accurately assess how much pleasure or pain —how much "utility"—they'll get from different outcomes and can estimate the likelihood of those outcomes with as much accuracy as the available information permits. People can also be counted on to pursue courses of action that will most likely advance their self-interest. Traditionally, economists have viewed the behavior of financial markets and the actions of individuals as they work, spend, save, and invest through the filter of these two assumptions.

"People who think money can't buy happiness don't know where to shop."

—BO DEREK

Psychologists know better. It's certainly true that people are often rational and can be counted on to pursue their self-interest reasonably well, most of the time. But human judgment is often distorted by predictable biases (see Chapter 4), and fortunately people are concerned about more than their own selfish interests (see Chapter 14). Knowing when and why people are likely to violate these twin assumptions of economics is essential to an accurate understanding of human economic behavior. Beginning in the 1980s, a group of psychologists and economists recognized that standard economic theory didn't address important shortcomings in individual judgment and decision making—shortcomings that could combine to influence the performance of the economy as a whole. They created a new field, referred to as **behavioral economics**, dedicated to taking insights from psychology about how the mind works and applying them to create more realistic, accurate models of economic behavior. Behavioral economics started out as a renegade area within economics and only gradually attracted supporters. After the severe recession in the fall of 2008, however, it has reached a much wider audience and won much greater acceptance. That recession served as something of an advertisement for the field of behavioral economics.

If people were entirely rational, one aspect of their economic behavior—their buy and sell decisions—would not be influenced by factors that have no bearing on the intrinsic value of what they're buying or selling. But such decisions *are* swayed by extraneous factors. For example, people sometimes try to lighten a bad mood by going shopping, only to end up buying things they regret. But maybe these attempts are, in fact, rational if they succeed in lifting a person's mood. Who's to say a better mood isn't worth the price of spending "too much" and experiencing later regret? Maybe "when the going gets tough, the tough go shopping" is an entirely rational strategy.

But what if people's moods influence their more deliberate investment decisions, or have an impact on entire markets? In such cases, it seems harder to defend the rationality of making such decisions based on mood. However, it turns out that important

The Stock Market Collapse
In the fall of 2008, housing and stock markets throughout the world experienced steep declines, sending the United States and much of the world into the worst economic downturn since the Great Depression.

financial transactions *are* influenced by such things as transitory, irrelevant mood states. Analyses of stock market performance in 26 countries over a 15-year period found that the amount of sunshine on a given day is positively correlated with market performance (Hirshleifer & Shumway, 2003; Kamstra, Kramer, & Levi, 2003). The market tends to go up more often on sunny days and down more often on gloomy days. The researchers maintain these results are due to investors attributing their good spirits to positive economic circumstances, rather than the true cause—sunshine. Another study found that a country's stock market tends to go down when their national soccer team is eliminated from important tournaments, such as the World Cup; similar dips occur following losses in other sports, such as cricket, rugby, and basketball (Edmans, Garcia, & Norli, 2007). It's hard to argue that these effects are rational.

Here's another example. It's difficult to maintain that it was rational for investors to bid up the stock of Computer Literacy Inc. by 33 percent in a single day simply because it changed its name to the edgier, more hip-sounding fatbrain.com. (Cooper, Dimitrov, & Rau, 2001; Zweig, 2007). The irrationality of stock movements (or at least the irrationality of *initial* stock movements) was further demonstrated in a study that examined the relationship between the name of a company newly listed on the stock exchange and its performance (Alter & Oppenheimer, 2006). Stocks in companies with easy-to-pronounce names (like Belden Inc. and Accenture Ltd.) performed better the day after, and 1 week after, they were listed than companies with names that were hard to pronounce (such as Magyar Tavkozlesi Rt. and Inspat International NV). Those who initially got taken in by the sound of a stock's name later paid a price for doing so, as the value of the easy-to-pronounce stock was not higher 6 months later. Eventually, the performance of the company—its profitability, not its name—carried the day.

Loss Aversion

Suppose that 10 years ago, your grandparents bought you 1,000 shares of stock in ABC corporation at $25 a share and 1,000 shares of XYZ corporation at $75 dollars a share. The stock of both companies is now selling for $50 a share. This means you own $50,000 of stock in each company—lucky you!

Now suppose you want to pay off your $25,000 student loan by selling some of your stock. You can sell shares in only one of the companies. Which would you sell: half your shares in ABC or half your shares in XYZ? Amazingly, the evidence suggests that most people would rather sell their stock in the company that had gone up in price (ABC, from $25 to $50) than sell stock in the company that had gone down (XYZ, from $75 to $50). People are more inclined to sell their winners, in other words, than their losers.

Although this example might seem fanciful, Terrance Odean (1998) found that people treat their investments precisely this way. He tracked the buy and sell decisions made by over 10,000 individuals who traded stocks with a discount brokerage firm. He found that investors were more likely to sell shares of the stocks that had gone up in value than the stocks that had gone down. And they paid a price for doing so. Over the next year, the stocks they sold (their winners) outperformed those they held onto (their losers) by 3.4 percent. Taking that 3.4 percent annual difference and compounding it over a lifetime can make the difference between being rich and just getting by.

Why would people make decisions that are so clearly to their disadvantage? The culprit appears to be the psychological phenomenon known as **loss aversion**—the tendency for a loss of a given magnitude (like losing $100) to have more psychological impact than an equivalent gain (winning $100). Loss aversion is a particular instance of the broader phenomenon discussed in Chapters 4 and 7 of bad things hurting more than equivalent good things feel good. Finding or winning $100 feels great, but not to the same degree that losing $100 feels bad. Because of loss aversion, people sometimes go to great lengths to avoid taking a loss—or at least to create the *illusion* that they haven't taken a loss.

If you sell shares of a stock that has gone up in price, you're realizing a gain. That feels good. But if you sell shares of a stock that has gone down in price, you're sustaining a loss. And that feels terrible. Some are willing to take a risk to avoid that feeling—the risk being that the losing stock will decline even more in value. (Note, by the way, that there are tax advantages of doing the opposite of what Odean's investors tended to do: selling stocks that have declined in value rather than those that have gone up. The amount of the loss, up to a certain point, can be deducted from your income.)

Construal, Framing, and Risk

Central to the principle of construal, which we've discussed throughout this book, is the idea that the same stimulus can be interpreted in different ways, and that how something is construed profoundly affects behavior. When it comes to economic transactions, the same outcome can be construed as a loss or a gain—depending on how it is framed.

It used to be illegal in the United States for commercial establishments to charge two different prices for a product: a higher price for a credit card transaction and a lower price for a cash transaction. But because merchants pay a fee to the credit card company, which they pass on to the customer in the form of higher prices, a single-price system could be considered unfair to those who pay cash. Cash customers end up subsidizing the credit transactions of others. As a result, Congress passed a law to permit a two-tiered pricing system. Credit card companies lobbied vigorously to control how the two-tiered system would be labeled (or framed). They preferred that it be called a "cash discount" rather than a "credit card surcharge." Because losses have greater psychological impact than gains, the credit card companies wisely reasoned that people would be less inclined to use their credit cards if they had to pay a surcharge to do so. Paying a surcharge is experienced, or construed, as a direct cost, or loss, whereas declining a cash discount is experienced as a forgone *gain*.

A few years ago, one of your textbook authors conducted a survey for a large life insurance company in which one group of respondents was asked whether they could comfortably save 20 percent of their income. Only half of them said they could. Another group was asked whether they could comfortably live on 80 percent of their income. Nearly 80 percent of them said they could. Of course, saving 20 percent means living on 80 percent, so rationally there should be no difference between the two groups. But saving 20 percent is construed as a loss of current spending resources, whereas living on 80 percent makes that missing 20 percent feel more like a forgone gain.

The asymmetry in people's reactions to outright losses versus forgone gains makes it easier for the government to pay for programs by granting tax breaks rather than by making cash payments. Paying for something (e.g., using tax dollars to pay for public housing) is experienced as a cost, or a loss. Granting a tax break (e.g., to companies that invest in public housing) is experienced as a forgone gain—tax revenue that would have been collected, but is not. This difference may help explain why populist reformers have made little headway in attacking "corporate welfare." Much of the voting public is easily riled by welfare to the poor because it involves direct payments from the government and is therefore construed as a loss. It's harder to get the public as upset over corporate welfare because it typically comes in the form of tax deductions rather than direct payments.

How economic outcomes are framed has a particularly strong effect on whether people are likely to make risky or conservative financial decisions. Consider the following example (adapted from Tversky & Kahneman, 1986):

You are first given $300 and then you must choose between:

- a sure gain of $100 or
- a 50-percent chance to gain $200 and a 50-percent chance to gain nothing

Nearly three-quarters of those who are presented with this problem say they would take the sure $100. They don't want to gamble; they are risk averse. But now consider the following, only slightly different, problem:

You are first given $500 and then you must choose between:

- a sure loss of $100 or
- a 50-percent chance to lose nothing and a 50-percent chance to lose $200

In this case, nearly two-thirds say they would take the gamble. They are risk seeking. This result is quite interesting, because if you look closely at both pairs of options, you'll notice they are objectively identical. In each problem, you must choose between having a final outcome of $400 for sure or a 50-percent chance of $500 and a 50-percent chance of $300. But one version forces you to think of the choice as being between two possible gains and the other as being between two possible losses. When choosing between possible gains, most people prefer the sure thing over a risky chance of a bigger prize.

This **risk aversion** when it comes to gains is due to what economists call diminishing marginal utility—that is, the more dollars you already own, the less utility you get from each additional dollar you receive. So, in this case, a gain of $100 is experienced as more than half as valuable as a gain of $200, so why gamble to get $200? Now consider the flip side: because diminishing marginal utility works for losses as well, people tend to be **risk seeking** when it comes to choosing between a sure loss of $100 and a risky chance to lose nothing or lose $200. A loss of $100 is more than half as painful as a loss of $200, so why not gamble on the possibility of avoiding a loss altogether?

The Sunk Cost Fallacy

Suppose that 6 months in advance, you paid $800 for airfare and lodging for a beach vacation with friends over spring break. Over those 6 months, however, you've had a falling out with two of your friends and you find it unpleasant to be around them. As the trip draws near, you're also not feeling well and you're at

risk aversion The reluctance to pursue an uncertain option with an average payoff that equals or exceeds the payoff attainable by another, certain option; the opposite of risk seeking.

risk seeking The tendency to forgo a guaranteed outcome in favor of a risky option; the opposite of risk aversion.

The Intensity of Possible Losses

In a study of loss aversion and framing, Tversky and Kahneman (1981) had one group of participants imagine that the United States is preparing for the outbreak of a rare disease expected to kill 600 people. Two alternative programs to combat the disease have been proposed:

- If program A is adopted, 200 people will be saved.
- If program B is adopted, there is a one-third probability that 600 people will be saved and a two-thirds probability that no one will be saved.

Among these participants, 72 percent preferred program A, the "safe" option. Saving 200 "for sure" is more appealing than trying to save all 600 lives at the risk of saving none.

Another group of participants was given the same introduction as before, but with the following options:

- If program C is adopted, 400 people will die.
- If program D is adopted, there is a one-third probability that nobody will die and a two-thirds probability that 600 people will die.

Of these participants, 78 percent preferred program D, the risky option. A one-third probability that no one will die is preferable to the certain death of 400 people. Note, however, that program A in the first version is identical to program C in the second version (200 people saved is equivalent to 400 people who die). Similarly, program B is identical to program D (a one-third probability that 600 people will be saved is equivalent to a one-third probability that nobody will die).

Chances are you found yourself thinking you'd make the same choice as the majority in each case. The first one, in fact, probably seemed like a no-brainer. If you can save 200 lives, better do it. End of story. In fact, as demonstrated in another study, when people in a brain scanner (fMRI machine) are choosing this option, their pattern of brain activity shows just how easy the choice is (Gonzalez, Dana, Koshino, & Just, 2005). When considering the sure gain, there is very little activity in the intraparietal sulcus, a region associated with imagining hypothetical events and their outcomes (**Figure A2.1**, top left). But when these participants consider the risky gain—trying to save all 600 lives at the risk of saving no one—the activity in the intraparietal sulcus is intense (Figure A2.1, top right). Most of us make the easy choice, the one less fraught with uncertainty and agitation.

But look what happens when participants think about losses. As the bottom of Figure A2.1 indicates, there is considerable activity in the intraparietal sulcus when they consider the smaller, certain loss or the larger, uncertain loss. Here the decision is more difficult and more stressful. They don't want to accept 400 deaths, but they also don't want to risk having 600 people die. For most people, the decision is resolved, and made easier, by seizing on the fact that a chance that no one will die feels better than the certainty that most of them will die.

These brain activation patterns show the neural foundation of both loss aversion (greater activity when considering losses rather than gains) and framing (outcomes described as gains yield a very different pattern of activity than identical outcomes described as losses).

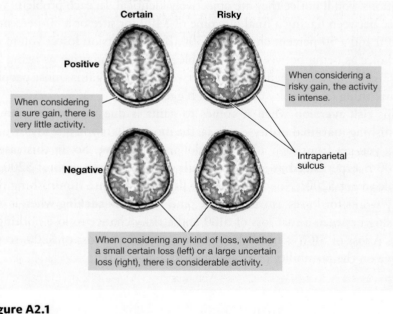

Certain   **Risky**

Positive

When considering a sure gain, there is very little activity.

When considering a risky gain, the activity is intense.

Intraparietal sulcus

Negative

When considering any kind of loss, whether a small certain loss (left) or a large uncertain loss (right), there is considerable activity.

Figure A2.1

The Neural Underpinnings of Loss Aversion

This study examined the brain activity that occurs when people consider sure and risky gains and losses.

SOURCE: Adapted from Gonzalez et al., 2005.

risk of slipping seriously behind in your coursework. Would you still go on the vacation, or would you stay home, get well, and take care of your studies?

Now suppose everything's the same, except that you won the airfare and lodging in a raffle. Would you still go on the trip?

Most people say they'd be much more likely to take the trip if they had paid for it than if they'd won it in a raffle. This is the **sunk cost fallacy**, a reluctance to "waste" money that leads people to look backward rather than forward when making decisions (loss aversion rearing its head again). In this case, whether the vacation was free or paid for makes no difference in whether it will be rewarding to go. If you paid in advance, you won't be getting the money back whether you go or not. The key question, in both scenarios, is whether your overall welfare, or utility, will be advanced more by staying home or by going on vacation. Rationally, historical costs should not factor into the decision. Only the future costs and benefits of different options should be weighed when deciding between them.

As this example illustrates, however, people are not always entirely rational. Most of us pay a great deal of attention to historical costs. Consider a study in which people interested in a season-ticket subscription to a campus theatrical program were randomly assigned to one of three groups (Arkes & Blumer, 1985). One group paid the regular ticket price ($15), another group was given a $2 discount on each ticket, and a third group received a $7 discount on each ticket. The investigators kept track of how often people in each group actually attended the theater after paying for all their tickets up front. Those who paid the most (regular ticket price) went to the theater more often than those who paid a bit less ($2 discount), and they, in turn, attended more often than those who paid even less ($7 discount). The more people paid for their tickets, the greater their sunk costs, and the more importance they attached to seeing the plays. A similar effect occurs in the area of health care and medicine. People benefit more from an inert pill—a placebo—the more they paid for it (Waber, Shiv, Carmon, & Ariely, 2008).

To drive home how irrational and yet how compelling the sunk cost fallacy is, Arkes and Blumer (1985) presented people with the following hypothetical scenario:

> On your way home you buy a TV dinner on sale for $3 at the local grocery store. A few hours later you decide it is time for dinner, so you get ready to put the TV dinner in the oven. Then you get an idea. You call up your friend to ask if he would like to come over for a quick TV dinner and then watch a good movie on TV. Your friend says sure. You go out to buy a second TV dinner. However, all the on-sale TV dinners are gone. You therefore have to spend $5 (the regular price) for the TV dinner identical to the one you just bought for $3. You go home and put both dinners in the oven. When the two dinners are fully cooked, you get a phone call. Your friend is ill and cannot come. You are not hungry enough to eat both dinners. You cannot freeze one. You must eat one and discard the other. Which one do you eat? (pp. 132–133)

Not surprisingly, most participants in this study expressed no preference. After all, everything is the same regardless of which TV dinner they eat; they'll have paid $8 and eaten one dinner. But a substantial minority said they would eat the $5 dinner, and only two said they'd eat the $3 dinner. Because of the sunk cost fallacy, throwing out the $5 dinner seems more wasteful than throwing out (the same) $3 dinner—even though, rationally, it is not.

sunk cost fallacy A reluctance to "waste" money that leads people to continue with an endeavor, whether it serves their future interests or not, because they have already invested money, effort, or time in it.

Mental Accounting

Suppose you decide to take a trip during spring break, and you go to the Bahamas, where there is casino gambling. You've allotted yourself $100 to gamble, and you sit down to play blackjack. How careful would you be with your bets? (Fairly careful, we hope.) Luck is with you, and soon you're ahead $100. You take your original $100 stake and put it in your pocket, and at this point you're going to limit yourself to playing with just the $100 you've won. How careful would you now be with your bets?

Many people report they would be more conservative initially when betting with their own money, but bolder when betting with the "house money." This scenario highlights another principle in behavioral economics known as **mental accounting**, the tendency to treat money differently depending on how it was acquired and the mental category to which it's attached. Note that the $100 a player wins at the casino is truly "her" money and should be treated every bit as seriously as the rest of her money. But when she thinks of it as "house money," it becomes much easier to treat frivolously. Easy come, easy go. (A casino never treats the money it receives from a player as "patron's money"; it's theirs the second the player loses it.)

The influence of mental accounting can also be seen in a thought experiment adapted from Richard Thaler (1980), one of the founders of behavioral economics. Imagine you've bought a $200 ticket to see a play, a sporting event, or a rock concert. As you approach the entrance, you realize you've lost your ticket. You can, however, fork over another $200 and get another ticket. Would you do so? Many people say they would not, on the grounds that $400 is too much to see a play, a sporting event, or a concert.

Now imagine a slightly different scenario. You have reserved a ticket and will pay the $200 when you arrive. But as you approach the entrance, you realize you've lost $200 somewhere in the parking lot. You still have enough money to buy your ticket to the event. Would you do so? In this case, most people say, "Of course. I want to see the event, it's worth $200 to me, and I have the money."

Notice that these two scenarios don't differ in any meaningful way. In both cases, the decision you face is the same. You're $200 poorer than you were a moment ago, and you have to decide whether it's worth it to pay $200 to attend—and you have the money to do so. Rationally, then, you should make the same choice in the two circumstances. But that's not what most people do. In one case, the lost $200 is mentally charged to the cost of the event, making it seem too steep at $400. In the other case, the lost $200 is mentally charged to some other "accident" or "general expenses" account, keeping the psychological cost of the ticket the same as it was originally—$200.

To make the best use of their money, economists advise people to integrate all their assets and liabilities into one overall account. But people nevertheless set up different mental accounts all the time, with rather peculiar—and important—implications for how they spend and invest the money they receive. For example, an economist at the Bank of Israel examined the economic behavior of a group of Israelis who were receiving regular payments from the German government as restitution for war crimes during World War II (Landsberger, 1966). Some of them received relatively large payments; others received relatively modest payments (depending on their family's financial situation back in Nazi Germany).

What he found was a striking example of mental accounting. Those who received the largest sums treated the money very seriously, spending relatively little and saving a lot. On average, they spent 23 cents of every dollar they received from the German government. Those who received smaller sums treated the money less seriously, spending a lot and saving little. In fact, these individuals spent $2 for every dollar they received in restitution money! Because the sums weren't large, they mentally assigned the money to some sort of "slush fund" or "every-day expense" account and spent it as quickly as spending opportunities arose. Those who received the larger payments mentally assigned the money to a more serious "asset" or "savings" account and therefore were reluctant to use it for more frivolous purposes.

This mistake comes in many guises. A friend of one of the authors was constantly getting parking tickets. She justified this expense by saying she didn't eat out at lunchtime, so she had a little nest egg to spend to avoid the trouble of rushing out to the parking meter in the middle of work. The parking tickets were "charged" to an entirely mental account funded by her thrifty lunchtime habits.

Consider the implications of this sort of mental accounting for national economic policy. On several occasions in the past few decades, the U.S. government has tried to stimulate the economy by giving people tax rebates. In 2001, for example, the government gave out $38 billion to taxpayers in the form of rebates of $300–$600; in 2008, the government gave $600–$1,200 in rebates. The rationale behind the rebate program is that people will spend more if they have more money to spend. Although this reasoning is true on some level, it seems that it's not as true as government officials hope. Neither the 2001 nor the 2008 rebate program was as successful as policy makers expected, and the culprit seems to have been mental accounting. By describing the money given out to taxpayers as "rebates," recipients were encouraged to think of it as their own money being returned to them. They thus treated it very seriously and put quite a bit of it in the bank. Given what we know about mental accounting, the government would have been better off labeling the payments "tax bonuses."

Such a simple change in wording has been shown to influence spending rather dramatically. In a study conducted at Harvard University, participants who showed up for an experiment were given, unexpectedly, a $50 check (Epley, Mak, & Idson, 2006). They were told it was from the investigator's research budget, which was financed by tuition dollars. The investigators described the check to some participants as a "rebate." Others were told it was a "bonus." A week later they asked the participants what they had done with the money. As **Figure A2.2** shows, those who'd received a "rebate" reported spending less than half as much ($9.55) as those who'd received a "bonus" ($22.04). The same effect was observed in a follow-up experiment in which participants could purchase items from a "Harvard lab store" on their way out. Those who'd received their money as a rebate spent substantially less of it than those whose money was described as a bonus.

Thus, the terminology people use to describe their money leads them to assign it to more serious or less serious mental accounts, with pronounced effects on their spending. As one of the authors of these studies put it, "Getting a rebate is more like being reimbursed for travel expenses than like getting a year-end bonus. Reimbursements send people on trips to the bank. Bonuses send people on trips to the Bahamas" (Epley, 2008, p. A27).

"The only way not to think about money is to have a great deal of it."

—EDITH WHARTON

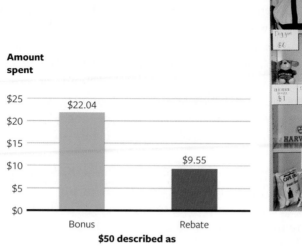

Amount
spent

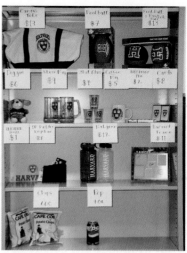

Figure A2.2

Mental Accounting

Participants in this study spent more of the money they received from the experimenter when it was described as a bonus rather than a rebate. The photo shows the lab store.

SOURCE: Adapted from Epley et al., 2006.

Decision Paralysis

Suppose you go to the grocery store to buy a pint of gourmet ice cream. Would you rather shop at a store that offers 45 flavors from 5 different vendors or a store with 18 flavors from 2 different vendors? It's a no-brainer, right? It's better to have more options so you can maximize your chances of getting *exactly* what you want. To economists, certainly, it's always better to have more options.

But psychologically, it's another story. Making decisions is hard, and we aren't equipped to deal with an abundance of choices all the time. With so many options, we can find ourselves suffering from decision paralysis, unable to decide which option to choose. Consider a study conducted in an upscale grocery store (Iyengar & Lepper, 2000). Catering to the local elite, the store offers its customers over 300 types of jams, 250 different mustards, and 75 varieties of olive oil. The store permitted two social psychologists to set up a tasting booth where they displayed a selection of jams. By rotating the selection every hour, they displayed 6 jams half the time and 24 jams the other half of the time. Shoppers who stopped by the booth were given a coupon for $1 off any jam purchased in the store. A bar code on the coupon tracked whether someone making a purchase had selected the jam when 6 items or 24 items were on display. The researchers were interested in whether shoppers would be stymied by more options—24 jams—unable to decide what to buy and hence less likely to make a purchase. They found that although many more people visited the booth when it had the large assortment of jams, ten times as many customers actually bought a jar when they examined the smaller set of choices. Having a large assortment looks good and draws a lot of customers, but it makes deciding hard—so hard, in fact, that many people never decide at all.

Failing to make a decision, however, is still a decision—often a costly one. To see how costly, consider the decision new employees must make in choosing whether and how to participate in their company's retirement plan. In the past, there was just *the* company retirement plan. No decision necessary. But in today's

The Effect of a Large or Small Choice Set

To examine the effect of the number of choices available on buying decisions, the researchers in this study (Iyengar & Lepper, 2000) displayed, at different times, (A) a small selection of 6 jams or (B) a large selection of 24 jams. A bar code tracking system enabled them to assess whether customers were more likely to make a purchase from a small choice set or a large one.

world, employees have to choose which 401(k) plan is best. In these plans, part of the employee's salary is invested in a stock, bond, or money market fund, often with the employer matching, dollar for dollar, what the employee contributes up to a certain amount (say, 5 percent of the employee's salary). For example, if you make $50,000 you might have $2,500 taken out of your paychecks over the year and invested in one of your company's 401(k) funds; your employer would then kick in an additional $2,500. Because of the employer match, it doesn't make economic sense not to participate. Failing to participate leaves "money on the table."

Employees have a bewildering array of funds in which to invest, and picking a fund, or the right mix of funds, can be daunting. Many people become overwhelmed, telling themselves, "I'll decide later." But many never do, depriving themselves of the "free money" that comes with the employer's match and severely hurting their long-term financial profile. The scope of the problem is shown in **Figure A2.3**, which depicts the percentage of employees in different

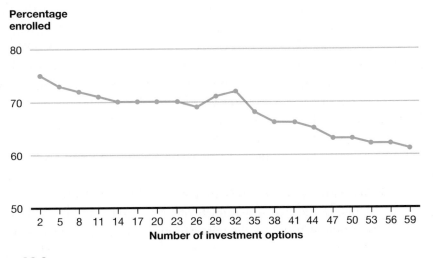

Figure A2.3

Overwhelmed by Choice

This study demonstrated that the larger the number of investment options for retirement plans, the harder it was for employees to make a decision to enroll.

SOURCE: Adapted from Sethi-Iyengar et al., 2004.

firms who enroll in their company's 401(k) plans as a function of how many plans the companies offer (Sethi-Iyengar, Huberman, & Jiang, 2004). As you can see, the more plans that are offered, the harder the choice becomes—so hard, in fact, that many people avoid making it, at considerable cost to their financial future. Sometimes having more options is not such a good thing.

Can anything be done to deal with this problem of decision paralysis when it comes to underenrollment in employee retirement plans? Behavioral economists have pointed to the powerful influence of defaults, or what happens if no action is taken. In this case, the usual default is that the employee is not enrolled in a savings plan. But an increasing number of companies have taken to switching the default; employees who do not make a decision are automatically enrolled in a 401(k) plan, usually one with a conservative investment strategy. Such policies have been a resounding success, leading to greater savings on the part of a substantial segment of the workforce at companies that have them (Beshears, Choi, Laibson, & Madrian, 2008).

A final example, one relevant to life on a college campus, should drive the point home even further. Researchers offered students $5 to complete a long questionnaire (Tversky & Shafir, 1992). Some were given 5 days to complete it, others were given 3 weeks, and a third group had no deadline. Of those who had only 5 days, 60 percent returned it on time versus 42 percent of those who had 3 weeks. And only 25 percent of those without a deadline ever returned it at all! Does this situation ring a bell? If so, you might consider asking your professors to set tight deadlines for all assignments. It seems that the more time we have to complete a task, the less pressure we feel to get started, so we often fail to get started at all.

Getting Started on Your Own Financial Planning

All the biases we've discussed in this module can lead you to make less than ideal decisions when you shop, save, borrow, and invest. What can you do about it? What should you keep in mind as you plan your own financial future? What can you do *now* to optimize your chances of being financially secure later in life? Five simple guidelines—call them the Five Pillars of Financial Wisdom—will improve anyone's financial prospects, regardless of their current economic situation.

Start Early

The key to having sufficient savings later in life is to start saving as soon as possible. The earlier you invest, the more the miracle of compound interest works in your favor. Belsky and Gilovich (1999) illustrate this idea with the following example:

> Meet Jill and John, 21-year-old twins who just graduated from college. Jill, immediately upon entering the workforce, began contributing $50 a month to a stock mutual fund and continued to do so for the next eight years, until she got married and found more pressing uses for her money. John, who married his college sweetheart immediately upon

graduating and soon after started a family, didn't start investing until he was 29. Still, he too contributed $50 a month to the same stock fund, but he continued doing so for 37 years until he retired at age 65. All told, John invested $22,200, while Jill contributed just $4,800. At age 65, which of the two siblings had the most money, assuming they earned an average of 10 percent a year? (p. 121)

The amazing result is that Jill, who invested just $4,800, ends up with more money ($256,650) than her brother John ($217,830), even though he invested over four times as much. If you get a late start on saving, it's hard to catch up. Let the math (compound interest) work for you, not against you.

Diversify

You have lived through two of the biggest boom-and-bust events in U.S. economic history—the stock market dive in 2001 and the collapse of the real estate market in 2008. Both episodes point to the difficulty of knowing when a particular class of investments is likely to do well or poorly, making you richer or poorer. But different assets—stocks, bonds, real estate, currency, even precious metals like gold—tend not to rise or fall in sync, so owning something in each class is a good way to protect your savings. A diversified portfolio of investments is less likely to suffer a wrenching decline even during historic busts like those of 2001 and 2008.

Invest in Mutual Funds

Of course, you probably don't have the financial resources to be able to buy a diverse group of stocks or an assortment of bonds, let alone property. But you don't have to. You can start by buying small pieces of each of these assets by purchasing shares in mutual funds. Mutual funds pool your money with that of other investors to buy stocks in a broad range of companies. Because of this variety and range, a mutual fund provides quite a bit of diversification on its own. You can also purchase mutual funds that invest in bonds or in combinations of different assets to further diversify your investments.

Mutual funds charge investors different fees for investing your money, and you should look for the ones with very low fees. Predicting market performance—which most mutual fund managers must do—is very difficult, and fund managers who do well one year often fail to do so the next. Therefore, paying the high fees that are often charged by "hot" funds with celebrity fund managers are typically not worth the extra expense. Index funds don't try to outfox the market; instead, they merely invest in a broad portfolio of stocks that mirror the market as a whole. Because they are not managed so actively, they typically have the lowest fees and hence represent particularly good investments.

Set Up a Payroll Deduction Plan

Once you get a job and start receiving a regular paycheck, you can enroll in a payroll deduction plan; it invests a portion of your wages, without your seeing the money first, into a savings account or a stock, bond, or money market mutual fund. Setting aside the money at the outset is much better than trying to do the saving and investing yourself. If you get your paycheck and then try to put some of it away for savings, the amount you save will feel like a loss of income. Instead, if it's automatically invested before you see your paycheck, the investment feels instead like a forgone gain—which, as discussed earlier, is easier to accept than an outright loss. If your employer matches your payroll deductions with an additional payment by the company, you should take the maximum allowable deduction. To do otherwise is to leave money on the table.

Pay Off Credit Card Debt

Many people have money in a savings account but don't use it to pay off the balance on their credit cards. It might sound reasonable ("I need some money stashed away for emergencies"), but it's not. Savings accounts earn very low interest (typically less than 2 percent as of this writing), but an unpaid credit card balance accrues hefty interest (a percentage often in the mid-teens). The difference between the two rates is money going out the door—from you to the credit card companies. If you don't pay off your credit cards, you're fighting the power of compound interest when you want it working for you. By all means you should be saving money, but not at the expense of absorbing the punishing interest charges on an unpaid credit card balance. If dipping into your savings still makes you nervous, note that those same credit card companies that want you to keep a balance on your card will be perfectly happy to lend you money should an emergency arise. And once you pay off your credit card, *then* you can start to put away money for emergencies.

Module Review

Online Study Materials

INQUIZITIVE   EBOOK

SUMMARY

Behavioral Economics and Financial Markets

- *Behavioral economics* is the effort by psychologists and economists to create more realistic economic models that take into account people's occasional irrationality when making financial decisions.
- Examples of irrationality can be found in the tendency of the stock market to go up on sunny days and down on cloudy days, and to go up in a country whose national sports team wins and down when it loses.

Loss Aversion

- *Loss aversion* is the tendency for a loss of a certain size to have more psychological impact than an equivalent gain.
- People tend to be *risk averse* for possible gains and *risk seeking* for possible losses. Framing choices as losses versus gains therefore yields irrationally inconsistent patterns of choice.
- People are susceptible to the *sunk cost fallacy*, being inclined to consume something (such as going to a play or a sporting event), even when it no longer has positive value to them, in order to be "economical" and not "waste" the money already paid for the item.

Mental Accounting

- *Mental accounting* is a tendency to treat money differently depending on how it is acquired and the mental category to which it is attached.
- People keep separate mental accounts when they would be better off integrating all their assets and liabilities in one overall mental category or account.

Decision Paralysis

- Having a great many choices can result in decision paralysis; the more options there are, the harder it can be to make any decision at all.

Getting Started on Your Own Financial Planning

- Five guidelines about handling money can have a big impact on anyone's financial security: save early and often, diversify, invest in mutual funds rather than specific stocks or bonds, set up a payroll deduction plan, and pay off credit card balances and avoid paying their high interest rates.

THINK ABOUT IT

1. Traditional economic models and theories were founded on the notion that people are rational in their economic decision making. However, research from the relatively new field of behavioral economics suggests that this assumption is not always valid. Describe at least three pieces of evidence presented in this module that supports the behavioral economists' assertion.

2. Jacob has racked up some serious credit card debt and decides to allocate $250 from his monthly paycheck to paying off the money he owes. For his birthday, Jacob's grandparents send him a check for $100. He has the opportunity to cut down on the interest he's paying to the credit card company if he puts the money toward paying off his bill. As the $100 was a gift, however, Jacob construes it as spending money and uses it to buy a new phone. Describe a behavioral economics principle that applies to Jacob's decision regarding how to spend the $100.

THE ANSWER GUIDELINES FOR THE THINK ABOUT IT QUESTIONS CAN BE FOUND AT THE BACK OF THE BOOK . . .

Social Psychology and Education

Overheard in Palo Alto, California: one European-American high school senior said to another, upon hearing of her friend's super-high SAT scores, "Good grief, Jessica, those scores are positively Asian."

On average, the academic achievements of Asian-American students are undeniably impressive, and Asians regularly outperform Americans in math and science. Why do you suppose that's true? What could be done to help European-American and African-American students perform at Asian levels? Or do you think such a thing is highly unlikely or impossible?

Social psychologists have studied why some students perform better in school than others. More important, they have investigated ways in which the findings of social psychologists might improve educational outcomes, especially for certain minority students, who often perform below their capacity.

Social psychology has provided excellent tools for improving the critical thinking skills of everyone—and these can be sharpened both by certain kinds of educational experiences and even by interventions that are remarkably brief but effective.

Pygmalion in the Classroom

How much influence does a teacher have on the academic progress of students? The idea that one person can transform another—even create an extraordinary person from ordinary raw material—has been a theme of literature going back to Greek mythology. A sculptor named Pygmalion made a statue so beautiful

that he fell in love with it, and with the help of the goddess Venus he brought it to life. A more recent version of the myth is the musical *My Fair Lady*, about an eccentric English phonetics professor who coaches a lowly flower girl in manners and accent, helping her pass for a lady in British high society.

Robert Rosenthal and Lenore Jacobson published a 1968 study, called *Pygmalion in the Classroom*, examining the effect of teacher expectations on the intellectual development and achievement of students. The study caused an uproar in the fields of both psychology and education. All students in a particular school took an IQ test. Allegedly on the basis of the test, the researchers told the teachers at the beginning of the school year that some of their students were "late bloomers"—that is, they were expected to show substantial IQ growth over the course of the year. About 20 percent of the children in each classroom were designated—ostensibly on the basis of the test, but in fact by random assignment—as being late bloomers. The investigators reported that the designated late bloomers made substantial IQ gains during a brief time period. The gains for young children were shockingly high—15 points for first-graders and 10 points for second-graders. These increases seemed to indicate that teachers' expectations for children operated as a powerful self-fulfilling prophecy: if the teacher believed the child was going to gain in intelligence, the teacher behaved toward the child in a way that such a gain would occur. An additional, and quite unnerving, finding was that the children in the control group who showed unexpected achievement gains were rated by the teacher as less interesting, less affectionate, and not as well adjusted (Rosenthal & Jacobson, 1968).

Education critics argued that the results showed that teacher bias, presumably in favor of white middle-class children, was a significant reason these children performed better in school and scored higher on IQ tests. Conversely, the scores of African-American, Hispanic-American, and children of lower socioeconomic status (SES) were being pulled down because of teachers' negative expectations for them.

The furor over the 1968 Rosenthal and Jacobson experiment persists to this day. Claims range from outright accusations of fraud to allegations that the results were an underestimate of what goes on in the classroom all the time. Lee Jussim and Kent Harber (2005) reviewed the almost 400 studies conducted in the first 35 years after the initial report and found several important patterns. (1) The extremely large effects Rosenthal and Jacobson found proved to be exceptional; subsequent investigators almost never found such large effects. (2) When expectations are manipulated, it's clear that teacher expectations sometimes do affect student IQ and academic performance. (If expectations are not manipulated, a correlation between teacher expectation and student performance could be due to accuracy on the teacher's part. Children who are believed to be—and are—more talented do better in school.) (3) Teacher expectation effects are rarely very strong; about three IQ points is typical, and often the effects of teacher expectations are literally zero. (4) Teacher expectation effects occur only if expectations are manipulated early in the school year, within the first 2 weeks. (5) Teacher expectation effects are greater for first-graders and second-graders than for older children. (6) Most important, teacher expectation effects can be genuinely large for low-achieving, lower-SES children and for African-American children.

In light of these findings a modified version of the original claims appears to be the correct one: a teacher's belief that lower-achieving, lower-SES, and African-American students can do well intellectually and academically can enhance the performance of those students.

Intelligence: Thing or Process?

Self-fulfilling prophecies can result not only from teachers' expectations but also from students' beliefs about their own intellectual abilities. Carol Dweck and her colleagues have shown that people have very different views about the nature of intelligence. They have proposed that there two kinds of theories different people hold (Dweck, 2007; Dweck & Leggett, 1988). Some believe intelligence is a malleable quality that can be improved with effort; these researchers call this an **incremental theory of intelligence**. Other people think intelligence is a fixed, predetermined "thing" that people have to one degree or another, and that there is not much they can do to change it; this is the **entity theory of intelligence**.

People who are incremental theorists believe they can increase their intellectual ability, and they attribute failure to lack of effort or to the difficulty of the task (Henderson & Dweck, 1990). As a result, they work more toward goals that will increase their ability, even at the risk of exposing their ignorance, and less toward trying to document their ability. In contrast, people who are entity theorists are less confident that what they do will make them any smarter. They blame their failures on a lack of intellectual ability, and they're inclined to feel

How to Tutor: The Five Cs

Social psychologist Mark Lepper made an intriguing discovery while studying college student tutors of elementary schoolchildren who were having trouble in math. Some tutors had a big—and fast—impact on their pupils. Others had no effect. Lepper then went to work to determine the difference between the effective and the ineffective tutors. Which of the following behaviors do you think would be helpful, and which unhelpful?

1. When a student starts to make even a minor mistake, stop the student immediately to avoid reinforcing the incorrect behavior.

2. If the student makes a mistake, carefully state the rule the student needs to know to successfully solve the problem.

3. Keep the problems simple, to avoid damaging self-esteem.

4. Praise the student often for doing work well.

5. Don't get emotionally involved with the student's difficulties, since this could create a dependent stance on the part of the student.

Actually, all these approaches are unhelpful and are avoided by effective tutors. They violate one or more of the strategies that characterize the successful tutor. Lepper and his colleagues offer Five Cs for effective tutoring (Lepper & Woolverton, 2001; Lepper, Woolverton, Mumme, & Gurtner, 1993):

1. Control. Foster a sense of control in the student, making the student feel she has command of the material.

2. Challenge. Challenge the student—but at a level of difficulty that's within the student's range of capability.

3. Confidence. Instill confidence by maximizing the student's success (expressing confidence by assuring the student the problem he or she just solved was a difficult one) and by minimizing failure (providing excuses for mistakes and emphasizing the part of the problem the student got right).

4. Curiosity. Encourage curiosity through Socratic methods (asking leading questions) and by linking the problem to other problems the student

has seen that appear on the surface to be different.

5. Contextualize. Place the problem in a real-world context, or in a context from a movie or TV show.

Expert tutors have a number of strategies that set them apart. They don't bother to correct minor errors like forgetting to write down a plus sign. If the student is about to make a mistake, they gently suggest a problem-solving path that would prevent it from occurring. Or sometimes they let the student make the mistake when they think it can provide a valuable learning experience. They never dumb down the material for the sake of self-esteem, but instead change the way they present it. Most of what good tutors do is ask questions. They ask students to explain their reasoning. They ask leading questions. They're actually less likely to give *positive* feedback than ineffective tutors are, because, Lepper theorizes, doing so makes the tutoring session feel too evaluative. And finally, expert tutors are always nurturing and empathetic.

they can do little to improve because they just don't have what it takes. Entity theorists also tend to choose tasks that seem likely to demonstrate positive views of their intellectual ability, but which provide no opportunity to learn something new. It should be clear which attitude would tend to result in increased intellectual skills, as well as improved self-esteem.

Henderson and Dweck (1990) found that students entering junior high school who were incremental theorists ended up getting better grades than students who were entity theorists. Moreover, incremental theorists got better grades regardless of prior academic achievement; whether they had a history of good or poor grades in elementary school, they got better grades in junior high if they believed their ability was under their control. In another study, researchers found that students who were about equal in their math performance at the beginning of junior high progressively increased their math grades over the course of 2 years in high school if they were incremental theorists, but tended not to improve their grades if they were entity theorists (Blackwell, Trzesniewski, & Dweck, 2007).

But who is right—the entity theorist or the incremental theorist? Neither—or rather, both. If you're an entity theorist, your intellectual skills probably won't improve as much as they could. So you're right: you don't believe your ability is under your control, so in fact it doesn't improve much, and your genes actually exert a greater influence on your ability than they would if you believed otherwise. On the other hand, if you're an incremental theorist, you're also right: you believe your ability is under your control and you act accordingly, thereby building on your genetic strengths and increasing your ability (Nisbett, 2009).

Culture and Achievement

Why do Asians—especially Chinese, Japanese, and Koreans and their Asian-American counterparts—tend to show above-average performance on academic tasks? Are they intrinsically smarter than people of European culture? Does something about their genes lead to intellectual superiority?

In fact, there is no good evidence that people of Asian heritage have a genetic advantage over Americans of Western origin. Cross-cultural comparisons of Asians with Westerners find no evidence that Asians have higher IQs, though admittedly it can be difficult to compare IQs across different cultures and languages (Flynn, 1991; Nisbett, 2009). A comparison of the IQs of children starting first grade in Minneapolis, Sendai (Japan), and in Taipei (Taiwan) found that the American children had slightly higher IQs than either group of Asian children (Stevenson et al., 1990). Considering the socialization practices of Asians and Americans, this finding shouldn't be surprising: Asians focus on social and emotional growth during the early years, and Americans, especially middle-class and upper-middle-class Americans, are more likely to focus on intellectual skills (Stevenson et al., 1990). By fifth grade, the IQ differences were gone, but the Asian children were far ahead of the Americans in math—partly a result of better teaching of math and longer school years in the Asian countries (Stevenson & Stigler, 1992), but also from the Asian children working harder at math (Stevenson & Lee, 1996). Asian (and Asian-American) students study many more hours a week on average than European-Americans do.

The best evidence available on the IQ differences between Asian-Americans and European-Americans comes from a massive study of the high school seniors of the class of 1966 (Flynn, 1991). Almost all these students were Americans, though some were first-generation Americans. The IQs of the Asian-Americans were trivially lower than those of the European-Americans—not surprising, given that many of them came from homes where English was not the native language. However, Asian-Americans' SAT scores were substantially higher. SAT scores, of course, are partly a reflection of the kinds of skills measured by IQ tests, and partly a reflection of work students have done. Even more striking, when the study participants were adults, fully 55 percent of the Chinese-Americans, the largest group of the Asian-Americans, ended up in professional, technical, or managerial positions. Only a third of European-Americans ended up in those jobs. The Asian-Americans capitalized on their ability to a far greater extent than the European-Americans.

"If there is no dark and dogged will, there will be no shining accomplishment; if there is no dull and determined effort, there will be no brilliant achievement."

—CHINESE SAYING

Confucius and Theories about Ability

Asian-Americans whose forebears came from the "Confucian cultures," such as China, Japan, and Korea, achieve at levels higher than predicted from their ability scores. Such outcomes could be expected based on ancient theories about talent. The Chinese teacher and philosopher Confucius—the founding father of modern East Asian cultures—said that although some of our ability is a gift from heaven, most of it is due to hard work. For 2,000 years, it was possible for a young person to go from being a poor peasant to being the highest magistrate in China by dint of study and hard work. In no other country until modern times has there been that degree of social mobility. It's no surprise that East Asians, and Americans who spring from that region, are devout incremental theorists. They believe, much more than European-Americans, that intellectual achievement is mostly a matter of hard work (Chen & Stevenson, 1995; Choi, Nisbett, & Norenzayan, 1999; Heine et al., 2001; Holloway, 1988; Stevenson et al., 1990). When Japanese and Canadians were told they had either succeeded or failed on a task that presumably measured creativity, the Canadians worked longer on a similar task if they had succeeded on the first one, thereby continuing to regard themselves as good at the task. The Japanese worked longer if they had failed, thus extending their abilities (Heine et al., 2001).

Confucius

Blocking Stereotype Threat in the Classroom

Other minority groups, such as African-Americans and Hispanic-Americans, have lower average IQ scores and lower academic achievement than either Asian-Americans or European-Americans. There are numerous social reasons for these differences. Most of these factors are in flux, however, and in recent years the IQ and achievement gaps have begun to lessen substantially (Nisbett, 2009).

To explore one of the factors suppressing academic success, Claude Steele and Joshua Aronson demonstrated that women and minorities often perform more poorly on ability tests because of stereotype threat, the fear of confirming stereotypes about the abilities of their group (see Chapter 11). With Catherine Good and Michael Inzlicht, Aronson decided to see what would happen if poor minority students could be convinced that their abilities were under their control. They performed an intervention with poor Hispanic-American students in Texas (Good, Aronson, & Inzlicht, 2003). All students in the study were assigned college student mentors. Experimental group mentors told their charges that intelligence was changeable and substantially under their control, and taught them how the brain can make new connections throughout life. A website reinforced the mentors' message. It showed pictures of the brain, including how neurons make new connections with one another, reflecting the learning that takes place when a person solves new problems. The mentors also helped the students design their own web pages, using their own words and pictures, which reinforced the message of the malleability of intelligence. Control group mentors gave the students cautionary information about drugs and encouraged them to avoid taking them.

The experimental intervention had a very large effect. On a statewide academic achievement test, the boys in the experimental group scored much higher in math than those in the control group. For the girls, who tend to worry that, because of their gender, they're naturally less talented in math, the difference was even greater. In tests of reading skills, both boys and girls in the experimental group did substantially better than students in the control group. The intervention worked by blocking, to a degree, the inhibitory effects of stereotype threat. For example, students spent less time making sure arithmetic calculations were correct—not the best use of time, though a way to avoid seeming they were utterly lacking in math ability.

Dweck and her colleagues performed a similar intervention with poor African-American and Latino seventh-grade students in New York City (Blackwell, Trzeniewski, & Dweck, 2007). As in the Texas project, the investigators presented convincing demonstrations of the changes in knowledge and intelligence that are produced by work and study. They taught them psychological theories about learning, showed changes in neurotransmission with learning, and showed them the kind of study skills that would be most likely to increase their knowledge and intelligence. Junior high is a difficult time for many students, but it seems to be particularly hard for disadvantaged minority children. The math performance of control students in the study grew worse as junior high school went on, but that didn't happen for students in the experimental group. They had held entity beliefs about intelligence and initially thought they were doomed to poor performance because they were incorrigibly unintelligent. Simply being made to believe their intelligence was under their control had a significant impact on their academic performance.

Daphna Oyserman and her colleagues carried out a different intervention with poor African-American junior high students in Detroit (Oyserman, Bybee, & Terry, 2006). They asked the students to think about what kind of future they wanted to have, what difficulties they might have along the way, how they could deal with those problems, and which of their friends would be most helpful. The researchers supplemented these sessions by having students work in small groups on how to respond to everyday problems, manage social difficulties and academic issues, and cope with the process of getting to high school graduation. The intervention had a modest effect on grade point average and on standardized tests, and a very large effect on the likelihood of being held back a grade in school.

A study by Geoffrey Cohen and his colleagues showed that simply having minority students write about their most important values at the beginning of middle school substantially improved their grades over the subsequent years (Cohen, Garcia, Apfel, & Master, 2006). The students were enrolled in a mostly middle-class integrated suburban school. As is often true in such schools, the African-American students in the past had had significantly lower grades than the white students. The African-American students were well aware of this, and the social psychologists who conducted the study assumed these students were subject to worries prompted by stereotype threat. The researchers reasoned that if the students were encouraged to think about their most important values, this self-affirmation in the school context would produce a sense of efficacy and

"Education is not filling a bucket but lighting a fire."

—WILLIAM B. YEATS

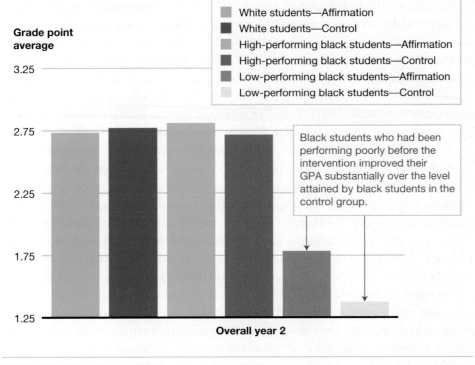

Grade point average

Legend:
- White students—Affirmation
- White students—Control
- High-performing black students—Affirmation
- High-performing black students—Control
- Low-performing black students—Affirmation
- Low-performing black students—Control

Black students who had been performing poorly before the intervention improved their GPA substantially over the level attained by black students in the control group.

3.25
2.75
2.25
1.75
1.25

Overall year 2

SOURCE: Adapted from Cohen et al., 2009.

Figure A3.1
Blocking Stereotype Threat
Mean GPA scores in core courses the year after some students experienced an affirmation intervention (by being asked to write out their most important values). Initially low-performing blacks improved their academic performance if exposed to the intervention.

belongingness. In fact, black students who were exposed to the affirmation intervention performed better over the term than black students in the control group (**Figure A3.1**). In the course in which the intervention took place, the students in the affirmation condition reduced the achievement gap with white students by 40 percent, and their likelihood of getting a D or worse was reduced by half.

Cohen and his colleagues followed the students over the next 2 years and found that the effects of the intervention were fully sustained (Cohen, Garcia, Purdie-Vaughns, Apfel, & Brzustoski, 2009). The likelihood of needing remediation was reduced from 18 percent to 5 percent. Interestingly, the intervention had no effect on black students who had performed well before entering middle school; presumably they were sufficiently confident that the affirmation manipulation was unnecessary. Nor did the affirmation manipulation have any effect on white students, whether previously high-performing or not.

Social Fears and Academic Achievement

Cohen, together with Gregory Walton, explored the effects of other types of concerns on the performance of minority students, this time in a college context (Walton & Cohen, 2007). Most first-year undergraduates worry about social acceptance and fitting in on campus, and this is particularly true for minorities. If they fail to make friends, because of the general lack of minority students and feeling uncomfortable with those from other backgrounds, they may begin to wonder whether they belong there. As a result, their motivation may flag, and their GPAs may suffer as well.

Walton and Cohen reasoned that lagging performance could be reversed if minority students knew that worries about social acceptance are common for all students, regardless of ethnicity, and that their experience was likely to improve in the future (Walton & Cohen, 2007). The researchers performed a modest intervention with black students at a prestigious private university. They invited black and white freshmen to participate in a psychology study at the end of their freshman year. They intended to convince an experimental group that worries about social acceptance were common for students of all ethnicities, but tended to vanish as time went on and they made more friends. The experimenters expected this information would help black students realize that the best way to understand their social difficulties was not in terms of their race ("I guess my kind of people don't really belong at this kind of place") but as part of the student experience common to everyone ("I guess everybody has these kinds of problems"). The researchers believed that recognition of the common problem—and its likely solution—would help keep the students from worrying about belonging, thereby enabling them to focus on academic achievement.

To drive the point home, Walton and Cohen had students in the experimental group write an essay about the likelihood that their social situation would improve in the future. Then they made a videotaped speech allegedly to be shown to new students, so the students could see what college would be like. This standard dissonance manipulation—getting them to say publicly something different from their own views—was intended to enhance the effects of the persuasive communications they had received.

The researchers measured student behavior related to academic achievement over the next week, as well as their GPAs the subsequent semester. The intervention had a large positive effect on blacks but not on whites. In the period after the intervention, blacks reported studying more, making more contacts with professors, and attending more review sessions and study group meetings. The subsequent term, grades of the black students in the experimental group reflected these behaviors: their grades were much higher than those of black students in the control group.

College is also a social challenge for those who are first-generation college students—the first in their working-class families to pursue education beyond high school. The attitudes and values they encounter are typically different from those they're used to in their families and neighborhoods. Working-class people are in general more interdependent than middle- and upper-middle-class people. For students of working-class origin, going to college is not so much an individual achievement as an accomplishment having deep social and interpersonal meaning.

To examine this issue, Nicole Stephens and her colleagues created two different welcome letters for new students (Stephens, Townsend, Markus, & Phillips, 2012). One, modeled on the actual university welcome letter, emphasized independent values such as exploring personal interests, expressing ideas and opinions, and participating in independent research. The other emphasized learning by being part of a community, working with and learning from others, and participating in collaborative research. Then the students were asked to give a 5-minute speech about their college goals. The investigators examined the students' stress levels during the speech by measuring blood cortisol (the stress hormone) and by the emotional content of the speech. The cortisol level of first-generation students who had read the independent welcome letter was greater during the speech than it was for those who had read the interdependent letter, whereas the type of letter had no effect on continuing-generation students. The emotional content of the speech reflected more emotional strain for first-generation students who read the independent letter than for those who read the interdependent letter, whereas the manipulation had no effect on the content of continuing-generation students' speeches. The researchers concluded that there is a mismatch between the values of working-class students and the new college environment—a mismatch that could impair academic performance.

Teaching with Entertainment-Education

Which reality television show depicting young people traveling around the countryside features such contests as how to repel the sexual advances of other young people? And in which states does the show air? You probably don't know. It's *Haath Se Haath Milaa* (*Hand in Hand Together*), and it's broadcast in the states of Rajasthan, Haryana, Delhi, Uttar Pradesh, and Uttaranchal—in India. It's designed to alert young people to the risks of HIV/AIDS, which exists in epidemic proportions in that country. The young people, by the way, travel in separate his-and-hers buses. The program is part of a worldwide network of TV shows collectively called entertainment-education.

Albert Bandura is a learning theorist, a scientist who studies how animals and humans learn connections between events in order to learn which events signal impending rewards and which signal impending punishments. He was one of the first such scientists to approach the question of how people learn appropriate and effective social behavior (Bandura, 1973). A fundamental principle of his theory is that people learn what to approach and what to avoid simply by watching relevant others. They observe other people's behavior and its consequences, and adopt the behaviors that seem to be successful and avoid those that are punished. People who are like themselves are role models for individuals.

The Mexican television producer Miguel Sabido read about Bandura's principles of social learning and decided to create TV shows that would educate people about effective and rewarding social behaviors and persuade them to avoid dangerous and unproductive ones. He produced the original entertainment-education telenovelas (similar to soap operas) in the 1970s and 1980s.

Sabido's telenovelas are yearlong stories that focus on a specific value. Each one presents three types of characters: positive role models, negative role models, and "doubters," those who fall in between (Singhal, Rogers, & Brown, 1993). There are typically four positive role models complemented by four negative role models. There is always a character who approves of the value being promoted (and one who disapproves), one who promotes the value (and one who does not), one who exercises the value (and one who does not), and one who validates the value (and one who does not). There are also three doubters. One of the doubters accepts the value about a third of the way through the series, one about two-thirds of the way through, and one never accepts the value. (The third doubter usually dies a painful death.) In general, those who accept the value are immediately rewarded, and those who don't are punished. Throughout the series, epilogues are inserted in which a famous individual speaks to the audience in order to reinforce the value.

Teaching with Telenovelas
These actors are running through a scene on the set of the Mexican telenovela *Heridas de Amor* (*Wounds of Love*).

These broadcasts clearly have an effect on behavior, although much of the early evidence has to be categorized as anecdotal, coming from Bandura's own account of their success (Bandura, 2004). One early telenovela by Sabido urged viewers to enroll in a literacy program. The day after it first appeared, about 25,000 people descended on the distribution center in downtown Mexico City to obtain their reading materials. The result was a monumental traffic jam in the city. The name of the series was *Ven Conmigo* (*Come With Me*), and in the year it aired, enrollment in literacy classes went up tenfold—from about 90,000 to about 900,000. Another drama, *Acompaname* (*Accompany Me*), emphasized family planning. Those who viewed the program were more inclined to think that having fewer children was likely to have social, economic, and psychological benefits. There was a 32 percent increase in new contraceptive users, and national sales of contraceptives went up markedly.

Sabido's telenovelas have been widely imitated. An Indian drama inspired by Sabido's work promoted female rights and family planning. Amazingly, the enrollment of girls in elementary schools rose from 10 percent to 38 percent during the year the series was broadcast. After a family planning telenovela aired in Kenya, contraception practices changed for people across all socioeconomic levels (Westoff & Rodriguez, 1995).

A radio soap opera designed to combat the spread of HIV in Tanzania spanned 4 years (Vaughn, Rogers, Singhal, & Swalehe, 2000). For the first 2 years the soap opera was not broadcast in a particular region in Tanzania, in order to provide a comparison group. The soap opera resulted in reducing the number of sexual partners and increasing condom use in the parts of Tanzania where the program was broadcast. The mediating factors that seemed to be crucial in producing behavior change were increased self-efficacy, increased communication about HIV, and increased risk awareness. In interviews, listeners said they identified with the characters in the soap opera and tried to emulate them, and this is consistent with social learning theory expectations.

Statistics, Social Science Methodology, and Critical Thinking

Consider the following two problems:

1. David is a high school senior choosing between two colleges. He has friends at both. His friends at college A like it a lot on social and academic grounds. His friends at college B are not as satisfied and are generally unenthusiastic about the college experience. David visits each college for a day. He meets some students at college A who are not very interesting and a professor who gives him a curt brushoff. He meets several students at college B who are lively and intelligent, and a couple of professors take a personal interest in him. Which college do you think he should go to? Why?

2. Medical research has established that drinking a moderate amount of alcohol is associated with a reduced risk of getting cancer or heart disease. Assume you are a teetotaler on economic and moral grounds. Should you start modest tippling?

Problem 1: If you said David should go to college B because he has to choose for himself (not let his friends choose for him), you're in good company with most undergraduates. However, you should also have considered the possibility that although David's samples of the two colleges were based on his own personal experience, the samples were not very large, and the experiences he could expect to have at the two colleges might be very different from his one-day visits. His friends, while they are not David, at least have the advantage of having much larger samples of the two schools. Their opinions ought to give David, and you, pause. Moreover, more energy may have been put into ensuring that David got a biased sample of events at college B than at college A. For example, if a friend at college B was particularly eager to get David to go there, he or she might have arranged things to impress David favorably.

Problem 2: If you said it might be best to keep your wallet in your pocket and your foot off the bar rail, then you recognized that correlation does not establish causation. Indeed, after decades of hearing from researchers that alcohol in moderation is a disease preventive, some scientists are now saying the association between moderate drinking and health may be a self-selection effect. People who don't drink at all may avoid it because their health is already poor or because their income discourages them from drinking (and income is strongly correlated with health). And people who drink a lot may be damaging their health.

As we've emphasized throughout this book, social psychology promotes the application of statistical and methodological analyses to everyday life events. Taking statistics courses and science courses that emphasize research principles is an excellent way to start being able to use those principles for solving everyday life problems and for critiquing media accounts of scientific research. But courses that teach those principles in the context of analyzing real-world events produce a big additional boost.

Darrin Lehman and Richard Nisbett (1990) studied the effects of 4 years in college for students majoring in the humanities, the natural sciences, psychology, and the social sciences. Students majoring in psychology and the social sciences showed a 65 percent improvement in their ability to reason using appropriate statistical and methodological principles like the ones just discussed. Students in the humanities and natural sciences improved by only about 25 percent. (Lest you think few advantages in reasoning come from studying the humanities and natural sciences, however, students in those fields improved by 65 percent in various kinds of logical reasoning, and students in psychology and the social sciences improved not at all.)

Two years of graduate-level training in psychology have a huge impact on people's ability to apply statistical and methodological principles to everyday life—particularly for students in the areas of psychology that deal with ordinary human behavior (Lehman, Lempert, & Nisbett, 1988). This includes the fields of social psychology, developmental psychology, and personality psychology. Improvements are less for students focusing mostly on the fields of biopsychology, cognitive psychology, or cognitive neuroscience, even though students in those fields are trained in statistics and methodology. Students of chemistry and law gain absolutely nothing in their ability to apply statistical and methodological reasoning to everyday life events.

Improving one's ability to apply statistical and scientific reasoning doesn't require immersion in higher education. Research by social psychologists shows that statistical and methodological principles, as well as economic concepts such as the cost-benefit principle, can be taught in very brief sessions (Fong, Krantz, & Nisbett, 1986; Larrick, Morgan, & Nisbett, 1990; Larrick, Nisbett, & Morgan, 1993; Nisbett, Fong, Lehman, & Cheng, 1987). For example, Richard Larrick and his colleagues (Larrick et al., 1990) taught participants, in sessions lasting less than an hour, about economic principles such as the sunk cost fallacy (doing something or consuming something that turns out to have little value just because a lot of money or effort was spent to obtain it; see Application Module 2). Several weeks later, the researchers phoned the participants in the guise of pollsters conducting an "opinion survey." The survey presented various personal and institutional dilemmas involving doing something undesirable that had already been paid for. The trained participants were much more likely to recognize that such behavior was actually uneconomical.

You've learned a great deal from this text, and the course you've just taken, about how to think critically about everyday life events, and also how to evaluate the thinking of others, including your friends and acquaintances as well as the media. This critical gift is one that keeps on giving: the more you use these critical-thinking principles, the more you're apt to invoke them in an ever-broadening range of circumstances.

SUMMARY

Pygmalion in the Classroom

- Teacher expectations about students can influence their academic achievement. Believing a child is talented, or is about to show a spurt in ability, may lead to a better performance. Expectation effects may be particularly large for lower-SES and minority students.

Intelligence: Thing or Process?

- According to the *incremental theory of intelligence*, people can improve their intelligence by working hard on challenging tasks.
- The *entity theory of intelligence* holds that intelligence is an unchangeable thing (entity) over which people have no control. Entity theorists tend to attribute failures to lack of ability, and are not likely to learn new things by taking on challenges.

- People can shift from being entity theorists to being incremental theorists, thereby improving their academic performance; this is especially true for minority students.

Culture and Achievement

- East Asians tend to be incremental theorists, and thereby gain the benefit of hard work and improved ability.

Blocking Stereotype Threat in the Classroom

- When minority group members are persuaded that their ability is under their control, they work harder and perform at higher levels. The same is true when they're asked to think about their goals in life and how to achieve them.

Social Fears and Academic Achievement

- Concerns about social acceptance can hold back minority students from engaging in college life and having academic success. Showing them that social acceptance improves results in greater well-being and higher grades.
- Colleges typically emphasize the value of an education in terms of independence goals for personal achievement. When they shift to an emphasis on interdependence values, the performance of first-generation students is likely to benefit.

Teaching with Entertainment-Education

- Entertainment-education, based on Bandura's social learning theory and the success of telenovelas, can have a big impact on the likelihood that people will avoid risky behavior and pursue beneficial goals.

Statistics, Social Science Methodology, and Critical Thinking

- Statistics and social science methodology, including methods used in social psychology, increase critical-thinking skills, enabling people to spot the mistakes in reported scientific studies and reducing errors of judgment in their own lives.

THINK ABOUT IT

1. On the first day of summer volleyball camp, if the camp counselors were told that the campers in Cabin 1 are on the verge of a growth and strength spurt, compared to the campers in Cabin 2, what is likely to happen? How large will the effect of this manipulation probably be? What factors would increase or reduce the impact of this manipulation?

2. Suppose Alex is choosing between two math classes for next semester. She can take either Math 301, which is outside her comfort zone but would teach her new skills, or Math 210, which is well within her domain of knowledge, and she'd probably get an A. If Alex were an entity theorist, which class would she likely select? Do you think entity versus incremental theorists differ in their overall GPA?

3. How would you change your college's Freshman Welcome program to help reduce achievement differences among students who are traditionally underrepresented in higher education (such as African-American and first-generation college students)?

THE ANSWER GUIDELINES FOR THE THINK ABOUT IT QUESTIONS CAN BE FOUND AT THE BACK OF THE BOOK . . .

Social Psychology and the Law

On a bright winter day in 1989, 29-year-old Eileen Franklin suddenly recalled a horror. She remembered that 20 years before, she had seen her best friend, 8-year-old Susan Nason, murdered. The murderer, silhouetted by the sun, lifted a heavy rock and crushed Susan Nason's skull. Eileen recalled covering her ears to block the sound of shattering bones. As her memory grew even sharper, she realized the murderer had been her own father, George Franklin. In the ensuing days, more details of the incident flooded her mind. She finally went to the police and told them about her recovered memory. Her father was ultimately sentenced to life imprisonment based solely on his daughter's testimony, even though some of Eileen's remarkably detailed memories were consistent with botched newspaper accounts rather than the actual facts of the case (Loftus & Ketcham, 1994). Franklin was convicted despite the testimony of psychologist Elizabeth Loftus that "recovered" memories can be utterly mistaken, and people can "remember" things that never happened. In fact, Eileen's memory *was* inaccurate. After serving 6 years in prison, Franklin was proven innocent and released. Loftus's testimony, which was at odds with views about memory held not only by the general public but also by many cognitive psychologists at the time, highlights the important role psychology can play in understanding the procedures that take place in a court of law.

The processes involved in a court case can be separated into three distinct phases: (1) pretrial events, including, in the case of criminal trials, eyewitness identification, attempts to elicit confessions, and efforts to distinguish lies from sincere efforts to tell the truth; (2) issues related to the trial itself, including jury selection, jury deliberation, and jury size; and (3) issues of punishment and

fairness. Social psychologists have made important contributions to each of these aspects of jurisprudence through their research, often by identifying flaws in existing practices and suggesting improvements. The criminal justice system has instituted quite a few changes in police practice and judicial procedures in response to these findings—a testimony to how the discoveries of social psychology can be used to improve an important social institution.

Before a Case Goes to Trial

You have probably seen many legal dramas on TV and in movies that unfold in a fairly predictable fashion: a crime occurs, the police investigate, witnesses identify one or more suspects, those suspects are interrogated, and the criminal does or does not confess. In real life, however, the process is not always so simple or straightforward.

Eyewitness Testimony

Almost nothing that comes before the jury in a criminal trial is more convincing than a witness who, pointing to the defendant, says, "I'm certain that is the man." (Or "the woman," but since the great majority of defendants are men, suspects and defendants are referred to here as men.) Every year, 75,000 eyewitnesses testify against suspects in criminal cases in the United States. But those identifications are wrong about a third of the time (Liptak, 2011). In fact, eyewitness errors have been found to be involved in more than half the cases of wrongful conviction (Kovera & Borgida, 2010). In some cases where people have been exonerated by DNA evidence establishing that they could not have been the person who committed the crime, more than one person had wrongly identified the convicted person as the perpetrator.

Social psychologists have studied many factors that can influence the accuracy of eyewitness testimony. Before you continue, however, take the following test. Indicate which of the statements seem to you to be true and which false. Write a T or F next to each statement to keep yourself honest before you check the answers on the next page. You don't want to fall prey to the "I-knew-it-all-along" effect!

1. Accurate eyewitnesses are generally more confident than inaccurate ones.
2. Witnesses are generally as accurate about identifying perpetrators of a race different from their own as they are in identifying perpetrators of their own race.
3. When the circumstances of a crime are highly stressful and arousing, the memory of an eyewitness is likely to be more accurate than when the events are less arousing.
4. Witnesses with correct memory for many details about the crime context (for example, how many doors were in the room) generally are more accurate in their testimony about perpetrators than witnesses with less correct memory for details.
5. Asking witnesses to help construct a face composite of the perpetrator generally improves the accuracy of identification of the perpetrator.
6. Asking witnesses to describe a perpetrator before they attempt to identify him from photos or a lineup generally increases the accuracy of recognition.
7. Witnesses who rapidly single out an individual from photos or a lineup are generally less accurate than those who take a longer time to consider who they believe to be the perpetrator.
8. Juries are generally capable of distinguishing correct testimony from incorrect testimony.

> "Memory can change the shape of a room; it can change the color of a car. And memories can be distorted. They're just an interpretation, they're not a record."
>
> —LEONARD SHELBY, PROTAGONIST IN THE FILM *MEMENTO*

The Effect of Misleading Questions
Participants in this study saw either the picture on the left or the one on the right. Many of those asked about the "stop sign" later reported that they had seen the stop sign even if they had actually seen the yield sign; many of those asked about the "yield sign" reported that they had seen the yield sign even if they had seen the stop sign.

SOURCE: Loftus et al., 1978.

The Persistence of Memory One of the greatest triumphs in the field of psychology is the discovery that memory is not a passive registry of the information a person has encountered. Instead, irrefutable evidence shows that memory is an active, constructive process in which inferences about "what must have been" guide memories of "what was." Through a series of ingenious studies beginning in the late 1970s and early 1980s, researchers have established that memories are inferences, not stored photographs or infallible representations, and that they can be affected by all kinds of information that becomes available after an event has occurred.

In one striking demonstration, Loftus and her colleagues showed participants a series of slides of an automobile accident (Loftus, Miller, & Burns, 1978). The image on one of the slides varied slightly from the others. A red Datsun was shown stopped at either a stop sign or a yield sign. Participants were asked questions about the accident they had "witnessed." One crucial question was different for two groups of participants. Participants were asked either "Did another car pass the red Datsun while it was stopped at the stop sign?" or "Did another car pass the red Datsun while it was stopped at the yield sign?" Later, the participants were shown the two pictures and asked which one they had actually seen before. Of those who'd been asked about the sign they had actually seen (stop sign or yield sign), 75 percent identified the correct picture. Of those who had been asked about the sign they hadn't actually seen, only 41 percent identified the correct picture.

In other research, Loftus and her colleagues found that people could be led to think a robber had a mustache when he didn't, and that a red light was green (Loftus, 2001). Of course, most of the time when investigators give misleading information to witnesses, they are not deliberately trying to mislead them. Instead, they often operate with patchy or mistaken details and may convey such misinformation to witnesses. In the courtroom, however, attorneys sometimes exercise poetic license in their phraseology in order to lead witnesses in a certain direction.

Research on eyewitness identification is relevant to the claims of psychotherapists that their patients have "recovered" memories that they had forgotten or repressed for decades. People have been convicted of heinous crimes based on reports of adults who are helped by their therapists to "remember" episodes of abuse or even murder. People are also sometimes convicted of child abuse based solely on the testimony of children who have been questioned by police.

Undoubtedly, some of these recovered memories are valid. But consider a demonstration reported by Loftus and Pickrell (1995), who successfully "implanted" memories in 24 university students. The researchers persuaded the students' relatives to tell stories about several events that occurred around the time the student in question was 5 years old. They were also asked to generate a plausible story about that child (the student) having been lost—although the event had not occurred. Six of the participants eventually "recalled" the event, sometimes providing substantial detail over the course of a series of interviews. Thus, 25 percent of randomly selected undergraduates were readily persuaded of the existence of a non-event—and could even provide details about it. Upon being told that one of the episodes never occurred, most of those students could not correctly identify which one it was.

In similar studies with children, Stephen Ceci and Maggie Bruck (1995) asked preschoolers to remember as much as they could, in weekly sessions for 10 weeks, about the time they went "to the hospital with a mousetrap on your finger."

Answers to Quiz on p. 602

1. *Confidence and accuracy.* Unless the perpetrator is extremely distinctive looking, confidence bears little relation to accuracy. Nevertheless, jurors are influenced by the degree of certainty expressed by witnesses (Wells, Memon, & Penrod, 2006).

2. *Race and accuracy of identification.* People are generally less accurate at identifying perpetrators of a different race (Brigham, Bennett, Meissner, & Mitchell, 2007; Johnson & Fredrickson, 2005) or age (Wright & Stroud, 2002) from their own.

3. *Stress and accuracy.* In one study, 500 soldiers in mock prisoner-of-war camps were deprived of food and sleep and subjected to interrogations of varying intensity. A day after the camp ended, soldiers subjected to mild stress correctly identified their interrogator 62 percent of the time; those subjected to extreme stress were correct only 30 percent of the time (Morgan et al., 2004).

4. *Memory for details and accuracy of perpetrator identification.* The *more* accurate eyewitnesses are about details of the crime scene, the *less* accurate they are about the criminal (Wells & Leippe, 1981). Jurors, however, tend to believe the opposite (Bell & Loftus, 1989).

5. *Constructing a face composite.* The resulting face composite usually doesn't look much like the suspect. More important, the very process of constructing the composite weakens the witness's memory for the actual suspect (Wells, Charman, & Olson, 2005).

6. *Verbally describing a perpetrator.* Witnesses who write a description of the perpetrator tend to be less able later on to spot the correct individual in a photo lineup (Schooler & Engstler-Schooler, 1990).

7. *Speed and accuracy of identification.* Rapid identifications are generally more accurate

than slower ones (Dunning & Stern, 1994), especially if the identification from a lineup is made within 12 seconds (Dunning & Perretta, 2002).

8. *Jurors' ability to tell whether eyewitness testimony is accurate.* Wells, Lindsay, and Ferguson (1979) faked thefts and asked participants serving as eyewitnesses to identify the thief from six photos. Other participants serving as jurors rated the testimony as accurate or inaccurate. Eyewitnesses were believed precisely 80 percent of the time—whether they were accurate or not.

"The best acting I ever did was in juvenile court."

—RAPPER, MODEL, AND ACTOR
MARK WAHLBERG

When they were interviewed later by another adult, 58 percent were able to tell detailed stories about the non-event. One boy remembered that "we went to the hospital, and my mommy, daddy, and Colin drove me there, to the hospital in our van, because it was far away. And the doctor put a bandage on this finger" (Ceci & Bruck, 1995, p. 219). Researchers including Loftus, Ceci, and their colleagues have thus established that memories, like perceptions and judgments, should be considered inferences rather than direct readouts of reality.

Factors Affecting Eyewitness Accuracy Given the generalization that memory is highly imperfect and highly susceptible to information provided after an event (or non-event) occurs, it's not surprising that eyewitness testimony is far from completely reliable. What factors influence whether such testimony is accurate and whether it is believed? Recall the statements about eyewitness testimony you read earlier. If you guessed that each statement was false, you were 100 percent correct. Otherwise, your intuitions fell short to one degree or another.

Improving Eyewitness Identification Procedures Fortunately, a massive amount of research by social psychologists on the accuracy of eyewitness testimony has had an equally significant effect on the law. In the 1990s, a panel of researchers, lawyers, and police from Canada and the United States developed a set of procedures to reduce eyewitness errors. A similar task force in the United States produced guidelines for best practices that are used by most U.S. law enforcement agencies today.

It is a great credit to psychologists that they have produced so much useful knowledge about the reliability of eyewitness testimony and the possible biases of jurors. It's also a great credit to policy makers that this research has been allowed to transform police and judicial practices.

Getting the Truth from Suspects

Guilty offenders sometimes confess their crimes, in which case the trial proceedings are relatively straightforward. Juries and judges simply attempt to arrive at a punishment that fits the admitted crime. But sometimes the guilty party does not admit to committing the crime. In the past, torture was frequently used to elicit confessions from the guilty. The assumption was that if people were truly innocent, they would never confess. But in fact people sometimes confess—even without torture—to crimes they did not commit.

False Confessions In 1989, five teenage boys were arrested for a horrific assault and rape of a woman who had been jogging in Central Park in New York. The woman was beaten nearly to death and was initially not expected to survive, although in a recovery regarded as miraculous she suffered only minor permanent damage. All five of the boys confessed to the crime, and they were given long prison sentences. Thirteen years after the crime, Matias Reyes, who was not one of the five boys, admitted to having been the sole perpetrator of the crime. DNA evidence, which had not been presented at the boys' trial, corroborated Reyes's admission.

Why would the boys have confessed to a crime they had not committed? They'd been up to no good in the park: they had been assaulting people, and during the interrogation they were probably in a state of extreme stress because they knew they were in fact guilty of something. In addition, they were subjected to pretty much standard operating police procedure. The suspect is placed

Certain, but Wrong

This account is excerpted from a *New York Times* article by Jennifer Thompson.

In 1984 I was a 22-year-old college student.... One night someone broke into my apartment, put a knife to my throat and raped me.

During my ordeal ... I studied every single detail on the rapist's face. I looked at his hairline; I looked for scars, for tattoos, for anything that would help me identify him. When and if I survived the attack, I was going to make sure that he was put in prison and he was going to rot.

... Looking at a series of police photos, I identified my attacker. I knew this was the man. I was completely confident. I was sure.

I picked the same man in a lineup. Again, I was sure. I knew it. I had picked the right guy, and he was going to go to jail. If there was the possibility of a death sentence, I wanted him to die. I wanted to flip the switch.

... Based on my testimony, Ronald Junior Cotton was sentenced to prison for life. It was the happiest day of my life because I could begin to put it all behind me....

Poole

Cotton

Bobby Poole and Ronald Cotton
Note the close resemblance between Poole, the perpetrator, and Cotton, the falsely accused man.

In 1995, 11 years after I had first identified Ronald Cotton, I was asked to provide a blood sample so that DNA tests could be run on evidence from the rape....

I will never forget the day I learned about the DNA results.... They [the detective and the prosecuting attorney] told me: "Ronald Cotton didn't rape you. It was Bobby Poole."

... The man I had identified so emphatically ... was absolutely innocent.

Ronald Cotton was released from prison after serving 11 years....

Ronald Cotton and I are the same age, so I knew what he had missed during those 11 years. My life had gone on. I had gotten married. I had graduated from college. I worked. I was a parent. Ronald Cotton hadn't gotten to do any of that.... (Thompson, 2000).

in a bare, soundproof room—a situation that has the effect of making the suspect feel alone and helpless. The most widely used manual for police interrogators advises a ninefold process for questioning suspects in that situation (Inbau, Reid, Buckley, & Jayne, 2001). (1) Insist that the suspect committed the crime; (2) give the suspect helpful excuses for why he might have committed the crime; (3) cut the suspect off when he tries to maintain his innocence; (4) defeat the suspect's objections to the charges; (5) don't let the increasingly silent suspect succeed in ignoring the interrogator; (6) express sympathy for why the suspect might have committed the crime in an effort to get him to admit the crime; (7) offer the suspect an explanation for the crime that would make him feel justified in committing it; (8) if possible, get the suspect to spell out details of the crime; (9) convert those details into a written confession. If those tactics don't suffice, police may offer sympathy and promise leniency in light of the supposed extenuating circumstances. These procedures often succeed in getting suspects to confess.

The problem, as in the case of the Central Park jogger, is that these police tactics can be altogether too effective, sometimes eliciting false confessions. In fact, in cases where defendants are convicted and later proved innocent by DNA tests, as many as one-fifth had confessed to the crime (Garrett, 2008). The young and inexperienced may be particularly susceptible. The five teenagers in the Central Park jogger case were interrogated for up to 30 hours before they gave their confessions, which were videotaped. The defendants later testified that they had been threatened and that promises of various kinds had been made if they would confess. (These charges were denied by the police.) Because of their naiveté, the boys reported believing they'd be allowed to go home if they just admitted to what they were said to have done.

Juries and Confessions Saul Kassin and Holly Sukel suspected that confessions made under dubious circumstances might still be taken at face value by jurors. To examine this hypothesis, they presented mock jurors with an account of a murder trial (Kassin & Sukel, 1997). In one condition, the suspect never admitted to the crime, and the jurors voted guilty 19 percent of the time. In a second condition, it was reported that the suspect had confessed, and the conviction rate rose to 62 percent. In a third condition, the suspect had confessed, but in a situation in which he was afraid and in pain while he was handcuffed behind his back. Although these participants generally recognized that the confession had been coerced, 50 percent of them voted for conviction anyway; they chose to believe the defendant's confession, even if it was forced, and even when they were told the judge ruled that it was inadmissible and should be ignored.

Can jurors recognize whether a confession is real or fake when they're allowed to watch a videotape of the interrogation? Not necessarily. In another study,

False Confession, Wrongful Conviction
(A) Yusef Salaam was one of five men sentenced to prison for their alleged role in the Central Park jogger case. (B) Matias Reyes admitted to being the sole perpetrator of the assault, thereby exonerating the five men who were wrongly convicted years earlier.

Kassin and his team videotaped prison inmates confessing either to a crime they had actually committed or to one they had not committed (Kassin, Meissner, & Norwick, 2005). College students and police investigators watched the video and indicated whether the inmate had or had not actually committed the crime. Neither the students nor the police were particularly accurate, but the police were for the most part quite confident in their judgments.

In response to research by Kassin and his colleagues as well as others, some state and local governments now require that the entire interrogation of suspects be videotaped. But as Kassin's research shows, doing so provides no guarantee that confessions are genuine or that jurors can recognize which confessions are genuine and which are not.

"Budget cuts—I'm good cop and bad cop."

Inside the Courtroom

The Sixth Amendment to the U.S. Constitution stipulates: "In all criminal prosecutions, the accused shall enjoy the right to a speedy and public trial, by an impartial jury of the State and district wherein the crime shall have been committed." How does the government in the relevant state and district assemble an impartial jury? And how large should the jury be? We typically think of juries of 12, but would a smaller number suffice? What decision rule should the jury follow in rendering a verdict? A unanimous decision is typically required, but some jurisdictions allow less stringent agreement. How do these differences affect the nature of the jury's deliberation and the kind of verdicts they deliver? Social psychologists have conducted research on all these questions in an effort to find out which procedures best serve the cause of justice.

Jury Selection

The first step in creating a jury takes place out of the public eye. Local governments—typically county or municipal courts—use a variety of public records, such as phone books and voter registration rolls, to compile a list of potential jurors. When a trial is coming up, the court randomly selects individuals from this list. Prospective jurors then appear in court and are interviewed by the judge, the prosecuting attorney, and the defense attorney in a jury-selection procedure known as **voir dire** (from old French, meaning "to speak the truth"). All three parties ask questions designed to find out whether a prospective juror is reasonably impartial, although the prosecution and defense are usually interested in ensuring that a juror is not biased *against* their side.

To weed out biased jurors, the prosecuting and defense attorneys consult their intuition about human nature and how certain types of people are likely to react to different types of arguments and evidence. Many attorneys believe, for instance, that engineers are stoic (and therefore not inclined to be moved by emotional appeals), that bearded men are unconventional (and therefore unlikely to be swayed by threats to the status quo), or that someone of German descent tends to be strict and conservative. Many attorneys also assume that particular types of jurors have special concerns that might lead them to be prejudiced for

voir dire The portion of a trial in U.S. courts in which prospective jurors are questioned about potential biases and a jury is selected.

scientific jury selection A statistical approach to jury selection whereby members of different demographic groups in the community are asked their attitudes toward various issues related to a trial, and defense and prosecuting attorneys try to influence the selection of jurors accordingly.

or against defendants in certain cases—for example, that mothers are especially sympathetic to claims about crimes involving children, the rich are sensitive to alleged crimes against property, and blacks are particularly moved by charges of police misconduct.

Based on the responses of prospective jurors to questions during voir dire, the defense and prosecution can ask the judge to excuse someone "for cause"—that is, because the person would not be impartial. Each side is also allowed a number of *peremptory challenges*—the right to exclude a prospective juror without offering any justification. Although a great deal of time and energy goes into the jury-selection process, psychological research shows that neither lawyers' intuitions about certain kinds of people nor jurors' responses to questions during voir dire are reliable guides to the decisions jurors are likely to reach (Kerr, Kramer, Carroll, & Alfini, 1991; Olczak, Kaplan, & Penrod, 1991; Zeisel & Diamond, 1978).

Scientific Jury Selection Recognizing the limits of their intuitions and the questionable value of prospective jurors' responses during voir dire, attorneys have turned increasingly to the practice of **scientific jury selection**, a statistical approach to selecting (or excluding) jurors likely to be predisposed to certain claims or appeals. Jury-selection specialists hired by defense and prosecuting attorneys conduct surveys and compile statistics on how demographic variables—such as age, gender, income, and ethnicity—are related to, for example, an inclination to trust the government, to admire corporate executives, to care about the environment, or to distrust the police. In the scientific jury-selection process, prospective jurors themselves are not questioned; instead, general associations between certain attitudes and demographic categories are established in the community at large. Research has demonstrated that the practice can be quite successful (Moran, Cutler, & DeLisa, 1994; Seltzer, 2006), enabling lawyers to know with reasonable accuracy, for instance, whether a prospective juror has a relatively pro-business or anti-business attitude (Hans, 2000).

Death-Qualified Juries As you are surely aware, the death penalty is a highly controversial component of the U.S. penal system. All but 14 states have the death penalty, although opponents question its effectiveness as a deterrent to crime, the consistency with which it is applied, and the very morality of its use. States with the death penalty do not have lower homicide rates than those without. And the homicide rate does not tend to go down when a state adopts the death penalty, nor does it go up when a state abolishes it (Costanzo, 1997; Haney & Logan, 1994). The overwhelming majority of those who are sentenced to death are poor and cannot afford the kind of defense that wealthy defendants use to maximize their chances of acquittal or, barring that, at least receiving a lesser sentence. In recent years, DNA evidence has exonerated many individuals who were convicted of capital crimes they did not commit.

In many jurisdictions, the jury decides not only the guilt or innocence of the individual charged with a capital crime, but also whether the death penalty is appropriate. If you were on a jury in a capital case that found the accused guilty, would you be willing to sentence the defendant to death? If the answer is no, should you be excluded from the sentencing phase of the trial? Indeed, should people with profound reservations about the death penalty be allowed to serve as jurors in capital cases at all?

"Ninety percent of all executions are carried out in just four countries: China, Iran, Saudi Arabia, and the United States."

—FORMER U.S. PRESIDENT JIMMY CARTER, *OUR ENDANGERED VALUES*

"Please read back that last remark in a more murdery voice."

Maintaining that it's not a good idea to have such people serve as jurors in capital cases, the courts allow the practice of death qualification, in which the judge may exclude prospective jurors who say they would never vote for the death sentence. But does the systematic exclusion of people with strong reservations about the death penalty alter the verdicts rendered by **death-qualified juries**? Psychological research indicates that it does indeed.

People who are willing to recommend the death penalty—and hence death-qualified juries as a whole—tend to be more concerned about crime and more trusting of police than people who are unwilling to recommend capital punishment. They also tend to be more skeptical of civil liberty procedures that protect the rights of the accused, and to have relatively negative views of defense lawyers (Fitzgerald & Ellsworth, 1984; Haney, Hurtado, & Vega, 1994). In experiments with participants assembled into mock juries who render a hypothetical verdict after looking at a videotape of a real trial, death-qualified juries are more likely to convict than juries in which those with reservations about the death penalty are not excluded (Cowan, Thompson, & Ellsworth, 1984). In another notable study, merely hearing the questions typically asked in the death-qualification part of the voir dire tended to bias the jurors toward conviction, presumably because such questions contain an implication of guilt (Haney, 1984). Given these differences between death-qualified and unqualified juries, many have questioned whether death-qualified juries really are impartial (Bersoff, 1987). Nevertheless, the U.S. Supreme Court has upheld the permissibility of death-qualified juries, first in *Witherspoon v. Illinois* (1968) and then again in *Lockhart v. McCree* (1986).

death-qualified jury A jury from which prospective jurors who would never recommend the death penalty have been excluded.

"Good news. Your execution was overturned on appeal."

Jury Deliberation

In fictional courtroom dramatizations, it's common for a steadfast and enlightened minority to overcome the impassioned but flawed view of the majority. Although this scenario makes good drama, it rarely happens in real life. In a landmark study of jury decision making, Kalven and Zeisel (1966) interviewed members of 225 juries. In 215 of them, a majority leaned in one direction or the other at the time of the initial straw vote; in 209 of these cases, the jury ended up handing down a verdict consistent with that initial majority. Also, in studies using mock juries, the initial majority almost always wins the day (Kerr, 1981; Stasser & Davis, 1981).

Given what social psychologists have learned about conformity pressures and social influence, it's no surprise that the initial majority so often gets its way. Indeed, studies on the nature of jury deliberation have found that the majority view prevails through the very processes of informational and normative social influence discussed in Chapter 9 (Kaplan & Schersching, 1981; Stasser & Davis, 1981). However, even though a minority rarely succeeds in producing the verdict they initially think is correct, they are able to persuade the majority to move in their direction a bit when it comes to sentencing (Pennington & Hastie, 1990).

Jury Size Most juries have 12 members, but that number is not specified in the U.S. Constitution, and some states allow smaller juries in noncapital cases. If you were convicted by a 6-person jury, would you think you had received a fair trial? Johnny Williams was in this very situation—convicted of robbery by a 6-person jury in Florida. He understandably thought the outcome might have been different with a larger jury, so he appealed. The Supreme Court, in *Williams v. Florida* (1970), upheld the conviction and affirmed the permissibility of 6-person juries, arguing that "there is no discernible difference between the results reached" by juries of different sizes. Later, in *Ballew v. Georgia* (1978), the Court reaffirmed its earlier opinion but ruled that juries of fewer than 6 people are unconstitutional.

In ruling that there is "no discernible difference" in the verdicts likely to be delivered by 6- and 12-person juries, the Supreme Court based its claim partly on conformity research. One concern of many legal scholars is guarding against the "tyranny of the majority"—that is, a nearly unanimous majority intimidating a slim minority into swallowing their convictions and caving in to the others. The Court maintained that research by Asch (1956) established that the amount of conformity pressure felt by the minority is proportional to the size of the majority. By this logic, minorities in a 5-to-1 or a 10-to-2 split are equally likely to give in to the majority. But that's not what Asch found (see Chapter 9). Having an ally makes an enormous difference in allowing the minority to stick to their convictions, so the lone holdout in a 5-to-1 split has a much harder time standing firm than either of the two jurors in a 10-to-2 split. And on purely numerical grounds, someone who dissents from the majority is more likely to have an ally—a bracing partner in dissent—in a group of 12 than in a group of 6. The Supreme Court simply misread the relevant evidence. Indeed, research conducted after the two Supreme Court verdicts has found that 6-person juries are more likely to arrive at a unanimous decision and do so with less deliberation (Saks & Marti, 1997).

Jury Decision Rule Recall that the Sixth Amendment guarantees anyone accused of a criminal offense "a speedy and public trial." Having juries with fewer than 12 members is one way to try to accelerate the flow of the large number of cases through the courts. Another way to speed up the pace of trials is to allow less than unanimous verdicts. The Supreme Court has twice upheld the permissibility of such decisions in state but not federal criminal trials. In *Apodaca, Cooper, and Madden v. Oregon* (1972), the Court upheld the convictions of three defendants found guilty using a 10-of-12 majority rule. In *Johnson v. Louisiana* (1972), the Court upheld a conviction obtained under a 9-of-12 decision rule. The Court maintained that a "conscientious juror" is concerned with justice, not with simply arriving at a verdict, so having a less than unanimous decision rule should not compromise either the length or the vigor of a jury's deliberation. Robust discussion, the Court argued, would continue well after a sufficiently large majority opinion has developed.

Jury Deliberation in Film

In the movie *12 Angry Men*, Henry Fonda plays the only juror who does not vote to convict the accused on the initial ballot. Slowly, employing one deft persuasion move after another, he wins over the other 11 members of the jury and engineers an acquittal.

At the heart of the Court's ruling, then, was an empirical claim, one that social psychologists quickly set out to test. In one ambitious study, researchers recruited over 800 people and assembled them into 69 mock juries (Hastie, Penrod, & Pennington, 1983). After watching a filmed reenactment of a real-world criminal trial, the mock juries rendered verdicts using three different decision rules: unanimous, 10-of-12, or 8-of-12. The results were clear-cut. Although the verdicts rendered by juries operating under different decision rules didn't vary by much, the juries that did not have to achieve unanimity spent much less time discussing the facts of the case and questions of law. The 8-of-12 juries, for example, typically deliberated for less than 5 minutes after reaching a majority of 8 or more. After the criterion was met, in other words, they all but ignored the holdouts, ended discussion, and announced their verdicts. Similar results were obtained from an analysis of videotaped civil trials with nonunanimous decision rules in Arizona. Minority opinions were given little attention once a sufficient majority view was reached (Diamond, Rose, & Murphy, 2006).

Note that these differences in how minority views are treated in juries with unanimous versus nonunanimous decision rules are important even if the two types of juries end up making the same decisions (as they often will if the case is relatively straightforward). The mock jurors in the Hastie et al. study (1983) later rated the quality of their deliberations, and those required to reach unanimity thought more highly of the thoroughness and seriousness of their discussions. Support for the legal system is enhanced when all participants come away convinced that justice has been served—a sentiment that is much more likely when a unanimous opinion must be reached.

Damage Awards Deciding the guilt or innocence of a defendant can sometimes be wrenchingly difficult, but at least there are only a few possible outcomes to consider—guilty versus not guilty, homicide versus manslaughter, and so on. In contrast, jurors in civil trials must often make decisions in which the response options are nearly boundless. For example, jurors must often decide how much a successful plaintiff should be paid in compensatory and punitive damages. How do jurors cope with such complexity, and how effective are they at awarding damages? Psychological research into these questions provides both encouraging and discouraging news (Kahneman, Schkade, & Sunstein, 1998; Sunstein, Kahneman, Schkade, & Ritov, 2002).

A compensatory damage award can be straightforward; it represents the amount the plaintiff should receive to compensate for any loss or harm sustained. The compensatory damages jurors can award are often tightly constrained by economic analyses of the harm done. Punitive damage awards are more subjective; they are designed to deter the defendant and others from acting in a similarly negligent manner or with similar intent in the future, and jurors often have much more discretion in what to award. What amount should a clothing manufacturer pay a child for burns she sustained because her pajamas were not sufficiently flame retardant? How much should a gas company pay if, in playing fast and loose with environmental laws, it contaminated local residents' drinking water?

Research indicates that jurors go about making such decisions by first consulting their sense of outrage at the defendant's behavior. As **Figure A4.1** shows, this sense of outrage tends to be affected by how recklessly the defendant behaved and how much malice seemed to be involved in the defendant's actions (Kahneman, Schkade, & Sunstein, 1998). Jurors then translate their sense of outrage into punitive intent, which is also influenced by the amount of harm the plaintiff experienced and by the plaintiff's identity (harm to children or koalas is likely to inspire more punitive intent than similar harm to CEOs or hyenas).

"Justice delayed is justice denied."

—BRITISH PRIME MINISTER WILLIAM GLADSTONE

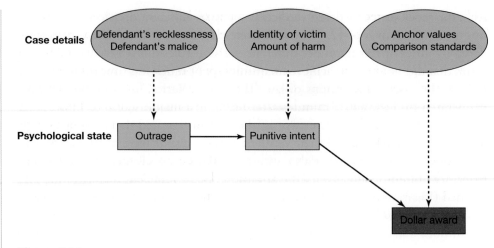

Figure A4.1
A Model of the Psychology of Punitive Damage Awards
When making punitive damage awards, jurors first assess how outraged they are by the facts of the case. Then, considering who the victim is and the amount of harm suffered, they develop a sense of their intent to punish. The translation of punitive intent can be difficult and is often influenced by such extraneous variables as an available anchor value or comparison standards that spring to mind.

SOURCE: Adapted from Kahneman et al., 1998.

The difficulty lies in the next step: translating one's sense of punitive intent into an actual dollar figure. How much more should someone pay if you feel strongly that he should be punished than if you merely believe he should be punished?

The good news is that people tend to agree about how outraged they are about a defendant's actions and their desire to punish. For instance, people generally agree that injuries to children merit more punishment than injuries to healthy retirees, that willful negligence calls for harsher treatment than simple carelessness, and that punishments that might deter the killing of dolphins or whales should be stiffer than those that might inhibit the killing of carp or mollusks.

The bad news is that the last step, translating punitive intent into an actual dollar amount, can be influenced by extraneous variables and therefore can be arbitrary. For example, various standards of comparison that are naturally evoked by a given case might introduce a degree of arbitrariness to the amount of a damage award. Suppose you hear about a company that allowed a toxic chemical to pollute the water supply that served a small nursing home, leading to the early deaths of several residents. You would no doubt be outraged, but your outrage would likely be affected by comparing this incident to other cases of lethal pollution you've heard about—cases involving larger communities and a wider range of victims, including very young children. Such comparisons might lead you to think that this case, though outrageous, is not as problematic as some, and therefore the punitive damages should not be as high. In fact, research has shown that people can end up recommending stiffer penalties for harming appealing animals such as dolphins than for harming human beings (Kahneman et al., 1998; Sunstein et al., 2002). Converting our moral sentiments into dollars is a difficult translation, one that is prone to predictable biases.

In certain civil cases an accessible anchor value, or a spontaneously invoked comparison, might influence the compensation awarded. In *Liebeck v. McDonald's Restaurants* (1994), a famous case that inspired calls for reform in civil trials, the jury voted to award 79-year-old Stella Liebeck $2.7 million because she suffered third-degree burns after spilling a cup of McDonald's coffee on her lap. The jury accepted Liebeck's attorneys' argument that McDonald's coffee was too hot (and inadequately labeled as hot), and they appeared to be influenced by her counsel's suggestion that McDonald's should be penalized an amount equal to 1–2 days of its average revenue from the sale of coffee ($1.35 million per day). But what would the award have been if another reasonable figure had been cited instead, such as 1–2 days of McDonald's *net profit* on coffee sales, or the average person's earnings during the period of Liebeck's recuperation? A different anchor value would almost certainly have yielded a different result. (The judge reduced the jury's recommended award to $480,000; Liebeck appealed that ruling and reached a settlement with McDonald's for an undisclosed amount believed to be less than $600,000.)

Punishment

Social psychologists have studied the nature of punishment—what societies do with those who break the rules—and the forms it has taken across time and cultures. Hunter-gatherer societies had no courts or juries, no judges or written laws, but individuals who transgressed tribal law—through stealing, cheating, or sexual infidelity, for example—were often subject to violent acts of revenge (Boehm, 1999). The Middle Ages and Renaissance in Europe were times of spectacularly brutal forms of punishment; beheadings, hangings, drawing and quartering, and whipping were regular practices, often in town squares for all community members to see. Even minor transgressions were subject to extreme punishment. In parts of Europe, if a baker sold bread that weighed less than advertised, he would receive the equivalent of today's water boarding. In fifteenth-century Scotland, individuals falsely posing as town fools were subject to having their ears nailed to a post or their fingers amputated.

Today, punishment largely has been subsumed by the criminal justice system, which determines the guilt or innocence of an individual alleged to have committed a crime and what the penalty should be if that person is convicted. Within the criminal justice system are people such as police officers, lawyers, judges, and jurors, who make judgments about guilt or innocence and about appropriate punishments. The latter is an act of the human mind, and social psychologists have uncovered important underpinnings of people's rationale for punishment—why we punish as we do and what makes punishments seem fair.

Motives and Kinds of Punishment: Just Desserts vs. Deterrence

Punishment is referred to as retributive justice, requiring people to make amends for harm and social transgressions. Within the realm of retributive justice, social psychologists differentiate between two motives that govern preferences for different kinds of punishment (Carlsmith, Darley, & Robinson, 2002; Weiner, Graham, & Reyna, 1997). One is the *just desserts* motive, commonly referred to as eye-for-an-eye justice; the goal is to avenge a prior evil deed rather than prevent future ones. Such punishments are calibrated to the moral offensiveness of the crime. Empirical studies of U.S. college students find that their recommended

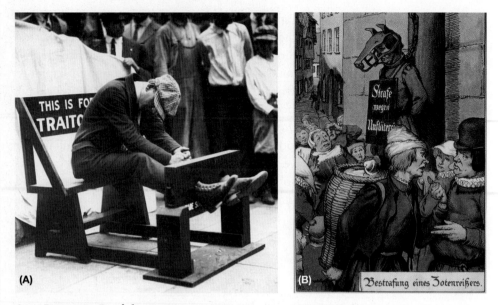

Just Desserts Punishments

(A) In earlier times, people who were guilty of various crimes were subjected to public ridicule by being kept in stocks in public venues. (B) Several hundred years ago in Europe, women who gossiped too much might be forced to wear a "shame mask" like this one. These punishments were guided by just desserts—the requirement that the punishment match the crime.

punishments closely track their feelings of moral outrage; people prefer punishments that match the perceived severity of the harm caused by the alleged crime (Carlsmith & Darley, 2008).

A second motive that can guide punitive judgments is *deterrence*, the goal of which is to reduce the likelihood of future crimes committed by the criminal or by others. People guided by the motive of deterrence assume that punishments change the cost-benefit analyses of committing crimes; they make more salient the costs of committing a crime (such as prison time or fines), which should outweigh any potential benefits, thereby deterring people from committing criminal acts in the future.

Punishments guided by the deterrence motive can take many forms. The criminal can be rehabilitated through special programs or engagement in the community. Incarceration (imprisonment) is an obvious way to prevent a convicted person from committing future crimes. More specific punishments practiced today, as well as those used in the past, reflect the deterrence motive. Lawyers who violate the law or their code of ethics are disbarred—prevented from practicing again. Priests are defrocked for immoral acts. Sex offenders have been castrated. In many countries in the past and present, thieves' hands have been cut off. The underlying logic is that these more specific punishments prevent the perpetrator from committing similar crimes in the future.

An Attributional Account of Punishment

The just desserts and deterrence motives are useful for thinking about people's rationale for punishment, and these motives may be at play in the pronounced variation in punishments handed out across different cultures. In Japan and Norway, for example, prisons are much more open, and prisoners are integrated

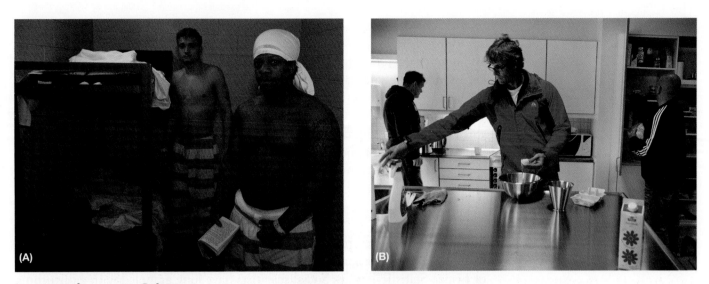

Incarceration across Cultures

(A) In the United States, prison sentences tend to be longer than in other developed countries, and the prisons themselves more aggressively segregate prisoners from the rest of the population. (B) In many other countries, such as Norway and Japan, prisoners are more readily integrated into local communities.

more readily into the nearby community. This approach to punishment appears to be guided by a deterrence-based practice of rehabilitation. The United States, by contrast, has much more severe sentencing practices, which might be in part the product of the greater influence of the just desserts motive (although it could readily be argued that severe sentences serve to deter criminals as well). What might account for such cultural variations, and, more generally, for preferences for just desserts versus deterrence-oriented punishments?

Bernard Weiner and his colleagues have offered one answer to this question. Their theory draws on the idea that emotion-based intuitions drive different punitive judgments (Weiner, Graham, & Reyna, 1997). According to their account, two attributions lead people to feel anger about a criminal act: (1) the belief that the perpetrator is responsible for the crime and intended it to happen, and (2) the belief that the crime reflects a stable part of the perpetrator's character. Numerous studies find that once angered, people prefer just desserts forms of punishment—they want the perpetrator to suffer in proportion to the harm caused (Lerner, Goldberg, & Tetlock, 1998).

A different set of attributions leads people to feel sympathy rather than anger toward the perpetrator of a criminal act. Specifically, people tend to feel sympathy when they believe that (1) situational factors, including the perpetrator's past history (such as being a victim of abuse), led to the crime, and (2) the crime does not reflect a stable part of the perpetrator's character. These two attributions reduce the inclination to see the perpetrator suffer in proportion to the harm caused (Rudolph, Roesch, Greitemeyer, & Weiner, 2004). Feeling sympathy also increases forgiveness and makes people prefer punishments that protect the criminal and society, such as forms of rehabilitation (Weiner et al., 1997).

Weiner and his colleagues have tested this framework in studies of teachers' attitudes toward punishing students for breaking rules, and U.S. citizens' attitudes toward punishing the famous football player O. J. Simpson when he was on trial for murdering his wife. The findings are in keeping with their analysis: attributions give rise to feelings of anger or sympathy, and these emotions lead to different punitive judgments. These principles are also at play in the legal strategies typically pursued by the prosecution (focusing on the responsibility and poor character of the defendant) and the defense (focusing on the role of circumstance). The same principles apply in recent debates about the relevance of a defendant's life history in the courtroom (Toobin, 2011). Many perpetrators of violent acts have suffered profound physical abuse as children, and increasingly this evidence is being considered in trials, particularly in death penalty cases. This kind of information, if allowed at trial, is likely to generate more sympathy for the defendant and more lenient punitive judgments.

Bias in the Criminal Justice System

The United States incarcerates a higher percentage of its citizens than any developed country except Russia. More than 1.5 million people are in prison (Bureau of Justice Statistics, 2013). Social scientists have long grappled with a disturbing fact: black and Latino men are represented in higher numbers in U.S. prisons than in the general population. Might this overrepresentation be due in part to bias in the system, to people's stereotypes and prejudices about blacks and Latinos? One fact might suggest that it is. Young blacks and Latinos are more likely to serve time for drug-related charges—the most common crime that sends people to prison—even though the most rigorous recent surveys indicate they are no more prone to using drugs than whites of comparable age and social class (Youth Risk Behavior Survey, 2007).

Social psychologists Jennifer Eberhardt, Phoebe Ellsworth, and Jack Glaser have argued in different ways that stereotype-based decision making may in part account for potential biases in the criminal justice system (Eberhardt, Davies, Purdie-Vaughns, & Johnson, 2006; Ellsworth, 2009; Glaser, 2012). Their reasoning is that cultural stereotypes of blacks and Latinos hold that they are more dangerous, prone to violence, and likely to use drugs. These stereotypes then guide the many decisions people in the criminal justice system make, thus giving rise to race-related biases in who is convicted and punished for different crimes (Plant & Peruche, 2005). Stereotypes, for example, are likely to influence which people police officers pull over and whether they search for drugs or write up a ticket for an offense. For similar reasons, stereotypes may shape how jurors assign responsibility for crimes, the degree to which they feel anger or sympathy, the likelihood of conviction, and sentencing length.

Evidence in support of a stereotype-based account of bias in the criminal justice system is mounting (for a summary, see Glaser, 2015). For example, the Supreme Court gives police officers ample latitude in terms of who they can pull over and search without probable cause. Bureau of Justice statistics indicate that blacks and Latinos are three times more likely to be searched when pulled over, even though these searches are not apt to yield incriminating evidence (Durose, Smith, & Langan, 2007; Plant & Peruche, 2005). Once on trial, blacks and Latinos may not receive treatment equal to that given other offenders; mock jurors are more likely to convict a black than a white defendant in a hypothetical trial for the same crime (Sommers & Ellsworth, 2001). Outside the laboratory, a summary of sentences given to 77,000 offenders found that blacks were given longer sentences than whites for similar crimes (Mustard, 2001). Collectively these findings suggest that racial stereotypes may partly explain racial biases in police behavior, conviction rates, and sentencing.

Perceptions of Fairness of the Criminal Justice System

procedural justice Assessments of whether the processes leading to legal outcomes are fair.

Theoretically, laws and punishments should instill a sense of order in society. In practice, the U.S. criminal justice system and the influence of its laws and punishments depend critically on another kind of justice social psychologists study—**procedural justice**, which refers to whether the processes resulting in the administration of rewards and punishments are perceived to be fair. Procedural justice depends on *how* rewards and punishments are determined. The concern with procedural justice is salient, for example, when considering whether employers use the same criteria to give bonuses to different employees, when there are conflicts about which criteria to use for admitting students to colleges and universities, or when there are concerns about whether the likelihood of arrest and the length of prison sentences depends on the race or social class of the individual.

Three factors shape a person's sense of procedural justice, according to social psychologist Tom Tyler (1994). The first involves assessments of the neutrality of the authority figure. When figure-skating judges give substantially higher scores to skaters from their own country, their neutrality is clearly in question, and the sense of procedural justice is undermined. With respect to punishment, a citizen's sense of procedural justice will depend critically on whether the legal system is seen as evenhanded. Second, there must be *trust* in the system. We must have confidence that authority figures—police officers, lawyers, judges— will be fair, that they will treat others according to consistent principles and standards. Third, the individual must feel that he or she is treated with *respect*. Do authority figures meting out justice—police officers giving out traffic tickets or judges delivering sentences, for example—treat those they are punishing politely? Respect on the part of authority figures, Tyler reasons, gives people a sense that the legal system is fair.

Tyler contends that these three facets of procedural justice have as much influence on the sense that outcomes—punishments and rewards in particular—are fair as does the actual content, good or bad, of the outcome itself (Tyler, 1994). In survey research, Tyler and colleagues have contacted people who have had recent experiences with authority figures. In one study, participants had recently received punishment for crimes they had committed, and they indicated what punishment they'd received, such as the length of their prison sentence (Tyler, 1987). Participants also indicated the extent to which they thought the authority figure had been neutral and trustworthy and had treated them with respect. The dependent measure of interest was the participant's feelings about the authority figure's fairness.

Two findings stand out. First, the magnitude of the punishment participants received in their recent experience with the criminal justice system was not correlated with their sense of procedural justice. This is an important finding because it suggests that people separate how the punishment is delivered from the punishment itself. Second, and perhaps more striking, their ratings of neutrality, trust, and respect were stronger determinants of their belief in the fairness of the criminal justice system than the actual punishment they received.

People's sense of justice thus revolves around more than personal gains or losses. People care profoundly about the neutrality of authority figures, the trustworthiness of the system, and the respect they receive from others. On the one hand, we might be encouraged by Tyler's findings. A society can build a prevailing sense of justice in groups and communities by ensuring that the distribution of reward and punishment is neutral, trustworthy, and respectful—and it can do so without changing the allocation of material resources. On the other hand, a more sinister implication of Tyler's findings is that authority figures might be responsible for all sorts of pernicious outcomes, from job layoffs to unwarranted prison sentences, without encountering protest, as long as they deliver them in a neutral, trustworthy, and respectful fashion.

Module Review

SUMMARY

Before a Case Goes to Trial

- Eyewitness testimony can be unreliable; even when trying their best to tell the truth, eyewitnesses can be mistaken when identifying perpetrators.
- The guesses of most people about the factors that influence witness accuracy can be wide of the mark. Because police investigators and jurors can't always assess witness accuracy, judicial procedures have recently been developed to minimize the likelihood of conviction due to mistaken identification.
- Suspects' confessions are sometimes false, even when coercion is not great, and, as a result, certain jurisdictions require videotaping of all interrogations. Jurors are poor judges of whether confessions are false or not.

Inside the Courtroom

- Jury selection begins with the process of *voir dire*, when the judge and the prosecuting and defense attorneys try to determine whether prospective jurors are impartial.
- Using *scientific jury selection*, attorneys accept or reject prospective jurors on the basis of demographic and statistical data. Whether only those jurors who would sentence a criminal to death should serve in capital cases is a controversial issue. *Death-qualified juries* are more likely to convict than those in which some jurors have reservations about the death penalty.
- When a minority of jurors dissent from the proposed verdict, the initial majority verdict usually prevails. While juries smaller than 12 people are allowed in some jurisdictions, larger juries are more likely to consider the opinions of a minority of jurors. When verdicts do not need to be unanimous, juries spend less time deliberating after the necessary majority is reached.
- Compensatory damage awards are intended to make up for any loss the plaintiff has suffered; punitive damage awards are intended to deter the defendant and others from acting similarly in the future. Compensatory damages are often straightforward, but punitive damages can be highly subjective and based on arbitrary comparisons and anchor values.

Punishment

- Two motives that guide punishment are the just desserts motive, intended to avenge a crime, and deterrence, intended to prevent the crime from happening again.
- Certain attributions and emotions lead to preferred forms of punishment. Believing that a criminal has acted willfully and is responsible for his actions leads to feelings of anger and a preference for just desserts forms of punishment. Believing that situational factors led, in large part, to the criminal act leads to sympathy and a preference for more deterrence-oriented punishment.
- Social psychology research has produced evidence of racial bias in the U.S. criminal justice system. Stereotypes about blacks and Latinos being more likely to commit crimes may lead to a greater likelihood that people in those groups will be investigated, convicted, and punished.

Perceptions of Fairness of the Criminal Justice System

- *Procedural justice* refers to people's assessments of whether the processes that result in the distribution of rewards and punishments are fair. If people feel the system is neutral and trustworthy and that they have been treated with respect, they are more likely to believe that outcomes are fair, regardless of the magnitude of the punishment or reward.

THINK ABOUT IT

1. Suppose your laptop was stolen from your dorm room one night, and a few of your neighbors caught a glimpse of a suspect as they were arriving home from a party. Your residence hall advisor (RA) brings in these neighbors individually to ask them about the suspect they saw. How should your RA pose his or her questions to your neighbors, in order to get the most accurate eyewitness testimony possible?

2. If you were in charge of establishing rules for jury deliberation, what could you do to increase the likelihood that minority opinions would be adequately considered? What research findings would you cite to back up your decisions?

3. Maria and Tanya are on the jury in a civil court case that has found the defendant guilty. They must now decide how the defendant should be punished. During their deliberations, it becomes clear that Maria is angered by the defendant's behavior, while Tanya feels sympathy. Using what you learned in this module, describe the differing attributions that might have led to Maria's anger compared to Tanya's sympathy. Which kind of punishment do you think each woman is likely to prefer?

4. Thais and Elisa both get speeding tickets, and are being punished by their parents. Thais's parents have a system of rules they follow for punishing all their children, and calmly but firmly explain to Thais that she will be grounded for 1 month. Elisa's parents, in contrast, favor her brothers over her, punish their children inconsistently from week to week, and scream at Elisa for her mistake, but only ground her for 1 week. Who is likely to feel their punishment is more just, and why: Elisa, with her shorter sentence, or Thais, with her longer sentence?

THE ANSWER GUIDELINES FOR THE THINK ABOUT IT QUESTIONS
CAN BE FOUND AT THE BACK OF THE BOOK . . .

ANSWER GUIDELINES FOR THINK ABOUT IT QUESTIONS

CHAPTER 1

1. How does social psychology differ from related disciplines, like personality psychology and sociology? How might a social psychologist, in contrast to researchers in other disciplines, try to understand the atrocities at Abu Ghraib?

ANSWER: Social psychology can be defined as the scientific study of the feelings, thoughts, and behaviors of individuals in social situations. Whereas personality psychologists study individual differences in behavior and sociologists study aggregate patterns of behavior, social psychologists study the influence of social factors on behavior. When seeking to explain the atrocities at Abu Ghraib, a social psychologist might consider social pressures the abusive guards may have faced from higher-ups, rather than simply assuming that the guards were "bad apples."

2. What does the Milgram experiment on obedience demonstrate about the power of the situation? What features of the experimental situation might have increased the likelihood that participants would continue to shock the learner even after the learner showed signs of pain?

ANSWER: The Milgram experiment demonstrated that, given the right situational factors, a majority of psychologically healthy adults were willing to continue shocking an innocent man even after he screamed and complained of a heart condition. Most of these participants were clearly not sadists, but rather were influenced by a powerful situation, which included the experimenter's insistence that they continue with the shocks, the intimidating setting (a prestigious university), and perhaps even the lack of a clear schema for how to politely discontinue participation.

3. Why are schemas so important for social interaction? What is your schema for being a student in a classroom? What might happen if you didn't have that schema?

ANSWER: To understand and navigate even the most seemingly simple social situations, like ordering food at a restaurant, we rely on complex systems of organized knowledge called schemas. A schema for being a student might consist of the expectation that a teacher will lead the class and that students should sit quietly in their seats, take notes, observe the teacher, and speak only when called upon. Without this schema, a confusing, embarrassing situation might ensue.

4. When trying to understand people's thoughts, feelings, and motivations, why don't researchers just ask them? What does research on automatic versus controlled processing tell us about people's awareness of their own mental states?

ANSWER: People tend to believe they have more conscious access to their mental processes than they really do. Research has shown that most mental processing happens nonconsciously—that is, outside of conscious awareness or control. For this reason, people's self-reports of their beliefs and motivations are not always accurate. Social psychology experiments can be designed in ways that tap into nonconscious processes. For example, one study showed that European-American participants who were reminded of African-Americans and then asked to read a brief description of someone whose race was not specified were more likely to rate that individual as more hostile, suggesting that they might implicitly associate African-Americans with hostility (Devine, 1989b). This was true even for participants who did not openly express negative attitudes toward African-Americans in a questionnaire.

5. How does evolution help explain social behavior? Which types of behaviors seem most likely to be explained by evolution, and which ones seem less likely?

ANSWER: Evolution operates through natural selection, the process whereby animals and plants that possess adaptive traits are more likely to survive and reproduce, and therefore pass on the genes that code for those traits to future generations. Many of the adaptive traits that humans almost universally possess, such as the capacity for language and the ability to form affectionate bonds, may have been shaped by natural selection. Traits that vary across cultures and individuals, such as valuing individual accomplishments over group accomplishments, are less likely to be explained by evolutionary theory.

6. What is the naturalistic fallacy, and why is it so important to avoid when considering evolutionary explanations?

ANSWER: The naturalistic fallacy refers to the erroneous claim that the way things *are* is the way they *should be*. Evolutionary theory as applied to human behavior is controversial in part because people have at times used evolutionary explanations to justify gender and racial inequality or to promote fascist ideology. The naturalistic fallacy can also lead people to believe that biology is destiny, and that there is little they can do to control their behavior. These beliefs are both destructive and inaccurate. Much of human civilization is based on the continual regulation and modification of biological predispositions, through medical interventions, education, and law enforcement.

7. How do Western and Eastern countries differ in their beliefs about the role of the self in relation to the group? How might these beliefs lead to different behaviors in an academic setting?

ANSWER: Research suggests that, on average, individuals in independent cultures, such as the United States and Great Britain, tend to focus more on their unique traits and accomplishments, whereas individuals in interdependent cultures, such as China and Korea, tend to focus more on their role within a group and their obligation to that group. In an academic setting, a member of a more independent culture might be more likely to strive to stand out among his or her classmates, whereas a member of a more interdependent culture may strive to blend in harmoniously with his or her peers.

8. Are evolutionary and cultural explanations for behavior compatible? How might these two perspectives complement each other when it comes to explaining gender differences in mate selection?

ANSWER: Evolutionary and cultural explanations for behavior are generally not mutually exclusive; they work together to provide a more complete picture. Evolution has provided humans with a broad array of tools and propensities that can be either cultivated through cultural practices or set aside if they are not useful in a given ecological or economic context. For example, although evolutionary forces may predispose women to prefer mates who have ample resources to support a family, in countries where women have greater financial resources themselves, this preference may no longer be as relevant, and mate preferences may shift.

CHAPTER 2

1. After reading this chapter, do you think it's important for students of social psychology to have a basic understanding of research methods? Why or why not?

ANSWER: Although this question asks for your opinion, it is essential for students of social psychology to have a basic understanding of research methods. This knowledge contributes to students' ability to both understand social psychological research, or almost any empirical research, and to think critically about the science involved. For example, without understanding that correlational research does not provide causal information, one might easily believe that certain claims have a causal connection, and therefore act on them. Consider parents of overweight children who read that attempts to control their diet will *cause* them to be overweight. If a parent new to research methods accepted this finding as fact, it would be reasonable for them to be overly permissive toward their child's eating habits, with potentially harmful consequences.

2. In an experiment on nonconscious processing, participants read a persuasive message in a room with either a fishy smell, an unpleasant smell that was not fishy, or no distinctive smell (Lee & Schwarz, 2012). The researchers measured the degree to which the participant was persuaded by the message, and discovered that participants were the least likely to be persuaded in the presence of a fishy smell (there was something "fishy" about the message). In this experiment, what was the independent variable? What was the dependent variable?

ANSWER: The independent variable is the variable the researcher manipulates—the hypothesized "cause." In this experiment it was the smell participants were exposed to, and it had three levels: a fishy smell, an unpleasant smell that was not fishy, and no distinctive smell. The dependent variable is what the researcher measures—the hypothesized "effect." In this experiment it was the degree to which the message persuaded the participants.

3. Suppose a group of researchers hypothesized that finding your romantic partner physically attractive contributes to feelings of satisfaction in your relationship. To evaluate this hypothesis, 100 participants completed a survey that included questions assessing their current relationship satisfaction, as well as ratings of how physically attractive they believed their partner to be. The researchers found that the more physically attractive participants rated their partners, the more satisfied they tended to be in their relationship. In this fictitious study, did the researchers employ a correlational or an experimental design? How do you know?

ANSWER: This study is correlational. The researchers evaluated whether a relationship exists between two naturally occurring variables: relationship satisfaction and perceived partner attractiveness. The researchers did not randomly assign participants to levels of the independent variable, and therefore it is not an experiment.

4. Consider the hypothetical study in question 3 again. The researchers found a relationship between perceptions of partner physical attractiveness and relationship satisfaction. With these data, can the researchers conclude that perceiving your partner as physically attractive causes you to become more satisfied in your relationship? Are there other potential explanations for these findings?

ANSWER: With these data, the researchers cannot determine a causal relationship between the two variables. For example, perceiving your partner to be attractive may cause you to be more satisfied. It is also possible, however, that being in a satisfying relationship causes you to be more attracted to your partner. Perhaps a third variable, such as being an optimistic person, causes you to be satisfied in your relationship and causes you to see your partner as attractive (the third variable problem). In order to rule out these possibilities, the researchers would have to conduct an experiment.

5. In Chapter 3, you will learn about research on the self, including self-esteem. Suppose the scatterplot below displays the relationship between self-esteem and academic success. How might you interpret this graph? Is the correlation between these two variables positive or negative? Try guessing the correlation coefficient.

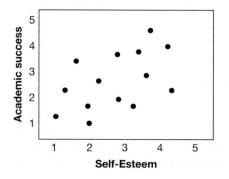

ANSWER: The graph shows that as self-esteem increases, so does academic success. This is a positive correlation. To know the correlation exactly, we would need to evaluate these results with mathematical formulas. It would be reasonable to guess, however, that the correlation is between .30 and .50.

6. In this textbook, you will learn about various studies evaluating social psychological phenomena using functional magnetic resonance imaging (fMRI), which measures activation in the brain while the participant lies immobile in a large metal tube, looking at a small computer screen. For example, in studying relationships, researchers may measure brain activation while participants experience a social rejection, or may look at how brain activation during a stressful experience is affected if a close friend holds the participant's hand. How would you characterize the external validity of such research?

ANSWER: Research using fMRI involves an unusual environment, one unlike any other a participant will experience in everyday life. For that reason, external validity is somewhat low. Unfortunately, questions about the connection between social experiences and reactivity in the brain cannot be answered by field research alone. Nevertheless, a thoughtful researcher can still set up a convincing psychological experience in a scanner. Is a perceived rejection any less real when experienced in the bore of the magnet? Social support from a friend may be particularly valuable in this stressful environment. (Think of a person being comforted by a spouse while undergoing an unusual or frightening medical procedure, not as part of an experiment, but during an actual course of treatment.) Moreover, consensus across studies lends additional support to the conclusion that a set of brain regions is involved under particular social psychological circumstances.

CHAPTER 3

1. According to research on the accuracy of self-knowledge, for what qualities are we the best judges of ourselves? For what qualities are others superior judges of us? How does motivation contribute to this asymmetry?

ANSWER: Although people predict that they are the best judges of themselves, when it comes to predicting behavior, others know us about as well as we know ourselves. However, we are superior judges of ourselves when it comes to private, inner qualities that are not easily observable (like our inner thoughts and feelings), whereas others are superior judges of us when it comes to qualities that are readily displayed in social settings (like our level of talkativeness and enthusiasm). Motivation contributes to the self/other knowledge asymmetry regarding qualities that have a positive or negative connotation. We are strongly motivated to see ourselves favorably, which may give us blind spots about our socially undesirable shortcomings. In these cases, others tend to know us more accurately than we know ourselves. (And thank goodness; you wouldn't want to be fully aware of your every flaw!)

2. Josie is a 13-year-old girl who thinks she's a funny person, and her friends and family generally think Josie is funny too. How would Cooley's notion of the "looking-glass self" explain how Josie's sense of herself as funny developed? As an adolescent, what does research suggest is likely occurring in Josie's brain when she thinks about her self-views?

ANSWER: Cooley (1902) would argue that Josie's sense of self developed from the way Josie thinks others perceive her, by using others' views as a mirror, or "looking glass," to perceive the self. Research suggests that among young adolescents, brain areas associated with perspective taking are especially active when contemplating one's self-views, so it seems likely that when Josie thinks about her self-views, regions of her brain that help her take the perspective of others will be activated. Thus, as an adolescent, Josie may be especially prone to incorporate what she thinks other people think of her into her self-concept.

3. How might a female undergraduate's working self-concept regarding her gender shift during a day on campus, as she attends her advanced math class (in which she is the only female), has a low-key lunch with a friend, and attends her gender studies class? Will her frequently shifting self-concept undermine her sense of having a coherent self?

ANSWER: The working self-concept shifts based on situational cues, such that in a given situation, especially relevant and/or distinctive self-aspects become part of the working self-concept. In her advanced math class, this young woman's gender identity is highly *distinctive* (as she is the only female), and in her gender studies class, her gender identity is highly *relevant* to the situation (discussing gender theory and struggles). Thus, both class contexts should highlight her gender identity in her working self-concept. During lunch, however, it's unlikely gender will be part of her working self-concept, being neither particularly relevant nor distinctive in that context. Despite these shifts in her working self-concept, she is probably not confused about her identity; she probably has a core set of self-aspects that define who she is regardless of her current working self-concept. Moreover, she is probably used to these fluctuations across her days on campus, which form a stable pattern of activation and deactivation of her gender in her working self-concept (feeling especially female in her math and gender studies classes, and less so at other times).

4. How do an individual's daily experiences in his or her contingent versus noncontingent domains affect his or her state self-esteem? Over time, how might these experiences translate to trait self-esteem?

ANSWER: Performance in contingent domains has consequences for state self-esteem, such that performing well in a contingent domain boosts state self-esteem, whereas performing poorly in a contingent domain diminishes state self-esteem. Performance in noncontingent domains has less influence upon state self-esteem. Over time, accumulating experiences of good versus poor performance may influence trait self-esteem, such that repeatedly performing poorly in contingent domains (threatening state self-esteem frequently) may ultimately reduce overall trait self-esteem. Similarly, regularly performing well in contingent domains (boosting state self-esteem repeatedly) may ultimately increase overall trait self-esteem. Performance over time in noncontingent domains is unlikely to affect trait self-esteem.

5. Do people from Eastern cultures generally feel worse about themselves than people from Western cultures? How do researchers interpret self-reported self-esteem differences between cultures?

ANSWER: Although members of Eastern cultures tend to report lower feelings of self-esteem than members of Western cultures, rather than reflecting an overall more negative view of the self, this difference may reflect differing cultural value systems. In East Asian and other non-Western cultures, views of the self are more interwoven with the social context. Accordingly, these cultures prioritize improving the self (perhaps to better fulfill one's obligations and duties in social relationships and systems) and meeting the goals of the group, rather than meeting the goals of being a self-confident and powerful individual (which Western cultures tend to prioritize). Thus, it may not be accurate to conclude that members of Eastern cultures feel worse about themselves than Westerners; they simply feel differently about the self as a whole.

6. Should people be more likely to display the better-than-average effect for their own intelligence before or after learning how intelligence is measured in scientific research? How do construals contribute to this process?

ANSWER: According to research on self-serving construals, the better-than-average effect is more prevalent for qualities with ambiguous or fuzzy definitions, but dissipates in strength when objective standards become apparent. Thus, before obtaining a clear definition of intelligence, people may be more prone to self-enhance with respect to their intelligence, in order to bolster their self-worth. In terms of construals, under these conditions of ambiguity, people may construe different qualities as being more or less important to intelligence, construing their own strengths (perhaps artistic or interpersonal skill) as key to intelligence, and their weaknesses as less relevant to intelligence. However, once people learn the precise scientific standards for intelligence, their tendency to display the better-than-average effect should reduce, by reducing people's freedom to construe their own best qualities as core to intelligence.

7. If you're fairly sure you are scatterbrained, but a friend tells you that you're organized and put-together, what will your cognitive reaction likely be? What will your emotional reaction likely be? Which motive (self-enhancement or self-verification) drives which set of reactions?

ANSWER: Self-verification, the need to be seen accurately by close others for important self-defining traits, should drive your cognitive reactions to this feedback, making you dubious about the quality of the feedback your friend has provided. In contrast, your emotional system, ruled more by self-enhancement, should register this as positive feedback and lead you to feel good about this feedback, even as your cognitive mind tells you it is inaccurate. Thus, you may think your friend is off-base in her compliment to you (perhaps making you question her competence as a judge of you), but you will still feel emotionally better about it than if she had confirmed your negative self-view of being scatterbrained.

8. Suppose two friends both have an actual self that is relatively happy, and a potential self that is extremely happy (happier than their actual self). If this discrepancy in happiness leads one friend to experience agitation, and the other friend to experience dejection as a result, what does this tell you? What theory would this evidence support?

ANSWER: Actual selves that are discrepant with ought selves produce agitation, whereas actual selves discrepant with ideal selves produce dejection. This suggests that for the agitated friend, the extremely happy potential self is an ought self, whereas for the dejected friend, the extremely happy potential self is an ideal self. In other words, the first friend feels that she really *should* be happier, whereas the second friend feels she would like to ideally be happier (but it's not a matter of "should"). This pattern of emotional responses would support self-discrepancy theory.

CHAPTER 4

1. How valid are snap judgments? Do brief exposures to a person's physical appearance or "thin slices" of their behavior provide meaningful information about what they are really like?

ANSWER: Snap judgments often contain a kernel of truth about a person, but not the whole truth. Research described in this chapter showed that snap judgments of a political candidate's competence, based on a brief look at the candidate's photo, were predictive of electoral success, suggesting that these judgments corresponded with the general consensus about the candidate based on larger samples of his or her behavior over time. There is no clear evidence, however, that snap judgments of competence reliably predict *actual* competence, and the same is true for judgments of most other traits. Therefore, it is best to avoid making important decisions solely on the basis of snap judgments.

2. What role might pluralistic ignorance play in the problem of binge drinking on college campuses? What could school administrators do to reduce pluralistic ignorance in this context?

ANSWER: College students who are privately concerned about the potential dangers of binge drinking may keep quiet because they assume most other students view binge drinking as acceptable, and they don't want to embarrass themselves by speaking out. But it's possible that many other students feel the same way and are not sharing their feelings for similar reasons. To counter this form of pluralistic ignorance, school administrators could launch an information campaign designed to show students that positive attitudes about binge drinking are not as widespread as they may seem.

3. How does the desire to entertain tend to bias the kinds of stories that are reported most frequently in the media? What effects might this bias have on people's beliefs about the world?

ANSWER: The media tend to overreport negative, violent, and sensational events because these types of stories attract viewers' attention more than positive, altruistic, and everyday events. Research shows that 80% of crime reported in the media is violent, whereas in reality only 20% of crime is violent. Unfortunately, this bias can lead people to fear victimization and view the world as a terribly dangerous place, especially if they live in an area where crime is more prevalent. This bad news bias can also prevent people from learning about inspiring, altruistic acts, such as relief efforts to help victims of natural disasters and ordinary citizens helping their neighbors through hard times.

4. If you were developing an advertising campaign for a fitness class, what kinds of framing strategies might you use to increase the chances of people signing up for the class? In particular, consider spin framing, positive and negative framing, and temporal framing.

ANSWER: An example of spin framing could be to highlight the low cost of the class: "Sign up now and save $20." An example of positive framing could be to describe the benefits of the class for physical appearance: "Get beach ready!" An example of negative framing (which generally has greater impact) could be to describe the potential health risks of not exercising: "Inactive people are nearly twice as likely to develop heart disease." An example of temporal framing could be to encourage people to sign up well in advance, before they have a chance to construe the class in potentially less pleasant, concrete terms (sweating, exhaustion, and so on).

5. Suppose you're about to go on a blind date when a mutual friend warns you that your date can be a little cold and unfriendly. According to research on the confirmation bias, how might this information influence the impression you ultimately form about your date?

ANSWER: If you expect your date to be cold and unfriendly, you might be more likely to pick up on behaviors that confirm your expectations; for example, you might notice that he or she is short with the waiter and frequently checks his or her phone. You might also be more likely to ask leading questions that elicit information consistent with your expectations; for example, if your date is a professor, you might ask, "So do your students drive you crazy?" As a result of your biased observations and behavior toward your date, your date may indeed reveal more cold and unfriendly characteristics, and you may consequently form a more negative impression of him or her that confirms your initial expectations.

6. Research on priming suggests that it is possible for a stimulus to activate a schema even if a person is not consciously aware of the stimulus. Can you think of ways that you might be able to use priming to influence others' behavior?

ANSWER: To increase creativity, you could have people work in a green or blue environment. To make someone more attracted to you, you could wear red or put a red border around a photo of yourself. To make people behave more honestly, you could put up a poster of something or someone with eyes, which makes people feel like they are being watched. To make people more concerned about preventing climate change, you could make your case about it in an especially hot room.

7. Imagine you're working on a group project with three other students and you are all asked to indicate your individual contribution to the project, relative to the other group members' contributions, in the form of a percentage. If you were to sum the individual percentages reported by each group member, would you expect it to add up to roughly 100%? Why or why not?

ANSWER: The sum of estimates would likely be above 100% due to the availability heuristic, a mental shortcut that leads people to overestimate their own contributions to joint or group efforts and to underestimate others' contributions. Examples of your own hard work are more available to you because you can experience them firsthand, whereas examples of others' hard work may be harder to bring to mind, making them seem less frequent. As a result, all four group members may estimate their individual contributions as over 25%, leading to an impossible total. Research indicates that people tend to overestimate their own contributions even when these contributions are negative (like starting arguments), suggesting that this phenomenon is not explained simply by a motivational bias to present oneself in a favorable light.

CHAPTER 5

1. Carla was the last person to be picked for dodgeball teams in her gym class. She thinks to herself, "Jeez, no one wants me for their team. I'm terrible at dodgeball. In fact, I'm terrible at all sports. No matter how much I work out or how hard I try, I'm never going to get any better." What are the three attribution dimensions that comprise explanatory style? Describe where Carla falls on these three dimensions. How do you know? Overall, what is Carla's explanatory style?

ANSWER: The three attribution dimensions that comprise explanatory style are internal/external, global/specific, and stable/unstable. In explaining why she got picked last for the team, Carla says she is terrible at dodgeball. This is an internal attribution. Carla also says she is terrible at all sports. Carla is going beyond this specific situation, and is therefore making a global attribution. Finally, Carla says that no matter how much she works out or how hard she tries, she will never get any better. In this way, Carla is making a stable attribution about her athletic abilities. Overall, Carla is displaying a pessimistic explanatory style. She is explaining a negative event as due to something internal about her, something global, that affects other areas of her life, and something stable, that cannot be changed.

2. Can you think of a time when you committed the fundamental attribution error? What happened? Why do you think you made this mistake?

ANSWER: We are all likely to commit the fundamental attribution error, and probably do so regularly. For example, consider when a friend's new girlfriend comes out with the gang for the first time. If the person is quiet and awkward, it's easy to assume she is an introverted person, thereby attributing the behavior to her disposition. But, being the odd person out in a group of close friends will make almost anyone feel a bit shy, right? Why don't we take into account this situation? The fundamental attribution error occurs for many reasons. For example, the just world hypothesis states that people want to believe that good things happen to good people. Believing that outcomes are determined by who a person is (her disposition) rather than factors outside of her control (the situation)—the fundamental attribution error, in other words—helps people maintain such just world beliefs. Another reason we commit the fundamental attribution error, is that a person's behavior is often more salient or obvious to us than the situational circumstances. We're more likely to notice the new girlfriend's awkward behavior than to be aware of the situation and how it will impact her (particularly because the situation is very different for us—comfortable and familiar). In addition, we know that it's easier to make dispositional attributions, whereas considering the situation takes more energy or effort. We can be lazy, so often the thoughtless dispositional attribution wins out.

3. Curtis, a busy guy with good taste in music, has a friend who raves about a new band. Curtis wants to know whether it's worth his time to listen: Is the band actually awesome (an external attribution) or is his friend not all that discerning about music (an internal attribution)? Curtis recalls that his friend raves about the band every time he listens to them, none of their other friends rave about the band, and his friend raves about every band. Describe the three components of the covariation principle, and explain how each one applies in this scenario. Based on this information, what should Curtis conclude? Is the band awesome or does his friend simply love all music?

ANSWER: We use the covariation principle to make attributions about a behavior. The three pieces of information we use are consensus (do other people respond similarly when they encounter the situation/stimulus), distinctiveness (does the person respond similarly to other situations/stimuli), and consistency (does the person respond the same way whenever they encounter the situation/stimulus). In this example, there is low consensus (other friends do not rave about the band), low distinctiveness (Curtis's friend raves about every band), and high consistency (Curtis's friend raves about the band every time he listens to them). Using this information, Curtis should conclude that the band is probably not awesome. Rather, his friend raves about the band because he simply loves all music—an internal attribution.

4. Imagine you are single and decide to go to a speed-dating event, in which you will have a series of 5-minute dates with many people. You really care about getting to know what your dates are like. Given this situation, which types of behaviors would strongly signal the type of person your date is? What types of behaviors might you discount, that is, chalk up to the demands of the speed-dating situation? Apply the augmentation and discounting principles in your analysis.

ANSWER: The situational demands in a speed-dating event are strong. For example, in this situation it's socially appropriate to act friendly, outgoing, and lighthearted. Therefore, if one of your dates acted friendly, outgoing, and lighthearted, it would be hard to tell whether she was truly that kind of person, or whether she was acting that way because the situation calls for such traits. This demonstrates the discounting principle, the idea that we should assign less weight to a cause of a behavior (your date's personality) if there are other possible causes that might have produced the behavior too (the demands of the speed-dating situation). In contrast, acting rude, introverted, or serious goes against the demands of the speed-dating situation. In this way, if one of your dates acted rude, introverted, or serious, it would strongly signal that this is the type of person your date is. This reflects the augmentation principle—the idea that we should assign greater weight to a cause of a behavior (your date's personality) if there are other causes present that normally produce the opposite behavior (the demands of the speed-dating situation).

5. Can you think of other aspects of one's identity (besides culture, religion, or social class) that might influence the types of attributions one makes? How so?

ANSWER: Many other aspects of our identity relate to the ways we make attributions, such as political affiliation, gender, and age, to name just a few. What about personality variables, like attachment style? In a study covered in this chapter, participants imagined their romantic partner engaging in a particular behavior and then made attributions regarding why the partner behaved that way. For example, the scenario "your partner brought you dinner when you were sick" could be attributed to "my partner is a caring and thoughtful person," or "my partner feels guilty about something and is trying to make up for it." Highly avoidant participants, those less comfortable with intimacy in their romantic relationships, were less likely to attribute the partner's behavior to caring intentions.

6. Mary, Travis, and Hussein stand to receive their awards at the National Spelling Bee. Mary, who won first place, receives her trophy with a smile on her face. The second-place winner, Travis, covers his face with his hands and sobs. Eventually, he politely receives his award despite the tears. When Hussein's name is called for the third-place prize, he grins and excitedly claims his award. Using what you learned in this chapter, explain Mary, Travis, and Hussein's (perhaps surprising) reactions to their respective prizes.

ANSWER: As the first-place winner, it's no surprise that Mary receives her award smiling. Travis and Hussein's reactions are more interesting, however. Travis, who won second place, is devastated, whereas, Hussein, who won third place, is thrilled. This nicely demonstrates a phenomenon discussed in this chapter regarding counterfactual thinking: considering what could or should have happened if only something small were different. If Travis engages in counterfactual thinking, he's likely to realize he was so close to first place. If only he hadn't made that last mistake. In this way, Travis feels devastated about just missing out. In contrast, if Hussein engages in counterfactual thinking, he's likely to realize that he almost didn't place in the competition. One more slip-up and he would have lost altogether. Thus, he is relieved and grateful he won third place.

CHAPTER 6

1. Humans appear to have a coordinated display of embarrassment that resembles appeasement signals in other species. What does this tell us about the function of embarrassment? Why do you feel embarrassed when you trip and fall in a full lecture hall? What effects should your resultant experience and display of embarrassment have on your classmates?

ANSWER: Emotions have myriad social functions, and embarrassment has a particularly interesting role in human relationships, signaling remorse for making social errors (like breaking norms or violating role constraints). Expressing embarrassment tells others in your social network that you're aware you committed a social transgression, recognize you may deserve punishment, and wish to be forgiven. Thus, when you trip and fall in lecture, you have violated an implicit social norm (not to trip and fall, or on the flipside, to be dignified and composed), and may in turn show a strong blush response and embarrassment display. These automatic signals communicate to your classmates that you know you've blundered, and should make them see you as more trustworthy and upstanding, if not especially graceful.

2. The relationship between culture and emotion is complex. Say you're seated at a wedding reception with an older European American man, who tells you that East Asians never get excited. How would you explain to him that he's mistaken, by drawing on the concepts of ideal emotions and display rules?

ANSWER: Excitement is an ideal emotion in Western cultures like America, where it is consistent with American cultural ideals, like readily expressing the self, and is thus highly valued. In contrast, many East Asian cultures more highly value calmness and contentedness, which are consistent with their cultural ideal of harmony. Moreover, display rules, which regulate expressions of emotion, could also be involved. Thus, even if an American and an East Asian experienced the same level of excitement, the American may play up his or her excitement more, augmenting its display, whereas the East Asian may regulate his or her excitement more, minimizing its display. Thus, excitement may simply be more valued and more commonly and readily displayed in America than in East Asia, but it certainly doesn't mean that East Asians never experience or express excitement.

3. Much communication today occurs distantly via electronic text, rather than face-to-face, whether in an online chat or text message, an e-mail, or a post on a social media site. Given what you know about the importance of emotions for social relationships, why do you think people frequently use emoticons and emojis in these communications? What social functions do they perform?

ANSWER: Emotion plays an important role in coordinating interactions, communicating our commitments and true feelings, and understanding what others are thinking and feeling. Emoticons and emojis can help us express and signal emotions in the online world, adding a layer of social color and richness to our digital interactions. Adding a smiley face, an uncertain face, a shocked face, or a face of relief can add emotional overtones to otherwise sterile textual conversations, helping us communicate our true intent and understand the nuances of others' statements. Perhaps they even provide social rewards for our conversation partners, and in group texts and conversations, perhaps they help us find and fill our social niche. Although emoticons cannot substitute for the rich language of touch, facial expressions, and vocal expressions of emotions, they may help make up for some of what is lost in a digital context.

4. Suppose you just got into a huge fight with your parents on the phone, and are feeling angry. You call up your romantic partner to talk about the fight, but just end up fighting with your partner. Using what you know about emotion's effects on perception, how would you explain this second fight, and perpetuated mood states more generally?

ANSWER: Anger makes us more attuned to signals of threat in the environment, and thus see more hostile intent in the actions of others. In this situation, the first fight made you angry, which likely colored your perception of the interaction with your romantic partner. Perhaps you saw him or her as more hostile and less understanding than you normally would, which made you quick to respond with even more anger. By altering perception, emotions may thus sometimes perpetuate themselves, leading to extended mood states. For instance, this chapter discusses how happiness makes people more prone to identifying happy words, and fear makes people believe future threats are more likely; in both cases, that emotion may enhance subsequent experiences of the same emotion.

5. If you were working as a canvasser collecting signatures for a petition to ban same-sex marriage, what strategies could you use to increase your signature count, given what you know about moral foundations theory and the effects of disgust on moral judgment?

ANSWER: Disgust intensifies judgments that impure acts are morally wrong. Gay men and lesbians are, unfortunately, seen as "impure" groups by some people, and same-sex marriage is thus a topic relevant to moral concerns about impurity. To collect more signatures, you might try to target people who are already feeling disgust about another stimulus. For instance, you could try standing next to a smelly garbage can, collecting signatures from people collecting trash on the side of the road. Or you could use a more traditional strategy of simply discussing the supposedly impure aspects of same-sex marriage prior to requesting a signature.

6. Would winning several million dollars in the lottery make you happier? What would research on affective forecasting predict? What does the research on money and happiness have to say? How should you spend your winnings to maximize happiness?

ANSWER: Based on affective forecasting research, although you might predict that winning the lottery would increase your happiness considerably, chances are you'd be less happy after winning the lottery than you'd predicted. This may occur because of focalism, such that you would focus on the salient aspects of winning the lottery (tons of money), but would neglect the possible detractors to this newfound happiness, like complicated taxes, sudden strange fame, and potentially strained relationships with family and friends. The research discussed in this chapter would also suggest that the lottery could indeed increase happiness for some people, but only if they already had an annual income below $75,000. In other words, money only makes people happier up to a point. To make yourself happiest with your newfound wealth, you should probably spend it on other people, and on experiences, rather than on yourself and on material goods.

CHAPTER 7

1. Consider an attitude object you feel strongly about, something you love or something you hate. Maybe you're passionate about soccer. Perhaps you are staunchly opposed to capital punishment. Describe this attitude along the three elements of affect, cognition, and behavior.

ANSWER: The three components of an attitude are affect (the degree to which you like or dislike the attitude object), cognition (thoughts, beliefs, memories, and images about the attitude object), and behavior (the tendency to approach or avoid the attitude object). Let's consider soccer as the attitude object from the perspective of someone who is passionate about the sport. With respect to affect, this person strongly likes soccer, or feels positive emotions, such as excitement, when engaging with soccer. With respect to cognition, he probably has a large store of knowledge about soccer, including the rules of the game and statistics about players, as well as a host of memories involving soccer. These affective and cognitive components reinforce behavioral tendencies, such as the desire to watch soccer, talk about soccer, and play soccer.

2. Suppose you're an attitude researcher and want to assess participant attitudes about the institution of marriage. Describe three methods you might use in your assessment.

ANSWER: Researchers interested in attitudes toward marriage can use a variety of measurement tools. With surveys, they can ask participants to report on a Likert scale the degree to which they believe marriage contributes to societal functioning. Measuring response latencies can indicate the strength, or accessibility, of an attitude, with participants responding faster to questions about more strongly held attitudes. To evaluate the centrality of attitudes about marriage to someone's belief system, researchers could ask a variety of questions related to the institution of marriage. For example, do you disapprove of divorce? Do you support traditional gender roles? Finally, researchers can also use implicit measures to access nonconscious attitudes toward marriage. For example, they could employ an IAT to determine the association between marriage and good versus bad, or look at brain activity when participants respond to marriage-related concepts. The latter implicit measures may be particularly useful if researchers want to study a more controversial aspect of marriage. For example, some participants may not be willing to report their attitudes about same-sex marriage.

3. You have two best friends who you like very much, Tanya and Amanda. Unfortunately, Tanya can't stand Amanda. This makes your life difficult as the three of you can never spend time together without Tanya getting irritated. Based on what you learned about cognitive dissonance theory, how might you go about getting Tanya to like Amanda more?

ANSWER: One way to make Tanya like Amanda is to get Tanya to behave in ways that suggest she does in fact like Amanda. For example, you might ask Tanya to give Amanda a ride home, to help you plan Amanda's birthday party, or to help out Amanda by picking up her laundry. If her attitudes toward Amanda (she doesn't like her) are inconsistent with her behavior toward Amanda (she behaves in a friendly way), Tanya is likely to experience cognitive dissonance and, therefore, to engage in dissonance-reduction tactics. Since the friendly behavior has already occurred and cannot be changed, Tanya's best option is to change her attitudes. In this way, she may come to hold more positive attitudes toward Amanda than she did before.

4. Although we readily assume that attitudes relate in meaningful ways to behavior, research suggests they don't always match up. Consider the dentist as the attitude object. Why might attitudes toward the dentist not necessarily predict behavioral responses to the dentist?

ANSWER: Attitudes toward the dentist may not predict behavioral responses to the dentist for a variety of reasons. First, attitudes do a poor job predicting behavior if there are other strong determinants of the behavior. Many people have negative attitudes about the dentist, but still make dental appointments for maintaining good health and a pleasing smile. Relatedly, attitudes do a poor job predicting behavior if the components of an attitude are in conflict. People may have negative feelings (affect) about the dentist, such as anxiety or fear, but positive thoughts (cognition), such as believing dentists are critical for maintaining good dental hygiene. Even if a person reports positive attitudes toward the dentist, they may still experience aversion at a gut level, particularly when seeing the drill! Often, these nonconscious or automatic responses to a stimulus are stronger determinants of behavior than more thoughtful, conscious beliefs. Attitudes may also do a poor job predicting behavior if the attitudes are measured at a different level of specificity than the behavior (attitude about dentists in general and behavior toward a particular dentist).

5. Suppose you're choosing between two vacation spots you think are equally amazing: Greece and Costa Rica. You have to pick one and elect to go to Costa Rica. Following your decision, Costa Rica starts to sound even more fantastic—zip-lining, cloud forests, and incredible wildlife. In contrast, Greece seems a little less special, it's expensive, and the beaches aren't really that nice. Describe a cognitive dissonance account of this change in your attitudes following the decision.

ANSWER: Cognitive dissonance theory states that inconsistencies between a person's attitudes and behavior can lead to an aversive emotional state called dissonance. After choosing Costa Rica for your vacation you may experience post-decision dissonance, because there is an inconsistency between your attitude (I like Greece) and your behavior (I did not choose Greece). To reduce this dissonance, you will probably change your attitude to better fit your behavior: you did not choose Greece (the behavior), so you must not have liked Greece very much after all (a change in your attitude). In this way, Greece starts to seem less exciting, while Costa Rica starts to seem like an even better choice.

6. Although your son already likes vegetables, you want him to eat even more vegetables. You decide to pay him $1 to spend at the toy store for every portion of vegetables he eats. Given what you learned about self-perception theory, is this a good approach? Why or why not?

ANSWER: Parents can use rewards and punishments to modify their children's behavior, such as offering their child $1 to spend at the toy store for each portion of vegetables he eats. Surely, that would entice him to eat more vegetables, right? However, there is a risk of the overjustification effect when strong rewards are given. According to this phenomenon, we tend to devalue activities we perform in order to get something else. So if you give your son $1 for eating vegetables, he may take notice of his behavior, "Hmm, I'm eating more and more veggies," but then recognize, "Oh! But I'm doing it to get the dollar." If your son started out liking vegetables, he will come to perceive himself as someone who eats vegetables—but who does so for the money. Once you stop paying him that dollar, he's likely to stop eating more vegetables, and he's even likely to eat *fewer* vegetables than he did before.

CHAPTER 8

1. A new boutique coffeehouse just opened in your neighborhood featuring coffee sustainably sourced from small organic farms around the world. Design two ads for the coffeehouse, one using the central (systematic) route to persuasion and one using the peripheral (heuristic) route. How do your ads differ?

ANSWER: The central route to persuasion occurs when the audience thinks carefully about the message's content—that is, when they have the motivation and ability to do so. An ad for the coffeehouse focusing on the central route will include strong arguments in support of the coffee and the shop itself. For example, your ad might state that sustainably sourced coffee is better for the environment, organic coffee is better for your health, in taste tests this coffee is preferred over those sold at other local shops, or the price is better.

The peripheral route to persuasion occurs when the audience has low motivation or ability to think critically about the message and they respond to superficial or easy-to-process features, such as the attractiveness or credibility of the message source. For example, you may recruit a famous chef or a trusted community leader to endorse the coffeehouse, or simply show an attractive person drinking the coffee. Alternatively, you might include colorful images of the coffee—factors that are easy to process and thus likely to persuade through the peripheral route.

2. Describe the three elements of a persuasive appeal, and give two examples of each element that influence persuasiveness.

ANSWER: The three elements of persuasion are source characteristics, message characteristics, and audience characteristics. Source characteristics are features of the person delivering the message. Attractive sources are more persuasive than unattractive sources. Credible sources, high in expertise and trustworthiness, are more apt to persuade, particularly in the present (less so with a delay—the sleeper effect). Certain or confident sources are also more likely to persuade than uncertain or less confident sources.

In terms of message characteristics, high-quality messages are more persuasive than low-quality messages, particularly if the audience is high in motivation and ability. Explicit messages are more likely to persuade than messages in which the take-home point isn't clear. Messages that overtly refute the opposition are more persuasive, as are messages in which the spokesperson argues in opposition to their own self-interest. Vivid, colorful, interesting, and memorable messages are typically persuasive, as are messages that induce fear to a moderate degree (particularly if coupled with information regarding how to counter the feared outcome). Finally, messages may vary in norms, values, and outlook, and may be especially persuasive if they match the cultural background of the target audience.

Audience characteristics are features of the person or group on the receiving end of the message. Audiences vary in their motivation and ability to process the message; those higher in motivation and ability are inclined to be persuaded by strong arguments, whereas people with low motivation and ability are more likely to be persuaded by superficial features of the message. Older participants and those with a stronger need for cognition tend to focus on argument quality when being persuaded. A person's mood can influence persuasion too. Finally, if the audience is large and diverse, abstract and general messages may be more persuasive than messages tailored to one particular group or type of person.

3. Suppose you are part of a global advertising team responsible for creating ads for oatmeal in both South Korea and the United States. Design an ad for each country, and explain why you designed the ads the way you did.

ANSWER: When designing an ad, advertising teams must consider the cultural backdrop for the message. One relevant variable is whether the culture encourages more independent or more interdependent construals of the self. Independent cultures, such as the United States, focus on individual uniqueness and self-actualization. Ads targeting such cultures should focus on the connection between the product and an individual's success or well-being. For example, an oatmeal ad in the United States might emphasize the ability of oatmeal to help *you* grow healthy and strong, and, therefore, to become the best version of yourself or achieve your hopes and dreams.

Interdependent cultures, such as South Korea, focus on social harmony. Ads targeting these cultures should focus on the connection between the product and one's social relationships. For example, an oatmeal ad in South Korea might encourage parents to buy oatmeal to help the *family* become healthy and strong.

4. What is the self-validation hypothesis? What aspects about our thoughts, besides the valence and number of thoughts we have on a topic, influence whether or not we are persuaded by them?

ANSWER: The self-validation hypothesis states that whether or not we are persuaded is influenced not only by the valence (direction) and number of thoughts we have on the issue or topic, but also on how confident we are about our thoughts. The more confident, the more we are likely to be persuaded by them. A few factors are known to influence thought confidence. The more valid we believe our thoughts are, the more easily we are able to come up with our thoughts, and the clearer our thoughts are, the more confident we'll be about our position, and the more we are likely to be persuaded.

5. Although your Uncle Ted watches hours of local news programming each night, he argues that "you young people" are way more susceptible to media messages than he is. Describe the phenomenon that Uncle Ted is exhibiting, and give an example of a study that scientifically supports the existence of such a phenomenon.

ANSWER: Uncle Ted is exhibiting the third-person effect, the assumption that other people are more easily influenced by persuasive messages (such as those in the media) than we ourselves are. In this case, Uncle Ted believes that young people are more susceptible to the media than he is, despite the fact that he watches hours of local news every night. In research described in this chapter, participants judged the impact of three media campaigns on themselves and on other participants. The campaigns included a political ad, a story about violence in the media, and a message against associating with those who drink and drive. In each case, participants believed others were more susceptible to these messages than they themselves were.

6. Tyrell and his girlfriend, Shea, have very different views on capital punishment: he opposes it, while she supports it. Even after Tyrell presents evidence that capital punishment is both financially wasteful and ineffective at preventing crime, Shea does not change her views. Using what you know about resistance to persuasion, how might Shea be staving off Tyrell's attempts to persuade her?

ANSWER: Persuasive attempts are often met with strong resistance. Even before Tyrell overtly presents her with counterattitudinal information, Shea is likely to engage in selective attention, tuning in to messages that reinforce her attitudes on capital punishment and tuning out information that contradicts them. She might seek out media outlets that support her perspective and avoid conversations with people who believe the contrary. Shea is also likely to selectively evaluate counterattitudinal messages, such as the information Tyrell presented. She might regard the arguments as weak and their sources as seriously lacking in credibility. Moreover, the more Shea knows about capital punishment, the more she will scrutinize Tyrell's messages in this way. Such processes are especially likely to occur if Shea made prior commitments to her attitudes, such as by joining a pro-capital punishment advocacy group or posting articles that support her beliefs on social media.

CHAPTER 9

1. What two reasons appear to explain why people so often mimic one another? How might each of these processes function differently in Hispanic versus Anglo-American cultures?

ANSWER: The two explanations for mimicry are as follows: (1) Because of ideomotor action, we are more likely to do something if it pops into our mind, by virtue of witnessing someone else do it. (2) Mimicry enhances rapport and prepares us to have smooth interactions. Research on cultural differences in mimicry suggests that Anglo-Americans are less sensitive to mimicry than Hispanic-Americans, due to Hispanic cultures placing more value on attunement to the emotions and the behaviors of others. Valuing attunement more might make Hispanics more likely to think about others, instigating more ideomotor action that matches others' behavior. But more important, greater attunement to others' emotions and behavior may also increase an individual's concern with rapport and having smooth interactions, which in turn is likely to foster mimicry.

2. Suppose your dining hall is having a contest, and you have to guess how many gumballs are in a giant jar (the closest guess wins). You and a few friends walk up to the gumball jar and tell your guesses to the volunteer running the contest. Your friends all say their guesses out loud, and you go last. You find yourself increasing your gumball estimate to be closer to those of your friends. How could each type of social influence (normative and informational) have affected your guess? How could you reduce the normative social influence in this situation?

ANSWER: Given that you're making a judgment about something uncertain (there's not an obvious right answer), you may have used your friends' guesses as a useful source of information, helping you arrive at a judgment that seemed more accurate; this is informational social influence. But given that you're also stating these judgments publicly, there is pressure to state a judgment that is similar to those of your friends, so you won't be seen as odd or clueless; this is normative social influence. You could reduce the normative social influence inherent in this situation by privately submitting your answers on pieces of paper, rather than stating them out loud.

3. In the battle for LGBT rights, what kind of social influence can minority LGBT groups exert on the majority? Should their goal be to engage public support or private internalization and acceptance of their arguments among members of the majority?

ANSWER: When minority groups influence majority groups to enact social change, it is typically via informational social influence, convincing members of the majority group to hear out their arguments and better understand their perspective. Normative social influence, which typically results in mere public compliance (without any private acceptance of LGBT arguments or positions), is a less powerful tool here, as the majority doesn't feel much pressure to conform and avoid public scorn; they largely control the public scorn, after all. Luckily, informational social influence is nonetheless a powerful force, one that is more likely to result in private acceptance and internalization of the minority perspective among members of the majority, which will likely aid the LGBT cause more in the long run.

4. Although they are distinct compliance strategies, the that's-not-all and door-in-the-face techniques share a common mechanism. What is it, and how does it work in each case?

ANSWER: Both strategies rely on the norm of reciprocity, a pervasive human norm whereby we are obligated to repay favors in order to maintain harmony and balance in social relationships and societies. In both techniques, the person seeking compliance (asking someone for a donation, for example) gives or gives up something to the target person, which then encourages that person to return the favor. In the door-in-the-face technique, the asker makes a concession by lowering their original ask, which then creates pressure for the target to also make a concession, in the form of complying (donating). In the that's-not-all technique, the asker keeps throwing in "free" gifts for the target, which creates pressure for the target to return the favor, in the form of complying (donating).

5. Suppose you want to increase voting rates among millennials (people born in the 1980s and 1990s). Describe one reason-based approach, one emotion-based approach, and one norm-based approach you could use to do so.

ANSWER: Reason-based approach: you could use a foot-in-the-door technique, asking eligible voters to do small volunteering duties for the election, which would highlight their sense of self as a politically engaged individual, hopefully leading to more behavior consistent with that sense of self, such as voting.

Emotion-based approach: you could give away cookies on the street on election day to induce positive emotion before reminding people to vote, which could lead them to construe the act of voting as not terribly inconvenient and make them more inclined to engage in a valued civic act to further or sustain their good mood.

Norm-based approach: you could create flyers that highlight how many people vote in certain neighborhoods and age groups, but you'd have to be careful not to advertise a norm of *not* voting, if rates were low. Adding a smiling face along with the numbers could help communicate that high voting rates are desirable.

6. In the context of the Milgram experiment, give an example of "tuning in the learner" and an example of "tuning out the experimenter," and explain how each one affects obedience rates.

ANSWER: "Tuning in the learner" means heightening the salience of the learner, and the consequences of the participant's actions for the learner's health and well-being. For example, having the participant hold the learner's hand against the shock plate while administering the shocks makes the participant more aware of what he's doing to another person by obeying the instructions of the experimenter, thereby reducing obedience rates. In contrast, "tuning out the experimenter" means reducing the salience of the experimenter, for instance by having the experimenter administer instructions over an intercom rather than in person. This tends to reduce the experimenter's authority and influence over the participant, thus reducing obedience.

CHAPTER 10

1. The need to belong is thought to be a fundamental human drive. Similar to physical drives like hunger, when people have their need to belong satisfied, they are unlikely to pursue this drive further. Based on this idea of drive satiation, who should be more likely to call up a friend to make plans: Betty, who's been spending lots of quality time with her children lately, or Blanche, who tends to stay home by herself?

ANSWER: If the need to belong resembles physical drives like hunger, the less belonging one feels, the more "socially hungry" one should feel, and the more motivated one should be to try to connect with others. This feeling of low belonging is like the feeling of an empty stomach, and it motivates a person to seek social contact. In this scenario, Blanche should be more hungry for social contact, and should be more apt to seek out connection with a friend, compared to Betty, who should have her fill of social contact from spending time with her children.

2. Sean and Mitch are just starting a relationship, but they seem to have different expectations about what each one deserves from a romantic partner. Sean thinks if his partner doesn't treat him extremely well, he's just not worth his time because there are better guys out there. Mitch, on the other hand, has been in several bad relationships and puts up with just about anything from a partner because he's deeply afraid of being alone. How would you describe Sean and Mitch's respective comparison levels and comparison levels for alternatives? What might the consequences of these levels be?

ANSWER: Sean appears to have a higher comparison level than Mitch, because he believes he deserves better treatment from his romantic partners than Mitch believes he himself does. Sean's comparison level for alternatives in this scenario is high, because he thinks there are better guys out there than a romantic partner who doesn't treat him extremely well. This suggests that Sean sees many potential rewards (high-quality partners) outside of his relationship. Coupled with his high comparison level, Sean may be quick to leave his relationship with Mitch if he doesn't get the treatment he thinks he deserves. Mitch's comparison level for alternatives in this scenario is about being alone (also an alternative to his current romantic situation), but it's low; he sees being alone as an undesirable alternative. This suggests that Mitch may put up with more bad behavior from a partner due to both his low comparison level and his low comparison level for alternatives; he doesn't expect much from his partner, and doesn't see many desirable alternatives to being in his current relationship.

3. If Jenny feels comfortable relying on and being close to her immediate family members, and she seeks extremely intimate, clingy romantic relationships but keeps her distance from her friends, not disclosing much to them or counting on them, how would you analyze her attachment styles? How would you describe her working models?

ANSWER: It sounds like Jenny has distinct attachment styles for the different types of relationships in her life. She has a secure attachment style with her family, because she feels comfortable trusting them and doesn't seem to worry about being close to them. But with her romantic partners, Jenny seeks extreme union and wants to be exceedingly close and intimate; this is characteristic of an anxious attachment style. With her friends, Jenny seems avoidant, seeking extreme independence and showing reluctance to be close and dependent. Jenny seems to have multiple attachment working models, for all three styles of attachment, that become activated and applied differently in various relationships.

4. Robert has a crush on Marilyn, but she doesn't seem to know he's alive. What could Robert do to make himself more attractive to Marilyn, based on the principles of proximity and similarity in terms of liking and attraction?

ANSWER: If Robert wanted to capitalize on proximity, he should find a way to get physically close to Marilyn, such as sitting by or near her in lecture, or moving to an apartment or dorm near hers. The more mere exposure Marilyn experiences with Robert, the more Marilyn should come to like him, so any way he can increase the probability of their paths crossing should help his cause. If he wanted to use similarity, Robert should highlight the ways he and Marilyn are similar, perhaps by altering the style of clothes he wears to more closely resemble hers, playing up the interests they have in common, or taking up new hobbies and causes she enjoys. The more similar Robert appears to be to her, the more rewarding their interactions will be, and the more Marilyn should feel validated about herself.

5. Suppose Alice wants to try an experiment about the halo effect of physical attractiveness on an online dating website. She sets up

two profiles for herself, making the content of the profiles identical except for her picture. On one profile, she uses a beautiful photo of herself as her profile photo, but on the other profile, she uses a horrible photo of herself. How might men respond to these two profiles, and how might Alice respond to them in turn?

ANSWER: Based on the halo effect, the high and low attractiveness photos should create self-fulfilling prophecies for Alice's experiences on each profile. Compared to the ugly profile, when men on the site are interacting with the pretty Alice profile, they may see her content as more charming and interesting and attractive, and in turn may write her more interesting, engaging messages, and see her responses to those messages as wittier and funnier. Moreover, Alice's responses could also be affected by the manipulation, such that she may feel more engaged with the men who are interacting with her pretty profile, and actually write better messages. In this way, the heightened expectations men have based on the pretty Alice profile may end up actually eliciting a better side of Alice, compared to Alice's behavior when interacting via the ugly profile.

6. How can the investment model of commitment help explain why people stay in long-term abusive relationships? How might an abusive partner manipulate the factors that contribute to commitment, to make an abuse victim stay in the relationship?

ANSWER: In abusive relationships, satisfaction is probably fairly low, since the costs are great. But satisfaction is not the only determinant of commitment; possible alternative partners and investments in the relationship are the other two. Investment in an abusive relationship may be high, if the partners are married, financially linked, have children and property together, and have intertwined lives. In any long-term relationship, many resources have been devoted to it over the years. It's possible an abusive romantic partner would deliberately increase investment on the part of a partner, for instance by having more children or making more joint commitments (such as loans), or would find ways to remind the partner of all the investments already made. Alternative partners may also come into play: perhaps partners in abusive relationships feel there are no other options, and that at least having the "good" times with the current partner is better than being alone or with some unknown other. Abusive partners could well manipulate perceptions of alternatives, such as making critical comments that make an abuse victim feel unworthy of love from anyone else. The cycle of abuse is powerful, and leaving is not always determined by something as simple as low satisfaction.

CHAPTER 11

1. Is it possible for people to be prejudiced without being aware of it? How have researchers addressed this question, and what evidence have they found?

ANSWER: Research suggests that it is indeed possible for people to be prejudiced without necessarily being aware of it. Implicit measures, such as the implicit association test (IAT), can reveal subtle, nonconscious prejudice even among those who sincerely believe they are not prejudiced. In research described in this chapter, participants whose IAT scores showed implicit prejudice toward African-Americans were more likely to show activation in a brain area associated with fear when they viewed African-American faces, but they were not more likely to report prejudiced beliefs on the Modern Racism Scale. These results suggest that people may hold attitudes they are either unable or unwilling to acknowledge.

2. Suppose every year, the male CEO of a small company always asks a female employee to take care of organizing the company's holiday party. When one female employee asks the CEO why he always gives this task to women, he says that women are better party planners than men. Is this an example of sexism? Why or why not? What adverse effects might the CEO's positive stereotype regarding women's party planning ability have on the female employees?

ANSWER: The CEO's characterization of women as skilled party planners is an example of benevolent sexism, which refers to positive stereotypes of outgroup members that can nonetheless lead to discrimination and impede social progress. Although the CEO's attitude toward women seems positive, it may also have negative components, such as the belief that women are not as effective as men in more important leadership roles. His attitude may also make his female employees feel they need to conform to traditional female gender roles in order to gain his approval. Another potential cost of the CEO's behavior is that his female employees may have to devote valuable time, which they could be spending on other work, to tasks that are not part of their job description and not helpful for advancing their career.

3. Describe the Robbers Cave experiment, and outline three important points this study revealed about intergroup relations.

ANSWER: After intense screening, the researchers enrolled 22 average boys into their summer camp. The boys were split into two groups and spent the first phase of the study developing a strong group identity through participation in games and activities. In the second phase, the two groups were brought together for a camp competition. The winner of the competition would receive a desirable prize, while the loser would receive nothing. The researchers evaluated intergroup relations and found that hostility between the groups was rampant. Following this competition phase, the researchers brought the groups together under friendlier circumstances. Intergroup conflict did not dissipate. Subsequently, the researchers staged various camp "crises" the boys had to solve by working together. Cooperation, here induced by external demands, did mitigate the conflict between the groups.

This study contributed important insights to the economic perspective, specifically realistic group conflict theory. Three important points from this study include the following. (1) Competition over resources fosters intergroup conflict. During the competition phase, the boys fought over material resources: a medal, along with a highly coveted pocketknife. Here, hostility abounded, involving name calling, food fights, cabin raids, and challenges to fight. (2) Defusing intergroup conflict cannot be accomplished through contact alone. During the third phase, the boys were brought together under noncompetitive circumstances, but name calling and fighting persisted. (3) Emphasizing superordinate goals relevant to both groups is necessary for contact to mitigate intergroup conflict. Once the boys worked together to solve the camp crises, including fixing a broken water pipe and pulling a broken down supply truck with a rope, hostility dissolved and friendships developed among the group members.

4. Imagine that a conversation about race relations in the United States develops during a family dinner. One of your relatives argues that given how ubiquitous stereotypes are, prejudice and discrimination are inevitable. Using research from the cognitive perspective, in particular automatic and controlling processing, how would you respond to this assertion? Are prejudice and

discrimination inevitable? Under which conditions are they more likely to emerge?

ANSWER: As your relative argues, research finds that even non-prejudiced people are aware of cultural stereotypes. Moreover, they are likely to be activated automatically, quickly, and reflexively. Research described in this chapter found that participants who were primed (outside of their conscious awareness) with words related to an African-American stereotype were more likely to perceive a target's behavior as hostile in a subsequent task. This automatic stereotyping effect was found even among people who were nonprejudiced, as measured with the Modern Racism Scale. These results, however, do not suggest that prejudice and discrimination are inevitable under all circumstances. If someone is motivated and has cognitive resources available, she can still engage in controlled processing to regulate these automatic tendencies. In a subsequent study, participants described characteristics of African-Americans. This task involved controlled processing. Participants had the time and energy to respond as they saw fit. Even though all participants were aware of negative African-American stereotypes (as demonstrated in the first study), nonprejudiced participants listed fewer negative characteristics than prejudiced participants. Collectively, these results suggest that although nonprejudiced people are aware of stereotypes, when controlled processing is possible they will take care not to use them; under such circumstances, prejudice and discrimination are not inevitable, contrary to your relative's argument.

5. Suppose a woman named Taylor was applying for a job at an accounting firm, and applicants had to complete a math test as part of the onsite interview process. If Taylor met her older male interviewer just prior to taking the math test and he (inappropriately) exclaimed, "You're Taylor? I was expecting, well, a man . . ." what impact might that have on Taylor's test performance, interview performance, and eventual likelihood of getting the job?

ANSWER: Taylor will likely experience stereotype threat during her math test, meaning she will become concerned that she will fulfill the stereotype that women are bad at math, and this concern will ultimately detract from her performance on the test, thus fulfilling the stereotype after all. She may also struggle during the interview if she believes her interviewer is biased against her, or if her interviewer is in fact biased against her, treating her differently than he would treat male applicants for the job. This may result in a self-fulfilling prophecy, wherein Taylor and/or Taylor's interviewer expects her to do poorly, she in turn does poorly, and ends up not getting the job.

6. Suppose you are a social psychologist and have been hired to help reduce prejudice and discrimination among students of different races, classes, cultures, and sexual orientations in a school system. What might you evaluate or implement in addressing this concern?

ANSWER: According to the contact hypothesis, bringing together students of different backgrounds is an important first step in reducing prejudice and discrimination. However, research suggests that simple contact between groups is not enough. For example, participants in the Robbers Cave experiment continued to display intergroup hostility after the competition phase, when the groups were brought together under friendlier circumstances. Additional conditions must be met for contact to work. Members of each group must have equal status. Teachers and administrators must not favor one group over another in the classroom or other institutional programs. This would be an important area of evaluation. Moreover, parents, teachers, and community members must support the contact, and

not endorse it begrudgingly. Evaluating and addressing these individuals' beliefs and behaviors is therefore as important as monitoring the students themselves. As the Robbers Cave experiment showed, superordinate goals that prompt cooperation among groups helps to reduce intergroup hostility and catalyzes the development of friendships. You may recommend that teachers institute a jigsaw classroom, in which students from different backgrounds are responsible for different parts of an assignment, and must, therefore, work together to complete it in total. In addition, one-on-one interactions help people to see others as more than just outgroup members. Assigning students from different backgrounds to work in pairs in the classroom, or during other school activities, could foster this kind of individualized contact.

CHAPTER 12

1. Open-plan offices, where large communal desks are used in place of private rooms or cubicles, are becoming increasingly popular. From the perspective of Zajonc's social facilitation theory, do you think open-plan offices are likely to facilitate or hinder performance and productivity? Why or why not? How might it depend on the type of work being conducted?

ANSWER: According to Zajonc's social facilitation theory, the presence of others tends to increase physiological arousal, which facilitates performance on well-learned, reflexive tasks but can impair performance on more complex tasks. Open-plan offices may therefore facilitate performance and productivity for employees who work at simple, repetitive tasks, whereas they may hinder performance for those who work on novel, unpredictable, and highly challenging tasks. For the latter group, private rooms may be more beneficial.

2. Can you think of any examples in your own life where groupthink has taken place? What factors contributed to groupthink in these situations? What kinds of safeguards could you put in place in similar future situations to promote better decision making?

ANSWER: Examples relevant to students could involve decisions made by a close group of friends, a student organization, a sports team, or a group working on a project together. Groupthink refers to the tendency for highly cohesive groups to make poor decisions when critical scrutiny of the issues at hand is subverted by social pressures to reach consensus. Factors that can contribute to groupthink include the presence of a strong leader, a sense of invulnerability and moral superiority, a narrow consideration of alternatives, and self-censorship of important information and conflicting viewpoints for fear of disrupting group harmony. Approaches that have been shown to reduce groupthink include designating "devil's advocates" to take alternative positions and point out weaknesses in the plan, welcoming outside input to protect against insularity, and having the group leader refrain from making his or her opinions or preferences known at the beginning of the discussion.

3. Suppose your company is trying to decide whether to make a risky new hire. Individually, most of the members of the hiring team lean toward hiring the candidate, as it could substantially increase revenues if it works out. When the hiring team gets together to discuss the potential hire, how might you predict that the attitudes of the individuals in the group will shift? What decision is likely to be made?

ANSWER: According to research on group polarization, group decisions tend to be more extreme than those made by individuals, and they tend to be extreme in whatever direction individuals are already leaning. In the hiring decision example, individuals are already leaning in favor of the risky hire, so the group discussion is likely to polarize individuals further in the direction of the hire and increase the likelihood that the hire will be made. Group polarization may be due in part to exposure to additional persuasive arguments from others, and in part to the desire to measure up favorably in comparison to others (that is, to appear even more comfortable with risk than others if riskiness is valued).

4. In *The Prince*, Machiavelli argued that people gain power through deception, manipulation, coercion, and the use of fear tactics. How does this perspective compare with research findings from about who rises to power?

ANSWER: People typically gain power by having knowledge and expertise that is relevant to the goals and identity of the group, by possessing strong social skills and building cooperative alliances among group members, and by demonstrating generosity and fairness. These findings suggest that Machiavelli's perspective may only apply some times and may not be generally accurate.

5. Do you think it's accurate to say that power corrupts? Why or why not? What factors influence the extent to which power leads to prosocial versus antisocial behavior?

ANSWER: Power involves the freedom to act on one's own wishes, without being constrained by others' wishes. According to the approach/inhibition theory of power, this lack of constraint and inhibition can lead high-power people to make impulsive decisions, stereotype others, feel less empathy, and engage in antisocial behaviors, such as sexual harassment and aggression. Low-power people, by contrast, need to be more cautious and socially attuned because their outcomes are more dependent on others. One factor that can counteract the disinhibiting effects of power is accountability, or a sense of responsibility toward others. Having a child, for example, can make powerful people less likely to engage in reckless behaviors. Another key factor is the extent to which a high-power individual has a communally oriented disposition to begin with: the acquisition of power can lead communally oriented individuals to behave more prosocially, rather than selfishly.

6. What does research on deindividuation show about why crime rates are so high on Halloween?

ANSWER: Deindividuation refers to a reduced sense of individual identity accompanied by diminished self-regulation that can occur in a large group. Deindividuation is fueled by anonymity, diffusion of responsibility, and high levels of arousal, all of which are common on Halloween, when people are disguised in masks and costumes, shrouded in darkness, and likely to move around in large packs. As a result, people might be more prone to engage in destructive and illegal behaviors that they would not have otherwise engaged in, such as vandalism, theft, or assault.

7. How could you use your knowledge of self-awareness theory to reduce cheating behavior on a test that relies on the honor system?

ANSWER: People are more likely to behave in line with their internal standards and values—and therefore behave more ethically—when they focus attention on themselves. One way to increase self-awareness and thereby reduce cheating could be to put a mirror in the testing room, or have students walk by a mirror before taking the test. Another approach could be to display objects that look like eyes or faces in the room so students have the implicit sense that their behavior is being monitored. This approach has been shown to be effective for promoting contributions to an "honest box" in exchange for the use of shared resources, such as coffee in an office setting.

CHAPTER 13

1. Describe the culture of honor, and provide two pieces of evidence that support this characterization. What might be the origin of these cultural tendencies?

ANSWER: A culture of honor, such as the one in parts of the U.S. South, is characterized by strong concerns regarding reputation. Acts of aggression or violence may be used to avenge insults or other threats to one's honor. According to research covered in this chapter, homicides resulting from perceived insult are more common in the South than the North, and people from the South have been found to react with greater emotion when insulted. This is not the case for other types of crimes. Cultures of honor are believed to grow out of societies that rely on animal herding as a main source of income, where a herder's entire livelihood would be lost if someone stole their animals.

2. According to the research described in this chapter, what kinds of attitudes and behaviors are more likely among men who dehumanize women as animals? Is this form of dehumanization a denial of human nature or a denial of human uniqueness?

ANSWER: Men who show faster response times to pairings of the concept of "woman" with animal-related words, indicating implicit dehumanization, are more likely to report a willingness to sexually harass and rape women, and to believe that women sometimes deserve to be raped. The association of women with animals is a denial of human uniqueness, or the attributes that distinguish humans from other species, such as civility, refinement, and complex cognitive capacities. Denial of human uniqueness is contrasted with denial of human nature, or the attributes that distinguish humans from inanimate entities, such as computers and robots.

3. Suppose you're the warden at a prison and can select the temperature setting for the master prison thermostat, but the thermostat didn't have enough settings, forcing you to choose between an uncomfortably cold setting and an uncomfortably hot setting. Which should you choose and why?

ANSWER: Given the strong connection between hot temperatures and aggressive behavior, you may want to set the thermostat a bit too cold, rather than too hot. If the temperature were too hot in the prison, the prisoners might start to exhibit increasingly aggressive behavior (due perhaps to attributing their discomfort to their fellow inmates, rather than the prison's temperature), which could result in more fights and potentially spiral toward a prison riot. It would be safer, at least in terms of levels of aggression, to err on the side of the prison being too cool.

4. Sometimes people respond to social rejection with physical aggression. How does the fundamental nature of our need for social connectedness help explain this tendency?

ANSWER: Humans are an inherently social species, and have evolved a fundamental system to maintain social connectedness, because it probably aided our early survival. Because social rejection was a kind of death sentence, we have a basic aversive response to it that activates a threat defense system. This system triggers responses normally cued by physical threats, such as surges in stress hormones, aroused fight-or-flight patterns, and increased defensive aggressive tendencies.

5. Suppose a friend said to you, "Well, men are just biologically hard-wired to be more aggressive than women." How would you respond? What nuances might this perspective miss?

ANSWER: First, women do exhibit aggression, but in different ways than men do. Women more commonly express relational aggression, which involves emotional rather than physical forms of harm, such as spreading rumors and damaging a reputation. Second, although some biological factors dictate gender differences in aggression, such as testosterone levels and overall size and strength, cultural factors also play a role. From a very young age, male and female children are treated differently, and aggressive behavior is both more readily perceived and more encouraged among males than females. Thus, any gender differences in physical aggression may not be purely biologically determined, but may be encouraged by cultural values as well.

6. What kinds of strategies have been shown to be most effective for reducing conflict and promoting peace, and why?

ANSWER: Face-to-face communication involving respectful dialogue and complex reasoning has been shown to facilitate conflict resolution by encouraging participants to find common ground and overcome misperceptions of the other group. It can also be helpful to understand that violence is often motivated not by blood lust but by a genuine sense of moral obligation, misguided as it may be; failure to recognize the motivation behind violence can lead to ineffective military interventions. Formal and informal reconciliation processes involving confession, apology, taking responsibility, and making reparations have been shown to be highly effective; for example, crime victims who participate in restorative justice programs report fewer thoughts of revenge.

CHAPTER 14

1. Someone might argue that as long as you're helping, your motives don't matter. Do you agree? Why or why not? In what situations might motives matter most?

ANSWER: There are three primary motives for helping. Two of them are egoistic: the desire for social rewards and the desire to reduce personal distress. The third is altruistic: empathic concern. Although the two egoistic motives can lead to helping behavior, they do so less consistently than empathic concern. Getting social rewards or reducing personal distress can be achieved many ways, not all of which involve helping; by contrast, empathic concern has been shown to consistently lead to helping, often at a cost to the self. A person who is motivated by social rewards and distress reduction may help only when rewards are available and when there are no other ways to reduce distress, but he or she may be less likely to help when helping behavior would be anonymous or when it's possible to easily escape the situation.

2. Based on what you've learned about bystander intervention and diffusion of responsibility, what actions could you take to increase the likelihood that someone would help you in an emergency that happens in front of a large crowd?

ANSWER: People are less likely to help when other people are around, presumably because they believe someone else will help. One way to reduce this diffusion of responsibility could be to single out one person and ask if she can help you. People hesitate to help when they don't know whether a situation is actually an emergency, and when they don't know what to do to help. To address this concern, you could clarify the situation by explicitly calling out and being specific about what you need people to do, such as helping you get up or calling an ambulance.

3. Research indicates that lower-class people tend to be more empathic and giving than upper-class people. What factors might explain this difference? How might they relate to what you learned about power and prosocial behavior?

ANSWER: Lower-class people are more attuned to those around them, in part because social attunement is necessary for adapting to unpredictable, stressful, and at times threatening environments. Upper-class people, by contrast, can be more independent from others because they enjoy greater resources and opportunities. This pattern is similar to that seen in the context of power. High-power people tend to be less empathic. Upper-class people may also be less likely to be regularly exposed to certain forms of suffering, but this can be remedied: research suggests, for example, that it's possible to increase compassion and prosocial behavior in upper-class people by exposing them to film clips portraying the suffering of children living in poverty.

4. According to evolutionary theory, behaviors that optimize survival and reproduction are favored by natural selection and therefore more likely to persist. How, then, can we explain the evolution of altruism, which is by definition costly to the self?

ANSWER: There are a number of possible evolutionary explanations for altruism, including kin selection, whereby evolution and natural selection favor behaviors that increase the chances of survival of genetic relatives. Kin selection can explain altruism toward relatives, but not non-kin. One explanation for altruism toward non-kin is reciprocity, or helping others with the expectation that they will reciprocate in the future. Reciprocal altruism can reduce the likelihood of conflict and facilitate resource sharing.

5. After learning about research on gossip, have your feelings about this behavior changed? Under what circumstances might gossip serve a useful purpose?

ANSWER: Gossip is a communicative act in which someone comments on the reputation of another person who is not present. This communication can be beneficial when it lets people learn about whom to trust and whom to avoid. Research suggests that when people have the opportunity to gossip, they are consequently more cooperative than when they don't. This may be because the threat of gossip serves as a warning that one's reputation could suffer if one behaves selfishly. Not all types of gossip are beneficial, however; mean-spirited comments about someone's appearance will not promote cooperation or goodwill.

6. In what ways could the tit-for-tat strategy be relevant in your life, such as a romantic relationship?

ANSWER: Tit-for-tat is a strategy to encourage mutual cooperation in the prisoner's dilemma game. This reciprocal strategy is cooperative, nonenvious, nonexploitable, forgiving, and easy to read. It helps maximize outcomes in potentially competitive situations that occur in real life. In the context of a romantic relationship, this strategy could involve being supportive and giving toward your partner initially, and continuing to do so as long as he is supportive and giving toward you, but not if he mistreats you.

APPLICATION MODULE 1: SOCIAL PSYCHOLOGY AND HEALTH

1. The experience of psychological stress typically triggers a host of physiological changes, including increased heart rate and blood pressure, sweating, and suppression of the immune system. When might these changes be helpful, and when are they more likely to be harmful?

ANSWER: The stress response evolved to help humans respond adaptively to threats in their environment and maximize their chance of survival. Increases in heart rate and blood pressure serve to distribute blood to appropriate muscle groups involved in fight-or-flight behavior, sweating helps regulate body temperature and may facilitate grasping motions, and the suppression of the immune system frees up resources for more pressing tasks. These physiological changes can be helpful for coping with short-term dangers, but when stress is chronic, they can lead to organ damage and the development of ulcers, heart disease, and cancer. Rumination, the tendency to think about a stressful event repeatedly, can contribute to chronic stress and increase health risks.

2. Who is more likely to suffer from health problems, a janitor or a Fortune 500 CEO, and why? How might each person's subjective construal of their position influence their health?

ANSWER: We might expect the janitor to be less healthy than the CEO, based on research showing that lower-SES individuals (having less family wealth and income, less education, and less prestigious jobs) are more likely to have health problems than higher-SES people. This difference can be explained by a number of factors, such as the presence of greater environmental toxins and less access to health care in lower-SES neighborhoods. Another explanation is that lower-SES people are more likely to feel they occupy a subordinate rank in society and therefore experience greater stress. In some cases, however, even someone in an objectively high position, like a CEO, may feel inferior relative to his or her peers and experience stress-related health issues as a result. By the same token, a janitor may enjoy high status within his or her community and experience good health as a result.

3. According to the tend-and-befriend theory, why might social support improve health?

ANSWER: When we tend to the needs of other people, the chemical oxytocin is released into our brain and bloodstream. Oxytocin has been shown to increase feelings of trust and love, and to reduce the stress hormone cortisol. Reduced cortisol levels can, in turn, benefit physical health. This research suggests that people may be able to improve their health by giving support to others, not just by receiving support.

4. Research indicates that optimistic people tend to enjoy better health. Can you conclude from these findings that becoming more optimistic will improve your health? Why or why not? If you were a researcher conducting a study on this topic, what other factors might you want to control for?

ANSWER: No, it is not possible to infer causality from a correlational study design. Optimistic people may enjoy better health in part because they had a better prognosis to begin with, among other reasons unrelated to optimism. As a researcher, it would be important to control for factors such as current health status, disease prognosis, and available financial and social resources. It would also be helpful to experimentally increase optimism in a group of randomly chosen participants and compare this group's health over time with that of a control group.

APPLICATION MODULE 2: SOCIAL PSYCHOLOGY AND PERSONAL FINANCE

1. Traditional economic models and theories were founded on the notion that people are rational in their economic decision making. However, research from the relatively new field of behavioral economics suggests that this assumption is wrong. Describe at least three pieces of evidence presented in the module that supports the behavioral economists' assertion.

ANSWER: Behavioral economics research indicates that people are often irrational in their financial decision making. Mood influences investments in the stock market, with markets rising on sunny days (presumably because investors are in a good mood) and declining on gloomy days (because the mood of many investors is less sunny). Because of loss aversion, people may make terrible financial decisions to avoid the feeling that they took a loss on an investment. The way a financial transaction is framed (such as a discount versus a surcharge or a payout versus a tax break) can lead people to make different decisions based on superficial features that should have no bearing on their choice. Given how unpleasant it feels to waste money, people will let financial decisions from the past guide their current behavior, even though only the future costs and benefits of a choice should be considered. This is the sunk cost fallacy. Behavioral economists have also demonstrated that people will treat money differently depending on its source, or their mental accounting. For example, money won at a casino may be spent more recklessly than money earned at the office. Finally, people can experience costly decision paralysis when they have too many options to choose from.

2. Jacob has racked up some serious credit card debt and decides to allocate $250 from his monthly paycheck to paying off the money he owes. For his birthday, Jacob's grandparents send him a check for $100. He has the opportunity to cut down on the interest he's paying to the credit card company if he puts the money toward paying off his bill. As the $100 was a gift, however, Jacob construes it as spending money and uses it to buy a new phone. Describe a behavioral economics principle that applies to Jacob's decision regarding how to spend the $100.

ANSWER: Mental accounting involves treating money differently as a function of the psychological category it has been assigned. Jacob has created a mental category for money for paying off his credit card debt. This is the $250 from his monthly paycheck. In contrast, Jacob assigns monetary gifts, such as the $100 his grandparents gave him, to the category of spending money. It might be wiser for Jacob to put the $100 gift toward his credit card debt, thereby lowering the amount of money he will pay in interest. Because the gift does not fall into the mental category for money for paying off credit card debt, however, he does not do so.

APPLICATION MODULE 3: SOCIAL PSYCHOLOGY AND EDUCATION

1. On the first day of summer volleyball camp, if the camp counselors were told that the campers in Cabin 1 are on the verge of a growth and strength spurt, compared to the campers in Cabin 2, what is likely to happen? How large will the effect of this manipulation probably be? What factors would increase or reduce the impact of this manipulation?

ANSWER: Based on the results of studies described in this module, the manipulated expectations should make the camp counselors expect and ultimately elicit stronger performance from the campers in Cabin 1. However, the effect might not be particularly strong, as many follow-up studies have demonstrated. The manipulation would have a smaller impact if the counselors were given this information halfway through the summer, but the manipulation could have a larger impact if the campers in Cabin 1 were low-achieving and/or beginners at volleyball.

2. Suppose Alex is choosing between two math classes for next semester. She can take either Math 301, which is outside her comfort zone but would teach her new skills, or Math 210, which is well within her domain of knowledge, and she'd probably get an A. If Alex were an entity theorist, which class would she likely select? Do you think entity versus incremental theorists differ in their overall GPA?

ANSWER: As an entity theorist, Alex would likely choose Math 210, an opportunity to document her existing ability, which she probably thinks of as being relatively fixed. Entity theorists usually don't take on challenging opportunities for growth, because these might indicate lack of adequate skills. If Alex were instead an incremental theorist, she would probably choose the "stretch" class (301), to help her learn new skills, which is consistent with her concept of her ability. If this pattern played out repeatedly across a student's college years, you *could* perhaps predict a lower GPA for incremental theorists, who would take on more challenging opportunities for growth, registering for classes that don't guarantee high grades. However, research demonstrates that incremental theorists actually end up with *higher* grades than entity theorists, perhaps due to greater effort expended on academic work.

3. How would you change your college's Freshman Welcome program to help reduce achievement differences among students who are traditionally underrepresented in higher education (such as African-American and first-generation college students)?

ANSWER: The research reviewed in this module suggests several potentially powerful factors that could help underrepresented students perform at their highest potential. First, teaching new students that they are in control of their performance, and that they can grow and change and improve their skill set and intelligence—essentially giving them an incremental mind-set about their abilities—could be very helpful. Second, assuring them that everyone has concerns about fitting in and finding friends on campus could help reduce the fear of not belonging, thus ultimately increasing their confidence and ability to achieve. Third, framing the college experience in a way that resonates with an interdependent mind-set (for example, focusing on community and collaboration) could help to make college a welcoming environment where their learning could be expected to increase their closeness to others.

APPLICATION MODULE 4: SOCIAL PSYCHOLOGY AND THE LAW

1. Suppose your laptop was stolen from your dorm room one night, and a few of your neighbors caught a glimpse of a suspect as they were arriving home from a party. Your residence hall advisor (RA) brings in these neighbors individually to ask them about the suspect they saw. How should your RA pose his or her questions to your neighbors, in order to get the most accurate eyewitness testimony possible?

ANSWER: Given the malleability of memory based on prompting, and given that the witnesses only caught a glimpse and may have been inebriated (and thus uncertain about what they saw), your RA should avoid leading the witnesses toward any specific details, such as asking any questions that suggest the perpetrator was of a specific gender, ethnicity, or stature, and avoid planting any details about what the person was wearing or carrying. For instance, it would be less problematic to ask "Can you describe the person's clothes?" than to ask a detail-specific question, like "Was the person wearing a blue sweatshirt?" Although it could be tempting to prod for such details, especially if another witness provided them initially, research shows that memory is highly suggestible and changeable, and that asking leading questions could alter the witnesses' memory significantly.

2. If you were in charge of establishing rules for jury deliberation, what could you do to increase the likelihood that minority opinions would be adequately considered? What research findings would you cite to back up your decisions?

ANSWER: You could require a minimum of 12 rather than 6 jurors, based on research showing that individuals with minority opinions are more likely to stick to their convictions, rather than quickly giving in to the majority view, if they have an ally. Just based on numbers, the likelihood that more than one juror will hold a minority opinion is greater in a group of 12 than in a group of 6. You could also require unanimous verdicts. Research suggests that juries that don't have to reach a unanimous verdict spend significantly less time discussing the case. Once they reach the minimum number of jurors required to come to a verdict, they tend to end their discussion and minority opinions are no longer considered.

3. Maria and Tanya are on the jury in a civil court case that has found the defendant guilty. They must now decide how the defendant should be punished. During their deliberations, it becomes clear that Maria is angered by the defendant's behavior, while Tanya feels sympathy. Using what you learned in this module, describe the differing attributions that might have led to Maria's anger compared to Tanya's sympathy. Which kind of punishment do you think each woman is likely to prefer?

ANSWER: According to research, the emotion an individual experiences in response to a criminal act, such as anger versus sympathy, drives the type of punishment that person prefers. The emotion depends on the attributions the juror makes about the defendant and his behavior. Maria, for example, is likely to experience anger to the degree that she (1) believes the defendant is responsible for the crime and intended for the crime to occur, and (2) believes the crime reflects a stable part of the defendant's character. In contrast, Tanya is likely to experience sympathy to the degree that she (1) believes that situational factors, including the defendant's upbringing and past history, influenced the crime, and (2) believes the crime does not reflect a stable part of the defendant's character—that is, for example, that the defendant has the potential to change. The emotion a juror experiences in response to the defendant and the crime influences the juror's sense of appropriate punishment. If a juror feels anger, like Maria, she is more likely to prefer just desserts punishment, wanting the defendant to suffer in proportion to the crime. In contrast, if a juror feels sympathy, like Tanya, she is more inclined to prefer deterrence, punishment that will deter the defendant from committing similar crimes in the future, such as rehabilitation or engagement with the community.

4. Thais and Elisa both get speeding tickets, and are being punished by their parents. Thais's parents have a system of rules they follow for punishing all their children, and calmly but firmly explain to Thais that she will be grounded for 1 month. Elisa's parents, in contrast, favor her brothers over her, punish their children inconsistently from week to week, and scream at Elisa for her mistake, but only ground her for 1 week. Who is likely to feel their punishment is more just, and why: Elisa, with her shorter sentence, or Thais, with her longer sentence?

ANSWER: Although Thais received a harsher penalty, her experience fits better with the principles of procedural justice. Her parents demonstrated neutrality and have a trustworthy system in place whose guidelines they follow impartially and consistently, and treated her with politeness and respect. Thus, Thais should see her punishment as fair, if a little harsh. Elisa, though she was only grounded for a week, probably feels her punishment is unjust, since her parents do not show neutrality (favoring her brothers), do not have a trustworthy or stable system of guidelines for punishment, and did not treat her with respect. Therefore, even though Thais got the harsher punishment, she may feel it was more just than Elisa feels about hers.

GLOSSARY

A

actor-observer difference A difference in attribution based on who is making the causal assessment: the actor (who is relatively inclined to make situational attributions) or the observer (who is relatively inclined to make dispositional attributions).

actual self The self that people believe they are. *See also* ideal self, ought self.

affective forecasting Predicting future emotions, such as whether an event will result in happiness or anger or sadness, and for how long.

agenda control Efforts of the media to select certain events and topics to emphasize, thereby shaping which issues and events people think are important.

altruism Unselfish behavior that benefits others without regard to consequences for oneself.

anxiety dimension of attachment A facet of attachment that captures the degree to which a person is worried about rejection and abandonment by relationship partners. *See also* avoidance dimension of attachment.

applied science Science or research concerned with solving important real-world problems. *See also* basic science.

appraisal process A component of emotion; patterns of construal for evaluating events and objects in the environment based on their relation to current goals.

approach/inhibition theory A theory maintaining that high-power individuals are inclined to go after their goals and make quick (and sometimes rash) judgments, whereas low-power individuals are more likely to constrain their behavior and pay careful attention to others.

artifact A spurious research result arising from a faulty method of investigation.

attachment theory The idea that early attachments with parents and other caregivers can shape relationships for a person's whole life.

attitude An evaluation of an object in a positive or negative fashion that includes three components: affect, cognition, and behavior.

attitude inoculation Small attacks on people's beliefs that engage their preexisting attitudes, prior commitments, and background knowledge, enabling them to counteract a subsequent larger attack and thus resist persuasion.

attribution theory A set of concepts explaining how people assign causes to the events around them and the effects of people's causal assessments.

audience characteristics Characteristics of those who receive a persuasive message, including need for cognition, mood, age, and audience size and diversity.

augmentation principle The idea that people should assign greater weight to a particular cause of behavior if other causes are present that normally would produce a different outcome. *See also* discounting principle.

authority Power that derives from institutionalized roles or arrangements.

availability heuristic The process whereby judgments of frequency or probability are based on how readily pertinent instances come to mind. *See also* representativeness heuristic.

avoidance dimension of attachment A facet of attachment that captures the degree to which a person is comfortable with intimacy and dependence on relationship partners. *See also* anxiety dimension of attachment.

B

base-rate information Information about the relative frequency of events or of members of different categories in a population.

basic science Science or research concerned with trying to understand some phenomenon in its own right, with a view toward using that understanding to build valid theories about the nature of some aspect of the world. *See also* applied science.

basking in reflected glory Taking pride in the accomplishments of other people in one's group, such as when sports fans identify with a winning team.

behavioral economics A discipline that uses insights from psychology to create more realistic and accurate models of economic behavior.

better-than-average effect The finding that most people think they are above average on various personality trait and ability dimensions.

bottom-up processes "Data-driven" mental processing, in which an individual forms conclusions based on the stimuli encountered in the environment. *See also* top-down processes.

broaden-and-build hypothesis The idea that positive emotions broaden thoughts and actions, helping people build social resources.

bystander intervention Assistance given by a witness to someone in need.

C

catharsis The release of a strong emotion, such as anger, by expressing it directly.

causal attribution Linking an event to a cause, such as inferring that a personality trait is responsible for a behavior.

central (systematic) route A route to persuasion wherein people think carefully and deliberately about the content of a persuasive message, attending to its logic and the strength of its arguments, as well as to related evidence and principles.

channel factors Situational circumstances that appear unimportant on the surface but that can have great consequences for behavior—facilitating it, blocking it, or guiding it in a particular direction.

cognitive dissonance theory The theory that inconsistencies among a person's thoughts, sentiments, and actions create an aversive emotional state (dissonance) that leads to efforts to restore consistency.

communal relationship A relationship in which the individuals feel a special responsibility for one another and give and receive according to the principle of need; such relationships are often long term. *See also* exchange relationship.

comparison level Expectations about what people think they deserve or expect to get out of a relationship.

comparison level for alternatives Expectations about what people think they can get out of alternative relationships.

complementarity The tendency for people to seek out others with characteristics that are different from, and complement, their own.

compliance Responding favorably to an explicit request by another person.

confirmation bias The tendency to test a proposition by searching for evidence that would support it.

conformity Changing one's behavior or beliefs in response to explicit or implicit pressure (real or imagined) from others.

consensus A type of covariation information: what most people would do in a given situation; that is, whether most people would behave the same way or few or no other people would behave that way. *See also* consistency, distinctiveness.

consistency A type of covariation: what an individual does in a given situation on different occasions; that is, whether next time, under the same circumstances, the person would behave the same or differently. *See also* consensus, distinctiveness.

construal An interpretation of or inference about the stimuli or situations people confront.

construal level theory A theory about the relationship between psychological distance and abstract or concrete thinking: Psychologically distant actions and events are thought about in abstract terms; actions and events that are close at hand are thought about in concrete terms.

contingencies of self-worth A perspective maintaining that self-esteem is contingent on successes and failures in domains on which a person has based his or her self-worth.

control condition A condition comparable to the experimental condition in every way except that it lacks the one ingredient hypothesized to produce the expected effect on the dependent variable.

correlational research Research that does not involve random assignment to different situations, or conditions, and that psychologists conduct to determine whether there is a relationship between the variables.

counterfactual thoughts Thoughts of what might have, could have, or should have happened "if only" something had occurred differently.

covariation principle The idea that behavior should be attributed to potential causes that occur along with the observed behavior.

culture of honor A culture defined by its members' strong concerns about their own and others' reputations, leading to sensitivity to insults and a willingness to use violence to avenge any perceived wrong.

D

death-qualified jury A jury from which prospective jurors who would never recommend the death penalty have been excluded.

debriefing In preliminary versions of an experiment, asking participants directly if they understood the instructions, found the setup to be reasonable, and so so. In later versions, debriefings are used to educate participants about the questions being studied.

deception research Research in which the participants are misled about the purpose of the research or the meaning of something that is done to them.

dehumanization The attribution of nonhuman characteristics and denial of human qualities to groups other than one's own.

deindividuation A reduced sense of individual identity accompanied by diminished self-regulation that comes over people when they are in a large group.

dependent variable In experimental research, the variable that is measured (as opposed to manipulated); it is hypothesized to be affected by manipulation of the independent variable.

descriptive norm The behavior exhibited by most people in a given context. *See also* prescriptive norm.

diffusion of responsibility A reduction of the sense of urgency to help someone involved in an emergency or dangerous situation, based on the assumption that others who are present will help.

discounting principle The idea that people should assign reduced weight to a particular cause of behavior if other plausible causes might have produced it. *See also* augmentation principle.

discrimination Unfair treatment of individuals based on their membership in a particular group.

display rule A culturally specific rule that governs how, when, to whom people express emotion.

dispositions Internal factors, such as beliefs, values, personality traits, and abilities, that guide behavior.

distinctiveness A type of covariation information: what an individual does in different situations; that is, whether the behavior is unique to a particular situation or occurs in all situations. *See also* consensus, consistency.

distraction-conflict theory A theory based on the idea that being aware of another person's presence creates a conflict between attending to that person and attending to the task at hand, and that this attentional conflict is arousing and produces social facilitation effects.

dominance Behavior enacted with the goal of acquiring or demonstrating power.

dominant response In a person's hierarchy of possible responses in any context, the response he or she is most likely to make.

duration neglect Giving relative unimportance of the length of an emotional experience, whether pleasurable or unpleasant, in judging and remembering the overall experience.

E

effort justification The tendency to reduce dissonance by justifying the time, effort, or money devoted to something that turned out to be unpleasant or disappointing.

ego depletion A state, produced by acts of self-control, in which people lack the energy or resources to engage in further acts of self-control.

elaboration-likelihood model (ELM) A model of persuasion maintaining that there are two different routes to persuasion: the central route and the peripheral route. *See also* heuristic-systematic model.

emotion A brief, specific response, both psychological and physiological, that helps people meet goals, many of which are social.

emotion accent A specific way people from different cultures express a particular emotion.

emotional amplification An increase in an emotional reaction to an event that is proportional to how easy it is to imagine the event not happening.

emotional intelligence (EQ) The ability to express, recognize, and use emotions well within social interactions.

empathic concern Identifying with someone in need, including feeling and understanding what that person is experiencing, accompanied by the intention to help the person.

encoding Filing information away in memory based on what information is attended to and the initial interpretation of the information.

entity theory of intelligence The belief that intelligence is something people are born with and cannot change. *See also* incremental theory of intelligence.

equity theory A theory that maintains that people are motivated to pursue fairness, or equity, in their relationship; a relationships is considered equitable when the benefits are proportionate to the effort both people put into it.

ethnocentrism Glorifying one's own group while vilifying other groups.

evaluation apprehension People's concern about how they might appear in the eyes of others, or be evaluated by them.

exchange relationship A relationship in which individuals feel little responsibility toward one another; giving and receiving are governed by concerns about equity and reciprocity; such relationships are usually short term. *See also* communal relationship.

experimental research In social psychology, research that randomly assigns people to different conditions, or situations, and that enables researchers to make strong inferences about how these different conditions affect behavior.

explanatory style A person's habitual way of explaining events, typically assessed along three dimensions: internal/external, stable/unstable, and global/specific.

external validity An indication of how well the results of an experiment generalize to contexts besides those of the study itself.

F

face The public image of ourself that we want others to believe.

field experiment An experiment set up in the real world, usually with participants who are not aware they are in a study of any kind.

fluency The feeling of ease (or difficulty) associated with processing information.

focal emotion An emotion that is especially common within a particular culture.

focalism A tendency to focus too much on a central aspect of an event while neglecting the possible impact of associated factors or other events.

foot-in-the-door technique A compliance approach that involves making an initial small request with which nearly everyone complies, followed by a larger request involving the real behavior of interest.

framing effect The influence on judgment resulting from the way information is presented, such as the order of presentation or the wording.

functional distance The influence of an architectural layout to encourage or inhibit certain activities, including contact between people.

fundamental attribution error The failure to recognize the importance of situational influences on behavior, and the corresponding tendency to overemphasize the importance of dispositions on behavior.

G

Gestalt psychology Based on the German word *gestalt*, meaning "form" or "figure," this approach stresses the fact that people perceive objects not by means of some automatic registering device but by active, usually nonconscious interpretation of what the object represents as a whole.

group polarization The tendency for group decisions to be more extreme than those made by individuals; whatever way the group as a whole is leaning, group discussion tends to make it lean further in that direction.

groupthink Faulty thinking by members of highly cohesive groups in which the critical scrutiny that should be devoted to the issues at hand is subverted by social pressures to reach consensus.

H

halo effect The common belief (accurate or not) that attractive individuals possess a host of positive qualities beyond their physical appearance.

heuristics Intuitive mental operations, performed quickly and automatically, that provide efficient answers to common problems of judgment.

heuristic-systematic model A model of persuasion maintaining that there are two different routes to persuasion: the systematic route and the heuristic route. *See also* elaboration-likelihood model.

hindsight bias People's tendency to be overconfident about whether they could have predicted a given outcome.

homophily The tendency for people to associate with similar others.

hostile aggression Behavior intended to harm another, either physically or psychologically, and motivated by feelings of anger and hostility. *See also* instrumental aggression.

hypothesis A prediction about what will happen under particular circumstances.

I

ideal self The self that embodies people's wishes and aspirations. *See also* actual self, ought self.

identifiable victim effect The tendency to be more moved by the vivid plight of a single individual than by a more abstract number of people.

ideomotor action The phenomenon whereby merely thinking about a behavior makes performing it more likely.

illusory correlation The belief that two variables are correlated when in fact they are not.

immune neglect The tendency for people to underestimate their capacity to be resilient in responding to difficult life events, which leads them to overestimate the extent to which life's problems will reduce their personal well-being.

implicit association test (IAT) A technique for revealing nonconscious attitudes toward different stimuli, including particular groups.

implicit attitude measure An indirect measures of attitudes that does not involve a self-report.

inclusive fitness According to evolutionary theory, the fitness of an individual based on reproductive success and the passing on of genes to future generations.

incremental theory of intelligence The belief that intelligence is something people can improve by working at it. *See also* entity theory of intelligence.

independent (individualistic) culture A culture in which people tend to think of themselves as distinct social entities, tied to each other by voluntary bonds of affection and organizational memberships but essentially separate from other people and having attributes that exist in the absence of any connection to others. *See also* interdependent culture.

independent variable In experimental research, the variable that is manipulated; it is hypothesized to be the cause of a particular outcome.

individuation An enhanced sense of individual identity produced by focusing attention on the self, which generally leads people to act carefully and deliberately and in accordance with their sense of propriety and values.

induced (forced) compliance Subtly compelling people to behave in a manner that is inconsistent with their beliefs, attitudes, or values, in order to elicit dissonance, and therefore a change in their original attitudes or values.

informational social influence The influence of other people that results from taking their comments or actions as a source of information about what is correct, proper, or effective. *See also* normative social influence.

informed consent A person's signed agreement to participate in a procedure or research study after learning all the relevant aspects.

institutional review board (IRB) A university committee that examines research proposals and makes judgments about the ethical appropriateness of the research.

instrumental aggression Behavior intended to harm another in the service of motives other than pure hostility (such as attracting attention, acquiring wealth, or advancing political or ideological causes). *See also* hostile aggression.

interdependent (collectivistic) culture A culture in which people tend to define themselves as part of a collective, inextricably tied to others in their group and placing less importance on individual freedom or personal control over their lives. *See also* independent culture.

internalization Private acceptance of a proposition, orientation, or ideology.

internal validity In experimental research, confidence that only the manipulated variable could have produced the results.

investment model of commitment A model of interpersonal relationships maintaining that three determinants make partners more committed to each other: relationship satisfaction, few alternative partners, and investments in the relationship.

J

just world hypothesis The belief that people get what they deserve in life and deserve what they get.

K

kin selection An evolutionary strategy that favors the reproductive success of one's genetic relatives, even at a cost to one's own survival and reproduction.

L

Likert scale A numerical scale used to assess people's attitudes; includes a set of possible answers with labeled anchors on each extreme.

loss aversion The tendency for a loss of a given magnitude to have more psychological impact than an equivalent gain.

M

measurement validity The correlation between some measure and some outcome the measure is supposed to predict.

mental accounting The tendency to treat money differently depending on how it is acquired and the mental category to which it is attached.

mere exposure effect The idea that repeated exposure to a stimulus, such as an object or a person, leads to greater liking of the stimulus.

message characteristics Aspects, or content, of a persuasive message, including the quality of the evidence and the explicitness of its conclusions.

metacognition Secondary thoughts that are reflections on primary cognitions.

minimal group paradigm An experimental paradigm in which researchers create groups based on arbitrary and seemingly meaningless criteria and then examine how the members of these "minimal groups" are inclined to behave toward one another.

modern racism Prejudice directed at other racial groups that exists alongside the rejection of explicitly racist beliefs.

moral foundations theory A theory proposing that there are five evolved, universal moral domains in which specific emotions guide moral judgments.

N

natural experiment A naturally occurring event or phenomenon having somewhat different conditions that can be compared with almost as much rigor as in experiments where the investigator manipulates the conditions.

natural selection An evolutionary process that molds animals and plants so that traits that enhance the probability of survival and reproduction are passed on to subsequent generations.

naturalistic fallacy The claim that the way things *are* is the way they *should be*.

negative state relief hypothesis The idea that people engage in certain actions, such as agreeing to a request, to relieve their negative feelings and feel better about themselves.

norm of reciprocity A norm dictating that people should provide benefits to those who benefit them.

normative social influence The influence of other people that comes from the desire to avoid their disapproval and other social sanctions (ridicule, barbs, ostracism). *See also* informational social influence.

O

obedience In an unequal power relationship, submitting to the demands of the person in authority.

ought self The self that is concerned with the duties, obligations, and external demands people feel they are compelled to honor. *See also* actual self, ideal self.

outgroup homogeneity effect The tendency for people to assume that within-group similarity is much stronger for outgroups than for ingroups.

P

paired distinctiveness The pairing of two distinctive events that stand out even more because they occur together.

parental investment The evolutionary principle that costs and benefits are associated with reproduction and the nurturing of offspring. Because these costs and benefits are different for males and females, one gender will normally value and invest more in each child than will the other.

peripheral (heuristic) route A route to persuasion wherein people attend to relatively easy-to-process, superficial cues related to a persuasive message, such as its length or the expertise or attractiveness of the source of the message. *See also* central (systematic) route.

personal distress A motive for helping others in distress that may arise from a need to reduce one's own distress.

planning fallacy The tendency for people to be unrealistically optimistic about how quickly they can complete a particular project, even when fully aware that they have often failed to complete similar projects on time in the past.

pluralistic ignorance Misperception of a group norm that results from observing people who are acting at variance with their private beliefs out of a concern for the social consequences; those actions reinforce the erroneous group norm.

power The ability to control our own outcomes and those of others; the freedom to act.

precarious manhood hypothesis The idea that a man's gender identity of strength and toughness is more easily lost in competition, and that such a loss can trigger aggressive behavior.

prejudice A negative attitude or affective response toward a certain group and its individual members.

prescriptive norm The way a person is supposed to behave in a given context. Also called *injunctive norm*. *See also* descriptive norm.

prevention focus Self-regulation of behavior with respect to ought self standards, or a focus on avoiding negative outcomes and avoidance-related behaviors. *See also* promotion focus.

primacy effect A type of order effect: the disproportionate influence on judgment by information presented first in a body of evidence. *See also* recency effect.

priming The presentation of information designed to activate a concept (such as a stereotype) and hence make it accessible. A prime is the stimulus presented to activate the concept in question.

prisoner's dilemma A situation involving payoffs to two people, who must decide whether to cooperate or defect. In the end, trust and cooperation lead to higher joint payoffs than mistrust and defection.

procedural justice Assessments of whether the processes leading to the distribution of resources and punishments are fair.

promotion focus Self-regulation of behavior with respect to ideal self standards, or a focus on attaining positive outcomes and approach-related behaviors. *See also* prevention focus.

psychological stress The sense that challenges and demands surpass one's current capacities, resources, and energies.

R

random assignment Assigning participants in experimental research to different groups randomly, so they are as likely to be assigned to one condition as to another.

rape-prone culture A culture in which rape tends to be used as an act of war against enemy women, as a ritual act, and as a threat against women to keep them subservient to men.

reactance theory The idea that people reassert their prerogatives in response to the unpleasant state of arousal they experience when they believe their freedoms are threatened.

reactive devaluation Attaching less value to an offer in a negotiation once the opposing group makes it.

realistic group conflict theory A theory that group conflict, prejudice, and discrimination are likely to arise over competition between groups for limited resources.

recency effect A type of order effect: the disproportionate influence on judgment by information presented last in a body of evidence. *See also* primacy effect.

reciprocal altruism Helping others with the expectation that they will probably return the favor in the future.

reciprocal concessions technique A compliance approach that involves asking someone for a very large favor that he or she will certainly refuse and then following that request with one for a smaller favor (which tends to be seen as a concession the target feels compelled to honor). Also called *door-in-the-face technique*.

reflected self-appraisal A belief about what others think of one's self.

regression effect The statistical tendency, when two variables are imperfectly correlated, for extreme values on one of them to be associated with less extreme values on the other.

regression fallacy The failure to recognize the influence of the regression effect and to offer a causal theory for what is really a simple statistical regularity.

regression to the mean The tendency of extreme scores on a variable to be followed by, or associated with, less extreme scores.

reliability The degree to which the particular way researchers measure a given variable is likely to yield consistent results.

replication The reproducing of the results of a scientific study.

representativeness heuristic The process whereby judgments of likelihood are based on assessments of similarity between individuals and group prototypes, or between cause and effect. *See also* availability heuristic.

reproductive fitness The capacity to pass one's genes on to subsequent generations.

reputation The collective beliefs, evaluations, and impressions people hold about an individual within a social network.

response latency The amount of time it takes to respond to a stimulus, such as an attitude question.

retrieval The extraction of information from memory.

risk aversion The reluctance to pursue an uncertain option with an average payoff that equals or exceeds the payoff attainable by another, certain option; the opposite of risk seeking.

risk seeking The tendency to forgo a certain outcome in favor of a risky option; the opposite of risk aversion.

risky shift The tendency for groups to make riskier decisions than individuals would.

rumination The tendency to think about some stressful event repeatedly.

S

schema A knowledge structure consisting of any organized body of stored information and which is used to help in understanding events.

scientific jury selection A statistical approach to jury selection whereby members of different demographic groups in the community are asked their attitudes toward various issues related to a trial, and defense and prosecuting attorneys try to influence the selection of jurors accordingly.

self-affirmation theory The idea that people can maintain an overall sense of self-worth following psychologically threatening information by affirming a valued aspect of themselves unrelated to the threat.

self-awareness theory A theory maintaining that when people focus their attention inward on themselves, they become concerned with self-evaluation and how their current behavior conforms to their internal standards and values.

self-censorship Withholding information or opinions in group discussions.

self-discrepancy theory A theory that behavior is motivated by standards reflecting ideal and ought selves. Falling short of these standards produces specific emotions: dejection-related emotions for actual-ideal discrepancies, and agitation-related emotions for actual-ought discrepancies.

self-distancing The ability to focus on one's feelings from the perspective of a detached observer.

self-enhancement The desire to maintain, increase, or protect one's positive self-views.

self-esteem The positive or negative evaluation an individual has of himself or herself.

self-evaluation maintenance (SEM) model The idea that people are motivated to view themselves favorably and that they do so through two processes: reflection and social comparison.

self-fulfilling prophecy The tendency for people to act in ways that bring about the very thing they expect to happen.

self-handicapping The tendency to engage in self-defeating behavior in order to have an excuse ready should one perform poorly or fail.

self-monitoring The tendency to monitor one's behavior to fit the current situation.

self-perception theory The theory that people come to know their own attitudes by looking at their behavior and the context in which it occurred, and inferring what their attitudes must be.

self-presentation Presenting the person we would like others to believe we are.

self-regulation Processes by which people initiate, alter, and control their behavior in the pursuit of goals, including the ability to resist short-term rewards that thwart the attainment of long-term goals.

self-schema A cognitive structure, derived from past experience, that represents a person's beliefs and feelings about the self in general and in specific situations.

self-selection In correlational research, a problem that arises when the participant, rather than the researcher, selects his or her level on each variable, bringing with this value unknown other properties that make causal interpretation of a relationship difficult.

self-serving attributional bias The tendency to attribute failure and other bad events to external circumstances, and to attribute success and other good events to oneself.

self-validation hypothesis The idea that the likelihood of attitude change can depend not only on the direction and amount of thoughts people have in response to a persuasive message, but also on the confidence with which they hold the thoughts.

self-verification theory The theory that people strive for stable, subjectively accurate beliefs about the self because such self-views give them a sense of coherence.

sleeper effect An effect that occurs when a persuasive message from an unreliable source initially exerts little influence but later causes attitudes to shift.

social class The amount of wealth, education, and occupational prestige individuals and their families have.

social comparison theory The hypothesis that people compare themselves to other people in order to obtain an accurate assessment of their own opinions, abilities, and internal states.

social exchange theory A theory based on the idea that how people feel about a relationship depends on their assessments of its costs and rewards.

social facilitation Initially a term for enhanced performance in the presence of others; now a broader term for the effect, positive or negative, of the presence of others on performance.

social identity theory The idea that a person's self-concept and self-esteem derive not only from personal identity and accomplishments but also from the status and accomplishments of the various groups to which the person belongs.

social influence The many ways people affect one another, including changes in attitudes, beliefs, feelings, and behavior resulting from the comments, actions, or even the mere presence of others. *See also* informational social influence, normative social influence.

social intuitionist model of moral judgment The idea that people first have fast, emotional reactions to morally relevant events, and then rely on reason to arrive at a judgment of right or wrong.

social loafing The tendency to exert less effort when working on a group task in which individual contributions cannot be monitored.

social psychology The scientific study of the feelings, thoughts, and behaviors of individuals in social situations.

social reward A benefit, such as praise, positive attention, something tangible, or gratitude, that may be gained from helping others, thus a motive for altruistic behavior.

sociometer hypothesis The idea that self-esteem is an internal, subjective index or marker of the extent to which a person is included or looked on favorably by others.

source characteristics Characteristics of the person who delivers a persuasive message, such as attractiveness, credibility, and certainty.

spotlight effect People's conviction that other people are attending to them (to their appearance and behavior) more than they actually are.

statistical significance A measure of the probability that a given result could have occurred by chance.

status The outcome of an evaluation of attributes that produces differences in respect and prominence, and which contributes to determining a person's power within a group.

stereotype The belief that certain attributes are characteristic of members of a particular group.

stereotype threat The fear of confirming the stereotypes others have about one's group.

subliminal stimulus A stimulus that is below the threshold of conscious awareness.

subtyping Explaining away exceptions to a given stereotype by creating a subcategory of the stereotyped group that can be expected to differ from the group as a whole.

sunk cost fallacy A reluctance to "waste" money that leads people to continue with an endeavor, whether it serves their future interests or not, because they have already invested money, effort, or time in it.

superordinate goal A goal that transcends the interests of any one group and can be achieved more readily by two or more groups working together.

system justification theory The theory that people are motivated to see the existing sociopolitical system as desirable, fair, and legitimate.

T

terror management theory (TMT) The theory that people deal with the potentially crippling anxiety associated with the knowledge of the inevitability of death by striving for symbolic immortality through preserving valued cultural worldviews and believing they have lived up to their standards.

that's-not-all technique A compliance approach that involves adding something to an original offer, thus creating some pressure to reciprocate.

theory A body of related propositions intended to describe some aspect of the world.

theory of mind The understanding that other people have beliefs and desires.

third variable In correlational research, a variable that exerts a causal influence on both variable 1 and variable 2.

third-person effect The assumption by most people that others are more prone to being influenced by persuasive messages (such as those in media campaigns) than they themselves are.

thought polarization hypothesis The hypothesis that more extended thought about a particular issue tends to produce a more extreme, entrenched attitude.

tit-for-tat strategy A strategy in the prisoner's dilemma game in which the player's first move is cooperative; thereafter, the player mimics the other person's behavior, whether cooperative or competitive. This strategy fares well when interacting with other strategies.

top-down processes "Theory-driven" mental processing, in which an individual filters and interprets new information in light of preexisting knowledge and expectations. *See also* bottom-up processes.

V

voir dire The portion of a trial in U.S. courts in which prospective jurors are questioned about potential biases and a jury is selected.

volunteerism Assistance a person regularly provides to another person or group with no expectation of compensation.

W

working self-concept A subset of self-knowledge that is brought to mind in a particular context.

REFERENCES

Aarts, H., & Dijksterhuis, A. (2003). The silence of the library: Environment, situational norm, and social behavior. *Journal of Personality and Social Psychology, 84*, 18–28.

Aarts, H., Gollwitzer, P. M., & Hassin, R. R. (2004). Goal contagion: Perceiving is for pursuing. *Journal of the Personality and Social Psychology, 87*, 23–37.

Abell, G. O. (1981). Astrology. In G. O. Abell & B. Singer (Eds.), *Science and the paranormal: Probing the existence of the supernatural.* New York: Charles Scribner's Sons.

Abrams, D., Viki, G. T., Masser, B., & Bohner, G. (2003). Perceptions of stranger and acquaintance rape: The role of benevolent and hostile sexism in victim blame and rape proclivity. *Journal of Personality and Social Psychology, 84*, 111–125.

Abu-Lughod, L. (1986). *Veiled sentiments.* Berkeley, CA: University of California Press.

Acevedo, B. P., & Aron, A. (2009). Does a long-term relationship kill romantic love? *Review of General Psychology, 13*, 59–65.

Ackerman, J. M., Griskevicius, V, & Li, N. P. (2011). Let's get serious: Communicating commitment in long-term relationships. *Journal of Personality and Social Psychology, 100*, 1079–1094.

Adler, N. E., Boyce, T., Chesney, M. A., Cohen, S., Folkman, S., Kahn, R. L., et al. (1994). Socioeconomic status and health: The challenge of the gradient. *American Psychologist, 49*, 15–24.

Agnew, C. R., Van Lange, P. A. M., Rusbult, C. E., & Langston, C. A. (1998). Cognitive interdependence: Commitment and the mental representation of close relationships. *Journal of Personality and Social Psychology, 74*, 939–954.

Ainsworth, M. D. S. (1993). Attachment as related to mother-infant interaction. *Advances in Infancy Research, 8*, 1–50.

Ainsworth, M. D. S., Blehar, M., Waters, E., & Wall, S. (1978). *Patterns of attachment.* Hillsdale, NJ: Erlbaum.

Ajzen, I. (1977). Intuitive theories of events and the effects of base-rate information on prediction. *Journal of Personality and Social Psychology, 35*, 303–314.

Ajzen, I. (1987). Attitudes, traits, and actions: Dispositional prediction of behavior in personality and social psychology. In L. Berkowitz (Ed.), *Advances in experimental social psychology* (Vol. 20, pp. 1–63). San Diego, CA: Academic Press.

Akerlof, G. A., Yellen, J. L., & Katz, M. L. (1996). An analysis of out-of-wedlock childbearing in the United States. *Quarterly Journal of Economics, 111*, 277–317.

Aldag, R. J., & Fuller, S. R. (1993). Beyond fiasco: A reappraisal of the groupthink phenomenon and a new model of group decision processes. *Psychological Bulletin, 113*, 533–552.

Alicke, M. D., & Govorun, O. (2005). The better-than-average effect. In M. D. Alicke, D. A. Dunning, & J. I. Krueger (Eds.), *The self in social judgment* (pp. 85–106). New York: Psychology Press.

Allan, G. A. (1979). *A sociology of friendship and kinship.* London: Allen & Unwin.

Allee, W. C., & Masure, R. H. (1936). A comparison of maze behavior in paired and isolated shell-parakeets (*Melopsittacus undulatus Shaw*) in a two-alley problem box. *Journal of Comparative Psychology, 3*, 159–182.

Allen, M., Emmers-Sommer, T. M., Gebhardt, L., & Giery, M. (1995). Pornography and rape myth acceptance. *Journal of Communication, 45*, 5–26.

Allen, V. L., & Wilder, D. A. (1979). Group categorization and attribution of belief similarity. *Small Group Behavior, 10*, 73–80.

Allport, F. H. (1920). The influence of the group upon association and thought. *Journal of Experimental Psychology, 3*, 159–182.

Alluisi, E. A., & Adams, O. S. (1962). Predicting letter preferences: Aesthetics and filtering in man. *Perceptual and Motor Skills, 14*, 123–131.

Alter, A. L., & Oppenheimer, D. M. (2006). Predicting stock price fluctuations using processing fluency. *Proceedings of the National Academy of Sciences, 103*, 9369–9372.

Alter, A. L., Oppenheimer, D. M., Epley, N., & Eyre, R. N. (2007). Overcoming intuition: Metacognitive difficulty activates analytic reasoning. *Journal of Experimental Psychology: General, 136*, 569–576.

Alterovitz, S. S., & Mendelsohn, G. A. (2009). Partner preferences across the life span: Online dating by older adults. *Psychology and Aging, 24*(2), 513–517.

Amato, P. R., & Keith, B. (1991). Parental divorce and well-being of children. *Psychological Bulletin, 110*, 26–46.

Ambady, N., Hallahan, M., & Conner, B. (1999). Accuracy of judgments of sexual orientation from thin slices of behavior. *Journal of Personality and Social Psychology, 77*(3), 538–547.

Ambady, N., Hallahan, M., & Rosenthal, R. (1995). On judging and being judged in zero-acquaintance situations. *Journal of Personality and Social Psychology, 69*, 518–529.

Ambady, N., & Rosenthal, R. (1993). Haifa minute: Predicting teacher evaluations from thin slices of nonverbal behavior and physical attractiveness. *Journal of Personality and Social Psychology, 64*, 431–441.

Amodio, D. M., & Devine, P. G. (2006). Stereotyping and evaluation in implicit race bias: Evidence for independent constructs and unique effects on behavior. *Journal of Personality and Social Psychology, 91*, 652–661.

Andersen, S. M., Glassman, N. S., Chen, S., & Cole, S. W. (1995). Transference in social perception: The role of chronic accessibility in significant-other representations. *Journal of Personality and Social Psychology, 69*, 41–57.

Andersen, S. M., & Ross, L. (1984). Self-knowledge and social influence I: The impact of cognitive/affective and behavioral data. *Journal of Personality and Social Psychology, 46*, 280–293.

Anderson, C., & Brown, C. E. (2010). The functions and dysfunctions of hierarchies. *Review of Organizational Behavior, 30*, 55–89.

Anderson, C., John, O. P., Keltner, D., & Kring, A. (2001). Social status in naturalistic face-to-face groups: Effects of personality and physical attractiveness in men and women. *Journal of Personality and Social Psychology, 81*, 1108–1129.

Anderson, C., Keltner, D., & John, O. P. (2003). Emotional convergence between people over time. *Journal of Personality and Social Psychology, 84*, 1054–1068.

Anderson, C., & Kilduff, G. J. (2009). Why do dominant personalities attain influence in face-to-face groups? The competence-signaling effects of trait dominance. *Journal of Personality and Social Psychology, 96*, 491–503.

Anderson, C. A. (1987). Temperature and aggression: Effects on quarterly, yearly, and city rates of violent and nonviolent crime. *Journal of Personality and Social Psychology, 52*, 1161–1173.

Anderson, C. A. (1989). Temperature and aggression: Ubiquitous effects of heat on occurrences of human violence. *Psychological Bulletin, 106*, 74–96.

Anderson, C. A. (1991). How people think about causes: Examination of the typical phenomenal organization of attributions for success and failure. *Social Cognition, 9*, 295–329.

Anderson, C. A., Berkowitz, L., Donnerstein, E., Huesmann, L. R., Johnson, J., Linz, D., et al. (2003). The influence of media violence on youth. *Psychological Science in the Public Interest, 4*, 81–110.

Anderson, C. A., & Bushman, B. J. (2001). Effects of violent video games on aggressive behavior, aggressive cognition, aggressive affect, physiological arousal, and prosocial behavior: A meta-analytic review of the scientific literature. *Psychological Science, 12*, 353–359.

Anderson, C. A., & Deuser, W. E. (1993). The primacy of control in causal thinking and attributional style: An attributional functionalism perspective. In G. Weary, F. Gleicher, & K. L. Marsh (Eds.), *Control motivation and social cognition* (pp. 94–121). New York: Springer-Verlag.

Anderson, C. A., & Dill, K. E. (2000). Video games and aggressive thoughts, feelings, and behavior in the laboratory and in life. *Journal of Personality and Social Psychology, 78*, 772–790.

Anderson, C. A., Krull, D. S., & Weiner, B. (1996). Explanations: Processes and consequences. In E. T. Higgins & A. W. Kruglanski (Eds.), *Social psychology: Handbook of basic principles* (pp. 271–296). New York: Guilford Press.

Anderson, C. A., Sakamoto, A., Gentile, D. A., Ihori, N., & Shibuya, A., Yukawa, S., Naito, M., & Kobayashi, K. (2008). Longitudinal effects of violent videogames aggression in Japan and the United States, *Pediatrics, 122*, e1067–e1072.

Anderson, C. A., Shibuya, A., Ihori, N., Swing, E. L., Bushman, B. J., Sakamoto, A., Rothstein, H. R., & Saleem, M. (2010). Violent video game effects on aggression, empathy, and prosocial behavior in Eastern and Western countries. *Psychological Bulletin, 136*, 151–173.

Anderson, J. L., Crawford, C. B., Nadeau, J., & Lindberg, T. (1992). Was the duchess of Windsor right? A cross-cultural review of the socioecology of ideals of female body shape. *Ethology and Sociobiology, 13*, 197–227.

Anderson, R., & Nida, S. A. (1978). Effect of physical attractiveness on opposite- and same-sex evaluations. *Journal of Personality, 46*, 401–413.

Anderson, R. C., & Pichert, J. W. (1978). Recall of previously unrecallable information following a shift in perspective. *Journal of Verbal Learning and Verbal Behavior, 17*, 1–12.

Anderson, T. A. (1993). *Den of lions: Memoirs of Seven Years.* New York: Crown Publishers.

Andrade, E. B., & Ho, T. (2007). How is the boss's mood today?: I want a raise. *Psychological Science, 18(8)*, 668–671.

Ansolabehere, S., & Iyengar, S. (1995). *Going negative: How political ads shrink and polarize the electorate.* New York: Free Press.

Antill, J. K. (1983). Sex role complementarity versus similarity in married couples. *Journal of Personality and Social Psychology, 45*, 145–155.

Archer, J. (2009). Does sexual selection explain human sex differences in aggression? *Behavioral and Brain Sciences, 32 (3-4)*, 249–311.

Arden, R., Gottfredson, L. S., Miller, G., & Pierce, A. (2008). Intelligence and semen quality are positively correlated [Electronic version]. *Intelligence.* Retrieved from 10.1016/j.intell.2008.11.001

Arendt, H. (1963). *Eichmann in Jerusalem: A report on the banality of evil.* New York: Viking Press.

Argyle, M. (1999). Causes and correlates of happiness. In D. Kahneman, E. Diener, & N. Schwarz (Eds.), *Well-being: The foundations of hedonic psychology* (pp. 353–373). New York: Russell Sage.

Arkes, H., & Blumer, C. (1985). The psychology of sunk cost. *Organizational Behavior and Human Decision Processes, 35*, 124–140.

Arkin, R. M., & Baumgardner, A. H. (1985). Basic issues in attribution theory and research. In J. H. Harvey & G. Weary (Eds.), *Self-handicapping* (pp. 169–202). New York: Academic Press.

Arkin, R. M., & Maruyama, G. M. (1979). Attribution, affect, and college exam performance. *Journal of Educational Psychology, 71*, 85–93.

Arndt, J., Schimel, J., & Goldenberg, J. L. (2003). Death can be good for your health: Fitness intentions as a proximal and distal defense against mortality salience. *Journal of Applied Social Psychology, 33*, 1726–1746.

Aron, A., & Aron, E. N. (1997). Self-expansion motivation and including the other in self. In S. Duck (Ed.), *Handbook of personal relationships: Theory, research, and interventions* (2nd ed., pp. 251–270). Chichester, England: Wiley.

Aron, A., Aron, E. N., & Allen, J. (1989). *The motivation for unrequited love: A self-expansion perspective.* Paper presented at the International Conference on Personal Relationships, Iowa City, IA.

Aron, A., Aron, E. N., Tudor, M., & Nelson, G. (1991). Close relationships as including other in self. *Journal of Personality and Social Psychology, 60*, 241–253.

Aron, A., & Fraley, B. (1999). Relationship closeness as including other in the self: Cognitive underpinnings and measures. *Social Cognition, 17*, 140–160.

Aron, A., Norman, C. C., Aron, E. N., McKenna, C., & Heyman, R. E. (2000). Couples' shared participation in novel and arousing activities and experienced relationship quality. *Journal of Personality and Social Psychology, 78,* 273–284.

Aronson, E. (1969). The theory of cognitive dissonance: A current perspective. In L. Berkowitz (Ed.), *Advances in experimental social psychology* (Vol. 4, pp. 1–34). New York: Academic Press.

Aronson, E., & Carlsmith, J. M. (1963). Effect of severity of threat in the devaluation of forbidden behavior. *Journal of Abnormal and Social Psychology, 66,* 584–588.

Aronson, E., Ellsworth, P. C., Carlsmith, J. M., & Gonzalez, M. H. (1990). *Methods of research in social psychology* (2nd ed.). New York: McGraw-Hill.

Aronson, E., Fried, C., & Stone, J. (1991). Overcoming denial and increasing the intention to use condoms through the induction of hypocrisy. *American Journal of Public Health, 81,* 1636–1638.

Aronson, E., & Mills, J. (1959). The effect of severity of initiation on liking for a group. *Journal of Abnormal and Social Psychology, 59,* 177–181.

Aronson, E., Stephan, C., Sikes, J., Blaney, N., & Snapp, M. (1978). *The jigsaw classroom.* Beverly Hills, CA: Sage.

Aronson, E., & Thibodeau, R. (1992). The jigsaw classroom: A co-operative strategy for reducing prejudice. In J. Lynch, C. Modgil, & S. Modgil (Eds.), *Cultural diversity in the schools* (pp. 110–118). London: Falmer Press.

Aronson, J., Fried, C. B., & Good, C. (2002). Reducing stereotype threat and boosting academic achievement of African-American students: The role of conceptions of intelligence. *Journal of Experimental Social Psychology, 38,* 113–125.

Aronson, J. M., Lustina, M. J., Good, C., Keough, K., Steele, C. M., & Brown, J. (1999). When white men can't do math: Necessary and sufficient factors in stereotype threat. *Journal of Experimental Social Psychology, 35,* 29–46.

Asch, S. E. (1940). Studies in the principles of judgments and attitudes: II. Determination of judgments by group and by ego standards. *Journal of Social Psychology, 12,* 584–588.

Asch, S. E. (1946). Forming impressions on personality. *Journal of Abnormal and Social Psychology, 41,* 258–290.

Asch, S. (1951). Effects of group pressure upon the modification and distortion of judgments. In G. Guetzkow (Ed.), *Groups, leadership, and men* (pp. 177–190). Pittsburgh, PA: Carnegie Press.

Asch, S. (1952). *Social psychology.* Englewood Cliffs, NJ: Prentice-Hall.

Asch, S. (1956). Studies of independence and conformity: A minority of one against a unanimous majority. *Psychological Monographs, 70* (Whole No. 416).

Asch, S. E., & Zukier, H. (1984). Thinking about persons. *Journal of Personality and Social Psychology, 46,* 1230–1240.

Asendorpf, J. B., Penke, L., & Back, M. D. (2011). From dating to mating and relating: Predictors of initial and long-term outcomes of speed-dating in a community sample. *European Journal of Personality, 25*(1), 16–30.

Ashburn-Nardo, L., Voils, C. I., & Monteith, M. J. (2001). Implicit associations as the seeds of intergroup bias: How easily do they take root? *Journal of Personality and Social Psychology, 81,* 789–799.

Aspinwall, L. G., & Taylor, S. E. (1993). Effects of social comparison direction, threat and self-esteem on affect, evaluation, and expected success. *Journal of Personality and Social Psychology, 64,* 708–722.

Aknin, L. B., Barrington-Leigh, C. P., Dunn, E. W., Helliwell, J. F., Burns, J., Biswas-Diener, R., & . . . Norton, M. I.

(2013). Prosocial spending and well-being: Cross-cultural evidence for a psychological universal. *Journal Of Personality And Social Psychology, 104*(4), 635–652.

Axelrod, R. (1984). *The evolution of cooperation.* New York: Basic Books.

Ayduk, O., Downey, G., Testa, A., Yen, Y., & Shoda, Y. (1999). Does rejection elicit hostility in rejection sensitive women? *Social Cognition, 17,* 245–271.

Ayduk, O., & Kross, E. (2008). Enhancing the pace of recovery: Differential effects of analyzing negative experiences from a self-distanced vs. self-immersed perspective on blood pressure reactivity. *Psychological Science, 19,* 229–231.

Bachorowski, J. A., & Owren, M. J. (2001). Not all laughs are alike: Voiced but not unvoiced laughter readily elicits positive affect. *Psychological Science, 12,* 252–257.

Back, M. D., Stopfer, J. M., Vazire, S., Gaddis, S., Schmukle, S. C., Egloff, B., & Gosling, S. D. (2010). Facebook profiles reflect actual personality, not self-idealization. *Psychological Science, 21,* 372–374.

Bain, L. L., Wilson, T., & Chaikind, E. (1989). Participant perceptions of exercise programs for overweight women. *Research Quarterly for Exercise and Sport, 60,* 134–143.

Baldwin, M. W., Keelan, J. P. R., Fehr, B., Enns, V., & Koh-Rangarajoo, E. (1996). Social-cognitive conceptualizations of attachment working models: Availability and accessibility effects. *Journal of Personality and Social Psychology, 71,* 94–109.

Bamshad, M. J., & Olson, S. E. (2003, December). Does race exist? *Scientific American,* 78–85.

Banaji, M., Hardin, C. C., & Rothman, A. J. (1993). Implicit stereotyping in person judgement. *Journal of Personality and Social Psychology, 65,* 272–281.

Bandura, A. (1973). *Social learning theory.* Englewood Cliffs, NJ: Prentice Hall.

Bandura, A. (2004). Social cognitive theory for personal and social change by enabling media. In M. J. Singhal, E. M. Cody, E. M. Rogers, & M. Sabido (Eds.), *Entertainment education and social change: History, research and practice* (pp. 75–96). Mahwah, NJ: Erlbaum.

Banks, T., & Dabbs, J. M., Jr. (1996). Salivary testosterone and cortisol in delinquents and violent urban culture. *Journal of Social Psychology, 136,* 49–56.

Bargh, J. A. (1996). Automaticity in social psychology. In E. T. Higgins & A. W. Kruglanski (Eds.), *Social psychology: Handbook of basic principles* (Vol. 1, pp. 1–40). New York: Guilford Press.

Bargh, J. A., Chaiken, S., Raymond, P., & Hymes, C. (1996). The automatic evaluation effect: Unconditional automatic activation with a pronunciation task. *Journal of Experimental Social Psychology, 31,* 104–128.

Bargh, J. A., Chen, M., & Burrows, L. (1996). Automaticity of social behavior: Direct effects of trait construct and stereotype activation on action. *Journal of Personality and Social Psychology, 71,* 230–244.

Bargh, J. A., Gollwitzer, P. M., Lee-Chai, A., Barndollar, K., & Trotschel, R. (2001). The automated will: Nonconscious activation and pursuit of behavioral goals. *Journal of Personality and Social Psychology, 81,* 1014–1027.

Bargh, J. A., & Pietromonaco, P. (1982). Automatic information processing and social perception: The influence of trait information presented outside of conscious awareness on impression formation. *Journal of Personality and Social Psychology, 43,* 437–449.

Bargh, J. A., Raymond, P., Pryor, J. B., & Strack, F. (1995). Attractiveness of the underling: An automatic power-sex association and its consequences for sexual harassment and aggression. *Journal of Personality and Social Psychology, 68*(5), 768–781.

Bar-Hillel, M. (1980). The base-rate fallacy in probability judgments. *Acta Psychologica, 44*, 211–233.

Bar-Hillel, M., & Fischhoff, B. (1981). When do base-rates affect predictions? *Journal of Personality and Social Psychology, 41*, 671–680.

Barker, R. G., & Wright, H. F. (1954). *Midwest and its children: The psychological ecology of an American town.* New York: Row, Peterson and Company.

Baron, R. S. (1986). Distraction-conflict theory: Progress and problems. In L. Berkowitz (Ed.), *Advances in experimental social psychology* (Vol. 19, pp. 1–40). New York: Academic Press.

Baron, R. S., Moore, D., & Sanders, G. S. (1978). Distraction as a source of drive in social facilitation research. *Journal of Personality and Social Psychology, 36*, 816–824.

Baron, R. S., Vandello, J. A., & Brunsman, B. (1996). The forgotten variable in conformity research: Impact of task importance on social influence. *Journal of Personality and Social Psychology, 71*, 915–927.

Barrett, L. F. (2006). Are emotions natural kinds? *Perspectives on Psychological Science, 1*, 28–58.

Barrett, L. F., Mesquita, B., Ochsner, K. N., & Gross, J. J. (2007). The experience of emotion. *Annual Review of Psychology, 58*, 373–403.

Barsalou, L. W. (2008). Grounded cognition. *Annual Review of Psychology, 59*, 617–645.

Bar-Tal, D. (1990). Causes and consequences of delegitimization: Models of conflict and ethnocentrism. *Journal of Social Issues, 46*, 65–81.

Bar-Tal, D., & Saxe, L. (1976). Perceptions of similarly and dissimilarly attractive couples and individuals. *Journal of Personality and Social Psychology, 33*, 772–781.

Bartholomew, K., & Horowitz, L. M. (1991). Attachment styles among young adults: A test for a four-category model. *Journal of Personality and Social Psychology, 61*, 226–244.

Bartholow, B. D., & Anderson, C. A. (2002). Effects of violent videogames on aggressive behavior: Potential sex differences. *Journal of Experimental Social Psychology, 38*, 283–290.

Bartholow, B. D., Anderson, C. A., Carnagey, N. L., & Benjamin, A. J. (2005). Interactive effects of life experience and situational cues on aggression: The weapons priming effect in hunters and nonhunters. *Journal of Experimental Social Psychology, 41*, 48–60.

Bartlett, F. A. (1932). *Remembering: A study in experimental psychology.* Cambridge, England: Cambridge University Press.

Bartsch, R A., Judd, C. M., Louw, D. A., Park, B., & Ryan, C. S. (1997). Cross-national outgroup homogeneity: United States and South African stereotypes. *South African Journal of Psychology, 27*(3), 166–170.

Bassili, J. N. (1996). Meta-judgmental versus operative indexes of psychological attributes: The case of measures of attitude strength. *Journal of Personality and Social Psychology, 71*, 637–653.

Bateson, M., Nettle, D., & Roberts, G. (2006). Cues of being watched enhance cooperation in a real-world setting. *Biology Letters, 2*(3), 412–414.

Batson, C. D., Engel, C. L., & Fridell, S. R. (1999). Value judgments: Testing the somatic-marker hypothesis using false physiological feedback. *Personality and Social Psychology Bulletin, 25*, 1021–1032.

Batson, C. D., O'Quin, K., Fultz, J., Vanderplas, M., & Isen, A. (1983). Self-reported distress and empathy and egoistic versus altruistic motivation for helping. *Journal of Personality and Social Psychology, 45*, 706–718.

Batson, C. D., & Shaw, L. L. (1991). Evidence for altruism: Toward a pluralism of prosocial motives. *Psychological Inquiry, 2*, 107–122.

Baumann, J., & DeSteno, D. (2010, August 23). Emotion Guided Threat Detection: Expecting Guns Where There Are None. *Journal of Personality and Social Psychology.* Advance online publication. doi: 10.1037/a0020665

Baumeister, R. F. (1982). A self-presentational view of social interaction. *Psychological Bulletin, 91*, 3–26.

Baumeister, R. F. (1987). How the self became a problem: A psychological review of historical research. *Journal of Personality and Social Psychology, 52*, 163–176.

Baumeister, R. F., Bratslavsky, E., Finkenauer, C., & Vohs, K. D. (2001). Bad is stronger than good. *Review of General Psychology, 5*, 323–370.

Baumeister, R. F., Bratslavsky, E., Muraven, M., & Tice, D. M. (1998). Ego depletion: Is the active self a limited resource? *Journal of Personality and Social Psychology, 74*, 1252–1265.

Baumeister, R. F., & Leary, M. R. (1995). The need to belong: Desire for interpersonal attachments as a fundamental human motivation. *Psychological Bulletin, 117*, 497–529.

Baumeister, R. F., Smart, L., & Boden, J. M. (1996). Relation of threatened egotism to violence and aggression: The dark side to high self-esteem. *Psychological Review, 103*, 5–33.

Baumeister, R. F., Stillwell, A. M., & Heatherton, T. F. (1994). Guilt: An interpersonal approach. *Psychological Bulletin, 115*, 243–267.

Baumeister, R. F., Vohs, K. D., & Tice, D. M. (2007). The strength model of self-control. *Current Directions in Psychological Science, 16*, 396–403.

Beaman, A. L., Klentz, B., Diener, E., & Svanum, S. (1979). Self-awareness and transgression in children: Two field studies. *Journal of Personality and Social Psychology, 37*, 1835–1946.

Beck, S. P., Ward-Hull, C. I., & McLear, P. M. (1976). Variables related to women's somatic preferences of the male and female body. *Journal of Personality and Social Psychology, 34*, 1200–1210.

Becker, E. (1973). *The denial of death.* New York: Simon & Schuster.

Becker, M. H., & Josephs, J. G. (1988). Aids and behavioral change to reduce risk: A review. *American Journal of Public Health, 78*, 394–410.

Beckman, L. (1970). Effects of students' performance on teachers' and observers' attributions of causality. *Journal of Educational Psychology, 61*, 76–82.

Beer, J., Heerey, E. A., Keltner, D., Scabini, D., & Knight, R. (2003). The regulatory function of self-conscious emotion: Insights from patients with orbitofrontal damage. *Journal of Personality and Social Psychology, 85*, 594–604.

Bell, B. E., & Loftus, E. F. (1989). Trivial persuasion in the courtroom: The power of (a few) minor details. *Journal of Personality and Social Psychology, 56*, 669–679.

Bell, S. T., Kuriloff, P. J., & Lottes, I. (1994). Understanding attributions of blame in stranger-rape and date-rape situations: An examination of gender, race, identification, and students' social perceptions of rape victims. *Journal of Applied Social Psychology, 24*, 1719–1734.

Belsky, G., & Gilovich, T. (1999). *Why smart people make big money mistakes, and how to correct them.* New York: Simon & Schuster.

Bem, D. J. (1967). Self-perception: An alternative interpretation of cognitive dissonance phenomena. *Psychological Review, 74*, 183–200.

Bem, D. J. (1972). Self-perception theory. In L. Berkowitz (Ed.), *Advances in experimental social psychology* (Vol. 6, pp. 1–62). New York: Academic Press.

Bem, S. L. (1993). *The lenses of gender: Transforming the debate on sexual inequality.* New Haven, CT: Yale University Press.

Benet-Martinez, V., Leu, J., Lee, F., & Morris, M. W. (2002). Negotiating biculturalism: Cultural frame switching in biculturals with oppositional versus compatible cultural identities. *Journal of Cross-Cultural Psychology, 33,* 492–516.

Ben-Zeev, T., Fein, S., & Inzlicht, M. (2005). Arousal and stereotype threat. *Journal of Experimental Social Psychology, 41,* 174–181.

Berg, J. H., & McQuinn, R. D. (1986). Attraction and exchange in continuing and noncontinuing dating relationships. *Journal of Personality and Social Psychology, 50,* 942–952.

Berger, J., Meredith, M., & Wheeler, S. C. (2010). Contextual priming: Where people vote affects how they vote. *Proceedings of the National Academy of Sciences, 105(26),* 8846–8849.

Berglas, S., & Jones, E. E. (1978). Drug choice as a self-handicapping strategy in response to non-contingent success. *Journal of Personality and Social Psychology, 36,* 405–417.

Berkman, L. F. (1995). The role of social relations in health promotion. *Psychosomatic Medicine, 57,* 245–254.

Berkman, L. F., & Syme, S. L. (1979). Social networks, host resistance, and mortality: A nine-year follow-up study of Alameda County residents. *American Journal of Epidemiology, 100,* 186–204.

Berkowitz, L. (1965). Some aspects of observed aggression. *Journal of Personality and Social Psychology, 2,* 359–369.

Berkowitz, L. (1989). The frustration-aggression hypothesis: An examination and reformulation. *Psychological Bulletin, 106,* 59–73.

Berkowitz, L. (1993). *Aggression.* New York: McGraw-Hill.

Berkowitz, L., & LePage, A. (1967). Weapons as aggression-eliciting stimuli. *Journal of Personality and Social Psychology, 7,* 202–207.

Berman, M., Jonides, J., & Kaplan, S. (2008). The cognitive benefits of interacting with nature. *Psychological Science, 19,* 1207–1212.

Bernieri, F. J., Zuckerman, M., Koestner, R., & Rosenthal, R. (1994). Measuring person perception accuracy: Another look at self-other agreement. *Personality and Social Psychology Bulletin, 20,* 367–378.

Bernstein, I. H., Lin, T., & McClellan, P. (1982). Cross- vs. within-racial judgments of attractiveness. *Perception and Psychophysics, 32,* 495–503.

Berry, D. S., & McArthur, L. Z. (1986). Perceiving character in faces: The impact of age-related craniofacial changes in social perception. *Psychological Bulletin, 100,* 3–18.

Berry, D. S., & Zebrowitz-McArthur, L. (1986). Perceiving character in faces: The impact of age-related craniofacial changes in social perception. *Psychological Bulletin, 100,* 3–18.

Berscheid, E. (2010). Love in the fourth dimension. *Annual Review of Psychology, 61,* 1–25.

Berscheid, E., Dion, K., Walster, E., & Walster, G. W. (1971). Physical attractiveness and dating choice: A test of the matching hypothesis. *Journal of Experimental Social Psychology, 7,* 173–189.

Berscheid, E., & Reis, H. T. (1998). Attraction and close relationships. In D. T. Gilbert, S. T. Fiske, & G. Lindzey (Eds.), *The handbook of social psychology* (4th ed., Vol. 2, pp. 193–281). New York: McGraw-Hill.

Bersoff, D. N. (1987). Social science data and the Supreme Court: Lockhart as a case in point. *American Psychologist, 42,* 52–58.

Beshears, J., Choi, J. J., Laibson, D. & Madrian, B. (2008). The importance of default options for retirement saving outcomes: Evidence from the USA. In S. J. Kay and T. Sinha (Eds.), *Lessons from pension reform in the Americas* (pp. 59–87). New York: Oxford University Press.

Bessenoff, G. R., & Sherman, J. W. (2000). Automatic and controlled components of prejudice toward fat people: Evaluation versus stereotype activation. *Social Cognition, 18,* 329–353.

Bettencourt, B. A., Brewer, M. B., Croak, M. R., & Miller, N. (1992). Cooperation and the reduction of intergroup bias: The role of reward structure and social orientation. *Journal of Experimental Psychology, 28,* 301–319.

Biernat, M., Manis, M., & Kobrynowicz, D. (1997). Simultaneous assimilation and contrast effects in judgments of self and others. *Journal of Personality and Social Psychology, 73,* 254–269.

Bird, K. (2002). Advertise or die: Advertising and market share dynamics revisited. *Applied Economic Letters, 9,* 763–767.

Blackwell, L., Trzesniewski, K., & Dweck, C. S. (2007). Implicit theories of intelligence predict achievement across an adolescent transition: A longitudinal study and an intervention. *Child Development, 78,* 246–263.

Blair, I. V., Judd, C. M., & Chapleau, K. M. (2004). The influence of Afrocentric facial features in criminal sentencing. *Psychological Science, 15,* 674–679.

Blair, I. V., Judd, C. M., & Fallman, J. L. (2004). The automaticity of race and Afrocentric facial features in social judgments. *Journal of Personality and Social Psychology, 87,* 763–778.

Blair, I. V., Judd, C., Sadler, M. S., & Jenkins, C. (2002). The role of Afrocentric features in person perception: Judging by features and categories. *Journal of Personality and Social Psychology, 83,* 5–25.

Blair, J., Mitchell, D., & Blair, K. (2005). *The psychopath: Emotion and the brain.* Malden, MA: Blackwell Publishing.

Blanton, H., Buunk, B. P., Gibbons, F. X., & Kuyper, H. (1999). When better-than-others compare upward: Choice of comparison and comparative evaluation as independent predictors of academic performance. *Journal of Personality & Social Psychology, 76,* 420–430.

Blanton, H., & Jaccard, J. (2008). Unconscious racism: A concept in pursuit of a measure. *Annual Review of Sociology, 34,* 277–297.

Blanton, H., Jaccard, J., Klick, J., Mellers, B., Mitchell, G., & Tetlock, P. E. (2009). Strong claims and weak evidence: Reassessing the predictive validity of the IAT. *Journal of Applied Psychology, 94,* 567–582.

Blanton, H., Pelham, B. W., De Hart, T., & Kuyper, H. (1999). When better-than-others compare upward: Choice of comparison and comparative evaluation as independent predictors of academic performance. *Journal of Personality and Social Psychology, 76,* 420–430.

Blascovich, J., & Mendes, W. B. (2001). Challenge and threat appraisals: The role of affective cues. In I. Forgas (Ed.), *Feeling and thinking: The role of affect in social cognition.* London: Cambridge University Press.

Blascovich, J., Mendes, W. B., Hunter, S. B., & Salomon, K. (1999). Social "facilitation" as challenge and threat. *Journal of Personality and Social Psychology, 77,* 68–77.

Blass, T. (1999). The Milgram paradigm after 35 years: Some things we now know about obedience to authority. *Journal of Applied Social Psychology, 29,* 955–978.

Blass, T. (2000). *Obedience to authority: Current perspectives on the Milgram paradigm.* Mahwah, NJ: Erlbaum.

Blass, T. (2004). *The man who shocked the world: The life and legacy of Stanley Milgram.* New York: Basic Books.

Bless, H., Clore, G. L., Schwarz, N., Golisano, V., Rabe, C., & Wölk, M. (1996). Mood and the use of scripts: Does a happy mood really lead to mindlessness? *Journal of Personality and Social Psychology, 71*(4), 665–679.

Block, J., & Robins, R. W. (1993). A longitudinal study of consistency and change in self-esteem from early adolescence to early adulthood. *Child Development, 64*, 909–923.

Bloom, B. L., White, S. W., & Asher, S. J. (1979). Marital disruption as a stressful life event. In G. Levinger & O. C. Moles (Eds.), *Divorce and separation: Context, causes, and consequences* (pp. 184–200). New York: Basic Books.

Bochner, S. (1994). Cross-cultural differences in the self-concept. *Journal of Cross-Cultural Psychology, 25*, 273–283.

Bodenhausen, G. V. (1988). Stereotypic biases in social decision making and memory: Testing process models of stereotype use. *Journal of Personality and Social Psychology, 55*, 726–737.

Bodenhausen, G. V. (1990). Stereotypes as judgmental heuristics: Evidence of circadian variations in discrimination. *Psychological Science, 1*, 319–322.

Bodenhausen, G. V., Macrae, C. N., & Sherman, J. W. (1999). On the dialectics of discrimination: Dual processes in social stereotyping. In S. Chaiken & Y. Trope (Eds.), *Dual process theories in social psychology* (pp. 271–290). New York: Guilford Press.

Bodenhausen, G., Sheppard, L., & Kramer, G. (1994). Negative affect and social judgment: The different impact of anger and sadness. *European Journal of Social Psychology, 24*, 45–62.

Boehm, C. (1999). *Hierarchy in the forest: The evolution of egalitarian behavior*. Cambridge, MA: Harvard University Press.

Boice, R., Quanty, C. B., & Williams, R. C. (1974). Competition and possible dominance in turtles, toads, and frogs. *Journal of Comparative and Physiological Psychology, 86*, 1116–1131.

Bond, M. H., & Cheung, T. (1983). College students' spontaneous self-concept. *Journal of Cross-Cultural Psychology, 14*, 154–171.

Bond, R., & Smith, P. B. (1996). Culture and conformity: A meta-analysis of studies using Asch's line judgment task. *Psychological Bulletin, 119*, 111–137.

Borg, J. S., Hyunes, C., Van Horn, J., Grafton, S., & Sinnott-Armstrong, W. (2006). Consequences, action, and intention as factors in moral judgments: An fMRI investigation. *Journal of Cognitive Neuroscience, 18*, 803–817.

Borg, J. S., Lieberman, D., & Kiehl, K. A. (2008). Infection, incest, and iniquity: Investigating the neural correlates of disgust and morality. *Journal of Cognitive Neuroscience, 20*, 1529–1546.

Borgida, E., Conner, C., & Manteufel, L. (1992). Understanding living kidney donations: A behavioral decision-making perspective. In S. Spacapan & S. Oskamp (Eds.), *Helping and being helped*. Newbury Park, CA: Sage.

Bornstein, R. F. (1989). Exposure and affect: Overview and meta-analysis of research, 1968–1987. *Psychological Bulletin, 106*, 265–289.

Bosson, J. K., & Vandello, J. A. (2011). Precarious manhood and its links to action and aggression. *Current Directions in Psychological Science, 20*, 82–86.

Boster, F. J., & Mongeau, P. (1984). Fear-arousing persuasive messages. In R. N. Bostrom (Ed.), *Communication yearbook* (Vol. 8, pp. 330–375). Beverly Hills, CA: Sage.

Boucher, J. D., & Brandt, M. E. (1981). Judgment of emotion: American and Malay antecedents. *Journal of Cross-Cultural Psychology, 12*, 272–283.

Bowlby, J. (1969). *Attachment and loss, Vol. 1: Attachment*. New York: Basic Books.

Bowlby, J. (1973). *Attachment and loss, Vol. 2: Separation*. New York: Basic Books.

Bowlby, J. (1980). *Attachment and loss, Vol. 3: Loss, sadness and depression*. New York: Basic Books.

Bowlby, J. (1982). *Attachment and loss* (2nd ed., Vol. 1). New York: Basic Books.

Boyd, R., & Richerson, P. J. (1985). Frequency-dependent bias and the evolution of cooperation. In R. Boyd & P. J. Richardson (Eds.), *Culture and the evolutionary process* (pp. 204–240). Chicago: University of Chicago Press.

Boyden, T., Carroll, J. S., & Maier, R. A. (1984). Similarity and attraction in homosexual males: The effects of age and masculinity-femininity. *Sex Roles, 10*, 939–948.

Brackett, M. A., Rivers, S. E. and Salovey, P. (2011), Emotional Intelligence: Implications for Personal, Social, Academic, and Workplace Success. *Social and Personality Psychology Compass, 5*: 88–103. doi: 10.1111/j.1751-9004.2010.00334.x

Bradbury, T. N., & Fincham, F. D. (1990). Attributions in marriage: Review and critique. *Psychological Bulletin, 107*, 3–33.

Bradbury, T. N., & Karney, B. R. (1993). Longitudinal study of marital interaction and dysfunction. *Clinical Psychology Review, 13*, 15–27.

Bradfield, A., & Wells, G. L. (2005). Not the same old hindsight bias: Outcome information distorts a broad range of retrospective judgments. *Memory and Cognition, 33*, 120–130.

Bransford, J. D., & Johnson, M. K. (1973). Considerations of some problems of comprehension. In W. G. Chase (Ed.), *Visual information processing* (pp. 383–438). New York: Academic Press.

Brauer, M., Chambres, P., Niedenthal, P. M., & Chatard-Pannetier, A. (2004). The relationship between expertise and evaluative extremity: The moderating role of experts' task characteristics. *Journal of Personality and Social Psychology, 86*, 5–18.

Brauer, M., & Er-rafiy, A. (2001). Increasing perceived variability reduces prejudice and discrimination. *Journal of Experimental Social Psychology, 47*(5), 871–881.

Breckler, S. J. (1984). Empirical validation of affect, behavior, and cognition as distinct components of attitude. *Journal of Personality and Social Psychology, 47*, 1191–1205.

Brehm, J. W. (1956). Post-decision changes in desirability of alternatives. *Journal of Abnormal and Social Psychology, 52*, 384–389.

Brendl, C. M., Higgins, E. T., & Lemm, K. M. (1995). Sensitivity to varying gains and losses: The role of self-discrepancies and event framing. *Journal of Personality and Social Psychology, 69*, 1028–1051.

Brendl, C. M., Markman, A. B., & Messner, C. (2001). How do indirect measures of evaluation work? Evaluating the inference of prejudice in the implicit association test. *Journal of Personality and Social Psychology, 81*, 760–773.

Brennan, K. A., Clark, C. L., & Shaver, P. R. (1998). Self-report measurement of adult attachment: An integrative overview. In J. A. Simpson & W. S. Rholes (Eds.), *Attachment theory and close relationships* (pp. 46–76). New York: Guilford Press.

Brennan, K. A., & Shaver, P. R. (1993). Attachment styles and parental divorce. *Journal of Divorce and Remarriage, 21*, 161–175.

Brewer, M. B. (1979). In-group bias in the minimal intergroup situation: A cognitive-motivational analysis. *Psychological Bulletin, 86*, 307–324.

Brewer, M. B. (1988). A dual process model of impression formation. In T. K. Srull & R. S. Wyer (Eds.), *Advances in social cognition*. Hillsdale, NJ: Erlbaum.

Brewer, M. B., & Brown, R. J. (1998). Intergroup relations. In D. T. Gilbert, S. T. Fiske, & G. Lindzey (Eds.), *The handbook of social psychology* (4th ed., Vol. 2, pp. 554–594). New York: McGraw-Hill.

Brewer, M. B., & Kramer, R. M. (1985). The psychology of intergroup attitudes and behavior. *Annual Review of Psychology, 36,* 219–243.

Brewer, M. B., & Miller, N. (1988). Contact and cooperation: When do they work? In P. Katz & D. Taylor (Eds.), *Eliminating racism: Profiles in controversy* (pp. 315–326). New York: Plenum Press.

Brewer, M. B., & Nakamura, G. V. (1984). The nature and functions of schemas. In R. S. Wyer & T. K. Srull (Eds.), *The handbook of social cognition* (Vol. 1). Hillsdale, NJ: Erlbaum.

Briggs, J. L. (1960). *Never in anger: Portrait of an Eskimo family.* Cambridge, MA: Harvard University Press.

Brigham, J. C. (1993). College students' racial attitudes. *Journal of Applied Social Psychology, 23,* 1933–1967.

Brigham, J., Bennett, L., Meissner, C., & Mitchell, T. (2007). The influence of race on eyewitness memory. In R. C. L. Lindsay, D. F. Ross, D. J. Read, & M. P. Toglia (Eds.), *The handbook of eyewitness psychology.* Mahwah, NJ: Erlbaum.

Brinker, L. Fox News, Michael Sam, and "Appropriate homophobia." *The advocate.com.* May 15, 2014. http://www.advocate.com /commentary/2014/05/15/op-ed-fox-news-michael-sam-and -appropriate-homophobia

Briñol, P., & DeMarree, K. G. (Eds.). (2012). *Social metacognition.* New York: Psychology Press.

Briñol, P. & Petty, R. E (2003). Overt head movements and persuasion: A self-validation analysis. *Journal of Personality and Social Psychology, 84,* 1123–1139.

Briñol, P., & Petty, R. E. (2009). Source factors in persuasion: A self-validation approach.
European Review of Social Psychology, 20, 49–96.

Brislin, R. W., & Lewis, S. A. (1968). Dating and physical attractiveness: Replication. *Psychological Reports, 22,* 976.

Brockner, J. (1979). The effects of self-esteem, success-failure, and self-consciousness on task performance. *Journal of Personality and Social Psychology, 37,* 1732–1741.

Broemer, P., & Diehl, M. (2003). What you think is what you get: Comparative evaluations of close relationships. *Personality and Social Psychology Bulletin, 29,* 1560–1569.

Brown, D. E. (1991). *Human universals.* New York: McGraw-Hill.

Brown, J. D. (1998). *The self.* New York: McGraw-Hill.

Brown, J. D., & Dutton, K. A. (1995). The thrill of victory, the complexity of defeat: Self-esteem and people's emotional reactions to success and failure. *Journal of Personality and Social Psychology, 68,* 712–722.

Brown, R. (1986). *Social psychology* (2nd ed.). New York: Free Press.

Brown, S. L., Nesse, R. M., Vinokur, A. D., & Smith, D. M. (2003). Providing social support may be more beneficial than receiving it: Results from a prospective study of mortality. *Psychological Science, 14*(4), 320–327.

Browning, C. R. (1992). *Ordinary men: Reserve police battalion 101 and the final solution in Poland.* New York: Aaron Asher.

Brownstein, A., Read, S. J., & Simon, D. (2004). Bias at the race-track: Effects of individual expertise and task importance on predecision reevaluation of alternatives. *Personality and Social Psychology Bulletin, 57,* 904–915.

Brownstein, A. L. (2003). Biased predecision processing. *Psychological Bulletin, 129,* 545–568.

Brumberg, J. J. (1997). *The body project: An intimate history of American girls.* New York: Random House.

Buehler, R., Griffin, D., & Ross, M. (1994). Exploring the "planning fallacy": Why people underestimate their task completion times. *Journal of Personality and Social Psychology, 67,* 366–381.

Bureau of Justice Statistics. (2011). Prisoner Statistics. *Correctional Population in the United States, 2011.* Retrieved from http://www .ojp.usdoj.gov/bjs/

Burger, J. M. (1981). Motivational biases in the attribution of responsibility for an accident: A meta-analysis of the defensive-attribution hypothesis. *Psychological Bulletin, 90,* 496–512.

Burger, J. M. (1986). Increasing compliance by improving the deal: The that's-not-all technique. *Journal of Personality and Social Psychology, 51,* 277–283.

Burger, J. M. (1999). The foot-in-the-door compliance procedure: A multiple process analysis and review. *Personality and Social Psychology Review, 3,* 303–325.

Burger, J. M. (2009). Replicating Milgram: Would people still obey today? *American Psychologist, 64,* 1–11.

Burger, J. M., Girgis, Z. M., & Manning, C. C. (2011). In their own words: Explaining obedience to authority through an examination of participants' comments. *Social Psychological and Personality Science, 2,* 460–466.

Burger, J. M., & Guadagno, R. E. (2003). Self-concept clarity and the foot-in-the-door procedure. *Basic and Applied Social Psychology, 25,* 79–86.

Burger, J. M., Reed, M., DeCesare, K., Rauner, S., & Rozolis, J. (1999). The effects of initial request size on compliance: More about the that's-not-all technique. *Basic and Applied Social Psychology, 21,* 243–249.

Burgess, E. W., & Wallin, P. (1953). *Engagement and marriage.* Philadelphia: Lippincott.

Burkhart, K. (1973). *Women in prison.* Garden City, NY: Doubleday.

Burnstein, E. (2005). Kin altruism: The morality of biological systems. In D. M. Buss (Ed.), *The handbook of evolutionary psychology* (pp. 528–551). New York: Wiley.

Burnstein, E., Crandall, C., & Kitayama, S. (1994). Some neo-Darwinian decision rules for altruism: Weighing cues for inclusive fitness as a function of the biological importance of the decision. *Journal of Personality and Social Psychology, 67,* 773–789.

Burnstein, E., & Vinokur, A. (1973). Testing two classes of theories about group-induced shifts in individual choice. *Journal of Experimental Social Psychology, 9,* 123–137.

Burnstein, E., Vinokur, A., & Trope, Y. (1973). Interpersonal comparison versus persuasive argumentation: A more direct test of alternative explanations for group-induced shifts in individual choice. *Journal of Experimental Social Psychology, 9,* 236–245.

Burt, R., Kilduff, M., & Tasselli, S. (2013). Social Network Analysis: Foundations and Frontiers on Advantage, *Annual Review of Psychology, 64,* 527–547.

Bushman, B. J. (2002). Does venting anger feed or extinguish the flame? Catharsis, rumination, distraction, anger, and aggressive responding. *Personality and Social Psychology Bulletin, 28(6),* 724–731. doi: 10.1177/0146167202289002

Buss, D. M. (1984). Toward a psychology of person-environment (PE) correlation: The role of spouse selection. *Journal of Personality and Social Psychology, 47,* 361–377.

Buss, D. M. (1989). Sex differences in human mate preference: Evolutionary hypothesis tested in 37 cultures. *Behavioral and Brain Sciences, 12,* 1–49.

Buss, D. M. (1994). *The evolution of desire: Strategies of human mating.* New York: Basic Books.

Byrne, D. (1961). Interpersonal attraction and attitude similarity. *Journal of Abnormal and Social Psychology, 62,* 713–715.

Byrne, D., Clore, G. L., & Smeaton, G. (1986). The attraction hypothesis: Do similar attitudes predict anything? *Journal of Personality and Social Psychology, 51,* 1167–1170.

Byrne, D., Griffitt, W., & Stefaniak, D. (1967). Attraction and similarity of personality characteristics. *Journal of Personality and Social Psychology, 5,* 82–90.

Byrne, D., & Nelson, D. (1965). Attraction as a linear function of proportion of positive reinforcements. *Journal of Abnormal and Social Psychology, 1,* 659–663.

Cacioppo, J. T., & Berntson, G. G. (1994). Relationship between attitudes and evaluative space: A critical review with emphasis on the separability of positive and negative substrates. *Psychological Bulletin, 115,* 401–423.

Cacioppo, J. T., & Gardner, W. L. (1999). Emotion. *Annual Review of Psychology, 50,* 191–214.

Cacioppo, J. T., Petty, R. E., Feinstein, J., & Jarvis, B. (1996). Individual differences in cognitive motivation: The life and times of people varying in need for cognition. *Psychological Bulletin, 119,* 197–253.

Cacioppo, J. T., Petty, R. E., & Morris, K. J. (1983). Effects of need for cognition on message evaluation, recall, and persuasion. *Journal of Personality and Social Psychology, 45,* 805–818.

Cacioppo, J. T., Petty, R. E., & Sidera, J. (1982). The effects of salient self-schema on the evaluation of proattitudinal editorials: Top-down versus bottom-up message processing. *Journal of Experimental Social Psychology, 18,* 324–338.

Cacioppo, J. T., Priester, J. R., & Berntson, G. G. (1993). Rudimentary determinants of attitude. II. Arm flexion and extension have differential effects on attitudes. *Journal of Personality and Social Psychology, 65,* 5–17.

Cadinu, M., Maass, A., Rosabianca, A., & Kiesner, J. (2005). Why do women underperform under stereotype threat? Evidence for the role of negative thinking. *Psychological Science, 16,* 572–578.

Cain, R. (1991). Stigma management and gay identity development. *Social Work, 36,* 67–73.

Campbell, D. T. (1975). On the conflicts between biological and social evolution and between psychology and moral tradition. *American Psychologist, 30,* 1103–1126.

Campbell, J. D., & Fairey, P. J. (1989). Informational and normative routes to conformity: The effect of faction size as a function of norm extremity and attention to the stimulus. *Journal of Personality and Social Psychology, 57,* 457–468.

Camposa, L., Ottab, E., & Siqueira, J. (2002). Sex differences in mate selection strategies: Content analyses and responses to personal advertisements in Brazil. *Evolution and Human Behavior 23,* 395–406.

Carli, L. L. (1999). Cognitive reconstruction, hindsight, and reactions to victims and perpetrators. *Personality and Social Psychology Bulletin, 25,* 966–979.

Carlsmith, J. M., & Gross, A. E. (1969). Some effects of guilt on compliance. *Journal of Personality and Social Psychology, 11,* 232–239.

Carlsmith, K. M., & Darley, J. M. (2008). Psychological aspects of retributive justice. *Advances in Experimental Social Psychology, 40,* 193–236.

Carlsmith, K. M., Darley, J. M., & Robinson, P. H. (2002). Why do we punish? Deterrence and just deserts as motives for punishment. *Journal of Personality and Social Psychology, 83,* 284–299.

Carlson, J. A., & Davis, C. M. (1971). Cultural values and the risky shift: A cross-cultural test in Uganda and the United States. *Journal of Personality and Social Psychology, 20,* 236–245.

Carlson, M., Charlin, V., & Miller, N. (1988). Positive mood and helping behavior: A test of six hypotheses. *Journal of Personality and Social Psychology, 55,* 211–229.

Carlston, D. E., & Skowronski, J. J. (1994). Savings in the relearning of trait information as evidence for spontaneous inference generation. *Journal of Personality and Social Psychology, 66,* 840–880.

Carnevale, P. J., & Isen, A. M. (1986). The influence of positive affect and visual access on the discovery of integrative solutions in bilateral negotiation. *Organizational Behavior and Human Decision Processes, 37,* 1–13.

Carney, D., Cuddy, A. J. C., & Yap, A. J. (2010). Power posing: Brief nonverbal displays affect neuroendocrine levels and risk tolerance. *Psychological Science, 21,* 1363–1368.

Carter, C. S. (1998). Neuroendocrine perspectives on social attachment and love. *Psychoneuroendocrinology, 23*(8), 779–818.

Carter, J., & Irons, M. (1991). Are economists different, and if so, why? *Journal of Economic Perspectives, 5,* 171–177.

Carter, T., Ferguson, M. J., & Hassin, R. R. (2011). A single exposure to the American flag shifts support toward Republicanism up to 8 months later. *Psychological Science, 22*(8), 341–359.

Carter, T. J., & Gilovich, T. (2010). The relative relativity of material and experiential purchases. *Journal of Personality and Social Psychology, 98*(1), 146–159.

Cartwright, D., & Zander, A. (1968). *Group dynamics: Research and theory.* New York: Harper & Row.

Carver, C. S. (1974). Facilitation of physical aggression through objective self-awareness. *Journal of Experimental Social Psychology, 10,* 365–370.

Carver, C. S., DeGregorio, E., & Gillis, R. (1980). Ego-defensive attribution among two categories of observers. *Personality and Social Psychology Bulletin, 6,* 4–50.

Carver, C. S., & Scheier, M. F. (1981). The self-attention-induced feedback loop and social facilitation. *Journal of Experimental Social Psychology, 17,* 545–568.

Carver, C. S., & Scheier, M. F. (1982). Control theory: A useful conceptual framework for personality-social, clinical, and health psychology. *Psychological Bulletin, 92,* 111–135.

Cash, T. F., & Duncan, N. C. (1984). Physical attractiveness stereotyping among black American college students. *Journal of Social Psychology, 122,* 71–77.

Cash, T. F., & Kilcullen, R. N. (1985). The eye of the beholder: Susceptibility to sexism and beautyism in the evaluation of managerial applicants. *Journal of Applied Social Psychology, 15,* 591–605.

Cash, T. F., & Trimer, C. A. (1984). Sexism and beautyism in women's evaluations of peer performance. *Sex Roles, 10,* 87–98.

Caspi, A., & Herbener, E. S. (1990). Continuity and change: Assortative marriage and the consistency of personality in adulthood. *Journal of Personality and Social Psychology, 58,* 250–258.

Caspi, A., McClay, J., Moffitt, T. E., Mill, J., Martin, J., Craig, I. W., et al. (2002). Role of genotype in the cycle of violence in maltreated children. *Science, 297,* 851–854.

Cate, R. M., Lloyd, S. A., Henton, J. M., & Larson, J. H. (1982). Fairness and reward level as predictors of relationship satisfaction. *Social Psychology Quarterly, 45,* 177–181.

Ceci, S. J., & Bruck, M. (1995). *Jeopardy in the courtroom: A scientific analysis of children's testimony.* Washington, DC: American Psychological Association.

Center for Media and Public Affairs. (July–August 2000). The media at the millennium: The networks' top topics, trends, and joke targets of the 1990s. *Media Monitor, 14,* 1–6.

Central Intelligence Agency. (2011). The World Factbook. Retrieved from https://www.cia.gov/library/publications/the-world-factbook/rankorder/2172rank.html

Cesario, J., Plaks, J. E., & Higgins, E. T. (2006). Automatic social behavior as motivated preparation to interact. *Journal of Personality and Social Psychology, 90,* 893–910.

Cha, J.-H., & Nam, K. D. (1985). A test of Kelley's cube theory of attribution: A cross-cultural replication of McArthur's study. *Korean Social Science Journal, 12,* 151–180.

Chagnon, N. A. (1997). *Yanomamö.* New York: Harcourt, Brace, Jovanovich.

Chaiken, S. (1980). Heuristic versus systematic information processing in the use of source versus message cues in persuasion. *Journal of Personality and Social Psychology, 39,* 752–766.

Chaiken, S., & Baldwin, M. W. (1981). Affective-cognitive consistency and the effect of salient behavioral information on the self-perception of attitudes. *Journal of Personality and Social Psychology, 41,* 1–12.

Chaiken, S., & Eagly, A. H. (1976). Communication modality as a determinant of persuasion: The role of communicator salience. *Journal of Personality and Social Psychology, 45,* 241–256.

Chaiken, S., Liberman, A., & Eagly, A. H. (1989). Heuristic and systematic processing within and beyond the persuasion context. In J. S. Uleman & J. A. Bargh (Eds.), *Unintended thought* (pp. 212–252). New York: Guilford Press.

Chaiken S., & Maheswaran, D. (1994). Heuristic processing can bias systematic processing: effects of source credibility, argument ambiguity, and task importance on attitude judgment. *Journal of Personality and Social Psychology, 66,* 460–473.

Chapman, L. J., & Chapman, J. (1967). Genesis of popular but erroneous diagnostic observations. *Journal of Abnormal Psychology, 72,* 193–204.

Charles, S. T. & Carstensen, L. L. (2009). Socioemotional selectivity theory. In H. Reis & S. Sprecher (Eds.) *Encyclopedia of Human Relationships.* Sage Publications.

Chartrand, T. L., & Bargh, J. A. (1999). The chameleon effect: The perception-behavior link and social interaction. *Journal of Personality and Social Psychology, 76,* 893–910.

Chen, C., Boucher, H., & Tapias, M. P. (2006). The relational self revealed: Integrative conceptualization and implications for interpersonal life. *Psychological Bulletin, 132*(2), 151–179.

Chen, C., & Stevenson, H. W. (1995). Motivation and mathematics achievement: A comparative study of Asian-American, Caucasian-American and East Asian high school students. *Child Development, 66,* 1215–1234.

Chen, M., & Bargh, J. A. (1999). Consequences of automatic evaluation: Immediate behavioral predispositions to approach or avoid the stimulus. *Personality and Social Psychology Bulletin, 25,* 215–224.

Chen, S., & Chaiken, S. (1999). The heuristic-systematic model in its broader context. In S. Chaiken & Y. Trope (Eds.), *Dual-process theories in social and cognitive psychology* (pp. 73–96). New York: Guilford Press.

Chen, S., Lee-Chai, A. Y., & Bargh, J. A. (2001). Relationship orientation as moderator of the effects of social power. *Journal of Personality and Social Psychology, 80,* 183–187.

Chen, S. C. (1937). Social modification of the activity of ants in nest-building. *Physiological Zoology, 10,* 420–436.

Cheng, P. W., & Novick, L. R. (1990). A probabilistic contrast model of causal induction. *Journal of Personality and Social Psychology, 58,* 545–567.

Cheryan, S., & Bodenhausen, G. V. (2000). When positive stereotypes threaten intellectual performance: The psychological hazards of "model minority" status. *Psychological Review, 11,* 399–402.

Cheung, F. M., Leung, K., Zhang, J. X., Sun, H. F., Gan, Y. Q., Song, W. Z., & Dong, X. (2001). Indigenous Chinese personality constructs: Is the five-factor model complete? *Journal of Cross-Cultural Psychology, 32,* 407–433.

Choi, I., & Nisbett, R. E. (1998). Situational salience and cultural differences in the correspondence bias and in the actor-observer bias. *Personality and Social Psychology Bulletin, 24,* 949–960.

Choi, I., Nisbett, R. E., & Norenzayan, A. (1999). Causal attribution across cultures: Variation and universality. *Psychological Bulletin, 125,* 47–63.

Choi, J., Laibson, D., & Madrian, B. (2009). Reducing the complexity costs of 401(k) participation through quick enrollment. In D. A. Wise (Ed.), *Research findings in the economics of aging* (pp. 57–82). Chicago: University of Chicago Press.

Choi, J. N., & Kim, M. U. (1999). The organizational application of groupthink and its limitations in organizations. *Journal of Applied Psychology, 84,* 297–306.

Chonody, J. M. (2013). Measuring sexual prejudice against gay men and lesbian women: Development of the Sexual Prejudice Scale (SPS). *Journal of Homosexuality, 60(6),* 895–926.

Christakis, N. A., & Fowler, J. H. (2009). *Connected.* New York: Little, Brown.

Christakis, N. A., & Fowler, J. H. (2013). Social contagion theory: Examining dynamic social networks and human behavior," *Statistics in Medicine, 32*(4), 556–577.

Chua, H., Leu, J., & Nisbett, R. E. (2005). Culture and the diverging views of social events. *Personality and Social Psychology Bulletin, 31,* 925–934.

Cialdini, R. B. (1984). *Influence: How and why people agree to things.* New York: Quill.

Cialdini, R. B., Borden, R. J., Thorne, A., Walker, M. R., Freeman, S., & Sloan, L. R. (1976). Basking in reflected glory: Three (football) field studies. *Journal of Personality and Social Psychology, 34,* 366–375.

Cialdini, R. B., Darby, B. L., & Vincent, J. E. (1973). Transgression and altruism: A case for hedonism. *Journal of Experimental Social Psychology, 9,* 502–516.

Cialdini, R. R., Demaine, L. J., Sagarin, B. J., Barrett, D. W., Rhoads, K., & Winters, K. (2006). Activating and aligning social norms for persuasive impact. *Social Influence, 1,* 3–15.

Cialdini, R. B., & Fultz, J. (1990). Interpreting the negative mood-helping literature via "mega" analysis: A contrarian view. *Psychological Bulletin, 107,* 210–214.

Cialdini, R. B., Kallgren, C. A., & Reno, R. R. (1991). A focus theory of normative conduct: A theoretical refinement and reevaluation of the role of norms in human behavior. In M. P. Zanna (Ed.), *Advances in experimental social psychology* (Vol. 24, pp. 201–234). San Diego, CA: Academic Press.

Cialdini, R. B., & Kenrick, D. T. (1976). Altruism as hedonism: A social development perspective on the relationship of negative mood state and helping. *Journal of Personality and Social Psychology, 34,* 907–914.

Cialdini, R. B., Schaller, M., Houlihan, D., Arps, K., Fultz, J., & Beaman, A. L. (1987). Empathy-based helping: Is it selflessly or selfishly motivated? *Journal of Personality and Social Psychology, 52,* 749–758.

Cialdini, R. B., & Trost, M. R. (1998). Social influence: Social norms, conformity, and compliance. In D. T. Gilbert, S. T. Fiske, & G. Lindzey (Eds.), *The handbook of social psychology* (4th ed., Vol. 2, pp. 151–192). New York: McGraw-Hill.

Cialdini, R. B., Vincent, J. E., Lewis, S. K., Catalan, J., Wheeler, D., & Darby, B. L. (1975). Reciprocal concessions procedure for inducing compliance: The door-in-the-face technique. *Journal of Personality and Social Psychology, 31,* 206–215.

Clancy, S. M., & Dollinger, S. J. (1993). Photographic depictions of the self: Gender and age differences in social connectedness. *Sex Roles, 15,* 145–158.

Clark, M., & Isen, A. M. (1982). Toward understanding the relationship between feeling states and social behavior. In A. H. Hastorf & A. M. Isen (Eds.), *Cognitive social psychology* (pp. 73–108). New York: Elsevier.

Clark, M. S. (1992). Research on communal and exchange relationships viewed from a functionalist perspective. In D. A. Owens & M. Wagner (Eds.), *Progress in modern psychology: The legacy of American functionalism* (pp. 241–258). Westport, CT: Praeger.

Clark, M. S., & Mills, J. (1979). Interpersonal attraction in exchange and communal relationships. *Journal of Personality and Social Psychology, 37,* 12–24.

Clark, M. S., & Mills, J. (1993). The difference between communal and exchange relationships: What is and is not. *Personality and Social Psychology Bulletin, 19,* 684–691.

Clark, R., Crockett, W., & Archer, R. (1971). Risk-as-value hypothesis: The relationship between perception of self, others, and the risky shift. *Journal of Personality and Social Psychology, 20,* 425–429.

Clark, R. D. I., & Word, L. E. (1972). Why don't bystanders help? Because of ambiguity? *Journal of Personality and Social Psychology, 24,* 392–400.

Clore, G. L. (1992). Cognitive phenomenology: Feelings and the construction of judgment. In L. L. Martin & A. Tesser (Eds.), *The construction of social judgments* (pp. 133–163). Hillsdale, NJ: Erlbaum.

Clore, G. L., & Byrne, D. (1974). A reinforcement-effect model of attraction. In T. L. Huston (Ed.), *Foundations of interpersonal attraction* (pp. 143–170). New York: Academic Press.

Clore, G. L., Gasper, K., & Garvin, E. (2001). Affect as information. In J. P. Forgas (Ed.), *Handbook of affect and social cognition* (pp. 121–144). Mahwah, NJ: Erlbaum.

Clore, G. L., & Gormly, J. B. (1974). Knowing, feeling, and liking: A psychophysical study of attraction. *Journal of Research in Personality, 8,* 218–230.

Clore, G. L., & Parrott, W. G. (1991). Moods and their vicissitudes: The informational properties of affective thoughts and feelings. In J. Forgas (Ed.), *Emotion and social judgments* (pp. 107–123). Elmsford, NY: Pergamon Press.

Coan, J. A., Schaefer, H. S., & Davidson, R. J. (2006). Lending a hand: Social regulation of the neural response to threat. *Psychological Science, 17,* 1032–1039.

Cohen, C. E. (1981). Person categories and social perception: Testing some boundaries of the processing effects of prior knowledge. *Journal of Personality and Social Psychology, 40,* 441–452.

Cohen, D., & Gunz, A. (2002). *As seen by the other . . . : The self from the "outside in" and the "inside out" in the memories and emotional perceptions of Easterners and Westerners.* Unpublished manuscript, University of Waterloo.

Cohen, D., & Nisbett, R. E. (1997). Field experiments examining the culture of honor: The role of institutions in perpetuating norms about violence. *Personality and Social Psychology Bulletin, 23,* 1188–1199.

Cohen, D., Nisbett, R. E., Bowdle, B., & Schwarz, N. (1996). Insult, aggression, and the Southern culture of honor: An "experimental ethnography." *Journal of Personality and Social Psychology, 70,* 945–960.

Cohen, G. L., Aronson, J., & Steele, C. M. (2000). When beliefs yield to evidence: Reducing biased evaluation by affirming the self. *Personality and Social Psychology Bulletin, 26,* 1151–1164.

Cohen, G. L., Garcia, J., Apfel, N., & Master, A. (2006). Reducing the racial achievement gap: A social-psychological intervention. *Science, 313,* 1307–1310.

Cohen, G. L., Garcia, J., Purdie-Vaughns, V., Apfel, N., & Brzustoski, P. (2009). Recursive processes in self-affirmation: Intervening to close the minority achievement gap. *Science, 324,* 400–403.

Cohen, S., Alper, C. M., Doyle, W. J., Adler, N., Treanor, J. J., & Turner, R. B. (2008). Objective and subjective socioeconomic status and susceptibility to the common cold. *Health Psychology, 27*(2), 268–274.

Cohen, S., & Herbert, T. B. (1996). Health psychology: Psychological factors and physical disease from the perspective of human psychoneuroimmunology. *Annual Review of Psychology, 47,* 113–142.

Cohen, T. R., Montoya, R. M., & Insko, C. A. (2006). Group morality and intergroup relations: Cross-cultural and experimental evidence. *Personality and Social Psychology Bulletin, 32,* 1559–1572.

Coie, J. D., Cillessen, A. H. N., Dodge, K. A., Hubbard, J. A., Schwartz, D., Lemerise, E. D., et al. (1999). It takes two to fight: A test of relational factors and a method for assessing aggressive dyads. *Developmental Psychology, 35,* 1179–1188.

Cole, S. W., Kemeny, M. E., Taylor, S. E., & Visscher, B. R. (1996). Accelerated course of human immunodeficiency virus infection in gay men who conceal their homosexual identity. *Psychosomatic Medicine, 58*(3), 219–231.

Collins, N. L., & Miller, L. C. (1994). Self-disclosure and liking: A meta-analytic review. *Psychological Bulletin, 116,* 457–475.

Collins, N. L., & Read, S. J. (1990). Adult attachment, working models, and relationship quality in dating couples, *Journal of Personality and Social Psychology, 58,* 644–663.

Collins, N. L., & Read, S. J. (1994). Cognitive representations of attachment: The structure and function of working models. In K. Bartholomew & D. Perlman (Eds.), *Attachment processes in adulthood: Advances in personal relationships* (Vol. 5, pp. 53–90). London: Kingsley.

Collins, R. L., Taylor, S. E., Wood, J. V., & Thompson, S. C. (1988). The vividness effect: Elusive or illusory? *Journal of Experimental Social Psychology, 24,* 1–18.

Columbus, C. (1492/1990). *Journal of the first voyage.* Warminster, England: Aris and Phillips Ltd.

Colvin, C. R., & Block, J. (1994). Do positive illusions foster mental health? An examination of the Taylor and Brown formulation. *Psychological Bulletin, 116,* 3–20.

Colvin, C. R., Block, J., & Funder, D. C. (1995). Overly positive self-evaluations and personality: Negative implications for mental health. *Journal of Personality and Social Psychology, 68,* 1152–1162.

Colvin, C. R., & Griffo, R. (2008). On the psychological costs of self-enhancement. In E. C. Chang (Ed.), *Self-criticism and self-enhancement: Theory, research, and clinical implications* (pp. 123–140). Washington, DC: American Psychological Association.

Condon, P., & DeSteno, D. (2011). Compassion for one reduces punishment for another. *Journal of Experimental Social Psychology, 47,* 698–701.

Condry, J., & Condry, S. (1976). Sex differences: A study of the eye of the beholder. *Child Development, 47,* 812–819.

Conley, T. D., Roesch, S. C., Peplau, L., & Gold, M. S. (2009). A test of positive illusions versus shared reality models of relationship satisfaction among gay, lesbian, and heterosexual couples. *Journal of Applied Social Psychology, 39(6),* 1417–1431.

Connolly, K. (1968). The social facilitation of preening behavior of *Drosophila melanogaster. Animal Behavior, 16,* 385–391.

Conway, L. G., & Schaller, M. (2002). On the verifiability of evolutionary psychological theories. *Personality and Social Psychology, 6,* 152–166.

Cooley, C. H. (1902). *Human nature and the social order.* New York: Charles Scribner's Sons.

Coontz, S. (2005). *Marriage, a history: From obedience to intimacy, or how love conquered marriage.* New York: Viking Press.

Cooper, J. (1971). Personal responsibility and dissonance: The role and foreseen consequences. *Journal of Personality and Social Psychology, 18,* 354–363.

Cooper, J., & Worchel, S. (1970). Role of undesired consequences in arousing cognitive dissonance. *Journal of Personality and Social Psychology, 16,* 199–206.

Cooper, J., Zanna, M. P., & Taves, T. A. (1978). Arousal as a necessary condition for attitude change following induced compliance. *Journal of Personality and Social Psychology, 36,* 1101–1106.

Cooper, M. J., Dimitrov, O., & Rau, P. R. (2001). A Rose.com by any other name. *Journal of Finance, 56,* 2371–2388.

Cooper, M. L., Shaver, P., & Collins, N. L. (1998). Attachment styles, emotion regulation, and adjustment in adolescence. *Journal of Personality and Social Psychology, 74,* 1380–1397.

Coriell, M., & Adler, N. E. (2001). Social ordering and health. In B. S. McEwen (volume Ed.) and H. M. Goodman (section Ed.), *Handbook of physiology. Section 7: The endocrine system* (pp. 533–546). New York: American Physiological Society and Oxford University Press.

Correll, J., & Park, B. (2005). A model of the ingroup as a social resource. *Personality and Social Psychology Review, 9,* 341–359.

Correll, J., Park, B., Judd, C. M., & Wittenbrink, B. (2002). The police officer's dilemma: Using ethnicity to disambiguate potentially threatening individuals. *Journal of Personality and Social Psychology, 83,* 1314–1329.

Correll, J., Park, B., Judd, C. M., Wittenbrink, B., Sadler, M. S., & Keesee, T. (2007). Across the thin blue line: Police officers and racial bias in the decision to shoot. *Journal of Personality and Social Psychology, 92(6),* 1006–1023.

Correll, J., Spencer, S. J., & Zanna, M. (2004). An affirmed self and an open mind: Self-affirmation and sensitivity to argument strength. *Journal of Experimental Social Psychology, 40,* 350–356.

Correll, J., Urland, G. R., & Ito, T. A. (2006). Event-related potentials and the decision to shoot: The role of threat perception and cognitive control. *Journal of Experimental Social Psychology, 42,* 120–128.

Cortes, B. P., Demoulin, S., Rodriguez, R. T., Rodriguez, A. P., & Leyens, J. P. (2005). Infrahumanization or familiarity? Attribution of uniquely human emotions to the self, the ingroup, and the outgroup. *Personality and Social Psychology Bulletin, 32(2),* 243–253.

Costanzo, M. (1997). *Just revenge: Costs and consequences of the death penalty.* New York: St. Martin's Press.

Cota, A. A., & Dion, K. L. (1986). Salience of gender and sex composition of ad hoc groups: An experimental test of the distinctiveness theory. *Journal of Personality and Social Psychology, 50,* 770–776.

Côté, S., & Miners, C. T. H. (2006). Emotional intelligence, cognitive intelligence, and job performance. *Administrative Science Quarterly, 51,* 1–28.

Cotterell, N., Eisenberger, R., & Speicher, H. (1992). Inhibiting effects of reciprocation wariness on interpersonal relationships. *Journal of Personality and Social Psychology, 62,* 658–668.

Cottrell, N. B., Wack, D. L., Sekerak, G. J., & Rittle, R. H. (1968). Social facilitation of dominant responses by the presence of an audience and the mere presence of others. *Journal of Personality and Social Psychology, 9,* 245–250.

Cousins, S. D. (1989). Culture and self-perception in Japan and the United States. *Journal of Personality and Social Psychology, 56,* 124–131.

Cowan, C. L., Thompson, W. C., & Ellsworth, P. C. (1984). The effects of death qualification on jurors' predisposition to convict and on the quality of deliberation. *Law and Human Behavior, 8,* 53–80.

Crandall, C. S. (1988). Social contagion of binge eating. *Journal of Personality and Social Psychology, 55,* 588–598.

Crandall, C. S., & Eshleman, A. (2003). A justification-suppression model of the expression and experience of prejudice. *Psychological Bulletin, 129,* 414–446.

Crandall, V. C., Katkovsky, W., & Crandall, V. J. (1965). Children's beliefs in their own control of reinforcements in intellectual-academic achievement situations. *Child Development, 36,* 91–109.

Crano, W. D. (1970). Effects of sex, response order, and expertise in conformity: A dispositional approach. *Sociometry, 33,* 239–252.

Critcher, C. R., & Ferguson, M. J. (2013). The costs of keeping it hidden: Decomposing concealment reveals what makes it depleting. *Journal of Experimental Psychology: General, 143,* 721–735.

Crocker, J. (1982). Biased questions in judgment of covariation studies. *Personality and Social Psychology Bulletin, 8,* 214–220.

Crocker, J., Hannah, D. B., & Weber, R. (1983). Person memory and causal attributions. *Journal of Personality and Social Psychology, 44,* 55–66.

Crocker, J., & Luhtanen, R. (1990). Collective self-esteem and ingroup bias. *Journal of Personality and Social Psychology, 58,* 60–67.

Crocker, J., Luhtanen, R. K., Cooper, M. L., & Bouvrette, A. (2003). Contingencies of self-worth in college students: Theory and measurement. *Journal of Personality and Social Psychology, 85,* 894–908.

Crocker, J., Major, B., & Steele, C. (1998). Social stigma. In D. T. Gilbert, S. T. Fiske, & G. Lindzey (Eds.), *The handbook of social psychology* (4th ed., Vol. 2, pp. 504–553). New York: McGraw-Hill.

Crocker, J., & Park, L. E. (2003). Seeking self-esteem: Construction, maintenance, and protection of self-worth. In M. R. Leary & J. P. Tangney (Eds.), *Handbook of self and identity* (pp. 291–313). New York: Guilford Press.

Crocker, J., & Park, L. E. (2004). The costly pursuit of self-esteem. *Psychological Bulletin, 130*, 392–414.

Crocker, J., Sommers, S. R., & Luhtanen, R. K. (2002). Hopes dashed and dreams fulfilled: Contingencies of self-worth and graduate school admissions. *Personality and Social Psychology Bulletin, 28*, 1275–1286.

Crocker, J., Voelkl, K., Testa, M., & Major, B. (1991). Social stigma: The affective consequences of attributional ambiguity. *Journal of Personality and Social Psychology, 60*, 218–228.

Crocker, J., & Wolfe, C. T. (2001). Contingencies of self-worth. *Psychological Review, 108*, 593–623.

Cross, H. A., Halcomb, C. G., & Matter, W. W. (1967). Imprinting or exposure learning in rats given early auditory stimulation. *Psychonomic Science, 7*, 233–234.

Cross, J. F., & Cross, J. (1971). Age, sex, race, and the perception of facial beauty. *Developmental Psychology, 5*, 433–459.

Cross, S. E., & Madson, L. (1997). Models of the self: Self-construals and gender. *Psychological Bulletin, 122*, 5–37.

Croyle, R. T., & Cooper, J. (1983). Dissonance arousal: Physiological evidence. *Journal of Personality and Social Psychology, 45*, 782–791.

Cullen, D. (2009). *Columbine.* New York: Twelve Publishing.

Cunningham, M. R., Roberts, A. R., Barbee, A. P., Druen, P. B., & Wu, C. (1995). "Their ideas of beauty are, on the whole, the same as ours": Consistency and variability in the cross-cultural perception of female physical attractiveness. *Journal of Personality and Social Psychology, 68*, 261–279.

Cunningham, W. A., Johnson, M. K., Raye, C. L., Gatenby, J. C., Gore, J. C., & Banaji, M. R. (2004). Separable neural components in the processing of black and white faces. *Psychological Science, 15*, 806–813.

Curran, J. P., & Lippold, S. (1975). The effects of physical attractiveness and attitude similarity on attraction in dating dyads. *Journal of Personality, 43*, 528–539.

Curry, R. L. (1988). Influence of kinship on helping behavior in Galápagos mockingbirds. *Behavioral Ecology and Sociobiology, 38*, 181–192.

Cutrona, C. E. (1982). Transition to college: Loneliness and the process of social adjustment. In L. A. Peplau & D. Perlman (Eds.), *Loneliness: A sourcebook of current theory, research, and therapy* (pp. 291–309). New York: Wiley.

Czopp, A. M., & Ashburn-Nardo, L. (2012). Interpersonal confrontations of prejudice. In D. W. Russell & A. Cristel (Eds.), *The psychology of prejudice: Interdisciplinary perspectives on contemporary issues* (pp. 175–201). Hauppauge, NY: Nova Science Publishers.

Czopp, A. M., & Monteith, M. J. (2006). Thinking well of African Americans: Measuring complimentary stereotypes and negative prejudice. *Basic and Applied Social Psychology, 28*, 233–250.

Dabbs, J. M., Jr. (2000). *Heroes, rogues and lovers.* New York: McGraw-Hill.

Daly, M., & Wilson, M. I. (1988). *Homicide.* New York: De Gruyter.

Daly, M., & Wilson, M. I. (1996). Violence against stepchildren. *Current Directions in Psychological Science, 5*, 77–81.

Daly, M., Wilson, M., & Vasdev, S. (2001). Income inequality and homicide rates in Canada and the United States. *Canadian Journal of Criminology*, 219–236.

Danner, D., Snowdon, D., & Friesen, W. (2001). Positive emotions in early life and longevity: Findings from the nun study. *Journal of Personality and Social Psychology, 80*, 804–813.

Danziger, S., Levav, J., & Avnaim-Pesso, L. (2011). Extraneous factors in judicial decisions. *Proceedings of the National Academy of Science, 10,:* 6889–6892.

Dardenne, B., Dumont, M., & Bollier T. (2007). Insidious dangers of benevolent sexism: Consequences for women's performance. *Journal of Personality and Social Psychology, 93(5)*, 764–779.

Darley, J. M., & Batson, C. D. (1973). From Jerusalem to Jericho: A study of situational and dispositional variables in helping behavior. *Journal of Personality and Social Psychology, 27*, 100–119.

Darley, J. M., & Berscheid, E. (1967). Increased liking as a result of the anticipation of personal contact. *Human Relations, 20*, 29–40.

Darley, J. M., & Gross, P. H. (1983). A hypothesis-confirming bias in labeling efects. *Journal of Personality and Social Psychology, 44*, 20–33.

Darley, J. M., & Latané, B. (1968). Bystander intervention in emergencies: Diffusion of responsibility. *Journal of Personality and Social Psychology, 8*, 377–383.

Darley, J. M., Teger, A. I., & Lewis, L. D. (1973). Do groups always inhibit individuals' responses to potential emergencies? *Journal of Personality and Social Psychology, 26*, 395–399.

Darlington, R. B., & Macker, C. E. (1966). Displacement of guilt-produced altruistic behavior. *Journal of Personality and Social Psychology, 4*, 442–443.

Darwin, C. (1871). *The descent of man, and selection in relation to sex.* London: John Murray.

Dasgupta, N., DeSteno, D., Williams, L. A., & Hunsinger, M. (2009). Fanning the flames: The influence of specific incidental emotions on implicit prejudice. *Emotion, 9*, 585–591.

Dashiell, J. F. (1930). An experimental analysis of some group effects. *Journal of Abnormal and Social Psychology, 25*, 190–199.

Davidson, R. J., & Begley, S. (2012). *The emotional life of your brain: How its unique patterns affect the way you think, feel, and live–and how you can change them.* New York: Hudson Street Press.

Davidson, R. J., Kabat-Zinn, J., Schumacher, J., Rosenkranz, M., Muller, D., Santorelli, S. F., et al. (2003). Alterations in brain and immune function produced by mindfulness meditation. *Psychosomatic Medicine, 65*, 564–570.

Davidson, R. J., Pizzagalli, D., Nitzschke, J. B., & Kalin, N. H. (2003). Parsing the subcomponents of emotion and disorders: Perspectives from affective neuroscience. In R. J. Davidson, K. Scherer, & H. H. Goldsmith (Eds.), *Handbook of affective science* (pp. 8–24). New York: Oxford University Press.

Davis, M. H., & Franzoi, S. L. (1991). Stability and change in adolescent self-consciousness and empathy. *Journal of Research in Personality, 25*, 70–87.

Davis, M. H., & Stephan, W. G. (1980). Attributions for exam performance. *Journal of Applied Social Psychology, 10*, 235–248.

Dawes, R. M. (1980). Social dilemmas. *Annual Review of Psychology, 31*, 169–193.

Dawes, R. M. (1988). *Rational choice in an uncertain world.* San Diego, CA: Harcourt, Brace, Jovanovich.

Dawson, E., Gilovich, T., & Regan, D. T. (2002). Motivated reasoning and performance on the Wason selection task. *Personality and Social Psychology Bulletin, 28*, 1379–1387.

de Waal, F. B. M. (1986). The integration of dominance and social bonding in primates. *Quarterly Review of Biology, 61*, 459–479.

de Waal, F. B. M. (1996). *Good natured: The origins of right and wrong in humans and other animals.* Cambridge, MA: Harvard University Press.

de Waal, F. B. M., & Lanting, F. (1997). *Bonobo: The forgotten ape.* Berkeley: University of California Press.

Dearing, J. W., & Rogers, E. M. (1996). *Agenda-setting.* Thousand Oaks, CA: Sage.

Deaux, K., & Emswiller, T. (1974). Explanations of successful performance on sex-linked tasks: What is skill for the male is luck for the female. *Journal of Personality and Social Psychology, 29,* 80–85.

Debner, J. A., & Jacoby, L. L. (1994). Unconscious perception: Attention, awareness, and control. *Journal of Experimental Psychology: Learning, Memory and Cognition, 20,* 304–317.

Decety, J., & Michalska, K. (2010). Neurodevelopmental changes in the circuits underlying empathy and sympathy from childhood to adulthood. *Developmental Science, 13,* 886–899.

Dechesne, M., Greenberg, J., Arndt, J., & Schimel, J. (2000). Terror management and sports fan affiliation: The effects of mortality salience on fan identification and optimism. *European Journal of Social Psychology, 30,* 813–835.

Dechesne, M., Pyszczynski, T., Arndt, J., Ransom, S., Sheldon, K. M., van Knippenberg, A., et al. (2003). Literal and symbolic immortality: The effect of evidence of literal immortality on self-esteem striving in response to mortality salience. *Journal of Personality and Social Psychology, 84,* 722–737.

Deci, E. L., & Ryan, R. M. (1985). *Intrinsic motivation and self-determination in human behavior.* New York: Plenum Press.

Dempster, F. N. (1992). The rise and fall of the inhibitory mechanism: Toward a unified theory of cognitive development and aging. *Developmental Review, 12,* 45–75.

Denes-Raj, V., & Epstein, S. (1994). Conflict between intuitive and rational processing: When people behave against their better judgment. *Journal of Personality and Social Psychology, 66,* 819–829.

DePaulo, B. M., & Friedman, H. S. (1998). Nonverbal communication. In D. T. Gilbert, S. T. Fiske, & G. Lindzey (Eds.), *Handbook of social psychology* (4th ed., Vol. 2, pp. 3–40). New York: McGraw-Hill.

DePaulo, B. M., Lanier, K., & Davis, T. (1983). Detecting the deceit of the motivated liar. *Journal of Personality and Social Psychology, 43,* 1096–1103.

Deppe, R. K., & Harackiewicz, J. M. (1996). Self-handicapping and intrinsic motivation: Buffering intrinsic motivation from the threat of failure. *Journal of Personality and Social Psychology, 70,* 868–876.

Dermer, M., & Theil, D. (1975). When beauty may fail. *Journal of Personality and Social Psychology, 31,* 1168–1177.

DeSteno, D., Dasgupta, N., Bartlett, M. Y., & Cajdric, A. (2004). Prejudice from thin air: The effect of emotion on automatic intergroup attitudes. *Psychological Science, IS,* 319–324.

DeSteno, D., Petty, R., Wegener, D., & Rucker, D. (2000). Beyond valence in the perception of likelihood: The role of emotion specificity. *Journal of Personality and Social Psychology, 78,* 397–416.

DeSteno, D. A., & Salovey, P. (1996). Jealousy and the characteristics of one's rival: A self-evaluation maintenance perspective. *Personality and Social Psychology, 22,* 920–932.

Deutsch, M., & Gerard, H. B. (1955). A study of normative and informational social influence upon individual judgment. *Journal of Abnormal and Social Psychology, 51,* 629–636.

Devine, P. G. (1989a). Automatic and controlled processes in prejudice: The roles of stereotypes and personal beliefs. In A. R. Pratkanis, S. J. Breckler, & A. G. Greenwald (Eds.), *Attitude structure and function.* Hillsdale, NJ: Erlbaum.

Devine, P. G. (1989b). Stereotypes and prejudice: Their automatic and controlled components. *Journal of Personality and Social Psychology, 56,* 5–18.

Devine, P. G., & Baker, S. M. (1991). Measurement of racial stereotype subtyping. *Personality and Social Psychology Bulletin, 17,* 44–50.

Devine, P. G., & Elliot, A. J. (1995). Are racial stereotypes really fading? The Princeton trilogy revisited. *Personality and Social Psychology Bulletin, 21,* 1139–1150.

Devine, P. G., & Monteith, M. J. (1999). Automaticity and control in stereotyping. In S. Chaiken & Y. Trope (Eds.), *Dual process theories in social psychology* (pp. 339–360). New York: Guilford Press.

Devine, P. G., Monteith, M. J., Zuwerink, J. R., & Elliot, A. J. (1991). Prejudice with and without compunction. *Journal of Personality and Social Psychology, 60,* 817–830.

Devine, P. G., Plant, E. A., Amodio, D. M., Harmon-Jones, E., & Vance, S. L. (2002). Exploring the relationship between implicit and explicit prejudice: The role of motivations to respond without prejudice. *Journal of Personality and Social Psychology, 82,* 835–848.

DeWall, C. N., Bushman, B. J., Giancola, P. R., & Webster, G. D. (2010). The big, the bad, and the boozed-up: Weight moderates the effect of alcohol on aggression. *Journal of Experimental Social Psychology, 46,* 619–623.

DeWall, C. N., MacDonald, G., Webster, G. D., Masten, C., Baumeister, R. F., Powell, C., et al. (2010). Acetaminophen reduces social pain: Behavioral and neural evidence. *Psychological Science, 21,* 931–937.

Dhawan, N., Roseman, I. J., Naidu, R. K., Thapa, K., & Rettek, S. I. (1995). Self-concepts across two cultures: India and the United States. *Journal of Cross-Cultural Psychology, 26,* 606–621.

Diamond, L. M. (2003). What does sexual orientation orient? A biobehavioral model distinguishing romantic love and sexual desire. *Psychological Review, 110,* 173–192.

Diamond, S. S., Rose, M. R., & Murphy, B. (2006). Revisiting the unanimity requirement: The behavior of the non-unanimous civil jury. *Northwestern Law Review, 100,* 201–230.

Dickerson, S. S., & Kemeny, M. E. (2004). Acute stressors and cortisol responses: A theoretical integration and synthesis of laboratory research. *Psychological Bulletin, 130,* 355–391.

Diener, E. (1980). Deindividuation: The absence of self-awareness and self-regulation in group members. In P. Paulus (Ed.), *The psychology of group influence* (pp. 209–242). Hillsdale, NJ: Erlbaum.

Diener, E. (2000). Subjective well-being: The science of happiness, and some policy implications. *American Psychologist, 55,* 34–43.

Diener, E., Fraser, S. C., Beaman, A. L., & Kelem, R. T. (1976). Effects of deindividuation variables on stealing among Halloween trick-or-treaters. *Journal of Personality and Social Psychology, 33,* 178–183.

Diener, E., & Wallbom, M. (1976). Effects of self-awareness on anti-normative behavior. *Journal of Research in Personality, 10,* 107–111.

Diener, E., Wolsic, B., & Fujita, F. (1995). Physical attractiveness and subjective well-being. *Journal of Personality and Social Psychology, 69,* 207–213.

Dienstbier, R. A., & Munter, P. O. (1971). Cheating as a function of the labeling of natural arousal. *Journal of Personality and Social Psychology, 17,* 208–213.

Dijksterhuis, A., Aarts, H., Bargh, J. A., & van Knippenberg, A. (2000). On the relation between associative strength and automatic behavior. *Journal of Experimental Social Psychology, 36,* 531–544.

Dijksterhuis, A., Aarts, H., & Smith, P. K. (2005). The power of the subliminal: On subliminal persuasion and other potential applications. In R. R. Hassin, J. S. Uleman, & J. A. Bargh (Eds.), *The new unconscious*. New York: Oxford University Press.

Dijksterhuis, A., Preston, J., Wegner, D. M., & Aarts, H. (2008). Effects of subliminal priming of self and God on self-attribution of authorship for events. *Journal of Experimental Social Psychology, 44(1)*, 2–9.

Dijksterhuis, A., & van Knippenberg, A. (1998). The relation between perception and behavior, or how to win a game of Trivial Pursuit. *Journal of Personality and Social Psychology, 74*, 865–877.

Dimberg, U., & Öhman, A. (1996). Behold the wrath: Psychophysiological responses to facial stimuli. *Motivation and Emotion, 20*, 149–182.

Dion, K. K., Berscheid, E., & Walster, E. (1972). What is a beautiful good? *Journal of Personality and Social Psychology, 24*, 285–290.

Dion, K. K., & Dion, K. L. (1993). Individualistic and collectivistic perspectives on gender and the cultural context of love and intimacy. *Journal of Social Issues, 49*, 53–69.

Ditto, P. H., Jemmott, J. B., & Darley, J. M. (1988). Appraising the threat of illness: A mental representational approach. *Health Psychology, 7*, 183–200.

Ditto, P. H., & Lopez, D. F. (1992). Motivated skepticism: Use of differential decision criteria for preferred and nonpreferred conclusions. *Journal of Personality and Social Psychology, 63*, 568–584.

Ditzen B., Schaer M., Gabriel B., Bodenmann G., Ehlert U., & Heinrichs M. (2009). Intranasal oxytocin increases positive communication and reduces cortisol levels during couple conflict. *Biological Psychiatry, 65*, 728–731.

Dodge, K. A., & Schwartz, D. (1997). Social information mechanisms in aggressive behavior. In D. M. Stoff & J. Breiling (Eds.), *Handbook of antisocial behavior* (pp. 171–180). New York: Wiley.

Dollard, J., Doob, L. W., Miller, N. E., Mowrer, H. H., & Sears, R. R. (1939). *Frustration and aggression*. New Haven: Yale University Press.

Donnellan, M. B., Trzesniewski, K. H., Robins, R. W., Moffitt, T. E., & Caspi, A. (2005). Low self-esteem is related to aggression, antisocial behavior, and delinquency. *Psychological Science, 16*, 328–335.

Donnerstein, E. (1980). Aggressive erotica and violence against women. *Journal of Personality and Social Psychology, 39*, 269–277.

Donnerstein, E., & Berkowitz, L. (1981). Victim reactions in aggressive erotic films as a factor in violence against women. *Journal of Personality and Social Psychology, 41*, 710–724.

Doob, A. N., & MacDonald, G. E. (1979). Television and fear of victimization: Is the relationship *causal? Journal of Personality and Social Psychology, 37*, 170–179.

Dovidio, J. F. (1984). Helping behavior and altruism: An empirical and conceptual overview. In L. Berkowitz (Ed.), *Advances in experimental social psychology* (pp. 361–427). New York: Academic Press.

Dovidio, J. F., & Gaertner, S. L. (1981). The effects of race, status, ability on helping behavior. *Social Psychology Quarterly, 44*, 192–203.

Dovidio, J. F., & Gaertner, S. L. (2004). Aversive racism. In M. P. Zanna (Ed.), *Advances in experimental social psychology* (Vol. 36, pp. 1–52). San Diego, CA: Elsevier.

Dovidio, J. F., Kawakami, K., & Gaertner, S. L. (2002). Implicit and explicit prejudice and interracial interaction. *Journal of Personality and Social Psychology, 82*, 62–68.

Dovidio, J. F., Smith, J. K., Donella, A. G., & Gaertner, S. L. (1997). Racial attitudes and the death penalty. *Journal of Applied Social Psychology, 27*, 1468–1487.

Dovidio, J. F., ten Vergert, M., Stewart, T. L., Gaertner, S. L., Johnson, J. D., Esses, V. M., et al. (2004). Perspective and prejudice: Antecedents and mediating mechanisms. *Personality and Social Psychology Bulletin, 30*, 1537–1549.

Downey, G., & Feldman, S. (1996). Implications of rejection sensitivity for intimate relationships. *Journal of Personality and Social Psychology, 70*, 1327–1343.

Downey, G., Feldman, S., & Ayduk, O. (2000). Rejection sensitivity and male violence in romantic relationships. *Personal Relationships, 7*, 45–61.

Downey, G., Freitas, A. L., Michaelis, B., & Khouri, H. (1998). The self-fulfilling prophecy in close relationships: Rejection sensitivity and rejection by romantic partners. *Journal of Personality and Social Psychology, 75*, 545–560.

Downing, C. J., Sternberg, R. J., & Ross, B. H. (1985). Multicausal inference: Evaluation of evidence in causally complex situations. *Journal of Experimental Psychology: General, 114*, 239–263.

Downing, J. W., Judd, C. M., & Brauer, M. (1992). Effects of repeated expression of attitudes on attitude extremity. *Journal of Personality and Social Psychology, 63*, 17–29.

Draine, S. C., & Greenwald, A. G. (1998). Replicable unconscious semantic priming. *Journal of Experimental Psychology: General, 127*, 286–303.

Duck, J. M., & Mullin, B. (1995). The perceived impact of the mass media: Reconsidering the third-person effect. *European Journal of Social Psychology, 25*, 77–93.

Duflo, E., & Saez, E. (2003). The role of information and social interactions in retirement plan decisions: Evidence from a randomized experiment. *Quarterly Journal of Economics, 118(3)*, 815–842.

Duncan, B. L. (1976). Differential social perception and attribution on intergroup violence: Testing the lower limits of stereotyping of blacks. *Journal of Personality and Social Psychology, 34*, 590–598.

Dunn, E. W., Aknin, L. B., & Norton, M. I. (2008). Spending money on others promotes happiness. *Science, 319*, 1687–1688.

Dunn, J., & Munn, P. (1985). Becoming a family member: Family conflict and the development of social understanding in the second year. *Child Development, 56*, 480–492.

Dunning, D., Heath, C., & Suls, J. (2004). Flawed self-assessment: Implications for health, education, and the workplace. *Psychological Science in the Public Interest, 5*, 69–106.

Dunning, D., Meyerowitz, J. A., & Holzberg, A. (1989). Ambiguity and self-evaluation: The role of idiosyncratic trait definitions in self-serving assessments of ability. *Journal of Personality and Social Psychology, 57*, 1082–1090.

Dunning, D., & Perretta, S. (2002). Automaticity and eyewitness accuracy: A 10-12-second rule for distinguishing accurate from inaccurate positive identifications. *Journal of Applied Psychology, 87*, 951–962.

Dunning, D., & Sherman, D. A. (1997). Stereotypes and tacit inference. *Journal of Personality and Social Psychology, 73*, 459–471.

Dunning, D., & Stern, L. B. (1994). Distinguishing accurate from inaccurate eyewitness identifications via inquiries about decision-making processes. *Journal of Personality and Social Psychology, 67*, 818–835.

Durose, M. R., Smith, E. L., & Langan, P. A. (2007). *Bureau of Justice Statistics Special Report: Contacts between police and the public, 2005*. Washington, DC: U.S. Department of Justice.

Dutton, D. G. (2002). The neurobiology of abandonment homicide. *Aggression and Violent Behavior, 7*, 407–421.

Dutton, D. G., & Aron, A. P. (1974). Some evidence for heightened sexual attraction under conditions of high anxiety. *Journal of Personality and Social Psychology, 30*, 510–517.

Duval, T. S., & Lalwani, N. (1999). Objective self-awareness and causal attributions for self-standard discrepancies: Changing self or changing standards of correctness. *Personality and Social Psychology Bulletin, 25,* 1220–1229.

Duval, T. S., & Wicklund, R. A. (1972). *A theory of objective self-awareness.* New York: Academic Press.

Dweck, C. S. (1975). The role of expectations and attributions in the alleviation of learned helplessness. *Journal of Personality and Social Psychology, 31,* 674–685.

Dweck, C. S. (1986). Motivational processes affecting learning. *American Psychologist, 41,* 1040–1048.

Dweck, C. S. (1999). *Self-theories: Their role in motivation, personality and development.* Philadelphia: Taylor and Francis/Psychology Press.

Dweck, C. S. (2007). *Mindset: The new psychology of success.* New York: Ballantine Books.

Dweck, C. S., Chiu, C., & Hong, Y. (1995). Implicit theories and their role in judgments and reactions: A world from two perspectives. *Psychological Inquiry, 6,* 267–285.

Dweck, C. S., Davidson, W., Nelson, S., & Enna, B. (1978). Sex differences in learned helplessness: (II) The contingencies of evaluative feedback in the classroom and (III) An experimental analysis. *Developmental Psychology, 14,* 268–276.

Dweck, C. S., Hong, Y. Y., & Chiu, C. Y. (1993). Implicit theories and individual differences in the likelihood and meaning of dispositional inference. *Personality and Social Psychology Bulletin, 19,* 644–656.

Dweck, C. S., & Leggett, E. L. (1988). A social-cognitive approach to motivation and personality. *Psychological Review, 95,* 256–273.

Dweck, C. S., & Reppucci, N. D. (1973). Learned helplessness and reinforcement responsibility in children. *Journal of Personality and Social Psychology, 25,* 109–116.

Eagly, A. H. (1987). *Sex differences in social behavior: A social-role interpretation.* Hillsdale, NJ: Erlbaum.

Eagly, A. H., Ashmore, R. D., Makhijani, M. G., & Longo, L. C. (1991). What is beautiful is good, but . . . : A meta-analytic review of research on the physical attractiveness stereotype. *Psychological Bulletin, 110,* 109–128.

Eagly, A. H., & Carli, L. L. (1981). Sex of researchers and sex-typed communications as determinants of sex differences in influenceability: A meta-analysis of social influence studies. *Psychological Bulletin, 110,* 109–128.

Eagly, A. H., & Chaiken, S. (1993). *The psychology of attitudes.* Fort Worth, TX: Harcourt Brace.

Eagly, A. H., & Chaiken, S. (1998). Attitude structure and function. In D. T. Gilbert, S. T. Fiske, & G. Lindzey (Eds.), *Handbook of social psychology* (4th ed., Vol. 1, pp. 269–322). New York: McGraw-Hill.

Eagly, A. H., & Chrvala, C. (2006). Sex differences in conformity: Status and gender role interpretations. *Psychology of Women Quarterly, 10,* 203–220.

Eagly, A. H., & Wood, W. (1999). The origins of sex differences in human behavior: Evolved dispositions vs. social roles. *American Psychologist, 54,* 408–423.

Eastwick, P. W., & Finkel, E. J. (2008). Sex differences in mate preferences revisited: Do people know what they initially desire in a romantic partner? *Journal of Personality and Social Psychology, 94(2),* 245–264.

Eastwick, P. W., Finkel, E. J., Mochon, D., & Ariely, D. (2007). Selective versus unselective romantic desire: Not all reciprocity is created equal. *Psychological Science, 18,* 317–319.

Eberhardt, J. L., Davies, P. G., Purdie-Vaughns, V. J., & Johnson, S. L. (2006). Looking deathworthy: Perceived stereotypicality of black defendants predicts capital sentencing outcomes. *Psychological Science, 17,* 383–386.

Eckland, B. (1968). Theories of mate selection. *Social Biology, 15,* 71–84.

Edmans, A., Garcia, D., & Norli, O. (2007). Sports sentiment and stock returns. *Journal of Finance, 62,* 1967–1998.

Efran, M. G. (1974). The effect of physical appearance on judgments of guilt, interpersonal attractiveness, and severity of recommended punishment in a simulated jury task. *Journal of Research in Personality, 8,* 45–54.

Ehrlinger, J., Plant, E. A., Eibach, R. P., Columb, C. J., Goplen, J. L., Kunstman, J. W., & Butz, D. A. (2011). How exposure to the Confederate flag affects willingness to vote for Barack Obama. *Political Psychology, 32(1),* 131–146.

Eibach, R. P., Libby, L. K., & Gilovich, T. (2003). When change in the self is mistaken for change in the world. *Journal of Personality and Social Psychology, 84,* 917–931.

Eibach, R. P., & Mock, S. E. (2011). Idealizing parenthood to rationalize parental investments. *Psychological Science, 22,* 203–208.

Eibl-Eibesfeldt, I. (1989). *Human ethology.* New York: Aldine de Gruyter Press.

Eisenberg, N., Fabes, R. A., Miller, P. A., Fultz, J., Shell, R., Mathy, R. M., et al. (1989). Relation of sympathy and distress to prosocial behavior: A multimethod study. *Journal of Personality and Social Psychology, 57,* 55–66.

Eisenberg, N., & Lennon, R. (1983). Sex differences in empathy and related capacities. *Psychological Bulletin, 94,* 100–131.

Eisenberger, N. I., & Lieberman, M. D. (2004). Why rejection hurts: A common neural alarm system for physical and social pain. *Trends in Cognitive Science, 8,* 294–300.

Eisenberger, N. I., Lieberman, M. D., & Williams, K. D. (2003). Does rejection hurt? An fMRI study of social exclusion. *Science, 302,* 290–292.

Ekman, P. (1984). Expression and the nature of emotion. In K. Scherer & P. Ekman (Eds.), *Approaches to emotion.* Hillsdale, NJ: Erlbaum.

Ekman, P. (1992). An argument for basic emotions. *Cognition and Emotion, 6,* 169–200.

Ekman, P. (1993). Facial expression and emotion. *American Psychologist, 48,* 384–392.

Ekman, P., & Davidson, R. J. (1993). Voluntary smiling changes regional brain activity. *Psychological Science, 4,* 342–345.

Ekman, P., Davidson, R. J., & Friesen, W. V. (1990). The Duchenne smile: Emotional expression and brain physiology II. *Journal of Personality and Social Psychology, 58,* 342–353.

Ekman, P., & Friesen, W. V. (1969). The repertoire of nonverbal behavior: Categories, origins, usage, and coding. *Semiotica, 1,* 49–98.

Ekman, P., & Friesen, W. V. (1971). Constants across cultures in the face and emotion. *Journal of Personality and Social Psychology, 17,* 124–129.

Ekman, P., Friesen, W. V., & Ellsworth, P. C. (1982a). *Emotion in the human face.* Cambridge, England: Cambridge University Press.

Ekman, P., Friesen, W. V., & Ellsworth, P. C. (1982b). What are the similarities and differences in facial behavior across cultures? In P. Ekman (Ed.), *Emotion in the human face.* Cambridge, England: Cambridge University Press.

Ekman, P., & O'Sullivan, M. (1991). Who can catch a liar? *American Psychologist, 46*, 913–920.

Ekman, P., O'Sullivan, M., Friesen, W. V., & Scherer, K. R. (1991). Face, voice and body in detecting deception. *Journal of Nonverbal Behavior, 15*, 125–135.

Ekman, P., Sorenson, E. R., & Friesen, W. V. (1969). Pan cultural elements in facial displays of emotions. *Science, 164*, 86–88.

Elfenbein, H. A., & Ambady, N. (2002). On the universality and cultural specificity of emotion recognition: A meta-analysis. *Psychological Bulletin, 128*, 203–235.

Elfenbein, H. A., & Ambady, N. (2003). Universal and cultural differences in recognizing emotions. *Current Directions in Psychological Science, 12*, 159–164.

Elgar, F. J., & Aitken, N. (2011). Income inequality, trust, and homicide in 33 countries. *European Journal of Public Health, 21(2),* 241–246.

Elkin, R. A., & Leippe, M. R. (1986). Physiological arousal, dissonance, and attitude change: Evidence for a dissonance-arousal link and a "don't remind me" effect. *Journal of Personality and Social Psychology, 51*, 55–65.

Elliot, A. J., & Devine, P. G. (1994). On the motivational nature of cognitive dissonance: Dissonance as psychological discomfort. *Journal of Personality and Social Psychology, 67*, 382–394.

Elliot, A. J., Kayser, D. N., Greitemeyer, T., Lichtenfeld, S. Gramzow, R. H., Maier, M. A., & Liu, H. (2012). Fertile green: Green facilitates creative performance. *Journal of Experimental Psychology: General, 139(3),* 399–417.

Ellis, B. (1992). The evolution of sexual attraction: Evaluative mechanisms in women. In J. H. Barkow, L. Cosmides, & J. Tooby (Eds.), *The adapted mind* (pp. 267–288). New York: Oxford University Press.

Ellsworth, P. C. (1994). Sense, culture and sensibility. In S. Kitayama & H. R. Markus (Eds.), *Emotion and culture.* Washington, DC: American Psychological Association.

Ellsworth, P. C. (2009). Race salience in juror decision-making: Misconceptions, clarifications, and unanswered questions. *Behavioral Science & Law, 27(4),* 599–609.

Ellyson, S. L., & Dovidio, J. F. (Eds.). (1985). *Power, dominance, and nonverbal behavior.* New York: Springer-Verlag.

eMarketer Inc. (2011). Retrieved from www.emarketer.com

Emler, N. (1994). Gossip, reputation, and social adaptation. In R. F. Goodman & A. Ben-Ze'ev (Eds.), *Good gossip* (pp. 117–138). Wichita: University Press of Kansas.

Emmons, R. A., McCullough, M. E., & Tsang, J. (2003). Counting blessings versus burdens: An experimental investigation of gratitude and subjective well-being in daily life. *Journal of Personality and Social Psychology, 84*, 377–389.

English, T., & Chen, S. (2007). Culture and self-concept stability: Consistency across and within contexts among Asian- and European-Americans. *Journal of Personality and Social Psychology, 93*, 478–490.

Epel, E. S., Blackburn, E. H., Lin, J., Dhabhar, F. S., Adler, N. E., Morrow, J. D., et al. (2004). Accelerated telomere shortening in response to life stress. *Proceedings of the National Academy of Sciences of the USA. 101*, 17312–17315.

Epley, N. (2008, January 31). Rebate psychology. *New York Times*, p. A27.

Epley, N., & Dunning, D. (2006). The mixed blessings of self-knowledge in behavioral prediction: Enhanced discrimination but exacerbated bias. *Personality and Social Psychology Bulletin, 32*, 641–655.

Epley, N., & Gilovich, T. (2004). Are adjustments insufficient? *Personality and Social Psychology Bulletin, 30*, 447–460.

Epley, N., Mak, D., & Idson, L. (2006). Bonus or rebate? The impact of income framing on spending and saving. *Journal of Behavioral Decision Making, 19*, 213–227.

Epley, N., Savitsky, K., & Gilovich, T. (2002). Empathy neglect: Reconciling the spotlight effect and the correspondence bias. *Journal of Personality and Social Psychology, 83*, 300–312.

Epstein, S. (1991). Cognitive-experiential self-theory: An integrative theory of personality. In R. Curtis (Ed.), *The self with others: Convergences in psychoanalytic, social, and personality psychology* (pp. 111–137). New York: Guilford Press.

Erber, R., & Tesser, A. (1994). Self-evaluation maintenance: A social psychological approach to interpersonal relationships. In R. Erber & R. Gilmour (Eds.), *Theoretical frameworks for personal relationships* (pp. 211–233). Hillsdale, NJ: Erlbaum.

Espinoza, P., Areas da Luz Fontes, A. B., & Arms-Chavez, C. J. (2014). Attributional gender bias: Teachers' ability and effort explanations for students' math performance. *Social Psychology of Education, 17(1),* 105–126.

Esser, J. K. (1998). Alive and well after 25 years: A review of groupthink research. *Organizational Behavior and Human Decision Processes, 73*, 116–141.

Esser, J. K., & Lindoerfer, J. S. (1989). Groupthink and the space shuttle *Challenger* accident: Toward a quantitative case analysis. *Journal of Behavioral Decision Making, 2*, 167–177.

Essock-Vitale, S. M., & McGuire, M. T. (1985). Women's lives viewed from an evolutionary perspective II. Patterns of helping. *Ethology and Sociobiology, 6*, 155–173.

Ettinger, R. F., Marino, C. J., Endler, N. S., Geller, S. H., & Natziuk, T. (1971). Effects of agreement and correctness on relative competence and conformity. *Journal of Personality and Social Psychology, 19*, 204–212.

Evans, J. St. B.T. (2007). *Hypothetical thinking: Dual processes in reasoning and judgment.* New York: Psychology Press.

Evans, R. (1980). *The making of social psychology.* New York: Gardner Press.

Fairchild, K. & Rudman, L.A. (2008). Everyday stranger harassment and women's objectification. *Social Justice Research, 21(3),* 338–357.

Fallon, A. (1990). Culture in the mirror: Sociocultural determinants of body image. In T. F. Cash & T. Pruzinsky (Eds.), *Body images: Development, deviance, and change* (pp. 80–109). New York: Guilford Press.

Fallon, A. E., & Rozin, P. (1985). Sex differences in perceptions of desirable body shape. *Journal of Abnormal Psychology, 94*, 102–105.

Farber, P. D., Khavari, K. A., & Douglass, F. M., IV. (1980). A factor analytic study of reasons for drinking: Empirical validation of positive and negative reinforcement dimensions. *Journal of Consulting and Clinical Psychology, 48*, 780–781.

Farley, F. (1986, May). The big *T* in personality. *Psychology Today*, pp. 44–52.

Fazio, R. H. (1995). Attitudes as object-evaluation associations: Determinants, consequences, and correlates of attitude accessibility. In R. E. Petty & J. A. Krosnick (Eds.), *Attitude strength: Antecedents and consequences* (pp. 247–282). Mahwah, NJ: Erlbaum.

Fazio, R. H., & Hilden, L. E. (2001). Emotional reactions to a seemingly prejudiced response: The role of automatically activated racial attitudes and motivation to control prejudiced reactions. *Personality and Social Psychology Bulletin, 27,* 538–549.

Fazio, R. H., Jackson, J. R., Dunton, B. C., & Williams, C. J. (1995). Variability in automatic activation as an unobtrusive measure of racial attitudes: A bona fide pipeline? *Journal of Personality and Social Psychology, 69,* 1013–1027.

Fazio, R. H., & Olson, M. A. (2003). Implicit measures in social cognition research: Their meaning and use. *Annual Review of Psychology, 54,* 297–327.

Fazio, R. H., Sanbonmatsu, D. M., Powell, M. C., & Kardes, F. R. (1986). On the automatic activation of attitudes. *Journal of Personality and Social Psychology, 50,* 229–238.

Fazio, R. H., & Williams, C. J. (1986). Attitude accessibility as a moderator of the attitude-perception and attitude-behavior relations: An investigation of the 1984 presidential election. *Journal of Personality and Social Psychology, 51,* 505–514.

Fazio, R. H., & Zanna, M. P. (1978). Attitudinal qualities relating to the strength of the attitude-behavior relationship. *Journal of Experimental Social Psychology, 14,* 398–408.

Fazio, R. H., Zanna, M., & Cooper, J. (1977). Dissonance and self-perception theory: An integrative view of each theory's proper domain of application. *Journal of Experimental Social Psychology, 13,* 464–479.

Fehr, B. (1994). Prototype-based assessment of laypeoples' views of love. *Personal Relationships, 1,* 309–331.

Fehr, E., & Gächter, S. (2001). Altruistic punishment in humans. *Nature, 415,* 137–140.

Fehr, B., & Russell, J. A. (1991). The concept of love viewed from a prototype perspective. *Journal of Personality & Social Psychology, 60,* 425–438.

Fehr, E., & Schmidt, K. M. (1999). A theory of fairness, competition, and cooperation. *Quarterly Journal of Economics, 114,* 817–868.

Feigenson, N., Park, J., & Salovey, P. (2001). The role of emotions in comparative negligence judgments. *Journal of Applied Social Psychology, 31,* 576–603.

Fein, S., & Spencer, S. (1997). Prejudice as a self-esteem maintenance: Affirming the self through derogating others. *Journal of Personality and Social Psychology, 73,* 31–44.

Feinberg, M., Willer, R., & Keltner, D. (2012). Flustered and faithful: Embarrassment as a signal of prosocial behavior. *Journal of Personality and Social Psychology, 102,* 81–97.

Feinberg, M., Willer, R., & Schultze, M. (2014). Gossip and ostracism promote cooperation in groups, *Psychological Science 25(3),* 656–664.

Feinberg, M., Willer, R., Stellar, J., & Keltner, D. (2012). The virtues of gossip: Reputational information sharing as prosocial behavior. *Journal of Personality and Social Psychology, 102,* 1015.

Feingold, A. (1984). Correlates of physical attractiveness among college students. *Journal of Social Psychology, 122,* 139–140.

Feingold, A. (1990). Gender differences in effects of physical attractiveness on romantic attraction: A comparison across five research paradigms. *Journal of Personality and Social Psychology, 59,* 981–993.

Feingold, A. (1992a). Gender differences in mate selection preferences: A test of the parental investment model. *Psychological Bulletin, 112,* 125–139.

Feingold, A. (1992b). Good-looking people are not what we think. *Psychological Bulletin, 111,* 304–341.

Felson, R. B. (1993). The somewhat social self: How others affect self-appraisals. In J. M. Suls (Ed.), *The self in social perspective* (pp. 1–26). Hillsdale, NJ: Erlbaum.

Fenigstein, A., Scheier, M. F., & Buss, A. H. (1975). Public and private self-consciousness: Assessment and theory. *Journal of Consulting and Clinical Psychology, 43,* 522–527.

Ferguson, C. J., & Kilburn, J. (2010). Much ado about nothing: The misestimation and overinterpretation of violent video game effects in Eastern and Western nations: Comment on Anderson et al. (2010). *Psychological Bulletin, 136,* 174–178. doi: 10.1037=a0018566

Ferguson, C. J., San Miguel, C. & Hartley, R.D. (2009). A multivariate analysis of youth violence and aggression: The influence of family, peers, depression, and media violence. *Journal of Pediatrics, 155,* 904–908.

Ferguson, M. J. (2008). On becoming ready to pursue a goal you don't know you have: Effects of nonconscious goals on evaluative readiness. *Journal of Personality and Social Psychology, 95,* 1268–1294.

Ferguson, M. J., & Bargh, J. A. (2008). Evaluative readiness: The motivational nature of automatic evaluation. In A. J. Elliott (Ed.), *Handbook of approach and avoidance motivation* (pp. 289–306). New York: Psychology Press.

Ferguson, M. J., Bargh, J. A., & Nayak, D. (2005). After-affects: How automatic evaluations influence the interpretation of subsequent, unrelated stimuli. *Journal of Experimental Social Psychology, 41,* 182–191.

Ferguson, M. J. & Zayas, V. (2009). Nonconscious evaluation. *Current Directions in Psychological Science, 18,* 362–366.

Festinger, L. (1954). A theory of social comparison processes. *Human Relations, 7,* 117–140.

Festinger, L. (1957). *A theory of cognitive dissonance.* Stanford, CA: Stanford University Press.

Festinger, L. (1964). *Conflict, decision, and dissonance.* Stanford, CA: Stanford University Press.

Festinger, L., & Carlsmith, J. M. (1959). Cognitive consequences of forced compliance. *Journal of Abnormal and Social Psychology, 47,* 382–389.

Festinger, L., Pepitone, A., & Newcomb, T. (1952). Some consequences of deindividuation in a group. *Journal of Abnormal and Social Psychology, 47,* 382–389.

Festinger, L., Schachter, S., & Back, K. (1950). *Social pressures in informal groups.* Stanford, CA: Stanford University Press.

Fiedler, K. (2000). Illusory correlations: A simple associative algorithm provides a convergent account of seemingly divergent paradigms. *Review of General Psychology, 4,* 25–58.

Fiedler, K. (2007). Construal level theory as an integrative framework for behavioral decision-making research and consumer psychology. *Journal of Consumer Psychology, 17(2),* 101–106.

Fiedler, K., & Freytag, P. (2004). Pseudocontingencies. *Journal of Personality and Social Psychology, 87,* 453–467.

Fiedler, K., Walther, E., & Nickel, S. (1999). Covariation-based attribution: On the ability to assess multiple covariations of an effect. *Personality and Social Psychology Bulletin, 25,* 607–622.

Finkel, E. J., & Eastwick, P. W. (2008). Speed-dating. *Current Directions in Psychological Science, 17,* 193–197.

Finkel E. J., Rusbult, C. E., Kumashiro, M., & P. A. Hannonn, (2002). Dealing with betrayal in close relationships: Does commitment promote forgiveness? *Journal of Personality and Social Psychology, 82,* 956–974.

Fishbach, A., Friedman, R. S., & Kruglanski, A. W. (2003). Leading us not unto temptation: Momentary allurements elicit overriding goal activation. *Journal of Personality and Social Psychology, 84*, 296–309.

Fishbach, A., & Shah, J. Y. (2006). Self control in action: Implicit dispositions toward goals and away from temptations. *Journal of Personality and Social Psychology, 90*, 820–832.

Fischhoff, B., Gonzalez, R., Lerner, J. S., & Small, D. A. (2005). Evolving judgments of terror risks: Foresight, hindsight, and emotion. *Journal of Applied Social Psychology, 23*, 124–139.

Fishbein, M., & Ajzen, I. (1975). *Belief, attitude, intention, and behavior: An introduction to theory and research.* Reading, MA: Addison-Wesley.

Fisher, H. E., Aron, A., & Brown, L. L. (2006). Romantic love: A mammalian brain system for mate choice. *Philosophical Transactions of the Royal British Society, 361*, 2173–2186.

Fiske, A. P. (1991). *Structures of social life: The four elementary forms of human relations.* New York: Free Press.

Fiske, A. P. (1992). The four elementary forms of sociality: Framework for a unified theory of social relations. *Psychological Review, 99*, 689–723.

Fiske, A. P., Kitayama, S., Markus, H. R., & Nisbett, R. E. (1998). The cultural matrix of social psychology. In D. T. Gilbert, S. T. Fiske, & G. Lindzey (Eds.), *Handbook of social psychology* (4th ed., pp. 915–981). New York: McGraw-Hill.

Fiske, A. P., & Rai, T. S. (2014). *Virtuous violence.* Cambridge, England.: Cambridge University Press.

Fiske, S. T. (1993). Controlling other people: The impact of power on stereotyping. *American Psychologist, 48*(6), 621–628.

Fiske, S. T., & Taylor, S. E. (1991). *Social cognition.* New York: McGraw-Hill.

Fitzgerald, R., & Ellsworth, P. C. (1984). Due process vs. crime control: Death qualification and jury attitudes. *Law and Human Behavior, 8*, 31–52.

Fivush, R. (1989). Exploring sex differences in the emotional content of mother-child conversations about the past. *Sex Roles, 20*, 675–691.

Fivush, R. (1991). Gender and emotion in mother-child conversations about the past. *Journal of Narrative and Life History, 1*, 325–341.

Fivush, R. (1992). Gender differences in parent-child conversations about past emotions. *Sex Roles, 27*, 683–698.

Flannery, K. V., & Marcus, J. (2012). *The creation of inequality: How our prehistoric ancestors set the stage for monarchy, slavery, and empire.* Cambridge: Harvard University Press.

Fleming, J. H., & Darley, J. M. (1989). Perceiving choice and constraint: The effects of contextual and behavioral cues on attitude attribution. *Journal of Personality and Social Psychology, 56*, 27–40.

Flynn, J. R. (1991). *Asian Americans: Achievement beyond IQ.* Hillsdale, NJ: Erlbaum.

Fong, C. (2001). Social preferences, self-interest, and the demand for redistribution. *Journal of Public Economics, 82*, 225–246.

Fong, G. T., Krantz, D. H., & Nisbett, R. E. (1986). The effects of statistical training on thinking about everyday problems. *Cognitive Psychology, 18*, 253–292.

Ford, C. S., & Beach, F. A. (1951). *Patterns of sexual behavior.* New York: Harper & Row.

Ford, T. E., & Kruglanski, A. (1995). Effects of epistemic motivations on the use of momentarily accessible constructs in social judgment. *Personality and Social Psychology Bulletin, 21*, 950–962.

Forgas, J. P. (1995). Mood and judgment: The affect infusion model (AIM). *Psychological Bulletin, 117*(1), 39–66.

Forgas, J. P. (1998a). Asking nicely? Mood effects on responding to more or less polite requests. *Personality and Social Psychology Bulletin, 24*, 173–185.

Forgas, J. P. (1998b). On being happy and mistaken: Mood effects on the fundamental attribution error. *Journal of Personality and Social Psychology, 75*(2), 318–331.

Forgas, J. P. (Ed.). (2000). *Feeling and thinking: The role of affect in social cognition.* New York: Cambridge University Press.

Forgas, J. P. (2003). Affective influences on attitudes and judgments. In R. J. Davidson, K. R. Scherer, & H. H. Goldsmith (Eds.), *Handbook of affective sciences* (pp. 596–618). New York: Oxford University Press.

Forgas, J. P., & Bower, G. H. (1987). Mood effects on person perception judgments. *Journal of Personality and Social Psychology, 53*, 53–60.

Forgas, J. P., & Moylan, S. (1987). After the movies: The effect of mood on social judgments. *Personality and Social Psychology Bulletin, 13*, 465–477.

Forsterling, F. (1985). Attributional retraining: A review. *Psychological Bulletin, 98*, 495–512.

Forsterling, F. (1989). Models of covariation and attribution: How do they relate to the analogy of analysis of variance? *Journal of Personality and Social Psychology, 57*, 615–625.

Fortune, J. L., & Newby-Clark, I. R. (2008). My friend is embarrassing me: Exploring the guilty by association effect. *Journal of Personality and Social Psychology, 95*, 1440–1449.

Foushee, M. C. (1984). Dyads and triads at 35,000 feet. *American Psychologist, 39*, 885–893.

Fowler, J., Baker, L. A., & Dawes, C. T. (2008). Genetic variation in political participation. *American Political Science Review, 102*, 233–248.

Fowler, J. H., & Christakis, N. A. (2010). Cooperative behavior cascades in social networks. *Proceedings of the National Academy of Sciences of the USA, 107*, 5334–5338.

Fowler, K. A., Lilienfeld, S. O., & Patrick, C. J. (2009). Detecting psychopathy from thin slices of behavior. *Psychological Assessment, 21(1)*, 68–78.

Fox, J. A., & Pierce, G. L. (1987). *Supplementary homicide reports 1976–1986* [Machine-readable data file]. Ann Arbor, Michigan.

Fraley, R. C., Hudson, N. W., Heffernan, M. E., & Segal, N. (2015). Are adult attachment styles categorical or dimensional? A taxometric analysis of general and relationship-specific attachment orientations. *Journal of Personality and Social Psychology.*

Fraley, R. C., & Spieker, S. J. (2003). Are infant attachment patterns continuously or categorically distributed? A taxometric analysis of strange situation behavior. *Developmental Psychology, 34*, 387–404.

Fraley, R. C., Vicary, A. M., Brumbaugh, C. C., & Roisman, G. I. (2011). Patterns of stability in adult attachment: An empirical test of two models of continuity and change. *Journal of Personality and Social Psychology, 101*, 974–992.

Fraley, R. C., Waller, N. G., & Brennan, K. A. (2000). An item response theory analysis of self-report measures of adult attachment. *Journal of Personality and Social Psychology, 78*, 350–365.

Francis, D., & Meaney, M. J. (1999). Maternal care and the development of stress responses. *Development, 9*, 128–134.

Frank, M. G., Ekman, P., & Friesen, W. V. (1993). Behavioral markers and recognizability of the smile of enjoyment. *Journal of Personality and Social Psychology, 64*, 83–93.

Frank, M. G., & Gilovich, T. (1988). The dark side of self and social perception: Black uniforms and aggression in professional sports. *Journal of Personality and Social Psychology, 54,* 74–85.

Frank, M. G., & Gilovich, T. (1989). The effect of memory perspective on retrospective causal attributions. *Journal of Personality and Social Personality, 57,* 399–403.

Frank, R. H. (1988). *Passions within reason.* New York: Norton.

Frank, R. H., Gilovich, T., & Regan, D. T. (1993). Does studying economics inhibit cooperation? *Journal of Economic Perspectives, 7,* 159–171.

Frank, R. H., Levine, A. S., & Dijk, O. (2014). Expenditure cascades. *Review of Behavioral Economics, 1,* 55–73. Franzen, A., & Pointner, S. (2013). The external validity of giving in the dictator game. A field experiment using the misdirected letter technique. *Experimental Economics, 16,* 155–169.

Franzen, A., & Pointner, S. (2013). The external validity of giving in the dictator game. *Experimental Economics,* 16:2, 155–169.

Frederick, S. (2005). Cognitive reflection and decision making. *Journal of Economic Perspectives, 19,* 24–42.

Fredrickson, B. L. (1998). What good are positive emotions? *Review of General Psychology, 2,* 300–319.

Fredrickson, B. L. (2001). The role of positive emotions in positive psychology: The broaden-and-build theory of positive emotions. *American Psychologist, 56,* 218–226.

Fredrickson, B. L., Cohn, M. A., Coffey, K. A., Pek, J., & Finkel, S. M. (2008). Open hearts build lives: Positive emotions, induced through loving-kindness meditation, build consequential personal resources. *Journal of Personality and Social Psychology, 95,* 1045–1062.

Fredrickson, B. L., & Kahneman, D. (1993). Duration neglect in retrospective evaluations of affective episodes. *Journal of Personality and Social Psychology, 65,* 45–55.

Fredrickson, B. L., & Roberts, T. (1997). Objectification theory: Toward understanding women's lived experiences and mental health risks. *Psychology of Women Quarterly, 21,* 173–206.

Freedman, J. L. (1965). Long-term behavioral effects of cognitive dissonance. *Journal of Experimental Social Psychology, 1,* 145–155.

Freedman, J. L., & Fraser, S. C. (1966). Compliance without pressure: The foot-in-the-door-technique. *Journal of Personality and Social Psychology, 4,* 195–203.

French, H. W. (2001, August 7). Hypothesis: A scientific gap. Conclusion: Japanese custom. *New York Times,* p. Al.

French, J., & Raven, B. (1959). The bases of social power. In D. Cartwright (Ed.), *Studies of social power* (pp. 150–167). Ann Arbor, MI: Institute for Social Research.

Frenkel, O. J., & Doob, A. N. (1976). Post-decision dissonance at the polling booth. *Canadian Journal of Behavioral Science, 8,* 347–350.

Friedman, R. S., & Forster, J. (2000). The effects of approach and avoidance motor actions on the elements of creative thought. *Journal of Personality and Social Psychology, 79,* 477–492.

Friese, M., Hofmann, W., & Schmitt, M. (2008). When and why do implicit measures predict behaviour? Empirical evidence for the moderating role of opportunity, motivation, and process reliance. *European Review of Social Psychology, 19,* 285–338.

Frieze, I. H., Olson, J. E., & Russell, J. (1991). Attractiveness and income for men and women in management. *Journal of Applied Social Psychology, 21,* 1039–1057.

Frijda, N. H., & Mesquita, B. (1994). The social roles and functions of emotions. In S. Kitayama & H. Markus (Eds.), *Emotion and culture: Empirical studies of mutual influence* (pp. 51–87). Washington, DC: American Psychological Association.

Frodi, A. (1975). The effect of exposure to weapons on aggressive behavior from a cross-cultural perspective. *International Journal of Psychology, 10,* 283–292.

Froming, W. J., Walker, G. R., & Lopyan, K. J. (1982). Public and private self-awareness: When personal attitudes conflict with societal expectations. *Journal of Experimental Social Psychology, 18,* 476–487.

Fujita, K., Henderson, M. D., Eng, J., Trope, Y., & Liberman, N. (2006). Spatial distance and mental construal of social events. *Psychological Science, 17,* 278–282.

Fultz, J., Batson, C. D., Fortenbach, V. A., McCarthy, P. M., & Varney, L. (1986). Social evaluation and the empathy-altruism hypothesis. *Journal of Personality and Social Psychology, 50,* 761–769.

Gable, S. L., Gonzaga, G., & Strachman, A. (2006). Will you be there for me when things go right? Social support for positive events. *Journal of Personality and Social Psychology, 91,* 904–917.

Gable, S. L., Reis, H. T., Impett, E. A., & Asher, E. R. (2004). What do you do when things go right? The intrapersonal and interpersonal benefits of sharing positive events. *Journal of Personality and Social Psychology, 87,* 228–245.

Gabrielidis, C., Stephan, W. G., Ybarra, O., Pearson, V. M. D. S., & Villareal, L. (1997). Preferred styles of conflict resolution, Mexico and the United States. *Journal of Cross-Cultural Psychology, 28*(6), 661–677.

Gaertner, L., Iuzzini, J., Witt, M., & Orina, M.M. (2006). Us without them: Evidence for an intragroup origin of positive ingroup regard. *Journal of Personality and Social Psychology, 90,* 426–439.

Gaertner, S. L., & Dovidio, J. F. (1977). The subtlety of white racism, arousal, and helping behavior. *Journal of Personality and Social Psychology, 35,* 691–707.

Gaertner, S. L., & Dovidio, J. F. (1986). The aversive form of racism. In J. F. Dovidio & S. L. Gaertner (Eds.), *Prejudice, discrimination, and racism* (pp. 61–89). Orlando, FL: Academic Press.

Gaertner, S. L., & Dovidio, J. F. (2000). Reducing intergroup bias: The common ingroup identity model. Philadelphia, PA: Psychology Press.

Gaertner, S. L., & Dovidio, J. F. (2009). A common intergroup identity: A categorization-based approach for reducing intergroup bias. In T.D. Nelson (Ed.), *Handbook of prejudice, stereotyping, and discrimination* (pp. 489–505). New York: Psychology Press.

Gaertner, S. L., Mann, J., Dovidio, J. F., Murrell, A., & Pomare, M. (1990). How does cooperation reduce intergroup bias? *Journal of Personality and Social Psychology, 59,* 692–704.

Gaertner, S. L., Murrell, A., & Dovidio, J. F. (1989). Reducing intergroup bias: The benefits of recategorization. *Journal of Personality and Social Psychology, 57,* 239–249.

Gailliot, M. T., Baumeister, R. F., DeWall, C. N., Maner, J. K., Plant, E. A., Tice, D. M., et al. (2007). Self-control relies on glucose as a limited energy source: Willpower is more than a metaphor. *Journal of Personality and Social Psychology, 92,* 325–336.

Galinsky, A. D., Stone, J., & Cooper, J. (2000). The reinstatement of dissonance and psychological discomfort following failed affirmations. *European Journal of Social Psychology, 30,* 123–147.

Gallo, L. C., Bogart, L. M., Vranceanu, A., & Matthews, K. A. (2005). Socioeconomic status, resources, psychological experiences, and emotional responses: A test of the reserve capacity model. *Journal of Personality and Social Psychology, 88*(2), 386–399.

Galton, F. (1878). Composite portraits. *Journal of the Anthropological Institute of Great Britain and Ireland, 8*, 132–142.

Gangestad, S. W., Simpson, J. A., Cousins, A. J., Garver-Apgar, C. E., & Christensen, P. N. (2004). Women's preferences for male behavioral displays change across the menstrual cycle. *Psychological Science, 15*, 203–207.

Gangestad, S. W., & Snyder, M. (2000). Self-monitoring: Appraisal and reappraisal. *Psychological Bulletin, 126*, 530–555.

Gangestad, S. W., & Thornhill, R. (1998). Menstrual cycle variation in women's preference for the scent of symmetrical men. *Proceedings of the Royal Society of London B, 265*, 727–733.

Garcia, J., Kimeldorf, D. J., & Koelling, R. A. (1955). Conditioned aversion to saccharin resulting from exposure to gamma radiation. *Science 122*(3160), 157–158.

Garcia-Marques, L., & Hamilton, D. L. (1996). Resolving the apparent discrepancy between the incongruency effect and the expectancy-based illusory correlation effect: The TRAP mode. *Journal of Personality and Social Psychology, 71*, 845–860.

Gardner, W. L., Gabriel, S., & Lee, A. Y. (1999). "I" value freedom, but "we" value relationships: Self-construal priming mirrors cultural differences in judgment. *Psychological Science, 10*, 321–326.

Garner, D. M., Garfinkel, P. E., Schwartz, D., & Thompson, M. (1980). Cultural expectations of thinness in women. *Psychological Reports, 47*, 483–491.

Garofalo, J. (1981). Crime and the mass media: A selective review of research. *Journal of Research in Crime and Delinquency, 18*, 319–350.

Garrett, B. (2008). Judging innocence. *Columbia Law Review, 108*, 55–142.

Gates, G. S. (1924). The effects of an audience upon performance. *Journal of Abnormal and Social Psychology, 18*, 334–342.

Gawronski, B. (2003). Implicational schemata and the correspondence bias: On the diagnostic value of situationally constrained behavior. *Journal of Personality and Social Psychology, 84*, 1154–1171.

Gawronski, B., Cunningham, W. A., LeBel, E. P., & Deutsch, R. (2010). Attentional influences on affective priming: Does categorization influence spontaneous evaluations of multiply categorizable objects? *Cognition and Emotion, 24*, 1008–1025.

Gawronski, B., & Payne, B. K. (Eds.). (2010). *Handbook of implicit social cognition: Measurement, theory, and applications.* New York: Guilford Press.

Geen, R. G. (1989). Alternative conceptions of social facilitation. In P. B. Paulus (Ed.), *Psychology of group influence* (2nd ed., pp. 15–51). Hillsdale, NJ: Erlbaum.

Geen, R. G. (1998). Aggression and antisocial behavior. In D. T. Gilbert, S. T. Fiske, & G. Lindzey (Eds.), *The handbook of social psychology* (4th ed., Vol. 2, pp. 317–356). New York: McGraw-Hill.

Geeraert, N. Y., Yzerbyt, V. Y., Corneille, O., & Wigboldus, D. (2004). The return of dispositionalism: On the linguistic consequences of dispositional suppression. *Journal of Experimental Social Psychology, 40*, 264–272.

Gelfand, M. J., Raver, J. L., Nishii, L., Leslie, L. M., Lun, J., Lim, B. C., . . . , & S. Yamaguchi. (2011). Differences between tight and loose cultures: A 33-nation study. *Science, 332*, 1100–1104.

Gentile, D. A. (2009). Pathological video game use among youth 8 to 18: A national study. *Psychological Science, 20*, 594–602.

Gerard, H. B., Wilhelmy, R. A., & Conolley, E. S. (1968). Conformity and group size. *Journal of Personality and Social Psychology, 8*, 79–82.

Gerber, A. S., & Rogers, T. (2009). Descriptive social norms and motivation to vote: Everyone's voting and so should you. *Journal of Politics, 71*, 178–191.

Gerbner, G., Gross, L., Morgan, M., & Signorielli, N. (1980). The "mainstreaming" of America: Violence profile no. 11. *Journal of Communication, 30*, 10–29.

Gerbner, G., Gross, L., Morgan, M., & Signorielli, N. (1986). Living with television: The dynamics of the cultivation process. In J. Bryant & D. Zillman (Eds.), *Perspectives on media effects* (pp. 17–40). Hillsdale, NJ: Erlbaum.

Gibbons, F. X. (1978). Sexual standards and reactions to pornography: Enhancing behavioral consistency through self-focused attention. *Journal of Personality and Social Psychology, 36*, 976–987.

Gigerenzer, G. (1991). How to make cognitive illusions disappear: Beyond "heuristics and biases." In W. Stroche & M. Hewstone (Eds.), *European review of social psychology* (Vol. 2, pp. 83–115). Chichester, England: Wiley.

Gilbert, D. T. (1989). Thinking lightly about others: Automatic components of the social inference process. In J. S. Uleman & J. A. Bargh (Eds.), *Unintended thought.* New York: Guilford Press.

Gilbert, D. T. (2002). Inferential correction. In T. Gilovich, D. W. Griffin, & D. Kahneman (Eds.), *Heuristics and biases: The psychology of intuitive judgment.* New York: Cambridge University Press.

Gilbert, D. T., Brown, R. P., Pinel, E. E., & Wilson, T. D. (2000). The illusion of external agency. *Journal of Personality and Social Psychology, 79*, 690–700.

Gilbert, D. T., & Jones, E. E. (1986). Perceiver-induced constraint: Interpretations of self-generated reality. *Journal of Personality and Social Psychology, 50*, 269–280.

Gilbert, D. T., & Malone, P. S. (1995). The correspondence bias. *Psychological Bulletin, 117*, 21–38.

Gilbert, D. T., Pinel, E. C., Wilson, T. D., Blumberg, S. J., & Wheatley, T. (1998). Immune neglect: A source of durability bias in affective forecasting. *Journal of Personality and Social Psychology, 75*, 617–638.

Gilbert, S. J. (1981). Another look at the Milgram obedience studies: The role of the gradated series of shocks. *Personality and Social Psychology Bulletin, 4*, 690–695.

Gilmour, T. M., & Reid, D. W. (1979). Locus of control and causal attribution for positive and negative outcomes on university examinations. *Journal of Research in Personality, 13*, 154–160.

Gilovich, T. (1981). Seeing the past in the present: The effect of associations to familiar events on judgments and decisions. *Journal of Personality and Social Psychology, 40*, 797–808.

Gilovich, T. (1983). Biased evaluation and persistence in gambling. *Journal of Personality and Social Psychology, 44*, 1110–1126.

Gilovich, T. (1991). *How we know what isn't so: The fallibility of human reason in everyday life.* New York: Free Press.

Gilovich, T., Griffin, D. W., & Kahneman, D. (Eds.). (2002). *Heuristics and biases: The psychology of intuitive judgment.* New York: Cambridge University Press.

Gilovich, T., Kruger, J., & Medvec, V. H. (2002). The spotlight effect revisited: Overestimating the manifest variability in our actions and appearance. *Journal of Experimental Social Psychology*, *38*, 93–99.

Gilovich, T., Medvec, V. H., & Savitsky, K. (2000). The spotlight effect in social judgment: An egocentric bias in estimates of the salience of one's own actions and appearance. *Journal of Personality and Social Psychology*, *79*, 211–222.

Gilovich, T., & Savitsky, K. (2002). Like goes with like: The role of representativeness in erroneous and pseudo-scientific beliefs. In T. Gilovich, D. W. Griffin, & D. Kahneman (Eds.), *Heuristics and biases: The psychology of intuitive judgment* (pp. 617–624). New York: Cambridge University Press.

Ginosar, Z., & Trope, Y. (1980). The effects of base rates and individuating information on judgments about another person. *Journal of Experimental Social Psychology*, *16*, 228–242.

Givens, D. B. (1983). *Love signals: How to attract a mate*. New York: Crown.

Gladwell, M. (2008). *Outliers*. New York: Little, Brown.

Glanz, J., & Schwartz, J. (2003, September 26). Dogged engineer's effort to assess shuttle damage. *New York Times*, p. Al.

Glaser, J. (2014). *Suspect race: Causes and consequences of racial profiling*. New York: Oxford University Press.

Glasman, L. R., & Albarracin, D. (2006). Forming attitudes that predict future behavior: A meta-analysis of the attitude-behavior relation. *Psychological Bulletin*, *132*, 778–822.

Glenn, N. D. (1991). The recent trend in marital success in the United States. *Journal of Marriage and the Family*, *53*, 261–270.

Glick, P., & Fiske, S. T. (2001a). Ambivalent sexism. In M. P. Zanna (Ed.), *Advances in experimental social psychology* (Vol. 33, pp. 115–188). Thousand Oaks, CA: Academic Press.

Glick, P., & Fiske, S. T. (2001b). An ambivalent alliance: Hostile and benevolent sexism as complementary justifications of gender inequality. *American Psychologist*, *56*, 109–118.

Glied, S., & Neidell, M. (2008). The economic value of teeth. National Bureau of Economic Research Working Paper 13879.

Glover, J. (1999). *Humanity*. New Haven, CT: Yale University Press.

Goethals, G. R., Cooper, J., & Naficy, A. (1979). Role of foreseen, foreseeable, and unforeseeable behavioral consequences in the arousal of cognitive dissonance. *Journal of Personality and Social Psychology*, *37*, 1179–1185.

Goetz, J., Keltner, D., & Simon-Thomas, E. (2010). Compassion: An evolutionary analysis and empirical review. *Psychological Bulletin*, *136*(3), 351–374.

Goff, P. A., Eberhardt, J. L., Williams, M., & Jackson, M. C. (2008). Not yet human: Implicit knowledge, historical dehumanization, and contemporary consequences. *Journal of Personality and Social Psychology*, *94*, 292–306.

Goffman, E. (1959). *The presentation of self in everyday life*. Garden City, NY: Doubleday.

Goffman, E. (1961). *Encounters: Two studies in the sociology of interaction*. New York: Penguin.

Goffman, E. (1966). *Behavior in public places*. New York: Free Press.

Goffman, E. (1967). *Interaction ritual: Essays on face-to-face behavior*. New York: Doubleday.

Goldberg, P. (1968, April). Are women prejudiced against women? *Trans-action: Social Science and Modern Society*, *5*, 28–30.

Goldin, C., & Rouse, C. (2000). Orchestrating impartiality: The impact of "blind" auditions on female musicians. *American Economic Review*, *90*, 715–741.

Goldman, W., & Lewis, P. (1977). Beautiful is good: Evidence that the physically attractive are more socially skillful. *Journal of Experimental Social Psychology*, *13*, 125–130.

Goldstein, N. J., Cialdini, R. B., & Griskevicius, V. (2008). A room with a viewpoint: Using social norms to motivate environmental conservation in hotels. *Journal of Consumer Research*, *35*, 472–482.

Goleman, D. (1985). *Vital lies, simple truths: The psychology of self-deception*. New York: Simon & Schuster.

Goleman, D. (1995.) *Emotional intelligence: Why it can matter more than IQ*. New York: Bantam Books.

Gologor, E. (1977). Group polarization in a non-risk-taking culture. *Journal of Cross-Cultural Psychology*, *8*, 331–346.

Gonzaga, G. C., Keltner, D., Londahl, E. A., & Smith, M. D. (2001). Love and the commitment problem in romantic relations and friendship. *Journal of Personality and Social Psychology*, *81*, 247–262.

Gonzaga, G. C., Keltner, D., & Ward, D. (2008). Power in mixed-sex interactions. *Cognition and Emotion*, *22*, 1555–1568.

Gonzalez, C., Dana, J., Koshino, H., & Just, M. (2005). The framing effect and risky decisions: Examining cognitive functions with fMRI. *Journal of Economic Psychology*, *26*, 1–20.

Gonzalez, R., & Griffin, D. (1997). On the statistics of interdependence: Treating dyadic data with respect. In S. Duck (Ed.), *Handbook of personal relationships: Theory, research, and interventions* (2nd ed., pp. 271–302). Chichester, England: Wiley.

Good, C., Aronson, J., & Inzlicht, M. (2003). Improving adolescents' standardized test performance: An intervention to reduce the effects of stereotype threat. *Applied Developmental Psychology*, *24*, 645–662.

Good, C., Rattan, A., & Dweck, C. S. (2012). Why do women opt out? Sense of belonging and women's representation in mathematics. *Journal of Personality and Social Psychology, 102*(4), 700–717.

Goodwin, S. A., Gubin, A., Fiske, S. T., & Yzerbyt, V. Y. (2000). Power can bias impression processes: Stereotyping subordinates by default and by design. *Group Processes and Intergroup Relations, 3*, 227–256.

Gordon, A. M., & Chen, S. (2013). Does power help or hurt? The moderating role of self-other focus on power and perspective-taking in romantic relationships. *Personality and Social Psychology Bulletin, 39*, 1097–1110.

Gosling, S. D., Ko, S. J., Mannarelli, T., & Morris, M. E. (2002). A room with a cue: Judgments of personality based on offices and bedrooms. *Journal of Personality and Social Psychology, 82*, 379–398.

Gottman, J. M. (1993). *Why marriages succeed or fail*. New York: Simon & Schuster.

Gottman, J. M., & Levenson, R. W. (1992). Marital processes predictive of later dissolution: Behavior, physiology, and health. *Journal of Personality and Social Psychology, 63*, 221–233.

Gottman, J. M., & Levenson, R. W. (1999). Rebound from marital conflict and divorce prediction. *Family Processes, 38*, 287–292.

Gottman, J. M., & Levenson, R. W. (2000). The timing of divorce: Predicting when a couple will divorce over a 14-year period. *Journal of Marriage and the Family, 62*, 737–745.

Gottschalk, J. Martin, J., Quish, H., & Rea, J. (2004). Sex differences in mate choice criteria are reflected in folktales from around the world and in historical European literature. *Evolution and Human Behavior, 205*,102–112.

Gouldner, A. W. (1960). The norm of reciprocity: A preliminary statement. *American Sociological Review, 25*, 161–178.

Gourevitch, P. (1998). *We wish to inform you that tomorrow we will be killed with our families.* New York: Picador Press.

Gove, W., Style, C., & Hughes, M. (1990). The effect of marriage on the well-being of adults: A theoretical analysis. *Journal of Family Issues, 11,* 4–35.

Graham, J., Haidt, J., Koleva, S., Motyl, M., Iyer, R., Wojcik, S., & Ditto, P. H. (2013). Moral Foundations Theory: The pragmatic validity of moral pluralism. *Advances in Experimental Social Psychology, 47,* 55–130.

Graham, J., Haidt, J., & Nosek, B. A. (2009). Liberals and conservatives rely on different sets of moral foundations. *Journal of Personality and Social Psychology, 96*(5), 1029.

Grant, A., & Gino, F. (2010). A little thanks goes a long way: Explaining why gratitude expressions motivate prosocial behavior. *Journal of Personality and Social Psychology, 98*(6), 946–955.

Green, D. P., Wong, J., & Strolovitch, D. (1996). *The effects of demographic change on hate crime.* New Haven: Institution for Social and Policy Studies, Yale University.

Greenberg, J., Eloul, L., Markus, H. R., & Tsai, J. (2012). *"Neither East nor West": Conformity and self-enhancement in the Muslim Middle East.* Stanford, CA: Stanford University.

Greenberg, J., Pyszczynski, T., & Solomon, S. (1982). The self-serving attributional bias: Beyond self-presentation. *Journal of Experimental Social Psychology, 18,* 56–67.

Greenberg, J., Pyszczynski, T., Solomon, S., Rosenblatt, A., Veeder, M., Kirkland, S., et al. (1990). Evidence for terror management theory II: The effects of mortality salience on reactions to those who threaten or bolster the cultural worldview. *Journal of Personality and Social Psychology, 58,* 308–318.

Greenberg, J., Simon, L., Porteus, J., Pyszczynski, T., & Solomon, S. (1995). Evidence of a terror management function of cultural icons: The effects of mortality salience on the inappropriate use of cherished cultural symbols. *Personality and Social Psychology Bulletin, 21,* 1221–1228.

Greene, D., Sternberg, B., & Lepper, M. R. (1976). Overjustification in a token economy. *Journal of Personality and Social Psychology, 34,* 1219–1234.

Greene, J. D., & Haidt, J. (2002). How (and where) does moral judgment work? *Trends in Cognitive Sciences, 6,* 517–523.

Greene, J. D., Sommerville, R. B., Nystrom, L. E., Darley, J. M., & Cohen, J. D. (2001). An fMRI investigation of emotional engagement in moral judgment. *Science, 293,* 2105–2108.

Greenspan, A. (1996). The challenge of central banking in a democratic society. Speech given to the American Enterprise Institute, December 5.

Greenwald, A. G. (1980). The totalitarian ego: Fabrication and revision of personal history. *American Psychologist, 35,* 603–618.

Greenwald, A. G., & Banaji, M. R. (1995). Implicit social cognition: Attitudes, self-esteem, and stereotypes. *Psychological Review, 102,* 4–27.

Greenwald, A. G., Klinger, M. R., & Liu, T. J. (1989). Unconscious processing of dichotically masked words. *Memory and Cognition, 17,* 35–47.

Greenwald, A. G., McGhee, D. E., & Schwartz, D. L. K. (1998). Measuring individual differences in implicit cognition: The Implicit Association Test. *Journal of Personality and Social Psychology, 74,* 1464–1480.

Greve, F. (2009, May 23). America's poor are its most generous. *The Seattle Times.* Retrieved from http://seattletimes.nwsource.com

Griffin, D., & Tversky, A. (1992). The weighing of evidence and the determinants of confidence. *Cognitive Psychology, 24,* 411–435.

Griffitt, W., & Veitch, R. (1971). Hot and crowded: Influences of population density and temperature on interpersonal affective behavior. *Journal of Personality and Social Psychology, 17,* 92–98.

Griffitt, W., & Veitch, R. (1974). Preacquaintance attitude similarity and attraction revisited: Ten days in a fall-out shelter. *Sociometry, 37,* 163–173.

Groff, B. D., Baron, R. S., & Moore, D. L. (1983). Distraction, attentional conflict, and drivelike behavior. *Journal of Experimental Social Psychology, 19,* 359–380.

Gross, J. J. (1998). Antecedent-and-response-focused emotion regulation: Divergent consequences for experience, expression, and physiology. *Journal of Personality and Social Psychology, 74,* 224–237.

Grossmann, I., & Kross, E. (2010). The impact of culture on adaptive versus maladaptive self-reflection. *Psychological Science, 21,* 1150–1157. doi:10.1177/0956797610376655

Grossmann, I. & Kross, E. (2014). Exploring "Solomon's paradox": Self-distancing eliminates the self-other asymmetry in wise reasoning about close relations in younger and older adults. *Psychological Science, 25*(8), 1571–1580.

Grossmann, I., & Varnum, M. (2011). Social class, culture and cognition. *Social Psychological and Personality Science, 2,* 81–89.

Grush, J. E. (1980). Impact of candidate expenditures, regionality, and prior outcomes on the 1976 presidential primaries. *Journal of Personality and Social Psychology, 38,* 337–347.

Guadagno, R. E., Rhoads, K. v. L., & Sagarin, B. J. (2011). Figural vividness and persuasion: Capturing the "elusive" vividness effect. *Personality and Social Psychology Bulletin, 37,* 626–638.

Guéguen, N. (2004). Nonverbal encouragement of participation in a course: The effect of touching. *Social Psychology of Education, 7*(1), 89–98.

Guerin, B. (1993). *Social facilitation.* New York: Cambridge University Press.

Guilbault, R. L., Bryant, F. B., Brockway, J. H., & Posavac, E. J. (2004). A meta-analysis of research on hindsight bias. *Basic and Applied Social Psychology, 26,* 103–117.

Guinote, A. (2007). Power and goal pursuit. *Personality and Social Psychology Bulletin, 33*(8), 1076–1087.

Guinote, A., Judd, C. M., & Brauer, M. (2002). Effects of power on perceived and objective group variability: Evidence that more powerful groups are more powerful. *Journal of Personality and Social Psychology, 82,* 708–721.

Gunnell, J., & Ceci, S. J. (2010). When emotionality trumps reason: A study of individual processing style and juror bias. *Behavioral Science and the Law, 28,* 850–877.

Gustavsson, L., Johnsson, J. I., & Uller, T. (2008). Mixed support for sexual selection theories of mate preferences in the Swedish population. *Evolutionary Psychology, 6*(4), 575–585.

Haberstroh, S., Oyserman, D., Schwarz, N., Kühnen, U., & Ji, L.-J. (2002). Is the interdependent self more sensitive to question context than the independent self? Self-construal and the observation of conversational norms. *Journal of Experimental Social Psychology, 38,* 323–329.

Haddock, G., Zanna, M. P., & Esses, V. M. (1993). Assessing the structure of prejudicial attitudes: The case of attitudes toward homosexuals. *Journal of Personality and Social Psychology, 65,* 1105–1118.

Hagger, M. S. & Chatzisarantis, N. L. D. (2013). The sweet taste of success: The presence of glucose in the oral cavity moderates the depletion of self-control resources. *Personality and Social Psychology Bulletin, 39*, 27–41.

Haidt, J. (2001). The emotional dog and its rational tail: A social intuitionist approach to moral judgment. *Psychological Review, 108*, 814–834.

Haidt, J. (2003). The moral emotions. In R. J. Davidson, K. R. Scherer, & H. H. Goldsmith (Eds.), *Handbook of affective sciences* (pp. 852–870). New York: Oxford University Press.

Haidt, J. (2012). *The righteous mind: Why good people are divided by politics and religion*. New York: Pantheon.

Haidt, J., & Joseph, C. (2004). Intuitive Ethics: How Innately Prepared Intuitions Generate Culturally Variable Virtues. *Daedalus*, pp. 55–66, Special issue on human nature.

Haidt, J., & Keltner, D. (1999). Culture and facial expression: Open-ended methods find more faces and a gradient of universality. *Cognition and Emotion, 13*, 225–266.

Haidt, J., Koller, S. H., & Dias, M. G. (1993). Affect, culture, and morality, or Is it wrong to eat your dog? *Journal of Personality and Social Psychology, 65*, 613–628.

Halberstadt, J. B., & Rhodes, G. (2000). The attractivenes of non-face averages: Implications for an evolutionary explanation of the attractiveness of average faces. *Psychological Science, 11*, 285–289.

Halberstadt, J. B., & Rhodes, G. (2003). It's not just average faces that are attractive: Computer-manipulated averageness makes birds, fish, and automobiles attractive. *Psychonomic Bulletin and Review, 10*, 149–156.

Halberstam, D. (1969). *The best and the brightest*. New York: Random House.

Haley, K., and Fessler, D. (2005). Nobody's watching? Subtle cues affect generosity in an anonymous economic game. *Evolution and Human Behavior, 26*, 245–256.

Hall, J. A. (1984). *Nonverbal gender differences: Accuracy of communication and expressive style*. Baltimore, MD: Johns Hopkins University Press.

Hamermesh, D. (2011). *Beauty pays: Why attractive people are more successful*. Princeton, NJ: Princeton University Press.

Hamermesh, D., & Biddle, J. (1994). Beauty and the labor market. *American Economic Review, 84*, 1174–1194.

Hamill, R., Wilson, T. D., & Nisbett, R. E. (1980). Insensitivity to sample bias: Generalizing from atypical cases. *Journal of Personality and Social Psychology, 39*, 578–589.

Hamilton, D. L., & Gifford, R. K. (1976). Illusory correlation in interpersonal perception: A cognitive basis of stereotypic judgments. *Journal of Experimental Social Psychology, 12*, 392–407.

Hamilton, D. L., & Sherman, S. J. (1989). Illusory correlations: Implications for stereotype theory and research. In D. Bar-Tal, C. F. Graumann, A. W. Kruglanski, & W. Stroebe (Eds.), *Stereotypes and prejudice: Changing conceptions* (pp. 59–82). New York: Springer-Verlag.

Hamilton, D. L., Stroessner, S., & Mackie, D. M. (1993). The influence of affect on stereotyping: The case of illusory correlations. In D. M. Mackie & D. L. Hamilton (Eds.), *Affect, cognition, and stereotyping: Interactive processes in group perception* (pp. 39–61). San Diego, CA: Academic Press.

Hamilton, D. L., & Zanna, M. P. (1974). Context effects in impression formation: Changes in connotative meaning. *Journal of Personality and Social Psychology, 29*, 649–654.

Hamilton, W. D. (1964). The genetical evolution of social behavior. *Journal of Theoretical Biology, 7*, 1–52.

Hampden-Turner, C., & Trompenaars, A. (1993). *The seven cultures of capitalism: Value systems for creating wealth in the United States, Japan, Germany, France, Britain, Sweden, and the Netherlands*. New York: Doubleday.

Han, S., & Shavitt, S. (1994). Persuasion and culture: Advertising appeals in individualistic and collectivistic societies. *Journal of Experimental Social Psychology, 30*, 326–350.

Haney, C. (1984). On the selection of capital juries: The biasing effects of the death-qualification process. *Law and Human Behavior, 8*, 121–132.

Haney, C., Banks, C., & Zimbardo, P. G. (1973). Interpersonal dynamics in a simulated prison. *International Journal of Criminology and Penology, 1*, 69–97.

Haney, C., Hurtado, A., & Vega, L. (1994). "Modern" death qualification: New data on its biasing effects. *Law and Human Behavior, 18*, 619–633.

Haney, C., & Logan, D. D. (1994). Broken promise: The Supreme Court's response to social science research on capital punishment. *Journal of Social Issues, 50*, 75–101.

Hanna, J. (1989, September 25). Sexual abandon: The condom is unpopular on the campus. *Maclean's*, p. 48.

Hans, V. P. (2000). *Business on trial: The civil jury and corporate responsibility*. New Haven, CT: Yale University Press.

Harackiewicz, J. M., Manderlink, G., & Sansone, C. (1984). Rewarding pinball wizardry: Effects of evaluation and cue value on intrinsic interest. *Journal of Personality and Social Psychology, 47*, 287–300.

Harari, H., Mohr, D., & Hosey, K. (1980). Faculty helpfulness to students: A comparison of compliance techniques. *Personality and Social Psychology Bulletin, 6*, 373–377.

Hardy, C. L., & van Vugt, M. (2006). Nice guys finish first: The competitive altruism hypothesis. *Personality and Social Psychology Bulletin, 32*, 1402–1413.

Hare, R. D. (1991). *The Hare Psychopathy Checklist—Revised*. Toronto, Ontario: Multi-Health Systems.

Harlow, H. F. (1959). Love in infant monkeys. *Scientific American, 200*, 68–86.

Harmon, A. (Dec 26, 2011). Navigating love and autism. *New York Times*.

Harmon-Jones, E. (2000). Cognitive dissonance and experienced negative affect: Evidence that dissonance increases experienced negative affect even in the absence of aversive consequences. *Personality and Social Psychology Bulletin, 26*, 1490–1501.

Harmon-Jones, E., Brehm, J. W., Greenberg, J., Simon, L., & Nelson, D. E. (1996). Evidence that the production of aversive consequences is not necessary to create cognitive dissonance. *Journal of Personality and Social Psychology, 70*, 5–16.

Harmon-Jones, E., Sigelman, J. D., Bohlig, A., & Harmon-Jones, C. (2003). Anger, coping, and frontal cortical activity: The effect of coping potential on anger-induced left frontal activity. *Cognition and Emotion, 17*, 1–24.

Harris, C. R. (2001). Cardiovascular responses of embarassment and effects of emotional suppression in a social setting. *Journal of Personality and Social Psychology, 81*, 886–897.

Harris, M. B. (1974). Mediators between frustration and aggression in a field experiment. *Journal of Experimental Social Psychology, 10*, 561–571.

Harris, R. J., Benson, S. M., & Hall, C. L. (1975). The effects of confession on altruism. *Journal of Social Psychology, 96*, 187–192.

Harrison, A. A., & Saeed, L. (1977). Let's make a deal: An analysis of revelations and stipulations in lonely hearts advertisements. *Journal of Personality and Social Psychology, 35*, 257–264.

Hart, D., Lucca-Irizarry, N., & Damon, W. (1986). The development of self-understanding in Puerto Rico and the United States. *Journal of Early Adolescence, 6*, 293–304.

Haslam, N., & Loughnan, S. (2014). Dehumanization and infrahumanization. *Annual Review of Psychology, 65*, 399–423.

Hass, R. G., & Linder, D. E. (1972). Counterargument availability and the effects of message structure on persuasion. *Journal of Personality and Social Psychology, 23*, 219–233.

Hassin, R. R., Ferguson, M. J., Shidlovsky, D., & Gross, T. (2007). Waved by invisible flags: The effects of subliminal exposure to flags on political thought and behavior. *Proceedings of the National Academy of Sciences of the USA, 104*, 19757–19761.

Hastie, R. (1981). Schematic principles in human memory. In E. T. Higgins, C. P. Herman, & M. P. Zanna (Eds.), *Social cognition: The Ontario Symposium* (Vol. 1, pp. 39–88). Hillsdale, NJ: Erlbaum.

Hastie, R., Penrod, S. D., & Pennington, N. (1983). *Inside the jury*. Cambridge, MA: Harvard University Press.

Hatala, M., & Prehodka, J. (1996). Content analysis of gay male and lesbian personal advertisements. *Psychological Reports, 78(2)*, 371–374.

Hatfield, E., Cacioppo, J. T., & Rapson, R. L. (1994). *Emotional contagion*. New York: Cambridge University Press.

Haugtvedt, C. P., & Petty, R. E. (1992). Personality and persuasion: Need for cognition moderates the persistence and resistance of attitude changes. *Journal of Personality and Social Psychology, 63*, 308–319.

Hauser, C. (2004, May 6). Many Iraqis are skeptical of Bush TV appeal. *New York Times*, p. 13.

Havas, D.A., Glenberg, A. M., Gutowski, K. A., Lucarelli, M. J., & Davidson, R. J. (2010). Cosmetic use of botulinum toxin-A affects processing of emotional language. *Psychological Science, 21*, 895–900.

Hazan, C., & Shaver, P. (1987). Romantic love conceptualized as an attachment process. *Journal of Personality and Social Psychology, 52*, 511–524.

Hazan, C., & Shaver, P. (1994). Attachment as an organizational framework for research on close relationships. *Psychological Inquiry, 5*, 1–22.

Heath, S. B. (1982). What no bedtime story means: Narrative skills at home and school. *Language in Society, 11*, 49–79.

Heath, S. B. (1983). *Ways with words*. Cambridge, England: Cambridge University Press.

Heatherton, T. F., Macrae, C. N., & Kelley, W. M. (2004). What the social brain sciences can tell us about the self. *Current Directions in Psychological Science, 13*, 190–193.

Heatherton, T. F., & Polivy, J. (1991). Development and validation of a scale for measuring state self-esteem. *Journal of Personality and Social Psychology, 60*, 895–910.

Heatherton, T. F., Wyland, C. L., McCrae, C. N., Demos, K. E., Denny, B. T., & Keley, W. M. (2006). Medial prefrontal activity differentiates self from close others. *Social Cognitive Affective Neuroscience, 1*, 18–25.

Hebl, M. R., Foster, J. B., Mannix, L. M., & Dovidio, J. F. (2002). Formal and interpersonal discrimination: A field study of bias toward homosexual applicants. *Personality and Social Psychology Bulletin, 28*, 815–825.

Hebl, M., & Heatherton, T. F. (1997). The stigma of obesity in women: The difference is black and white. *Personality and Social Psychology Bulletin, 24*, 417–426.

Hedden, T., Ji, L., Jing, Q., Jiao, S., Yao, C., Nisbett, R. E., et al. (2000). *Culture and age differences in recognition memory for social dimensions*. Paper presented at the Cognitive Aging Conference, Atlanta, GA.

Hedden, T., Ketay, S., Aron, A., Markus, H. R., & Gabrieli, J. D. E. (2008). Cultural influences on neural substrates of attentional control. *Psychological Science, 19*, 12–17.

Heider, F. (1958). *The psychology of interpersonal relations*. New York: Wiley.

Heine, S. J. (2005). Constructing good selves in Japan and North America. In *Culture and social behavior: The Tenth Ontario Symposium* (pp. 115–143). Hillsdale, NJ: Erlbaum.

Heine, S. J., Kitayama, S., Lehman, D. R., Takata, T., Ide, E., Leung, C., & Matsumoto, H. (2001). Divergent consequences of success and failure in Japan and North America: An investigation of self-improving motivations and malleable selves. *Journal of Personality and Social Psychology, 81*, 599–615.

Heine, S. J., & Lehman, D. R. (1997). Culture, dissonance, and self-affirmation. *Personality and Social Psychology Bulletin, 23*, 389–400.

Heine, S. J., & Lehman, D. R. (2003). Move the body, change the self: Acculturative effects on the self-concept. In M. Schaller & C. S. Crandall (Eds.), *Psychological foundations of culture* (pp. 305–331). Mahwah, NJ: Erlbaum.

Heine, S. J., Lehman, D. R., Markus, H. R., & Kitayama, S. (1999). Is there a universal need for positive self-regard? *Psychological Review, 106*, 766–794.

Helgeson, V. S., & Mickelson, K. D. (1995). Motives for social comparison. *Personality and Social Psychology Bulletin, 21*, 1200–1209.

Helliwell, J. F., & Putnam, R. D. (2004). The social context of well-being. Philosophical Transactions of the Royal Society B: *Biological Sciences*, 359(1449), 1435–1446. doi:10.1098/rstb.2004.1522

Henderson, V. L., & Dweck, C. S. (1990). Achievement and motivation in adolescence: A new model and data. In S. Feldman & G. Elliott (Eds.), *At the threshold: The developing adolescent*. Cambridge, MA: Harvard University Press.

Hendrix, K. S., & Hirt, E. R.(2009).Stressed out over possible failure: The role of regulatory fit on claimed self-handicapping. *Journal of Experimental Social Psychology, 45*, 51–59.

Henley, N. M., & LaFrance, M. (1984). Gender as culture: Difference and dominance in nonverbal behavior. In A. Wolfgang (Ed.), *Nonverbal behavior: Perspectives, applications, intercultural insights*. Lewiston, NY: C. J. Hogrefe.

Henningsen, D. D., Henningsen, M. L. M., Eden, J., & Cruz, M. G. (2006). Examining the symptoms of groupthink and retrospective sensemaking. *Small Group Research, 37*, 36–64.

Henrich, J., & Boyd, R. (1998). The evolution of conformist transmission and the emergence of between-group differences. *Evolution and Human Behavior, 19*, 215–242.

Henrich, J., Boyd, R., Bowles, S., Camerer, C., Gintis, H., McElreath, R., et al. (2001). In search of *Homo economicus*: Experiments in 15 small-scale societies. *American Economic Review, 91(2)*, 73–79.

Henrich, J., Heine, S. J., & Norenzayan, A. (2010). The weirdest people in the world? *Behavioral and Brain Sciences, 33*, 61–83.

Hepworth, J. T., & West, S. G. (1988). Lynchings and the economy: A time-series reanalysis of Hovland and Sears (1940). *Journal of Personality and Social Psychology, 55*, 239–247.

Herek, G. M. (1998). *Stigma and sexual orientation: Understanding prejudice against lesbians, gay men, and bisexuals*. Thousand Oaks, CA: Sage.

Herr, P. M. (1986). Consequences of priming: Judgment and behavior. *Journal of Personality and Social Psychology, 51,* 1106–1115.

Hertenstein, M. J. (2002). Touch: Its communicative functions in infancy. *Human Development, 45,* 70–94.

Hertenstein, M. J., Keltner, D., App, B., Bulleit, B. A., & Jaskolka, A. R. (2006). Touch communicates distinct emotions. *Emotion, 6,* 528–533.

Hess, U., Banse, R., & Kappas, A. (1995). The intensity of facial expression is determined by underlying affective states and social situations. *Journal of Personality and Social Psychology, 69,* 280–288.

Hewstone, M., & Jaspers, J. (1983). A re-examination of the roles of consensus, consistency, & distinctiveness: Kelley's cube revisited. *British Journal of Social Psychology, 22,* 41–50.

Hewstone, M., & Jaspers, J. (1987). Covariation and causal attribution: A logical model of the intuitive analysis of variance. *Journal of Personality and Social Psychology, 53,* 663–672.

Higgins, E. T. (1987). Self discrepancy: A theory relating self and affect. *Psychological Review, 94,* 319–340.

Higgins, E. T. (1996). Ideals, oughts, and regulatory focus: Affect and motivation from distinct pains and pleasures. In P. M. Gollwitzer & J. A. Bargh (Eds.), *The psychology of action: Linking cognition and motivation to behavior* (pp. 91–114). New York: Guilford Press.

Higgins, E. T. (1999). Promotion and prevention as motivational duality: Implications for evaluative processes. In S. Chaiken & Y. Trope (Eds.), *Dual-process theories in social psychology.* New York: Guilford Press.

Higgins, E. T., & Brendl, M. (1995). Accessibility and applicability: Some "activation rules" influencing judgment. *Journal of Experimental Social Psychology, 31,* 218–243.

Higgins, E. T., King, G. A., & Mavin, G. H. (1982). Individual construct accessibility and subjective impressions and recall. *Journal of Personality and Social Psychology, 43,* 35–47.

Higgins, E. T., Rholes, W. S., & Jones, C. R. (1977). Category accessibility and impression formation. *Journal of Experimental Social Psychology, 13,* 141–154.

Higgins, E. T., Shah, J., & Friedman, R. (1997). Emotional responses to goal attainment: Strength of regulatory focus as a moderator. *Journal of Personality and Social Psychology, 72,* 515–525.

Hilton, D. J., & Slugoski, B. R. (1986). Knowledge-based causal attribution: The abnormal conditions focus model. *Psychological Review, 93,* 75–88.

Hilton, D. J., Smith, R. H., & Kim, S. H. (1995). Process of causal explanation and dispositional attribution. *Journal of Personality and Social Psychology, 68,* 377–387.

Hinsz, V. B., Tindale, R. S., & Vollrath, D. A. (1997). The emerging conceptualization of groups as information processors. *Psychological Bulletin, 121,* 43–64.

Hirshleifer, D., & Shumway, T. (2003). Good day sunshine: Stock returns and the weather. *Journal of Finance, 58*(3), 1009–1032.

Hirt, E. R. (1990). Do I see only what I expect? Evidence for an expectancy-guided retrieval model. *Journal of Personality and Social Psychology, 58,* 937–951.

Hirt, E. R., MacDonald, H. E., & Erikson, G. A. (1995). How do I remember thee? The role of encoding set and delay in reconstructive memory processes. *Journal of Experimental Social Psychology, 31,* 379–409.

Hirt, E. R., McCrea, S. M., & Kimble, C. E. (2000). Public self-focus and sex differences in behavioral self-handicapping: Does increasing self-threat still make it just a man's game? *Personality and Social Psychology Bulletin, 26,* 1131–1141.

Hirt, E. R., Zillman, D., Erickson, G. A., & Kennedy, C. (1992). Costs and benefits of allegiance: Changes in fans' self-ascribed competencies after team victory versus defeat. *Journal of Personality and Social Psychology, 63,* 724–738.

Ho, C., & Jackson, J. W. (2001). Attitudes toward Asian Americans: Theory and measurement. *Journal of Applied Social Psychology, 31,* 1553–1581.

Hobart, C. (1991). Conflict in remarriages. *Journal of Divorce and Remarriage, 15,* 69–86.

Hodson, G., Dovidio, J. F., & Gaertner, S. L. (2002). Processes in racial discrimination: Differential weighting of conflicting information. *Personality and Social Psychology Bulletin, 28,* 460–471.

Hoeksema-van Orden, C. Y. D., Gaillard, A. W. K., & Buunk, B. P. (1998). Social loafing under fatigue. *Journal of Personality and Social Psychology, 75,* 1179–1190.

Hofstede, G. (1980). *Culture's consequences: International differences in work-related values.* Beverly Hills, CA: Sage.

Holland, R. W., Hendricks, M., & Aarts, H. (2005). Smells like clean spirit: Nonconscious effects of scent on cognition and behavior. *Psychological Science, 16,* 689–693.

Holloway, S. (1988). Concepts of ability and effort in Japan and the United States. *Review of Educational Research, 58,* 327–345.

Holtgraves, T., & Lasky, B. (1999). Linguistic power and persuasion. *Journal of Language and Social Psychology, 18,* 196–205.

Holyoak, K. J., & Thagard, P. (1995). *Mental leaps: Analogy in creative thought.* Cambridge, MA: MIT Press.

Homans, G. C. (1965). Group factors in worker productivity. In H. Proshansky & L. Seidenberg (Eds.), *Basic studies in social psychology.* New York: Holt.

Hong, Y., Chiu, C., & Kung, T. (1997). Bringing culture out in front: Effects of cultural meaning system activation on social cognition. In K. Leung, U. Kim, S. Yamaguchi, & Y. Kashima (Eds.), *Progress in Asian social psychology* (Vol. 1, pp. 135–146). Singapore: Wiley.

Hoorens, V., & Ruiter, S. (1996). The optimal impact phenomenon: Beyond the third person effect. *European Journal of Social Psychology, 26,* 599–610.

Horberg, E. J., Oveis, C., Keltner, D., & Cohen, A. B. (2009). Disgust and the moralization of purity. *Journal of Personality and Social Psychology, 97,* 963–976.

Hosey, G. R., Wood, M., Thompson, R. J., & Druck, P. L. (1985). Social facilitation in a non-social animal, the centipede *Lithobius forficatus. Behavioral Processes, 10,* 123–130.

Hoshino-Browne, E., Zanna, A. S., Spencer, S. J., & Zanna, M. P. (2004). Investigating attitudes cross-culturally: A case of cognitive dissonance among East Asians and North Americans. In G. Haddock & G. R. Maio (Eds.), *Contemporary perspectives on the psychology of attitudes* (pp. 375–397). East Sussex, England: Psychology Press.

Hosman, L. A. (1989). The evaluative consequences of hedges, hesitations, and intensifiers: Powerful and powerless speech styles. *Human Communication Research, 15,* 383–406.

Hovland, C. I., Janis, I. L., & Kelley, H. H. (1953). *Communication and persuasion: Psychological studies of opinion change.* New Haven, CT: Yale University Press.

Hovland, C. J., Lumsdaine, A. A., & Sheffield, F. D. (1949). *Experiments on mass communication.* Princeton, NJ: Princeton University Press.

Hovland, C. J., & Sears, R. R. (1940). Minor studies in aggression: VI. Correlation of lynchings with economic indices. *Journal of Abnormal and Social Psychology, 9,* 301–310.

Hovland, C. J., & Weiss, W. (1951). The influence of source credibility on communication effectiveness. *Public Opinion Quarterly, 15,* 635–660.

Howard, J. W., & Rothbart, M. (1980). Social categorization and memory for ingroup and outgroup behavior. *Journal of Personality and Social Psychology, 38,* 301–310.

Hrdy, S. B. (1999). *Mother nature: A history of mothers, infants, and natural selection.* New York: Pantheon.

Hsiang, S. M., Meng, K. C., & Cane, M. A. (2011). Civil conflicts are associated with the global climate. *Nature, 476,* 438–441.

Hsu, F. L. K. (1953). *Americans and Chinese: Two ways of life.* New York: Schuman.

Hubschman, J. H., & Stack, M. A. (1992). Parasite-induced changes in *Chironomus decorus* (Diptera: Chironomidae). *Journal of Parasitology, 78,* 872–875.

Huesmann, L. R. (1986). Psychological processes promoting the relations between exposure to media violence and aggressive behavior by the viewer. *Journal of Social Issues, 42,* 125–139.

Huesmann, L. R., Moise-Titus, J., Podolski, C.-L., & Eron, L. D. (2003). Longitudinal relations between children's exposure to TV violence and their aggressive and violent behavior in young adulthood: 1977–1992. *Developmental Psychology, 39,* 201–221.

Hughes, M. E., & Waite, L. J. (2009). Marital biography and health at midlife. *Journal of Health and Social Behavior, 50*(3), 344–358.

Hugo, P., & Dominus, S. (2014). Portraits of reconciliation. *New York Times Interactive Magazine,* April 6, 2014.

Huguet, P., Galvaing, M. P., Monteil, J. M., & Dumas, F. (1999). Social presence effects in the Stroop task: Further evidence for an attentional view of social facilitation. *Journal of Personality and Social Psychology, 77,* 1011–1025.

Humphrey, R. (1985). How work roles influence perception: Structural-cognitive processes and organizational behavior. *American Sociological Review, 50,* 242-252.

Hunter, J. E., & Hunter, R. F. (1984). Validity and utility of alternative predictors of job performance. *Psychological Bulletin, 96,* 72–98.

Huntley, J. (1990). *The elements of astrology.* Shaftesbury, Dorset, England: Element Books Unlimited.

Ijerman, H., & Semin, G. R. (2009). The thermometer of social relations: Mapping social proximity on temperature. *Psychological Science, 20,* 1214–1210.

Iliffe, A. H. (1960). A study of preferences in feminine beauty. *British Journal of Psychology, 51,* 267–273.

Inagaki, T. K., & Eisenberger, N. (2013). Shared neural mechanisms underlying social and physical warmth. *Psychological Science, 24,* 2272–2280.

Inbar, Y., Pizarro, D.A., & Bloom (2012). Disgusting smells cause decreased liking of gay men. *Emotion, 12,* 23-27.Inbau, F. E., Reid, J. E., Buckley, J. P., & Jayne, B. C. (2001). *Criminal interrogation and confessions* (4th ed.). Gaithersburg, MD: Aspen.

Independent Sector. (2002). *Giving and volunteering in the United States.* Washington, DC: Independent Sector.

Innes, J. M., & Zeitz, H. (1988). The public's view of the impact of the mass media: A test of the "third person" effect. *European Journal of Social Psychology, 18,* 457–463.

Insel, T. R., Young, L., & Zuoxin, W. (1997). Molecular aspects of monogamy. In C. S. Carter & I. I. Lederhendler (Eds.), *Annals of the New York Academy of Sciences* (Vol. 807, pp. 302–316). New York: New York Academy of Sciences.

Insko, C. A., Smith, R. H., Alicke, M. D., Wade, J., & Taylor, S. (1985). Conformity and group size: The concern with being right and the concern with being liked. *Personality and Social Psychology Bulletin, 11,* 41–50.

Inzlicht, M., Aronson, J., & Mendoza-Denton, R. (2009). On being the target of prejudice: Educational implications. In F. Butera & J. Levine (Eds.) *Coping with minority status: Responses to exclusion and inclusion* (pp. 13–37). Cambridge, England: Cambridge University Press.

Inzlicht, M., & Ben-Zeev, T. (2000). A threatening intellectual environment: Why females are susceptible to experiencing problem-solving deficits in the presence of males. *Psychological Science, 11,* 365–371.

Inzlicht, M., Schmeichel, B. J., & Macrae, C. N. (2014). Why self-control seems (but may not be) limited. *Trends in Cognitive Sciences, 18,* 127–133.

Ip, G. W. M., & Bond, M. H. (1995). Culture, values, and the spontaneous self-concept. *Asian Journal of Psychology, 1,* 29–35.

Isen, A. M. (1987). Positive affect, cognitive processes, and social behavior. In L. Berkowitz (Ed.), *Advances in experimental social psychology* (pp. 203–253). New York: Academic Press.

Isen, A. M. (1993). Positive affect and decision making. In M. Lewis & J. M. Haviland-Jones (Eds.), *Handbook of emotions* (pp. 261–278). New York: Guilford Press.

Isen, A. M. (1999). Positive affect. In T. Dalgleish & M. J. Power (Eds.), *Handbook of cognition and emotion* (pp. 521–539). Chichester, England: Wiley.

Isen, A. M., Clark, M., & Schwartz, M. F. (1976). Duration of the effect of good mood on helping: Footprints on the sands of time. *Journal of Personality and Social Psychology, 34,* 385–393.

Isen, A. M., & Levin, P. F. (1972). Effect of feeling good on helping: Cookies and kindness. *Journal of Personality and Social Psychology, 21,* 384–388.

Ito, T. A., Larsen, J. T., Smith, N. K., & Cacioppo, J. T. (1998). Negative information weighs more heavily on the brain: The negativity bias in evaluative categorizations. *Journal of Personality and Social Psychology, 75,* 887–900.

Iyengar, S. (2004). Engineering consent: The renaissance of mass communications research in politics. In J. T. Jost, M. R. Banaji, & D. Prentice (Eds.), *Perspectives in social psychology: The yin and the yang of scientific progress: Perspectives on the social psychology of thought systems.* Washington, DC: APA Press.

Iyengar, S., & Kinder, D. (1987). *News that matters: Television and American opinion.* Chicago: University of Chicago Press.

Iyengar, S. S., & Lepper, M. R. (2000). When choice is demotivating: Can one desire too much of a good thing? *Journal of Personality and Social Psychology, 79,* 995–1006.

Izard, C. E. (1971). *The face of emotion.* New York: Appleton -Century-Crofts.

Izard, C. E. (1994). Innate and universal facial expressions: Evidence from developmental and cross-cultural research. *Psychological Bulletin, 115,* 288–299.

Jackson, L. A., Hunter, J. E., & Hodge, C. N. (1995). Physical attractiveness and intellectual competence: A meta-analytic review. *Social Psychology Quarterly, 58,* 108–122.

Jacobson, G. C. (1978). The effects of campaign spending in house elections. *American Political Science Review, 72,* 469–1191.

Jacoby, L. L., & Dallas, M. (1981). On the relationship between autobiographical memory and perceptual learning. *Journal of Experimental Psychology, 3,* 306–340.

Jacoby, L. L., Woloshyn, V., & Kelley, C. (1989). Becoming famous without being recognized: Unconscious influences of memory produced by dividing attention. *Journal of Experimental Psychology: General, 118*, 115–125.

James, W. (1884). What is an emotion? *Mind, 9*, 188–205.

James, W. (1890). *Principles of psychology*. New York: Holt.

Janes, L. M., & Olson, J. M. (2000). Jeer pressure: The behavioral effects of observing ridicule of others. *Personality and Social Psychology Bulletin, 26*, 474–485.

Janis, I. L. (1972). *Victims of groupthink*. Boston: Houghton Mifflin.

Janis, I. L. (1982). *Groupthink: Psychological studies of policy decisions and fiascos* (2nd ed.). Boston: Houghton Mifflin.

Janis, I. L., & Mann, L. (1977). *Decision making*. New York: Free Press.

Jeffery, R. W. (1996). Does weight cycling present a health risk? *American Journal of Clinical Nutrition, 63*, 452S–455S.

Jellison, J. M., & Riskind, J. (1970). A social comparison of abilities interpretation of risk-taking behavior. *Journal of Personality and Social Psychology, 15*, 375–390.

Jemmott, J. B. III, Jemmott, L. S., Braverman, P. K., & Fong, G. T. (2005). HIV/STD risk reduction interventions for African American and Latino adolescent girls at an inner-city adolescent medicine clinic: A randomized controlled trial. *Archives of Pediatrics and Adolescent Medicine, 159*, 440–449.

Jemmott, J. B. III, Jemmott, L. S., & Fong, G. T. (1998). Abstinence and safer sex: A randomized controlled trial of HIV sexual risk-reduction interventions for young African American adolescents. *Journal of the American Medical Association, 279*, 1529–1536.

Jenni, K., & Loewenstein, G. (1997). Explaining the identifiable victim effect. *Journal of Risk and Uncertainty, 14*(3), 235–257.

Ji, L., Schwarz, N., & Nisbett, R. E. (2000). Culture, autobiographical memory, and social comparison: Measurement issues in cross-cultural studies. *Personality and Social Psychology Bulletin, 26*, 585–593.

Ji, L. J., Nisbett, R. E., & Su, Y. (2001). Culture, change, and prediction. *Psychological Science, 12*, 450–456.

Ji, L. J., Zhang, Z., & Guo, T. (2008). To buy or to sell: Cultural differences in stock market decisions based on stock price trends. *Journal of Behavioral Decision Making, 21*, 399–413.

Job, R. F. S. (1988). Effective and ineffective use of fear in health promotion campaigns. *American Journal of Public Health, 78*, 163–167.

Job, V., Dweck, C. S., & Walton, G. M. (2010). Ego depletion—Is it all in your head?: Implicit theories about willpower affect self-regulation . *Psychological Science, 21*, 1686–1693.

Joel, S., Gordon, A. M., Impett, E. A., MacDonald, G., & Keltner, D. (2013). The things you do for me: Perceptions of a romantic partner's investments promote gratitude and commitment. *Personality and Social Psychology Bulletin, 39*, 1333–1345.

John, O. P., & Robins, R. W. (1994). Accuracy and bias in self-perception: Individual differences in self-enhancement and the role of narcissism. *Journal of Personality & Social Psychology, 66*(1), 206–219.

Johnson, J. T. (1986). The knowledge of what might have been: Affective and attributional consequences of near outcomes. *Personality and Social Psychology Bulletin, 12*, 51–62.

Johnson, K. J., & Fredrickson, B. L. (2005). We all look the same to me: Positive emotions eliminate the own-race-bias in face recognition. *Psychological Science, 16*, 875–881.

Jones, C., & Aronson, E. (1973). Attribution of fault to a rape victim as a function of the respectability of the victim. *Journal of Personality and Social Psychology, 26*, 415–419.

Jones, E. E. (1964). *Ingratiation*. New York: Appleton-Century-Crofts.

Jones, E. E., & Berglas, S. (1978). Control of attributions about the self through self-handicapping strategies: The appeal of alcohol and the role of underachievement. *Personality and Social Psychology Bulletin, 4*, 200–206.

Jones, E. E., & Davis, K. E. (1965). From acts to dispositions: The attribution process in person perception. In L. Berkowitz (Ed.), *Advances in experimental social psychology* (Vol. 2, pp. 219–266). New York: Academic Press.

Jones, E. E., Davis, K. E., & Gergen, K. J. (1961). Role-playing variations and their informational value for person perception. *Journal of Abnormal and Social Psychology, 63*, 302–310.

Jones, E. E., Farina, A., Hastorf, A. H., Markus, H., Miller, D. T., & Scott, R. A. (1984). *Social stigma: The psychology of marked relationships*. New York: Freeman.

Jones, E. E., & Harris, V. A. (1967). The attribution of attitudes. *Journal of Experimental Social Psychology, 3*, 1–24.

Jones, E. E., & Nisbett, R. E. (1972). The actor and the observer: Divergent perceptions of the causes of behavior. In E. E. Jones, D. E. Kanouse, H. H. Kelley, R. E. Nisbett, S. Valins, & B. Weiner (Eds.), *Attribution: Perceiving the causes of behavior*. Morristown, NJ: General Learning Press.

Joshi, P., & Wakslak, C. J. (2014) Communicating with the crowd: Speakers use abstract messages when addressing larger audiences. *Journal of Experimental Psychology: General, 143*, 351–362.

Jost, J. T. (1997). An experimental replication of the depressed entitlement effect among women. *Psychology of Women Quarterly, 21*, 387–393.

Jost, J. T., & Banaji, M. R. (1994). The role of stereotyping in system justification and the production of false consciousness. *British Journal of Social Psychology, 33*, 1–27.

Jost, J. T., Banaji, M. R., & Nosek, B. A. (2004). A decade of system justification theory: Accumulated evidence of conscious and unconscious bolstering of the status quo. *Political Psychology, 25*, 881–919.

Jost, J. T., & Kay, A. C. (2005). Exposure to benevolent sexism and complementary gender stereotypes: Consequences for specific and diffuse forms of system justification. *Journal of Personality and Social Psychology, 88*, 498–509.

Jost, J. T., Pelham, B. W., Sheldon, O., & Sullivan, B. N. (2003). Social inequality and the reduction of ideological dissonance on behalf of the system: Evidence of enhanced system justification among the disadvantaged. *European Journal of Social Psychology, 33*, 13–36.

Jost, J. T., & van der Toorn, J. (2012). System justification theory. In P. A. M. Van Lange, A. W. Kruglanski, & E. T. Higgins (Eds), *Handbook of theories of social psychology* (Vol. 2, pp. 313–343). Thousand Oaks, CA: Sage Publications.

Jostmann, N. B., Lakens, D., & Schubert, T. W. (2009). Weight as an embodiment of importance. *Psychological Science, 20*(9), 1169–1174.

Jourard, S. M. (1966). An exploratory study of body accessibility. *British Journal of Social and Clinical Psychology, 5*, 221–231.

Judd, C. M., Blair, I. V., & Chapleau, K. M. (2004). Automatic stereotypes vs. automatic prejudice: Sorting out the possibilities in the Payne (2001) weapon paradigm. *Journal of Experimental Social Psychology, 40*, 75–81.

Judd, C. M., Drake, R. A., Downing, J. W., & Krosnick, J. A. (1991). Some dynamic properties of attitude structures: Context induced responses facilitation and polarization. *Journal of Personality and Social Psychology, 60,* 193–202.

Judd, C. M., & Lusk, C. M. (1984). Knowledge structures and evaluative judgments: Effects of structural variables on judgment extremity. *Journal of Personality and Social Psychology, 46,* 1193–1207.

Judd, C. M., & Park, B. (1993). The assessment of accuracy of social stereotypes. *Psychological Review, 100,* 109–128.

Judge, T. A., Bono, J. E., Hies, R., & Gerhardt, M. W. (2002). Personality and leadership: A qualitative and quantitative review. *Journal of Applied Psychology, 87,* 765–780.

Jung, C. G. (1960). *Synchronicity: An acausal connecting principle.* Princeton, NJ: Princeton University Press.

Jussim, L. (1986). Self-fulfilling prophecies: A theoretical and integrative review. *Psychological Review, 93,* 429–445.

Jussim, L., Eccles, J., & Madon, S. J. (1996). Social perception, social stereotypes, and teacher expectations: Accuracy and the quest for the powerful self-fulfilling prophecy. *Advances in Experimental Social Psychology, 29,* 281–388.

Jussim, L., & Harber, K. (2005). Teacher expectations and self-fulfilling prophecies: Knowns and unknowns, resolved and unresolved controversies. *Personality and Social Psychology Review, 9,* 131–155.

Kahneman, D. (1999). Objective happiness. In D. Kahneman, E. Diener, & N. Schwarz (Eds.), *Hedonic psychology.* New York: Cambridge University Press.

Kahneman, D., & Frederick, S. (2002). Representativeness revisited: Attribute substitution in intuitive judgment. In T. Gilovich, D. W. Griffin, & D. Kahneman (Eds.), *Heuristics and biases: The psychology of intuitive judgment* (pp. 49–81). New York: Cambridge University Press.

Kahneman, D., & Lovallo, D. (1993). Timid choices and bold forecasts: A cognitive perspective on risk taking. *Management Science, 39,* 17–31.

Kahneman, D., & Miller, D. T. (1986). Norm theory: Comparing reality to its alternatives. *Psychological Review, 93,* 136–153.

Kahneman, D., Schkade, D., & Sunstein, C. R. (1998). Shared outrage and erratic awards: The psychology of punitive damages. *Journal of Risk and Uncertainty, 16,* 49–86.

Kahneman, D., Slovic, P., & Tversky, A. (1982). *Judgment under uncertainty: Heuristics and biases.* New York: Cambridge University Press.

Kahneman, D., & Tversky, A. (1972). Subjective probability: A judgment of representativeness. *Cognitive Psychology, 3,* 430–454.

Kahneman, D., & Tversky, A. (1973a). Availability: A heuristic for judging frequency and probability. *Cognitive Psychology, 4,* 207–232.

Kahneman, D., & Tversky, A. (1973b). On the psychology of prediction. *Psychological Review, 80,* 237–251.

Kahneman, D., & Tversky, A. (1982a). The simulation heuristic. In D. Kahneman, P. Slovic, & A. Tversky (Eds.), *Judgment under certainty: Heuristics and biases* (pp. 201–208). New York: Cambridge University Press.

Kahneman, D., & Tversky, A. (1982b). Variants of uncertainty. *Cognition, 11,* 143–157.

Kahneman, D., & Tversky, A. (1995). On the reality of cognitive illusions. *Psychological Review, 103,* 582–591.

Kaid, L. L. (1981). Political advertising. In D. D. Nimmo & K. R. Sanders (Eds.), *Handbook of political communication.* Beverly Hills, CA: Sage.

Kalven, H., & Zeisel, H. (1966). *The American jury.* Boston: Little, Brown.

Kamarck, T. W., Manuch, S., & Jennings, J. R. (1990). Social support reduces cardiovascular reactivity to psychological challenge: A laboratory model. *Psychosomatic Medicine, 52,* 42–58.

Kamstra, M. J., Kramer, L. A., & Levi, M. D. (2003). Winter blues: Seasonal affective disorder (SAD) and stock market returns. *American Economic Review, 93,* 324–343.

Kaplan, M. F., & Schersching, C. (1981). Juror deliberation: An information integration analysis. In B. Sales (Ed.), *The trial process* (pp. 235–262). New York: Plenum.

Karau, S. J., & Williams, K. D. (1995). Social loafing: Research findings, implications, and future directions. *Current Directions in Psychological Science, 4,* 134–140.

Karmarkar, U. R., & Tormala, Z. L. (2010). Believe me, I have no idea what I'm talking about: The effects of source certainty on consumer involvement and persuasion. *Journal of Consumer Research, 36,* 1033–1049.

Karney, B. R., & Bradbury, T. N. (1995). The longitudinal course of marital quality and stability: A review of theory, method, and research. *Psychological Bulletin, 118,* 3–34.

Karney, B. R., & Bradbury, T. N. (1997). Neuroticism, marital interaction, and the trajectory of marital satisfaction. *Journal of Personality and Social Psychology, 72,* 1075–1092.

Karney, B. R., & Bradbury, T. N. (2000). Attributions in marriage: State or trait? A growth curve analysis. *Journal of Personality and Social Psychology, 78,* 295–309.

Karney, B. R., Bradbury, T. N, Fincham, F. D., & Sullivan, K. T. (1994). The role of negative affectivity in the association between attributions and marital satisfaction. *Journal of Personality and Social Psychology, 66,* 413–424.

Karpinski, A., & Hilton, J. L. (2001). Attitudes and the Implicit Association Test. *Journal of Personality and Social Psychology, 81,* 774–788.

Kashima, Y., Siegal, M., Tanaka, K., & Kashima, E. S. (1992). Do people believe behaviours are consistent with attitudes? Towards a cultural psychology of attribution processes. *British Journal of Social Psychology, 37,* 111–124.

Kashima, Y., Yamaguchi, S., Kim, U., Choi, S.-C, Gelfand, M. J., & Yuki, M. (1995). Culture, gender, and self: A perspective from individualism-collectivism research. *Journal of Personality and Social Psychology, 69,* 925–937.

Kasof, J. (1993). Sex bias in the naming of stimulus persons. *Psychological Bulletin, 113,* 140–165.

Kasser, T., & Sheldon, K. M. (2000). Of wealth and death: Materialism, mortality salience, and consumption behavior. *Psychological Science, 11,* 348–351.

Kassin, S. (1985). Eyewitness identification: Retrospective self-awareness and the accuracy-confidence correlation. *Journal of Personality and Social Psychology, 49,* 878–893.

Kassin, S. M., Goldstein, C. C., & Savitsky, K. (2003). Behavioral confirmation in the interrogation room: On the dangers of presuming guilt. *Law and Human Behavior, 27(2),* 187–203.

Kassin, S. M., Meissner, C., & Norwick, R. J. (2005). "I'd know a false confession if I saw one": A comparative study of college students and police investigators. *Law and Human Behavior, 29,* 211–227.

Kassin, S. M., & Sukel, H. (1997). Coerced confessions and the jury: An experimental test of the "harmless error" rule. *Law and Human Behavior, 21,* 27–46.

Katz, I., Glucksberg, S., & Krauss, R. (1960). Need satisfaction and Edwards PPS scores in married couples. *Journal of Consulting Psychology, 24,* 205–208.

Kay, A. C., & Jost, J. T. (2003). Complementary justice: Effects of "poor but happy" and "poor but honest" stereotype exemplars on system justification and implicit activation of the justice motive. *Journal of Personality and Social Psychology, 85,* 823–837.

Kay, A. C., Wheeler, S. C., Bargh, J. A., & Ross, L. (2004). Material priming: The influence of mundane physical objects on situation construal and competitive behavioral choice. *Organizational Behavior and Human Decision Processes, 95,* 83–96.

Kelley, H. H. (1967). Attribution theory in social psychology. In D. Levine (Ed.), *Nebraska Symposium on Motivation* (Vol. 15, pp. 192–238). Lincoln: University of Nebraska Press.

Kelley, H. H. (1973). The processes of causal attribution. *American Psychologist, 28,* 107–128.

Kelley, H. H., & Thibaut, J. W. (1978). *Interpersonal relations: A theory of interdependence.* New York: Wiley.

Kelman, H. C. (1958). Compliance, identification, and internalization: Three processes of attitude change. *Journal of Conflict Resolution, 2,* 51–60.

Keltner, D. (1995). The signs of appeasement: Evidence for the distinct displays of embarrassment, amusement, and shame. *Journal of Personality and Social Psychology, 68,* 441–454.

Keltner, D., & Anderson, C. (2000). Saving face for Darwin: Functions and uses of embarrassment. *Current Directions in Psychological Science, 9,* 187–191.

Keltner, D., & Bonanno, G. A. (1997). A study of laughter and dissociation: The distinct correlates of laughter and smiling during bereavement. *Journal of Personality and Social Psychology, 73,* 687–702.

Keltner, D., & Buswell, B. N. (1997). Embarrassment: Its distinct form and appeasement functions. *Psychological Bulletin, 122,* 250–270.

Keltner, D., Capps, L. M., Kring, A. M., Young, R. C., & Heerey, E. A. (2001). Just teasing: A conceptual analysis and empirical review. *Psychological Bulletin, 127,* 229–248.

Keltner, D., Ellsworth, P. C., & Edwards, K. (1993). Beyond simple pessimism: Effects of sadness and anger on social perception. *Journal of Personality and Social Psychology, 64,* 740–752.

Keltner, D., Gruenfeld, D. H., & Anderson, C. A. (2003). Power, approach, and inhibition. *Psychological Review, 110,* 265–284.

Keltner, D., & Haidt, J. (1999). Social functions of emotions at four levels of analysis. *Cognition and Emotion, 13,* 505–521.

Keltner, D., & Haidt, J. (2003). Approaching awe: A moral, spiritual, and aesthetic emotion. *Cognition and Emotion, 17,* 297–314.

Keltner, D., Kogan, A., Piff, P., & Saturn, S. (2014). The Sociocultural Appraisal, Values, and Emotions (SAVE) Model of Prosociality: Core Processes from Gene to Meme. *Annual Review of Psychology, 65,* 425–460.

Keltner, D., Locke, K. D., & Audrain, P. C. (1993). The influence of attributions on the relevance of negative feelings to personal satisfaction. *Personality and Social Psychology Bulletin, 19,* 21–29.

Keltner, D., Moffitt, T., & Stouthamer-Loeber, M. (1995). Facial expressions of emotion and psychopathology in adolescent boys. *Journal of Abnormal Psychology, 104,* 644–652.

Keltner, D., Van Kleef, G. A., Chen, S., & Kraus, M. W. (2008). A reciprocal influence model of social power: Emerging principles and lines of inquiry. *Advances in Experimental Social Psychology, 40,* 151–192.

Keltner, D., Young, R. C., Heerey, E. A., Oemig, C., & Monarch, N. D. (1998). Teasing in hierarchial and intimate relations. *Journal of Personality and Social Psychology, 75,* 1231–1247.

Kemper, T. D. (1991). Predicting emotions from social relations. *Social Psychology Quarterly, 54,* 330–342.

Kenny, D. A., & DePaulo, B. M. (1993). Do people know how others view them? An empirical and theoretical account. *Psychological Bulletin, 114,* 145–161.

Kenrick, D. T., & Keefe, R. C. (1992). Age preferences in mates reflect sex differences in reproductive strategies. *Behavioral and Brain Sciences, 15,* 75–133.

Kenrick, D. T., & MacFarlane, S. W. (1984). Ambient temperature and horn-honking: A field study of the heat/aggression relationship. *Environment and Behavior, 18,* 179–191.

Kernis, M. H. (2005). Measuring self-esteem in context: The importance of stability of self-esteem in psychological functioning. *Journal of Personality, 73,* 1569–1605.

Kernis, M. H., Cornell, D. P., Sun, C. R., & Harlow, T. (1993). There's more to self-esteem than whether it is high or low: the importance of stability of self-esteem. *Journal of Personality and Social Psychology, 65,* 190–204.

Kerr, N. L. (1981). Social transition schemes: Charting the group's road to agreement. *Journal of Personality and Social Psychology, 41,* 684–702.

Kerr, N. L., Kramer, G. P., Carroll, J. S., & Alfini, J. J. (1991). On the effectiveness of voir dire in criminal cases with prejudicial pretrial publicity: An empirical study. *American University Law Review, 40,* 665–701.

Kerr, N. L., MacCoun, R. J., & Kramer, G. P. (1996). Bias in judgment: Comparing individuals and groups. *Psychological Review, 103,* 687–719.

Ketelaar, T. (2005). Emotions and economic decision-making: The role of moral sentiments in experimental economics. In D. De Cremer, K. Murnighan, &. M. Zeelenberg, (Eds.), *Social psychology and experimental economics.* Mahwah, NJ: Erlbaum.

Kiecolt-Glaser, J. K., & Glaser, R. (1995). Psychoneuroimmunology and health consequences: Data and shared mechanisms. *Psychosomatic Medicine, 57,* 269–274.

Kiecolt-Glaser, J. K., Malarkey, W. B., Cacioppo, J. T., & Glaser, R. (1994). Stressful personal relationships: Immune and endocrine function. In R. Glaser & Kiecolt-Glaser (Eds.), *Handbook of human stress and immunity* (pp. 321–339). San Diego, CA: Academic Press.

Kiesler, S. B. (1971). *The psychology of commitment: Experiments linking behavior to belief.* New York: Academic Press.

Kiesler, S. B., & Mathog, R. (1968). The distraction hypothesis in attitude change. *Psychological Reports, 23,* 1123–1133.

Kim, H., & Baron, R. S. (1988). Exercise and illusory correlation: Does arousal heighten stereotypic processes? *Journal of Experimental Social Psychology, 24,* 366–380.

Kim, H., & Markus, H. R. (1999). Deviance or uniqueness, harmony or conformity? A cultural analysis. *Journal of Personality and Social Psychology, 77,* 785–800.

Kimmel, M. S. (2004). *The gendered society* (2nd ed.). New York: Oxford University Press.

Kinder, D. R., & Sears, D. O. (1981). Prejudice and politics: Symbolic racism versus racial threats to the good life. *Journal of Personality and Social Psychology, 40*, 414–431.

King, E. B., Knight, J. L., & Hebl, M. R. (2010). The influence of economic conditions on aspects of stigmatization. *Journal of Social Issues, 66*, 446–460.

King, L. A., & Miner, K. N. (2000). Writing about the perceived benefits of traumatic events: Implications for physical health. *Personality and Social Psychology Bulletin, 26*, 220–230.

Kitayama, S., Duffy, S., Kawamura, T., & Larsen, J. T. (2002). Perceiving an object in its context in different cultures: A cultural look at the New Look. *Psychological Science, 14*, 201–206.

Kitayama, S., Karasawa, M., & Mesquita, B. (2004). Collective and personal processes in regulating emotions: Emotion and self in Japan and the United States. In P. Philipot & R. S. Feldman (Eds.), *The regulation of emotion* (pp. 251–273). Hillsdale, NJ: Erlbaum.

Kitayama, S., Markus, H. R., & Kurokawa, M. (2000). Culture, emotion, and well-being: Good feelings in Japan and the United States. *Cognition and Emotion, 14*, 93–124.

Kitayama, S., Markus, H. R., Matsumoto, H., & Norasakkunkit, V. (1997). Individual and collective processes in the construction of the self: Self-enhancement in the United States and self-depreciation in Japan. *Journal of Personality and Social Psychology, 72*, 1245–1267.

Kitayama, S., & Masuda, T. (1997). Shaiaiteki ninshiki no bunkateki baikai model: taiousei bias no bunkashinrigakuteki kentou. [Cultural psychology of social inference: The correspondence bias in Japan.] In K. Kashiwagi, S. Kitayama, & H. Azuma (Eds.), *Bunkashinrigaju: riron tojisho. [Cultural psychology: Theory and evidence]*. Tokyo: University of Tokyo Press.

Kitayama, S., Mesquita, B., & Karasawa, M. (2005). *Culture and emotional experience: Socially engaging and disengaging emotions in Japan and the United States*. Unpublished manuscript.

Kitayama, S., Snibbe, A. C., Markus, H. R., & Suzuki, T. (2004). Is there any "free" choice? Self and dissonance in two cultures. *Psychological Science, 15*, 527–533.

Klauer, K. C., & Meiser, T. (2000). A source-monitoring analysis of illusory correlations. *Personality and Social Psychology Bulletin, 26*, 1074–1093.

Klayman, J., & Ha, Y. (1987). Confirmation, disconfirmation, and information in hypothesis testing. *Psychological Review, 94*, 211–228.

Kleinhesselink, R. R., & Edwards, R. E. (1975). Seeking and avoiding belief-discrepant information as a function of its perceived refutability. *Journal of Personality and Social Psychology, 31*, 787–790.

Klinger, M. R., Burton, P. C., & Pitts, G. S. (2000). Mechanisms of unconscious priming I: Response competition, not spreading activation. *Journal of Experimental Psychology: Learning, Memory, and Cognition, 26*, 441–455.

Klohnen, E. C., & Bera, S. J. (1998). Behavioral and experiential patterns of avoidantly and securely attached women across adulthood: A 30-year longitudinal perspective. *Journal of Personality and Social Psychology, 74*, 211–223.

Kniffin, K. M., & Wilson, D. S. (2004). The effect of nonphysical traits on the perception of physical attractiveness: Three naturalistic studies. *Evolution and Human Behavior, 25*, 88–101.

Knox, R. E., & Inkster, J. A. (1968). Postdecision dissonance [at post] time. *Journal of Personality and Social Psychology, 8*,

Knutson, B. (1996). Facial expressions of emotion influence interpersonal trait inferences. *Journal of Nonverbal Behavior, 20*, 165–182.

Knutson, B., Wimmer, G. E., Rick, S., Hollon, N. G., Prelec, D., & Loewenstein, G. (2008). Neural antecedents of the endowment effect. *Neuron, 58*, 814–822.

Kogut. T. (2011). Someone to blame: When identifying a victim decreases helping. *Journal of Experimental Social Psychology, 47*, 748–755.

Kogut T., & Ritov, I. (2005). The "identified victim" effect: An identified group, or just a single individual? *Organizational Behavior and Human Decision Processes, 97*, 106–116.

Kohn, M. L. (1969). Class and conformity: A study in values. Homewood, IL: Dorsey Press.

Kolbert, E. (2009, November 9). The things people say. *The New Yorker*, p. 112.

Konner, M. (2003). *The tangled wing: Biological constraints on the human spirit*. New York: Holt.

Korpela, U., & Kinnunen, K. (2009). How is leisure time interacting with nature related to the need for recovery from work demands? Testing multiple mediators. *Leisure Sciences, 33*, 1–14.

Koslowsky, M., & Schwarzwald, J. (2001). The power interaction model: Theory, methodology, and empirical applications. In A. Y. Lee-Chai & J. A. Bargh (Eds.), *The use and abuse of power: Multiple perspectives on the causes of corruption* (pp. 195–214). Philadelphia: Psychology Press.

Kovera, M.B., & Borgida, E. (2010). Social psychology and law. In D.T. Gilbert and S.T. Fiske (eds.), The handbook of social psychology (5th edition, pp. 1343-1385). Hoboken, NJ: John Wiley & Sons.

Kraus, M. W., Côté, S., & Keltner, D. (2010). Social class, contextualism, and empathic accuracy, *Psychological Science, 21*, 1716–1723.

Kraus, M. W., Huang, C., & Keltner, D. (2010). Tactile communication, cooperation, and performance: An ethological study of the NBA, *Emotion, 10*, 745–749.

Kraus, M. W., Piff, P. K., & Keltner, D. (2009). Social class, sense of control, and social explanation, *Journal of Personality and Social Psychology, 97*, 992–1004.

Kraus, M. W., Piff, P. K., & Keltner, D. (2011). Social class as culture: The convergence of resources and rank in the social realm. *Current Directions in Psychological Science, 100*, 246–250.

Kremer, M., & Levy, D. M. (2003). Peer effects and alcohol use among college students. *NBER Working Papers*. Cambridge, MA: Harvard University Press.

Kristof, N. D. (2014). When whites just don't get it, part 5. *New York Times*, Nov. 30, Sunday Review, p. 9.

Kristof, N. D., & WuDunn, S. (2009). *Half the sky*. New York: Knopf.

Krosch, A. R. & Amodio, D. M. (2014). Economic scarcity alters the perception of race. *Proceedings of the National Academy of Sciences, 111(25)*, 9079-9084.

Krosnick, J. A. (1988). The role of attitude importance in social evaluation: A study of policy preferences, presidential candidate evaluations, and voting behavior. *Journal of Personality and Social Psychology, 55*, 196–210.

Krosnick, J. A., Betz, A. L., Jussim, L. J., & Lynn, A. R. (1992). Subliminal conditioning of attitudes. *Personality and Social Psychology Bulletin, 18*, 152–162.

Krosnick, J. A., & Petty, R. E. (1995). Attitude strength: An overview. In R. E. Petty & J. A. Krosnick (Eds.), *Attitude strength: Antecedents and consequences* (pp. 1–24). Mahwah, NJ: Erlbaum.

Kross, E., & Ayduk, O. (2008). Facilitating adaptive emotional analysis: Distinguishing distanced-analysis of depressive experiences from immersed-analysis and distraction. *Personality and Social Psychology Bulletin, 34*, 924–938.

Kross, E., Ayduk, O., & Mischel, W. (2005). When asking "why" does not hurt: Distinguishing rumination from reflective processing of negative emotions. *Psychological Science, 16*, 709–715.

Kruger, J., Wirtz, D., & Miller, D. (2005). Counterfactual thinking and the first instinct fallacy. *Journal of Personality and Social Psychology, 88*, 725–735.

Kruger, J. M., & Dunning, D. (1999). Unskilled and unaware of it: How difficulties in recognizing one's own incompetence lead to inflated self-assessments. *Journal of Personality and Social Psychology, 77*, 1121–1134.

Kruglanski, A. W., & Mayseless, O. (1990). Classic and current social comparison research: Expanding the perspective. *Psychological Bulletin, 108*(2), 195–208.

Kruglanski, A. W., & Webster, D. M. (1991). Group members' reactions to opinion deviates and conformists at varying degrees of proximity to decision deadline and of environmental noise. *Journal of Personality and Social Psychology, 61*, 212–225.

Kruglanski, A. W., & Webster, D. M. (1996). Motivated closing of the mind: "Seizing" and "freezing." *Psychological Review, 103*, 263–283.

Krull, D. S. (1993). Does the grist change the mill? The effect of the perceiver's inferential goal on the process of social inference. *Personality and Social Psychology Bulletin, 19*, 340–348.

Krull, D. S., & Dill, J. C. (1996). On thinking first and responding fast: Flexibility in social inference processes. *Personality and Social Psychology Bulletin, 22*, 949–959.

Krull, D. S., & Erickson, D. J. (1995). Inferential hopscotch: How people draw social inferences from behavior. *Current Directions in Psychological Science, 4*, 35–38.

Krull, D. S., Loy, M., Lin, J., Wang, C.-F., Chen, S., & Zhao, X. (1996). *The fundamental attribution error: Correspondence bias in independent and interdependent cultures.* Paper presented at the 13th Congress of the International Association for Cross-Cultural Psychology, Montreal, Quebec, Canada.

Kteily, N. S., Sidanius, J., & Levin, S. (2011). Social dominance orientation: Cause or 'mere effect'? Evidence for SDO as a causal predictor of prejudice and discrimination against ethnic and racial outgroups. *Journal of Experimental Social Psychology, 47*, 208–214.

Kuhlmeier, V., Wynn, K., & Bloom, P. (2003). Attribution of dispositional states by 12-month-olds. *Psychological Science, 5*, 402–408.

Kuhn, M. H., & McPartland, T. S. (1954). An empirical investigation of self-attitudes. *American Sociological Review, 19*, 68–76.

Kühnen, U., & Oyserman, D. (2002). *Thinking about the self influences thinking in general: Cognitive consequences of salient self-concept.* Ann Arbor: University of Michigan Press.

Kulik, J. A. (1983). Confirmatory attribution and the perpetuation of social beliefs. *Journal of Personality and Social Psychology, 44*, 1171–1181.

Kunda, Z. (1990). The case for motivated reasoning. *Psychological Bulletin, 108*, 480–496.

Kunda, Z., & Oleson, K. C. (1995). Maintaining stereotypes in the face of disconfirmation: Constructing grounds for subtyping deviants. *Journal of Personality and Social Psychology, 68*, 565–579.

Kunda, Z., & Sherman-Williams, B. (1993). Stereotypes and the construal of individuating information. *Personality and Social Psychology Bulletin, 19*, 90–99.

Kunda, Z., & Thagard, P. (1996). Forming impressions from stereotypes, traits, and behaviors: A parallel-constraint-satisfaction theory. *Psychological Review, 103*, 646–657.

Kunstman, J., & Maner, J. K. (2011). Sexual overperception: Power, mating goals, and biases in social judgment. *Journal of Personality and Social Psychology, 100*, 282–294.

Kunz, P. R., & Woolcott, M. (1976). Season's greetings: From my status to yours. *Social Research, 5*, 269–278.

Kuo, F. E., & Sullivan, W. C. (2001). Environment and crime in the inner city. Does vegetation reduce crime? *Environment and Behavior, 33*, 343–367.

Kuo, F. E., & Sullivan, W. C. (2001). Aggression and violence in the inner city: Effects of environment via mental fatigue. *Environment and Behavior, 33*, 543–571.

Kurdek, L. A. (1993). Predicting marital dissolution: A 5-year prospective longitudinal study of newlywed couples. *Journal of Personality and Social Psychology, 64*, 221–242.

Kurzban, R. (2001). The social psychophysics of cooperation: Nonverbal communication in a public goods game. *Journal of Nonverbal Behavior, 25*, 241–259.

LaBrie, J. W., Hummer, J. F., Neighbors, C., & Pedersen, E. R. (2008). Live interactive group-specific normative feedback reduces misperceptions and drinking in college students: A randomized cluster trial. *Psychology of Addictive Behaviors, 22*, 141–148.

LaFrance, M., Henley, N. M., Hall, J. A., & Halberstadt, A. G. (1997). Nonverbal behavior: Are women's superior skills caused by their oppression? In M. R. Walsh (Ed.), *Women, men, and gender: Ongoing debates.* New Haven: Yale University Press.

Lakin, J. L., & Chartrand, T. L. (2003). Using nonconscious behavioral mimicry to create affiliation and rapport. *Psychological Science, 14*, 334–339.

Lakoff, G. (2004). *Don't think of an elephant: Know your values and frame the debate.* White River Junction, VT: Chelsea Green Publishing.

Lakoff, G., & Johnson, M. (1980). *Metaphors we live by.* Chicago: University of Chicago Press.

Lambert, A. J., Burroughs, T., & Nguyen, T. (1999). Perceptions of risk and the buffering hypothesis: The role of just world beliefs and right-wing authoritarianism. *Personality and Social Psychology Bulletin, 25*, 643–656.

Lammers, J., Stapel, D. A., & Galinsky, A. D. (2011). Power increases hypocrisy: Moralizing in reasoning, immorality in behavior. *Psychological Science, 21*, 737–744.

Landau, M. J., Solomon, S., Greenberg, J., Cohen, F., & Pyszczynski, T. (2004). Deliver us from evil: The effects of mortality salience and reminders of 9/11 on support for President George W. Bush. *Personality and Social Psychology Bulletin, 30*, 1136–1150.

Landes, E. M., & Rosenfield, A. M. (1994). Durability of advertising revisited. *Journal of Industrial Economics, 43*, 263–277.

Landsberger, M. (1966). Windfall income and consumption: Comment. *American Economic Review, 56*, 534–540.

Landy, D., & Sigall, H. (1974). Beauty is talent: Task evaluation as a function of the performer's physical attractiveness. *Journal of Personality and Social Psychology, 29*, 299–304.

Lane, K. A., Banaji, M. R., Nosek, B. A., & Greenwald, A. G. (2007). Understanding and using the Implicit Association Test: IV: Procedures and validity. In B. Wittenbrink & N. Schwarz (Eds.), *Implicit measures of attitudes: Procedures and controversies* (pp. 59–102). New York: Guilford Press.

Langer, E. J., & Rodin, J. (1976). The effects of choice and enhanced personal responsibility for the aged: A field experiment in an institutional setting. *Journal of Personality and Social Psychology, 34,* 191–198.

Langlois, J. H., Kalakanis, L., Rubenstein, A. J., Larson, A., Hallam, M., & Smoot, M. (2000). Maxims or myths of beauty? A meta-analytic review and theoretical review. *Psychological Bulletin, 126,* 390–423.

Langlois, J. H., Ritter, J. M., Roggman, L. A., & Vaughn, L. S. (1991). Facial diversity and infant preferences for attractive faces. *Developmental Psychology, 27,* 79–84.

Langlois, J. H., & Roggman, L. A. (1990). Attractive faces are only average. *Psychological Science, 1,* 115–121.

Langlois, J. H., Roggman, L. A., Casey, R. J., Ritter, J. M., Rieser-Danner, L. A., & Jenkins, V. Y. (1987). Infant preferences for attractive faces: Rudiments of a stereotype. *Developmental Psychology, 23,* 363–369.

LaPiere, R. T. (1934). Attitudes versus actions. *Social Forces, 13,* 230–237.

Larrick, R. P., Morgan, J. N., & Nisbett, R. E. (1990). Teaching the use of cost-benefit reasoning in everyday life. *Psychological Science, 1,* 362–370.

Larrick, R. P., Nisbett, R. E., & Morgan, J. N. (1993). Who uses the cost-benefit rules of choice? Implications for the normative status of microeconomic theory. *Organizational Behavior and Human Decision Processes, 56,* 331–347.

Larrick, R. P., Timmerman, T. A., Carton, A. M., & Abrevaya, J. (2011). Temper, temperature, and temptation: Heat-related retaliation in baseball. *Psychological Science, 22,* 423–428.

Lassiter, G. D., Geers, A. L., Munhall, P. J., Ploutz-Snyder, R. J., & Breitenbecher, D. L. (2002). Illusory causation: Why it occurs. *Psychological Science, 13,* 299–305.

Latané, B., & Darley, J. M. (1968). Group inhibition of bystander intervention in emergencies. *Journal of Personality and Social Psychology, 10,* 215–221.

Latané, B., & Nida, S. (1981). Ten years of research on group size and helping. *Psychological Bulletin, 89,* 308–324.

Latané, B., Williams, K., & Harkins, S. (1979). Many hands make the work light: The causes and consequences of social loafing. *Journal of Personality and Social Psychology, 37,* 822–832.

Lau, G., Kay, A. C., & Spencer, S. J. (2008). Loving those who justify inequality: The effects of system threat on attraction to women who embody benevolent sexist ideals. *Psychological Science, 19*(1), 20–21.

Lau, R. R., & Russell, D. (1980). Attributions in the sports pages: A field test of some current hypotheses about attribution research. *Journal of Personality and Social Psychology, 39,* 29–38.

Laughlin, P. R. (1988). Collective induction: Group performance, social combination processes, and mutual majority and minority influence. *Journal of Personality and Social Psychology, 54,* 254–267.

Laughlin, P. R., & Ellis, A. L. (1986). Demonstrability and social combination processes on mathematical intellective tasks. *Journal of Experimental Social Psychology, 22,* 177–189.

Laughlin, P. R., Hatch, E. C., Silver, J. S., & Boh, L. (2006). Groups perform better than the best individuals on letters-to-numbers problems: Effects of group size. *Journal of Personality and Social Psychology, 90,* 644–651.

Lawler, K. A., Younger, J. W., Piferi, R. L., Billington, E., Jobe, R., Edmondson, K., et al. (2003). A change of heart: Cardiovascular correlates of forgiveness in response to interpersonal conflict. *Journal of Behavioral Medicine, 26,* 373–393.

Lazarus, R. S. (1966). *Psychological stress and the coping process.* New York: McGraw-Hill.

Lazarus, R. S. (1991). *Emotion and adaptation.* New York: Oxford University Press.

Lea, M., Spears, R., & de Groot, D. (2001). Knowing me, knowing you: Anonymity effects on social identity processes within groups. *Personality and Social Psychology Bulletin, 27,* 526–537.

Leary, M. R. (2007). Motivational and emotional aspects of the self. *Annual Review of Psychology, 58,* 317–344.

Leary, M. R., & Jones, J. L. (1993). The social psychology of tanning and sunscreen use: Self-presentational motives as a predictor of health risk. *Journal of Applied Social Psychology, 23,* 1390–1406.

Leary, M. R., & Kowalski, R. M. (1990). Impression management: A literature review and two-component model. *Psychological Bulletin, 107,* 34–47.

Leary, M. R., Kowalski, R. M., Smith, L., & Phillips, S. (2003). Teasing, rejection, and violence: Case studies of the school shootings. *Aggressive Behavior, 29,* 202–214.

Leary, M. R., Tambor, E. S., Terdal, S. K., & Downs, D. L. (1995). Self-esteem as an interpersonal monitor: The sociometer hypothesis. *Journal of Personality and Social Psychology, 68,* 518–530.

Leary, M. R., Tchividjian, L. R., & Kraxberger, B. E. (1994). Self-presentation can be hazardous to your health: Impression management and health risk. *Health Psychology, 13,* 451–470.

LeBon, G. (1895). *The crowd.* London: Unwin.

LeDoux, J. E. (1989). Cognitive-emotional interactions in the brain. *Cognition and Emotion, 3,* 267–289.

LeDoux, J. E. (1993). Emotional networks in the brain. In M. Lewis & J. M. Haviland (Eds.), *Handbook of emotions* (pp. 109–118). New York: Guilford Press.

LeDoux, J. E. (1996). *The emotional brain.* New York: Simon & Schuster.

Lee, A., Aaker, J., & Gardner, W. (2000). The pleasures and pains of distinct self-construals: The role of interdependence in regulatory focus, *Journal of Personality and Social Psychology, 78,* 1122–1134.

Lee, F., Hallahan, M., & Herzog, T. (1996). Explaining real-life events: How culture and domain shape attributions. *Personality and Social Psychology Bulletin, 22,* 732–741.

Lee, S. W. S., & Schwarz, N. (2011). Clean slate effects: The psychological consequences of physical cleansing. *Current Directions in Psychological Science, 20,* 307–311.

Lee, S. W. S., & Schwarz, N. (2012). Bidirectionality, mediation, and moderation of metaphorical effects: The embodiment of social suspicion and fishy smells. *Journal of Personality and Social Psychology, 103,* 737–749.

Lee, Y., Jussim, L., & McCauley, C. R. (1995). *Stereotype accuracy: Toward appreciating group differences.* Washington, DC: American Psychological Association.

Legate, N., Ryan, R. M., & Weinstein, N. (2012). Is coming out always a "good thing"? Exploring the relations of autonomy support, outness, and wellness for lesbian, gay, and bisexual individuals. *Social Psychological and Personality Science, 3,* 145–152.

Lehman, B. J., Taylor, S. E., Kiefe, C. I., & Seeman, T. E. (2005). Relation of childhood socioeconomic status and family environment to adult metabolic functioning in the CARDIA study. *Psychosomatic Medicine, 67,* 846–854.

Lehman, D. R., Lempert, R. O., & Nisbett, R. E. (1988). The effects of graduate training on reasoning: Formal discipline and thinking about everyday life events. *American Psychologist, 43,* 431–443.

Lehman, D. R. and Nisbett, R. E. (1990). A longitudinal study of the effects of undergraduate education on reasoning. *Developmental Psychology, 26,* 952–960.

Leighton, J., Bird, G., Orsini, C., & Heyes, C. (2010). Social attitudes modulate automatic imitation. *Journal of Experimental Social Psychology, 46,* 905–910.

Leippe, M. R., & Elkin, R. A. (1987). When motives clash: Issue involvement and response involvement as determinants of persuasion. *Journal of Personality and Social Psychology, 52,* 269–278.

Lemyre, L., & Smith, P. M. (1985). Intergroup discrimination and self-esteem in the minimal group paradigm. *Journal of Personality and Social Psychology, 49,* 660–670.

Lepore, L., & Brown, R. (1997). Category and stereotype activation: Is prejudice inevitable? *Journal of Personality and Social Psychology, 72,* 275–287.

Lepore, S. J., Allen, K. M., & Evans, G. W. (1993). Social support lowers cardiovascular reactivity to an acute stressor. *Psychosomatic Medicine, 55,* 518–524.

Lepper, M. R. (1973). Dissonance, self-perception, and honesty in children. *Journal of Personality and Social Psychology, 23,* 65–74.

Lepper, M. R., & Greene, D. (1978). *The hidden costs of reward.* Hillsdale, NJ: Erlbaum.

Lepper, M. R., Greene, D., & Nisbett, R. E. (1973). Undermining children's intrinsic interest with extrinsic reward: A test of the overjustification hypothesis. *Journal of Personality and Social Psychology, 28,* 129–137.

Lepper, M. R., Sagotsky, G., Dafoe, J., & Greene, D. (1982). Consequences of superfluous social constraints: Effect on young children's social inferences and subsequent intrinsic interest. *Journal of Personality and Social Psychology, 42,* 51–65.

Lepper, M. R., & Woolverton, M. (2001). The wisdom of practice: Lessons learned from the study of highly effective tutors. In J. Aronson (Ed.), *Improving academic achievement: Contributions of social psychology.* Orlando, FL: Academic Press.

Lepper, M. R., Woolverton, M., Mumme, D. L., & Gurtner, J.-L. (1993). Motivational techniques of expert human tutors: Lessons for the design of computer-based tutors. In S. P. Lajoie & S. J. Derry (Eds.), *Computers as cognitive tools.* Hillsdale, NJ: Erlbaum.

Lerner, J. S., Goldberg, J. H., & Tetlock, P. E. (1998). Sober second thoughts: The effects of accountability, anger, and authoritarianism on attributions of responsibility. *Personality and Social Psychology Bulletin, 24,* 563–574.

Lerner, J. S., & Gonzalez, R. M. (2005). Forecasting one's future based on fleeting subjective experiences. *Personality and Social Psychology Bulletin, 31*(4), 454–466.

Lerner, J. S., Gonzalez, R. M., Small, D. A., & Fischhoff, B. (2003). Effects of fear and anger on perceived risks of terrorism: A national field experiment. *Psychological Science, 14*(2), 144–150.

Lerner, J. S., & Keltner, D. (2001). Fear, anger, and risk. *Journal of Personality and Social Psychology, 81,* 146–159.

Lerner, M. J. (1980). *The belief in a just world: A fundamental delusion.* New York: Plenum Press.

Lerner, M. J., & Miller, D. T. (1978). Just world research and the attribution process: Looking back and ahead. *Psychological Bulletin, 85,* 1030–1051.

Lerner, M. J., & Simmons, C. H. (1966). Observer's reactions to the "innocent victim": Compassion or rejection? *Journal of Personality and Social Psychology, 4,* 203–210.

Leslie, A. (2000). "Theory of mind" as a mechanism of selective attention. In M. S. Gazzaniga (Ed.), *The new cognitive neurosciences* (pp. 1235–1247). Cambridge, MA: MIT Press.

Levenson, R. W. (2003). Autonomic specificity and emotion. In R. J. Davidson, K. R. Scherer, & H. H. Goldsmith (Eds.), *Handbook of affective sciences* (pp. 212–224). New York: Oxford University Press.

Levenson, R. W., & Gottman, J. M. (1983). Marital interaction: Physiological linkage and affective exchange. *Journal of Personality and Social Psychology, 45,* 587–597.

Leventhal, H. (Ed.). (1970). *Findings and theory in the study of fear communications.* New York: Academic Press.

Leventhal, H., Singer, R. P., & Jones, S. H. (1965). The effects of fear and specificity of recommendation upon attitudes and behavior. *Journal of Personality and Social Psychology, 2,* 20–29.

Leventhal, H., Watts, J. C., & Pagano, F. (1967). Effects of fear and instructions on how to cope with danger. *Journal of Personality and Social Psychology, 6,* 313–321.

Levin, I. P., & Gaeth, G. J. (1988). Framing of attribute information before and after consuming the product. *Journal of Consumer Research, 15,* 374–378.

Levine, J. M. (1989). Reaction to opinion deviance in small groups. In P. B. Paulus (Ed.), *Psychology of group influence* (2nd ed., pp. 187–231). Hillsdale, NJ: Erlbaum.

Levine, J. M., Higgins, E. T., & Choi, H. S. (2000). Development of strategic norms in groups. *Organizational Behavior and Human Decision Processes, 82,* 88–101.

Levine, J. M., & Moreland, R. L. (1990). Progress in small group research. *Annual Review of Psychology, 41,* 585–634.

Levine, J. M., & Moreland, R. L. (1998). Small groups. In D. T. Gilbert, S. T. Fiske, & G. Lindzey (Eds.), *The handbook of social psychology* (4th ed., Vol. 2, pp. 415–469). New York: McGraw-Hill.

LeVine, R. A., & Campbell, D. T. (1972). *Ethnocentrism.* New York: Wiley.

Levinger, G. (1964). Note on need complementarity in marriage. *Psychological Bulletin, 61,* 153–157.

Levinger, G., & Schneider, D. J. (1969). Test of the "risk as a value" hypothesis. *Journal of Personality and Social Psychology, 11,* 165–169.

Levinger, G., Senn, D. J., & Jorgensen, B. W. (1970). Progress toward permanence in courtship: A test of the Kerckhoff-Davis hypothesis. *Sociometry, 33,* 427–433.

Levitt, S., List, J., 2007a. What do laboratory experiments measuring social preferences reveal about the real world? *Journal of Economic Perspectives* 21 (2), 153–174.

Levitt, S. D. (1994). Using repeat challengers to estimate the effect of campaign spending on election outcomes in the U.S. House. *Journal of Political Economy, 102,* 777–798.

Lewin, K. (1935). The conflict between Aristotelian and Galilean modes of thought in contemporary psychology. *Journal of General Psychology, 5,* 141–177.

Lewin, K. (1952). Group decision and social change. In G. E. Swanson, T. M. Newcomb, & E. L. Hartley (Eds.), *Readings in social psychology.* New York: Holt.

Lewis, M., & Sullivan, M. W. (2005). The development of self-conscious emotions. In A. J. Elliot & C. S. Dweck (Eds.),

Handbook of competence and motivation. New York: Guilford Press.

Lewis, M. A., & Neighbors, C. (2004). Gender-specific misperceptions of college student drinking norms. *Psychology of Addictive Behaviors, 18*, 334–339.

Leyens, J. P., Camino, L., Parke, R. D., & Berkowitz, L. (1975). Effects of movie violence on aggression in a field setting as a function of group dominance and cohesion. *Journal of Personality and Social Psychology, 32*, 346–360.

Leyens, J. P., Cisneros, T., & Hossay, J. F. (1976). Decentration as a means of reducing aggression after exposure to violent stimuli. *European Journal of Social Psychology, 6*, 459–473.

Leyens, J. P., & Picus, S. (1973). Identification with the winner of a fight and name mediation: Their differential effects upon subsequent aggressive behavior. *British Journal of Social and Clinical Psychology, 12*, 374–377.

Li, J., Wang, L., & Fischer, K. W. (2004). The organization of Chinese shame concepts. *Cognition and Emotion, 18*(6), 767–797.

Li, Y., Johnson, E. J., & Zaval, L. (2011). Local warming: Daily temperature change influences belief in global warming. *Psychological Science, 22*, 454–459.

Li, Y. J., Johnson, K. A., Cohen, A. B., Williams, M. J., Knowles, E. D., & Chen, Z. (2011). Fundamental(ist) attribution error: Protestants are dispositionally focused. *Journal of Personality and Social Psychology*. Retrieved from http://psycnet.apa.org/journals/psp/102/2/281/.

Libby, L. K., & Eibach, R. P. (2011). Visual perspective in mental imagery: A representational tool that functions in judgment, emotion, and self-insight. In J. M. Olson & M. P. Zanna (Eds.), *Advances in experimental social psychology* (Vol. 44, pp. 185–245). Burlington, VT: Academic Press.

Libby, L. K., Shaeffer, E. M., Eibach, R. P., & Slemmer, J. A. (2007). Picture yourself at the polls: Visual perspective in mental imagery affects self-perception and behavior. *Psychological Science, 18*, 199–203.

Libby, L. K., Valenti, G., Pfent, A., & Eibach, R. P. (2011). Seeing failure in your life: Third-person imagery causes self-esteem to shape reactions to recalled and imagined failure. Manuscript under review.

Liberman, N., Sagristano, M., & Trope, Y. (2002). The effect of temporal distance on level of construal. *Journal of Experimental Social Psychology, 38*, 523–535.

Liberman, V., Samuels, S. M., & Ross, L. (2002). The name of the game: Predictive power of reputations vs. situational labels in determining Prisoner's Dilemma game moves. *Personality and Social Psychology Bulletin, 30*, 1175–1185.

Lichtenfeld, S., Elliot, A., Maier, M. A., & Pekrun, R. (2012). Fertile green: Green facilitates creative performance. *Personality and Social Psychology Bulletin, 38*, 784–797.

Lieberman, M. D. (2007). Social cognitive neuroscience: A review of core processes. *Annual Review of Psychology, 58*, 259–289.

Lieberman, M.D. (2013). *Social: Why our brains are wired to connect*. New York, NY: Crown Publishers.

Lieberman, M. D., Hariri, A., Jarcho, J. M., Eisenberger, N. I., & Bookheimer, S. Y. (2005). An fMRI investigation of race-related amygdala activity in African-American and Caucasian-American individuals. *Nature Neuroscience, 8*, 720–722.

Linder, D. E., Cooper, J., & Jones, E. E. (1967). Decision freedom as a determinant of the role of incentive magnitude in attitude change. *Journal of Personality and Social Psychology, 6*, 245–254.

Linville, P. W. (1982). The complexity-extremity effect and age-based stereotyping. *Journal of Personality and Social Psychology, 42*, 193–211.

Linville, P. W. (1987). Self-complexity as a cognitive buffer against stress-related illness and depression. *Journal of Personality and Social Psychology, 52*, 663–676.

Linville, P. W., & Carlston, D. E. (1994). Social cognition of the self. In P. G. Devine, D. L. Hamilton, & T. M. Ostrom (Eds.), *Social Cognition: Impact on Social Psychology* (pp. 143–193). San Diego: Academic Press.

Linville, P. W., Fischer, G. W., & Fischhoff, B. (1993). AIDS risk perceptions and decision biases. In J. B. Pryor and G. D. Reeder (Eds.), *The social psychology of HIV infection* (pp. 5–38). Hillsdale, NJ: Erlbaum.

Linville, P. W., Fischer, G. W., & Salovey, P. (1989). Perceived distributions of the characteristics of in-group and out-group members: Empirical evidence and a computer simulation. *Journal of Personality and Social Psychology, 57*, 165–188.

Lipkus, I. M., Dalbert, C., & Siegler, I. C. (1996). The importance of distinguishing the belief in a just world for self versus for others: Implications for psychological well-being. *Personality and Social Psychology Bulletin, 22*, 666–677.

Lippa, R. A. (2007). The preferred traits of mates in a cross-national study of heterosexual and homosexual men and women: An examination of biological and cultural influences. *Archives of Sexual Behavior, 36*(2), 193–208.

Lippmann, W. (1922). *Public opinion*. New York: Harcourt Brace.

Liptak, A. (2011, August 23). 34 years later, Supreme Court will revisit eyewitness IDs. *New York Times*. Retrieved from http://www.nytimes.com/2011/08/23/us/23bar.html?scp=1&sq=eyewitness%20identification&st=cse

Little, A. C., Burris, R. P., Jones, B. & Roberts, S.C. (2007). Facial appearance affects voting decisions. *Evolution and Human Behavior, 28(1),* 18–27.

Livingston, R. W., & Brewer, M. B. (2002). What are we really priming? Cue-based versus category-based processing of facial stimuli. *Journal of Personality and Social Psychology, 82*, 5–18.

Livshits, G., & Kobyliansky, E. (1991). Fluctuating asymmetry as a possible measure of developmental homeostasis in humans: A review. *Human Biology, 63*, 441–466.

Locke, K. D., & Horowitz, L. M. (1990). Satisfaction in interpersonal interactions as a function of similarity in level of dysphoria. *Journal of Personality and Social Psychology, 58*, 823–831.

Lockwood, P. (2002). Could it happen to you? Predicting the impact of downward social comparisons on the self. *Journal of Personality and Social Psychology, 82*, 343–358.

Loewenstein, G., & Lerner, J. S. (2003). The role of affect in decision making. In R. J. Davidson, K. R. Scherer, & H. H. Goldsmith (Eds.), *Handbook of affective sciences* (pp. 619–642). New York: Oxford University Press.

Loftus, E. F. (1993). The reality of repressed memories. *American Psychologist, 48*, 518–537.

Loftus, E. F. (2001). Imagining the past. *The Psychologist, 14*, 584–587.

Loftus, E. F. (2003). The dangers of memory. In R. J. Sternberg (Ed.), *Psychologists defying the crowd: Stories of those who battled the establishment and won* (pp. 105–117). Washington, DC: American Psychological Association.

Loftus, E. F., & Ketcham, K. (1994). *The myth of repressed memory*. New York: St. Martin's Press.

Loftus, E. F., Miller, D. G. & Burns, H. J. (1978). Semantic integration of verbal information into a visual memory. *Human Learning and Memory, 4*, 19–31.

Loftus, E. F., & Pickrell, J. E. (1995). The formation of false memories. *Psychiatric Annals, 25*, 720–725.

Longley, J., & Pruitt, D. G. (1980). Groupthink: A critique of Janis' theory. In L. Wheeler (Ed.), *Review of personality and social psychology*. Beverly Hills, CA: Sage.

Lord, C. G., Desforges, D. M., Ramsey, S. L., Trezza, G. R., & Lepper, M. R. (1991). Typicality effects in attitude-behavior — consistency: Effects of category discrimination and category knowledge. *Journal of Experimental Social Psychology, 27*, 550–575.

Lord, C. G., Lepper, M. R., & Mackie, D. (1984). Attitude prototypes as determinants of attitude-behavior consistency. *Journal of Personality and Social Psychology, 46*, 1254–1266.

Lord, C., Ross, L., & Lepper, M. (1979). Biased assimilation and attitude polarization: The effects of prior theories on subsequently considered evidence. *Journal of Personality and Social Psychology, 37*, 2098–2109.

Lord, C. G., Scott, K. O., Pugh, M. A., & Desforges, D. M. (1997). Leakage beliefs and the correspondence bias. *Personality and Social Psychology Bulletin, 23*, 824–836.

Lorenz, K. (1971/1950). Part and parcel in animal and human societies. In *Studies in animal and human behaviour* (Vol. 2, pp. 115–195). Cambridge, MA: Harvard University Press.

Losch, M. E., & Cacioppo, J. T. (1990). Cognitive dissonance may enhance sympathetic tonus, but attitudes are changed to reduce negative affect rather than arousal. *Journal of Experimental Social Psychology, 26*, 289–304.

Lott, A. J., & Lott, B. E. (1961). Group cohesiveness, communication level, and conformity. *Journal of Abnormal and Social Psychology, 62*, 408–412.

Lott, A. J., & Lott, B. E. (1974). The role of reward in formation of positive interpersonal attitudes. In T. L. Huston (Ed.), *Foundations of interpersonal attraction* (pp. 171–189). New York: Academic Press.

Lowery, B. S., Unzueta, M. M., Knowles, E. D., & Goff, P. A. (2006). Concern for the ingroup and opposition to affirmative action. *Journal of Personality and Social Psychology, 90*, 961–974.

Luo, S., & Zhang, G. (2009). What leads to romantic attraction: Similarity, reciprocity, security, or beauty? Evidence from a speed-dating study. *Journal of Personality, 77*(4), 933–964.

Lutz, C. A. (1988). *Unnatural emotions: Everyday sentiments on a Micronesian atoll and their challenge to Western theory.* Chicago: University of Chicago Press.

Lydon, J., Zanna, M. P., & Ross, M. (1988). Bolstering attitudes by autobiographical recall: Attitude persistence and selective memory. *Personality and Social Psychology Bulletin, 14*, 78–86.

Lynam, D. R., Milich, R., Zimmerman, R., Novak, S. P., Logan, T. K., Martin, C. E., et al. (1999). Project DARE: No effects at 10-year follow-up. *Journal of Consulting and Clinical Psychology, 67*, 590–593.

Lynch, J. J. (1979). *The broken heart: The medical consequences of loneliness.* New York: Basic Books.

Lyubomirsky, S. (2007). *The how of happiness.* New York: Penguin Press.

Lyubomirsky, S., King, L., & Diener, E. (2005). The benefits of frequent positive affect: Does happiness lead to success? *Psychological Bulletin, 131*, 803–855.

Lyubomirsky, S., & Nolen-Hoeksema, S. (1995). Effects of self-focused rumination on negative thinking and interpersonal problem solving. *Journal of Personality and Social Psychology, 69*, 176–190.

Lyubomirsky, S., Sheldon, K. M., & Schkade, D. (2005). Pursuing happiness: The architecture of sustainable change. *Review of General Psychology, 9*, 111–131.

Ma, D. S., & Correll, J. (2011). Target prototypicality moderates racial bias in the decision to shoot. *Journal of Experimental Social Psychology, 47*, 391–396.

Ma, V., & Schoeneman, T. J. (1997). Individualism versus collectivism: A comparison of Kenyan and American self-concepts. *Basic and Applied Social Psychology, 19*, 261–273.

Maass, A., & Clark, R. D. III (1983). Internalization versus compliance: Different processes underlying minority influence and conformity. *European Journal of Social Psychology, 13*, 197–215.

Maass, A., Salvi, D., Arcuri, L., & Semin, G. (1989). Language use in intergroup contexts: The linguistic intergroup bias. *Journal of Personality and Social Psychology, 57*, 981–993.

Maccoby, E. E. (1990). Gender and relationships: A developmental account. *American Psychologist, 45*, 513–520.

Maccoby, E. E., & Jacklin, C. N. (1974). *The psychology of sex differences.* Stanford, CA: Stanford University Press.

MacCoun, R. (1993). Blaming others to a fault. *Chance, 6*, 31–33.

MacDonald, G., & Leary, M. R. (2005). Why does social exclusion hurt? The relationship between social and physical pain. *Psychological Bulletin, 131*(2), 202–223.

Machiavelli, N. (1532/2003). *The prince* (G. Bull, Trans.). New York: Penguin Classics.

Macintyre, S., Maciver, S., & Solomon, A. (1993). Area, class, and health: Should we be focusing on places or people? *Journal of Social Policy, 22*, 213–234.

Mackie, D. M. (1987). Systematic and nonsystematic processing of majority and minority persuasive communications. *Journal of Personality and Social Psychology, 53*, 41–52.

Mackie, D. M., Silver, L. A., & Smith, E. R. (2004). Intergroup emotions: Emotion as an intergroup phenomenon. In L. Z. Tiedens & C. W. Leach (Eds.), *The social life of emotions* (pp. 227–246). New York: Cambridge University Press.

Mackie, D. M., & Worth, L. T. (1989). Cognitive deficits and the mediation of positive affect in persuasion. *Journal of Personality and Social Psychology, 57*, 27–40.

Macrae, C. N., Alnwick, K. A., Milne, A. B., & Schloerscheidt, A. M. (2002). Person perception across the menstrual cycle: Hormonal influences on social-cognitive functioning. *Psychological Science, 13*, 532–536.

Macrae, C. N., & Bodenhausen, G. V. (2000). Social cognition: Thinking categorically about others. *Annual Review of Psychology, 51*, 93–120.

Macrae, C. N., Hewstone, M., & Griffiths, R. J. (1993). Processing load and memory for stereotype-based information. *European Journal of Social Psychology, 23*, 77–87.

Macrae, C. N., Milne, A. B., & Bodenhausen, G. V. (1994). Stereotypes as energy-saving devices: A peek inside the cognitive toolbox. *Journal of Personality and Social Psychology, 66*, 37–47.

Macrae, C. N., Stangor, C., & Milne, A. B. (1994). Activating social stereotypes: A functional analysis. *Journal of Experimental Social Psychology, 30*, 370–389.

Madrian, B. C., & Shea, D. F. (2001). The power of suggestion: Inertia in 401(k) participation and savings behavior. *Quarterly Journal of Economics, 116* , 1149–1187.

Magee, J. C., Galinsky, A. D., Inesi, M. E., & Gruenfeld, D. H. (2006). Power and perspectives not taken. *Psychological Science, 17*(12), 1068–1074.

Magnay, J. (2002). Thorpe straight as the line on the bottom of the pool. *Sydney Morning Herald*, November 18. http://www.smh.com.au/articles/2002/11/17/1037490052340.html

Major, B. (1994). From social inequality to personal entitlement: The role of social comparisons, legitimacy appraisals, and group membership. *Advances in Experimental Social Psychology, 26*, 293–355.

Malle, B. F. (1999). How people explain behavior: A new theoretical framework. *Personality and Social Psychology Review, 3*, 23–48.

Malle, B. F. (2001). Folk explanations of intentional actions. In B. F. Malle, L. J. Moses, & D. A. Baldwin (Eds.), *Intentions and intentionality: Foundations of social cognition.* Cambridge, MA: MIT Press.

Malle, B. F. (2006). The actor-observer asymmetry in causal attribution: A (surprising) meta-analysis. *Psychological Bulletin, 132*, 895–919.

Malle, B. F., Moses, L. J., & Baldwin, D. A. (2001). *Intentions and intentionality: Foundations of social cognition.* Cambridge, MA: MIT Press.

Mann, L. (1981). The baiting crowd in episodes of threatened suicide. *Journal of Personality and Social Psychology, 41*, 703–709.

Manning, J. T., & Hartley, M. A. (1991). Symmetry and ornamentation are correlated in the peacock's train. *Animal Behavior, 42*, 1020–1021.

Maret, S. M. (1983). Attractiveness ratings of photographs of blacks by Cruzans and Americans. *Journal of Psychology, 115*, 113–116.

Maret, S. M., & Harling, G. A. (1985). Cross cultural perceptions of physical attractiveness: Ratings of photos of whites by Cruzans and Americans. *Perceptual and Motor Skills, 60*, 163–166.

Margolin, L., & White, L. (1987). The continuing role of physical attractiveness in marriage. *Journal of Marriage and the Family, 49*, 21–27.

Markow, T. A., & Ricker, J. P. (1992). Male size, developmental stability, and mating success in natural populations on three *Drosophila* species. *Heredity, 69*, 122–127.

Markus, H. (1977). Self-schemata and processing information about the self. *Journal of Personality and Social Psychology, 35*, 63–78.

Markus, H. (1978). The effect of mere presence on social facilitation. An unobtrusive test. *Journal of Experimental Social Psychology, 14*, 389–397.

Markus, H. R., & Kitayama, S. (1991). Culture and the self: Implications for cognition, emotion, and motivation. *Psychological Review, 98*, 224–253.

Markus, H., & Wurf, E. (1987). The dynamic self-concept: A social psychological perspective. *Annual Review in Psychology, 38*, 299–337.

Marmot, M. G., Shipley, S., & Rose, G. (1984). Inequalities in death—Specific explanations of a general pattern. *Lancet, 1*, 1003–1006.

Marsh, H. L. (1991). A comparative analysis of crime coverage in newspapers in the United States and other countries from 1960–1989: A review of the literature. *Journal of Criminal Justice, 19*, 67–79.

Marsh, H. W., & Parker, J. W. (1984). Determinants of student self-concept: Is it better to be a relatively large fish in a small pond even if you don't learn to swim as well? *Journal of Personality and Social Psychology, 47*, 213–231.

Marshall, S. L. A. (1947). Men under Fire: The Problem of Battle Command in Future War. New York: William Morrow.

Martin, G. G., & Clark, R. D. I. (1982). Distress crying in infants: Species and peer specificity. *Developmental Psychology, 18*, 3–9.

Martin, T., & Bumpass, L. (1989). Recent trends in marital disruption. *Demography, 26*, 37–52.

Martinie, M., Olive, T., Milland, L., Joule, R. & Capa, R. L. (2013). Evidence that dissonance arousal is initially undifferentiated and only later labeled as negative. *Journal of Experimental Social Psychology, 49*, 767–770.

Maruyama, G., & Miller, N. (1980). Physical attractiveness, race, and essay evaluation. *Personality and Social Psychology Bulletin, 6*, 384–390.

Marwell, G., & Ames, R. (1981). Economists free ride, does anyone else? Experiments on the provision of public goods, IV. *Journal of Public Economics, 15*, 295–310.

Masuda, T., Ellsworth, P. C., Mesquita, B., Leu, J., Tanida, S., & Van de Veerdonk, E. (2008). Placing the face in context: Cultural differences in the perception of facial emotion. *Journal of Personality and Social Psychology, 94*, 365–381.

Mathur, V. A., Harada, T., Lipke, T., & Chiao, J. Y. (2010). Neural basis of extraordinary empathy and altruistic motivation. *Neuroimage, 51*, 1468–1475.

Matsumoto, D., & Willingham, B. (2006). The thrill of victory and the agony of defeat: Spontaneous expressions of medal winners of the 2004 Athens Olympic games. *Journal of Personality and Social Psychology, 91*, 568–581.

Matza, D. (1964). *Delinquency and drift.* New York: Wiley.

Mauro, R., Sato, K., & Tucker, J. (1992). The role of appraisal in human emotions: A cross-cultural study. *Journal of Personality and Social Psychology, 62*, 301–317.

Mayer, J. D., Barsade, S. G., & Roberts, R. D. (2008). Human abilities: Emotional intelligence. *Annual Review of Psychology, 59*, 507–536.

McAdams, D. P. (2008). Personal narratives and the life story. In O. P. John, R. Robins, & L. Pervin (Eds.), *Handbook of personality: Theories and research* (3rd ed., pp. 242–262). New York: Guilford Press.

McArthur, L. Z. (1972). The how and what of why: Some determinants and consequences of causal attribution. *Journal of Personality and Social Psychology, 13*, 733–742.

McArthur, L. Z., & Baron, R. M. (1983). Toward an ecological theory of social perception. *Psychological Review, 90*, 215–238.

McCauley, C. (1989). The nature of social influence in groupthink: Compliance and internalization. *Journal of Personality and Social Psychology, 57*, 250–260.

McCauley, C. (1998). Group dynamics in Janis's theory of groupthink: Backward and forward. *Organizational Behavior and Human Decision Processes, 73*, 142–162.

McConahay, J. B. (1986). Modern racism, ambivalence, and the modern racism scale. In J. F. Dovidio & S. L. Gaertner (Eds.), *Prejudice, discrimination, and racism* (pp. 91–126). Orlando, FL: Academic Press.

McConahay, J. B., Hardee, B. B., & Batts, V. (1981). Has racism declined in America? It depends upon who is asking and what is asked. *Journal of Conflict Resolution, 25*, 563–579.

McConnell, A. R., & Leibold, J. M. (2001). Relations among the implicit association test, discriminatory behavior, and explicit measures of racial attitudes. *Journal of Experimental Social Psychology, 37*, 435–442.

McCoy, S. K., & Major, B. (2003). Group identification moderates emotional responses to perceived prejudice. *Personality and Social Psychology Bulletin, 29*, 1005–1017.

McCrae, R. R., Costa, P. T., & Yik, M. S. M. (1996). Universal aspects of Chinese personality structure. In M. H. Bond (Ed.), *The handbook of Chinese psychology* (pp. 189–207). Hong Kong: Oxford University Press.

McCullough, M. C., Kilpatrick, S. D., Emmons, R. A., & Larson, D. B. (2001). Is gratitude a moral affect? *Psychological Bulletin, 127*, 249–266.

McCullough, M. E. (2008). *Beyond revenge: The evolution of the forgiveness instinct.* New York: Basic Books.

McCullough, M. E., Fincham, F. D., & Tsang, J. (2003). Forgiveness, forbearance, and time: The temporal unfolding of transgression-related interpersonal motivations. *Journal of Personality and Social Psychology, 84*, 540–557.

McFayden-Ketchum, M., Bates, S. A., Dodge, K. A., & Pettit, G. S. (1996). Patterns of change in early childhood aggressive-disruptive behavior: Gender differences in predictions from early coercive and affectionate mother-child interactions. *Child Development, 67*, 2417–2433.

McGill, A. L. (1989). Context effects in judgments of causation. *Journal of Personality and Social Psychology, 57*, 189–200.

McGlone, M. S., & Tofighbakhsh, J. (2000). Birds of a feather flock conjointly(?): Rhyme as reason in aphorisms. *Psychological Science, 11*, 424–428.

McGrath, J. (1984). *Groups: Interaction and performance.* Englewood Cliffs, NJ: Prentice-Hall.

McGuire, W. J. (1985). Attitudes and attitude change. In G. Lindzey & E. Aronson (Eds.), *Handbook of social psychology* (3rd ed., Vol. 2, pp. 233–346). New York: Random House.

McGuire, W. J. (1986). The myth of massive media impact: Savagings and salvagings. *Public Communication and Behavior, 1*, 173–257.

McGuire, W. J., & Padawer-Singer, A. (1978). Trait salience in the spontaneous self-concept. *Journal of Personality and Social Psychology, 33*, 743–754.

McGuire, W. J., & Papageorgis, D. (1961). The relative efficacy of various types of prior belief-defense in producing immunity against persuasion. *Journal of Abnormal and Social Psychology, 62*, 327–337.

McMahon, D. M. (2006). *Happiness: A history.* New York: Grove Press.

McNeil, B. J., Pauker, S. G., Sox, H. C., & Tversky, A. (1982). On the elicitation of preferences for alternative therapies. *New England Journal of Medicine, 306*, 1259–1262.

McNulty, J. K., & Karney, B. R. (2001). Attributions in marriage: Integrating specific and global evaluations of a relationship. *Personality and Social Psychology Bulletin, 27*, 943–955.

McNulty, J. K., Olson, M. A., Meltzer, A. L., & Shaffer, M. J. (2013). Though they may be unaware, newlyweds implicitly know whether their marriage will be satisfying. *Science, 342*, 1119–1120.

McPherson, K. (1983). Opinion-related information seeking: Personal and situational variables. *Personality and Social Psychology Bulletin, 9*, 116–124.

McQueen, A., & Klein, W. (2006). Experimental manipulations of self-affirmation: A systematic review. *Self and Identity, 5*, 289–354.

Mead, G. H. (1934). *Mind, self, and society.* Chicago: University of Chicago Press.

Medcoff, J. W. (1990). PEAT: An integrative model of attribution processes. In M. P. Zanna (Ed.), *Advances in experimental social psychology* (Vol. 23, pp. 111–209). New York: Academic Press.

Medvec, V. H., Madey, S. F., & Gilovich, T. (1995). When less is more: Counterfactual thinking and satisfaction among Olympic medalists. *Journal of Personality and Social Psychology, 69*, 603–610.

Mehrabian, A., & Williams, M. (1969). Nonverbal concomitants of perceived and intended persuasiveness. *Journal of Personality and Social Psychology, 13*, 37–58.

Mehta, P. H., & Josephs, R. A. (2010). Testosterone and cortisol jointly regulate dominance: Evidence for a dual-hormone hypothesis. *Hormones and Behavior, 58*, 898–906.

Mehta, R., & Zhu, R. J. (2009). Blue or red? Exploring the effect of color on cognitive performances. Science, 323, 1226–1229.

Meltzer, A. L., McNulty, J. K., Jackson, G. L., & Karney, B. R. (2014). Men still value physical attractiveness in a long-term mate more than women: Rejoinder to Eastwick, Neff, Finkel, Luchies, and Hunt. *Journal of Personality and Social Psychology106*, 435–440.

Merton, R. (1957). *Social theory and social structure.* Glencoe, IL: Free Press.

Mesquita, B. (2001). Emotions in collectivist and individualist contexts. *Journal of Personality and Social Psychology, 80*, 68–74.

Mesquita, B. (2003). Emotions as dynamic cultural phenomena. In R. J. Davidson, K. R. Scherer, & H. H. Goldsmith (Eds.), *Handbook of affective sciences* (pp. 871–890). New York: Oxford University Press.

Mesquita, B., & Ellsworth, P. C. (2001). The role of culture in appraisal. In K. R. Scherer & A. Schorr (Eds.), *Appraisal processes in emotion: Theory, methods, research.* New York: Oxford University Press.

Mesquita, B., & Frijda, N. H. (1992). Cultural variations in emotions: A review. *Psychological Bulletin, 112*, 179–204.

Mesquita, B., & Karasawa, M. (2002). Different emotional lives. *Cognition and Emotion, 16*, 127–141.

Mesquita, B., & Leu, J. (2007). The cultural psychology of emotion. In S. Kitayama & D. Cohen (Eds.), *The handbook of cultural psychology* (pp. 734–759). New York: Guilford Press.

Meyer, J. P., & Pepper, S. (1977). Need compatibility and marital adjustment in young married couples. *Journal of Personality and Social Psychology, 35*, 331–342.

Michaels, J. W., Blommel, J. M., Brocato, R. M., Linkous, R. A., & Rowe, J. S. (1982). Social facilitation and inhibition in a natural setting. *Replications in Social Psychology, 2*, 21–24.

Mikulincer, M. (1998). Attachment working models and the sense of trust: An exploration of interaction goals and affect regulation, *Journal of Personality and Social Psychology, 74*, 1209–1224.

Mikulincer, M., & Shaver, P. R. (2003). The attachment behavioral system in adulthood: Activation, psychodynamics, and interpersonal processes. In M. P. Zanna (Ed.), *Advances in experimental social psychology* (Vol. 35, pp. 53–152). New York: Academic Press.

Mikulincer, M., Shaver, P. R., Gillath, O., & Nitzberg, R. E. (2005). Attachment, caregiving, and altruism: Boosting attachment security increases compassion and helping. *Journal of Personality and Social Psychology, 89*, 817–839.

Milgram, S. (1961). Nationality and conformity. *Scientific American, 205*, 45–51.

Milgram, S. (1963). Behavioral study of obedience. *Journal of Abnormal and Social Psychology, 67*, 371–378.

Milgram, S. (1965). Some conditions of obedience and disobedience to authority. *Human Relations, 18*, 57–75.

Milgram, S. (1970). The experience of living in cities. *Science, 167*, 1461–1468.

Milgram, S. (1974). *Obedience to authority: An experimental view.* New York: Harper & Row.

Millar, M., & Tesser, A. (1986). Effects of affective and cognitive focus on the attitude-behavior relation. *Journal of Personality and Social Psychology, 51*, 270–276.

Miller, A. G. (1986). *The obedience experiments: A case study of controversy in social science.* New York: Praeger.

Miller, A. G., Ashton, W., & Mishal, M. (1990). Beliefs concerning the features of constrained behavior: A basis for the fundamental attribution error. *Journal of Personality and Social Psychology, 59*, 635–650.

Miller, A. G., Jones, E. E., & Hinkle, S. (1981). A robust attribution error in the personality domain. *Journal of Experimental Social Psychology, 17*, 587–600.

Miller, D. T., & McFarland, C. (1986). Counterfactual thinking and victim compensation: A test of norm theory. *Personality and Social Psychology Bulletin, 12*, 513–519.

Miller, D. T., & McFarland, C. (1991). When social comparison goes awry: The case of pluralistic ignorance. In J. M. Suls & T. A. Wills (Eds.), *Social comparison: Contemporary theory and research* (pp. 287–313). Hillsdale, NJ: Erlbaum.

Miller, D. T., & Taylor, B. R. (1995). Counterfactual thought, regret, and superstition: How to avoid kicking yourself. In N. J. Roese & J. M. Olson (Eds.), *What might have been: The social psychology of counterfactual thinking.* Mahwah, NJ: Erlbaum.

Miller, N., & Brewer, M. B. (1986). Categorization effects on ingroup and outgroup perception. In J. F. Dovidio & S. L. Gaertner (Eds.), *Prejudice, discrimination, and racism* (pp. 209–230). Orlando, FL: Academic Press.

Miller, N. E. (1941). The frustration-aggression hypothesis. *Psychological Review, 48*, 337–342.

Miller, N. E., & Bugelski, R. (1948). Minor studies of aggression: II. The influence of frustrations imposed by the in-group on attitudes expressed toward out-groups. *Journal of Psychology, 25*, 437–442.

Miller, R. S. (1992). The nature and severity of self-reported embarrassing circumstances. *Personality and Social Psychology Bulletin, 18*, 190–198.

Miller, R. S. (1996). *Embarrassment: Poise and peril in everyday life.* New York: Guilford Press.

Miller, R. S., & Leary, M. R. (1992). Social sources and interactive functions of embarrassment. In M. Clark (Ed.), *Emotion and social behavior.* Newbury Park, CA: Sage.

Miller, R. S., & Tangney, J. P. (1994). Differentiating embarrassment from shame. *Journal of Social and Clinical Psychology, 13*, 273–287.

Miller, S. L., & Maner, J. K. (2010). Scent of a woman: Men's testosterone responses to olfactory ovulation cues. *Psychological Science, 21*(2), 276–283.

Miller, S. L., & Maner, J. K. (2011). Ovulation as a male mating prime: Subtle signs of women's fertility influence men's mating cognition and behavior. *Journal of Personality and Social Psychology, 100*(2), 295–308.

Mineka, S., Rafaeli, E., & Yovel, I. (2003). Cognitive biases in emotional disorders: Information processing and social-cognitive perspectives. In R. J. Davidson, K. R. Scherer, & H. H. Goldsmith (Eds.), *Handbook of affective sciences* (pp. 976–1009). New York: Oxford University Press.

Miranda, J., & Storms, M. (1989). Psychological adjustment of lesbians and gay men. *Journal of Counseling & Development, 68*, 41–45.

Mischel, W., & Shoda, Y. (1995). A cognitive-affective system theory of personality: Reconceptualizing situations, dispositions, dynamics, and invariance in personality structures. *Psychological Review, 102*, 246–268.

Mita, T. H., Dermer, M., & Knight, J. (1977). Reversed facial images and the mere-exposure hypothesis. *Journal of Personality and Social Psychology, 35*, 597–601.

Mithen, S. (1996). *The prehistory of the mind: The cognitive origins of art and science.* London: Thames and Hudson.

Mohr, J. J., Selterman, D., & Fassinger, R. E. (2013). Romantic attachment and relationship functioning in same-sex couples. *Journal of Counseling Psychology, 60*(1), 72–82.

Molden, D. C., Hui, C. M., Scholer, A. A., Meier, B. P., Noreen, E. E., D'Agostino, P. R. & Martin, V. (2012). Motivational versus metabolic effects of carbohydrates on self-control. *Psychological Science, 23*, 1137–1144.

Moller, A. P. (1992a). Female swallow preference for symmetrical male sexual ornaments. *Nature, 357*, 238–240.

Moller, A. P. (1992b). Parasites differentially increase the degree of fluctuating asymmetry in secondary sexual characteristics. *Journal of Evolutionary Biology, 5*, 691–699.

Moore, J. S., Graziano, W. G., & Millar, M. G. (1987). Physical attractiveness, sex role orientation, and the evaluation of adults and children. *Personality and Social Psychology Bulletin, 13*, 95–102.

Moran, G., Cutler, B. L., & De Lisa, A. (1994). Attitudes toward tort reform, scientific jury selection, and juror bias: Verdict inclination in criminal and civil trials. *Law and Psychology Review, 18*, 309–328.

Moreland, R. L., & Beach, S. R. (1992). Exposure effects in the classroom: The development of affinity among students. *Journal of Experimental Social Psychology, 28*, 255–276.

Moreland, R. L., & Levine, J. M. (1989). Newcomers and oldtimers in small groups. In P. Paulus (Ed.), *Psychology of group influence* (2nd ed., pp. 143–186). Hillsdale, NJ: Erlbaum.

Morelli, G. A., & Rothbaum, F. (2007). Situating the child in context: Attachment relationships and self-regulation in different cultures. In *Handbook of Cultural Psychology* (pp. 500–527). New York: Guilford Press.

Morenoff, J. D., Sampson, R. J., & Raudenbush, S. (2001). Neighborhood inequality, collective efficacy, and the spatial dynamics of urban violence. *Criminology, 39*, 517–560.

Morgan, C. A., III, Hazlett, G., Doran, A., Garrett, S., Hoyt, G., et al. (2004). Accuracy of eyewitness memory for persons encountered during exposure to highly intense stress. *International Journal of Law and Psychiatry, 27*, 265–279.

Morris, M. W., & Peng, K. (1994). Culture and cause: American and Chinese attributions for social and physical events. *Journal of Personality and Social Psychology, 67*, 949–971.

Morrow, J., & Nolen-Hoeksema, S. (1990). Effects of responses to depression on the remediation of depressive affect. *Journal of Personality and Social Psychology, 58*, 519–527.

Moscovici, S. (1985). Social influence and conformity. In G. Lindzey & E. Aronson (Eds.), *The handbook of social psychology* (3rd ed., Vol. 2, pp. 347–412). New York: Random House.

Moscovici, S., Lage, E., & Naffrechoux, M. (1969). Influences of a consistent minority on the responses of a majority in a color perception task. *Sociometry, 32*, 365–380.

Moscovici, S., & Zavalloni, M. (1969). The group as a polarizer of attitudes. *Journal of Personality and Social Psychology, 12*, 125–135.

Moskowitz, D. S. (1994). Cross-situational generality and the interpersonal circumplex. *Journal of Personality and Social Psychology, 66*, 921–933.

Moskowitz, J. T., Epel, E. S., & Acree, M. (2008). Positive affect uniquely predicts lower risk of mortality in people with diabetes. *Health Psychology, 27*, 73–82.

Mountain, L. (2006). Safety cameras: Stealth tax or life-savers? *Significance, 3(3),* 111–113.

Mullen, B., & Riordan, C. A. (1988). Self-serving attributions for performance in naturalistic settings: A meta-analytic review. *Journal of Applied Social Psychology, 18*, 3–22.

Munro, D. (1985). Introduction. In D. Munro (Ed.), *Individualism and holism: Studies in Confucian and Taoist values* (pp. 1–34). Ann Arbor: Center for Chinese Studies, University of Michigan.

Muraven, M., & Slessareva, E. (2003). Mechanisms of self-control failure: Motivation and limited resources. *Personality and Social Psychology Bulletin, 29*, 894–906.

Muraven, M., Tice, D. M., & Baumeister, R. F. (1998). Self-control as a limited resource: regulatory depletion patterns. *Journal of Personality and Social Psychology, 74*, 774–789.

Muraven, M. R., & Baumeister, R. F. (2000). Self-regulation and depletion of limited resources: Does self-control resemble a muscle? *Psychological Bulletin, 126*, 247–259.

Murphy, S. T., & Zajonc, R. B. (1993). Affect, cognition, and awareness: Affective priming with optimal and suboptimal stimulus exposures. *Journal of Personality and Social Psychology, 64*, 723–739.

Murray, S. L., & Holmes, J. G. (1993). Seeing virtues in faults: Negativity and the transformation of interpersonal narratives in close relationships. *Journal of Personality and Social Psychology, 65*, 707–723.

Murray, S. L., & Holmes, J. G. (1997). A leap of faith? Positive illusions in romantic relationships. *Personality and Social Psychology Bulletin, 23*, 586–604.

Murray, S. L., & Holmes, J. G. (1999). The (mental) ties that bind: Cognitive structures that predict relationship resilience. *Journal of Personality and Social Psychology, 77*, 1228–1244.

Murray, S. L., Holmes, J. G., Dolderman, D., & Griffin, D. W. (2000). What the motivated mind sees: Comparing friends' perspectives to married partners' views of each other. *Journal of Experimental Social Psychology, 36*, 600–620.

Murray, S. L., Holmes, J. G., & Griffin, D. W. (1996). The benefits of positive illusions: Idealization and the construction of satisfaction in close relationships. *Journal of Personality and Social Psychology, 70*, 79–98.

Murray, S. L., Holmes, J. G., MacDonald, G., & Ellsworth, P. C. (1998). Through the looking glass darkly? When self-doubts turn into relationship insecurities. *Journal of Personality and Social Psychology, 75*, 1459–1480.

Muscatell, K. A., & Eisenberger, N. I. (2012). A social neuroscience perspective on stress and health. *Social and Personality Psychology Compass, 6*, 890–904.

Mustard, D. B. (2001). Racial, ethnic, and gender disparities in sentencing: Evidence from the U.S. federal courts. *Journal of Law and Economics, 19*, 285–314.

Mwaniki, M. K. (1973). *The relationship between self-concept and academic achievement in Kenyan pupils.* Unpublished doctoral dissertation, Stanford University, California.

Myers, D. G. (1999). Close relationships and quality of life. In K. Kahneman, E. Diener, & N. Schwarz (Eds.), *Well-being: The foundations of hedonic psychology* (pp. 374–391). New York: Russell Sage Foundation.

Myers, D. G. (2000a). *The American paradox.* New Haven: Yale University Press.

Myers, D. G. (2000b). The funds, friends, and faith of happy people. *American Psychologist, 55*, 56–67.

Myers, D. G., & Bishop, G. D. (1971). Enhancement of dominant attitudes in group discussion. *Journal of Personality and Social Psychology, 20*, 386–391.

Na, J., & Kitayama, S. (2011). Spontaneous trait inference is culture-specific: Behavioral and neural evidence. *Psychological Science, 22*, 1025–1032.

Nahemow, L., & Lawton, M. P. (1975). Similarity and propinquity in friendship formation. *Journal of Personality and Social Psychology, 32*, 205–213.

Neff, L. A., & Karney, B. R. (2002). Judgments of a relationship partner: Specific accuracy but global enhancement. *Journal of Personality, 70*, 1079–1112.

Neighbors, C., Larimer, M. E., & Lewis, M. A. (2004). Targeting misperceptions of descriptive drinking norms: Efficacy of a computer-delivered personalized normative feedback intervention. *Journal of Consulting and Clinical Psychology, 72*, 434–447.

Neimeyer, R. A., & Mitchell, K. A. (1988). Similarity and attraction: A longitudinal study. *Journal of Social and Personal Relationships, 5*, 131–148.

Nel, E., Helmreich, R., & Aronson, E. (1969). Opinion change in the advocate as a function of the persuasibility of his audience: A clarification on the meaning of dissonance. *Journal of Personality and Social Psychology, 12*, 117–124.

Nelson, L. D., & Morrison, E. L. (2005). Judgments of food and finances influence preferences for potential partners. *Psychological Science, 16*, 167–173.

Nemeroff, C., & Rozin, P. (1989). "You are what you eat": Applying the demand-free "impressions" technique to an unacknowledged belief. *Ethos, 17*, 50–69.

Nemeth, C. (1986). Differential contributions of majority and minority influence. *Psychological Review, 93*, 23–32.

Nesse, R. (1990). Evolutionary explanations of emotions. *Human Nature, 1*, 261–289.

Neuberg, S. L. (1988). Behavioral implications of information presented outside of conscious awareness: The effect of subliminal presentation of trait information on behavior in the Prisoner's Dilemma game. *Social Cognition, 6*, 207–230.

Neuberg, S. L., & Fiske, S. T. (1987). Motivational influences on impression formation: Outcome dependency, accuracy-driven attention, and individuating processes. *Journal of Personality and Social Psychology, 53*, 431–444.

Newcomb, T. M. (1956). The prediction of interpersonal attraction. *American Psychologist, 1*, 575–586.

Newcomb, T. M. (1961). *The acquaintance process.* New York: Holt, Rinehart and Winston.

Newman, L. S. (1991). Why are traits inferred spontaneously? A developmental approach. *Social Cognition, 9*, 221–253.

Newman, L. S. (1993). How individualists interpret behavior: Idiocentrism and spontaneous trait inference. *Social Cognition, 11*, 243–269.

Nickerson, D. W. (2008) Is voting contagious? Evidence from two field experiments. *American Political Science Review, 102,* 49–57.

Niedenthal, P. M. (2008). Emotion concepts. In M. Lewis, J. M. Haviland-Jones, & L. F. Barrett (Eds.), *Handbook of emotions* (pp. 587–600). New York: Guilford Press.

Niedenthal, P. M., Barsalou, L. W., Winkielman, P., Krauth-Gruber, S., & Ric, F. (2005). Embodiment in attitudes, social perception, and emotion. *Personality and Social Psychology Review, 9*, 184–211.

Niedenthal, P. M., Mermillod, M., Maringer, M., & Hess, U (2010). The Simulation of Smiles (SIMS) model: Embodied simulation and the meaning of facial expression. *Behavioral and Brain Sciences, 33*, 417–433.

Niedenthal, P.M., & Setterlund, M .B. (1994). Emotion congruence in perception. *Personality and Social Psychology Bulletin, 20*, 401–410.

Niedenthal, P. M., Winkielman, P. Mondillon, L., & Vermeulen, N. (2009). Embodiment of emotional concepts: Evidence from EMG measures. *Journal of Personality and Social Psychology, 96*, 1120–1136.

Nier, J. A., Gaertner, S. L., Dovidio, J. F., Banker, B. S. & Ward, C. M. (2001). Changing interracial evaluations and behavior: The benefits of a common ingroup identity. *Group Processes and Intergroup Relations, 4*, 299–316.

Nisbett, R. E. (1993). Violence and U.S. regional culture. *American Psychologist, 48*, 441–449.

Nisbett, R. E. (2003). *The geography of thought: Why we think the way we do.* New York: Free Press.

Nisbett, R. E. (2009). *Intelligence and how to get it: Why schools and cultures count.* New York: Norton.

Nisbett, R. E. (2015). *Mindware: Tools for Smart Thinking.* New York: Farrar, Straus & Giroux.

Nisbett, R. E., Caputo, C., Legant, P., & Maracek, J. (1973). Behavior as seen by the actor and as seen by the observer. *Journal of Personality and Social Psychology, 27*, 154–164.

Nisbett, R. E., & Cohen, D. (1996). *Culture of honor: The psychology of violence in the South.* Boulder, CO: Westview Press.

Nisbett, R. E., Fong, G. T., Lehman, D. R., & Cheng, P. W. (1987). Teaching reasoning. *Science, 238*, 625–631.

Nisbett, R. E., & Ross, L. (1980). *Human inference: Strategies and shortcomings of social judgment.* Englewood Cliffs, NJ: Prentice-Hall.

Nisbett, R. E., & Wilson, T. D. (1977). Telling more than we can know: Verbal reports on mental processes. *Psychological Review, 84*, 231–259.

Nolen-Hoeksema, S. (1987). Sex differences in unipolar depression: Evidence and theory. *Psychological Bulletin, 101*, 259–282.

Nolen-Hoeksema, S. (2003). *Women who think too much.* New York: Holt.

Norenzayan, A., Choi, I., & Nisbett, R. E. (1999). Eastern and Western perceptions of causality for social behavior: Lay theories about personalities and social situations. In D. Prentice & D. Miller (Eds.), *Cultural divides: Understanding and overcoming group conflict* (pp. 239–272). New York: Russell Sage Foundation.

Norenzayan, A., & Heine, S. J. (2004). *Psychological universals: What are they and how can we know?* Vancouver: University of British Columbia.

Norenzayan, A., & Shariff, A. F. (2008). The origin and evolution of religious prosociality. *Science, 322*, 58–62.

North, A. C., Hargreaves, D. J., and McKendrick, J. (1999). The influence of in-store music on wine selections. *Journal of Applied Psychology, 84*, 271–276.

Norton, M. I., Monin, B., Cooper, J., & Hogg, M. (2003). Vicarious dissonance: Attitude change from the inconsistency of others. *Journal of Personality and Social Psychology, 85*, 47–62.

Nosek, B. A., Banaji, M. R., & Greenwald, A. G. (2002). Harvesting implicit group attitudes and beliefs from demonstration web site. *Group Dynamics: Theory, Research, and Practice, 6*, 101–115.

Nosek, B. A., Greenwald, A. G., & Banaji, M. R. (2005). Understanding and using the Implicit Association Test: II. Method variables and construct validity. *Personality and Social Psychology Bulletin, 31*, 166–180.

Nowak, M. A., Page, K. M., & Sigmund, K. (2000). Fairness versus reason in the ultimatum game. *Science, 289*, 1773–1775.

Nowak, M. A., & Sigmund, K. (2005). Evolution of indirect reciprocity. *Nature, 437* (7063), 1291–1298.

Oakes, J. M., & Rossi, R. H. (2003). The measurement of SES in health research: Current practice and steps toward a new approach. *Social Science and Medicine, 56*, 769–784.

Oakes, P. J., & Turner, J. C. (1980). Social categorization and intergroup behavior: Does minimal intergroup discrimination make social identity more positive? *European Journal of Social Psychology, 10*, 295–301.

Oatley, K. (1993). Social construction in emotion. In M. Lewis & J. Haviland (Eds.), *Handbook of emotions* (pp. 342–352). New York: Guilford Press.

Oatley, K. (2003). Creative expression and communication of emotions in the visual and narrative arts. In R. J. Davidson, K. R. Scherer, & H. H. Goldsmith (Eds.). *Handbook of affective sciences* (pp. 481–502). New York: Oxford University Press.

Oatley, K., & Johnson-Laird, P. N. (2011). Basic emotions in social relationships, reasoning, and psychological illnesses. *Emotion Review, 3*, 424–433.

Oatley, K. (2004). *Emotions: A brief history.* Malden, MA: Blackwell.

Oatley, K., & Jenkins, J. M. (1992). Human emotions: Function and dysfunction. *Annual Review of Psychology, 43*, 55–85.

Oatley, K., Keltner, D., & Jenkins, J. (2006). *Understanding emotions* (2nd ed.). Malden, MA: Blackwell.

Ochsner, K. N., & Lieberman, M. D. (2001). The emergence of social cognitive neuroscience. *American Psychologist, 56*, 717–734.

Odean, T. (1998). Are investors reluctant to realize their losses? *Journal of Finance, 53*, 1775–1798.

O'Donovan, A., Lin, J., Dhabhar, F. S., Wolkowitz, O., Tillie, J. M., Blackburn, E., et al. (2009). Pessimism correlates with leukocyte telomere shortness and elevated interleukin-6 in post-menopausal women. *Brain Behavior Immunology, 23*(4), 446–449.

Ogbu, J. U. (1991). Low performance as an adaptation: The case of blacks in Stockton, California. In M. A. Gibson & J. U. Ogbu (Eds.), *Minority status and schooling* (pp. 249–285). New York: Garland.

Ogbu, J. U., & Davis, A. (2003). *Black American students in an affluent suburb: A study of academic disengagement.* Mahwah, NJ: Erlbaum.

Öhman, A. (1986). Face the beast and fear the face: Animal and social fears as prototypes for evolutionary analysis of emotions. *Psychophysiology, 23*, 123–145.

O'Keefe, D. J., & Figgé, M. (1997). A guilt-based explanation of the door-in-the-face influence strategy. *Human Communication Research, 24*, 64–81.

O'Keefe, D. J., & Hale, S. L. (1998). The door-in-the-face influence strategy: A random-effects meta-analytic review. In M. E. Roloff (Ed.), *Communication yearbook* (Vol. 21, pp. 1–33). Thousand Oaks, CA: Sage.

O'Keefe, D. J., & Hale, S. L. (2001). An odds-ratio-based meta-analysis of research on the door-in-the-face influence strategy. *Communication Reports, 14*, 31–38.

Olczak, P. V., Kaplan, M. F., & Penrod, S. (1991). Attorneys' lay psychology and its effectiveness in selecting jurors: Three empirical studies. *Journal of Social Behavior and Personality, 6*, 431–452.

Oliner, S., & Oliner, P. (1988). *The altruistic personality.* New York: Free Press.

Omoto, A. M., Malsch, A. M., & Barraza, J. A. (2009). Compassionate acts: Motivations for and correlates of volunteerism among older adults. In B. Fehr, S. Sprecher, & L. G. Underwood (Eds.), *The science of compassionate love: Theory, research, and applications* (pp. 257–282). Malden, MA: Wiley-Blackwell.

Omoto, A. M., & Snyder, M. (1995). Sustained helping without obligation: Motivation, longevity of service, and perceived attitude change among AIDS volunteers. *Journal of Personality and Social Psychology, 68*, 671–686.

Oppenheimer, D. M. (2008). The secret life of fluency. *Trends in Cognitive Sciences, 12*, 237–241.

Ostrom, T. M., & Sedikides, C. (1992). Out-group homogeneity effects in natural and minimal groups. *Psychological Bulletin, 112*, 536–552.

Oveis, C., Horberg, E. J., & Keltner, D. (2010). Compassion, pride, and social intuitions of self-other similarity. *Journal of Personality and Social Psychology, 98*, 618–630.

Oxman, T. E., & Hull, J. G. (1997). Social support, depression, and activities of daily living in older heart surgery patients. *Journal of Gerontology: Psychological Sciences, 52*, 1–14.

Oyserman, D., Bybee, D., & Terry, K. (2006). Possible selves and academic outcomes: How and when possible selves impel action. *Journal of Personality and Social Psychology, 91*, 188–204.

PA Consulting Group & UCL (2005). The national safety camera programme: Four-year evaluation report. http://www.dft.gov .uk/stellent/groups/dft_rdsafety/documents/downloadable/dft _rdsafety_610816.pdf.

Pallak, M. S., Mueller, M., Dollar, K., & Pallak, J. (1972). Effects of commitment on responsiveness to an extreme consonant communication. *Journal of Personality and Social Psychology, 23*, 429–436.

Park, B., & Judd, C. M. (1990). Measures and models of perceived group variability. *Journal of Personality and Social Psychology, 59*, 173–191.

Park, B., & Rothbart, M. (1982). Perception of out-group homogeneity and levels of social categorization: Memory for the subordinate attributes of in-group and out-group members. *Journal of Personality and Social Psychology, 42*, 1051–1068.

Parrott, W. G. (2001). Implications of dysfunctional emotions for understanding how emotions function. *Review of General Psychology, 5*, 180–186.

Parrott, W. G., & Smith, S. F. (1991). Embarrassment: Actual vs. typical cases, classical vs. prototypical representations. *Cognition and Emotion, 5*, 467–488.

Payne, B. K. (2001). Prejudice and perception: The role of automatic and controlled processes in misperceiving a weapon. *Journal of Personality and Social Psychology, 81*, 181–192.

Payne, B. K. (2006). Weapons bias: Split-second decisions and unintended stereotyping. *Current Directions in Psychological Science, 15*, 287–291.

Payne, B. K., Lambert, A.J., & Jacoby, L. L. (2002). Best laid plans: Effect of goals on accessibility bias and cognitive control in race-based misperceptions of weapons. *Journal of Experimental Social Psychology, 38*, 384–396.

Pearson, C. M., & Porath, C. L. (1999). *Workplace incivility: The target's-eye view.* Paper presented at the Annual Meeting of the Academy of Management, Chicago.

Peng, K., & Knowles, E. (2003). Culture, ethnicity and the attribution of physical causality. *Personality and Social Psychology Bulletin, 29*, 1272–1284.

Pennebaker, J. W. (1989). Confession, inhibition, and disease. In L. Berkowitz (Ed.), *Advances in experimental social psychology* (Vol. 22, pp. 211–244). New York: Academic Press.

Pennebaker, J. W. (1993). Putting stress into words: Health, linguistic and therapeutic implications. *Behavioral Research and Therapy, 31*, 539–548.

Pennebaker, J. W., Hughes, C. F., & O'Heeron, R. C. (1987). The psychophysiology of confession: Linking inhibitory and psychosomatic processes. *Journal of Personality and Social Psychology, 52*, 781–793.

Pennebaker, J. W., Mayne, T. J., & Francis, M. (1997). Linguistic predictors of adaptive bereavement. *Journal of Personality and Social Psychology, 72*, 863–871.

Pennebaker, J. W., & Roberts, T. A. (1992). Toward a his and hers theory of emotion: Gender differences in visceral perception. *Journal of Social and Clinical Psychology, 11*, 199–212.

Penner, L. A., Dovidio, J. F., Piliavin, J. A., & Schroeder, D. A. (2005). Prosocial behavior: Multi-level perspectives. *Annual Review of Psychology, 56*, 365–392.

Pennington, N., & Hastie, R. (1990). Practical implications of psychological research on juror and jury decision making. *Personality and Social Psychology Bulletin, 16*, 90–105.

Penton-Voak, I. S., Perrett, D. I., Castles, D. L., Kobayashi, T., Burt, D. M., Murray, L. K., et al. (1999). Menstrual cycle alters face preference. *Nature, 399*, 741–742.

Peplau, L. A., & Fingerhut, A. W. (2007). The close relationships of lesbians and gay men. *Annual Review of Psychology, 58,* 10.1–10.20.

Peplau, L. A., Frederick, D. A., Yee, C., Maisel, N., Lever, J., & Ghavami, N. (2009). Body image satisfaction in heterosexual, gay, and lesbian adults. *Archives of Sexual Behavior, 38(5)*, 713–725.

Pérez-Benítez, C. I., O'Brien, W. H., Carels, R. A., Gordon, A. K., & Chiros, C. E. (2007). Cardiovascular correlates of disclosing homosexual orientation. *Stress and Health, 23(3)*, 141–152.

Perkins, H. W., & Craig, D. W. (2006). A successful social norms campaign to reduce alcohol misuse among college student-athletes. *Journal of Studies on Alcohol, 67*, 880–889.

Perkins, H. W., Haines, M. P., & Rice, R. (2005). Misperceiving the college drinking norm and related problems: A nationwide study of exposure to prevention information, perceived norms and student alcohol misuse. *Journal of Studies on Alcohol, 66*, 470–478.

Perloff, R. M. (1993). Third-person effect research 1983–1992: A review and synthesis. *International Journal of Public Opinion Research, 5*, 167–184.

Perner, J., Frith, U., Leslie, A. M., & Leekam, S. R. (1989). Exploration of the autistic child's theory of mind: Knowledge, belief and communication. *Child Development, 60*, 689–700.

Perper, T. (1985). *Sex signals: The biology of love.* Philadelphia: ISI Press.

Perrett, D. I., Lee, K., Penton-Voak, I., Burt, D. M., Rowland, D., Yoshikawa, S., et al. (1998). Sexual dimorphism and facial attractiveness. *Nature, 394,* 884–886.

Perrett, D. I., May, K. A., & Yoshikawa, S. (1994). Facial shape and judgments of female attractiveness. *Nature, 368,* 239–242.

Perrin, S., & Spencer, C. (1981). Independence of conformity in the Asch experiment as a reflection of cultural or situational factors. *British Journal of Social Psychology, 20,* 205–209.

Pessin, J. (1933). The comparative effects of social and mechanical stimulation on memorizing. *American Journal of Psychology, 45,* 263–270.

Pessin, J., & Husband, R. W. (1933). Effect of social stimulation on human maze learning. *Journal of Abnormal and Social Psychology, 28,* 148–154.

Peterson, C. (2000). The future of optimism. *American Psychologist, 55,* 44–55.

Peterson, C., & Barrett, L. C. (1987). Explanatory style and academic performance among university freshmen. *Journal of Personality and Social Psychology, 53,* 603–607.

Peterson, C., Maier, S., & Seligman, M. E. P. (1993). *Learned helplessness.* New York: Oxford University Press.

Peterson, C., Seligman, M. E. P., & Vaillant, G. E. (1988). Pessimistic explanatory style is a risk factor for physical illness: A thirty-five-year longitudinal study. *Journal of Personality and Social Psychology, 55,* 23–27.

Petrocelli, J. V., Tormala, Z. L., & Rucker, D. D. (2007). Unpacking attitude certainty: Attitude clarity and attitude correctness. *Journal of Personality and Social Psychology, 92,* 30–41.

Pettigrew, T. (1979). The ultimate attribution error: Extending Allport's cognitive analysis to prejudice. *Personality and Social Psychology Bulletin, 5,* 461–476.

Pettigrew, T. F., & Tropp, L. R. (2000). Does intergroup contact reduce prejudice? Recent meta-analytic findings. In S. Oskamp (Ed.), *Reducing prejudice and discrimination: The Claremont Symposium on Applied Social Psychology* (pp. 93–114). Mahwah, NJ: Erlbaum.

Pettigrew, T. F., & Tropp, L. R. (2006). A meta-analytic test of intergroup contact theory. *Journal of Personality and Social Psychology, 90,* 751–783.

Pettigrew, T. F., & Tropp, L. R. (2008). How does intergroup contact reduce prejudice? Meta-analytic tests of three mediators. *European Journal of Social Psychology, 38,* 922–934.

Petty, R.E. (1997). The evolution of theory and research in social psychology: From single to multiple effect and process models. In C. McGarty & S. A. Haslam (Eds.), *The message of social psychology: Perspectives on mind in society* (pp. 268–290). Oxford, England: Blackwell.

Petty, R. E., & Brinol, P. (2008). Persuasion: From single to multiple to metacognitive processes. *Perspectives on Psychological Science, 3,* 137–147.

Petty, R. E., Briñol, P., & Tormala, Z. L. (2002). Thought confidence as a determinant of persuasion: The self-validation hypothesis. *Journal of Personality and Social Psychology, 82,* 722–741.

Petty, R. E., Briñol, P., Tormala, Z. L., & Wegener, D. T. (2007). The role of metacognition in social judgment. In E. T. Higgins & A. W. Kruglanski, (Eds.) *Social psychology: A handbook of basic principles* (2nd ed., pp. 254–284). New York: Guilford Press.

Petty, R. E., & Cacioppo, J. T. (1979). Issue involvement can increase or decrease persuasion by enhancing message-relevant cognitive responses. *Journal of Personality and Social Psychology, 37,* 1915–1926.

Petty, R. E., & Cacioppo, J. T. (1984). The effects of involvement on responses to argument quantity and quality: Central and peripheral routes to persuasion. *Journal of Personality and Social Psychology, 46,* 69–81.

Petty, R. E., & Cacioppo, J. T. (1986). The elaboration likelihood model of persuasion. In L. Berkowitz (Ed.), *Advances in experimental social psychology* (Vol. 19, pp. 123–205). New York: Academic Press.

Petty, R. E., Cacioppo, J. T., & Goldman, R. (1981). Personal involvement as a determinant of argument-based persuasion. *Journal of Personality and Social Psychology, 41,* 847–855.

Petty, R. E., Cacioppo, J. T., & Schumann, D. W. (1983). Central and peripheral routes to advertising effectiveness: The moderating role of involvement. *Journal of Consumer Research, 10,* 135–146.

Petty, R. E., Haugtvedt, C. P., & Smith, S. M. (1995). Elaboration as a determinant of attitude strength. In R. E. Petty & J. A. Krosnick (Eds.), *Attitude strength: Antecedents and consequences* (pp. 93–130). Mahwah, NJ: Erlbaum.

Petty, R. E., & Wegener, D. (1998). Attitude change: Multiple roles for persuasion variables. In D. T. Gilbert, S. T. Fiske, & G. Lindzey (Eds.), *Handbook of social psychology* (4th ed., pp. 323–390). New York: McGraw-Hill.

Pew Research Center. (2007, January 9). How young people view their lives, futures, and politics: A portrait of "generation next."

Pfeifer, J. H., Masten, C. L., Borofsky, L. A., Dapretto, M., Fuligni, A. J., & Lieberman, M. D. (2009). Neural correlates of direct and reflected self-appraisals in adolescents and adults: When social perspective taking informs self-perception. *Child Development, 80,* 1016–1038.

Phelps, E. A., O'Connor, K. J., Cunningham, W. A., Funayama, E. S., Gatenby, J. C., Gore, J. C., et al. (2000). Performance on indirect measure of race evaluation predicts amygdala activation. *Journal of Cognitive Neuroscience, 12,* 729–738.

Phillips, D. P. (1986). Natural experiments on the effects of mass media violence on fatal aggression: Strengths and weakness of a new approach. In L. Berkowitz (Ed.), *Advances in experimental social psychology* (Vol. 19, pp. 207–250). Orlando, FL: Academic Press.

Piaget, J., & Inhelder, B. (1958). *The growth of logical thinking from childhood to adolescence.* New York: Basic Books.

Piedmont, R. L., & Chase, J. H. (1997). Cross-cultural generality of the five-factor model of personality: Development and validation of the NEO-PI-R for Koreans. *Journal of Cross-Cultural Psychology, 28,* 131–155.

Pietromonaco, P. R., & Feldman-Barrett, L. (2000). Internal working models: What do we know about knowing the self in relation to others? *Review of General Psychology, 4,* 155–175.

Piff, P. K., Kraus, M. W., Côté, S., Cheng, B., & Keltner, D. (2010). Having less, giving more: The influence of social class on prosocial behavior, *Journal of Personality and Social Psychology, 99,* 771–784.

Piliavin, J. A., & Piliavin, I. M. (1972). The effects of blood on reactions to a victim. *Journal of Personality and Social Psychology, 23,* 253–261.

Piliavin, J. A., Piliavin, I. M., & Broll, L. (1976). Time of arousal at an emergency and likelihood of helping. *Personality and Social Psychology Bulletin, 2,* 273–276.

Pinel, E. (1999). Stigma consciousness: The psychological legacy of social stereotypes. *Journal of Personality and Social Psychology, 76,* 114–128.

Pinker, S. (1994). *The language instinct.* New York: HarperCollins.

Pinker, S. (2002). *The blank slate: The modern denial of human nature.* New York: Viking.

Pinker, S. (2003). *The blank slate: The modern denial of human nature.* London: Penguin Books.

Pinker, S. (2007). A history of violence [Electronic version]. *The New Republic Online.* Retrieved March 16, 2009.

Pinker, S. (2011). *The better angels of our nature: Why violence has declined.* New York: Viking.

Place, S. S., Todd, P. M., Penke, L., & Asendorpf, J. B. (2009). The ability to judge the romantic interest of others. *Psychological Science, 20(1),* 22–26.

Plaks, J. E., & Higgins, E. T. (2000). Pragmatic use of stereotyping in teamwork: Social loafing and compensation as a function of inferred partner–situation fit. *Journal of Personality and Social Psychology, 79,* 962–974.

Plant, E. A., & Devine, P. G. (1998). Internal and external motivation to respond without prejudice. *Journal of Personality and Social Psychology, 75,* 811–832.

Plant, E. A., Kling, K. C., & Smith, G. L. (2004). The influence of gender and social role on the interpretation of facial expressions. *Sex Roles, 51,* 187–196.

Plant, E. A., & Peruche, B. M. (2005). The consequences of race for police officers' responses to criminal suspects. *Psychological Science, 16,* 180–183.

Plant, E. A., Peruche, B. M., & Butz, D. A. (2005). Eliminating automatic racial bias: Making race non-diagnostic for responses to criminal suspects. *Journal of Experimental Social Psychology, 41,* 141–156.

Platania, J., & Moran, G. P. (2001). Social facilitation as a function of the mere presence of others. *Journal of Social Psychology, 141,* 190–197.

Platt, J. J., & James, W. T. (1966). Social facilitation of eating behavior in young opossums: I. Group vs. solitary feeding. *Psychonomic Science, 6,* 421–422.

Platt, J. J., Yaksh, T., & Darby, C. L. (1967). Social facilitation of eating behavior in armadillos. *Psychological Reports, 20,* 1136.

Plous, S. (1985). Perceptual illusions and military realities. *Journal of Conflict Resolution, 29,* 363–389.

Podratz, K. E., Halverson, S. K., & Dipboye, R. L. (2004). Physical attractiveness biases in ratings of employment suitability: Tracking down the "beauty is beastly." Manuscript submitted for publication.

Polak, M. (1993). Parasitic infection increases fluctuating asymmetry of male *Drosophila nigrospiracula:* Implications for sexual selection. *Genetica, 89,* 255–265.

Pollock, C. L., Smith, S. D., Knowles, E. S., & Bruce, H. J. (1998). Mindfulness limits compliance with the that's-not-all technique. *Personality and Social Psychology Bulletin, 24,* 1153–1157.

Postmes, T., & Spears, R. (1998). Deindividuation and antinormative behavior: A meta-analysis. *Psychological Bulletin, 123,* 238–259.

Pound, N., Penton-Voak, I. S., & Brown, W. M. (2007). Facial symmetry is positively associated with self-reported extraversion. *Personality and Individual Differences, 43,* 1572–1582.

Pratkanis, A. R., Greenwald, A. G., Leippe, M. R., & Baumgardner, M. H. (1988). In search of reliable persuasion effects: III. The sleeper effect is dead. Long live the sleeper effect. *Journal of Personality and Social Psychology, 54,* 203–218.

Pratto, F., & Bargh, J. A. (1991). Stereotyping based upon apparently individuating information: Trait and global components of sex stereotypes under attention overload. *Journal of Experimental Psychology, 27,* 26–47.

Prentice, D. A. (1990). Familiarity and differences in self- and other-representations. *Journal of Personality and Social Psychology, 59,* 369–383.

Prentice, D. A., & Miller, D. T. (1993). Pluralistic ignorance and alcohol use on campus: Some consequences of misperceiving the social norm. *Journal of Personality and Social Psychology, 64,* 243–256.

Prentice-Dunn, S., & Rogers, R. W. (1989). Deindividuation and self-regulation of behavior. In P. Paulus (Ed.), *The psychology of group influence* (2nd ed., pp. 87–109). Hillsdale, NJ: Erlbaum.

Preston, C. E., & Harris, S. (1965). Psychology of drivers in traffic accidents. *Journal of Applied Psychology, 49,* 284–288.

Preston, S. D., & de Waal, F. B. M. (2002). Empathy: Its ultimate and proximate bases. *Behavioral and Brain Sciences, 25,* 1–72.

Preuschoft, S. (1992). "Laughter" and "smile" in Barbary macaques (*Macaca sylvanus*). *Ethology, 91,* 220–236.

Price, K. H., Harrison, D. A., & Gavin, J. H. (2006). Withholding inputs in team contexts: Member composition, interaction processes, evaluation structure, and social loafing. *Journal of Applied Social Psychology, 90,* 197–209.

Pronin, E., Berger, J., & Molouki, S. (2007). Alone in a crowd of sheep: Asymmetric perceptions of conformity and their roots in an introspection illusion. *Journal of Personality and Social Psychology, 92,* 585–595.

Pronin, E., Gilovich, T., & Ross, L. (2004). Objectivity in the eye of the beholder: Divergent perceptions of bias in self versus others. *Psychological Review, 111,* 781–799.

Pronin, E., Kruger, J., Savitsky, K., & Ross, L. (2001). You don't know me, but I know you: The illusion of asymmetric insight. *Journal of Personality and Social Psychology, 81,* 639–656. Pronin, E., Lin, D. Y., & Ross, L. (2002). The bias blind spot: Perceptions of bias in self versus others. *Personality and Social Psychology Bulletin, 28,* 369–381.

Provine, R. R. (1992). Contagious laughter: Laughter is a sufficient stimulus for laughs and smiles. *Bulletin of the Psychonomic Society, 30,* 1–4.

Ptacek, J. T., & Dodge, K. L. (1995). Coping strategies and relationship satisfaction in couples. *Personality and Social Psychology Bulletin, 21,* 76–84.

Puts, D. A. (2005). Mating context and menstrual phase affect women's preferences for male voice pitch. *Evolution and Human Behavior, 26,* 388–397.

Pyszczynski, T., Abdollahi, A., Solomon, S., Greenberg, J., Cohen, F., & Weise, D. (2006). Mortality salience, martyrdom, and military might: The great Satan versus the Axis of Evil. *Personality and Social Psychology Bulletin, 32,* 525–537.

Pyszczynski, T., & Greenberg, J. (1987). Toward an integration of cognitive and motivational perspectives on social inference: A biased hypothesis-testing model. In L. Berkowitz (Ed.), *Advances in experimental social psychology* (Vol. 20, pp. 297–340). New York: Academic Press.

Quattrone, G. A., & Jones, E. E. (1980). The perception of variability within in-groups and out-groups: Implications for the law of small numbers. *Journal of Personality and Social Psychology, 38,* 141–152.

Queller, S., & Smith, E. R. (2002). Subtyping versus bookkeeping in stereotype learning and change: Connectionist simulations and empirical findings. *Journal of Personality and Social Psychology, 82,* 300–313.

Quigley, B., & Tedeschi, J. (1996). Mediating effects of blame attributions on feelings of anger. *Personality and Social Psychology Bulletin, 22,* 1280–1288.

Rajecki, D. W., Bledsoe, S. B., & Rasmussen, J. L. (1991). Successful personal ads: Gender differences and similarities in offers, stipulations, and outcomes. *Basic and Applied Psychology, 12,* 457–469.

Rajecki, D. W., Ickes, W., Corcoran, C., & Lenerz, K. (1977). Social facilitation of human performance: Mere presence effects. *Journal of Social Psychology, 102,* 297–310.

Rand, D. G., Arbesman, S., & Christakis, N. A. (2011). Dynamic networks promote cooperation in experiments with humans. *Proceedings of the National Academy of Sciences, 108,* 19193–19198.

Rand, D. G., & Epstein, Z. G. (2014). Risking your life without a second thought: Intuitive decision-making and extreme altruism, *PLoS ONE,* 9 e109687.

Rand, D. G., & Nowak, M. A. (2013) Human cooperation. *Trends in Cognitive Sciences, 17,* 413–425.

Rasinski, H., Geers, A. L., & Czopp, A. M. (2013). "I guess what he said wasn't that bad": Dissonance in nonconfronting targets of prejudice. *Personality and Social Psychology Bulletin, 39,* 856–869.

Raz, N., Gunning, F. M., Head, D., Dupuis, J. H., McQuain, J., Briggs, S. D., et al. (1997). Selective aging of the human cerebral cortex observed in vivo: Differential vulnerability of the prefrontal gray matter. *Cerebral Cortex, 7,* 268–282.

Read, A. W., et al. (1978). *Funk and Wagnalls new comprehensive international dictionary of the English language.* New York: Publishers Guild Press.

Read, S. J. (1984). Analogical reasoning social judgment: The importance of causal theories. *Journal of Personality and Social Psychology, 46,* 14–25.

Read, S. J. (1987). Similarity and causality in the use of social analogies. *Journal of Experimental Social Psychology, 23,* 189–207.

Read, S. J., & Urada, S. I. (2003). A neural network simulation of the outgroup homogeniety effect. *Personality and Social Psychology Review, 7,* 146–159.

Realo, A., & Allik, J. (1999). A cross-cultural study of collectivism: A comparison of American, Estonian, and Russian students. The Journal of Social Psychology, 139, 133–142.

Reber, R., Schwarz, N., & Winkielman, P. (2004). Processing fluency and aesthetic pleasure: Is beauty in the perceiver's processing experience? *Personality and Social Psychology Review, 8,* 364–382.

Reber, R., Winkielman, P., & Schwarz, N. (1998). Effects of perceptual fluency on affective judgments. *Psychological Science, 9,* 45–48.

Redelmeier, D. A., Katz, J., & Kahneman, D. (2003). Memories of colonoscopy: A randomized trial. *Pain, 104,* 187–194.

Reed, J. (1981). Below the Smith and Wesson line: Reflections on Southern violence. In M. Black & J. Reed (Eds.), *Perspectives on the American South: An annual review of society, politics, and culture.* New York: Gordon and Breach Science Publications.

Reed, J. S. (1990). Billy, the fabulous moolah, and me. In J. S. Reed (Ed.), *Whistling Dixie* (pp. 119–122). San Diego, CA: Harcourt Brace Jovanovich.

Reeder, G. D., Monroe, A. E., & Pryor, J. B. (2008). Impressions of Milgram's obedient teachers: Situational cues inform inferences about motives and traits. *Journal of Personality and Social Psychology, 95,* 1–17.

Reeves, R. A., Baker, G. A., Boyd, J. G., & Cialdini, R. B. (1991). The door-in-the-face technique: Reciprocal concessions vs. self-presentational explanations. *Journal of Social Behavior and Personality, 6,* 645–658.

Reeves-Sanday, P. (1997). The socio-cultural context of rape: A cross-cultural study. In L. L. O'Toole (Ed.), *Gender violence: Interdisciplinary perspectives.* New York: New York University Press.

Regan, D. T. (1971). Effects of a favor and liking on compliance. *Journal of Experimental Social Psychology, 7,* 627–639.

Regan, D. T., & Kilduff, M. (1988). Optimism about elections: Dissonance reduction at the ballot box. *Political Psychology, 9,* 101–107.

Regan, D. T., Williams, M., & Sparling, S. (1972). Voluntary expiation of guilt: A field experiment. *Journal of Personality and Social Psychology, 24,* 42–45.

Regan, J. W. (1971). Guilt, perceived injustice, and altruistic behavior. *Journal of Personality and Social Psychology, 18,* 124–132.

Reifman, A. S., Larrick, R. P., & Fein, S. (1991). Temper and temperature on the diamond: The heat-aggression relationship in major league baseball. *Personality and Social Psychology Bulletin, 17,* 580–585.

Reis, H. T., Maniaci, M.R., Caprariello, P.A., Eastwick, P.W., Finkel, E.J. (2011). Familiarity does indeed promote attraction in live interaction. *Journal of Personality and Social Psychology, 101,* 557–570.

Reis, H. T., Nezlek, J., & Wheeler, L. (1980). Physical attractiveness in social interaction. *Journal of Personality and Social Psychology, 38,* 604–617.

Reis, H. T., Wheeler, L., Speigel, N., Kernis, M. H., Nezlek, J., & Perri, M. (1982). Physical attractiveness in social interaction: 2. Why does appearance affect social experience? *Journal of Personality and Social Psychology, 43,* 979–996.

Remley, A. (1988, October). From obedience to independence. *Psychology Today,* 56–59.

Rhee, E., Uleman, J. S., Lee, H. K., & Roman, R. J. (1995). Spontaneous self-descriptions and ethnic identities in individualistic and collectivist cultures. *Journal of Personality and Social Psychology, 69,* 142–152.

Rhine, R. J., & Severance, L. J. (1970). Ego-involvement, discrepancy, source credibility, and attitude *change. Journal of Personality and Social Psychology, 16,* 175–190.

Rhodes, G. (2006). The evolutionary psychology of facial beauty. *Annual Review of Psychology, 57,* 199–226.

Rhodes, G., Yoshikawa, S., Clark, A., Lee, K., McKay, R., & Akamatsu, S. (2001). Attractiveness of facial averageness and symmetry in non-Western cultures: In search of biologically based standards of beauty. *Perception, 30,* 611–625.

Richards, Z., & Hewstone, M. (2001). Subtyping and subgrouping: Processes for the prevention and promotion of stereotype change. *Personality and Social Psychology Review, 5,* 52–73.

Rigdon, M., Ishii, K., Watabe, M., & Kitayama, S. (2009). Minimal social cues in the dictator game. *Journal of Economic Psychology, 30,* 358–367.

Riggio, R. E., & Friedman, H. S. (1983). Individual differences and cues to deception. *Journal of Personality and Social Psychology, 45,* 899–915.

Riggio, R. E., & Woll, S. B. (1984). The role of nonverbal cues and physical attractiveness in the selection of dating partners. *Journal of Social and Personal Relationships, 1,* 347–357.

Rilling, J. K., Gutman, D. A., Zeh, T. R., Pagnoni, G., Berns, G. S., & Kilts, C. D. (2002). A neural basis for cooperation. *Neuron, 35,* 395–405.

Risen, J. L., & Critcher, C. R. (2011). Visceral fit: While in a visceral state, associated states of the world seem more likely. *Journal of Personality and Social Psychology, 100,* 777–785.

Risen, J. L., & Gilovich, T. (2007). Another look at why people are reluctant to exchange lottery tickets. *Journal of Personality and Social Psychology, 93,* 12–22.

Risen, J. L., & Gilovich, T. (2008). Why people are reluctant to tempt fate. *Journal of Personality and Social Psychology, 95,* 293–307.

Risen, J. L., Gilovich, T., & Dunning, D. (2007). One-shot illusory correlations and stereotyping. *Personality and Social Psychology Bulletin, 33,* 1492–1502.

Ritov, I. & Kogut, T. (2011). Ally or adversary: the effect of identifiability in inter-group conflict situations. *Organizational Behavior and Human Decision Process, 116,* 96–103.

Robberson, M. R., & Rogers, R. W. (1988). Beyond fear appeals: Negative and positive persuasive appeals to health and self-esteem. *Journal of Applied Social Psychology, 18,* 277–287.

Roberts, T. A., & Pennebaker, J. W. (1995). Gender differences in perceiving internal state: Toward a his-and-hers model of perceptual cue use. In M. Zanna (Ed.), *Advances in experimental social psychology* (Vol. 27, pp. 143–176). New York: Academic Press.

Robins, R. W., & Beer, J. S. (2001). Positive illusions about the self: Short-term benefits and long-term costs. *Journal of Personality and Social Psychology, 80,* 340–352.

Robinson, J., & McArthur, L. Z. (1982). Impact of salient vocal qualities on causal attribution for a speaker's behavior. *Journal of Personality and Social Psychology, 43,* 236–247.

Robinson, R., Keltner, D., Ward, A., & Ross, L. (1995). Actual versus assumed differences in construal: "Naive realism" in intergroup perception and conflict. *Journal of Personality and Social Psychology, 68,* 404–417.

Rodeheffer, C. D., Hill, S. E., & Lord, C. G. (2012). Does this recession make me look black? The effect of resource scarcity on the categorization on biracial faces. *Psychological Science, 23(12),* 1476–1478.

Rodriguez Mosquera, P. M., Fischer, A. H., & Manstead, A. S. R. (2000). The role of honor-related values in the elicitation, experience, and communication of pride, shame, and anger: Spain and the Netherlands compared. *Personality and Social Psychology Bulletin, 26,* 833–844.

Rodriguez Mosquera, P. M., Fischer, A. H., & Manstead, A. S. R. (2004). Inside the heart of emotion: On culture and relational concerns. In L. Z. Tiedens & C. W. Leach, *The social life of emotions* (pp. 187–202). New York: Cambridge University Press.

Roesch, S. C., & Amirkhan, J. H. (1997). Boundary conditions for self-serving attributions: Another look at the sports pages. *Journal of Applied Social Psychology, 27,* 245–261.

Roese, N. J. (1997). Counterfactual thinking. *Psychological Bulletin, 121,* 133–148.

Roese, N. J., & Olson, J. M. (Eds.). (1995). *What might have been: The social psychology of counterfactual thinking.* Mahwah, NJ: Erlbaum.

Rogers, R. W., & Mewborn, C. R. (1976). Fear appeals and attitude change: Effects of a threat's noxiousness, probability of occurrence and the efficacy of coping responses. *Journal of Personality and Social Psychology, 34,* 54–61.

Rohrer, J. H., Baron, S. H., Hoffman, E. L., & Swander, D. V. (1954). The stability of autokinetic judgments. *Journal of Abnormal and Social Psychology, 49,* 595–597.

Rolls, E. T. (2000). The orbitofrontal cortext and reward. *Cerebral Cortex, 10,* 284–294.

Roseman, I. J. (1991). Appraisal determinants of discrete emotions. *Cognition and Emotion, 5,* 161–200.

Rosenberg, L. A. (1961). Group size, prior experience, and conformity. *Journal of Abnormal and Social Psychology, 63,* 436–437.

Rosenberg, M. (1965). *Society and the adolescent self-image.* Princeton, NJ: Princeton University Press.

Rosenblatt, A., & Greenberg, J. (1988). Depression and interpersonal attraction: The role of perceived similarity. *Journal of Personality and Social Psychology, 55,* 112–119.

Rosenblatt, A., Greenberg, J., Solomon, S., Pyszczynski, T., & Lyon, D. (1989). Evidence for terror management theory I: The effects of mortality salience on reactions to those who violate or uphold cultural values. *Journal of Personality and Social Psychology, 57,* 681–690.

Rosenthal, R., & Jacobson, L. (1968). *Pygmalion in the classroom: Teacher expectation and student intellectual development.* New York: Holt, Rinehart, and Winston.

Ross, C., Mirowsky, J., & Goldsteen, K. (1990). The impact of the family on health: The decade in review. *Journal of Marriage and the Family, 52,* 1059–1078.

Ross, L. (1977). The intuitive psychologist and his shortcomings. In L. Berkowitz (Ed.), *Advances in experimental social psychology* (Vol. 10, pp. 173–220). New York: Academic Press.

Ross, L. (1988). Situationist perspectives on the obedience experiments. *Contemporary Psychology, 33,* 101–104.

Ross, L., Amabile, T. M., & Steinmetz, J. L. (1977). Social roles, social control, and biases on social-perception processes. *Journal of Personality and Social Psychology, 35,* 485–494.

Ross, L., Bierbrauer, G., & Hoffman, S. (1976). The role of attribution process in conformity and dissent: Revisiting the Asch situation. *American Psychologist, 31,* 148–157.

Ross, L., & Stillinger, C. (1991). Barriers to conflict resolution. *Negotiation Journal, 8,* 389–404.

Ross, L., & Ward, A. (1995). Psychological barriers to dispute resolution. In M. P. Zanna (Ed.), Advances in experimental social psychology (Vol. 27, pp. 255–304). San Diego, CA: Academic Press.

Ross, L., & Ward, A. (1996). Naive realism in everyday life: Implications for social conflict and misunderstanding. In T. Brown, E. S. Reed, & E. Turiel (Eds.), *Values and knowledge.* The Jean Piaget Symposium Series (pp. 103–135). Hillsdale, NJ: Erlbaum.

Ross, M., & Sicoly, F. (1979). Egocentric biases in availability and attribution. *Journal of Personality and Social Psychology, 32,* 880–892.

Ross, M. W. (1990). The relationship between life events and mental health in homosexual men. *Journal of Clinical Psychology, 46,* 402–411.

Ross, S., & Ross, J. G. (1949). Social facilitation of feeding behavior in dogs: I. Group and solitary feeding. *Journal of Genetic Psychology, 74,* 97–108.

Roszell, P., Kennedy, D., & Grabb, E. (1989). Physical attractiveness and income attainment among Canadians. *Journal of Psychology, 123,* 547–559.

Rothbart, M., Evans, M., & Fulero, S. (1979). Recall for confirming events: Memory processes and the maintenance of social stereotyping. *Journal of Experimental Social Psychology, 15,* 343–355.

Rothberg, J. M., & Jones, F. D. (1987). Suicide in the U.S. Army: Epidemiological and periodic aspects. *Suicide and Life-Threatening Behavior, 17,* 119–132.

Rozin, P. (1996). Towards a psychology of food and eating: From motivation to module to model to marker, morality, meaning, and metaphor. *Current Directions in Psychological Science, 5,* 18–24.

Rozin, P., Lowery, L., Imada, S., & Haidt, J. (1999). The CAD triad hypothesis: A mapping between three moral emotions (contempt, anger, and disgust) and three moral codes (community, autonomy, divinity). *Journal of Personality and Social Psychology, 66,* 870–881.

Rozin, P., & Royzman, E. B. (2001). Negativity bias, negativity dominance, and contagion. *Personality and Social Psychology Review, 5,* 296–320.

Rozin, P., & Singh, L. (1999). The moralization of cigarette smoking in America. *Journal of Consumer Behavior, 8,* 321–337.

Ruch, W. (1995). Will the real relationship between facial expression and affective experience please stand up? The case of exhilaration. *Cognition and Emotion, 9,* 33–58.

Rudman, L. A., & Ashmore, R. D. (2007). Discrimination and the IAT. *Group Processes and Intergroup Relations, 10,* 359–372.

Rudman, L. A., & Borgida, E. (1995). The afterglow of construct accessibility: The behavioral consequences of priming men to view women as sexual objects. *Journal of Experimental Social Psychology, 31,* 493–517.

Rudman, L. A., & Mescher, K. (2012). Of animals and objects: Men's implicit dehumanization of women and male sexual aggression. *Personalty and Social Psychology Bulletin, 38,* 734–746.

Rudolph, U., Roesch, S. C., Greitemeyer, T., & Weiner, B. (2004). A meta-analytic review of help giving and aggression from an attributional perspective: Contributions to a general theory of motivation. *Cognition and Emotion, 18,* 815–848.

Rusbult, C. E. (1980). Commitment and satisfaction in romantic associations: A test of the investment model. *Journal of Experimental Social Psychology, 17,* 172–186.

Rusbult, C. E. (1983). A longitudinal test of the investment model: The development (and deterioration) of satisfaction and commitment in heterosexual involvements. *Journal of Personality and Social Psychology, 45,* 101–117.

Rusbult, C. E., Martz, J. M., and Agnew, C. R. (1998). The investment model scale: Measuring commitment level, satisfaction level, quality of alternatives, and investment size. *Personal Relationships, 5,* 357–391.

Rushton, J. P., & Bons, T. A. (2005). Mate choice and friendship in twins: Evidence for genetic similarity. *Psychological Science, 16,* 555–559.

Russell, E. M., DelPriore, D. J, Butterfield, M. E. & Hill, S. E. (2013). Friends with Benefits, but Without the Sex: Straight Women and Gay Men Exchange Trustworthy Mating Advice. *Evolutionary Psychology, 11,* 132–147.

Russell, J. A. (2003). Core affect and the psychological construction of emotion. *Psychological Review, 110,* 145–172.

Russo, J. E., Medvec, V. H., & Meloy, M. G. (1996). The distortion of information during decisions. *Organizational Behavior and Human Decision Processes, 66,* 102–110.

Russo, J. E., Meloy, M. G., & Medvec, V. H. (1998). Predecisional distortion of product information. *Journal of Marketing Research, 35,* 438–452.

Ryckman, D. B., & Peckham, P. (1987). Gender differences in attributions for success and failure situations across subject areas. *Journal of Educational Research, 81,* 120–125.

Sabini, J. (1995). *Social psychology* (2nd ed.). New York: Norton.

Sagar, H. A., & Schofield, J. W. (1980). Racial and behavioral cues in black and white children's perceptions of ambiguously aggressive acts. *Journal of Personality and Social Psychology, 39,* 590–598.

Said, C. P., & Todorov, A. (2011). A statistical model of facial attractiveness. *Psychological Science, 22*(9), 1183–1190.

Sakai, H. (1981). Induced compliance and opinion change. *Japanese Psychological Research, 23,* 1–8.

Saks, M. J., & Marti, M. W. (1997). A meta-analysis of the effects of jury size. *Law and Human Behavior, 21,* 451–468.

Salancik, G., & Meindl, J. R. (1984). Corporate attributions as strategic illusions of management control. *Administrative Science Quarterly, 29,* 238–254.

Salovey, P., & Mayer, J. D. (1990). Emotional intelligence. *Imagination, Cognition, and Personality, 9*(3), 185–211.

Salovey, P., & Rodin, J. (1989). Envy and jealousy in close relationships. *Review of Personality and Social Psychology, 10,* 221–246.

Salovey, P., & Rothman, A. J. (1991). Jealousy and envy: Self and society. In P. Salovey (Ed.), *The psychology of jealousy and envy* (pp. 271–286). New York: Guilford Press.

Sampson, R. J., Raudenbush, S., & Earls, F. (1997). Neighborhoods and violent crime: A multilevel study of collective efficacy. *Science, 277,* 918–924.

Samuels, C. A., & Ewy, R. (1985). Aesthetic perception of faces during infancy. *British Journal of Developmental Psychology, 3,* 221–228.

Sanchez-Burks, J. (2002). Protestant relational ideology and (in) attention to relational cues in work settings. *Journal of Personality and Social Psychology, 83*(4), 919–929.

Sanchez-Burks, J. (2004). Protestant relational ideology: The cognitive underpinnings and organizational implications of an American anomaly. In B. Staw & R. Kramer (Eds.), *Research in organizational behavior* (Vol. 26, pp. 265–305). San Diego, CA: Elsevier, JAI Press.

Sanchez-Burks, J., Bartel, C. A., & Blount, S. (2009). Performance in intercultural interactions at work: Cross-cultural differences in response to behavioral mirroring. *Journal of Applied Psychology, 94,* 216–223.

Sanchez-Burks, J., Nisbett, R. E., & Ybarra, O. (2000). Cultural styles, relationship schemas, and prejudice against outgroups. *Journal of Personality and Social Psychology, 79,* 174–189.

Sanday, P. R. (1981). The socio-cultural context of rape: A cross-cultural study. Journal *of Social Issues, 37,* 5–27.

Sanday, P. R. (1997). The socio-cultural context of rape: A cross-cultural study. In L. L. O'Toole (Ed.), *Gender violence: Interdisciplinary perspectives.* New York: New York University Press.

Sanders, G. S. (1981). Driven by distraction: An integrative review of social facilitation theory and research. *Journal of Experimental Social Psychology, 17,* 227–251.

Sanders, G. S., & Baron, R. S. (1975). The motivating effects of distraction on task performance. *Journal of Personality and Social Psychology, 32,* 956–963.

Sanna, L. J. (1992). Self-efficacy theory: Implications for social facilitation and social loafing. *Journal of Personality and Social Psychology, 62,* 774–786.

Sansone, C., & Harackiewicz, J. M. (Eds.). (2000). *Intrinsic and extrinsic motivation: The search for optimal motivation and performance.* San Diego, CA: Academic Press.

Sapolsky, R. M. (1982). The endocrine stress-response and social status in the wild baboon. *Hormones and Behavior, 16*(3), 279–292.

Sapolsky, R. M. (1994). *Why zebras don't get ulcers*. New York: Freeman.

Sastry, J., & Ross, C. E. (1998). Asian ethnicity and the sense of personal control. *Social Psychology Quarterly, 61*, 101–120.

Saucier, D. A., Miller, C. T., & Doucet, N. (2005). Differences in helping whites and blacks: A meta-analysis. *Personality and Social Psychology Review, 9*, 2–16.

Saulnier, K., & Perlman, D. (1981). The actor-observer bias is alive and well in prison: A sequel to Wells. *Personality and Social Psychology Bulletin, 7*, 559–564.

Savani, K., Markus, H. R., & Conner, A. L. (2008). Let your preference be your guide: Preferences and choices are more tightly linked for North Americans than for Indians. *Journal of Personality and Social Psychology, 95*, 861–876.

Savin-Williams, R. C. (1977). Dominance in a human adolescent group. *Animal Behavior, 25*, 400–406.

Savitsky, K., Epley, N., & Gilovich, T. (2001). Is it as bad as we fear? Overestimating the extremity of others' judgments. *Journal of Personality and Social Psychology, 81*, 44–56.

Schachter, S. (1951). Deviation, rejection and communication. *Journal of Abnormal and Social Psychology, 46*, 190–207.

Schachter, S., & Singer, J. E. (1962). Cognitive, social and psychological determinants of emotional state. *Psychological Review, 69*, 379–399.

Schacter, D. L. (2001). *The seven sins of memory: How the mind forgets and remembers*. Boston: Houghton Mifflin.

Schaller, M., Simpson, J. A., & Kenrick, D. T. (2006). *Evolution and social psychology*. New York: Psychology Press.

Schanie, C. F., & Sundel, M. (1978). A community mental health innovation in mass media preventive education: The alternative project. *American Journal of Community Psychology, 6*(6), 573–581.

Schank, R., & Abelson, R. P. (1977). *Scripts, plans, goals, and understanding: An inquiry into human knowledge structures*. Hillsdale, NJ: Erlbaum.

Schaumberg, R., & Flynn, F. (2012). Uneasy lies the head that wears the crown: The link between guilt-proneness and leadership. *Journal of Personality and Social Psychology, 103*: 327–342.

Scheib, J. E., Gangestad, S. W., & Thornhill, R. (1999). Facial attractiveness, symmetry, and cues of good genes. *Proceedings of the Royal Society London B, 266*, 1913–1917.

Scheier, M. F., Fenigstein, A., & Buss, A. H. (1974). Self-awareness and physical aggression. *Journal of Experimental Social Psychology, 10*, 264–273.

Schelling, T. C. (1978). *Micromotives and macrobehavior*. New York: Norton.

Scherer, K. R. (1997). The role of culture in emotion-antecedent appraisal. *Journal of Personality and Social Psychology, 73*, 902–922.

Scherer, K. R., Johnstone, T., & Klasmeyer, G. (2003). Vocal expression of emotion. In R. J. Davidson, K. R. Scherer, & H. H. Goldsmith (Eds.), *Handbook of affective science* (pp. 433–456). New York: Oxford University Press.

Schick, T., & Vaughn, L. (1995). *How to think about weird things: Critical thinking for a new age*. Mountain View, CA: Mayfield.

Schimmack, U., Oishi, S., & Diener, E. (2002). Cultural influences on the relation between pleasant emotions and unpleasant emotions: Asian dialectic philosophies or individualism-collectivism? *Cognition and Emotion, 16*, 705–719.

Schlenker, B. R. (1980). *Impression management: The self-concept, social identity, and interpersonal relations*. Monterey, CA: Brooks/Cole.

Schlenker, B. R., & Leary, M. R. (1982). Social anxiety and self-presentation: A conceptualization and a model. *Psychological Bulletin, 92*, 641–669.

Schmeichel, B. J., & Martens, A. (2005). Self-affirmation and mortality salience: Affirming values reduces worldview defense and death-thought accessibility. *Personality and Social Psychology Bulletin, 31*, 658–667.

Schmitt, B. H., Gilovich, T., Goore, N., & Joseph, L. (1986). Mere presence and social facilitation: One more time. *Journal of Experimental Social Psychology, 22*, 242–248.

Schmitt, D. P. (2003). Universal sex differences in the desire for sexual variety: Tests from 52 nations, 6 continents, and 13 islands. *Journal of Personality and Social Psychology, 85*, 85–104.

Schnall, E., Wassertheil-Smoller, S., Swencionis, C., Zemon, V., Tinker, L., O'Sullivan, J., et. al. (2008). The relationship between religion and cardiovascular outcomes and all-cause mortality in the women's health initiative observational study [Electronic version]. *Psychology and Health*, 1–15. Retrieved from http://dx.doi .org/10.1080/08870440802311322

Schoeneman, T. J., & Rubanowitz, D. E. (1985). Attributions in the advice columns: Actors and observers, causes and reasons. *Personality and Social Psychology Bulletin, 11*, 315–325.

Schooler, J. W., & Engstler-Schooler, T. Y. (1990). Verbal overshadowing of visual memories: Some things are better left unsaid. *Cognitive Psychology, 22*, 36–71.

Schroeder, C. M., & Prentice, D. A. (1998). Exposing pluralistic ignorance to reduce alcohol use among college students. *Journal of Applied Social Psychology, 28*, 2150–2180.

Schroeder, D. A., Penner, L. A., Dovidio, J. F., & Piliavin, J. A. (1995). *The psychology of helping and altruism*. New York: McGraw-Hill.

Schroeder, J., & Risen, J. L. (2014). Befriending the enemy: Outgroup friendship longitudinally predicts intergroup attitudes in a co-existence program for Israelis and Palestinians. *Group Processes and Intergroup Relations*. DOI: 10.1177/1368430214542257

Schulthiess, O.C. (2013). The hormonal correlates of implicit motives. *Social and Personality Psychology Compass 7 (1)*, 52–65.

Schultz, P. W., Nolan, J. M., Cialdini, R. B., Goldstein, N. J., & Griskevicius, V. (2007). The constructive, destructive, and reconstructive power of social norms. *Psychological Science, 18*, 429–434.

Schwartz, J. (2004, May 6). Simulated prison in '71 showed a fine line between "normal" and "monster." *New York Times*, A14.

Schwartzwald, J., Bizman, A., & Raz, M. (1983). The foot-in-the-door paradigm: Effects of second request size on donation probability and donor generosity. *Personality and Social Psychology Bulletin, 9*, 443–450.

Schwarz, N., & Bless, H. (1992). Constructing reality and its alternatives: An inclusion/exclusion model of assimilation and contrast in social judgment. In L. L. Martin & A. Tesser (Eds.), *The construction of social judgments* (pp. 217–245). Hillsdale, NJ: Erlbaum.

Schwarz, N., Bless, H., Strack, F., Klumpp, G., Rittenauer-Schatka, H., & Simons, A. (1991). Ease of retrieval as information: Another look at the availability heuristic. *Journal of Personality and Social Psychology, 61*, 195–202.

Schwarz, N., & Clore, G. L. (1983). Mood, misattribution, and judgments of well-being: Informative and directive functions of affective states. *Journal of Personality and Social Psychology, 45*, 513–523.

Schwarz, N., & Vaughn, L. A. (2002). The availability heuristic revisited: Ease of recall and content of recall as distinct sources of information. In T. Gilovich, D. W. Griffin, & D. Kahneman (Eds.), *Heuristics and biases: The psychology of intuitive judgment* (pp. 103–119). New York: Cambridge University Press.

Searle, J. R. (1983). *Intentionality: An essay in the philosophy of mind.* Cambridge, England: Cambridge University Press.

Sears, D. O. (1986). College students in the laboratory: Influences of a narrow database on social psychology's view of human nature. *Journal of Personality and Social Psychology, 51,* 515–530.

Sears, D. O. (1988). Symbolic racism. In P. A. Katz & D. A. Taylor (Eds.), *Eliminating racism: Profiles in controversy* (pp. 53–84). New York: Plenum Press.

Sears, D. O., & Henry, P. J. (2005). Over thirty years later: A contemporary look at symbolic racism. In M. P. Zanna (Ed.), *Advances in experimental social psychology* (Vol. 37, pp. 95–150). San Diego, CA: Elsevier.

Sears, D. O., & Kinder, D. R. (1985). Whites' opposition to busing: On conceptualizing and operationalizing group conflict. *Journal of Personality and Social Psychology, 48,* 1141–1147.

Sedikides, C., & Brewer, M. B. (2001). *Individual self, relational self, collective self.* Philadelphia: Psychology Press.

Sedikides, C., & Gregg, A. (2008). Self-enhancement: Food for thought. *Perspectives on Psychological Science, 3,* 102–116.

Segal, N. L. (1984). Cooperation, competition, and altruism within twin sets: A reappraisal. *Ethology and Sociobiology, 5,* 163–177.

Seibt, B., & Forster, J. (2004). Stereotype threat and performance: How self-stereotypes influence processing by inducing regulatory foci. *Journal of Personality and Social Psychology, 87,* 38–56.

Select Committee on Intelligence. United States Senate. (2004). Report on the U.S. intelligence community's prewar intelligence assessments on Iraq. Ordered reported on July 7, 2004. 108th Congress.

Seligman, M. E. P. (1970). On the generality of the laws of learning. *Psychological Review, 77,* 127–190.

Seligman, M. E. P. (1988). Boomer blues. *Psychology Today, 22,* 50–53.

Seligman, M. E. P., Maier, S. F., & Geer, J. H. (1968). Alleviation of learned helplessness in the dog. *Journal of Abnormal Psychology, 73,* 256–262.

Seltzer, R. (2006). Scientific jury selection: Does it work? *Journal of Applied Social Psychology, 36,* 2417–2435.

Semin, G. R., & Manstead, A. S. R. (1982). The social implications of embarrassment displays and restitution behavior. *European Journal of Social Psychology, 12,* 367–377.

Sen, A. (1990, January 20). More than 100 million women are missing. *The New York Review of Books.*

Seta, C. E., & Seta, J. J. (1992). Increments and decrements in mean arterial pressure levels as a function of audience composition: An averaging and summation analysis. *Personality and Social Psychology Bulletin, 18,* 173–181.

Sethi-Iyengar, S., Huberman, G., and Jiang, W. (2004). How much choice is too much? Contributions to 401(k) retirement plans. In O. S. Mitchell & S. Utkus (Eds.), *Pension design and structure: New lessons from behavioral finance* (pp. 83–95). New York: Oxford University Press.

Shah, J., & Higgins, E. T. (2001). Regulatory concerns and appraisal efficiency: The general impact of promotion and prevention. *Journal of Personality and Social Psychology, 80,* 693–705.

Shah, J. Y. (2003). Automatic for the people: How representations of significant others implicitly affect goal pursuit. *Journal of Personality and Social Psychology, 84,* 661–681.

Shapin, S. (2006, January 16). Eat and run. *The New Yorker,* 76–82.

Shapiro, D. H., Schwartz, C. E., & Astin, J. A. (1996). Controlling ourselves, controlling our world. *American Psychologist, 51,* 1213–1230.

Shariff, A. F., & Norenzayan, A. (2007). God is watching you: Priming God concepts increases prosocial behavior in an anonymous economic game. *Psychological Science, 18,* 803–809.

Sharot, T., Fleming, S. M., Yu, X., Koster, R., & Dolan, R. J. (2012). Is choice-induced preference change long lasting? *Psychological Science, 23,* 1123–1129.

Shaver, P. R., & Brennan, K. A. (1992). Attachment style and the "big five" of personality traits: Their connections with each other and with romantic relationship outcomes. *Personality and Social Psychology Bulletin, 18,* 536–545.

Shavitt, S., Sanbonmatsu, D. M., Smittipatana, S., & Posavac, S. S. (1999). Broadening the conditions for illusory correlation formation: Implications for judging minority groups. *Basic and Applied Social Psychology, 21,* 263–279.

Shearn, D., Bergman, E., Hill, K., Abel, A., & Hinds, L. (1992). Blushing as a function of audience size. *Psychophysiology, 29,* 431–436.

Shedler, L., & Manis, M. (1986). Can the availability heuristic explain vividness effects? *Journal of Personality and Social Psychology, 51,* 26–36.

Sheley, J. F., & Askins, C. D. (1981). Crime, crime news, and crime views. *Public Opinion Quarterly, 45,* 492–506.

Shelley, H. P. (1965). Eating behavior: Social facilitation or social inhibition. *Psychonomic Science, 3,* 521–522.

Shelton, J. N., Alegre, J. M., & Son, D. (2010). Social stigma and disadvantage: Current themes and future prospects. *Journal of Social Issues, 66,* 618–633.

Shelton, J. N, & Richeson, J. A. (2005). Intergroup contact and pluralistic ignorance. *Journal of Personality and Social Psychology, 88,* 91–107.

Shelton, J. N., Richeson, J. A., & Salvatore, J. (2005). Expecting to be the target of prejudice: Implications for interethnic interactions. *Personality and Social Psychology Bulletin, 31,* 1189–1202.

Shepperd, J. A. (1995). Remedying motivation and productivity loss in collective settings. *Current Directions in Psychological Science, 4,* 131–134.

Shepperd, J. A., & Taylor, K. M. (1999). Social loafing and expectancy-value theory. *Personality and Social Psychology Bulletin, 25,* 1147–1158.

Sherif, M. (1936). *The psychology of social norms.* New York: Harper.

Sherif, M., Harvey, O. J., White, B. J., Hood, W., & Sherif, C. (1961). *Intergroup conflict and cooperation: The robbers cave experiment.* Norman: University of Oklahoma Institute of Group Relations.

Sherman, D. A. K., Nelson, L. D., & Steele, C. M. (2000). Do messages about health risks threaten the self: Increasing the acceptance of threatening health messages via self-affirmation. *Personality and Social Psychology Bulletin, 26,* 1046–1058.

Sherman, D. K., & Cohen, G. L. (2002). Accepting threatening information: Self-affirmation and the reduction of defensive biases. *Current Directions in Psychological Science, 11,* 119–123.

Sherman, D. K., & Cohen, G. L. (2006). The psychology of self-defense: Self-affirmation theory. In M. P. Zanna (Ed.), *Advances in experimental social psychology* (Vol. 38, pp. 183–242). San Diego, CA: Academic Press.

Sherman, J. W., Gawronski, B., Gonsalkorale, K., Hugenberg, K., Allen, T. J., & Groom, C. J. (2008). The self-regulation of automatic associations and behavioral impulses. *Psychological Review, 115,* 314–335.

Sherman, L., & Strang, H. (2007). *Restorative justice: The evidence.* London: Smith Institute.

Sherman, P. W. (1985). Alarm calls of Belding's ground squirrels to aerial predators: Nepotism or self-preservation? *Behavioral Ecology and Sociobiology, 17,* 313–323.

Sherman, S. J., & Gorkin, L. (1980). Attitude bolstering when behavior is inconsistent with central attitudes. *Journal of Experimental Social Psychology, 16,* 388–403.

Sherman, S. J., Mackie, D. M., & Driscoll, D. M. (1990). Priming and the differential use of dimensions in evaluation. *Personality and Social Psychology Bulletin, 16,* 405–418.

Shermer, M. (1997). *Why people believe weird things: Pseudoscience, superstition, and other contusions of our time.* New York: Freeman.

Shih, M., Pittinsky, T. L., & Ambady, N. (1999). Stereotype susceptibility: Identity salience and shifts in quantitative performance. *Psychological Science, 10(1),* 80–83.

Shiller, R. J. (2000). *Irrational exuberance.* Princeton, NJ: Princeton University Press.

Shimamura, A.P. (1994). Neuropsychological perspectives on memory and cognitive decline in normal human aging. *Seminars in the Neurosciences, 6,* 387–394.

Shook, N. J., & Fazio, R. H. (2008). An experimental field test of the contact hypothesis. *Psychological Science, 19,* 717–723.

Showers, C. (1992). Compartmentalization of positive and negative self-knowledge: Keeping bad apples out of the bunch. *Journal of Personality and Social Psychology, 62,* 1036–1049.

Shrauger, J. S., & Shoeneman, T. J. (1979). Symbolic interactionist view of self-concept: Through the looking glass darkly. *Psychological Bulletin, 86,* 549–573.

Shweder, R. A., & Bourne, E. J. (1984). Does the concept of the person vary cross-culturally? In R. A. Shweder & R. A. LeVine (Eds.), *Culture theory: Essays on mind, self, and emotion* (pp. 158–199). Cambridge, England: Cambridge University Press.

Shweder, R. A., Jensen, L. A., & Goldstein, W. M. (1995). Who sleeps by whom revisited: A method for extracting moral goods implicit in practice. *New Directions in Child Development, 67,* 21–39.

Sidanius, J., & Pratto, F. (1999). *Social dominance: An intergroup theory of social hierarchy and oppression.* New York: Cambridge University Press.

Sieverding, M., Decker, S., & Zimmermann, F. (2010). Information about low participation in cancer screening demotivates other people. *Psychological Science, 21,* 941–943.

Sigall, H., & Ostrove, N. (1975). Beautiful but dangerous: Effects of offender attractiveness and nature of the crime on juridic judgment. *Journal of Personality and Social Psychology, 31,* 410–414.

Silverstein, B., Perdue, L., Peterson, L., & Kelly, E. (1986). The role of the mass media in promoting a thin standard of bodily attractiveness for women. *Sex Roles, 14,* 519–532.

Simon, B., Mlicki, P., Johnston, L., Caetano, A., Warowicki, M., Van Knippenberg, A., et al. (1990). The effects of ingroup and outgroup homogeneity on ingroup favouritism, stereotyping, and overestimation of relative ingroup size. *European Journal of Social Psychology, 20(6),* 519–523.

Simon, D., Krawczyk, D. C., & Holyoak, K. J. (2004). Construction of preferences by constraint satisfaction. *Psychological Science, IS,* 331–336.

Simon, D., Pham, L. B., Le, Q. A., & Holyoak, K. J. (2001). The emergence of coherence over the course of decision making. *Journal of Experimental Psychology: Learning, Memory and Cognition, 27,* 1250–1260.

Simons, D. J., & Chabris, C. F. (1999). Gorillas in our midst: Sustained inattentional blindness for dynamic events. *Perception, 28,* 1059–1074.

Simpson, G. E., & Yinger, J. M. (1985). *Racial and cultural minorities: An analysis of prejudice and discrimination.* New York: Plenum Press.

Simpson, J. A. (1987). The dissolution of romantic relationships: Factors involved in relationship stability and emotional distress. *Journal of Personality and Social Psychology, S3,* 683–692.

Simpson, J. A., & Rholes, W. S. (1998). *Attachment theory and close relationships.* New York: Guilford Press.

Sinaceur, M., & Tiedens, L. Z. (2006). Get mad and get more than even: When and why anger expression is effective in negotiations. *Journal of Experimental Social Psychology, 42(3),* 314–322.

Sinclair, L., & Kunda, Z. (1999). Reactions to a black professional: Motivated inhibition and activation of conflicting stereotypes. *Journal of Personality and Social Psychology, 77,* 885–904.

Singer, J. E., Brush, C. A., & Lublin, S. C. (1965). Some aspects of deindividuation: Identification and conformity. *Journal of Experimental Social Psychology, 1,* 356–378.

Singer, T., Seymour, B., O'Doherty, J., Kaube, H., Dolan, R. J., & Frith, C. D. (2004). Empathy for pain involves the affective but not sensory components of pain. *Science, 303,* 1157–1162.

Singh, D. (1993). Adaptive significance of female physical attractiveness: Role of waist-to-hip ratio. *Journal of Personality and Social Psychology, 65,* 293–307.

Singhal, A., Rogers, E. M., & Brown, W. J. (1993). Harnessing the potential of entertainment-education telenovelas. *Gazette, 51,* 1–18.

Singh-Manoux, A., Adler, N. E., & Marmot, M. G. (2003). Subjective social status: Its determinants and its association with measures of ill health in the Whitehall II study. *Social Science & Medicine, 56(6),* 1321–1333.

Sistrunk, F., & McDavid, J. W. (1971). Sex variable in conforming behavior. *Journal of Personality and Social Psychology, 17,* 200–207.

Skov, R. B., & Sherman, S. J. (1986). Information-gathering processes: Diagnosticity, hypothesis-confirmatory strategies, and perceived hypothesis confirmation. *Journal of Experimental Social Psychology, 22,* 93–121.

Slater, A., von der Shulenburg, C., Brown, E., Badenoch, M., Butterworth, G., Parsons, S., et al. (1998). Newborn infants prefer attractive faces. *Infant Behavior and Development, 21,* 345–354.

Slavin, R. E. (1995). *Cooperative learning: Theory, research, and practice* (2nd ed.). Boston: Allyn & Bacon.

Sloman, S. A. (2002). Two systems of reasoning. In T. Gilovich, D. W. Griffin, & D. Kahneman (Eds.), *Heuristics and biases: The psychology of intuitive judgement* (pp. 379–396). New York: Cambridge University Press.

Slovic, P., Fischoff, B., & Lichtenstein, S. (1982). Facts versus fears: Understanding perceived risk. In D. Kahneman, P. Slovic, & A. Tversky (Eds.), *Judgment under uncertainty: Heuristics and biases* (pp. 463–489). New York: Cambridge University Press.

Small Arms Survey. (2011). *The Small Arms Survey 2011: States of security.* Retrieved from http://en.wikipedia.org/wiki /List_of_countries_by_gun_ownership

Small, D. A., Loewenstein, G. & Slovic, P. (2007). Sympathy and callousness: The impact of deliberative thought on donations to identifiable and statistical victims. *Organizational Behavior and Human Decision Processes, 102(2),* 143–153.

Smith, A. (1776/1998). *The wealth of nations*. Washington, DC: Regnery Publishing.

Smith, A. E., Jussim, L., & Eccles, J. S. (1999). Do self-fulfilling prophecies accumulate, dissipate, or remain stable over time? *Journal of Personality and Social Psychology, 77*, 548–565.

Smith, C., & Ellsworth, P. (1985). Patterns of cognitive appraisal in emotion. *Journal of Personality and Social Psychology, 48*, 813–838.

Smith, E. R., & Miller, F. D. (1979). Salience and the cognitive mediation of attribution. *Journal of Personality and Social Psychology, 37*, 2240–2252.

Smith, E. R., & Zarate, M. A. (1990). Exemplar and prototype use in social categorization. *Social Cognition, 8*, 243–262.

Smith, P. K., Jostmann, N. B., Galinsky, A. D., & van Dijk, W. W (2008). Lacking power impairs executive functions. *Psychological Science, 19*(5), 441–447.

Smith, P. K., & Trope, Y. (2006). You focus on the forest when you're in charge of the trees: Power priming and abstract information processing. *Journal of Personality and Social Psychology, 90*, 578–596.

Smith, S. M., & Shaffer, D. R. (2000). Vividness can undermine or enhance message processing: The moderating role of vividness congruency. *Personality and Social Psychology Bulletin, 26*, 769–779.

Smith, S. S., & Richardson, D. (1983). Amelioration of deception and harm in psychological research: The important role of debriefing. *Journal of Personality and Social Psychology, 44*, 1075–1082.

Smith, T. W. (2009). Loving and caring in the United States: Trends and correlates of empathy, altruism, and related constructs. In B. Fehr, S. Sprecher, & L. G. Underwood (Eds.), *The science of compassionate love: Theory, research, and applications* (pp. 81–120). Malden, MA: Wiley-Blackwell.

Smoski, M. J., & Bachorowski, J.-A. (2003). Antiphonal laughter between friends and strangers. *Cognition and Emotion, 17*, 327–340.

Smyth, J. M. (1998). Written emotional expression: Effect sizes, outcome types, and moderating variables. *Journal of Consulting and Clinical Psychology, 66*, 174–184.

Snibbe, A. C., & Markus, H. R., (2005). You can't always get what you want: Educational attainment, agency, and choice. *Journal of Personality and Social Psychology, 88*, 703–720.

Snyder, M. (1974). Self-monitoring of expressive behavior. *Journal of Personality and Social Psychology, 30*, 526–537.

Snyder, M. (1979). Self-monitoring processes. In L. Berkowitz (Ed.), *Advances in experimental social psychology* (Vol. 12, pp. 85–128). New York: Academic Press.

Snyder, M., & Swann, W. B. (1978). Hypothesis-testing in social interaction. *Journal of Personality and Social Psychology, 36*, 1202–1212.

Snyder, M., Tanke, E. D., & Berscheid, E. (1977). Social perception and interpersonal behavior: On the self-fulfilling nature of social stereotypes. *Journal of Personality and Social Psychology, 35*, 656–666.

Sommers, S. R. (2006). On racial diversity and group decision making: Identifying multiple effects of racial composition on jury deliberations. *Journal of Personality and Social Psychology, 90*, 597–612.

Sommers, S. R., & Ellsworth, P. C. (2001). White juror bias: An investigation of prejudice against black defendants in the American courtroom. *Psychology and Public Policy & Law, 7*(1), 201–229.

Song, H., & Schwarz, N. (2008). If it's hard to read, it's hard to do. *Psychological Science, 19*, 986–988.

Spears, R. (2011). Group identities: The social identity perspective. In S. J. Schwartz, K. Luyckx, & V. L. Vignoles (Eds.), *Handbook of identity theory and research* (Vols. 1 and 2; pp. 201–224). New York: Springer.

Speer, N. K., Reynolds, J. R., Swallow, K. M., & Zacks, J. M. (2009). Reading stories activates neural representations of visual and motor experiences. *Psychological Science, 20*, 989–999.

Spellman, B. A., & Holyoak, K. J. (1992). If Saddam is Hitler then who is George Bush? Analogical mapping between systems of social roles. *Journal of Personality and Social Psychology, 62*, 913–933.

Spencer, S. J., Steele, C. M., & Quinn, D. M. (1999). Stereotype threat and women's math performance. *Journal of Experimental Social Psychology, 35*, 4–28.

Sperber, D. (1996). *Explaining culture: A naturalistic approach*. Oxford, England: Blackwell.

Spiegel, D., Bloom, J. R., Kraemer, H. C., & Gottheil, E. (1989). Effect of psychosocial treatment on survival of patients with metastatic breast cancer. *Lancet, 2*, 888–891.

Spivey, C. B., & Prentice-Dunn, S. (1990). Assessing the directionality of deindividuated behavior: Effects of deindividuation, modeling, and private self-consciousness on aggressive and pro-social responses. *Basic and Applied Psychology, 11*, 387–403.

Sprecher, S., & Regan, P. C. (1998). Passionate and companionate love in courting and young married couples. *Sociological Inquiry, 68*, 163–185.

Sritharan, R., & Gawronski, B. (2010). Changing implicit and explicit prejudice: Insights from the associative-propositional evaluation model. *Social Psychology, 41*(3), 113–123.

Srull, T. K., & Wyer, R. S. (1979). The role of category accessibility in the interpretation of information about persons: Some determinants and implications. *Journal of Personality and Social Psychology, 37*, 1660–1672.

Srull, T. K., & Wyer, R. S. (1980). Category accessibility and social perception: Some implications for the study of person memory and interpersonal judgments. *Journal of Personality and Social Psychology, 38*, 841–856.

Stangor, C., & Duan, C. (1991). Effects of multiple task demands upon memory for information about social groups. *Journal of Experimental Social Psychology, 27*, 357–378.

Stangor, C., & Lange, J. E. (1994). Mental representation of social groups: Advances in understanding stereotypes and stereotyping. In M. P. Zanna (Ed.), *Advances in experimental social psychology* (Vol. 26). San Diego, CA: Academic Press.

Stangor, C., & McMillan, D. (1992). Memory for expectancy-congruent and expectancy-incongruent information: A review of the social and social developmental literatures. *Psychological Bulletin, 111*, 42–61.

Stanovich, K. E., & West, R. F. (2002). Individual differences in reasoning: Implications for the rationality debate. In T. Gilovich, D. W. Griffin, & D. Kahneman (Eds.), *Heuristics and biases: The psychology of intuitive judgment* (pp. 421–440). New York: Cambridge University Press.

Stapel, D. A., Koomen, W., & van der Plight, J. (1997). Categories of category accessibility: The impact of trait versus exemplar priming on person judgments. *Journal of Experimental Social Psychology, 33* 44–76.

Stasser, G., & Davis, J. H. (1981). Group decision making and social influence: A social interaction sequence model. *Psychological Review, 88*, 523–551.

Staub, E. (1989). *The roots of evil: The origins of genocide and other group violence*. Cambridge, England: Cambridge University Press.

Steblay, N. M. (1987). Helping behavior in rural and urban environments: A meta-analysis. *Psychological Bulletin, 102*, 346–356.

Steele, C. M. (1988). The psychology self-affirmation: Sustaining the integrity of the self. In L. Berkowitz (Ed.), *Advances in experimental social psychology* (Vol. 21, pp. 261–302). New York: Academic Press.

Steele, C. M. (1997). A threat in the air: How stereotypes shape intellectual identity and performance. *American Psychologist, 52,* 613–629.

Steele, C. M., & Aronson, J. (1995). Stereotype threat and the intellectual test performance of African Americans. *Journal of Personality and Social Psychology, 69,* 797–811.

Steele, C. M., Spencer, S. J., & Aronson, J. (2002). Contending with group image: The psychology of stereotype and social identity threat. In M. P. Zanna (Ed.), *Advances in experimental social psychology* (Vol. 34, pp. 379–440). San Diego, CA: Academic Press.

Steele, C. M., Spencer, S. J., & Lynch, M. (1993). Self-image resilience and dissonance: The role of affirmational resources. *Journal of Personality and Social Psychology, 64,* 885–896.

Stel, M., van Baaren, R. B., Blascovich, J., van Dijk, E., McCall, C., Pollmann, M. M. H., . . . , & Vonk, R. (2010). Effects of a priori liking on the elicitation of mimicry. *Experimental Psychology, 57*(6), 412–418.

Stephan, W. G. (1986). The effect of school desegregation: An evaluation 30 years after *Brown.* In M. J. Saks & L. Saxe (Eds.), *Advances in applied social psychology* (Vol. 3, pp. 181–206). Hillsdale, NJ: Erlbaum.

Stephan, W. G., & Stephan, C. W. (1996). *Intergroup relations.* Madison, WI: Brown & Benchmark.

Stephens, N., Fryberg, S., Markus, H. R., Johnson, C., & Covarrubias, R. (2012). Unseen disadvantage: How American universities' focus on independence undermines the academic performance of first-generation college students. *Journal of Personality and Social Psychology, 102,* 1178–1197.

Stephens, N. , Markus, H. R., & Phillips, L. T. (2014). Social class culture cycles: How three gateway contexts shape selves and fuel inequality. *Annual Review of Psychology. 65,* 611–634.

Stephens, N. M., Fryberg, S. A., & Markus, H. R. (2011). When choice does not equal freedom: A sociocultural analysis of agency in working-class American contexts. *Social and Personality Psychology Science, 2,* 33–41.

Stephens, N. M., Hamedani, M. G., & Destin, M. (2014). Closing the social-class achievement gap: A difference-education intervention improves first-generation students' academic performance and all students' college transition. *Psychological Science, 25,* 943–953.

Stephens, N. M., Hamedani, M. G., Markus, H. R., Bergsieker, H. B., & Eloul, L. (2009). Why did they "choose" to stay? Perspectives of Hurricane Katrina observers and survivors. *Psychological Science, 20,* 878–886.

Stephens, N. M., Markus, H. R., & Townsend, S. S. M. (2007). Choice as an act of meaning: The case of social class. *Journal of Personality and Social Psychology, 93,* 814–830.

Stephens, N. M., Townsend, S. S. M., Markus, H. R., & Phillips, L. T. (2012). A cultural mismatch: Independent cultural norms contribute to increased stress among first-generation college students in American universities. Evanston, IL: Northwestern University.

Sternberg, R. J. (1986). A triangular theory of love. *Psychological Review, 93,* 119–135.

Sternberg, R. J. (1988). Triangulating love. In R. J. Sternberg & M. L. Barnes (Eds.), *The psychology of love.* New Haven, CT: Yale University Press.

Stevenson, H. W., & Lee, S. (1996). The academic achievement of Chinese students. In M. H. Bond (Ed.), *The handbook of Chinese psychology* (pp. 124–142). New York: Oxford University Press.

Stevenson, H. W., Lee, S. Y., Chen, C., Stigler, J. W., Hsu, C. C., & Kitamura, S. (1990). Contexts of achievement: A study of American, Chinese and Japanese children. *Monographs of the Society for Research in Child Development, 55,* 1–2, Serial No. 221.

Stevenson, H. W., & Stigler, J. W. (1992). *The learning gap: Why our schools are failing and what can we learn from Japanese and Chinese education.* New York: Summit Books.

Stewart, J. E. (1980). Defendant's attractiveness as a factor in the outcome of criminal trials: An observational study. *Journal of Applied Social Psychology, 10,* 348–361.

Stone, J., Lynch, C. I., Sjomeling, M., & Darley, J. M. (1999). Stereotype threat effects on black and white athletic performance. *Journal of Personality and Social Psychology, 77,* 1213–1227.

Stone, J., Perry, Z., & Darley, J. (1997). "White men can't jump": Evidence for perceptual confirmation of racial stereotypes following a basketball game. *Basic and Applied Social Psychology, 19,* 291–306.

Stoner, J. A. F. (1961). *A comparison of individual and group decisions involving risk.* Unpublished Master's thesis, MIT, Cambridge, Massachusetts.

Storms, M. D. (1973). Videotape and the attribution process: Reversing actors' and observers' points of view. *Journal of Personality and Social Psychology, 27,* 165–175.

Strack, F., & Deutsch, R. (2004). Reflective and impulsive determinants of social behavior. *Personality and Social Psychology Review, 8,* 220–247.

Strack, F., Martin, L. L., & Schwarz, N. (1988). Priming and communication: The social determinants of information use in judgments of life satisfaction. *European Journal of Social Psychology, 18,* 429–442.

Strack, F., Martin, L. L., & Stepper, S. (1988). Inhibiting and facilitating conditions of the human smile: A nonobtrusive test of the facial feedback hypothesis. *Journal of Personality and Social Psychology, 53,* 768–777.

Strahan, E. J., Spencer, S. J., & Zanna, M. P. (2002). Subliminal priming and persuasion: Striking while the iron is *hot. Journal of Experimental Social Psychology, 38,* 556–568.

Strauman, T. J., & Higgins, E. T. (1987). Automatic activation of self-discrepancies and emotional syndromes: When cognitive structures influence affect. *Journal of Personality and Social Psychology, 53,* 1004–1014.

Strobel, M. G. (1972). Social facilitation of operant behavior in satiated rats. *Journal of Comparative Physiological Psychology, 80,* 502–508.

Stroebe, K., Spears, R., & Lodewijkx, H. (2007) Contrasting and integrating social identity and interdependence approaches to intergroup discrimination in the minimal group paradigm. In M. Hewstone, H. A. W. Schut, J. B. F. De Wit, K. Van Den Bos, & M. S. Stroebe (Eds.), *The scope of social psychology: Theory and applications* (pp. 173–190). New York: Psychology Press.

Strohmetz, D., Rind, B., Fisher, R. & Lynn, M. (2002). Sweetening the till: The use of candy to increase restaurant tipping. *Journal of Applied Social Psychology, 32,* 300–309.

Studd, M. V. (1996). Sexual harassment. In D. M. Buss & N. M. Malamuth (Eds.), *Sex, power, and conflict: Evolutionary and feminist perspectives.* New York: Oxford University Press.

Suedfeld, P., & Tetlock, P. E. (1977). Integrative complexity of communications in international crises. *Journal of Conflict Resolution, 21,* 169–184.

Suh, E., Diener, E., Oishi, S., & Triandis, H. C. (1998). The shifting basis of life satisfaction judgments across cultures: Emotions versus norms. *Journal of Personality and Social Psychology, 74,* 482–493.

Sulloway, F. J. (1996). *Born to rebel: Birth order, family dynamics, and creative lives.* New York: Pantheon Books.

Sulloway, F. J. (2001). Birth order, sibling competition, and human behavior. In H. R. Halcomb III (Ed.), *Conceptual challenges in evolutionary psychology: Innovative research strategic Studies in cognitive systems* (Vol. 27, pp. 39–83). Dordrecht, the Netherlands: Kluwer Academic Publishers.

Suls, J., Martin, R., & Wheeler, L. (2002). Social comparison: Why, with whom and with what effect? *Current Directions in Psychological Science, 11*(5), 159–163.

Suls, J. M., & Wheeler, L. (2000). *Handbook of social comparison: Theory and research.* New York: Kluwer Academic/Plenum.

Summers, G., & Feldman, N. S. (1984). Blaming the victim versus blaming the perpetrator: An attributional analysis of spouse abuse. *Journal of Applied Social and Clinical Psychology, 2,* 339–347.

Sunstein, C. R., Kahneman, D., Schkade, D., & Ritov, I. (2002). Predictably incoherent judgments. *Stanford Law Review, 54,* 1153–1215.

Svenson, O. (1981). Are we all less risky and more skillful than our fellow drivers? *Acta Psychologica, 47,* 143–148.

Swann, W. B., Jr. (1990). To be adored or to be known: The interplay of self-enhancement and self-verification. In R. M. Sorrentino & E. T. Higgins (Eds.). *Handbook of motivation and cognition* (Vol. 2, pp. 408–448). New York: Guilford Press.

Swann, W. B., Jr., De La Ronde, C., & Hixon, J. G. (1994). Authenticity and positivity strivings in marriage and courtship. *Journal of Personality and Social Psychology, 66,* 857–869.

Swann, W. B., Griffin, J. J., Predmore, S. C., & Gaines, B. (1987). The cognitive-affective cross: When self-consistency confronts self-enhancement. *Journal of Personality and Social Psychology, 52,* 881–889.

Swann, W. B., Jr., & Read, S. J. (1981). Self-verification processes: How we sustain our self-conceptions. *Journal of Experimental Social Psychology, 17,* 351–372.

Swann, W. B., Jr., Wenzlaff, R. M., Krull, D. S., & Pelham, B. W. (1992). The allure of negative feedback: Self-verification strivings among depressed persons. *Journal of Abnormal Psychology, 101,* 293–306.

Sweeney, P. D., & Gruber, K. L. (1984). Selective exposure: Voter information preferences and the Watergate affair. *Journal of Personality and Social Psychology, 46,* 1208–1221.

Swim, J. K., Aikin, K. J., Hall, W. S., & Hunter, B. A. (1995). Sexism and racism: Old-fashioned and modern prejudices. *Journal of Personality and Social Psychology, 68,* 199–214.

Swim, J. K., & Sanna, L. (1996). He's skilled, she's lucky: A meta-analysis of observers' attributions for women's and men's successes and failures. *Personality and Social Psychology Bulletin, 22,* 507–519.

Szymanski, D. M., Chung, Y., & Balsam, K. F. (2001). Psychosocial correlates of internalized homophobia in lesbians. *Measurement And Evaluation In Counseling And Development, 34*(1), 27–38.

Tajfel, H., & Billig, M. G. (1974). Familiarity and categorization in intergroup behavior. *Journal of Experimental Social Psychology, 10,* 159–170.

Tajfel, H., Billig, M. G., Bundy, R. P., & Flament, C. (1971). Social categorization and intergroup behavior. *European Journal of Social Psychology, 1,* 149–177.

Tajfel, H., & Turner, J. (1979). An integrative theory of intergroup conflict. In W. G. Austin & S. Worchel (Eds.), *The social psychology of intergroup relations.* Monterey, CA: Brooks/Cole.

Tan, D. T. Y., & Singh, R. (1995). Attitudes and attraction: A developmental study of the similarity-attraction dissimilarity-repulsion hypotheses. *Personality and Social Psychology Bulletin, 21,* 975–986.

Tangney, J. P., Miller, R. S., Flicker, L., & Barlow, D. H. (1996). Are shame, guilt, and embarrassment distinct emotions? *Journal of Personality and Social Psychology, 70,* 1256–1264.

Taubman-Ben-Ari, O., Florian, V., & Mikulincer, M. (1999). The impact of mortality salience on reckless driving—A test of terror management mechanisms. *Journal of Personality and Social Psychology, 76,* 35–45.

Taylor, A. F., & Kuo, F. E. (2009). Children with attention deficits concentrate better after a walk in the park. *Journal of Attention Disorders, 12,* 402–409.

Taylor, D. M., & Jaggi, V. (1974). Ethnocentrism and causal attribution in a South Indian context. *Journal of Cross-Cultural Psychology, 5,* 162–171.

Taylor, S. E. (1983). Adjustment to threatening events: A theory of cognitive adaptation. *American Psychologist, 38,* 1161–1173.

Taylor, S. E. (1991). Asymmetrical effects of positive and negative events: The mobilization-minimization hypothesis. *Psychological Bulletin, 110,* 67–85.

Taylor, S. E. (2002). *The tending instinct.* New York: Holt.

Taylor, S. E., & Brown, J. D. (1988). Illusion and well-being: A social psychological perspective on mental health. *Psychological Bulletin, 103,* 193–210.

Taylor, S. E., & Brown, J. D. (1994). Positive illusions and well-being revisited: Separating fact from fiction. *Psychological Bulletin, 116,* 21–27.

Taylor, S. E., Burklund, L. J., Eisenberger, N. I., Lehman, B. J., Hilmert, C. J., & Lieberman, M. D. (2008). Neural bases of moderation of cortisol stress responses by psychosocial resources. *Journal of Personality and Social Psychology, 95,* 197–211.

Taylor, S. E., & Crocker, J. (1981). Schematic bases of social information processing. In E. T. Higgins, C. P. Herman, & M. P. Zanna (Eds.), *Social cognition: The Ontario Symposium* (Vol. 1, pp. 89–134). Hillsdale, NJ: Erlbaum.

Taylor, S. E., & Fiske, S. T. (1975). Point of view and perceptions of causality. *Journal of Personality and Social Psychology, 32,* 439–445.

Taylor, S. E., Kemeny, M., Aspinwall, L. G., Schneider, S. G., Rodriguez, R., & Herbert, M. (1992). Optimism, coping, psychological distress, and high-risk sexual behavior among men at risk for AIDS. *Journal of Personality and Social Psychology, 63,* 460–473.

Taylor, S. E., Klein, L. C., Lewis, B. P., Gruenewal, T. L., Gurung, R. A. R., & Updegraff, J. A. (2000). Biobehavioral responses to stress in females: Tend-and-befriend, not fight-or-flight. *Psychological Review, 107,* 411–429.

Taylor, S. E., Lerner, J. S., Sherman, D. K., Sage, R. M., & McDowell, N. K. (2003). Are self-enhancing cognitions associated with healthy or unhealthy biological profiles? *Journal of Personality and Social Psychology, 85,* 605–615.

Taylor, S. E., Lichtman, R. R., & Wood, J. V. (1984). Attributions, beliefs about control, and adjustment to breast cancer. *Journal of Personality and Social Psychology, 46,* 489–502.

Taylor, S. E., & Lobel, M. (1989). Social comparison activity under threat: Downward evaluation and upward contacts. *Psychological Review, 96*, 569–575.

Taylor, S. E., & Thompson, S. C. (1982). Stalking the elusive "vividness" effect. *Psychological Review, 89*, 155–181.

Taylor, S. E., Wood, J. V., & Lichtman, R. R. (1983). It could be worse: Selective evaluation as a response to victimization. *Journal of Social Issues, 39*, 19–40.

Teger, A. I., & Pruitt, D. G. (1967). Components of group risk taking. *Journal of Experimental Social Psychology, 3*, 189–205.

Tenney, E. R., MacCoun, R. J., Spellman, B. A., & Hastie, R. (2007). Calibration trumps confidence as a basis for witness credibility. *Psychological Science, 18*, 46–50.

Tesser, A. (1988). Toward a self-evaluation maintenance model of social behavior. In L. Berkowitz (Ed.), *Advances in experimental social psychology* (Vol. 21, pp. 181–227). San Diego, CA: Academic Press.

Tesser, A. (1993). The importance of heritability in psychological research: The case of attitudes. *Psychological Review, 100*, 129–142.

Tesser, A., Campbell, J. D., & Mickler, S. (1983). The role of social pressure, attention to the stimulus, and self-doubt in conformity. *European Journal of Social Psychology, 13*, 217–233.

Tesser, A., & Conlee, M. C. (1975). Some effects of time and thought on attitude polarization. *Journal of Personality and Social Psychology, 31*, 262–270.

Tesser, A., Martin, L., & Mendolia, M. (1995). The impact of thought on attitude extremity and attitude-behavior consistency. In R. E. Petty & J. Krosnick (Eds.), *Attitude strength: Antecedents and consequences.* Mahwah, NJ: Erlbaum.

Tesser, A., & Smith, J. (1980). Some effects of friendship and task relevance on helping: You don't always help the one you like. *Journal of Experimental Social Psychology, 16*, 582–590.

Tetlock, P. E. (1981). Pre- to post-election shifts in presidential rhetoric: Impression management or cognitive adjustment. *Journal of Personality and Social Psychology, 41*, 207–212.

Tetlock, P. E. (1984). Cognitive style and political belief systems in the British House of Commons. *Journal of Personality and Social Psychology, 46*, 365–375.

Tetlock, P. E., Peterson, R. S., McGuire, C., Chang, S., & Feld, P. (1992). Assessing political group dynamics: A test of the groupthink model. *Journal of Personality and Social Psychology, 20*, 142–146.

Thakerar, J. N., & Iwawaki, S. (1979). Cross-cultural comparisons in interpersonal attraction of females toward males. *Journal of Social Psychology, 108*, 121–122.

Thaler, R. H. (1980). Toward a positive theory of consumer choice. *Journal of Economic Behavior and Organization, 1*, 39–60.

Thomas, S. L., Skitka, L. J., Christen, S., & Jurgena, M. (2002). Social facilitation and impression formation. *Basic and Applied Social Psychology, 24*, 67–70.

Thompson, J. (2000, June 18). "I was certain, but I was wrong." New York Times, June 18, 2000. Retrieved from http://www.nytimes.com/2000/06/18/opinion/i-was-certain-but-i-was-wrong.html

Thompson, L. (2005). *The heart and mind of the negotiator* (3rd ed.). Upper Saddle River, NJ: Pearson Education.

Thompson, L., & Hrebec, D. (1996). Lose-lose arguments in interdependent decision making. *Psychological Bulletin, 120*, 396–409.

Thornhill, R., & Gangestad, S. W. (1993). Human facial beauty: Averageness, symmetry, and parasite resistance. *Human Nature, 4*, 237–269.

Thornhill, R., & Gangestad, S. W. (1999). The scent of symmetry: A human sex pheromone that signals fitness? *Evolution and Human Behavior, 20*, 175–201.

Thornhill, R., & Gangestad, S. W. (2005). Facial sexual dimorphism, developmental stability, and susceptibilty to disease in men and women. *Evolution and Human Behavior, 27*, 131–144.

Thornhill, R., Gangestad, S. W., Miller, R., Scheyd, G., McCollough, J., & Franklin, M. (2003). MHC, symmetry and body scent attractiveness in men and women (*Homo sapiens*). *Behavioral Ecology, 14*, 668–768.

Tice, D. M. (1993). Self-concept change and self-presentation: The looking glass self is also a magnifying glass. *Journal of Personality and Social Psychology, 63*, 435–451.

Tice, D. M., Baumeister, R. F., Shmueli, D., & Muraven, M. (2007). Restoring the self: Positive affect helps improve self-regulation following ego depletion. *Journal of Experimental Social Psychology, 43*, 379–384.

Tice, D. M., & Wallace, H. M. (2005). The reflected self: Creating yourself as (you think) others see you. In M. R. Leary & J. P. Tangney (Eds.), *Handbook of self and identity* (pp. 91–105). New York: Guilford Press.

Tiedens, L. Z. (2001). Anger and advancement versus sadness and subjugation: The effect of negative emotion expressions on social status conferral. *Journal of Personality and Social Psychology, 80(1)*, 86–94.

Tiedens, L. Z., & Leach, C. W. (2004). *The social life of emotions.* New York: Cambridge University Press.

Todorov, A., & Bargh, J. A. (2002). Automatic sources of aggression. *Aggression and Violent Behavior, 7*, 53–68.

Todorov, A., Mandisodza, A. N., Goren, A., & Hall, C. C. (2005). Inferences of competence from faces predict election outcomes. *Science, 308*, 1623–1626.

Todorov, A., Said, C. P., Engell, A. D., & Oosterhof, N. N. (2008). Understanding evaluation of faces on social dimensions. *Trends in Cognitive Sciences, 12*, 455–460.

Todorov, A., & Uleman, J. S. (2003). The efficiency of binding spontaneous trait inferences to actors' faces. *Journal of Experimental Social Psychology, 39*, 549–562.

Tom, S. M., Fox, C. R., Trepel, C., & Poldrack, R. A. (2007). The neural basis of loss aversion in decision-making under risk. *Science, 315*, 515–518.

Toma, C.L. & Hancock, J.T. (2010). Looks and lies: The role of physical attractiveness in online dating self-presentation and deception. *Communication Research 37(3)*, 335–351.

Tomkins, S. S. (1962). *Affect, imagery, consciousness: I. The positive affects.* New York: Springer.

Tomkins, S. S. (1963). *Affect, imagery, consciousness: II. The negative affects.* New York: Springer.

Toobin, J. (2011, May 9). The mitigator: A new way of looking at the death penalty. *The New Yorker.*

Tooby, J., & Cosmides, L. (1992). The psychological foundations of culture. In J. H. Barkow, L. Cosmides, & J. Tooby (Eds.), *The adapted mind: Evolutionary psychology and the generation of culture.* New York: Oxford University Press.

Tormala, Z. L., Briñol, P., & Petty, R. E. (2006). When credibility attacks: The reverse impact of source credibility on persuasion. *Journal of Experimental Social Psychology, 42*, 684–691.

Tormala, Z. L., Brinol, P., & Petty, R. E. (2007). Multiple roles for source credibility under high elaboration: It's all in the timing. *Social Cognition, 25*, 536–552.

Tormala, Z. L., Clarkson, J. J., & Petty, R. E. (2006). Resisting persuasion by the skin of one's teeth: The hidden success of resisted persuasive messages. *Journal of Personality and Social Psychology, 91,* 423–435.

Tormala, Z. L., & Petty, R. E. (2002). What doesn't kill me makes me stronger: The effects of resisting persuasion on attitude certainty. *Journal of Personality and Social Psychology, 83,* 1298–1313.

Tormala, Z. L., Petty, R. E., & Briñol, P. (2002). Ease of retrieval effects in persuasion: A self-validation analysis. *Personality and Social Psychology Bulletin, 28,* 1700–1712.

Torrance, E. P. (1955). Some consequences of power differences in decision making in permanent and temporary 3-man groups. In A. P. Hare, E. F. Bogatta, & R. F. Bales (Eds.), *Small groups: Studies in social interaction.* New York: Knopf.

Tourangeau, R., Rasinski, K., & Bradburn, N. (1991). Measuring happiness in surveys: A test of the subtraction hypothesis. *Public Opinion Quarterly, 55,* 255–266.

Tower, R. K., Kelly, C., & Richards, A. (1997). Individualism, collectivism and reward allocation: A cross-cultural study in Russia and Britain. *British Journal of Social Psychology, 36,* 331–345.

Tracy, J. L., & Matsumoto, D. (2008). The spontaneous display of pride and shame: Evidence for biologically innate nonverbal displays. *Proceedings of the National Academy of Sciences of the USA, 105,* 11655–11660.

Tracy, J. L., & Robins, R. W. (2004). Show your pride: Evidence for a discrete emotion expression. *Psychological Science, 15,* 94–97.

Tracy, J. L., & Robins, R. W. (2007). Emerging insights into the nature and function of pride. *Current Directions in Psychological Science, 16,* 147–150.

Trafimow, D., Triandis, H. C., & Goto, S. G. (1991). Some tests of the distinction between the private self and the collective self. *Journal of Personality and Social Psychology, 60,* 649–655.

Travis, L. E. (1925). The effect of a small audience upon eye-hand coordination. *Journal of Abnormal and Social Psychology, 20,* 142–146.

Trawalter, S., Richeson, J. A., & Shelton, J. N. (2009). Predicting behavior during interracial interactions: A stress and coping approach. *Personality and Social Psychology Review, 13,* 243–268.

Triandis, H. C. (1987). Individualism and social psychological theory. In C. Kagitcibasi (Ed.), *Growth and progress in cross-cultural psychology* (pp. 78–83). New York: Swets North America.

Triandis, H. C. (1989). The self and social behavior in differing cultural contexts. *Psychological Review, 96,* 269–289.

Triandis, H. C. (1994). *Culture and social behavior.* New York: McGraw-Hill.

Triandis, H. C. (1995). *Individualism and collectivism.* Boulder, CO: Westview Press.

Triandis, H. C., Bontempo, R., Villareal, M. J., Asai, M., & Lucca, N. (1988). Individualism and collectivism: Cross-cultural perspectives on self-ingroup relationships. *Journal of Personality and Social Psychology, 54*(2), 323–338.

Triandis, H. C., McCusker, C., & Hui, C. H. (1990). Multimethod probes of individualism and collectivism. *Journal of Personality and Social Psychology, 56,* 1006–1020.

Triplett, N. (1898). The dynamogenic factors in pacemaking and competition. *American Journal of Psychology, 9,* 507–533.

Trivers, R. L. (1971). The evolution of reciprocal altruism. *Quarterly Review of Biology, 46,* 35–57.

Trivers, R. L. (1985). *Social evolution.* Menlo Park, CA: Benjamin Cummings.

Trope, Y. (1986). Identification and inferential processes in dispositional attribution. *Psychological Review, 93,* 239–257.

Trope, Y., & Liberman, N. (2003). Temporal construal. *Psychological Review, 110,* 403–421.

Trope, Y., & Liberman, N. (2010). Construal-level theory of psychological distance. *Psychological Review, 117,* 440–463.

Tsai, J. L. (2007). Ideal affect: Cultural causes and behavioral consequences. *Perspectives on Psychological Science, 2,* 242–259.

Tsai, J. L., Knutson, B., & Fung, H. H. (2006). Cultural variation in affect valuation. *Journal of Personality and Social Psychology, 90,* 288–307.

Tsai, J. L., & Levenson, R. W. (1997). Cultural influences on emotional responding: Chinese American and European American dating couples during interpersonal conflict. *Journal of Cross-Cultural Psychology, 28,* 600–625.

Turnbull, C. (1965). *Wayward servants.* New York: Natural History Press.

Turner, C., & Leyens, J. (1992). The weapons effect revisited: The effects of firearms on aggressive behavior. In P. Suedfeld & P. E. Tetlock (Eds.), *Psychology and social policy* (pp. 201–221). New York: Hemisphere.

Turner, M. E., & Pratkanis, A. R. (1998). Twenty-five years of groupthink theory and research: Lessons from the evaluation of a theory. *Organizational Behavior and Human Decision Processes, 73,* 105–115.

Tversky, A., & Kahneman, D. (1974). Judgment under uncertainty: Heuristics and biases. *Science, 185,* 1124–1131.

Tversky, A., & Kahneman, D. (1981). The framing of decisions and the psychology of choice. *Science, 211,* 453–458.

Tversky, A., & Kahneman, D. (1982). Evidential impact of base rates. In D. Kahneman, P. Slovic, & A. Tversky (Eds.), *Judgment under uncertainty: Heuristics and biases* (pp. 153–160). New York: Cambridge University Press.

Tversky, A., & Kahneman, D. (1986). Rational choice and the framing of decisions. *Journal of Business, 59,* 5251–5278.

Tversky, A., & Shafir, E. (1992). Choice under conflict: The dynamics of deferred decision. *Psychological Science, 3*(6), 358–361.

Twenge, J. M. (2002). Birth cohort, social change, and personality: The interplay of dysphoria and individualism in the 20th century. In D. Cervone & W. Mischel (Eds.), *Advances in personality science.* New York: Guilford Press.

Twenge, J. M., Baumeister, R. F., Tice, D. M., & Stucke, T. S. (2001). If you can't join them, beat them: Effects of social exclusion on aggressive behavior. *Journal of Personality and Social Psychology, 81,* 1058–1069.

Twenge, J. M., & Campbell, W. K. (2001). Age and birth cohort differences in self-esteem: A cross-temporal analysis. *Personality and Social Psychology Review, 5,* 321–344.

Tyler, T. R. (1984). Assessing the risk of crime victimization: The integration of personal victimization experience and socially transmitted information. *Journal of Social Issues, 40,* 27–38.

Tyler, T. R. (1987). Conditions leading to value-expressive effects in judgments of procedural justice: A test of four models. *Journal of Personality and Social Psychology, 52,* 333–344.

Tyler, T. R. (1994). Psychological models of the justice motive: Antecedents of distributive and procedural justice. *Journal of Personality and Social Psychology, 67,* 850–863.

Tyler, T. R., & Caine, A. (1981). The influence of outcomes and procedures on satisfaction with formal leaders. *Journal of Personality and Social Psychology, 41,* 642–655.

Uchino, B. N., Cacioppo, J. T., & Kiecolt-Glaser, J. K. (1996). The relationship between social support and physiological process: A review with emphasis on underlying mechanisms and implications for health. *Psychological Bulletin, 119*, 88–531.

Uematsu, T. (1970). Social facilitation of feeding behavior in freshwater fish. I. *Rhodeus, Acheilognathus* and *Rhinogobius. Annual of Animal Psychology, 20*, 87–95.

Uleman, J. S. (1987). Consciousness and control: The case of spontaneous trait inferences. *Personality and Social Psychology Bulletin, 13*, 337–354.

Umberson, D., & Hughes, M. (1987). The impact of physical attractiveness on achievement and psychological well-being. *Social Psychology Quarterly, 50*, 227–236.

UN Women. (2011). Virtual Knowledge Centre to End Violence against Women and Girls. Retrieved from www.endvawnow.org

Updegraff, J. A., & Taylor, S. E. (2000). From vulnerability to growth: Positive and negative effects of stressful life events. In J. H. Harvey & E. D. Miller (Eds.), *Loss and trauma: General and close relationship perspectives* (pp. 3–28). New York: Brunner-Routledge.

Uranowitz, S. W. (1975). Helping and self-attributions: A field experiment. *Journal of Personality and Social Psychology, 31*, 852–854.

Uskul, A. K., Sherman, D. K., & Fitzgibbon, J. (2009). The cultural congruency effect: Culture, regulatory focus, and the effectiveness of gain- vs. loss-framed health messages. *Journal of Experimental Social Psychology, 45*, 535–541.

Vaes, J., Paladino, M. P., Castelli, L., Leyens, J. Ph., Giovanazzi, A. (2003). On the behavioral consequences of infra-humanization: The implicit role of uniquely human emotions in intergroup relations. *Journal of Personality and Social Psychology, 85*, 1016–1034

Valdesolo, P., & DeSteno, D. (2011). Synchrony and the social tuning of compassion. *Emotion, 11*, 262–266.

Valenti, A. C., & Downing, L. L. (1975). Differential effects of jury size on verdicts following deliberations as a function of the apparent guilt of a defendant. *Journal of Personality and Social Psychology, 32*, 655–663.

Vallacher, R. R., & Wegner, D. M. (1987). What do people think they're doing? Action identification and human behavior. *Psychological Review, 94*, 3–15.

Vallone, R. P., Ross, L., & Lepper, M. R. (1985). The hostile media phenomenon: Biased perception and perceptions of media bias in *coverage* of the Beirut massacre. *Journal of Personality and Social Psychology, 49*, 577–585.

Van Baaren, R. B., Holland, R. W., Kawakami, K., & van Knippenberg, A. (2004). Mimicry and pro-social behavior. *Psychological Science, 15*, 71–74.

Van Baaren, R. B., Holland, R. W., Steenaert, B., & van Knippenberg, A. (2003). Mimicry for money: Behavioral consequences of imitation. *Journal of Experimental Social Psychology, 39*, 393–398.

Van Boven, L., & Campbell, M., & Gilovich, T. (2010). Stigmatizing materialism: On stereotypes and impressions of materialistic versus experiential pursuits. *Personality and Social Psychology Bulletin, 36*, 551–563.

Van Boven, L., Kamada, A., & Gilovich, T. (1999). The perceiver as perceived: Everyday intuitions about the correspondence bias. *Journal of Personality and Social Psychology, 77*, 1188–1199.

van Dijk, C., de Jong, P. J., & Peters, M. L. (2009). The remedial value of blushing in the context of transgressions and mishaps. *Emotion, 9*, 287–291.

Van Dort, B. E., & Moos, R. H. (1976). Distance and the utilization of a student health *center. Journal of the American College Health Association, 24*, 159–162.

Van Kleef, G. A. (2009). How emotions regulate social life: The emotions as social information (EASI) model. *Current Directions in Psychological Science, 18*, 184-188.

Van Kleef, G. A., De Dreu, C. K. W., Pietroni, D., & Manstead, A. S. R. (2006). Power and emotion in negotiation: Power moderates the interpersonal effects of anger and happiness on concession making. *European Journal of Social Psychology*: Special issue on social power, *36*, 557–581.

Van Lange, P. A. M., Agnew, C. R., Harinck, F., & Steemers, G. E. M. (1997). From game theory to real life: How social value orientation affects willingness to sacrifice in ongoing close relationships. *Journal of Personality and Social Psychology, 82*, 956–974.

Van Vugt, M., & Spisak, B. R. (2008). Sex differences in the emergence of leadership during competitions within and between groups. *Psychological Science, 19(9)*, 854–858.

Vandals ignite 400 fires in Detroit. (1984). *Washington Post*, p. A18.

Vandello, J., & Cohen, D. (1999). Patterns of individualism and collectivism across the United States. *Journal of Personality and Social Psychology, 77*, 279–292.

Vanneman, R. D., & Pettigrew, T. F. (1972). Race and relative deprivation in the urban United States. *Race, 13*, 461–486.

Varnum, M., Grossmann, I., Katunar, D., Nisbett, R. E., & Kitayama, S. (2008). Holism in a European cultural context: Differences in cognitive style between Central and East Europeans and Westerners. *Journal of Cognition and Culture, 8(3)*, 321–333.

Vasquez, K., Keltner, D., Ebenbach, D. H., & Banaszynski, T. L. (2001). Cultural variation and similarity in moral rhetorics: Voices from the Philippines and United States. *Journal of Cross-Cultural Psychology, 32*, 93–120.

Vasquez, N. A., & Buehler, R. (2007). Seeing future success: Does imagery perspective influence achievement motivation? *Personality and Social Psychology Bulletin, 33*, 1392–1405.

Vaughn, P. W., Rogers, E. M., Singhal, A., & Swalehe, R. M. (2000). Entertainment-education and HIV/AIDS prevention: A field experiment in Tanzania. *Journal of Health Communication, 5*, 81–100.

Vazire, S. (2010). Who knows what about a person? The Self-Other Knowledge Asymmetry (SOKA) model. *Journal of Personality and Social Psychology, 98*, 281–300.

Vazire, S., & Carlson, E. N. (2011). Others sometimes know us better than we know ourselves. *Current Directions in Psychological Science, 20*, 104–108.

Vazire, S., & Mehl, M. R. (2008). Knowing me, knowing you: The accuracy and unique predictive validity of self-ratings and other-ratings of daily behavior. *Journal of Personality and Social Psychology, 95*, 1202–1216.

Vescio, T. K., Gervais, S. J., Heidenreich, S., & Snyder, M. (2006). The effects of prejudice level and social influence strategy on powerful people's responding to racial outgroup members. *European Journal of Social Psychology, 36*, 435–450.

Vescio, T. K., Gervais, S. J., Snyder, M., & Hoover, A. (2005). Power and the creation of patronizing environments: The stereotype-based behaviors of the powerful and their effects on female performance in masculine domains. *Journal of Personality and Social Psychology, 88(4)*, 658–672.

Vescio, T. K., Snyder, M., & Butz, D. (2003). Power in stereotypically masculine domains: A social influence strategy × stereotype match model. *Journal of Personality and Social Psychology, 85*(6), 1062–1078.

von Hippel, W., Sekaquaptewa, D., & Vargas, P. (1995). On the role of encoding processes in stereotype maintenance. In M. P. Zanna (Ed.), *Advances in experimental social psychology* (Vol. 27, pp. 177–254). San Diego, CA: Academic Press.

Vonk, R. (1999). Effects of outcome dependency on the correspondence bias. *Personality and Social Psychology Bulletin, 25*, 382–389.

Vonk, R. (2002). Self-serving interpretations of flattery: Why ingratiation works. *Journal of Personality and Social Psychology, 82*, 515–526.

Waber, R., Shiv, B., Carmon, Z., & Ariely, D. (2008). Commercial features of placebo and therapeutic efficacy. *Journal of the American Medical Association, 299*(9), 1016–1017.

Waggoner, A. S., Smith, E. R., & Collins, E. C. (2009). Person perception by active verses passive perceivers. *Journal of Experimental Social Psychology, 45*, 1028–1031.

Wagner, R. C. (1975). Complementary needs, role expectations, interpersonal attraction, and the stability of work relationships. *Journal of Personality and Social Psychology, 32*, 116–124.

Wallach, M. A., Kogan, N., & Bem, D. J. (1962). Group influences on individual risk taking. *Journal of Abnormal and Social Psychology, 65*, 75–86.

Wallerstein, J. S., Lewis, J., & Blakeslee, S. (2000). *The unexpected legacy of divorce: The 25-year landmark study.* New York: Hyperion.

Walster, E. (1966). Assignment of responsibility for an accident. *Journal of Personality and Social Psychology, 3*, 73–79.

Walster, E., Aronson, E., & Abrahams, D. (1966). On increasing the persuasiveness of a low prestige communicator. *Journal of Experimental Social Psychology, 2*, 325–342.

Walster, E., Aronson, V., Abrahams, D., & Rottman, L. (1966). Importance of physical attractiveness in dating behavior. *Journal of Personality and Social Psychology, 4*, 508–516.

Walster, E., Walster, G. W., & Berscheid, E. (1978). *Equity: Theory and research.* Boston: Allyn & Bacon.

Walton, G. M., & Cohen, G. L. (2007). A question of belonging: Race, social fit, and achievement. *Journal of Personality and Social Psychology, 92*, 82–96.

Warneken, F., & Tomasello, M. (2006). Altruistic helping in human infants and young chimpanzees. *Science, 311*, 5765, 1301–1303.

Waterman, C. K. (1969). The facilitating and interfering effects of cognitive dissonance on simple and complex paired associates learning tasks. *Journal of Experimental Social Psychology, 5*, 31–42.

Watson, D. (1982). The actor and the observer: How are their perceptions of causality divergent? *Psychological Bulletin, 92*, 682–700.

Watson, R. I. (1973). Investigation into deindividuation using a cross-cultural survey technique. *Journal of Personality and Social Psychology, 25*, 342–345.

Waugh, C. E., & Fredrickson, B. L. (2006). Nice to know you: Positive emotions, self-other overlap, and complex understanding in the formation of a new relationship. *Journal of Positive Psychology, 1*, 93–106.

Waytz, A., & Epley, N. (2012). Social connection enables dehumanization. *Journal of Experimental Social Psychology, 48,* 70–76.

Weber, M. (1947). *The theory of social and economic organization* (A. M. Henderson & T. Parsons, Trans.). New York: Oxford University Press.

Weber, R., & Crocker, J. (1983). Cognitive processes in the revision of stereotypic beliefs. *Journal of Personality and Social Psychology, 45*, 961–977.

Wedekind, C., & Milinski, M. (2000). Cooperation through image scoring in humans. *Science, 288*, 850–852.

Wegener, D. T., & Petty, R. E. (1994). Mood management across affective states: The hedonic contingency hypothesis. *Journal of Personality and Social Psychology, 66*, 1034–1048.

Wegener, D. T., Petty, R. E., & Smith, S. M. (1995). Positive mood can increase or decrease message scrutiny: The hedonic contingency view of mood and message processing. *Journal of Personality and Social Psychology, 69*, 5–15.

Wegner, D. M. (1994). Ironic processes of mental control. *Psychological Review, 101*, 34–52.

Wegner, D. M., Ansfield, M., & Pilloff, D. (1998). The putt and the pendulum: Ironic effects of the mental control of action. *Psychological Science, 9*, 196–199.

Weiner, B. (1986). *An attributional theory of achievement and motivation.* New York: Springer-Verlag.

Weiner, B., Graham, S., & Reyna, C. (1997). An attributional examination of retributive versus utilitarian philosophies of punishment. *Social Justice Research, 10*, 431–452.

Wellman, H. M. (1990). *The child's theory of mind.* Cambridge, MA: MIT Press.

Wells, G. L., Charman, S. D., & Olson, E. A. (2005). Building face composites can harm lineup identification performance. *Journal of Experimental Psychology, 11*, 147–156.

Wells, G. L., Ferguson, T. J., & Lindsay, R. C. L. (1981). The tractability of eyewitness confidence and its implications for triers of fact. *Journal of Applied Psychology, 66*, 688–696.

Wells, G. L., & Gavanski, I. (1989). Mental simulation of causality. *Journal of Personality and Social Psychology, 56*, 161–169.

Wells, G. L., & Leippe, M. R. (1981). How do triers of fact enter the accuracy of eyewitness identification? *Journal of Applied Psychology, 66*, 682–687.

Wells, G. L., Lindsay, R. C. L., & Ferguson, T. (1979). Accuracy, confidence and juror perceptions in eyewitness identification. *Journal of Applied Psychology, 64*, 440–448.

Wells, G. L., Memon, A., & Penrod, S. D. (2006). Eyewitness evidence: Improving its probative value. *Psychological Science in the Public Interest, 7*, 45–75.

Wells, G. L., & Petty, R. E. (1980). The effects of overt head movements on persuasion: Compatibility and incompatibility of responses. *Basic and Applied Social Psychology, 1*, 219–230.

West, S. G., & Brown, T. J. (1975). Physical attractiveness, the severity of the emergency, and helping: A field experiment and interpersonal simulation. *Journal of Experimental Social Psychology, 11*, 531–538.

West, T. V., Pearson, A. R., Dovidio, J. F., Shelton, J. N., & Trail, T. E. (2009). Superordinate identity and intergroup roommate friendship development. *Journal of Experimental Social Psychology, 45*, 1266–1272.

Westoff, C. F., & Rodriguez, G. (1995). The mass media and family planning in Kenya. *International Family Planning Perspectives, 21*(1), 26–31, 35.

Wetzel, C. G. (1982). Self-serving biases in attribution: A Bayesian analysis. *Journal of Personality and Social Psychology, 43*, 197–209.

Whatley, M. A., Webster, J. M., Smith, R. H., & Rhodes, A. (1999). The effect of a favor on public and private compliance: How internalized is the norm of reciprocity? *Basic and Applied Social Psychology, 21,* 251–259.

Wheatley, T., & Haidt, J. (2005). Hypnotic disgust makes moral judgments more severe. *Psychological Science, 16,* 780–785.

Wheeler, L., & Kim, Y. (1997). What is beautiful is culturally good: The physical attractiveness stereotype has different content in collectivistic cultures. *Personality and Social Psychology Bulletin, 23,* 795–800.

Wheeler, L., & Nezlek, J. (1977). Sex differences in social participation. *Journal of Personality and Social Psychology, 35,* 742–754.

White, G. L., & Kight, T. D. (1984). Misattribution of arousal and attraction: Effects of salience of explanations of arousal. *Journal of Experimental Social Psychology, 20,* 55–64.

White, H. (1997). Longitudinal perspective on alcohol and aggression during adolescence. In M. Galanter (Ed.), *Recent developments in alcoholism: Alcohol and violence: Epidemiology, neurobiology, psychology, and family issues* (Vol. 13, pp. 81–103). New York: Plenum Press.

White, L. K., & Booth, A. (1991). Divorce over the life course: The role of marital happiness. *Review of Personality and Social Psychology, 12,* 265–289.

White, P. A. (2002). Causal attribution from covariation information: The evidential evaluation model. *European Journal of Social Psychology, 32,* 667–684.

Whitley, B. E. (1990). The relationship of heterosexuals' attributions for the causes of homosexuality to attitudes towards lesbians and gay men. *Personality and Social Psychology Bulletin, 16,* 369–377.

Whitley, B. E., & Frieze, I. H. (1985). Children's causal attributions for success and failure in achievement settings: A meta-analysis. *Journal of Educational Psychology, 77(5),* 608–616.

Whittlesea, B. W., & Leboe, J. P. (2000). The heuristic basis of remembering and classification: Fluency, generation, and resemblance. *Journal of Experimental Psychology: General, 129,* 84–106.

Wicker, A. W. (1969). Attitudes versus actions: The relationship of verbal and overt behavioral responses to attitude objects. *Journal of Social Issues, 25,* 41–78.

Wienke, C., & Hill, G. J. (2009). Does the 'marriage benefit' extend to partners in gay and lesbian relationships? Evidence from a random sample of sexually active adults. *Journal of Family Issues, 30(2),* 259–289.

Wigboldus, D. H. J., Sherman, J. W., Franzese, H. L., & van Knippenberg, A. (2004). Capacity and comprehension: Spontaneous stereotyping under cognitive load. *Social Cognition, 22,* 292–309.

Wiggins, J. S., Wiggins, N., & Conger, J. C. (1968). Correlates of heterosexual somatic preference. *Journal of Personality and Social Psychology, 10,* 82–90.

Wilder, D. A. (1984). Predictions of belief homogeneity and similarity following social categorization. *British Journal of Social Psychology, 23,* 323–333.

Wilder, D. A. (1986). Social categorization: Implications for creation and reduction of intergroup bias. In L. Berkowitz (Ed.), *Advances in experimental social psychology* (Vol. 19, pp. 291–355). San Diego, CA: Academic Press.

Wiley, M. G., Crittenden, K. S., & Birg, L. D. (1979). Why a rejection? Causal attribution of a career achievement event. *Social Psychology Quarterly, 42,* 214–222.

Wilkinson, F., & Pickett, K. (2009). *Spirit level: Why greater equality makes societies stronger.* New York: Bloomsbury Press.

Wilkinson, G. (1990, February). Food sharing in vampire bats. *Scientific American,* 76–82.

Wilier, R. (2004). The effects of government-issued terror warnings on presidential approval ratings. *Current Research in Social Psychology, 10,* 1–12.

Willer, R. (2009). Groups reward individual sacrifice: The status solution to the collective action problem. *American Sociological Review, 74,* 23–43.

Williams, D. R., & Collins, C. (1995). U.S. socioeconomic and racial differences in health: Patterns and explanations. *Annual Review of Sociology, 21,* 349–386.

Williams, E. F., & Gilovich, T. (2012). The better-than-my-average effect: The relative impact of peak and typical performances in judging the self and others. *Journal of Experimental Social Psychology, 48,* 556–561.

Williams, E. F., Gilovich, T., & Dunning, D. (2012). Being all that you can be: How potential performances influence assessments of self and others. *Personality and Social Psychology Bulletin, 38(2),* 143–154.

Williams, J. R., Insel, T. R., Harbaugh, C. R., & Carter, C. S. (1994). Oxytocin administered centrally facilitates formation of a partner preference in female prairie voles (*Microtus ochrogaster*). *Journal of Neuroendocrinology, 6,* 247–250.

Williams, K. D. (2007). Ostracism. *Annual Review of Psychology, 58,* 425–452.

Williams, K. D., Harkins, S., & Latané, B. (1981). Identifiability as a deterrent to social loafing: Two cheering experiments. *Journal of Personality and Social Psychology, 40,* 303–311.

Willis, F. N., & Hamm, H. K. (1980). The use of interpersonal touch in securing compliance. *Journal of Nonverbal Behavior, 5(1),* 49–55.

Willis, J., & Todorov, A. (2006). First impressions: Making up your mind after a 100-ms exposure to a face. *Psychological Science, 17,* 592–598.

Wilson, M. I., Daly, M., & Weghorst, S. J. (1980). Household composition and the risk of child abuse and neglect. *Journal of Biological Science, 12,* 333–340.

Wilson, R. E., Gosling, S. D., & Graham, L. T. (2012). A review of Facebook research in the social sciences. *Perspectives on Psychological Science, 7,* 203–220.

Wilson, T., & Brekke, N. (1994). Mental contamination and mental correction: Unwanted influences on judgments and evaluations. *Psychological Bulletin, 116,* 117–142.

Wilson, T., Centerbar, D., & Brekke, N. (2002). Mental contamination and the debiasing problem. In T. Gilovich, D. W. Griffin, & D. Kahneman (Eds.), *Heuristics and biases: The psychology of intuitive judgment* (pp. 185–200). New York: Cambridge University Press.

Wilson, T. D. (2002). *Strangers to ourselves: Discovering the adaptive unconscious.* Cambridge, MA: Harvard University Press.

Wilson, T. D., & Dunn, D. S. (1986). Effects of introspection on attitude-behavior consistency: Analyzing reasons versus focusing on feelings. *Journal of Experimental Social Psychology, 22,* 249–263.

Wilson, T. D., Dunn, D. S., Bybee, J. A., Hyman, D. B., & Rotondo, J. A. (1984). Effects of analyzing reasons on attitude-behavior consistency. *Journal of Personality and Social Psychology, 47,* 5–16.

Wilson, T. D., & Dunn, E. (2004). Self-knowledge: Its limits, value, and potential for improvement. *Annual Review of Psychology, 55,* 493–518.

Wilson, T. D., & Gilbert, D. T. (2008). Explaining why. A model of affective adaptation. *Perspectives in Psychological Science, 3,* 372–388.

Wilson, T. D., Lisle, D., Schooler, J. W., Hodges, S. D., Klaaren, K. J., & LaFleur, S. J. (1993). Introspecting about reasons can reduce post-choice satisfaction. *Personality and Social Psychology Bulletin, 19,* 331–339.

Wilson, T. D., & Schooler, J. W. (1991). Thinking too much: Introspection can reduce the quality of preferences and decisions. *Journal of Personality and Social Psychology, 60,* 181–192.

Wilson, T. D., Wheatley, T., Kurtz, J., Dunn, & Gilbert, D. T. (2004). When to fire: Anticipatory versus postevent reconstrual of uncontrollable events. *Personality and Social Psychology Bulletin, 30,* 1–12.

Wilson, T. D., Wheatley, T., Meyers, J. M., Gilbert, D. T., & Axson, D. (2000). Focalism: A source of durability bias in affective forecasting. *Journal of Personality and Social Psychology, 78,* 821–836.

Winch, R. F. (1955). The theory of complementary needs in mate selection: A test of one kind of complementariness. *American Sociological Review, 20,* 52–56.

Winch, R. F., Ktanes, T., & Ktanes, V. (1954). The theory of complementary needs in mate selection: An analytic and descriptive study. *American Sociological Review, 19,* 241–249.

Winch, R. F., Ktanes, T., & Ktanes, V. (1955). Empirical elaboration of the theory of complementary needs in mate selection. *Journal of Abnormal and Social Psychology, 51,* 508–513.

Windhauser, J., Seiter, J., & Winfree, T. (1991). Crime news in the Louisiana press. *Journalism Quarterly, 45,* 72–78.

Winkielman, P., & Cacioppo, J. T. (2001). Mind at ease puts a smile on the face: Psychophysiological evidence that processing facilitation increases positive affect. *Journal of Personality and Social Psychology, 81,* 989–1000.

Winter, D. G. (1973). *The power motive.* New York: Free Press.

Winter, D. G. (1988). The power motive in women and men. *Journal of Personality and Social Psychology, 54,* 510–519.

Winter, D. G., & Barenbaum, N. B. (1985). Responsibility and the power motive in women and men. *Journal of Personality, 53,* 335–355.

Winter, L., & Uleman, J. S. (1984). When are social judgments made? Evidence for the spontaneousness of trait inferences. *Journal of Personality and Social Psychology, 47,* 237–252.

Wiseman, C. V., Gray, J. J., Mosimann, J. E., & Ahrens, A. H. (1992). Cultural expectations of thinness in women: An update. *International Journal of Eating Disorders, 11,* 85–89.

Wisman, A., and Goldenberg, J. (2005). From the grave to the cradle: Evidence that mortality salience engenders a desire for offspring. *Journal of Personality and Social Psychology, 89,* 46–61.

Wittenbrink, B. (2004). Ordinary forms of prejudice. *Psychological Inquiry, 15,* 306–310.

Wittenbrink, B., Judd, C. M., & Park, B. (1997). Evidence for racial prejudice at the implicit level and its relationship with questionnaire measures. *Journal of Personality and Social Psychology, 72,* 262–274.

Wittenbrink, B., & Schwarz, N. (Eds.). (2007). *Implicit measures of attitudes.* New York: Guilford Press.

Wolf, S. (1985). Manifest and latent influence on majorities and minorities. *Journal of Personality and Social Psychology, 48,* 899–908.

Wolfe, T. (1979). *The right stuff.* New York: Farrar, Straus & Giroux.

Wolfe, T. (1987). *The bonfire of the vanities.* New York: Farrar, Straus & Giroux.

Woll, S. (1986). So many to choose from: Decision strategies in videodating. *Journal of Social and Personal Relationships, 3,* 43–52.

Wood, J. V. (1996). What is social comparison and how should we study it? *Personality and Social Psychology Bulletin, 22,* 520–537.

Wood, W. (1982). Retrieval of attitude-relevant information from memory: Effects of susceptibility to persuasion and on intrinsic motivation. *Journal of Personality and Social Psychology, 42,* 798–810.

Wood, W., & Eagly, A. H. (2002). A cross-cultural analysis of the behavior of women and men: Implications for the origin of sex differences. *Psychological Bulletin, 126,* 699–727.

Wood, W., & Kallgren, C. A. (1988). Communicator attributes and persuasion: Recipients access to attitude-relevant information in memory. *Personality and Social Psychology Bulletin, 14,* 172–182.

Wood, W., Lundgren, S., Ouellette, J. A., Busceme, S., & Blackstone, T. (1994). Minority influence: A meta-analytic review of social influence processes. *Psychological Bulletin, 115,* 323–345.

Wooley, S. C., & Wooley, O. W. (1980). Eating disorders: Obesity and anorexia. In A. M. Brodsky & R. T. Hare-Mustin (Eds.), *Women and psychotherapy: An assessment of research and practice* (pp. 135–158). New York: Guilford Press.

Woolger, R. J. (1988). *Other lives, other selves: A Jungian psychotherapist discovers past lives.* New York: Bantam.

Worchel, S. (1974). The effects of three types of arbitrary thwarting on the instigation to aggression. *Journal of Personality, 42,* 301–318.

Word, C. O., Zanna, M. P., & Cooper, J. (1974). The nonverbal mediation of self-fulfilling prophecies in interracial interaction. *Journal of Experimental Social Psychology, 10,* 109–120.

Wright, D. B., & Stroud, J. N. (2002). Age differences in lineup identification accuracy: People are better with their own age. *Law and Human Behavior, 26,* 641–654.

Wright, R. (2000). *Nonzero: The logic of human destiny.* New York: Pantheon Books.

Wright, S., Aron, A., McLaughlin-Volpe, T., & Ropp, S. (1997). The extended contact effect: Knowledge of cross-group friendships and prejudice. *Journal of Personality and Social Psychology, 73,* 73–90.

Wu, C., & Shaffer, D. R. (1987). Susceptibility to persuasive appeals as a function of source credibility and prior experience with the attitude object. *Journal of Personality and Social Psychology, 52,* 677–688.

Wyer, R. S., & Srull, T. K. (1981). Category accessibility: Some theoretical and empirical issues concerning the processing of social stimulus information. In E. T. Higgins, C. P. Herman, & M. P. Zanna (Eds.), *Social cognition: The Ontario Symposium* (pp. 161–197). Hillsdale, NJ: Erlbaum.

Wyer, R. S., Srull, T. K., Gordon, S. E., & Hartwick, J. (1982). Effects of processing objectives on the recall of prose material. *Journal of Personality and Social Psychology, 43,* 674–688.

Yamagishi, T., Mifune, N., Liu, J. H., & Pauling, J. (2008). Exchanges of group-based favors: Ingroup bias in the prisoner's dilemma game with minimal groups in Japan and New Zealand. *Asian Journal of Social Psychology, 11*(3), 196–207.

Yang, M. H., & Bond, M. H. (1990). Exploring implicit personality theories with indigenous or imported constructs: The Chinese case. *Journal of Personality and Social Psychology, 58,* 1087–1095.

Yoeli, E., Hoffman, M., Rand, D. G., & Nowak, M. A. (2013) Powering up with indirect reciprocity in a large-scale field experiment. *Proceedings of the National Academy of Sciences, 110,* 10424–10429.

Youth Risk Behavior Survey. (2007). *Health risk behaviors by race/ethnicity.* Atlanta, GA: Centers for Disease Control.

Yuchida, Y., & Kitayama, S. (2009). *Happiness and unhappiness in East and West.* Kyoto, Japan: Kyoto University.

Yudko, E., Blanchard, D., Henne, J., & Blanchard, R. (1997). Emerging themes in preclinical research on alcohol and aggression. In M. Galanter (Ed.), *Recent developments in alcoholism: Alcohol and violence: Epidemiology, neurobiology, psychology, and family issues* (Vol. 13, pp. 123–138). New York: Plenum Press.

Zadny, J., & Gerard, H. B. (1974). Attributed intentions and informational selectivity. *Journal of Experimental Social Psychology, 10*, 34–52.

Zajonc, R. B. (1965). Social facilitation. *Science, 149*, 269–274.

Zajonc, R. B. (1968). The attitudinal effects of mere exposure. *Journal of Personality and Social Psychology, 9* (monographs), 1–27.

Zajonc, R. B. (1980). Feeling and thinking: Preferences need no inferences. *American Psychologist, 35*, 151–175.

Zajonc, R. B. (2001). Mere exposure: A gateway to the subliminal. *Current Directions in Psychological Science, 10*, 224–228.

Zajonc, R. B. (2002). The zoomorphism of human collective violence. In L. S. Newman & R. Erber (Eds.), *Understanding genocide: The social psychology of the Holocaust* (pp. 222–240). New York: Oxford University Press.

Zajonc, R. B., Adelmann, P. K., Murphy, S. T., & Niedenthal, P. M. (1987). Convergence in the physical appearance of spouses. *Motivation and Emotion, 11*, 335–346.

Zajonc, R. B., Heingartner, A., & Herman, E. M. (1969). Social enhancement and impairment of performance in the cockroach. *Journal of Personality and Social Psychology, 13*, 83–92.

Zanna, M. P., & Cooper, J. (1974). Dissonance and the pill: An attribution approach to studying the arousal properties of dissonance. *Journal of Personality and Social Psychology, 29*, 703–709.

Zanna, M. P., & Rempel, J. K. (1988). Attitudes: A new look at an old concept. In D. Bar-Tal & A. W. Kruglanski (Eds.), *The social psychology of knowledge* (pp. 315–334). Cambridge, England: Cambridge University Press.

Zarate, M. A., Uleman, J. S., & Voils, C. I. (2001). Effects of culture and processing goals on the activation and binding of trait concepts. *Social Cognition, 19*, 295–323.

Zebrowitz, L. (1997). *Reading faces: Window to the soul?* Boulder, CO: Westview Press.

Zebrowitz, L. A., & McDonald, S. M. (1991). The impact of litigants' babyfacedness and attractiveness on adjudications in small claims courts. *Law and Human Behavior, 15*, 603–624.

Zebrowitz, L. A., & Montepare, J. M. (2005). Appearance DOES matter. *Science, 308*, 1565–1566.

Zebrowitz, L. A., Olson, K., & Hoffman, K. (1993). Stability of babyfaceness and attractiveness across the life span. *Journal of Personality and Social Psychology, 64*, 453–466.

Zebrowitz, L. A., Tenenbaum, D. R., & Goldstein, L. H. (1991). The impact of job applicants' facial maturity, gender, and academic achievement on hiring recommendations. *Journal of Applied Social Psychology, 21*, 525–548.

Zebrowitz, L. A., Voinescu, L., & Collins, M. A. (1996). "Wide-eyed" and "crooked-faced": Determinants of perceived and real honesty across the life span. *Personality and Social Psychology Bulletin, 22*, 1258–1269.

Zeisel, H., & Diamond, S. (1978). The effect of peremptory challenges on jury and verdict: An experiment in a federal district court. *Stanford Law Review, 30*, 491–531.

Zentner, M. & Mitura, K. (2012). Stepping out of the caveman's shadow: Nations' Gender Gap predicts degree of sex differentiation in mate preferences. *Psychological Science, 23*, 1176–1185.

Zhong, C. B., & Leonardelli, G. J. (2008). Cold and lonely: Does social exclusion literally feel cold? *Psychological Science, 19*, 838–842.

Zhong, C. B., & Liljenquist, K. (2006). Washing away your sins: Threatened morality and physical cleansing. *Science, 313*, 1451–1452.

Zhu, Y., Zhang, L., Fan, J., & Han, S. (2007). Neural basis of cultural influences on self-representation. *Neuroimage, 34*, 1310–1316.

Zimbardo, P. G. (1970). *The human choice: Individuation, reason and order versus deindividuation, impulse and chaos.* Paper presented at the Nebraska Symposium on Motivation (1969), Lincoln, Nebraska.

Zimbardo, P. G. (1990). Shyness: What it is what to do about it. Cambridge, MA: Da Capo Press.

Zimbardo, P. G., & Leippe, M. R. (1991). *The psychology of attitude change and social influence.* New York: McGraw-Hill.

Zimet, G., Dalhem, W., Zimet, S. & Farley, G. (1988). The Multidimensional Scale of Perceived Social Support. *Journal of Personality Assessment, 52*(1), 30–41.

Zuber, J. A., Crott, H. W., & Werner, J. (1992). Choice shift and group polarization: An analysis of the status of arguments and social decision schemes. *Journal of Personality and Social Psychology, 62*, 50–61.

Zusne, L., & Jones, W. H. (1982). *Anomalistic psychology.* Hillsdale, NJ: Erlbaum.

Zuwerink, J. R., & Devine, P. G. (1996). Attitude importance and resistance to persuasion: It's not just the thought that counts. *Journal of Personality and Social Psychology, 70*, 931–944.

Zweig, J. (2007). *Your money and your brain.* New York: Simon & Schuster.

CREDITS

CHAPTER 1

Photos: p. 2: Qilai Shen/Panos Pictures; p. 4: The Granger Collection, New York; p. 5 (top left): AP Photo/Charles Rex Arbogast, File; p. 5 (top right): AP Photo/Andy Manis; p. 5 (bottom left): Nicole Bengiveno/The New York Times/Redux; p. 6 (left): Public Domain/Wikimedia; p. 6 (right): Photo from the Zimbardo Simulated Prison Study, August 15–20, 1971; p. 7: Tony Freeman/Photo Edit; p. 10 (left and right): From the film Obedience, © 1965 by Stanley Milgram and distributed by Penn State Media Sales; p. 13: © Karl Eelmaa/Alamy; p. 15: 2005 Salvador Dali Museum, Inc. © 2015 Salvador Dali, Gala-Salvador Dali Foundation/Artists Rights Society (ARS), New York; p. 16 (left): Mark L. Stephenson/Corbis; p. 16 (right): Steve Prezant/Corbis; p. 17: Iconica/Getty Images; p. 19: Stone/Getty Images; p. 20 (left): © Diane Auckland/Arcaid/Corbis; p. 20 (right): AP Photo/Frank Franklin II, File; p. 22: Robert Leighton/The New Yorker Collection/The Cartoon Bank; p. 24 (left): Tom Brakefield/Corbis; p. 24 (center): AP Photo/Charles Krupa; p. 24 (right): © Stephanie Howard / Alamy; p. 25: Matt Slaby/Luceo for TIME; p. 27: Barbara Smaller/The New Yorker Collection/The Cartoon Bank; p. 30 (left and right): McCain Library and Archives, University of Southern Mississippi; p. 35 (far left): © BOB STRONG/Reuters/Corbis; p. 35 (center left): Michael Gottschalk/Photothek/Getty Images; p. 35 (center right): © INTS KALNINS/Reuters/Corbis; p. 35 (far right): © Martin H. Simon/Corbis.

Drawn Art: Fig. 1.3: Kanizsa, G. From "Subjective Contours," *Scientific American* 234. Copyright © 1976. Reprinted by permission of Jerome Kuhl.

CHAPTER 2

Photos: p. 40: © Chronicle/Alamy; p. 42: The Granger Collection, New York; p. 45: Courtesy Larry Sugiyama; p. 46: Courtesy Everett Collection; p. 50: PARS International; p. 52: From '49 Up,' A Granada Television Production, Photo Courtesy of First Run Features from the Up Series; p. 54: Cohen, Nisbett, and Schwartz 1996; p. 60: Tony Freeman/Photo Edit.

CHAPTER 3

Photos: p. 66: KMazur/WireImage/Getty; p. 68 (left): Nicky J. Sims/Redferns/Getty; p. 68 (center): © Frank Trapper/Corbis;

p. 68 (right): Larry Busacca/Getty Images For The Recording Academy; p. 71: Robert Weber/The New Yorker Collection/The Cartoon Bank; p. 73 (left): Rex Features via AP Images; p. 73 (right): Ian Gavan WPA Pool/Getty Images; p. 75 (left and right): From the film *Zelig*; p. 79 (left and right): Masuda et al. Placing the face in context: Cultural differences in the perception of facial emotion. Journal of Personality and Social Psychology 94.3 (Mar 2008): 365–381., Images Courtesy Takahiro Masuda; p. 83 (left): Justin Sullivan/Getty Images; p. 83 (right): Mike Ehrmann/Getty Images; p. 86: Duomo/Corbis; p. 87: Mike Twohy/The New Yorker Collection/The Cartoon Bank; p. 90: Alamy; p. 95: Mike Flanagan/www.CartoonStock.com; p. 96 (left): © Kai Chiang/Golden Pixels LLC/Corbis; p. 96 (right): © Uden Graham/Redlink/Corbis; p. 99 (left): Bildagentur Zoonar GmbH/Shutterstock; p. 99 (right): Robert Linton/Getty Images; p. 102 (top): Jesse Moss, Mile End Films, Inc.; p. 102 (bottom left): REX USA/MCP; p. 102 (bottom right): LOIC VENANCE/AFP/Getty Images; p. 103: Alamy.

Table 3.1: Morris Rosenberg, "Rosenberg Self Esteem Scale" from *Society and the Adolescent Self-Image*, revised edition. Middletown, CT: Wesleyan University Press (1989). Reprinted with permission of Dr. Florence Rosenberg and the Morris Rosenberg Foundation.

CHAPTER 4

Photos: p. 108: © Reuters/CORBIS; p. 110: AP Photo/Mike Albans; p. 113 (top): JGI/Jamie Grill; p. 113 (center): Rick Gomez/Radius Images/Getty Images; p. 113 (bottom left): Andy Roberts/Getty Images; p. 113 (bottom center): Harald Sund/Getty Images; p. 113 (bottom right): © DLILLC/Corbis; p. 115: diane39/istock; p. 116: Aldo Murillo/Getty Images; p. 117: Richard Cline/The New Yorker Collection/The Cartoon Bank; p. 118 (top): AFP/Getty Images; p. 118 (bottom): © CBS/Courtesy Everett Collection; p. 121 (top): ADEK BERRY/AFP/Getty Images; p. 121 (bottom left and right): © Patti McConville/Alamy; p. 123 (left): Jim Purdum/Getty Images; p. 123 (right): YinYang/Getty Images; p. 125: David Callow/Sports Illustrated/Getty Images; p. 126: Jonathan Fickies/Getty Images; p. 128 (all images): Pion Press; figures provided by Daniel J. Simons; p. 130: © Martin Benik/Westend61/Corbis; p. 131 (left): Hulton-Deutsch Collection/Corbis; p. 131 (right): Julio Donoso/Sygma/Corbis; p. 133: Scott Olson/

Getty Images; p. 137 (left): Eric Nguyen/Jim Reed Photography/Corbis; p. 137 (right): MGM/Photofest; p. 140: David L. Ryan/The Boston Globe via Getty Images; p. 141: © Max Wanger/Corbis; p. 142 (left): Harry E. Walker/ MCT /LANDOV; p. 142 (right): SAUL LOEB/AFP/Getty Images; p. 146 (left): Charles & Josette Lenars/Corbis; p. 146 (right): REUTERS/Lockheed Martin/Randy A. Crites/Handout; p. 147: Dorling Kindersley/Getty Images; p. 149 (all images): © Ikon Images/Corbis; p. 150: Dana Fradon/The New Yorker Collection/The Cartoon Bank.

CHAPTER 5

Photos: p. 154: Tania Lee; p. 156 (left): © Deborah Feingold/Corbis; p. 156 (right): © MAURIZIO GAMBARINI/epa/Corbis; p. 157: © Tim Pannell/Corbis; p. 160: © Bettmann/Corbis; p. 162: Leo Cullum/The New Yorker Collection/The Cartoon Bank; p. 164: GV Cruz/WireImage/Getty Images; p. 167: Al Bello/Getty Images; p. 168 (left): From Yiyo y Sanchez Cubero. Photo: Nuñez; p. 168 (right): Reuters/Corbis; p. 169: Frank Cotham/The New Yorker Collection/The Cartoon Bank; p. 170 (top): David Sipress/www.cartoonbank.com; p. 170 (bottom left): Kyle Terada-USA TODAY Sports/Reuters; p. 170 (bottom right): Rich Sugg/Kansas City Star/MCT/Getty Images; p. 175: Thomas Schmidt/Getty Images; p. 176 (left): Joe Raedle/Getty Images; p. 176 (right): REUTERS/Robert Galbraith RG/CN; p. 177: Leo Cullum/The New Yorker Collection/The Cartoon Bank; p. 178: Klaus Vedfelt/Getty Images; p. 181: Ariel Skelley/Getty Images; p. 186 (left): Uwe Anspach/dpa/picturealliance/Newscom; p. 186 (right): SHIN WON-GUN/AFP/Getty Images; p. 188 (far left): Wes Thompson Photography/Corbis; p. 188 (center left): Dale C. Spartas/Corbis; p. 188 (center right): Imagemore Co., Ltd./Corbis; p. 188 (far right): Chris Heller/Corbis.

Drawn art: Fig. 5.8: Kitayama, et al. From "Perceiving an object in its context in different cultures," *Psychological Science* 14.3 (May 2003) 201–206. Reprinted by permission of Wiley-Blackwell Ltd.

CHAPTER 6

Photos: p. 194: © LOUAFI LARBI/Reuters/Corbis; p. 196: © Bettmann/CORBIS; p. 198 (left): Laura Romin & Larry Dalton/Alamy; p. 198 (right): Monika Graff/Getty Images; p. 200 (left and right): © Ekman 1975–2004; p. 201 (top and center): From The Expression of the Emotions in Man and Animals by Charles Darwin; p. 201 (bottom): Pictorial Press Ltd/Alamy; p. 202 (all images top left): Adapted from Ekman, Sorenson, & Friesen (1969); p. 202 (all images bottom right): Photographs courtesy Professor Dacher Keltner; p. 203 (top left): Steve Bloom Images/Alamy; p. 203 (top right): M. Watson/ardea.com; p. 203 (bottom): © Bettmann/CORBIS; p. 204 (top left): © Radius Images/Corbis; p. 204 (top right): Courtesy of Frans de Waal; p. 205 (left and right): Haidt & Keltner, 1999; p. 207: Joe Giron/Corbis; p. 208: Alamy; p. 209 (top): AP/Corbis; p. 209 (bottom): ImageState/Alamy; p. 210: Courtesy of Nu Life; p. 211 (top): © Pierre Lahalle/TempSport/Corbis; p. 211 (bottom): Mike Twohy/The New Yorker Collection/The Cartoon Bank; p. 212: Courtesy of Matt Jones; p. 214: Whitney Curtis/The New York Times/Redux.

Drawn art: Fig. 6.5: Graham, Haidt & Nosek, Figure 1 from "Liberals and conservatives use different sets of moral foundations," *Journal of Personality and Social Psychology 96*, 1029-1046. Copyright © 2009, American Psychological Association.

CHAPTER 7

Photos: p. 228: © Bettmann/CORBIS; p. 230 (top left): Bettmann/Corbis; p. 230 (top right): AP/Wide World Photos; p. 230 (bottom): culliganphoto/Alamy; p. 233: © Dennis, David M./Animals Animals/Superstock; p. 234: Looper5920/Wikimedia Commons; p. 236: Timothy A. Clary/AFP/Getty Images; p. 237: AP Photo/Wally Santana; p. 239: Rob Rogers, © 1994 The Pittsburgh Post-Gazette/Distributed by United Feature Syndicate, Inc.; p. 240: Kevin R. Morris/Corbis; p. 241: 1982 Karen Zebuion, Courtesy New School Public Relations Department; p. 242: Kim Warp/The New Yorker Collection/The Cartoon Bank; p. 243: Photo courtesy of Terp Weekly Edition; p. 245: Universal Images Group/Superstock; p. 247: DILBERT, © 1999 Scott Adams/Distributed by United Feature Syndicate, Inc.; p. 254 (left): © Steve Starr/CORBIS; p. 254 (right): REUTERS/Lucas Jackson; p. 257: © David Young-Wolff/PHOTO EDIT; p. 258 (top left and right): Courtesy of W.W. Norton & Co., Inc.; p. 258 (bottom): Bill Frakes/Sports Illustrated/Getty Images; p. 261: © JGI/Tom Grill/Blend Images/Corbis; p. 262 (top): Bill Woodman/The New Yorker Collection/The Cartoon Bank; p. 262 (bottom): Damian Dovarganes/Ap.

CHAPTER 8

Photos: p. 266: Jesse Mendoza/Valley Morning Star/Harlingen, Texas; p. 268: Don't mess with Texas ® is a registered service and trademark owned by the Texas Department of Transportation. Use of this trademark is by permission only authorized by the Texas Department of Transportation; p. 269: Carl Rose/The New Yorker Collection/The Cartoon Bank; p. 271: Peter Steiner/The New Yorker Collection/The Cartoon Bank; p. 274: Reuters/Corbis; p. 275: Jason Tanner/UNHCR/Getty Images; p. 276: Hulton-Deutsch Collection/Corbis; p. 278: AP/Wide World Photos/Daily Sentinel; p. 279 (left): Taro Yamasaki/The LIFE Images Collection/Getty Images; p. 279 (right): Eric Draper/WireImage/Getty; p. 280: © Howard Davies/Corbis; p. 282 (left): Swim Ink 2, LLC/Corbis; p. 282 (right): Courtesy U.S. Army; p. 283: Corbis; p. 284: © Design Pics Inc./Alamy; p. 285: Sidney Harris/CartoonStock; p. 288 (left and right): © Michael Prince/CORBIS; p. 290 (left): BRENDON O'HAGAN/AFP/Getty Images; p. 290 (right): Henrik Kettunen/Bloomberg via Getty Images; p. 291 (top left): REUTERS/Chris Keane; p. 291 (top right): Gordon M. Grant/Alamy; p. 291 (bottom): Courtesy of the National Youth Anti-Drug Media Campaign and Ogilvy & Mather; p. 294: Mick Stevens/The New Yorker Collection/The Cartoon Bank.

Drawn art: Fig. 8.5: Zakary L. Tormala, et al. Figure 1 from "When credibility attacks: The reverse impact of source credibility on persuasion," *Journal of Experimental Social Psychology* 42 (5), September 2006, 684–691. Copyright © 2006. Reprinted with permission from Elsevier Limited.

CHAPTER 9

Photos: p. 302: Nisarg Lakhmani/Alamy; p. 304 (top): Dynamic spread of happiness in a large social network: longitudinal analysis over 20 years in the Framingham Heart Study, James H Fowler, associate professor, 1 Nicholas A Christakis, professor 2; BMJ 2008;337:a2338 doi:10.1136/bmj.a2338; p. 304 (bottom left): © Trinity Mirror/Mirrorpix/Alamy; p. 304 (bottom center): Peter Kramer/NBC/NBC NewsWire via Getty Images; p. 304 (bottom right): Gregg DeGuire/FilmMagic/Getty Images; p. 306 (left): Al Fenn/Contributor/Time & Life Pictures/Getty Images; p. 306

(right): © David M. Grossman/The Image Works; p. 307: Mick Stevens/The New Yorker Collection/The Cartoon Bank; p. 309 (left): Barbara Kinney/William J. Clinton Presidential Library and Museum; p. 309 (right): Keystone-France/Gamma-Keystone via Getty Images; p. 311: Courtesy of Swathmore College; p. 312 (all images): Adapted from Asch (1956); p. 313: Nick Doan/WireImage for Relevent PR/Getty Images; p. 317: Stephen Chernin/Getty Images; p. 318 (left): Aurora Photos/Alamy; p. 318 (right): Mauricio Piffer/AP Photo; p. 320 (left and center): Bettmann/Corbis; p. 320 (right): © Terry Schmitt/San Francisco Chronicle/Corbis; p. 322: Herbert Kehrer/Fuse/Getty Images; p. 325: Alamy; p. 326: Stephen Lovekin/Getty Images for UNICEF; p. 327: United States Holocaust Memorial Museum, courtesy of Avi Granot; p. 330: © Chuck Savage/Corbis; p. 331: Alamy; p. 332: Pars International; p. 333: Alexandra Milgram; p. 334 (left and right): From the film Obedience, © 1965 by Stanley Milgram and distributed by Penn State Media Sales; p. 335: From the film Obedience, © 1965 Stanley Milgram and distributed by Penn State Media Sales; p. 336: © Paul J Fearn/Alamy; p. 339 (left and right): Courtesy of Jerry Burger; p. 341 (left): From Obedience to Authority: An Experimental View by Stanley Milgram, Harper & Row, Publishers; p. 341 (right): © 1974 by Stanley Milgram.

CHAPTER 10

Photos: p. 346: Guylain Doyle/Lonely Planet Images/Getty Images; p. 348: Alamy; p. 350 (left and right): Harlow 1959; p. 351 (top left): David Katzenstein; p. 351 (top center): Eleonora Ghioldi; p. 351 (top right): Ralph Reinhold/Photolibrary; p. 351 (bottom): Gallo Images/Corbis; p. 352: Mischa Richter/The New Yorker Collection/The Cartoon Bank; p. 355 (top): Ed Koren/The New Yorker Collection/The Cartoon Bank; p. 355 (All images at bottom): Courtesy the Estate of Mary Ainsworth; p. 362 (left): Natalie Fobes/Corbis; p. 362 (right): Craig Lovell/Corbis; p. 363 (left and right): FRANCIS R. MALASIG/AFP/Getty Images; p. 364: Glowimages/Getty Images; p. 365: Barbara Smaller/The New Yorker Collection/The Cartoon Bank; p. 366: Rob & Sas/Corbis; p. 368: Marisa Acocella Marchetto/The New Yorker/The Cartoon Bank; p. 370: Trevor Hoey/The New Yorker Collection/The Cartoon Bank; p. 371 (far left): Erich Lessing/Art Resource; p. 371 (center left): Nimatallah/Art Resource; p. 371 (center right): Sunset Boulevard/Corbis; p. 371 (far right): Frank Trapper/Corbis; p. 373 (top left): Archivo Iconografico, S.A./Corbis; p. 373 (top right): Evan Agostini/Getty Images; p. 373 (center left and bottom): Professor Judith Hall Langlois, University of Texas at Austin; p. 374 (top images): Copyright 1994 Macmillan Publishers, Ltd. Photos courtesy of Professor David Perrett, University of St. Andrews, Scotland; p. 374 (bottom): From TIME Magazine, 11/18/1993 © 1993 Time Inc. Used under license; p. 376: Frank Cotham/The New Yorker Collection/The Cartoon Bank; p. 380: Menstrual cycles alters face preference, I. S. Penton-Voak, D. I. Perrett, D. L. Castles, T. Kobayashi, D. M. Burt, L. K. Murray & R. Minamisawa, Nature 399, 741-742 (24 June 1999), Fig.1; p. 382 (left): Wally Herbert/AgeFotostock; p. 382 (center): R. Matina/AgeFotostock; p. 382 (right): Tao Images/AgeFotostock; p. 384: Image Source/Newscom; p. 386: Robert Weber/The New Yorker Collection/The Cartoon Bank; p. 389 (left): Cavan Images/Offset; p. 389 (right): Redchopsticks Collect/AgeFotostock.

CHAPTER 11

Photos: p. 394: Courtesy of We Are Part Of You.org; p. 396: Stapleton Collection/Corbis; p. 398 (top): Yellow Dog Productions/Getty Images; p. 398 (bottom): © Janine Wiedel/Photolibrary/Alamy; p. 404 (top): drbimages/iStock; p. 404 (bottom): Luis Alvarez/Getty Images; p. 406 (left and right): Archives of the History of American Psychology, University of Akron; The Carolyn and Muzafer Sherif Papers; p. 407 (left and right): Archives of the History of American Psychology, University of Akron; The Carolyn and Muzafer Sherif Papers; p. 409: Scott Olson/Getty Images; p. 413 (left): Scott J. Ferrell/Congressional Quarterly/Getty Images; p. 413 (right): Alamy; p. 414: © Dustin Bradford/Icon SMI/Corbis; p. 415: © Sonja Pacho/Corbis; p. 419: David Sipress/The New Yorker Collection/The Cartoon Bank; p. 420: John Becker/Courtesy of Norm Ball; p. 423 (left): Long Hoang/Getty Images; p. 423 (right): Image Source/Alamy; p. 426: Scott Olson/Getty Images; p. 427 (left): Laura Barrera/Getty Images; p. 427 (right): ROBERTO CARLI/AFP/Getty Images; p. 429 (top left): Paul Panayiotou/Corbis; p. 429 (top right): Monty Rakusen/Getty Images; p. 429 (center left): © Roberto Westbrook/Blend Images/Corbis; p. 429 (center right): © Amer Alfaj/Demotix/Corbis; p. 429 (bottom left): © Hill Street Studios/Blend Images/Corbis; p. 429 (bottom right): Ryan McVay/Getty Images; p. 431: Payne, Lambert, & Jacoby 2002; p. 433: © Mike Stewart/Sygma/Corbis; p. 435: Corbis; p. 440 (left): AP Photo/Robert F. Bukaty; p. 440 (right): Derek Davis/Portland Press Herald via Getty Images.

CHAPTER 12

Photos: p. 444: Michael Blann/Getty Images; p. 446 (left): © Corbis/Corbis; p. 446 (right): AP Photo/Mark Duncan; p. 448: © Tim Anger/Demotix/Corbis; p. 449: Hazel Markus; p. 450: Rubes cartoon by permission of Leigh Rubin and Creators Syndicate, Inc; p. 455: © LWA/Dann Tardif/Blend Images/Corbis; p. 456: Allison Michael Orenstein/ Getty Images; p. 458: AP Photo/Pablo Martinez Monsivais; p. 460: AP/Wide World Photos; p. 462: Mike Twohy/The New Yorker Collection/The Cartoon Bank; p. 465 (left): © Douglas Kirkland/Corbis; p. 465 (right): © Kimberly White/Corbis; p. 466: © Corbis; p. 467 (all images): George Tames/The New York Times/Redux; p. 468 (left): © Wally McNamee/CORBIS; p. 468 (center):© Ron Sachs/CNP/Corbis; p. 468 (right): © Antoine Gyori/AGP/Corbis; p. 469 (left and right): Warren Goldswain/Shutterstock; p. 471 (left): F. Carter Smith/Bloomberg via Getty Images; p. 471 (right): James Nielsen/Getty Images; p. 472 (left): Alamy; p. 472 (right): Image Source/Getty Images; p. 473: Leo Cullum/The New Yorker Collection/The Cartoon Bank; p. 475 (left): Roger Ressmeyer/Corbis; p. 475 (right): John Storey/San Francisco Chronicle; p. 476: Yoshikazu Tsuno/AFP/Getty Images; p. 477: REUTERS/Jim Young; p. 478: Chris Graythen/Getty Images; p. 479: Doug Steley/Alamy; p. 481 (left and right): Oleksiy Maksymenko/Alamy; p. 482: Corbis.

Drawn art: Fig. 12.2: Zajonc, et al., Figure from "Social enhancement and impairment of performance in the cockroach," *Journal of Personality and Social Psychology* 13.2, 83–92. Copyright © 1969, American Psychological Association.

NAME INDEX

Note: Material in figures or tables is indicated by italic page numbers.

Fleming, J. H., 173
Fleming, S. M., 241
Florian, V., 263
Flynn, F., 208
Flynn, J. R., 588
Fonda, H., *610*
Fong, C., 261
Fong, G. T., 37, 291, 596
Ford, C. S., 370
Ford, T. E., 132
Forgas, J. P., 213, 215, 326
Forster, J., 258, 436
Fortenbach, V. A., 527
Fortune, J. L., 482
Foster, J., 492
Foster, J. B., 425
Fosterling, F., 160, 162, 163
Fowler, J., 296
Fowler, J. H., 304, *304, 549*
Fowler, K. A., 114
Fox, C. R., 27
Fraley, B., 383
Fraley, R. C., 357
Frank, M. G., 183, 200, 500, *500,* 517
Frank, R. H., 208, 223, 550
Franklin, B., 73, 547
Franklin, E., 600
Franklin, G., 600
Franzen, A., 548
Franzese, H. L., 417
Franzoi, S. L., 81
Fraser, S. C., 255, 324, 480
Frederick, D. A., 370
Frederick, S., 135, 141
Frederick the Great of Prussia, 397
Fredrickson, B. L., 215, 224, 225, 370, 603
Freedman, J. L., 245, 255, 324
Freitas, A. L., 386
French, H. W., 460
French, J., 466, 468
Frenkel, O. J., 240
Freytag, P., 421
Fridell, S. R., 216
Fried, C., 268
Fried, C. B., 61
Friedman, H. S., 279, 472
Friedman, R., 98
Friedman, R. S., 100, 258
Friese, M., 404
Friesen, W. V., 200, 201, 202, 207, 209, 220, 279
Frieze, I. H., 160, 368
Frijda, N. H., 197, 198
Frith, U., 25
Frodi, A., 501
Fromm, E., 353
Fryberg, S. A., 34
Fujita, F., 369
Fujita, K., 124
Fukuyama, F., 31
Fulero, S., 129
Fuller, M., 88
Fuller, S. R., 458
Fultz, J., 327, 525, 526, 527, *528*
Funder, D. C., 94
Fung, H. H., 206

G

Gable, S. L., 389
Gabriel, S., 34
Gabrieli, J. D. E., 184
Gabrielidis, C., 30
Gächter, S. 208
Gaertner, S. L., 398, 399, 404, 409, 430, 439, 533
Gaeth, G. J., 122

Gaillard, A. W. K., 456
Gailliot, M. T., 99
Gaines, B., 96
Galinsky, A. D., 253, 469, 470, 471
Gallo, L. C., 560
Galton, F., 373
Galvaing, M. P., 454
Gandhi, M., 73, 268
Gangestad, S. W., 103, 374, 379, 380
Garcia, D., 571
Garcia, J., 590, 591
Garcia-Marques, L., 421
Gardner, W., 98, 281
Gardner, W. L., 34, 233
Garfinkel, P. E., 371
Garner, D. M., 371
Garner, E., 396
Garofalo, J., 117
Garrett, B., 606
Garver-Apgar, C. E., 380
Garvin, E., 213
Gasper, K., 213
Gates, B., 155, 156, *156,* 538
Gates, G. S., 448
Gavanski, I., 166, *166*
Gavin, J. H., 456
Gawronski, B., 172, 402, 404, 428
Gebhardt, L., 492
Geen, R. G., 452, 492
Geer, G. H., 160
Geeraert, N. Y., 180
Geers, A. L., 177, 250
Gelfand, M. J., 317, 318
Geller, S. H., 316
Genghis Khan, 375
Genovese, K., 530, *530*
Gentile, D. A., 493
Gerard, H. B., 129, 311, 312, 314
Gerber, A. S., 331
Gerbner, G., 117, 118, 292, 491
Gergen, K. J., 165, *165*
Gerhardt, M. W., 467
Gervais, S. J., 470
Ghavami, N., 370
Giambologna, *506*
Giancola, P. R., 510
Gibbons, F. X., 84, 481
Gifford, R. K., 422, *422,* 423, 424
Gigerenzer, G., 145
Gilbert, D., 13, 424
Gilbert, D. T., 172, 173, 178, 179, 180, *180,* 198, 220, 221, *221,* 241, 342
Gillath, O., 532
Gillis, R., 169
Gilmour, T. M., 169
Gilovich, T., 14, 37, 91, 125, 126, 137, 147, 167, 168, 173, 174, 183, 223, 258, 292, 293, 423, 454, 482, 483, 500, *500,* 550, 580
Gino, F., 543, 544
Ginosar, Z., 143
Girgis, Z. M., 335, 339
Givens, D. B., 209
Gladstone, W., 611
Gladwell, M., 155
Glanz, J., 457
Glaser, J., 432, 616
Glaser, R., 385, 562
Glasman, L. R., 235
Glenn, N. D., 385
Glick, P., 400
Glied, S., 370
Glucksberg, S., 367
Goethals, G. R., 249
Goetz, J., 198

Goff, P. A., 398, 502
Goffman, E., 102, 103, 104, 335, 353
Gogorun, O., 91
Gold, M. S., 390
Goldberg, J. H., 615
Goldberg, P., 401
Goldenberg, J., 261
Goldenberg, J. L., 263
Goldin, C., 401
Goldman, R., 272, 276
Goldman, W., 369
Goldsteen, K., 351
Goldstein, C., 116
Goldstein, L. H., 112, *113*
Goldstein, N. J., 328
Goldstein, W. M., 358
Goleman, D., 129, 212
Gollwitzer, P. M., 131, 132
Gologor, E., 465
Gonzaga, G., 389
Gonzaga, G. C., 383, 469
Gonzalez, C., 574, *574*
Gonzalez, M. H., 55
Gonzalez, R., 43, 348
Gonzalez, R. M., 214
Good, C., 61, 160, 589
Goodwin, S. A., 469
Goore, N., 454
Gordon, A. K., 437
Gordon, A. M., 384, 474
Gordon, S. E., 129
Gore, A., 274
Goren, A., 114
Gorkin, L., 247
Gosling, S. D., 96, 104, 132
Goto, S. G., 34
Gottheil, E., 563
Gottman, J. M., 219, 220, 386, 387, 388, *388*
Gottschalk, J., 377
Gouldner, A. W., 322, 543
Gourevitch, P., 487
Gove, W., 351
Grabb, E., 368
Grafton, S., 27
Graham, J., 216, *218*
Graham, L. T., 104
Graham, S., 613, 615
Grandin, T., *25*
Grant, A., 543, 544
Granville, J., 115, 116
Gray, J. J., 371
Graziano, W. G., 369
Green, B., *525*
Green, T., *467*
Greenberg, J., 30, 126, 169, 254, 262, 263
Greene, D., 255, 256, 257
Greene, J., 328
Greene, J. D., 27, 216, 217
Greenspan, A., 568
Greenwald, A. G., 18, 71, 133, 277, 402, 403
Gregg, A., 90
Greitemeyer, T., 615
Greve, F., 538
Griffin, D., 145, 146, 348
Griffin, D. W., 137, 390
Griffin, J. J., 96
Griffit, W., 366
Griffiths, H., 417
Griffitt, W., 366
Griffo, R., 94
Griskevicius, V., 328, 383
Groff, B. D., 454
Gross, A. E., 327
Gross, J. J., 198

Gross, L., 117, 292, 491
Gross, P. H., 419
Gross, T., 132
Grossmann, I., 30, 77, 503
Gruber, K. L., 294
Gruenfeld, D. H., 468, 469
Guadagno, R. E., 280
Gubin, A., 469
Guéguen, N., 211
Guerin, B., 452, 454
Guilbault, R. L., 43
Guinote, A., 468, 471
Gunnell, J., 368
Gunz, A., 78
Guo, T., 147
Gurtner, J.-L., 587
Gustavsson, L., 376

H

Ha, Y., 124
Haberstroh, S., 119
Habyarimana, J., 487
Hacker, A., 277
Haddock, G., 399
Hagger, M. S., 100
Haidt, J., 197, 205, *205,* 213, 215, 216, 217, *218,* 219
Haines, M. P., 329
Halberstadt, A. G., 469
Halberstadt, J. B., 364
Halberstam, D., 229
Halcomb, C. G., 362, *363*
Hale, S. L., 323
Haley, K., 134
Hall, C. C., 114
Hall, C. L., 327
Hall, J. A., 81, 469
Hall, W. S., 399
Hallahan, M., 81, 114, 184
Halverson, S. K., 369
Hamedani, M. G., 82, 176
Hamermesh, D., 368
Hamill, R., 278, 280
Hamilton, A., *42*
Hamilton, D. L., 120, 421, 422, *422, 423,* 424
Hamilton, W. D., 542
Hampden-Turner, C., 32, 33
Han, S., 79, 281
Hancock, J. T., 105
Haney, C., 608, 609
Hanna, J., 104
Hannah, D. B., 426
Hannity, S., 293
Hannon, P. A., 385
Hans, V. P., 608
Harackiewicz, J. M., 103, 257
Harada, T., 534
Harbaugh, C. R., 208
Harber, K., 586
Hardee, B. B., 400
Hardin, C. C., 404
Hardy, C. L., 525
Hare, R. D., 512
Hargreaves, D. J., 131
Harinck, F., 385
Harkins, S., 456
Harling, G. A., 372
Harlow, H. F., 350
Harlow, T., 89
Harmon, A., 207
Harmon-Jones, C., 198
Harmon-Jones, E., 18, 198, 253, 254
Harris, C. R., 203
Harris, E., 493, *494, 495*
Harris, R. J., 327
Harris, S., 91

SUBJECT INDEX

Note: Material in figures or tables is indicated by italic page numbers.

nucleus accumbens, cooperation and, 546
nursing home patients, personal control study, 565–66, *566*